UNIVERSITY CASEBOOK SERIES®

SEXUALITY, GENDER, AND THE LAW

FOURTH EDITION

WILLIAM N. ESKRIDGE JR.
John A. Garver Professor of Jurisprudence
Yale Law School

NAN D. HUNTER
Professor of Law
Georgetown University Law Center

COURTNEY G. JOSLIN
Professor of Law
University of California, Davis, School of Law

FOUNDATION
PRESS

University Casebook Series is a trademark registered in the U.S. Patent and Trademark Office.

© 1997, 2004 FOUNDATION PRESS
© 2011 by THOMSON REUTERS/FOUNDATION PRESS
© 2018 LEG, Inc. d/b/a West Academic
  444 Cedar Street, Suite 700
  St. Paul, MN 55101
  1-877-888-1330

Printed in the United States of America

ISBN: 978-1-63460-529-8

Dedicated to the Memory of
Rhonda Copelon
Mary Dunlap
Paula Ettelbrick
Tyron Garner
Franklin Kameny
John Lawrence
Herma Hill Kay
Del Martin
Sylvia Rivera
Tom Stoddard
Edie Windsor

ACKNOWLEDGMENTS

We are grateful for critical comments from many friends and colleagues who have used earlier editions, and who have contributed immeasurably to this edition by sharing their experiences in teaching from the book. Our respective deans deserve credit for their material and collegial support: Georgetown University Law Center Deans Alex Aleinikoff, Judy Areen, and Bill Treanor; Yale Law School Deans Robert Post and Heather Gerken; and UC-Davis Law Dean Kevin Johnson. The Williams Institute provided us with up-to-date data that enriched the project as well.

We could not have updated this swiftly changing field without the work of student research assistants at the three schools. For this edition, we express our appreciation to Eric Baudry (Yale Class of 2019), Courtney Lee (Georgetown Class of 2016), Yena Lee (Yale Class of 2019), Charlotte Schwartz (Yale Class of 2019), Daniel Strunk (Yale Class of 2019), and Todd Venook (Yale Class of 2019).

We dedicate this book to colleagues and pioneers whose lives have ended since this casebook was first published in 1997: Rhonda Copelon, Mary Dunlap, Paula Ettelbrick, Tyron Garner, Franklin Kameny, Herma Hill Kay, John Lawrence, Del Martin, Sylvia Rivera, Tom Stoddard, and Edie Windsor.

WILLIAM N. ESKRIDGE JR.
NEW HAVEN, CT

NAN D. HUNTER
WASHINGTON, DC

COURTNEY G. JOSLIN
DAVIS, CA

INTRODUCTION

A major part of the excitement of writing—and, we hope, using—this book lies in the emerging—and fresh—nature of the field. Twenty years on from the first edition, the study of sexuality, gender, and the law continues to generate exciting new scholarly writing and academic offerings together with the emergence of the kind of canon that characterizes more mature fields. In this casebook, we seek to introduce students to these topics in a way that conveys the richness of the issues it encompasses, while also providing conceptual handles for understanding and organizing what can be disparate areas of law and scholarship. The book is decidedly interdisciplinary but also deeply grounded in law.

In the past, we envisioned the book as an extended claim for the centrality of this field, but that no longer seems necessary. The intellectual territory that one traverses in analyzing state regulation of sexuality and gender is no longer thought to be marginal to "core" law. These issues provide the critical defining line for the public-private boundary in law, and shape many of the most important questions in constitutional interpretation. This is true in substantive due process doctrine, in the development of an equal liberty jurisprudence of individual rights, in distinguishing between protected and unprotected speech under the First Amendment, in questions of whether state action constitutes a subsidy or penalty, and in adjudications of whether certain "private" information can be classified as newsworthy.

The co-incidence is not simply coincidental. In the last century, the state has taken on the function not only of regulating sexuality, but also of contributing to its very production, through a multitude of discursive interventions. In turn, these interventions help shape the contours of people's core identities and what they believe to be the appropriate role of the state. A mutually constitutive dynamic operates between sexuality and the state, just as one operates between the market and the state.

One way to teach a sexuality and gender course would be to use it as the focus of an advanced constitutional law course. Most teachers will opt for either a broad survey of sexuality, gender, and law or for a course that highlights either sexual orientation or gender. The book is designed so that it can be used as the basis for any of these three frameworks. To paraphrase Justice Blackmun's dissent in *Bowers v. Hardwick*, there are *many* "right" ways of teaching sexuality, gender, and the law.

The book begins with constitutional doctrine. Chapter 1 is a doctrinal introduction to substantive due process, equal protection, and expression and association rights. Chapter 2 treats recent landmark Supreme Court decisions—the *Casey to Whole Woman's Health* line of cases, *Lawrence v. Texas*, and *Obergefell v. Hodges*. Following each, the text presents relevant questions that remain in their wake. Chapter 3 introduces the student to a variety of theoretical approaches, stressing the dialectic between feminism and some post-modern philosophies, and closing with a section on how law operates as a mechanism of social construction as to sexuality and gender. Chapter 4 explores, in still greater detail, what we believe is now the most acute clash of rights that courts address today: the tension between the anti-discrimination norm and the liberty claims raised by those seeking exemptions based on religious beliefs.

The remainder of this casebook applies the doctrinal and/or theoretical precepts of Chapters 1–4 to a variety of institutional settings important to our society: the workplace (Chapter 5), the family (Chapters 6–7), schools (Chapter 8), and the armed forces and prisons (Chapter 9).

Throughout, we emphasize doctrine, theory, and practice, drawing on nonlegal as well as legal materials The appendices include statutory provisions, administrative documents, and ballot question materials. In addition to notes following the major cases, we include several extended problems in each chapter, which can serve as the focus for class discussions or assignments. These are intended to probe current questions that are particularly difficult and to inspire lively debate among any group of students.

Although one can slice the field (or this text) in numerous ways, we view sexuality and gender as so inextricably linked as to cast doubt on the ability to separate them completely and still attain a thorough understanding of either. One theme of the book is that debates over gender now lie at the heart of the most serious disputes over sex discrimination doctrine. Thus we concentrate on those aspects of discrimination "based on sex" that most clearly illustrate its linkages to gender—for example, the attempt by Virginia to preserve the Virginia Military Institute's training of young men in the ways of masculinity and the lively debates over employment policies related to pregnancy and the inclusion of sexual orientation and gender identity within the frame of sex discrimination.

We consider "sexuality" in its broadest sense. One enterprise in these pages is the deconstruction and analysis of sexual identity, and we do not limit that to gay, lesbian, bisexual, and transgender identities. We explore how the law constructs homosexuality *and* heterosexuality in diacritical relationship to each other. We explicate at some length the law's impact on stigmatized sexualities, but we also examine aspects of sexuality—such as pregnancy and assault—that help constitute social and legal understandings of heterosexuality. We use this approach to achieve two goals: to render visible the lives of lesbians, gay men, and bisexual and transgender persons, who are often invisible in the law, and at the same time to analyze the social meanings of heterosexuality, which often passes as the unquestioned norm in our culture and law.

WILLIAM N. ESKRIDGE JR.
NEW HAVEN, CT

NAN D. HUNTER
WASHINGTON, DC

COURTNEY G. JOSLIN
DAVIS, CA

SUMMARY OF CONTENTS

ACKNOWLEDGMENTS...V

INTRODUCTION VII

TABLE OF CASES.. XXIX

Chapter 1. Constitutional Frameworks: Liberty, Equality, Expression...1
Section 1. Liberty and Its Limits 3
Section 2. Bounded Equality...49
Section 3. Expression and Identity..125

Chapter 2. Watershed Decisions and the Rise of Equal Liberty 189
Section 1. Access to Abortion: From *Casey* to *Whole Woman's Health*
    and Beyond...191
Section 2. The Regulation of Sexual Conduct: *Lawrence v. Texas* and
    Beyond 225
Section 3. Liberty, Equality, and Marriage..............................277

Chapter 3. Theories of Sexuality, Gender, and the Law...................345
Section 1. Natural Law Theories of Sexuality, Gender, and the Law........349
Section 2. Modern or Liberal Theories of Sexuality, Gender, and the
    Law 365
Section 3. Post-Liberal Theories of Sexuality, Gender, and the Law........421

Chapter 4. Clashes Between Religious Liberty and Sexual and Gender Equality...507
Section 1. Religious Freedom Restoration Acts 513
Section 2. Specific Religious Exemptions from Antidiscrimination
    Laws...539
Section 3. Religious Liberty vs. LGBT Equality Clashes in Schools..........559

Chapter 5. Sexuality and Gender in the Workplace.........................601
Section 1. Cultural and Legal Discourses at Work....................605
Section 2. Pregnancy and Parenthood..621
Section 3. Sexual and Gender Harassment 659
Section 4. Gender Performance..685
Section 5. The Scope of "Because of Sex".................................709

Chapter 6. Relationships We Choose: Privatization and Plurality in Family Law...751
Section 1. The Privatization of Family Law...............................759
Section 2. Common Law Regulation of Cohabiting Relationships..........789
Section 3. The Emerging Menu of Relationship Recognition.....807

Chapter 7. Parents and Children 853
Section 1. Custody and Visitation..857
Section 2. Adoption and Foster Care 877

Section 3. Establishing Parentage...897
Section 4. Polyparenting 957

Chapter 8. Sexuality, Gender, and Education **971**
Section 1. Regulating Expressions of Sexuality and Gender.....................973
Section 2. Sexuality and Gender-Based Harassment and
    Discrimination..991
Section 3. Sex and Sexuality Education.....................................1045

Chapter 9. Military, Prisons, and the Construction of
    Manhood **1083**
Section 1. Exclusions and Segregation in the U.S. Armed Forces 1085
Section 2. Sexual Harassment, Sexual Violence, and Sexual Conduct
    in the U.S. Armed Forces 1133
Section 3. Due Process and Equal Protection in Prison...........................1147
Section 4. Sexual Harassment, Sexual Violence, and Sexual Conduct
    in Prison 1163
Section 5. Access to Health Care in Prison.................................1185

Appendix 1. Individual Rights Provisions from the
    Amendments to the Constitution of the United States...........**1207**

Appendix 2. Title VII of the Civil Rights Act of 1964 as
    Amended (Excerpts) **1211**

Appendix 3. The Proposed Equality Act (Excerpts) **1219**

Appendix 4. The Attorney General's Letter Supporting
    Heightened Scrutiny for Sexual Orientation
    Discrimination **1225**

Appendix 5. The District of Columbia Human Rights Act
    (Excerpts) **1231**

Appendix 6. Texas Sex Crimes Statutes **1239**

Appendix 7. The Ballot Pamphlet Supporting Amendment 2
    to the Colorado Constitution (1992) **1253**

Appendix 8. Proposition 8 Ballot Materials....................................**1261**

TOPIC INDEX...1275

TABLE OF CONTENTS

ACKNOWLEDGMENTS...V

INTRODUCTION VII

TABLE OF CASES.. XXIX

Chapter 1. Constitutional Frameworks: Liberty, Equality, Expression..1

Section 1. Liberty and Its Limits..3
A.   Controls on Contraception..4
    1.   *New York v. Sanger*...5
    2.   Sanger, Early Feminists and "Doctors Only"..................................6
        Paul and Pauline Poe et al. v. Abraham Ullman............................9
        Estelle Griswold et al. v. Connecticut.......................................11
        Notes on *Griswold* and the Right of Sexual Privacy.....................14
        Problem 1-1 Sex, Law, and Public Policy 16
    3.   Foundational Critiques of the Right of Privacy 17
        Robert Bork, "Neutral Principles and Some First Amendment
            Problems"...17
        Thomas Eisenstadt v. William Baird.......................................18
        Notes on *Eisenstadt* and the Expanding Privacy Right 21
B.   The Right to Choose Abortion 22
    Jane Roe v. Henry Wade 23
    Notes on *Roe* and the Right to Abortion...25
    Problem 1-2 Stupak Amendment in the Affordable Care Act of
        2010..29
C.   The Era of Sodomy Law...29
    Note on the Medicalization of Homosexuality 31
    Michael Bowers v. Michael Hardwick et al.....................................34
    Notes on *Bowers v. Hardwick* 41

Section 2. Bounded Equality 49
A.   Discrimination Based on Sex 50
    1.   Seeking Stricter Scrutiny 52
        Sharron Frontiero and Joseph Frontiero v. Elliot Richardson 52
        Notes on Arguments for Heightened Scrutiny for
            Classifications Based on Sex 56
        Notes on the Initial Pregnancy Discrimination Cases 57
    2.   *Craig*, Backlash, and the Court's Post-*Craig* Sex
        Discrimination Jurisprudence...59
        Curtis Craig v. David Boren..59
    3.   The Ginsburg Formulation...61
        United States v. Virginia..61
        Notes on the *VMI* Case and the Disaggregation of Sex from
            Gender..71
        Notes on State Justifications for Certain Sex Discriminations 74
B.   Discrimination Based on Sexual Orientation 76
    1.   Liberty-Based Arguments Against Discrimination 77

2. From Liberty to Equal Protection Claims 80
    John Singer v. U.S. Civil Service Commission.............................81
    Notes on *Singer* and the Fall of the Civil Service Exclusion.........83
    Notes on Equality After *Hardwick* 84
    Roy Romer v. Richard Evans...86
    Notes on *Romer v. Evans*..98
    Note on the Immutability "Requirement" for Suspect
        Classifications and Its Relevance to Sexual Orientation 100
3. The Sex and Sexual Orientation Relationship in Equal
    Protection Law 102
    Andrew Koppelman, "Why Discrimination Against Lesbians
        and Gay Men is Sex Discrimination"................................102
    Notes on the Sex Discrimination Argument in Equal
        Protection Law 104

C. Discrimination Based on Gender Identity 106
    1. Do Clothes Make the (Wo)Man: Cross-Dressing Laws.................106
    2. The Rise of the Medical Model....................................108
        City of Chicago v. Wallace Wilson and Kim Kimberley 110
        Notes on Law and the Medical Model.............................111
        Note on Competing Discourses 112
        Susan Etta Keller, "Crisis of Authority: Medical Rhetoric and
            Transsexual Identity" 112
        Problem 1-3 Client Narrative and Legal Strategy...............115
        Notes and Questions on Disability Law and Gender Identity....116
        Problem 1-4 Assessing the Medical Model 116
    3. The Sex Discrimination Theory 117
        Vandiver Elizabeth Glenn v. Sewell R. Brumby..................117
        Notes and Questions...122
        Note on Intersex Persons......................................122

Section 3. Expression and Identity....................................**125**
A. From Obscenity to Political Speech 130
    Gay Students Organization of the University of New Hampshire v.
        Thomas Bonner 130
    Gay Law Students Association et al. v. Pacific Telephone and
        Telegraph Co. 134
    Notes on "Coming out" as Political Activity 136
B. Feminist Pornography Debates 138
    American Booksellers Association, Inc. v. William Hudnut, III.........141
    Note on the Indianapolis Pornography Case 146
    Problem 1-5 What Should Be Labeled Pornographic?.....................147
    Note on the Racialization of Sexual Speech 147
    Note on Incoherence in the Public-Private Distinction for Sexual
        Expression 151
    David Cole, "Playing By Pornography's Rules: The Regulation of
        Sexual Expression" 151
C. Public Funding and Sexual Speech 153
    Nan D. Hunter, "Identity, Speech and Equality" 155
    Problem 1-6 Deconstructing "Public" "Sex"............................157

D.   Identity Speech and Expressive Association.....................................157
     John Hurley v. Irish-American Gay, Lesbian, and Bisexual Group
         of Boston 158
     Notes on the Boston Parade Case...161
     Note on Expressive Association 165
     Boy Scouts of America et al. v. James Dale 166
     Notes on the Boy Scouts Case..179
     1.   Freedom of Association Redux 181
          Donald H. Rumsfeld v. Forum for Academic and Institutional
              Rights, Inc. et al. 182
          Note on the *FAIR* Case and the Limits of *Hurley* and *Dale*........187

Chapter 2. Watershed Decisions and the Rise of Equal Liberty 189

Section 1. Access to Abortion: From *Casey* to *Whole Woman's*
**   *Health* and Beyond...191**
A.   The Center Holds 191
     Planned Parenthood of Southeastern Pennsylvania v. Robert
         Casey..191
     Notes on *Casey* 199
B.   The State's Interest in Fetal Life...200
     Alberto R. Gonzales v. Leroy Carhart et al. 201
     Notes on *Carhart* and the Evolving Right to Privacy.........................208
C.   Clarifying "Undue Burden" 210
     Whole Woman's Health et al. v. Hellerstedt, Commissioner,
         Texas Dep't of State Health Services, et al. 211
     Notes and Questions...222
     Problem 2-1 "Informed Consent" 223

Section 2. The Regulation of Sexual Conduct: *Lawrence v. Texas*
**   and Beyond 225**
Washington v. Harold Glucksberg...225
A.   The Repudiation of *Bowers v. Hardwick* 226
     John Geddes Lawrence and Tyron Garner v. Texas............................227
     Notes and Questions...245
     Note on Sodomy Laws Outside the U.S..250
     Problem 2-2 State Regulation of Sexual Conduct After *Lawrence* 251
B.   State Regulation of Sex Work 252
     Note on Current Proposals for the Regulation of Sex Work 254
     Terri Jean Bedford, et al. v. Attorney General of Canada (Attorney
         General) v. Terri-Jean Bedford et al. 256
     Notes and Questions...261
     Vivid Entertainment, LLC, et al. v. Jonathan Fielding, Director of
         Los Angeles County Department of Public Health, et al.............263
     Notes and Questions...265
     Problem 2-3 The Demand Side...266
C.   The Consent Paradigm 267
     Regina v. Anthony Brown et al. 267
     Notes and Questions...270

Problem 2-4 Sex and Risk 272
Notes on Age of Consent: Not as Clear Cut as You Think 272

Section 3. Liberty, Equality, and Marriage **277**
A.   State Law Marriage Exclusions 277
Richard and Mildred Loving v. Virginia 277
Notes and Questions 280
Notes and Questions 284
In re Marriage Cases 286
Notes and Questions 295
Kristin M. Perry, Sandra B. Stier, Paul T. Katami and Jeffrey J.
Zarrillo, and the City and County of San Francisco v. Arnold
Schwarzenegger (Governor), Edmund G. Brown Jr. (Attorney
General) et al. 296
Problem 2-5 Byproducts of the State Marriage Cases 297
B.   The Rise and Fall of the Defense of Marriage Act 297
United States v. Edith Windsor 300
Notes and Questions 308
C.   *Obergefell* and Beyond 309
Notes on Post-*Windsor* Cases 310
James Obergefell et al. v. Richard Hodges et al. 312
Notes and Questions 332
Problem 2-6 The Scope of *Obergefell* 336
Note on the Politics and Future of Marriage 336
Paula L. Ettelbrick, "Since When Is Marriage a Path to
Liberation?" 337
Thomas Stoddard, "Why Gay People Should Seek the Right to
Marry" 338
Notes and Questions 340
Problem 2-7 Next Generation Marriage Law 343

Chapter 3. Theories of Sexuality, Gender, and the Law **345**
Problem 3-1 Application of Theory to Constitutional Issues of Sexuality
and Gender 347

**Section 1. Natural Law Theories of Sexuality, Gender, and the
Law** **349**
Notes on Implications of the New Natural Law for State Regulation 353
Stephen Macedo, "Homosexuality and the Conservative Mind" 357
Robert George & Gerard Bradley, "Marriage and the Liberal
Imagination" 358
Notes on a Newer Natural Law Open to Sexual Minorities 359
Notes on a Different Kind of Natural Law Theory: Evolutionary
Psychology (Sociobiology) 360

**Section 2. Modern or Liberal Theories of Sexuality, Gender,
and the Law** **365**
A.   Economic Theories 370
Richard Posner, Sex and Reason 370
Gary Becker, A Treatise on the Family 372

Notes on Economic Theories of Sex and the Family...........................374
Problem 3-2 Application of Economic Theory to Legal Issues
         Involving Transgender and Intersex Persons 377
Carol Rose, "Women and Property: Gaining and Losing Ground" 377
Notes on the Consequences of Women's "Taste for Cooperation".......379
B.   Feminist Theories 380
     1.   Formal Equality 381
          Wendy Webster Williams, "The Equality Crisis: Some
               Reflections on Culture, Courts, and Feminism"...................382
     2.   Anti-Subordination 384
          Catharine A. MacKinnon, "Feminism, Marxism, Method, and
               the State: An Agenda for Theory" 384
          Notes on Radical Feminism and the Relationship Between
               Compulsory Heterosexuality and Patriarchy......................387
          Gayle Rubin, "Thinking Sex: Note for a Radical Theory of the
               Politics of Sexuality" 391
          Notes on the Debate Between MacKinnon's and Rubin's
               Theories of Sexuality, Gender, and the Law 397
          Robin West, "The Difference in Women's Hedonic Lives: A
               Phenomenological Critique of Feminist Legal Theory".......399
     3.   Intersectionality 401
          Kimberlé Crenshaw, Demarginalizing the Intersection of Race
               and Sex: A Black Feminist Critique of Antidiscrimination
               Doctrine, Feminist Theory, and Antiracist Politics 402
          Notes on Intersectionality and Its Implications for the
               Constitutional Politics of Sexuality and Gender.................404
          Elisabeth Young-Bruehl, The Anatomy of Prejudices 409
          Notes on Young-Bruehl's Theory of Prejudice and Implications
               for Constitutional Rights 411
C.   Transgender and Intersex Voices in Feminist Debates 412
     Notes on Trans Theory: Critiquing Oppositional and Traditional
          Sexism..414
     Problem 3-3 Mary Dunlap's Proposal for Sex-Choice..........................416
     Notes on Feminist Theory and Intersex Persons................................416
     Problem 3-4 The Intersex Olympian?...419

**Section 3. Post-Liberal Theories of Sexuality, Gender, and the
     Law**..421
A.   Social Constructionist Theories 424
     1.   Sexuality as a Social Construction (Michel Foucault)................424
          Problem 3-5 Foucauldian Strategies for Understanding Laws
               Regulating Sex, Gender, and Sexuality...............................429
          Jed Rubenfeld, "The Right to Privacy" 429
          Notes on Foucault and Constitutional Discourse 431
          Note on Feminism and Foucault..432
          Problem 3-6 Foucault, Feminism, Rape, Statutory Rape, and
               Incest...434
          State v. Marvin Kaiser..435
          Notes on Foucault and Incest, Statutory Rape, and Rape 437

2. Gender and Sex as Social Constructions 440
Judith Butler, Gender Trouble: Feminism and the Subversion
    of Identity 440
Price Waterhouse v. Ann Hopkins 442
Notes on *Hopkins* and Law's Invocation of Gender 447
Note on Identity Politics and Social Constructionist
    Thinking... 449
J. Jack Halberstam, Gaga Feminism: Sex, Gender, and the
    End of Normal 451
3. Constructing Sexuality Through Disease and Disability 453
Linda Singer, "Bodies—Pleasures—Powers" 455
Note on AIDS and Productive Discourses 457
Alain Giami & Christopher Perrey, "Transformations in the
    Medicalization of Sex: HIV Prevention between Discipline
    and Biopolitics"... 459
Russell K. Robinson, "Racing the Closet" 460
Note on the Raced Closet and AIDS Policy 462
Robert McRuer, "Disabling Sex: Notes for a Crip Theory of
    Sexuality"... 463
Note on Disability and Sexuality 465
Problem 3-7 A Right to Sex or a Right to Privacy? 466
B. Post-Liberal Theories of Identity and Strategies of Empowerment ... 466
Erving Goffman, Stigma: Notes on the Management of a Spoiled
    Identity 467
Note on Goffmanian Strategies for Dealing with Stigma: Passing,
    Covering, and Microperformances 469
Eve Kosofsky Sedgwick, The Epistemology of the Closet 471
Note on Binaries, Double Binds, and the Law............................... 477
Marjorie Rowland v. Mad River Local School District 479
Notes on the *Mad River* Case, the Construction of Heterosexuality,
    and the Erasure of Bisexuality 480
Note on Minoritizing Versus Universalizing Strategies for Sex,
    Gender, and Sexual Minorities 482
Sonia Katyal, "Exporting Identity"... 484
C. The Role of Law in the Social Construction Process 488
Ellen Ross and Rayna Rapp, "Sex and Society: A Research Note
    From Social History and Anthropology" 489
Dean Spade, "Documenting Gender"... 491
Noa Ben-Asher, "The Necessity of Sex Change: A Struggle for
    Intersex and Transsex Liberties"... 496
Notes on Constitutional Resistance to Law's Regimentation of
    Transsex and Intersex Persons 497
Jasbir Puar, Terrorist Assemblages: Homonationalism in Queer
    Times.. 500
Notes on Abu Ghraib and Theories of Sexuality, Gender, and the
    Law.. 504

**Chapter 4. Clashes Between Religious Liberty and Sexual and
  Gender Equality**..**507**
Problem 4-1 Devising a Balance Between Religious Liberty and LGBT
  Equality 511

Section 1. Religious Freedom Restoration Acts **513**
Sylvia Mathews Burwell, Secretary of Health and Human Services v.
  Hobby Lobby Stores, Inc., et al. 513
Notes on the Broad Reach of RFRA..531
Problem 4-2 Executive Order Barring Sexual Orientation and Gender
  Identity Discrimination by Federal Contractors 534
Notes on Post-*Hobby Lobby* Efforts to Update Junior-RFRAs 535

**Section 2. Specific Religious Exemptions from
  Antidiscrimination Laws**...**539**
Robin Fretwell Wilson, "When Governments Insulate Dissenters from
  Social Change: What *Hobby Lobby* and Abortion Conscience
  Clauses Teach Us About Specific Exemptions"....................................539
Note on Statutory Exemptions for Religious Organizations.......................542
Elane Photography, LLC v. Vanessa Willock 543
Charlie Craig and David Mullins v. Masterpiece Cakeshop......................548
Lexington Fayette Urban County Human Rights Commission v. Hands
  On Originals, Inc...551
Notes on First Amendment Protection for Small Businesses Declining
  to Collaborate with Gay Events 553
Proposed Marriage Conscience Protection Act 556
Problem 4-3 Applying the Proposed Exemption Law 557

**Section 3. Religious Liberty vs. LGBT Equality Clashes in
  Schools** **559**
A. Public School LGBT Students Burdened by No Promo Homo and
    Anti-Trans Policies 559
    Clifford Rosky, "Anti-Gay Curriculum Laws" 560
    Problem 4-4 The North Carolina Public Schools Bathroom Law 562
B. Private Schools Burdened by Education Antidiscrimination Laws....564
    Gay Rights Coalition of Georgetown University Law Center et al.
      v. Georgetown University 564
    Notes on the Georgetown Case and the Interaction of Conduct,
      Status, and Viewpoint...574
C. Public School Religious Students (and Their Parents) Burdened by
    Nondiscrimination Policies...577
    Christian Legal Society Chapter of the University of California,
      Hastings College of the Law v. Leo Martinez 577
    Notes on the Christian Legal Society Case 584
    David Parker; Tonia Parker; Joshua Parker; Jacob Parker; Joseph
      Robert Wirthlin; Robin Wirthlin; Joseph Robert Wirthlin Jr. v.
      William Hurley et al. 586
    Notes on the Free Exercise of Religion and Liberty-Based
      Objections to Marriage Equality...590

Note on California's Education Anti-Discrimination Laws 590
Tyler Chase Harper v. Poway Unified School District 591
Notes on High School Censorship in the "T-Shirt Wars" 596
Note on Proposition 8 and Liberty-Protecting Arguments Against
    Marriage Equality 598

Chapter 5. Sexuality and Gender in the Workplace **601**

Section 1. Cultural and Legal Discourses at Work **605**
A. No Sex at Work? 606
    Rosemary Pringle, "Sexuality at Work" 606
    Vicki Schultz, "The Sanitized Workplace" 611
B. Federal Law Protection Against Workplace Discrimination 613
C. State Law Protections 618

Section 2. Pregnancy and Parenthood **621**
Problem 5-1 The Big Picture 621
A. Adding Pregnancy to Title VII 621
    Dwight Geduldig v. Carolyn Aiello 622
    General Electric v. Gilbert 623
    Note on the Equal Treatment/Special Treatment Debate 625
    California Federal Savings and Loan Association v. Mark Guerra ... 626
    Notes and Questions 629
    Note on the Comparator Question 630
    Peggy Young v. United Parcel Service, Inc. 630
    Notes and Questions 638
    Note on Discrimination and (Re)Distribution 640
B. Pregnancy, Marriage and the BFOQ 641
    Problem 5-2 Role Model Jobs 641
    Leigh Cline v. Catholic Diocese of Toledo 642
    Crystal Chambers v. Omaha Girls Club, Inc. 645
    Notes and Questions 649
C. Parenting and Work 650
    Nevada Department of Human Resources v. William Hibbs 650
    Elana Back v. Hastings on Hudson Union Free School District,
        et al. 652
    Notes and Questions 656

Section 3. Sexual and Gender Harassment **659**
A. Core Concepts: Unwelcomeness and Harm 660
    Marcia Hocevar v. Purdue Frederick Co. 660
    Julie Gallagher v. C.H. Robinson Worldwide, Inc. 669
    Notes and Questions 672
B. Competing Paradigms 673
    Problem 5-3 Applying Theory to Practice 675
C. Same-Sex Harassment 675
    Joseph Oncale v. Sundowner Offshore Services, Inc., et al. 675
    Notes and Questions 679
    Medina Rene v. MGM Grand Hotel, Inc. 679
    Notes and Questions 683

Section 4. Gender Performance...**685**
A.   Stereotyping 685
     Price Waterhouse v. Ann Hopkins...685
     Notes and Questions...689
B.   When Is Gender Itself a BFOQ? 692
     Teamsters Local No. 117 v. Washington Dep't of Corrections...........693
     Problem 5-4 The Trans Prison Guard 695
C.   Sex @ Work...696
     Darlene Jespersen v. Harrah's Operating Co., Inc. 696
     Jacqueline Schiavo, et al. v. Marina District Development Co...........702
     Notes and Questions...707

Section 5. The Scope of "Because of Sex".......................................**709**
A.   From Sex to Gender to Gender Identity....................................709
     Diane Schroer v. James H. Billington, Librarian of Congress...........712
     Vandiver Elizabeth Glenn v. Sewell R. Brumby.......................716
     Mia Macy v. Eric Holder..716
     Notes and Questions...718
B.   From Gender to Sexual Orientation 719
     David Baldwin v. Anthony Foxx, Secretary, Dept. of
          Transportation 720
     Notes and Questions...722
     Kimberly Hiveley v. Ivy Tech Community College of Indiana............723
     Jameka J. Evans v. Georgia Regional Hospital.........................733
     Notes and Questions...737
C.   From Gender Identity Coverage to the Bathroom Access Question...741
     Julienne Goins v. West Group..741
     Krystal Etsitty v. Utah Transit Authority 743
     Tamara Lusardi v. John M. McHugh, Secretary, Department of
          the Army 745
     Notes and Questions on Bathroom Access 748
     Problem 5-5 Bathroom Access...749

**Chapter 6. Relationships We Choose: Privatization and
     Plurality in Family Law**...**751**
Martha Albertson Fineman, The Neutered Mother, the Sexual Family,
     and Other Twentieth Century Tragedies....................................752
Problem 6-1 State Recognition of Horizontal Partnerships? 755

Section 1. The Privatization of Family Law **759**
Jana Singer, "The Privatization of Family Law"...................................760
William N. Eskridge Jr., "Family Law Pluralism: The Guided-Choice
     Regime of Menus, Default Rules, and Override Rules".....................767
Notes on the Deinstitutionalization of Marriage: Cause for Concern?
     What Can Be Done?...770
Note on Feminist Thinking About Privatization 777
Problem 6-2 Constitutional Protection for Polyamorous
     Relationships? 778
Kody Brown et al. v. Jeffrey R. Buhman...779

Notes on Bigamy/Polygamy and the Constitution 784
Note on the American Law Institute's Principles of the Law of Family
    Dissolution (2002) 786

Section 2. Common Law Regulation of Cohabitating
    Relationships...**789**
Michelle Marvin v. Lee Marvin 790
Notes on *Marvin* and Judicial Treatment of Contractual Claims by
    Cohabiting Partners 792
Blumenthal v. Brewer 797
American Law Institute, Principles of the Law of Family Dissolution......798
Note on the ALI's Proposed "Domestic Partnership" Status 800
Note on Rights of Cohabiting Partners After *Obergefell*............................801
Melissa Murray, "*Obergefell v. Hodges* and Nonmarriage Inequality"......802
Courtney Joslin, "The Gay Rights Canon and the Right to
    Nonmarriage" 803
Problem 6-3 Constitutionalizing the Rights of Unmarried Couples?.........804
Miguel Braschi v. Stahl Associates Company 805

Section 3. The Emerging Menu of Relationship Recognition **807**
A.   Domestic Partnerships 807
    Milagros Irizarry v. Board of Education of City of Chicago 811
    Note on Domestic Partnerships Discriminating Against Straight
        Couples 816
    Joseph R. Diaz v. Janice K. Brewer, Governor of the State of
        Arizona...818
    Note on the Arizona Domestic Partnership Case 820
    Note on Federal Benefits for Domestic Partners.................................821
    Problem 6-4 Defining Eligibility for Partner Benefits 823
    Douglas NeJaime, "Before Marriage: The Unexplored History of
        Nonmarital Recognition and Its Relationship to Marriage".......824
B.   Reciprocal Beneficiaries, Designated Beneficiaries, and Civil
    Unions...826
    1.   Reciprocal and Designated Beneficiaries 827
        Colorado Designated Beneficiary Agreements Act of 2009.........830
        Notes on the Colorado Designated Beneficiaries Law.................834
    2.   Marriage Equivalent Statuses 835
        Problem 6-5 The Future of Civil Unions?....................................837
    3.   Interstate and Federal Recognition of New Family Law
        Institutions? 837
        Problem 6-6 Interstate Recognition of Designated
            Beneficiaries 839
        Note on Federal Recognition of Nonmarital Families.................840
        Revenue Ruling 2013–17..840
        Problem 6-7 Civil Unions Under the Internal Revenue Code
            and Other Federal Statutes..845
C.   The Emerging Regime: A Menu of State-Recognized Family
    Forms...847

William N. Eskridge Jr., Equality Practice: Civil Unions and the
 Future of Gay Rights 847
Notes on the Expanding Menu of State-Recognized Family Forms ...850
Problem 6-8 Create a Legal Regime for Partnered Relationships......852

Chapter 7. Parents and Children **853**

Section 1. Custody and Visitation...**857**
A.   Child Custody as a Form of Morals Regulation..................................857
     Notes on the Implications of *Palmore v. Sidoti*.................................858
B.   Sexual Orientation and Custody...859
     Notes on the Nexus Approach in Operation: The Perseverance of
      Anti-Homosexual Tropes 860
     Note on *D.W.W.* and the Modernization and Sedimentation of
      Antigay Discourse 864
     In re the Marriage of: Rachelle K. Black and Charles W. Black 865
     Problem 7-1 The *Black* Case on Remand 868
C.   Gender Identity and Custody...868
     Note on *Daly* and Discrimination Against Transgender Parents.......871
D.   LGBT Parenting: What Do We Know About It? 872
     Note on Studies of Children Raised by Transgender Parents 874

Section 2. Adoption and Foster Care...**877**
A.   Sexual Orientation and Adoption 877
     Notes on LGBT People and Adoption 878
     Steven Lofton et al. v. Secretary of the Department of Children
      and Social Services et al. 879
     Problem 7-2 Indirect Ways to Head off Lesbian and Gay
      Adoptions 882
     Arkansas Department of Human Services v. Sheila Cole et al. 883
     Note on Discriminatory Adoption and Foster Care Policies 885
     Note on Race and Adoption 887
B.   Second-Parent Adoptions 887
     In re M.M.D. & B.H.M. 889
     Notes on Race, Sexual Orientation, and Second-Parent Adoptions ...892
     Note on Interstate Recognition of Adoptions and Other Parentage
      Judgments 895

Section 3. Establishing Parentage **897**
Problem 7-3 Policy: Best Rule for Determining Parentage?.....................898
A.   Parentage and Married LGBT Couples...898
     Introductory Notes on Parenting..898
     Marisa N. Pavan, et al. v. Nathaniel Smith......................................902
     Notes on *Pavan* 905
     Problem 7-4 Policy: Best Rule for the Marital Presumption...............910
B.   Surrogacy..911
     In the Matter of Baby M..912
     Notes on Critiques and Defenses of Surrogacy.................................916
     Problem 7-5 The Constitutionality of Criminal Surrogacy Laws 919
C.   Parentage and Un-Married LGBT People..919

Bani Chatterjee v. Taya King 921
Notes on the "Holding out" Provision 925
D.   Gamete Providers 926
In re Thomas S. v. Robin Y. 927
Notes on *Thomas S.* and Sperm Donors.......................... 933
Note on Ova Sharing 936
E.   Equitable Parenthood.. 938
V.C. v. M.J.B. 939
Notes on Equitable Parentage 949
Problem 7-6 Who Is a Parent? 950
Notes on Critiques of Equitable Parentage.................... 951
Problem 7-7 Equitable Parentage in a Post-*Obergefell* World........... 952
Douglas NeJaime, "The Nature of Parenthood" 953
Problem 7-8 Policy: Best Rules for Determining Parentage 955

Section 4. Polyparenting **957**
A.   Equitable Parentage and Numerosity.............................. 957
K.A.F. v. D.L.M. 958
B.   More than Two Legal Parents... 962
S.M. v. E.C.. 963
Notes on *S.M. v. E.C.* 969

Chapter 8. Sexuality, Gender, and Education **971**

Section 1. Regulating Expressions of Sexuality and Gender **973**
A.   Inculcation, Critical Thinking, and the First Amendment 973
Bethel School District No. 403 v. Matthew Fraser, a Minor, and
    E.L. Fraser, Guardian Ad Litem.............................. 977
Notes on *Tinker, Fricke,* and *Fraser* 981
Problem 8-1 Gender Identity and the First Amendment 985
B.   Protecting Anti-Gay Speech 986
Tyler Chase Harper v. Poway Unified School District 987
Notes on the High School T-Shirt Wars 987
Notes on Student Clubs in Public High Schools 988

Section 2. Sexuality and Gender-Based Harassment and
Discrimination **991**
A.   Sex-Based Harassment in Schools.................................... 992
Notes on Title IX and Sex-Based Harassment.................. 992
Montgomery v. Independent Sch. Dist. No. 709 996
Problem 8-2 Protection for LGB Students Under Title IX 1001
Notes About Transgender Students and Title IX 1001
Problem 8-3 Protection for Transgender Students Under Title
    IX.. 1004
Whitaker v. Kenosha Unified School District No. 1 1004
Problem 8-4 Bathroom Access and Sex Discrimination.............. 1011
Note on LGBT Students and the Equal Protection Clause.............. 1011
B.   Clash of Free Speech and Anti-Discrimination 1014
David Warren Saxe et al. v. State College Area School District
    (SCASD) et al. 1014

Problem 8-5 Sexual Harassment as a Limit on Academic
    Freedom?...1019
C.   Sexual Violence 1020
    Notes on Sexual Violence 1020
    Problem 8-6 Sexual Misconduct on Campus 1023
D.   The Revolutionary Expansion of Athletic Programs for Female
    Students...1024
    Amy Cohen et al. v. Brown University et al......................1025
    Note on *Cohen* 1030
    Notes on Proposals to Change the Department of Education's
       Rules on Intercollegiate Athletics 1032
    Note on Transgender Students and Sex-Segregated Athletic
       Teams..1033
E.   Structural Reform: Same-Sex or All-LGBT Schools? 1034
    Notes on Proposals for Female- or LGBT-Only Classes and
       Schools 1036
    United States v. Virginia...1040
    Notes on the Impact of the *VMI* Case on the Legality of Same-Sex
       Educational Institutions...1042
    Problem 8-7 Defending a Single-Sex Public School 1043

Section 3. Sex and Sexuality Education **1045**
A.   Students' Right to Factually Accurate Instruction? 1046
    Notes on *Pico* and Students' Right to Know.....................1050
B.   Teachers' Right to Teach?...1053
    Note on Academic Freedom 1053
    Problem 8-8 Access to Information About Sex and Sexuality in
       Schools 1057
C.   Parental Rights 1060
    Notes About Parental Rights and School Curriculum........1060
    Ignacia Alfonso et al. v. Joseph Fernandez et al...............1061
    Notes on the Legality of Condom Distribution Programs and
       Parents' Constitutional Rights in Their Children's
       Upbringing..1066
    Note on HIV/AIDS Instruction as Possibly Creating a Hostile
       School Environment for Some Students 1067
    Comparative Law Note: American Versus European Sex
       Education Policies 1068
D.   LGBT Issues in the Classroom...1069
    Notes on the Evolution of Discourse Relating to LGBT Issues in
       Secondary Schools 1070
    Arizona Revised Statutes § 15–716, Instruction on Acquired
       Immune Deficiency Syndrome 1074
    Problem 8-9 State HIV/AIDS Education and the Policy Against
       Promoting Homosexuality 1075
    Gay Men's Health Crisis et al. v. Dr. Louis Sullivan 1075
    Notes on Constitutional Challenges to Anti-LGBT Curriculum
       Policies 1080
    Note on California's Education Antidiscrimination Laws.....1080

Chapter 9. Military, Prisons, and the Construction of Manhood 1083

Section 1. Exclusions and Segregation in the U.S. Armed Forces 1085
A. Racial Exclusions and Segregation 1085
    Kenneth L. Karst, "The Pursuit of Manhood and the
        Desegregation of the Armed Forces" 1085
    Notes on Racial Segregation in the U.S. Armed Forces (1940s) 1094
B. The Exclusion of Women 1096
    1. Women in the Military, 1861–1971 1096
    2. Partial Integration of Women in the Armed Forces,
        1971–81 1099
        Sharron Frontiero and Joseph Frontiero v. Elliott
            Richardson 1099
        Constitutional Issues for Women in the Military After
            Frontiero 1099
    3. Elimination of Women's Combat Exclusion 1102
        Note on Congressional and Administrative Deliberation over
            the Women-in-Combat Issue 1103
        Problem 9-1 Reconsideration of *Rostker*? 1105
C. The Military's Exclusions of LGBT People 1105
    1. The Exclusion of "Sodomites" and Sexual "Deviates" 1105
    2. Don't Ask, Don't Tell, 1993–2011 1111
        Policy Concerning Homosexuality in the Armed Forces:
            Hearings Before the Senate Committee on Armed
            Services 1111
        Note on the Aftermath of the Gays in the Military Hearings:
            The Don't Ask, Don't Tell Statute and Regulations 1115
        Notes on Discharges Under the Don't Ask, Don't Tell
            Regime 1116
        Michelle Benecke and Kristin Dodge, "Military Women in
            Nontraditional Fields: Casualties of the Armed Forces'
            War on Homosexuals" 1117
        Notes on Challenges to DADT and the Deference Issue 1121
        Note on Harassment of LGB People in the Armed Forces 1123
    3. The Demise of DADT and Its Aftermath 1123
        Notes on First Amendment Attacks on DADT 1127
        Note on Transgender and Intersex Persons in the U.S. Armed
            Forces 1128
        Problem 9-2 Openly Transgender Servicemembers 1131

Section 2. Sexual Harassment, Sexual Violence, and Sexual Conduct in the U.S. Armed Forces 1133
A. Sexual Harassment in the Military 1133
    Introductory Notes on Sexual Harassment in the Armed Forces 1133
    Military EO Policy, Department of Defense, Directive 1350.2,
        "The Defense Military Equal Opportunity Program" 1136
    Notes on the Armed Forces' EO Policy 1137

B. The Regulation of Sexual Conduct in the U.S. Armed Services 1138
    1. Pregnancy and Abortion for Military Personnel 1138
        Problem 9-3 Family Choice Rights for Military Personnel 1140
    2. Criminalization of Sexual Conduct in the U.S. Armed
        Forces 1141
        Notes on *Marcum* and Sex Crimes by Military Personnel 1144

Section 3. Due Process and Equal Protection in Prison 1147
A. Prisons and Fundamental Rights 1148
    William R. Turner v. Leonard Safley, et al. 1149
    Notes on Prisons and Fundamental Rights 1154
B. Prisons and Equal Protection 1156
    Garrison S. Johnson v. California, et al. 1157
    Notes on Prisons and Equal Protection 1160

**Section 4. Sexual Harassment, Sexual Violence, and Sexual
Conduct in Prison** **1163**
A. What's Happening and What Do Prison Officials Have to Do
    About It? 1163
    Notes on Sexual Victimization in Prison 1163
    Ashley A. Diamond v. Brian Owens, et al. 1165
    Problem 9-4 Condom Access and the Eighth Amendment 1169
B. Segregation and Sexual Violence 1170
    Notes on the Use of Isolation 1170
    Estate of Miki Ann DiMarco v. Wyoming Department of
        Corrections, Division of Prisons, et al. 1172
    Note on LGBT Inmates and Isolation 1177
C. The Placement of Trans Prisoners 1178
    Patti Hammond Shaw v. District of Columbia, et al. 1179
    Problem 9-5 Trangender Detainees and Placement Decisions 1183

Section 5. Access to Health Care in Prison **1185**
A. Access to Transition-Related Care 1186
    Andrea Fields v. Judy P. Smith 1186
    Notes on Transition-Related Medical Care in Prisons 1191
    Note on Medical Care for HIV-Positive Inmates 1194
B. Access to Reproductive Health Care in Prison 1194
    Notes on Reproductive Care in Prison 1195
    Juana Villegas v. Metropolitan Gov't of Nashville, et al. 1197
    Notes on *Villegas* 1205

**Appendix 1. Individual Rights Provisions from the
Amendments to the Constitution of the United States** **1207**

**Appendix 2. Title VII of the Civil Rights Act of 1964 as
Amended (Excerpts)** **1211**

Appendix 3. The Proposed Equality Act (Excerpts) **1219**

Appendix 4. The Attorney General's Letter Supporting
    Heightened Scrutiny for Sexual Orientation
    Discrimination 1225

Appendix 5. The District of Columbia Human Rights Act
    (Excerpts) 1231

Appendix 6. Texas Sex Crimes Statutes 1239

Appendix 7. The Ballot Pamphlet Supporting Amendment 2
    to the Colorado Constitution (1992) 1253

Appendix 8. Proposition 8 Ballot Materials 1261

TOPIC INDEX...1275

TABLE OF CASES

The principal cases are in bold type.

A.C. v. C.B., 923
A.E., In the Interest of, 899, 907
A.G.R. v. D.R.H. & S.H., 915
A.O.V. v. J.R.V., 861
Able v. United States, 1121
Acosta, Matter of, 102
Adarand Constructors, Inc. v. Peña, 1158, 1226
Agency for International Development v. Alliance for Open Society International, Inc., 263
Akron v. Akron Center for Reproductive Health, 27
Albright v. Albright, 862
Alderson v. Alderson, 794
Alexander v. DeAngelo, 374
Alfonso v. Fernandez, 1061
Alison D., In re v. Virginia M., 938
Alvarez, United States v., 125
Amalgamated Food Employees Local 590 v. Logan Valley Plaza, Inc., 161
American Booksellers Association, Inc. v. Hudnut, 141
American Federation of State, County, and Municipal Employees v. State of Washington, 617
Andersen v. King County, 295
Anderson, In re, 1156
Andrews v. Drew Mun. Separate Sch. Dist., 641, 648
Angel Lace M., In Interest of, 888
Ankenbrandt v. Richards, 301
Appeal in Pima County Juvenile Action B-10489, In re, 878
Appleby, Commonwealth v., 270
Arkansas Department of Human Services v. Cole, 883
Arlene's Flowers, Inc., State v., 548
Ashcroft v. The Free Speech Coalition, 147
Atlanta, City of v. McKinney, 810
Atlanta, City of v. Morgan, 810
Avery v. Homewood City Board of Education, 648
Baby M., In the Matter of, 912
Baby Z., In re Adoption of, 893
Back v. Hastings on Hudson Union Free School District, 652
Baehr v. Lewin, 104, 281, 315, 827
Baird v. Eisenstadt, 20
Baird, Commonwealth v., 18
Baker by Thomas v. General Motors Corp., 895
Baker v. Nelson, 60, 280, 316

Baker v. State of Vermont, 104, 281, 312
Baldwin v. Foxx, 720
Barnae v. Barnae, 923
Barnes v. City of Cincinnati, 119, 712
Barnes v. Glen Theatre, Inc., 151
Barse v. Pasternek, 906
Baskin v. Bogan, 309, 377
Beck v. Beck, 945
Bedford v. Attorney General of Canada, 256
Beecham v. Henderson County, Tennessee, 252
Belcher v. Kirkwood, 793
Bell v. Wolfish, 1150
Bellotti v. Baird, 274
Bennett v. Clemens, 859
Ben-Shalom v. Marsh, 1228
Berg v. Claytor, 1109
Beswick v. City of Philadelphia, 796
Bethel School District No. 403 v. Fraser, 977
Bezio v. Patenaude, 859
Big Mama Rag, Inc. v. United States, 1077
Binns v. Fredendall, 796
Birdsall v. Birdsall, 861
Bishop v. Smith, 309
Bitty, United States v., 253
Black v. Zaring Homes, Inc., 666
Black, In re Marriage of, 865
Blackmore v. Kalamazoo County, 1199
Blackwell v. U.S. Dep't of the Treasury, 111
Blatt v. Cabela's Retail, 116
Blau v. Fort Thomas Pub. Sch. Dist., 588
Block v. Rutherford, 1150
Blum v. Gulf Oil Corp., 733
Blumenthal v. Brewer, 797
Board of Directors of Rotary Int'l v. Rotary Club of Duarte, 174
Board of Education of the Highland Local Sch. Dist. v. United States Dep't of Educ., 1002
Board of Education v. Mergens, 988
Board of Education, Island Trees Union Free School District No. 26 v. Pico, 1047
Bob Jones Univ. v. United States, 335, 510, 553, 1041
Boerne, City of v. Flores, 510
Boland v. Catalano, 793
Bolling v. Sharpe, 49, 302
Bonadio, Commonwealth v., 252
Bono v. Saxbe, 1171

Boos v. Barry, 1016
Boseman v. Jarrell, 888
Bostic v. Schaefer, 309
Boswell v. Boswell, 861
Boutilier v. INS, 32, 482
Bowen v. Gilliard, 1226
Bowen v. Kendrick, 154
Bowers v. Hardwick, 34, 1227
**Boy Scouts of America v. Dale,
166**, 355, 575, 579, 1227
Boyd County High School Gay
   Straight Alliance v. Bd. of Educ. of
   Boyd County, Ky., 989
Boyd v. United States, 12
Boyer, In re Estate of, 794
Bradley, Commonwealth v., 859
Bradwell v. Illinois, 381, 602
Bragdon v. Abbott, 463, 1171
Brandenburg v. Ohio, 90, 97, 133,
   144
Braschi v. Stahl Associates Company,
   805
Brawley v. Washington, 1201, 1205
Bray v. Alexandria Women's Health
   Clinic, 390
Britell v. United States, 1140
Broadrick v. Oklahoma, 133, 1016,
   1128
Brockett v. Spokane Arcades, Inc.,
   138
Brooke S.B. v. Elizabeth A.C.C., 938,
   953
Brown v. Board of Education, 982,
   1055, 1158
Brown v. Buhman, 779
Brown v. Glines, 1127
Brown v. Henderson, 656
Brown v. Hot, Sexy and Safer
   Productions, Inc., 1068
Brown, Regina v., 267
Brown, United States v., 1143
Burkett v. Zablocki, 408
Burlington Indus. v. Ellerth, 659
Burns v. Burns, 838
Burton v. Wilmington Parking Auth.,
   161
**Burwell v. Hobby Lobby Stores,
   Inc., 513**
Butler, Regina v., 146
C.N. v. Ridgewood Bd. of Educ., 589,
   1061
Caban v. Mohammed, 75, 760
Califano v. Goldfarb, 321
Califano v. Webster, 62
Califano v. Westcott, 321
**California Federal Savings and
   Loan Association v. Guerra, 62,
   626**
Caminetti v. United States, 253
Campaign for S. Equal. v. Mississippi
   Dep't of Human Servs., 878
Campbell v. Sundquist, 234

Cannon v. University of Chicago, 991
Carcaño v. McCrory, 563
Carey v. Population Services,
   International, 21, 35, 1065
Carlson v. Olson, 793
Carolene Products, United States v.,
   49
Carson v. Heigel, 901
Cary, In re Marriage of, 792
Case v. Unified School District No.
   233, 1051
Caudillo ex rel. Caudillo v. Lubbock
   Independent School Dist., 989
Centola v. Potter, 721
Chadwick v. Wellpoint, Inc., 656
**Chambers v. Omaha Girls Club,
   Inc., 645**
Chaplinsky v. New Hampshire, 987
Charles B., In re Adoption of, 878
Chatterjee v. King, 921
Chicago, City of v. Wilson, 110
Childers v. Dallas Police
   Department, 84
**Christian Legal Society Chapter
   of the University of California,
   Hastings College of the Law v.
   Martinez**, 450, 549, **577**
Christian Legal Society v. Martinez,
   989
Christian Legal Society v. Wu, 586
Christiansen v. Omnicom Group Inc.,
   740
Church of the Holy Trinity v. United
   States, 715
Church of the Lukumi Babalu Aye,
   Inc. v. City of Hialeah, 587, 782
Citizens for Equal Prot. v. Bruning,
   1228
Citizens for Parental Rights v. San
   Mateo County Bd. of Educ., 1045
Citizens United v. Federal Election
   Comm'n, 527
Civil Rights Cases, 87, 91
Clark v. Jeter, 1228
Cleburne, City of v. Cleburne Living
   Center, 50, 85, 118, 121, 1226,
   1227, 1229
Cleveland Board of Education v.
   LaFleur, 57, 316, 603, 622
Clifton v. Eubank, 1196, 1197
**Cline v. Catholic Diocese of
   Toledo, 642**
Cohen v. Brown University, 1025,
   1026
Cohen v. California, 138, 978, 1056
Cohen v. San Bernardino Valley
   College, 1019
Coker v. Whittington, 252
Coleman v. Caddo Parish School
   Board, 1060
Colin v. Orange Unified Sch. Dist.
   Bd. of Educ., 989

Collins v. Davis, 793
Collins v. Harker Heights, 328, 329
Conaway v. Deane, 295
Conkel v. Conkel, 859
Conover v. Conover, 953
Cook v. Cook, 793
Cook v. Gates, 1124, 1228
Cooper, In re, 806
Cordero v. Coughlin, 1171
Corporation of Presiding Bishop of
  Church of Jesus Christ of Latter-
  day Saints v. Amos, 527
Craft v. Metromedia, Inc., 704
Craig and Mullins v. Masterpiece
  Cakeshop, 548
Craig v. Boren, 59, 120, 1028, 1100
Craig v. Yale Univ. School of
  Medicine, 616
Crooke v. Gilden, 795
Croskey v. Cty. of St. Louis, 1197
Cruzan v. Director, Mo. Dep't of
  Health, 499
Cytron v. Malinowitz, 795
D.C. and M.S. v. City of St. Louis,
  107
D.G. v. K.S., 957
D.M.T. v. T.M.H., 937
D.W.W., Ex parte, 862
Daly v. Daly, 868
Damron v. Damron, 861
Dandridge v. Williams, 94
Davis v. Beason, 90, 97
Davis v. Monroe Cty. Bd. of Educ.,
  994
De Burgh v. De Burgh, 287
De Sylva v. Ballentine, 301
Dean v. District of Columbia, 893
DeAngelis v. El Paso Mun. Police
  Officers Ass'n, 1015
DeBoer v. Snyder, 310
Debra H. v. Janice R., 838, 952
DeGraffenreid v. General Motors,
  403
Demers v. Austin, 1055
Dennett, United States v., 7
Department of Agriculture v.
  Moreno, 302
DeSantis v. Pac. Tel. & Tel. Co., 710
DeShaney v. Winnebago County
  Dept. of Social Servs., 330
Devine v. Devine, 854, 857
Diamond v. Owens, 1165, 1192
Diaz v. Brewer, 818, 821
**DiMarco, Estate of v. Wyoming
  Department of Corrections,
  Division of Prisons, 1172**
Doe ex rel. Doe v. Yunits, 984
Doe v. Arpaio, 1195
Doe v. Attorney General, 919
Doe v. Bell, 113
Doe v. Belleville, 677, 680
Doe v. Burkland, 793, 795
Doe v. George Mason University, 271
Doe v. Irwin, 1066
Doe v. U.S. Postal Service, 111
Doe v. University of Michigan, 1019
Doe, In re Adoption of, 881
Dominguez v. Cruz, 793
Donovan v. Poway Unified Sch. Dist.,
  1081
Dothard v. Rawlinson, 382, 647, 692
Dragovich v. U.S. Department of the
  Treasury, 1226
Dred Scott v. Sandford, 1085
Dudgeon v. United Kingdom, 250
Dugan v. Dugan, 787
Duncan v. Louisiana, 315
Dunn v. Blumstein, 91
Dunphy v. Gregor, 796
Edmonson v. Leesville Concrete Co.,
  161
Edward J. DeBartolo Corp. v. Fla.
  Gulf Coast Bldg. & Constr. Trades
  Council, 842
Edwards v. South Carolina, 158
Eisenstadt v. Baird, 18, 316, 819
**Elane Photography, LLC v.
  Willock,** 531, **543**
Elden v. Sheldon, 796
Elisa B. v. Superior Court, 922, 924,
  925
Embry v. Ryan, 896
Employment Division v. Smith, 509,
  517, 526, 548, 780
Enriquez v. West Jersey Health
  Systems, 117
Epperson v. Arkansas, 1047, 1054
Equal Employment Opportunity
  Commission v. Sage Realty Corp.,
  705
Equality Foundation of Greater
  Cincinnati, Inc. v. City of
  Cincinnati, 1227, 1228
Erie, City of v. Pap's A.M., 153
Eriksen, In re Estate of, 793
Erznoznik v. City of Jacksonville, 133
Estelle v. Gamble, 1185, 1190, 1202
**Etsitty v. Utah Transit Authority,
  743**
Evancho v. Pine-Richland Sch. Dist.,
  1003, 1013
**Evans v. Georgia Regional
  Hospital, 733**
Evans v. Romer, 87, 89, 98
Evans-Marshall v. Bd. of Educ. of
  Tipp City Exempted Vill. Sch.
  Dist., 1055, 1056, 1057
F.S. Royster Guano Co. v. Virginia,
  89
Faragher v. City of Boca Raton, 398,
  659
Farmer v. Brennan, 1165, 1182, 1200
FCC v. Pacifica Foundation, 138, 979
Featherston v. Steinhoff, 793

Feliciano v. Rosemar Silver Co., 796
Ferguson v. McKiernan, 934, 935
Ferguson v. Skrupa, 3
Fesel v. Masonic Home of Delaware, 692
Fields v. Smith, 1186, 1189
Finstuen v. Crutcher, 896
First National Bank of Boston v. Bellotti, 1047
Flagg Brothers, Inc. v. Brooks, 161
Flores v. Morgan Hill Unified Sch. Dist., 1012
Foster v. Florida, 241
Frank G. v. P.F., 957
Franklin v. Gwinnett County Public Schools, 993
Fricke v. Lynch, 596, 974
Friede, People v., 128
Frontiero v. Richardson, 52, 321, 381, **1099**, 1227
Fulk v. Fulk, 862
Furnco Constr. Corp. v. Waters, 635
G.G. ex rel. Grimm v. Gloucester County Sch. Bd., 1003
Gallagher v. C.H. Robinson Worldwide, Inc., 669
Ganzy v. Allen Christian School, 645
Garcetti v. Ceballos, 1054, 1056, 1057
Garrett v. Board of Education, 1042
Gartner v. Dep't of Public Health, 901
Gay Alliance of Students v. Matthews, 132
Gay and Lesbian Students Ass'n v. Gohn, 132
Gay Law Students Association v. Pacific Telephone and Telegraph Co., 134
Gay Lesbian Bisexual Alliance v. Pryor, 986
Gay Lesbian Bisexual Alliance v. Sessions, 986
Gay Lib v. University of Mo., 132
Gay Men's Health Crisis v. Dr. Louis Sullivan, 156, **1075**
Gay Rights Coalition of Georgetown University v. Georgetown University, 564, 571
Gay Students Organization of the University of New Hampshire v. Bonner, 130
Gay Students Servs. v. Texas A & M Univ., 132
Gaylord v. Tacoma School Dist. No. 10, 84
Gay-Straight Alliance of Yulee High School v. School Board of Nassau, 989
Gebser v. Lago Vista Indep. Sch. Dist., 993
Geduldig v. Aiello, 58, 383, 622, 623

General Electric v. Gilbert, 383, 623, 634
Geneva College v. Secretary, U.S. Dept. of Health and Human Services, 533
Gerber v. Hickman, 1154
Gerdom v. Continental Airlines, Inc., 697
Gfrerer v. Lemcke, 793
Giancaspro v. Congleton, 896
Gill v. Office of Personnel Management, 1226
Gillespie-Linton v. Miles, 796
Ginsberg v. New York, 979
Glasgo v. Glasgo, 793
Gleason v. Mesirow Fin., Inc., 666
Glenn v. Brumby, 117, 716, 1013
Gloucester County School Bd. v. G.G. ex rel. Grimm, 1003
GMHC v. Sullivan, 1075
Goesaert v. Cleary, 50, 603
Goins v. West Group, 741
Goldman v. Weinberger, 1124
Gomez v. Perez, 923
Gonzales v. Carhart, 201, 1190
Good News Club v. Milford Central School, 579, 988, 1060
Goodridge v. Department of Public Health, 281, 315
Gormley v. Robertson, 795
Graves v. Estabrook, 796
Greece, Town of v. Galloway, 325
Gregory v. Chicago, 158
Griggs v. Duke Power Co., 615, 627
Griswold v. Connecticut, 11, 21, 316, 329
Griswold v. Fresenius USA, Inc., 679
Grotts v. Zahner, 796
Grutter v. Bollinger, 1158
Gryczan v. State, 234
Guzman-Martinez v. Corrections Corp. of America, 1182
H.S.H.-K., In re Custody of, 938
Haas v. Lewis, 796
Haddock v. Haddock, 301
Hague v. Committee for Industrial Organization, 160
Hall v. Gus Const. Co., 665, 666
Harper v. Poway Unified School District, 591, 597, **987**
Harris v. Forklift Sys., Inc., 660, 676, 678
Harris v. McRae, 28, 1140
Harris v. Thispen, 1171
Harvey v. YWCA, 642
Hastie v. Rodriguez, 796
Hay v. Hay, 793
Hazelwood School District v. Kuhlmeier, 981, 1054
Healy v. James, 577
Heldreth v. Marrs, 796
Heller v. Doe, 89

Henderson v. Adams, 901
Hernandez v. Coughlin, 1156
Hernandez v. Robles, 295, 806
Hernandez-Montiel v. INS, 102
Herring v. State, 38
Hewitt v. Hewitt, 792
Higgins v. New Balance Athletic
  Shoe, Inc., 719, 1000
High Tech Gays v. Defense Indust.
  Sec. Clearance Office, 1228
Hinds County School Board, United
  States v., 1039
Hirabayashi v. United States, 279
Hislop v. Salt River Project Agric.
  Improvement & Power Dist., 796
**Hiveley v. Ivy Tech Community
  College of Indiana**, 448, 478,
  723, 740, 816, 1008
Hobbs v. Smith, 784
**Hocevar v. Purdue Frederick Co.,
  660**
Hodgson v. Minnesota, 274
Hoffman, In re, 161
Hollingsworth v. Perry, 105, 297
Holloway v. Arthur Andersen & Co.,
  710
Holm, State v., 780
Holmes v. California Army Nat'l
  Guard, 1121
Hopkins v. Price Waterhouse, 446
Hosanna-Tabor Evangelical
  Lutheran Church & School v.
  EEOC, 508, 527
Howard v. Burns Bros. Inc., 665
Hoyt v. Florida, 50, 381
Hudson v. DeLonjay, 793
Hudson View Props. v. Weiss, 806
**Hurley v. Irish-American Gay,
  Lesbian, and Bisexual Group of
  Boston**, 87, **158**, 547, 575
Immerman v. Immerman, 859
International Union, UAW v.
  Johnson Controls, 692
Ireland v. Flanagan, 795
**Irizarry v. Board of Education of
  City of Chicago**, **811**
J.A.L. v. E.P.H., 950
J.E.B. v. Alabama, 121
J.M., In re, 251
J.N., In re Commitment of, 893
Jacob v. Shultz-Jacob, 958
Jacob, Matter of, 888
Jacobson v. Massachusetts, 1067
James v. Lieb, 796
James v. Strange, 49
Janice M. v. Margaret K., 953
Jeffries v. Harris Cnty. Community
  Action Ass'n, 616
Jegley v. Picado, 234, 883
**Jespersen v. Harrah's Operating
  Co., Inc., 696**
Jessica N., In re Adoption of, 893

Jhordan C. v. Mary K., 926
Joan S. v. John S., 793
Johnson v. California, 1157
Johnson v. Calvert, 918
Johnson v. Johnson, 1228
Johnson v. Transportation Agency,
  Santa Clara Cty., 676
Johnston v. Missouri Department of
  Social Services, 885
Jones v. Barlow, 938
Jones v. Daly, 795
Jones v. Hallahan, 280
Jones v. North Carolina Prisoners'
  Union, 1150
Jones v. T.H., 1063
Jordan v. Fed. Bureau of Prisons,
  1174
K.A.F. v. D.L.M., 958
K.M. v. E.G., 936
K.S.P., In re Adoption of, 888
Kadrmas v. Dickinson Public Schools,
  91
Kaemmerling v. Lappin, 528
Kaiser, State v., 435
Kameny v. Brucker, 80
Kandu, In re, 1226
Kansas v. Matthew R. Limon, 275
Kentucky, Commonwealth of v.
  Wasson, 226, 234
Kerrigan v. Comm'r of Pub. Health,
  295
Keyishian v. Board of Regents, 1053
Kimble v. Wisconsin Dep't of
  Workforce Development, 616
Kingsley International Pictures Corp.
  v. Regents of the University of the
  State of New York, 128
Kinkenon v. Hue, 793
Kinnison v. Kinnison, 793
Kirchberg v. Feenstra, 321
Kitchen v. Herbert, 309
Knapp v. Northwestern University,
  1188
Knauer v. Knauer, 793
Korematsu v. United States, 279
Kosilek v. Spencer (Kosilek II), 1193
Kosilek v. Spencer (Kosilek III), 1193
Kosilek v. Spencer (Kosilek IV), 1193
Kothmann v. Rosario, 1192
Koushal v. Naz Foundation, 251
Kozlowski v. Kozlowski, 793
Krizek v. Board of Education of
  Cicero-Stickney Township High
  School District No. 201, 1057
LaChapelle v. Denise Mitten, 958
Lalli v. Lalli, 189
Lamb v. Maschner, 1179, 1191, 1192
Lamb's Chapel v. Center Moriches
  Union Free School Dist., 579
Lamont v. Postmaster General, 1048
Lane v. Lane, 899
Langan v. St. Vincent's Hosp., 838

Laskey, Jaggard and Brown v.
    United Kingdom, 270
Late Corp. of The Church of Jesus
    Christ of Latter-Day Saints v.
    United States, 780
Latham v. Latham, 793
Latta v. Otter, 105, 309
Lawlis v. Thompson, 793
Lawrence v. Texas, **227**, 331, 779,
    820, 1148, 1156, 1226, 1227
Laws v. Griep, 796
Layton v. Layton, 793
Lee v. Washington, 1158
Lee, United States v., 508, 521
Leebaert v. Harrington, 1061
Lehr v. Robertson, 61, 72, 76, 761,
    932, 942
Leibovitz v. New York City Transit
    Auth., 666
Lemon v. Kurtzman, 1060
Levenson, In re, 1226
Levy v. Louisiana, 760
Lewis v. Casey, 1159
Lewis v. Harris, 295
Li v. State, 295
Liberta, People v., 765
Lindahl v. Air France, 690
Lindsey v. Visitec, Inc., 796
Little Forest Medical Center of Akron
    v. Ohio Civil Rights Com'n, 692
Littleton v. Prange, 112
Lloyd Corp. v. Tanner, 161
Lochner v. New York, 3, 325
**Lofton v. Secretary of the
    Department of Children and
    Social Services**, 877, **879**, 1156,
    1228
Log Cabin Republicans v. United
    States, 1126
Los Angeles Dept. of Water and
    Power, City of v. Manhart, 688,
    724
Louisville Gas & Elec. Co. v.
    Coleman, 90, 302
Loving v. Virginia, 22, 104, 277, 316,
    1152
Lovisi v. Slayton, 252
Lovisi v. Zahradnick, 252
Lugar v. Edmondson Oil Co., 161
Luke Records, Inc. et al. v. Nick
    Navarro, 148
Lusardi v. McHugh, **745**
M.F., In re Paternity of, 935
M.L.B. v. S.L.J., 316
M.M.D. & B.H.M., In re, **889**
M.T. v. J.T., 111
Mabior, Regina v., 272
Macy v. Holder, **716**
Madelyn B., In re Guardianship of,
    925
Madrid v. Gomez, 1171
Madrone, In re, 920

Maggert v. Hanks, 377, 1188
Magnuson v. Magnuson, 871, 872
Maher v. Roe, 355, 407
Mallard v. Boring, 135
Manual Enterprises v. Day, 129
Mapp v. Ohio, 12
Marchioli v. Garland Co., Inc., 651
Marcum, United States v., 1141
Margolies v. Hopkins, 793
Marriage Cases, In re, **286**
Martin v. Struthers, 1048
Martin v. Ziherl, 251
Marvin v. Marvin, **790**, 792
Mason v. Rostad, 793
Massachusetts Bd. of Retirement v.
    Murgia, 94
Massachusetts v. U.S. Dep't of
    Health and Human Services, 299,
    303
Massey v. Banning Unified Sch.
    Dist., 1012
Mathews v. Eldridge, 1177
Matlovich v. Secretary of the Air
    Force, 1109
Mauricio Archibald, People of the
    State of New York v., 107
Maynard v. Hill, 319, 326, 762
McCoy v. Nev. Dep't of Prisons, 1161
McDonnell Douglas Corp. v. Green,
    631
McLaughlin v. Florida, 22, 278, 290
McLaughlin v. Jones, 905, 906, 908
McWilliams v. Fairfax County Board
    of Supervisors, 677
Meacham v. Fano, 3
Medina v. Income Support Div., 719
Meritor Savings Bank v. Vinson, 660,
    676, 678, 681
Meriwether v. Faulkner, 1188, 1191,
    1192
Merrill v. Davis, 793
Meyer v. Nebraska, 3, 4, 316, 871,
    1060, 1061
Miami Herald Publishing Co. v.
    Tornillo, 184
Michael H. v. Gerald D., 854
Michael M. v. Superior Court of
    Sonoma County, 60, 273, 382
Milberger v. KBHL, L.L.C., 796
Miles v. Denver Public Schools, 1057
Miller v. Albright, 71
Miller v. California, 138, 148
Miller v. Civil City of South Bend,
    151
Miller v. Miller, 968
Miller v. Mitchell, 147
Miller v. Ratner, 793
Miller v. Vesta, Inc., 679
Milliken v. Bradley, 66
Minnesota ex rel. McClure, In re, 530
Miranda v. Arizona, 435

Mississippi University for Women v. Hogan, 59, 120, 1039
Modinos v. Cyprus, 234, 250
Monmouth Cnty. Corr. Instit. Inmates v. Lanzaro, 1195
Montgomery v. Independent Sch. Dist. No. 709, 996
Moore v. East Cleveland, 36, 329
Moore v. Hughes Helicopter, Inc., 403
Moore v. Mabus, 1171
Morales v. Pallito, 1156
Morales, State v., 232, 237
Morone v. Morone, 793
Morrison, United States v., 390
Morse v. Frederick, 597, 983
Mount Healthy City School District Bd. of Educ. v. Doyle, 445
Mozert v. Hawkins County Board of Education, 588
Mugler v. Kansas, 3
Muhammad v. Carlson, 1171
Muller v. Oregon, 381, 603
Murphy v. Ramsey, 253, 326
Music v. Rachford, 938
NAACP v. Alabama, 12, 135, 165
NAACP v. Button, 135
Nabozny v. Podlesny, 1011
Naim v. Naim, 277
National Coalition for Gay and Lesbian Equality v. The Minister of Justice, 190, 250
National Endowment for the Arts v. Finley, 157
National Gay Task Force v. Board of Education of the City of Oklahoma City, 132
National Socialist Party of America v. Skokie, 159
Neal v. Board of Trustees of the Calif. State Univs., 1030
Nehra, Matter of v. Uhlar, 929
Nelson v. Correctional Medical Services, 1200, 1201, 1202, 1205
Nevada Commission on Ethics v. Carrigan, 550
Nevada Department of Human Resources v. Hibbs, 121, 650, 651
New State Ice Co. v. Liebman, 285
New York City Transit Authority v. Beazer, 94
New York Times Co. v. Sullivan, 144
New York Times Co. v. United States, 144
New York v. Ferber, 147
Newman v. Piggie Park Enterprises, Inc., 530
Newport News Shipbuilding and Dry Dock Co. v. EEOC, 624, 634, 717
Neyman v. Buckley, 838
Nguyen v. INS, 71, 761, 907
Nicholas H., In re, 924

Nichols v. Azteca Restaurant Enterprises, Inc., 682
Nichols v. Frank, 684
Norris v. Ireland, 234, 250
Norsworthy v. Beard, 1193
Norton v. Greene Cty., Tenn., 1197
Norton v. Macy, 78
Nugent v. Bauermeister, 796
Nuxoll ex rel. Nuxoll v. Indian Prairie Sch. Dist. No. 204, 596, 987
O'Brien v. O'Brien, 787
O'Brien, United States v., 153, 170, 974
O'Connor v. Sobol, 1057
Obergefell v. Hodges, 277, 312, 773, 801, 868, 902, 903, 906, 907, 1080
Ohio ex rel. Popovici v. Agler, 301
Olmstead v. United States, 4
Oncale v. Sundowner Offshore Services, Inc., 675, 715, 717, 722, 995, 1008
One Book Entitled "Ulysses", United States v., 128
One Package, United States v., 8
One, Inc. v. Olesen, 128
Onofre, People v., 42
Orr v. Orr, 120, 321, 382, 766
Owens v. Brown, 1101
P.G. & J.H. v. United Kingdom, 234
Pace v. Alabama, 278
Pacific Gas & Elec. Co. v. Public Util. Comm'n of Cal., 184
Padula v. Webster, 1228
Palko v. Connecticut, 17, 24
Palmen, In re Estate of, 794
Palmore v. Sidoti, 858, 868, 1229
Parentage of L.B., In re, 950, 951
Parental Responsibilities of A.R.L., In re, 925
Parham v. Hughes, 75
Paris Adult Theatre I v. Slaton, 38, 39
Parker v. Hurley, 586, 591
Parr v. Woodmen of the World Life Ins. Co., 712
Pavan v. Smith, 335, 901, 902
Payne v. Travenol, 403
Pedersen v. OPM, 843, 1226
Pell v. Procunier, 1150, 1152
Pennington v. Pennington, 800
Perez v. Lippold, 290
Perkins v. Kansas Department of Corrections, 1194
Perry Ed. Assn. v. Perry Local Educators' Assn., 579
Perry v. Brown, 105, 297
Perry v. Schwarzenegger, 105, 296
Personnel Administrator v. Feeney, 58, 89
Phillips v. Martin Marietta Corp., 690

Phillips v. Michigan Dep't of Corr., 1192

Piantanida v. Wyman Ctr., Inc., 652

Pickering v. Board of Education, 1053

Pidgeon v. Turner, 335

Pierce v. Society of Sisters, 4, 948, 1060

Pitts v. Thornburg, 1161

Planned Parenthood Ass'n v. Chicago Transit Authority, 145

Planned Parenthood of Southeastern Pennsylvania v. Casey, 191, 199, 524

Planned Parenthood of Wis., Inc. v. Schimel, 217

Planned Parenthood of Wis., Inc. v. Van Hollen, 217

Planned Parenthood Southeast, Inc. v. Strange, 217

Plessy v. Ferguson, 86

Poe v. Levy's Estate, 793

Poe v. Ullman, 9

Poelker v. Doe, 407

Police Department v. Mosley, 131, 132, 161

Ponton v. Newport News School Board, 648

Pool v. Sebastian Cty., Ark, 1197

Posik v. Layton, 795

Post v. State, 230

Powell v. State, 226, 234

Price Waterhouse v. Hopkins, 118, **442**, **685**, 689, 717, 1008

Priests for Life v. U.S. Dept. of Health and Human Services, 533

Prince v. Massachusetts, 11, 951, 1060

Procunier v. Martinez, 1149

Prowel v. Wise Business Forms, Inc., 719

PruneYard Shopping Center v. Robins, 184, 573

Quillin v. Walcott, 761

Quong Wing v. Kirkendall, 603

R.A.V. v. City of St. Paul, 1128

R.W. v. D.W.W., 862

Raffaelli v. Committee of Bar Examiners, 292

Railway Express Agency v. New York, 49, 238

Ramey v. Sutton, 950

Randles v. Hester, 1169

Reed v. Reed, 26, 52, 321, 1099

Reeves v. C.H. Robinson Worldwide, Inc., 670

Regents of the Univ. of Cal. v. Bakke, 1027

Regents of Univ. of Michigan v. Ewing, 1053

Reliable Consultants, Inc., v. Earle, 250

Rene v. MGM Grand Hotel, Inc., 679

Reno v. Flores, 327

Renton, City of v. Playtime Theatres, 138

Reynolds v. United States, 780, 785

Rhoades v Iowa, 271

Richardson v. Ramirez, 91, 97

Richenberg v. Perry, 1121

Robert O., Matter of v. Russell K., 932

Roberts v. United States Jaycees, 165, 579

Robins v. Pruneyard Shopping Center, 161

Roccamonte, In re Estate of, 793

Roe v. Crawford, 1195

Roe v. Patton, 898, 901

Roe v. Wade, 23

Romer v. Evans, 86, 301, 381, 1229

Romero v. Bd. of Cty. Commissioners for the Cty. of Curry, 1171

Rorie v. United Parcel Serv., 665

Rosa v. Park West Bank & Trust Co., 117, 119

Rosenberger v. Rector and Visitors of the University of Virginia, 163, 574, 577, 1053

Rosengarten v. Downes, 838

Rostker v. Goldberg, 60, 382, 1100

Roth v. United States, 128

Rowland v. Cal. Men's Colony, Unit II Men's Advisory Council, 843

Rowland v. Mad River Local School District, 479, 481, 559, 1070

Rumsfeld v. Forum for Academic and Institutional Rights, Inc., 182

Rust v. Sullivan, 154, 842, 1059

Rutan v. Republican Party of Ill., 68

S.M. v. E.C., 963

Safley v. Turner, 1149

Sail'er Inn, Inc. v. Kirby, 51

Salzman v. Bachrach, 793, 834

Samuels, People v., 271

San Antonio Independent School Dist. v. Rodriguez, 330

Sandin v. Conner, 1171, 1173, 1174, 1179

Sanger v. People of State of New York, 6

Santiago-Ramos v. Centennial P.R. Wireless Corp., 655

Sawatzky v. City of Oklahoma City, 251

Sawyer v. Bailey, 796

Saxe v. State College Area School District (SCASD), 1014

Schiavo v. Marina District Development Co., 702

Schlesinger v. Ballard, 1028, 1100

Schmid, State v., 161

Schroeder ex rel. Schroeder v. Maumee Bd. of Educ., 1012

Schroer v. Billington, 712

Schuster v. Schuster, 859

Schwegmann v. Schwegmann, 793

Schwenk v. Hartford, 117, 119, 716, 1165

Schwimmer, United States v., 583

Scoby, United States v., 1142

Scusa v. Nestle U.S.A. Co., 667

Sees v. Baber, 912

Segmiller v. Laverkin City, 782

Seminole Tribe of Fla. v. Florida, 1040

Sessions v. Morales-Santana, 74, 75

Shaw v. District of Columbia, 1179

Shaw v. Murphy, 1159

Shaw v. Reno, 1158, 1159

Sheehan v. Donlen Corp., 655

Shelley v. Kraemer, 90

Sherbert v. Verner, 509, 885

Shunn v. State, 765

Silver v. Starrett, 795

Singer v. Hara, 104, 280

Singer v. U.S. Civil Service Commission, 81

Singson v. Commonwealth, 251

Skidmore v. Swift & Co., 719

Skinner v. State of Oklahoma, 10, 26, 90, 189, 190, 279, 316

Small v. Harper, 793

Smelt v. County of Orange, 1226

Smith v. City of Salem, 117, 119, 1008

Smith v. Org. of Foster Families for Equal. & Reform, 879

Smith v. Pavan, 901

Smith v. Salem, 711, 712

Smith v. Toney, 796

Smith, State v., 765

SmithKline Beecham Corp. v. Abbott Laboratories, 310, 311

Snyder v. Massachusetts, 327

Sosna v. Iowa, 301

Sostock v. Reiss, 796

South v. Gomez, 1192

Spafford v. Coats, 793

Spencer v. Bouchard, 1200

Spencer v. World Vision, Inc., 531

St. Mary v. Damon, 937

Stanley v. Georgia, 1047

Stanley v. Illinois, 55, 760

Stanton v. Stanton, 59, 120, 382

State Division of Human Rights v. Xerox Corp., 114

Steffan v. Perry, 1111, 1121, 1227

Stenberg v. Carhart, 201

Stroman v. Williams, 860

Stromberg v. California, 159

Struck v. Secretary of Defense, 621, 1138

Student Coalition for Gay Rights v. Austin Peay Univ., 132

Students v. United States Department of Education, 1002

Sturgis v. Attorney General, 18

Sullivan v. County of Pierce, 1194

Supre v. Ricketts, 1191

Sweatt v. Painter, 66, 90

Sweezy v. New Hampshire, 1053

Taylor v. Small, 704

Taylor, In re, 1180

Teamsters Local No. 117 v. Washington Dep't of Corrections, 693

Texas Dept. of Community Affairs v. Burdine, 635

Texas v. United States, 1003

Thomas S., In re v. Robin Y., 927

Thomas v. Board of Education, Granville Central School Dist., 978

Thomasson v. Perry, 1121

Thompson, State v., 251

Thornburgh v. Abbott, 1159

Thornburgh v. American College of Obstetricians and Gynecologists, 27, 191, 199

Thurmon v. Sellers, 796

Tileston v. Ullman, 8

Tinker v. Des Moines Independent Community School District, 135, 159, 592, 973

Trammel v. United States, 765

Tremblay v. Carter, 796

Trombetta v. Conkling, 796

Trombley v. Starr-Wood Cardiac Group, P.C., 796

Troxel v. Granville, 588, 946, 1060

Trustees of Dartmouth College v. Woodward, 526

Trutalli v. Meraviglia, 790

Turner v. Safley, 281, 316, 1149, 1156, 1159, 1160

Turner v. Steiner, 906, 909

U.S. Department of Agriculture v. Moreno, 50, 91, 818

Ulane v. Eastern Airlines, Inc., 711, 1007

Union Pacific Ry. v. Botsford, 3

University of Pennsylvania v. EEOC, 1053

Urbano v. Cont'l Airlines, Inc., 630

V.C. v. M.J.B., 939, 959, 960

V.L. v. E.L., 895, 896

Vallera v. Vallera, 791

Van Ooteghem v. Gray, 84

Varnum v. Brien, 285

Veney v. Wyche, 1228

Vickers v. Fairfield Med. Ctr., 719

Victoria W. v. Larpenter, 1195

Villegas v. Metropolitan Gov't of Nashville, 1197
Virginia, United States v., **61**, 118, 121, **1040**, 1226, 1228
Vivid Entertainment, LLC v. Fielding, 263
Vorchheimer v. School Dist., 1039
Waldie v. Schlesinger, 1099
Washington v. Davis, 58, 820
Washington v. Glucksberg, 225, 781
Washington v. Harper, 1156, 1159, 1161
Washington v. Seattle School Dist. No. 1, 1159
Waters v. Ricketts, 901
Watkins v. United States Army, 85
Wayte v. United States, 1125
Weaver v. Nebo School District, 986
Weber v. Aetna Casualty & Surety Co., 54
Webster v. Reproductive Health Servs., 27
Weinberger v. Wiesenfeld, 59, 120, 321, 382
Wengler v. Druggists Mut. Ins. Co., 321
West Virginia Board of Education v. Barnette, 39, 143, 159, 176, 183, 508, 588
Whaley v. Whaley, 857
Wheaton College v. Burwell, 532, 533
Whitaker v. Kenosha Unified School District No. 1, **1004**
Whole Woman's Health v. Cole, 214
Whole Woman's Health v. Hellerstedt, **211**
Whole Woman's Health v. Lakey, 214
Whorton v. Dillingham, 795
Wicklund, In re Marriage of, 867
Widmar v. Vincent, 577
Wilkinson v. Austin, 1173, 1177
Williams v. Attorney General of Alabama, 249
Williams v. McNair, 1043
Williams v. North Carolina, 301
Williamson v. A.G. Edwards & Sons, Inc., 719
Williamson v. Lee Optical, Co., 49
Williams-Yulee v. Florida Bar, 221
Wilson v. Ake, 1226
Windsor v. United States, 1225
Windsor, United States v., **300**
Wisconsin v. Mitchell, 1125
Wisconsin v. Yoder, 144, 588
Witt v. Department of the Air Force, 1126
Women Prisoners of D.C. Dep't of Corr. v. Dist. of Columbia, 1200, 1202
Wood v. Davison, 132
Woodward v. United States, 1227
Wooley v. Maynard, 183

Wrightson v. Pizza Hut of America, 677
X.X.G. and N.R.G., In re Matter of Adoption of, 880
X-Citement Video, Inc., United States v., 842
Yates v. Stalder, 1161
Yick Wo v. Hopkins, 90, 238
Young v. United Parcel Service, Inc., **630**, 632
Yovino v. Big Bubba's BBQ, L.L.C., 796
Z.J.H., In re, 938
Zablocki v. Redhail, 280, 316, 1152
Zamecnik v. Indian Prairie School Dist. No. 204, 987
Zarda v. Altitude Express, 723
Zzyym v. Kerry, 498

SEXUALITY, GENDER, AND THE LAW

FOURTH EDITION

CHAPTER 1

CONSTITUTIONAL FRAMEWORKS: LIBERTY, EQUALITY, EXPRESSION

SECTION 1   Liberty and Its Limits
SECTION 2   Bounded Equality
SECTION 3   Expression and Identity

Chapter 1 sets the stage for the remainder of the book in two ways. First, it provides historical context for the rapidly increasing importance of sexuality and gender issues in American law, covering developments through approximately the end of the twentieth century. Second, it introduces you to the triple helix of constitutional doctrine that has dominated the field: the interwoven strands of liberty, equality, and expression. Each of the three sections of Chapter 1 analyzes one of these doctrinal strands. For each, consider the extent to which social movements for greater sexual freedom and gender equality have shaped the broader law in each area.

As an active reader, also try to identify additional themes in the materials. One example might be that courts have shifted away from enforcing the categorical rules that metaphorically banished deviants from the realm of law (such as the criminalization of sodomy and obscene speech) and toward incorporating greater use of the analogic reasoning and balancing tests that characterize all fields of constitutional doctrine. Or one might characterize the prevailing discursive tropes supporting repressive policies as shifting from sin to disease to traditional values, with a corresponding conceptual shift by those seeking greater freedom, from tolerance to therapy to rights. A third theme might be how legal and societal changes have affected understandings of the dynamic between (sexual) acts and (sexual) identities. Can you identify other cross-cutting themes?

SECTION 1

LIBERTY AND ITS LIMITS

The Fifth and Fourteenth Amendments prohibit "deprivation of . . . liberty without due process of law." Liberty, wrote Justice Stevens, is "one of the cardinal inalienable rights. . . . [the] basic freedom which the Due Process Clause protects." *Meacham v. Fano*, 427 U.S. 215, 230 (1976) (Stevens, J., dissenting). "Substantive due process" arose from the tension between liberty rights that may be inalienable, as Justice Stevens said, but also were unenumerated in the Constitution.

Beginning in the second half of the nineteenth century, courts began to recognize common law-based individual rights asserted against government intrusion into aspects of life that are central in some way to one's sense of selfhood. In *Union Pacific Ry. v. Botsford*, 141 U.S. 250, 251 (1891), the Supreme Court found that the "right to possession and control of [one's] own person" protected an individual litigant from having to undergo a forced medical examination. In 1897, the Supreme Court ruled that the inherent authority of states to preserve public order (known as the "police powers") was not a blank check, and that the Due Process Clause required courts to "look at the substance of things" when a statute was challenged. *Mugler v. Kansas*, 123 U.S. 623, 661 (1897). Thus was born the doctrine of substantive due process, the examination of whether a governmental action intruded too deeply into the realm of personal liberty, regardless of how much process (such as legislative debate and enactment) accompanied the law. The Court built substantive due process into a bridge too far in *Lochner v. New York*, 198 U.S. 45 (1905), by ruling that New York infringed the economy liberty rights of business owners with enactment of a maximum hours law. The Court later pulled back, and adopted the principle of combining deference to social and economic regulation, while reserving closer scrutiny for infringements of political and civil rights. See *Ferguson v. Skrupa*, 372 U.S. 726, 729–32 (1963).

In *Meyer v. Nebraska*, 262 U.S. 390 (1923), the Court struck down a law prohibiting the teaching of foreign languages except in high schools. Emphasizing the right of parents to control the education of their children, the Court described the "liberty" guaranteed by the Due Process Clause as follows:

> Without doubt it denotes not merely freedom from bodily restraint, but also the right of the individual to contract, to engage in any of the common occupations of life, to acquire useful knowledge, to marry, establish a home and bring up children, to worship God according to the dictates of his own conscience, and, generally, to enjoy those privileges long

3

recognized at common law as essential to the orderly pursuit of happiness by free men. (262 U.S. at 399.)

In *Pierce v. Society of Sisters*, 268 U.S. 510, 535 (1925), the Court struck down an Oregon law forbidding private schools, quoting the passage above and declaring that "[t]he fundamental theory of liberty * * * excludes any power of the state to standardize its children."

Meanwhile, the concept of privacy was also in its nascent years. An 1890 law review essay by Samuel Warren and Louis Brandeis that focused on tort law famously called for "a general right to privacy for thoughts, emotions, and sensations." "The Right to Privacy," 4 *Harv. L. Rev.* 193 (1890). As a Supreme Court Justice, Brandeis noted that the "makers of our Constitution undertook to secure conditions favorable to the pursuit of happiness." He pressed for "a right to be let alone" from government intrusion, "the most comprehensive of rights." *Olmstead v. United States*, 277 U.S. 438, 478 (1928) (dissenting from ruling that Fourth Amendment did not protect against wiretapping of telephone calls).

Thus, by the early decades of the twentieth century, the Supreme Court had established the principle that courts could evaluate the substantive weight of liberty interests as compared to the state's goals, when assessing the constitutionality of government actions. The Court denominated the most important personal liberties as fundamental rights, the abridgement of which required that the government demonstrate a compelling state interest served by a narrowly tailored restriction on liberty.

As Justice Brandeis had hoped, one branch of fundamental rights law became known as the right to privacy. In the realm of sexuality, the articulation of a right to privacy grew directly out of the birth control movement. More than any other individual, Margaret Sanger—that movement's founder—transformed a demand for women's bodily autonomy into a liberty right protected by the Constitution.

A. CONTROLS ON CONTRACEPTION

Margaret Higgins Sanger was born to a poor Irish family in Corning, New York in 1879. Convinced that her mother's ill health and eventual death resulted from bearing eleven children, Sanger developed a fierce belief in women's right to sexual and reproductive autonomy. For her, the means to this end were legalized birth control and greater public candor about sexuality. A nurse before she became a reformer, Sanger attacked a social structure that denied information to women about even simple methods of birth control. Lacking the power to control pregnancy led to enormous hardships for women, ranging from the economic strain of large families to early death or impaired health.

Sanger's first writings about sex education were published in *The Call*, a socialist newspaper. Sanger soon started her own magazine, *The*

Woman Rebel, which led to a federal indictment in 1914 for sending indecent material through the mails. Sanger was charged under the Comstock law, a federal obscenity statute. While under indictment, Sanger wrote and disseminated *Family Limitation*, a pamphlet detailing birth control methods and encouraging women to seek their own gratification in heterosexual relations. At the time, prosecutions under the federal Comstock law and analogous state obscenity statutes were common. Sanger fled to Europe to avoid arrest. There she worked with sexologist Havelock Ellis and other reformers, and visited the world's first birth control clinic in the Netherlands. Upon her return the following year, growing public sympathy for the birth control movement led the U.S. Attorney's office to drop the charges against her.

1. *NEW YORK V. SANGER*

Sanger opened the first birth control clinic in the United States in 1916 in Brooklyn, New York. She notified local press and police, and distributed announcements that read: "Mothers! Can you afford to have a large family? Do you want any more children? If not, why do you have them? Do not kill, Do not take life, But Prevent. Safe, harmless information can be obtained of trained nurses. * * * All mothers welcome." After nine days of providing services, during which 464 women came for help, Sanger and her staff were arrested for violating the New York obscenity law. Sanger decided to seek change by constitutional challenges to the laws rather than by lobbying legislatures.

Sanger's trial drew enormous public attention, including a rally at Carnegie Hall. The courtroom was packed each day with press, clinic patients, and wealthy society women whom Sanger had adroitly solicited for financial support. Both the prosecution and the defense relied on former patients as witnesses, with the District Attorney eliciting testimony that women visited the clinic to "have her stop the babies," and Sanger's attorney having them describe their experiences of miscarriages, sickness, and poverty.

The New York obscenity statute under which she was prosecuted made it a misdemeanor "to sell, or give away, or to advertise or offer for sale, any instrument or article, drug or medicine, for the prevention of conception, or to give information orally, stating when, where, or how such an instrument, article, or medicine can be purchased or obtained." The law contained an exception under which physicians could provide contraceptives to prevent or cure "disease." Previously, this exception had applied only to venereal disease and the distribution of condoms. "In that case," Sanger wrote, "the intent was to protect the man. * * * I wanted the interpretation to be broadened into the intent to protect women from ill health as the result of excessive childbearing and, equally important, to have the right to control their own destinies."

Sanger was convicted, and served 30 days in a women's prison. New York's highest court affirmed, but interpreted "disease" to be broadly defined as "any alteration in the state of body which caused or threatened pain or sickness." *People v. Sanger*, 222 N.Y. 192, 118 N.E. 637, 638 (1918). This ruling expanded the meaning of "disease" to include pregnancy in addition to sexually transmitted diseases. With this decision, Sanger achieved one of her goals, although indirectly by statutory rather than constitutional interpretation. Her lawyers pressed for review in the Supreme Court in an effort to secure a ruling that would allow birth control services for non-health reasons as well, arguing in their brief that "compulsory motherhood" violated women's right to liberty as ensured by the Due Process Clause. The Supreme Court dismissed the appeal. 251 U.S. 537 (1919) (*per curiam*).

You ought to be ashamed, I said, to look so antique.
(And her only thirty-one)
I can't help it, she said, pulling a long face.
It's them pills I took, to bring it off, she said.
(She's had five already, and nearly died of young George.)
The chemist said it would be all right, but I've never been the same.
You are a proper fool, I said.
Well, if Albert won't leave you alone, there it is, I said.
What you get married for if you don't want children?

T.S. Eliot, *The Waste Land* (1922)

2.   SANGER, EARLY FEMINISTS AND "DOCTORS ONLY"

In the early twentieth century, the women's movement divided between the suffragist wing, which sought equality in public realms such as voting and employment, and maternalist or welfare feminism, which emphasized the special needs of mothers and young children. For both, sexual propriety was an important characteristic of the respectable woman.

Sanger and her allies upset feminists in both camps by arguing that women had a right to heterosexual gratification: "a mutual and satisfied sexual act is of great benefit to the average woman." The very technology of diaphragms (the only birth control available at the time for use by women) was controversial: their *only* function was to prevent conception, rather than infections. Diaphragms were the first birth control technology to enable women to affirmatively engage in intercourse for pleasure and intimacy, without fear of pregnancy.

Using the "disease" exception recognized by the New York court, Sanger developed a "doctors only" strategy, based on a two-part compromise: access to birth control would be made available only by prescription, but doctors' discretion to prescribe would be expanded. This approach created an important alliance between feminists and supportive elements of the medical profession, and dominated birth control reform strategy for decades. Restricting access through physician intermediaries also reassured those who feared that easier access would facilitate sexual freedom for women, especially outside of marriage. (Sanger's lawyers had conceded that the New York law was a reasonable regulation in its application to unmarried women.) The downside of this strategy was that it encouraged the pathologizing of contraception, reinforced an income barrier for women who could not afford doctors, and dampened consciousness of birth control as a political issue. Despite—or because of—its shortcomings, the "doctors only" argument largely succeeded.

The African-American community took a different approach. In 1918, the Women's Political Association of Harlem included birth control as a topic in its lecture series. In 1919, W.E.B. DuBois published an essay arguing that a woman "must have the right of motherhood at her own discretion." Black community organizations started and supported birth control clinics throughout the United States, and debate about whether birth control was good for the community or destructive of its future was a common theme in the African-American press. In 1941, the National Council of Negro Women became the first national women's organization to endorse birth control. Its resolution argued that birth control should be used to help families have as many children as they could afford. Racial betterment, rather than individual freedom, was the predominant theme of birth control advocates within the African-American community.

Less successfully, Mary Ware Dennett, a rival of Sanger's in the birth control movement, opposed the concept of a doctors only exception because it left contraceptive information classified as obscene. Dennett unsuccessfully attempted to repeal first the New York obscenity statute and then the federal Comstock Law as those laws applied to contraception.

Issues of racism muddied the debates from the beginning. Some birth control supporters in the North seized the argument that providing access to birth control for the poor would help curb population growth among immigrants. Birth control opponents made racist claims from a different angle, asserting that because upper-class women were more likely to use birth control, the "fit" stock would die off. Southern racists were divided. Some southern state agencies offered contraceptive services to whites only; others funded birth control selectively for African-Americans as a method of limiting growth in the black population. Opponents from the left argued that the duty of women, especially in minority racial and ethnic groups, was to bear children.

Meanwhile, birth control advocates gained greater breathing space in the law. In 1930, the Second Circuit reversed Dennett's obscenity conviction for having mailed copies of a sex education pamphlet she had written for her own two children. *United States v. Dennett*, 39 F.2d 564 (2d Cir.1930). The *Dennett* decision cleared the way for development of formal sex education curricula. The same court then held that physicians' goal of promoting health, including by importing diaphragms, was not "immoral" under the Comstock law. *United States v. One Package*, 86 F.2d 737 (2d Cir.1936). *One Package* effectively removed all federal law obstacles limiting private physicians' access to birth control information and supplies.

Starting in the Depression years of the 1930s, pressure mounted on government agencies to include birth control information in their services for the poor and as part of public health programs. Funding for contraception began under the Federal Emergency Relief Administration, Title V of the Social Security Act of 1938 (for maternal and child health services), and the Venereal Disease Control Act of 1939. Implementation of the legislation occurred only after Eleanor Roosevelt intervened with agency officials, however. These laws were the forerunners of Title X of the Public Health Service Act (introduced by then Representative George H.W. Bush and signed by President Richard Nixon in 1970). Title X assured federal monetary support for family planning by unmarried as well as married persons.

At the state level, birth control advocates invoked the reasoning of *One Package* to challenge the constitutionality of statutes that prohibited access to birth control information and devices. By 1960, Massachusetts and Connecticut were the only states left with statutes that banned contraception without providing for a physician exception. The first birth control case to reach the U.S. Supreme Court was *Tileston v. Ullman*, 318 U.S. 44 (1943) (*per curiam*). The plaintiff in that case was a doctor who argued that the Connecticut statute prevented him from providing health-and life-saving medical advice to his patients. *Tileston* presented the Court with Sanger's doctor-oriented arguments, but the Court skirted the substantive issue. The Court ruled instead that Tileston did not assert a harm personal to himself and did not have standing to assert the rights of third parties, his patients.

In the next case, *Poe v. Ullman*, plaintiffs were married women who asserted that they were denied needed medical advice by the statute. This case reflected a fusion of Sanger's doctors only strategy with the early privacy cases based on rights of the women plaintiffs, and it met the standing requirements of *Tileston*. The Supreme Court still declined to reach the merits, this time on ripeness grounds, but Justice Harlan's dissent was a breakthrough for birth control arguments. (See below.) The Court finally reached the merits in the third Connecticut contraception case that came before it, *Griswold v. Connecticut*, decided almost 50 years after Margaret Sanger served her 30-day prison sentence.

Paul and Pauline Poe et al. v. Abraham Ullman

United States Supreme Court, 1961.
367 U.S. 497, 81 S.Ct. 1752, 6 L.Ed.2d 989.

■ [MR. JUSTICE FRANKFURTER announced the judgment of the Court, holding that the lawsuit was not ripe for adjudication because the plaintiffs were not prevented from obtaining and using contraceptives. He relied on the availability of contraceptives in Connecticut drug stores and on his belief that only one person had ever been arrested under the 1879 law, and no one recently.]

■ MR. JUSTICE HARLAN, dissenting. [Justice Harlan began his argument by asserting that the Due Process Clause safeguards more than procedural rights.]* * *

Due process has not been reduced to any formula; its content cannot be determined by reference to any code. The best that can be said is that through the course of this Court's decisions it has represented the balance which our Nation, built upon postulates of respect for the liberty of the individual, has struck between that liberty and the demands of organized society. * * * No formula could serve as a substitute, in this area, for judgment and restraint.

It is this outlook which has led the Court continuously to perceive distinctions in the imperative character of Constitutional provisions, since that character must be discerned from a particular provision's larger context. And inasmuch as this context is one not of words, but of history and purposes, the full scope of the liberty guaranteed by the Due Process Clause cannot be found in or limited by the precise terms of the specific guarantees elsewhere provided in the Constitution. This "liberty" is not a series of isolated points pricked out * * *. It is a rational continuum which, broadly speaking, includes a freedom from all substantial arbitrary impositions and purposeless restraints, and which also recognizes, what a reasonable and sensitive judgment must, that certain interests require particularly careful scrutiny of the state needs asserted to justify their abridgment.

* * * For it is the purposes of those guarantees and not their text, the reasons for their statement by the Framers and not the statement itself, which have led to their present status in the compendious notion of "liberty" embraced in the Fourteenth Amendment.

* * * [T]he very inclusion of the category of morality among state concerns indicates that society is not limited in its objects only to the physical well-being of the community, but has traditionally concerned itself with the moral soundness of its people as well. Indeed to attempt a line between public behavior and that which is purely consensual or solitary would be to withdraw from community concern a range of subjects with which every society in civilized times has found it necessary to deal. The laws regarding marriage which provide both when the sexual powers may be used and the legal and societal context in which children

are born and brought up, as well as laws forbidding adultery, fornication and homosexual practices which express the negative of the proposition, confining sexuality to lawful marriage, form a pattern so deeply pressed into the substance of our social life that any Constitutional doctrine in this area must build upon that basis.

It is in this area of sexual morality, which contains many proscriptions of consensual behavior having little or no direct impact on others, that the State of Connecticut has expressed its moral judgment that all use of contraceptives is improper. Appellants cite an impressive list of authorities who, from a great variety of points of view, commend the considered use of contraceptives by married couples. What they do not emphasize is that not too long ago the current of opinion was very probably quite the opposite, and that even today the issue is not free of controversy. Certainly, Connecticut's judgment is no more demonstrably correct or incorrect than are the varieties of judgment, expressed in law, on marriage and divorce, on adult consensual homosexuality, abortion, and sterilization, or euthanasia and suicide. If we had a case before us which required us to decide simply, and in abstraction, whether the moral judgment implicit in the application of the present statute to married couples was a sound one, the very controversial nature of these questions would, I think, require us to hesitate long before concluding that the Constitution precluded Connecticut from choosing as it has among these various views.

* * * Precisely what is involved here is this: the State is asserting the right to enforce its moral judgment by intruding upon the most intimate details of the marital relation with the full power of the criminal law. Potentially, this could allow the deployment of all the incidental machinery of the criminal law, arrests, searches and seizures; inevitably, it must mean at the very least the lodging of criminal charges, a public trial, and testimony as to the *corpus delicti*. Nor could any imaginable elaboration of presumptions, testimonial privileges, or other safeguards, alleviate the necessity for testimony as to the mode and manner of the married couples' sexual relations, or at least the opportunity for the accused to make denial of the charges. In sum, the statute allows the State to enquire into, prove and punish married people for the private use of their marital intimacy.

This, then, is the precise character of the enactment whose Constitutional measure we must take. The statute must pass a more rigorous Constitutional test than that going merely to the plausibility of its underlying rationale. This enactment involves what, by common understanding throughout the English-speaking world, must be granted to be a most fundamental aspect of "liberty," the privacy of the home in its most basic sense, and it is this which requires that the statute be subjected to "strict scrutiny." [*Skinner v. Oklahoma*, 316 U.S. 535, 541 (1942)]. * * *

Of course, just as the requirement of a warrant is not inflexible in carrying out searches and seizures, so there are countervailing considerations at this more fundamental aspect of the right involved. "[T]he family * * * is not beyond regulation," *Prince v. Massachusetts*, [321 U.S. 158, 166 (1944)], and it would be an absurdity to suggest either that offenses may not be committed in the bosom of the family or that the home can be made a sanctuary for crime. The right of privacy most manifestly is not an absolute. Thus, I would not suggest that adultery, homosexuality, fornication and incest are immune from criminal enquiry, however privately practiced. So much has been explicitly recognized in acknowledging the State's rightful concern for its people's moral welfare. But not to discriminate between what is involved in this case and either the traditional offenses against good morals or crimes which, though they may be committed anywhere, happen to have been committed or concealed in the home, would entirely misconceive the argument that is being made.

Adultery, homosexuality and the like are sexual intimacies which the State forbids altogether, but the intimacy of husband and wife is necessarily an essential and accepted feature of the institution of marriage, an institution which the State not only must allow, but which always and in every age it has fostered and protected. It is one thing when the State exerts its power either to forbid extra-marital sexuality altogether, or to say who may marry, but it is quite another when, having acknowledged a marriage and the intimacies inherent in it, it undertakes to regulate by means of the criminal law the details of that intimacy.

In sum, even though the State has determined that the use of contraceptives is as iniquitous as any act of extra-marital sexual immorality, the intrusion of the whole machinery of the criminal law into the very heart of marital privacy, requiring husband and wife to render account before a criminal tribunal of their uses of that intimacy, is surely a very different thing indeed from punishing those who establish intimacies which the law has always forbidden and which can have no claim to social protection. * * *

Estelle Griswold et al. v. Connecticut

United States Supreme Court, 1965.
381 U.S. 479, 85 S.Ct. 1678, 14 L.Ed.2d 510.

■ JUSTICE DOUGLAS delivered the opinion of the Court [striking down the 1879 Connecticut law prohibiting the sale or use of contraceptives].

[W]e are met with a wide range of questions that implicate the Due Process Clause of the Fourteenth Amendment. * * * This law * * * operates directly on an intimate relation of husband and wife and their physician's role in one aspect of that relation.

The association of people is not mentioned in the Constitution nor in the Bill of Rights. The right to educate a child in a school of the parents' choice—whether public or private or parochial—is also not mentioned. Nor is the right to study any particular subject or any foreign language. Yet the First Amendment has been construed to include certain of those rights. [The Court then reviewed *Meyer v. Nebraska* and *Pierce v. Society of Sisters*, as well as First Amendment cases dealing with freedom of association.]

The foregoing cases suggest that specific guarantees in the Bill of Rights have penumbras, formed by emanations from those guarantees that help give them life and substance. Various guarantees create zones of privacy. * * *

The Fourth and Fifth Amendments were described in *Boyd v. United States*, 116 U.S. 616, 630, as protection against all governmental invasions "of the sanctity of a man's home and the privacies of life." We recently referred in *Mapp v. Ohio*, 367 U.S. 643, 656, to the Fourth Amendment as creating a "right to privacy, no less important than any other right carefully and particularly reserved to the people." * * *

The present case, then, concerns a relationship lying within the zone of privacy created by several fundamental constitutional guarantees. And it concerns a law which, in forbidding the use of contraceptives rather than regulating their manufacture or sale, seeks to achieve its goals by means having a maximum destructive impact upon that relationship. Such a law cannot stand in light of the familiar principle, so often applied by this Court, that a "governmental purpose to control or prevent activities constitutionally subject to state regulation may not be achieved by means which sweep unnecessarily broadly and thereby invade the area of protected freedoms." *NAACP v. Alabama*, 377 U.S. 288, 307. Would we allow the police to search the sacred precincts of marital bedrooms for telltale signs of the use of contraceptives? The very idea is repulsive to the notions of privacy surrounding the marriage relationship.

We deal with a right of privacy older than the Bill of Rights—older than our political parties, older than our school system. Marriage is a coming together for better or for worse, hopefully enduring, and intimate to the degree of being sacred. It is an association that promotes a way of life, not causes; a harmony in living, not political faiths; a bilateral loyalty, not commercial or social projects. Yet it is an association for as noble a purpose as any involved in our prior decisions. * * *

■ JUSTICE GOLDBERG, joined by CHIEF JUSTICE WARREN and JUSTICE BRENNAN, concurred.

* * * The language and history of the Ninth Amendment reveal that the Framers of the Constitution believed that there are additional fundamental rights, protected from governmental infringement, which exist alongside those fundamental rights specifically mentioned in the first eight constitutional amendments. * * *

I [do not] mean to state that the Ninth Amendment constitutes an independent source of rights protected from infringement by either the States or the Federal Government. Rather, the Ninth Amendment shows a belief of the Constitution's authors that fundamental rights exist that are not expressly enumerated in the first eight amendments and an intent that the list of rights included there not be deemed exhaustive. * * *

In determining which rights are fundamental, judges are not left at large to decide cases in light of their personal and private notions. Rather, they must look to the 'traditions and (collective) conscience of our people' to determine whether a principle is 'so rooted (there) * * * as to be ranked as fundamental.' The inquiry is whether a right involved is of such a character that it cannot be denied without violating those 'fundamental principles of liberty and justice which lie at the base of all our civil and political institutions' * * *

* * * Of this whole 'private realm of family life' it is difficult to imagine what is more private or more intimate than a husband and wife's marital relations.

The entire fabric of the Constitution and the purposes that clearly underlie its specific guarantees demonstrate that the rights to marital privacy and to marry and raise a family are of similar order and magnitude as the fundamental rights specifically protected.

* * * The fact that no particular provision of the Constitution explicitly forbids the State from disrupting the traditional relation of the family—a relation as old and as fundamental as our entire civilization—surely does not show that the Government was meant to have the power to do so. Rather, as the Ninth Amendment expressly recognizes, there are fundamental personal rights such as this one, which are protected from abridgment by the Government though not specifically mentioned in the Constitution. * * *

In sum, I believe that the right of privacy in the marital relation is fundamental and basic-a personal right 'retained by the people' within the meaning of the Ninth Amendment. * * *

■ [JUSTICE HARLAN concurred in the Court's judgment, and largely repeated his dissenting opinion in *Poe v. Ullman.*]

■ JUSTICE WHITE, concurring in the judgment.

* * * [T]he statute is said to serve the State's policy against all forms of promiscuous or illicit sexual relationships, be they premarital or extramarital, concededly a permissible and legitimate legislative goal.

Without taking issue with the premise that the fear of conception operates as a deterrent to such relationships in addition to the criminal proscriptions Connecticut has against such conduct, I wholly fail to see how the ban on the use of contraceptives by married couples in any way reinforces the State's ban on illicit sexual relationships. Connecticut does not bar the importation or possession of contraceptive devices; they are not considered contraband material under state law, and their availability in that State is not seriously disputed. The only way Connecticut seeks to limit or control the availability of such devices is through its general aiding and abetting statute whose operation in this context has been quite obviously ineffective and whose most serious use has been against birth-control clinics rendering advice to married, rather than unmarried, persons. * * *

In these circumstances one is rather hard pressed to explain how the ban on use by married persons in any way prevents use of such devices by persons engaging in illicit sexual relations and thereby contributes to the State's policy against such relationships. Neither the state courts nor the State before the bar of this Court has tendered such an explanation. It is purely fanciful to believe that the broad proscription on use facilitates discovery of use by persons engaging in a prohibited relationship or for some other reason makes such use more unlikely and thus can be supported by any sort of administrative consideration. * * * At most the broad ban is of marginal utility to the declared objective. * * * I find nothing in this record justifying the sweeping scope of this statute, with its telling effect on the freedoms of married persons, and therefore conclude that it deprives such persons of liberty without due process of law.

■ [The dissenting opinions of JUSTICE BLACK and JUSTICE STEWART objected to the Court's creation of a constitutional right to "privacy" that is not moored in a firmer constitutional text. Although JUSTICE STEWART found this an "uncommonly silly law," he and JUSTICE BLACK found that it did not violate any provision of the Constitution.]

NOTES ON *GRISWOLD* AND THE RIGHT OF SEXUAL PRIVACY

1. *What Was the Best Constitutional Basis for the Result in* Griswold? In particular, which opinion best states a constitutional basis for a right of privacy? How do the jurisprudential approaches of Justices Douglas, Goldberg, and Harlan differ? All three approaches create a right that is not clearly instantiated in the Constitution's text. Douglas' penumbral theory is the most creative, for he implies an underlying constitutional right from the emanations of existing provisions. Goldberg's reliance on the Ninth Amendment is only slightly less creative. Although he relies on actual text in the Constitution, the Ninth Amendment is worded as a residual "catch-all" provision, difficult to delineate. Harlan's invocation of the Due Process Clause likewise relies on a specific provision, but expands text that on its face refers only to process into a substantive provision with considerable constitutional bite.

Critics have accused the Court of becoming a "super-legislature" with this decision (see the Bork excerpt following these notes). Which approach (penumbras, Ninth Amendment, due process) best avoids this difficulty by tying the Court's decision to "principled" criteria that have a defensible connection to the Constitution? What do you think of Justice White's focus on the irrationality of the means? What are the pro's and con's of a broader opinion?

2. *The Justices' Reticence About Sex.* In a part of Justice Goldberg's concurrence that we did not excerpt, he remarked that "it may shock some of my Brethren that the Court today holds that the Constitution protects the right of marital privacy." Note that the Court employs numerous euphemisms referring to sexual relations. The opinion stops just short of holding that the right of spouses to sexual relations is a fundamental right. Indeed, explicitness may be part of the problem. Perhaps one reason *Griswold* is so frustratingly vague is that the Court could not bring itself to be sexually explicit. What is *Griswold* primarily about? Marriage? Sex? Procreation?

3. *The Claim to Sexual Freedom.* The briefs in the case were more direct. The petitioners' brief argued that "the inner core of the privacy right" lay in "the sanctity of the home and the intimacies of the sexual relationship in marriage." The briefs in *Griswold* apparently drew on the language of some of the briefs that had been filed in *Poe*. The *Poe* briefs were the first to articulate a right of privacy for "sexual union and the right to bear and raise a family." In *Poe*, the petitioner's brief, written by Fowler Harper of the Yale Law School (formerly a colleague of Professor Alfred Kinsey, who authored the famous empirical studies of sex in America), argued that "sexual pleasure" is an important end in itself, and frustration of one's preferred sexual outlet, by the state or otherwise, is psychologically harmful to the individual as well as the family. The ACLU amicus brief, written by Melvin Wulf, argued that the Connecticut law forced married couples to choose between planning the size of their family and engaging in sexual intercourse, which "is no choice at all."

In *Griswold*, counsel for Planned Parenthood represented the petitioner. Planned Parenthood's brief in *Poe* had centered on the rights of doctors, but in its *Griswold* brief, the organization switched directions, beginning its brief with a claim for "privacy," based on Harlan's dissent. The *Griswold* brief referred repeatedly to sexual relations and the "sex drive," cited Kinsey's study on sexuality, and argued that restricting sexual intercourse to procreation is not a legitimate state purpose. Like the earlier briefs, it carefully linked sexuality to marriage, however. The brief framed the privacy right as one to engage in marital sexual relations *and* to make a conscious decision about whether to have children. Given the one-way operation of the statute, the phrasing about decisionmaking is euphemistic for having sexual relations and *not* having children. The *Griswold* briefs marked a major reframing of reproductive rights arguments, with less emphasis on doctors and more on the privacy rights of the individuals seeking care.

4. *Marriage and Sex: Estoppel Against the State?* Are there other contexts in which the state recognizes a right to sexual relations in marriage? And indeed enforces it? "The point is that the state has undertaken to sponsor one institution that has at its core the love-sex relationship. That relationship demands liberty in the practice of the sexual act." Harry Wellington, "Common Law Rules and Constitutional Double Standards:

Some Notes on Adjudication," 83 *Yale L.J.* 221, 292 (1973). The practical import of the Connecticut statute would be to force married couples to modify the frequency of intercourse in order to avoid pregnancy, a result which, according to Wellington, "smacks of fraud." *Id.* at 293.

5.   *"Safer Sex" for Women? The Forgotten Equality Argument.* In today's terms, we might refer to birth control as "safer sex" for heterosexual women. Is a sex discrimination claim possible on the facts of *Griswold*? If so what would it be? Why was its possibility not mentioned in either *Griswold* or *Poe*? See Section 2A, *infra*, for a discussion of sex discrimination law at that time.

6.   *The Public-Private Dynamic and the Role of Clinics.* The problem that the plaintiffs in both the Connecticut cases had in formulating a test case was that there had never been a prosecution against private doctors for violating the law, although their activities in prescribing contraceptives were well known. Nor had any but a few been prosecuted for purchasing condoms. What the law did succeed in doing, however, was to prevent the establishment of an openly operating birth control clinic in Connecticut.

Note several ironies. The right recognized in *Griswold* purports to protect "private" sphere activities in the spirit of John Stuart Mill and Louis Brandeis. Because the contraceptive gendarmerie did not patrol bedrooms and contraceptives were available in drug stores, the private sphere (the marital bedroom) was essentially unregulated, leaving only the public sphere (birth control clinics) to actual regulation. But look again. The public sphere for men's access to condoms was apparently not policed; only the clinics (which prescribed diaphragms and pills for women) were. Most women in Connecticut found it hard to practice birth control (private sphere) without access to birth control clinics that could provide information (public sphere). A final look: The Roman Catholic Church, which had spearheaded political opposition to repealing anti-contraception laws, believed that the anti-procreation features of contraception (private sphere) had profound implications for the institution of marriage and religious community (public sphere). In the Church's view, the availability of contraception, whether private or public, undermined the private as well as public (procreative) goals of marriage. In short, the concept of "privacy" is easy to deconstruct. Does this ease of deconstruction vitiate the usefulness of the concept?

PROBLEM 1-1
SEX, LAW, AND PUBLIC POLICY

Imagine yourself to be an AIDS activist in the 1980s. A scary new sexually transmitted disease is generating proposals for repressive laws. Some proposals include (a) registration of persons infected with the HIV virus that causes AIDS; (b) closure of "bath houses" where gay men were known to engage in sexual activities that posed high risks of infection; and (c) mandatory HIV testing for the adult population or some subset. Compare the role of AIDS lawyers in the 1980s to that of birth control lawyers in earlier decades. How do you frame your arguments on behalf of persons with this disease? What are the advantages and disadvantages of invoking medical expertise? Consider how the strategies of the birth control movement evolved from 1916 to the 1960s—do any carry over to AIDS legal work? How do the strands of the triple helix of legal concepts—liberty, equality and expression—play out in the context of AIDS?

3. FOUNDATIONAL CRITIQUES OF THE RIGHT OF PRIVACY

Probably the most controversial debate triggered by *Griswold* has been that over what process the judiciary should use to identify and recognize a substantive due process right, *i.e.*, an intrinsic component of liberty under the Due Process Clause. Since 1937, the Court has defined those rights as "implicit in the concept of ordered liberty . . . principle[s] of justice so rooted in the traditions and conscience of our people as to be ranked as fundamental." *Palko v. Connecticut*, 302 U.S. 319, 325 (1937). Debate soon arose, and continues today, over how to identify the "traditions" of American "liberty" and thereby recognized fundamental substantive rights.

The primary academic criticism of *Griswold* came from Professor, later Judge, Robert Bork, who wrote a scathing critique of it as an "unprincipled" decision.

Robert Bork, "Neutral Principles and Some First Amendment Problems"
47 *Indiana Law Journal* 1, 8–9 (1971).*

[In *Griswold*, Justice Douglas] performed a miracle of transsubstantiation. He called the first amendment's penumbra a protection of "privacy." He had no better reason to use the word "privacy" than that the individual is free within these zones, free to act in public as well as in private. None of these penumbral zones—from the first, third, fourth or fifth amendments, all of which he cited, along with the ninth—covered the case before him. One more leap was required. Justice Douglas asserted that these various "zones of privacy" created an independent right of privacy, a right not lying within the penumbra of any specific amendment. He did not disclose, however, how a series of specified rights combined to create a new and unspecified right. * * *

Griswold, then, is an unprincipled decision, both in the way in which it derives a new constitutional right and in the way it defines that right, or rather fails to define it. We are left with no idea of the sweep of the right of privacy and hence no notion of the cases to which it may or may not be applied in the future. * * *

One of my colleagues refers to [the Court's] conclusion, not without sarcasm, as the "Equal Gratification Clause." The phrase is apt, and I accept it, though not the sarcasm. Equality of human gratifications, where the document does not impose a hierarchy, is an essential part of constitutional doctrine because of the necessity that judges be principled.

---

*   Copyright 1971 Indiana Law Journal. Reprinted by permission.

To be perfectly clear on the subject, I repeat that the principle is not applicable to legislatures. Legislation requires value choice and cannot be principled in the sense under discussion. Courts must accept any value choice the legislature makes unless it clearly runs contrary to a choice made in the framing of the Constitution.

* * * In *Lochner*, Justice Peckham, defending liberty from what he conceived as a mere meddlesome interference, asked, "[A]re we all . . . at the mercy of legislative majorities?" The correct answer, where the Constitution does not speak, must be "yes." * * *

In the following case, consider how the Court handles the issue of whether a right of sexual privacy exists outside of marriage. How does Justice Brennan's opinion sidestep the conflict between traditional state regulation of morality and a right to engage in private sexual conduct?

Thomas Eisenstadt v. William Baird

United States Supreme Court, 1972.
405 U.S. 438, 92 S.Ct. 1029, 31 L.Ed.2d 349.

■ JUSTICE BRENNAN delivered the opinion of the Court.

Appellee William Baird was convicted * * * first, for exhibiting contraceptive articles in the course of delivering a lecture on contraception to a group of students at Boston University and, second, for giving a young woman a package of Emko vaginal foam at the close of his address. * * *

[The relevant state statutes] make it a felony for anyone, other than a registered physician or pharmacist * * * to dispense any article with the intention that it be used for the prevention of conception. The statutory scheme distinguishes among three distinct classes of distributees—first, married persons may obtain contraceptives to prevent pregnancy, but only from doctors or druggists on prescription; second, single persons may not obtain contraceptives from anyone to prevent pregnancy; and, third, married or single persons may obtain contraceptives from anyone to prevent, not pregnancy, but the spread of disease. This construction of state law is, of course, binding on us.

The legislative purposes that the statute is meant to serve are not altogether clear. In *Commonwealth v. Baird*, [247 N.E.2d 574, 578 (1969)], the [Massachusetts] Supreme Judicial Court noted only the State's interest in protecting the health of its citizens * * * In a subsequent decision, *Sturgis v. Attorney General*, 260 N.E.2d 687, 690 (1970), the court, however, found "a second and more compelling ground for upholding the statute"—namely, to protect morals through "regulating the private sexual lives of single persons." The [U.S.]Court of Appeals, for reasons that will appear, did not consider the promotion of health or the protection of morals through the deterrence of fornication to be the legislative aim. Instead, the court concluded that the statutory goal was to limit contraception in and of itself—a purpose that the court held conflicted "with fundamental human rights" under *Griswold* * * *

We agree that the goals of deterring premarital sex and regulating the distribution of potentially harmful articles cannot reasonably be regarded as legislative aims of §§ 21 and 21A. And we hold that the statute, viewed as a prohibition on contraception *per se*, violates the rights of single persons under the Equal Protection Clause of the Fourteenth Amendment. * * *

* * * The question for our determination in this case is whether there is some ground of difference that rationally explains the different treatment accorded married and unmarried persons under Massachusetts General Laws Ann., c. 272, §§ 21 and 21A. For the reasons that follow, we conclude that no such ground exists.

First. Section 21 stems from Mass. Stat. 1879, c. 159, § 1, which prohibited without exception, distribution of articles intended to be used as contraceptives. In [1917], the Massachusetts Supreme Judicial Court explained that the law's "plain purpose is to protect purity, to preserve chastity, to encourage continence and self restraint, to defend the sanctity of the home, and thus to engender in the State and nation a virile and virtuous race of men and women." Although the State clearly abandoned that purpose with the enactment of § 21A, at least insofar as the illicit sexual activities of married persons are concerned, the court reiterated in *Sturgis*, that the object of the legislation is to discourage premarital sexual intercourse. Conceding that the State could, consistently with the Equal Protection Clause, regard the problems of extramarital and premarital sexual relations as "[e]vils . . . of different dimensions and proportions, requiring different remedies," we cannot agree that the deterrence of premarital sex may reasonably be regarded as the purpose of the Massachusetts law. * * *

* * * Even conceding the legislature a full measure of discretion in fashioning means to prevent fornication, and recognizing that the State may seek to deter prohibited conduct by punishing more severely those who facilitate than those who actually engage in its commission, we, like the Court of Appeals, cannot believe that in this instance Massachusetts has chosen to expose the aider and abetter who simply *gives away* a contraceptive to *20* times the *90-day* sentence of the offender himself. The very terms of the State's criminal statutes, coupled with the *de minimis* effect of §§ 21 and 21A in deterring fornication, thus compel the conclusion that such deterrence cannot reasonably be taken as the purpose of the ban on distribution of contraceptives to unmarried persons.

Second. Section 21A was added to the Massachusetts General Laws by Stat. 1966, c. 265, § 1. The Supreme Judicial Court in *Baird* held that the purpose of the amendment was to serve the health needs of the community by regulating the distribution of potentially harmful articles.

It is plain that Massachusetts had no such purpose in mind before the enactment of § 21A. As the Court of Appeals remarked, "Consistent with the fact that the statute was contained in a chapter dealing with 'Crimes Against Chastity, Morality, Decency and Good Order,' it was cast only in terms of morals. A physician was forbidden to prescribe contraceptives even when needed for the protection of health." Nor did the Court of Appeals "believe that the legislature [in enacting § 21A] suddenly reversed its field and developed an interest in health. Rather, it merely made what it thought to be the precise accommodation necessary to escape the *Griswold* ruling." * * *

Third. If the Massachusetts statute cannot be upheld as a deterrent to fornication or as a health measure, may it, nevertheless, be sustained simply as a prohibition on contraception? The Court of Appeals analysis "led inevitably to the conclusion that, so far as morals are concerned, it is contraceptives *per se* that are considered immoral." 429 F.2d 1398, 1401–02 (1st Cir. 1970). [The Court of Appeals upheld a fundamental right to contraception that the state cannot invade.] We need not, however, decide that important question in this case because, whatever the rights of the individual to access to contraceptives may be, the rights must be the same for the unmarried and the married alike.

If under *Griswold* the distribution of contraceptives to married persons cannot be prohibited, a ban on distribution to unmarried persons would be equally impermissible. It is true that in *Griswold* the right of privacy in question inhered in the marital relationship. Yet the marital couple is not an independent entity with a mind and heart of its own, but an association of two individuals each with a separate intellectual and emotional makeup. If the right of privacy means anything, it is the right of the *individual*, married or single, to be free from unwarranted governmental intrusion into matters so fundamentally affecting a person as the decision whether to bear or beget a child.

On the other hand, if *Griswold* is no bar to a prohibition on the distribution of contraceptives, the State could not, consistently with the Equal Protection Clause, outlaw distribution to unmarried but not to married persons. In each case the evil, as perceived by the State, would be identical, and the underinclusion would be invidious. * * * We hold that by providing dissimilar treatment for married and unmarried persons who are similarly situated, Massachusetts General Laws Ann., c. 272, §§ 21 and 21A, violate the Equal Protection Clause.

■ MR. JUSTICE POWELL and MR. JUSTICE REHNQUIST took no part in the consideration or decision of this case.

■ [MR. JUSTICE DOUGLAS concurred in the result on the ground that Baird's act of passing around a sample of vaginal foam was protected as ancillary to his free speech rights. MR. JUSTICE WHITE and MR. JUSTICE BLACKMUN concurred in the result, on the grounds that there was no evidence to suggest that medical supervision was necessary to protect health when the contraceptive being distributed was, as here, vaginal foam; nor was there record evidence as to the recipient's marital status.]

■ [MR. CHIEF JUSTICE BURGER dissented on the ground that "the choice of a means of birth control, although a highly personal matter, is also a health matter in a very real sense, and I see nothing arbitrary in a requirement of medical supervision."]

NOTES ON *EISENSTADT* AND THE EXPANDING PRIVACY RIGHT

1. *What Was the State's Interest Underlying This Statute?* In *Griswold*, Justice Brennan joined Justice Goldberg's concurring opinion which "in no way interferes with a State's proper regulation of sexual promiscuity or misconduct." 381 U.S. at 498–99. In *Eisenstadt*, Justice Brennan sidesteps contradicting his earlier implicit endorsement of a state's right to regulate for those purposes by refusing to accept either sexual morality or a health concern as the basis for the statute because he found both to be so imperfectly related to the impact of the law. In its brief and in oral argument, the state had claimed both justifications.

Essentially the same questions regarding the legitimacy of the state's interest in using anti-contraceptive laws to discourage sexual activity arose five years later in the context of a New York statute prohibiting distribution of contraceptives to persons younger than 16, except by a physician. *Carey v. Population Services, International*, 431 U.S. 678 (1977). In *Carey*, four Justices joined a plurality opinion, written by Justice Brennan, holding that minors have a privacy right that includes access to contraceptives, and that a state cannot impose restrictions on contraception for the purpose of deterring sexual activity by increasing the hazards of engaging in it. *Id.* at 694–95. Justice Stevens concurred, but derided as "frivolous" the plurality's argument "that a minor has the constitutional right to put contraceptives to their intended use." Nonetheless, Stevens concurred in the plurality's result, on the ground that the state could not communicate its policy against teenage sexuality by imposing a risk of physical harm, regardless of whether minors had an underlying constitutional right.

2. *From Sex to Procreation in Three Easy Steps.* Justice Brennan found that the "real" state interest was that the legislature had considered "contraceptives *per se*" to be immoral. In other words, he rejected the notion that the state's interest in morality was the instrumental one of deterring nonmarital sexual activities, but rather was the intrinsic immorality of preventing new life. Apply Brennan's over-and under-inclusiveness analyses to this rationale—how does it fare? This first step eliminated any need to scrutinize the sexual morality justification.

Both the plaintiffs and *amicus* Planned Parenthood had argued that even if the state could criminalize nonmarital sexual conduct, it could not penalize it by the less direct, but harsher, method of forcing individuals to risk pregnancy as a result. Such a means to that end, they argued, was arbitrary and capricious. Brennan sidestepped the question of what means could be utilized toward that end, however, by step two: finding that "whatever the rights of the individual to access to contraceptives may be, the rights must be the same for the unmarried and married alike." Thus, equal protection doctrine decides the case.

In step three, the Court returns, unnecessarily, to privacy. Brennan elaborated the holding with what is the most quoted portion of the opinion, the "[i]f the right of privacy means anything" sentence. At the end of that sentence, we have arrived at "the right to decide whether to bear or beget a child." With marriage absent from the case, Brennan ignored those aspects of *Griswold* that focused on sexuality, and instead grounded this opinion solely in the decision-making aspects of procreation. By step three, the Court had substituted procreation for sexuality or sexual morality. Does that work? Is the conclusion supported by the cases Brennan cites? Is it a euphemistic cop-out or an artful dodge?

Note that Justice Kennedy's opinion in *Lawrence v. Texas* (Chapter 2, Section 2) answers the question of whether consenting adults have a right of privacy outside the context of procreative decision-making, and, in doing so, cites this language in *Eisenstadt* as support, thus obviating the linguistic minuet from 30 years earlier.

3.   *Another Invocation of Equal Protection to Avoid a Controversial Liberty Right.* During the same 1964 Term in which *Griswold* was argued, the Court also struck down a Florida law forbidding interracial cohabitation. McLaughlin v. Florida, 379 U.S. 184 (1964). Florida defended the provision as auxiliary to another section of the same statute that prohibited interracial marriage. The Court declined to examine whether the state's purpose of deterring interracial sexual relations was valid, but instead held that a race-neutral fornication law served that purpose as well as a race-specific one. It therefore found that Florida's inter-racial cohabitation law violated the Equal Protection Clause, but did not address whether its criminalization of sexual relations between unmarried persons violated a fundamental liberty right. (Two terms later, the Court tackled the miscegenation issue head-on and ruled the Virginia law unconstitutional in *Loving v. Virginia*, 388 U.S. 1 (1967). See Chapter 2, Section 3C).

4.   *Law on the Ground.* After the decision in *Eisenstadt*, what if anything has changed in the Massachusetts law regarding fornication? Consider how powerful the indirect, as well as direct, regulation of sexuality can be. Compare the real life impact of a fornication law on women versus its impact on men.

B. THE RIGHT TO CHOOSE ABORTION

By the time the last contraception laws were off the books, a powerful "pro-choice" social movement had formed around the issue of abortion: when contraception was not available or was unable to prevent pregnancy before the fact, abortion ought to be available after the fact. Doctors (fearful of prosecution) as well as feminists supported reform of abortion laws. In thirteen states abortion laws were amended to allow an exception for the woman's health, and four states had repealed their laws altogether by 1972. As the civil rights and birth control movements had done, the pro-choice movement went to court. The case that reached the

Supreme Court and defined the right to choose began with a women's liberation group at the University of Texas in which the members first sought to provide counseling for women who wanted abortions, and then decided to challenge the law itself. The plaintiff's lawyers in *Roe v. Wade* maintained that state bars to, and even regulation of, abortion violated *Griswold's* privacy right. Because "a pregnancy to a woman is perhaps one of the most determinative aspects of her life," argued Sarah Weddington for the unmarried pregnant plaintiff, it is of fundamental importance that a woman have the freedom to terminate it. Texas argued that its interest in human life justified broad regulatory authority. The state's brief contained eight pages of photographs of the human fetus *in utero* to make its point.

Jane Roe v. Henry Wade

United States Supreme Court, 1973.
410 U.S. 113, 93 S.Ct. 705, 35 L.Ed.2d 147.

■ MR. JUSTICE BLACKMUN delivered the opinion of the Court.

This [appeal presents] constitutional challenges to state criminal abortion legislation. The Texas statutes under attack here [which make procuring an abortion a crime except "by medical advice for the purpose of saving the life of the mother"] are typical of those that have been in effect in many states for approximately a century. * * *

Three reasons have been advanced to explain historically the enactment of criminal abortion laws in the 19th century and to justify their continued existence.

It has been argued occasionally that these laws were the product of a Victorian social concern to discourage illicit sexual conduct. Texas, however, does not advance this justification in the present case, and it appears that no court or commentator has taken the argument seriously. * * *

A second reason is concerned with abortion as a medical procedure. When most criminal abortion laws were first enacted, the procedure was a hazardous one for the woman. Thus, it has been argued that a State's real concern in enacting a criminal abortion law was to protect the pregnant woman, that is, to restrain her from submitting to a procedure that placed her life in serious jeopardy.

Modern medical techniques have altered this situation. * * * Mortality rates for women undergoing early abortions [appear] to be as low as or lower than the rates for normal childbirth. * * * Of course, important state interests in the areas of health and medical standards do remain. The State has a legitimate interest in seeing to it that abortion, like any other medical procedure, is performed under circumstances that insure maximum safety for the patient. * * * Thus, the State retains a definite interest in protecting the woman's own health and safety when an abortion is proposed at a late stage of pregnancy.

The third reason is the State's interest—some phrase it in terms of duty—in protecting prenatal life. Some of the argument for this justification rests on the theory that a new human life is present from the moment of conception. * * * In assessing the State's interest, recognition may [also] be given to the less rigid claim that as long as at least *potential* life is involved, the state may assert interests beyond the protection of the pregnant woman. * * *

The Constitution does not explicitly mention any right of privacy. [But] the Court has recognized that a right of personal privacy, or a guarantee of certain areas or zones of privacy, does exist under the Constitution. In varying contexts, the Court or individual Justices have, indeed, found at least the roots of that right in the First Amendment; in the Fourth and Fifth Amendments; in the penumbras of the Bill of Rights; or in the concept of liberty guaranteed by the first section of the Fourteenth Amendment. [All of these arguments were made by parties and amici in *Roe*.] These decisions make it clear that only personal rights deemed "fundamental" or "implicit in the concept of ordered liberty," *Palko v. Connecticut*, 302 U.S. 319, 325 (1937), are included in this guarantee of personal privacy. * * *

This right of privacy, whether it be founded in the Fourteenth Amendment's concept of personal liberty and restrictions upon state action, as we feel it is, or, as the District Court determined, in the Ninth Amendment's reservation of rights to the people, is broad enough to encompass a woman's decision whether or not to terminate her pregnancy. The detriment that the State would impose upon the pregnant woman by denying this choice altogether is apparent. Specific and direct harm medically diagnosable even in early pregnancy may be involved. Maternity, or additional offspring, may force upon the woman a distressful life and future. Psychological harm may be imminent. Mental and physical health may be taxed by child care. There is also the distress, for all concerned, associated with the unwanted child, and there is the problem of bringing a child into a family already unable, psychologically and otherwise, to care for it. In other cases, [the] additional difficulties and continuing stigma of unwed motherhood may be involved. All these are factors the woman and her responsible physician necessarily will consider in consultation.

On the basis of elements such as these, appellant and some *amici* argue that the woman's right is absolute and that she is entitled to terminate her pregnancy at whatever time, in whatever way, and for whatever reason she alone chooses. With this we do not agree. * * * The Court's decisions recognizing a right of privacy also acknowledge that some state regulation in areas protected by that right is appropriate. As noted above, a State may properly assert important interests in safeguarding health, in maintaining medical standards, and in protecting potential life. * * *

[Laws that limit exercise of a fundamental right must be justified by a "compelling state interest" and "narrowly drawn to express only the legitimate state interests at stake."]

* * * [T]he State does have an important and legitimate interest in preserving and protecting the health of the pregnant woman, and * * * another important and legitimate interest in protecting the potentiality of human life. These interests are separate and distinct. Each grows in substantiality as the woman approaches term and, at a point during pregnancy, each becomes "compelling."

[Justice Blackmun set the "compelling" point, where the state can begin regulation with the goal of preserving fetal life, at approximately the end of the first trimester, when the fetus "quickens" in the old common law sense. During the first trimester the state cannot interfere with decisions by "the attending physician, in consultation with his patient." During the second trimester the state can set licensing and other medical regulations to protect the safety of the mother and to recognize the potential life.]

■ [We omit the separate concurring opinions of JUSTICES STEWART and DOUGLAS and of CHIEF JUSTICE BURGER and the separate dissenting opinion of JUSTICE REHNQUIST.]

■ JUSTICES WHITE and REHNQUIST, dissenting.

* * * I find nothing in the language or history of the Constitution to support the Court's judgments. The Court simply fashions and announces a new constitutional right for pregnant women and, with scarcely any reason or authority for its action, invests that right with sufficient substance to override most existing state abortion statutes. The upshot is that the people and the legislatures of the 50 States are constitutionally disentitled to weigh the relative importance of the continued existence and development of the fetus, on the one hand, against a spectrum of possible impacts on the mother, on the other hand. As an exercise of raw judicial power, the Court perhaps has authority to do what it does today; but in my view its judgment is an improvident and extravagant exercise of the power of judicial review that the Constitution extends to this Court.

The Court apparently values the convenience of the pregnant woman more than the continued existence and development of the life or potential life that she carries. Whether or not I might agree with that marshaling of values, I can in no event join the Court's judgment because I find no constitutional warrant for imposing such an order of priorities on the people and legislatures of the States. * * *

NOTES ON *ROE* AND THE RIGHT TO ABORTION

1. *Procreation as the Core of Privacy.* With the Court's decision in *Roe*, the privacy line of cases became firmly grounded in matters related to reproduction. The pendency of *Roe* almost certainly shaped the way the

Court structured its opinion in the precursor decision of *Eisenstadt*, with its holding that the right to privacy must encompass the individual's right "to be free from unwarranted governmental intrusion into * * * the decision whether to bear or beget a child." The Court heard arguments in *Eisenstadt* in November 1971, followed less than a month later by the first arguments in *Roe*. *Eisenstadt* was decided in the term prior to the decision in *Roe*, only because *Roe* was held over for a second round of arguments.

2.   *Finally a Constitutional Home for the Right to Privacy.* After roosting in the penumbras of the Bill of Rights (the Douglas opinion in *Griswold*), the Ninth Amendment (the Goldberg concurrence), and even the Equal Protection Clause [*Eisenstadt* and, earlier, *Skinner v. Oklahoma*, 316 U.S. 535 (1942), the Court in *Roe* finally gave the right of privacy its constitutional home in the jurisprudential location that Justice Harlan's *Poe v. Ullman* opinion had outlined: the Due Process Clause's protection of "liberty." The Joint Opinion of Justices O'Connor, Kennedy, and Souter in *Planned Parenthood v. Casey* in 1992 reaffirmed that placement. (Chapter 2, Section 1A.) And there it remains today.

3.   *The Missing Argument: Sex Discrimination.* Many commentators have opined that the abortion right would have been more strongly grounded in the Constitution and in social reality had it been based on a theory of sex discrimination, rather than of privacy. In fact, a sex discrimination argument was made to the Court in *Roe* in an *amicus* brief filed by Nancy Stearns for the Center for Constitutional Rights. The CCR brief argued that abortion laws were a way to punish unmarried women for being heterosexually active. Another *amicus* brief, filed by Joan Bradford for the California Committee to Legalize Abortion, argued that forced childbearing was a form of involuntary servitude, prohibited under the Thirteenth Amendment. These arguments apparently had little impact on the Justices, who were in the midst of wrestling with the question of how to analyze classifications based on sex under the Equal Protection Clause. The Supreme Court's 1971–72 term also included *Reed v. Reed,* 404 U.S. 71 (1971), in which the Court struck down a sex-based classification as unconstitutional for the first time in history.

4.   *The Logic of Biological Determinism. Roe* also marked the apex to date of the medicalization of the law of reproductive decision-making, both in its consideration of medical history and in its vesting of decisional authority in "the woman and her responsible physician." In an extensive critique of *Roe*, Reva Siegel argues that this medicalization served as a mask for using "[f]acts about women's bodies * * * to justify regulation enforcing judgments about women's roles."

> *Roe* * * * defines [the state's] regulatory interest in potential life physiologically, without reference to the sorts of constitutional considerations that normally attend the use of state power against a citizen. In the Court's reasoning, facts concerning the physiological development of the unborn provide "logical and biological justifications" both limiting and legitimating state action directed against the pregnant woman. * * * [T]he Court has never described the state's interest in protecting potential life as an

interest in forcing women to bear children. *Roe's* physiological reasoning obscures that simple social fact. * * *

Abortion-restrictive regulation is state action compelling pregnancy and motherhood, and this simple fact cannot be evaded by invoking nature or a woman's[a] choices to explain the situation in which the pregnant woman subject to abortion restrictions finds herself. A pregnant woman seeking an abortion has the practical capacity to terminate a pregnancy, which she would exercise but for the community's decision to prevent or deter her. If the community successfully effectuates its will, it is the state, and not nature, which is responsible for causing her to continue the pregnancy. * * *

Reva Siegel, "Reasoning From the Body: A Historical Perspective on Abortion Regulation and Questions of Equal Protection," 44 *Stan. L. Rev.* 261, 276–77, 350–51 (1992).

5. *The Withering of a Fundamental Right.* In *Akron v. Akron Center for Reproductive Health*, 462 U.S. 416 (1983), the Court reaffirmed its strict review of infringements on the abortion right, striking down a series of impediments, including a 24-hour waiting period and the requirement that doctors read abortion patients a lengthy, biased script as a prerequisite for informed consent. What emerged from *Akron* as the opinion of greatest lasting consequence, however, was not the majority opinion, but the dissent by then recently appointed Justice Sandra Day O'Connor. Justice O'Connor proffered a compromise between the standard of review established in *Roe* (strict scrutiny to protect a fundamental right) and the one urged by the dissent in *Roe* (any regulation of abortion with a rational basis was acceptable). Because of the "limited nature of the fundamental right" of abortion, she argued, strict scrutiny should be used if a regulation created an "unduly burdensome interference" with the woman's decision, and rational basis review should be used if it did not.

In the decade that followed, as more Justices skeptical of *Roe* were appointed to the Court, support for the fundamental right/strict scrutiny approach of *Roe* and *Akron* dwindled. The original holding, joined by seven Justices in 1973, was affirmed by a majority of six in 1983 (*Akron*), and by a majority of five in 1986 (*Thornburgh v. American College of Obstetricians and Gynecologists*, 476 U.S. 747). In *Webster v. Reproductive Health Servs.*, 492 U.S. 490 (1989), with four Reagan-appointed Justices on the Court, both the state (Missouri) and the Solicitor General asked the Court to overrule *Roe*. The *Webster* Court reached only the statute before it (upholding a requirement that doctors test for viability before performing an abortion after the twentieth week of pregnancy), with five Justices filing separate opinions. In a concurring opinion, Justice O'Connor noted that "[w]hen the constitutional invalidity of a State's abortion statute actually turns on the

---

[a] See, e.g., Sylvia Law, "Rethinking Sex and the Constitution," 132 U. Rev. 955 (1984); Ruth Bader Ginsburg, "Some Thoughts on Autonomy and Equality in Relation to *Roe v. Wade*, 63 *N.C.L Rev* 375 (1985); Donald Regan, "Rewriting *Roe v. Wade*," 77 *Mich. L. Rev.* 1569, 1621–45 (1979).

constitutional validity of *Roe v. Wade*, there will be time enough to reexamine *Roe*." We will pick up this story again in Chapter 2, Section 1A.

6. *The Absence of a Positive Right.* One major critique of privacy, especially in the abortion context, has been its susceptibility to the claim that, under a negative rights analysis, the state is compelled only to refrain from creating obstacles to choosing abortion, but has no duty to assist in the effectuation of that right, by, for example, including abortion within the realm of medical procedures provided to indigent women in the Medicaid program. In the 40 years since *Roe v. Wade*, Congress and state legislatures have enacted—and the Supreme Court has upheld—a series of restrictions on the use of public funds to support abortion. Most important have been those affecting the use of Medicaid funds. Medicaid is the federal-state safety net program that pays for health services for indigent persons. The Hyde Amendment (named for its author, Rep. Henry Hyde of Illinois) barred use of Medicaid program funds to cover abortions unless the pregnant woman's life was endangered or the pregnancy resulted from rape or incest. (Consider the message implicit in that exception: the fetus is no more or less human than in any other pregnancy, but the woman is allowed to opt out of mandatory motherhood only if she lacks responsibility for the sexual encounter that led to the pregnancy. Otherwise, presumably the "punishment" fits the "crime.")

In **Harris v. McRae, 448 U.S. 297, 100 S.Ct. 2671, 65 L.Ed.2d 784 (1980),** the Supreme Court upheld the validity of the Hyde Amendment, finding that it "places no governmental obstacle in the path of a woman who chooses to terminate her pregnancy, but rather, by means of unequal subsidization of abortion and other medical services, encourages alternative activity deemed in the public interest. * * * [I]t simply does not follow that a woman's freedom of choice carries with it a constitutional entitlement to the financial resources to avail herself of the full range of protected choices. * * * [A]lthough government may not place obstacles in the path of a woman's exercise of her freedom of choice, it need not remove those not of its own creation. Indigency falls in the latter category. The financial constraints that restrict an indigent woman's ability to enjoy the full range of constitutionally-protected freedom of choice are the product not of governmental restrictions on access to abortions, but rather of her indigency. Although Congress has opted to subsidize medically necessary services generally, but not certain medically necessary abortions, the fact remains that the Hyde Amendment leaves an indigent woman with at least the same range of choice in deciding whether to obtain a medically necessary abortion as she would have had if Congress had chosen to subsidize no health care costs at all."

Justice Brennan, joined in dissent by Justices Marshall and Blackmun, wrote that "the Court fails to appreciate * * * that it is not simply the woman's indigency that interferes with her freedom of choice, but the combination of her own poverty and the government's unequal subsidization of abortion of childbirth."

The Hyde Amendment, with slight variations, still applies.

PROBLEM 1-2
STUPAK AMENDMENT IN THE AFFORDABLE CARE ACT OF 2010

The absence under Medicaid of coverage for abortion (unless a state government pays the entire cost) has consequences beyond that one program. In 2010, when health reform legislation was before Congress, the question of whether abortion would be covered by federally funded subsidies to low-income persons purchasing insurance on the exchanges became a major issue. What emerged was the Stupak Amendment. Based on the Hyde Amendment, and adopted as part of the overall bill, it provides in part:

(a) IN GENERAL—No funds authorized or appropriated by this Act * * * may be used to pay for any abortion or to cover any part of the costs of any health [insurance] plan that includes coverage of abortion, except in the case where a woman suffers from a physical disorder, physical injury, or physical illness that would, as certified by a physician, place the woman in danger of death unless an abortion is performed, including a life-endangering physical condition caused by or arising from the pregnancy itself, or unless the pregnancy is the result of an act of rape or incest.

(b) OPTION TO PURCHASE SEPARATE SUPPLEMENTAL COVERAGE OR PLAN—Nothing in this section shall be construed as prohibiting any nonfederal entity (including an individual or a State or local government) from purchasing supplemental coverage for abortions for which funding is prohibited under this section, or a plan that includes such abortions [so long as the coverage is not purchased with federal funds, tax credits, or matching funds that trigger federal payments].

Can you structure a subsidy system to assist low-income persons to purchase health insurance from private insurance companies that avoids this issue? Compare issues with the contraceptive mandate portion of the Affordable Care Act. See Chapter 4, Section 1.

C. THE ERA OF SODOMY LAW

Given the intensity of the battles that developed over state regulation of sodomy, one might assume that the combatants on both sides would have been clear as to exactly what conduct they were fighting about so strenuously. Not true. Sodomy laws came to be seen as prohibitions of "gay sex," and even as "traditional" prohibitions of gay sex, which is wrong as an historical matter. At common law, sodomy laws targeted a type of conduct, not a category of persons. They prohibited anal (and later oral) sex between any two partners, not (any kind of) sex between gay men or lesbians. The "crime against nature," as sodomy was often euphemistically called in older statutes, came into being not as a crime against heterosexuality, but instead as a crime against any sexual conduct without the possibility of procreation. See William Eskridge Jr.,

Dishonorable Passions: Sodomy Law in America, 1861–2003 chs. 1–3 (2008) (history of sodomy laws through World War II).

Even if incorrect, however, misreadings of sodomy law were not without reason: as the stigma for heterosexual sex outside of (especially prior to) marriage diminished during the twentieth century, coupled with cultural backlash against an increasingly larger and more visible lesbian and gay rights movement, the *meaning* of sodomy changed. This shift in social meaning produced shifts in understandings of the law, even at the Supreme Court.

The contestation over the criminal status of "gay sex" developed slowly in post-World War II America. The first major cultural breakthrough was the publication of two books: Alfred Kinsey, et al., *Sexual Behavior in the Human Male* (1948) and *Report on Sexual Behavior in the Human Female* (1953). Professor Kinsey, an entomologist who made his scientific reputation in a definitive study of the gall wasp, brought an astringent empiricism to the study of human sexuality. Although later studies have produced more scientifically reliable estimates of the percentage of Americans who engage in various sexual acts, Kinsey's studies were shocking as much because of the non-judgmental frame in which they were presented as because of the specific numbers. Among his most dramatic findings were that many more men than was commonly believed had significant homosexual experience, including 10 per cent who had been more or less exclusively homosexual for at least three years; half of the married men and a quarter of the married women had engaged in adulterous sexual relations, and significantly more had engaged in pre-marital sex (which was then a crime in 35 states); and that women, rather than being merely passive, asexual partners, experienced orgasm, often through masturbation as well as during sex with other women. The two Kinsey Reports became best sellers; their publication triggered complaints of moral decay, but also allied scientific rationalism with sexual non-judgmentalism in U.S. culture.

During the 1950s and 1960s, the legal profession in both the U.S. and England undertook major efforts toward decriminalization. In 1962, the American Law Institute adopted the proposed Model Penal Code (MPC), which endorsed the decriminalization of private consensual adultery, fornication, and sodomy. Meanwhile in Great Britain, motivated by concern about an increasing number of street arrests for sexual activity, the Office of the Home Secretary commissioned *The Report of the Wolfenden Committee on Homosexual Offences and Prostitution*, published in 1957. *The Wolfenden Report* recommended the decriminalization of private consensual homosexual conduct, concluding that "[t]here must remain a realm of private morality and immorality which is, in brief and crude terms, not the law's business." At the same time, however, it recommended an increase in penalties for prostitution. The logic of the Report was that both homosexuality and prostitution were repugnant, but that society's interests would best be served by concentrating the prohibitions of law on the public manifestations of these behaviors. Parliament largely followed the *Wolfenden* recommendations, increasing the maximum sentence for open prostitution in the Street Offences Act of 1959, and in 1967 repealing the prohibition against private consensual sodomy in the Sexual Offences Act. (Adultery and fornication had been dropped from the British criminal code prior to *The Wolfenden Report*.)

The Wolfenden Report triggered a famous debate between Lord Patrick Devlin and Professor H.L.A. Hart over the proper role of the state in regulating sexual conduct. In a 1959 lecture later published as *The Enforcement of Morals*, Lord Devlin argued that the use of law to enforce widely held moral judgments was essential to society. "[A]n established morality is as necessary as good government to the welfare of society." Therefore, Devlin wrote, "society is justified in taking the same steps to preserve its moral code as it does to preserve its government and other essential institutions." Devlin asserted that a society's moral consensus could be based on the beliefs of the "reasonable man."

In 1963, Professor Hart responded to Devlin with his equally classic text, *Law, Liberty and Morality*. Hart elaborated on principles first articulated by Jeremy Bentham and John Stuart Mill, who had argued that the state had no legitimate right to intrude in individual conduct unless that conduct threatened to harm others. Hart agreed with Devlin that "*some* shared morality is essential to the existence of any society" (emphasis in the original), but argued that the responsibility of government was to secure the safety and liberty necessary for citizens to debate and continuously re-assess what they wished the moral code of their society to be. Such a code was better protected by non-governmental institutions and private actions than by coercion based on enforcement of the law.

Note that the period of the development of both the MPC and *The Wolfenden Report* coincided with the litigation of *Ullman* and *Griswold*. How might these events in Britain have influenced the approaches of the Justices? In 1961, the same year that *Ullman* was decided, Illinois became the first state to repeal its sodomy law, by adopting a draft version of the MPC. The next sodomy law repeal occurred in 1969 (Connecticut), and many states followed suit through the 1970s and 1980s. Most repeals occurred when states modernized their entire criminal codes; dropping or lightening of penalties for consensual sexual practices was often part of a larger overhaul of the statutory scheme.

NOTE ON THE MEDICALIZATION OF HOMOSEXUALITY

Criminal law provides the most direct and obvious means for the state to regulate sexual behavior, but not necessarily the most powerful. Other modes of surveillance and discipline abounded in twentieth century America. Laws controlling access to birth control, immigration law, employment law and family law all played a role. Although they were premised on the categorization of certain sexual conduct as unlawful, they extended the reach of state authority far beyond criminal law. Two developments between the 1950s and the 1970s stand out: first, the use of a medical or therapeutic model to frame homosexuality as mental illness, as a liberal substitute for the prosecution-oriented model, and second, the increasing engagement of the federal government. In the following case, for example, decided two years after *Griswold v. Connecticut*, consider how immigration law contributed to the legal construction of homosexuality.

Clive Michael Boutilier v. Immigration and Naturalization Service, 387 U.S. 118 (1967), involved a Canadian immigrant who had been arrested on morals charges involving sexual activities with other men. The INS ordered him deported on the ground that he should not have been allowed to enter the country in the first place, because federal law barred entry of immigrants "afflicted with psychopathic personality," which the INS interpreted to include all "homosexuals and sex perverts." Boutilier challenged his deportation. Affidavits from psychiatrists claimed that he was reasonably well-adjusted and not psychopathic; moreover, he was not a "homosexual," as he enjoyed sex with women as well as men. He also claimed that the statute was unconstitutionally vague if that statutory language were applied to bar him.

The issue presented was whether Congress intended to include "homosexuals and other sex perverts"—"such as petitioner"—in the deportable category of persons with a "psychopathic personality." The Court, in an opinion by **Justice Clark**, traced the legislative history of the phrase and found that Congress did intend to exclude gay people, and that Boutilier fell into that category:

> The Public Health Service doctors found and certified that at the time of his entry petitioner 'was afflicted with a class A condition, namely, psychopathic personality, sexual deviate.' * * * Having substantial support in the record, we do not now disturb that finding, especially since petitioner admitted being a homosexual at the time of his entry. The existence of this condition over a continuous and uninterrupted period prior to and at the time of petitioner's entry clearly supports the ultimate finding upon which the order of deportation was based. * * *

Justice Brennan dissented, quoting the Court of Appeals opinion statement, "Had the petitioner known that sexual deviation at the time of entry would be automatic grounds for exclusion, there is considerable reason to believe that he could have modified his behavior so that he could not be considered a deviate * * * While he had engaged in homosexual acts from the age of 16 to the age of 21, he had also had sexual relations with women three or four times during this period. * * *

Justice Douglas, joined by **Justice Fortas**, also dissented. He, like the dissenting judge below and Justice Brennan, believed that the term "psychopathic personality" was not intended to cover "every person who ever had a homosexual experience." Reflecting the dominance of Freudian thought at that time, Justice Douglas wrote:

> The homosexual is one, who by some freak, is the product of an arrested development: "All people have originally bisexual tendencies which are more or less developed and which in the course of time normally deviate either in the direction of male or female. This may indicate that a trace of homosexuality, no matter how weak it may be, exists in every human being. It is present in the adolescent stage, where there is a considerable amount of undifferentiated sexuality." Abrahamsen, *Crime and the Human Mind* 117 (1944). * * *

Justice Douglas also relied on the report of a psychiatrist retained by Boutilier who stated: [Boutilier's] "sexual structure still appears fluid and immature so that he moves from homosexual to heterosexual interests as well as abstinence with almost equal facility. His homosexual orientation seems secondary to a very constricted, dependent personality pattern rather than occurring in the context of a psychopathic personality. My own feeling is that his own need to fit in and be accepted is so great that it far surpasses his need for sex in any form." * * *

Query. Based on this opinion, would you say that Boutilier was "gay"? Although it is treacherous to project current labels and concepts backward in time, today he might self-identify as bisexual. Note that the dissenting Justices all appeared to believe that Boutilier could have chosen to have only women partners, in an effort to control his "illness."

––––––––––

At the 1970 and 1971 conventions of the American Psychiatric Association (APA), protesters challenged the psychiatrists to "delist" homosexuality as a psychiatric disorder in its *Diagnostic and Statistical Manual* (DSM). On December 15, 1973, the APA's Nomenclature Committee voted to drop homosexuality's classification as a disease in *DSM-II.* The Committee's decision survived an unprecedented referendum vote among APA members instigated by adherents to the traditional view. As a result of an emerging consensus among medical professionals that homosexuality is not per se a mental disease, the Public Health Service (PHS), which jointly administered the medical bases for excluding immigrants with the INS, announced in 1979 that it would no longer cooperate in the exclusion of lesbians, gay men, and bisexuals as people afflicted with "psychopathic personality" or "sexual deviation" (a term added by Congress in 1965). Although the INS continued to follow *Boutilier*, it did little to enforce the exclusion, and Congress repealed "the homosexual exclusion" in 1990. Pub. L. No. 101–649, § 601, 104 Stat. 4978, 5067.

In the generation after *Boutilier*, a proliferation of rights claims in the courts and in the streets upended the assumption that homosexuality was either a sin or a sickness. See William Eskridge Jr., *Dishonorable Passions: Sodomy Law in America, 1861–2003,* chs. 5–7 (2008) (detailed description of state and federal law reform efforts, including constitutional litigation). Nonetheless, in the case that advocates had hoped would amount to judicial adoption of a Wolfenden-like resolution of sexual morality debates, the Supreme Court instead narrowly opted to side with Lord Devlin.

Michael Bowers v. Michael Hardwick et al.

United States Supreme Court, 1986.
478 U.S. 186, 106 S.Ct. 2841, 92 L.Ed.2d 140.

■ JUSTICE WHITE delivered the opinion of the Court.

In August 1982, respondent [Michael Hardwick] was charged with violating the Georgia statute criminalizing sodomy[1] by committing that act with another adult male in the bedroom of respondent's home.[b] After a preliminary hearing, the District Attorney decided not to present the matter to the grand jury unless further evidence developed.

Respondent then brought suit in the Federal District Court, challenging the constitutionality of the statute insofar as it criminalized consensual sodomy.[2] He asserted that he was a practicing homosexual, that the Georgia sodomy statute, as administered by the defendants, placed him in imminent danger of arrest, and that the statute for several reasons violates the Federal Constitution. The District Court granted the defendants' motion to dismiss for failure to state a claim * * *. [The Eleventh Circuit Court of Appeals reversed.]

This case does not require a judgment on whether laws against sodomy between consenting adults in general, or between homosexuals in particular, are wise or desirable. It raises no question about the right or propriety of state legislative decisions to repeal their laws that criminalize homosexual sodomy, or of state-court decisions invalidating those laws on state constitutional grounds. The issue presented is

---

[1]   Georgia Code Ann. § 16–6–2 (1984) provides, in pertinent part, as follows:

"(a)   A person commits the offence of sodomy when he performs or submits to any sexual act involving the sex organs of one person and the mouth or anus of another. . .

(b)   A person convicted of the offense of sodomy shall be punished by imprisonment for not less than one nor more than 20 years. . . "

[b]   Michael Hardwick later told an interviewer that the police had come to his home to serve an arrest warrant, issued for drinking in public, by a police officer who saw him leaving a gay bar. (The warrant had expired.) Hardwick strongly suspected that this incident, and an unexplained physical assault shortly before his arrest, were engineered by police wanting to harass him for being gay. Peter Irons. "What Are You Doing in My Bedroom?," in *The Courage of Their Convictions* 392 (1988).

[2]   John and Mary Doe were also plaintiffs in this action. They alleged that they wished to engage in sexual activity prohibited by § 16–6–2 in the privacy of their home, and that they had been "chilled and deterred" from engaging such activity by both the existence of the statute and Hardwick's arrest. The District Court held, however, that because had neither sustained, nor were in immediate danger of sustaining, any direct injury from the enforcement of the statute, they did not have proper standing to maintain the action. The Court of Appeals affirmed * * * and the Does do not challenge that holding in this Court.

The only claim properly before the Court, therefore, is Hardwick's challenge to the Georgia statute as applied to consensual homosexual sodomy. We express no opinion on the constitutionality of the Georgia statute as applied to other acts of sodomy.

whether the Federal Constitution confers a fundamental right upon homosexuals to engage in sodomy and hence invalidates the laws of the many States that still make such conduct illegal and have done so for a very long time. The case also calls for some judgment about the limits of the Court's role in carrying out its constitutional mandate.

We first register our disagreement with the Court of Appeals and with respondent that the Court's prior cases have construed the Constitution to confer a right of privacy that extends to homosexual sodomy and for all intents and purposes have decided this case. The reach of this line of cases was sketched in *Carey v. Population Services International,* 431 U.S. 678, 685 (1977) [striking down a state bar to making contraceptives available to minors]. *Pierce* [*v. Society of* Sisters] and *Meyer* [*v. Nebraska*] were described as dealing with child rearing and education; *Prince* [*v. Massachusetts*], with family relationships; *Skinner* [*v. Oklahoma*] with procreation; *Loving* [*v. Virginia*] with marriage; *Griswold* and *Eisenstadt* with contraception; and *Roe v. Wade* with abortion. The latter three cases were interpreted as construing the Due Process Clause of the Fourteenth Amendment to confer a fundamental individual right to decide whether or not to beget or bear a child. *Carey.*

Accepting the decisions in these cases and the above description of them, we think it evident that none of the rights announced in those cases bears any resemblance to the claimed constitutional right of homosexuals to engage in acts of sodomy that is asserted in this case. No connection between family, marriage, or procreation on the one hand and homosexual activity on the other has been demonstrated, either by the Court of Appeals or by respondent. Moreover, any claim that these cases nevertheless stand for the proposition that any kind of private sexual conduct between consenting adults is constitutionally insulated from state proscription is unsupportable. Indeed, the Court's opinion in *Carey* twice asserted that the privacy right, which the *Griswold* line of cases found to be one of the protections provided by the Due Process Clause, did not reach so far.

Precedent aside, however, respondent would have us announce, as the Court of Appeals did, a fundamental right to engage in homosexual sodomy. This we are quite unwilling to do. It is true that despite the language of the Due Process Clauses of the Fifth and Fourteenth Amendments, which appears to focus only on the processes by which life, liberty, or property is taken, the cases are legion in which those Clauses have been interpreted to have substantive content, subsuming rights that to a great extent are immune from federal or state regulation or proscription. Among such cases are those recognizing rights that have little or no textual support in the constitutional language. *Meyer, Prince,* and *Pierce* fall in this category, as do the privacy cases from *Griswold* to *Carey.*

Striving to assure itself and the public that announcing rights not readily identifiable in the Constitution's text involves much more than the imposition of the Justices' own choice of values on the States and the Federal Government, the Court has sought to identify the nature of the rights qualifying for heightened judicial protection. In *Palko v. Connecticut* it was said that this category includes those fundamental liberties that are "implicit in the concept of ordered liberty," such that "neither liberty nor justice would exist if [they] were sacrificed." A different description of fundamental liberties appeared in *Moore v. East Cleveland*, 431 U.S. 494, 503 (1977) (opinion of Powell, J.) where they are characterized as those liberties that are "deeply rooted in this Nation's history and tradition."

It is obvious to us that neither of these formulations would extend a fundamental right to homosexuals to engage in acts of consensual sodomy. Proscriptions against that conduct have ancient roots. Sodomy was a criminal offense at common law and was forbidden by the laws of the original 13 States when they ratified the Bill of Rights. In 1868, when the Fourteenth Amendment was ratified, all but 5 of the 37 States in the Union had criminal sodomy laws. In fact, until 1961, all 50 States outlawed sodomy, and today, 24 States and the District of Columbia continue to provide criminal penalties for sodomy performed in private and between consenting adults. Against this background, to claim that a right to engage in such conduct is "deeply rooted in this Nation's history and tradition" or "implicit in the concept of ordered liberty" is, at best, facetious.

Nor are we inclined to take a more expansive view of our authority to discover new fundamental rights imbedded in the Due Process Clause. The Court is most vulnerable and comes nearest to illegitimacy when it deals with judge-made constitutional law having little or no cognizable roots in the language or design of the Constitution. * * * There should be, therefore, great resistance to expand the substantive reach of those Clauses, particularly if it requires redefining the category of rights deemed to be fundamental. Otherwise, the Judiciary necessarily takes to itself further authority to govern the country without express constitutional authority. The claimed right pressed on us today falls far short of overcoming this resistance. * * *

Even if the conduct at issue here is not a fundamental right, respondent asserts that there must be a rational basis for the law and that there is none in this case other than the presumed belief of a majority of the electorate in Georgia that homosexual sodomy is immoral and unacceptable. This is said to be an inadequate rationale to support the law. The law, however, is constantly based on notions of morality, and if all laws representing essentially moral choices are to be invalidated under the Due Process Clause, the courts will be very busy indeed. Even respondent makes no such claim, but insists that majority sentiments about the morality of homosexuality should be declared inadequate. We do not agree, and are unpersuaded that the sodomy laws of some 25 States should be invalidated on this basis.[8] * * *

■ CHIEF JUSTICE BURGER, concurring. * * *

As the Court notes, the proscriptions against sodomy have very "ancient roots." Decisions of individuals relating to homosexual conduct have been subject to state intervention throughout the history of Western Civilization. Condemnation of these practices is firmly rooted in Judeo-Christian moral and ethical standards. Homosexual sodomy was a capital crime under Roman law. During the English Reformation when powers of the ecclesiastical courts were transferred to the King's Courts, the first English statute criminalizing sodomy was passed. Blackstone described "the infamous crime against nature" as an offense of "deeper malignity" than rape, an heinous act "the very mention of which is a disgrace to human nature," and "a crime not fit to be named." The common law of England, including its prohibition of sodomy, became the received law of Georgia and the other Colonies. In 1816 the Georgia Legislature passed the statute at issue here, and that statute has been continuously in force in one form or another since that time. To hold that the act of homosexual sodomy is somehow protected as a fundamental right would be to cast aside millennia of moral teaching. * * *

■ JUSTICE POWELL, concurring.

I join the opinion of the Court. I agree with the Court that there is no fundamental right—i.e., no substantive right under the Due Process Clause—such as that claimed by respondent, and found to exist by the Court of Appeals. This is not to suggest, however, that respondent may not be protected by the Eighth Amendment of the Constitution. The Georgia statute at issue in this case authorizes a court to imprison a person for up to 20 years for a single private, consensual act of sodomy. In my view, a prison sentence for such conduct—certainly a sentence of long duration—would create a serious Eighth Amendment issue. * * *

In this case, however, respondent has not been tried, much less convicted and sentenced. Moreover, respondent has not raised the Eighth Amendment issue below. For these reasons this constitutional argument is not before us.

■ JUSTICE BLACKMUN, with whom JUSTICE BRENNAN, JUSTICE MARSHALL, and JUSTICE STEVENS join, dissenting.

This case is no more about "a fundamental right to engage in homosexual sodomy," as the Court purports to declare, than *Stanley* was about a fundamental right to watch obscene movies, or *Katz v. United States* was about a fundamental right to place interstate bets from a telephone booth. Rather, this case is about "the most comprehensive of

---

[8] Respondent does not defend the judgment below based on the Ninth Amendment, the Equal Protection Clause, or the Eighth Amendment.

rights and the right most valued by civilized men," namely, "the right to be let alone." *Olmstead* (Brandeis, J., dissenting). * * *

* * * I believe we must analyze respondent's claim in the light of the values that underlie the constitutional right to privacy. If that right means anything, it means that, before Georgia can prosecute its citizens for making choices about the most intimate aspects of their lives, it must do more than assert that the choice they have made is an " 'abominable crime not fit to be named among Christians.' " *Herring v. State*, 46 S.E. 876, 882 (Ga.1904). * * *

[T]he Court's almost obsessive focus on homosexual activity is particularly hard to justify in light of the broad language Georgia has used. Unlike the Court, the Georgia Legislature has not proceeded on the assumption that homosexuals are so different from other citizens that their lives may be controlled in a way that would not be tolerated if it limited the choices of those other citizens. The sex or status of the persons who engage in the act is irrelevant as a matter of state law. * * * I therefore see no basis for the Court's decision to treat this case as an "as applied" challenge to § 16–6–2, or for Georgia's attempt, both in its brief and at oral argument, to defend § 16–6–2 solely on the grounds that it prohibits homosexual activity. * * *

The Court concludes today that none of our prior cases dealing with various decisions that individuals are entitled to make free of governmental interference "bears any resemblance to the claimed constitutional right of homosexuals to engage in acts of sodomy that it asserted in this case." While it is true that these cases may be characterized by their connection to protection of the family, the Court's conclusion that they extend no further than this boundary ignores the warning in *Moore v. East Cleveland*, against "clos[ing] our eyes to the basic reasons why certain rights associated with the family have been accorded shelter under the Fourteenth Amendment's Due Process Clause." We protect those rights not because they contribute, in some direct and material way, to the general public welfare, but because they form so central a part of an individual's life. * * *

Only the most willful blindness could obscure the fact that sexual intimacy is "a sensitive, key relationship of human existence, central to family life, community welfare, and the development of human personality," *Paris Adult Theatre I v. Slaton*, 413 U.S. 49, 63 (1973). The fact that individuals define themselves in a significant way through their intimate sexual relationships with others suggests, in a Nation as diverse as ours, that there may be many "right" ways of conducting those relationships, and that much of the richness of a relationship will come from the freedom an individual has to *choose* the form and nature of these intensely personal bonds. See Karst, "The Freedom of Intimate Association," 89 *Yale L.J.* 624, 637 (1980). * * *

* * * "The right of the people to be secure in their . . . houses," expressly guaranteed by the Fourth Amendment, is perhaps the most

"textual" of the various constitutional provisions that inform our understanding of the right to privacy, and thus I cannot agree with the Court's statement that "[t]he right pressed upon us here has no . . . support in the text of the Constitution." Indeed, the right of an individual to conduct intimate relationships in the intimacy of his or her own home seems to me to be the heart of the Constitution's protection of privacy.

The Court's failure to comprehend the magnitude of the liberty interests at stake in this case leads it to slight the question whether petitioner, on behalf of the State, has justified Georgia's infringement on these interests. I believe that neither of the two general justifications for § 16–6–2 that petitioner has advanced warrants dismissing respondent's challenge for failure to state a claim.

[Justice Blackmun rejects the argument that homosexual acts may spread communicable diseases or foster other criminal activity.] "Inasmuch as this case was dismissed by the District Court on the pleadings, it is not surprising that the record before us is barren of any evidence to support petitioner's claim. * * * Nothing in the record before the Court provides any justification for finding the activity forbidden by § 16–6–2 to be physically dangerous, either to the persons engaged in it or to others.

The core of petitioner's defense * * *, however, is that respondent and others who engage in the conduct prohibited by § 16–6–2 interfere with Georgia's exercise of the " 'right of the Nation and of the States to maintain a decent society,' " *Paris Adult Theatre I v. Slaton*, 413 U.S. at 59–60. * * *

I cannot agree that either the length of time a majority has held its convictions or the passions with which it defends them can withdraw legislation from this Court's scrutiny. *Roe v. Wade*; *Loving v. Virginia*; *Brown v. Board of Education*. As Justice Jackson wrote so eloquently for the Court in *West Virginia Board of Education v. Barnette*, 319 U.S. 624, 641–42 (1943), " * * * [F]reedom to differ is not limited to things that do not matter much. The test of its substance is the right to differ as to things that touch the heart of the existing order." It is precisely because the issue raised by this case touches the heart of what makes individuals what they are that we should be especially sensitive to the rights of those whose choices upset the majority. * * *

■ JUSTICE STEVENS, with whom JUSTICE BRENNAN and JUSTICE MARSHALL join, dissenting.

 * * * Sodomy was condemned as an odious and sinful type of behavior during the formative period of the common law. That condemnation was equally damning for heterosexual and homosexual sodomy. Moreover, it provided no special exemption for married couples. The license to cohabit and to produce legitimate offspring simply did not include any permission to engage in sexual conduct that was considered a "crime against nature." * * * The history of the Georgia statute before

us clearly reveals this traditional prohibition of heterosexual, as well as homosexual, sodomy. * * *

Because the Georgia statute expresses the traditional view that sodomy is an immoral kind of conduct regardless of the identity of the persons who engage in it, I believe that a proper analysis of its constitutionality requires consideration of two questions: First, may a State totally prohibit the described conduct by means of a neutral law applying without exception to all persons subject to its jurisdiction? If not, may the State save the statute by announcing that it will only enforce the law against homosexuals? * * *

Our prior cases make two propositions abundantly clear. First, the fact that the governing majority in a State has traditionally viewed a particular practice as immoral is not a sufficient reason for upholding a law prohibiting the practice; neither history nor tradition could save a law prohibiting miscegenation from constitutional attack. Second, individual decisions by married persons, concerning the intimacies of their physical relationship, even when not intended to produce offspring, are a form of "liberty" protected by the Due Process Clause * * *

If the Georgia statute cannot be enforced as it is written—if the conduct it seeks to prohibit is a protected form of liberty for the vast majority of Georgia's citizens—the State must assume the burden of justifying a selective application of its law. Either the persons to whom Georgia seeks to apply its statute do not have the same interest in "liberty" that others have, or there must be a reason why the State may be permitted to apply a generally applicable law to certain persons that it does not apply to others.

The first possibility is plainly unacceptable. Although the meaning of the principle that "all men are created equal" is not always clear, it surely must mean that every free citizen has the same interest in "liberty" that the members of the majority share. From the standpoint of the individual, the homosexual and the heterosexual have the same interest in deciding how he will live his own life, and, more narrowly, how he will conduct himself in his personal and voluntary associations with his companions. State intrusion into the private conduct of either is equally burdensome.

The second possibility is similarly unacceptable. A policy of selective application must be supported by a neutral and legitimate interest— something more substantial than a habitual dislike for, or ignorance about, the disfavored group. Neither the State nor the Court has identified any such interest in this case. The Court has posited as a justification for the Georgia statute "the presumed belief of a majority of the electorate in Georgia that homosexual sodomy is immoral and unacceptable." But the Georgia electorate has expressed no such belief— instead, its representatives enacted a law that presumably reflects the belief that *all sodomy* is immoral and unacceptable. Unless the Court is prepared to conclude that such a law is constitutional, it may not rely on the work product of the Georgia Legislature to support its holding. For the Georgia statute does not single out homosexuals as a separate class meriting special disfavored treatment. * * *

NOTES ON *BOWERS V. HARDWICK*

1.   *The Shadow of* Roe. The majority opinion can be read as a signal that *Roe v. Wade* was in trouble. The Justices rejected an "expansive view of our authority to discover new fundamental rights imbedded in the Due Process Clause. The Court is most vulnerable and comes nearest to illegitimacy when it deals with judge-made constitutional law having little or no cognizable roots in the language or design of the Constitution." The backlash against *Roe* was in full flower in the mid-1980s. Justice Blackmun, the author of *Roe*, uses his *Hardwick* dissent to frame the rights at issue in those cases as analogous in their centrality to individual flourishing. Justice Stevens articulates the kernel of what will become the theme of equal liberty, which will eventually dominate the doctrine in this area.

2.   *Misreading History and Culture.* "All of the Justices seem to have assumed that 'homosexuality' has been an invariant reality, outside of history. In fact, however, like most ways of describing aspects of the human condition, 'homosexuality' is a cultural and historical artifact. No attitude toward 'homosexuals' or 'homosexuality' can really be identified before the mid-nineteenth century because the concept [and even the word 'homosexual'] did not exist until then. * * * Thus, by referring to 'homosexual sodomy' in ancient times, in 1791, and even in 1868, White and Burger were inserting their modern understanding of 'homosexuality' anachronistically into systems of values organized on other principles, obscuring the relative novelty of the distinction between 'homosexuality' and 'heterosexuality' with a myth about its antiquity." Anne Goldstein, "History, Homosexuality and Public Values: Searching for the Hidden Determinants of *Bowers v. Hardwick*," 97 *Yale L. J.* 1073, 1087–89 (1988).

Supplementing Professor Goldstein's account, William Eskridge Jr., "*Hardwick* and Historiography," 1999 *U. Ill. L. Rev.* 631, demonstrated that contrary to the Court's account, the crime against nature at common law did not include oral sex; it was not until 1879 that any state made consensual oral sex a crime, and some states never criminalized oral sex between women. Moreover, the historical purpose of sodomy laws was regulation of public or predatory sexual behaviors, not private consensual activities. Reported American sodomy decisions in the nineteenth century involved either predatory or public conduct by the defendant, to the extent one can tell from reading the reported cases. Indeed, state criminal codes categorized the crime against nature as either a crime against the person (with rape and other forms of unconsented assault) or a crime against *public* decency (with unlawful cohabitation, indecent exposure in public places, and other public misconduct). Indeed, common law rules of evidence rendered such prosecutions virtually impossible: when the crime against nature involved a consenting adult, the state could not rely on the testimony of the legal "accomplice" and had to corroborate it with independent evidence, presumably unobtainable if the acts were committed in the defendant's home or another private place.

3. *Judicial Discomfort and the Near Miss.* Justice Powell's original vote was reportedly with Justice Blackmun, which would have meant five votes to invalidate the Georgia statute, but Justice Powell changed his mind. John Calvin Jeffries, Jr., Powell's biographer, writes that Powell agonized over his decision in the case and was aware of his ignorance about homosexuality. Jeffries, *Lewis F. Powell, Jr.* 313–30 (1993). At one point he engaged in a discussion of the matter with one of his law clerks, who tried to explain to the Justice that "homosexuals" are normal human beings who are part of the everyday environment of virtually everyone. Justice Powell apparently found it hard to understand how this could be and confessed to the clerk that he had never met a "homosexual" that he knew of. In truth, however, several of Justice Powell's clerks had been gay, including the law clerk to whom he made this confession, but apparently none had come out to him.

4. *Supreme Court Hall of Shame.* *Hardwick* quickly became one of the most criticized opinions in the history of the Court, with virtually no defenders in the academy or established bar. (We are aware of no decision of the Court *upholding* a statute that was the object of such immediate and overwhelming criticism as the decision in *Bowers*.) Doctrinally, it may be read as simply drawing a line beyond which the much-criticized reasoning of *Griswold* and *Roe*, in finding a right of privacy implied in the Constitution, would not venture. Yet the contemptuous tone of its language seems, ironically, to have created its own undoing as a legitimate attempt at interpretation. Compare the majority in *Hardwick* with the dissent in *People v. Onofre*, 51 N.Y.2d 476 (1980) for example. The latter comes to the same conclusion, as to a New York statute that was virtually identical to the Georgia law. Yet the language of the *Onofre* dissent simply continues the public-private morality debate in measured tones, whereas the *Hardwick* opinion reads as an anti-gay screed. One critical difference between the two opinions was that the New York Court of Appeals had consolidated several cases, including two involving heterosexual sex, into the ruling in *Onofre*.

5. *The Double Bind Critique.* Janet Halley, "Reasoning about Sodomy: Act and Identity in and after *Bowers v. Hardwick*," 79 *Va. L. Rev.* 1721 (1993), compared the rhetoric of the Court's fundamental rights holding with the rhetoric of its rational basis discussion as an example of "the systematic ways in which acts and identities generate incoherence and instability. In his fundamental rights analysis, Justice White (cheered on by Chief Justice Burger) exploited the rhetoric of acts to make plausible his claim that sodomy has been, transhistorically and without surcease, the object of intense social disapprobation. In the rational basis holding, on the other hand, Justice White moved into a rhetoric of identities, holding that Georgia's sodomy statute rationally implements popular condemnation of *homosexuality*." Halley argues that Justice White's ability to jump back and forth between act and identity created a "double bind" for gay people:

> "In everyday language, you are in a double bind when you cannot win because your victorious opponent is willing to be a hypocrite and to 'damn you if you do and damn you if you don't.'

More strictly examined, a double bind involves a systematic arrangement of symbolic systems with at least three characteristics. First, two conceptual systems (or 'discourses') are matched in their opposition to one another; one is consistently understood to be not only different from but the logical alternative of the other. Second, the preferred discourse actually requires the submerged one to make it work. It is at this point that a naive deconstructive claim is often made, that the secret inclusion of the nonpreferred discourse as a prerequisite for the smooth operation of the express one reveals the whole system to be fatally unstable. But third, that very instability can be the source of suppleness and resilience, because the two stacked discourses can be flipped: the one that was submerged and denied can become express, and it in turn can be covertly supported by the one that was preferred. The master of a double bind always has somewhere to go."

Hence, Justice White could rely on the ancient pedigree of sodomy law's disapproval of certain nonprocreative acts to refute Hardwick's claim that his conduct was protected by traditional liberty-based norms. Taken too far, such rhetoric could create anxiety among his Brethren, many of whom probably had committed sodomy in their own bedrooms—and so Justice White's history ignored the possibility of "heterosexual sodomy" and totalized the crime around "homosexuality." This illustrates the close relationship between the dominant (acts) and the subordinate (identity) categories. In the rational basis analysis, the categories are flipped, with homosexual identity being the dominant theme. Underlying Georgians' presumed morality that demonizes homosexuality as a degraded identity is their disgust at homosexual acts.

6. *The Normative Critique.* The lawyers' strategy in the *Hardwick* litigation was to deemphasize the fact that Hardwick was a gay man having sex with another man and to situate the case as similar to heterosexual non-procreative sex protected in *Griswold* and subsequent cases. One effect of this strategy was to reinforce the impression that everyone was ashamed of Hardwick's activities and, perhaps also, his homosexuality. This was a mistake, argued political philosopher Michael Sandel, in "Moral Argument and Liberal Toleration," 77 *Calif. L. Rev.* 521 (1989). "Like Blackmun and Stevens, the [Eleventh Circuit] appeals court [in *Hardwick*] constructed an analogy between privacy in marriage and privacy in homosexual relations. But unlike the Supreme Court dissenters, it did not rest the analogy on voluntarist grounds," namely, the argument that government should be neutral among competing concepts of morality, alone. "It argued instead that both practices may realize important human goods." The appeals court reasoned that the moral good of marriage is the "unsurpassed opportunity for mutual support and self-expression that it provides." Rather than relying so strongly on *Stanley,* which protected private viewing of pornography, Hardwick's attorneys should have emphasized that the human goods of homosexual relations are the same as those enjoyed by the married couple protected in *Griswold.*

Professor Sandel's article was not just a challenge to the litigators' strategy in *Bowers,* but also to a *tolerance-based* theory of the privacy right. "The problem with the neutral case for toleration is the opposite side of its appeal; it leaves wholly unchallenged the adverse views of homosexuality itself. Unless those views can be plausibly addressed, even a Court ruling in their favor is unlikely to win for homosexuals more than a thin and fragile toleration. A fuller respect would require, if not admiration, at least some appreciation of the lives homosexuals live. Such appreciation, however, is unlikely to be cultivated by a legal and political discourse conducted in terms of autonomy rights alone."

Hardwick's lawyers would have responded that there was no way to win the case with Sandel's arguments. Most of the Justices in 1986 would have been flabbergasted to hear that "homosexual intimacy" was similar to "heterosexual marriage" as a human good, and Justice Powell (the critical fifth Justice) was appalled by that very comparison. See Eskridge, *Dishonorable Passions,* 243–46. How might advocates have used an argument so far ahead of its time?

7. *The Social Constructionist Critique.* The following article was one of the first articulations of a critique of *Bowers v. Hardwick* grounded in the work of French philosopher Michel Foucault. It argues that the personhood arguments of liberals such as Justice Blackmun incorporate an implicit, self-defeating essentialism and that the harm of a decision like *Hardwick* comes less from the conduct it prohibits than from the life choices it indirectly coerces. Do you agree? Consider the further materials on Michel Foucault's philosophy of sexuality in Chapter 3, Section 3.

Jed Rubenfeld, "The Right of Privacy" 102 *Harvard Law Review* **737, 777–800 passim (1989).*** The individualistic concept of privacy embedded in *Griswold* and in the *Hardwick* dissents is an imprisoning strategy. "Let us look carefully at personhood's stance on homosexuality. The personhood position, as we have seen, is that homosexual sex should receive constitutional protection because it is so essential to an individual's self-definition—to his identity. * * *

"There is, however, an ambiguity in the idea that homosexual sex is central to the identity of those who engage in it. Is homosexual sex said to be self-definitive simply because it is sex, or especially because it is homosexual sex? In fact, proponents of personhood appear to argue for the second proposition. One reason for this is that the first version of the argument would be quite difficult to sustain. To begin with, it would * * * be required to claim that prostitution, for example, is an exercise of one's constitutional rights. (Personhood could, of course, choose to defend this position.) Moreover, it simply seems implausible to assert that the act of sex on any given occasion is necessarily fundamental in defining the identity of the person engaging in it.

" * * * Prohibiting homosexual sex, personhood can say, violates the right to privacy because homosexual sex is for homosexuals 'expressive of innermost traits of being.' It 'touches the heart of what makes individuals what they are.' * * *

"Without doubt, personhood's arguments for homosexual rights are intended to show and to seek the highest degree of respect for those on behalf of whom they are made. Nevertheless, in the very concept of a homosexual identity there is something potentially disserving—if not disrespectful—to the cause advocated. There is something not altogether liberating. Those who engage in homosexual sex may or may not perceive themselves as bearing a 'homosexual identity.' Their homosexual relations may be a pleasure they take or an intimacy they value without constituting—at least qua homosexual relations—something definitive of their identity. At the heart of personhood's analysis is the reliance upon a sharply demarcated 'homosexual identity' to which a person is immediately consigned at the moment he seeks to engage in homosexual sex. For personhood, that is, homosexual relations are to be protected to the extent that they fundamentally define a species of person that is, by definition, to be strictly distinguished from the heterosexual. Persons may have homosexual sex only because they have elected to define themselves as 'homosexuals'—because homosexuality lies at 'the heart of . . . what they are.' Thus, even as it argues for homosexual rights, personhood becomes yet another turn of the screw that has pinned those who engage in homosexual sex into a fixed identity specified by their difference from 'heterosexuals.' * * *

" * * * Obviously, differences of sexuality, gender, and race exist among us. These are not, however, differences in *identity* until we make them so. Moreover, it is the desire to count oneself 'superior' to another, or even to count oneself 'normal,' that converts such differences into those specified identities in opposition to which we define ourselves. To protect the rights of 'the homosexual' would of course be a victory; doing so, however, because homosexuality is essential to a person's identity is no liberation, but simply the flip side of the same rigidification of sexual identities by which our society simultaneously inculcates sexual roles, normalizes sexual conduct, and vilifies 'faggots.'

" * * * We must reject the personhood thesis, then, not because the concept of 'self-definition' is analytically incoherent, nor because it is too 'individualistic,' but ultimately because it betrays privacy's—if not personhood's own—political aspirations. By conceiving of the conduct that it purports to protect as 'essential to the individual's identity,' personhood inadvertently reintroduces into privacy analysis the very premise of the invidious uses of state power it seeks to overcome.

"Perhaps the example of abortion can best serve to drive this point home. Personhood must defend the right to abortion on the ground that abortion is essential to the woman's self-definition. But underlying the idea that a woman is *defining her identity* by determining not to have a child is the very premise of those institutionalized sexual roles through which the subordination of women has for so long been maintained. Only if it were 'natural' for a woman to want to bear children—and unnatural if she did not—would it make sense to insist that the decision not to have a child at one given moment was centrally definitive of a woman's identity. Those of us who believe that a woman has a right to abort her pregnancy must defend the position on other grounds. The claim that an abortion is a fundamental act of self-definition is nothing other than a corollary to the insistence that motherhood, or at least the desire to be a mother, is the fundamental, inescapable, natural backdrop of womanhood against which every woman is defined.

"Women should be able to abort their pregnancies so that they may *avoid being forced into an identity*, not because they are defining their identities through the decision itself. Resisting an enforced identity is not the same as defining oneself. Therein lies the real flaw of the personhood account of privacy—and therein the core of the alternative view of privacy advanced in what follows.

"Anti-abortion laws produce motherhood: they take diverse women with every variety of career, life-plan, and so on, and make mothers of them all. To be sure, motherhood is no unitary phenomenon that is experienced alike by all women. Nonetheless, it is difficult to imagine a state-enforced rule whose ramifications within the actual, everyday life of the actor are more far-reaching. For a period of months and quite possibly years, forced motherhood shapes women's occupations and preoccupations in the minutest detail it creates a perceived identity for women and confines them to it; and it gathers up a multiplicity of approaches to the problem of being a woman and reduces them all to the single norm of motherhood. * * *

"Now, it is quite clear that *Roe v. Wade* had something to do with control over the body; indeed, it has become conventional to interpret *Roe* as resting at least in part on women's right to 'bodily integrity' or to 'control their own bodies.' This supposed right of bodily control, however, has been either poorly articulated or simply misunderstood. The right to control one's body cannot possibly be a right to do as one pleases with it even where the state can rationally identify harms being caused thereby; otherwise common law crimes or torts would be constitutionally immunized. Nor, however, should the bodily control theme in *Roe* be reduced to the woman's interest in deciding whether a certain surgical operation is to be performed upon her. In fact, anti-abortion laws produce a far more affirmative and pronounced bodily intervention: the compulsion to carry a fetus to term, to deliver the baby, and to care for the child in the first years of its life. All of these processes, in their real daily effects, involve without question the most intimate and strenuous exercises of the female body. The woman's body will be subjected to a continuous regimen of diet, exercise, medical examination, and possibly surgical procedures. Her most elemental biological and psychological impulses will be enlisted in the process. In these ways, anti-abortion laws exert power productively over a woman's body and, through the uses to which her body is put, forcefully reshape and redirect her life. * * *

"Thus it is difficult to imagine a single proscription with a greater capacity to shape lives into singular, normalized, functional molds than the prohibition of abortions. Even if the propensity of anti-abortion laws to exert power over the body and to instrumentalize women is discounted, it remains the case that such laws radically and affirmatively redirect women's lives. Indeed it is difficult to conceive of a particular legal prohibition with a more total effect on the life and future of the one enjoined. It is no exaggeration to say that mandatory childbearing is a totalitarian intervention into a woman's life. With regard to the occupation and direction of lives, the positive ramifications of anti-abortion laws are unparalleled. *Roe v. Wade* was, in this view, correctly decided." * * *

In Chapter 2, we will pick up the development of substantive due process law in reproductive rights, sexual conduct, and [what Justice White described as "at best facetious"] same-sex marriage by analyzing the Supreme Court's most important decisions in each field.

SECTION 2

BOUNDED EQUALITY

The Fourteenth Amendment guarantees all persons the "equal protection of the law" against infringement by state and local governments. The context for its adoption was the Reconstructionist effort to void state laws denying African Americans basic rights. Since then, the Equal Protection Clause has been extended in two ways: to apply to the federal government, by incorporation into the Due Process Clause of the Fifth Amendment, *Bolling v. Sharpe*, 347 U.S. 497 (1954); and to cover classifications other than those based on race. See *infra*.

The modern history of the Equal Protection Clause has focused on the tension between its mandate for equal treatment and the need in many areas of the law to create classifications. In constitutional law's most famous footnote, the Supreme Court distinguished categories routinely created to regulate markets and address other economic issues, from classifications reflecting "prejudice against discrete and insular minorities." *United States v. Carolene Products*, 304 U.S. 144, 152–53 n.4 (1938). Normally, the Court said, deference to legislative majorities should protect the former category from stringent judicial review, so long as the lines drawn embodied a rational basis for distinctions related to legitimate state interests. For the latter category of anti-minority laws, however, the Court endorsed a more rigorous judicial approach.

The deferential rational basis standard developed into one line of cases, under which the Court balked at striking down what may have seemed like questionable distinctions so long as some plausible reason for them might have motivated the legislature to act as did. *See Railway Express Agency v. New York*, 336 U.S. 106 (1949) (upholding ban on all vehicular advertising unless for a business of vehicle's owner); *Williamson v. Lee Optical Co.*, 348 U.S. 483 (1955) (upholding law requiring opticians from transferring lenses to new frames without a prescription from an optometrist or ophthalmologist). A handful of cases found that the state's justification for a classification failed even the rational basis standard. *See, e.g., James v. Strange*, 407 U.S. 128 (1972) (striking law denying indigent defendant, in action by the state to recoup legal defense fees, certain exemptions available to other judgment debtors).

An increasing number of civil rights cases comprised the second strand of more robust equal protection law. The Court solidified the *Carolene Products* concern with race-based classifications by developing a strict scrutiny method, under which a law using an inherently "suspect" classification (e.g., race) would be struck down unless the government could demonstrate that the use of race was narrowly tailored and necessary to achieve a compelling state interest. In a highly influential

49

book, John Hart Ely argued that the counter-majoritarian power of strict scrutiny review was justified because it was necessary to protect those groups ("discrete and insular minorities") whose stigmatization rendered them unable to compete as other groups did in the legislative process. *Democracy and Distrust: A Theory of Judicial Review* (1980). Professor Ely's "representation-reinforcement" theory aligned neatly with the racial and religious minorities with which the Court was concerned in 1938 (as it watched the rise of European fascism). How well does it apply to women, a group with a numerical majority? Or to minorities dispersed throughout the population? For women, the Court developed an intermediate standard of judicial review. *See Craig v. Boren, infra.*

Finally, as the twentieth century drew to a close, the Court began to decide some equal protection challenges by using rational basis-style language, but paired with much closer examination of the history, logic, purposes, and effects of certain classifications. Called "rational basis with bite" or "heightened rational basis," this new and unacknowledged approach could produce invalidation of laws even in the absence of suspect classifications. *See, e.g., U.S. Dep't of Agriculture v. Moreno*, 413 U.S. 528 (1973) (denial of Food Stamp benefits to a household unless all residents were related to each other); *City of Cleburne v. Cleburne Living Center*, 473 U.S. 432 (1985) (denial of zoning variance to a group home for mentally disabled persons). In time, heightened rational basis was used in sexual orientation cases as well.

A. DISCRIMINATION BASED ON SEX

After ratification in 1920 of the Nineteenth Amendment granting women the right to vote, the question of women's equality under the law remained mostly dormant until the 1960s. See, e.g., *Goesaert v. Cleary*, 335 U.S. 464 (1948) (upholding law prohibiting women from working as bartenders unless the daughter or wife of a male bar owner). In 1961, the Supreme Court unanimously upheld Florida's opt-in system for women to serve on juries, based on what the Court considered to be a reasonable reflection of the conventional wisdom that women should be occupied with domestic matters rather than called up for jury duty. *Hoyt v. Florida*, 368 U.S. 57, 62 (1961) (noting that "woman is still regarded as the center of home and family life"). The decision in *Hoyt* maintained the Court's record of never having invalidated a law that discriminated based on sex on the ground that it violated the Equal Protection Clause.

In 1961, President John Kennedy established the President's Commission on the Status of Women, which served as a consciousness-raising and idea-sharing forum for feminist lawyers and thinkers. Pauli Murray, a civil rights lawyer working toward her J.S.D. at Yale Law School, drafted a remarkable memorandum for the Commission. The memorandum argued that the Equal Protection Clause could be interpreted to question sex-based discriminations for the same reasons the Court had deployed it against race-based discriminations: sex discriminations (like race discriminations) rested upon a natural law understanding of "inherent differences" that had been deployed to support disadvantages and social inferiority of women; the naturalized view of sex differences rested upon unproven stereotypes or myths about women that were usually an irrational basis for subordinating them; like blacks, women needed to mobilize against pervasive state discrimination through the formation of an organization like the NAACP. Murray's arguments persuaded the Commission to endorse (albeit at a highly general level) the principle that "equality of rights under the law for all persons, male or female, is so basic to democracy and its commitment to the ultimate value of the individual that it must be reflected in the fundamental law of the land." Her memorandum bridged the concerns of various civil rights activists: her Fourteenth Amendment strategy sought equality for women (desired by liberal ERA feminists), but without sacrificing laws genuinely remedying women's disadvantages in the workplace (desired by labor feminists and ERA opponents). Murray, an African American who had been active in the civil rights movement, sought to unite blacks and women in a common campaign against prejudice and discrimination.

Murray's arguments found their way into the congressional debates through the addition of sex discrimination to the jobs title of the 1964 Civil Rights Act. Although ironically it was anti-civil rights Representative Howard Smith of Virginia who proposed the amendment to add "sex," Murray and other feminists supported it and ensured that it was preserved in the final statute. The EEOC refused to make sex discrimination a priority in its enforcement of the new law, a stance that drew strong protests. When officials ignored their complaints at a 1966 conference on women's status, Murray, Betty Friedan, and other feminists stormed out in protest and went on to found the National Organization for Women (NOW). The feminist political energy harnessed by NOW sought adoption of an Equal Rights Amendment (ERA), which would assure constitutional equality; serious enforcement of the Equal Pay Act and Title VII, to assure equality in the workplace; liberalization or repeal of restrictive abortion laws; and adoption of legislation barring sex discrimination in education, accomplished with the enactment of Title IX in 1972.

In 1971, the ACLU established its Women's Rights Project, headed by Professor Ruth Bader Ginsburg. Representing a new generation of litigators, Ginsburg pressed courts to rule that women had the same legal rights and duties as men. The first case of the new wave to reach the Supreme Court challenged an Idaho statute that preferred male relatives over female ones for purposes of appointment to administer estates of intestate decedents. The ACLU sought a ruling that sex was a suspect classification, as the California Supreme Court had just declared in *Sail'er Inn, Inc. v. Kirby*, 5 Cal.3d 1, 485 P.2d 529 (1971). The U.S. Supreme Court was not prepared to go that far, however. Chief Justice

Burger's opinion for a unanimous Court in *Reed v. Reed*, 404 U.S. 71 (1971) rested upon the statute's arbitrariness. The *Reed* opinion did not specify which standard of review the Court was relying on, leading to the presumption that the statute had failed under a rational basis standard.

1. SEEKING STRICTER SCRUTINY

In March 1972, Congress approved a proposed Equal Rights Amendment (ERA) by a large bipartisan majority and sent it to the states for ratification. Section 1 of the ERA provided that "Equality of rights under the law shall not be denied or abridged by the United States or by any State on account of sex." By 1973, the follow-up case to *Reed v. Reed*, with Ginsburg pressing for strict scrutiny, was before the Supreme Court.

Sharron Frontiero and Joseph Frontiero
v. Elliot Richardson

United States Supreme Court, 1973.
411 U.S. 677, 93 S.Ct. 1764, 36 L.Ed.2d 583.

■ MR. JUSTICE BRENNAN announced the judgment of the Court in an opinion in which MR. JUSTICE DOUGLAS, MR. JUSTICE WHITE, and MR. JUSTICE MARSHALL join.

The question before us concerns the right of a female member of the uniformed services to claim her spouse as a "dependent" for the purposes of obtaining increased quarters allowances and medical and dental benefits under 37 U.S.C. §§ 401, 403, and 10 U.S.C. §§ 1072, 1076, on an equal footing with male members. Under these statutes, a serviceman may claim his wife as a "dependent" without regard to whether she is in fact dependent upon him for any part of her support. A servicewoman, on the other hand, may not claim her husband as a "dependent" under these programs unless he is in fact dependent upon her for over one-half of his support. Thus, the question for decision is whether this difference in treatment constitutes an unconstitutional discrimination against servicewomen in violation of the [Equal Protection component of the] Due Process Clause of the Fifth Amendment. * * *

Although the legislative history of these statutes sheds virtually no light on the purposes underlying the differential treatment accorded male and female members, a majority of the three-judge District Court surmised that Congress might reasonably have concluded that, since the husband in our society is generally the "breadwinner" in the family—and the wife typically the "dependent" partner—"it would be more economical to require married female members claiming husbands to prove actual dependency than to extend the presumption of dependency to such members." Indeed, given the fact that approximately 99% of all members of the uniformed services are male, the District Court speculated that such differential treatment might conceivably lead to a "considerable saving of administrative expense and manpower."

At the outset, appellants contend that classifications based upon sex, like classifications based upon race, alienage, and national origin, are inherently suspect and must therefore be subjected to close judicial scrutiny. We agree and, indeed, find at least implicit support for such an approach in our unanimous decision only last Term in *Reed*. * * *

The Court [in *Reed*] noted that the Idaho statute "provides that different treatment be accorded to the applicants on the basis of their sex; it thus establishes a classification subject to scrutiny under the Equal Protection Clause." Under "traditional" equal protection analysis, a legislative classification must be sustained unless it is "patently arbitrary" and bears no rational relationship to a legitimate governmental interest.

In an effort to meet this standard, appellee contended that the statutory scheme was a reasonable measure designed to reduce the workload on probate courts by eliminating one class of contests. Moreover, appellee argued that the mandatory preference for male applicants was in itself reasonable since "men (are) as a rule more conversant with business affairs than . . . women." Indeed, appellee maintained that "it is a matter of common knowledge, that women still are not engaged in politics, the professions, business or industry to the extent that men are." And the Idaho Supreme Court, in upholding the constitutionality of this statute, suggested that the Idaho Legislature might reasonably have "concluded that in general men are better qualified to act as an administrator than are women."

Despite these contentions, however, the Court held the statutory preference for male applicants unconstitutional. In reaching this result, the Court implicitly rejected appellee's apparently rational explanation of the statutory scheme, and concluded that, by ignoring the individual qualifications of particular applicants, the challenged statute provided "dissimilar treatment for men and women who are . . . similarly situated." The Court therefore held that, even though the State's interest in achieving administrative efficiency "is not without some legitimacy," "[t]o give a mandatory preference to members of either sex over members of the other, merely to accomplish the elimination of hearings on the merits, is to make the very kind of arbitrary legislative choice forbidden by the [Constitution][.]" This departure from "traditional" rational-basis analysis with respect to sex-based classifications is clearly justified.

There can be no doubt that our Nation has had a long and unfortunate history of sex discrimination. Traditionally, such discrimination was rationalized by an attitude of "romantic paternalism" which, in practical effect, put women, not on a pedestal, but in a cage. * * *

As a result of notions such as these, our statute books gradually became laden with gross, stereotyped distinctions between the sexes and, indeed, throughout much of the 19th century the position of women in our society was, in many respects, comparable to that of blacks under the pre-Civil War slave codes. Neither slaves nor women could hold office, serve on juries, or bring suit in their own names, and married women traditionally were denied the legal capacity to hold or convey property or to serve as legal guardians of their own children. And although blacks were guaranteed the right to vote in 1870, women were denied even that right * * * until adoption of the Nineteenth Amendment half a century later.

It is true, of course, that the position of women in America has improved markedly in recent decades. Nevertheless, it can hardly be doubted that, in part because of the high visibility of the sex characteristic, women still face pervasive, although at times more subtle, discrimination in our educational institutions, in the job market and, perhaps most conspicuously, in the political arena.

Moreover, since sex, like race and national origin, is an immutable characteristic determined solely by the accident of birth, the imposition of special disabilities upon the members of a particular sex because of their sex would seem to violate "the basic concept of our system that legal burdens should bear some relationship to individual responsibility. . . ." *Weber v. Aetna Casualty & Surety Co.*, 406 U.S. 164, 175 (1972). And what differentiates sex from such non-suspect statuses as intelligence or physical disability, and aligns it with the recognized suspect criteria, is that the sex characteristic frequently bears no relation to ability to perform or contribute to society. As a result, statutory distinctions between the sexes often have the effect of invidiously relegating the entire class of females to inferior legal status without regard to the actual capabilities of its individual members.

We might also note that, over the past decade, Congress has itself manifested an increasing sensitivity to sex-based classifications. In Title VII of the Civil Rights Act of 1964, for example, Congress expressly declared that no employer, labor union, or other organization subject to the provisions of the Act shall discriminate against any individual on the basis of "race, color, religion, *sex*, or national origin." Similarly, the Equal Pay Act of 1963 provides that no employer covered by the Act "shall discriminate . . . between employees on the basis of sex." And § 1 of the Equal Rights Amendment, passed by Congress on March 22, 1972, and submitted to the legislatures of the States for ratification, declares that "[e]quality of rights under the law shall not be denied or abridged by the United States or by any State on account of sex." Thus, Congress itself has concluded that classifications based upon sex are inherently invidious, and this conclusion of a coequal branch of Government is not without significance to the question presently under consideration.

With these considerations in mind, we can only conclude that classifications based upon sex, like classifications based upon race, alienage, or national origin, are inherently suspect, and must therefore be subjected to strict judicial scrutiny. Applying the analysis mandated by that stricter standard of review, it is clear that the statutory scheme now before us is constitutionally invalid.

The sole basis of the classification established in the challenged statutes is the sex of the individuals involved. * * * [A] female member of the uniformed services seeking to obtain housing and medical benefits for her spouse must prove his dependency in fact, whereas no such burden is imposed upon male members. In addition, the statutes operate so as to deny benefits to a female member, such as appellant Sharon Frontiero, who provides less than one-half of her spouse's support, while at the same time granting such benefits to a male member who likewise provides less than one-half of his spouse's support. Thus, to this extent at least, it may fairly be said that these statutes command "dissimilar treatment for men and women who are . . . similarly situated." *Reed.*

Moreover, the Government concedes that the differential treatment accorded men and women under these statutes serves no purpose other than mere "administrative convenience." In essence, the Government maintains that, as an empirical matter, wives in our society frequently are dependent upon their husbands, while husbands rarely are dependent upon their wives. Thus, the Government argues that Congress might reasonably have concluded that it would be both cheaper and easier simply conclusively to presume that wives of male members are financially dependent upon their husbands, while burdening female members with the task of establishing dependency in fact.

The Government offers no concrete evidence, however, tending to support its view that such differential treatment in fact saves the Government any money. In order to satisfy the demands of strict judicial scrutiny, the Government must demonstrate, for example, that it is actually cheaper to grant increased benefits with respect to all male members, than it is to determine which male members are in fact entitled to such benefits and to grant increased benefits only to those members whose wives actually meet the dependency requirement. Here, however, there is substantial evidence that, if put to the test, many of the wives of male members would fail to qualify for benefits. And in light of the fact that the dependency determination with respect to the husbands of female members is presently made solely on the basis of affidavits rather than through the more costly hearing process, the Government's explanation of the statutory scheme is, to say the least, questionable.

In any case, our prior decisions make clear that, although efficacious administration of governmental programs is not without some importance, "the Constitution recognizes higher values than speed and efficiency." *Stanley v. Illinois*, 405 U.S. 645, 656 (1972). And when we enter the realm of "strict judicial scrutiny," there can be no doubt that "administrative convenience" is not a shibboleth, the mere recitation of which dictates constitutionality. On the contrary, any statutory scheme which draws a sharp line between the sexes, *solely* for the purpose of achieving administrative convenience, necessarily commands "dissimilar treatment for men and women who are . . . similarly situated," and therefore involves the "very kind of arbitrary legislative choice forbidden by the [Constitution] . . ." *Reed*. We therefore conclude that, by according differential treatment to male and female members of the uniformed services for the sole purpose of achieving administrative convenience, the challenged statutes violate the Due Process Clause of the Fifth Amendment insofar as they require a female member to prove the dependency of her husband.

■ MR. JUSTICE STEWART concurs in the judgment, agreeing that the statutes before us work an invidious discrimination in violation of the Constitution. *Reed*.

■ [We omit the dissenting opinion of MR. JUSTICE REHNQUIST and the opinion of MR. JUSTICE POWELL (joined by MR. CHIEF JUSTICE BURGER and MR. JUSTICE BLACKMUN) concurring in the judgment. JUSTICE POWELL's concurring opinion argued that the statute's sex discrimination was invalid under *Reed* and that it was premature for the Court to decide whether sex is a suspect classification so long as the ERA was pending.]

NOTES ON ARGUMENTS FOR HEIGHTENED SCRUTINY FOR CLASSIFICATIONS BASED ON SEX

Because Justice Brennan's opinion drew only four votes, the effort to secure strict scrutiny fell short. The level of scrutiny question had been conceptualized and argued almost entirely on the grounds of whether sex was sufficiently analogous to race to justify the most stringent review. The two situations shared a history of invidious motivations and starkly unfair results, but there were also complexities. Consider the following:

1. *The Paradoxical Effects of Political Progress.* Recall that the justification of strict scrutiny for race-based classifications derived, at least in part, from the *Carolene Products* idea that special constitutional protection should be extended to "discrete and insular minorities" subjected to systemic discrimination in the political process. Working inside this framework, and realizing that women are neither insular nor a minority, the *Frontiero* litigants generated an argument that used the successes of women in the political process (e.g., enactment of employment protections) to demonstrate congressional acknowledgment of the seriousness of discrimination against women, while still insisting that women's continuing lack of political power justified strict scrutiny review. Was this argument persuasive? At what point, if ever, will it cease to be persuasive? The question of how to measure political power for Equal Protection purposes is still unanswered: especially when a group includes a majority of voters, what should the criteria be for political powerlessness?

2. *Stereotypes and "Real" Differences.* By the 1960s, no reputable scientist argued that intrinsic race-based differences were meaningful. But sex-based physical differences—primarily the biological fact that only women can become pregnant and bear children—were undeniable, and were considered legitimate reasons to treat men and women differently in some contexts. (Indeed, this is still the case; *see Nguyen v. INS, infra.*) On the other hand, courts were beginning to accept the premise that women were held back by cognitive *stereotypes*—even if not by prejudice or animus—with the same net result of a pattern male dominance. Much of the sex discrimination jurisprudence the 45 years since *Frontiero* has wrestled with how to denaturalize "real differences," beginning in earnest with the early pregnancy discrimination cases, *infra.*

3. *The Role of Immutability and the Analogy to Race.* Another aspect of the "real differences" theme arose from defendants' arguments that nature, not law, rendered women less fit than men for certain roles. Ginsburg flipped this defense into an argument that sex, like race, is immutable and that it was fundamentally unfair to penalize an individual for a condition over which she had no control. In general, the debate over whether sex could properly be analogized to race for Equal Protection Clause purposes dominated the era of the early cases. See generally, Serena Mayeri, *Reasoning From Race: Feminism, Law, and the Civil Rights Revolution* (2011).

Since the 1970s, the immutability argument has become significantly more complex for at least two reasons. First, there is now widespread recognition that gender transition is possible, although atypical. Second, most scholars agree that equality guarantees should not necessarily be weaker for characteristics for which change is commonplace (e.g., religious affiliation) or for which change occurs for reasons not yet fully understood (see note on immutability and sexual orientation, *infra*). In a world in which individuals do transition between sexes and often express themselves sexually in different ways over the course of a lifetime, what should the ramifications be of immutability in an equal protection case? What *is* immutability?

NOTES ON THE INITIAL PREGNANCY DISCRIMINATION CASES

The most important equality issue for women's rights advocates after winning *Frontiero* was discrimination on the basis of pregnancy. Government programs excluded pregnant women, and private as well as public employers either discharged female employees who became pregnant or required them to take unpaid leaves. Public schools often conclusively presumed that pregnant teachers were unable to work after a particular point in their pregnancies. Cleveland, Ohio, for example, required all pregnant teachers to take mandatory leaves starting five months before their due dates and continuing until three months after delivery. Justice Stewart's opinion for the Court ruled that the policy was an irrebuttable presumption that violated the Due Process Clause because it was often not factually justified. *Cleveland Board of Education v. LaFleur,* 414 U.S. 632 (1974).

Representing pregnant women who were excluded from coverage under a state disability insurance program in *Geduldig v. Aiello*, 417 U.S. 484 (1974), Wendy Webster Williams maintained that "the individual who receives a benefit or suffers a detriment because of a physical characteristic unique to one sex benefits or suffers because he or she belongs to one or the other sex. * * * Those who would make these unique physical differences a touchstone for unscrutinized differential treatment offer nothing other than the modern version of the historical rationales which were for so long the source of women's second class citizenship under the law."

Denying the constitutional claims, Justice Stewart again wrote for the Court in *Geduldig v. Aiello,* 417 U.S. 484 (1974). His main justification was that the pregnancy exclusion was cost-based and not aimed at excluding women from the state benefit system; indeed, Stewart found, women's claim rates were *higher* than men's, even with the pregnancy exclusion. In an important footnote (number 20), Justice Stewart also stated that the majority did not consider pregnancy exclusions to be sex discrimination: the exclusion did not distinguish all men from all women, but merely men and non-pregnant women from pregnant women. Three Justices (Douglas, Brennan, and Marshall) dissented on the ground that the exclusion was adverse treatment based on sex that was no more defensible than those the Court had struck down in *Reed* and *Frontiero*.

The reasoning in footnote 20 illuminated a serious shortcoming in the formal equality approach (likes must be treated alike) of the Court's Equal Protection Clause jurisprudence. By 1973, the Court understood that race discrimination was unconstitutional under the liberal model, because there were no material differences between the races. But only women could become pregnant and bear children. That created a space for Justices to understand pregnancy as a *real difference*, and not as an *invidious discrimination*. This was a key reason why Justices Powell, Blackmun, and Stewart balked at treating all sex-based discriminations like race-based ones. Equality is denied rather than satisfied if different things are treated the same. (We will pick up the story of pregnancy discrimination law when we move into the realm of statutory, rather than constitutional, protections in the workplace materials in Chapter 5.)

During the same period, the Court also restricted the scope of Equal Protection Clause jurisprudence more generally. It held that if a law was facially neutral, plaintiffs had to prove that there was a discriminatory *intent* behind the law. In other words, whether related to race or sex, laws without an explicit classification but with a discriminatory or disparate impact would not be invalidated on that basis alone. *Washington v. Davis*, 426 U.S. 229 (1976); *Personnel Administrator v. Feeney*, 442 U.S. 256 (1979). After this point, disparate impact claims were no longer viable if based on the Constitution, although the Court continues to recognize that some statutes— such as Title VII of the 1964 Civil Rights Act—provide a disparate impact cause of action. (See Chapter 5.)

2. *CRAIG*, BACKLASH, AND THE COURT'S POST-*CRAIG* SEX DISCRIMINATION JURISPRUDENCE

Curtis Craig v. David Boren, 429 U.S. 190 (1976). Oklahoma law allowed 18-year-old girls to buy low-alcohol (2%) beer but required boys to be 21 years old. Because this beer-purchase law rested upon the stereotypes of " 'reckless' young men" and responsible young women, the Court found that it violated the Equal Protection Clause. **Justice Brennan**'s opinion for the Court (joined by six Justices) fixed upon a formula for evaluating sex discrimination claims:

"To withstand constitutional challenge, previous cases establish that classifications by gender must serve important governmental objectives and must be substantially related to achievement of those objectives. Thus, in *Reed*, the objectives of 'reducing the workload on probate courts' and 'avoiding intrafamily controversy' were deemed of insufficient importance to sustain use of an overt gender criterion in the appointment of administrators of intestate decedents' estates. Decisions following *Reed* similarly have rejected administrative ease and convenience as sufficiently important objectives to justify gender-based classifications. * * *

"*Reed v. Reed* has also provided the underpinning for decisions that have invalidated statutes employing gender as an inaccurate proxy for other, more germane bases of classification. Hence, 'archaic and overbroad' generalizations * * * concerning the financial position of servicewomen, *Frontiero*, and working women, *Weinberger v. Wiesenfeld*, [420 U.S. 636 (1975)], could not justify use of a gender line in determining eligibility for certain governmental entitlements. Similarly, increasingly outdated misconceptions concerning the role of females in the home rather than in the 'marketplace and world of ideas' were rejected as loose-fitting characterizations incapable of supporting state statutory schemes that were premised upon their accuracy. [*Stanton v. Stanton*, 421 U.S. 7 (1975).] In light of the weak congruence between gender and the characteristic or trait that gender purported to represent, it was necessary that the legislatures choose either to realign their substantive laws in a gender-neutral fashion, or to adopt procedures for identifying those instances where the sex-centered generalization actually comported with fact."

In *Mississippi University for Women v. Hogan*, 458 U.S. 718 (1982), Justice Sandra Day O'Connor, the first woman to serve on the Court, wrote the opinion for a 5–4 Court striking down a state law allowing only women to enroll at the state nursing college. When a law adopts a sex-based classification, she reasoned, the state has a burden of showing an " 'exceedingly persuasive justification for the classification,' " a burden that cannot be met by post-hoc rationalizations by counsel or policies that ultimately rest upon gender stereotypes.

The victories for women's rights in the early 1970s catalyzed the formation of an anti-feminist countermovement in the later part of that decade. Like the feminist movement, the countermovement made strongly normative arguments, expressed in the language of constitutionalism. Its tenets included the following: (1) sex-neutral and abortion-protective rules imposed by nine Justices were at war with the values of localism, where the family and the state are the primary situs for rules relating to gender-normative roles in bearing and raising children, without interference from the national government; (2) under a proper separation of powers, the popularly elected legislature is both the most legitimate and the most institutionally competent state entity to handle complex, delicate moral and family issues; and (3) the rights articulated on behalf of fetuses and parents should be considered as fundamental liberties.

The Equal Rights Amendment, which went before state legislatures for ratification during this time, became a vehicle for anti-feminists. Phyllis Schlafly and others argued that the ERA was a bad idea because it would undermine the family and deprive states of their ability to legislate morality, would empower unaccountable federal judges to impose their own elite views on an unconsenting populace, and would deprive wives and parents of fundamental rights needed for the preservation of families.

Among Mrs. Schlafly's most popular charges against the ERA were that it would empower the Supreme Court to subject women to the draft and military service, to invalidate gendered statutory rape laws, and to require states to recognize same-sex marriages and other "homosexual rights." Many Americans in the 1970s agreed with Mrs. Schafly on these issues. By 1982, when the period for ERA ratification by state legislatures expired, the Supreme Court had reaffirmed or suggested sympathy with all of the foregoing forms of sex discrimination, substantially following the constitutional logic of Mrs. Schlafly and her allies. In *Rostker v. Goldberg*, 453 U.S. 57 (1981), the Court refused to extend draft registration to women. Justice Rehnquist's opinion held that "the decision to exempt women from registration was not the 'accidental by-product of a traditional way of thinking about females.'" Instead, the decision was a corollary of the proposition that women were barred from combat roles, a bar not challenged by the plaintiffs: because the goal of registration was to prepare for combat mobilization, it was reasonable to limit registration to men. The Court also upheld a statutory rape law that criminalized consensual conduct only by the male, not by the young woman, in *Michael M. v. Superior Court of Sonoma County*, 450 U.S. 464 (1981), reasoning that the state could find that "natural sanctions" (fear of pregnancy) sufficed to deter females. And in *Baker v. Nelson*, 409 U.S. 810 (1972), the Court declined to review (for lack of a substantial federal question) a decision by the Minnesota Supreme Court that the state ERA did not invalidate the exclusion of same-sex couples from marriage.

The Supreme Court accepted traditionalist arguments in the areas of greatest social anxiety about sex equality—women in combat, same-sex marriage, and adolescent sexuality. At the same time, however, it in effect adopted a watered down version of the ERA through enforcing the compromise level of heightened scrutiny adopted in *Craig*. After an extraordinary period in the early 1970s of subjecting sex-based classifications to meaningful constitutional review for the first time, the Court proceeded with a *sub silentio* compromise. It substituted the intermediate level standard in *Craig* for a strict scrutiny standard that women's rights groups had sought, and it acquiesced to conservative cultural norms in the most controversial arenas. After that, the constitutional debates over sex equality abated. From 1983 [*Lehr v. Robertson*, 463 U.S. 248 (1983)] to 1996, the Court decided no Equal Protection Clause-based sex discrimination cases.

3. THE GINSBURG FORMULATION

United States v. Virginia

United States Supreme Court, 1996.
518 U.S. 515, 116 S.Ct. 2264, 135 L.Ed.2d 735.

■ JUSTICE GINSBURG delivered the opinion of the Court.

[Virginia Military Institute (VMI) was the sole single-sex school among Virginia's public institutions of higher learning. VMI's distinctive mission was to produce "citizen-soldiers," men prepared for leadership in civilian life and in military service. Using an "adversative," or constantly challenging and doubting, method of training not available elsewhere in Virginia, VMI endeavored to instill physical and mental discipline in its cadets and to impart to them a strong moral code. The adversative method has yielded a large number of civilian and military leaders in Virginia; VMI alumni have been unusually bonded to one another and to the school. Their school loyalty is legendary, and as a consequence VMI has had one of the largest per-student endowments of all undergraduate institutions in the Nation.

[The United States sued Virginia and VMI, alleging that VMI's exclusively male admission policy violated the Equal Protection Clause. The District Court ruled in VMI's favor. The Fourth Circuit reversed and ordered Virginia to remedy the constitutional violation. In response, Virginia proposed a parallel program for women: Virginia Women's Institute for Leadership (VWIL), located at Mary Baldwin College, a private liberal arts school for women. In lieu of VMI's adversative method, the VWIL Task Force favored "a cooperative method which reinforces self-esteem." In addition to the standard bachelor of arts program offered at Mary Baldwin, VWIL students would take courses in leadership, complete an off-campus leadership externship, participate in community service projects, and assist in arranging a speaker series.

[On remand, the District Court found that Virginia's proposal satisfied the Constitution's equal protection requirement, and the Fourth Circuit affirmed. The appeals court deferentially reviewed Virginia's plan and determined that provision of single-sex educational options was a legitimate objective. Maintenance of single-sex programs, the court concluded, was essential to that objective. The court recognized, however, that its analysis risked bypassing equal protection scrutiny, so it fashioned an additional test, asking whether VMI and VWIL students would receive "substantively comparable" benefits. Although the Court of Appeals acknowledged that the VWIL degree lacked the historical benefit and prestige of a VMI degree, the court nevertheless found the educational opportunities at the two schools sufficiently comparable.]

* * * To summarize the Court's current directions for cases of official classification based on gender: Focusing on the differential treatment or denial of opportunity for which relief is sought, the reviewing court must determine whether the proffered justification is "exceedingly persuasive." The burden of justification is demanding and it rests entirely on the State. See *Mississippi Univ. for Women v. Hogan*. The State must show "at least that the [challenged] classification serves 'important governmental objectives and that the discriminatory means employed' are 'substantially related to the achievement of those objectives.'" *Id*. The justification must be genuine, not hypothesized or invented *post hoc* in response to litigation. And it must not rely on overbroad generalizations about the different talents, capacities, or preferences of males and females.

The heightened review standard our precedent establishes does not make sex a proscribed classification. Supposed "inherent differences" are no longer accepted as a ground for race or national origin classifications. Physical differences between men and women, however, are enduring: "[T]he two sexes are not fungible; a community made up exclusively of one [sex] is different from a community composed of both." *Ballard v. United States*.

"Inherent differences" between men and women, we have come to appreciate, remain cause for celebration, but not for denigration of the members of either sex or for artificial constraints on an individual's opportunity. Sex classifications may be used to compensate women "for particular economic disabilities [they have] suffered," *Califano v. Webster*, 430 U.S. 313, 320 (1977) (*per curiam*), to "promot[e] equal employment opportunity," see *California Federal Sav. & Loan Assn. v. Guerra*, 479 U.S. 272, 289 (1987), to advance full development of the talent and capacities of our Nation's people. But such classifications may not be used, as they once were, to create or perpetuate the legal, social, and economic inferiority of women.

Measuring the record in this case against the review standard just described, we conclude that Virginia has shown no "exceedingly persuasive justification" for excluding all women from the citizen-soldier training afforded by VMI. We therefore affirm the Fourth Circuit's initial judgment, which held that Virginia had violated the Fourteenth Amendment's Equal Protection Clause. Because the remedy proffered by Virginia—the Mary Baldwin VWIL program—does not cure the constitutional violation, i.e., it does not provide equal opportunity, we reverse the Fourth Circuit's final judgment in this case.

The Fourth Circuit initially held that Virginia had advanced no state policy by which it could justify, under equal protection principles, its determination "to afford VMI's unique type of program to men and not to women." Virginia challenges that "liability" ruling and asserts two justifications in defense of VMI's exclusion of women. First, the Commonwealth contends, "single-sex education provides important educational benefits," and the option of single-sex education contributes to "diversity in educational approaches." Second, the Commonwealth argues, "the unique VMI method of character development and leadership training," the school's adversative approach, would have to be modified were VMI to admit women. We consider these two justifications in turn.

Single-sex education affords pedagogical benefits to at least some students, Virginia emphasizes, and that reality is uncontested in this litigation. Similarly, it is not disputed that diversity among public educational institutions can serve the public good. But Virginia has not shown that VMI was established, or has been maintained, with a view to diversifying, by its categorical exclusion of women, educational opportunities within the State. In cases of this genre, our precedent instructs that "benign" justifications proffered in defense of categorical exclusions will not be accepted automatically; a tenable justification must describe actual state purposes, not rationalizations for actions in fact differently grounded. * * *

[Justice Ginsburg's review of the record of single-sex education in Virginia revealed that it originated in the state's belief that only men would benefit from higher education. Virginia persisted in that belief much longer than other states; its public university, the University of Virginia, did not admit female students until 1970. The only deliberative effort by the state to express its policy since 1970 was the report of the Virginia Commission on the University of the 21st Century, which found: "Because colleges and universities provide opportunities for students to develop values and learn from role models, it is extremely important that they deal with faculty, staff, and students without regard to sex, race, or ethnic origin." VMI's reexamination of its policy after *Mississippi University for Women* offered "no persuasive evidence" that diversity was the state's goal in maintaining VMI as a single-sex college. Justice Ginsburg then addressed the state's second justification: preserving the adversative method of education.]

* * * The District Court forecast from expert witness testimony, and the Court of Appeals accepted, that coeducation would materially affect

"at least these three aspects of VMI's program—physical training, the absence of privacy, and the adversative approach." And it is uncontested that women's admission would require accommodations, primarily in arranging housing assignments and physical training programs for female cadets. It is also undisputed, however, that "the VMI methodology could be used to educate women." The District Court even allowed that some women may prefer it to the methodology a women's college might pursue. "[S]ome women, at least, would want to attend [VMI] if they had the opportunity," the District Court recognized, and "some women," the expert testimony established, "are capable of all of the individual activities required of VMI cadets." * * *

In support of its initial judgment for Virginia, a judgment rejecting all equal protection objections presented by the United States, the District Court made "findings" on "gender-based developmental differences." These "findings" restate the opinions of Virginia's expert witnesses, opinions about typically male or typically female "tendencies." For example, "[m]ales tend to need an atmosphere of adversativeness," while "[f]emales tend to thrive in a cooperative atmosphere." "I'm not saying that some women don't do well under [the] adversative model," VMI's expert on educational institutions testified, "undoubtedly there are some [women] who do"; but educational experiences must be designed "around the rule," this expert maintained, and not "around the exception." * * *

It may be assumed, for purposes of this decision, that most women would not choose VMI's adversative method. As Fourth Circuit Judge Motz observed, however, in her dissent from the Court of Appeals' denial of rehearing en banc, it is also probable that "many men would not want to be educated in such an environment." (On that point, even our dissenting colleague might agree.) Education, to be sure, is not a "one size fits all" business. The issue, however, is not whether "women—or men—should be forced to attend VMI"; rather, the question is whether the State can constitutionally deny to women who have the will and capacity, the training and attendant opportunities that VMI uniquely affords.

The notion that admission of women would downgrade VMI's stature, destroy the adversative system and, with it, even the school, is a judgment hardly proved, a prediction hardly different from other "self-fulfilling prophec[ies]," see *Mississippi Univ. for Women*, routinely used to deny rights or opportunities. When women first sought admission to the bar and access to legal education, concerns of the same order were expressed. For example, in 1876, the Court of Common Pleas of Hennepin County, Minnesota, explained why women were thought ineligible for the practice of law. Women train and educate the young, the court said, which

> "forbids that they shall bestow that time (early and late) and labor, so essential in attaining to the eminence to which the true lawyer should ever aspire. It cannot therefore be said that the

opposition of courts to the admission of females to practice . . . is to any extent the outgrowth of . . . 'old fogyism[.]' . . . [I]t arises rather from a comprehension of the magnitude of the responsibilities connected with the successful practice of law, and a desire to *grade up* the profession." In re Application of Martha Angle Dorsett to Be Admitted to Practice as Attorney and Counselor at Law (Minn. C.P. Hennepin Cty., 1876), in *The Syllabi*, Oct. 21, 1876, pp. 5, 6 (emphasis added).

A like fear, according to a 1925 report, accounted for Columbia Law School's resistance to women's admission, although

"[t]he faculty . . . never maintained that women could not master legal learning. . . . No, its argument has been . . . more practical. If women were admitted to the Columbia Law School, [the faculty] said, then the choicer, more manly and red-blooded graduates of our great universities would go to the Harvard Law School!" *The Nation*, Feb. 18, 1925, p. 173.

Medical faculties similarly resisted men and women as partners in the study of medicine. More recently, women seeking careers in policing encountered resistance based on fears that their presence would "undermine male solidarity"; deprive male partners of adequate assistance; and lead to sexual misconduct. Field studies did not confirm these fears.

Women's successful entry into the federal military academies, and their participation in the Nation's military forces, indicate that Virginia's fears for the future of VMI may not be solidly grounded. The State's justification for excluding all women from "citizen-soldier" training for which some are qualified, in any event, cannot rank as "exceedingly persuasive," as we have explained and applied that standard. * * *

The State's misunderstanding and, in turn, the District Court's, is apparent from VMI's mission: to produce "citizen-soldiers," individuals

" 'imbued with love of learning, confident in the functions and attitudes of leadership, possessing a high sense of public service, advocates of the American democracy and free enterprise system, and ready . . . to defend their country in time of national peril.' " 766 F. Supp., at 1425 (quoting Mission Study Committee of the VMI Board of Visitors, Report, May 16, 1986).

Surely that goal is great enough to accommodate women, who today count as citizens in our American democracy equal in stature to men. Just as surely, the State's great goal is not substantially advanced by women's categorical exclusion, in total disregard of their individual merit, from the State's premier "citizen-soldier" corps. Virginia, in sum, "has fallen far short of establishing the 'exceedingly persuasive justification,' " *Mississippi Univ. for Women*, that must be the solid base for any gender-defined classification. * * *

[Justice Ginsburg then turned to the remedial plan, the constitutionality of which had been upheld in the lower courts. The Supreme Court's race discrimination precedents establish that the remedial decree must closely fit the constitutional violation; it must be shaped to place persons unconstitutionally denied an opportunity or advantage in "the position they would have occupied in the absence of [discrimination]." See *Milliken v. Bradley*, 433 U.S. 267, 280 (1977). Justice Ginsburg found that the establishment of the VWIL did not practically remedy the discrimination, in large part because the women's program was qualitatively different and quantitatively inferior to that retained for males at VMI. Tangible differences included fewer courses for VWIL students, less qualified faculty members, lower admissions standards for students, no comparable athletic facilities, a much smaller educational endowment, and incomplete access to VMI's impressive alumni network. Intangible differences included loss of the adversative method and the bonding it seems to achieve.] "[T]he most important aspects of the VMI educational experience occur in the barracks," the District Court found, yet Virginia deemed that core experience nonessential, indeed inappropriate, for training its female citizen-soldiers. * * *

Virginia maintains that these methodological differences are "justified pedagogically," based on "important differences between men and women in learning and developmental needs," "psychological and sociological differences" Virginia describes as "real" and "not stereotypes." The Task Force charged with developing the leadership program for women, drawn from the staff and faculty at Mary Baldwin College, "determined that a military model and, especially VMI's adversative method, would be wholly inappropriate for educating and training most women." The Commonwealth embraced the Task Force view, as did expert witnesses who testified for Virginia.

As earlier stated, generalizations about "the way women are," estimates of what is appropriate for *most women*, no longer justify denying opportunity to women whose talent and capacity place them outside the average description. Notably, Virginia never asserted that VMI's method of education suits *most men*. It is also revealing that Virginia accounted for its failure to make the VWIL experience "the entirely militaristic experience of VMI" on the ground that VWIL "is planned for women who do not necessarily expect to pursue military careers." By that reasoning, VMI's "entirely militaristic" program would be inappropriate for men in general or *as a group*, for "[o]nly about 15% of VMI cadets enter career military service." * * *

Virginia's VWIL solution is reminiscent of the remedy Texas proposed 50 years ago, in response to a state trial court's 1946 ruling that, given the equal protection guarantee, African Americans could not be denied a legal education at a state facility. See *Sweatt v. Painter*, 339 U.S. 629 (1950). Reluctant to admit African Americans to its flagship

University of Texas Law School, the State set up a separate school for [Herman] Sweatt and other black law students. As originally opened, the new school had no independent faculty or library, and it lacked accreditation. Nevertheless, the state trial and appellate courts were satisfied that the new school offered Sweatt opportunities for the study of law "substantially equivalent to those offered by the State to white students at the University of Texas."

[The Supreme Court struck down the remedy on the ground that the tangible facilities and faculty of the new law school were distinctly inferior and that there was an even greater disparity in "those qualities which are incapable of objective measurement but which make for greatness" in a school, including "reputation of the faculty, experience of the administration, position and influence of the alumni, standing in the community, traditions and prestige."] Facing the marked differences reported in the *Sweatt* opinion, the Court unanimously ruled that Texas had not shown "substantial equality in the [separate] educational opportunities" the State offered. Accordingly, the Court held, the Equal Protection Clause required Texas to admit African Americans to the University of Texas Law School. In line with *Sweatt*, we rule here that Virginia has not shown substantial equality in the separate educational opportunities the State supports at VWIL and VMI. * * *

A prime part of the history of our Constitution * * * is the story of the extension of constitutional rights and protections to people once ignored or excluded. VMI's story continued as our comprehension of "We the People" expanded. There is no reason to believe that the admission of women capable of all the activities required of VMI cadets would destroy the Institute rather than enhance its capacity to serve the "more perfect Union." * * *

■ JUSTICE THOMAS took no part in the consideration of this case.

■ [CHIEF JUSTICE REHNQUIST concurred in the judgment. He maintained that the six-Justice Court had departed from the traditional test for evaluating sex-based classifications. The approach taken in earlier cases requires the state to offer only an "important government objective" that is "substantially related" to the sex-based classification. The CHIEF JUSTICE believed that the Court's requirement of an "exceedingly persuasive justification" subtly altered the analysis. CHIEF JUSTICE REHNQUIST also objected to the Court's examination of Virginia's long history of excluding women from higher education on the basis of stereotypes about women's abilities and role. He maintained that the Court should only examine Virginia's justifications since *Mississippi University for Women*, decided in 1982, as it was only with that decision that states could have been on notice that single-sex institutions required any justification beyond tradition. Nonetheless, the CHIEF JUSTICE found that Virginia had not offered a substantial justification borne out by the evidence in the case and agreed with the Court's judgment.]

■ JUSTICE SCALIA, dissenting. * * *

Much of the Court's opinion is devoted to deprecating the closed-mindedness of our forebears with regard to women's education, and even with regard to the treatment of women in areas that have nothing to do with education. Closed-minded they were—as every age is, including our own, with regard to matters it cannot guess, because it simply does not consider them debatable. The virtue of a democratic system with a First Amendment is that it readily enables the people, over time, to be persuaded that what they took for granted is not so, and to change their laws accordingly. That system is destroyed if the smug assurances of each age are removed from the democratic process and written into the Constitution. So to counterbalance the Court's criticism of our ancestors, let me say a word in their praise: they left us free to change. The same cannot be said of this most illiberal Court, which has embarked on a course of inscribing one after another of the current preferences of the society (and in some cases only the counter-majoritarian preferences of the society's law-trained elite) into our Basic Law. Today it enshrines the notion that no substantial educational value is to be served by an all-men's military academy—so that the decision by the people of Virginia to maintain such an institution denies equal protection to women who cannot attend that institution but can attend others. Since it is entirely clear that the Constitution of the United States—the old one—takes no sides in this educational debate, I dissent.

* * * [I]n my view the function of this Court is to *preserve* our society's values regarding (among other things) equal protection, not to *revise* them; to prevent backsliding from the degree of restriction the Constitution imposed upon democratic government, not to prescribe, on our own authority, progressively higher degrees. For that reason it is my view that, whatever abstract tests we may choose to devise, they cannot supersede—and indeed ought to be crafted so as to reflect—those constant and unbroken national traditions that embody the people's understanding of ambiguous constitutional texts. More specifically, it is my view that "when a practice not expressly prohibited by the text of the Bill of Rights bears the endorsement of a long tradition of open, widespread, and unchallenged use that dates back to the beginning of the Republic, we have no proper basis for striking it down." *Rutan v. Republican Party of Ill.*, 497 U.S. 62, 95 (1990) (Scalia, J., dissenting). The same applies, *mutatis mutandis*, to a practice asserted to be in violation of the post-Civil War Fourteenth Amendment. * * *

[Justice Scalia then launched into a series of criticisms: the Court was silently replacing the intermediate scrutiny standard traditionally applied in sex-discrimination cases with a strict scrutiny standard akin to that in race-discrimination cases; the Court's requirement that VMI must open its adversative method to women so long as there are any women who would benefit from it imported a least-restrictive-means requirement characteristic only of strict scrutiny and not of intermediate scrutiny as articulated in precedents such as *Mississippi University for Women* and, even more prominently, *Rostker v. Goldberg*; and the Court's approach destabilized equal protection law, and without any firm theoretical basis. With respect to his last criticism, Justice Scalia adverted to *Carolene Products'* justification for judicial review when "prejudice against discrete and insular minorities may be a special condition, which tends seriously to curtail the operation of those political processes ordinarily to be relied upon to protect minorities, and which may call for a correspondingly more searching judicial inquiry."]

It is hard to consider women a "discrete and insular minorit[y]" unable to employ the "political processes ordinarily to be relied upon," when they constitute a majority of the electorate. And the suggestion that they are incapable of exerting that political power smacks of the same paternalism that the Court so roundly condemns. Moreover, a long list of legislation proves the proposition false. See, e.g., Equal Pay Act of 1963, 29 U.S.C. § 206(d); Title VII of the Civil Rights Act of 1964, 42 U.S.C. § 2000e–2; Title IX of the Education Amendments of 1972, 20 U.S.C. § 1681; Women's Business Ownership Act of 1988, Pub. L. 100–533, 102 Stat. 2689; Violence Against Women Act of 1994, Pub. L. 103–322, Title IV, 108 Stat. 1902. * * *

* * * [B]esides its single-sex constitution, VMI is different from other colleges in another way. It employs a "distinctive educational method," sometimes referred to as the "adversative, or doubting, model of education." "Physical rigor, mental stress, absolute equality of treatment, absence of privacy, minute regulation of behavior, and indoctrination in desirable values are the salient attributes of the VMI educational experience." No one contends that this method is appropriate for all individuals; education is not a "one size fits all" business. Just as a State may wish to support junior colleges, vocational institutes, or a law school that emphasizes case practice instead of classroom study, so too a State's decision to maintain within its system one school that provides the adversative method is "substantially related" to its goal of good education.* * *

* * * In an odd sort of way, it is precisely VMI's attachment to such old-fashioned concepts as manly "honor" that has made it, and the system it represents, the target of those who today succeed in abolishing public single-sex education. The record contains a booklet that all first-year VMI students (the so-called "rats") were required to keep in their possession at all times. Near the end there appears the following period-piece, entitled "The Code of a Gentleman":

"* * * A Gentleman . . .

Does not discuss his family affairs in public or with acquaintances.

Does not speak more than casually about his girl friend.

Does not go to a lady's house if he is affected by alcohol. He is temperate in the use of alcohol.

Does not lose his temper; nor exhibit anger, fear, hate, embarrassment, ardor or hilarity in public.

Does not hail a lady from a club window.

A gentleman never discusses the merits or demerits of a lady.* * *

I do not know whether the men of VMI lived by this Code; perhaps not. But it is powerfully impressive that a public institution of higher education still in existence sought to have them do so. I do not think any of us, women included, will be better off for its destruction. * * *

Katherine Franke, "The Central Mistake of Sex Discrimination Law: The Disaggregation of Sex from Gender" 144 *U. Pa. L. Rev.* 1–3 (1995).* "Contemporary sex discrimination jurisprudence accepts as one of its foundational premises the notion that sex and gender are two distinct aspects of human identity. That is, it assumes that the identities male and female are different from the characteristics masculine and feminine. Sex is regarded as a product of nature, while gender is understood as a function of culture. This disaggregation of sex from gender represents a central mistake of equality jurisprudence.

"Antidiscrimination law is founded upon the idea that sex, conceived as biological difference, is prior to, less normative than, and more real than gender. Yet in every way that matters, sex bears an epiphenomenal relationship to gender; that is, under close examination, almost every claim with regard to sexual identity or sex discrimination can be shown to be grounded in normative gender rules and roles. Herein lies the mistake. In the name of avoiding the 'grossest discrimination,' that is, 'treating things that are different as though they were exactly alike,' sexual equality jurisprudence has uncritically accepted the validity of biological sexual differences. By accepting these biological differences, equality jurisprudence reifies as foundational *fact* that which is really an *effect* of normative gender ideology. This jurisprudential error not only produces obvious absurdities at the margin of gendered identity, but it also explains why sex discrimination laws have been relatively ineffective in dismantling profound sex segregation in the wage-labor market, in shattering "glass ceilings" that obstruct women's entrance into the upper echelons of corporate management, and in increasing women's wages, which remain a fraction of those paid men.

"The targets of antidiscrimination law, therefore, should not be limited to the 'gross, stereotyped distinctions between the sexes' but should also include the social processes that construct and make coherent

---

the categories male and female. In many cases, biology operates as the excuse or cover for social practices that hierarchize individual members of the social category 'man' over individual members of the social category 'woman.' In the end, biology or anatomy serve as metaphors for a kind of inferiority that characterizes society's view of women."

NOTES ON THE *VMI* CASE AND THE DISAGGREGATION OF SEX FROM GENDER

Writing in 1984, Sylvia Law questioned whether the Constitution would be interpreted so that women could "claim equality only insofar as they are like men." Sylvia A. Law, "Rethinking Sex and the Constitution," 132 *U. Pa. L. Rev.* 955, 1007 (1984). The VMI case presented that issue in sharp relief. The Court's opinion questions whether toughness/aggression necessarily correlates with the biological category of maleness, and argues that women who seek an education grounded in stereotypically masculine, adversative methods of learning, even if few in number, should have the same opportunity as men to do so. But the Court did not engage the more radical critique that Professor Franke advocates: that biological difference is more metaphor than reality. Indeed, Justice Ginsburg says that differences between males and females are to be "celebrated." Many interpretations of this language are possible. Was this aside needed to cajole six Justices to join the opinion for the Court? Is it meant to rebuff any attempt to examine the relationship between sex and gender?

Nor does the decision question the state's valorization of traditionally masculine traits as the ones most useful as leadership qualities. Is it unfair to characterize the VMI case as standing for the constitutional proposition that women have the right to switch genders, culturally if not literally, in order to achieve equal opportunity?

The VMI case can also be read as a powerful rejection of gender stereotypes. For an analysis of how stereotypes have lurked beneath the surface of virtually every Equal Protection decision regarding women, see Judge Rosemary Barkett's decision for the Eleventh Circuit in *Glenn v. Brumby*, Part C3 of this section, *infra*.

Tuan Anh Nguyen v. INS, **533 U.S. 53 (2001).** The Supreme Court rejected a challenge to a federal statute, 8 U.S.C. § 1409(a)(4), that accorded American citizenship automatically, upon birth, to a child born out of wedlock in a foreign country to an American mother, but denied citizenship to such a child whose only American parent was her father, unless the child had been legally legitimated or paternity had been established in a court of law or by paternal oath before the child's eighteenth birthday. In *Miller v. Albright*, 523 U.S. 420 (1998), a divided Court had failed to resolve the constitutionality of § 1409(a)(4), because two Justices believed that the child plaintiff seeking a declaration of citizenship did not have standing to raise her father's sex discrimination claim. In *Nguyen*, both the child and the father were plaintiffs, so there was no problem of standing. All the Justices recognized that the statute was a sex discrimination requiring strong justification under *Craig* and the VMI case.

Justice Kennedy's opinion for the Court found the sex discrimination justified by two governmental interests. "The first governmental interest to be served is the importance of assuring that a biological parent-child relationship exists. In the case of the mother, the relation is verifiable from the birth itself. The mother's status is documented in most instances by the birth certificate or hospital records and the witnesses who attest to her having given birth.

"In the case of the father, the uncontestable fact is that he need not be present at the birth. If he is present, furthermore, that circumstance is not incontrovertible proof of fatherhood. See *Lehr v. Robertson*, 463 U.S. 248, 260 n.16 (1983). Fathers and mothers are not similarly situated with regard to the proof of biological parenthood. The imposition of a different set of rules for making that legal determination with respect to fathers and mothers is neither surprising nor troublesome from a constitutional perspective. Section 1409(a)(4)'s provision of three options for a father seeking to establish paternity—legitimation, paternity oath, and court order of paternity—is designed to ensure an acceptable documentation of paternity. * * *

"[T]o require Congress to speak without reference to the gender of the parent with regard to its objective of ensuring a blood tie between parent and child would be to insist on a hollow neutrality. * * * Congress could have required both mothers and fathers to prove parenthood within 30 days or, for that matter, 18 years, of the child's birth. Given that the mother is always present at birth, but that the father need not be, the facially neutral rule would sometimes require fathers to take additional affirmative steps which would not be required of mothers, whose names will appear on the birth certificate as a result of their presence at the birth, and who will have the benefit of witnesses to the birth to call upon. The issue is not the use of gender specific terms instead of neutral ones. Just as neutral terms can mask discrimination that is unlawful, gender specific terms can mark a permissible distinction. The equal protection question is whether the distinction is lawful. Here, the use of gender specific terms takes into account a biological difference between the parents. The differential treatment is inherent in a sensible statutory scheme, given the unique relationship of the mother to the event of birth.

"The second important governmental interest furthered in a substantial manner by § 1409(a)(4) is the determination to ensure that the child and the citizen parent have some demonstrated opportunity or potential to develop not just a relationship that is recognized, as a formal matter, by the law, but one that consists of the real, everyday ties that provide a connection between child and citizen parent and, in turn, the United States. In the case of a citizen mother and a child born overseas, the opportunity for a meaningful relationship between citizen parent and child inheres in the very event of birth, an event so often critical to our constitutional and statutory understandings of citizenship. The mother knows that the child is in being and is hers and has an initial point of contact with him. There is at least an opportunity for mother and child to develop a real, meaningful relationship.

"The same opportunity does not result from the event of birth, as a matter of biological inevitability, in the case of the unwed father. Given the 9-month interval between conception and birth, it is not always certain that a father will know that a child was conceived, nor is it always clear that even the mother will be sure of the father's identity. This fact takes on particular significance in the case of a child born overseas and out of wedlock. One concern in this context has always been with young people, men for the most part, who are on duty with the Armed Forces in foreign countries." Justice Kennedy finally concluded that the statutory differentiation was narrowly enough tailored to fit this asserted interest, as well as the first.

Justice Scalia, joined by **Justice Thomas**, concurred in the Court's opinion but reiterated their view, stated in *Miller*, that Congress has plenary and unreviewable power in the arena of immigration and naturalization.

Justice O'Connor, joined by **Justices Souter**, **Ginsburg**, and **Breyer**, dissented. Justice O'Connor maintained that the Court's approach deviated from the heightened scrutiny its precedents bound it to apply in sex discrimination cases, such as the VMI case. Specifically, she criticized the Court's first justification (proof of parental relationship) as insufficient because (1) there was scant evidence that this was the actual reason for the sex-based classification; (2) the requirements of § 1409(a)(4) add nothing to what § 1409(a)(1) already requires, namely, a blood test showing a parental relationship between the American father and the child claiming citizenship; and (3) sex-neutral criteria, such as the blood-test requirement of § 1409(a)(1) for the child-claimant whatever the sex of its American parent, would fully serve the asserted governmental interest. Justice O'Connor suggested that the Court's willingness to attribute a rational goal to Congress and to allow much leeway in the fit between the statutory criterion and the valid state interest was more characteristic of rational basis review than heightened scrutiny as required by the VMI case and other precedents.

Justice O'Connor made two of the same criticisms of the Court's second justification ("opportunity" of the American parent and foreign-born child to develop a relationship): It was hypothetical and could be met by a more direct, and ungendered, statutory criterion (*e.g.*, the child and the parent, whatever the gender, have enjoyed a relationship). By stressing an "opportunity" for a relationship, the Court was more successful in creating a closer fit between the end and the means—but at the expense of creating an end that is not sufficiently important to justify a statutory sex discrimination.

"The claim that § 1409(a)(4) substantially relates to the achievement of the goal of a 'real, practical relationship' thus finds support not in biological differences but instead in a stereotype—*i.e.*, 'the generalization that mothers are significantly more likely than fathers . . . to develop caring relationships with their children.' *Miller* (Breyer, J., dissenting). Such a claim relies on 'the very stereotype the law condemns,' *J.E.B.*, 'lends credibility' to the generalization, [*Hogan*], and helps to convert that 'assumption' into 'a self-fulfilling prophecy,' *ibid.* Indeed, contrary to this stereotype, Boulais [the father] has reared Nguyen, while Nguyen apparently has lacked a relationship with his mother. * * *

"In denying petitioner's claim that § 1409(a)(4) rests on stereotypes, the majority articulates a misshapen notion of 'stereotype' and its significance in our equal protection jurisprudence. The majority asserts that a 'stereotype' is 'defined as a frame of mind resulting from irrational or uncritical analysis.' This Court has long recognized, however, that an impermissible stereotype may enjoy empirical support and thus be in a sense 'rational.' See, e.g., *J.E.B.* ('We have made abundantly clear in past cases that gender classifications that rest on impermissible stereotypes violate the Equal Protection Clause, even when some statistical support can be conjured up for the generalization'); *Craig* (invalidating a sex-based classification even though the evidence supporting the distinction was 'not trivial in a statistical sense'). Indeed, the stereotypes that underlie a sex-based classification 'may hold true for many, even most, individuals.' *Miller* (Ginsburg, J., dissenting). But in numerous cases where a measure of truth has inhered in the generalization, 'the Court has rejected official actions that classify unnecessarily and overbroadly by gender when more accurate and impartial functional lines can be drawn.' *Ibid.*

NOTES ON STATE JUSTIFICATIONS FOR CERTAIN SEX DISCRIMINATIONS

1. *Justice Ginsburg's Limitation of* Nguyen. In *Sessions v. Morales-Santana*, 137 S.Ct. 1678 (2017), the Court struck down a law that imposed more stringent requirements on a child who is born outside the U.S. to an unmarried citizen father than it does on a child born outside the U.S. to an unmarried citizen mother. This statutory provision is related to, but different from, the provision at issue in *Nguyen*. The earlier case involved a paternal-acknowledgment requirement, which the father in the *Morales-Santana* case had satisfied by marrying the mother (after the child's birth). In the 2017 case, the father had failed to satisfy a requirement for the duration of the non-citizen parent's residency in the U.S. prior to the child's birth. For noncitizen unmarried fathers, five years residence was required, while the rule for noncitizen unmarried mothers was one year.

In an opinion by Justice Ginsburg, the Court held that "[l]aws granting or denying benefits 'on the basis of the sex of qualifying parent' * * *differentiate on the basis of gender, and therefore attract heightened review under the Constitution's equal protection guarantee." 137 S.Ct. at

1689. "Unlike the paternal-acknowledgment requirement * * *, the physical-presence requirements * * * relate solely to the duration of the parent's pre-birth residency in the United States, not to the parent's filial tie to the child." *Id.* at 1694. Ginsburg cited the VMI Case's standard of review, and went on to emphasize the "classification must serve an important governmental interest *today*" (emphasis in the original), citing *Obergefell v. Hodges* for the principle that " 'new insights and society understandings can reveal unjustified inequality . . . that once passed unnoticed and unchallenged.' " *Id.* at 1690. See Chapter 2, Section 3C.

Underlying Ginsburg's reasoning is limiting the *Nguyen* result to a "justifiable, easily met means of ensuring the existence of a biological parent-child relationship which the mother satisfies by giving birth." *Id.* at 1694. Ginsburg then distinguishes a provision that creates a distinction between the parents based on sex rather than one based on the nature of the biological link to the child. She traces the stereotype behind the law at issue in *Morales-Santana* to the belief that the child of unmarried parents was the "natural" responsibility of the mother, so that that if only the unmarried father was a U.S. citizen, there would be little likelihood that the child would grow up with a sense of being American, unless the father had a strong link to the U.S. as reflected in residence for a significant period. However, because the five-year physical-presence requirement is the general rule, i.e., applicable to married couples in which one spouse is a citizen and the other is not, the Court held that its best reading of legislative intent led it to eliminate the one-year rule for unmarried mothers (created as an exception to the general rule), rather than extend it to unmarried fathers.

2. *Standing to Sue and Adoption.* In a parallel line of cases, the Court has ruled on state laws treating mothers of nonmarital children differently from fathers. In *Parham v. Hughes*, 441 U.S. 347 (1979), for example, the Court upheld a Georgia law allowing the mother but not the father of a child born outside of marriage to bring suit for the child's wrongful death. The 5–4 Court found that men and women are not similarly situated in such a case: the mother is automatically considered the child's parent, while the father is not unless he has gone through a legitimation proceeding. "Since fathers who do legitimate their children can sue for wrongful death in precisely the same circumstances as married fathers whose children were legitimate *ab initio*, the statutory classification does not discriminate against fathers as a class but instead distinguishes between fathers who have legitimated their children and those who have not." Contrast *Caban v. Mohammed*, 441 U.S. 380 (1979), where a different 5–4 majority struck down a New York law requiring the consent of the mother, but not the father, for the adoption of their nonmarital child. The Court treated the statutory classification as a routine discrimination on the basis of sex and rejected the "real differences" argument (mothers are more bonded to their children than fathers) on the ground that, even if generally true, it was not true in *Caban*, where the father had bonded with the child. New York responded to *Caban* with a statute requiring the mother of a child born outside of marriage to be notified of any proposed adoption and allowing her to veto the adoption, but not according either notice or veto power to the biological father unless he had claimed paternity by registering with the state or had established a substantial relationship with the child. A divided Court upheld this law in *Lehr v. Robertson*, 463 U.S. 248 (1983). Note how *Lehr* provides key precedential support for Justice Kennedy in *Nguyen*. Although the Court does not discuss these cases in *Morales-Santana*, the issue of biological evidence of a filial tie could link *Parham* and *Lehr* to *Nguyen*.

3. *Institutional Context Matters.* The sex-based classification in *Nguyen* survived in part because the issue arose under Congress's plenary authority over immigration and naturalization. Contrast earlier cases, like *Craig* and the VMI case, where the Court was reviewing odd state laws. The Court will rarely invalidate an immigration and naturalization statute. The opinion in *Nguyen* provides an example of deference for institutional reasons. In contrast to Justice Ginsburg's opinion in the other two cases, Justice Kennedy's opinion does not hold the federal government to the originally stated reasons for the sex discrimination, does not impute the stereotype-grounded objectives suggested by the history of the discrimination, and does not require that the government show an important interest that could not be met by a non-sex classification. In *Morales-Santana*, Justice Ginsburg limits that deferential approach, even for an immigration and naturalization statute, to the context of proving a biological relationship.

B. DISCRIMINATION BASED ON SEXUAL ORIENTATION

The formation of communities of people whose erotic desires marked them as a minority cannot be understood apart from the broader context of U.S. history. The key time period was the second half of the nineteenth century, which saw an explosion in the number, variety and harshness of mechanisms for state regulation of sexuality and gender. As we saw from the history of abortion laws described in *Roe v. Wade*, the movement to increase penalties for abortion, led by the newly formed American Medical Association, began in the 1870s. The federal Comstock Act, enacted in 1873, outlawed birth control materials anywhere in the U.S. as obscene, and essentially deployed the Post Office as a national censorship agency for all expressions of sexual liberty. The word "homosexual" first appeared in English language medical literature in 1892, but dance hall owners in New York City had begun hiring powdered and rouged men, sometimes dressed in women's clothes, to entertain customers in the late 1870s. (See Part C1, *infra,* for history of laws prohibiting gender impersonation.) For women, some new mechanisms of regulation took the form of liberalization. For example, during the same period, the women's suffrage movement gained strength, and state legislatures enacted Married Women's Property Acts. Women began to attend college and to move into the public sphere worlds of political and economic engagement in significant numbers.

There is that in me—I do not know what it is—but I know it is in me.

Walt Whitman, Leaves of Grass (1892 ed.)

What explains this ferment? Especially in the North and Midwest, enormous population change occurred during the half century following the Civil War, resulting from both internal and foreign migration patterns. Millions of young adults left rural areas and small towns in search of both the economic opportunities being created by large-scale industrialization and the greater personal liberty available in cities, away from family control. Waves of immigrants from Europe and Asia also arrived, especially in New York, Boston and San Francisco, creating dense pockets of unfamiliar cultural norms and triggering a backlash by resident whites that included stereotyping of (often imagined) sexual practices. In the economically depressed South, whites latched onto myths of hypersexualized African-Americans as part of a violent campaign to end Reconstruction and build apartheid regimes with Jim Crow laws. By the end of World War I, the Great Migration of African-Americans out of the South to cities like New York and Chicago had begun.

During the first half of the twentieth century, a number of subordinated groups began formal advocacy organizations. The National Organization for the Advancement of Colored People (NAACP) began in 1909 in New York. Alice Paul founded the National Women's Party in 1913. Margaret Sanger launched the American Birth Control League and Birth Control Clinical Research Bureau in 1921. Those two groups merged in 1942 to become the Birth Control Federation of America, renamed Planned Parenthood. The first "homophile" organization in the United States—the Society for Human Rights—began in Chicago in 1924, but lasted only a year. Henry Hay started the longer-lived Mattachine Society in 1950 in Los Angeles, and Del Martin and Phyllis Lyons founded the Daughters of Bilitis in 1955 in San Francisco.

1. LIBERTY-BASED ARGUMENTS AGAINST DISCRIMINATION

"It was 2:00 a.m. on a Tuesday night in the fall of 1963, and Washington's principal downtown gay bars, the Chicken Hut and the Derby Room, had just closed. On his way home, Clifford Norton, a budget analyst with the National Aeronautics and Space Administration, decided to drive by nearby Lafayette Park, a popular meeting and trysting site for gay men since the early part of the century. Seeing Madison Proctor standing on the corner, Norton stopped his car, rolled down the window and struck up a conversation. After inviting Proctor home for a drink, he drove him to his nearby parked car. Norton then drove home to his Southwest Washington apartment, and Proctor followed. When they arrived, however, they discovered they had been followed by two District of Columbia police officers assigned to the Morals

Division. Outside the parking lot, the officers questioned Norton and Proctor about their interaction at the park and, because they had trailed them at speeds exceeding 45 miles per hour, brought the two in to police headquarters on a 'traffic violation.' "

"At headquarters, Roy Blick, chief of the Morals Division, interrogated Norton and Proctor for two hours concerning their activities that night and their sexual histories in general. 'How long have you been a homosexual?' Blick repeatedly asked the NASA employee. Norton refused to answer. Blick eventually relented and issued Norton only a traffic summons. But since Norton had revealed his place of employment, Blick telephoned NASA's security director, who came to police headquarters and continued to interrogate Norton about his sexual history until 6:30 a.m. Several days later, despite a 15-year record of exemplary government service, NASA discharged Norton for 'immoral, indecent and disgraceful conduct.' Although they acknowledged that issues of national security were not involved, NASA officials claimed that a recurrence of this type of activity might "embarrass" the agency. The Civil Service Commission concurred and determined that Norton's dismissal would promote 'the efficiency of the service.' " David Johnson, "Homosexual Citizens: Washington's Gay Community Confronts the Civil Service," *Wash. History*, Fall/Winter 1994–95, at 45–46.

Clifford Norton's 1963 arrest reflected the risks run by sexually active gay men and lesbians all over America. "Homosexuals and other sex perverts" were considered outlaws because of their presumed sodomy, and they were pervasively discriminated against by state, local, and federal governments. The gay man caught cruising for partners could not only be arrested for solicitation, but also faced dismissal from his job in the public or private sector, loss of his professional license to practice law or medicine, eviction from the apartment he was renting, termination of visitation rights to his children from a prior marriage, exclusion from jury service, and even deportation from the United States if he were a noncitizen (*e.g.*, *Boutilier*). *See* William N. Eskridge Jr., *Dishonorable Passions: Sodomy Law in America, 1861–2003*, at 99–108 (2008); David Johnson, *The Lavender Scare: The Cold War Persecution of Gays and Lesbians in the Federal Government* (2003).

***Clifford Norton v. John Macy et al.*, 417 F.2d 1161 (D.C. Cir. 1969).** A panel of the D.C. Circuit ruled that Norton's discharge violated the Due Process Clause of the Fifth Amendment. **Chief Judge Bazelon**'s opinion noted that Congress has provided that protected civil servants shall not be dismissed except "for such cause as will promote the efficiency of the service." The Civil Service Commission's regulations provide that an appointee may be removed, inter alia, for "infamous * * *, immoral, or notoriously disgraceful conduct" and for "any * * * other disqualification which makes the individual unfit for the service." Chief Judge Bazelon questioned whether Norton's homosexuality rendered him "unfit for the service."

"The Government's obligation to accord due process sets at least minimal substantive limits on its prerogative to dismiss its employees: it forbids all dismissals which are arbitrary and capricious. These constitutional limits may be greater where, as here, the dismissal imposes a 'badge of infamy,' disqualifying the victim from any further Federal employment, damaging his prospects for private employ, and fixing upon him the stigma of an official defamation of character." Chief Judge Bazelon also opined that this constitutional protection "may also cut deeper into the Government's discretion where a dismissal involves an intrusion upon that ill-defined area of privacy which is increasingly if indistinctly recognized as a foundation of several specific constitutional protections. [*Griswold*.]"

"Preliminarily, we must reject [Macy's] contention that once the label 'immoral' is plausibly attached to an employee's off-duty conduct, our inquiry into the presence of adequate rational cause for removal is at an end. A pronouncement of 'immorality' tends to discourage careful analysis because it unavoidably connotes a violation of divine, Olympian, or otherwise universal standards of rectitude. However, the Civil Service Commission has neither the expertise nor the requisite anointment to make or enforce absolute moral judgments, and we do not understand that it purports to do so. Its jurisdiction is at least confined [by the statute] to the things which are Caesar's, and its avowed standard of 'immorality' is no more than 'the prevailing mores of our society.' "

"Accordingly, a finding that an employee has done something immoral or indecent could support a dismissal without further inquiry only if all immoral or indecent acts of an employee have some ascertainable deleterious effect on the efficiency of the service. The range of conduct which might be said to affront prevailing mores is so broad and varied that we can hardly arrive at any such conclusion without reference to specific conduct. Thus, we think the sufficiency of the charges against appellant must be evaluated in terms of the effects on the service of what in particular he has done or has been shown to be likely to do."

Homosexuality in the abstract is not related to the efficiency of governmental operations, but, according to Chief Judge Bazelon, it might be if the employee were being blackmailed or evidenced "an unstable personality unsuited for certain kinds of work." Finally, "[i]f an employee makes offensive overtures while on the job, or if his conduct is notorious, the reactions of other employees and of the public with whom he comes in contact in the performance of his official functions may be taken into account." Norton's dismissal rested upon none of these possibly permissible grounds; indeed, the supervisor who dismissed him said that Norton was a "competent employee" doing "very good work."

On appeal, the most the government could say was that Norton's arrest was an "embarrassment" to NASA—a far too nebulous reason under the statute. "A claim of possible embarrassment might, of course, be a vague way of referring to some specific potential interference with an agency's performance; but it might also be a smokescreen hiding personal antipathies or moral judgments which are excluded by statute as grounds for dismissal. A reviewing court must at least be able to discern some reasonably foreseeable, specific connection between an employee's potentially embarrassing conduct and the efficiency of the service. Once the connection is established, then it is for the agency and the Commission to decide whether it outweighs the loss to the service of a particular competent employee."

"In the instant case [NASA] has shown us no such specific connection. Indeed, on the record appellant is at most an extremely infrequent offender, who neither openly flaunts nor carelessly displays his unorthodox sexual conduct in public. Thus, even the potential for the embarrassment the agency fears is minimal. * * * [I]f the statute is to have any force, an agency cannot support a dismissal as promoting the efficiency of the service merely by turning its head and crying 'shame.'" (**Judge Tamm** dissented on the ground that homosexuals in the civil service "present targets for public reproach and private extortion" and therefore represent a threat to the efficient functioning of a government agency such as NASA.)

2.   FROM LIBERTY TO EQUAL PROTECTION CLAIMS

As *Norton* illustrates, it was due process/liberty notions of "arbitrary" treatment that did the work of delinking homosexuality and the presumed threat to national security, a necessary step before an equal protection claim could be plausible to judges and the broader society. With the model of the civil rights movement for racial justice at hand, however, advocates had already begun to fashion a demand for equal rights. Its earliest known appearance in a legal document was the unsuccessful cert petition filed by Franklin Kameny, a U.S. Army astronomer who challenged his own firing by the federal government. *Kameny v. Brucker*, 365 U.S. 843 (1961). Kameny argued that gay people were persecuted because of prejudice and stereotyping no different from the racist prejudices and stereotypes that were the objects of the civil rights revolution. For the same reasons that the Supreme Court ruled that race is a suspect classification, he argued that sexual orientation is a suspect classification that the state cannot deploy without compelling justification. (Kameny, who founded the Mattachine Society of Washington in 1961, was honored in 2009 at a ceremony at which Office of Personnel Management Director John Berry apologized on behalf of the federal government for how Kameny had been treated five decades earlier.)

John Singer v. U.S. Civil Service Commission

United States Court of Appeals for the Ninth Circuit, 1976.
530 F.2d 247, *vacated*, 429 U.S. 1034, 97 S.Ct. 725, 50 L.Ed.2d 744 (1977).

■ JAMESON, DISTRICT JUDGE. * * *

On August 2, 1971, Singer was hired by the Seattle Office of the Equal Employment Opportunity Commission (EEOC) as a clerk typist. Pursuant to 5 C.F.R. § 315.801 *et seq.,* he was employed for one year on probationary status, subject to termination if "his work performance or conduct during this period (failed) to demonstrate his fitness or his qualifications for continued employment" (§ 315.804). At the time he was hired Singer informed the Director of EEOC that he was a homosexual.

On May 12, 1972, an investigator for the Civil Service Commission sent a letter to Singer inviting him "to appear voluntarily for an interview to comment upon, explain or rebut adverse information which has come to the attention of the Commission" as a result of its investigation to determine Singer's "suitability for employment in the competitive Federal service." The interview was set for May 19. Singer appeared at the appointed time with his counsel. Singer was advised that the investigation by the Commission disclosed that "you are homosexual. You openly profess that you are homosexual and you have received wide-spread publicity in this respect in at least two states." Specific acts were noted, which may be summarized as follows:

(1) During Singer's previous employment with a San Francisco mortgage firm Singer had "flaunted" his homosexuality by kissing and embracing a male in front of the elevator in the building where he was employed and kissing a male in the company cafeteria;

(2) The *San Francisco Chronicle* wrote an article on Singer in November of 1970 in which he stated his name and occupation and views on "closet queens";

(3) At the Seattle EEOC office Singer openly admitted being "gay" and indicated by his dress and demeanor that he intended to continue homosexual activity as a "way of life";

(4) On September 20, 1971, Singer and another man applied to the King County Auditor for a marriage license, which was eventually refused by the King County Superior Courta

(5) As a result of the attempt to obtain the marriage license Singer was the subject of extensive television, newspaper and magazine publicity;

(6) Articles published in the Seattle papers of September 21, 1971 included Singer's identification as a typist employed by

---

a   Singer's marriage license application was denied, and the Washington courts rejected Singer's constitutional challenge to the marriage exclusion. See Chapter 2, Section 3A.

EEOC and quoted Singer as saying, in part, that he and the man he sought to marry were "two human beings who happen to be in love and want to get married for various reasons"; * * *

[By a letter dated June 26, 1972 the Chief of the Investigations Division of the Seattle office of the Civil Service Commission notified Singer that by reason of his "immoral and notoriously disgraceful conduct" he was disqualified under the Civil Service Regulations, 5 C.F.R. § 731.201(b). The letter stated: "The information developed by the investigation, taken with your reply, indicate that you have flaunted and broadcast your homosexual activities and have sought and obtained publicity in various media in pursuit of this goal. * * * Your activities in these matters are those of an advocate for a socially repugnant concept. * * * In determining that your employment will not promote the efficiency of the service, the Commission has considered such pertinent factors as the potential disruption of service efficiency because of the possible revulsion of other employees to homosexual conduct and/or their apprehension of homosexual advances and solicitations; the hazard that the prestige and authority of a Government position will be used to foster homosexual activity, particularly among youth; the possible use of Government funds and authority in furtherance of conduct offensive to the mores and law of our society; and the possible embarrassment to, and loss of public confidence in, your agency and the Federal civil service."

[The Hearing Officer rejected Singer's appeal. Although Singer's coworkers and supervisor had voiced no complaint about Singer's job performance, the overall "efficiency of the service" was compromised by "notoriously disgraceful conduct." The Civil Service Commission, Board of Appeals and Review affirmed, saying:

> There is evidence in the file which indicated that appellant's actions establish that he has engaged in immoral and notoriously disgraceful conduct, openly and publicly flaunting his homosexual way of life and indicating further continuance of such activities. Activities of the type he has engaged in are such that general public knowledge thereof reflects discredit upon the Federal Government as his employer, impeding the efficiency of the service by lessening general public confidence in the fitness of the Government to conduct the public business with which it is entrusted.]

Appellant contends that he was discharged because of his status as a homosexual without the Commission showing any "rational nexus" between his homosexual activities and the efficiency of the service, in violation of the Due Process Clause of the Fifth Amendment; and that he has been denied freedom of expression and the right to petition the Government for redress of grievances, in violation of the First Amendment. [The court held that the scope of judicial review was extremely narrow, because Singer was a probationary employee; such employees generally have no right to continued employment, only a right to be shielded from arbitrary and capricious action.]

With the foregoing principles and trends in mind, we turn to those cases which have considered homosexual activities as a basis for dismissal of Civil Service employees. The leading case is *Norton v. Macy* * * *. The court noted, however, that homosexual conduct cannot be ignored as a factor in determining fitness for federal employment since it might "bear on the efficiency of the service in a number of ways." More specifically the court said: "If an employee makes offensive overtures while on the job, or if his conduct is notorious, the reactions of other employees and of the public with whom he comes in contact in the performance of his official functions may be taken into account. Whether or not such potential consequences would justify removal, they are at least broadly relevant to 'the efficiency of the service." * * *

We conclude from a review of the record in its entirety that appellant's employment was not terminated because of his status as a homosexual or because of any private acts of sexual preference. The statements of the Commission's investigation division, hearing examiner, and Board of Appeals make it clear that the discharge was the result of appellant's "openly and publicly flaunting his homosexual way of life and indicating further continuance of such activities," while identifying himself as a member of a federal agency. The Commission found that these activities were such that "general public knowledge thereof reflects discredit upon the Federal Government as his employer, impeding the efficiency of the service by lessening public confidence in the fitness of the Government to conduct the public business with which it was entrusted."

[The court denied Singer's First Amendment claim on the ground that cases protecting speech about homosexuality had not "involved the open and public flaunting or advocacy of homosexual conduct."]

NOTES ON *SINGER* AND THE FALL OF THE CIVIL SERVICE EXCLUSION

1. *The Subsequent History of Singer's Case.* The Ninth Circuit opinion was vacated by the Supreme Court, which remanded the case to the Civil Service Commission for reconsideration in light of new Civil Service regulations adopted during the pendency of the case. In 1978, the Federal Employee Appeals Authority (FEAA) canceled the personnel action that caused Singer's dismissal. The FEAA found a "complete absence of any evidence which indicates that appellant's presence on the rolls of the agency impeded the agency's ability to carry out its missions" and concluded that the dismissal had been based on "unsubstantiated conclusions." Rhonda Rivera, "Sexual Preference Law," 30 *Drake L. Rev.* 317–18 (1980–81).

2. *The Evolving Civil Service Regulations.* Singer was discharged and sued in 1972. The Civil Service Bulletin adopting a *Norton* (nexus) approach was issued at the end of 1973. The district court dismissed the case in 1974. Final

Civil Service regulations were issued in 1975. The court of appeals affirmed in 1976. (The commission's new guidelines were not dispositive in *Singer* because they were issued subsequent to judgment and during pendency of the appeal. The court of appeals decision was based on the record before it, which included only the guidelines in place at the time of the discharge.)

In a May 12, 1980 memorandum, Alan K. Campbell, Director of the Office of Personnel Management, elaborated on the application of the statutory provision barring consideration of non-job-related conduct in federal employment matters. He stated, "Thus, applicants and employees are to be protected against inquiries into, or actions based upon, non-job-related conduct, such as religious, community or social affiliations, or sexual orientation." A February 17, 1994 memorandum from OPM Director James B. King stated, "The 1980 memorandum continues to reflect the Federal Government's longstanding policy on the matter of discrimination based on non-job-related conduct." In 1998, President Clinton amended Executive Order No. 11,478, which mandates anti-discrimination protections for federal government employees, by adding sexual orientation to the list of prohibited bases for discrimination. Executive Order No. 13,087 (May 29, 1998).

3. *"Flaunting."* Through the 1970s and 1980s, many courts adopted the rationale that state and local governments could not penalize public employees for being gay but could penalize them for public announcements of homosexuality. Illustrative of that era is *Childers v. Dallas Police Department*, 513 F.Supp. 134 (N.D.Tex.1981), which upheld the police department's refusal to promote Childers because of his pro-gay activism. Relying specifically on *Singer*, Judge Porter held that because "Childers was in no way inclined to be discreet about his homosexuality," his expressive activity would undermine the community respect needed for police work and the efficiency of the department (the latter because Childers' gay activism would "foment controversy and conflict within the department"). See also *Gaylord v. Tacoma School Dist. No. 10*, 88 Wash.2d 286, 559 P.2d 1340, *cert. denied*, 434 U.S. 879 (1977), in which the court ruled that negative reactions to a gay teacher's homosexuality by students, teachers and parents justified his firing. More abstract speech on issues related to homosexuality, such as the need to repeal or enact various laws, garnered greater protection. *E.g.*, *Van Ooteghem v. Gray*, 654 F.2d 304 (5th Cir. 1981) (holding that county employee could not be fired for speech urging legislators to adopt civil rights law).

NOTES ON EQUALITY AFTER *HARDWICK*

When the Supreme Court upheld the Georgia sodomy law in *Bowers v. Hardwick* in 1986, equal protection litigation hit a roadblock. If the conduct (sodomy) that arguably defined the class (of homosexuals) could be criminalized, how could lesser forms of discrimination based on that classification be suspect? For the decade following *Hardwick*, until the Supreme Court decided *Romer v. Evans*, *infra*, many lesbian and gay rights advocates pressed for a status/conduct distinction, arguing that even if sexual conduct could be criminalized, the persons in the group could not be made targets for discrimination. For those ten years, the relationship between, and the legal meaning of, acts and identities became a central issue.

In the leading case, ***Perry Watkins v. United States Army***, 847 F.2d 1329, vacated en banc, 875 F.2d 699 (9th Cir. 1989), a panel of Ninth Circuit judges held that an Army sergeant could not be discharged for his sexual orientation. Moreover, the panel ruled that sexual orientation is a suspect classification. Even though he agreed that Watkins had been treated arbitrarily, **Judge Stephen Reinhardt** dissented from the equal protection analysis. "I believe that after *Hardwick* the government may outlaw homosexual sodomy even though it fails to regulate the private sexual conduct of heterosexuals. In *Hardwick* the Court took great care to make clear that it was saying only that homosexual sodomy is not constitutionally protected, and not that all sexual acts—both heterosexual and homosexual— that fall within the definition of sodomy can be prohibited."

Writing for the panel majority, **Judge William A. Norris** responded that "nothing in *Hardwick* actually holds that the state may make invidious distinctions when regulating sexual conduct. * * * We cannot read *Hardwick* as standing for the proposition that government may outlaw sodomy only when committed by a disfavored class of persons. Surely, for example, *Hardwick* cannot be read as a license for the government to outlaw sodomy only when committed by blacks. If government insists on regulating private sexual conduct between consenting adults, it must, at a minimum, do so evenhandedly—prohibiting all persons from engaging in the proscribed sexual acts rather than placing the burden of sexual restraint solely on a disfavored minority."

As the case caption reveals, the *Watkins* decision was vacated *en banc*. The full Ninth Circuit reached the same result as the panel, but on a narrower theory. The *en banc* court ruled that Watkins was entitled to reinstatement based on an estoppel theory because the Army had repeatedly re-enlisted him throughout his career, while knowing that he was gay. Judge Reinhardt wrote a concurring opinion, expressing relief that justice could be done for Sergeant Watkins without the court having to settle on the one true meaning of *Hardwick* or resolve what seemed like a highly artificial distinction between homosexuality and homosexual conduct.

Although not obvious at the time, by 1985 the Supreme Court appears to have closed the door on heightened scrutiny for any classifications—not just sexual orientation—not already recognized as suspect. In *City of Cleburne v. Cleburne Living Center, Inc.*, 473 U.S. 432 (1985), the Court rejected a Court of Appeals ruling that applied heightened scrutiny to the city's decision to deny a zoning permit for location of a group home for intellectually disabled persons. In addition to reasoning that differential treatment of disabled persons was often justified by relative capacities and sometimes originated in benign motives, the Court also indicated that it did not want to analyze whether every group arguably victimized by discrimination met the criteria for heightened scrutiny. "We are reluctant to set out on that course, and we decline to do so." *Id.* at 446. Consider how the Court reconciled its hostility to higher tiers of scrutiny with an openly anti-gay law in the following case.

Roy Romer v. Richard Evans

United States Supreme Court, 1996.
517 U.S. 620, 116 S.Ct. 1620, 134 L.Ed.2d 855.

■ JUSTICE KENNEDY delivered the opinion of the Court.

One century ago, the first Justice Harlan admonished this Court that the Constitution "neither knows nor tolerates classes among citizens." *Plessy v. Ferguson*, 163 U.S. 537, 559 (1896) (dissenting opinion). Unheeded then, those words now are understood to state a commitment to the law's neutrality where the rights of persons are at stake. The Equal Protection Clause enforces this principle and today requires us to hold invalid a provision of Colorado's Constitution.

The enactment challenged in this case is an amendment to the Constitution of the State of Colorado, adopted in a 1992 statewide referendum. The parties and the state courts refer to it as "Amendment 2," its designation when submitted to the voters. The impetus for the amendment and the contentious campaign that preceded its adoption came in large part from ordinances that had been passed in various Colorado municipalities. For example, the cities of Aspen and Boulder and the City and County of Denver each had enacted ordinances which banned discrimination in many transactions and activities, including housing, employment, education, public accommodations, and health and welfare services. Denver Rev. Municipal Code, Art. IV §§ 28–91 to 28–116 (1991); Aspen Municipal Code § 13–98 (1977); Boulder Rev. Code §§ 12–1–1 to 12–1–11 (1987). What gave rise to the statewide controversy was the protection the ordinances afforded to persons discriminated against by reason of their sexual orientation. Amendment 2 repeals these ordinances to the extent they prohibit discrimination on the basis of "homosexual, lesbian or bisexual orientation, conduct, practices or relationships." Colo. Const., Art. II, § 30b.

Yet Amendment 2, in explicit terms, does more than repeal or rescind these provisions. It prohibits all legislative, executive or judicial action at any level of state or local government designed to protect the named class, a class we shall refer to as homosexual persons or gays and lesbians.[b] [Justice Kennedy quoted Amendment 2.]

The State's principal argument in defense of Amendment 2 is that it puts gays and lesbians in the same position as all other persons. So, the State says, the measure does no more than deny homosexuals special rights. This reading of the amendment's language is implausible. We rely

---

[b]   Amendment 2 provided as follows: "No Protected Status Based on Homosexual, Lesbian or Bisexual Orientation. Neither the State of Colorado, through any of its branches or departments, nor any of its agencies, political subdivisions, municipalities or school districts, shall enact, adopt or enforce any statute, regulation, ordinance or policy whereby homosexual, lesbian or bisexual orientation, conduct, practices or relationships shall constitute or otherwise be the basis of or entitle any person or class of persons to have or claim any minority status, quota preferences, protected status or claim of discrimination. This Section of the Constitution shall be in all respects self-executing."

not upon our own interpretation of the amendment but upon the authoritative construction of Colorado's Supreme Court. The state court, deeming it unnecessary to determine the full extent of the amendment's reach, found it invalid even on a modest reading of its implications. The critical discussion of the amendment, set out in *Romer* I, is as follows:

> "The immediate objective of Amendment 2 is, at a minimum, to repeal existing statutes, regulations, ordinances, and policies of state and local entities that barred discrimination based on sexual orientation. * * *

> "The 'ultimate effect' of Amendment 2 is to prohibit any governmental entity from adopting similar, or more protective statutes, regulations, ordinances, or policies in the future unless the state constitution is first amended to permit such measures." 854 P.2d, at 1284–1285, and n. 26.

Sweeping and comprehensive is the change in legal status effected by this law. So much is evident from the ordinances that the Colorado Supreme Court declared would be void by operation of Amendment 2. Homosexuals, by state decree, are put in a solitary class with respect to transactions and relations in both the private and governmental spheres. The amendment withdraws from homosexuals, but no others, specific legal protection from the injuries caused by discrimination, and it forbids reinstatement of these laws and policies.

The change that Amendment 2 works in the legal status of gays and lesbians in the private sphere is far-reaching, both on its own terms and when considered in light of the structure and operation of modern anti-discrimination laws. That structure is well illustrated by contemporary statutes and ordinances prohibiting discrimination by providers of public accommodations. "At common law, innkeepers, smiths, and others who 'made profession of a public employment,' were prohibited from refusing, without good reason, to serve a customer." *Hurley v. Irish-American Gay, Lesbian and Bisexual Group of Boston, Inc.*, 515 U.S. 557, 571 (1995) (Section 3C, *infra*). The duty was a general one and did not specify protection for particular groups. The common law rules, however, proved insufficient in many instances, and it was settled early that the Fourteenth Amendment did not give Congress a general power to prohibit discrimination in public accommodations, *Civil Rights Cases*, 109 U.S. 3, 25 (1883). In consequence, most States have chosen to counter discrimination by enacting detailed statutory schemes.

Colorado's state and municipal laws typify this emerging tradition of statutory protection and follow a consistent pattern. The laws first enumerate the persons or entities subject to a duty not to discriminate. The list goes well beyond the entities covered by the common law. The Boulder ordinance, for example, has a comprehensive definition of entities deemed places of "public accommodation." They include "any place of business engaged in any sales to the general public and any place that offers services, facilities, privileges, or advantages to the general public or that receives financial support through solicitation of the general public or through governmental subsidy of any kind." * * *

These statutes and ordinances also depart from the common law by enumerating the groups or persons within their ambit of protection. Enumeration is the essential device used to make the duty not to discriminate concrete and to provide guidance for those who must comply. In following this approach, Colorado's state and local governments have not limited anti-discrimination laws to groups that have so far been given the protection of heightened equal protection scrutiny under our cases. Rather, they set forth an extensive catalogue of traits which cannot be the basis for discrimination, including age, military status, marital status, pregnancy, parenthood, custody of a minor child, political affiliation, physical or mental disability of an individual or of his or her associates—and, in recent times, sexual orientation.

Amendment 2 bars homosexuals from securing protection against the injuries that these public-accommodations laws address. That in itself is a severe consequence, but there is more. Amendment 2, in addition, nullifies specific legal protections for this targeted class in all transactions in housing, sale of real estate, insurance, health and welfare services, private education, and employment.

Not confined to the private sphere, Amendment 2 also operates to repeal and forbid all laws or policies providing specific protection for gays or lesbians from discrimination by every level of Colorado government. The State Supreme Court cited two examples of protections in the governmental sphere that are now rescinded and may not be reintroduced. The first is Colorado Executive Order D0035 (1990), which forbids employment discrimination against " 'all state employees, classified and exempt' on the basis of sexual orientation." Also repealed, and now forbidden, are "various provisions prohibiting discrimination based on sexual orientation at state colleges." The repeal of these measures and the prohibition against their future reenactment demonstrates that Amendment 2 has the same force and effect in Colorado's governmental sector as it does elsewhere and that it applies to policies as well as ordinary legislation.

Amendment 2's reach may not be limited to specific laws passed for the benefit of gays and lesbians. It is a fair, if not necessary, inference from the broad language of the amendment that it deprives gays and lesbians even of the protection of general laws and policies that prohibit arbitrary discrimination in governmental and private settings. At some point in the systematic administration of these laws, an official must determine whether homosexuality is an arbitrary and, thus, forbidden basis for decision. Yet a decision to that effect would itself amount to a policy prohibiting discrimination on the basis of homosexuality, and so would appear to be no more valid under Amendment 2 than the specific prohibitions against discrimination the state court held invalid.

If this consequence follows from Amendment 2, as its broad language suggests, it would compound the constitutional difficulties the law creates. The state court did not decide whether the amendment has this effect, however, and neither need we. In the course of rejecting the argument that Amendment 2 is intended to conserve resources to fight discrimination against suspect classes, the Colorado Supreme Court made the limited observation that the amendment is not intended to affect many anti-discrimination laws protecting non-suspect classes, *Romer II*, 882 P.2d at 1346, n.9. In our view that does not resolve the issue. In any event, even if, as we doubt, homosexuals could find some safe harbor in laws of general application, we cannot accept the view that Amendment 2's prohibition on specific legal protections does no more than deprive homosexuals of special rights. To the contrary, the amendment imposes a special disability upon those persons alone. Homosexuals are forbidden the safeguards that others enjoy or may seek without constraint. They can obtain specific protection against discrimination only by enlisting the citizenry of Colorado to amend the State Constitution or perhaps, on the State's view, by trying to pass helpful laws of general applicability. This is so no matter how local or discrete the harm, no matter how public and widespread the injury. We find nothing special in the protections Amendment 2 withholds. These are protections taken for granted by most people either because they already have them or do not need them; these are protections against exclusion from an almost limitless number of transactions and endeavors that constitute ordinary civic life in a free society.

The Fourteenth Amendment's promise that no person shall be denied the equal protection of the laws must co-exist with the practical necessity that most legislation classifies for one purpose or another, with resulting disadvantage to various groups or persons. *Personnel Administrator of Mass. v. Feeney*, 442 U.S. 256, 271–272 (1979); *F.S. Royster Guano Co. v. Virginia*, 253 U.S. 412, 415 (1920). We have attempted to reconcile the principle with the reality by stating that, if a law neither burdens a fundamental right nor targets a suspect class, we will uphold the legislative classification so long as it bears a rational relation to some legitimate end. See, *e.g.*, *Heller v. Doe*, 509 U.S. 312, 319–320 (1993).

Amendment 2 fails, indeed defies, even this conventional inquiry. First, the amendment has the peculiar property of imposing a broad and undifferentiated disability on a single named group, an exceptional and, as we shall explain, invalid form of legislation. Second, its sheer breadth is so discontinuous with the reasons offered for it that the amendment seems inexplicable by anything but animus toward the class that it affects; it lacks a rational relationship to legitimate state interests.

Taking the first point, even in the ordinary equal protection case calling for the most deferential of standards, we insist on knowing the relation between the classification adopted and the object to be attained.

The search for the link between classification and objective gives substance to the Equal Protection Clause; it provides guidance and discipline for the legislature, which is entitled to know what sorts of laws it can pass; and it marks the limits of our own authority. In the ordinary case, a law will be sustained if it can be said to advance a legitimate government interest, even if the law seems unwise or works to the disadvantage of a particular group, or if the rationale for it seems tenuous. * * * By requiring that the classification bear a rational relationship to an independent and legitimate legislative end, we ensure that classifications are not drawn for the purpose of disadvantaging the group burdened by the law. * * *

Amendment 2 confounds this normal process of judicial review. It is at once too narrow and too broad. It identifies persons by a single trait and then denies them protection across the board. The resulting disqualification of a class of persons from the right to seek specific protection from the law is unprecedented in our jurisprudence. The absence of precedent for Amendment 2 is itself instructive; "[d]iscriminations of an unusual character especially suggest careful consideration to determine whether they are obnoxious to the constitutional provision." *Louisville Gas & Elec. Co. v. Coleman*, 277 U.S. 32, 37–38 (1928).

It is not within our constitutional tradition to enact laws of this sort. Central both to the idea of the rule of law and to our own Constitution's guarantee of equal protection is the principle that government and each of its parts remain open on impartial terms to all who seek its assistance. " 'Equal protection of the laws is not achieved through indiscriminate imposition of inequalities.' " *Sweatt v. Painter*, 339 U.S. 629, 635 (1950) (quoting *Shelley v. Kraemer*, 334 U.S. 1, 22 (1948)). Respect for this principle explains why laws singling out a certain class of citizens for disfavored legal status or general hardships are rare. A law declaring that in general it shall be more difficult for one group of citizens than for all others to seek aid from the government is itself a denial of equal protection of the laws in the most literal sense. "The guaranty of 'equal protection of the laws is a pledge of the protection of equal laws.' " *Skinner v. Oklahoma ex rel. Williamson*, 316 U.S. 535, 541 (1942) (quoting *Yick Wo v. Hopkins*, 118 U.S. 356, 369 (1886)).

[The Court next responded to the analogy argued by the dissent to *Davis v. Beason*, 133 U.S. 333 (1890), which upheld "an Idaho territorial statute denying Mormons, polygamists, and advocates of polygamy the right to vote and to hold office because, as the Court construed the statute, it 'simply excludes from the privilege of voting, or of holding any office of honor, trust or profit, those who have been convicted of certain offences, and those who advocate a practical resistance to the laws of the Territory and justify and approve the commission of crimes forbidden by it.' "] To the extent *Davis* held that persons advocating a certain practice may be denied the right to vote, it is no longer good law. *Brandenburg v.*

Ohio, 395 U.S. 444 (1969) (per curiam). To the extent it held that the groups designated in the statute may be deprived of the right to vote because of their status, its ruling could not stand without surviving strict scrutiny, a most doubtful outcome. *Dunn v. Blumstein*, 405 U.S. 330, 337 (1972). To the extent *Davis* held that a convicted felon may be denied the right to vote, its holding is not implicated by our decision and is unexceptionable. See *Richardson v. Ramirez*, 418 U.S. 24 (1974).

A second and related point is that laws of the kind now before us raise the inevitable inference that the disadvantage imposed is born of animosity toward the class of persons affected. "[I]f the constitutional conception of 'equal protection of the laws' means anything, it must at the very least mean that a bare . . . desire to harm a politically unpopular group cannot constitute a *legitimate* governmental interest." *Department of Agriculture v. Moreno*, 413 U.S. 528, 534 (1973). Even laws enacted for broad and ambitious purposes often can be explained by reference to legitimate public policies which justify the incidental disadvantages they impose on certain persons. Amendment 2, however, in making a general announcement that gays and lesbians shall not have any particular protections from the law, inflicts on them immediate, continuing, and real injuries that outrun and belie any legitimate justifications that may be claimed for it. We conclude that, in addition to the far-reaching deficiencies of Amendment 2 that we have noted, the principles it offends, in another sense, are conventional and venerable; a law must bear a rational relationship to a legitimate governmental purpose, *Kadrmas v. Dickinson Public Schools*, 487 U.S. 450, 462 (1988), and Amendment 2 does not.

The primary rationale the State offers for Amendment 2 is respect for other citizens' freedom of association, and in particular the liberties of landlords or employers who have personal or religious objections to homosexuality. Colorado also cites its interest in conserving resources to fight discrimination against other groups. The breadth of the Amendment is so far removed from these particular justifications that we find it impossible to credit them. We cannot say that Amendment 2 is directed to any identifiable legitimate purpose or discrete objective. It is a status-based enactment divorced from any factual context from which we could discern a relationship to legitimate state interests; it is a classification of persons undertaken for its own sake, something the Equal Protection Clause does not permit. "[C]lass legislation . . . [is] obnoxious to the prohibitions of the Fourteenth Amendment. . . ." *Civil Rights Cases*, 109 U.S., at 24.

We must conclude that Amendment 2 classifies homosexuals not to further a proper legislative end but to make them unequal to everyone else. This Colorado cannot do. A State cannot so deem a class of persons a stranger to its laws. Amendment 2 violates the Equal Protection Clause, and the judgment of the Supreme Court of Colorado is affirmed.

■ JUSTICE SCALIA, with whom THE CHIEF JUSTICE [REHNQUIST] and JUSTICE THOMAS join, dissenting.

The Court has mistaken a Kulturkampf for a fit of spite. The constitutional amendment before us here is not the manifestation of a " 'bare . . . desire to harm' " homosexuals, but is rather a modest attempt by seemingly tolerant Coloradans to preserve traditional sexual mores against the efforts of a politically powerful minority to revise those mores through use of the laws. That objective, and the means chosen to achieve it, are not only unimpeachable under any constitutional doctrine hitherto pronounced (hence the opinion's heavy reliance upon principles of righteousness rather than judicial holdings); they have been specifically approved by the Congress of the United States and by this Court.

In holding that homosexuality cannot be singled out for disfavorable treatment, the Court contradicts a decision, unchallenged here, pronounced only 10 years ago, see *Hardwick*, and places the prestige of this institution behind the proposition that opposition to homosexuality is as reprehensible as racial or religious bias. Whether it is or not is *precisely* the cultural debate that gave rise to the Colorado constitutional amendment (and to the preferential laws against which the amendment was directed). Since the Constitution of the United States says nothing about this subject, it is left to be resolved by normal democratic means, including the democratic adoption of provisions in state constitutions. This Court has no business imposing upon all Americans the resolution favored by the elite class from which the Members of this institution are selected, pronouncing that "animosity" toward homosexuality, is evil. I vigorously dissent.

Let me first discuss [the Court's rejection of] the State's arguments that Amendment 2 "puts gays and lesbians in the same position as all other persons," and "does no more than deny homosexuals special rights." The Court concludes that this reading of Amendment 2's language is "implausible" under the "authoritative construction" given Amendment 2 by the Supreme Court of Colorado.

[Justice Scalia quoted the decision of the Colorado Supreme Court, which construed Amendment 2 as follows: "[It] seeks only to prevent the adoption of antidiscrimination laws intended to protect gays, lesbians, and bisexuals."] The clear import of the Colorado court's conclusion that it is not affected is that "general laws and policies that prohibit arbitrary discrimination" would continue to prohibit discrimination on the basis of homosexual conduct as well. This analysis, which is fully in accord with (indeed, follows inescapably from) the text of the constitutional provision, lays to rest such horribles, raised in the course of oral argument, as the prospect that assaults upon homosexuals could not be prosecuted. The amendment prohibits *special treatment* of homosexuals, and nothing more. It would not affect, for example, a requirement of state law that pensions be paid to all retiring state employees with a certain length of service; homosexual employees, as well as others, would be entitled to that benefit. But it would prevent the State or any municipality from making death-benefit payments to the "life partner" of a homosexual when it does not make such payments to the long-time roommate of a non-homosexual employee. Or again, it does not affect the requirement of the State's general insurance laws that customers be afforded coverage without discrimination unrelated to anticipated risk. Thus, homosexuals could not be denied coverage, or charged a greater premium, with respect to auto collision insurance; but neither the State nor any municipality could require that distinctive health insurance risks associated with homosexuality (if there are any) be ignored.

Despite all of its hand-wringing about the potential effect of Amendment 2 on general antidiscrimination laws, the Court's opinion ultimately does not dispute all this, but assumes it to be true. The only denial of equal treatment it contends homosexuals have suffered is this: They may not obtain *preferential* treatment without amending the State Constitution. That is to say, the principle underlying the Court's opinion is that one who is accorded equal treatment under the laws, but cannot as readily as others obtain *preferential* treatment under the laws, has been denied equal protection of the laws. If merely stating this alleged "equal protection" violation does not suffice to refute it, our constitutional jurisprudence has achieved terminal silliness.

The central thesis of the Court's reasoning is that any group is denied equal protection when, to obtain advantage (or, presumably, to avoid disadvantage), it must have recourse to a more general and hence more difficult level of political decisionmaking than others. The world has never heard of such a principle, which is why the Court's opinion is so long on emotive utterance and so short on relevant legal citation. And it seems to me most unlikely that any multilevel democracy can function under such a principle. For *whenever* a disadvantage is imposed, or conferral of a benefit is prohibited, at one of the higher levels of democratic decisionmaking (*i.e.*, by the state legislature rather than local government, or by the people at large in the state constitution rather than the legislature), the affected group has (under this theory) been denied equal protection. * * *

I turn next to whether there was a legitimate rational basis for the substance of the constitutional amendment—for the prohibition of special protection for homosexuals. It is unsurprising that the Court avoids discussion of this question, since the answer is so obviously yes. The case most relevant to the issue before us today is not even mentioned in the Court's opinion: In *Bowers v. Hardwick*, we held that the Constitution does not prohibit what virtually all States had done from the founding of the Republic until very recent years—making homosexual conduct a crime. That holding is unassailable, except by those who think that the Constitution changes to suit current fashions. But in any event it is a given in the present case: Respondents' briefs did not urge overruling *Bowers*, and at oral argument respondents' counsel expressly disavowed any intent to seek such overruling. If it is constitutionally permissible for a State to make homosexual conduct criminal, surely it is constitutionally permissible for a State to enact other laws merely *disfavoring* homosexual conduct. * * * And *a fortiori* it is constitutionally permissible for a State to adopt a provision *not even* disfavoring homosexual conduct, but merely prohibiting all levels of state government from bestowing *special protections* upon homosexual conduct. Respondents (who, unlike the Court, cannot afford the luxury of ignoring inconvenient precedent) counter *Bowers* with the argument that a greater-includes-the-lesser rationale cannot justify Amendment 2's application to individuals who do not engage in homosexual acts, but are merely of homosexual "orientation." * * *

But assuming that, in Amendment 2, a person of homosexual "orientation" is someone who does not engage in homosexual conduct but merely has a tendency or desire to do so, *Bowers* still suffices to establish a rational basis for the provision. If it is rational to criminalize the conduct, surely it is rational to deny special favor and protection to those with a self-avowed tendency or desire to engage in the conduct. Indeed, where criminal sanctions are not involved, homosexual "orientation" is an acceptable stand-in for homosexual conduct. A State "does not violate the Equal Protection Clause merely because the classifications made by its laws are imperfect," *Dandridge v. Williams*, 397 U.S. 471, 485 (1970). Just as a policy barring the hiring of methadone users as transit employees does not violate equal protection simply because *some* methadone users pose no threat to passenger safety, see *New York City Transit Authority v. Beazer*, 440 U.S. 568 (1979), and just as a mandatory retirement age of 50 for police officers does not violate equal protection even though it prematurely ends the careers of many policemen over 50 who still have the capacity to do the job, see *Massachusetts Bd. of Retirement v. Murgia*, 427 U.S. 307 (1976) (*per curiam*), Amendment 2 is not constitutionally invalid simply because it could have been drawn more precisely so as to withdraw special antidiscrimination protections only from those of homosexual "orientation" who actually engage in homosexual conduct. * * *

The foregoing suffices to establish what the Court's failure to cite any case remotely in point would lead one to suspect: No principle set forth in the Constitution, nor even any imagined by this Court in the past 200 years, prohibits what Colorado has done here. But the case for Colorado is much stronger than that. What it has done is not only unprohibited, but eminently reasonable, with close, congressionally approved precedent in earlier constitutional practice.

First, as to its eminent reasonableness. The Court's opinion contains grim, disapproving hints that Coloradans have been guilty of "animus" or "animosity" toward homosexuality, as though that has been established as un-American. Of course it is our moral heritage that one should not hate any human being or class of human beings. But I had thought that one could consider certain conduct reprehensible—murder, for example, or polygamy, or cruelty to animals—and could exhibit even "animus" toward such conduct. Surely that is the only sort of "animus" at issue here: moral disapproval of homosexual conduct, the same sort of moral disapproval that produced the centuries-old criminal laws that we held constitutional in *Bowers*. The Colorado amendment does not, to speak entirely precisely, prohibit giving favored status to people who are *homosexuals*; they can be favored for many reasons—for example, because they are senior citizens or members of racial minorities. But it prohibits giving them favored status *because of their homosexual conduct*—that is, it prohibits favored status *for homosexuality*.

But though Coloradans are, as I say, *entitled* to be hostile toward homosexual conduct, the fact is that the degree of hostility reflected by Amendment 2 is the smallest conceivable. The Court's portrayal of Coloradans as a society fallen victim to pointless, hate-filled "gay-bashing" is so false as to be comical. Colorado not only is one of the 25 States that have repealed their antisodomy laws, but was among the first to do so. See 1971 Colo. Sess. Laws, ch. 121, § 1. But the society that eliminates criminal punishment for homosexual acts does not necessarily abandon the view that homosexuality is morally wrong and socially harmful; often, abolition simply reflects the view that enforcement of such criminal laws involves unseemly intrusion into the intimate lives of citizens. * * *

There is a problem, however, which arises when criminal sanction of homosexuality is eliminated but moral and social disapprobation of homosexuality is meant to be retained. The Court cannot be unaware of that problem; it is evident in many cities of the country, and occasionally bubbles to the surface of the news, in heated political disputes over such matters as the introduction into local schools of books teaching that homosexuality is an optional and fully acceptable "alternate life style." The problem (a problem, that is, for those who wish to retain social disapprobation of homosexuality) is that, because those who engage in homosexual conduct tend to reside in disproportionate numbers in certain communities, see Record, Exh. MMM, have high disposable income, see *ibid.*; App. 254 (affidavit of Prof. James Hunter), and, of course, care about homosexual-rights issues much more ardently than the public at large, they possess political power much greater than their numbers, both locally and statewide. Quite understandably, they devote this political power to achieving not merely a grudging social toleration, but full social acceptance, of homosexuality. * * *

By the time Coloradans were asked to vote on Amendment 2, their exposure to homosexuals' quest for social endorsement was not limited to newspaper accounts of happenings in places such as New York, Los Angeles, San Francisco, and Key West. Three Colorado cities—Aspen, Boulder, and Denver—had enacted ordinances that listed "sexual orientation" as an impermissible ground for discrimination, equating the moral disapproval of homosexual conduct with racial and religious bigotry. The phenomenon had even appeared statewide: the Governor of Colorado had signed an executive order pronouncing that "in the State of Colorado we recognize the diversity in our pluralistic society and strive to bring an end to discrimination in any form," and directing state agency-heads to "ensure non-discrimination" in hiring and promotion based on, among other things, "sexual orientation." Executive Order No. D0035 (Dec. 10, 1990). I do not mean to be critical of these legislative successes; homosexuals are as entitled to use the legal system for reinforcement of their moral sentiments as are the rest of society. But they are subject to being countered by lawful, democratic countermeasures as well.

That is where Amendment 2 came in. It sought to counter both the geographic concentration and the disproportionate political power of homosexuals by (1) resolving the controversy at the statewide level, and (2) making the election a single-issue contest for both sides. It put directly, to all the citizens of the State, the question: Should homosexuality be given special protection? They answered no. The Court today asserts that this most democratic of procedures is unconstitutional. Lacking any cases to establish that facially absurd proposition, it simply asserts that it *must* be unconstitutional, because it has never happened before. * * * As I have noted above, this is proved false every time a state law prohibiting or disfavoring certain conduct is passed, because such a law prevents the adversely affected group—whether drug addicts, or smokers, or gun owners, or motorcyclists—from changing the policy thus established in "each of [the] parts" of the State. What the Court says is even demonstrably false at the constitutional level. The Eighteenth Amendment to the Federal Constitution, for example, deprived those who drank alcohol not only of the power to alter the policy of prohibition *locally* or through *state legislation*, but even of the power to alter it through *state constitutional amendment* or *federal legislation*. The Establishment Clause of the First Amendment prevents theocrats from having their way by converting their fellow citizens at the local, state, or federal statutory level; as does the Republican Form of Government Clause prevent monarchists.

But there is a much closer analogy, one that involves precisely the effort by the majority of citizens to preserve its view of sexual morality statewide, against the efforts of a geographically concentrated and politically powerful minority to undermine it. The Constitutions of the States of Arizona, Idaho, New Mexico, Oklahoma, and Utah *to this day* contain provisions stating that polygamy is "forever prohibited." Polygamists, and those who have a polygamous "orientation," have been "singled out" by these provisions for much more severe treatment than merely denial of favored status; and that treatment can only be changed by achieving amendment of the state constitutions. The Court's disposition today suggests that these provisions are unconstitutional, and that polygamy must be permitted in these States on a state-legislated, or perhaps even local-option, basis—unless, of course, polygamists for some reason have fewer constitutional rights than homosexuals. * * *

I cannot say that this Court has explicitly approved any of these state constitutional provisions; but it has approved a territorial statutory provision that went even further, depriving polygamists of the ability even to achieve a constitutional amendment, by depriving them of the power to vote. In *Davis v. Beason*, 133 U.S. 333 (1890), Justice Field wrote for a unanimous Court:

> "In our judgment, § 501 of the Revised Statutes of Idaho Territory, which provides that 'no person . . . who is a bigamist or polygamist or who teaches, advises, counsels, or encourages any person or persons to become bigamists or polygamists, or to commit any other crime defined by law, or to enter into what is known as plural or celestial marriage, or who is a member of any order, organization or association which teaches, advises, counsels, or encourages its members or devotees or any other persons to commit the crime of bigamy or polygamy, or any other crime defined by law . . . is permitted to vote at any election, or to hold any position or office of honor, trust, or profit within this Territory,' *is not open to any constitutional or legal objection.*" *Id.*, at 346–347 (emphasis added).

To the extent, if any, that this opinion permits the imposition of adverse consequences upon mere abstract advocacy of polygamy, it has of course been overruled by later cases. See *Brandenburg v. Ohio*, 395 U.S. 444 (1969) (*per curiam*). But the proposition that polygamy can be criminalized, and those engaging in that crime deprived of the vote, remains good law. See *Richardson v. Ramirez*, 418 U.S. 24, 53 (1974). *Beason* rejected the argument that "such discrimination is a denial of the equal protection of the laws." Among the Justices joining in that rejection were the two whose views in other cases the Court today treats as equal-protection lodestars [Justices Harlan and Bradley]. * * *

* * * Has the Court concluded that the perceived social harm of polygamy is a "legitimate concern of government," and the perceived social harm of homosexuality is not?

I strongly suspect that the answer to the last question is yes, which leads me to the last point I wish to make: The Court today, announcing that Amendment 2 "defies . . . conventional [constitutional] inquiry," and "confounds [the] normal process of judicial review," employs a constitutional theory heretofore unknown to frustrate Colorado's reasonable effort to preserve traditional American moral values. * * *

When the Court takes sides in the culture wars, it tends to be with the knights rather than the villeins—and more specifically with the Templars, reflecting the views and values of the lawyer class from which the Court's Members are drawn. How that class feels about homosexuality will be evident to anyone who wishes to interview job applicants at virtually any of the Nation's law schools. The interviewer may refuse to offer a job because the applicant is a Republican; because he is an adulterer; because he went to the wrong prep school or belongs to the wrong country club; because he eats snails; because he is a womanizer; because she wears real-animal fur; or even because he hates the Chicago Cubs. But if the interviewer should wish not to be an associate or partner of an applicant because he disapproves of the applicant's homosexuality, *then* he will have violated the pledge which the Association of American Law Schools requires all its member schools to exact from job interviewers: "assurance of the employer's willingness" to hire homosexuals. This law-school view of what "prejudices" must be stamped out may be contrasted with the more plebeian attitudes that apparently still prevail in the United States Congress, which has been unresponsive to repeated attempts to extend to homosexuals the protections of federal civil rights laws, see, e.g., Employment Non-Discrimination Act of 1994, S. 2238, 103d Cong., 2d Sess. (1994); Civil Rights Amendments of 1975, H.R. 5452, 94th Cong., 1st Sess. (1975), and which took the pains to exclude them specifically from the Americans with Disabilities Act of 1990, see 42 U.S.C. § 12211(a) (1988 ed., Supp. V).

Today's opinion has no foundation in American constitutional law, and barely pretends to. The people of Colorado have adopted an entirely reasonable provision which does not even disfavor homosexuals in any substantive sense, but merely denies them preferential treatment. Amendment 2 is designed to prevent piecemeal deterioration of the sexual morality favored by a majority of Coloradans, and is not only an appropriate means to that legitimate end, but a means that Americans have employed before. Striking it down is an act, not of judicial judgment, but of political will. I dissent.

NOTES ON *ROMER V. EVANS*

1. *What Is the Holding of* Romer v. Evans? What exactly was wrong with Amendment 2? Some possibilities:

    (a) It deprived gay people of the right to participate equally in the political process;[c]

    (b) The law was a denial of the "equal protection of the laws" in the most literal sense, as it closed off state process to one vulnerable group;[d]

    (c) The state cannot, without justification, single out one social group for "pariah" status by creating a constitutional right to discriminate against that group,[e] or the state has an obligation

---

[c]   This was the theory below. *Evans v. Romer*, 854 P.2d 1270 (Colo. 1993).

[d]   "Scholars' amicus brief," by Laurence Tribe, et al., filed in Supreme Court.

[e]   Daniel Farber & Suzanna Sherry, "The Pariah Principle," 13 *Const. Comm.* 257 (1996).

to remedy pervasive discrimination against a vulnerable group similar to those the state does protect;[f]

(d) The law's goal—state action reflecting widespread animus against gay people—was impermissible "class legislation";[g]

(e) The measure, unprecedented in its sweep, was overbroad.[h]

Which is the *best* (most persuasive) basis for *Romer v. Evans*?

2. *Identity and Conduct; Animus und Kulturkampf.* Echoing Judge Norris in *Watkins*, Justice Kennedy in *Romer v. Evans* reads Amendment 2 through the lens of identity and a history of persecution. Unlike Norris, Kennedy places some emphasis on motive: Amendment 2 was a product of "animus," not rationality. Animus plays an ambiguous role in the opinion. Colorado had presented itself as a tolerant state, because it had long ago shed its consensual sodomy law, and the amendment was a mild "no promo homo" measure—rather than putting LGB people in jail, Colorado tolerates them but signals its preference for heterosexuality. Why did the Court not accept this presentation? (Review the ballot materials in Appendix 7. Do they suggest antigay animus?) How should courts distinguish between morals regulations and laws motivated by animus?

Justice Scalia reads Amendment 2 through the lens of conduct and a history of morals regulation. Not only does Scalia accept Colorado's self-presentation as tolerant, he also scorns the Court's finding of "animus," though he does so in an odd way. Consider his rhetoric. *Kulturkampf* is "culture *war*" conducted by the state to erase an unpopular minority. (The original *Kulturkampf* was Chancellor Bismarck's effort to domesticate the Roman Catholic Church in Germany.) Scalia's invocation of the anti-Mormon cases makes the violence explicit, for the federal government's campaign to destroy the Church of Latter-Day Saints was premised on the Church's support of polygamy. Not only did polygamists go to jail for consensual adult activities, but people advocating tolerance of polygamy lost the right to vote and serve on juries, and the Church's property was confiscated. Does the majority in *Romer* overrule *Beason*?

One can read the dissent as a rhetorical invitation for states to accommodate "cultural wars" against gay people, and the majority opinion to be an insistence that the courts should not permit *Kulturkampf*. Scalia seems to consign gay people to a state of nature (the essence of *Kulturkampf* if you are the persecuted minority), while the opening reference to the *Plessy* dissent suggests that the Court was invoking a pluralist idea that the majority may not deploy the state to suppress an unpopular minority.

---

[f]   Louis Michael Seidman, "*Romer*'s Radicalism: The Unexpected Revival of Warren Court Activism," 1996 *Sup. Ct. Rev.* 67; Jane Schacter, "*Romer v. Evans* and Democracy's Domain," 50 *Vand. L. Rev.* 361 (1997).

[g]   Eskridge, *Gaylaw* 205–18; Andrew Koppelman, "*Romer v. Evans* and Invidious Intent," 6 *Wm. & Mary Bill of Rights J.* 89 (1997); Cass Sunstein, "The Supreme Court, 1995 Term—Foreword: Leaving Things Undecided," 110 *Harv. L. Rev.* 4, 62 (1996).

[h]   Richard Duncan, "The Narrow and Shallow Bite of *Romer* and the Eminent Rationality of Dual-Gender Marriage, 6 *Wm. & Mary Bill of Rights J.* 147 (1997).

One reason the case is complex is that Justice Kennedy's text performs multiple functions simultaneously. Most dramatically, it reverses what lower federal courts had interpreted as a rule of categorical inequality in *Bowers v. Hardwick, i.e.*, despite the absence of an equal protection ruling in *Hardwick*, many judges followed Judge Reinhardt's lead in *Watkins* to conclude that it permitted a virtual blank check for adverse treatment. Instead, the decision in *Romer* substituted the requirement of some reasonable nexus between the classification and a legitimate legislative purpose, and it held that, at least some of the time for some purposes, laws enacted to foster disapprobation of homosexuality were fatally flawed.

3. *Standard of Review?* Although there is a brief reference to equal protection in the Court's decision striking down the exclusion of same-sex couples from marriage (see Chapter 2, Section 3A, *infra*), *Romer* remains the leading Supreme Court decision in which the Court has found legislation to be unconstitutional on equality grounds. Like *Reed v. Reed*, the Court's silence on standard of review in *Romer* has led lower courts to conclude that it was applying a rational basis test—or perhaps more precisely, a heightened rational basis standard. See Justice O'Connor's concurring opinion in *Lawrence v. Texas*, Chapter 2, Section 2A *infra*.

NOTE ON THE IMMUTABILITY "REQUIREMENT" FOR SUSPECT CLASSIFICATIONS AND ITS RELEVANCE TO SEXUAL ORIENTATION

One of the persistent questions in the analysis of sexual orientation discrimination claims under the Equal Protection Clause is whether homosexuality is immutable. The various theories are presented and critically examined in Edward Stein, *The Mismeasure of Desire: The Science, Theory, and Ethics of Sexual Orientation* (1999). The most famous hypothesis is that there is a genetic cause contributing directly or indirectly toward homosexuality. This hypothesis has had an enduring appeal among scientists, policymakers, and some gay people, but has been resistant to proof.

Studies of twins and adopted siblings have been particular favorites of researchers looking for genetic influence in sexual orientation. Since identical twins theoretically share all of their genes, and fraternal twins only one-half, one would expect that a genetically-influenced trait would show up significantly more often in the former than the latter. This was the result found in studies of both female and male twins by Michael Bailey and Richard Pillard. In Bailey & Pillard, "A Genetic Study of Male Sexual Orientation," 48 *Archives Gen. Psychiatry* 1089 (1991), subjects were recruited through advertisements in gay publications for gay or bisexual men over eighteen who had male siblings. Based upon reports of their own and their siblings' sexual orientation, checked with the latter where possible, Bailey and Pillard found that identical twin brothers were concordant for sexual orientation (*i.e.*, if one brother was gay, so was the other) 52% of the time, as compared to 22% for fraternal twins, 9% for non-twin brothers and 11% for adoptive brothers. Bailey et al., "Heritable Factors Influence Sexual Orientation in Women," 50 *Archives Gen. Psychiatry* 217 (1993), found that identical twin sisters were concordant for sexual orientation 71% of the time, as compared to 37% for fraternal twins, 33% for adoptive sisters, and 14% for non-twin sisters. Subsequent work by Bailey and other colleagues has found lower numbers for both twin brothers (20–38% concordance for sexual orientation) and twin sisters (24–36%). The twins studies make it clear that sexual orientation cannot be *purely* genetic, because if it were the expected concordance rate for identical twins would be near 100%. Instead, the range of heritability estimates from these studies is from 30–70%. For other criticisms, see William Byne & Bruce Parsons, "Human Sexual Orientation: The Biological Theories Reappraised," 50 *Archives Gen. Psychiatry* 228–39 (1993).

The genetic thesis got perhaps its strongest, or best-publicized, support from Dean Hamer et al., "A Linkage Between DNA Markers on the X Chromosome and Male Sexual Orientation," 261 *Science* 321–27 (1993), elaborated in Dean Hamer & Peter Copeland, *The Science of Desire: The Search for the Gay Gene and the Biology of Behavior* (1994). The authors, researchers at the National Cancer Institute of the National Institutes of Health (NIH), claimed to have found a location on the X chromosome (Xq28, to be precise) where a "gay gene" would likely be found. The study concentrated on pairs of brothers in which both were gay, reasoning that if being gay was genetic, then families with pairs of gay brothers would be more "loaded" with the gay gene than others and would be the best place to look. The NIH group first found that among these families, the maternal uncles and male cousins were more likely to be gay than the general population or the paternal relatives; this pattern suggests a trait linked to the X chromosome, which men get from their mother but not their father. They then examined 40 pairs of gay brothers, and found that 33 of them shared the same markers in the Xq28 region of the X chromosome, a result significantly higher than the 50% one would expect from random distribution. Based on this data, the NIH group concluded (cautiously) that "at least one subtype of male sexual orientation is genetically influenced." This NIH study has been criticized on a number of fronts, and its results have not been satisfactorily replicated.

While *determinist theories* of sexual orientation (such as the gay gene) remain unproven, *voluntarist theories* (such as those of reparative therapists) have found virtually no support among scientists. Leading reparative therapists have conceded that their therapy rarely purges the patient of all homosexual desires, and there is no hard empirical evidence that it has any long-term effects on any patients. The professional organizations in psychiatry and psychology have disavowed reparative therapy as sectarian rather than scientific and as unethical in its asserted manipulation of patients. Other theories are *quasi-determinist*. The most famous is Freud's theory that homosexuality is the result of family psychodynamics (the Oedipus Complex). Some scientists maintain that childhood gender deviation (sissy boys and tomboys) correlates with adult sexual deviation. These theories enjoy the greatest empirical support but are subject to the chicken-and-the-egg problem: Does the gender deviation cause or contribute to the sexual deviation? Or do they both derive from the same biological or developmental roots?

Of what consequence should these debates be to legal questions? Assume that the scientific evidence establishes that sexual orientation can be influenced if not completely chosen. How, if at all, would that change the legal analysis under the Equal Protection Clause? Consider the approach under immigration law: The United Nations Protocol Relating to the Status of Refugees provides that states grant asylum to persons who face persecution in their home country because of membership in a "particular social group." American law has defined that phrase to mean "an individual who is a member of a group of persons all of whom share a common, immutable characteristic." *Matter of Acosta*, 19 I. & N. Dec. 211, 233, 1985 WL 56042 (BIA 1985). Can an LGBT person meet that definition? *See Hernandez-Montiel v. Immigration and Naturalization Service*, 225 F.3d 1084 (9th Cir. 2000) (defining "immutable" to include "an innate characteristic that is so fundamental of the identities or consciences of its members that members either cannot or should not be required to change it.") Reread *Boutilier* and consider how these arguments relate to bisexuality.

3. THE SEX AND SEXUAL ORIENTATION RELATIONSHIP IN EQUAL PROTECTION LAW

The first scholar to argue that a law discriminating against lesbians and gay men should fall on sex discrimination grounds was Sylvia A. Law, in "Homosexuality and the Social Meaning of Gender, 1988 *Wis. L. Rev.* 187, in which the focus was on sodomy law. The following article elaborated on social meanings of sexual orientation and gender.

Andrew Koppelman, "Why Discrimination Against Lesbians and Gay Men is Sex Discrimination"

69 *New York University Law Review* 197, 202, 218 (1994).*

* * * Laws that discriminate against gays rest upon a normative stereotype: the bald conviction that certain behavior—for example, sex with women—is appropriate for members of one sex, but not for members of the other sex. Such laws therefore flatly violate the constitutional prohibition on sex discrimination as it has been interpreted by the Supreme Court. Since intermediate scrutiny of gender-based classifications is appropriate, and laws that discriminate against gays cannot withstand intermediate scrutiny, our legal argument is concluded. A court applying received doctrine should invalidate any statute that singles out gays for unequal treatment.

* * * Much of the connection between sexism and the homosexuality taboo lies in social meanings that are accessible to everyone. It should be clear from ordinary experience that the stigmatization of the homosexual has *something* to do with the homosexual's supposed deviance from traditional sex roles. "Our society," Joseph Pleck observes, "uses the male heterosexual-homosexual dichotomy as a central symbol for *all* the

---

*   Copyright 1994 NYU Law Review; reprinted by permission.

rankings of masculinity, for the division on *any* grounds between males who are 'real men' and have power and males who are not. Any kind of powerlessness or refusal to compete becomes imbued with the imagery of homosexuality." Similarly, the denunciation of feminism as tantamount to lesbianism is depressingly familiar. * * *

Most Americans learn no later than high school that one of the nastier sanctions that one will suffer if one deviates from the behavior traditionally deemed appropriate for one's sex is the imputation of homosexuality. The two stigmas, sex-inappropriateness and homosexuality, are virtually interchangeable, and each is readily used as a metaphor for the other. There is nothing esoteric or sociologically abstract in the claim that the homosexuality taboo enforces traditional sex roles. Everyone knows that it is so. The recognition that in our society homosexuality is generally understood as a metaphor for failure to live up to the norms of one's gender resembles the recognition that segregation stigmatizes blacks, in that both are "matters of common notoriety, matters not so much for judicial notice as for the background knowledge of educated men who live in the world."

* * * Just as the hierarchy of whites over blacks is greatly strengthened by extreme differentiation of the races, so the hierarchy of males over females is greatly strengthened by extreme differentiation of the sexes. The element of both differentiations that promotes hierarchy is the idea that certain anatomical features *necessarily* entail certain social roles: one's status in society is obviously and unproblematically determined by the color of one's skin or the shape of one's reproductive organs. Blacks are supposed to defer to whites and obey whites' wishes because that is what blacks do. Women are supposed to defer to men and obey men's wishes because that is what women do.

The reification of socially constructed reality is always useful for the maintenance of that reality. But such reification takes on added urgency in modern Western civilization, with its radically egalitarian philosophy that manifests itself in, among other things, the fourteenth amendment of the U.S. Constitution. Thus the miscegenation taboo ultimately could not be justified in terms of its real purpose, and ended its days rationalized as a eugenic measure, on the basis of the shabbiest kind of pseudo-science. Where hierarchies based on birth are illegitimate, their survival is greatly enhanced by invisibility. Overt homosexuality is thus a greater danger to gender hierarchy in our society than it has been in other, more stable cultures. It threatens the hierarchy of the sexes because its existence suggests that even in a realm where a person's sex has been regarded as absolutely determinative, anatomy has less to do with destiny than one might have supposed. It is therefore unsurprising that, as we shall shortly see, the courts, which have enforced both of these putatively "natural" prohibitions, have struggled to conceal their socially constructed character.

The point of emphasizing this socially constructed character is not to argue that since social contexts—taken for granted meanings and habitual practices—can be revealed to be social constructions that restrict human possibilities, they ought to be smashed. Rather, the point is that *certain* meanings and practices operate in furtherance of morally indefensible ends. Where this is true, exposure of those meanings and practices as socially constructed deprives them of the invisibility provided by the appearance of "naturalness" and makes them subject to criticism. In order to survive, these systems of social construction have to lie. * * *

NOTES ON THE SEX DISCRIMINATION ARGUMENT IN EQUAL PROTECTION LAW

As a formal matter, marriage laws that excluded same-sex couples made distinctions on the basis of *sex*, rather than *sexual orientation*, i.e., whether two people could marry, for example, technically turned on the sex of the partners. In most instances, though, courts have rejected the sex discrimination claim. (The sex discrimination argument has gained significant ground in Title VII cases, however; see Chapter 5, Section 5.) Why do you think that it has been such a hard sell to judges in the realm of constitutional litigation?

In *Singer v. Hara*, 11 Wash. App. 247, 522 P.2d 1187, review denied, 84 Wash.2d 1008 (1974), the court rejected a sex discrimination argument on definitional grounds. Unlike *Loving v. Virginia*, 388 U.S. 1 (1967), in which the Supreme Court refused to accept the argument that anti-miscegenation laws passed muster because both whites and blacks were equally prohibited from marrying someone of the other race, the Washington court held that a statute that barred both males and females from marrying someone of the same sex was lawful. "The operative distinction lies in the relationship which is described by the term 'marriage' itself, and that relationship is the legal union of one man and one woman. Washington statutes, specifically those relating to marriage and marital (community) property, are clearly founded upon the presumption that marriage, as a legal relationship, may exist only between one man and one woman who are otherwise qualified to enter that relationship."

In *Baehr v. Lewin*, 74 Haw. 530, 852 P.2d 44 (1993), the sex discrimination claim under the state constitution prevailed. A plurality of Justices (two of the three in the majority) held that the exclusion of same-sex couples from marriage was presumptively unconstitutional, and remanded the case for a trial to give the state the opportunity to demonstrate a compelling interest to justify it. Appeals of the trial court ruling (in favor of plaintiffs) were cut short by a 1998 referendum in which voters adopted a state constitutional amendment allowing the exclusion of same-sex couples.

The Vermont Supreme Court struck down its marriage discrimination against lesbian and gay couples in *Baker v. Vermont*, 170 Vt. 194, 744 A.2d 864 (1999), based on the Common Benefits Clause of the Vermont constitution. Justice Denise Johnson concurred in *Baker* on the ground that the exclusion was unconstitutional as sex discrimination:

> "[C]onsider the following example. Dr. A and Dr. B both want to marry Ms. C, an X-ray technician. Dr. A may do so because Dr. A is a man. Dr. B may not because Dr. B is a woman. Dr. A and Dr. B are people of opposite sexes who are similarly situated in the sense that they both want to marry a person of their choice. The statute disqualifies Dr. B from marriage solely on the basis of her sex and treats her differently from Dr. A, a man. This is sex discrimination."

Justice Johnson then argued that "[if] the sex-based classification contained in the marriage laws is unrelated to any valid purpose, but rather is a vestige of sex-role stereotyping that applies to both men and women, the classification is still unlawful sex discrimination even if it applies equally to men and women." One of the state's justifications for excluding same-sex couples was "uniting men and women to celebrate the 'complementarity' (sic) of the sexes and providing male and female role models for children," which Justice Johnson found to be "based on broad and vague generalizations about the roles of men and women that reflect outdated sex-role stereotyping. The State contends that (1) marriage unites the rich physical and psychological differences between the sexes; (2) sex differences strengthen and stabilize a marriage; (3) each sex contributes differently to a family unit and to society; and (4) uniting the different male and female qualities and contributions in the same institution instructs the young of the value of such a union. The State relies on social science literature, such as Carol Gilligan's *In a Different Voice: Psychological Theory and Women's Development* (1982), to support its contention that there are sex differences that justify the State requiring two people to be of opposite sex to marry." Justice Johnson rejected this argument as "sex stereotyping of the most retrograde sort."

Justice Johnson "conclude[d] that the classification is a vestige of the historical unequal marriage relationship that more recent legislative enactments and our own jurisprudence have unequivocally rejected. The protections conferred on Vermonters by the [state constitution] cannot be restricted by the outmoded conception that marriage requires one man and one woman, creating one person—the husband."

Allegations of sex discrimination have arisen most often in the marriage cases immediately prior to *Obergefell*. In an extended analysis, Ninth Circuit Judge Marsha Berzon rejected the defense claim that there was no Equal Protection violation when the two groups—men and women—were both subject to the prohibition because individuals were treated differently based on sex. *Latta v. Otter*, 771 F. 3d 456, 482–84 (9th Cir. 2014) (Berzon, J., concurring). Judge Berzon also found that the ban on same-sex marriage sought "to preserve an outmoded, sex-role-based vision of the marriage institution." *Id.* at 487. See also, *Perry v. Schwarzenegger*, 704 F.Supp.2d 921, 996 (N.D. Cal, 2010), *aff'd sub. nom. Perry v. Brown*, 671 F.3d 1052 (9th Cir. 2012), *vacated and remanded sub. nom. Hollingsworth v. Perry*, 133 S. Ct. 2652 (2013).

The fundamental reason for the reluctance of other courts to rule on sex discrimination grounds may be that sex discrimination arguments are "risky." They "ask decisionmakers to revisit and unsettle deeply rooted or widespread social norms and practices. That is, they not only seek a desired practical outcome but also aim to shift a court's conceptualization of the problem at issue. * * * [T]hese arguments take direct aim at the presence of discrimination in longstanding laws and practices that tend to be treated, uncritically, as part of the 'natural order.'" Suzanne B. Goldberg, "Risky Arguments in Social-Justice Litigation: The Case of Sex Discrimination and Marriage Equality," 114 *Colum. L. Rev.* 2087, 2089 (2014). Assuming that Professor Goldberg is correct, how should litigators use the sex discrimination argument in future cases?

C. DISCRIMINATION BASED ON GENDER IDENTITY

In *Transgender History*, Professor Susan Stryker offers a definition of "transgender," taking into account the relative newness and dynamic nature of this category:

> * * * people who move away from the gender they were assigned at birth, people who cross over (trans-) the boundaries constructed by their culture to define and contain that gender. * * *[I]t is *the movement across a socially imposed boundary away from an unchosen starting place*—rather than any particular destination or mode of transition—that best characterizes the concept of "transgender."

(Emphasis in the original). The legal system first took note of nonconforming gender presentation in the growing urban areas of late nineteenth century America.

1. DO CLOTHES MAKE THE (WO)MAN: CROSS-DRESSING LAWS

Laws against wearing the clothes of the other sex were first enacted as municipal ordinances, probably because the phenomenon was associated with urban life. Typical was the ordinance adopted by St. Louis in 1864:

> Whoever shall, in this city, appear in any public place in a state of nudity, or in a dress not belonging to his or her sex, or in an indecent or lewd dress; or shall make an indecent exposure of his or her person, or be guilty of an indecent or lewd act or behavior; or shall exhibit, sell or offer to sell, any indecent or lewd book, picture or other thing; or shall exhibit or perform any indecent, immoral, or lewd play or other representation, shall be deemed guilty of a misdemeanor.

Chicago had adopted a similar regulation in 1851, Charleston in 1858, Kansas City in 1860, and Memphis in 1863. Following the Civil War, more laws against cross-dressing were enacted in San Francisco in 1866,

Minneapolis in 1877, Oakland in 1879, Dallas in 1880, Nashville in 1881, San José in 1882, Tucson in 1883, Butte in 1885, and Denver in 1886. Municipal ordinances prohibiting cross-dressing proliferated further in the first half of the twentieth century, reaching Los Angeles, Houston, Detroit, Miami, Miami Beach, Cincinnati and Columbus. See Eskridge, *Gaylaw*, 338–41.

No state law specifically targeted cross-dressing per se, but "disguise" laws were sometimes applied to cross dressers. A New York statute of 1845 defined as an unlawful vagrant "[a] person who, having his face painted, discolored, covered, or concealed, or being otherwise disguised, in a manner calculated to prevent his being identified, appears in a road or public highway." New York Laws 1845, ch. 3, § 6. California in 1873 adopted a law prohibiting the concealment of one's identity by wearing a masque or disguise. California Laws 1873–74, ch. 614, p. 426, § 15. Anecdotal evidence and police records document that police invoked these laws to arrest cross-dressing women and men.

At whom were the laws aimed, and who was prosecuted? Most of the earliest cross-dressing statutes were framed as prohibitions of disguise or deceit. Some may have reflected social anxiety about images and press reports that began to appear of women wearing trousers or men's suits, sometimes as a lark, sometimes as part of attempts to escape social confinements by passing as male. One of us has classified such cases as about "gender fraud" as women sought to covertly secure the advantages of male privilege. Increasing urbanization provided space for displays of male effeminacy as well, and the attention of the state came to focus on cross-dressing as a signal of gender deviance.

Police records substantiating how many people were arrested for violating such ordinances are difficult to locate, and existing ones may be incomplete. We do know that in St. Louis, for example, approximately half a dozen people a year (including males and females in roughly equal numbers) were arrested for "appearing in dress not belonging to [his] sex" between 1887 and 1920, after which such arrests disappear from the records. The laws themselves, however, continued. St. Louis' ordinance against cross-dressing remained on the books and enforced until 1986, when a federal court ruled both it and the law against lewd behavior invalid on vagueness grounds. *D.C. and M.S. v. City of St. Louis*, 795 F.2d 652 (8th Cir.1986).

In New York, police adapted a nineteenth century anti-disguise law to police gender presentation and homosexuality until well into the twentieth century. *People of the State of New York v. Mauricio Archibald*, 58 Misc.2d 862, 296 N.Y.S.2d 834 (App. Term. 1968), aff'd, 27 N.Y.2d 504, 260 N.E.2d 871 (1970). Returning home from a masquerade party, Mauricio Archibald appeared in public wearing a white evening dress, high heel shoes, blonde wig, female undergarments, and facial makeup. While he was waiting for his train at a subway station, the police arrested Archibald as a "vagrant," defined by statute to include anyone "who * * *

[has] his face painted, discolored, covered or concealed, or being otherwise disguised, in a manner calculated to prevent his being identified." The defendant argued that he was not a "vagrant" under the common meaning of the term, because he had visible means of support; he also argued that he was not a vagrant under the statute because he was not cross-dressing in order to commit an illegal act. In a per curiam disposition, the appellate division rejected those arguments on the ground that the statute did not impose either requirement.

In dissent, Judge Markowitz argued that Archibald's attire did not fall within the original 1845 statute, which "was enacted as part of an over-all policy aimed at ending the anti-rent riots, an armed insurrection by farmers in the Hudson Valley. The rioting had reached such intensity that a state of insurrection had been declared. This particular statute was addressed to a specific group of insurrectionists who, while disguised as 'Indians,' murdered law enforcement officers attempting to serve writs upon the farmers. The 'Indians' were in fact farmers, who as part of their costumes, wore women's calico dresses to further conceal their identities."

Judge Markowitz observed that the 1845 law had been updated and readopted, with a more modern aim to discourage "overt homosexuality in public places which is offensive to public morality" as well as disguises used to cover criminal activities." But Archibald was not engaged in criminal activities, nor was he, as far as the record showed, gay. Mere "masquerading" without harming third parties is not a crime in New York, suggested Judge Markowitz.

"If appellant's conviction was correct then circus clowns, strangely attired 'hippies,' flowing-haired 'yippies' and every person who would indulge in the Halloween tradition of 'Trick or Treat' ipso facto may be targets for criminal sanctions as vagrants. Today women are wearing their hair increasingly shorter, and men are wearing their hair increasingly longer. Facial makeup, hair dyeing and cosmetic treatment are no longer the exclusive province of women. Men's and women's clothing styles are becoming increasingly similar. Thus, carrying the majority view to its logical conclusion, a young man or woman could possibly be convicted under this section as a vagrant merely for venturing into the street in his or her normal attire, which is otherwise acceptable in society today."

2.   THE RISE OF THE MEDICAL MODEL

The identification and naming of transsexualism as a medical condition grew out of the work of early sexologists who saw gender inversion as one branch of homosexuality. Gradually the two concepts differentiated, into one based on sexual desire and the other based on gender identity. The term "transsexual" derives from Magnus Hirschfield's work in Germany, was mentioned by Kinsey in his 1948 book's discussion of male homosexuality, then developed as an independent category by physician/sexologist David O. Cauldwell beginning in 1949, and eventually popularized when Dr. Harry Benjamin, an endocrinologist, published *The Transsexual Phenomenon* in 1966. As defined by psychiatrist Robert J. Stoller, in *Sex and Gender* (1968), "[t]ranssexualism is the conviction * * * of being a member of the opposite sex * * * [often] accompanied by requests for surgical and endocrinological procedures that change anatomical appearance to that of the opposite sex." As you read through this section, note how the vocabulary and the definitions have shifted over time.

The first American to receive significant public notice for surgery to change her sex was Christine Jorgensen. Born to Danish-American parents in New York, Jorgensen learned while visiting family members in Copenhagen that such medical treatment had become available there. After surgery, she returned to New York in 1952 and was the subject of a front-page article in the New York Daily News ("Ex-GI Becomes Blonde Bombshell").

In the United States, Dr. John Money, of Johns Hopkins University, pioneered sex reassignment surgery (SRS)—now called gender correction surgery—beginning in the 1960s. In response, almost all states either have enacted statutes, such as the one mentioned in *Wilson, infra*, that allow persons to seek an amended birth certificate after SRS, or have developed procedures allowing for such an amendment. One state— Tennessee—statutorily prohibits recording a change in the gender on a birth certificate. Two other states—Idaho and Ohio—do not construe their records statutes to allow changes after SRS, and a court in Puerto Rico barred such changes.

The year 1980 marked a turning point in social understandings about what was then called transsexuality. The American Psychiatric Association published the third edition of its *Diagnostic and Statistical Manual of Mental Disorders* (*DSM-III*), which included "transsexualism" for the first time. In 1993, the next edition of *DSM* dropped transsexualism and substituted "gender identity disorder," an apparent recognition that not all transsexuals needed psychiatric treatment. According to *DSM-IV*:

> Adults with Gender Identity Disorder are preoccupied with their wish to live as a member of the other sex. This preoccupation may be manifested as an intense desire to adopt the social role of the other sex through hormonal or surgical manipulation.

DSM-IV also listed gender disorder (childhood) and transvestic fetishism, as separate conditions.

The current edition (DSM-V), released in 2013, substituted "gender dysphoria" for "gender identity disorder" in an effort to destigmatize the classification and focus on the distress (dysphoria) experienced by transgender people. Gender dysphoria is defined as "a marked incongruence between one's experienced/expressed gender and assigned gender, of at least 6 months duration" and "associated with clinically significant distress or impairment in social, occupational, or other important areas of functioning." *DSM-V* also replaced "transvestic fetishism" with "transvestic disorder."

City of Chicago v. Wallace Wilson and Kim Kimberley

Illinois Supreme Court, 1978.
75 Ill.2d 525, 27 Ill.Dec. 458, 389 N.E.2d 522.

■ THOMAS J. MORAN, JUSTICE.

Defendants were arrested on February 18, 1974, minutes after they emerged from a restaurant where they had had breakfast. Defendant Wilson was wearing a black, knee-length dress, a fur coat, nylon stockings and a black wig. Defendant Kimberley had a bouffant hair style and was wearing a pants suit, high-heeled shoes and cosmetic makeup. Defendants were taken to the police station and were required to pose for pictures in various stages of undress. Both defendants were wearing brassieres and garter belts; both had male genitals. * * *

At trial, the defendants testified that they were transsexuals, and were, at the time of their arrests, undergoing psychiatric therapy in preparation for a sex reassignment operation. As part of this therapy, both defendants stated, they were required to wear female clothing and to adopt a female life-style. Kimberley stated that he had explained this to the police at the time of his arrest. Both defendants said they had been transsexuals all of their lives and thought of themselves as females. [Both were convicted and fined $100 each under a municipal ordinance making it a misdemeanor for"[a]ny person who shall appear in a public place * * * in a dress not belonging to his or her sex, with intent to conceal his or her sex." On appeal, the defendants challenged the constitutionality of the ordinance.] * * *

In this court, the city has asserted four reasons for the total ban against cross-dressing in public: (1) to protect citizens from being misled or defrauded; (2) to aid in the description and detection of criminals; (3) to prevent crimes in washrooms; and (4) to prevent inherently antisocial conduct which is contrary to the accepted norms of our society. The record, however, contains no evidence to support these reasons. * * *

* * * In its brief, however, the city has not articulated the manner in which the ordinance is designed to protect the public morals. It is presumably believed that cross-dressing in public is offensive to the general public's aesthetic preference. There is no evidence, however, that cross-dressing, when done as a part of a preoperative therapy program or otherwise, is, in and of itself, harmful to society. In this case, the aesthetic preference of society must be balanced against the individual's well-being.

Through the enactment of section 17(1)(d) of the Vital Records Act, which authorizes the issuance of a new certificate of birth following sex-reassignment surgery, the legislature has implicitly recognized the necessity and validity of such surgery. It would be inconsistent to permit sex-reassignment surgery yet, at the same time, impede the necessary therapy in preparation for such surgery. Individuals contemplating such surgery should, in consultation with their doctors, be entitled to pursue the therapy necessary to insure the correctness of their decision.

* * * [We] find that section 192–8 as applied to the defendants is an unconstitutional infringement of their liberty interest. * * *

NOTES ON LAW AND THE MEDICAL MODEL

In 1973, Congress enacted the Rehabilitation Act, 29 U.S.C. § 794, which prohibited discrimination, by government agencies and by private entities that have contracts with the federal government, against persons with "handicaps." Advocates in the 1980s put *DSM-III* and the statute together, and began to argue that persons who had been diagnosed as having any of the officially-recognized disorders, including transsexuality, were protected from discrimination under the Rehabilitation Act. See, e.g., *Blackwell v. U.S. Dep't of the Treasury*, 830 F.2d 1183 (D.C. Cir. 1987); *Doe v. U.S. Postal Service*, 37 F.E.P. Cases 1867, 1985 WL 9446 (D.D.C. 1985). Congress eliminated that avenue of relief in 1990. In enacting the Americans with Disabilities Act that year, Congress explicitly excluded transsexuality, transvestism "and gender identity disorders not resulting from physical impairments" as disabilities, 42 U.S.C. § 12211(b)(1); and for good measure also amended the Rehabilitation Act to exclude coverage of those conditions under that statute as well. 29 U.S.C. § 706(8)(F)(i).

The medical model approach found some traction in family law, involving challenges to the validity of a marriage (typically arising upon divorce or in probate) when one spouse had transitioned prior to the marriage. The first reported case in the United States was **M.T. v. J.T., 140 N.J.Super. 77, 355 A.2d 204 (1976)**, which recognized the validity of gender transition:

> [I]t has been established that an individual suffering from the condition of transsexualism is one with a disparity between his or her genitalia or anatomical sex and his or her gender, that is, the individual's strong and consistent emotional and psychological sense of sexual being. A transsexual in a proper case can be treated medically by certain supportive measures and through surgery to remove and replace existing genitalia with sex organs which will coincide with the person's gender. If such sex reassignment surgery is successful and the postoperative transsexual is, by virtue of medical treatment, thereby possessed of the full capacity to function sexually as a male or female, as the case may be, we perceive no legal barrier, cognizable social taboo, or reason grounded in public policy to prevent that person's identification at least for purposes of marriage to the sex finally indicated. * * *

In this case the transsexual's gender and genitalia are no longer discordant; they have been harmonized through medical treatment. Plaintiff has become physically and psychologically unified and fully capable of sexual activity consistent with her reconciled sexual attributes of gender and anatomy. Consequently, plaintiff should be considered a member of the female sex for marital purposes. * * *

The decisions on this point are split, however. On essentially identical facts, the Court of Appeals of Texas reached the opposite conclusion in *Littleton v. Prange*, 9 S.W.3d 223 (Tex.App. 1999):

* * * Christie [Littleton] was created and born a male. Her original birth certificate, an official document of Texas, clearly so states. [Plaintiff completed sex reassignment surgery.] During the pendency of this suit, Christie amended the original birth certificate to change the sex and name. * * * The facts contained in the original birth certificate were true and accurate, and the words contained in the amended certificate are not binding on this court.

There are some things we cannot will into being. They just are.

We hold, as a matter of law, that Christie Littleton is a male. * * *

NOTE ON COMPETING DISCOURSES

You might be wondering whether transgender advocates agree that being transgender *is* a disability, or should be considered as one. Doesn't building a lawsuit around a diagnosis reify transgender status as pathology? Or is that concern itself a marker of the misguided view that disability is synonymous with stigma? How, if at all, should reform strategies guide choices for the doctrinal framing of litigation? Recall the differing arguments made against consensual sodomy laws by Professors Michael Sandel and Jed Rubenfeld, and consider how they might apply to gender identity claims.

Susan Etta Keller, "Crisis of Authority: Medical Rhetoric and Transsexual Identity"

11 *Yale Journal of Law & Feminism* 51, 51–57, 59, 69–70 (1999).*

* * *[A] reliance on a medical model of transsexuality, despite its disempowering potential, is often deemed necessary for the provision of public and private medical insurance benefits for transsexuals, adequate treatment in prison, relief from arrest, and other benefits as well as a justification for the gender reassignment surgery sought by transsexuals. The term "crisis of authority" describes this conflict between the perception of the medical model's practical importance and the countervailing perception of its disempowering effects. * * *

This conflict creates a crisis not just because reliance on medical authority generates both positives and negatives, but also because such

---

reliance presents a challenge to transsexuals for an agentic image of identity. If transsexual identity is constructed through the medical model, yet the model disempowers transsexuals, there seems to be no choice (i.e., either abandoning or retaining the model) that promises a complete and empowering identity for transsexuals unless they abandon the very concept of transsexuality. Because of the role law plays in reinforcing the medical model and because of the protection it at least potentially offers transsexuals against various forms of negative societal sanction, the choice is even more complicated. * * *

Like judges, transsexuals are faced with choices more difficult than they appear. It may seem as if the choice transsexuals face is simply whether to rely on a medical rhetoric that brings positive practical benefits, as the cases demonstrate, but negative consequences for identity, as some have argued. However, the choice is actually more complicated. First, because medical authorities do not always reach conclusions beneficial to transsexuals, and because the courts rely on these authorities when deciding whether to provide positive practical benefits, the positive side of the equation is not reliably constant. Second, * * * the medical model may hold positive as well as negative consequences for transsexual identity. More precisely, the inclusion of transsexuality as a diagnostic category in medical texts such as the DSM may have very different meaning for transsexual identity construction than the inclusion of homosexuality had for lesbian and gay identity construction. * * *

* * * The decision by the American Psychiatric Association to remove homosexuality from the DSM was the result of intense activism by gay and lesbian advocates. A strong motivation for this activism was indeed the negative association of identity with pathology. But it is also clear from accounts of the series of political actions and meetings leading to the removal that for lesbians and gay men, inclusion of their status in the DSM offered no positive benefits whatsoever to counterbalance the negative impact. Because inclusion of homosexuality led to treatment protocols that sought to undermine or alter sexual orientation, such inclusion was seen as both a denial of the identity claims of those who sought no treatment and also the justification for numerous discriminatory practices in the world at large. For transsexuals, by contrast, inclusion of their condition in the DSM provides a basis for treatment protocols, such as sex-reassignment surgery, that bolster their identity claims. * * *

In the Matter of Jean Doe, By Her Next Friend, David Pumo v. William C. Bell, As Commissioner of New York City Administration of Children's Services, **194 Misc.2d 774, 754 N.Y.S.2d 846 (Sup. Ct. 2003).** A 17-year-old teenager, in foster care since age 9, Jean Doe was born a male but identified as a female. Because she was uncomfortable dressing as a male, she had run away from prior foster care placements in which she was forced to dress like a man. A qualified physician diagnosed Doe with GID and prescribed a treatment plan whereby Doe would wear girls' clothing, make-up, and accessories. According to the doctor, "[t]he goal is to facilitate acceptance of the gender identity of a transgendered person by allowing her to dress in a manner consistent with her internal identity. Research has found that forcing youths with GID to dress in conflict with their identity, though it may be in harmony with their biological attributes, causes significant anxiety, psychological harm, and antisocial behavior."

Atlantic Transitional, a state foster care facility for boys aged 15 to 21, did not allow Doe to wear women's clothing within the facility. The Administration for Children's Services declined to change this policy, and Doe sued for relief under New York law barring discrimination in public facilities because of a "disability." Within a month of the lawsuit, the facility (with the approval of ACS) announced new written dress standards for residents of Atlantic Transitional. Residents "must wear pants, or in warm weather, loose-fitting shorts that extend at least to mid-thigh. Shirts (or blouses) must also be worn at all times and must not expose the chest or midriff." Atlantic residents are prohibited from wearing "clothing that is sexually provocative, that is, excessively short or tight fitting, or which is see thru, but "[r]esidents who wish to wear female attire may do so as long as the above guidelines are respected." Under the new rules, Jean Doe could wear scarves, "nails," breast enhancers and brassieres, hair weaves, and make-up at the facility but could not wear skirts or dresses.

Judge Louise Gruner Gans found that even the revised policy denied Jean Doe rights because of a disability. The state human rights law defined disability as "a physical, mental or medical impairment resulting from anatomical, physiological, genetic, or neurological conditions which prevents the exercise of a normal bodily function or is demonstrable by medically accepted clinical or laboratory diagnostic techniques." N.Y. Exec. Law § 292(21). The New York Court of Appeals had interpreted disability to include any kind of medical impairment that "prevents the exercise of a normal bodily function" and is "demonstrable by medically accepted clinical or diagnostic techniques." *State Division of Human Rights v. Xerox Corp.*, 65 N.Y.2d 213, 218–19, 491 N.Y.S.2d 106, 480 N.E.2d 695.

Judge Gans ruled that ACS and Atlantic should have accommodated Doe's disability by exempting her from the facility's prohibition on her wearing skirts and dresses. Wearing women's attire is necessary for Doe's mental well-being, and she cannot enjoy the benefits of the facility without that accommodation.

"ACS asserts that its dress policy is necessary to protect the safety of residents and staff. According to Dr. Antoine, it was necessary to restrict the kind of dress worn by Jean Doe because a male in feminine clothing creates a 'sexual dynamic . . . that can lead to unsafe and emotionally harmful sexual behavior.' Further, at the facility, 'there are many boys who are not emotionally mature and who feel confused or threatened by the presence of a transgendered boy among them and are prone to act out when Jean is nearby.'

"The Court is not persuaded that Mr. Antoine's concerns render the accommodation sought by Jean Doe an unreasonable one. The premise of respondents' argument is that cross-dressing by a resident can lead to unsafe sexual behavior and other inappropriate conduct. But respondents permit Jean Doe to wear a number of different kinds of feminine clothing without jeopardizing the safety of the facility and its residents. * * * Respondents cannot explain why she may safely wear these feminine items of clothing and accessories, but may not wear skirts or dresses without endangering the safety of the facility and its residents. * * * There is simply no rational basis for treating dresses and skirts differently than the other feminine accoutrements which Jean Doe may now wear. In these circumstances, the City's purported safety concerns provide no basis for rejecting Doe's accommodation as unreasonable."

PROBLEM 1-3
CLIENT NARRATIVE AND LEGAL STRATEGY

You are a lawyer with the Transgender Legal Services Office in your city. A 20-year-old undergraduate comes to you for help, explaining that she wants to transition to being male. Among her questions is whether she can obtain sex reassignment surgery. As a practical matter, the surgery will be contingent on whether her health insurance policy will pay for it, and that in turn will depend on whether a physician certifies that the surgery is medically necessary. (Her insurance policy is unusual in not specifically excluding such surgery from its scope of coverage.) You anticipate that there might be a fight over whether SRS meets the standards for medical necessity. When you ask for more information about her background, she says the following:

> I've worked hard to not engage the gay childhood narrative—I never talk about tomboyish behavior as an antecedent to my lesbian identity, I don't tell stories about cross-dressing or crushes on girls, and I intentionally fuck with the assumption of it by telling people how I used to be straight and have sex with boys like any sweet trashy rural girl. I see these narratives as strategic, and I've always rejected the strategy that adopts some theory of innate sexuality and forecloses the possibility that anyone, gender troubled childhood or not, could transgress sexual and gender norms at any time. I don't want to participate in an idea that only some people have to struggle to learn gender norms in childhood.

Dean Spade, "Resisting Medicine, Re/Modeling Gender," 18 *Berkeley Women's L. J.* 15 (2003).

How do you advise your client?

NOTES AND QUESTIONS ON DISABILITY LAW AND GENDER IDENTITY

1.   *The Disability Paradigm for Trans Anti-Discrimination Cases.* To plead a case of disability discrimination under the ADA, one must allege that the plaintiff is disabled, has a history of disability or is perceived as having a disability. Disability is defined as a "physical or mental impairment" that "substantially limits a major life activity," including but not limited to working. 42 U.S.C. § 12102. Assume that broader concepts such as social interaction are also treated as major life activities within the meaning of the ADA. Further assume that there is medical disagreement about whether gender dysphoria or gender identity disorder is a "physical or mental impairment." To what principles should a court turn in interpreting the statutory language?

2.   *The Scope of the ADA Exclusion.* In *Blatt v. Cabela's Retail*, 2017 WL 2178123 (E.D. Pa. 2017), the court ruled that the exclusionary language in the ADA includes only trans-identified persons who lacked "actually disabling" conditions such as gender identity disorder or gender dysphoria. The ADA excludes from its protection "transvestism, transsexualism, [or] gender identity disorders not resulting from physical impairments." *Blatt* was originally brought in part to press a claim that the exclusion of trans people from disability coverage under the ADA violated their equal protection rights. The District Court in *Blatt* avoided the constitutional issue by adopting a novel statutory interpretation offered in an *amicus* brief from the Justice Department, i.e., that the exclusion was intended to cover only disabilities without a physical basis and that "a growing body of scientific evidence suggests that gender dysphoria may 'result[ ] from [a] physical impairment[ ].'" See 2015 WL 9872493. Does this interpretation effectively create a distinction between persons with and without a formal diagnosis? It is unclear whether the Justice Department will continue to advance this argument under the Trump administration.

3.   *The Constitutionality of the ADA's Exclusion.* How would you construct the argument that the trans exclusion from disability law is an independent equal protection violation (i.e., separately from whether gender identity discrimination is a variant of sex discrimination)? What would be the primary obstacles to achieving strict scrutiny for classifications based on gender identity without using a sex discrimination argument? What would the advantages be of pursuing this theory?

PROBLEM 1-4
ASSESSING THE MEDICAL MODEL

The single strongest advantage of using a medicalized argument for pursuing anti-discrimination claims by trans persons may be the simplest: at least in some courts, it may enhance your client's chance of success. What are the longer-term implications? Imagine that the (hypothetical) Trans Legal Defense Alliance asks you to develop a comprehensive review of whether the disability framework is likely to prove problematic for trans equality. Compare arguments for and against using disability-based claims in, respectively, Jennifer L. Levi, "Clothes Don't Make the (Wo)Man, But Gender Identity Might," 15 *Colum. J. Gender and L.* 90 (2006) and Jonathan L. Koenig, "Distributive Consequences of the Medical Model," 48 *Harv. C.R.-C.L. L. Rev.* 619 (2011).

3. THE SEX DISCRIMINATION THEORY

Federal courts remained almost uniformly hostile to discrimination claims by trans persons until the late 1990s. There was virtually no litigation under the Equal Protection Clause. The early breakthroughs came from assertions that anti-trans discrimination was a form of sex discrimination in violation of federal statutes. *Smith v. City of Salem*, 378 F.3d 566 (6th Cir. 2004) (Title VII); *Rosa v. Park West Bank & Trust Co.*, 214 F.3d 213 (1st Cir. 2000) (Equal Credit Opportunity Act). Cf. *Schwenk v. Hartford*, 204 F.3d 1187 (9th Cir. 2000) (transgender persons protected by Gender Motivated Violence Act). Litigants also pursued sex discrimination claims based on state statutes. See, e.g., *Enriquez v. West Jersey Health Systems*, 342 N.J. Super. 501, 777 A.2d 365 (Super. Ct. App. Div. 2001) (finding that firing plaintiff when she began gender transition violated state anti-discrimination law on both sex and disability grounds).

In the following case, the transgender plaintiff brought an employment discrimination claim. Because she worked for a public agency, she relied on an Equal Protection argument. When job discrimination cases—generally covered by Title VII—involve public sector defendants—also covered by the Equal Protection Clause—courts look to both constitutional and Title VII precedent.

Vandiver Elizabeth Glenn v. Sewell R. Brumby
United States Court of Appeals for the Eleventh Circuit, 2011.
663 F.3d 1312.

■ BARKETT, CIRCUIT JUDGE.

Sewell R. Brumby appeals from an adverse summary judgment in favor of Vandiver Elizabeth Glenn on her complaint seeking declaratory and injunctive relief pursuant to 42 U.S.C. § 1983 for alleged violations of her rights under the Equal Protection Clause of the Fourteenth Amendment of the U.S. Constitution. Glenn claimed that Brumby fired her from her job as an editor in the Georgia General Assembly's Office of Legislative Counsel ("OLC") because of sex discrimination, thus violating the Equal Protection Clause. The district court granted summary judgment in Glenn's favor on this claim. * * *

Vandiver Elizabeth Glenn was born a biological male. Since puberty, Glenn has felt that she is a woman, and in 2005, she was diagnosed with GID, a diagnosis listed in the American Psychiatric Association's Diagnostic and Statistical Manual of Mental Disorders.

Starting in 2005, Glenn began to take steps to transition from male to female under the supervision of health care providers. This process included living as a woman outside of the workplace, which is a prerequisite to sex reassignment surgery. In October 2005, then known as Glenn Morrison and presenting as a man, Glenn was hired as an editor by the Georgia General Assembly's OLC. Sewell Brumby is the head of the OLC and is responsible for OLC personnel decisions, including the decision to fire Glenn.

In 2006, Glenn informed her direct supervisor, Beth Yinger, that she was a transsexual and was in the process of becoming a woman. On Halloween in 2006, when OLC employees were permitted to come to work wearing costumes, Glenn came to work presenting as a woman. When Brumby saw her, he told her that her appearance was not appropriate and asked her to leave the office. Brumby deemed her appearance inappropriate "[b]ecause he was a man dressed as a woman and made up as a woman." Brumby stated that "it's unsettling to think of someone dressed in women's clothing with male sexual organs inside that clothing," and that a male in women's clothing is "unnatural." Following this incident, Brumby met with Yinger to discuss Glenn's appearance on Halloween of 2006 and was informed by Yinger that Glenn intended to undergo a gender transition.

In the fall of 2007, Glenn informed Yinger that she was ready to proceed with gender transition and would begin coming to work as a woman and was also changing her legal name. Yinger notified Brumby, who subsequently terminated Glenn because "Glenn's intended gender transition was inappropriate, that it would be disruptive, that some people would view it as a moral issue, and that it would make Glenn's coworkers uncomfortable." * * *

[The Court explains heightened scrutiny for sex discrimination claims in Equal Protection Clause analysis, citing *City of Cleburne v. Cleburne Living Ctr., Inc.*, 473 U.S. 432 (1985) and *United States v. Virginia*, 518 U.S. 515 (1996), and notes that the Supreme Court has used the terms "sex" and "gender" interchangeably.]

The question here is whether discriminating against someone on the basis of his or her gender non-conformity constitutes sex-based discrimination under the Equal Protection Clause. For the reasons discussed below, we hold that it does.

In *Price Waterhouse v. Hopkins*, 490 U.S. 228 (1989), the Supreme Court held that discrimination on the basis of gender stereotype is sex-based discrimination. * * * The Court noted that "[a]s for the legal relevance of sex stereotyping, we are beyond the day when an employer could evaluate employees by assuming or insisting that they matched the stereotypes associated with their group. . . ." *Id.* at 251.

A person is defined as transgender precisely because of the perception that his or her behavior transgresses gender stereotypes.

"[T]he very acts that define transgender people as transgender are those that contradict stereotypes of gender-appropriate appearance and behavior." Ilona M. Turner, *Sex Stereotyping Per Se: Transgender Employees and Title VII*, 95 Cal. L. Rev. 561, 563 (2007); *see also* Taylor Flynn, *Transforming the Debate: Why We Need to Include Transgender Rights in the Struggles for Sex and Sexual Orientation Equality*, 101 Colum. L. Rev. 392, 392 (2001) (defining transgender persons as those whose "appearance, behavior, or other personal characteristics differ from traditional gender norms"). There is thus a congruence between discriminating against transgender and transsexual individuals and discrimination on the basis of gender-based behavioral norms.

Accordingly, discrimination against a transgender individual because of her gender-nonconformity is sex discrimination, whether it's described as being on the basis of sex or gender. Indeed, several circuits have so held. For example, in *Schwenk v. Hartford*, the Ninth Circuit concluded that a male-to-female transgender plaintiff who was singled out for harassment because he presented and defined himself as a woman had stated an actionable claim for sex discrimination under the Gender Motivated Violence Act because "the perpetrator's actions stem from the fact that he believed that the victim was a man who 'failed to act like one.' " 204 F.3d 1187, 1198–1203 (9th Cir. 2000). The First Circuit echoed this reasoning in *Rosa v. Park West Bank & Trust Co.*, where it held that a transgender plaintiff stated a claim by alleging that he "did not receive [a] loan application because he was a man, whereas a similarly situated woman would have received [a] loan application. That is, the Bank . . . treat[s] . . . a woman who dresses like a man differently than a man who dresses like a woman." 214 F.3d 213, 215–16 (1st Cir. 2000). These instances of discrimination against plaintiffs because they fail to act according to socially prescribed gender roles constitute discrimination under Title VII according to the rationale of *Price Waterhouse*.

The Sixth Circuit likewise recognized that discrimination against a transgender individual because of his or her gender non-conformity is gender stereotyping prohibited by Title VII and the Equal Protection Clause. *See Smith v. City of Salem*, 378 F.3d 566 (6th Cir. 2004). The court concluded that a transsexual firefighter could not be suspended because of "his transsexualism and its manifestations," *id.* at 569, because to do so was discrimination against him "based on his failure to conform to sex stereotypes by expressing less masculine, and more feminine mannerisms and appearance." *Id.* at 572; *see Barnes v. City of Cincinnati*, 401 F.3d 729 (6th Cir. 2005) (holding that transsexual plaintiff stated a claim for sex discrimination "by alleging discrimination . . . for his failure to conform to sex stereotypes"). * * *

All persons, whether transgender or not, are protected from discrimination on the basis of gender stereotype. For example, courts have held that plaintiffs cannot be discriminated against for wearing jewelry that was considered too effeminate, carrying a serving tray too gracefully, or taking too active a role in child-rearing. An individual cannot be punished because of his or her perceived gender-nonconformity. Because these protections are afforded to everyone, they cannot be denied to a transgender individual. The nature of the discrimination is the same; it may differ in degree but not in kind, and discrimination on this basis is a form of sex-based discrimination that is subject to heightened scrutiny under the Equal Protection Clause. Ever since the Supreme Court began to apply heightened scrutiny to sex-based classifications, its consistent purpose has been to eliminate discrimination on the basis of gender stereotypes.

In *Frontiero v. Richardson*, the Court struck down legislation requiring only female service members to prove that their spouses depended upon them financially in order to receive certain benefits for married couples. The plurality applied heightened scrutiny to sex-based classifications by referring to the pervasiveness of gender stereotypes (noting a tradition of " 'romantic paternalism' " that "put women [ ] not on a pedestal, but in a cage"), and held that gender-based classifications are "inherently suspect," because they are often animated by "stereotyped distinctions between the sexes." Two years later, the Court applied this heightened level of scrutiny to a Utah statute setting a lower age of majority for women and concluded that the statute could not be sustained by the stereotypical assumption that women tend to marry earlier than men. *See Stanton v. Stanton*, 421 U.S. 7, 14 (1975). The Court again rejected gender stereotypes, holding that " 'old notions' " about men and women's behavior provided no support for the State's classification. That same year, the Court confronted a provision of the Social Security Act that allowed certain benefits to widows while denying them to widowers. *See Weinberger v. Wiesenfeld*, 420 U.S. 636, 637 (1975). The Court again used heightened scrutiny to strike at gender stereotype, concluding that "the Constitution also forbids gender-based differentiation" premised on the stereotypical assumption that a husband's income is always more important to the wife than is the wife's to the husband.

In each of these foundational cases, the Court concluded that discriminatory state action could not stand on the basis of gender stereotypes. *See also Craig v. Boren*, 429 U.S. 190, 199 (explaining that "the weak congruence between gender and the characteristic or trait that gender purported to represent" necessitated applying heightened scrutiny); *Orr v. Orr*, 440 U.S. 268, 282 ("Legislative classifications which distribute benefits and burdens on the basis of gender carry the risk of reinforcing stereotypes about the 'proper place' of women. . . ."). The Court's more recent cases reiterate that the Equal Protection Clause does not tolerate gender stereotypes. *See Mississippi Univ. for Women v. Hogan*, 458 U.S. 718, 726 (1982) (explaining that "the purpose" of heightened scrutiny is to ensure that sex-based classifications rest upon "reasoned analysis rather than . . . traditional, often inaccurate, assumptions about the proper roles of men and women."); *see also Virginia,* 518 U.S. at 533 ("[The government] must not rely on overbroad generalizations about the different talents, capacities, or preferences of males and females."); *cf. Nevada Dep't of Human Res. v. Hibbs,* 538 U.S. 721, 735 (2003) (holding that Congress may enact remedial measures under Section Five of the Fourteenth Amendment to counteract sex-based stereotypes). Accordingly, governmental acts based upon gender stereotypes—which presume that men and women's appearance and behavior will be determined by their sex—must be subjected to heightened scrutiny because they embody "the very stereotype the law condemns." *J.E.B. v. Alabama,* 511 U.S. 127, 138 (1994) (internal quotation marks omitted) (declaring unconstitutional a government attorney's use of peremptory juror strikes based on the presumption that potential jurors' views would correspond to their sexes).

We conclude that a government agent violates the Equal Protection Clause's prohibition of sex-based discrimination when he or she fires a transgender or transsexual employee because of his or her gender non-conformity.

We now turn to whether Glenn was fired on the basis of gender stereotyping. * * * Brumby testified at his deposition that he fired Glenn because he considered it "inappropriate" for her to appear at work dressed as a woman and that he found it "unsettling" and "unnatural" that Glenn would appear wearing women's clothing. Brumby testified that his decision to dismiss Glenn was based on his perception of Glenn as "a man dressed as a woman and made up as a woman," and Brumby admitted that his decision to fire Glenn was based on "the sheer fact of the transition." Brumby's testimony provides ample direct evidence to support the district court's conclusion that Brumby acted on the basis of Glenn's gender non-conformity.

If this were a Title VII case, the analysis would end here. * * * However, because Glenn's claim is based on the Equal Protection Clause, we must, under heightened scrutiny, consider whether Brumby succeeded in showing an "exceedingly persuasive justification," *Virginia,* 518 U.S. at 546 (internal quotation marks omitted), that is, that there was a "sufficiently important governmental interest" for his discriminatory conduct, *Cleburne,* 473 U.S. at 441. This burden "is demanding and it rests entirely on the State." *Virginia,* 518 U.S. at 533. The defendant's burden cannot be met by relying on a justification that is "hypothesized or invented post hoc in response to litigation." *Id.*

On appeal, Brumby advances only one putative justification for Glenn's firing: his purported concern that other women might object to Glenn's restroom use. However, Brumby presented insufficient evidence to show that he was actually motivated by concern over litigation regarding Glenn's restroom use. To support the justification that he now argues, Brumby points to a single statement in his deposition where he referred to a speculative concern about lawsuits arising if Glenn used the women's restroom. The district court recognized that this single reference, based on speculation, was overwhelmingly contradicted by specific evidence of Brumby's intent, and we agree. Indeed, Brumby testified that he viewed the possibility of a lawsuit by a co-worker if Glenn were retained as unlikely and the record indicates that the OLC, where Glenn worked, had only single-occupancy restrooms. Brumby advanced this argument before the district court only as a *conceivable* explanation for his decision to fire Glenn under rational basis review. The fact that such a hypothetical justification may have been sufficient to withstand rational-basis scrutiny, however, is wholly irrelevant to the heightened scrutiny analysis that is required here. * * *

NOTES AND QUESTIONS

1.   *The Sex Discrimination Paradigm for Trans Anti-Discrimination Cases.* The Title VII/sex discrimination theory has proven to be the most successful basis to date for securing protection for persons fired because of their gender identity. Unlike disability discrimination arguments, which have succeeded in some state courts under state law, the sex discrimination argument has been adopted by a number of federal courts, beginning more than 15 years ago in *Smith*, and by the EEOC. However, the Supreme Court has never ruled on the validity of the sex discrimination theory. Meanwhile, all attempts to secure federal legislation explicitly banning discrimination based on gender identity (or sexual orientation) have failed. Imagine that you are asked to consider strategic options for the Trans Legal Defense Alliance? What would you advise?

2.   *More on Sex.* This book picks up the analysis of cases using sex discrimination theory to challenge anti-trans policies in the materials on workplace discrimination in Chapter 5, Section 5.

NOTE ON INTERSEX PERSONS

Intersexuality is a different condition, found in persons whose physical sex is in some way ambiguous at birth. Typically, the somatic characteristics of the two sexes align: chromosomes (women XX, men XY), genitalia (women vaginas, men penises), internal organs (women ovaries, men testes), and hormones (women estrogen, men androgen). Some persons do not have XX or XY chromosomal patterns. People with Turner's syndrome have only 45 chromosomes rather than 46; people with Klinefelter's syndrome have XXY chromosomes. See John Money, *Venuses Penises: Sexology, Sexosophy and Exigency Theory* ch. 6 (1986).

Moreover, many people with XX or XY chromosomes do not unambiguously display female or male sex characteristics, respectively. Anne Fausto-Sterling, "The Five Sexes: Why Male and Female Are Not Enough," *The Sciences*, March/April 1993, at 20–24, calls these people "intersexual" and divides them into the following groups. "True hermaphrodites" possess both a testis and an ovary and usually have ambiguous external genitalia, often a small penis as well as a vagina. "Male pseudohermaphrodites" have testes and some manifestations of female genitalia but no ovaries. "Female pseudohermaphrodites" have ovaries and some manifestations of male genitalia but no testes. She thinks that as many as 4% of human births are intersex.

An early landmark piece on intersex persons was John Money, Joan Hampson & John Hampson, "An Examination of Some Basic Sexual Concepts: The Evidence of Human Hermaphroditism," 97 *Bulletin of the Johns Hopkins Hospital* 301 (1955). The authors, researchers at Johns Hopkins, examined 76 persons who had "mismatched" markers (such as chromosomes of one sex but external genitalia and/or internal organs of another). They not only found the subjects functional in modern society but, further, found that the subjects had happily assumed the gender roles that had been assigned them by their parents. This research and the ensuing clinical practice have become quite controversial, however. Adults who, as children, underwent surgery to conform their bodies to suit medical and parental preferences, assert that they have been misunderstood, deceived, and mutilated. See, e.g., John Colapinto, *As Nature Made Him: The Boy Who Was Raised as a Girl* (2000); Angela Moreno, as told to Jan Goodwin, "Am I a Woman or a Man?," *Mademoiselle*, Mar. 1998, at 178–81, 208. See generally, Julie A. Greenberg, *Intersexuality and the Law: Why Sex Matters* (2012). For more background, see the website of the Intersex Society of North America: www.isna.org (viewed Dec. 16, 2016).

SECTION 3

EXPRESSION AND IDENTITY

Unlike the privacy right, but like the equality right, the free speech right has a secure foundation in the text of the Constitution, namely, the First Amendment. The First Amendment is first in more ways than one. It is not simply the first in the list of rights added to the Constitution. It is in many ways the first and most fundamental principle of a democracy: that individuals can voice their opinions without fear that government will punish them for their views. Justice Kennedy described the basic concepts behind protection for speech and other forms of expression in a recent case (the citations in this excerpt are omitted):

[A]s a general matter, the First Amendment means that government has no power to restrict expression because of its message, its ideas, its subject matter, or its content." As a result, the Constitution "demands that content-based restrictions on speech be presumed invalid * * * and that the Government bear the burden of showing their constitutionality."

In light of the substantial and expansive threats to free expression posed by content-based restrictions, this Court has rejected as "startling and dangerous" a "free-floating test for First Amendment coverage [based on] an ad hoc balancing of relative social costs and benefits." Instead, content-based restrictions on speech have been permitted, as a general matter, only when confined to the few " 'historic and traditional categories [of expression] long familiar to the bar.' " Among these categories are advocacy intended, and likely, to incite imminent lawless action; obscenity; defamation; speech integral to criminal conduct; so-called "fighting words" [insults so harsh that they can be expected to trigger a violent response]; child pornography; fraud; true threats; and speech presenting some grave and imminent threat the government has the power to prevent, although a restriction under the last category is most difficult to sustain. These categories have a historical foundation in the Court's free speech tradition. The vast realm of free speech and thought always protected in our tradition can still thrive, and even be furthered, by adherence to those categories and rules. * * *

The Nation well knows that one of the costs of the First Amendment is that it protects the speech we detest as well as the speech we embrace.

United States v. Alvarez, 567 U.S. 709, 715–18, 729 (2012). This quotation provides insights into three key aspects of First Amendment law:

- The government cannot censor speech because of the viewpoint or message that it expresses. Restrictions that are based on content other than political viewpoint (advertising, for example) are also subjected to searching review, although courts are somewhat less stringent in those situations. Courts frequently categorize laws that regulate expressive activities as content-based or content-neutral, or viewpoint-based or viewpoint neutral.

- The second main point of the quoted passage is that it furnishes a list of kinds of speech that are categorically excluded from First Amendment protection, such as defamation, fraud or pornography depicting children. While there can be questions about whether particular examples of speech fall into or outside the boundaries of these categories, the list of categories that are excluded from First Amendment shelter has remained stable for some time.

- The third principle is the statement that for restrictions based on the content of the speech being restrained, "the Government bear[s] the burden of showing their constitutionality." This refers to the understanding that the government will have the burden of persuading a judge or jury that the restrictions being challenged are justified. For highly protected forms of speech, such as political expression, the test for doing so is quite high: the government must demonstrate that the restriction is necessary to serve a compelling state interest and that it is narrowly drawn to achieve that goal.

In addition to what we learn from the passage from *Alvarez*, two other important principles emerge from First Amendment case law. First, location and context can be significant. For example, wearing a button that urges votes for candidate X when walking down the street is essentially immune from regulation as the expression of an individual's political beliefs, but if a government employee wears the same button, regulation may be permissible because it is reasonable for the government acting as an employer to limit divisive speech in the workplace. Second, conduct as well as speech can be expressive. Picketing and protest marches are classic examples. When expressive conduct is involved, the analysis shifts slightly, but the focus remains on whether regulation is content- or viewpoint-neutral. Often, the courts examine whether laws create time, place and manner rules that apply to everyone equally.

The separate right of "expressive association" is not mentioned in the First Amendment's text (though a right of assembly is). It is, like the privacy right, culled from the penumbras of the First Amendment's explicit dimensions; indeed, the right of association was one of the foundations for recognition of a constitutional right to privacy in *Griswold*.

As with the privacy and equality rights explored above, it might be useful to consider some prominent theories of the First Amendment: Why are free speech and association so valuable in our constitutional polity?

One theory is its instrumental value for individuals: expression is an essential feature of an individual's flourishing, and the freedom to express oneself is a cherished liberty that has few parallels. *E.g.*, Thomas Emerson, *The System of Freedom of Expression* (1970). Even communitarian theorists support the same idea, perhaps indirectly: the state and the community should be encouraging individualism, nonconformity, and anti-authoritarianism, the very values that a liberal finds in the First Amendment. *E.g.*, Steven Shiffrin, *Dissent, Injustice, and the Meanings of America* (1999).

A second theoretical support for the First Amendment is substantive. The best way for a polity or society to reach correct answers is to assure a free and open debate, where all points of view are heard. John Milton, *Areopagitica* (1644), may have originated the notion that there is a marketplace of ideas, where the good ones will dominate the bad ones over time. *Accord*, John Stuart Mill, *On Liberty* (1859). Today's dissenting opinion will be tomorrow's truth. Relatedly, the First Amendment may contribute to a social culture that is tolerant rather than dogmatic, a great boon to social robustness. *E.g.*, Lee Bollinger, *The Tolerant Society: Freedom of Speech and Extremist Speech in America* (1986).

Finally, the First Amendment arguably serves democratic values. The lesson of Alexander Meiklejohn's classic, *Free Speech and Its Relation to Self-Government* (1948), is that a robust democracy requires that the channels of communication and public debate be open. Professor Meiklejohn took the town hall meeting as the democratic ideal protected by the First Amendment. John Hart Ely's *Democracy and Distrust: A Theory of Judicial Review* (1980) argues that protection of speech and association is one of the few areas where judges should aggressively enforce rights under his representation-reinforcing theory of judicial review.

How do any of these grand theories apply to sexualized speech? Until the middle of the twentieth century, non-condemnatory speech about homosexuality or sexuality outside of marriage was considered to be immoral rather than political. Under the then-prevailing definition of obscenity, immoral speech was classified as obscene, and obscenity lacked any First Amendment protection. Examples:

- Obscenity laws were the primary mechanism used to suppress birth control information and devices.

- A New York court banned the classic lesbian novel *The Well of Loneliness* on the ground that "it seeks to justify the right of a pervert to prey upon normal members of a community and to uphold such relationship as noble and lofty. Although it pleads for tolerance, it does not argue for repression or moderation of insidious impulses." *People v. Friede*, 133 Misc. 611, 233 N.Y.S. 565, 567 (Mag. Ct. 1929) (ultimately overturned on appeal). The court was particularly offended by the lesbian protagonist's statement "there's no shame in me."

- Other literary victims of the ban on obscenity included *An American Tragedy, Lady Chatterly's Lover, God's Little Acre, Strange Fruit,* and *Memoirs of Hecate County.* An early watershed in the acceptance of explicit sexuality in serious literature came with Judge Augustus Hand's decision allowing the importation of James Joyce's *Ulysses. United States v. One Book Entitled "Ulysses,"* 72 F.2d 705 (2d Cir. 1934).

- In a case involving the film version of *Lady Chatterly's Lover,* the Supreme Court invalidated a New York statute that required the denial of a license to exhibit motion pictures "which are immoral in that they portray 'acts of sexual immorality as desirable, acceptable or proper patterns of behavior.'" *Kingsley International Pictures Corp. v. Regents of the University of the State of New York,* 360 U.S. 684, 687 (1959) (quoting the lower court, 4 N.Y.2d 349, 151 N.E.2d 197, 197 (1958)). The New York Court of Appeals had found that the film was not obscene, but that, taken as a whole, it "alluringly portrays adultery as proper behavior." The Supreme Court found that the propriety of adultery was an idea, the advocacy of which was protected.

In *Roth v. United States*, 354 U.S. 476 (1957), the Supreme Court abandoned the traditional definition of obscenity as material that tended to corrupt morals. (We will pick up the story of how the definition has evolved since then in Part B, *infra.*) One immediate consequence of *Roth* was the reversal of a Ninth Circuit decision in which *One,* the monthly magazine of the Mattachine Society and the first major homophile publication in the U.S., was found to be obscene. Because it was obscene, the Court of Appeals upheld the decision of the Post Office to seize copies that had been mailed to subscribers, which essentially shut down what constituted the forerunner to the gay press. *One, Inc. v. Olesen,* 241 F.2d 772 (9th Cir. 1957), *reversed per curiam,* 355 U.S. 371 (1958). Consider the lower court's reasoning:

" * * * Plaintiff, as publisher, states on the second page of the magazine that it is published for the purpose of dealing primarily with homosexuality from the scientific, historical and critical point of view-to sponsor educational programs, lectures and concerts for the aid and benefit of social variants and to promote among the general public an interest, knowledge and understanding of the problems of [sexual] variation. The story "Sappho Remembered," appearing on pages 12 to 15 of the magazine, the poem "Lord Samuel and Lord Montagu" on pages 18 and 19, and the information given on page 29 as to where to obtain "The Circle," a magazine "with beautiful photos," do not comport with the lofty ideals expressed on page 2 by the publishers.

"The article "Sappho Remembered" is the story of a lesbian's influence on a young girl only twenty years of age * * * in her struggle to choose between a life with the lesbian, or a normal married life with her childhood sweetheart. The lesbian's affair with her room-mate while in college, resulting in the lesbian's expulsion from college, is recounted to bring in the jealousy angle. The climax is reached when the young girl gives up her chance for a normal married life to live with the lesbian. This article is nothing more than cheap pornography calculated to promote lesbianism. It falls far short of dealing with homosexuality from the scientific, historical and critical point of view.

"The poem "Lord Samuel and Lord Montagu" is about the alleged homosexual activities of Lord Montagu and other British Peers and contains a warning to all males to avoid the public toilets while Lord Samuel is "sniffing round the drains" of Piccadilly (London). The poem pertains to sexual matters of such a vulgar and indecent nature that it tends to arouse a feeling of disgust and revulsion. It is dirty, vulgar and offensive to the moral senses. * * *

"An examination of "The Circle" clearly reveals that it contains obscene and filthy matter which is offensive to the moral senses, morally depraving and debasing, and that it is designed for persons having lecherous and salacious proclivities. * * * "

Blocked by the Supreme Court ruling in *One, Inc.* from confiscating pro-gay textual material, the Post Office nonetheless continued to seize the gay male equivalent of pin-up publications. In *Manual Enterprises v. Day*, 370 U.S. 478 (1962), the Supreme Court stopped Post Office censorship of male physique magazines. Stanley Dietz, the lawyer for Manual Enterprises, argued that gay erotica should be treated the same as comparable material for heterosexuals and that homosexuality as such was not intrinsically evil. In other words, if Americans had a right to buy *Playboy*, they should be equally allowed to subscribe to magazines with photographs of muscular young men. The Court agreed that the depictions of male nudes were not any more obscene than comparable images of female nudes, but noted that the magazines were "dismally unpleasant, uncouth, and tawdry." *Id.* at 490.

In Section 1 of this chapter, we saw how the development of a liberty/autonomy right regarding reproductive decision making led to the demise of obscenity law as a method to block access to birth control, especially for women. Beginning in the late 1960s, the demand for equal rights for LGBT people spread, especially in urban and university centers. With the diffusion of this new idea, the transformation of what had traditionally been considered obscene speech into core political (although still unpopular) speech was complete.

A. FROM OBSCENITY TO POLITICAL SPEECH

Gay Students Organization of the University of New Hampshire v. Thomas Bonner

United States Court of Appeals for the First Circuit, 1974.
509 F.2d 652.

■ COFFIN, CHIEF JUDGE.

The Gay Students Organization (GSO) was officially recognized as a student organization at the University of New Hampshire in May, 1973, and on November 9, 1973 the group sponsored a dance on campus. The dance itself was held without incident, but media coverage of the event and criticism by Governor Meldrim Thomson, Jr., led the University's Board of Trustees to reconsider its treatment of the organization. The next day, November 10, 1973, the Board issued a "Position Statement" which indicated that the University would attempt to have determined the "legality and appropriateness of scheduling social functions by the Gay Students Organization" and which "directed that in the interim the University administration would schedule no further social functions by the Gay Students Organization until the matter is legally resolved." The University subsequently filed a declaratory judgment action in Strafford County Superior Court on November 21, 1973.

When the GSO requested permission to sponsor a play on December 7 and have a social function afterward, the University permitted the play but denied permission for the social function. The play was given as scheduled, and the GSO held a meeting following it. Sometime during the evening copies of two "extremist" homosexual publications were distributed by individuals over whom the GSO claims it had no control. Governor Thomson wrote an open letter to the trustees after the play, warning that if they did not "take firm, fair and positive action to rid your campuses of socially abhorrent activities" he would "stand solidly against the expenditure of one more cent of taxpayers' money for your institutions." Dr. Thomas N. Bonner, President of the University, then issued a public statement condemning the distribution of the homosexual literature and announcing that a repetition of the behavior would cause him to seek suspension of the GSO as a student organization. Bonner also revealed that he had "ordered that the current Trustee ban on GSO social functions be interpreted more strictly by administrative authorities than had been the case before December 7, 1973." * * *

* * * [W]e are conscious of the tension between deeply felt, conflicting values or moral judgments, and the traditional legal method of extracting and applying principles from decided cases. * * * [T]he campus group sought to be regulated stands for sexual values in direct conflict with the deeply imbued moral standards of much of the community whose taxes support the university.

The underlying question, usually not articulated, is whether * * * group activity promoting values so far beyond the pale of the wider community's values is also beyond the boundaries of the First Amendment, at least to the extent that university facilities may not be used by the group to flaunt its credo. If visceral reactions suggest an affirmative answer, the next task for judges is to devise a standard which, while damping down the First Amendment on a university campus, is generally applicable and free from the dangers of arbitrariness. At this point troubles arise. * * * [W]e are unable to devise a tolerable standard exempting this case at the threshold from general First Amendment precedents. * * *

* * * Communicative conduct is subject to regulation as to "time, place and manner" in the furtherance of a substantial governmental interest, so long as the restrictions imposed are only so broad as required in order to further the interest and are unrelated to the content and subject matter of the message communicated. *Police Department v. Mosley*, 408 U.S. 92 (1972).

There can be no doubt that expression, assembly and petition constitute significant aspects of the GSO's conduct in holding social events. The GSO was created, as its Statement of Purpose attests, to promote the free exchange of ideas among homosexuals and between homosexuals and heterosexuals, and to educate the public about bisexuality and homosexuality. GSO claims that social events in which discussion and exchange of ideas can take place in an informal atmosphere can play an important part in this communication. It would seem that these communicative opportunities are even more important for it than political teas, coffees, and dinners are for political candidates and parties, who have much wider access to the media, being more highly organized and socially accepted. And beyond the specific communications at such events is the basic "message" GSO seeks to convey—that homosexuals exist, that they feel repressed by existing laws and attitudes, that they wish to emerge from their isolation, and that public understanding of their attitudes and problems is desirable for society.

Perhaps these claims, being self-serving, fall short of establishing the speech-relatedness of GSO social events. But they receive the strongest corroboration from the interpretation placed on these events by the outside community, as related by appellants. Appellants have relied heavily on their obligation and right to prevent activities which the people of New Hampshire find shocking and offensive. In the brief for President Bonner and the University administrators we are told that the "activity of the GSO was variously labelled a spectacle, an abomination and similar terms of disapprobation" after the GSO dance on November 8, 1973; that the University has an obligation to prevent activity which affronts the citizens of the University and the town and which violates breach of the peace statutes; that the GSO dance constituted "grandstanding"; that recognition of the GSO inflamed a large segment of the people of the state; that the organization cannot be permitted to use its unpopularity without restriction to undermine the University within the state; and that "the ban on social functions reflects the distaste with which homosexual organizations are regarded in the State".

We do not see how these statements can be interpreted to avoid the conclusion that the regulation imposed was based in large measure, if not exclusively, on the content of the GSO's expression. It is well established that "above all else the First Amendment means that government has no power to restrict expression because of its message, its ideas, its subject matter, or its content." *Mosley*, 408 U.S. at 95. * * *

Postscript. *Bonner* was an early example of the single most successful line of cases that gay rights advocates brought in the twentieth century: challenges to the denials of recognition of student organizations by universities. See *Gay and Lesbian Students Ass'n v. Gòhn*, 850 F.2d 361 (8th Cir. 1988); *Gay Students Servs. v. Texas A & M Univ.*, 737 F.2d 1317 (5th Cir. 1984); *Gay Lib v. University of Mo.*, 558 F.2d 848 (8th Cir. 1977), *cert. denied*, 434 U.S. 1080 (1978); *Gay Alliance of Students v. Matthews*, 544 F.2d 162 (4th Cir. 1976); *Student Coalition for Gay Rights v. Austin Peay Univ.*, 477 F.Supp. 1267 (M.D.Tenn. 1979); and *Wood v. Davison*, 351 F.Supp. 543 (N.D.Ga. 1972). What about the framing of a First Amendment claim might make courts hospitable to the arguments by lesbian and gay plaintiffs, even in a time of widespread hostility to homosexuality?

***National Gay Task Force v. Board of Education of the City of Oklahoma City*, 729 F.2d 1270 (10th Cir. 1984), aff'd by an equally divided Court, 470 U.S. 903 (1985).** Oklahoma adopted a statute requiring the discharge of public school teachers who engaged in either "public homosexual activity" (i.e., same-sex sodomy that is "indiscreet and not practiced in private") or "public homosexual conduct" (i.e., "advocating, soliciting, imposing, encouraging or promoting public or private homosexual activity in a manner that creates a substantial risk that such conduct will come to the attention of school children or school employees") and who are rendered "unfit" for public service because of such activity or conduct. In the unfitness inquiry, the legislature instructed administrators to consider the circumstances of the activity/conduct, the likelihood of repetition, and "[w]hether the conduct or activity is of a repeated or continuing nature which tends to encourage or dispose school children toward similar conduct or activity."

The Task Force challenged the statute on its face, as a violation of teacher's First Amendment rights to speak out in favor of toleration or rights for gay people. The trial court held that the statute reached protected speech but upheld the constitutionality of the statute by reading a "material and substantial disruption" test into it. On appeal Chief Judge Logan reversed. Facial challenges based on First Amendment overbreadth are "strong medicine" and should be used "sparingly and only as a last resort." *Broadrick v. Oklahoma*, 413 U.S. 601, 613 (1973). Nonetheless, Chief Judge Logan concluded, "invalidation is an appropriate remedy in the instant case because [the bar to "public homosexual conduct"] is overbroad, is 'not readily subject to a narrowing construction by the state courts,' and 'its deterrent effect on legitimate expression is both real and substantial.' *Erznoznik v. City of Jacksonville*, 422 U.S. 205, 216 (1975). Also, we must be especially willing to invalidate a statute for facial overbreadth when, as here, the statute regulates 'pure speech.' "

"The First Amendment protects 'advocacy' even of illegal conduct except when 'advocacy' is 'directed to inciting or producing imminent lawless action and is likely to incite or produce such action.' *Brandenburg v. Ohio*, 395 U.S. 444, 447 (1969). The First Amendment does not permit someone to be punished for advocating illegal conduct at some indefinite future time.

" 'Encouraging' and 'promoting,' like 'advocating,' do not necessarily imply incitement to imminent action. A teacher who went before the Oklahoma legislature or appeared on television to urge the repeal of the Oklahoma anti-sodomy statute would be 'advocating,' 'promoting,' and 'encouraging' homosexual sodomy and creating a substantial risk that his or her speech would come to the attention of school children or school employees if he or she said, 'I think it is psychologically damaging for people with homosexual desires to suppress those desires. They should act on those desires and should be legally free to do so.' Such statements, which are aimed at legal and social change, are at the core of First Amendment protections. As in *Erznoznik*, the statute by its plain terms is not easily susceptible of a narrowing construction. The Oklahoma legislature chose the word 'advocacy' despite the Supreme Court's interpretation of that word in *Brandenburg*. Finally, the deterrent effect of [the statute] is both real and substantial. It applies to all teachers, substitute teachers, and teachers' aides in Oklahoma. To protect their jobs they must restrict their expression. Thus, the § 6–103.15 proscription of advocating, encouraging, or promoting homosexual activity is unconstitutionally overbroad."

Judge Barrett dissented. "Sodomy is *malum in se*, i.e., immoral and corruptible in its nature without regard to the fact of its being noticed or punished by the law of the state. It is not *malum prohibitum*, i.e., wrong *only* because it is forbidden by law and not involving moral turpitude. It is on this principle that I must part with the majority's holding that the 'public homosexual conduct' portion of the Oklahoma statute is overbroad. Any teacher who advocates, solicits, encourages or promotes the practice of *sodomy* 'in a manner that creates a substantial risk that such conduct will come to the attention of school children or school employees' is in fact and in truth *inciting* school children to participate in the abominable and detestable crime against nature. * * * A teacher advocating the practice of sodomy to school children is without First Amendment protection. This statute furthers an important and substantial government interest, as determined by the Oklahoma legislature, unrelated to the suppression of free speech. The incidental restriction on alleged First Amendment freedom is no greater than is essential to the furtherance of that interest."

Judge Barrett concluded that to "require proof that advocacy of the act of sodomy will substantially interfere or disrupt normal school activities is a bow to permissiveness. To the same extent, the advocacy of violence, sabotage and terrorism as a means of effecting political reform held in *Brandenburg* to be protected speech unless demonstrated as directed to and likely to incite or produce such action *did not* involve advocacy of a crime *malum in se* to school children by a school teacher."

Postscript. On review before the Supreme Court, the Justices split four to four; in that event, the court of appeals decision is affirmed. Justice Powell took no part in the case.

Gay Law Students Association et al. v. Pacific Telephone and Telegraph Co.

California Supreme Court, 1979.
24 Cal.3d 458, 156 Cal.Rptr. 14, 595 P.2d 592.

■ Tobriner, Justice.

[Plaintiffs, four individuals and two associations organized to promote equal rights for homosexual persons, sued Pacific Telephone and Telegraph Company (PT & T), alleging that PT & T practiced discrimination against homosexuals in the hiring, firing and promotion of employees, and seeking both injunctive and monetary relief under the California Labor Code. The trial court sustained defendant's demurrer and held that California statutory law did not give plaintiffs a claim for relief. The California Supreme Court reversed.]

Over 60 years ago the California Legislature, recognizing that employers could misuse their economic power to interfere with the political activities of their employees, enacted Labor Code sections 1101 and 1102 to protect the employees' rights. Labor Code section 1101 provides that "No employer shall make, adopt, or enforce any rule, regulation, or policy: (a) Forbidding or preventing employees from engaging or participating in politics. . . . (b) Controlling or directing, or tending to control or direct the political activities of affiliations of employees." Similarly, section 1102 states that "No employer shall coerce or influence or attempt to coerce or influence his employees through or by means of threat of discharge or loss of employment to adopt or follow or refrain from adopting or following any particular course or line of political action or political activity." These sections serve to protect "the fundamental right of employees in general to engage in political activity without interference by employers."

These statutes cannot be narrowly confined to partisan activity. As explained in *Mallard v. Boring* (1960) 182 Cal.App.2d 390, 395: "The term 'political activity' connotes the espousal of a candidate *or a cause*, and some degree of action to promote the acceptance thereof by other persons." (Emphasis added.) The Supreme Court has recognized the political character of activities such as participation in litigation (*N.A.A.C.P. v. Button* (1963) 371 U.S. 415, 429), the wearing of symbolic armbands (*Tinker v. Des Moines School Dist.* (1969) 393 U.S. 503), and the association with others for the advancement of beliefs and ideas (*N.A.A.C.P. v. Alabama* (1958) 357 U.S. 449).

Measured by these standards, the struggle of the homosexual community for equal rights, particularly in the field of employment, must be recognized as a political activity. Indeed the subject of the rights of homosexuals incites heated political debate today, and the "gay liberation movement" encourages its homosexual members to attempt to convince other members of society that homosexuals should be accorded the same fundamental rights as heterosexuals. The aims of the struggle for homosexual rights, and the tactics employed, bear a close analogy to the continuing struggle for civil rights waged by blacks, women, and other minorities.

A principal barrier to homosexual equality is the common feeling that homosexuality is an affliction which the homosexual worker must conceal from his employer and his fellow workers. Consequently one important aspect of the struggle for equal rights is to induce homosexual individuals to "come out of the closet," acknowledge their sexual preferences, and to associate with others in working for equal rights.

In light of this factor in the movement for homosexual rights, the allegations of plaintiffs' complaint assume a special significance. Plaintiffs allege that PT & T discriminates against "manifest" homosexuals and against persons who make "an issue of their homosexuality." The complaint asserts also that PT & T will not hire anyone referred to them by plaintiff Society for Individual Rights, an organization active in promoting the rights of homosexuals to equal employment opportunities. These allegations can reasonably be construed as charging that PT & T discriminates in particular against persons who identify themselves as homosexual, who defend homosexuality, or who are identified with activist homosexual organizations. So construed, the allegations charge that PT & T has adopted a "policy . . . tending to control or direct the political activities or affiliations of employees" in violation of section 1101, and has "attempt[ed] to coerce or influence . . . employees . . . to . . . refrain from adopting [a] particular course or line of political . . . activity" in violation of section 1102. * * *

■ RICHARDSON, JUSTICE, dissenting. * * *

* * * [T]he complaint herein fails to allege *any* attempted control or coercion by PT & T of any employee or applicant with respect to any "*political*" activity whatever. Significantly, plaintiffs' appellate briefs do not even raise the point. They cite neither section 1101 nor 1102 in support of their complaint. The "political" argument has never been advanced nor apparently even thought of by either lawyers or litigants.

The gist of plaintiffs' allegations in the complaint herein is that plaintiffs have been damaged by reason of PT & T's alleged refusal to hire or promote "manifest homosexuals." As the "introduction" to the first amended complaint alleges, "PT & T has, since at least 1971, had an articulated policy of excluding homosexuals from employment opportunities with its organization." Again, in the "fact allegations" of the complaint, it is alleged that ". . . PT & T has maintained and enforced a policy of employment discrimination against homosexuals. . . . PT & T refuses to hire any 'manifest homosexual' which [*sic*] may apply to it for employment at any occupational level or category." Nowhere in the complaint, from beginning to end, do plaintiffs allege that PT & T's asserted policy of discrimination is directed toward any of plaintiffs' *political* activity or affiliations. Rather, plaintiffs contend, and the gravamen of their complaint is, that employment discrimination is based solely on the overt and manifest nature of their sexual orientation itself. * * *

NOTES ON "COMING OUT" AS POLITICAL ACTIVITY

1. *Identity Speech.* The Oklahoma statute challenged in *NGTF* was identical in substance to the Briggs Initiative (sponsored by state Senator John Briggs), which California voters rejected in a referendum.[a] (The fight over the Briggs Initiative provided the central plot line in the film *Milk*.) The campaign produced the first large-scale consideration of a gay rights issue in electoral politics. Its focus was what one of us has called "identity speech":

> The Briggs Initiative appeared on the November 1978 California state ballot as a referendum question. * * * It was widely understood to be a vote on whether the state should fire gay teachers and thus purge that group from the schools and from contact with children. * * *

---

[a] The initiative provided that a public school teacher, teacher's aide, administrator, or counselor could be fired if the employee was found to have engaged in either (1) "public homosexual activity," which the initiative defined as an act of homosexual sex which was "not discreet and not practiced in private, whether or not such act, at the time of its commission, constituted a crime," or (2) "public homosexual conduct," which the initiative defined as "the advocating, soliciting, imposing, encouraging or promoting of private or public homosexual activity directed at, or likely to come to the attention of, schoolchildren and/or other employees."

But the Briggs Initiative was configured to play a double role. It was framed in terms of banning a viewpoint, the "advocating" or "promoting" of homosexuality, rather than the exclusion of a group of persons. Lesbians and gay men easily fell within this proscription because to come out is to implicitly, or often explicitly, affirm the value of homosexuality. For that reason, a Briggs-style law could be used to target all lesbian and gay school employees who had expressed their sexual orientation, except in the most furtive contexts.

The viewpoint target made the initiative more complicated, however. It threatened anyone, gay or straight, who voiced the forbidden ideas. Thus it simultaneously discriminated against gay people while extending its aim to everyone not gay who supported them.

The proposed law did not merely include the two distinct elements of viewpoint bias and group classification. It merged them into one new concept. This merger—what I would describe as the formation of a legal construct of identity that incorporates both viewpoint and status—would come to dominate both the right-wing strategy against gay rights and the claims of the lesbian and gay community for equality.

* * * The Briggs Initiative referendum campaign marked the moment when American politics began to treat homosexuality as something more than deviance, conduct, or lifestyle; it marked the emergence of homosexuality as an openly political claim and as a viewpoint. That, in turn, laid the foundation for the emergence of a new analysis of speech about homosexuality. Instead of treating such speech as the advocacy of conduct, courts shifted to a consideration of gay speech as the advocacy of ideas. The once-bright boundary between sexual speech and political speech began to fade.

Nan D. Hunter, "Identity, Speech and Equality," 79 *Va. L. Rev.* 1695, 1703–05 (1993).

2.   *Category Contest.* Drafters of the Oklahoma statute at issue in *NGTF* labeled "encouraging," "promoting," and "advocating" certain illegal conduct (sodomy) as "public homosexual conduct." What is the rhetorical strategy behind that phrase? Analyze its three components: What must be "public" for the behavior to be prohibited? Which Oklahoma statutes are and are not limited to "homosexual" activity? What is the "conduct" at issue? By contrast, plaintiffs framed the statute as endangering pure political speech and relied on its potential scope extending to out-of-classroom speech. What if the statute had been limited to in-classroom speech? (See Chapter 8, Section 1.)

3.   *Personal (Speech) as Political.* Note the timing of the decision in *PT & T*, namely, the year after defeat of the Briggs Initiative. The case eventually settled with a $5 million payment to the plaintiff class and the adoption by defendant of an antidiscrimination policy. Leonard, *Sexuality and the Law* 417 (1992). Under *PT & T*, would it be political speech to put a photograph of one's same-sex lover on one's desk at work? What about a photo of one's different-sex partner? How could the first act be political speech if the second is not also?

B. FEMINIST PORNOGRAPHY DEBATES

Although the law no longer consigns all sexual speech to the obscenity category, First Amendment doctrine nonetheless continues to invoke the premise that sexual expression is less worthy than political expression. The Court allows government to regulate sexual expression in ways that it flatly forbids for political speech. For example, sexual expression can be zoned to remote parts of town, *City of Renton v. Playtime Theatres*, 475 U.S. 41 (1986), and denied access to the airwaves until late at night, *FCC v. Pacifica Foundation*, 438 U.S. 726 (1978). By contrast, the state is generally barred from regulating political expression, even if a majority of the public finds it offensive. *Cohen v. California*, 403 U.S. 15 (1971) (wearing a jacket that said "Fuck the Draft").

The Supreme Court settled on its current definition of obscenity in *Miller v. California*, 413 U.S. 15, 24 (1973), holding that classification as obscene could apply only to "works which, taken as a whole, appeal to the prurient interest in sex, which portray sexual conduct in a patently offensive way, and which, taken as a whole, do not have serious literary, artistic, political, or scientific value." What is "the prurient interest in sex"? The Court upheld a Washington statute that defined prurient interest as "that which incites lasciviousness or lust" by narrowly construing "lust" to cover only "that which appeals to a shameful or morbid interest in sex." *Brockett v. Spokane Arcades, Inc.*, 472 U.S. 491, 504–05 (1985). The Court did not define "normal," "unhealthy," "shameful," or "morbid."

In the mid-1980s, feminists debated whether pornography should be considered a civil rights harm to women. Implementing their view that pornography legitimates and may cause violence against women, Professor Catharine MacKinnon and feminist author Andrea Dworkin secured the passage of an anti-pornography ordinance in Indianapolis. Professor MacKinnon explained the theory behind the ordinance:

> * * * In pornography, there it is, in one place, all of the abuses that women had to struggle so long even to begin to articulate, all the *unspeakable* abuse: the rape, the battery, the sexual harassment, the prostitution, and the sexual abuse of children. Only in the pornography it is called something else: sex, sex, sex, sex, and sex, respectively. Pornography sexualizes rape, battery, sexual harassment, prostitution, and child sexual abuse; it thereby celebrates, promotes, authorizes, and legitimizes them. More generally, it eroticizes the dominance and submission that is the dynamic common to them all. It makes hierarchy sexy and calls that "the truth about sex" or just

a mirror of reality. Through this process, pornography constructs what a woman is as what men want from sex. This is what the pornography means. * * *

Pornography constructs what a woman is in terms of its view of what men want sexually, such that acts of rape, battery, sexual harassment, prostitution, and sexual abuse of children become acts of sexual equality. Pornography's world of equality is a harmonious and balanced place. Men and women are perfectly complementary and perfectly bipolar. Women's desire to be fucked by men is equal to men's desire to fuck women. All the ways men love to take and violate women, women love to be taken and violated. The women who most love this are most men's equals, the most liberated; the most participatory child is the most grown-up, the most equal to an adult. Their consent merely expresses or ratifies these preexisting facts. * * *

What pornography *does* goes beyond its content: It eroticizes hierarchy, it sexualizes inequality. It makes dominance and submission sex. Inequality is its central dynamic; the illusion of freedom coming together with the reality of force is central to its working. Perhaps because this is a bourgeois culture, the victim must look free, appear to be freely acting. Choice is how she got there. Willing is what she is when she is being equal. It seems equally important that then and there she actually be forced and that forcing be communicated on some level, even if only through still photos of her in postures of receptivity and access, available for penetration. Pornography in this view is a form of forced sex, a practice of sexual politics, an institution of gender inequality.

From this perspective, pornography is neither harmless fantasy nor a corrupt and confused misrepresentation of an otherwise natural and healthy sexual situation. It institutionalizes the sexuality of male supremacy, fusing the erotization of dominance and submission with the social construction of male and female. To the extent that gender is sexual, pornography is part of constituting the meaning of that sexuality. Men treat women as who they see women as being. Pornography constructs who that is. Men's power over women means that the way men see women defines who women can be. Pornography is that way. Pornography is not imagery in some relation to a reality elsewhere constructed. It is not a distortion, reflection, projection, expression, fantasy, representation, or symbol either. It is a sexual reality.

Catharine MacKinnon, "Pornography, Civil Rights, and Speech," 20 *Harv. C.R.-C.L. L. Rev.* 1 (1985)

Another set of feminist advocates (including one of us) opposed the ordinance on the ground that its stated purposes masked an unintended resurrection of moralism that harmed women's interests:

* * * Although proponents claim that the Minneapolis and Indianapolis ordinances represent a new way to regulate pornography, the strategy is still laden with our culture's old, repressive approach to sexuality. The implementation of such laws hinges on the definition of pornography as interpreted by the judiciary. The definition provided in the Minneapolis legislation is vague, leaving critical phrases such as "the sexually explicit subordination of women," "postures of sexual submission," and "whores by nature" to the interpretation of the citizen who files a complaint and to the judge who hears the case. The legislation does not prohibit just the images of rape and abusive sexual violence that most supporters claim to be its target, but instead drifts toward covering an increasingly wide range of sexually explicit material. * * *

At its heart, this analysis implies that heterosexual sex itself is sexist, that women do not engage in it of their own volition, and that behavior pleasurable to men is intrinsically repugnant to women. In some contexts, for example, the representation of fellatio and multiple partners can be sexist, but are we willing to concede that they always are? If not, then what is proposed as actionable under the Indianapolis law includes merely sexually explicit representation (the traditional target of obscenity laws), which proponents of the legislation vociferously insist they are not interested in attacking. * * *

Certain troubling questions arise here, for if one claims, as some anti-pornography activists do, that there is a direct relationship between images and behavior, why should images of violence against women or scenarios of sexism in general not be similarly proscribed? Why is sexual explicitness singled out as the cause of women's oppression? For proponents to exempt violent and sexist images, or even sexist images, from regulation is inconsistent, especially since they are so pervasive. * * *

* * * [W]hat underlies this legislation, and the success of its analysis in blurring and exceeding boundaries, is an appeal to a very traditional view of sex: Sex is degrading to women. By this logic, any illustrations or descriptions of explicit sexual acts that involve women are in themselves affronts to women's dignity. In its brief, the City of Indianapolis was quite specific about this point: "The harms caused by pornography are by no means limited to acts of physical aggression. The mere existence of pornography in society degrades and demeans all women." Embedded in this view are several other familiar themes: that sex is degrading to women, but not to men; that men are raving

beasts; that sex is dangerous for women; that sexuality is male, not female; that women are victims, not sexual actors; that men inflict "it" on women; that penetration is submission; that heterosexual sexuality, rather than the institution of heterosexuality, is sexist.

These assumptions, in part intended, in part unintended, lead us back to the traditional target of obscenity law: sexually explicit material. What initially appeared novel, then, is really the reappearance of a traditional theme. It is ironic that a feminist position on pornography incorporates most of the myths about sexuality that feminism has struggled to displace. * * *

Lisa Duggan, Nan D. Hunter & Carole Vance, "False Promises: Feminist Anti-Pornography Legislation," first published in *Women and Censorship* (Varda Burstyn, ed. 1985), republished in 38 *New York Law School Law Review* 133 (1993). (Reprinted by permission)

American Booksellers Association, Inc. v. William Hudnut, III

United States Court of Appeals for the Seventh Circuit, 1985.
771 F.2d 323, *aff'd mem.*, 475 U.S. 1001 (1986).

■ EASTERBROOK, CIRCUIT JUDGE.

Indianapolis enacted an ordinance defining "pornography" as a practice that discriminates against women. "Pornography" is to be redressed through the administrative and judicial methods used for other discrimination. The City's definition of "pornography" is considerably different from "obscenity," which the Supreme Court has held is not protected by the First Amendment. * * *

"Pornography" under the ordinance is "the graphic sexually explicit subordination of women, whether in pictures or in words, that also includes one or more of the following:

(1) Women are presented as sexual objects who enjoy pain or humiliation; or

(2) Women are presented as sexual objects who experience sexual pleasure in being raped; or

(3) Women are presented as sexual objects tied up or cut up or mutilated or bruised or physically hurt, or as dismembered or truncated or fragmented or severed into body parts; or

(4) Women are presented as being penetrated by objects or animals; or

(5) Women are presented in scenarios of degradation, injury, abasement, torture, shown as filthy or inferior, bleeding,

bruised, or hurt in a context that makes these conditions sexual; or

(6)   Women are presented as sexual objects for domination, conquest, violation, exploitation, possession, or use, or through postures or positions of servility or submission or display."

Indianapolis Code § 16–3(q). The statute provides that the "use of men, children, or transsexuals in the place of women in paragraphs (1) through (6) above shall also constitute pornography under this section." The ordinance as passed in April 1984 defined "sexually explicit" to mean actual or simulated intercourse or the uncovered exhibition of the genitals, buttocks or anus. An amendment in June 1984 deleted this provision, leaving the term undefined.

The Indianapolis ordinance does not refer to the prurient interest, to offensiveness, or to the standards of the community. It demands attention to particular depictions, not to the work judged as a whole. It is irrelevant under the ordinance whether the work has literary, artistic, political, or scientific value. The City and many *amici* point to these omissions as virtues. They maintain that pornography influences attitudes, and the statute is a way to alter the socialization of men and women rather than to vindicate community standards of offensiveness. * * *

Civil rights groups and feminists have entered this case as *amici* on both sides. Those supporting the ordinance say that it will play an important role in reducing the tendency of men to view women as sexual objects, a tendency that leads to both unacceptable attitudes and discrimination in the workplace and violence away from it. Those opposing the ordinance point out that much radical feminist literature is explicit and depicts women in ways forbidden by the ordinance and that the ordinance would reopen old battles. It is unclear how Indianapolis would treat works from James Joyce's *Ulysses* to Homer's *Iliad*; both depict women as submissive objects for conquest and domination.

We do not try to balance the arguments for and against an ordinance such as this. The ordinance discriminates on the ground of the content of the speech. Speech treating women in the approved way—in sexual encounters "premised on equality" (MacKinnon, *supra*, at 22)—is lawful no matter how sexually explicit. Speech treating women in the disapproved way—as submissive in matters sexual or as enjoying humiliation—is unlawful no matter how significant the literary, artistic, or political qualities of the work taken as a whole. The state may not ordain preferred viewpoints in this way. The Constitution forbids the state to declare one perspective right and silence opponents. * * *

"If there is any fixed star in our constitutional constellation, it is that no official, high or petty, can prescribe what shall be orthodox in politics, nationalism, religion, or other matters of opinion or force citizens to confess by word or act their faith therein." *West Virginia State Board of Education v. Barnette*, 319 U.S. 624, 642 (1943). Under the First Amendment the government must leave to the people the evaluation of ideas. Bald or subtle, an idea is as powerful as the audience allows it to be. A belief may be pernicious—the beliefs of Nazis led to the death of millions, those of the Klan to the repression of millions. A pernicious belief may prevail. Totalitarian governments today rule much of the planet, practicing suppression of billions and spreading dogma that may enslave others. One of the things that separates our society from theirs is our absolute right to propagate opinions that the government finds wrong or even hateful. * * *

Under the ordinance graphic sexually explicit speech is "pornography" or not depending on the perspective the author adopts. Speech that "subordinates" women and also, for example, presents women as enjoying pain, humiliation, or rape, or even simply presents women in "positions of servility or submission or display" is forbidden, no matter how great the literary or political value of the work taken as a whole. Speech that portrays women in positions of equality is lawful, no matter how graphic the sexual content. This is thought control. It establishes an "approved" view of women, of how they may react to sexual encounters, of how the sexes may relate to each other. Those who espouse the approved view may use sexual images; those who do not, may not.

Indianapolis justifies the ordinance on the ground that pornography affects thoughts. Men who see women depicted as subordinate are more likely to treat them so. Pornography is an aspect of dominance. It does not persuade people so much as change them. It works by socializing, by establishing the expected and the permissible. In this view pornography is not an idea; pornography is the injury.

There is much to this perspective. Beliefs are also facts. People often act in accordance with the images and patterns they find around them. People raised in a religion tend to accept the tenets of that religion, often without independent examination. People taught from birth that black people are fit only for slavery rarely rebelled against that creed; beliefs coupled with the self-interest of the masters established a social structure that inflicted great harm while enduring for centuries. Words and images act at the level of the subconscious before they persuade at the level of the conscious. Even the truth has little chance unless a statement fits within the framework of beliefs that may never have been subjected to rational study.

Therefore we accept the premises of this legislation. Depictions of subordination tend to perpetuate subordination. The subordinate status of women in turn leads to affront and lower pay at work, insult and injury at home, battery and rape on the streets. In the language of the legislature, "[p]ornography is central in creating and maintaining sex as a basis of discrimination. Pornography is a systematic practice of exploitation and subordination based on sex which differentially harms women. The bigotry and contempt it produces, with the acts of aggression it fosters, harm women's opportunities for equality and rights [of all kinds]." Indianapolis Code § 16–1(a)(2).

Yet this simply demonstrates the power of pornography as speech. All of these unhappy effects depend on mental intermediation. Pornography affects how people see the world, their fellows, and social relations. If pornography is what pornography does, so is other speech. Hitler's orations affected how some Germans saw Jews. Communism is a world view, not simply a *Manifesto* by Marx and Engels or a set of speeches. Efforts to suppress communist speech in the United States were based on the belief that the public acceptability of such ideas would increase the likelihood of totalitarian government. Religions affect socialization in the most pervasive way. The opinion in *Wisconsin v. Yoder*, 406 U.S. 205 (1972), shows how a religion can dominate an entire approach to life, governing much more than the relation between the sexes. Many people believe that the existence of television, apart from the content of specific programs, leads to intellectual laziness, to a penchant for violence, to many other ills. The Alien and Sedition Acts passed during the administration of John Adams rested on a sincerely held belief that disrespect for the government leads to social collapse and revolution—a belief with support in the history of many nations. Most governments of the world act on this empirical regularity, suppressing critical speech. In the United States, however, the strength of the support for this belief is irrelevant. Seditious libel is protected speech unless the danger is not only grave but also imminent. See *New York Times Co. v. Sullivan*, 376 U.S. 254 (1964); cf. *Brandenburg v. Ohio*, [395 U.S. 444 (1969)]; *New York Times Co. v. United States*, 403 U.S. 713 (1971) [the Pentagon Papers Case].

Racial bigotry, anti-semitism, violence on television, reporters' biases—these and many more influence the culture and shape our socialization. None is directly answerable by more speech, unless that speech too finds its place in the popular culture. Yet all is protected as speech, however insidious. Any other answer leaves the government in control of all of the institutions of culture, the great censor and director of which thoughts are good for us.

Sexual responses often are unthinking responses, and the association of sexual arousal with the subordination of women therefore may have a substantial effect. But almost all cultural stimuli provoke unconscious responses. Religious ceremonies condition their participants. Teachers convey messages by selecting what not to cover; the implicit message about what is off limits or unthinkable may be more powerful than the messages for which they present rational argument. Television scripts contain unarticulated assumptions. People may be conditioned in subtle ways. If the fact that speech plays a role in a process of conditioning were enough to permit governmental regulation, that would be the end of freedom of speech. * * *

Much of Indianapolis's argument rests on the belief that when speech is "unanswerable," and the metaphor that there is a "marketplace of ideas" does not apply, the First Amendment does not apply either. The metaphor is honored; Milton's *Aeropagitica* and John Stuart Mill's *On Liberty* defend freedom of speech on the ground that the truth will prevail, and many of the most important cases under the First Amendment recite this position. The Framers undoubtedly believed it. As a general matter it is true. But the Constitution does not make the dominance of truth a necessary condition of freedom of speech. To say that it does would be to confuse an outcome of free speech with a necessary condition for the application of the amendment.

A power to limit speech on the ground that truth has not yet prevailed and is not likely to prevail implies the power to declare truth. At some point the government must be able to say (as Indianapolis has said): "We know what the truth is, yet a free exchange of speech has not driven out falsity, so that we must now prohibit falsity." If the government may declare the truth, why wait for the failure of speech? Under the First Amendment, however, there is no such thing as a false idea, so the government may not restrict speech on the ground that in a free exchange truth is not yet dominant. * * *

We come, finally, to the argument that pornography is "low value" speech, that it is enough like obscenity that Indianapolis may prohibit it. Some cases hold that speech far removed from politics and other subjects at the core of the Framers' concerns may be subjected to special regulation. [Citing *Pacifica; Mini Theatres; Chaplinsky*.] These cases do not sustain statutes that select among viewpoints, however. In *Pacifica* the FCC sought to keep vile language off the air during certain times. The Court held that it may; but the Court would not have sustained a regulation prohibiting scatological descriptions of Republicans but not scatological descriptions of Democrats, or any other form of selection among viewpoints. See *Planned Parenthood Ass'n v. Chicago Transit Authority*, 767 F.2d 1225, 1232–33 (7th Cir.1985).

At all events, "pornography" is not low value speech within the meaning of these cases. Indianapolis seeks to prohibit certain speech because it believes this speech influences social relations and politics on a grand scale, that it controls attitudes at home and in the legislature. This precludes a characterization of the speech as low value. True, pornography and obscenity have sex in common. But Indianapolis left out of its definition any reference to literary, artistic, political, or scientific value. The ordinance applies to graphic sexually explicit subordination in works great and small. The Court sometimes balances the value of speech against the costs of its restriction, but it does this by category of speech and not by the content of particular works. Indianapolis has created an approved point of view and so loses the support of these cases.

Any rationale we could imagine in support of this ordinance could not be limited to sex discrimination. Free speech has been on balance an ally of those seeking change. Governments that want stasis start by restricting speech. Culture is a powerful force of continuity; Indianapolis paints pornography as part of the culture of power. Change in any complex system ultimately depends on the ability of outsiders to challenge accepted views and the reigning institutions. Without a strong guarantee of freedom of speech, there is no effective right to challenge what is. * * *

NOTE ON THE INDIANAPOLIS PORNOGRAPHY CASE

Consider Judge Easterbrook's opinion in light of the purposes allegedly served by the First Amendment, described at the beginning of this section. The constitutional goals served by strong protections for speech would include allowing truth to triumph in the marketplace of ideas, fostering democracy and self-government, and enhancing individual autonomy and flourishing. Consider the three perspectives you have read concerning the anti-pornography ordinance: how does each invoke, refute, or re-interpret these interests? What new or additional First Amendment interests do they propose?

Feminist efforts to suppress pornography have largely dissipated in the U.S. since the *Hudnut* decision, but their arguments have acquired greater purchase elsewhere. In Canada, the Supreme Court upheld the national obscenity law on the ground that it was reasonably related to promoting equality. *Regina v. Butler*, [1992] 1 S.C.R. 452, 89 D.L.R.4th 449. Justice Sopinka, writing for the court, based his reasoning on an earlier case finding that hate speech was not entitled to protection, and concluded that

> * * * Parliament was entitled to have a "reasoned apprehension of harm" resulting from the desensitization of individuals exposed to materials which depict violence, cruelty, and dehumanization in sexual relations. Accordingly, I am of the view that there is a sufficiently rational link between the criminal sanction, which demonstrates our community's disapproval of the dissemination of materials which potentially victimize women and which restricts the negative influence which such materials have on changes in attitudes and behavior, and the objective.

Ironically, the first prosecution for obscenity after the *Butler* ruling was against the owners of a gay bookstore for the sale of *Bad Attitude*, a lesbian sex magazine published in Boston. They were found guilty, with the court ruling that the combination in one short story of "bondage in various forms, the pulling of hair, a hard slap and explicit sex" met the *Butler* test. *R. v. Scythes*, Ontario Court (Provincial Division) (Feb. 16, 1993) (unreported). Canadian Customs also relied on *Butler*'s definition of obscenity to seize shipments of, *inter alia*, *Trash* by Dorothy Allison, *Querelle* by Jean Genet, *Macho Sluts* by Pat Califia and the cartoon book, *Hot head Paisan*. See Janine Fuller & Stuart Blackley, *Restricted Entry: Censorship On Trial* (1995).

PROBLEM 1-5
WHAT SHOULD BE LABELED PORNOGRAPHIC?

Conventional objections to restricting pornography often invoke the slippery slope to Shakespeare—the argument deployed by Judge Easterbrook in *Hudnut* that it is virtually impossible to draw a defensible boundary specifying which non-obscene sexual speech should be heavily policed without threatening other sexual speech that is worthy of protection. Following are examples of explicit speech that could be suppressed under the Indianapolis ordinance—consider how they should be resolved under each of the three theories of the First Amendment, including your interpretation of how each applies to sexually explicit speech:

(a) *Is Gay Porn Different?* The Indianapolis ordinance would have included materials that depicted only men, so long as a male was being portrayed in a "subordinate" position. Compare Jeffrey Sherman, "Love Speech: The Social Utility of Pornography," 47 *Stan. L. Rev.* 661 (1995) (defending gay male porn in part by arguing that pornography serves strong First Amendment purposes for gay male adolescents in particular) and Scott Tucker, *Radical Feminism and Gay Male Porn* (1983) (similar) with John Stoltenberg, *Refusing To Be A Man: Essays on Sexual Justice* 132 (1989) (arguing that gay male pornography "eroticizes domination and subordination of * * * effeminacy").

(b) *Is Filming* Lolita *Different?* It is well established that depictions of sexual acts involving children can be prohibited. *New York v. Ferber*, 458 U.S. 747 (1982). It is equally clear that a novel, such as *Lolita*, which has literary merit cannot be banned because it describes sexual acts by a minor. What of realistic visual images created by the use of software or other methods that do not involve actual children? Congress enacted the Child Pornography Prevention Act of 1996, 18 U.S.C. § 2251 et seq. to reach precisely those materials, but it was struck down in *Ashcroft v. The Free Speech Coalition*, 535 U.S. 234 (2002).

(c) *Is Sexting Different?* When a minor takes a nude or semi-nude photograph of herself or himself and texts the photo to a friend, should the law step in? A district attorney in Pennsylvania threatened several local teenagers with felony child pornography charges unless they agreed to probation and participation in counseling. The parents of two of the girls who were threatened with prosecution obtained an injunction against the prosecutor. *Miller v. Mitchell*, 598 F.3d 139 (3d Cir. 2010). Should the prosecutor have done something else? Nothing?

NOTE ON THE RACIALIZATION OF SEXUAL SPEECH

In the spring of 1990, responding to citizens' complaints, a deputy sheriff in Broward County, Florida (Fort Lauderdale) purchased a copy of 2 Live Crew's hit album, "As Nasty As They Wanna Be." The sheriff's department secured a declaratory judgment in state court that the album's lyrics were obscene, and thus any store selling it could be prosecuted. Music stores all over south Florida (and perhaps elsewhere) removed it from the shelves. The record company and the musicians sued in federal court.

Luke Records, Inc. et al. v. Nick Navarro, 960 F.2d 134 (11th Cir. 1992). Luke Records challenged the lower court's judgment that 2 Live Crew's rap-music recording "As Nasty As They Wanna Be" was criminally obscene under *Miller v. California*, 413 U.S. 15 (1973). Under *Miller*, the standard for determining obscenity was whether the item lacked serious literary, artistic, political or scientific value. The *Luke Records* case may have been the first time a federal court of appeals applied the *Miller* test to a musical composition.

In the lower court, 2 Live Crew's attorneys called expert witnesses who testified that the song had serious musical value. Dr. Carlton Long testified that "As Nasty As They Wanna Be" contained three oral traditions, or musical conventions, known as call and response, doing the dozens, and boasting. Long testified that these oral traditions derive their roots from certain segments of black culture and that certain portions of the song were statements of political significance or exemplified numerous literary conventions.

In a *per curiam* opinion, the Eleventh Circuit assumed without deciding that the lower court's familiarity with contemporary community standards was sufficient to carry the case as to the first two prongs of the *Miller* test (*i.e.,* prurient interest and patent offensiveness). But the court found the record insufficient "to satisfy the last prong of the *Miller* analysis, which requires determination of whether a work 'lacks serious artistic, scientific, literary or political value.'" The court cited Supreme Court precedent for the principle "that whether a work possesses serious value was not a question to be decided by contemporary community standards. * * * We reject the argument that simply by listening to this musical work, the judge could determine that it had no serious artistic value."

Kimberlé Williams Crenshaw, "Mapping The Margins: Intersectionality, Identity Politics, and Violence Against Women of Color" 43 *Stan. L. Rev.* 1241, 1285–95 (1991).* Professor Crenshaw argues that "race played some role in distinguishing 2 Live Crew as the first group ever to be prosecuted for obscenity in connection with a musical recording, and one of a handful of recording artists to be prosecuted for a live performance. Recent controversies about sexism, racism, and violence in popular culture point to a vast range of expression that might have provided targets for censorship, but was left untouched. Madonna has acted out masturbation, portrayed the seduction of a priest, and insinuated group sex on stage, but she has never been prosecuted for obscenity. While 2 Live Crew was performing in Hollywood, Florida, Andrew Dice Clay's recordings were being sold in stores and he was performing nationwide on HBO. Well-known for his racist 'humor,' Clay is also comparable to 2 Live Crew in sexual explicitness and misogyny. In his show, for example, Clay offers, 'Eenie, meenie, minee, mo/Suck my [expletive] and swallow slow,' and 'Lose the bra,

---

bitch.' Moreover, graphic sexual images—many of them violent—were widely available in Broward County where the performance and trial took place. According to the testimony of a Broward County vice detective, 'nude dance shows and adult bookstores are scattered throughout the county where 2 Live Crew performed.' "

Professor Crenshaw makes a more general point about *Miller*: by making "community standards" the primary test for obscenity, the Court invites racially motivated prosecutions such as this one. "Negative reactions to the sexual conduct of Black men have traditionally had racist overtones, especially where that conduct threatens to 'cross over' into the mainstream community. So even if the decision to prosecute did reflect a widespread community perception of the purely prurient character of 2 Live Crew's music, that perception itself might reflect an established pattern of vigilante attitudes directed toward the sexual expression of Black men. In short, the appeal to community standards does not undercut a concern about racism; rather, it underscores that concern.

"A second troubling dimension of the case brought against 2 Live Crew was the [trial] court's apparent disregard for the culturally rooted aspects of 2 Live Crew's music. Such disregard was essential to a finding of obscenity given the third prong of the *Miller* test requiring that material judged obscene must, taken as a whole, lack literary, artistic, or political value. 2 Live Crew argued that this criterion of the *Miller* test was not met in the case of *Nasty* since the recording exemplified such African-American cultural modes as 'playing the dozens,' 'call and response,' and 'signifying.' The court denied each of the group's claims of cultural specificity, recharacterizing in more generic terms what 2 Live Crew contended was distinctly African American. According to the court, 'playing the dozens' is 'commonly seen in adolescents, especially boys, of all ages'; 'boasting' appears to be 'part of the universal human condition'; and the cultural origins of 'call and response'— featured in a song on Nasty about fellatio in which competing groups chanted 'less filling' and 'tastes great'—were to be found in a Miller beer commercial, not in African-American cultural tradition. The possibility that the Miller beer commercial may have itself evolved from an African-American cultural tradition was apparently lost on the court.

"In disregarding the arguments made on behalf of 2 Live Crew, the court denied that the form and style of *Nasty* and, by implication, rap music in general had any artistic merit. This disturbing dismissal of the cultural attributes of rap and the effort to universalize African-American modes of expression are a form of colorblindness that presumes to level all significant racial and ethnic differences in order to pass judgment on intergroup conflicts. The court's analysis here also manifests a frequently encountered strategy of cultural appropriation. African-American contributions that have been accepted by the mainstream culture are eventually absorbed as simply 'American' or found to be 'universal.' Other modes associated with African-American culture that resist absorption remain distinctive and are either neglected or dismissed as 'deviant.'

"The court apparently rejected as well the possibility that even the most misogynistic rap may have political value as a discourse of resistance. The element of resistance found in some rap is in making people uncomfortable, thereby challenging received habits of thought and action. Such challenges are potentially political, as are more subversive attempts to contest traditional rules by becoming what is most feared. Against a historical backdrop in which the Black male as social outlaw is a prominent theme, 'gangsta' rap' might be taken as a rejection of a conciliatory stance aimed at undermining fear through reassurance, in favor of a more subversive form of opposition that attempts to challenge the rules precisely by becoming the very social outlaw that society fears and attempts to proscribe. Rap representations celebrating an aggressive Black male sexuality can be easily construed as discomforting and oppositional. Not only does reading rap in this way preclude a finding that *Nasty* lacks political value, it also defeats the court's assumption that the group's intent was to appeal solely to prurient interests" * * *.

"The point here is not that the distinction between sex and violence should be rigorously maintained in determining what is obscene or, more specifically, that rap artists whose standard fare is more violent ought to be protected. To the contrary, these more violent groups should be much more troubling than 2 Live Crew. My point instead is to suggest that obscenity prosecutions of rap artists do nothing to protect the interests of those most directly implicated in rap—Black women. On the one hand, prevailing notions of obscenity separate out sexuality from violence, which has the effect of shielding the more violently misogynistic groups from prosecution; on the other, historical linkages between images of Black male sexuality and violence permit the singling out of 'lightweight' rappers for prosecution among all other purveyors of explicit sexual imagery."

"While concerns about racism fuel my opposition to the obscenity prosecution of 2 Live Crew, the uncritical support for, and indeed celebration of, 2 Live Crew by other opponents of the prosecution is extremely troubling as well. If the rhetoric of antisexism provided an occasion for racism, so, too, the rhetoric of antiracism provided an occasion for defending the misogyny of 2 Live Crew. That defense took two forms, one political, the other cultural, both advanced prominently by Henry Louis Gates. Gates's political defense argues that 2 Live Crew advances the antiracist agenda by exaggerating stereotypes of Black male sexuality 'to show how ridiculous [they] are.' The defense contends that by highlighting to the extreme the sexism, misogyny, and violence stereotypically associated with Black male sexuality, 2 Live Crew represents a postmodern effort to 'liberate' us from the racism that perpetuates these stereotypes."

Professor Gates's defense has a kernel of truth—2 Live Crew were probably trying to be funny—but is no more persuasive than earlier efforts to defend the racist humor of Andrew Dice Clay as an effort to poke fun at racism. "The claim that a representation is meant simply as a joke may be true, but the joke functions as humor within a specific social context in which it frequently reinforces patterns of social power. Though racial humor may sometimes be intended to ridicule racism, the close relationship between the stereotypes and the prevailing images of marginalized people complicates this strategy. And certainly, the humorist's positioning vis-à-vis a targeted group colors how the group interprets a potentially derisive stereotype or gesture. Although one could argue that Black comedians have broader license to market stereotypically racist images, that argument has no force here. 2 Live Crew cannot claim an in-group privilege to perpetuate misogynist humor against Black women: the members of 2 Live Crew are not Black women, and more importantly, they enjoy a power relationship over them."

NOTE ON INCOHERENCE IN THE PUBLIC-PRIVATE DISTINCTION FOR SEXUAL EXPRESSION

Section 35–45–4–1 of the Indiana Code prohibits nudity in a public place and defines "nudity" to include wearing less than a G-string, not covering female breast nipples with "pasties," or showing male genitals "in a discernibly turgid state." This statute was the basis for prosecution of the Kitty Kat Lounge, where female go-go dancers took off all their clothes, and Glen Theatre, an adult bookstore offering booths where patrons could watch female strippers through glass windows. Defendants claimed that erotic dance, including nudity, involved "expressive conduct" protected by the First Amendment. The Seventh Circuit agreed. *Miller v. Civil City of South Bend*, 904 F.2d 1081 (1990) (en banc). Judge Posner wrote a concurring opinion containing a learned discussion of erotic art and dancing. *Id.* at 1089–1104.

In *Barnes v. Glen Theatre, Inc.,* 501 U.S. 560 (1991), the Supreme Court reversed the Seventh Circuit. As described in the excerpt that follows, there was no majority for a standard of review or a single rationale for upholding the statute.

David Cole, "Playing By Pornography's Rules: The Regulation of Sexual Expression"

143 *University of Pennsylvania Law Review* 111, 143–50, 176–77 (1994).*

The most recent example of the Court's sanctioning of public/private policing is *Barnes v. Glen Theatre, Inc.*, in which the Court upheld an Indiana "public nudity" statute that required nude dancers to wear pasties and a G-string. This case is about nothing but the public/private line; as Justice Scalia noted, "Indiana bans nudity in public places, but not within the privacy of the home." The Court's judgment in *Barnes* rested tenuously on three separate opinions * * *. Virtually the only point of agreement [among] the five Justices who made up the majority was that Indiana's law was unrelated to the suppression of expression. Reaching this conclusion was necessary to uphold the statute because the Court had previously recognized nude dancing as expressive conduct, and had recently reaffirmed that where regulation of expressive conduct is related to its communicative aspects, it violates the First Amendment absent a compelling state interest. But the conclusion is highly dubious.

[Chief Justice] Rehnquist and [Justice] Scalia reasoned that the state's interest in regulating public nudity was unrelated to expression because the state sought to protect "societal order and morality." Neither Justice explained, however, *how* public nudity harms public morality other than by virtue of what it expresses. Scalia insisted that the ban was unrelated to expression because it "generally" prohibited public nudity, irrespective of its message. But Scalia's use of "generally" is question-begging. The Indiana law does not "generally" prohibit all nudity, but singles out *public* nudity, that is, nudity communicated to others in public.

Ordinarily, where government selectively regulates public but not private conduct or expression, there is reason to suspect that the government is attempting to suppress the message communicated to the public, and strict scrutiny is triggered. * * *

Justice Souter's rationale for finding the Indiana law "unrelated to the suppression of expression" is no less strained. He reasoned that because Indiana might have determined that forbidding nude barroom dancing would further its "interest in preventing prostitution, sexual assault, and associated crimes," the public nudity law should be viewed as directed at those secondary effects, and not at nude dancing's expressive elements. In order to reach this result, Souter had to clear several hurdles.

First, there was no indication that Indiana actually sought to further these interests. Second, there was no basis for believing that the secondary effects Justice Souter identified as flowing from nude dancers would be mitigated by pasties and a G-string. If bars featuring nude dancing attract "prostitution, sexual assault, and associated crime," it is difficult to see why bars featuring nude dancing under a pasties-and-G-string regime would not. Third, the public nudity law on its face extended beyond nude barroom dancing, reaching instances of public nudity—such as skinny-dipping, nude sunbathing, and "streaking"—with no connection to the secondary effects Souter posited as the law's justification. * * * In essence, the Justices upheld different laws. The nude dancing law Souter upheld would fail under Rehnquist and Scalia's analysis, which was predicated on the law generally banning all public nudity. And the law that Rehnquist and Scalia upheld would have failed Justice Souter's test, because Indiana could not possibly demonstrate secondary effects with respect to *all* public nudity. * * *

Left unstated is *how* requiring otherwise nude dancers to don pasties and G-strings will uphold the morals of the community. The moral difference between an entirely nude dancer and a dancer wearing pasties and a G-string is not immediately apparent. But the pasties and G-string do serve an important symbolic function: they insist that the law is present in this public space, very literally enforcing a line, albeit a very fine one. The thinness of the line is ultimately less important than the fact that the line exists. The statute regulates the public sphere precisely by demanding that dancers keep their "private parts" private, but only in the most minimal sense. Thus, the pasties and G-string are an apt metaphor for the regulation of sexual expression: they symbolically police the public sphere by barring certain "private" topics from surfacing, even as they permit (and possibly even increase the desirability of) *regulated* sexual expression in the public sphere. They reflect society's compromise on sexual expression: such expression may remain relatively free in the private sphere, but its public expression, although far from forbidden altogether, must be subject to legal regulation. The Court has in turn sanctioned that compromise, but in order to do so it has had to invert the First Amendment. * * *

Postscript. In *City of Erie, et al. v. Pap's A.M. tdba "Kandyland,"* 529 U.S. 277 (2000), five Justices agreed that "governmental restrictions on public nudity * * * should be evaluated under the framework set forth in [*United States v. O'Brien*, 391 U.S. 367 (1968)] for content-neutral restrictions on symbolic speech." Under *O'Brien*, the state interest behind a law prohibiting expressive conduct must be unrelated to the suppression of speech and must prohibit no more speech than is necessary to further that interest.

C. PUBLIC FUNDING AND SEXUAL SPEECH

When government creates a forum in which individuals and other entities may speak, it is almost always prohibited from favoring or disfavoring speakers based on the viewpoint being expressed. When government expresses its own views, however, it is not required to give equal time to all perspectives. Consider whether it is possible for there to be an "official" version of scientific and normative principles related to sexuality. This in turn raises the question of whether the First Amendment places limits on which messages the state may promote. We assume that it is acceptable for the government to condemn communism. The Supreme Court has also ruled that states may take positions in favor of childbirth and against abortion. See Section 1A, *supra.* May it also disfavor homosexuality? For examination of this question in the context of public schools, see Chapter 8, Section 3.

In some instances, the Establishment Clause of the First Amendment performs a free expression function. In 1981, Congress enacted the Adolescent Family Life Act (AFLA), which provided funds for pilot projects designed to promote "self discipline and other prudent approaches to the problem of adolescent premarital sexual relations," in part through education and counseling services. Religious groups were eligible to apply, and several received grants. The ACLU challenged the statute on the ground that direct federal funding of religious entities to conduct programs on the topic of premarital sexual relations virtually invited a violation of the Establishment Clause.

In **Bowen v. Kendrick**, **487 U.S. 589 (1988)**, the Supreme Court upheld the AFLA as constitutional on its face and remanded for further evidence as to how it was applied. (The Department of Health and Human Services had not renewed grants for the most flagrantly sectarian programs after the lawsuit was initiated.) **Chief Justice Rehnquist**, writing for the Court, rejected the facial challenge on the ground that "we do not think the possibility that AFLA grants may go to religious institutions that can be considered 'pervasively sectarian' is sufficient to conclude that no grants whatsoever can be given under the statute to religious organizations. * * * [T]he possibility or even the likelihood that some of the religious institutions who receive AFLA funding will agree with the message that Congress intended to deliver to adolescents through the AFLA is insufficient to warrant a finding that the statute on its face has the primary effect of advancing religion." *Id.* at 612. On the as applied claim, the Court ruled that "although there is no dispute that the record contains evidence of specific incidents of impermissible behavior by AFLA grantees, we feel that this lawsuit should be remanded to the District Court for consideration of the evidence presented by appellees insofar as it sheds light on the manner in which the statute is presently being administered." *Id.* at 620–21.

The 1980s and early 1990s were filled with battles over sexualized speech that had some measure of government financial support. Opponents of such speech characterized it loosely as "pornography," a handy term since in the public mind that category often blurred into obscenity, even though the former had no defined legal meaning, while the latter existed outside the bounds of First Amendment protection.

Drawing on the line between public and private realms that justified the denial of Medicaid funds for poor women's abortions in *Harris v. McRae*, Section 1A *supra*, the Court in **Rust v. Sullivan**, **500 U.S. 173 (1991)**, upheld regulations that prohibited federally-funded family planning clinics from engaging in activities that "encourage, promote or advocate abortion." Doctors employed by the clinics sought to preserve the ability to discuss abortion with their patients. The Court held that the regulations were a permissible implementation of the statutory provision (Title X of the Public Health Service Act) that prohibited funding "programs where abortion is a method of family planning." The Court reasoned that

> The challenged regulations * * * are designed to ensure that the limits of the federal program are observed. [Similarly, a] doctor who wished to offer prenatal care to a project patient who became pregnant could properly be prohibited from doing so because such service is outside the scope of the federally funded program. * * * This is not a case of the Government "suppressing a dangers idea," but of a prohibition on a project grantee or its employees from engaging in activities outside of its scope.

The question of viewpoint suppression in the context of government-funded health education programs arose with a vengeance in the context of HIV/AIDS.

Nan D. Hunter, "Identity, Speech and Equality"
79 *Va. L. Rev.* 1695, 1706, 1710–14 (1993).

* * * With the advent of the HIV epidemic in the early 1980s, gay male sexuality became a topic of widespread political discussion and debate. Although legal and social reaction ostensibly focused on the disease, the disease itself was so closely associated with gay men in the first years of the epidemic that much of the reaction seemed a euphemism for opinions of male homosexuality.

In a narrow sense, most of the case law generated by and about HIV falls outside the category of gay rights law. * * * But in a broader and deeper sense, courts, Congress and state legislatures had begun a fight over which new social understanding about homosexuality would supersede silence. At issue was the question of what information would comprise public knowledge, and how the government would define and enforce the boundaries of public discourse. * * *

In 1985, the CDC began funding educational programs aimed at behavior change, which included support for some innovative programs undertaken by the Gay Men's Health Crisis ("GMHC"), a New York City group that provides education and other services to people infected with HIV. GMHC and other AIDS service organizations had always used private funds to develop their most provocative materials, which sought to eroticize condom use and other safe-sex practices. Officials at CDC became alarmed, however, by the potential for conservative backlash against the agency for supporting a gay organization engaged in controversial work. In January 1986, the CDC first promulgated restrictions on the content of federally funded programs, requiring that all such materials must use language that "would be judged by a reasonable person to be unoffensive to most educated adults." In 1987, this issue reached Congress. In October, Senator Jesse Helms introduced an amendment to the appropriations bill for the Department of Health and Human Services that forbade use of any CDC funds "to provide AIDS education, information, or prevention materials and activities that promote or encourage, directly or indirectly, homosexual sexual activities" * * * Opponents succeeded only in deleting the term "indirectly," thus arguably limiting its scope to the most graphic materials. * * *The debate on adoption of the Helms Amendment centered on objections raised by Senator Helms to AIDS education efforts within the gay male community, specifically those of the GMHC. Senator Helms made clear, repeatedly, that his objections were based on his views of what was moral and that the purpose of his amendment was to insure that the content of AIDS education be made to conform to what he believed to be moral precepts of behavior, which for him meant absolute opposition to homosexuality or any tolerance for it.

Senator Helms paraphrased the GMHC proposal, noting that AIDS education sessions (all of which were specifically targeted for gay male participants) included discussions of "a positive sense of gay pride." He continued:

> Then . . . we get to session 5 and session 6. . . . This is entitled "Guidelines for Healthy Sex." . . . The behavioral objectives of these two sessions included the ability to "list satisfying, erotic alternatives to high-risk sexual practices; identify erogenous areas of the body,"—and here is here [sic] I get embarrassed—"other than the genitals, that produce an erotic response."
>
> Oh boy * * *
>
> There is no mention of any moral code * * * I may throw up.

Senator Helms reiterated throughout the debate his intent that the amendment was designed to forbid publicly funded AIDS education materials from advocacy of homosexuality: "Yes, it will require us to make a moral judgment. I think it is about time we started making some moral judgments and stop playing around with all those esoteric things and saying 'Yes but.' I believe, * * * it is time to draw the line." * * *

In *Gay Men's Health Crisis et al. v. Dr. Louis Sullivan*, 792 F. Supp. 278 (S.D.N.Y. 1992), plaintiff challenged the following requirements for federal funding of HIV/AIDS prevention materials:

> Written materials, audiovisual materials, and pictorials should not include terms, descriptors, or displays which will be offensive to a majority of the intended audience or to a majority of adults outside the intended audience unless, in the judgment of the Program Review Panel [PRP], the potential offensiveness of such materials is outweighed by the potential effectiveness in communicating an important HIV prevention message. 55 *Fed.Reg.* 23414 (June 7, 1990).

Judge Shirley Kram found this provision void for vagueness: "[P]laintiffs are correct when they assert that the Revised Grant Terms provide no way of answering questions such as: Can educational material be offensive simply because it mentions homosexuality? Because it depicts an interracial couple? Can a proposed AIDS education project be offensive because it traps a captive audience, such as subway riders, and forces them to look at a condom? Does offensive apply to all descriptions of sexual behavior, graphic depictions of sexual behavior, or descriptions of unusual sexual behavior?" (The Department of Justice did not appeal Judge Kram's decision.)

The last of the 1990s public funding of sexual speech cases involved four artists, who were selected for National Endowment for the Arts grants that were later rescinded by the NEA Director. The "NEA 4" challenged the statute directing the agency to consider "general standards of decency and respect for the diverse beliefs and values of the American public" in its deliberations over which applications to fund. The Supreme Court upheld the provision, ruling that it did not constitute viewpoint discrimination. *National Endowment for the Arts v. Finley*, **524 U.S. 569 (1998). Justice O'Connor**'s opinion for the Court accepted the NEA's argument that the provision was "merely hortatory" and found that "the provision does not introduce considerations that, in practice, would effectively preclude or punish the expression of particular views. * * * [I]t seems unlikely that this provision will introduce any greater element of selectivity than the determination of 'artistic excellence' itself." **Justice Scalia** concurred in the result, but wrote that the Court had sustained the statute "by gutting it. * * * By its terms, it establishes content-and viewpoint-based criteria upon which grant applications are to be evaluated. And that is perfectly constitutional." The government, he wrote, may allocate competitive funding as it sees fit; such decisions do not "abridge" free speech. **Justice Souter** dissented alone. He agreed with Justice Scalia that the provision amounted to viewpoint discrimination, and found that its legislative history demonstrated that Congress's purpose "was to prevent the funding of art that conveys an offensive message. * * * [A] statute that mandates the consideration of viewpoint [when government decides whether to fund private speech] is quite obviously unconstitutional."

PROBLEM 1-6
DECONSTRUCTING "PUBLIC" "SEX"

In Chapter 3, Section 3, *infra*, you will consider the intersection of gender and sexuality law with deconstructionist theory. Consider how that approach might apply to the category of cases involving the use of public funds to support sexualized speech, whether in health programs or arts funding. In almost all these decisions, courts upheld restrictions, finding no viewpoint bias. In what ways might this reasoning have been influenced *sub silentio* by the context of sexuality? Recall that in the *NGTF v. Board of Education* case at the beginning of this part, a statute defined "public sexual conduct" to include sexual speech (in the context of public schools). Can you deconstruct the proposition that public money can transform speech into public sex?

D. IDENTITY SPEECH AND EXPRESSIVE ASSOCIATION

Identity can be constituted as much by what one is *not* as by what one *is*. The duality of identity formation often finds its way into the public arena, as when one group wants to self-identify in a context in which the perceived self-identity of another group is threatened. When a group believes that exclusion of another group is central to its own coherency, norms of expression and anti-discrimination clash.

John Hurley v. Irish-American Gay, Lesbian, and Bisexual Group of Boston

United States Supreme Court, 1995.
515 U.S. 557, 115 S.Ct. 2338, 132 L.Ed.2d 487.

■ JUSTICE SOUTER delivered the opinion of the Court.

[Since 1947, the South Boston Allied War Veterans Council, a private group, has been granted authority by the City of Boston to organize the annual St. Patrick's Day Parade, an event of special significance to people of Irish ancestry. Every year the Council has applied for and been granted a permit for the parade. In 1992, a court ordered the Council to include the Irish-American Gay, Lesbian, and Bisexual Group of Boston (GLIB), the respondents. In 1993, GLIB sued the Council for violating the state law which prohibits discrimination on account of sexual orientation (*inter alia*) in the admission of individuals to a place of public accommodation. The state courts interpreted the public accommodations law to require that GLIB be included and overruled the Council's claim that such an interpretation violated the First Amendment. The Supreme Court reversed.]

If there were no reason for a group of people to march from here to there except to reach a destination, they could make the trip without expressing any message beyond the fact of the march itself. Some people might call such a procession a parade, but it would not be much of one. Real "[p]arades are public dramas of social relations, and in them performers define who can be a social actor and what subjects and ideas are available for communication and consideration." S. Davis, *Parades and Power: Street Theatre in Nineteenth-Century Philadelphia* 6 (1986). Hence, we use the word "parade" to indicate marchers who are making some sort of collective point, not just to each other but to bystanders along the way. Indeed a parade's dependence on watchers is so extreme that nowadays, as with Bishop Berkeley's celebrated tree, "if a parade or demonstration receives no media coverage, it may as well not have happened." *Id.*, at 171. Parades are thus a form of expression, not just motion, and the inherent expressiveness of marching to make a point explains our cases involving protest marches. In *Gregory v. Chicago*, 394 U.S. 111, 112 (1969), for example, petitioners had taken part in a procession to express their grievances to the city government, and we held that such a "march, if peaceful and orderly, falls well within the sphere of conduct protected by the First Amendment." Similarly, in *Edwards v. South Carolina*, 372 U.S. 229 (1963), where petitioners had joined in a march of protest and pride, carrying placards and singing The Star Spangled Banner, we held that the activities "reflect an exercise of these basic constitutional rights in their most pristine and classic form."

The protected expression that inheres in a parade is not limited to its banners and songs, however, for the Constitution looks beyond written or spoken words as mediums of expression. Noting that "symbolism is a primitive but effective way of communicating ideas," *West Virginia Bd. of Ed. v. Barnette*, 319 U.S. 624, 632 (1943), our cases have recognized that the First Amendment shields such acts as saluting a flag (and refusing to do so), wearing an arm band to protest a war, *Tinker v. Des Moines Independent Community School Dist.*, 393 U.S. 503, 505–506 (1969), displaying a red flag, *Stromberg v. California*, 283 U.S. 359, 369 (1931), and even "[m]arching, walking or parading" in uniforms displaying the swastika, *National Socialist Party of America v. Skokie*, 432 U.S. 43 (1977). As some of these examples show, a narrow, succinctly articulable message is not a condition of constitutional protection, which if confined to expressions conveying a "particularized message," would never reach the unquestionably shielded painting of Jackson Pollock, music of Arnold Schönberg, or Jabberwocky verse of Lewis Carroll.

Not many marches, then, are beyond the realm of expressive parades, and the South Boston celebration is not one of them. [W]e agree with the state courts that in spite of excluding some applicants, the Council is rather lenient in admitting participants. But a private speaker does not forfeit constitutional protection simply by combining multifarious voices, or by failing to edit their themes to isolate an exact message as the exclusive subject matter of the speech. Nor, under our precedent, does First Amendment protection require a speaker to generate, as an original matter, each item featured in the communication. * * *

Respondents' participation as a unit in the parade was equally expressive. GLIB was formed for the very purpose of marching in it, as the trial court found, in order to celebrate its members' identity as openly gay, lesbian, and bisexual descendants of the Irish immigrants, to show that there are such individuals in the community, and to support the like men and women who sought to march in the New York parade. * * * GLIB understandably seeks to communicate its ideas as part of the existing parade, rather than staging one of its own. * * *

* * * The petitioners disclaim any intent to exclude homosexuals as such, and no individual member of GLIB claims to have been excluded from parading as a member of any group that the Council has approved to march. Instead, the disagreement goes to the admission of GLIB as its own parade unit carrying its own banner. Since every participating unit affects the message conveyed by the private organizers, the state courts' application of the statute produced an order essentially requiring petitioners to alter the expressive content of their parade. Although the state courts spoke of the parade as a place of public accommodation, once the expressive character of both the parade and the marching GLIB contingent is understood, it becomes apparent that the state courts' application of the statute had the effect of declaring the sponsors' speech itself to be the public accommodation. Under this approach any contingent of protected individuals with a message would have the right to participate in petitioners' speech, so that the communication produced

by the private organizers would be shaped by all those protected by the law who wished to join in with some expressive demonstration of their own. But this use of the State's power violates the fundamental rule of protection under the First Amendment, that a speaker has the autonomy to choose the content of his own message. * * *

Petitioners' claim to the benefit of this principle of autonomy to control one's own speech is as sound as the South Boston parade is expressive. Rather like a composer, the Council selects the expressive units of the parade from potential participants, and though the score may not produce a particularized message, each contingent's expression in the Council's eyes comports with what merits celebration on that day. Even if this view gives the Council credit for a more considered judgment than it actively made, the Council clearly decided to exclude a message it did not like from the communication it chose to make, and that is enough to invoke its right as a private speaker to shape its expression by speaking on one subject while remaining silent on another. The message it disfavored is not difficult to identify. Although GLIB's point (like the Council's) is not wholly articulate, a contingent marching behind the organization's banner would at least bear witness to the fact that some Irish are gay, lesbian, or bisexual, and the presence of the organized marchers would suggest their view that people of their sexual orientations have as much claim to unqualified social acceptance as heterosexuals and indeed as members of parade units organized around other identifying characteristics. The parade's organizers may not believe these facts about Irish sexuality to be so, or they may object to unqualified social acceptance of gays and lesbians or have some other reason for wishing to keep GLIB's message out of the parade. But whatever the reason, it boils down to the choice of a speaker not to propound a particular point of view, and that choice is presumed to lie beyond the government's power to control. * * *

It might, of course, have been argued that a broader objective is apparent: that the ultimate point of forbidding acts of discrimination toward certain classes is to produce a society free of the corresponding biases. Requiring access to a speaker's message would thus be not an end in itself, but a means to produce speakers free of the biases, whose expressive conduct would be at least neutral toward the particular classes, obviating any future need for correction. But if this indeed is the point of applying the state law to expressive conduct, it is a decidedly fatal objective. Having availed itself of the public thoroughfares "for purposes of assembly [and] communicating thoughts between citizens," the Council is engaged in a use of the streets that has "from ancient times, been a part of the privileges, immunities, rights, and liberties of citizens." *Hague v. Committee for Industrial Organization*, 307 U.S. 496, 515 (1939) (opinion of Roberts, J.). Our tradition of free speech commands that a speaker who takes to the street corner to express his views in this way should be free from interference by the State based on the content of what he says. See, e.g., *Police Department of Chicago v. Mosley*, 408 U.S. 92, 95 (1972); cf. H. Kalven, Jr., *A Worthy Tradition* 6–19 (1988); O. Fiss, "Free Speech and Social Structure," 71 *Iowa L. Rev.* 1405, 1408–1409 (1986). The very idea that a noncommercial speech restriction be used to produce thoughts and statements acceptable to some groups or, indeed, all people, grates on the First Amendment, for it amounts to nothing less than a proposal to limit speech in the service of orthodox expression. The Speech Clause has no more certain antithesis. While the law is free to promote all sorts of conduct in place of harmful behavior, it is not free to interfere with speech for no better reason than promoting an approved message or discouraging a disfavored one, however enlightened either purpose may strike the government. * * *

NOTES ON THE BOSTON PARADE CASE

1. *State Action.* GLIB had challenged the exclusions of gays on the basis of the First Amendment as well as the state public accommodations law. They lost their initial claim on the ground that the First Amendment (like the other individual rights protections of the Constitution) applies only to "state action" and there was no "state actor" in this case (the Veterans Council being a private group). GLIB did not appeal this issue, and it was not before the Supreme Court.

Seeking to expand the scope of state action was one possible response. On the one hand, many state courts have interpreted free speech provisions in state constitutions to be applicable to large-scale private as well as public actors, on the ground that institutions such as shopping centers, *e.g.*, *Robins v. Pruneyard Shopping Center*, 23 Cal.3d 899, 153 Cal.Rptr. 854, 592 P.2d 341 (1979), *aff'd*, 447 U.S. 74 (1980), universities, *e.g.*, *State v. Schmid*, 84 N.J. 535, 423 A.2d 615 (1980), appeal dismissed, 455 U.S. 100 (1982), and train stations, *e.g.*, *In re Hoffman*, 67 Cal.2d 845, 64 Cal.Rptr. 97, 434 P.2d 353 (1967), exercise the functional equivalent of public power. Compare *Amalgamated Food Employees Local 590 v. Logan Valley Plaza, Inc.*, 391 U.S. 308 (1968) (similar analysis under the First Amendment), overruled by *Lloyd Corp. v. Tanner*, 407 U.S. 551 (1972). GLIB could have made a similar pitch under the Massachusetts Constitution.

Even under federal constitutional law, a private actor may be deemed a state actor when "conspiring" with a state official, *e.g.*, *Lugar v. Edmondson Oil Co.*, 457 U.S. 922 (1982), or when delegated to perform state functions, *e.g.*, *Flagg Brothers, Inc. v. Brooks*, 436 U.S. 149 (1978) (dictum), or when closely intermingled with the state, *e.g.*, *Burton v. Wilmington Parking Auth.*, 365 U.S. 715 (1961). The Court in *Edmonson v. Leesville Concrete Co.*, 500 U.S. 614 (1991), said that "in determining whether a particular action or course of conduct is governmental in character, it is relevant to examine * * * the extent to which the actor relies on government assistance and benefits; whether the actor is performing a traditional governmental function; and whether the injury caused is aggravated in a unique way by the incidents of governmental authority." What arguments did GLIB have for the proposition that the Veterans Council was so intermingled with the City that its parade could be treated as a "public" event?

Note how the dynamics of the litigation changes if GLIB is able to tag the Veterans Council as a state actor. The Council would then be in a dilemma: if it claims the parade is an expressive event, it violates the First Amendment by excluding lesbian, gay, and bisexual speakers; but if it doesn't claim expressiveness, it has no defense to the public accommodations law.

2. *The Reach of Public Accommodations Laws.* The Massachusetts anti-discrimination law defines "public accommodation" as "any place * * * which is open to and accepts or solicits the patronage of the general public and, without limiting the generality of this definition, whether or not it be * * * (6) a boardwalk or other public highway [or] (8) a place of public amusement, recreation, sport, exercise or entertainment." Is a parade a public accommodation under this law? Should it be? (This was an issue of state law, and Justice Souter's opinion accepted as settled the Massachusetts Supreme Judicial Court's decision that a parade did fall within this statute.) The large majority of states and cities have statutes prohibiting discrimination by public accommodations. The anti-discrimination statutes of 21 states plus the District of Columbia prohibit discrimination by public accommodations on the basis of sexual orientation: California (initially as an interpretation of the Unruh Act, then by statute enacted in 2001); Colorado (2007); Connecticut (1991); Delaware (2009); the District of Columbia (regulation adopted 1973, statute 1977); Hawaii (limited scope, 1991); Illinois (2005); Iowa (2007); Maine (2005); Maryland (2001); Massachusetts (1989); Minnesota (1991); New Hampshire (1997); New Jersey (1991, the statute applied in *Dale, infra*); New Mexico (2003); New York (2003); Oregon (2008); Rhode Island (1995); Vermont (1991); Washington (2006) and Wisconsin (1982). Dozens and probably hundreds of cities have similar prohibitions against public accommodation discrimination based on sexual orientation, including Baltimore (ordinance adopted 1988), Boston (1984), Chicago (1988), Cleveland (1984), Detroit (1979), Denver (1990), Los Angeles (1979), New Orleans (1991), New York City (1986), Philadelphia (1982), Portland (1991), St. Louis (1992), San Diego (1990), and San Francisco (1978). Most of the statutes and ordinances define "public accommodation" broadly, and this breadth has generated not only questions of statutory interpretation, but also constitutional problems.

3. *The Identity-Speech Dichotomy.* Viewed sympathetically, the Council contended that it excluded GLIB because of its expression. GLIB contended that it was excluded because of its members' sexual orientation. The state trial court found that GLIB was "excluded because of its values and its message, *i.e.*, its members' sexual orientation." Appendix to Petition for Cert., at B4 n.5. It is not so easy to distinguish these two factors, because for gay people they are interconnected. Unlike race and sex, sexual orientation is ordinarily an invisible characteristic. If women march in this parade, they are conveying a message (women are Irish and proud of it!) by their very presence. Lesbians and gay men can only be known by more explicit signals.

For them to participate in a parade in the same way that women participate, they need some device to uncloset themselves.

Consider these complexities. The Council maintained that it was happy to have gay people participate, just not as a group. (Don't ask, don't tell!) Say the Council said the same thing to women—we shall let you march only in groups with men, and not as your own group. Could the state constitutionally prohibit this? At oral argument, GLIB's attorney noted that GLIB was not asking to carry pro-homosexual signs (therefore nothing like "Gay Is Good"); it was only asking to be included as a self-identified group, and the only signs it was asking to carry were signs identifying the group. GLIB was even willing to abandon its signs if the Council adopted a general ban on signs. Does this undermine Justice Souter's effort to create a gulf between expression and identity?

In the final question at oral argument, Justice Breyer asked the Council's attorney whether he thought GLIB's goal was identity or speech. Chester Darling, the attorney for the Council, exclaimed that it was "self-proclamation," expression, self-identity. Justice Breyer sighed wearily.

The distinction is treacherous in part because the strongest protections against governmental intrusion into speech rights attaches when state action targets particular viewpoints, an issue that often arises in the context of a particular venue for expression.

In a series of cases, the Supreme Court has addressed the question of whether the government may favor or disfavor certain speech when acting in its capacity of either creating a forum for others to speak or providing funding for private speech. (By contrast, when the government itself speaks or funds others to disseminate a message on behalf of the government, it is free to endorse one viewpoint or another; it does not have to maintain neutrality on, for example, whether terrorism is good or bad.) In *Rosenberger v. Rector and Visitors of the Univ. of Virginia*, **515 U.S. 819, 115 S.Ct. 2510, 132 L.Ed.2d 700 (1995),** a public university refused to authorize disbursements from its Student Activities Fund (SAF) to finance the printing of an evangelistic Christian student newspaper ["Wide Awake"]. The refusal was based on a university guideline that prohibited funding for activities that "primarily promote or manifest a particular belief in or about a deity." **Justice Kennedy**'s opinion for the Court held that by subsidizing the SAF, the University had created a *limited public forum*. When an arm of the state creates such a forum, it may impose restrictions on the content of speech allowed, so long as they are reasonably designed to preserve the limited subject matter of the forum. "[O]n the other hand, viewpoint discrimination, * * * is presumed impermissible when directed against speech otherwise within the forum's limitations. * * *

"[I]t must be acknowledged, the distinction is not a precise one. It is, in a sense, something of an understatement to speak of religious thought and discussion as just a viewpoint, as distinct from a comprehensive body of thought. The nature of our origins and destiny and their dependence upon the existence of a divine being have been subjects of philosophic inquiry throughout human history. We conclude, nonetheless, that here, * * * viewpoint discrimination is the proper way to interpret the University's objections to Wide Awake. By the very terms of the SAF prohibition, the University does not exclude religion as a subject matter but selects for disfavored treatment those student journalistic efforts with religious editorial viewpoints. Religion may be a vast area of inquiry, but it also provides, as it did here, a specific premise, a perspective, a standpoint from which a variety of subjects may be discussed and considered. The prohibited perspective, not the general subject matter, resulted in the refusal to make third-party payments, for the subjects discussed were otherwise within the approved category of publications. * * *

Justice Kennedy acknowledged that "we have recognized special Establishment Clause dangers where the government makes direct money payments to sectarian institutions," but held that payment of printing costs for Wide Awake would not run afoul of that principle. "The University provides printing services to a broad spectrum of student newspapers * * *. Any benefit to religion is incidental to the government's provision of secular services for secular purposes on a religion-neutral basis. Printing is a routine, secular, and recurring attribute of student life."

Justice O'Connor provided the decisive fifth vote for the majority. She conditioned her finding in favor of Wide Awake on several facts: that all student organizations operated independently of the university; that the procedures for reimbursement insured that funds would be paid directly to third-party vendors; and that the context "makes improbable any perception of government endorsement of the religious message."

Justice Souter, writing in dissent for himself and **Justices Stevens, Ginsburg and Breyer**, accused the majority of a category error: the confusion of an appropriate content limitation, necessitated by the prohibitions of the Establishment Clause, with viewpoint discrimination. Here, Justice Souter argued, "the regulation is being applied, not to deny funding for those who discuss issues in general from a religious viewpoint, but to those engaged in promoting or opposing religious conversion and religious observances as such. If this amounts to viewpoint discrimination, the Court has all but eviscerated the line between viewpoint and content."

4.   *Anti-Gay Speech as a Protected Viewpoint.* Much of the normative luster of the First Amendment is its function as a guardian of unpopular speech. As public opinion shifted to be more supportive of equal rights for LGBT persons and politicians in some jurisdictions sought to appeal to LGBT voters, social conservatives became the minority voices in some contexts. This issue becomes more important with the increasing tension between religious liberty and equality claims, and we explore it in depth in Chapter 4. Consider the highly practical and frequently recurring issue of student attire in public schools. Can a school allow wearing of T-shirts that say "gay is good" without allowing T-shirts saying "gay is sinful"? What if a T-shirt displays only the citation to a Bible verse without quoting it (e.g., Romans 1:27)? Must there be equal rules for displays of support and opposition to ideas of "diversity" and "tolerance"? For an examination of how the institutional context of public schools affects expressive rights, see Chapter 8.

NOTE ON EXPRESSIVE ASSOCIATION

Although the First Amendment does not explicitly protect rights of association, the Supreme Court held such rights protected by implication in *NAACP v. Alabama*, 357 U.S. 449 (1958). Justice Harlan's opinion reasoned that associational rights are prerequisites for rights to speak and publish that are explicitly protected. The Court disallowed a state's effort to obtain NAACP membership lists, because the disclosure of membership by an unpopular group would surely chill entry into the group. That sort of reasoning was just as applicable to homophile groups that had formed in the 1950s, particularly the Daughters of Bilitis and the Mattachine Society. Not only did the homophile groups promise to keep their membership hidden from the authorities, but many and perhaps most members of the group were also disinclined to reveal their real names and identities to the group itself! Hence, even though *NAACP v. Alabama* did not involve lesbian and gay plaintiffs, its holding was critically important for homophile groups.

More recent cases have confirmed and broadened the associational feature of the First Amendment recognized in *NAACP*. "[T]he Court has recognized a right to associate for the purpose of engaging in those activities protected by the First Amendment—speech, assembly, petition for the redress of grievances, and the exercise of religion. The Constitution guarantees freedom of association of this kind as an indispensable means of preserving other individual liberties." *Roberts v. United States Jaycees*, 468 U.S. 609, 618 (1984). Under what circumstances, if any, can the state limit people's rights of association? Consider the following cases.

Kathryn Roberts v. United States Jaycees, 468 U.S. 609, 104 S.Ct. 3244, 82 L.Ed.2d 462 (1984). The Minnesota Human Rights Act, as amended in 1973, made it illegal for a "public accommodation" to "deny any person the full and equal enjoyment of the goods, services, facilities, privileges, advantages, and accommodations * * * because of race, color, creed, religion, disability, national origin or sex." The national Jaycees, a network of all-male civic clubs, disciplined its Minnesota chapters for admitting women pursuant to the state law, and the state courts held the national chapter in violation of the law. The Jaycees challenged the statute, as construed, on the ground that it violated the right of association in the First Amendment. The Supreme Court affirmed.

Justice Brennan's opinion for the Court recognized that "certain kinds of personal bonds have played a critical role in the culture and traditions of the Nation by cultivating and transmitting shared ideals and beliefs; they thereby foster diversity and act as critical buffers between the individual and the power of the State. * * * Protecting these relationships from unwarranted state interference therefore safeguards the ability independently to define one's identity that is critical to any concept of liberty." The core protection of this feature of the right of association is the family, "distinguished by such attributes as relative smallness, a high degree of selectivity in decisions to begin and maintain the affiliation, and seclusion from others in critical aspects of the relationship. * * * Conversely, an association lacking these qualities—such as a large business enterprise—seems remote from the concerns giving rise to the constitutional protection."

According to findings of fact in the record, the Jaycees were large and sprawling, relatively unselective in choosing members (essentially accepting everyone except women and a few other minorities), and casual in member interaction. Even when associational interests were stronger, infringements can be justified by "regulations adopted to serve compelling state interests, unrelated to the suppression of ideas, that cannot be achieved through means significantly less restrictive of associational freedoms." Justice Brennan found that for Minnesota, a "compelling interest in eradicating discrimination against its female citizens justifies the impact that application of the statute to the Jaycees may have on the male members' associational freedoms." He found it important that the statute did not discriminate "on the basis of viewpoint" and was not administered arbitrarily.

There was no dissent, but **Justice O'Connor** wrote an opinion concurring only in the Court's judgment. **(Justice Rehnquist** concurred in the Court's judgment, but without stating his reasons.) She maintained that the majority's approach swept too broadly, threatening traditionalist associations for which some discrimination was important for the group's functioning—including the example of the Girl Scouts. Nonetheless, she agreed with the Court that the anti-discrimination law could be constitutionally applied to the Jaycees—but because they were more like a commercial business than a truly private organization. Her concurring opinion suggested that the more like a business the institution is, the less inclined courts should be to recognize First Amendment defenses against anti-discrimination laws.

Boy Scouts of America et al. v. James Dale

United States Supreme Court, 2000.
530 U.S. 640, 120 S.Ct. 2446, 147 L.Ed.2d 554.

■ CHIEF JUSTICE REHNQUIST delivered the opinion of the Court.

Petitioners are the Boy Scouts of America and the Monmouth Council, a division of the Boy Scouts of America (collectively, Boy Scouts). The Boy Scouts is a private, not for profit organization engaged in instilling its system of values in young people. The Boy Scouts asserts that homosexual conduct is inconsistent with the values it seeks to instill. Respondent is James Dale, a former Eagle Scout whose adult membership in the Boy Scouts was revoked when the Boy Scouts learned that he is an avowed homosexual and gay rights activist. The New Jersey Supreme Court held that New Jersey's public accommodations law requires that the Boy Scouts admit Dale. This case presents the question whether applying New Jersey's public accommodations law in this way violates the Boy Scouts' First Amendment right of expressive association. We hold that it does. * * *

In *Roberts v. United States Jaycees*, we observed that "implicit in the right to engage in activities protected by the First Amendment" is "a corresponding right to associate with others in pursuit of a wide variety of political, social, economic, educational, religious, and cultural ends." This right is crucial in preventing the majority from imposing its views on groups that would rather express other, perhaps unpopular, ideas. Government actions that may unconstitutionally burden this freedom may take many forms, one of which is "intrusion into the internal structure or affairs of an association" like a "regulation that forces the group to accept members it does not desire." Forcing a group to accept certain members may impair the ability of the group to express those views, and only those views, that it intends to express. Thus, "[f]reedom of association . . . plainly presupposes a freedom not to associate."

The forced inclusion of an unwanted person in a group infringes the group's freedom of expressive association if the presence of that person affects in a significant way the group's ability to advocate public or private viewpoints. But the freedom of expressive association, like many freedoms, is not absolute. We have held that the freedom could be overridden "by regulations adopted to serve compelling state interests, unrelated to the suppression of ideas that cannot be achieved through means significantly less restrictive of associational freedoms." *Roberts*.

To determine whether a group is protected by the First Amendment's expressive associational right, we must determine whether the group engages in "expressive association." The First Amendment's protection of expressive association is not reserved for advocacy groups. But to come within its ambit, a group must engage in some form of expression, whether it be public or private.

Because this is a First Amendment case where the ultimate conclusions of law are virtually inseparable from findings of fact, we are obligated to independently review the factual record to ensure that the state court's judgment does not unlawfully intrude on free expression. The record reveals the following. The Boy Scouts is a private, nonprofit organization. [According to its mission statement, the Boy Scouts' mission is "to serve others by helping to instill values in young people," including the values in the Scout Oath "[t]o help other people at all times; [t]o keep myself physically strong, mentally awake, and morally straight."]

Thus, the general mission of the Boy Scouts is clear: "[T]o instill values in young people." The Boy Scouts seeks to instill these values by having its adult leaders spend time with the youth members, instructing and engaging them in activities like camping, archery, and fishing. During the time spent with the youth members, the scoutmasters and assistant scoutmasters inculcate them with the Boy Scouts' values—both expressly and by example. It seems indisputable that an association that seeks to transmit such a system of values engages in expressive activity.

Given that the Boy Scouts engages in expressive activity, we must determine whether the forced inclusion of Dale as an assistant scoutmaster would significantly affect the Boy Scouts' ability to advocate public or private viewpoints. This inquiry necessarily requires us first to explore, to a limited extent, the nature of the Boy Scouts' view of homosexuality.

The values the Boy Scouts seeks to instill are "based on" those listed in the Scout Oath and Law. The Boy Scouts explains that the Scout Oath and Law provide "a positive moral code for living; they are a list of 'do's' rather than 'don'ts.' " Brief for Petitioners 3. The Boy Scouts asserts that homosexual conduct is inconsistent with the values embodied in the Scout Oath and Law, particularly with the values represented by the terms 'morally straight' and 'clean.' "

Obviously, the Scout Oath and Law do not expressly mention sexuality or sexual orientation. And the terms "morally straight" and "clean" are by no means self defining. Different people would attribute to those terms very different meanings. For example, some people may believe that engaging in homosexual conduct is not at odds with being "morally straight" and "clean." And others may believe that engaging in homosexual conduct is contrary to being "morally straight" and "clean." The Boy Scouts says it falls within the latter category.

The New Jersey Supreme Court analyzed the Boy Scouts' beliefs and found that the "exclusion of members solely on the basis of their sexual orientation is inconsistent with Boy Scouts' commitment to a diverse and 'representative' membership ... [and] contradicts Boy Scouts' overarching objective to reach 'all eligible youth.' " The court concluded that the exclusion of members like Dale "appears antithetical to the organization's goals and philosophy." But our cases reject this sort of inquiry; it is not the role of the courts to reject a group's expressed values because they disagree with those values or find them internally inconsistent.

The Boy Scouts asserts that it "teach[es] that homosexual conduct is not morally straight," Brief for Petitioners 39, and that it does "not want to promote homosexual conduct as a legitimate form of behavior," Reply Brief for Petitioners 5. We accept the Boy Scouts' assertion. We need not inquire further to determine the nature of the Boy Scouts' expression with respect to homosexuality. But because the record before us contains written evidence of the Boy Scouts' viewpoint, we look to it as instructive, if only on the question of the sincerity of the professed beliefs.

A 1978 position statement to the Boy Scouts' Executive Committee, signed by Downing B. Jenks, the President of the Boy Scouts, and Harvey L. Price, the Chief Scout Executive, expresses the Boy Scouts' "official position" with regard to "homosexuality and Scouting":

"Q. May an individual who openly declares himself to be a homosexual be a volunteer Scout leader?

"A. No. The Boy Scouts of America is a private, membership organization and leadership therein is a privilege and not a right. We do not believe that homosexuality and leadership in Scouting are appropriate. We will continue to select only those who in our judgment meet our standards and qualifications for leadership."

Thus, at least as of 1978—the year James Dale entered Scouting—the official position of the Boy Scouts was that avowed homosexuals were not to be Scout leaders. [The Chief Justice also relied on a position statement promulgated by the Boy Scouts in 1991: "We believe that homosexual conduct is inconsistent with the requirement in the Scout Oath that a Scout be morally straight and in the Scout Law that a Scout be clean in word and deed, and that homosexuals do not provide a desirable role model for Scouts." In the 1980s, the Boy Scouts took this position in litigation under California's public accommodations law.]

We must then determine whether Dale's presence as an assistant scoutmaster would significantly burden the Boy Scouts' desire to not "promote homosexual conduct as a legitimate form of behavior." Reply Brief for Petitioners 5. As we give deference to an association's assertions regarding the nature of its expression, we must also give deference to an association's view of what would impair its expression. That is not to say that an expressive association can erect a shield against antidiscrimination laws simply by asserting that mere acceptance of a member from a particular group would impair its message. But here Dale, by his own admission, is one of a group of gay Scouts who have "become leaders in their community and are open and honest about their sexual orientation." Dale was the co-president of a gay and lesbian organization at college and remains a gay rights activist. Dale's presence in the Boy Scouts would, at the very least, force the organization to send a message, both to the youth members and the world, that the Boy Scouts accepts homosexual conduct as a legitimate form of behavior.

[The Chief Justice analogized the Boy Scouts to the parade organizers in *Hurley*.] As the presence of GLIB in Boston's St. Patrick's Day parade would have interfered with the parade organizers' choice not to propound a particular point of view, the presence of Dale as an assistant scoutmaster would just as surely interfere with the Boy Scouts' choice not to propound a point of view contrary to its beliefs.

[The New Jersey Supreme Court reasoned that the Boy Scouts' ability to disseminate its message was not significantly affected by the forced inclusion of Dale as an assistant scoutmaster because homosexuality is not an announced theme of the association, which discourages its leaders from disseminating any views on sexual issues and includes sponsors and members who subscribe to different views in respect of homosexuality. Again, the Chief Justice ruled that the Court had rejected precisely that argument in *Hurley*.] [E]ven if the Boy Scouts discourages Scout leaders from disseminating views on sexual issues—a fact that the Boy Scouts disputes with contrary evidence—the First Amendment protects the Boy Scouts' method of expression. If the Boy Scouts wishes Scout leaders to avoid questions of sexuality and teach only by example, this fact does not negate the sincerity of its belief discussed above.

[Moreover], the First Amendment simply does not require that every member of a group agree on every issue in order for the group's policy to be "expressive association." The Boy Scouts takes an official position with respect to homosexual conduct, and that is sufficient for First Amendment purposes. In this same vein, Dale makes much of the claim that the Boy Scouts does not revoke the membership of heterosexual Scout leaders that openly disagree with the Boy Scouts' policy on sexual orientation. But if this is true, it is irrelevant. The presence of an avowed homosexual and gay rights activist in an assistant scoutmaster's uniform sends a distinctly different message from the presence of a heterosexual assistant scoutmaster who is on record as disagreeing with Boy Scouts policy. The Boy Scouts has a First Amendment right to choose to send one message but not the other. The fact that the organization does not trumpet its views from the housetops, or that it tolerates dissent within its ranks, does not mean that its views receive no First Amendment protection.

Having determined that the Boy Scouts is an expressive association and that the forced inclusion of Dale would significantly affect its expression, we inquire whether the application of New Jersey's public accommodations law to require that the Boy Scouts accept Dale as an assistant scoutmaster runs afoul of the Scouts' freedom of expressive association. We conclude that it does.

[The Chief Justice started with the observation that the understanding of what is a "public accommodation" in state anti-discrimination laws has dramatically expanded from commercial entities, such as restaurants, bars, and hotels, to membership organizations such as the Boy Scouts. With such expansion, "the potential for conflict between state public accommodations laws and the First Amendment rights of organizations has increased." In *Roberts* and other cases, the Court recognized that states have "a compelling interest in eliminating discrimination against women in public accommodations. But in each of these cases we went on to conclude that the enforcement of these statutes would not materially interfere with the ideas that the organization sought to express." *Hurley*, of course, came out the other way.] So in these cases, the associational interest in freedom of expression has been set on one side of the scale, and the State's interest on the other.

Dale contends that we should apply the intermediate standard of review enunciated in *United States v. O'Brien*, 391 U.S. 367 (1968), to evaluate the competing interests. There the Court enunciated a four part test for review of a governmental regulation that has only an incidental effect on protected speech—in that case the symbolic burning of a draft card. A law prohibiting the destruction of draft cards only incidentally affects the free speech rights of those who happen to use a violation of that law as a symbol of protest. But New Jersey's public accommodations law directly and immediately affects associational rights, in this case associational rights that enjoy First Amendment protection. Thus, *O'Brien* is inapplicable.

In *Hurley*, we applied traditional First Amendment analysis to hold that the application of the Massachusetts public accommodations law to a parade violated the First Amendment rights of the parade organizers. Although we did not explicitly deem the parade in *Hurley* an expressive association, the analysis we applied there is similar to the analysis we apply here. We have already concluded that a state requirement that the Boy Scouts retain Dale as an assistant scoutmaster would significantly burden the organization's right to oppose or disfavor homosexual conduct. The state interests embodied in New Jersey's public accommodations law do not justify such a severe intrusion on the Boy Scouts' rights to freedom of expressive association. That being the case, we hold that the First Amendment prohibits the State from imposing such a requirement through the application of its public accommodations law.

Justice Stevens' dissent makes much of its observation that the public perception of homosexuality in this country has changed. Indeed, it appears that homosexuality has gained greater societal acceptance. But this is scarcely an argument for denying First Amendment protection to those who refuse to accept these views. The First Amendment protects expression, be it of the popular variety or not. And the fact that an idea may be embraced and advocated by increasing numbers of people is all the more reason to protect the First Amendment rights of those who wish to voice a different view. * * *

■ JUSTICE STEVENS, with whom JUSTICE SOUTER, JUSTICE GINSBURG, and JUSTICE BREYER join, dissenting. * * *

In this case, Boy Scouts of America contends that it teaches the young boys who are Scouts that homosexuality is immoral. Consequently, it argues, it would violate its right to associate to force it to admit homosexuals as members, as doing so would be at odds with its own shared goals and values. This contention, quite plainly, requires us to look at what, exactly, are the values that BSA actually teaches.

BSA's mission statement reads as follows: "It is the mission of the Boy Scouts of America to serve others by helping to instill values in young people and, in other ways, to prepare them to make ethical choices over their lifetime in achieving their full potential." Its federal charter declares its purpose is "to promote, through organization, and cooperation with other agencies, the ability of boys to do things for themselves and others, to train them in scoutcraft, and to teach them patriotism, courage, self reliance, and kindred values, using the methods which were in common use by Boy Scouts on June 15, 1916." 36 U.S.C. § 23. BSA describes itself as having a "representative membership," which it defines as "boy membership [that] reflects proportionately the characteristics of the boy population of its service area." In particular, the group emphasizes that "[n]either the charter nor the bylaws of the Boy Scouts of America permits the exclusion of any boy. . . . To meet these responsibilities we have made a commitment that our membership shall be representative of all the population in every community, district, and council." * * *

To bolster its claim that its shared goals include teaching that homosexuality is wrong, BSA directs our attention to two terms appearing in the Scout Oath and Law. The first is the phrase "morally straight," which appears in the Oath ("On my honor I will do my best . . . To keep myself . . . morally straight"); the second term is the word "clean," which appears in a list of 12 characteristics together comprising the Scout Law.

The Boy Scout Handbook defines "morally straight," as such:

"To be a person of strong character, guide your life with honesty, purity, and justice. Respect and defend the rights of all people. Your relationships with others should be honest and open. Be clean in your speech and actions, and faithful in your religious beliefs. The values you follow as a Scout will help you become virtuous and self reliant."

The Scoutmaster Handbook emphasizes these points about being "morally straight":

"In any consideration of moral fitness, a key word has to be 'courage.' A boy's courage to do what his head and his heart tell him is right. And the courage to refuse to do what his heart and his head say is wrong. Moral fitness, like emotional fitness, will clearly present opportunities for wise guidance by an alert Scoutmaster."

[As for the term "clean," the Boy Scout Handbook admonishes against "foul language and harmful thoughts," as well as "[s]wear words, profanity, and dirty stories," and "racial slurs and jokes making fun of ethnic groups or people with physical or mental limitations. A Scout knows there is no kindness or honor in such mean spirited behavior. He avoids it in his own words and deeds. He defends those who are targets of insults."]

It is plain as the light of day that neither one of these principles— "morally straight" and "clean"—says the slightest thing about homosexuality. Indeed, neither term in the Boy Scouts' Law and Oath expresses any position whatsoever on sexual matters.

BSA's published guidance on that topic underscores this point. Scouts, for example, are directed to receive their sex education at home or in school, but not from the organization: "Your parents or guardian or a sex education teacher should give you the facts about sex that you must know." Boy Scout Handbook (1992). To be sure, Scouts are not forbidden from asking their Scoutmaster about issues of a sexual nature, but Scoutmasters are, literally, the last person Scouts are encouraged to ask: "If you have questions about growing up, about relationships, sex, or making good decisions, ask. Talk with your parents, religious leaders, teachers, or Scoutmaster." Moreover, Scoutmasters are specifically directed to steer curious adolescents to other sources of information. * * *

[Justice Stevens criticizes the Court's effort "to fill the void" in BSA's expressive association claim. The 1978 internal letter, for example, does not support the Court's inference when read in its entirety. The letter says that BSA does "not knowingly employ homosexuals as professionals or non professionals. We are unaware of any present laws which would prohibit this policy." In response to the next question, whether BSA would terminate an openly "homosexual" officer or employee, the letter said: "Yes, *in the absence of any law to the contrary.* At the present time we are unaware of any statute or ordinance in the United States which prohibits discrimination against individual's employment upon the basis of homosexuality. *In the event that such a law was applicable, it would be necessary for the Boy Scouts of America to obey it, in this case as in Paragraph 4 above.* It is our position, however, that homosexuality and professional or non professional employment in Scouting are not appropriate." (*Emphasis added* by Justice Stevens.) Not only was the letter not a public statement of BSA's expressive mission, but the primary commitment in the letter was to obey local anti-discrimination laws such as the New Jersey law in the Dale litigation.]

The majority also relies on four other policy statements that were issued between 1991 and 1993. All of them were written and issued *after* BSA revoked Dale's membership. Accordingly, they have little, if any, relevance to the legal question before this Court. In any event, they do not bolster BSA's claim.

In 1991, BSA issued two statements both stating: "We believe that homosexual conduct is inconsistent with the requirement in the Scout Oath that a Scout be morally straight and in the Scout Law that a Scout be clean in word and deed, and that homosexuals do not provide a desirable role model for Scouts." A third statement issued in 1992 was substantially the same. By 1993, however, the policy had changed:

BSA Position

"The Boy Scouts of America has always reflected the expectations that Scouting families have had for the organization.

"We do not believe that homosexuals provide a role model consistent with these expectations.

"Accordingly, we do not allow for the registration of avowed homosexuals as members or as leaders of the BSA."

Aside from the fact that these statements were all issued after Dale's membership was revoked, there are four important points relevant to them. First, while the 1991 and 1992 statements tried to tie BSA's exclusionary policy to the meaning of the Scout Oath and Law, the 1993 statement abandoned that effort. Rather, BSA's 1993 homosexual exclusion policy was based on its view that including gays would be contrary to "the expectations that Scouting families have had for the organization." * * * It was simply an exclusionary membership policy, similar to those we have held insufficient in the past.

Second, even during the brief period in 1991 and 1992, when BSA tried to connect its exclusion of homosexuals to its definition of terms found in the Oath and Law, there is no evidence that Scouts were actually taught anything about homosexuality's alleged inconsistency with those principles. * * *

Third, BSA never took any clear and unequivocal position on homosexuality. Though the 1991 and 1992 policies state one interpretation of "morally straight" and "clean," the group's published definitions appearing in the Boy Scout and Scoutmaster Handbooks take quite another view. And BSA's broad religious tolerance combined with its declaration that sexual matters are not its "proper area" render its views on the issue equivocal at best and incoherent at worst. We have never held, however, that a group can throw together any mixture of contradictory positions and then invoke the right to associate to defend any one of those views. At a minimum, a group seeking to prevail over an antidiscrimination law must adhere to a clear and unequivocal view.

Fourth, at most the 1991 and 1992 statements declare only that BSA believed "homosexual *conduct* is inconsistent with the requirement in the Scout Oath that a Scout be morally straight and in the Scout Law that a Scout be clean in word and deed." (emphasis added). But New Jersey's law prohibits discrimination on the basis of sexual orientation. And when Dale was expelled from the Boy Scouts, BSA said it did so because of his sexual orientation, not because of his sexual conduct. * * *

* * * It speaks volumes about the credibility of BSA's claim to a shared goal that homosexuality is incompatible with Scouting that since at least 1984 it had been aware of this issue indeed, concerned enough to twice file amicus briefs before this Court yet it did nothing in the intervening six years (or even in the years after Dale's expulsion) to explain clearly and openly why the presence of homosexuals would affect its expressive activities, or to make the view of "morally straight" and "clean" taken in its 1991 and 1992 policies a part of the values actually instilled in Scouts through the Handbook, lessons, or otherwise.

BSA's claim finds no support in our cases. * * * Several principles are made perfectly clear by *Jaycees* and [*Board of Directors of Rotary Int'l v. Rotary Club of Duarte*, 481 U.S. 537 (1987), where the Court applied *Jaycees* to a similar application to a Rotary Club]. First, to prevail on a claim of expressive association in the face of a State's antidiscrimination law, it is not enough simply to engage in *some kind* of expressive activity. Both the Jaycees and the Rotary Club engaged in expressive activity protected by the First Amendment, yet that fact was not dispositive. Second, it is not enough to adopt an openly avowed exclusionary membership policy. Both the Jaycees and the Rotary Club did that as well. Third, it is not sufficient merely to articulate *some* connection between the group's expressive activities and its exclusionary policy. The Rotary Club, for example, justified its male only membership policy by pointing to the "'aspect of fellowship ... that is enjoyed by the [exclusively] male membership'" and by claiming that only with an exclusively male membership could it "'operate effectively'" in foreign countries.

Rather, in *Jaycees*, we asked whether Minnesota's Human Rights Law requiring the admission of women "impose[d] any *serious burdens*" on the group's "collective effort on behalf of [its] *shared goals*." (emphases added). Notwithstanding the group's obvious publicly stated exclusionary policy, we did not view the inclusion of women as a "serious burden" on the Jaycees' ability to engage in the protected speech of its choice. Similarly, in *Rotary Club*, we asked whether California's law would "affect in any *significant* way the existing members' ability" to engage in their protected speech, or whether the law would require the clubs "to abandon their *basic goals*." (emphases added). * * * Accordingly, it is necessary to examine what, exactly, are BSA's shared goals and the degree to which its expressive activities would be burdened, affected, or restrained by including homosexuals.

The evidence before this Court makes it exceptionally clear that BSA has, at most, simply adopted an exclusionary membership policy and has no shared goal of disapproving of homosexuality. BSA's mission statement and federal charter say nothing on the matter; its official membership policy is silent; its Scout Oath and Law—and accompanying definitions are devoid of any view on the topic; its guidance for Scouts and Scoutmasters on sexuality declare that such matters are "not construed to be Scouting's proper area," but are the province of a Scout's parents and pastor; and BSA's posture respecting religion tolerates a wide variety of views on the issue of homosexuality. Moreover, there is simply no evidence that BSA otherwise teaches anything in this area, or that it instructs Scouts on matters involving homosexuality in ways not conveyed in the Boy Scout or Scoutmaster Handbooks. In short, Boy Scouts of America is simply silent on homosexuality. There is no shared goal or collective effort to foster a belief about homosexuality at all—let alone one that is significantly burdened by admitting homosexuals.

As in *Jaycees*, there is "no basis in the record for concluding that admission of [homosexuals] will impede the [Boy Scouts'] ability to engage in [its] protected activities or to disseminate its preferred views" and New Jersey's law "requires no change in [BSA's] creed." And like

Rotary Club, New Jersey's law "does not require [BSA] to abandon or alter any of" its activities. * * *

The majority pretermits this entire analysis. It finds that BSA in fact " 'teach[es] that homosexual conduct is not morally straight.' " This conclusion, remarkably, rests entirely on statements in BSA's briefs. Moreover, the majority insists that we must "give deference to an association's assertions regarding the nature of its expression" and "we must also give deference to an association's view of what would impair its expression." So long as the record "contains written evidence" to support a group's bare assertion, "[w]e need not inquire further." Once the organization "asserts" that it engages in particular expression, "[w]e cannot doubt" the truth of that assertion.

This is an astounding view of the law. I am unaware of any previous instance in which our analysis of the scope of a constitutional right was determined by looking at what a litigant asserts in his or her brief and inquiring no further. It is even more astonishing in the First Amendment area, because, as the majority itself acknowledges, "we are obligated to independently review the factual record." It is an odd form of independent review that consists of deferring entirely to whatever a litigant claims. * * *

* * * If this Court were to defer to whatever position an organization is prepared to assert in its briefs, there would be no way to mark the proper boundary between genuine exercises of the right to associate, on the one hand, and sham claims that are simply attempts to insulate nonexpressive private discrimination, on the other hand. Shielding a litigant's claim from judicial scrutiny would, in turn, render civil rights legislation a nullity, and turn this important constitutional right into a farce. Accordingly, the Court's prescription of total deference will not do. * * *

[In the next part of his opinion, Justice Stevens discussed BSA's separate argument that it had a "First Amendment right to refrain from including debate and dialogue about homosexuality as part of its mission to instill values in Scouts." Cf. *West Virginia Bd. of Ed. v. Barnette*, 319 U.S. 624 (1943), where the Court protected religious minorities who wanted to remain silent when the Pledge of Allegiance was recited in school. Although the Court did not distinguish between BSA's expressive association and free (non)speech claims, Justice Stevens viewed them as separate. He rejected the constitutional claim, because there was no evidence that James Dale intended to use his position as Associate Scoutmaster as a platform to advance political viewpoints of any sort, much less those inconsistent with the BSA mission. There was no example in the record where BSA had expelled a Scoutmaster for being a member of a religious denomination that proselytizes outsiders to join their faith community.

[In its expressive association discussion, the Court cited *Hurley* to adopt BSA's claim that "Dale's mere presence among the Boy Scouts will itself force the group to convey a message about homosexuality—even if Dale has no intention of doing so." Justice Stevens found *Hurley* inapposite.] First, it was critical to our analysis that GLIB was actually conveying a message by participating in the parade—otherwise, the parade organizers could hardly claim that they were being forced to include any unwanted message at all. Our conclusion that GLIB was conveying a message was inextricably tied to the fact that GLIB wanted to march in a parade, as well as the manner in which it intended to march. We noted the "inherent expressiveness of marching [in a parade] to make a point," and in particular that GLIB was formed for the purpose of making a particular point about gay pride. * * * Indeed, we expressly distinguished between the members of GLIB, who marched as a unit to express their views about their own sexual orientation, on the one hand, and homosexuals who might participate as individuals in the parade without intending to express anything about their sexuality by doing so.

Second, we found it relevant that GLIB's message "would likely be perceived" as the parade organizers' own speech. That was so because "[p]arades and demonstrations . . . are not understood to be so neutrally presented or selectively viewed" as, say, a broadcast by a cable operator, who is usually considered to be "merely 'a conduit' for the speech" produced by others. Rather, parade organizers are usually understood to make the "customary determination about a unit admitted to the parade."

Dale's inclusion in the Boy Scouts is nothing like the case in *Hurley*. His participation sends no cognizable message to the Scouts or to the world. Unlike GLIB, Dale did not carry a banner or a sign; he did not distribute any fact sheet; and he expressed no intent to send any message. If there is any kind of message being sent, then, it is by the mere act of joining the Boy Scouts. Such an act does not constitute an instance of symbolic speech under the First Amendment. * * * Indeed, if merely joining a group did constitute symbolic speech; and such speech were attributable to the group being joined; and that group has the right to exclude that speech (and hence, the right to exclude that person from joining), then the right of free speech effectively becomes a limitless right to exclude for every organization, whether or not it engages in *any* expressive activities. That cannot be, and never has been, the law.

The only apparent explanation for the majority's holding, then, is that homosexuals are simply so different from the rest of society that their presence alone—unlike any other individual's—should be singled out for special First Amendment treatment. Under the majority's reasoning, an openly gay male is irreversibly affixed with the label "homosexual." That label, even though unseen, communicates a message that permits his exclusion wherever he goes. His openness is the sole and sufficient justification for his ostracism. Though unintended, reliance on such a justification is tantamount to a constitutionally prescribed symbol of inferiority. As counsel for the Boy Scouts remarked, Dale "put a banner around his neck when he . . . got himself into the newspaper. . . . He created a reputation. . . . He can't take that banner off. He put it on himself and, indeed, he has continued to put it on himself." See Tr. of Oral Arg. 25.

Another difference between this case and *Hurley* lies in the fact that *Hurley* involved the parade organizers' claim to determine the content of the message they wish to give at a particular time and place. The standards governing such a claim are simply different from the standards that govern BSA's claim of a right of expressive association. Generally, a private person or a private organization has a right to refuse to broadcast a message with which it disagrees, and a right to refuse to contradict or garble its own specific statement at any given place or time by including the messages of others. An expressive association claim, however, normally involves the avowal and advocacy of a consistent position on some issue over time. This is why a different kind of scrutiny must be given to an expressive association claim, lest the right of expressive association simply turn into a right to discriminate whenever some group can think of an expressive object that would seem to be inconsistent with the admission of some person as a member or at odds with the appointment of a person to a leadership position in the group.

Furthermore, it is not likely that BSA would be understood to send any message, either to Scouts or to the world, simply by admitting someone as a member. Over the years, BSA has generously welcomed over 87 million young Americans into its ranks. In 1992 over one million adults were active BSA members. The notion that an organization of that size and enormous prestige implicitly endorses the views that each of those adults may express in a non-Scouting context is simply mind boggling. * * * For an Olympic gold medal winner or a Wimbledon tennis champion, being "openly gay" perhaps communicates a message—for example, that openness about one's sexual orientation is more virtuous than concealment; that a homosexual person can be a capable and virtuous person who should be judged like anyone else; and that homosexuality is not immoral—but it certainly does not follow that they necessarily send a message on behalf of the organizations that sponsor the activities in which they excel. * * *

[Justice Stevens closed his dissenting opinion with a prophecy that the classic animus against gay people, which the Court in *Bowers* celebrated for having "ancient roots," was giving way all across the nation to the tolerant attitude that New Jersey's anti-discrimination law reflected.]

■ [JUSTICE SOUTER, the author of *Hurley,* wrote a separate dissent, joined by JUSTICES GINSBURG and BREYER. He suggested that the First Amendment rights of "rearguard" beliefs are just as protected as those with "vanguard" beliefs and opined that "there may well be circumstances in which the antidiscrimination law must yield * * * It is certainly possible for an individual to become so identified with a position as to epitomize it publicly. When that position is at odds with a group's advocated position, applying an antidiscrimination statute to require the group's acceptance of the individual in a position of group leadership could so modify or muddle or frustrate the group's advocacy as to violate the expressive associational right."]

NOTES ON THE BOY SCOUTS CASE

1. *The Meaning of Outness.* The Court made two critical holdings as to the impact of the mere presence of an openly gay Scoutmaster. First, that "Dale's presence * * * would, at the very least, force the organization to send a message * * * that the Boy Scouts accepts homosexual conduct as a form of behavior." Second, that "the presence of an avowed homosexual and gay rights activist in an assistant scoutmaster's uniform sends a distinctly different message from the presence of a heterosexual assistant scoutmaster who is on record disagreeing with Boy Scouts policy." Do you agree? What are the ramifications of holding that compliance with an anti-discrimination law expresses a message? The dissent argues that mere presence "sends no cognizable message" and that the majority's ruling creates for an openly gay person a "label ... that permits his exclusion wherever he goes." Is the majority's analysis limited to identity-group situations? Scholars are divided on what to make of *Dale*.[b]

2. *The Meaning of* Hurley *After* Dale? Doctrinally, the Chief Justice's opinion introduces confusion. The Boy Scouts' briefs in *Dale* presented two kinds of claims—a forced speech claim governed by *Hurley* and an expressive association claim governed by *Roberts*. The Chief Justice conflated the two claims, so that much of his analysis of the expressive association claim focuses on *Hurley* and ignores *Roberts*.

As the Chief Justice saw the case, the decision in *Dale* turns on how *Hurley* should be interpreted. The majority relies primarily on *Hurley*'s exclusion of lesbian and gay marchers as support for the proposition that "forced inclusion" of an openly gay person would have the same impact as the inclusion sought by the lesbian, gay, and bisexual Irish-American group in the St. Patrick's Day Parade. The dissent argues that there is a "wide gulf" between *Dale* and *Hurley*. Which is the better argument?

3. *Status/Conduct Redux.* As the dissent notes, counsel for the Boy Scouts acknowledged during oral argument that their objection to Dale's presence

---

[b]   For conflicting interpretations of the case, see Dale Carpenter, "Freedom of Expressive Association and Antidiscrimination Law After *Dale*: A Tripartite Approach," 85 *Minn. L. Rev.* (2001) (case was correctly decided; its central principle is important to lesbian and gay organizations); Richard Epstein, "The Constitutional Perils of Moderation: The Case of the Boy Scouts," 74 *S. Cal. L. Rev.* 119 (2000) (the Court ruled correctly but too narrowly; anti-discrimination laws should never apply to private associations that do not possess monopoly power); and Nan D. Hunter, "Accommodating the Public Sphere: Beyond the Market Model," 85 *Minn. L. Rev.* (2001) (the Court's unstated premises regarding sexuality and gender limited Dale's claim to full citizenship, which public accommodations laws have historically extended into the non-government realm). For an analysis of the conundrum that has arisen in the law because of its inability to harmonize equality claims with their intrinsic communicative elements, see Nan D. Hunter, "Expressive Identity: Recuperating Dissent for Equality," 35 *Harv. C.R.-.C.L. L. Rev.* 1 (1999).

was not based on concern that he would engage in inappropriate conduct as a Scoutmaster. The dissent frames the case as one in which Dale's openness is simply an aspect of his presence, *i.e.,* of his civil rights claim. The majority refers to the Scouts' rejection of "homosexual conduct as a form of behavior." Presumably, the reference is to sexual conduct. Implicitly, though, the majority also suggests that Dale's conduct in coming out in discussing his homosexuality in the press also disqualified him; see the reference to him as "an avowed homosexual and gay rights activist." Note how this framing helps constitute the Boy Scouts' defense, based significantly on its right to condemn conduct.

4.   *Gender as Subtext.* Although there is no sex discrimination argument as such used in *Dale,* gender is a subtextual issue in several respects. First, doctrinally, the parties argued over the applicability of cases like *Roberts,* in which women sought admission to previously male only clubs: Were the Scouts more like the Jaycees in *Roberts* or the St. Patrick's Day Parade in *Hurley*? Does the presence of an openly gay person affect the BSA's expressive capacity more than the presence of women did for the Jaycees?

Second, one question lurking in the case was whether, if the Scouts could be forced to admit gay youth, could they be forced by the same statute to admit girls? In fact, that was the first question posed during oral argument (before the end of his third sentence) to Evan Wolfson, counsel for Lambda Legal Defense and Education Fund, who represented Dale, by Justice O'Connor. Wolfson answered by noting that the New Jersey statute itself provided certain exemptions for same-sex organizations, and also argued that a clearly boys only group might have an expressive association defense as well. Justice Ginsburg remarked, "[T]here's a certain irony in that you're relying on the *Jaycees* case and the *Rotary* case." 2000 U.S. Trans Lexis 44. In a footnote we omitted from the excerpt, Justice Stevens' dissent noted the existence of the exemption.

Lastly, gender is a powerful cultural factor in the case. In their petition for certiorari, the Scouts argued that the presence of gay Scouts created a conflict with their message about "what it means to be a man." Pet. for Cert. at 18.

5.   *An Alternative Theory.* Jed Rubenfeld argues that the case was simple: "[T]here is no such thing as a free speech immunity based on the claim that someone wants to break an otherwise constitutional law for expressive purposes. The actor's purposes are not relevant to free speech analysis. The state's purposes, on the other hand, are dispositive. When a law is otherwise constitutional, and when an actor has not been singled out because of his expression, the actor has no free speech claim. The Boy Scouts were not singled out in this way. As a result, the Scouts' First Amendment claim should have been taken no more seriously than that of a tax protestor * * * who is also prevented from communicating a message he wants to communicate and who is also forced, as much as the Scouts are, to send a message he does not want to send—support for the United States government. The tax protestor's most effective means (perhaps his only effective means) of communicating his lack of support for the United States might be his refusal to pay his taxes. But he does not for this reason obtain an immunity from the tax code." Jed Rubenfeld, "The First Amendment's Purpose," 53 *Stan. L. Rev.* 767, 769, 808–09 (2001).

One interesting question raised by Rubenfeld's argument is whether a pure speech First Amendment claim—like that of the tax protestor—is given additional weight by the presence of a linked expressive associational claim. Should organizations that constitute civil society have a stronger claim in this sort of case? Building on Robert Cover's concept of "nomic communities," or intentionally-formed communities of people who share common beliefs as to normative values, one of us has argued that the law ought to accord such groups the widest possible berth: "The state must allow individual nomic communities to flourish or wither as they may, and the state cannot as a normal matter become the means for the triumph of one community over all others." When a collision of principles cannot be avoided, an excellent model for resolution would be to accommodate the essential needs of the two communities in conflict. William N. Eskridge Jr., "A Jurisprudence of 'Coming Out': Religion, Homosexuality and Collisions of Liberty and Equality in American Public Law," 106 *Yale L. J.* 2411, 2415 (1997).

1. FREEDOM OF ASSOCIATION REDUX

Starting in 1977 (at NYU), most American law schools adopted policies barring employers from access to their placement services unless the employers certified that they did not discriminate on the basis of sexual orientation (in addition to sex, race, and other criteria). In 1990, the American Association of Law Schools (AALS) required all accredited law schools to include sexual orientation in their non-discrimination policies. AALS member schools were thereafter prohibited from extending use of career services facilities to employers who discriminate based on sexual orientation.

In 1994, Representative Gerald Solomon successfully introduced an amendment to Department of Defense appropriations bills that denied federal grants or contracts (including student aid) to any educational institution preventing military recruiters access to campus, students on campus, or student directory information. 10 U.S.C.A. § 983. After 1994, the Solomon Amendment was revised on numerous occasions, generally expanding its ambit to impose cutoffs of millions of dollars in federal research funds upon universities whose law schools did not allow military recruiters to interview under exactly the same terms as the most favored employers. (The Solomon Amendment exempted institutions that barred military recruiters for religious reasons.)

Donald H. Rumsfeld v. Forum for Academic and Institutional Rights, Inc. et al.

United States Supreme Court, 2006.
547 U.S. 47, 126 S.Ct. 1297, 164 L.Ed.2d 156.

■ CHIEF JUSTICE ROBERTS delivered the opinion for the Court.

[The Forum for Academic & Institutional Rights (FAIR), an association of law schools formed to protect academic freedom, challenged the Department of Defense's (DOD's) enforcement of the Solomon Amendment. As amended in 2004, § 983 provides that if any part of an institution of higher education denies military recruiters access equal to that provided other recruiters, the entire institution would lose certain federal funds. The lower court ruled that the Solomon Amendment violated the First Amendment rights of FAIR's members and remanded to the trial court to enter an injunction against terminating federal funds to universities with non-complying law schools. The Supreme Court reversed.]

[III. DOD had argued that the federal government has greater authority to condition the receipt of funds upon the recipient's agreement to behave in a certain way than it has to regulate the conduct directly. The Chief Justice declined to address that argument, because he found that the First Amendment allows the federal government to impose the Solomon Amendment's equal access requirement directly on universities.]

A.   The Solomon Amendment neither limits what law schools may say nor requires them to say anything. Law schools remain free under the statute to express whatever views they may have on the military's congressionally mandated employment policy, all the while retaining eligibility for federal funds. See Tr. of Oral Arg. 25 (Solicitor General acknowledging that law schools "could put signs on the bulletin board next to the door, they could engage in speech, they could help organize student protests"). As a general matter, the Solomon Amendment regulates conduct, not speech. It affects what law schools must *do*-afford equal access to military recruiters-not what they may or may not *say*.

Nevertheless, the Third Circuit concluded that the Solomon Amendment violates law schools' freedom of speech in a number of ways. First, in assisting military recruiters, law schools provide some services, such as sending e-mails and distributing flyers, that clearly involve speech. The Court of Appeals held that in supplying these services law schools are unconstitutionally compelled to speak the Government's message. Second, military recruiters are, to some extent, speaking while they are on campus. The Court of Appeals held that, by forcing law schools to permit the military on campus to express its message, the Solomon Amendment unconstitutionally requires law schools to host or accommodate the military's speech. Third, although the Court of Appeals thought that the Solomon Amendment regulated speech, it held in the alternative that, if the statute regulates conduct, this conduct is expressive and regulating it unconstitutionally infringes law schools' right to engage in expressive conduct. We consider each issue in turn.

Some of this Court's leading First Amendment precedents have established the principle that freedom of speech prohibits the government from telling people what they must say. In *West Virginia Bd. of Ed. v. Barnette*, 319 U.S. 624, 642 (1943), we held unconstitutional a state law requiring schoolchildren to recite the Pledge of Allegiance and to salute the flag. And in *Wooley v. Maynard*, 430 U.S. 705, 717 (1977), we held unconstitutional another that required New Hampshire motorists to display the state motto-"Live Free or Die"-on their license plates.

The Solomon Amendment does not require any similar expression by law schools. Nonetheless, recruiting assistance provided by the schools often includes elements of speech. For example, schools may send e-mails or post notices on bulletin boards on an employer's behalf. Law schools offering such services to other recruiters must also send e-mails and post notices on behalf of the military to comply with the Solomon Amendment. As FAIR points out, these compelled statements of fact ("The U.S. Army recruiter will meet interested students in Room 123 at 11 a.m."), like compelled statements of opinion, are subject to First Amendment scrutiny.

This sort of recruiting assistance, however, is a far cry from the compelled speech in *Barnette* and *Wooley*. The Solomon Amendment, unlike the laws at issue in those cases, does not dictate the content of the speech at all, which is only "compelled" if, and to the extent, the school provides such speech for other recruiters. There is nothing in this case approaching a Government-mandated pledge or motto that the school must endorse.

The compelled speech to which the law schools point is plainly incidental to the Solomon Amendment's regulation of conduct, and "it has never been deemed an abridgment of freedom of speech or press to make a course of conduct illegal merely because the conduct was in part initiated, evidenced, or carried out by means of language, either spoken, written, or printed." Congress, for example, can prohibit employers from discriminating in hiring on the basis of race. The fact that this will require an employer to take down a sign reading "White Applicants Only" hardly means that the law should be analyzed as one regulating the employer's speech rather than conduct. Compelling a law school that sends scheduling e-mails for other recruiters to send one for a military recruiter is simply not the same as forcing a student to pledge allegiance, or forcing a Jehovah's Witness to display the motto "Live Free or Die" and it trivializes the freedom protected in *Barnette* and *Wooley* to suggest that it is.

Our compelled-speech cases are not limited to the situation in which an individual must personally speak the government's message. We have also in a number of instances limited the government's ability to force one speaker to host or accommodate another speaker's message. See *Hurley* (state law cannot require a parade to include a group whose message the parade's organizer does not wish to send); *Pacific Gas & Elec. Co. v. Public Util. Comm'n of Cal.,* 475 U.S. 1, 20–21 (1986) (state agency cannot require a utility company to include a third-party newsletter in its billing envelope); *Miami Herald Publishing Co. v. Tornillo,* 418 U.S. 241 (1974) (right-of-reply statute violates editors' right to determine the content of their newspapers). Relying on these precedents, the Third Circuit concluded that the Solomon Amendment unconstitutionally compels law schools to accommodate the military's message "[b]y requiring schools to include military recruiters in the interviews and recruiting receptions the schools arrange."

The compelled-speech violation in each of our prior cases, however, resulted from the fact that the complaining speaker's own message was affected by the speech it was forced to accommodate. The expressive nature of a parade was central to our holding in *Hurley*. We concluded that because "every participating unit affects the message conveyed by the [parade's] private organizers," a law dictating that a particular group must be included in the parade "alter[s] the expressive content of th[e] parade." As a result, we held that the State's public accommodation law, as applied to a private parade, "violates the fundamental rule of protection under the First Amendment, that a speaker has the autonomy to choose the content of his own message." * * *

In this case, accommodating the military's message does not affect the law schools' speech, because the schools are not speaking when they host interviews and recruiting receptions. Unlike a parade organizer's choice of parade contingents, a law school's decision to allow recruiters on campus is not inherently expressive. Law schools facilitate recruiting to assist their students in obtaining jobs. A law school's recruiting services lack the expressive quality of a parade, a newsletter, or the editorial page of a newspaper; its accommodation of a military recruiter's message is not compelled speech because the accommodation does not sufficiently interfere with any message of the school.

The schools respond that if they treat military and nonmilitary recruiters alike in order to comply with the Solomon Amendment, they could be viewed as sending the message that they see nothing wrong with the military's policies, when they do. We rejected a similar argument in *PruneYard Shopping Center v. Robins,* 447 U.S. 74 (1980). In that case, we upheld a state law requiring a shopping center owner to allow certain expressive activities by others on its property. We explained that there was little likelihood that the views of those engaging in the expressive activities would be identified with the owner, who remained free to disassociate himself from those views and who was "not . . . being compelled to affirm [a] belief in any governmentally prescribed position or view."

The same is true here. Nothing about recruiting suggests that law schools agree with any speech by recruiters, and nothing in the Solomon Amendment restricts what the law schools may say about the military's policies. We have held that high school students can appreciate the difference between speech a school sponsors and speech the school permits because legally required to do so, pursuant to an equal access policy. Surely students have not lost that ability by the time they get to law school.

Having rejected the view that the Solomon Amendment impermissibly regulates *speech*, we must still consider whether the expressive nature of the *conduct* regulated by the statute brings that conduct within the First Amendment's protection. In *O'Brien*, we recognized that some forms of " 'symbolic speech' " were deserving of First Amendment protection. But we rejected the view that "conduct can be labeled 'speech' whenever the person engaging in the conduct intends thereby to express an idea." Instead, we have extended First Amendment protection only to conduct that is inherently expressive. In *Texas v. Johnson*, for example, we applied *O'Brien* and held that burning the American flag was sufficiently expressive to warrant First Amendment protection.

Unlike flag burning, the conduct regulated by the Solomon Amendment is not inherently expressive. Prior to the adoption of the Solomon Amendment's equal-access requirement, law schools "expressed" their disagreement with the military by treating military recruiters differently from other recruiters. But these actions were expressive only because the law schools accompanied their conduct with speech explaining it. For example, the point of requiring military interviews to be conducted on the undergraduate campus is not "overwhelmingly apparent." *Johnson*. An observer who sees military recruiters interviewing away from the law school has no way of knowing whether the law school is expressing its disapproval of the military, all the law school's interview rooms are full, or the military recruiters decided for reasons of their own that they would rather interview someplace else.

The expressive component of a law school's actions is not created by the conduct itself but by the speech that accompanies it. The fact that such explanatory speech is necessary is strong evidence that the conduct at issue here is not so inherently expressive that it warrants protection under *O'Brien*. If combining speech and conduct were enough to create expressive conduct, a regulated party could always transform conduct into "speech" simply by talking about it. For instance, if an individual announces that he intends to express his disapproval of the Internal Revenue Service by refusing to pay his income taxes, we would have to apply *O'Brien* to determine whether the Tax Code violates the First Amendment. Neither *O'Brien* nor its progeny supports such a result. * * *

B.   The Solomon Amendment does not violate law schools' freedom of speech, but the First Amendment's protection extends beyond the right to speak. We have recognized a First Amendment right to associate for the purpose of speaking, which we have termed a "right of expressive association." See, *e.g.*, *Dale*. The reason we have extended First Amendment protection in this way is clear: The right to speak is often exercised most effectively by combining one's voice with the voices of others. If the government were free to restrict individuals' ability to join together and speak, it could essentially silence views that the First Amendment is intended to protect.

FAIR argues that the Solomon Amendment violates law schools' freedom of expressive association. According to FAIR, law schools' ability to express their message that discrimination on the basis of sexual orientation is wrong is significantly affected by the presence of military recruiters on campus and the schools' obligation to assist them. Relying heavily on our decision in *Dale*, the Court of Appeals agreed.

In *Dale*, we held that the Boy Scouts' freedom of expressive association was violated by New Jersey's public accommodations law, which required the organization to accept a homosexual as a scoutmaster. After determining that the Boy Scouts was an expressive association, that "the forced inclusion of Dale would significantly affect its expression," and that the State's interests did not justify this intrusion, we concluded that the Boy Scouts' First Amendment rights were violated.

The Solomon Amendment, however, does not similarly affect a law school's associational rights. To comply with the statute, law schools must allow military recruiters on campus and assist them in whatever way the school chooses to assist other employers. Law schools therefore "associate" with military recruiters in the sense that they interact with them. But recruiters are not part of the law school. Recruiters are, by definition, outsiders who come onto campus for the limited purpose of trying to hire students-not to become members of the school's expressive association. This distinction is critical. Unlike the public accommodations law in *Dale*, the Solomon Amendment does not force a law school " 'to accept members it does not desire.' " [*Dale*, quoting *Roberts*.] The law schools *say* that allowing military recruiters equal access impairs their own expression by requiring them to associate with the recruiters, but just as saying conduct is undertaken for expressive purposes cannot make it symbolic speech, so too a speaker cannot "erect a shield" against laws requiring access "simply by asserting" that mere association "would impair its message." [*Dale*.]

FAIR correctly notes that the freedom of expressive association protects more than just a group's membership decisions. For example, we have held laws unconstitutional that require disclosure of membership lists for groups seeking anonymity, or impose penalties or withhold benefits based on membership in a disfavored group. Although these laws did not directly interfere with an organization's composition, they made group membership less attractive, raising the same *First Amendment* concerns about affecting the group's ability to express its message.

The Solomon Amendment has no similar effect on a law school's associational rights. Students and faculty are free to associate to voice their disapproval of the military's message; nothing about the statute affects the composition of the group by making group membership less desirable. The Solomon Amendment therefore does not violate a law school's First Amendment rights. A military recruiter's mere presence on campus does not violate a law school's right to associate, regardless of how repugnant the law school considers the recruiter's message. * * *

In this case, FAIR has attempted to stretch a number of First Amendment doctrines well beyond the sort of activities these doctrines protect. The law schools object to having to treat military recruiters like other recruiters, but that regulation of conduct does not violate the First Amendment. To the extent that the Solomon Amendment incidentally affects expression, the law schools' effort to cast themselves as just like the schoolchildren in *Barnette*, the parade organizers in *Hurley*, and the Boy Scouts in *Dale* plainly overstates the expressive nature of their activity and the impact of the Solomon Amendment on it, while exaggerating the reach of our First Amendment precedents. * * *

■ JUSTICE ALITO took no part in the deliberation or decision of this case.

NOTE ON THE *FAIR* CASE AND THE LIMITS OF *HURLEY* AND *DALE*

The Forum for Academic & Institutional Rights (FAIR) sought to apply the principles of *Hurley* and *Dale* to protect law schools' expressive conduct (*Hurley*) and expressive association (*Dale*) critical of the Department of Defense's exclusion of openly lesbian and gay service personnel. As FAIR and the lower court had argued, the Chief Justice's opinion characterized *Hurley* as a case where the state had "sought to force one speaker to host or accommodate another speaker's message." But the Court found *Hurley* different, because "the complaining speaker's own message was affected by the speech it was forced to accommodate." The law schools' career service offices were not engaged in expressive activities when they arranged and publicized employer interviews with their law students, the Court found. In short, a job fair does not have the expressive qualities of a parade. Would that be true if the Boy Scouts held a job fair?

The Chief Justice's opinion characterized *Dale* as a case where the state sought to control the *membership* of an expressive association, an intrusion deeper than the Solomon Amendment's effort to regulate law schools' interaction with *outsiders*. The Court says: "A military recruiter's mere presence on campus does not violate a law school's freedom to associate, regardless of how repugnant the law school considers the recruiter's message." True in all contexts?

CHAPTER 2

WATERSHED DECISIONS AND THE RISE OF EQUAL LIBERTY

SECTION 1   Access to Abortion: From *Casey* to *Whole Women's Health* and
             Beyond
SECTION 2   The Regulation of Sexual Conduct: *Lawrence v. Texas* and Beyond
SECTION 3   Liberty, Equality, and Marriage

As the twentieth century drew to a close, three issues dominated constitutional questions regarding state regulation of sexuality and gender: abortion, criminalization of certain sexual conduct, and exclusionary marriage laws. In a period of roughly 20 years, the Supreme Court addressed all three, in the cases that we will read in this chapter.

By this time, it appeared clear that the Court's openness to expanding the use of heightened scrutiny in reviewing infringements on either liberty or equality had come to an end. The Court's most recent decisions holding that a form of discrimination would be subject to intermediate scrutiny occurred in the late 1970s. *Craig v. Boren* (sex) (Chapter 1, Section 2A); *Lalli v. Lalli*, 439 U.S. 259 (1978) (birth to unmarried parents). For questions of liberty protected by the Due Process Clause, the Court refused to find a fundamental right to consensual sexual relations in *Bowers v. Hardwick* (Chapter 1, Section 1C) and signaled that it might diminish the level of scrutiny in abortion cases.

As the Court's unwillingness to extend explicitly heightened scrutiny has continued, the substitute that has emerged is a vaguely articulated principle of equal liberty. The typical equal liberty case involves laws that burden the exercise of an important personal freedom *and* that impose burdens in ways that further disadvantage stigmatized groups of persons. Neither the liberty interest nor the classification falls into a heightened scrutiny category, but the joinder elicits greater care from the Court than traditional rational basis review, which is highly deferential. In equal liberty cases, the Court has demonstrated a willingness to closely examine the purposes behind, and the effects of, the challenged law or policy without specifying which level of review it is using.

The equal liberty model has been most fully developed in the cases in this chapter, but its antecedents stretch back to at least the mid-twentieth century. In *Skinner v. Oklahoma*, 316 U.S. 535 (1942), the Court struck down a law that provided for sterilization of "habitual criminals," defined as persons convicted more than twice of "felonies involving moral turpitude." The Court held that the law violated the Equal Protection Clause, because it exempted persons convicted of embezzlement or tax law violations, but included those convicted of other types of larceny, regardless of the amounts involved. As its reason for finding inequality, the Court relied more on the nature of the liberty deprivation than on a suspect class approach:

> We are dealing here with legislation which involves one of the basic civil rights of man. Marriage and procreation are fundamental to the very existence and survival of the race. * * * There is no redemption for the individual whom the law touches. * * * He is forever deprived of a basic liberty. * * * [S]trict scrutiny of the classification which a State makes in a sterilization law is essential, lest unwittingly or otherwise invidious discriminations are made against groups or types of individuals in violation of the constitutional guaranty of just and equal laws.

Id. at 541. Under *Skinner* and its progeny, strict scrutiny applies to any classification that differentiates among groups of persons in the exercise of a fundamental right. What contemporary law has added to this calculus is a heightened level of scrutiny when the liberty right has not been denominated as fundamental.

The animating principle behind equal liberty analysis was well stated by South African Constitutional Court Justice Sachs in his concurring opinion in the decision that struck down the sodomy law in that country:

> * * * [E]quality and privacy cannot be separated * * * [T]he negation by the state of different forms of intimate personal behaviour becomes the foundation for the repudiation of equality. Human rights are better approached and defended in an integrated rather than a disparate fashion. The rights must fit the people, not the people the rights. This requires looking at rights and their violations from a person-centered rather than a formula-based position, and analysing them contextually rather than abstractly. * * *

The National Coalition for Gay and Lesbian Equality v. The Minister of Justice, 1999 (1) SA 6 (CC) (S. Afr.).

From the perspective of statecraft, how well do these opinions serve the function of a court seeking to navigate the dynamics in a pluralist society in which abortion and homosexuality are bitterly divisive moral issues? How has the state's power to regulate sexuality been diminished or enhanced?

SECTION 1

ACCESS TO ABORTION: FROM *CASEY* TO *WHOLE WOMAN'S HEALTH* AND BEYOND

By the 1990s, support for the fundamental rights approach to abortion that the Supreme Court established in *Roe v. Wade* had significantly weakened. (See Chapter 1, Section 1B.) Whereas *Roe v. Wade* had commanded a 7–2 split of the Justices, by the time of the Court's opinion in *Thornburgh v. American College of Obstetricians and Gynecologists*, 476 U.S. 747 (1986), Chief Justice Burger and Justice O'Connor joined *Roe* dissenting Justices White and Rehnquist to indicate their willingness to either overrule or weaken what *Roe* had declared to be a fundamental right. *Roe*'s fate seemed sealed when two strongly pro-choice Justices—Brennan and Marshall—left the Court in 1990–91 and were replaced by Justices David Souter and Clarence Thomas.

A. THE CENTER HOLDS

In response to Planned Parenthood's challenge to Pennsylvania's extensive regulation of women's decision-making about abortions, the state urged the Court to overrule *Roe*, as did Solicitor General Kenneth Starr. Planned Parenthood argued to the Court that no section of the statute could be upheld without overturning *Roe*, in effect gambling that an explicit overruling would be better politically than further dilution.

Planned Parenthood of Southeastern Pennsylvania v. Robert Casey

United States Supreme Court, 1992.
505 U.S. 833, 112 S.Ct. 2791, 120 L.Ed.2d 674.

■ JUSTICE O'CONNOR, JUSTICE KENNEDY, and JUSTICE SOUTER announced the judgment of the Court and delivered the opinion of the Court with respect to Parts I, II, III, V-A, V-C, and VI, an opinion with respect to Part V-E, in which JUSTICE STEVENS joins, and an opinion with respect to Parts IV, V-B, and V-D.

[I.] Liberty finds no refuge in a jurisprudence of doubt. Yet 19 years after our holding that the Constitution protects a woman's right to terminate her pregnancy in its early stages, that definition of liberty is still questioned. Joining the respondents as *amicus curiae,* the United States, as it has done in five other cases in the last decade, again asks us to overrule *Roe v. Wade.* * * *

After considering the fundamental constitutional questions resolved by *Roe,* principles of institutional integrity, and the rule of *stare decisis,* we are led to conclude this: the essential holding of *Roe v. Wade* should be retained and once again reaffirmed. [The Joint Opinion characterized the first part of "Roe's essential holding" as a recognition of "the right of the woman to choose to have an abortion before viability and to obtain it without undue interference from the State."]

[II.] Constitutional protection of the woman's decision to terminate her pregnancy derives from the Due Process Clause of the Fourteenth Amendment. It declares that no State shall "deprive any person of life, liberty, or property, without due process of law." The controlling word in the cases before us is "liberty." * * *

Men and women of good conscience can disagree, and we suppose some always shall disagree, about the profound moral and spiritual implications of terminating a pregnancy, even in its earliest stage. * * * Our obligation is to define the liberty of all, not to mandate our own moral code. The underlying constitutional issue is whether the State can resolve these philosophic questions in such a definitive way that a woman lacks all choice in the matter, except perhaps in those rare circumstances in which the pregnancy is itself a danger to her own life or health, or is the result of rape or incest.

It is conventional constitutional doctrine that where reasonable people disagree the government can adopt one position or the other. That theorem, however, assumes a state of affairs in which the choice does not intrude upon a protected liberty. * * *

* * * At the heart of liberty is the right to define one's own concept of existence, of meaning, of the universe, and of the mystery of human life. Beliefs about these matters could not define the attributes of personhood were they formed under compulsion of the State.

These considerations begin our analysis of the woman's interest in terminating her pregnancy but cannot end it, for this reason: though the abortion decision may originate within the zone of conscience and belief, it is more than a philosophic exercise. Abortion is a unique act. It is an act fraught with consequences for others: for the woman who must live with the implications of her decision; for the persons who perform and assist in the procedure; for the spouse, family, and society which must confront the knowledge that these procedures exist, procedures some deem nothing short of an act of violence against innocent human life; and, depending on one's beliefs, for the life or potential life that is aborted. Though abortion is conduct, it does not follow that the State is entitled to proscribe it in all instances. That is because the liberty of the woman is at stake in a sense unique to the human condition and so unique to the law. The mother who carries a child to full term is subject to anxieties, to physical constraints, to pain that only she must bear. That these sacrifices have from the beginning of the human race been endured by woman with a pride that ennobles her in the eyes of others and gives to the infant a bond of love cannot alone be grounds for the State to insist she make the sacrifice. Her suffering is too intimate and personal for the State to insist, without more, upon its own vision of the woman's role, however dominant that vision has been in the course of our history and our culture. The destiny of the woman must be shaped to a large extent on her own conception of her spiritual imperatives and her place in society.

[III.]   [W]hen this Court reexamines a prior holding, its judgment is customarily informed by a series of prudential and pragmatic considerations designed to test the consistency of overruling a prior decision with the ideal of the rule of law, and to gauge the respective costs of reaffirming and overruling a prior case. * * *

So in this case we may enquire whether *Roe*'s central rule has been found unworkable; whether the rule's limitation on state power could be removed without serious inequity to those who have relied upon it or significant damage to the stability of the society governed by it; whether the law's growth in the intervening years has left *Roe*'s central rule a doctrinal anachronism discounted by society; and whether *Roe*'s premises of fact have so far changed in the ensuing two decades as to render its central holding somehow irrelevant or unjustifiable in dealing with the issue it addressed.

1.   Although *Roe* has engendered opposition, it has in no sense proven "unworkable," representing as it does a simple limitation beyond which a state law is unenforceable. While *Roe* has, of course, required judicial assessment of state laws affecting the exercise of the choice guaranteed against government infringement, and although the need for such review will remain as a consequence of today's decision, the required determinations fall within judicial competence.

2.   The inquiry into reliance counts the cost of a rule's repudiation as it would fall on those who have relied reasonably on the rule's continued application. * * *

* * * Abortion is customarily chosen as an unplanned response to the consequence of unplanned activity or to the failure of conventional birth control, and except on the assumption that no intercourse would have occurred but for *Roe*'s holding, such behavior may appear to justify no reliance claim. Even if reliance could be claimed on that unrealistic assumption, the argument might run, any reliance interest would be *de minimis*. This argument would be premised on the hypothesis that reproductive planning could take virtually immediate account of any sudden restoration of state authority to ban abortions.

To eliminate the issue of reliance that easily, however, one would need to limit cognizable reliance to specific instances of sexual activity. But to do this would be simply to refuse to face the fact that for two decades of economic and social developments, people have organized intimate relationships and made choices that define their views of themselves and their places in society, in reliance on the availability of abortion in the event that contraception should fail. The ability of women to participate equally in the economic and social life of the Nation has been facilitated by their ability to control their reproductive lives. The Constitution serves human values, and while the effect of reliance on *Roe* cannot be exactly measured, neither can the certain cost of overruling *Roe* for people who have ordered their thinking and living around that case be dismissed.

3.   No evolution of legal principle has left *Roe's* doctrinal footings weaker than they were in 1973. No development of constitutional law since the case was decided has implicitly or explicitly left *Roe* behind as a mere survivor of obsolete constitutional thinking.

It will be recognized, of course, that *Roe* stands at an intersection of two lines of decisions, but in whichever doctrinal category one reads the case, the result for present purposes will be the same. The *Roe* Court itself placed its holding in the succession of cases most prominently exemplified by *Griswold v. Connecticut.* When it is so seen, *Roe* is clearly in no jeopardy, since subsequent constitutional developments have neither disturbed, nor do they threaten to diminish, the scope of recognized protection accorded to the liberty relating to intimate relationships, the family, and decisions about whether or not to beget or bear a child.

Roe, however, may be seen not only as an exemplar of *Griswold* liberty but as a rule (whether or not mistaken) of personal autonomy and bodily integrity, with doctrinal affinity to cases recognizing limits on governmental power to mandate medical treatment or to bar its rejection. If so, our cases since *Roe* accord with *Roe's* view that a State's interest in the protection of life falls short of justifying any plenary override of individual liberty claims. * * *

4.   We have seen how time has overtaken some of *Roe's* factual assumptions: advances in maternal health care allow for abortions safe to the mother later in pregnancy than was true in 1973, and advances in neonatal care have advanced viability to a point somewhat earlier. But these facts go only to the scheme of time limits on the realization of competing interests, and the divergences from the factual premises of 1973 have no bearing on the validity of *Roe's* central holding, that viability marks the earliest point at which the State's interest in fetal life is constitutionally adequate to justify a legislative ban on nontherapeutic abortions. The soundness or unsoundness of that constitutional judgment in no sense turns on whether viability occurs at approximately 28 weeks, as was usual at the time of *Roe,* at 23 to 24 weeks, as it sometimes does today, or at some moment even slightly earlier in pregnancy, as it may if fetal respiratory capacity can somehow be enhanced in the future. Whenever it may occur, the attainment of viability may continue to serve as the critical fact, just as it has done since *Roe* was decided; which is to say that no change in *Roe's* factual

underpinning has left its central holding obsolete, and none supports an argument for overruling it.

5. The sum of the precedential enquiry * * * shows *Roe*'s underpinnings unweakened in any way affecting its central holding. While it has engendered disapproval, it has not been unworkable. An entire generation has come of age free to assume *Roe*'s concept of liberty in defining the capacity of women to act in society, and to make reproductive decisions; no erosion of principle going to liberty or personal autonomy has left *Roe*'s central holding a doctrinal remnant; *Roe* portends no developments at odds with other precedent for the analysis of personal liberty; and no changes of fact have rendered viability more or less appropriate as the point at which the balance of interests tips. Within the bounds of normal *stare decisis* analysis, then, and subject to the considerations on which it customarily turns, the stronger argument is for affirming *Roe*'s central holding, with whatever degree of personal reluctance any of us may have, not for overruling it.

[IV.]   *Roe* established a trimester framework to govern abortion regulations. Under this elaborate but rigid construct, almost no regulation at all is permitted during the first trimester of pregnancy; regulations designed to protect the woman's health, but not to further the State's interest in potential life, are permitted during the second trimester; and during the third trimester, when the fetus is viable, prohibitions are permitted provided the life or health of the mother is not at stake. * * *

Though the woman has a right to choose to terminate or continue her pregnancy before viability, it does not at all follow that the State is prohibited from taking steps to ensure that this choice is thoughtful and informed. Even in the earliest stages of pregnancy, the State may enact rules and regulations designed to encourage her to know that there are philosophic and social arguments of great weight that can be brought to bear in favor of continuing the pregnancy to full term and that there are procedures and institutions to allow adoption of unwanted children as well as a certain degree of state assistance if the mother chooses to raise the child herself. It follows that States are free to enact laws to provide a reasonable framework for a woman to make a decision that has such profound and lasting meaning. This, too, we find consistent with *Roe*'s central premises, and indeed the inevitable consequence of our holding that the State has an interest in protecting the life of the unborn.

We reject the trimester framework, which we do not consider to be part of the essential holding of *Roe*. Measures aimed at ensuring that a woman's choice contemplates the consequences for the fetus do not necessarily interfere with the right recognized in *Roe*, although those measures have been found to be inconsistent with the rigid trimester framework announced in that case. A logical reading of the central holding in *Roe* itself, and a necessary reconciliation of the liberty of the woman and the interest of the State in promoting prenatal life, require, in our view, that we abandon the trimester framework as a rigid prohibition on all pre-viability regulation aimed at the protection of fetal life. The trimester framework suffers from these basic flaws: in its formulation it misconceives the nature of the pregnant woman's interest; and in practice it undervalues the State's interest in potential life, as recognized in *Roe*. * * *

* * * Numerous forms of state regulation might have the incidental effect of increasing the cost or decreasing the availability of medical care, whether for abortion or any other medical procedure. The fact that a law which serves a valid purpose, one not designed to strike at the right itself, has the incidental effect of making it more difficult or more expensive to procure an abortion cannot be enough to invalidate it. Only where state regulation imposes an undue burden on a woman's ability to make this decision does the power of the State reach into the heart of the liberty protected by the Due Process Clause. * * *

A finding of an undue burden is shorthand for the conclusion that a state regulation has the purpose or effect of placing a substantial obstacle in the path of a woman seeking an abortion of a nonviable fetus. A statute with this purpose is invalid because the means chosen by the State to further the interest in potential life must be calculated to inform the woman's free choice, not hinder it. And a statute which, while furthering the interest in potential life or some other valid state interest, has the effect of placing a substantial obstacle in the path of a woman's choice cannot be considered a permissible means of serving its legitimate ends. To the extent that the opinions of the Court or of individual Justices use the undue burden standard in a manner that is inconsistent with this analysis, we set out what in our view should be the controlling standard. In our considered judgment, an undue burden is an unconstitutional burden. Understood another way, we answer the question, left open in previous opinions discussing the undue burden formulation, whether a law designed to further the State's interest in fetal life which imposes an undue burden on the woman's decision before fetal viability could be constitutional. The answer is no.

Some guiding principles should emerge. What is at stake is the woman's right to make the ultimate decision, not a right to be insulated from all others in doing so. Regulations which do no more than create a structural mechanism by which the State, or the parent or guardian of a minor, may express profound respect for the life of the unborn are permitted, if they are not a substantial obstacle to the woman's exercise of the right to choose. Unless it has that effect on her right of choice, a state measure designed to persuade her to choose childbirth over abortion will be upheld if reasonably related to that goal. Regulations designed to foster the health of a woman seeking an abortion are valid if they do not constitute an undue burden. * * *

[Pennsylvania required a woman seeking an abortion to wait 24 hours (except in a medical emergency), so that she could consider information regarding the nature and risks of the procedure and the probable gestational age of the fetus, which the law required the physician to provide. The law required minors to obtain the consent of one parent, with a judicial-bypass option. Married women were required to notify their spouses. The Joint Opinion found only the spousal notification requirement unconstitutional, because it alone constituted an "undue burden" on the woman's right to choose an abortion.]

■ [We omit the opinions of JUSTICES BLACKMUN and STEVENS. They concurred in the Joint Opinion's refusal to overrule *Roe v. Wade* and its invalidation of the spousal notification requirement but dissented from the Joint Opinion's narrowing of *Roe v. Wade* and its upholding of the waiting period, informed consent, and parental consent requirements.]

■ CHIEF JUSTICE REHNQUIST, with whom JUSTICE WHITE, JUSTICE SCALIA, and JUSTICE THOMAS join, concurring in the judgment in part and dissenting in part.

* * * In *Roe v. Wade,* the Court recognized a "guarantee of personal privacy" which "is broad enough to encompass a woman's decision whether or not to terminate her pregnancy." We are now of the view that, in terming this right fundamental, the Court in *Roe* read the earlier opinions upon which it based its decision much too broadly. Unlike marriage, procreation, and contraception, abortion "involves the purposeful termination of a potential life." The abortion decision must therefore "be recognized as *sui generis*, different in kind from the others that the Court has protected under the rubric of personal or family privacy and autonomy." One cannot ignore the fact that a woman is not isolated in her pregnancy, and that the decision to abort necessarily involves the destruction of a fetus.

Nor do the historical traditions of the American people support the view that the right to terminate one's pregnancy is "fundamental." The common law which we inherited from England made abortion after "quickening" an offense. At the time of the adoption of the Fourteenth Amendment, statutory prohibitions or restrictions on abortion were commonplace; in 1868, at least 28 of the then-37 States and 8 Territories had statutes banning or limiting abortion. By the turn of the century virtually every State had a law prohibiting or restricting abortion on its books. By the middle of the present century, a liberalization trend had set in. But 21 of the restrictive abortion laws in effect in 1868 were still in effect in 1973 when *Roe* was decided, and an overwhelming majority of the States prohibited abortion unless necessary to preserve the life or health of the mother. On this record, it can scarcely be said that any deeply rooted tradition of relatively unrestricted abortion in our history supported the classification of the right to abortion as "fundamental" under the Due Process Clause of the Fourteenth Amendment.

We think, therefore, both in view of this history and of our decided cases dealing with substantive liberty under the Due Process Clause, that the Court was mistaken in *Roe* when it classified a woman's decision to terminate her pregnancy as a "fundamental right" that could be abridged only in a manner which withstood "strict scrutiny." * * *

We believe that the sort of constitutionally imposed abortion code of the type illustrated by our decisions following *Roe* is inconsistent "with the notion of a Constitution cast in general terms, as ours is, and usually speaking in general principles, as ours does." The Court in *Roe* reached too far when it analogized the right to abort a fetus to the rights involved in *Pierce*, *Meyer*, *Loving*, and *Griswold*, and thereby deemed the right to abortion fundamental. * * *

The joint opinion discusses several *stare decisis* factors which, it asserts, point toward retaining a portion of *Roe*. Two of these factors are that the main "factual underpinning" of *Roe* has remained the same, and that its doctrinal foundation is no weaker now than it was in 1973. Of course, what might be called the basic facts which gave rise to *Roe* have remained the same—women become pregnant, there is a point somewhere, depending on medical technology, where a fetus becomes viable, and women give birth to children. But this is only to say that the same facts which gave rise to *Roe* will continue to give rise to similar cases. It is not a reason, in and of itself, why those cases must be decided in the same incorrect manner as was the first case to deal with the question. And surely there is no requirement, in considering whether to depart from *stare decisis* in a constitutional case, that a decision be more wrong now than it was at the time it was rendered. If that were true, the most outlandish constitutional decision could survive forever, based simply on the fact that it was no more outlandish later than it was when originally rendered. * * *

The joint opinion thus turns to what can only be described as an unconventional—and unconvincing—notion of reliance, a view based on the surmise that the availability of abortion since *Roe* has led to "two decades of economic and social developments" that would be undercut if the error of *Roe* were recognized. The joint opinion's assertion of this fact is undeveloped and totally conclusory. In fact, one cannot be sure to what economic and social developments the opinion is referring. Surely it is dubious to suggest that women have reached their "places in society" in reliance upon *Roe*, rather than as a result of their determination to obtain higher education and compete with men in the job market, and of society's increasing recognition of their ability to fill positions that were previously thought to be reserved only for men.

[The CHIEF JUSTICE and the other dissenters would have upheld the entire statute and so concurred in the Joint Opinion's judgment upholding the waiting period, informed consent, and parental consent requirements. They dissented from the judgment striking down the spousal notification requirement. We omit the separate dissenting opinion of JUSTICE SCALIA.]

NOTES ON *CASEY*

1. *Rewriting* Roe. Although the Court stopped short of reversing *Roe v. Wade*, the *Casey* decision weakened women's right to have an abortion in significant ways. Doctrinally, there were two key steps, one involving the trimester framework used in *Roe* and the other involving the standard of review. Identify those two steps and then consider the practical effects of these changes. What kinds of laws that were invalid under the standards of *Roe* and *Akron* became permissible after *Casey*? What were the impacts of such laws?

2. *Reproductive Rights and Women's Full Citizenship.* Recall that *Roe v. Wade* was framed as about individual autonomy and medical professionalism, and did not link control over reproduction to women's equality or their ability to participate in economic and social life as full citizens. (See Chapter 1, Section 1B.)

After *Roe*, in a series of law review articles and briefs in abortion cases, feminists laid the groundwork for understanding sex equality to be a foundational doctrine supporting reproductive choice. The arguments slowly seeped into decisions. In *Thornburgh v. American College of Obstetricians and Gynecologists*, 476 U.S. 747 (1986), the Court referred to the Constitution's "promise that a certain private sphere of individual liberty will be kept largely beyond the reach of government," adding the equal liberty note: "That promise extends to women as well as to men." *Id.* at 772.

By the time of *Casey*, the Court's Joint Opinion addressed the impact of reproductive choice on the capacity of women to function in civil society as equals to men as a key factor in its stare decisis reasoning. Justice Blackmun's concurring and dissenting opinion in *Casey* went further and briefly suggested an explicit sex discrimination argument. In his concurring opinion, Justice Stevens wrote that the mandatory 24-hour delay between counseling and the actual abortion that was upheld by the Court "rests on outmoded and unacceptable assumptions about the decisionmaking capacity of women." *Casey*, 505 U.S. at 918. David Gans expanded on this point:

> * * *[T]he state interest in protecting the fetus by forcing reconsideration of the abortion decision merge[s] into an attempt to force women to be mothers. The statute questions women's decision-making power *insofar as women seek to free themselves from the vision of women as mothers*. If a woman does not want to follow the role society has chosen for her, the state discourages that choice, requiring her to make additional trips to the clinic, forcing her to pay for the extra travel, and exposing her to further loss of confidentiality.
>
> This becomes apparent when one compares the abortion context to other procedures in which a woman's decision will affect the life of another. In other matters of "life" and "death," the state does not second-guess a woman's decision or require her to wait a specified time period before effectuating her decision. For example, a pregnant woman may refuse medical treatment even though the fetus will not survive without such treatment. * * * Unlike the

decision to choose abortion, these other decisions about the type of medical care she will use do not implicate the state's vision of her proper social role. Such treatment may have the effect of ending a pregnancy, but it is not the purpose of the treatment to end a pregnancy. In the case of abortion, however, the state requires a woman to rethink her decision because she is violating social understandings of women's proper roles by using a treatment designed to end her pregnancy. Only in this context, where assumptions about women's proper roles are central, does the state allow fetal life to trump the rights of the woman to make decisions about her medical care.

David H. Gans, Note, "Stereotyping and Difference: *Planned Parenthood v. Casey* and the Future of Sex Discrimination Law," 104 *Yale L. J.* 1875, 1903–04 (1995) (emphasis in the original).

3. *The Construction of a Backlash.* By the time Casey was decided 25 years ago, it had become conventional wisdom that *Roe v. Wade* exemplified judicial overreach. The backlash against *Roe*, many believed, necessitated a jurisprudential and political correction, which the Joint Opinion in *Casey* supplied. Recent scholarship by Professors Reva Siegel and Linda Greenhouse, however, calls into question the understanding that the backlash originated as a kind of natural reaction to an extreme decision. There was little criticism of *Roe*, outside the Roman Catholic Church, for the first several years after it was announced. According to Siegel and Greenhouse, social conservatives then began framing it as a symbol and rallying point against a cluster of women's autonomy issues, including the ERA. (See Chapter 1, Section 2A.) "Traditional values" movements grew most rapidly among conservative Protestants, who then adopted anti-abortion positions for the first time. Linda Greenhouse and Reva B. Siegel, "Before (and After) *Roe v. Wade*: New Questions About Backlash," 120 *Yale L. J.* 2028 (2011). Consider the trajectory of so-called morality issues in U.S. politics, including jurisprudential movements, since *Casey* was decided in 1992. In what ways has the *Casey* compromise succeeded, or not, in fostering deliberative pluralism?

4. *What Is an "Undue Burden"?* After *Casey*, states continued to enact laws that impose various kinds of restrictions on access to abortion. For example, does the state impose an "undue burden" if it makes the process of securing an abortion significantly more expensive for the woman? How much more expensive would the process have to be for strict scrutiny to kick in? What if state regulators imposed new rules on abortion clinics that, indirectly, raised costs for women seeking abortions and/or made it much more difficult for women to find a local provider? The "jurisprudence of doubt" left in the wake of *Casey* lasted until the *Whole Woman's Health* case in Part C, *infra*.

B. THE STATE'S INTEREST IN FETAL LIFE

Under the *Roe v. Wade* regime, the state had no legitimate interest in promoting or protecting fetal life until after the point of viability. *Casey* jettisoned that rule, and opened the door for the state to "further its interest in potential life" at any point in the pregnancy so long as the methods chosen did not constitute an undue burden on the woman's "right to make the ultimate decision." This change provided the opportunity for legislatures to adopt laws that sought to indirectly channel women away from abortion even in the first trimester, through mechanisms such as required viewing of ultrasound images or prescriptive "informed consent" warnings.

A more direct method has been to outlaw certain forms of abortion after the fetus has begun to form. Second trimester abortions involve different medical techniques than those used in early abortions. An increasing number of first trimester abortions are non-surgical and occur after the patient takes a pill, a process somewhat confusingly called medical abortion. Other first trimester methods are vacuum aspiration and dilation and curettage (D&C); the latter involves scraping the uterus with a surgical tool called a curette. Dilation and extraction (D&E or D&X), the most controversial method, involves extracting the fetus from the uterus into the vagina. From there, the doctor either removes the fetal material in pieces or shrinks the head by aspiration and then removes the fetus intact.

Although only 11% of abortions are performed after the first trimester, the women who seek them tend to be younger, less economically secure and less educated than the women who obtain early abortions. Failure to realize that one is pregnant and greater distance from a provider are often associated with later abortions. Abortions because of serious fetal anomalies, though relatively rare, almost always occur during the second trimester because fetal testing is usually inconclusive before that time. Rachel K. Jones & Jenna Jerman, "Characteristics and Circumstances of U.S. Women Who Obtain Very Early and Second-Trimester Abortions," 12 *PLoS ONE* 1 (2017); Lawrence Finer et al., "Timing of Steps and Reasons for Delays in Obtaining Abortions in the United States," 74 *Contraception* 334 (2006).

Alberto R. Gonzales v. Leroy Carhart et al.

United States Supreme Court, 2007.
550 U.S. 124, 127 S.Ct. 1610, 167 L.Ed.2d 480.

■ JUSTICE KENNEDY delivered the opinion of the Court.

[In *Stenberg v. Carhart,* 530 U.S. 914 (2000), the Court overturned a Nebraska partial-birth abortion law that banned intact D & E (often termed D & X) procedures. The Court found two constitutional problems: first, the law was vague as to what procedures it actually criminalized; second, there was no exception to protect the health of the mother. After *Stenberg,* Congress passed a national Partial-Birth Abortion Ban Act of 2003. The federal statute prohibits "knowingly perform[ing] a partial-birth abortion . . . that is [not] necessary to save the life of a mother." There is no exclusion for abortions needed to protect the mother's health.

The statute defines a partial birth abortion as a procedure in which the doctor "(A) deliberately and intentionally vaginally delivers a living fetus until, in the case of a head-first presentation, the entire fetal head is outside the [mother's] body * * * or, in the case of breech presentation, any part of the fetal trunk past the navel is outside the [mother's] body * * * for the purpose of performing an overt act that the person knows will kill the partially delivered living fetus," and "(B) performs the overt act, other than completion of delivery, that kills the fetus."]

[I. Justice Kennedy opened his majority with a detailed description of the intact D & E (or D & X) procedures. He started with an "abortion doctor's clinical description," followed by "another description from a nurse who witnessed the same method performed on a 26-week fetus and who testified before the Senate Judiciary Committee":

> Dr. Haskell went in with forceps and grabbed the baby's legs and pulled them down into the birth canal. Then he delivered the baby's body and the arms—everything but the head. The doctor kept the head right inside the uterus.

> The baby's little fingers were clasping and unclasping, and his little feet were kicking. Then the doctor stuck the scissors in the back of his head, and the baby's arms jerked out, like a startle reaction, like a flinch, like a baby does when he thinks he is going to fall.

> The doctor opened up the scissors, stuck a high-powered suction tube into the opening, and sucked the baby's brains out. Now the baby went completely limp. . . .

> He cut the umbilical cord and delivered the placenta. He threw the baby in a pan, along with the placenta and the instruments he had just used.

Based upon testimony such as this, Congress found that "[a] moral, medical, and ethical consensus exists that the practice of performing a partial-birth abortion * * * is a gruesome and inhumane procedure that is never medically necessary and should be prohibited." Congressional Findings, 117 Stat. 1202, notes following 18 U.S.C. § 1531.]

[II.] The principles set forth in the joint opinion in [Casey] did not find support from all those who join the instant opinion. Whatever one's views concerning the Casey joint opinion, it is evident a premise central to its conclusion—that the government has a legitimate and substantial interest in preserving and promoting fetal life—would be repudiated were the Court now to affirm the judgments of the Courts of Appeals. * * *

We assume the following principles for the purposes of this opinion. Before viability, a State "may not prohibit any woman from making the ultimate decision to terminate her pregnancy." Casey (plurality [joint] opinion). It also may not impose upon this right an undue burden, which exists if a regulation's "purpose and effect is to place a substantial obstacle in the path of a woman seeking an abortion before the fetus obtains viability." On the other hand, "[r]egulations which do no more than create a structural mechanism by which the State, or the parent or the guardian of a minor, may express profound respect for the life of the unborn are permitted, if they are not a substantial obstacle to the woman's exercise of the right to choose." *Casey*, in short, struck a balance. The balance was central to its holding. We now apply its standard to the cases at bar. * * *

[The Court found that the statute was not unconstitutionally vague because it specified an "anatomical landmark" in the process of delivery that marked criminal liability, unlike the statute at issue in *Stenberg*, which referred to delivery of a "substantial portion" of the fetus. In addition, intent was an element of the crime in the newer statute: "a doctor performing a D & E will not face criminal liability if he or she delivers a fetus beyond the prohibited point by mistake."]

[III.C.] We next determine whether the Act imposes an undue burden, as a facial matter, because its restrictions on second-trimester abortions are too broad. A review of the statutory text discloses the limits of its reach. The Act prohibits intact D & E; and, notwithstanding respondents' arguments, it does not prohibit the D & E procedure in which the fetus is removed in parts. * * *

The Act excludes most D & E's in which the fetus is removed in pieces, not intact. If the doctor intends to remove the fetus in parts from the outset, the doctor will not have the requisite intent to incur criminal liability. A doctor performing a standard D & E procedure can often "tak[e] about 10–15 'passes' through the uterus to remove the entire fetus." Removing the fetus in this manner does not violate the Act because the doctor will not have delivered the living fetus to one of the anatomical landmarks or committed an additional overt act that kills the fetus after partial delivery. § 1531(b)(1). * * *

[IV. Finally, Justice Kennedy considered the *Casey*—based argument that the Act imposed a substantial obstacle to late-term but pre-viability abortions.]

[IV.A.] The Act's purposes are set forth in recitals preceding its operative provisions. A description of the prohibited abortion procedure demonstrates the rationale for the congressional enactment. The Act proscribes a method of abortion in which a fetus is killed just inches before completion of the birth process. Congress stated as follows: "Implicitly approving such a brutal and inhumane procedure by choosing not to prohibit it will further coarsen society to the humanity of not only newborns, but all vulnerable and innocent human life, making it increasingly difficult to protect such life." Congressional Findings. The Act expresses respect for the dignity of human life. * * *

Respect for human life finds an ultimate expression in the bond of love the mother has for her child. The Act recognizes this reality as well.

Whether to have an abortion requires a difficult and painful moral decision. *Casey.* While we find no reliable data to measure the phenomenon, it seems unexceptionable to conclude some women come to regret their choice to abort the infant life they once created and sustained. See Brief for Sandra Cano et al. as *Amici Curiae.* Severe depression and loss of esteem can follow. See *ibid.*

In a decision so fraught with emotional consequence some doctors may prefer not to disclose precise details of the means that will be used, confining themselves to the required statement of risks the procedure entails. From one standpoint this ought not to be surprising. Any number of patients facing imminent surgical procedures would prefer not to hear all details, lest the usual anxiety preceding invasive medical procedures become the more intense. This is likely the case with the abortion procedures here in issue.

It is, however, precisely this lack of information concerning the way in which the fetus will be killed that is of legitimate concern to the State. *Casey* (plurality opinion). The State has an interest in ensuring so grave a choice is well informed. It is self-evident that a mother who comes to regret her choice to abort must struggle with grief more anguished and sorrow more profound when she learns, only after the event, what she once did not know: that she allowed a doctor to pierce the skull and vacuum the fast-developing brain of her unborn child, a child assuming the human form.

It is a reasonable inference that a necessary effect of the regulation and the knowledge it conveys will be to encourage some women to carry the infant to full term, thus reducing the absolute number of late-term abortions. The medical profession, furthermore, may find different and less shocking methods to abort the fetus in the second trimester, thereby accommodating legislative demand. The State's interest in respect for life is advanced by the dialogue that better informs the political and legal systems, the medical profession, expectant mothers, and society as a whole of the consequences that follow from a decision to elect a late-term abortion.

It is objected that the standard D & E is in some respects as brutal, if not more, than the intact D & E, so that the legislation accomplishes little. What we have already said, however, shows ample justification for the regulation. Partial-birth abortion, as defined by the Act, differs from a standard D & E because the former occurs when the fetus is partially outside the mother to the point of one of the Act's anatomical landmarks. It was reasonable for Congress to think that partial-birth abortion, more than standard D & E, "undermines the public's perception of the appropriate role of a physician during the delivery process, and perverts a process during which life is brought into the world." Congressional Findings. * * * In sum, we reject the contention that the congressional purpose of the Act was "to place a substantial obstacle in the path of a woman seeking an abortion." *Casey* (plurality opinion).

[IV.B.]   The Act's furtherance of legitimate government interests bears upon, but does not resolve, the next question: whether the Act has the effect of imposing an unconstitutional burden on the abortion right because it does not allow use of the barred procedure where " 'necessary, in appropriate medical judgment, for [the] preservation of the . . . health of the mother.' " [W]hether the Act creates significant health risks for women has been a contested factual question. The evidence presented in the trial courts and before Congress demonstrates both sides have medical support for their position.

[For example, "abortion doctors" testified that intact D & E is safer for the pregnant woman, because it poses less risk of cervical laceration or uterine perforation and of leaving fetal material in the uterus. On the other hand, Justice Kennedy pointed to trial and congressional testimony "by other doctors" that D & E is "always" a safe alternative to intact D & E. "There is documented medical disagreement whether the Act's prohibition would ever impose significant health risks on women."]

The question becomes whether the Act can stand when this medical uncertainty persists. The Court's precedents instruct that the Act can survive this facial attack. The Court has given state and federal legislatures wide discretion to pass legislation in areas where there is medical and scientific uncertainty.

This traditional rule is consistent with *Casey*, which confirms the State's interest in promoting respect for human life at all stages in the pregnancy. Physicians are not entitled to ignore regulations that direct them to use reasonable alternative procedures. The law need not give abortion doctors unfettered choice in the course of their medical practice, nor should it elevate their status above other physicians in the medical community. * * *

Medical uncertainty does not foreclose the exercise of legislative power in the abortion context any more than it does in other contexts. The medical uncertainty over whether the Act's prohibition creates significant health risks provides a sufficient basis to conclude in this facial attack that the Act does not impose an undue burden. * * *

In reaching the conclusion the Act does not require a health exception we reject certain arguments made by the parties on both sides of these cases. On the one hand, the Attorney General urges us to uphold the Act on the basis of the congressional findings alone. Although we review congressional factfinding under a deferential standard, we do not in the circumstances here place dispositive weight on Congress' findings. The Court retains an independent constitutional duty to review factual findings where constitutional rights are at stake.

As respondents have noted, and the District Courts recognized, some recitations in the Act are factually incorrect. Whether or not accurate at the time, some of the important findings have been superseded. * * *

On the other hand, relying on the Court's opinion in *Stenberg*, respondents contend that an abortion regulation must contain a health exception "if 'substantial medical authority supports the proposition that banning a particular procedure could endanger women's health.' " As illustrated by respondents' arguments and the decisions of the Courts of Appeals, *Stenberg* has been interpreted to leave no margin of error for legislatures to act in the face of medical uncertainty.

A zero tolerance policy would strike down legitimate abortion regulations, like the present one, if some part of the medical community were disinclined to follow the proscription. This is too exacting a standard to impose on the legislative power, exercised in this instance under the Commerce Clause, to regulate the medical profession. Considerations of marginal safety, including the balance of risks, are within the legislative competence when the regulation is rational and in pursuit of legitimate ends. When standard medical options are available, mere convenience does not suffice to displace them; and if some procedures have different risks than others, it does not follow that the State is altogether barred from imposing reasonable regulations. The Act is not invalid on its face where there is uncertainty over whether the barred procedure is ever necessary to preserve a woman's health, given the availability of other abortion procedures that are considered to be safe alternatives. * * *

■ [JUSTICE THOMAS, joined by JUSTICE SCALIA, concurred in JUSTICE KENNEDY's opinion. They reiterated their view that "the Court's abortion jurisprudence, including *Casey* and *Roe v. Wade*, has no basis in the Constitution." JUSTICE THOMAS also noted that the parties had not raised the question of whether the statute exceeded Congress's Article I powers and, therefore, that the validity of Congress's exercising jurisdiction over this issue was not before the Court.]

■ JUSTICE GINSBURG, with whom JUSTICE STEVENS, JUSTICE SOUTER, and JUSTICE BREYER join, dissenting. * * *

Today's decision is alarming. It refuses to take *Casey* and *Stenberg* seriously. It tolerates, indeed applauds, federal intervention to ban nationwide a procedure found necessary and proper in certain cases by the American College of Obstetricians and Gynecologists (ACOG). It blurs the line, firmly drawn in *Casey*, between previability and postviability abortions. And, for the first time since *Roe*, the Court blesses a prohibition with no exception safeguarding a woman's health.

I dissent from the Court's disposition. Retreating from prior rulings that abortion restrictions cannot be imposed absent an exception safeguarding a woman's health, the Court upholds an Act that surely would not survive under the close scrutiny that previously attended state-decreed limitations on a woman's reproductive choices. * * *

[I.] As *Casey* comprehended, at stake in cases challenging abortion restrictions is a woman's "control over her own destiny." * * * [L]egal challenges to undue restrictions on abortion procedures do not seek to vindicate some generalized notion of privacy; rather, they center on a woman's autonomy to determine her life's course, and thus to enjoy equal citizenship stature. See, e.g., Siegel, Reasoning from the Body: A Historical Perspective on Abortion Regulation and Questions of Equal Protection, 44 Stan. L. Rev. 261 (1992); Law, Rethinking Sex and the Constitution, 132 U. Pa.L. Rev. 955, 1002–28 (1984).

In keeping with this comprehension of the right to reproductive choice, the Court has consistently required that laws regulating abortion, at any stage of pregnancy and in all cases, safeguard a woman's health. *Stenberg.*

[Justice Ginsburg noted that the federal statute had no health exception, based upon incorrect assumptions, such as the congressional finding that "[t]here is no credible medical evidence that partial-birth abortions are safe or are safer than other abortion procedures." Yet ACOG and other medical associations attested to Congress and the trial courts that "intact D & E carries meaningful safety advantages over other methods." Intact D & E minimizes the number of times a physician must insert instruments through the cervix and into the uterus, a minimization that helps the woman avoid risks of tearing and infection. Intact D & E reduces the risk that fetal material will be left in the uterus, which can cause infection, hemorrhage, and infertility. Intact D & E diminishes the chances of exposing the woman's tissues to sharp bony fragments sometimes resulting from dismemberment of the fetus. Intact D & E takes less operating time, thereby reducing risks of complications relating to anesthesia. Justice Ginsburg maintained that there was no reasonable basis to believe otherwise, as reflected in the trial record.]

[II.] The Court offers flimsy and transparent justifications for upholding a nationwide ban on intact D & E *sans* any exception to safeguard a women's health. Today's ruling, the Court declares, advances "a premise central to [*Casey's*] conclusion"—*i.e.,* the Government's "legitimate and substantial interest in preserving and promoting fetal life." But the Act scarcely furthers that interest: The law saves not a single fetus from destruction, for it targets only a *method* of performing abortion. And surely the statute was not designed to protect the lives or health of pregnant women. In short, the Court upholds a law that, while doing nothing to "preserv[e] . . . fetal life," bars a woman from choosing intact D & E although her doctor "reasonably believes [that procedure] will best protect [her]." * * *

Ultimately, the Court admits that "moral concerns" are at work, concerns that could yield prohibitions on any abortion. Notably, the concerns expressed are untethered to any ground genuinely serving the Government's interest in preserving life. By allowing such concerns to carry the day and case, overriding fundamental rights, the Court dishonors our precedent.

Revealing in this regard, the Court invokes an antiabortion shibboleth for which it concededly has no reliable evidence: Women who have abortions come to regret their choices, and consequently suffer from "[s]evere depression and loss of esteem." Because of women's fragile emotional state and because of the "bond of love the mother has for her child," the Court worries, doctors may withhold information about the nature of the intact D & E procedure. The solution the Court approves, then, is *not* to require doctors to inform women, accurately and adequately, of the different procedures and their attendant risks. Instead, the Court deprives women of the right to make an autonomous choice, even at the expense of their safety.

This way of thinking reflects ancient notions about women's place in the family and under the Constitution—ideas that have long since been discredited.

Though today's majority may regard women's feelings on the matter as "self-evident," this Court has repeatedly confirmed that "[t]he destiny of the woman must be shaped . . . on her own conception of her spiritual imperatives and her place in society." *Casey.* * * *

* * * In candor, the Act, and the Court's defense of it, cannot be understood as anything other than an effort to chip away at a right declared again and again by this Court—and with increasing comprehension of its centrality to women's lives. * * *

NOTES ON *CARHART* AND THE EVOLVING RIGHT TO PRIVACY

1. *Is There a Core to the Privacy Right?* Does Justice Kennedy have persuasive answers to Justice Ginsburg's arguments that the Court is departing from precedent in various ways, including *Stenberg*'s holding that state limits on pre-viability abortion methods must include a mother's health exception and *Casey*'s holding that the state cannot impose undue burdens on women seeking pre-viability abortions? The Court responds that *Casey* set a "balance," and the woman's liberty is just one prong of that balance. But the question remains whether the Court is departing from reasoning essential to these precedents.

Justice Ginsburg's dissenting opinion essentially accuses the majority—five politically conservative male Justices—of writing their gendered morality into the Constitution. Implicit in the background for her dissent (which she chose to read aloud when the decision was announced) was alarm at the replacement of Justice O'Connor, who joined the *Stenberg* majority in finding that statute to be unconstitutional, with Justice Alito, who was in the *Carhart* majority.

After *Carhart*, women may still have a "liberty" to choose abortions, but not with the safest procedure for later but still pre-viability abortions. Although we have edited the majority opinion's extensive description of the intact D & E procedure, the nurse's description of it in our excerpt conveys to you the palpable disgust that Justice Kennedy must feel toward the procedure. Bluntly, intact D & E looks too much like infanticide for the nurse and the Justices in the majority to find it acceptable.

2. *The Relationship of Carhart to Lawrence.* Consider the similarities between *Carhart* and *Lawrence* (Section 2A, *infra*). Justice Kennedy, the author of five-Justice majority opinions in both cases, overruled (*Lawrence*) or narrowly construed *(Carhart)* recent precedents, abandoned the "fundamental rights" framework and treated privacy as simply a due process "liberty" that can be regulated in a number of ways, but not "too much."

The differences between the two opinions are also notable and might help us understand the limits of *Lawrence* as well as the normative problems with *Carhart*. First, equal citizenship played a key role in *Lawrence*, as a reason to give bite to the privacy right, while it was not only ignored but rhetorically inverted in *Carhart*. Justice Ginsburg's dissent not only emphasized the relationship of abortion choice to women's equal citizenship, but also charged that the Court's rhetoric revealed a slanted perspective. Women appear in the majority opinion more frequently as body parts than as subjects, and in describing their agency, Justice Kennedy presented women as prone to regret.

In addition, morality played a different role in the two cases. *Lawrence* announced that sectarian morality cannot justify invading gay people's privacy—but *Carhart* said that the same kind of natural law morality can require women seeking late-term abortions to fall back on riskier procedures. Virtually all women who decide to terminate a pregnancy prefer to have the procedure done as early as possible, but encounter various barriers. Should that matter? Does *Carhart* suggest that in certain circumstances, a state's view of morality can justify restrictions on a woman's right to choose a pre-viability abortion?

Justice Kennedy co-authored the Joint Opinion in *Casey*, so he has put himself on record that women's abortion choices cannot be completely foreclosed by moral views. But, thirdly, he seems moved by disgust, which played a different role in the two cases. In *Lawrence*, Justice Kennedy said nothing about what actually goes on in the homosexual bedroom, while his *Carhart* opinion laid out the process of partial-birth abortion from the perspective of a nurse who viewed it as killing a helpless baby. Most readers will be disgusted by what they read in Part I of *Carhart*, but only the most dedicated homophobe would be disgusted by the sanitized presentation of gay relationships in *Lawrence*.

All three points are related. Social scientists have found that people's moral opinions are shaped by what "disgusts" them, and public morality is shaped by creating disgusting images and associating them with certain people (homosexuals) or practices (sodomy) or both (the homosexual is always a disgusting sodomite). Reflecting modern social attitudes, *Lawrence* disrupts that process for homosexuals and sodomy, but *Carhart* initiates a new process that partially reverses what *Roe* and *Casey* were trying to do, namely, disaggregate women's life choices from the view of abortion as infanticide.

3. *Operation Outcry.* The argument that women regret abortions has been an important theme of the pro-life social movement since the 1980s, if not before. See Reva Siegel, "The New Politics of Abortion: An Equality Analysis of Woman-Protecting Abortion Restrictions," 2007 *U. Ill. L. Rev.* 992. As early as 1981, pro-life thinkers were referring to "post-abortion syndrome," a variant of post-traumatic stress disorder. Although post-abortion syndrome was rejected as a medical concept by (pro-life) Surgeon General C. Everett Koop and has never been recognized by a professional medical association, it has achieved status as folk wisdom. See Emily Bazelon, "Is There a Post-Abortion Syndrome?," N.Y. Times Magazine, Jan. 21, 2007.

Founded in Texas, the Justice Foundation created *Operation Outcry* as a project "to end legal abortion by exposing the truth about its devastating impact on women and families. We believe this will be accomplished through prayer and with testimonies of mothers who have taken the life of their own unborn babies and of others who have suffered harm from abortion." (Source: www.operationoutcry.org) Operation Outcry collected sworn affidavits from thousands of women, most of whom submitted their testimonies through the operation's website. These sworn affidavits were the factual basis for an abortion ban adopted by the South Dakota Legislature in 2005 (later revoked by a popular referendum) and for the amicus brief Justice Kennedy credited in *Carhart*.

The methodology of Operation Outcry bears some similarity to the consciousness-raising method of some feminist political campaigns, such as the anti-pornography campaigns in Minneapolis and Indianapolis in the early 1980s. It has thus far attracted little support within mainstream medical science. "The best studies available on psychological responses to unwanted pregnancy terminated by abortion in the United States suggest that severe negative reactions are rare, and they parallel those following other normal life stresses." N.E. Adler et al., "Psychological Factors in Abortion: A Review," *American Psychologist*, Oct. 1992, 1194, 1202. A five-year follow-up study found that a history of mental health problems and traumatic experiences, such as child abuse, were the most significant factors predictive of adverse mental health outcomes following abortion. M. Antonia Biggs et. al., "Women's Mental After Having or Being Denied an Abortion," *JAMA Psychiatry online*, Dec. 14, 2016. What are the strongest arguments for and against deferring to state legislatures that cite psychological damage from regret as a basis for restrictive laws?

C. CLARIFYING "UNDUE BURDEN"

What test should courts use to determine when a state-imposed burden on having an abortion becomes "undue"? According to recent data, the concentration of abortion among poor women is not only intense, but also is increasing, even as the overall number and rate of abortions is decreasing. In 2000, 27% of women having abortions were poor. The percentage shot up to 42% in 2008 and to 49% in 2014. [The study defines poverty as a family income up to the Federal Poverty Level (FPL). As of 2017, the FPL was set at $24,600 for a family of four.] Among poor women, Black and Hispanic women were overrepresented. Jenna Jerman et al., "Characteristics of U.S. Abortion Patients in 2014 and

Changes Since 2008," Guttmacher Institute (2016). These figures do not represent poor women having an increasing number of abortions. Rather, they indicate that more economically secure women are having fewer and that abortion is more and more an issue of poverty as well as women's rights.

Access is critical, especially for low-income women. As of 2014, 90% of counties, with 39% of the population, had no abortion provider. The effect was to create a geographically skewed map for access to services: 55% of women in the Midwest lived in counties without a provider, as did 51% of women in the South. By comparison, the figure was 23% for women in the Northeast and 17% for women in the West.

Whole Woman's Health et al. v. Hellerstedt, Commissioner, Texas Dep't of State Health Services, et al.

United States Supreme Court, 2016.
___ U.S. ___, 136 S.Ct. 2292, 195 L.Ed.2d 665.

■ JUSTICE BREYER delivered the opinion of the Court.

In *Planned Parenthood of Southeastern Pa. v. Casey*, a plurality of the Court concluded that there "exists" an "undue burden" on a woman's right to decide to have an abortion, and consequently a provision of law is constitutionally invalid, if the "*purpose or effect*" of the provision "*is to place a substantial obstacle*" in the path of a woman seeking an abortion before the fetus attains viability. (Emphasis added.) The plurality added that "[u]nnecessary health regulations that have the purpose or effect of presenting a substantial obstacle to a woman seeking an abortion impose an undue burden on the right."

We must here decide whether two provisions of Texas' House Bill 2 violate the Federal Constitution as interpreted in *Casey*. The first provision, which we shall call the "*admitting-privileges requirement*," says that

> "[a] physician performing or inducing an abortion . . . must, on the date the abortion is performed or induced, have active admitting privileges at a hospital that . . . is located not further than 30 miles from the location at which the abortion is performed or induced." * * *

The second provision, which we shall call the "*surgical-center requirement*," says that

> "the minimum standards for an abortion facility must be equivalent to the minimum standards adopted under [the Texas Health and Safety Code section] for ambulatory surgical centers."

We conclude that neither of these provisions offers medical benefits sufficient to justify the burdens upon access that each imposes. Each places a substantial obstacle in the path of women seeking a previability abortion, each constitutes an undue burden on abortion access, *Casey*, and each violates the Federal Constitution.

[I.] * * * The District Court received stipulations from the parties and depositions from the parties' experts. The court conducted a 4-day bench trial. It heard, among other testimony, the opinions from expert witnesses for both sides. On the basis of the stipulations, depositions, and testimony, that court reached the following conclusions

1.   Of Texas' population of more than 25 million people, "approximately 5.4 million" are "women" of "reproductive age," living within a geographical area of "nearly 280,000 square miles."

2.   "In recent years, the number of abortions reported in Texas has stayed fairly consistent at approximately 15–16% of the reported pregnancy rate, for a total number of approximately 60,000–72,000 legal abortions performed annually."

3.   Prior to the enactment of H.B. 2, there were more than 40 licensed abortion facilities in Texas, which "number dropped by almost half leading up to and in the wake of enforcement of the admitting-privileges requirement that went into effect in late-October 2013."

4.   If the surgical-center provision were allowed to take effect, the number of abortion facilities, after September 1, 2014, would be reduced further, so that "only seven facilities and a potential eighth will exist in Texas."

5.   Abortion facilities "will remain only in Houston, Austin, San Antonio, and the Dallas/Fort Worth metropolitan region." These include "one facility in Austin, two in Dallas, one in Fort Worth, two in Houston, and either one or two in San Antonio."

6.   "Based on historical data pertaining to Texas's average number of abortions, and assuming perfectly equal distribution among the remaining seven or eight providers, this would result in each facility serving between 7,500 and 10,000 patients per year. Accounting for the seasonal variations in pregnancy rates and a slightly unequal distribution of patients at each clinic, it is foreseeable that over 1,200 women per month could be vying for counseling, appointments, and follow-up visits at some of these facilities."

7.   The suggestion "that these seven or eight providers could meet the demand of the entire state stretches credulity."

8.   "Between November 1, 2012 and May 1, 2014," that is, before and after enforcement of the admitting-privileges requirement, "the decrease in geographical distribution of abortion facilities" has meant that the number of women of reproductive age living more than 50 miles from a clinic has doubled (from 800,000 to over 1.6 million); those living more than 100 miles has increased by 150% (from 400,000 to 1 million); those living more than 150 miles has increased by more than 350% (from

86,000 to 400,000); and those living more than 200 miles has increased by about 2,800% (from 10,000 to 290,000). After September 2014, should the surgical-center requirement go into effect, the number of women of reproductive age living significant distances from an abortion provider will increase as follows: 2 million women of reproductive age will live more than 50 miles from an abortion provider; 1.3 million will live more than 100 miles from an abortion provider; 900,000 will live more than 150 miles from an abortion provider; and 750,000 more than 200 miles from an abortion provider.

9.   The "two requirements erect a particularly high barrier for poor, rural, or disadvantaged women."

10.   "The great weight of evidence demonstrates that, before the act's passage, abortion in Texas was extremely safe with particularly low rates of serious complications and virtually no deaths occurring on account of the procedure."

11.   "Abortion, as regulated by the State before the enactment of House Bill 2, has been shown to be much safer, in terms of minor and serious complications, than many common medical procedures not subject to such intense regulation and scrutiny." (describing risks in colonoscopies, vasectomy, endometrial biopsy, and plastic surgery).

12.   "Additionally, risks are not appreciably lowered for patients who undergo abortions at ambulatory surgical centers as compared to nonsurgical-center facilities."

13.   "[W]omen will not obtain better care or experience more frequent positive outcomes at an ambulatory surgical center as compared to a previously licensed facility."

14.   "[T]here are 433 licensed ambulatory surgical centers in Texas," of which "336 . . . are apparently either "grandfathered" or enjo[y] the benefit of a waiver of some or all" of the surgical-center "requirements."

15.   The "cost of coming into compliance" with the surgical-center requirement "for existing clinics is significant," "undisputedly approach[ing] 1 million dollars," and "most likely exceed[ing] 1.5 million dollars," with "[s]ome . . . clinics" unable to "comply due to physical size limitations of their sites." The "cost of acquiring land and constructing a new compliant clinic will likely exceed three million dollars."

On the basis of these and other related findings, the District Court determined that the surgical-center requirement "imposes an undue burden on the right of women throughout Texas to seek a previability abortion," and that the "admitting-privileges requirement, . . . in conjunction with the ambulatory-surgical-center requirement, imposes an undue burden on the right of women in the Rio Grande Valley, El Paso, and West Texas to seek a previability abortion." The District Court concluded that the "two provisions" would cause "the closing of almost all abortion clinics in Texas that were operating legally in the fall of 2013," and thereby create a constitutionally "impermissible obstacle as applied to all women seeking a previability abortion" by "restricting access to previously available legal facilities." On August 29, 2014, the court enjoined the enforcement of the two provisions. [46 F.Supp.3d 673 (W.D.Tex. 2014).] * * *

On June 9, 2015, the Court of Appeals reversed the District Court on the merits. [790 F.3d 563 (5th Cir. 2015.] Because the Court of Appeals' decision rests upon alternative grounds and fact-related considerations, we set forth its basic reasoning in some detail. The Court of Appeals concluded:

- The District Court was wrong to hold the admitting-privileges requirement unconstitutional because (except for the clinics in McAllen and El Paso) the providers had not asked them to do so, and principles of res judicata barred relief.

- Because the providers could have brought their constitutional challenge to the surgical-center provision in their earlier lawsuit, principles of res judicata also barred that claim.

- In any event, a state law "regulating previability abortion is constitutional if: (1) it does not have the purpose or effect of placing a substantial obstacle in the path of a woman seeking an abortion of a nonviable fetus; and (2) it is reasonably related to (or designed to further) a legitimate state interest."

- "[B]oth the admitting privileges requirement and" the surgical-center requirement "were rationally related to a legitimate state interest," namely, "rais[ing] the standard and quality of care for women seeking abortions and . . . protect[ing] the health and welfare of women seeking abortions."

- The "[p]laintiffs" failed "to proffer competent evidence contradicting the legislature's statement of a legitimate purpose."

- "[T]he district court erred by substituting its own judgment [as to the provisions" effects] for that of the legislature, albeit . . . in the name of the undue burden inquiry."

- Holding the provisions unconstitutional on their face is improper because the plaintiffs had failed to show that either of the provisions "imposes an undue burden on a large fraction of women."

- The District Court erred in finding that, if the surgical-center requirement takes effect, there will be too few abortion providers in Texas to meet the demand. That factual determination was based upon the finding of one of plaintiffs" expert witnesses (Dr. Grossman) that abortion providers in Texas" "will not be able to go from providing approximately 14,000 abortions annually, as they currently are, to providing the 60,000 to 70,000 abortions that are done each year in Texas once all" "of the clinics failing to meet the surgical-center requirement" "are forced to close." But Dr. Grossman's opinion is (in the Court of Appeals" view)" "*ipse dixit*"; the "record lacks any actual evidence regarding the current or future capacity of the eight clinics"; and there is no "evidence in the record that" "the providers that currently meet the surgical-center requirement" "are operating at full capacity or that they cannot increase capacity." * * *

[II. The Court found that Plaintiffs" claims were not precluded because the regulations at issue here had changed from those at issue in a prior round of litigation.]

[III. *Undue Burden—Legal Standard.*] We begin with the standard, as described in *Casey*. We recognize that the "State has a legitimate interest in seeing to it that abortion, like any other medical procedure, is performed under circumstances that insure maximum safety for the patient." *Roe v. Wade*. But, we added, "a statute which, while furthering [a] valid state interest, has the effect of placing a substantial obstacle in the path of a woman's choice cannot be considered a permissible means of serving its legitimate ends." *Casey* (plurality opinion). Moreover, "[u]nnecessary health regulations that have the purpose or effect of presenting a substantial obstacle to a woman seeking an abortion impose an undue burden on the right."

The Court of Appeals wrote that a state law is "constitutional if: (1) it does not have the purpose or effect of placing a substantial obstacle in the path of a woman seeking an abortion of a nonviable fetus; and (2) it is reasonably related to (or designed to further) a legitimate state interest." The Court of Appeals went on to hold that "the district court erred by substituting its own judgment for that of the legislature" when it conducted its "undue burden inquiry," in part because "medical uncertainty underlying a statute is for resolution by legislatures, not the courts."

The Court of Appeals' articulation of the relevant standard is incorrect. The first part of the Court of Appeals" test may be read to imply that a district court should not consider the existence or nonexistence of medical benefits when considering whether a regulation of abortion constitutes an undue burden. The rule announced in *Casey*, however, requires that courts consider the burdens a law imposes on abortion access together with the benefits those laws confer. And the second part of the test is wrong to equate the judicial review applicable to the regulation of a constitutionally protected personal liberty with the less strict review applicable where, for example, economic legislation is at issue. The Court of Appeals" approach simply does not match the standard that this Court laid out in *Casey*, which asks courts to consider whether any burden imposed on abortion access is "undue."

The statement that legislatures, and not courts, must resolve questions of medical uncertainty is also inconsistent with this Court's case law. Instead, the Court, when determining the constitutionality of laws regulating abortion procedures, has placed considerable weight upon evidence and argument presented in judicial proceedings. In *Casey*, for example, we relied heavily on the District Court's factual findings and the research-based submissions of *amici* in declaring a portion of the law at issue unconstitutional. And, in *Gonzales* [v. *Carhart*], the Court, while pointing out that we must review legislative "factfinding under a deferential standard," added that we must not "place dispositive weight" on those "findings." *Gonzales* went on to point out that the "*Court retains an independent constitutional duty to review factual findings where constitutional rights are at stake.*" (emphasis added). Although there we upheld a statute regulating abortion, we did not do so solely on the basis of legislative findings explicitly set forth in the statute, noting that "evidence presented in the District Courts contradicts" some of the legislative findings. In these circumstances, we said, "[u]ncritical deference to Congress' factual findings . . . is inappropriate."

Unlike in *Gonzales*, the relevant statute here does not set forth any legislative findings. Rather, one is left to infer that the legislature sought to further a constitutionally acceptable objective (namely, protecting women's health). For a district court to give significant weight to evidence in the judicial record in these circumstances is consistent with this Court's case law. As we shall describe, the District Court did so here. It did not simply substitute its own judgment for that of the legislature. It considered the evidence in the record—including expert evidence, presented in stipulations, depositions, and testimony. It then weighed the asserted benefits against the burdens. We hold that, in so doing, the District Court applied the correct legal standard.

[IV. *Undue Burden—Admitting-Privileges Requirement*] * * * The purpose of the admitting-privileges requirement is to help ensure that women have easy access to a hospital should complications arise during an abortion procedure. But the District Court found that it brought about no such health-related benefit. The court found that "[t]he great weight of evidence demonstrates that, before the act's passage, abortion in Texas was extremely safe with particularly low rates of serious complications and virtually no deaths occurring on account of the procedure." Thus, there was no significant health-related problem that the new law helped to cure.

The evidence upon which the court based this conclusion included [peer-reviewed studies and multiple experts.] * * *

We add that, when directly asked at oral argument whether Texas knew of a single instance in which the new requirement would have holpod over one woman obtain better treatment, Texas admitted that there was no evidence in the record of such a case. This answer is consistent with the findings of the other Federal District Courts that have considered the health benefits of other States" similar admitting-privileges laws. See *Planned Parenthood of Wis., Inc. v. Van Hollen*, 94 F. Supp. 3d 949, 953 (W.D. Wis. 2015), aff'd *sub nom. Planned Parenthood of Wis., Inc. v. Schimel*, 806 F. 3d 908 (7th Cir. 2015); *Planned Parenthood Southeast, Inc. v. Strange*, 33 F. Supp. 3d 1330, 1378 (M.D. Ala. 2014).

At the same time, the record evidence indicates that the admitting-privileges requirement places a "substantial obstacle in the path of a woman's choice." The District Court found, as of the time the admitting-privileges requirement began to be enforced, the number of facilities providing abortions dropped in half, from about 40 to about 20. Eight abortion clinics closed in the months leading up to the requirement's effective date. Eleven more closed on the day the admitting-privileges requirement took effect.

Other evidence helps to explain why the new requirement led to the closure of clinics. We read that other evidence in light of a brief filed in this Court by the Society of Hospital Medicine. That brief describes the undisputed general fact that "hospitals often condition admitting privileges on reaching a certain number of admissions per year." * * * In a word, doctors would be unable to maintain admitting privileges or obtain those privileges for the future, because the fact that abortions are so safe meant that providers were unlikely to have any patients to admit. * * *

In our view, the record contains sufficient evidence that the admitting-privileges requirement led to the closure of half of Texas' clinics, or thereabouts. Those closures meant fewer doctors, longer waiting times, and increased crowding. Record evidence also supports the finding that after the admitting-privileges provision went into effect, the "number of women of reproductive age living in a county . . . more than 150 miles from a provider increased from approximately 86,000 to 400,000 . . . and the number of women living in a county more than 200 miles from a provider from approximately 10,000 to 290,000." We recognize that increased driving distances do not always constitute an "undue burden." See *Casey*. But here, those increases are but one additional burden, which, when taken together with others that the closings brought about, and when viewed in light of the virtual absence of any health benefit, lead us to conclude that the record adequately supports the District Court's "undue burden" conclusion. * * *

[V. *Undue Burden—Surgical-Center Requirement*] The second challenged provision of Texas' new law sets forth the surgical-center requirement. Prior to enactment of the new requirement, Texas law required abortion facilities to meet a host of health and safety requirements. Under those pre-existing laws, facilities were subject to annual reporting and recordkeeping requirements, a quality assurance program, personnel policies and staffing requirements, physical and environmental requirements, infection control standards, disclosure requirements, patient-rights standards, and medical- and clinical-services standards, including anesthesia standards. These requirements are policed by random and announced inspections, at least annually, as well as administrative penalties, injunctions, civil penalties, and criminal penalties for certain violations.

H.B. 2 added the requirement that an "abortion facility" meet the "minimum standards . . . for ambulatory surgical centers" under Texas law. The surgical-center regulations include, among other things, detailed specifications relating to the size of the nursing staff, building dimensions, and other building requirements. The nursing staff must comprise at least "an adequate number of [registered nurses] on duty to meet the following minimum staff requirements: director of the department (or designee), and supervisory and staff personnel for each service area to assure the immediate availability of [a registered nurse] for emergency care or for any patient when needed," as well as "a second individual on duty on the premises who is trained and currently certified in basic cardiac life support until all patients have been discharged from the facility" for facilities that provide moderate sedation, such as most abortion facilities. Facilities must include a full surgical suite with an operating room that has "a clear floor area of at least 240 square feet" in which "[t]he minimum clear dimension between built-in cabinets, counters, and shelves shall be 14 feet." There must be a preoperative patient holding room and a postoperative recovery suite. The former "shall be provided and arranged in a one-way traffic pattern so that patients entering from outside the surgical suite can change, gown, and move directly into the restricted corridor of the surgical suite," and the latter "shall be arranged to provide a one-way traffic pattern from the restricted surgical corridor to the postoperative recovery suite, and then to the extended observation rooms or discharge." Surgical centers must meet numerous other spatial requirements, including specific corridor widths. Surgical centers must also have an advanced heating, ventilation, and air conditioning system, and must satisfy particular piping system and plumbing requirements. Dozens of other sections list additional requirements that apply to surgical centers.

There is considerable evidence in the record supporting the District Court's findings indicating that the statutory provision requiring all abortion facilities to meet all surgical-center standards does not benefit patients and is not necessary. The District Court found that "risks are not appreciably lowered for patients who undergo abortions at ambulatory surgical centers as compared to nonsurgical-center facilities." The court added that women "will not obtain better care or experience more frequent positive outcomes at an ambulatory surgical center as compared to a previously licensed facility." And these findings are well supported.

The record makes clear that the surgical-center requirement provides no benefit when complications arise in the context of an abortion produced through medication. That is because, in such a case, complications would almost always arise only after the patient has left the facility. The record also contains evidence indicating that abortions taking place in an abortion facility are safe—indeed, safer than numerous procedures that take place outside hospitals and to which Texas does not apply its surgical-center requirements. * * * Nationwide, childbirth is 14 times more likely than abortion to result in death, but Texas law allows a midwife to oversee childbirth in the patient's own home. Colonoscopy, a procedure that typically takes place outside a hospital (or surgical center) setting, has a mortality rate 10 times higher than an abortion.

The upshot is that this record evidence, along with the absence of any evidence to the contrary, provides ample support for the District Court's conclusion that "[m]any of the building standards mandated by the act and its implementing rules have such a tangential relationship to patient safety in the context of abortion as to be nearly arbitrary." That conclusion, along with the supporting evidence, provides sufficient support for the more general conclusion that the surgical-center requirement "will not [provide] better care or . . . more frequent positive outcomes." The record evidence thus supports the ultimate legal conclusion that the surgical-center requirement is not necessary.

At the same time, the record provides adequate evidentiary support for the District Court's conclusion that the surgical-center requirement places a substantial obstacle in the path of women seeking an abortion. The parties stipulated that the requirement would further reduce the number of abortion facilities available to seven or eight facilities, located in Houston, Austin, San Antonio, and Dallas/Fort Worth. In the District Court's view, the proposition that these "seven or eight providers could meet the demand of the entire State stretches credulity." We take this statement as a finding that these few facilities could not 'meet' that "demand." * * *

Finally, the District Court found that the costs that a currently licensed abortion facility would have to incur to meet the surgical-center requirements were considerable, ranging from $1 million per facility (for facilities with adequate space) to $3 million per facility (where additional land must be purchased). This evidence supports the conclusion that more surgical centers will not soon fill the gap when licensed facilities are forced to close.

We agree with the District Court that the surgical-center requirement, like the admitting-privileges requirement, provides few, if any, health benefits for women, poses a substantial obstacle to women seeking abortions, and constitutes an "undue burden" on their constitutional right to do so.

[VI. * * * "Texas claims that the provisions at issue here do not impose a substantial obstacle because the women affected by those laws are not a "large fraction" of Texan women "of reproductive age," which Texas reads *Casey* to have required. But *Casey* used the language "large fraction" to refer to "a large fraction of cases in which [the provision at issue] is *relevant*," a class narrower than "all women," "pregnant women," or even "the class of *women seeking abortions* identified by the State." (emphasis added). Here, as in *Casey*, the relevant denominator is "those [women] for whom [the provision] is an actual rather than an irrelevant restriction." * * *

■ JUSTICE GINSBURG, concurring.

* * * Given [the medical safety of legal abortion], it is beyond rational belief that H.B. 2 could genuinely protect the health of women, and certain that the law "would simply make it more difficult for them to obtain abortions." *Planned Parenthood of Wis. v. Schimel*. When a State severely limits access to safe and legal procedures, women in desperate circumstances may resort to unlicensed rogue practitioners, *faute de mieux*, at great risk to their health and safety. So long as this Court adheres to *Roe v. Wade* and *Planned Parenthood of Southeastern Pa. v. Casey*, Targeted Regulation of Abortion Providers laws like H.B. 2 that "do little or nothing for health, but rather strew impediments to abortion," *Planned Parenthood of Wis.*, cannot survive judicial inspection.

■ JUSTICE THOMAS, dissenting.

I remain fundamentally opposed to the Court's abortion jurisprudence. Even taking *Casey* as the baseline, however, the majority radically rewrites the undue-burden test in three ways. First, today's decision requires courts to "consider the burdens a law imposes on abortion access together with the benefits those laws confer." Second, today's opinion tells the courts that, when the law's justifications are medically uncertain, they need not defer to the legislature, and must instead assess medical justifications for abortion restrictions by scrutinizing the record themselves. Finally, even if a law imposes no "substantial obstacle" to women's access to abortions, the law now must have more than a "reasonabl[e] relat[ion] to . . . a legitimate state interest." These precepts are nowhere to be found in *Casey* or its successors, and transform the undue-burden test to something much more akin to strict scrutiny.

The majority's furtive reconfiguration of the standard of scrutiny applicable to abortion restrictions also points to a deeper problem. The undue-burden standard is just one variant of the Court's tiers-of-scrutiny approach to constitutional adjudication. And the label the Court affixes to its level of scrutiny in assessing whether the government can restrict a given right—be it "rational basis," intermediate, strict, or something else—is increasingly a meaningless formalism. As the Court applies whatever standard it likes to any given case, nothing but empty words separates our constitutional decisions from judicial fiat. * * *

These labels now mean little. Whatever the Court claims to be doing, in practice it is treating its "doctrine referring to tiers of scrutiny as guidelines informing our approach to the case at hand, not tests to be mechanically applied." *Williams-Yulee* [*v. Florida Bar*, 135 S.Ct. 1656, 1673 (2015)] (BREYER, J., concurring). The Court should abandon the pretense that anything other than policy preferences underlies its balancing of constitutional rights and interests in any given case. * * *

In 1938, seven Justices heard a constitutional challenge to a federal ban on shipping adulterated milk in interstate commerce. Without economic substantive due process, the ban clearly invaded no constitutional right. See *United States v. Carolene Products Co.* Within Justice Stone's opinion for the Court, however, was a footnote that just three other Justices joined—the famous *Carolene Products* Footnote 4. The footnote's * * * third and most familiar paragraph raised the question "whether prejudice against discrete and insular minorities may be a special condition, which tends seriously to curtail the operation of those political processes ordinarily to be relied upon to protect minorities, and which may call for a correspondingly more searching judicial inquiry."

Though the footnote was pure dicta, the Court seized upon it to justify its special treatment of certain personal liberties like the First Amendment and the right against discrimination on the basis of race—but also rights not enumerated in the Constitution. As the Court identified which rights deserved special protection, it developed the tiers of scrutiny as part of its equal protection (and, later, due process) jurisprudence as a way to demand extra justifications for encroachments on these rights. And, having created a new category of fundamental rights, the Court loosened the reins to recognize even putative rights like abortion, which hardly implicate "discrete and insular minorities." * * *

■ JUSTICE ALITO, with whom THE CHIEF JUSTICE and JUSTICE THOMAS join, dissenting.

The constitutionality of laws regulating abortion is one of the most controversial issues in American law, but this case does not require us to delve into that contentious dispute. Instead, the dispositive issue here concerns * * * whether the present case is barred by res judicata. [The dissenting opinion found that plaintiffs' claims should have been litigated in an earlier lawsuit that had also challenged House Bill 2. See 769 F.3d 285 (5th Cir. 2014). The Alito dissent contended that the] Court's patent refusal to apply well-established law in a neutral way is indefensible and will undermine public confidence in the Court as a fair and neutral arbiter. [In addition, the dissenters found that plaintiff providers could not rely solely on evidence of harm to patients to support their own standing, and that the provisions in House Bill 2 were severable and should not have been enjoined in their entirety.]

NOTES AND QUESTIONS

1. *A New* Casey. Although it left a number of questions unanswered, *Whole Woman's Health* marked the first time in more than 15 years that the Supreme Court struck down a restriction on abortion as constituting too heavy a burden to survive constitutional review. Watershed? Aberration?

The only two Justices still on the Court in 2016 who had participated in *Casey* were Justices Kennedy and Thomas. In *Whole Woman's Health*, Justice Kennedy provided the critical fifth vote by endorsing a carefully crafted opinion of the Court (note the meticulous, repeated use of quotations from earlier cases and from the record). The authorship role went to Justice Breyer, who also wrote *Stenberg v. Carhart* in 2000, a decision that was largely eviscerated seven years later by Justice Kennedy's decision in *Gonzalez v. Carhart*. Might Breyer become the new leading voice on abortion issues? Justice Thomas took the occasion of *Whole Woman's Health* not only to reiterate his opposition to abortion, but also his disagreement with according heightened judicial review to infringements on personal liberty (any more than on economic rights). *Whole Woman's Health* was decided when there were eight Justices on the Court (because of the death of Justice Scalia in February 2016). What might the future hold? Note that Justice Neil Gorsuch has taken Justice Scalia's seat and seems to share the late Justice's philosophy regarding the Court's jurisprudence of sexuality, gender, and the law. The three oldest Justices (all 80 or older) are in the majority for *Whole Woman's Health*.

2. *The Standard of Review.* Texas took the position in this case that, to meet the "undue burden" standard set in *Casey*, the impact of the law had to be so severe as to take away from the pregnant woman "the ultimate decision" whether to continue the pregnancy. Mindful that *Casey* had cut back on what had been considered a fundamental right, the plaintiffs characterized the right to an abortion as a "fundamental liberty." How did the Supreme Court in *Whole Woman's Health* characterize the standard of review? Why do you think the Court approached the standard of review issue the way that it did? Is Justice Thomas correct that this is strict scrutiny in disguise?

3. *Balancing Act.* For future cases, the Court upholds the role of courts in weighing the benefits against the burdens imposed by a restrictive law, and rejects the argument that courts should always defer to legislative assessment of what constitutes an undue burden. In *Casey*, however, the Court upheld a 24-hour waiting period, saying that it was permissible for a state to try to persuade a woman not to have an abortion by using a "structural mechanism" such as a waiting period, even though there was an "incidental [negative] effect" on access. Does *Whole Woman's Health* cast that portion of *Casey* into doubt? Are waiting periods *per se* constitutional? Or does a restrictive law have to approach the impact of House Bill 2—

eliminating half the providers in a state—before it runs afoul of the undue burden standard?

4. *Singling out Abortion.* Plaintiffs sought a ruling that states could not regulate abortion providers more stringently than providers of other procedures with comparable medical risk. This seems to have been the point of Justice Ginsburg's concurrence. How far did the Court go toward adopting this argument?

5. *The De-Constitutionalization Critique.* Robin West advocates a structural rethinking of the right to abortion. She argues that feminists should move away from a negative individual right as the conceptual model and from adjudication as the enforcement venue. Rather than either privacy or equality as a constitutional framework, West argues for a legislative approach that seeks a broader understanding of reproductive justice and the establishment of a network of support for the processes of reproduction. Robin West, "From Choice to Reproductive Justice: De-Constitutionalizing Abortion Rights," 118 *Yale L. J.* 1394 (2009). Assuming that such legislation would be politically achievable, consider how the trade-offs intrinsic to the legislative process differ from those intrinsic to litigation and constitutional argument. What are the strengths and weaknesses of using political versus judicial institutions to make reproductive rights law?

PROBLEM 2-1
"INFORMED CONSENT"

Texas defended the regulation of clinics at issue in *Whole Woman's Health* as based on its interest in protecting the health of women seeking abortions, whereas the law at issue in *Carhart* was squarely premised on the state's desire to promote fetal life. In both cases, the Court was interpreting and applying its 1992 decision in *Casey*. In light of those three decisions, how would you analyze the following state statute:

Consent to an abortion is voluntary and informed only if, before any sedative or anesthesia is administered and before the abortion is performed:

(1) The physician (or a certified sonographer) performs a sonogram on the pregnant woman on whom the abortion is to be performed;

(2) The physician displays the sonogram images in a manner that the pregnant woman may view them;

(3) The physician provides a verbal explanation of the results of the sonogram images, including a medical description of the dimensions of the embryo or fetus, the presence of cardiac activity, and the presence of external members and internal organs; and

(4) The physician (or a certified sonographer) makes audible the heart auscultation for the pregnant woman to hear, if it is present, and provides a simultaneous verbal explanation.

THE REGULATION OF SEXUAL CONDUCT: *LAWRENCE V. TEXAS* AND BEYOND

Aside from *Planned Parenthood v. Casey*, the most significant substantive due process case decided by the Supreme Court in the 17 years between *Hardwick* and *Lawrence v. Texas* was **Washington v. Harold Glucksberg, 521 U.S. 702, 117 S.Ct. 2258, 138 L.Ed.2d 772 (1997).** *Glucksberg* involved a challenge to laws prohibiting assisted suicide by doctors and others of what its supporters call "aid in dying." The various opinions provide a window into how the Justices were approaching the doctrinal questions that they would face in *Lawrence*.

In *Glucksberg*, the Court unanimously rejected the claim for a due process right to assisted suicide. **Chief Justice Rehnquist**'s opinion for the Court was grounded in a conservative understanding of the right to privacy line of cases. "[W]e 'ha[ve] always been reluctant to expand the concept of substantive due process because guideposts for responsible decision making in this uncharted area are scarce and open-ended.' " * * *

"Our established method of substantive-due-process analysis has two primary features: First, we have regularly observed that the Due Process Clause specially protects those fundamental rights and liberties which are, objectively, 'deeply rooted in this Nation's history and tradition,' and 'implicit in the concept of ordered liberty,' such that 'neither liberty nor justice would exist if they were sacrificed.' Second, we have required in substantive-due-process cases a 'careful description' of the asserted fundamental liberty interest. Our Nation's history, legal traditions, and practices thus provide the crucial 'guideposts for responsible decisionmaking' and direct and restrain our exposition of the Due Process Clause." The Chief Justice noted that both common law and statutory law had long regulated both suicide and assisting suicide. Hence, there was no fundamental right, and the state statute easily survived rational basis review.

Justice Souter, concurring in the Court's judgment, provided the primary challenge to Chief Justice Rehnquist's framework. Souter set forth a "living tradition" understanding of the right to privacy, drawing from Justice Harlan's *Poe* dissent (Chapter 1, Section 1). He explicitly linked this to the common law method of analogy and case-by-case evolution, with this difference: unlike common law, constitutional law can proceed only cautiously, for it takes an issue away from the political process, and only when the Court is certain that a statutory policy unreasonably burdens traditionally recognized liberty interests. "It is only when the legislation's justifying principle, critically valued, is so far from being commensurable with the individual interest as to be arbitrarily or pointlessly applied that the statute must give way. Only if this standard points against the statute can the individual claimant be said to have a constitutional right." Under this standard as applied to the facts in *Glucksberg*, Justice Souter believed a constitutional right premature and that the interests identified by the state were "commensurable" to the restriction on liberty imposed by the statutes. Similar concurring opinions were written by **Justices Stevens**, **Ginsburg**, and **Breyer**, none of whom joined the Rehnquist opinion, although all concurred in the judgment.

In response, Chief Justice Rehnquist's opinion specifically rejected the *Poe* approach to substantive due process and refused to read *Casey* to require that methodology. **Justice O'Connor** joined the Chief Justice's opinion (giving him five votes) and also wrote separately to say that the cases before the Court did not settle "the narrower question whether a mentally competent person who is experiencing great suffering has a constitutionally cognizable interest in controlling the circumstances of his or her imminent death." Because we all know that we shall face death but cannot know the circumstances of it, Justice O'Connor was confident that the democratic process would reach suitable accommodations between "the interests of terminally ill, mentally competent individuals who would seek to end their suffering and the State's interests in protecting those who might seek to end life mistakenly or under pressure." Justices Ginsburg and Breyer joined her concurring opinion except insofar as it joined the opinion of the Court.

Under the *Glucksberg* approach, how would you have expected the Court to rule when advocates sought to reverse *Hardwick*?

A. THE REPUDIATION OF *BOWERS V. HARDWICK*

While the Justices continued to debate the contours of the constitutional privacy right, the law of sodomy was changing at the state level. The intensely negative reaction to *Bowers v. Hardwick* in America's law schools and the changing public perceptions of LGB people more generally encouraged lawyers to launch a new wave of constitutional challenges—but under state constitutions rather than the U.S. Constitution. This new wave produced judicial invalidations of sodomy laws in some states, including, ironically, Georgia. *Powell v. State*, 270 Ga. 327, 510 S.E.2d 18 (1998). The most expansive state court victory came in Kentucky, where the state supreme court held that a sodomy law limited to same-sex partners violated the protections for privacy and equal treatment in the state constitution. *Commonwealth of Kentucky v. Wasson*, 842 S.W.2d 487 (Ky. 1992).

When *Lawrence v. Texas* reached the Supreme Court, only 12 of the 25 sodomy laws that had been in effect in 1986, when *Hardwick* was decided, were still being enforced. Four jurisdictions had repealed sodomy laws legislatively (Arizona, the District of Columbia, Nevada, and Rhode Island). The highest court in five states had found such laws unconstitutional under the state constitution (Arkansas, Georgia, Kentucky, Montana, and Tennessee). In four additional states, lower courts had ruled the law unconstitutional, and the state chose not to appeal (Maryland, Michigan, Minnesota, and Missouri).

In addition to the changes in sodomy laws, there had been a second enormous change at the state level: the adoption of civil rights protections that included sexual orientation. Only one (Wisconsin) existed in 1986. When *Lawrence* came before the Court, 13 states had expanded their prohibitions on discrimination to include sexual orientation, a number equal to that of the states that prohibited sodomy.

John Geddes Lawrence and Tyron Garner v. Texas

United States Supreme Court, 2003.
539 U.S. 558, 123 S.Ct. 2472, 156 L.Ed.2d 508.

■ JUSTICE KENNEDY delivered the opinion of the Court.

Liberty protects the person from unwarranted government intrusions into a dwelling or other private places. In our tradition the State is not omnipresent in the home. And there are other spheres of our lives and existence, outside the home, where the State should not be a dominant presence. Freedom extends beyond spatial bounds. Liberty presumes an autonomy of self that includes freedom of thought, belief, expression, and certain intimate conduct. The instant case involves liberty of the person both in its spatial and more transcendent dimensions.

[Acting on a report of a possible burglary, the Harris County Police entered the apartment of John Lawrence and found him engaging in anal sex with another adult man, Tyron Garner. The police arrested and detained the men overnight for violating Texas's "Homosexual Conduct law." Tex. Penal Code Ann. § 21.06(a) (2003). The law provides: "A person commits an offense if he engages in deviate sexual intercourse with another individual of the same sex." The statute defines deviate sexual intercourse to include oral and anal sex. The defendants pleaded *nolo contendere*, were fined $200 apiece (plus court costs of $141.25), and appealed their convictions, on the ground that the Homosexual Conduct law was unconstitutional. The Texas courts rejected their federal constitutional claims, largely on the authority of *Bowers v. Hardwick*.]

[II.] We conclude the case should be resolved by determining whether the petitioners were free as adults to engage in the private conduct in the exercise of their liberty under the Due Process Clause of the Fourteenth Amendment to the Constitution. For this inquiry, we deem it necessary to reconsider the Court's holding in *Bowers*.

* * * [T]he most pertinent beginning point is our decision in *Griswold v. Connecticut*. In *Griswold* * * * [t]he Court described the protected interest as a right to privacy and placed emphasis on the marriage relation and the protected space of the marital bedroom.

After *Griswold*, it was established that the right to make certain decisions regarding sexual conduct extends beyond the marital relationship. *Eisenstadt v. Baird*. * * * The opinions in *Griswold* and *Eisenstadt* were part of the background for the decision in *Roe v. Wade*. * * * *Roe* recognized the right of a woman to make certain fundamental decisions affecting her destiny. * * *

The Court began its substantive discussion in *Bowers* as follows: "The issue presented is whether the Federal Constitution confers a fundamental right upon homosexuals to engage in sodomy and hence invalidates the laws of the many States that still make such conduct illegal and have done so for a very long time." That statement, we now conclude, discloses the Court's own failure to appreciate the extent of the liberty at stake. To say that the issue in *Bowers* was simply the right to engage in certain sexual conduct demeans the claim the individual put forward, just as it would demean a married couple were it to be said marriage is simply about the right to have sexual intercourse. The laws involved in *Bowers* and here are, to be sure, statutes that purport to do no more than prohibit a particular sexual act. Their penalties and purposes, though, have more far-reaching consequences, touching upon the most private human conduct, sexual behavior, and in the most private of places, the home. The statutes do seek to control a personal relationship that, whether or not entitled to formal recognition in the law, is within the liberty of persons to choose without being punished as criminals.

This, as a general rule, should counsel against attempts by the State, or a court, to define the meaning of the relationship or to set its boundaries absent injury to a person or abuse of an institution the law protects. It suffices for us to acknowledge that adults may choose to enter upon this relationship in the confines of their homes and their own private lives and still retain their dignity as free persons. When sexuality finds overt expression in intimate conduct with another person, the conduct can be but one element in a personal bond that is more enduring. The liberty protected by the Constitution allows homosexual persons the right to make this choice.

Having misapprehended the claim of liberty there presented to it, and thus stating the claim to be whether there is a fundamental right to engage in consensual sodomy, the *Bowers* Court said: "Proscriptions against that conduct have ancient roots." In academic writings, and in many of the scholarly *amicus* briefs filed to assist the Court in this case, there are fundamental criticisms of the historical premises relied upon by the majority and concurring opinions in *Bowers*. Brief for Cato Institute as *Amicus Curiae* 16–17; Brief for American Civil Liberties

Union et al. as *Amici Curiae* 15–21; Brief for Professors of History et al. as *Amici Curiae* 3–10. We need not enter this debate in the attempt to reach a definitive historical judgment, but the following considerations counsel against adopting the definitive conclusions upon which *Bowers* placed such reliance.

At the outset it should be noted that there is no longstanding history in this country of laws directed at homosexual conduct as a distinct matter. [Both English and early American crime against nature laws regulated relations between men and women as well as between men.] The absence of legal prohibitions focusing on homosexual conduct may be explained in part by noting that according to some scholars the concept of the homosexual as a distinct category of person did not emerge until the late 19th century. See, *e.g.*, J. Katz, *The Invention of Heterosexuality* 10 (1995); J. D'Emilio & E. Freedman, *Intimate Matters: A History of Sexuality in America* 121 (2d ed. 1997) ("The modern terms *homosexuality* and *heterosexuality* do not apply to an era that had not yet articulated these distinctions"). Thus early American sodomy laws were not directed at homosexuals as such but instead sought to prohibit nonprocreative sexual activity more generally. This does not suggest approval of homosexual conduct. It does tend to show that this particular form of conduct was not thought of as a separate category from like conduct between heterosexual persons.

Laws prohibiting sodomy do not seem to have been enforced against consenting adults acting in private. A substantial number of sodomy prosecutions and convictions for which there are surviving records were for predatory acts against those who could not or did not consent, as in the case of a minor or the victim of an assault. As to these, one purpose for the prohibitions was to ensure there would be no lack of coverage if a predator committed a sexual assault that did not constitute rape as defined by the criminal law. Thus the model sodomy indictments presented in a 19th-century treatise, [2 Joseph Chitty, *A Practical Treatise on Criminal Law* 49 (1847)], addressed the predatory acts of an adult man against a minor girl or minor boy. Instead of targeting relations between consenting adults in private, 19th-century sodomy prosecutions typically involved relations between men and minor girls or minor boys, relations between adults involving force, relations between adults implicating disparity in status, or relations between men and animals.

To the extent that there were any prosecutions for the acts in question, 19th-century evidence rules imposed a burden that would make a conviction more difficult to obtain even taking into account the problems always inherent in prosecuting consensual acts committed in private. Under then-prevailing standards, a man could not be convicted of sodomy based upon testimony of a consenting partner, because the partner was considered an accomplice. A partner's testimony, however, was admissible if he or she had not consented to the act or was a minor, and therefore incapable of consent. See, *e.g.,* F. Wharton, *Criminal Law* 443 (2d ed. 1852); 1 F. Wharton, *Criminal Law* 512 (8th ed. 1880). The rule may explain in part the infrequency of these prosecutions. In all events that infrequency makes it difficult to say that society approved of a rigorous and systematic punishment of the consensual acts committed in private and by adults. The longstanding criminal prohibition of homosexual sodomy upon which the *Bowers* decision placed such reliance is as consistent with a general condemnation of nonprocreative sex as it is with an established tradition of prosecuting acts because of their homosexual character.

The policy of punishing consenting adults for private acts was not much discussed in the early legal literature. We can infer that one reason for this was the very private nature of the conduct. Despite the absence of prosecutions, there may have been periods in which there was public criticism of homosexuals as such and an insistence that the criminal laws be enforced to discourage their practices. But far from possessing "ancient roots," *Bowers*, American laws targeting same-sex couples did not develop until the last third of the 20th century. The reported decisions concerning the prosecution of consensual, homosexual sodomy between adults for the years 1880–1995 are not always clear in the details, but a significant number involved conduct in a public place. See Brief for American Civil Liberties Union et al. as *Amici Curiae* 14–15, and n. 18.

It was not until the 1970s that any State singled out same-sex relations for criminal prosecution, and only nine States have done so. See 1977 Ark. Gen. Acts no. 828; 1983 Kan. Sess. Laws p. 652; 1974 Ky. Acts p. 847; 1977 Mo. Laws p. 687; 1973 Mont. Laws p. 1339; 1977 Nev. Stats. p. 1632; 1989 Tenn. Pub. Acts ch. 591; 1973 Tex. Gen. Laws ch. 399; see also *Post* v. *State*, 715 P. 2d 1105 (Okla. Crim. App. 1986) (sodomy law invalidated as applied to different-sex couples). Post-*Bowers* even some of these States did not adhere to the policy of suppressing homosexual conduct. Over the course of the last decades, States with same-sex prohibitions have moved toward abolishing them.

In summary, the historical grounds relied upon in *Bowers* are more complex than the majority opinion and the concurring opinion by Chief Justice Burger indicate. Their historical premises are not without doubt and, at the very least, are overstated.

It must be acknowledged, of course, that the Court in *Bowers* was making the broader point that for centuries there have been powerful voices to condemn homosexual conduct as immoral. The condemnation has been shaped by religious beliefs, conceptions of right and acceptable behavior, and respect for the traditional family. For many persons these are not trivial concerns but profound and deep convictions accepted as ethical and moral principles to which they aspire and which thus determine the course of their lives. These considerations do not answer the question before us, however. The issue is whether the majority may use the power of the State to enforce these views on the whole society through operation of the criminal law. "Our obligation is to define the liberty of all, not to mandate our own moral code." *Casey*.

Chief Justice Burger joined the opinion for the Court in *Bowers* and further explained his views as follows: "Decisions of individuals relating to homosexual conduct have been subject to state intervention throughout the history of Western civilization. Condemnation of those practices is firmly rooted in Judeo-Christian moral and ethical standards." As with Justice White's assumptions about history, scholarship casts some doubt on the sweeping nature of the statement by Chief Justice Burger as it pertains to private homosexual conduct between consenting adults. See, *e.g.,* Eskridge, Hardwick and Historiography, 1999 U. Ill. L. Rev. 631, 656. In all events we think that our laws and traditions in the past half century are of most relevance here. These references show an emerging awareness that liberty gives substantial protection to adult persons in deciding how to conduct their private lives in matters pertaining to sex. "[H]istory and tradition are the starting point but not in all cases the ending point of the substantive due process inquiry." *County of Sacramento* v. *Lewis* (Kennedy, J., concurring).

This emerging recognition should have been apparent when *Bowers* was decided. In 1955 the American Law Institute promulgated the Model Penal Code and made clear that it did not recommend or provide for "criminal penalties for consensual sexual relations conducted in private." ALI, Model Penal Code § 213.2, Comment 2, p. 372 (1980). It justified its decision on three grounds: (1) The prohibitions undermined respect for the law by penalizing conduct many people engaged in; (2) the statutes regulated private conduct not harmful to others; and (3) the laws were arbitrarily enforced and thus invited the danger of blackmail. ALI, Model Penal Code, Commentary 277–280 (Tent. Draft No. 4, 1955). In 1961 Illinois changed its laws to conform to the Model Penal Code. Other States soon followed. Brief for Cato Institute as *Amicus Curiae* 15–16.

In *Bowers* the Court referred to the fact that before 1961 all 50 States had outlawed sodomy, and that at the time of the Court's decision 24 States and the District of Columbia had sodomy laws. Justice Powell pointed out that these prohibitions often were being ignored, however. Georgia, for instance, had not sought to enforce its law for decades.

The sweeping references by Chief Justice Burger to the history of Western civilization and to Judeo-Christian moral and ethical standards did not take account of other authorities pointing in an opposite direction. A committee advising the British Parliament recommended in 1957 repeal of laws punishing homosexual conduct. The Wolfenden Report: Report of the Committee on Homosexual Offenses and Prostitution (1963). Parliament enacted the substance of those recommendations 10 years later. Sexual Offences Act 1967, § 1.

Of even more importance, almost five years before *Bowers* was decided the European Court of Human Rights considered a case with parallels to *Bowers* and to today's case. An adult male resident in Northern Ireland alleged he was a practicing homosexual who desired to engage in consensual homosexual conduct. The laws of Northern Ireland forbade him that right. He alleged that he had been questioned, his home had been searched, and he feared criminal prosecution. The court held that the laws proscribing the conduct were invalid under the European Convention on Human Rights. *Dudgeon* v. *United Kingdom*, 45 Eur. Ct. H. R. (1981) ¶ 52. Authoritative in all countries that are members of the Council of Europe (21 nations then, 45 nations now), the decision is at odds with the premise in *Bowers* that the claim put forward was insubstantial in our Western civilization.

In our own constitutional system the deficiencies in *Bowers* became even more apparent in the years following its announcement. The 25 States with laws prohibiting the relevant conduct referenced in the *Bowers* decision are reduced now to 13, of which 4 enforce their laws only against homosexual conduct. In those States where sodomy is still proscribed, whether for same-sex or heterosexual conduct, there is a pattern of nonenforcement with respect to consenting adults acting in private. The State of Texas admitted in 1994 that as of that date it had not prosecuted anyone under those circumstances. *State* v. *Morales*, 869 S. W. 2d 941, 943.

Two principal cases decided after *Bowers* cast its holding into even more doubt. In *Casey*, the Court reaffirmed the substantive force of the liberty protected by the Due Process Clause. The *Casey* decision again confirmed that our laws and tradition afford constitutional protection to personal decisions relating to marriage, procreation, contraception, family relationships, child rearing, and education. In explaining the respect the Constitution demands for the autonomy of the person in making these choices, we stated as follows:

> "These matters, involving the most intimate and personal choices a person may make in a lifetime, choices central to personal dignity and autonomy, are central to the liberty protected by the Fourteenth Amendment. At the heart of liberty is the right to define one's own concept of existence, of meaning, of the universe, and of the mystery of human life. Beliefs about these matters could not define the attributes of personhood were they formed under compulsion of the State."

Persons in a homosexual relationship may seek autonomy for these purposes, just as heterosexual persons do. The decision in *Bowers* would deny them this right.

The second post-*Bowers* case of principal relevance is *Romer v. Evans* [Chapter 1, Section 2B]. There the Court struck down class-based legislation directed at homosexuals as a violation of the Equal Protection Clause. *Romer* invalidated an amendment to Colorado's constitution which named as a solitary class persons who were homosexuals, lesbians, or bisexual either by "orientation, conduct, practices or relationships," and deprived them of protection under state antidiscrimination laws. We concluded that the provision was "born of animosity toward the class of persons affected" and further that it had no rational relation to a legitimate governmental purpose.

As an alternative argument in this case, counsel for the petitioners and some *amici* contend that *Romer* provides the basis for declaring the Texas statute invalid under the Equal Protection Clause. That is a tenable argument, but we conclude the instant case requires us to address whether *Bowers* itself has continuing validity. Were we to hold the statute invalid under the Equal Protection Clause some might question whether a prohibition would be valid if drawn differently, say, to prohibit the conduct both between same-sex and different-sex participants.

Equality of treatment and the due process right to demand respect for conduct protected by the substantive guarantee of liberty are linked in important respects, and a decision on the latter point advances both interests. If protected conduct is made criminal and the law which does so remains unexamined for its substantive validity, its stigma might remain even if it were not enforceable as drawn for equal protection reasons. When homosexual conduct is made criminal by the law of the State, that declaration in and of itself is an invitation to subject homosexual persons to discrimination both in the public and in the private spheres. The central holding of *Bowers* has been brought in question by this case, and it should be addressed. Its continuance as precedent demeans the lives of homosexual persons.

The stigma this criminal statute imposes, moreover, is not trivial. The offense, to be sure, is but a class C misdemeanor, a minor offense in the Texas legal system. Still, it remains a criminal offense with all that imports for the dignity of the persons charged. The petitioners will bear on their record the history of their criminal convictions. * * * We are advised that if Texas convicted an adult for private, consensual homosexual conduct under the statute here in question the convicted person would come within the [sex offender] registration laws of a least four States were he or she to be subject to their jurisdiction. This underscores the consequential nature of the punishment and the state-sponsored condemnation attendant to the criminal prohibition. Furthermore, the Texas criminal conviction carries with it the other collateral consequences always following a conviction, such as notations on job application forms, to mention but one example.

The foundations of *Bowers* have sustained serious erosion from our recent decisions in *Casey* and *Romer*. When our precedent has been thus weakened, criticism from other sources is of greater significance. In the United States criticism of *Bowers* has been substantial and continuing, disapproving of its reasoning in all respects, not just as to its historical assumptions. See, *e.g.,* C. Fried, *Order and Law: Arguing the Reagan Revolution—A Firsthand Account* 81–84 (1991); R. Posner, *Sex and Reason* 341–350 (1992). The courts of five different States have declined to follow it in interpreting provisions in their own state constitutions parallel to the Due Process Clause of the Fourteenth Amendment, see *Jegley* v. *Picado*, 349 Ark. 600, 80 S. W. 3d 332 (2002); *Powell* v. *State*, 270 Ga. 327, 510 S. E. 2d 18, 24 (1998); *Gryczan* v. *State*, 283 Mont. 433, 942 P. 2d 112 (1997); *Campbell* v. *Sundquist*, 926 S. W. 2d 250 (Tenn. App. 1996); *Commonwealth* v. *Wasson*, 842 S. W. 2d 487 (Ky. 1992).

To the extent *Bowers* relied on values we share with a wider civilization, it should be noted that the reasoning and holding in *Bowers* have been rejected elsewhere. The European Court of Human Rights has followed not *Bowers* but its own decision in *Dudgeon* v. *United Kingdom*. See *P. G. & J. H.* v. *United Kingdom*, App. No. 00044787/98, ¶ 56 (Eur. Ct. H. R., Sept. 25, 2001); *Modinos* v. *Cyprus*, 259 Eur. Ct. H. R. (1993); *Norris* v. *Ireland*, 142 Eur. Ct. H. R. (1988). Other nations, too, have taken action consistent with an affirmation of the protected right of homosexual adults to engage in intimate, consensual conduct. See Brief for Mary Robinson et al. as *Amici Curiae* 11–12. The right the petitioners seek in this case has been accepted as an integral part of human freedom in many other countries. There has been no showing that in this country the governmental interest in circumscribing personal choice is somehow more legitimate or urgent.

The doctrine of *stare decisis* is essential to the respect accorded to the judgments of the Court and to the stability of the law. It is not, however, an inexorable command. In *Casey* we noted that when a Court is asked to overrule a precedent recognizing a constitutional liberty interest, individual or societal reliance on the existence of that liberty cautions with particular strength against reversing course. The holding in *Bowers*, however, has not induced detrimental reliance comparable to some instances where recognized individual rights are involved. Indeed, there has been no individual or societal reliance on *Bowers* of the sort that could counsel against overturning its holding once there are compelling reasons to do so. *Bowers* itself causes uncertainty, for the precedents before and after its issuance contradict its central holding.

The rationale of *Bowers* does not withstand careful analysis. In his dissenting opinion in *Bowers* Justice Stevens came to these conclusions:

"Our prior cases make two propositions abundantly clear. First, the fact that the governing majority in a State has traditionally viewed a particular practice as immoral is not a sufficient reason for upholding a law prohibiting the practice; neither history nor tradition could save a law prohibiting miscegenation from constitutional attack. Second, individual decisions by married persons, concerning the intimacies of their physical relationship, even when not intended to produce offspring, are a form of 'liberty' protected by the Due Process Clause of the

Fourteenth Amendment. Moreover, this protection extends to intimate choices by unmarried as well as married persons."

Justice Stevens' analysis, in our view, should have been controlling in *Bowers* and should control here.

Bowers was not correct when it was decided, and it is not correct today. It ought not to remain binding precedent. *Bowers* v. *Hardwick* should be and now is overruled.

The present case does not involve minors. It does not involve persons who might be injured or coerced or who are situated in relationships where consent might not easily be refused. It does not involve public conduct or prostitution. It does not involve whether the government must give formal recognition to any relationship that homosexual persons seek to enter. The case does involve two adults who, with full and mutual consent from each other, engaged in sexual practices common to a homosexual lifestyle. The petitioners are entitled to respect for their private lives. The State cannot demean their existence or control their destiny by making their private sexual conduct a crime. Their right to liberty under the Due Process Clause gives them the full right to engage in their conduct without intervention of the government. "It is a promise of the Constitution that there is a realm of personal liberty which the government may not enter." *Casey*. The Texas statute furthers no legitimate state interest which can justify its intrusion into the personal and private life of the individual.

Had those who drew and ratified the Due Process Clauses of the Fifth Amendment or the Fourteenth Amendment known the components of liberty in its manifold possibilities, they might have been more specific. They did not presume to have this insight. They knew times can blind us to certain truths and later generations can see that laws once thought necessary and proper in fact serve only to oppress. As the Constitution endures, persons in every generation can invoke its principles in their own search for greater freedom. * * *

■ JUSTICE O'CONNOR, concurring in the judgment.

[Justice O'Connor, who had joined the Court's opinion in *Bowers*, was not willing to join the Court's opinion overruling that precedent. But, she concluded, the Texas Homosexual Conduct Law did violate the Equal Protection Clause.] When a law exhibits such a desire to harm a politically unpopular group, we have applied a more searching form of rational basis review to strike down such laws under the Equal Protection Clause.

We have been most likely to apply rational basis review to hold a law unconstitutional under the Equal Protection Clause where, as here, the challenged legislation inhibits personal relationships. In *Department of Agriculture* v. *Moreno*, for example, we held that a law preventing those households containing an individual unrelated to any other member of the household from receiving food stamps violated equal protection because the purpose of the law was to " 'discriminate against hippies.' " The asserted governmental interest in preventing food stamp fraud was not deemed sufficient to satisfy rational basis review. In *Eisenstadt v. Baird*, we refused to sanction a law that discriminated between married and unmarried persons by prohibiting the distribution of contraceptives to single persons. Likewise, in *Cleburne*, we held that it was irrational for a State to require a home for the mentally disabled to obtain a special use permit when other residences—like fraternity houses and apartment buildings—did not have to obtain such a permit. And in *Romer* v. *Evans,* we disallowed a state statute that "impos[ed] a broad and undifferentiated disability on a single named group"—specifically, homosexuals. The dissent apparently agrees that if these cases have *stare decisis* effect, Texas' sodomy law would not pass scrutiny under the Equal Protection Clause, regardless of the type of rational basis review that we apply.

The statute at issue here makes sodomy a crime only if a person "engages in deviate sexual intercourse with another individual of the same sex." Tex. Penal Code Ann. § 21.06(a) (2003). Sodomy between opposite-sex partners, however, is not a crime in Texas. That is, Texas treats the same conduct differently based solely on the participants. Those harmed by this law are people who have a same-sex sexual orientation and thus are more likely to engage in behavior prohibited by § 21.06.

The Texas statute makes homosexuals unequal in the eyes of the law by making particular conduct—and only that conduct—subject to criminal sanction. It appears that prosecutions under Texas' sodomy law are rare. This case shows, however, that prosecutions under § 21.06 *do* occur. And while the penalty imposed on petitioners in this case was relatively minor, the consequences of conviction are not. As the Court notes, petitioners' convictions, if upheld, would disqualify them from or restrict their ability to engage in a variety of professions, including medicine, athletic training, and interior design. See, *e.g.,* Tex. Occ. Code Ann. § 164.051(a)(2)(B) (2003 Pamphlet) (physician); § 451.251 (a)(1) (athletic trainer); § 1053.252(2) (interior designer). Indeed, were petitioners to move to one of four States, their convictions would require them to register as sex offenders to local law enforcement. See, *e.g.,* Idaho Code § 18–8304 (Cum. Supp. 2002); La. Stat. Ann. § 15:542 (West Cum. Supp. 2003); Miss. Code Ann. § 45–33–25 (West 2003); S. C. Code Ann. § 23–3–430 (West Cum. Supp. 2002).

And the effect of Texas' sodomy law is not just limited to the threat of prosecution or consequence of conviction. Texas' sodomy law brands all homosexuals as criminals, thereby making it more difficult for homosexuals to be treated in the same manner as everyone else. Indeed, Texas itself has previously acknowledged the collateral effects of the law, stipulating in a prior challenge to this action that the law "legally sanctions discrimination against [homosexuals] in a variety of ways unrelated to the criminal law," including in the areas of "employment, family issues, and housing." *State* v. *Morales*, 826 S. W. 2d 201, 203 (Tex. App. 1992).

Texas attempts to justify its law, and the effects of the law, by arguing that the statute satisfies rational basis review because it furthers the legitimate governmental interest of the promotion of morality. In *Bowers*, we held that a state law criminalizing sodomy as applied to homosexual couples did not violate substantive due process. We rejected the argument that no rational basis existed to justify the law, pointing to the government's interest in promoting morality. The only question in front of the Court in *Bowers* was whether the substantive component of the Due Process Clause protected a right to engage in homosexual sodomy. *Bowers* did not hold that moral disapproval of a group is a rational basis under the Equal Protection Clause to criminalize homosexual sodomy when heterosexual sodomy is not punished.

This case raises a different issue than *Bowers:* whether, under the Equal Protection Clause, moral disapproval is a legitimate state interest to justify by itself a statute that bans homosexual sodomy, but not heterosexual sodomy. It is not. Moral disapproval of this group, like a bare desire to harm the group, is an interest that is insufficient to satisfy rational basis review under the Equal Protection Clause. See, *e.g., Moreno*; *Romer*. Indeed, we have never held that moral disapproval, without any other asserted state interest, is a sufficient rationale under the Equal Protection Clause to justify a law that discriminates among groups of persons.

Moral disapproval of a group cannot be a legitimate governmental interest under the Equal Protection Clause because legal classifications must not be "drawn for the purpose of disadvantaging the group burdened by the law." [*Romer*.] Texas' invocation of moral disapproval as a legitimate state interest proves nothing more than Texas' desire to criminalize homosexual sodomy. But the Equal Protection Clause prevents a State from creating "a classification of persons undertaken for its own sake." And because Texas so rarely enforces its sodomy law as applied to private, consensual acts, the law serves more as a statement of dislike and disapproval against homosexuals than as a tool to stop criminal behavior. The Texas sodomy law "raise[s] the inevitable inference that the disadvantage imposed is born of animosity toward the class of persons affected." [*Romer*.] * * *

A State can of course assign certain consequences to a violation of its criminal law. But the State cannot single out one identifiable class of citizens for punishment that does not apply to everyone else, with moral disapproval as the only asserted state interest for the law. The Texas sodomy statute subjects homosexuals to "a lifelong penalty and stigma. A legislative classification that threatens the creation of an underclass . . . cannot be reconciled with" the Equal Protection Clause. *Plyler* v. *Doe* (Powell, J., concurring).

Whether a sodomy law that is neutral both in effect and application, see *Yick Wo* v. *Hopkins,* 118 U.S. 356 (1886), would violate the substantive component of the Due Process Clause is an issue that need not be decided today. I am confident, however, that so long as the Equal Protection Clause requires a sodomy law to apply equally to the private consensual conduct of homosexuals and heterosexuals alike, such a law would not long stand in our democratic society. In the words of Justice Jackson:

> "The framers of the Constitution knew, and we should not forget today, that there is no more effective practical guaranty against arbitrary and unreasonable government than to require that the principles of law which officials would impose upon a minority be imposed generally. Conversely, nothing opens the door to arbitrary action so effectively as to allow those officials to pick and choose only a few to whom they will apply legislation and thus to escape the political retribution that might be visited upon them if larger numbers were affected." *Railway Express Agency, Inc.* v. *New York,* 336 U.S. 106, 112–113 (1949) (concurring opinion).

That this law as applied to private, consensual conduct is unconstitutional under the Equal Protection Clause does not mean that other laws distinguishing between heterosexuals and homosexuals would similarly fail under rational basis review. Texas cannot assert any legitimate state interest here, such as national security or preserving the traditional institution of marriage. Unlike the moral disapproval of same-sex relations—the asserted state interest in this case—other reasons exist to promote the institution of marriage beyond mere moral disapproval of an excluded group. * * *

■ JUSTICE SCALIA, with whom THE CHIEF JUSTICE [REHNQUIST] and JUSTICE THOMAS join, dissenting.

"Liberty finds no refuge in a jurisprudence of doubt." *Casey.* That was the Court's sententious response, barely more than a decade ago, to those seeking to overrule *Roe v. Wade.* The Court's response today, to those who have engaged in a 17-year crusade to overrule *Bowers* v. *Hardwick* is very different. The need for stability and certainty presents no barrier.

Most of the rest of today's opinion has no relevance to its actual holding—that the Texas statute "furthers no legitimate state interest which can justify" its application to petitioners under rational-basis review. Though there is discussion of "fundamental proposition[s]," and "fundamental decisions," nowhere does the Court's opinion declare that homosexual sodomy is a "fundamental right" under the Due Process Clause; nor does it subject the Texas law to the standard of review that would be appropriate (strict scrutiny) if homosexual sodomy *were* a "fundamental right." Thus, while overruling the *outcome* of *Bowers,* the Court leaves strangely untouched its central legal conclusion:

"[R]espondent would have us announce . . . a fundamental right to engage in homosexual sodomy. This we are quite unwilling to do." Instead the Court simply describes petitioners' conduct as "an exercise of their liberty"—which it undoubtedly is—and proceeds to apply an unheard-of form of rational-basis review that will have far-reaching implications beyond this case.

[I.] Today's approach to *stare decisis* invites us to overrule an erroneously decided precedent (including an "intensely divisive" decision) *if:* (1) its foundations have been "eroded" by subsequent decisions; (2) it has been subject to "substantial and continuing" criticism; and (3) it has not induced "individual or societal reliance" that counsels against overturning. The problem is that *Roe* itself—which today's majority surely has no disposition to overrule—satisfies these conditions to at least the same degree as *Bowers*.

[Justice Scalia maintained that, like *Bowers*, *Roe* has been (1) "eroded" by the Court's decision in *Washington v. Glucksburg* and, indeed, by *Casey* itself, which jettisoned large chunks of *Roe*'s approach; (2) subjected to unrelenting criticism, including acid critique from Professor Fried and Judge Posner, whose books the Court cited as examples of academic critique of *Bowers*; and (3) the object of no less reliance than *Bowers*, which has been the foundation for much of the nation's public policy, including its ban of gay people in the armed forces, as well as state laws against bigamy, same-sex marriage, adult incest, prostitution, masturbation, adultery, fornication, bestiality, and obscenity.]

What a massive disruption of the current social order, therefore, the overruling of *Bowers* entails. Not so the overruling of *Roe*, which would simply have restored the regime that existed for centuries before 1973, in which the permissibility of and restrictions upon abortion were determined legislatively State-by-State. *Casey*, however, chose to base its *stare decisis* determination on a different "sort" of reliance. "[P]eople," it said, "have organized intimate relationships and made choices that define their views of themselves and their places in society, in reliance on the availability of abortion in the event that contraception should fail." This falsely assumes that the consequence of overruling *Roe* would have been to make abortion unlawful. It would not; it would merely have *permitted* the States to do so. Many States would unquestionably have declined to prohibit abortion, and others would not have prohibited it within six months (after which the most significant reliance interests would have expired). Even for persons in States other than these, the choice would not have been between abortion and childbirth, but between abortion nearby and abortion in a neighboring State.

To tell the truth, it does not surprise me, and should surprise no one, that the Court has chosen today to revise the standards of *stare decisis* set forth in *Casey*. It has thereby exposed *Casey*'s extraordinary deference to precedent for the result-oriented expedient that it is. * * *

[III. Justice Scalia defended the correctness of *Bowers'* holdings that only interests traditionally recognized in American law can be "fundamental" and that the right to engage in consensual sodomy (homosexual or otherwise) is not one of those traditional rights.] Whether homosexual sodomy was prohibited by a law targeted at same-sex sexual relations or by a more general law prohibiting both homosexual and heterosexual sodomy, the only relevant point is that it *was* criminalized—which suffices to establish that homosexual sodomy is not a right "deeply rooted in our Nation's history and tradition." * * *

Next, the Court makes the claim, again unsupported by any citations, that "[l]aws prohibiting sodomy do not seem to have been enforced against consenting adults acting in private." The key qualifier here is "acting in private"—since the Court admits that sodomy laws *were* enforced against consenting adults (although the Court contends that prosecutions were "infrequent"). I do not know what "acting in private" means; surely consensual sodomy, like heterosexual intercourse, is rarely performed on stage. If all the Court means by "acting in private" is "on private premises, with the doors closed and windows covered," it is entirely unsurprising that evidence of enforcement would be hard to come by. (Imagine the circumstances that would enable a search warrant to be obtained for a residence on the ground that there was probable cause to believe that consensual sodomy was then and there occurring.) Surely that lack of evidence would not sustain the proposition that consensual sodomy on private premises with the doors closed and windows covered was regarded as a "fundamental right," even though all other consensual sodomy was criminalized. There are 203 prosecutions for consensual, adult homosexual sodomy reported in the West Reporting system and official state reporters from the years 1880–1995. See W. Eskridge, *Gaylaw: Challenging the Apartheid of the Closet* 375 (1999) (hereinafter *Gaylaw*). There are also records of 20 sodomy prosecutions and 4 executions during the colonial period. J. Katz, *Gay/Lesbian Almanac* 29, 58, 663 (1983). *Bowers'* conclusion that homosexual sodomy is not a fundamental right "deeply rooted in this Nation's history and tradition" is utterly unassailable.

Realizing that fact, the Court instead says: "[W]e think that our laws and traditions in the past half century are of most relevance here. These references show *an emerging awareness* that liberty gives substantial protection to adult persons in deciding how to conduct their private lives *in matters pertaining to sex*." (Emphasis added.) Apart from the fact that such an "emerging awareness" does not establish a "fundamental right," the statement is factually false. States continue to prosecute all sorts of crimes by adults "in matters pertaining to sex": prostitution, adult incest, adultery, obscenity, and child pornography. Sodomy laws, too, have been enforced "in the past half century," in which there have been 134 reported cases involving prosecutions for consensual, adult, homosexual sodomy. *Gaylaw* 375. In relying, for evidence of an "emerging recognition," upon the American Law Institute's 1955 recommendation not to criminalize " 'consensual sexual relations conducted in private,' " the Court ignores the fact that this recommendation was "a point of resistance in most of the states that considered adopting the Model Penal Code." *Gaylaw* 159.

In any event, an "emerging awareness" is by definition not "deeply rooted in this Nation's history and tradition[s]," as we have said "fundamental right" status requires. Constitutional entitlements do not spring into existence because some States choose to lessen or eliminate criminal sanctions on certain behavior. Much less do they spring into existence, as the Court seems to believe, because *foreign nations* decriminalize conduct. The *Bowers* majority opinion *never* relied on "values we share with a wider civilization," but rather rejected the claimed right to sodomy on the ground that such a right was not " 'deeply rooted in *this Nation's* history and tradition' " (emphasis added). *Bowers'* rational-basis holding is likewise devoid of any reliance on the views of a "wider civilization." The Court's discussion of these foreign views (ignoring, of course, the many countries that have retained criminal prohibitions on sodomy) is therefore meaningless dicta. Dangerous dicta, however, since "this Court . . . should not impose foreign moods, fads, or fashions on Americans." *Foster v. Florida*, 537 U.S. 990, 991 (2002) (Thomas, J., concurring in denial of certiorari).

[IV.]   I turn now to the ground on which the Court squarely rests its holding: the contention that there is no rational basis for the law here under attack. This proposition is so out of accord with our jurisprudence—indeed, with the jurisprudence of *any* society we know— that it requires little discussion.

The Texas statute undeniably seeks to further the belief of its citizens that certain forms of sexual behavior are "immoral and unacceptable," *Bowers*—the same interest furthered by criminal laws against fornication, bigamy, adultery, adult incest, bestiality, and obscenity. *Bowers* held that this was a legitimate state interest. The Court today reaches the opposite conclusion. The Texas statute, it says, "furthers no legitimate state interest which can justify its intrusion into the personal and private life of the individual" (emphasis added). The Court embraces instead Justice Stevens' declaration in his Bowers dissent, that "the fact that the governing majority in a State has traditionally viewed a particular practice as immoral is not a sufficient reason for upholding a law prohibiting the practice." This effectively decrees the end of all morals legislation. If, as the Court asserts, the promotion of majoritarian sexual morality is not even a *legitimate* state interest, none of the above-mentioned laws can survive rational-basis review.

[V.] Finally, I turn to petitioners' equal-protection challenge, which no Member of the Court save Justice O'Connor embraces: On its face § 21.06(a) applies equally to all persons. Men and women, heterosexuals and homosexuals, are all subject to its prohibition of deviate sexual intercourse with someone of the same sex. To be sure, § 21.06 does distinguish between the sexes insofar as concerns the partner with whom the sexual acts are performed: men can violate the law only with other men, and women only with other women. But this cannot itself be a denial of equal protection, since it is precisely the same distinction regarding partner that is drawn in state laws prohibiting marriage with someone of the same sex while permitting marriage with someone of the opposite sex.

The objection is made, however, that the anti-miscegenation laws invalidated in *Loving* v. *Virginia* similarly were applicable to whites and blacks alike, and only distinguished between the races insofar as the *partner* was concerned. In *Loving*, however, we correctly applied heightened scrutiny, rather than the usual rational-basis review, because the Virginia statute was "designed to maintain White Supremacy." A racially discriminatory purpose is always sufficient to subject a law to strict scrutiny, even a facially neutral law that makes no mention of race. No purpose to discriminate against men or women as a class can be gleaned from the Texas law, so rational-basis review applies. That review is readily satisfied here by the same rational basis that satisfied it in *Bowers*—society's belief that certain forms of sexual behavior are "immoral and unacceptable." This is the same justification that supports many other laws regulating sexual behavior that make a distinction based upon the identity of the partner—for example, laws against adultery, fornication, and adult incest, and laws refusing to recognize homosexual marriage.

Justice O'Connor argues that the discrimination in this law which must be justified is not its discrimination with regard to the sex of the partner but its discrimination with regard to the sexual proclivity of the principal actor. * * * Of course the same could be said of any law. A law against public nudity targets "the conduct that is closely correlated with being a nudist," and hence "is targeted at more than conduct"; it is "directed toward nudists as a class." But be that as it may. Even if the Texas law *does* deny equal protection to "homosexuals as a class," that denial *still* does not need to be justified by anything more than a rational basis, which our cases show is satisfied by the enforcement of traditional notions of sexual morality.

Justice O'Connor simply decrees application of "a more searching form of rational basis review" to the Texas statute. The cases she cites do not recognize such a standard, and reach their conclusions only after finding, as required by conventional rational-basis analysis, that no conceivable legitimate state interest supports the classification at issue. Nor does Justice O'Connor explain precisely what her "more searching form" of rational-basis review consists of. It must at least mean, however, that laws exhibiting " 'a . . . desire to harm a politically unpopular group,' " are invalid *even though* there may be a conceivable rational basis to support them.

This reasoning leaves on pretty shaky grounds state laws limiting marriage to opposite-sex couples. Justice O'Connor seeks to preserve them by the conclusory statement that "preserving the traditional institution of marriage" is a legitimate state interest. But "preserving the traditional institution of marriage" is just a kinder way of describing the State's *moral disapproval* of same-sex couples. Texas's interest in § 21.06 could be recast in similarly euphemistic terms: "preserving the traditional sexual mores of our society." In the jurisprudence Justice O'Connor has seemingly created, judges can validate laws by characterizing them as "preserving the traditions of society" (good); or invalidate them by characterizing them as "expressing moral disapproval" (bad).

Today's opinion is the product of a Court, which is the product of a law-profession culture, that has largely signed on to the so-called homosexual agenda, by which I mean the agenda promoted by some homosexual activists directed at eliminating the moral opprobrium that has traditionally attached to homosexual conduct. I noted in an earlier opinion the fact that the American Association of Law Schools (to which any reputable law school *must* seek to belong) excludes from membership any school that refuses to ban from its job-interview facilities a law firm (no matter how small) that does not wish to hire as a prospective partner a person who openly engages in homosexual conduct. See *Romer* [dissenting opinion].

One of the most revealing statements in today's opinion is the Court's grim warning that the criminalization of homosexual conduct is "an invitation to subject homosexual persons to discrimination both in the public and in the private spheres." It is clear from this that the Court has taken sides in the culture war, departing from its role of assuring, as neutral observer, that the democratic rules of engagement are observed. Many Americans do not want persons who openly engage in homosexual conduct as partners in their business, as scoutmasters for their children, as teachers in their children's schools, or as boarders in their home. They view this as protecting themselves and their families from a lifestyle that they believe to be immoral and destructive. The Court views it as "discrimination" which it is the function of our judgments to deter. So imbued is the Court with the law profession's anti-anti-homosexual culture, that it is seemingly unaware that the attitudes of that culture are not obviously "mainstream"; that in most States what the Court calls "discrimination" against those who engage in homosexual acts is perfectly legal; that proposals to ban such "discrimination" under Title VII have repeatedly been rejected by Congress, see Employment Non-Discrimination Act of 1994, S. 2238, 103d Cong., 2d Sess. (1994); Civil Rights Amendments, H. R. 5452, 94th Cong., 1st Sess. (1975); that in some cases such "discrimination" is *mandated* by federal statute, see 10 U. S. C. § 654(b)(1) (mandating discharge from the armed forces of any service member who engages in or intends to engage in homosexual acts);

and that in some cases such "discrimination" is a constitutional right, see *Boy Scouts of America* v. *Dale* [Chapter 1, Section 3D].

Let me be clear that I have nothing against homosexuals, or any other group, promoting their agenda through normal democratic means. Social perceptions of sexual and other morality change over time, and every group has the right to persuade its fellow citizens that its view of such matters is the best. That homosexuals have achieved some success in that enterprise is attested to by the fact that Texas is one of the few remaining States that criminalize private, consensual homosexual acts. But persuading one's fellow citizens is one thing, and imposing one's views in absence of democratic majority will is something else. I would no more *require* a State to criminalize homosexual acts—or, for that matter, display *any* moral disapprobation of them—than I would *forbid* it to do so. What Texas has chosen to do is well within the range of traditional democratic action, and its hand should not be stayed through the invention of a brand-new "constitutional right" by a Court that is impatient of democratic change. It is indeed true that "later generations can see that laws once thought necessary and proper in fact serve only to oppress;" and when that happens, later generations can repeal those laws. But it is the premise of our system that those judgments are to be made by the people, and not imposed by a governing caste that knows best.

One of the benefits of leaving regulation of this matter to the people rather than to the courts is that the people, unlike judges, need not carry things to their logical conclusion. The people may feel that their disapprobation of homosexual conduct is strong enough to disallow homosexual marriage, but not strong enough to criminalize private homosexual acts—and may legislate accordingly. The Court today pretends that it possesses a similar freedom of action, so that we need not fear judicial imposition of homosexual marriage, as has recently occurred in Canada (in a decision that the Canadian Government has chosen not to appeal). At the end of its opinion—after having laid waste the foundations of our rational-basis jurisprudence—the Court says that the present case "does not involve whether the government must give formal recognition to any relationship that homosexual persons seek to enter." Do not believe it. More illuminating than this bald, unreasoned disclaimer is the progression of thought displayed by an earlier passage in the Court's opinion, which notes the constitutional protections afforded to "personal decisions relating to *marriage*, procreation, contraception, family relationships, child rearing, and education," and then declares that "[p]ersons in a homosexual relationship may seek autonomy for these purposes, just as heterosexual persons do" (emphasis added). Today's opinion dismantles the structure of constitutional law that has permitted a distinction to be made between heterosexual and homosexual unions, insofar as formal recognition in marriage is concerned. If moral disapprobation of homosexual conduct is "no legitimate state interest" for purposes of proscribing that conduct; and if, as the Court coos (casting aside all pretense of neutrality), "[w]hen sexuality finds overt expression in intimate conduct with another person, the conduct can be but one element in a personal bond that is more enduring;" what justification could there possibly be for denying the benefits of marriage to homosexual couples exercising "[t]he liberty protected by the Constitution?" Surely not the encouragement of procreation, since the sterile and the elderly are allowed to marry. This case "does not involve" the issue of homosexual marriage only if one entertains the belief that principle and logic have nothing to do with the decisions of this Court. Many will hope that, as the Court comfortingly assures us, this is so.

The matters appropriate for this Court's resolution are only three: Texas's prohibition of sodomy neither infringes a "fundamental right" (which the Court does not dispute), nor is unsupported by a rational relation to what the Constitution considers a legitimate state interest, nor denies the equal protection of the laws. I dissent.

■ JUSTICE THOMAS, dissenting.

* * * I write separately to note that the law before the Court today "is ... uncommonly silly." *Griswold* v. *Connecticut* (Stewart, J., dissenting). If I were a member of the Texas Legislature, I would vote to repeal it. Punishing someone for expressing his sexual preference through noncommercial consensual conduct with another adult does not appear to be a worthy way to expend valuable law enforcement resources.

Notwithstanding this, * * * just like Justice Stewart, I "can find [neither in the Bill of Rights nor any other part of the Constitution a] general right of privacy," [*id.*], or as the Court terms it today, the "liberty of the person both in its spatial and more transcendent dimensions."

NOTES AND QUESTIONS

1. *Standard of Review.* The major question with which lower courts have struggled since *Lawrence* is what standard of review the Supreme Court was using. On this point, Justice Kennedy's opinion seems intentionally opaque. The power of the rhetoric in *Lawrence* makes it easy to lose sight of the fact that, unlike in the contraception or abortion cases from the 1960s and 1970s, there is no *fundamental* right explicitly recognized as such. Is it a fair inference from the citations in the opinion to those earlier cases that the Court here is also using a fundamental right analysis? Or is that a bridge too far?

The Court seems to proceed by reasoning that Americans have a liberty interest in private sexual conduct and that Texas has no rational basis for criminalizing such conduct. What are the pro's and con's of using a rational basis test? To have a law fail this lowest level test makes the Court's conclusion even more powerful in certain respects: the interests proffered by Texas are found to be not even rational, much less compelling. It also lowers the stakes for describing the individual's right: the Court's text makes clear that it is somehow a core right, but never crosses the line into denominating it as fundamental, with the attendant doctrinal consequence of heightened scrutiny. At the same time, however, using a rational basis test makes a strong decision potentially easier to distinguish in future cases: the Court can always return to an approach that gives much greater deference to state laws, as the typical rational basis test does, while claiming not to step outside of precedent.

Meanwhile, what happened to *Glucksberg*? Justice Scalia cites it in a brief section of his dissent (which we omitted) for the principle that only fundamental rights receive heightened scrutiny and that such a right must be an essential ingredient of liberty. Neither Justice Kennedy nor Justice O'Connor mentions *Glucksberg* here, but note that this question returns in *Obergefell*, *infra*, leaving the status of tiered review unclear under the Due Process Clause as it is under the Equal Protection Clause.

2.   *"Liberty," Not "Privacy."* There are many references to "private" sexual conduct in the decision, but nowhere except in citing older cases does the Court describe the right at issue here as "privacy." The same is true of *Casey*. Ironically, *Lawrence* may mark the end of a "right of privacy" in formal constitutional taxonomy, even as it validates its core principles. Perhaps the Court, while sounding like it is writing to praise privacy, has come to bury it, by substituting references to "liberty," a word that—unlike "privacy"— does have an unambiguous mooring in constitutional text.

It is difficult to know how much to make of this semantic shift, or whether "privacy" as such will reappear in future decisions. (The word has such widespread popular appeal that it may be impossible for the Court to put this cat back into the constitutional bag, even if the majority wants to.) But it is noteworthy that the Court resuscitates from *Hardwick* not the classic defense of privacy in Justice Blackmun's dissent, but the equal liberty analysis of Justice Stevens. (Re-read the Stevens dissent.) The Court in *Lawrence* invokes the contraception-abortion line of cases as protection for choice, control of one's "destiny," and the principle of "autonomy." The language of an individual's right of "choice" and to "choose"—words used three times in five sentences—connects this decision to that earlier line of cases.

3.   *Major and Minor Chords.* In some respects, recognition of the individual liberty of adults to engage in consensual sexual acts in private seems merely like the long overdue culmination of principles from the Model Penal Code and The Wolfenden Report, both documents from the 1950s. The Court has settled a very old and narrow debate; the same outcome could have occurred in the Eisenhower era. And while this might aptly summarize the Court's holding, it would not capture the full social meaning of the case, because the *Lawrence* decision combines a utilitarian holding with the strong rhythms of dignitarian reasoning.

"Liberty" is the Court's major chord. As the opening paragraph states, this case is about "unwarranted government intrusions," about both private and public realms where government should not go. Correlatively, where government does not intrude or impede, protections for individual freedom are not triggered. Certainly nothing in this decision undermines the negative liberty logic of *Harris v. McRae*. (Chapter 1, Section 1B *supra*.) This is classic libertarian philosophy.

But the civil rights-style rhetoric which forms the Court's minor chord suggests that this is libertarianism with a new inflection, where the desire to erect a buffer against government may be the primary, but is not the sole, driving force. Certainly it sounds nothing like the language of those 1950s texts, which assumed that homosexuality was repugnant, and sought only to argue that criminal law was not the method of choice for deterring it. In *Lawrence*, we have a Court opposed to the existence of sodomy laws because they "demean" gay people and create "stigma" for a group that deserves "respect" for the "choices" made in their "private lives."

The combination of these two discursive chords yields a complementarity of liberty and equality, a cultural and political zone where the new libertarians and the neo-egalitarians of the early twenty-first century can meet. The invocation of both strains—liberty as doctrine, equality as rhetoric—also produces an opinion that seems more holistic and connected to social experience and practice than might have been the case if the Court had separated its analyses of substantive due process and equal protection into distinct segments. Although the opinion of the Court says nothing *per se* about equal protection, the concept of equality is woven into the text.

In dissent, Justice Scalia appreciates that his colleagues in the majority are not following the old libertarian script, and that *Lawrence* represents a new recognition by the Court that gay people have equality rights as well as freedom from state intrusions. The sarcastic tone of his dissenting opinion suggests outrage as well as skepticism. Almost as much as he did in his *Romer* dissent, Justice Scalia accuses the majority of enforcing a lawless constitutional version of political correctness. He is accusing the majority of taking sides in the "culture wars," and the vigor and intensity of the dissenting opinion leave little doubt that Justice Scalia thought that the Court has taken the *wrong* side. Would his dissents here and in *Romer* have been more effective if they had not been so emotional? Contrast Justice Thomas's dissent: he disrespects the Texas Homosexual Conduct Law as "silly," but maintains that the Constitution does not authorize him to strike down every inane thing that a legislature does.

In the conclusion of his dissenting opinion, Justice Scalia also maintains that, by swallowing the "homosexual [privacy] agenda" in *Lawrence*, the Court was essentially writing the "homosexual [equality] agenda" into the Constitution as well. While this might have just been rhetorical flourish on Scalia's part, we think he was suggesting that once the state could not premise antigay discrimination on presumptively illegal conduct, the remaining defenses for antigay discriminations were vulnerable.

4. *Arguments Based upon Morality Cannot Be Used to Create an Underclass.* Justice O'Connor's concurring opinion repeats the proportionality principle of *Romer v. Evans*, that the law cannot target a group of persons for a broad range of disfavored treatment based on a single characteristic bearing little or no relationship to the particular policies at issue. See Nan D. Hunter, "Proportional Equality: Readings of *Romer*," 89 Ky. L. J.885 (2001). On this reasoning, the Court in *Romer* could and presumably would have written the same decision if the group in question had been burglars rather than gay people. O'Connor's opinion takes *Romer* one logical step further, by finding that "moral disapproval of a group cannot be a legitimate governmental interest." In *Romer*, Colorado (which had long ago repealed its sodomy law) did not claim morality as a state interest in support of Amendment 2, and the opinion of the Court did not declare whether morality could comprise a proper basis for such a law. In *Lawrence*, Texas did claim morality as the interest behind its sodomy law. It seemed clear even at the time of *Romer*—and is obvious now—that the six-Justice majority in that case would have rejected a claim of morality alone as basis for Amendment 2, so O'Connor's reasoning is not a surprise. But Justice O'Connor's opinion does serve to complete the logic of the *Romer* analysis. It also complements *Romer* by its focus on the argument that the law creates an "underclass."

The debate between Justices O'Connor and Scalia was a debate about rationality itself. Scalia argued that protection or expression of public morality is a rational state interest. O'Connor argued that expression of public dislike of a class of people is not a rational state interest. This is the tension between *Bowers v. Hardwick*, which held moral disapproval could be a rational basis, and *Romer v. Evans*, which held that animus against gay people could not be. O'Connor joined both opinions and seems to reaffirm both in *Lawrence*. Can they be reconciled?

5.   *Assessing History.* Even though they essentially rely on the same secondary sources, the majority and dissent read the history very differently. Without defending the simplistic history in Justice White's opinion, Justice Scalia seeks to rehabilitate *Hardwick*: Forget about the details of sodomy law evolution and the fact that "homosexual sodomy" was not the focus of such laws before the nineteenth century, he says. The thing to emphasize is that sodomy has been a prohibited activity for all of American history, and that alone precludes its being protected by the right to privacy. Recall that Justice Scalia demands a long and unbroken history of affirmative protection before he will acknowledge some kind of fundamental right protection—but that view of the relationship between history and substantive due process was rejected in *Griswold, Roe, Casey*, and *Loving v. Virginia*. Justice Scalia argued that an "evolving tradition" gives judges and the citizenry insufficient guidance in understanding what are the contours of individual liberty. Note how in *Lawrence* this argument is turned around: Justice Kennedy demonstrates that "unevolving tradition" was just as malleable in *Bowers* as "evolving tradition" would be. Moreover, Justice Kennedy provides examples of objective benchmarks for evolving tradition—the ALI's Model Penal Code, the adoption of its principle in the next generation of state legislative and judicial deliberation, the experience of other Western countries.

Another way to understand the Court's deployment of tradition is examining the level of generality. Justice Kennedy emphasizes a higher level of generality than Justice Scalia does. Scalia can hardly question that American constitutionalism has traditionally valued the integrity of the home, one's freedom to control one's own body, and (perhaps) our liberty to form relationships with one another. Kennedy starts with those principles and then announces that "homosexuals" are not exempt from their protection—a point Scalia disputes on the ground that "homosexuals" and their activities have not been *specifically protected* by any American tradition and, indeed, have been *specifically targeted* by the state throughout the twentieth century.

Justice Scalia argued that the Court is taking moral issues away from the democratic process; We the People rather than We the Court should be deciding the great moral issues of the day. Kennedy's response, subtly articulated in the opinion, is that consensual sodomy is no longer a great moral issue—it has been decided by consensus, and the Court is engaged in a mop-up operation.

Underlying Kennedy's approach is not the idea that the Court should decide great moral issues, but that the Court and its constitutional discourse contribute to a well-managed pluralism. America is a nation of social groups who constantly come into conflict. The political process is the arena where their conflicts are worked out, most of the time. But constitutionalism can serve a useful purpose of managing and channeling intergroup conflict. It can prevent the state from being deployed as a means whereby a minority is turned into an outlaw group. That is not only an unfair deployment of the state, but creates resentments and the risk that the outlaws (and the in-laws) will go outside normal politics to fight.

6. *"Domesticated Liberty"?* The most influential critique of *Lawrence* has been that the opinion is framed too narrowly to effectively shelter any sexual conduct except the respectable, marriage-like relationships of couples. "The price of the victory in *Lawrence* has been to trade sexuality for domesticity." Katherine M. Franke, "The Domesticated Liberty of *Lawrence v. Texas*," 104 *Colum. L. Rev.* 1399, 1409 (2004). Using a different lens, one of us has argued that, as a practical matter, *Lawrence* brought a formal end to the era in which lesbian and gay Americans were, literally, outlaws and empowered this minority to challenge other discriminations, including their exclusion from civil marriage. William N. Eskridge Jr., *Dishonorable Passions: The Crime Against Nature in America, 1861–2003* (2008). Another of us made the Foucauldian prediction that with the end of criminalization, "the state, through its judicial and social service arms, will be more, not less, involved with the regulation of homosexuality." Nan D. Hunter, "Sexual Orientation and the Paradox of Heightened Scrutiny," 102 *Mich. L. Rev.* 1502, 1534 (2004). Consider, e.g., the possibilities inherent in divorce law. With the decision now roughly 15 years old, how would you assess its broader impacts?

7. *The Sex Toy Saga.* In *Williams v. Attorney General of Alabama*, 378 F.3d 1232 (11th Cir. 2004), the ACLU challenged an Alabama law that prohibited the sale or distribution of devices "useful primarily for the stimulation of human genital organs." The Court of Appeals for the Eleventh Circuit ruled that *Lawrence* did not recognize a fundamental right to consensual sexual activity; instead, the court consulted *Glucksberg* to ask whether there was a history and tradition of protecting the right to use sexual devices. Judge Rosemary Barkett in dissent fired back that "the *Lawrence* Court held that the petitioners' 'right to liberty under the Due Process Clause gives them the full right to engage in their [private sexual] conduct without intervention of the government.'" The Supreme Court denied certiorari. 543 U.S. 1152 (2005). Further litigation ensued, but in the end, the statute remains on the books, Ala. Code § 13A–12–200.2, as does the same prohibition in Mississippi, Miss. Code Ann. § 97–29–105.

The neighboring Fifth Circuit reached the opposite conclusion in *Reliable Consultants, Inc., v. Earle*, 517 F.3d 738, *reh'g denied* 538 F.3d 355 (5th Cir. 2008). The Fifth Circuit struck down a Texas law banning the sale or promotion of sex toys (defined as in the Alabama law), ruling that the statute could not be distinguished from *Lawrence* on the ground that it reached public, rather than private, conduct. "The State's primary justifications for the statute are 'morality based.' The asserted interests include 'discouraging prurient interests in autonomous sex and the pursuit of sexual gratification unrelated to procreation and prohibiting the commercial sale of sex.' * * * Just as in *Lawrence*, the State here wants to use its laws to enforce a public moral code by restricting private intimate conduct. The case is * * * about controlling what people do in the privacy of their own homes because the State is morally opposed to a certain type of consensual private intimate conduct. This is an insufficient justification for the statute after *Lawrence*. It follows that the Texas statute cannot define sexual devices themselves as obscene and prohibit their sale." Texas did not seek certiorari.

NOTE ON SODOMY LAWS OUTSIDE THE U.S.

In most other nations, the elimination of sodomy laws has occurred by legislative action. Laws against same-sex sexual conduct were repealed in Great Britain (1967), Canada (1969), Germany (1968 in what was then East Germany and 1969 in what was then West Germany), Norway (1972), Spain (1979), Israel (1988), Japan (1989), and China (1993). In Australia, with a federal system similar to that of the U.S., state-by-state decriminalization began in 1975 and ended in 1997. In a number of other countries, such as France, criminal prohibitions of sodomy ended in the nineteenth century, although police did not stop using other laws to harass gay people until much later.

Litigation challenges to sodomy laws began in the 1980s in courts around the world. Courts invalidated sodomy laws in Northern Ireland, *Dudgeon v. United Kingdom*, 45 Eur. Ct. H.R. (ser. A) (1981); Ireland, *Norris v. Ireland*, 142 Eur. Ct. H.R. (ser. A) (1988); Cyprus, *Modinos v. Cyprus*, 259 Eur. Ct. H.R. (ser. A) (1993); Colombia, *Sentencia No. C–098/96* (Corte Constitucional, 1996); Ecuador, Constitutional Tribunal, Ecuador, *Sentencia No. 111-97-TC* in Registro Oficial (Official Registry), Supp. No. 203, Nov. 27, 1997; and South Africa, *National Coalition for Gay and Lesbian Equality v. Minister of Justice*, 1999 (1) SA 6 (CC) (S. Afr.). Not every challenge was successful. In India, an appeals court decision invalidating the colonial-era sodomy law inherited from the British was reversed by the Supreme Court. Koushal v. Naz Foundation, (2014) 1 SCC 1.

Professor Sonia Katyal argues that there is a cultural and constitutional diaspora at work in the formation of identity for many LGBT persons of color, both for those outside the U.S. and for those who are immigrants to the U.S. Sonia K. Katyal, "The Dissident Citizen," 57 *UCLA L. Rev.* 1415 (2010). Identity constructions that differ from those in the U.S. can enhance understandings of non-western cultures of sexuality and also enrich jurisprudential approaches. What are the challenges for developing such global perspectives?

PROBLEM 2-2
STATE REGULATION OF SEXUAL CONDUCT AFTER *LAWRENCE*

In his dissenting opinion, Justice Scalia predicted that *Lawrence* would mark the end of state morals regulation. Was he right? Consider what you believe is the interpretation most faithful to *Lawrence*, and apply that principle to the examples below. (In the remaining parts of this section, *infra*, we will consider two other examples in greater detail: sex work and the capacity to consent.)

For the questions in this Problem, assume that **A** and **B** are adults who have sexual relations in a private place (such as a home), unless specified otherwise. The state makes their activity a crime. Would prosecution be constitutional after *Lawrence*? Are there state interests that justify criminalization?

1. *Fornication.* **A** and **B** are unmarried, and the state prosecutes them for the misdemeanor of fornication. At the time *Lawrence* was decided, fornication was criminal in seven states; in seven other states, such acts were criminal when "open and notorious" or where the parties were cohabiting. These may be anomalous statutes, i.e., now unenforceable even though unrepealed. See *Martin v. Ziherl*, 269 Va. 35, 607 S.E.2d 367 (2005) and *In re J.M.*, 276 Ga. 88, 575 S.E.2d 441 (2003). (See Chapter 6, Section 1 on cohabitation laws.)

2. *Solicitation for Sex in a Private Place.* **A** solicits **B** in a public park to return to **A**'s house for private, consensual (and uncompensated) sexual activities. Even prior to *Lawrence*, jurisdictions divided on whether it was constitutional to criminalize solicitation for a "lewd" act such as oral or anal sex. *Compare, Sawatzky v. City of Oklahoma City,* 906 P.2d 785 (Okla. Crim. App. 1995) (upholding statute); *State v. Thompson,* 95 Ohio St.3d 264, 767 N.E.2d 251 (2002) (striking law as unconstitutional). Would a characteristic other than sexual orientation—e.g., whether one party intended to pay for the encounter—justify criminalization?

3. *Solicitation for Sex in a Quasi-Public Place.* It may make a difference where the solicitation and the proposed sexual encounter take place. Does *Lawrence* protect a man who asks another man in a restroom for oral sex behind the closed door of a bathroom stall? See *Singson v. Commonwealth,* 46 Va.App. 724, 621 S.E.2d 682 (2005) (upholding conviction).

4. *Adultery.* **A** is married to **C** but is having consensual sex with **B**, who is unmarried. At the time *Lawrence* was decided, about half the states criminalized adultery between consenting adults, usually as a misdemeanor. Can adultery between consenting adults still be prosecuted after *Lawrence*? Most cases involving adultery involve terminations of employment rather than criminal prosecutions. Even since *Lawrence*, firing for this reason has been upheld, especially if the individual's job involved law enforcement or the judicial system. Coker v. Whittington, 858 F.3d 304 (5th Cir. 2017) (sheriff's department); Beecham v. Henderson County, Tennessee, 422 F.3d 373 (6th Cir. 2005) (office of the clerk of court).

5. *Sex Between Related Adults.* **A** and **B** are adults and first cousins by blood. Sexual relations between first cousins is a crime in 22 states. Is that constitutional after *Lawrence*? Does it make a difference that before the Civil War no state made sexual relations between first cousins a crime and that states later made first-cousin intercourse a crime based upon eugenics-based theories that have in the late twentieth century been largely discredited? See Martin Ottenheimer, *Forbidden Relatives: The American Myth of Cousin Marriages* (1996). In 2014, the German Ethics Council, an official body that reports to the Bundestag, recommended that sexual relations between adult siblings be decriminalized. (Opinion available at http://www.ethikrat.org/files/opinion-incest-prohibition.pdf.) Consensual adult incest is not a crime in many jurisdictions, including France, Belgium, Spain, Russia, China, Japan, South Korea, Brazil, and Argentina. What is your view?

6. *Consensual Sex in a Private Location Involving More than Two Persons.* Could the state have validly convicted Lawrence and Garner if a third party had joined them for sexual activities? Cf. *Lovisi v. Slayton*, 539 F.2d 349 (4th Cir.) (en banc), *cert. denied sub nom. Lovisi v. Zahradnick*, 429 U.S. 977 (1976) (ruling that a married couple's right of privacy had been waived by their invitation to a third party to join them in a *ménage à trois*).

7. *Sexual Acts in a Commercial Space Open to the Public, but Sequestered Except for Those Who Knowingly Enter.* Can the state prohibit sex clubs? Membership-only sex clubs? Clubs or venues where sex is implicitly encouraged or tolerated? See *Commonwealth v. Bonadio*, 490 Pa. 91, 415 A.2d 47 (1980). Most states rely on zoning laws to control such entities. *See* Britt Cramer, "Zoning Adult Businesses: Evaluating the Secondary Effects Doctrine," 86 *Temp. L. Rev.* 577 (2014).

B. STATE REGULATION OF SEX WORK

One point on which American law has moved very little since *Lawrence* is the continuing criminalization of prostitution. Recall that the authors of *The Wolfenden Report* (Chapter 1, Section 1C) called for longer sentences for public prostitution at the same time that they were recommending de-criminalization of sodomy by consenting adults in private. The public/private boundary reflected in *The Wolfenden Report* spoke to what many persons saw as the problem of prostitution. "[P]rostitution, like obscenity and like other sexual offenses, should be viewed as a nuisance offense whose gravamen is not the act itself, or even the accompanying commercial transaction, but rather its status as a public indecency." Herbert Packer, *The Limits of the Criminal Sanction* 330 (1968). Social conservatives rejected this view as inadequate, refusing to accept that the state cannot reach beyond the public sphere to enforce morality. Progressive reformers wanted to eliminate prostitution as they would a naturally occurring disease, considering it a disease in the body politic. Feminists have pointed out the gender blindness in framing prostitution as a problem only because of its public dimension, and have been split over how the state and the world of commercial sex should interact, arguing primarily over what would be best for the women involved.

The Act of March 3, 1875, § 3, 18 Stat. 477, federalized immigration law and forbade the "importation into the United States of women for the purposes of prostitution." Immigration policy in general during this period was based on establishing and enforcing "quality" standards for persons seeking to enter the U.S., and immigration law-making became a venue for discourses of sexualized and racialized concepts of citizenship. In 1908 the Supreme Court, in construing the federal statute, described prostitutes as living lives hostile to "the idea of the family, as consisting in and springing from the union for life of one man and one woman in the holy estate of matrimony; the sure foundation of all that is stable and noble in our civilization, the best guaranty of that reverent morality which is the source of all beneficent progress in social and political improvement." *United States v. Bitty*, 208 U.S. 393, 401 (1908) (quoting *Murphy v. Ramsey*, 114 U.S. 15, 45 (1885)).

At the beginning of the twentieth century, public attention focused on how young women, both foreign and native, began working as prostitutes. What emerged from Congress was the White Slave Traffic Act of 1910, 36 Stat. 825, codified at 18 U.S.C. § 2421 (known as the Mann Act, after its author, Representative James Mann). Section 2 made it a federal crime to transport a woman or girl in interstate or foreign commerce "for the purpose of prostitution or debauchery, or for any other immoral purpose, or with the intent and purpose to induce, entice, or compel such woman or girl to become a prostitute or to give herself up to debauchery, or to engage in any other immoral practice." Section 3 prohibited any person from persuading or forcing, or assisting in either, a woman to travel in interstate or foreign commerce for the same prohibited purposes ("prostitution, debauchery or any other immoral purpose").

The question soon arose of whether the statute applied to interstate transportation of women for noncommercial but nonetheless "immoral" purposes. In *Caminetti v. United States*, 242 U.S. 470, 486 (1917), the Supreme Court found prostitution was not a necessary component of the conduct prohibited by the Mann Act:

> To cause a woman or girl to be transported for the purposes of
> debauchery, and for an immoral purpose, to wit, becoming a

concubine or mistress, * * * would seem by the very statement of the facts to embrace transportation for purposes denounced by the act, and therefore fairly within its meaning. * * *

According to Professor David Langum's study [*Crossing Over the Line: Legislating Morality and the Mann Act* (1994)], most of the Mann Act prosecutions between 1917 and 1928 were noncommercial fornication cases; lots of people, including many women, went to jail for consensual adult intercourse. Beginning in the late 1920s, juries stopped convicting defendants for simple intercourse, and prosecutors stopped bringing noncommercial cases unless there was an aggravating factor (*e.g.*, the woman was a minor or was tricked) or the defendant was someone the feds targeted for other reasons. Among the first celebrity defendants the Department of Justice went after was African-American boxing champion Jack Johnson, who was prosecuted for his relationship with a white woman, and served a year in prison.

Congress revised the Mann Act in minor ways in 1978 and more significantly in 1986. It now criminalizes interstate transportation of "any individual * * * with intent that such individual engage in prostitution, or in any sexual activity for which any person can be charged with a criminal offense." Public Law No. 99–628, § 5(b)(1), 100 Stat. 3511 (1986), amending 18 U.S.C. § 2421. Who other than those involved in sex-for-compensation activities could be prosecuted today?

NOTE ON CURRENT PROPOSALS FOR THE REGULATION OF SEX WORK

The effort to develop a legal regime that both respects and protects sex workers has bedeviled feminists for several generations, producing not only different but also inconsistent approaches. While law reform in this field has largely stalled in the U.S., there has been substantial movement outside the U.S. and in some states, especially California, where the adult film industry is based. The most significant proposals offer new variations on themes that one can trace back to Mills and Bentham. Following are the primary schools of thought about how state power should be deployed:

- The traditional emphasis on punishing prostitution as a crime of immorality, especially when it is publicly visible, continues in most jurisdictions within the U.S. and in most nations. Although the avowed goal is elimination of prostitution, there is often tacit agreement to allow other forms of sex work, and even some street prostitutes, in undesirable locations or low-income neighborhoods.

- Modern abolitionism campaigns, often led by feminists, also seek to eliminate prostitution but by prosecuting customers and pimps, rather than the sex workers themselves. This is often referred to as the Swedish model because of its origins. Non-prostitution forms of sex work are heavily policed. From this perspective, all sex workers are viewed as victims of trafficking.

- In weak legalization regimes, neither customers nor sex workers are subject to criminal penalties, but geographic containment renders activities socially invisible except to those who seek them out. State authority is deployed primarily to combat sexually transmitted diseases through regular testing programs. Nevada, where state-licensed brothels are located in rural areas, is an example of this approach.

- Where the conduct itself is legal, feminists may pursue assimilationist or regulatory goals, seeking to extend workplace health and safety rules to sex work. The objective is to treat this activity as a labor market in which greater regulation is needed for the protection of the workers. Existing government agencies expand their portfolios to incorporate sexual entertainment businesses. The adult film industry is regulated in this manner.

- Amnesty International framed sex work policy in international human rights terms in 2016, calling for decriminalization of consensual sex work; protection of workers "from harm, exploitation and coercion; the participation of sex workers in the development of laws that affect their lives and safety; an end to discrimination and access to education and employment options for all." (See https://www.amnesty.org/en/documents/pol30/4062/2016/en/.) The statement also emphasized opposition to all forms of human trafficking. Accord, World Health Organization, Sexual health, human rights and the law 27–29 (2016).

- Libertarians argue that the state should minimize any government oversight of sex work, with a possible exception for STD testing. The primary goal is decriminalization and maximization of individual freedom.

No consensus has emerged as to whether criminal law, employment law, health law, or human rights law should serve as the dominant paradigm for state policy in this field. The cases below focus on what we consider to be the most important approaches today in the U.S.: abolitionist/criminal law and assimilationist/employment law perspectives.

Terri Jean Bedford, et al. v. Attorney General of Canada (Attorney General) v. Terri-Jean Bedford et al.

Supreme Court of Canada, 2013.
2013 SCC 72.

■ MCLACHLIN C.J.C. (LEBEL, FISH, ABELLA, ROTHSTEIN, CROMWELL, MOLDAVER, KARAKATSANIS and WAGNER JJ. concurring)

* * * Three applicants, all current or former prostitutes, brought an application seeking declarations that three provisions of the *Criminal Code*, R.S.C. 1985, c. C–46, are unconstitutional.

The three impugned provisions criminalize various activities related to prostitution. They are primarily concerned with preventing public nuisance, as well as the exploitation of prostitutes. Section 210 makes it an offence to be an inmate of a bawdy-house, to be found in a bawdy-house without lawful excuse, or to be an owner, landlord, lessor, tenant, or occupier of a place who knowingly permits it to be used as a bawdy-house. Section 212(1)(*j*) makes it an offence to live on the avails of another's prostitution. Section 213(1)(*c*) makes it an offence to either stop or attempt to stop, or communicate or attempt to communicate with, someone in a public place for the purpose of engaging in prostitution or hiring a prostitute.

* * * [P]rostitution itself is not illegal. It is not against the law to exchange sex for money. * * *

The applicants allege that all three provisions infringe s. 7 of the *Canadian Charter of Rights and Freedoms* by preventing prostitutes from implementing certain safety measures—such as hiring security guards or "screening" potential clients—that could protect them from violent clients. [Section 7 states, "Everyone has the right to life, liberty and security of the person and the right not to be deprived thereof except in accordance with the principles of fundamental justice."] * * *

The bawdy-house provisions make it an offence to [to sell sex for money] in any "place" that is "kept or occupied" or "resorted to" for the purpose of prostitution. * * *

The practical effect of s. 210 is to confine lawful prostitution to two categories: street prostitution and out-calls. In-calls, where the john comes to the prostitute's residence, are prohibited. Out-calls, where the prostitute goes out and meets the client at a designated location, such as the client's home, are allowed. Working on the street is also permitted, though the practice of street prostitution is significantly limited by the prohibition on communicating in public.

The application [trial court] judge found, on a balance of probabilities, that the safest form of prostitution is working independently from a fixed location. She concluded that indoor work is far less dangerous than street prostitution—a finding that the evidence amply supports. She also concluded that out-call work is not as safe as in-call work, particularly under the current regime where prostitutes are precluded by virtue of the living on the avails provision from hiring a driver or security guard. Since the bawdy-house provision makes the safety-enhancing method of in-call prostitution illegal, the application judge concluded that the bawdy-house prohibition materially increased the risk prostitutes face under the present regime. I agree.

First, the prohibition prevents prostitutes from working in a fixed indoor location, which would be safer than working on the streets or meeting clients at different locations, especially given the current prohibition on hiring drivers or security guards. This, in turn, prevents prostitutes from having a regular clientele and from setting up indoor safeguards like receptionists, assistants, bodyguards and audio room monitoring, which would reduce risks. Second, it interferes with provision of health checks and preventive health measures. Finally * * * the bawdy-house prohibition prevents resort to safe houses, to which prostitutes working on the street can take clients. In Vancouver, for example, "Grandma's House" was established to support street workers in the Downtown Eastside, at about the same time as fears were growing that a serial killer was prowling the streets—fears which materialized in the notorious Robert Pickton. Street prostitutes—who the application judge found are largely the most vulnerable class of prostitutes, and who face an alarming amount of violence—were able to bring clients to Grandma's House. However, charges were laid under s. 210, and although the charges were eventually stayed—four years after they were laid—Grandma's House was shut down. For some prostitutes, particularly those who are destitute, safe houses such as Grandma's House may be critical. For these people, the ability to work in brothels or hire security, even if those activities were lawful, may be illusory. * * *

Section 212(1)(*j*) criminalizes living on the avails of prostitution of another person, wholly or in part. While targeting parasitic relationships, it has a broad reach. As interpreted by the courts, it makes it a crime for anyone to supply a service to a prostitute, because she is a prostitute. In effect, it prevents a prostitute from hiring bodyguards, drivers and receptionists. The application judge found that by denying prostitutes access to these security-enhancing safeguards, the law prevented them from taking steps to reduce the risks they face and negatively impacted their security of the person. As such, she found that the law engages s. 7 of the *Charter*.

The evidence amply supports the judge's conclusion. Hiring drivers, receptionists, and bodyguards, could increase prostitutes' safety, but the law prevents them from doing so. * * *

Section 213(1)(*c*) prohibits communicating or attempting to communicate for the purpose of engaging in prostitution or obtaining the sexual services of a prostitute, in a public place or a place open to public view. The provision extends to conduct short of verbal communication by prohibiting stopping or attempting to stop any person for those purposes.

The application judge found that face-to-face communication is an "essential tool" in enhancing street prostitutes' safety. Such communication, which the law prohibits, allows prostitutes to screen prospective clients for intoxication or propensity to violence, which can reduce the risks they face. This conclusion, based on the evidence before her, sufficed to engage security of the person under s. 7. * * *

For the reasons discussed above, the application judge concluded— and I agree—that the impugned laws negatively impact and thus engage security of the person rights of prostitutes. However, the appellant Attorneys General contend that s. 7 is not engaged because there is an insufficient causal connection between the laws and the risks faced by prostitutes. * * *

The Attorneys General of Canada and Ontario argue that prostitutes choose to engage in an inherently risky activity. They can avoid both the risk inherent in prostitution and any increased risk that the laws impose simply by choosing not to engage in this activity. They say that choice— and not the law—is the real cause of their injury.

The Attorneys General contend that Parliament is entitled to regulate prostitution as it sees fit. Anyone who chooses to sell sex for money must accept these conditions. If the conditions imposed by the law prejudice their security, it is their choice to engage in the activity, not the law, that is the cause.

What the applicants seek, the Attorneys General assert, is a constitutional right to engage in risky commercial activities. Thus the Attorney General of Ontario describes the s. 7 claim in this case as a "veiled assertion of a positive right to vocational safety". * * *

The Attorneys General buttress this argument by asserting that if this Court accepts that these laws can be viewed as causing prejudice to the applicants' security, then many other laws that leave open the choice to engage in risky activities by only partially or indirectly regulating those activities will be rendered unconstitutional.

Finally, in a variant on the argument that the impugned laws are not the cause of the applicants' alleged loss of security, the Attorneys General argue that the source of the harm is third parties—the johns who use and abuse prostitutes and the pimps who exploit them.

For the following reasons, I cannot accept the argument that it is not the law, but rather prostitutes' choice and third parties, that cause the risks complained of in this case.

First, while some prostitutes may fit the description of persons who freely choose (or at one time chose) to engage in the risky economic activity of prostitution, many prostitutes have no meaningful choice but to do so. * * * Whether because of financial desperation, drug addictions, mental illness, or compulsion from pimps, they often have little choice but to sell their bodies for money. Realistically, while they may retain some minimal power of choice—what the Attorney General of Canada called "constrained choice"—these are not people who can be said to be truly "choosing" a risky line of business.

Second, even accepting that there are those who freely choose to engage in prostitution, it must be remembered that prostitution—the exchange of sex for money—is not illegal. The causal question is whether the impugned laws make this lawful activity more dangerous. An analogy could be drawn to a law preventing a cyclist from wearing a helmet. That the cyclist chooses to ride her bike does not diminish the causal role of the law in making that activity riskier. The challenged laws relating to prostitution are no different.

Nor is it accurate to say that the claim in this case is a veiled assertion of a positive right to vocational safety. The applicants are not asking the government to put into place measures making prostitution safe. Rather, they are asking this Court to strike down legislative provisions that aggravate the risk of disease, violence and death.

It makes no difference that the conduct of pimps and johns is the immediate source of the harms suffered by prostitutes. The impugned laws deprive people engaged in a risky, but legal, activity of the means to protect themselves against those risks. The violence of a john does not diminish the role of the state in making a prostitute more vulnerable to that violence. * * *

I have concluded that the impugned laws deprive prostitutes of security of the person, engaging s. 7. The remaining step in the s. 7 analysis is to determine whether this deprivation is in accordance with the principles of fundamental justice. If so, s. 7 is not breached.

The principles of fundamental justice set out the minimum requirements that a law that negatively impacts on a person's life, liberty, or security of the person must meet. * * * In this case, we are concerned with the basic values against arbitrariness, overbreadth, and gross disproportionality. * * *

The case law on arbitrariness, overbreadth and gross disproportionality is directed against two different evils. The first evil is the absence of a connection between the infringement of rights and what the law seeks to achieve—the situation where the law's deprivation of an individual's life, liberty, or security of the person is not connected to the purpose of the law. The first evil is addressed by the norms against arbitrariness and overbreadth, which target the absence of connection between the law's purpose and the s. 7 deprivation.

The second evil lies in depriving a person of life, liberty or security of the person in a manner that is grossly disproportionate to the law's objective. The law's impact on the s. 7 interest is connected to the purpose, but the impact is so severe that it violates our fundamental norms. * * *

The appellant Attorneys General argue that the object of this provision, considered alone and in conjunction with the other prohibitions, is to deter prostitution. The record does not support this contention; on the contrary, it is clear from the legislative record that the purpose of the prohibition is to prevent community harms in the nature of nuisance. * * *

The harms identified by the courts below are grossly disproportionate to the deterrence of community disruption that is the object of the law. Parliament has the power to regulate against nuisances, but not at the cost of the health, safety and lives of prostitutes. A law that prevents street prostitutes from resorting to a safe haven such as Grandma's House while a suspected serial killer prowls the streets, is a law that has lost sight of its purpose. * * *

* * * [T]he living on the avails provision * * * punishes everyone who lives on the avails of prostitution without distinguishing between those who exploit prostitutes (for example, controlling and abusive pimps) and those who could increase the safety and security of prostitutes (for example, legitimate drivers, managers, or bodyguards). It also includes anyone involved in business with a prostitute, such as accountants or receptionists. In these ways, the law includes some conduct that bears no relation to its purpose of preventing the exploitation of prostitutes. The living on the avails provision is therefore overbroad. * * *

The object of the communicating provision * * * responds to the concerns of home-owners, businesses, and the residents of urban neighbourhoods. Public solicitation for the purposes of prostitution is closely associated with street congestion and noise, oral harassment of non-participants and general detrimental effects on passers-by or bystanders, especially children. * * *

It is certainly conceivable * * * that some street prostitutes would not refuse a client even if communication revealed potential danger. It is also conceivable that the danger may not be perfectly predicted in advance. However, that does not negate the application judge's finding that communication is an essential tool that can decrease risk. The assessment is qualitative, not quantitative. If screening could have prevented one woman from jumping into Robert Pickton's car, the severity of the harmful effects is established. * * *

The provision's negative impact on the safety and lives of street prostitutes is a grossly disproportionate response to the possibility of nuisance caused by street prostitution. * * *

Parliament [not] is precluded from imposing limits on where and how prostitution may be conducted. Prohibitions on keeping a bawdy-house, living on the avails of prostitution and communication related to prostitution are intertwined. They impact on each other. Greater latitude in one measure—for example, permitting prostitutes to obtain the assistance of security personnel—might impact on the constitutionality of another measure—for example, forbidding the nuisances associated with keeping a bawdy-house. The regulation of prostitution is a complex and delicate matter. It will be for Parliament, should it choose to do so, to devise a new approach, reflecting different elements of the existing regime.

This raises the question of whether the declaration of invalidity should be suspended and if so, for how long.

On the one hand, immediate invalidity would leave prostitution totally unregulated while Parliament grapples with the complex and sensitive problem of how to deal with it. How prostitution is regulated is a matter of great public concern, and few countries leave it entirely unregulated. Whether immediate invalidity would pose a danger to the public or imperil the rule of law may be subject to debate. However, it is clear that moving abruptly from a situation where prostitution is regulated to a situation where it is entirely unregulated would be a matter of great concern to many Canadians.

On the other hand, leaving [these] prohibitions in their present form leaves prostitutes at increased risk for the time of the suspension—risks which violate their constitutional right to security of the person.

The choice between suspending the declaration of invalidity and allowing it to take immediate effect is not an easy one. Neither alternative is without difficulty. However, considering all the interests at stake, I conclude that the declaration of invalidity should be suspended for one year.

NOTES AND QUESTIONS

1. *Greater Criminalization.* The *Bedford* litigation began as an effort to decriminalize associated activity in order to enhance the safety of sex workers, but the saga ended (at least for now) when the Ministry of Justice proposed new legislation in response to the Supreme Court opinion that *increases* criminalization of activities related to sex work, with the goal of ending prostitution. Bill C–36, the Protection of Communities and Exploited Persons Act, took effect in December 2014. S.C. 2014, c.25.

The Ministry described the new law as "a significant paradigm shift away from the treatment of prostitution as 'nuisance', as found by the Supreme Court of Canada in *Bedford*, toward treatment of prostitution as a form of sexual exploitation that disproportionately and negatively impacts on women and girls" and as a "made-in-Canada model, which directly targets the demand for this dangerous activity." The Ministry published a technical paper categorizing four activities covered by the new law, as follows:

(A) Purchasing

"Bill C–36 criminalizes, for the first time in Canadian criminal law, the purchase of sexual services. This new offence makes prostitution itself an illegal practice; every time prostitution takes place, regardless of venue, an offence is committed. In criminalizing those who create the demand for prostitution, Bill C–36 furthers its overall objective to reduce that demand, with a view to ultimately abolishing prostitution to the greatest extent possible."

A contract or agreement involving an expectation of payment between the seller and the purchaser involves "sexual services for consideration." This can include lap-dancing; masturbation of a client in the context of a massage; sado-masochistic activities if sexually stimulating or gratifying; and activities that do not involve physical contact, such as self-masturbation.

(B) Advertising

Bill C–36 also criminalizes advertising the sale of sexual services for the first time in Canada. Advertising includes print media and web sites; publishers or website administrators can be prosecuted for knowingly communicating such messages. Courts may order the seizure of print materials or their removal from the internet.

(C) Receiving Material Benefit

Bill C–36 creates a new material benefit offense to "modernize" the living on the avails of prostitution offense found unconstitutional by the lower court in Bedford. Bill C–36 criminalizes receiving a financial or other material benefit obtained by or derived from the commission of the purchasing offense.

(D) Procuring

The new law criminalizes "procuring [i.e., inducing or recruiting] a person to offer or provide sexual services for consideration, or recruiting, holding, concealing or harbouring a person who offers or provides sexual services for consideration, or exercising control, direction or influence over the movements of that person, for the purpose of facilitating the purchasing offence." This provision requires the active involvement of a third party in the prostitution and not just receiving material gains from it.

The new Canadian law also preserves some aspects of the court decision that were designed to protect sex workers. Individuals are allowed to advertise or negotiate the sale of their own sexual services, except near spaces where children congregate, such as school grounds. (Communications to purchase sexual services, however, are criminalized in any space, public or private.) Individuals, such as bodyguards, who provide protective services for sex workers cannot be prosecuted for receiving a material benefit from prostitution, unless there are exploitative circumstances.

Criticism of the new statute has come from multiple sources, including the Ontario Women's Justice Network and Human Rights Watch. The Vancouver Police Department issued guidelines saying that it would enforce laws regarding sex work "while paying particular attention to the safety of the sex worker." (See http://vancouver.ca/police/assets/pdf/reports-policies/

sex-enforcement-guidelines.pdf.) The City of Vancouver called for reconsideration of the legislation.

2. *U.S. Constitutional Law. Bedford* was decided under Canada's Charter of Rights, which the Supreme Court of Canada has interpreted to require a rule of proportionality for liberty restrictions. Canadian courts weigh whether the state's interest is weighty enough to justify a particular liberty deprivation. How would these kinds of challenges be framed under the U.S. Constitution? Does *Lawrence* create a constitutional space for federal courts to strike down anti-prostitution laws, either on their face or as applied?

The strongest, although indirect, support for *Bedford*-style efforts in the U.S. may come from the First Amendment. A law to fund AIDS/HIV treatment in Africa barred organizations from eligibility unless they had a policy explicitly opposing prostitution. The Supreme Court struck down the "prostitution pledge," as it was called, on First Amendment grounds, as the imposition of a government-dictated viewpoint. *Agency for International Development v. Alliance for Open Society International, Inc.*, ___U.S.___, 133 S.Ct. 2321 (2013).

3. *Therapeutic Justice?* In 2013, New York established Human Trafficking Intervention Courts (HTIC's) in 11 locations throughout the state. The HTIC's hear all prostitution-related offenses regardless of whether the incidents involve trafficking. Defendants in the HTIC system become eligible for dismissed or reduced charges if they complete programs offered by social service providers. Services are designed to assist individuals in leaving sex work; persons who do not make that commitment are not eligible for the assistance. See Aya Gruber, Amy J. Cohen & Kate Mogulescu, "Penal Welfare and the New Human Trafficking Intervention Courts," 68 *Fla. L. Rev.* 1333 (2016). HTIC's also exist in other states.

Vivid Entertainment, LLC, et al. v. Jonathan Fielding, Director of Los Angeles County Department of Public Health, et al.

United States Court of Appeals for the Ninth Circuit, 2014.
774 F.3d 566.

■ GRABER, CIRCUIT JUDGE.

[By voter initiative in 2012, Los Angeles County adopted the Safer Sex in the Adult Film Industry Act (commonly known as Measure B).] Measure B imposes a permitting system and additional production obligations on the makers of adult films, including a requirement that performers wear condoms in [activities that expose the actors to the exchange of bodily fluids]. Plaintiffs sued for declaratory and injunctive relief, arguing that Measure B burdens their freedom of expression in violation of the First Amendment. * * *

* * * Under Measure B, producers of adult films must obtain a newly designated "public health permit" before shooting an adult film in Los Angeles County. * * * [T]o obtain such a permit, producers of adult films

must pay a fee, provide the Department with proof that certain employees have completed a county-approved training program concerning blood-borne pathogens, display the permit while filming, post a notice at the film site that the use of condoms is required, report to the Department any changes in the permitted business, and comply with all applicable laws, including [a regulation that] mandates barrier protection for all employees who are exposed to blood-borne pathogens, which Measure B interprets to require condoms for performers who engage in vaginal or anal intercourse. * * *

[Plaintiffs argue that the condom mandate should be subject to strict scrutiny under the First Amendment because it is content-based regulation. The court acknowledges that "nearly all regulation of the adult entertainment industry is content based," but cites Circuit precedent for the application of intermediate scrutiny instead of strict scrutiny when speech "is sexual or pornographic in nature" and "the primary motivation behind the regulation [is] to prevent secondary effects. But even if those two conditions are met, strict scrutiny may still apply if the regulation amounts to a complete ban on expression."]

* * * [Measure B meets both those criteria. Nonetheless,] Plaintiffs argue that * * * the district court should have applied strict scrutiny because the condom mandate amounts to a complete ban on their protected expression. * * * Plaintiffs' argument presupposes that their relevant expression for First Amendment purposes is the depiction of condomless sex. * * *

* * * Plaintiffs submitted declarations stating that condomless sex differs from sex generally because condoms remind the audience about real-world concerns such as pregnancy and disease. Under this view, films depicting condomless sex convey a particular message about sex in a world without those risks. * * *

* * * The requirement that actors in adult films wear condoms while engaging in sexual intercourse might have "some minimal effect" on a film's erotic message, but that effect is certainly no greater than the effect of pasties and G-strings on the erotic message of nude dancing. [Citing *City of Erie v. Pap's A.M.*; see Chapter 1, Section 3A.] * * * [A] de minimis restriction on expression is, by definition, not a complete ban on expression, and so does not trigger strict scrutiny.

[Under the intermediate scrutiny test, plaintiffs contend that the condom mandate is not sufficiently tailored to serve the government's interest in protecting public health.]

Plaintiffs' narrow-tailoring argument rests largely on the proposition that Measure B duplicates a voluntary testing and monitoring scheme that already is in place in the industry. The adult film industry and its trade associations have established the Adult Protection Health & Safety Service, which has implemented a program whereby performers are tested, either monthly or more frequently, and the test results are made available in a database. In addition, if the Safety Service receives notification of a positive test result, it must inform the Department of Public Health. Adult film producers and performers have access to the database in order to verify that performers have been tested and that those tests have been negative. Certain employers require their performers, by contract, to submit to testing at various intervals. For example, Plaintiff Kross' contract requires testing every 15 days, Plaintiff Pierce is tested every 14 days, and all of Plaintiff Vivid Entertainment's performers are tested at least once every 28 days.

* * * Plaintiff Vivid Entertainment allows participation in the production only by performers with a current test status and a negative result. Plaintiffs Kross and Pierce declare that they undertake this screening process before every explicit scene in which they perform, and both Plaintiffs Kross and Pierce declare that they would not take part in an explicit scene if the screening measures were not in place. Plaintiffs also provided testimony from industry officials that this testing system is effective.

The district court considered Plaintiffs' evidence and weighed it against contradictory evidence that the industry's testing scheme is ineffective. * * * The Findings and Declaration section of Measure B refers specifically to documentation by the Los Angeles County Department of Public Health of the spread of HIV/AIDS and other sexually transmitted infections in the adult film industry.

In [a] 2009 letter, the Department of Public Health reported that its analysis of 2008 data showed a markedly higher rate of sexually transmitted infections for performers within the adult film industry, 20%, than for the general public, 2.4%, and even for the county area with the highest rate of infection, 4.5%. The Department of Public Health also found that 20.2% of performers in adult films diagnosed with an infection were reinfected within one year. * * *

The district court weighed all the evidence before it and, finding the 2009 letter especially compelling, held that Plaintiffs were unlikely to succeed on the merits in their First Amendment challenge to the condom mandate. In so doing, the district court did not abuse its discretion. * * *

NOTES AND QUESTIONS

1.   *Sex, Money and Videotape.* Battles over enforcement of the mandate for condom use in the adult film industry continue. A statewide version of Measure B—called Proposition 60—was on the California ballot in 2016, but voters rejected it by a 54 to 46% margin. Both the Democratic and Republican Parties opposed Proposition 60, as well as a number of LGBT and AIDS service organizations. Opponents mixed assimilationist and libertarian themes in their arguments, asserting that existing state regulations already protected sex workers and that the provision in Proposition 60 for a private right of action for performers would create a "lawsuit bonanza." Meanwhile, the California Occupational and Health Standards Board continues to study

whether it should craft a new standard for bloodborne pathogens with respect to the adult film industry or maintain the same standards for filming as for medical offices and hospitals. Information is sparse as to how (and whether) enforcement actually occurs and how well the industry's post-Measure B policies protect performers. *See, e.g.*, Peter Hartlaub, "Proposition 60 Would Require Condoms in Porn," *San Francisco Chronicle* (Oct. 4, 2016) (available at http://www.sfchronicle.com/electionsredesign/article/Proposition-60-would-require-condoms-in-porn-9695930.php).

2. *The New Zealand Model.* New Zealand is the only nation to have adopted a comprehensive regulatory model for sex work. The 2003 Prostitution Reform Act decriminalized all aspects of sex work, unless there has been coercion or the individual is younger than 18. The PRA requires use of condoms or other appropriate protection, requires brothels to obtain permits, authorizes the occupational health and safety agency to regulate and conduct inspections, and prohibits denial of social security benefits because of an individual's participation in sex work. (See text at http://www. legislation.govt.nz/act/public/2003/0028/latest/whole.html.) The legislation also provided for review of the impact of the PRA. Analysts from the Department of Health at the University of Otago, Christchurch found that the law had positive effects on the health and safety of sex workers and that there was little, if any, increase in the number of sex workers. (See http:// www.otago.ac.nz/christchurch/otago018607.pdf.)

3. *Regulation Through Rose-Colored Glasses.* In a trenchant analysis, Adrienne Davis criticizes assimilationists for failing to address how sex work differs from other employment. Davis argues that while many health and safety regulations and protections against management abuses could be easily applied to venues for sex work, advocates must remember that

> professional sex is not like "most" work. [P]articularities of sex work [include]: the culture of alcohol, drinking, and drugs; the homosocial "mob" context [of customers in clubs]; the blurred line between legitimate renegotiations and criminal assaults; a similarly blurred line between on-site/off-site (that is, on-duty/off-duty) identities; and employer expectations of "free" services * * *. Nor does most work entail the stigma and resulting isolation or threaten entrenched liberal norms of autonomy in the same way.

Adrienne D. Davis, "Regulating Sex Work: Erotic Assimilationism, Erotic Exceptionalism, and the Challenge of Intimate Labor" 103 *Cal. L. Rev.* 1195, 1250 (2015). To be effective, regulation must take account of these differences. Analyze the text of New Zealand's Prostitution Reform Act; does it pass muster?

PROBLEM 2-3
THE DEMAND SIDE

In her article, Professor Davis also criticizes feminist abolitionists for trying to eliminate sex work through criminalization of the conduct of demand-side actors such as customers without addressing the complexity of forces behind the demand. "Something has to give: either we use Title VII and other discrimination law to impose tight restrictions on demand and ban sexual preferences and fantasies for gender, race, ability, and age for inevitably more vanilla sex markets, or we carve a narrow exemption from Title VII and allow these preferences * * * " *Id.* at 1271. Her argument recalls the attempt by the plaintiffs in *Vivid Entertainment* to assert that condomless sex carried its own specific message. Would such a ban on advertisements for sex work survive a strict scrutiny analysis? Intermediate scrutiny?

C. THE CONSENT PARADIGM

Historically, consent has never been a simple or self-evident concept in the law, for many reasons. For example, consent under the law has been heavily racialized. During the Jim Crow era, African-American men could be lynched for the slightest indication of sexual interest in white women, real or imagined, while white men who coerced African-American women into sexual relations were effectively immune from prosecution. Although the regime of apartheid has ended, racially skewed reactions to sexuality and sexual representation continue. See Chapter 1, Section 3.

There is also the ancient canard that women cannot be trusted to tell the truth, especially about sex. State laws still vary in whether and under what circumstances a married woman can allege sexual assault against her husband. Most states have eliminated the traditional blanket marital exemption from prosecution for rape, but some states treat sexual violence between spouses differently than the same conduct between unmarried persons, by requiring actual force rather than threat of force, deception or drugging the victim. See, e.g., Idaho (Code § 18–6107) and Ohio (Ohio Rev. Code Ann. § 2907.02).

Lastly, sexual acts that are disfavored, even if lawful, may give rise to a differential treatment of what courts will consider as consent.

Regina v. Anthony Brown et al.
United Kingdom, The House of Lords, 1993.
[1994] 1 AC 212, [1993] 2 All ER 75, [1993] 2 WLR 556.

[The appellants mutually participated in the commission of violent acts for the sexual pleasure engendered from the giving and receiving of pain. The complainant had willingly joined the group's activities. The defendants were convicted under the Offenses against the Person Act of 1861, specifically sections 20 ("unlawfully and maliciously wound[ing] or inflict[ing] any grievous bodily harm upon any other person, either with or without any weapon or instrument") and 47 ("assault occasioning actual bodily harm"). The Court of Appeal (Criminal Division) dismissed the appeal. A divided (3–2) panel of the House of Lords dismissed the appeal.]

■ Lord Templeman.

*** My Lords, the authorities dealing with the intentional infliction of bodily harm do not establish that consent is a defence to a charge under the Act of 1861. They establish that the courts have accepted that consent is a defence to the infliction of bodily harm in the course of some lawful activities. The question is whether the defence should be extended to the infliction of bodily harm in the course of sado-masochistic encounters. [The issue is essentially one of public policy, because the legal authorities do not squarely address it.]

Counsel for some of the appellants argued that the defence of consent should be extended to the offence of occasioning actual bodily harm under section 47 of the Act of 1861 but should not be available to charges of serious wounding and the infliction of serious bodily harm under section 20. I do not consider that this solution is practicable. Sado-masochistic participants have no way of foretelling the degree of bodily harm which will result from their encounters. The differences between actual bodily harm and serious bodily harm cannot be satisfactorily applied by a jury in order to determine acquittal or conviction.

Counsel for [other] appellants argued that consent should provide a defence to charges under both section 20 and section 47 because, it was said, every person has a right to deal with his body as he pleases. I do not consider that this slogan provides a sufficient guide to the policy decision which must now be made. It is an offence for a person to abuse his own body and mind by taking drugs. Although the law is often broken, the criminal law restrains a practice which is regarded as dangerous and injurious to individuals and which if allowed and extended is harmful to society generally. In any event the appellants in this case did not mutilate their own bodies. They inflicted bodily harm on willing victims. Suicide is no longer an offence but a person who assists another to commit suicide is guilty of murder or manslaughter. ***

The evidence disclosed that drink and drugs were employed to obtain consent and increase enthusiasm. The victim was usually manacled so that the sadist could enjoy the thrill of power and the victim could enjoy the thrill of helplessness. The victim had no control over the harm which the sadist, also stimulated by drink and drugs, might inflict. In one case a victim was branded twice on the thigh and there was some doubt as to whether he consented to or protested against the second branding. The dangers involved in administering violence must have been appreciated by the appellants because, so it was said by their counsel, each victim was given a code word which he could pronounce when excessive harm or pain was caused. The efficiency of this precaution, when taken, depends on the circumstances and on the personalities involved. No one can feel the pain of another. The charges against the appellants were based on genital torture and violence to the buttocks, anus, penis, testicles and nipples. The victims were degraded and humiliated, sometimes beaten, sometimes wounded with instruments and sometimes branded. Bloodletting and the smearing of human blood produced excitement. There were obvious dangers of serious personal injury and blood infection. Prosecuting counsel informed the trial judge against the protests of defence counsel, that although the appellants had not contracted AIDS, two members of the group had died from AIDS and one other had contracted an HIV infection although not necessarily from the practices of the group. Some activities involved excrement. The assertion that the instruments employed by the sadists were clean and sterilized could not have removed the danger of infection, and the assertion that care was taken demonstrates the possibility of infection. Cruelty to human beings was on occasions supplemented by cruelty to animals in the form of bestiality. It is fortunate that there were no permanent injuries to a victim though no one knows the extent of harm inflicted in other cases. It is not surprising that a victim does not complain to the police when the complaint would involve him in giving details of acts in which he participated. * * *

In principle there is a difference between violence which is incidental and violence which is inflicted for the indulgence of cruelty. The violence of sado-masochistic encounters involves the indulgence of cruelty by sadists and the degradation of victims. Such violence is injurious to the participants and unpredictably dangerous. I am not prepared to invent a defence of consent for sado-masochistic encounters which breed and glorify cruelty and result in offenses under sections 47 and 20 of the Act of 1861. * * *

■ [LORD JAUNCEY of Tullichettle and LORD LOWRY concurred with this judgment in separate opinions.]

■ LORD MUSTILL.

My Lords, this is a case about the criminal law of violence. In my opinion it should be a case about the criminal law of private sexual relations, if about anything at all. * * * [W]hatever the outsider might feel about the subject matter of the prosecutions—perhaps horror, amazement or incomprehension, perhaps sadness—very few could read even a summary of the other activities without disgust. The House has been spared the video tapes, which must have been horrible. If the criminality of sexual deviation is the true ground of these proceedings, one would have expected that these above all would have been the subject of attack. Yet the picture is quite different. * * *

* * * [T]he involvement of the Act of 1861 was adventitious. This impression is reinforced when one considers the title of the statute under which the appellants are charged, "Offenses against the Person." Conduct infringing [sections] 18, 20 and 47 of the 1861 Act comes before the Crown Courts every day. Typically it involves brutality, aggression and violence, of a kind far removed from the appellants' behavior which, however worthy of censure, involved no animosity, no aggression, no personal rancour on the part of the person inflicting the hurt towards the recipient and no protest by the recipient. In fact, quite the reverse. Of

course we must give effect to the statute if its words capture what the appellants have done, but in deciding whether this is really so it is in my opinion legitimate to assume that the choice of the 1861 Act as the basis for the relevant counts in the indictment was made only because no other statute was found which could conceivably be brought to bear upon them. * * *

* * * [T] decks are clear for the House to tackle completely anew the question whether the public interest requires [section] 47 of the 1861 Act to be interpreted as penalising an infliction of harm which is at the level of actual bodily harm, but not grievous bodily harm; which is inflicted in private (by which I mean that it is exposed to the view only of those who have chosen to view it); which takes place not only with the consent of the recipient but with his willing and glad co-operation; which is inflicted for the gratification of sexual desire, and not in a spirit of animosity or rage; and which is not engaged in for profit.

* * * When proposing that the conduct is not rightly so charged I do not invite your Lordships' House to endorse it as morally acceptable. Nor do I pronounce in favour of a libertarian doctrine specifically related to sexual matters. Nor in the least do I suggest that ethical pronouncements are meaningless, that there is no difference between right and wrong, that sadism is praiseworthy, or that new opinions on sexual morality are necessarily superior to the old, or anything else of the same kind. What I do say is that these are questions of private morality; that the standards by which they fall to be judged are not those of the criminal law; and that if these standards are to be upheld the individual must enforce them upon himself according to his own moral standards, or have them enforced against him by moral pressures exerted by whatever religious or other community to whose ethical ideals he responds. * * *

* * * The only question is whether these consensual private acts are offenses against the existing law of violence. To this question I return a negative response. * * *

■ [LORD SLYNN of Hadley also dissented from the Court's judgment in a separate opinion.]

NOTES AND QUESTIONS

1.   *Postscript.* The European Court of Human Rights affirmed the decision, ruling that it did not violate Article 8 of the European Convention on Human Rights, which protects "respect for . . . private life." *Laskey, Jaggard and Brown v. United Kingdom*, 24 E.H.H.R. 39 (1997). "[T]he state is unquestionably entitled to regulate, through the operation of the criminal law, activities which involve the infliction of physical harm." *Id.* at 58. The Court also found that determination of the tolerable level of harm where the victim consented was primarily a matter for the state's authorities. The Court found no anti-gay bias, and concluded that the decision was based "on the extreme nature of the practices." *Id.* at 59. American courts have ruled to the same effect: *Commonwealth v. Appleby*, 402 N.E.2d 1051 (Mass. 1980);

People v. Samuels, 250 Cal.App.2d 501, 58 Cal. Rptr. 439 (Ct. App. 1st Dist. 1967).

2. *BDSM Versus "More Traditional Sex."* In *Doe v. George Mason University*, 149 F.Supp.3d 602 (E.D.Va. 2016), a student who was expelled for sexual misconduct challenged the decision on the ground that administrators had treated what he alleged was consensual BDSM as misconduct per se. Doe asserted that when his partner said "no" during a sexual encounter, he continued his actions because the two had a prior agreement that only the safe word "red" signaled that the activity should stop. The court read *Glucksberg* and *Lawrence* together as justification for rejecting plaintiff's claim:

> Under the *Lawrence* methodology, * * * courts must consider not only the history and tradition of freedom to engage in certain conduct, but also any history and tradition of impermissible animus that motivates the legislative restriction on the freedom in order to weigh with appropriate rigor whether the government's interest in limiting some liberty is a justifiable use of state power or an arbitrary abuse of that power. In this respect, the conclusion reached here under the *Glucksberg* line of reasoning that there is no deeply rooted history or tradition of BDSM sexual activity remains relevant and important to the analysis. Also relevant and important to the analysis is the *absence* of a history of impermissible animus as the basis for the restriction at issue here. Sexual activity that involves binding and gagging or the use of physical force such as spanking or choking poses certain inherent risks to personal safety not present in more traditional types of sexual activity. Thus, as in * * * *Glucksberg*, a legislative restriction on BDSM activity is justifiable by reference to the state's interest in the protection of vulnerable persons, *i.e.* sexual partners placed in situations with an elevated risk of physical harm. Accordingly, * * * plaintiff has no constitutionally protected and judicially enforceable fundamental liberty interest under the Due Process Clause of the Fourteenth Amendment to engage in BDSM sexual activity. * * *

Id. at 633–34. Virginia, where GMU is located, prohibits assault but does not criminalize BDSM sexual activities specifically. Could it constitutionally do so? (Doe was not charged with a crime.)

3. *Nondisclosure of HIV Status.* Another example of when consent is contested arises when one partner fails to disclose, or misrepresents, positive HIV status to the other partner. Most states criminalize such behavior and consider it to be non-consensual sex, on the theory that the unknowing partner's consent was vitiated by the lack of disclosure. Generally, these laws apply regardless of whether the sexual act placed the partner at actual risk. *See, e.g.*, Rhoades v Iowa, 848 N.W.2d 22, 33 (Iowa 2014) ("[T]here is a question of whether it was medically true [that] a person with a nondetectable viral load could transmit HIV through * * * blood, semen or vaginal fluid or whether transmission was merely theoretical.")

PROBLEM 2-4
SEX AND RISK

Imagine that you are a legislator in the newly created state of East Illinois. Local press reports of a young woman who became HIV positive during a relationship with a man whom she did not know was infected have fueled demands for a legal response. What are the advantages and disadvantages of a criminal law, a civil law, or no law? What should the definition of consent be in such a situation? How should the law calibrate the *mens rea* requirement in such a situation: should proof of a specific mental state or intent to cause harm be required? Alternatively, should recklessness or negligence suffice? How much difference should it make if the exposure occurred, but there was no transmission? Consider the Canadian approach in *Regina v. Mabior*, 2012 SCC 47 [2012] 2 S.C.R. 584, and draft legislation to address the issue of withholding this information vitiates the other partner's consent.

NOTES ON AGE OF CONSENT: NOT AS CLEAR CUT AS YOU THINK

Most people believe that the law's regulation of sex with children is simple: there is a standard "age of consent," and any sexual intercourse with a person under that age is illegal. This vision of the law serves a useful regulatory function (i.e., adults know that underage people are sexual "jailbait"), but it is multifariously erroneous. State law today defies easy characterization.[a]

To begin with, in most states it is a misnomer to say that a minor can never "consent" to sex. In Pennsylvania, for example, a complex law provides that it is "statutory rape" only if the adult is at least 18 years old and the minor is less than 15 years old. However, an adult of 18 can lawfully have sex with a 15 year old; a 15 year old can have sex with a 13 year old; and a 13 year old can have sex with another 13 year old. See 18 Pa. Const. Stat. §§ 3122.1, 3121.

Second, many states have adopted a nuanced statutory scheme that penalizes by reference to both age and the type of sexual conduct (such as penetrative intercourse or nonpenetrative contact). For example, in Rhode Island penetrative sexual intercourse (i.e., vaginal, oral, and anal intercourse) with a person 14 years old or younger is first degree "child molestation sexual assault," a felony carrying a sentence of 25 years to life in prison. R.I. Gen. Laws § 11–37–8.1–8.2. It is second degree child molestation sexual assault if the defendant has nonpenetrative sexual contact with a person 14 years old or younger. Id. § 11–37–8.3. It is third degree sexual assault for a defendant older than age 18 to engage in penetrative sexual intercourse with a person between the ages of 14 and 16 years old. Id. § 11–37–6.

Third, in some states the age of the minor affects the severity of an offense and thus the penalty. The Tennessee criminal code contains

---

[a]   In the third edition of this casebook, Chapter 2, Section 3D contained a table of all state age of consent laws as of 2010.

categories of statutory rape, "aggravated statutory rape," and mitigated statutory rape. Tenn. Code Ann. § 39–13–506. Other states—and there are several examples in the preceding chart—allow a small age differential to be a defense or an affirmative defense.

Fourth, many states include special rules for situations where the adult is in a relation of trust or authority over the minor. In South Carolina, for example, criminal sexual conduct with a minor in the second degree includes intercourse with a minor between 14 and 16 if the actor is in a position of "familial, custodial, or official authority to coerce the victim to submit or is older than the victim." S.C. Code Ann. § 16–3–655 (B)(2).

Fifth, virtually all of the state age of consent laws exempt married persons. That is, if an adult wants to marry a 15-year-old and can obtain parental consent (usually a prerequisite for underage marriages), the adult can have sex with his or her spouse.

Lastly, the enforcement of statutory rape laws and of other laws trenching on sexuality and minors has historically been an arena in which courts have accorded gender and sexual stereotypes greater latitude than in other areas of law. Examples include:

1. *Risk of Pregnancy as a "Natural" Basis for Gender Distinctions.* In **Michael M. v. Superior Court of Sonoma County, 450 U.S. 464, 101 S.Ct. 1200, 67 L.Ed.2d 437 (1981),** the Court upheld California's "statutory rape" law, even though it made only males criminally liable for the act of sexual intercourse. "Because virtually all of the significant harmful and inescapably identifiable consequences of teenage pregnancy fall on the young female, a legislature acts well within its authority when it elects to punish only the participant who, by nature, suffers few of the consequences of his conduct. It is hardly unreasonable for a legislature acting to protect minor females to exclude them from punishment. Moreover, the risk of pregnancy itself constitutes a substantial deterrence to young females. No similar natural sanctions deter males. A criminal sanction imposed solely on males thus serves to roughly 'equalize' the deterrents on the sexes." After this decision, the California legislature amended the law to provide for gender-neutral punishment.

2. *Enhancing Parental Control of Adolescent Girls.* One aspect of teenage sexuality with which the Supreme Court has had to engage frequently since its decision in *Roe v. Wade* is whether a pregnant teenager who is still a minor can consent to abortion. Abortion decisions require young women to negotiate what are sometimes difficult relations with parents and boyfriends, at a moment of acute stress. The result may be a critical struggle for power and control between young women and others in their world. From the parent's point of view, learning of a daughter's desire to have an abortion may present a threefold jolt. The parent realizes that: (1) the daughter is sexually active, (2) she is pregnant, and (3) she desires an abortion. For many parents, this notice may be the first time that they know or acknowledge that their daughter is sexually active. *See* Rosalind Petchesky, *Abortion and Woman's Choice: The State, Sexuality and Reproductive Freedom* 209–22 (1990). Should a pregnant teenager have the option to tell only one parent?

Studies indicate that those teenagers who communicate with a parent about sexuality and pregnancy are far more likely to confer with a mother than a father. Professor Petchesky concludes that "a requirement that both parents be informed affirms [specifically] paternal authority and power over young women's sexual lives." *Id.* at 307.

In **Bellotti v. Baird, 443 U.S. 622 (1979),** the Court struck down a law requiring either parental consent to a minor's abortion, or parental notification plus judicial approval. Writing for four Justices, **Justice Powell** concluded that the state could legislate to insure at least some parental involvement in the minor's decision, but found that the statute before the Court was defective because the requirement of parental involvement was absolute. He wrote that the statute could have passed muster if it had allowed the minor to obtain an abortion by using the "judicial bypass" without parental notification. This balancing preserved the belief, "deeply rooted in our Nation's history and tradition * * * that the parental role implies a substantial measure of authority over one's children. * * * Properly understood, then, the tradition of parental authority is not inconsistent with our tradition of individual liberty; rather, the former is one of the basic presuppositions of the latter."

The Powell plurality opinion in *Bellotti* still sets the boundaries for requirements of parental consent or notification for a minor's abortion, and has produced a new jurisdictional category for family courts around the nation: petitions for authorization of abortion. In **Jane Hodgson, et al. v. Minnesota, et al, 497 U.S. 417, 110 S.Ct. 2926, 111 L.Ed.2d 344 (1990),** the Supreme Court rejected an as applied challenge to such a system. The District Court had found a judicial bypass process did not provide additional protection for the minor nor did it enhance family integrity, especially in situations in which there was discord between the parents. The Supreme Court reversed on the ground that the provision of a judicial bypass option cured any infringement of the minor's liberty interests.

Statutes such as the Minnesota law instantiate socially appropriate notions of female sexuality and gender. The law effectively creates social identities for pregnant minors with normatively loaded consequences. The girl may carry the pregnancy to term with no social restriction, thus receiving society's endorsement of the identity of mother. Should she desire to terminate the pregnancy, she must go to court seeking a ruling that she is a "mature minor," marking the sexually active teenage girl as lawbreaker. If a judge finds that the girl is too immature to be treated as an adult for decision-making purposes, she must seek parental approval to proceed with the termination of a pregnancy.

The association of the judicial bypass process with the notion of criminality is evident to teenagers. Thus, "some teenagers feel that they don't belong in the court system, that they are ashamed, embarrassed and somehow that they are being punished for the situation they are in. I had a teenager tell me last week when I was describing to her the location of the building, when I said the Juvenile Justice Center she said I feel like a criminal and I think that is pretty typical of the reaction that the kids have when they find out they have to go to court. They see court as a place for teenagers who have done something wrong." Trial Testimony Excerpts of Susanne Smith, Supervisor of Guardian Ad Litem Program in Hennepin County, Minnesota, Joint Appendix, Part 1, *Hodgson*.

3. *Gay/Straight Differential in Age of Consent Laws.* In **Kansas v. Matthew R. Limon, 280 Kan. 275, 122 P.3d 22 (2005),** the state supreme court struck down an unlawful voluntary sexual relations statute on equal protection grounds because it punished the same sexual conduct between members of the opposite sex less harshly than the same conduct between members of the same sex. Commonly referred to as the Romeo and Juliet statute, the law reduced the possible penalties for statutory rape when the "offender" was 18 or younger and the "victim" was at least 14, but only if they were of the opposite sex. Limon's conviction was based on conduct that met all of the elements of the Romeo and Juliet statute but for the fact that the other participant was also male. The state argued that *Lawrence* did not control because Justice Kennedy's opinion covered only adults. The Kansas Supreme Court disagreed:

> Undoubtedly, the State has broad powers to protect minors. * * * [However,] even when the articulated interest is the protection of minors, there still must be a connection between the State's interest and the classification and, if the burden would not be allowed if placed upon an adult, the State's interest must be unique to children. So, unless the justifications for criminalizing homosexual activity between teenagers more severely than heterosexual activity between teenagers are somehow different than the justifications for criminalizing adult homosexual activity, those justifications must fail.

4. *Harm and Taboo.* As repugnant as we find the idea of coercive sexual contacts between adults and children, from a Foucauldian point of view, law's intense interest in the sexuality of minors is more likely to *incite* sexual interest than to *suppress* it (See Chapter 3, Section 3A). Child abuse laws present an agonizing legal conundrum: they punish actions that most Americans consider deeply immoral and harmful, yet the operation of the law can deepen or even create harm to victims and their families. William N. Eskridge Jr., *Gaylaw: Challenging the Apartheid of the Closet* ch. 6 (1999). The legal system is too much of a blunt instrument to treat the most complex situations with intelligence and sensitivity. A young adolescent's sexual curiosity can create dangers, for example, but empirical research does not support the conclusion that *all* sexual encounters are *always* harmful to *all* children. See, e.g., Claudia Konker, "Rethinking Child Sexual Abuse: An Anthropological Perspective," 62 *Amer. J. Orthopsychiatry* 147 (1992). Konker argues that "psychological damage resulting from [sexual interaction between adults and adolescents] may be related not simply to the physical contact per se, but to other family and interpersonal variables or to the stigmatization and punitive responses that can follow the disclosure of such behavior." The point is not that predators should be given excuses, but that the minors should not be assumed to be forever damaged.

SECTION 3

LIBERTY, EQUALITY, AND MARRIAGE

Perhaps the most stunning single victory for LGBT rights advocates was the Supreme Court decision that required all states to allow and recognize same-sex marriages. *Obergefell v. Hodges*, ___ U.S. ___, 135 S.Ct. 2584, 192 L.Ed.2d 609 (2015). Many people expected that the effort to secure this goal would take much longer than it did, in part because it confounded the standard left-right division in American politics. For social conservatives, the very concept of marriage between two men or two women seemed radical, unnatural and a violation of religious beliefs. Many progressives believed that seeking access to marriage was a profoundly conservative goal for an equality movement. To the mass of Americans in the middle, the prospect of same-sex marriage changed from an outlandish idea to one whose time had come. The story of the role played by lawyers and the legal system in changing the social meaning of marriage involves all branches and levels of government. In this section, we trace that 40-year campaign.

A. STATE LAW MARRIAGE EXCLUSIONS

The most important marriage case in U.S. law is **Richard and Mildred Loving v. Virginia, 388 U.S. 1, 87 S.Ct. 1817, 18 L.Ed.2d 1010 (1967).** In 1958, an African-American woman (Mildred Jeter) and a European-American man (Richard Loving), both residents of Virginia, married one another in the District of Columbia. Upon returning to their home in Virginia, the Lovings were prosecuted for violating the state anti-miscegenation law. After they pleaded guilty in 1959, the Virginia trial judge imposed a one-year jail sentence, but suspended it on condition that the Lovings leave Virginia and not return together for 25 years. The state courts later denied the Lovings' motion to vacate the conviction and sentence on the ground that the anti-miscegenation law was unconstitutional. The state supreme court followed its prior decision, upholding the state's "racial integrity" statute against equal protection challenge, in *Naim v. Naim*, 197 Va. 80, 87 S.E.2d 749 (1955).[a]

The Supreme Court reversed, in a unanimous opinion by **Chief Justice Warren.** The Chief Justice first dispatched the argument that an anti-miscegenation law does not "discriminate" on the basis of race, because such "statutes punish equally both the white and the Negro

---

[a] In *Naim*, the state court concluded that the State's legitimate purposes were "to preserve the racial integrity of its citizens," and to prevent "the corruption of blood," "a mongrel breed of citizens," and "the obliteration of racial pride," obviously an endorsement of the doctrine of White Supremacy.

participants in an interracial marriage." Virginia argued that the Framers of the Fourteenth Amendment did not intend for it to invalidate state anti-miscegenation laws. "Many of the statements alluded to by the State concern the debates over the Freedmen's Bureau Bill, which President Johnson vetoed, and the Civil Rights Act of 1866, 14 Stat. 27, enacted over his veto. While these statements have some relevance to the intention of Congress in submitting the Fourteenth Amendment, it must be understood that they pertained to the passage of specific statutes and not to the broader, organic purpose of a constitutional amendment. As for the various statements directly concerning the Fourteenth Amendment, we have said in connection with a related problem, that although these historical sources 'cast some light' they are not sufficient to resolve the problem; '[a]t best, they are inconclusive.' The most avid proponents of the post-War Amendments undoubtedly intended them to remove all legal distinctions among 'all persons born or naturalized in the United States.' Their opponents, just as certainly, were antagonistic to both the letter and the spirit of the Amendments and wished them to have the most limited effect.' *Brown*. We have rejected the proposition that the debates in the Thirty-ninth Congress or in the state legislatures which ratified the Fourteenth Amendment supported the theory advanced by the State, that the requirement of equal protection of the laws is satisfied by penal laws defining offenses based on racial classifications so long as white and Negro participants in the offense were similarly punished. *McLaughlin v. Florida*, 379 U.S. 184 (1964).

"The State finds support for its 'equal application' theory in the decision of the Court in *Pace v. Alabama*, 106 U.S. 583 (1883). In that case, the Court upheld a conviction under an Alabama statute forbidding adultery or fornication between a white person and a Negro which imposed a greater penalty than that of a statute proscribing similar conduct by members of the same race. The Court reasoned that the statute could not be said to discriminate against Negroes because the punishment for each participant in the offense was the same. However, as recently as the 1964 Term, in rejecting the reasoning of that case, we stated '*Pace* represents a limited view of the Equal Protection Clause which has not withstood analysis in the subsequent decisions of this Court.' *McLaughlin*. As we there demonstrated, the Equal Protection Clause requires the consideration of whether the classifications drawn by any statute constitute an arbitrary and invidious discrimination. The clear and central purpose of the Fourteenth Amendment was to eliminate all official state sources of invidious racial discrimination in the States.

"There can be no question but that Virginia's miscegenation statutes rest solely upon distinctions drawn according to race. The statutes proscribe generally accepted conduct if engaged in by members of different races. Over the years, this Court has consistently repudiated '[d]istinctions between citizens solely because of their ancestry' as being 'odious to a free people whose institutions are founded upon the doctrine of equality.' *Hirabayashi v. United States*, 320 U.S. 81 (1943). At the very least, the Equal Protection Clause demands that racial classifications, especially suspect in criminal statutes, be subjected to the 'most rigid scrutiny,' *Korematsu v. United States*, 323 U.S. 214 (1944), and, if they are ever to be upheld, they must be shown to be necessary to the accomplishment of some permissible state objective, independent of the racial discrimination which it was the object of the Fourteenth Amendment to eliminate."

Chief Justice Warren struck down the race-based classification based upon strict scrutiny. "There is patently no legitimate overriding purpose independent of invidious racial discrimination which justifies this classification. The fact that Virginia prohibits only interracial marriages involving white persons demonstrates that the racial classifications must stand on their own justification, as measures designed to maintain White Supremacy.[11] We have consistently denied the constitutionality of measures which restrict the rights of citizens on account of race. There can be no doubt that restricting the freedom to marry solely because of racial classifications violates the central meaning of the Equal Protection Clause."

In addition, the Court identified an alternative ground for its holding. "These statutes also deprive the Lovings of liberty without due process of law in violation of the Due Process Clause of the Fourteenth Amendment. The freedom to marry has long been recognized as one of the vital personal rights essential to the orderly pursuit of happiness by free men. Marriage is one of the 'basic civil rights of man,' fundamental to our very existence and survival. *Skinner v. State of Oklahoma*, 316 U.S. 535 (1942). To deny this fundamental freedom on so unsupportable a basis as the racial classifications embodied in these statutes, classifications so directly subversive of the principle of equality at the heart of the Fourteenth Amendment, is surely to deprive all the State's citizens of liberty without due process of law."

---

[11] Appellants point out that the State's concern in these statutes, as expressed in the words of the 1924 Act's title, "An Act to Preserve Racial Integrity," extends only to the integrity of the white race. While Virginia prohibits whites from marrying any nonwhite (subject to the exception for the descendants of Pocahontas), Negroes, Orientals, and any other racial class may intermarry without statutory interference. Appellants contend that this distinction renders Virginia's miscegenation statutes arbitrary and unreasonable even assuming the constitutional validity of an official purpose to preserve "racial integrity." We need not reach this contention because we find the racial classifications in these statutes repugnant to the Fourteenth Amendment, even assuming an even-handed state purpose to protect the "integrity" of all races. [*Editors' note*: The Virginia statutes stated that "the term 'white person' shall apply only to such person as has no trace whatever of any blood other than Caucasian; but persons who have one-sixteenth or less of the blood of the American Indian and have no other non-Caucasic blood shall be deemed to be white persons." In an earlier footnote, Chief Justice Warren explained this exception by quoting a 1925 publication by a state official, who wrote that it reflected " 'the desire of all to recognize as an integral and honored part of the white race the descendants of John Rolfe and Pocahontas.' "]

NOTES AND QUESTIONS

1. Loving *as the Guide.* The Court applied heightened scrutiny under both the Equal Protection Clause (Part I of the Court's opinion) and the Due Process Clause (Part II), but Part I contains the bulk of the opinion. Consider what this emphasis says about the Court's primary goals in eliminating anti-miscegenation laws. When you read *Obergefell*, *infra*, compare your notes to the Court's approach in that case. Of what significance are the differences in emphasis?

2. *Early Challenges to the Exclusion of Same-Sex Couples. Loving* inspired early lesbian and gay activists to think that same-sex couples, like different-race couples, had a constitutional right to state recognition of their relationships. The first such constitutional challenge was brought by a Minnesota couple, Jack Baker and Michael McConnell. The Minnesota Supreme Court rejected their claim in *Baker v. Nelson*, 291 Minn. 310, 191 N.W.2d 185 (1971), and Michael Wetherbee of the local ACLU chapter filed an appeal with the U.S. Supreme Court. Doctrinally, Wetherbee made the key constitutional arguments that LGBT rights lawyers honed for the next 44 years. First, exclusionary laws deny lesbian and gay couples their fundamental right to marry. If the state creates an institution with as many legal entitlements as civil marriage, it must have a compelling justification for excluding a class of citizens from its benefits. Second, the marriage bar also denies such couples the important property and economic rights that accompany spousal status as a matter of law. Third, the state's discrimination was one "based on gender." By a unanimous vote, the Supreme Court dismissed the appeal for lack of a substantial federal question in *Baker v. Nelson*, 409 U.S. 810 (1972) (No. 71–1027). Soon after, a different state's appeals court rejected the sex discrimination argument as brought under a state ERA. See *Singer v. Hara*, 11 Wash.App. 247, 522 P.2d 1187, review denied, 84 Wash.2d 1008 (1974).

As recently as 1993, not a single judge had concluded that same-sex couples must have access to marriage under federal or state statutory or constitutional law. The primary reasoning was definitional. As the court said in *Jones v. Hallahan*, 501 S.W.2d 588, 589 (Ky.App.1973),

> Marriage was a custom long before the state commenced to issue licenses for that purpose. For a time the records of marriage were kept by the church. * * * [M]arriage has always been considered as the union of a man and a woman and we have been presented with no authority to the contrary. * * * It appears that appellants are prevented from marrying, not by the statutes of Kentucky or the refusal of the County Clerk of Jefferson County to issue them a license, but rather by their own incapability of entering into a marriage as that term is defined.

3. *Other Barriers to Marriage Fall.* Even as lower courts were uniformly rejecting marriage claims by lesbian, gay, and transgender couples, the Supreme Court ruled that the constitutional right to marry barred states from preventing remarriages by fathers who owed child support, see *Zablocki* *v. Redhail*, 434 U.S. 374 (1978), and from barring marriages by incarcerated prisoners, see *Turner v. Safley*, 482 U.S. 78 (1987).

4. *New Fights, New Venues.* Beginning in the mid-1990s, after the Supreme Court had found that a voter initiative barring anti-discrimination coverage for lesbians and gay men violated the Equal Protection Clause (*Romer v. Evans*, Chapter 1, Section 2B), social conservatives turned to marriage as the next issue around which to frame the opportunity for voters to express their opposition to LGBT rights. The first initiative came in Hawaii, after state courts found that the exclusion of same-sex couples required strict scrutiny and that none of the state's arguments amounted to a compelling state interest. *Baehr v. Lewin*, 74 Haw. 530, 852 P.2d 44 (1993), on remand, *Baehr v. Miike*, 1996 WL 694235 (Hawai'i Cir. Ct. 1996). In response, in a popular vote referendum in 1998, voters amended the Hawaii state constitution to allow the exclusion of same-sex couples from marriage. For almost two decades after the Hawaii experience, state after state enacted new state constitutional amendments and statutes to bar same-sex marriage.

5. *Vermont Creates a New Status.* In *Baker v. State*, 744 A.2d 864 (Vt. 1999), the Vermont Supreme Court unanimously ruled that the exclusion of lesbian and gay couples from all the rights, benefits, and duties of marriage violated the Common Benefits Clause of the state constitution. The justices found the definition of marriage argument circular, the defense of marriage and children argument unsupported by any evidence, and the no promo homo argument inconsistent with the state's statutory commitment to equal treatment of lesbian and gay citizens. Hence, without ruling that sexual orientation is a suspect classification, the court found the discrimination unconstitutional—but four of the five justices also ruled that the court would rely on the legislature to remedy the discriminatory exclusion. In 2000, the Vermont Legislature created *civil unions*, with all the legal benefits and duties of marriage, but not the name (see Chapter 6, Section 2). Then came *Lawrence*—and immediately after *Lawrence* came another landmark state court decision.

Hillary Goodridge et al. v. Department of Public Health, 440 Mass. 309, 798 N.E.2d 941 (2003). Seven lesbian and gay couples sued the state to invalidate its exclusion of same-sex couples from marriage. **Chief Justice Margaret Marshall** delivered the opinion of a closely (4–3) divided court striking down the discrimination under the Massachusetts Constitution. "Whether and whom to marry, how to express sexual intimacy, and whether and how to establish a family—these are among the most basic of every individual's liberty and due process rights. And central to personal freedom and security is the assurance that the laws will apply equally to persons in similar situations. The liberty interest in choosing whether and whom to marry would be hollow if the Commonwealth could, without sufficient justification, foreclose an individual from freely choosing the person with whom to share an exclusive commitment in the unique institution of civil marriage." Notwithstanding this language, Chief Justice Marshall concluded that the Court need not reach the issue whether to apply heightened scrutiny, for the discrimination had no rational basis.

"The department posits three legislative rationales for prohibiting same-sex couples from marrying: (1) providing a 'favorable setting for procreation'; (2) ensuring the optimal setting for child rearing, which the department defines as 'a two-parent family with one parent of each sex'; and (3) preserving scarce State and private financial resources."

The Chief Justice found the first reason a justifiable state interest, but not one advanced by excluding lesbian and gay couples from marriage. "General Laws c. 207 contains no requirement that the applicants for a marriage license attest to their ability or intention to conceive children by coitus. Fertility is not a condition of marriage, nor is it grounds for divorce. People who have never consummated their marriage, and never plan to, may be and stay married. People who cannot stir from their deathbed may marry. While it is certainly true that many, perhaps most, married couples have children together (assisted or unassisted), it is the exclusive and permanent commitment of the marriage partners to one another, not the begetting of children, that is the *sine qua non* of civil marriage. * * *

"The 'marriage is procreation' argument singles out the one unbridgeable difference between same-sex and opposite-sex couples, and transforms that difference into the essence of legal marriage. Like Amendment 2 to the Constitution of Colorado, which effectively denied homosexual persons equality under the law and full access to the political process, the marriage restriction impermissibly 'identifies persons by a single trait and then denies them protection across the board.' *Romer v. Evans.* In so doing, the State's action confers an official stamp of approval on the destructive stereotype that same-sex relationships are inherently unstable and inferior to opposite-sex relationships and are not worthy of respect.

"The department's first stated rationale, equating marriage with unassisted heterosexual procreation, shades imperceptibly into its second: that confining marriage to opposite-sex couples ensures that children are raised in the 'optimal' setting. Protecting the welfare of children is a paramount State policy. Restricting marriage to opposite-sex couples, however, cannot plausibly further this policy. * * * Moreover, we have repudiated the common-law power of the State to provide varying levels of protection to children based on the circumstances of birth. The 'best interests of the child' standard does not turn on a parent's sexual orientation or marital status.

"The department has offered no evidence that forbidding marriage to people of the same sex will increase the number of couples choosing to enter into opposite-sex marriages in order to have and raise children. There is thus no rational relationship between the marriage statute and the Commonwealth's proffered goal of protecting the 'optimal' child rearing unit. Moreover, the department readily concedes that people in same-sex couples may be 'excellent' parents. These couples (including four of the plaintiff couples) have children for the reasons others do—to love them, to care for them, to nurture them. But the task of child rearing for same-sex couples is made infinitely harder by their status as outliers to the marriage laws. * * *

"The third rationale advanced by the department is that limiting marriage to opposite-sex couples furthers the Legislature's interest in conserving scarce State and private financial resources. The marriage restriction is rational, it argues, because the General Court logically could assume that same-sex couples are more financially independent than married couples and thus less needy of public marital benefits, such as tax advantages, or private marital benefits, such as employer-financed health plans that include spouses in their coverage.

"An absolute statutory ban on same-sex marriage bears no rational relationship to the goal of economy. First, the department's conclusory generalization—that same-sex couples are less financially dependent on each other than opposite-sex couples—ignores that many same-sex couples, such as many of the plaintiffs in this case, have children and other dependents (here, aged parents) in their care. The department does not contend, nor could it, that these dependents are less needy or deserving than the dependents of married couples. Second, Massachusetts marriage laws do not condition receipt of public and private financial benefits to married individuals on a demonstration of financial dependence on each other; the benefits are available to married couples regardless of whether they mingle their finances or actually depend on each other for support.

"The department suggests additional rationales for prohibiting same-sex couples from marrying, which are developed by some *amici*. It argues that broadening civil marriage to include same-sex couples will trivialize or destroy the institution of marriage as it has historically been fashioned. Certainly our decision today marks a significant change in the definition of marriage as it has been inherited from the common law, and understood by many societies for centuries. But it does not disturb the fundamental value of marriage in our society.

"Here, the plaintiffs seek only to be married, not to undermine the institution of civil marriage. They do not want marriage abolished. They do not attack the binary nature of marriage, the consanguinity provisions, or any of the other gate-keeping provisions of the marriage licensing law. Recognizing the right of an individual to marry a person of the same sex will not diminish the validity or dignity of opposite-sex marriage, any more than recognizing the right of an individual to marry a person of a different race devalues the marriage of a person who marries someone of her own race. If anything, extending civil marriage to same-sex couples reinforces the importance of marriage to individuals and communities. That same-sex couples are willing to embrace marriage's solemn obligations of exclusivity, mutual support, and commitment to one another is a testament to the enduring place of marriage in our laws and in the human spirit.

" * * * Alarms about the imminent erosion of the 'natural' order of marriage were sounded over the demise of antimiscegenation laws, the expansion of the rights of married women, and the introduction of 'no-fault' divorce. Marriage has survived all of these transformations, and we have no doubt that marriage will continue to be a vibrant and revered institution."

In a concurring opinion, **Justice Greaney** concluded that the case should be decided on a different constitutional basis, namely, that the marriage law discriminated on the basis of sex and, hence, should have been subjected to strict scrutiny (as in *Loving*) In dissent, **Justice Spina** argued that the court should not have resolved the validity of the marriage statute, but left it for the legislature "to effectuate social change without interference from the courts." Another dissent, by **Justice Sosman**, found that the primary basis for the majority's opinion was that the benefits of civil marriage could not be withheld from same-sex couples raising children; she argued that the legislature had a rational basis for limiting those benefits to marital households because marriages were the only environment proven to support healthy child-rearing.

Justice Cordy's dissenting opinion made the argument that traditional marriage has been linked to procreation, and that linkage has been a source of strength for the institution. "As long as marriage is limited to opposite-sex couples who can at least theoretically procreate, society is able to communicate a consistent message to its citizens that marriage is a (normatively) necessary part of their procreative endeavor; that if they are to procreate, then society has endorsed the institution of marriage as the environment for it and for the subsequent rearing of their children; and that benefits are available explicitly to create a supportive and conducive atmosphere for those purposes. If society proceeds similarly to recognize marriages between same-sex couples who cannot procreate, it could be perceived as an abandonment of this claim, and might result in the mistaken view that civil marriage has little to do with procreation: just as the potential of procreation would not be necessary for a marriage to be valid, marriage would not be necessary for optimal procreation and child rearing to occur. In essence, the Legislature could conclude that the consequence of such a policy shift would be a diminution in society's ability to steer the acts of procreation and child rearing into their most optimal setting."

NOTES AND QUESTIONS

1.   *The Functions of Marriage.* Chief Justice Marshall's opinion is an exercise in liberal theory: marriage is depicted as state institution that functions much as a public good. Two individuals who agree to assume its responsibilities can secure its rights. While the state can define those rights and duties, it must adopt neutral criteria for who can qualify. Justice Cordy's

dissenting opinion, which became quite influential in subsequent state court challenges to marriage laws, imagined marriage as a channeling device that aimed its sticks and carrots structure at different-sex couples. Same-sex couples seem almost beside the point in his analysis, their exclusion a kind of collateral damage. What is the best response to Justice Cordy's argument?

2. *State Constitutional Law.* From the late 1990s to *Perry v. Hollingsworth, infra,* all but one of the marriage equality cases were based solely on claims arising under state constitutions. (The Supreme Court will not review a state court decision based on adequate and independent state law grounds.) In avoiding the federal court system, with its path on appeal leading to the U.S. Supreme Court, LGBT rights advocates were re-using the strategy that proved successful in the years between *Bowers v. Hardwick* and *Lawrence v. Texas*: a state-by-state approach that eventually could help persuade the Supreme Court that the nation was ready for same-sex marriage. In Massachusetts, the court relied on concepts and precedent from federal law, but the holding did not apply beyond the state law grounds pled by plaintiffs. By comparison, in the *Baker* case, *supra,* the Vermont Supreme Court used the opportunity to develop a new interpretation of the state constitution's Common Benefits Clause.

3. *The Role of the Judiciary.* Are there advantages to the strategy of reliance on state law beyond the ability to insulate an issue from a Supreme Court that appears to be hostile? Although Justice Brandeis's suggestion that states could serve as "laboratories" of democracy in *New State Ice Co. v. Liebman* [285 U.S. 262, 387 (1932)] usually applies to statutory law, state judiciaries might be called laboratories of judicial review or of countermajoritarianism. For marriage equality advocates, the lab results were mixed. In Massachusetts, they beat back an effort to put the question on a statewide ballot that would have amended the state constitution to prohibit same-sex marriage, as had occurred in Hawaii. In the worst case of retribution against the judicial branch, three of the Iowa Supreme Court justices who joined in a unanimous opinion in favor of marriage equality [*Varnum v. Brien,* 763 N.W.2d 862 (2009)] were defeated in a retention election held the next year. Arguments about same-sex marriage reinvigorated debate about the role of the judiciary, even when it was more homegrown than federal courts are perceived to be. Accusations of "judicial activism" became the backbeat for arguments against same-sex marriage, culminating in Chief Justice Roberts' dissenting opinion in *Obergefell v. Hodges, infra.*

4. *Organizing and Litigating.* Both the Vermont and Massachusetts cases were brought by Gay and Lesbian Advocates and Defenders (GLAD). Taking to heart the adage that lawsuits are ultimately won or lost in the court of public opinion, GLAD selected Vermont for its first case in part because that state's process for a voter initiative to amend the state constitution is cumbersome, and thus a victory in court would be less vulnerable to backlash. In both states, GLAD began working with local advocacy groups on outreach and public education projects to build public support several years before filing the complaints to initiate litigation. See William N. Eskridge Jr., *Equality Practice: Civil Unions and the Future of Gay Rights*

(2002). This election campaign-style organizing work became an increasingly important component of the marriage equality toolkit. See Nan D. Hunter, "Varieties of Constitutional Experience: On Social Movements and Direct Democracy," 64 *UCLA L. Rev.*, forthcoming 2017.

5. *National Reaction.* The decision in *Goodridge* was announced less than four months after the ruling in *Lawrence*, and almost exactly one year before the 2004 presidential election. Although *Lawrence* was a nationwide decision, it incited relatively mild reactions from social conservative groups. The primary criticism followed the lead of Justice Scalia's dissenting opinion, a dire (and accurate) prediction that the logic of *Lawrence* would topple barriers to same-sex marriage. By contrast, when *Goodridge* was announced, although it applied to only one state, traditionalist values groups seized on "gay marriage" as a mobilizing issue for the election. In February 2004, President George W. Bush endorsed a federal constitutional amendment to limit the definition of marriage. Ballot questions asking whether marriage should be restricted to one man and one woman were offered in 13 states during 2004; voters approved all of them.

In re Marriage Cases

California Supreme Court, 2008.
43 Cal.4th 757, 183 P.3d 384, 76 Cal.Rptr.3d 683.

■ CHIEF JUSTICE GEORGE delivered the opinion for the Court.

[These appeals consolidated six cases where lesbian and gay couples sought recognition of their committed relationships as *marriages*. Since statehood in 1850, California's family law had implicitly limited civil marriage to different-sex relationships. A 1977 statute limited marriage to unions between one man and one woman, and a 2000 initiative reaffirmed the limitation of marriage to different-sex couples and provided that the state would not recognize out-of-state same-sex marriages. Plaintiffs argued that the discrimination against their relationships violated the equality guarantees of the California Constitution. They argued that the discrimination was subject to strict scrutiny for three independent reasons: the exclusion of same-sex couples from state marriage law rested upon two "suspect" classifications, namely, (1) sex and (2) sexual orientation and, moreover, (3) denied those couples a "fundamental" interest in marriage.]

[Part IV of the Chief Justice's opinion held that the plaintiff lesbian and gay couples have a "fundamental right to marry." Unlike the U.S. Constitution, the California Constitution mentions privacy rights, in Article I, section 1, which provides: "All people are by nature free and independent and have inalienable rights. Among these are enjoying and defending life and *liberty*, acquiring, possessing, and protecting property, and pursuing and obtaining safety, happiness, and *privacy*." (Added 1972, emphasis added.) Like the U.S. Constitution, however, the California Constitution does not explicitly protect a fundamental right to marry, but the state supreme court has inferred such a right from the

1972 amendment, which was meant to codify *Griswold v. Connecticut* in the state constitution.

[The lower court had rejected plaintiffs' claim on the ground that lesbian and gay couples enjoyed no "fundamental right to marriage," because marriage had traditionally not included them. Although all other state appeals courts had accepted or acquiesced in a similar argument, Chief Justice George rejected it as circular.] In *Perez v. Sharp*, this court's 1948 decision holding that the California statutory provisions prohibiting interracial marriage were unconstitutional—the court did not characterize the constitutional right that the plaintiffs in that case sought to obtain as "a right to interracial marriage" and did not dismiss the plaintiffs' constitutional challenge on the ground that such marriages never had been permitted in California. Instead, the *Perez* decision focused on the *substance* of the constitutional right at issue—that is, the importance to an individual of the freedom "to join in marriage *with the person of one's choice*"—in determining whether the statute impinged upon the plaintiffs' fundamental constitutional right. * * * And, in addressing a somewhat analogous point, the United States Supreme Court in *Lawrence v. Texas* concluded that its prior decision in *Bowers v. Hardwick* had erred in narrowly characterizing the constitutional right sought to be invoked in that case as the right to engage in intimate *homosexual* conduct, determining instead that the constitutional right there at issue properly should be understood in a broader and more neutral fashion so as to focus upon the substance of the interests that the constitutional right is intended to protect.

[When understood at the proper level of generality, the question becomes, why marriage is so important. *Perez* and other cases established a] linkage between marriage, establishing a home, and raising children in identifying civil marriage as the means available to an individual to establish, with a loved one of his or her choice, an officially recognized family relationship. In *De Burgh v. De Burgh* (1952) 39 Cal.2d 858, for example, in explaining "the public interest in the institution of marriage," this court stated: "The family is the basic unit of our society, the center of the personal affections that ennoble and enrich human life. It channels biological drives that might otherwise become socially destructive; it ensures the care and education of children in a stable environment; it establishes continuity from one generation to another; it nurtures and develops the individual initiative that distinguishes a free people. Since the family is the core of our society, the law seeks to foster and preserve marriage."

[In response to the argument that marriage had traditionally been reserved for different-sex couples only, the Chief Justice noted that the same kind of argument had been rejected in *Perez*. The point of constitutional review is to subject tradition to normative scrutiny.] There can be no question but that, in recent decades, there has been a fundamental and dramatic transformation in this state's understanding and legal treatment of gay individuals and gay couples. California has repudiated past practices and policies that were based on a once common viewpoint that denigrated the general character and morals of gay individuals, and at one time even characterized homosexuality as a mental illness rather than as simply one of the numerous variables of our common and diverse humanity. This state's current policies and conduct regarding homosexuality recognize that gay individuals are entitled to the same legal rights and the same respect and dignity afforded all other individuals and are protected from discrimination on the basis of their sexual orientation, and, more specifically, recognize that gay individuals are fully capable of entering into the kind of loving and enduring committed relationships that may serve as the foundation of a family and of responsibly caring for and raising children.

[*Amici* argued that the main point of marriage is procreation, and that the valid state interest in channeling reproductive activity into marriage justified the omission of same-sex couples, who could not produce children through their sexual activities. The Chief Justice was unpersuaded, in part because as many as 70,000 children were being raised in California by same-sex couples. Some of these children were adopted, others came through surrogates and artificial insemination, but the fact remained, for the Court, that even this traditional value of marriage was not served by excluding so many families from the state marriage law.]

* * * The personal enrichment afforded by the right to marry may be obtained by a couple whether or not they choose to have children, and the right to marry never has been limited to those who plan or desire to have children. Indeed, in *Griswold v. Connecticut*—one of the seminal federal cases striking down a state law as violative of the federal constitutional right of privacy—the high court upheld a married couple's right to use contraception *to prevent procreation*, demonstrating quite clearly that the promotion of procreation is not the sole or defining purpose of marriage. Similarly, in *Turner v. Safley*, the court held that the constitutional right to marry extends to an individual confined in state prison—even a prisoner who has no right to conjugal visits with his would—be spouse—emphasizing that "[m]any important attributes of marriage remain . . . after taking into account the limitations imposed by prison life . . . [including the] expressions of emotional support and public commitment [that] are an important and significant aspect of the marital relationship." Although *Griswold* and *Turner* relate to the right to marry under the federal Constitution, they accurately reflect the scope of the state constitutional right to marry as well. Accordingly, this right cannot properly be defined by or limited to the state's interest in fostering a favorable environment for the procreation and raising of children.

The Proposition 22 Legal Defense Fund and the Campaign also rely upon several academic commentators who maintain that the constitutional right to marry should be viewed as inapplicable to same-sex couples because a contrary interpretation assertedly would sever the link that marriage provides between procreation and child rearing and would "send a message" to the public that it is immaterial to the state whether children are raised by their biological mother and father. Although we appreciate the genuine concern for the wellbeing of children underlying that position, we conclude this claim lacks merit. Our recognition that the core substantive rights encompassed by the constitutional right to marry apply to same-sex as well as opposite-sex couples does not imply in any way that it is unimportant or immaterial to the state whether a child is raised by his or her biological mother and father. By recognizing this circumstance we do not alter or diminish either the legal responsibilities that biological parents owe to their children or the substantial incentives that the state provides to a child's biological parents to enter into and raise their child in a stable, long-term committed relationship. Instead, such an interpretation of the constitutional right to marry simply confirms that a stable two-parent family relationship, supported by the state's official recognition and protection, is equally as important for the numerous children in California who are being raised by same-sex couples as for those children being raised by opposite-sex couples (whether they are biological parents or adoptive parents). This interpretation also guarantees individuals who are in a same-sex relationship, and who are raising children, the opportunity to obtain from the state the official recognition and support accorded a family by agreeing to take on the substantial and long-term mutual obligations and responsibilities that are an essential and inseparable part of a family relationship.

[Finally, the Chief Justice rejected the Attorney General's argument that the Domestic Partnership Act, as amended to provide virtually all the legal benefits and duties of marriage for same-sex couples, satisfied the constitutional marriage right.] Whether or not the name "marriage," in the abstract, is considered a core element of the state constitutional right to marry, one of the core elements of this fundamental right is the right of same-sex couples to have their official family relationship accorded the same dignity, respect, and stature as that accorded to all other officially recognized family relationships. The current statutes—by drawing a distinction between the name assigned to the family relationship available to opposite-sex couples and the name assigned to the family relationship available to same-sex couples, and by reserving the historic and highly respected designation of marriage exclusively to opposite-sex couples while offering same-sex couples only the new and unfamiliar designation of domestic partnership—pose a serious risk of denying the official family relationship of same-sex couples the equal dignity and respect that is a core element of the constitutional right to marry. As observed by the City [and County] of San Francisco at oral argument, this court's conclusion in *Perez* that the statutory provision barring interracial marriage was unconstitutional, undoubtedly would have been the same even if alternative nomenclature, such as "transracial union," had been made available to interracial couples. * * *

[IV.A.   The Sex Discrimination Argument.] * * * In drawing a distinction between opposite-sex couples and same-sex couples, the challenged marriage statutes do not treat men and women differently. Persons of either gender are treated equally and are permitted to marry only a person of the opposite gender. In light of the equality of treatment between genders, the distinction prescribed by the relevant statutes plainly does not constitute discrimination on the basis of sex as that concept is commonly understood. * * *

The decisions in [*Perez v. Lippold*, 32 Cal.2d 711 (1948) (holding California's anti-miscegenation statute unconstitutional] and *Loving v. Virginia* * * * are clearly distinguishable from this case, because the antimiscegenation statutes at issue in those cases plainly treated members of minority races differently from White persons, prohibiting only intermarriage that involved White persons in order to prevent (in the undisguised words of the defenders of the statute in *Perez*) "the Caucasian race from being contaminated by races whose members are by nature physically and mentally inferior to Caucasians." (*Perez*; see also *Loving*.) Under these circumstances, there can be no doubt that the reference to race in the statutes at issue in *Perez* and *Loving* unquestionably reflected the kind of racial discrimination that always has been recognized as calling for strict scrutiny under equal protection analysis.

In *Perez, Loving*, and a number of other decisions (see, e.g., *McLaughlin v. Florida* (1964) 379 U.S. 184, 192), courts have recognized that a statute that treats a couple differently based upon whether the couple consists of persons of the same race or of different races generally reflects a policy disapproving of the integration or close relationship of individuals of different races in the setting in question, and as such properly is viewed as embodying an instance of *racial discrimination* with respect to the interracial couple and both of its members. By contrast, past judicial decisions, in California and elsewhere, virtually uniformly hold that a statute or policy that treats men and women equally but that accords differential treatment either to a couple based upon whether it consists of persons of the same sex rather than opposite sexes, or to an individual based upon whether he or she generally is sexually attracted to persons of the same gender rather than the opposite gender, is more accurately characterized as involving differential treatment on the basis of *sexual orientation* rather than an instance of *sex discrimination*, and properly should be analyzed on the *former* ground. These cases recognize that, in realistic terms, a statute or policy that treats same-sex couples differently from opposite-sex couples, or that treats individuals who are sexually attracted to persons of the same gender differently from individuals who are sexually attracted to persons of the opposite gender, does not treat an individual man or an individual woman differently *because of* his or her *gender* but rather accords differential treatment *because of* the individual's *sexual orientation.* * * *

Although plaintiffs further contend that the difference in treatment prescribed by the relevant statutes should be treated as sex discrimination for equal protection purposes because the differential treatment reflects illegitimate gender-related stereotyping based on the view that men are attracted to women and women are attracted to men, this argument again improperly conflates two concepts—discrimination on the basis of sex, and discrimination on the basis of sexual orientation—that traditionally have been viewed as distinct phenomena. Under plaintiffs' argument, discrimination on the basis of sexual orientation always would constitute a subset of discrimination on the basis of sex. * * *

Accordingly, we conclude that in the context of California's equal protection clause, the differential treatment prescribed by the relevant statutes cannot properly be found to constitute discrimination on the basis of sex, and thus that the statutory classification embodied in the marriage statutes is not subject to strict scrutiny on that ground.

[IV.B.   Sexual Orientation Discrimination.] * * * Having concluded that the California marriage statutes treat persons differently on the basis of sexual orientation, we must determine whether sexual orientation should be considered a "suspect classification" under the California equal protection clause, so that statutes drawing a distinction on this basis are subject to strict scrutiny. * * *

In addressing this issue, the majority in the Court of Appeal stated: "For a statutory classification to be considered 'suspect' for equal protection purposes, generally three requirements must be met. The defining characteristic must (1) be based upon an 'immutable trait'; (2) 'bear[ ] no relation to [a person's] ability to perform or contribute to society'; and (3) be associated with a 'stigma of inferiority and second class citizenship,' manifested by the group's history of legal and social disabilities. (*Sail'er Inn*.) While the latter two requirements would seem to be readily satisfied in the case of gays and lesbians, the first is more controversial." Concluding that "whether sexual orientation is immutable presents a factual question" as to which an adequate record had not been presented in the trial court, the Court of Appeal ultimately held that "[l]acking guidance from our Supreme Court or decisions from our sister Courts of Appeal," the court would review the marriage statutes under the rational basis, rather than the strict scrutiny, standard. * * *

We disagree, however, with the Court of Appeal's conclusion that it is appropriate to reject sexual orientation as a suspect classification, in applying the California Constitution's equal protection clause, on the ground that there is a question as to whether this characteristic is or is not "immutable." Although we noted in *Sail'er Inn* that generally a person's gender is viewed as an immutable trait, immutability is not invariably required in order for a characteristic to be considered a suspect classification for equal protection purposes. California cases establish that a person's religion is a suspect classification for equal protection purposes, and one's religion, of course, is not immutable but is a matter over which an individual has control. (See also *Raffaelli v. Committee of Bar Examiners* (1972) 7 Cal.3d 288, 292 [alienage treated as a suspect classification notwithstanding circumstance that alien can become a citizen].) Because a person's sexual orientation is so integral an aspect of one's identity, it is not appropriate to require a person to repudiate or change his or her sexual orientation in order to avoid discriminatory treatment.

In his briefing before this court, the Attorney General does not maintain that sexual orientation fails to satisfy the three requirements for a suspect classification discussed by the Court of Appeal, but instead argues that a *fourth* requirement should be imposed before a characteristic is considered a constitutionally suspect basis for classification for equal protection purposes—namely, that "a 'suspect' classification is appropriately recognized only for minorities who are unable to use the political process to address their needs." The Attorney General's brief asserts that "[s]ince the gay and lesbian community in California is obviously able to wield political power in defense of its interests, this Court should not hold that sexual orientation constitutes a suspect classification."

Although some California decisions in discussing suspect classifications have referred to a group's "political powerlessness" (see, e.g., *Raffaelli*), our cases have not identified a group's *current* political powerlessness as a necessary *prerequisite* for treatment as a suspect class. Indeed, if a group's *current* political powerlessness were a prerequisite to a characteristic's being considered a constitutionally suspect basis for differential treatment, it would be impossible to justify the numerous decisions that continue to treat sex, race, and religion as suspect classifications. Instead, our decisions make clear that the most important factors in deciding whether a characteristic should be considered a constitutionally suspect basis for classification are whether the class of persons who exhibit a certain characteristic historically has been subjected to invidious and prejudicial treatment, and whether society now recognizes that the characteristic in question generally bears no relationship to the individual's ability to perform or contribute to society. Thus, "courts must look closely at classifications based on that characteristic lest *outdated* social stereotypes result in invidious laws or practices." (*Sail'er Inn.*) This rationale clearly applies to statutory classifications that mandate differential treatment on the basis of sexual orientation. In sum, we conclude that statutes imposing differential treatment on the basis of sexual orientation should be viewed as constitutionally suspect under the California Constitution's equal protection clause. * * *

There is no persuasive basis for applying to statutes that classify persons on the basis of the suspect classification of sexual orientation a standard less rigorous than that applied to statutes that classify on the basis of the suspect classifications of gender, race, or religion. Because sexual orientation, like gender, race, or religion, is a characteristic that frequently has been the basis for biased and improperly stereotypical treatment and that generally bears no relation to an individual's ability to perform or contribute to society, it is appropriate for courts to evaluate with great care and with considerable skepticism any statute that embodies such a classification. The strict scrutiny standard therefore is applicable to statutes that impose differential treatment on the basis of sexual orientation. * * *

[IV.D. Interests of the state.] [I]n circumstances, as here, in which the strict scrutiny standard of review applies, the state bears a heavy burden of justification. In order to satisfy that standard, the state must demonstrate not simply that there is a rational, constitutionally legitimate interest that supports the differential treatment at issue, but instead that the state interest is a *constitutionally compelling* one that justifies the disparate treatment prescribed by the statute in question. Furthermore, unlike instances in which the rational basis test applies, the state does not meet its burden of justification under the strict scrutiny standard merely by showing that the classification established by the statute is rationally or reasonably related to such a compelling state interest. Instead, the state must demonstrate that the distinctions drawn by the statute (or statutory scheme) are *necessary* to further that interest.

[The Chief Justice summarily rejected the argument made by the Proposition 22 Legal Defense Fund that the California Constitution required the Legislature to follow the traditional definition of "marriage" as one man, one woman, as well as the Attorney General's argument that constitutional separation of powers precluded the judiciary from second-guessing legislative policy judgments. The Court gave greater attention to the argument that it ought to defer to the popular judgment, reflected in the Knight Initiative approved by a large majority in 2000, that the state ought to preserve the traditional definition of marriage.]

Although defendants maintain that this court has an obligation to defer to the statutory definition of marriage contained in section 308.5 because that statute—having been adopted through the initiative process—represents the expression of the "people's will," this argument fails to take into account the very basic point that the provisions of the California Constitution itself constitute the ultimate expression of the people's will, and that the fundamental rights embodied within that Constitution for the protection of all persons represent restraints that the people themselves have imposed upon the statutory enactments that may be adopted either by their elected representatives or by the voters through the initiative process. * * *

After carefully evaluating the pertinent considerations in the present case, we conclude that the state interest in limiting the designation of marriage exclusively to opposite-sex couples, and in excluding same-sex couples from access to that designation, cannot properly be considered a compelling state interest for equal protection purposes. To begin with, the limitation clearly is not necessary to preserve the rights and benefits of marriage currently enjoyed by opposite-sex couples. Extending access to the designation of marriage to same-sex couples will not deprive any opposite-sex couple or their children of any of the rights and benefits conferred by the marriage statutes, but simply will make the benefit of the marriage designation available to same-sex couples and their children. As Chief Judge Kaye of the New York Court of Appeals succinctly observed in her dissenting opinion in *Hernandez v. Robles*: "There are enough marriage licenses to go around for everyone." Further, permitting same-sex couples access to the designation of marriage will not alter the substantive nature of the legal institution of marriage; same-sex couples who choose to enter into the relationship with that designation will be subject to the same duties and obligations to each other, to their children, and to third parties that the law currently imposes upon opposite-sex couples who marry. Finally, affording same-sex couples the opportunity to obtain the designation of marriage will not impinge upon the religious freedom of any religious organization, official, or any other person; no religion will be required to change its religious policies or practices with regard to same-sex couples, and no religious officiant will be required to solemnize a marriage in contravention of his or her religious beliefs.

While retention of the limitation of marriage to opposite-sex couples is not needed to preserve the rights and benefits of opposite-sex couples, the exclusion of same-sex couples from the designation of marriage works a real and appreciable harm upon same-sex couples and their children. As discussed above, because of the long and celebrated history of the term "marriage" and the widespread understanding that this word describes a family relationship unreservedly sanctioned by the community, the statutory provisions that continue to limit access to this designation exclusively to opposite-sex couples—while providing only a novel, alternative institution for same-sex couples—likely will be viewed as an official statement that the family relationship of same-sex couples is not of comparable stature or equal dignity to the family relationship of opposite-sex couples. Furthermore, because of the historic disparagement of gay persons, the retention of a distinction in nomenclature by which the term "marriage" is withheld only from the family relationship of same-sex couples is all the more likely to cause the new parallel institution that has been established for same-sex couples to be considered a mark of second-class citizenship. Finally, in addition to the potential harm flowing from the lesser stature that is likely to be afforded to the family relationships of same-sex couples by designating them domestic partnerships, there exists a substantial risk that a judicial decision upholding the differential treatment of opposite-sex and same-sex couples would be understood as *validating* a more general proposition that our state by now has repudiated: that it is permissible, under the law, for society to treat gay individuals and same-sex couples differently from, and less favorably than, heterosexual individuals and opposite-sex couples. * * *

■ [We omit the concurring opinion of JUSTICE KENNARD as well as the concurring and dissenting opinions of JUSTICE BAXTER and JUSTICE CORRIGAN. Four Justices joined the opinion for the Court; three dissented.]

NOTES AND QUESTIONS

1. *Second in Line.* California was the next state, after Massachusetts, to require access to marriage for same-sex couples as a result of litigation. In the five years between *Goodridge* and the California decision, other state courts rejected arguments for marriage equality. *Conaway v. Deane*, 932 A.2d 571 (Md. 2007); *Lewis v. Harris*, 908 A.2d 196 (N.J. 2006) (following *Baker*, to require equal treatment but not necessarily civil marriage); *Hernandez v. Robles*, 855 N.E.2d 1 (N.Y. 2006); *Li v. State*, 110 P.3d 91 (Or. 2005); *Andersen v. King County*, 138 P.3d 963 (Wash. 2006). Shortly after the California decision, Connecticut became the third state high court to require access to marriage. *Kerrigan v. Comm'r of Pub. Health*, 957 A.2d 407 (Conn. 2008).

2. *Doctrinal Differences.* Compare Chief Justice Marshall's opinion in *Goodridge* to Chief Justice George's opinion. *Goodridge* illustrates what we call the equal liberty approach, with a structure similar to that of the *Lawrence* opinion, in that it utilizes both liberty and equality themes but identifies liberty as the primary ground on which it relies. The California decision, by contrast, breaks new ground by finding sexual orientation to be a suspect classification under the state's constitution. (The court also finds that a fundamental liberty interest is violated.)

Consider a possible paradox in the strengths of each approach. Constitutional lawyers have traditionally treated an explicitly stringent standard of review as the most powerful dimension of a ruling. For both the Massachusetts and California courts, however, the acid test for the durability of its opinion was neither doctrinal nor jurisprudential, but political: whether the decision would be reversed by popular referendum. By that measure, *Goodridge* remained intact, while Chief Justice George's opinion suffered a popular rejection. (See below.)

3. *Sex Discrimination.* In rejecting the sex discrimination argument, the court took the side of legal scholars who have argued that the formal basis of a classification (sex) is less significant than the defining characteristic of the persons being targeted for adverse treatment (sexual orientation). See discussion in Chapter 1, Section 1B. In so doing, however, the court also rejected the theory that gender stereotyping provides the conceptual foundation for sexual orientation discrimination. Would the opinion have been weakened or strengthened by accepting sex discrimination as an alternative basis for an equal protection violation? Revisit this point when you read Chapter 5, Section 5, *infra.*

4. *Is the State Required to Establish Marriage or to Use That Term?* As you saw from the opinion, the Attorney General had argued that same-sex couples were adequately protected by the state's registered domestic partnership system, which accorded them all of the rights and duties of marriage under state law. While the case was pending, the court asked the parties to brief the question of whether "the terms 'marriage' or 'marry' themselves have constitutional significance." The Justices appeared to be considering whether the state's duty to treat different-sex and same-sex couples equally could be fulfilled by eliminating the term "marriage" and providing a differently named status for both kinds of couples. Plaintiffs opposed that approach. See Respondents Supplemental Brief, 2007 WL 2733221. How would you have answered the court's question?

5. *Popular Constitutionalism and Proposition 8.* We omitted Justice Baxter's dissenting opinion, which objected that the Court's result not only ran against the state's traditional understanding of the definition of marriage and affirmations of that traditional understanding in legislative enactments, but also against the specific will of the people. The Chief Justice responded that the Constitution itself is a supermajoritarian expression of the people's will, and that it trumped the 2000 initiative by which voters had amended the Family Code to bar same-sex marriage.

Justice Baxter's concerns turned out to be prophetic. Less than six months after the decision in *The Marriage Cases*, a proposal to amend the state constitution to override the Court—Proposition 8—appeared on the November 2008 ballot. Proposition 8 stated, "Only marriage between a man and a woman is valid or recognized in California." One of the most effective arguments used by supporters of Proposition 8 was that the legality of same-sex marriage would lead to children being taught beliefs about homosexuality in school that contradicted their parents' beliefs. (See Appendix 8.) Proposition 8 passed by a 52% to 48% margin.

Breaking with the strategy by national LGBT rights groups to seek judicial invalidations of state marriage laws in state courts, a Los Angeles-based group called the American Federation for Equality Rights (AFER), challenged Prop 8 on federal constitutional grounds in a case filed in the Northern District of California. ***Kristin M. Perry, Sandra B. Stier, Paul T. Katami and Jeffrey J. Zarrillo, and the City and County of San Francisco v. Arnold Schwarzenegger (Governor), Edmund G. Brown Jr. (Attorney General) et al.,*** **704 F. Supp. 2d 921 (N.D. Cal. 2010).** The California Governor and Attorney General declined to defend Proposition 8, and the court allowed a group of persons who had been its official proponents for purposes of securing its qualification for the ballot to intervene as defendants. **Judge Vaughn Walker** insisted that the parties go to trial and build a factual record, rather than have the court resolve the case on pretrial motions. Theodore Olson, a top Republican lawyer and former Department of Justice official, and David Boies, a top lawyer for the Democratic Party, were lead co-counsel for the plaintiffs. In a lengthy opinion reviewing the record, Judge Walker found that Proposition 8 lacked even a rational basis, and violated both the Due Process and Equal Protection Clauses.

The Ninth Circuit's Opinion in Perry. The Ninth Circuit affirmed Judge Walker on narrow grounds. *Perry v. Brown*, 681 F.3d 1065 (9th Cir. 2012). Specifically, the Ninth Circuit ruled that Proposition 8 was illegitimate caste legislation for the same reasons the Supreme Court gave for striking down Amendment 2 in *Romer v. Evans* (Chapter 1, Section 2B). The Ninth Circuit also emphasized that Proposition 8 was a constitutional take-back: *after* the state had recognized marriage equality as constitutionally fundamental, the voters had taken back that fundamental right from lesbian and gay couples. Most observers saw the Ninth Circuit's reframing of the case as an attempt to suggest narrow grounds on which the Supreme Court might affirm.

The Supreme Court's Decision in Perry. Instead of the merits, however, the Supreme Court in *Perry* resolved the case on standing. The Ninth Circuit had also held that the proponents of Proposition 8 had Article III standing to pursue an appeal from Judge Walker's judgment. In *Hollingsworth v. Perry*, 133 S. Ct. 2652 (2013), the Supreme Court reversed the Ninth Circuit on the standing point, holding that the supporters of Proposition 8 did not have Article III standing. This proved decisive, because the named defendants—the Governor, the Attorney General, and two county clerks— had declined to appeal. The net effect was to leave Judge Walker's trial court ruling in place. In the end, the *Perry* litigation succeeded in eliminating Proposition 8 but had no impact on marriage laws nationwide, as the plaintiffs had originally sought.

PROBLEM 2-5
BYPRODUCTS OF THE STATE MARRIAGE CASES

As of 2017, the Supreme Judicial Court of Massachusetts has not altered its state constitutional analysis of sexual orientation classifications since *Goodridge*. The holding that the exclusion of same-sex couples from marriage failed to pass a rational basis test remains good law, and no more stringent level of scrutiny has been adopted. California presents the opposite twist: its holding that such classifications must be considered suspect under the state constitution also remains good law, although voters enacted a marriage exception to that principle which a federal district court then contravened. Assume that both states enact a law allowing religiously-affiliated adoption services to place children only with different-sex couples. How might each state craft a defense of such a law?

B. THE RISE AND FALL OF THE DEFENSE OF MARRIAGE ACT

Flash back to the marriage litigation in Hawaii in the 1990s— National social conservative groups, chastened by the loss in *Romer v. Evans* of a method to put anti-gay measures before voters for popular approval, saw in the Hawaiian campaign for same-sex marriage an opportunity to deploy the same tactic of referenda as in Colorado, using the even more powerful issue of marriage. The issue moved from advocacy groups to national political parties when Republicans introduced the Defense of Marriage Act (DOMA) just prior to the 1996 election. The GOP's insight that officeholders of both parties would be afraid to support marriage equality proved correct.

During House hearings on the proposed DOMA, the Department of Justice opined that the measure "would be sustained as constitutional," but stated no reasons in support of that view. Reacting to the decision in *Romer*, the House Judiciary Committee and the bill's sponsors sought to justify DOMA's discrimination against same-sex spouses. H.R. Rep. No. 104–664, reprinted in 1996 USCCAN 2905. The committee posited that the federal government has "an interest in maintaining and protecting the institution of heterosexual marriage because it has a deep and abiding interest in encouraging responsible procreation and child-rearing." As the committee's report went on, the families-with-children objective morphed into an argument that marriage was an imperiled institution needing defense from gay rights groups, who were prepared to flood Hawaii with same-sex couples who would then demand recognition of their marriages from sister states. This was a major theme of the floor debates as well.

"Closely related to this interest in protecting traditional marriage is a corresponding interest in promoting heterosexuality," the House Judiciary Committee opined. This was a deeper reason for the bill. "Civil laws that permit only heterosexual marriage reflect and honor a collective moral judgment about human sexuality. This judgment entails both moral disapproval of homosexuality, and a moral conviction that heterosexuality better comports with traditional (especially Judeo-Christian) morality." On the floor of the House, DOMA supporters emphasized the no promo homo argument. As Representative Funderburk put it, "homosexuals" were demanding much more than tolerance; they were "aiming for government and corporate mandated acceptance," which must be resisted because homosexuality is "inherently wrong and harmful to individuals, families, and societies." 142 Cong. Rec. 17075 (July 12, 1996). According to Representative Canady, a key question was "whether the law of this country should treat homosexual relationships as morally equivalent to heterosexual relationships." He thought not and posed this question: "Should this Congress tell the children of America that it is a matter of indifference whether they establish families with a partner of the opposite sex or cohabit with someone of the same sex?" 142 Cong. Rec. 16976 (July 11, 1996) and 17079 (July 12, 1996) (same language on two different days of debate). No promo homo was also a theme in the Senate debates: "[W]hen we prefer traditional marriage and family in our law, it is not intolerance. Tolerance does not require us to say that all lifestyles are morally equal." 142 Cong. Rec. 22451 (Sept. 10, 1996) (Sen. Coats).

DOMA critics claimed that the legislation was premature, as no state had adopted same-sex marriage, and an excessive response even if the problem were imminent. Representative John Lewis, one of America's most distinguished civil rights leaders, observed, "I have known racism. [This] bill stinks of the same fear, hatred and intolerance." 142 Cong. Rec. 16972 (July 11, 1996). DOMA supporters responded that the bill did not reflect prejudice or bigotry and, instead, reflected a genuine threat to the nation's values. Representative Robert Barr, the House sponsor, opened the second day of debate with a fear that the "flames of hedonism, the flames of narcissism, the flames of self-centered morality are licking at the very foundation of our society: the family unit." 142 Cong. Rec. 17070 (July 12, 1996). Representative Tom Coburn supported DOMA because his constituents felt "homosexuals" are "immoral" and "promiscuous." The issue, he said, "is not diversity"—the issue is "perversity." He warned of the social consequences of "homosexuality and the perversion which it" brings. 142 Cong. Rec. 16972 (July 11, 1996). Opening the Senate debate, Senator Robert Byrd urged that DOMA was an emergency measure because of the concerted campaign by gay people to force same-sex marriage upon the country. This was followed by a denunciation of homosexuality—a proposition for which Senator Byrd, like the House Judiciary Committee, cited only the Bible. 142 Cong. Rec. 22447 (Sept. 10, 1996).

DOMA sailed through Congress by margins of 342–67 in the House and 85–14 in the Senate. President Clinton signed it in a midnight ceremony. Pub. L. No. 104–199, 110 Stat. 2419 (1996). A General Accounting Office report documented that DOMA implicated 1,138 federal laws, including those related to entitlement programs, such as Social Security; health benefits; and taxation. U.S. Gov. Accountability Office, GAO–04–353R Defense of Marriage Act (2004), *available at* http://www.gao.gov/new.items/d04353r.pdf.

Challenges to DOMA began in 2009. GLAD sought relief on behalf of persons who had lawfully married in Massachusetts but were denied federal benefits because of DOMA. The Commonwealth of Massachusetts then filed its own challenge, alleging possible denial of federal monies to joint federal-state programs in which the state recognized the validity of same-sex marriages. On a consolidated appeal, the First Circuit held DOMA unconstitutional, reasoning that the Supreme Court had begun to move away from the traditionally deferential rational basis standard of review, and had adopted examination of the "case-specific nature of the discrepant treatment, the burden imposed, and the infirmities of the justifications offered" in *Romer* and similar cases. *Massachusetts v. U.S. Dep't of Health and Human Services*, 682 F.3d 1, 10 (1st Cir. 2012).

In 2010, two challenges to DOMA were filed in District Courts within the Second Circuit, which had no circuit precedent on the standard of review for sexual orientation classifications. The Department of Justice had defended DOMA in the Massachusetts cases based on circuit precedent that rational basis was the controlling standard. There was no such limitation in the Second Circuit, and the Justice Department had to determine what position it would take on the correct standard of review. In a letter to Congress, Attorney General Eric Holder announced that the Department would thereafter support heightened review for sexual orientation classifications. (See Appendix 4).

In the intervening period, Solicitor General Elena Kagan had been appointed to the Supreme Court. Because she had played a role in fashioning the Administration's position in the Massachusetts cases and thus would have to recuse herself from participation in reviewing them, the Court granted certiorari in the leading Second Circuit case in order to assure resolution of the questions presented by the full nine-member Court.

United States v. Edith Windsor

United States Supreme Court, 2013.
___ U.S. ___, 133 S. Ct. 2675, 186 L.Ed.2d 808.

■ JUSTICE KENNEDY delivered the opinion for the Court.

[Edith Windsor was legally married in Canada to her life partner, Thea Spyer, at the time her partner died. New York, the spouses' domicile, recognized their out-of-state marriage even before that state authorized marriage licenses for same-sex couples. Because of the Defense of Marriage Act (DOMA), however, Windsor did not have the benefit of the spousal exclusion for federal estate tax purposes and had to pay $363,000 in estate taxes that a different-sex married couple would have owed. DOMA § 3, discussed in Casebook, pp. 316–18. Windsor challenged DOMA § 3 as an unconstitutional discrimination against her. Agreeing with Windsor, the Second Circuit ruled that DOMA § 3 violated the equal protection component of the Fifth Amendment's Due Process Clause. The Supreme Court affirmed, but on somewhat different grounds than the Second Circuit. Part II of Justice Kennedy's opinion ruled that the United States, represented by the Department of Justice, had constitutional standing under Article III to pursue this appeal, even though the Department agreed with the decision below on the merits.]

[III.] * * * By history and tradition the definition and regulation of marriage, as will be discussed in more detail, has been treated as being within the authority and realm of the separate States. Yet it is further established that Congress, in enacting discrete statutes, can make determinations that bear on marital rights and privileges. [Thus, for immigration and social security law, Congress does not follow state marriage law.]

* * * DOMA has a far greater reach; for it enacts a directive applicable to over 1,000 federal statutes and the whole realm of federal regulations. And its operation is directed to a class of persons that the laws of New York, and of 11 other States, have sought to protect. [This is

significant, because "regulation of domestic relations" is "an area that has long been regarded as a virtually exclusive province of the States." *Sosna v. Iowa*, 419 U.S. 393, 404 (1976).]

The recognition of civil marriages is central to state domestic relations law applicable to its residents and citizens. See *Williams v. North Carolina*, 317 U.S. 287, 298 (1942) ("Each state as a sovereign has a rightful and legitimate concern in the marital status of persons domiciled within its borders"). The definition of marriage is the foundation of the State's broader authority to regulate the subject of domestic relations with respect to the "[p]rotection of offspring, property interests, and the enforcement of marital responsibilities." *Ibid.* "[T]he states, at the time of the adoption of the Constitution, possessed full power over the subject of marriage and divorce . . . [and] the Constitution delegated no authority to the Government of the United States on the subject of marriage and divorce." *Haddock v. Haddock*, 201 U.S. 562, 575 (1906).

[For this reason, the large majority of federal statutes defer to state policy decisions with respect to domestic relations. E.g., *De Sylva v. Ballentine*, 351 U.S. 570 (1956) (Copyright Act). See also *Ankenbrandt v. Richards*, 504 U.S. 689, 703 (1992) (affirming the domestic relations exception "which divests the federal courts of power to issue divorce, alimony, and child custody decrees"). From the very beginning of the Nation,] the common understanding was that the domestic relations of husband and wife and parent and child were matters reserved to the States." *Ohio ex rel. Popovici v. Agler*, 280 U.S. 379, 383–384 (1930). [Accordingly, each state has constructed the eligibility and rules for marriage in distinctive ways.]

Against this background DOMA rejects the long established precept that the incidents, benefits, and obligations of marriage are uniform for all married couples within each State, though they may vary, subject to constitutional guarantees, from one State to the next. Despite these considerations, it is unnecessary to decide whether this federal intrusion on state power is a violation of the Constitution because it disrupts the federal balance. The State's power in defining the marital relation is of central relevance in this case quite apart from principles of federalism. Here the State's decision to give this class of persons the right to marry conferred upon them a dignity and status of immense import. When the State used its historic and essential authority to define the marital relation in this way, its role and its power in making the decision enhanced the recognition, dignity, and protection of the class in their own community. DOMA, because of its reach and extent, departs from this history and tradition of reliance on state law to define marriage. "[D]iscriminations of an unusual character especially suggest careful consideration to determine whether they are obnoxious to the constitutional provision." *Romer v. Evans*, 517 U.S. 620, 633 (1996) (quoting *Louisville Gas & Elec. Co. v. Coleman*, 277 U.S. 32, 37–38 (1928)). * * *

The States' interest in defining and regulating the marital relation, subject to constitutional guarantees, stems from the understanding that marriage is more than a routine classification for purposes of certain statutory benefits. * * * By its recognition of the validity of same-sex marriages performed in other jurisdictions and then by authorizing same-sex unions and same-sex marriages, New York sought to give further protection and dignity to that bond. For same-sex couples who wished to be married, the State acted to give their lawful conduct a lawful status. This status is a far-reaching legal acknowledgment of the intimate relationship between two people, a relationship deemed by the State worthy of dignity in the community equal with all other marriages. It reflects both the community's considered perspective on the historical roots of the institution of marriage and its evolving understanding of the meaning of equality.

[IV.] DOMA seeks to injure the very class New York seeks to protect. By doing so it violates basic due process and equal protection principles applicable to the Federal Government. See U.S. Const., Amdt. 5; *Bolling v. Sharpe*, 347 U.S. 497 (1954). The Constitution's guarantee of equality "must at the very least mean that a bare congressional desire to harm a politically unpopular group cannot" justify disparate treatment of that group. *Department of Agriculture v. Moreno*, 413 U.S. 528, 534–535 (1973). In determining whether a law is motived by an improper animus or purpose, " '[d]iscriminations of an unusual character' " especially require careful consideration. DOMA cannot survive under these principles. The responsibility of the States for the regulation of domestic relations is an important indicator of the substantial societal impact the State's classifications have in the daily lives and customs of its people. DOMA's unusual deviation from the usual tradition of recognizing and accepting state definitions of marriage here operates to deprive same-sex couples of the benefits and responsibilities that come with the federal recognition of their marriages. This is strong evidence of a law having the purpose and effect of disapproval of that class. The avowed purpose and practical effect of the law here in question are to impose a disadvantage, a separate status, and so a stigma upon all who enter into same-sex marriages made lawful by the unquestioned authority of the States.

The history of DOMA's enactment and its own text demonstrate that interference with the equal dignity of same-sex marriages, a dignity conferred by the States in the exercise of their sovereign power, was more than an incidental effect of the federal statute. It was its essence. The House Report announced its conclusion that "it is both appropriate and necessary for Congress to do what it can to defend the institution of traditional heterosexual marriage. . . . H. R. 3396 is appropriately entitled the 'Defense of Marriage Act.' The effort to redefine 'marriage' to extend to homosexual couples is a truly radical proposal that would fundamentally alter the institution of marriage." H.R. Rep. No. 104–664, pp. 12–13 (1996). The House concluded that DOMA expresses "both moral disapproval of homosexuality, and a moral conviction that heterosexuality better comports with traditional (especially Judeo-Christian) morality." *Id.*, at 16 (footnote deleted). The stated purpose of the law was to promote an "interest in protecting the traditional moral teachings reflected in heterosexual-only marriage laws." *Ibid.* Were there any doubt of this far-reaching purpose, the title of the Act confirms it: The Defense of Marriage.

The arguments put forward by BLAG [the Bipartisan Legislative Advisory Group in Congress] are just as candid about the congressional purpose to influence or interfere with state sovereign choices about who may be married. As the title and dynamics of the bill indicate, its purpose is to discourage enactment of state same-sex marriage laws and to restrict the freedom and choice of couples married under those laws if they are enacted. The congressional goal was "to put a thumb on the scales and influence a state's decision as to how to shape its own marriage laws." [*Massachusetts v. United States Dept. of Health and Human Servs.*, 682 F. 3d 1, 12–13 (CA1 2012).] The Act's demonstrated purpose is to ensure that if any State decides to recognize same-sex marriages, those unions will be treated as second-class marriages for purposes of federal law. This raises a most serious question under the Constitution's Fifth Amendment.

DOMA's operation in practice confirms this purpose. When New York adopted a law to permit same-sex marriage, it sought to eliminate inequality; but DOMA frustrates that objective through a system-wide enactment with no identified connection to any particular area of federal law. DOMA writes inequality into the entire United States Code. The particular case at hand concerns the estate tax, but DOMA is more than a simple determination of what should or should not be allowed as an estate tax refund. Among the over 1,000 statutes and numerous federal regulations that DOMA controls are laws pertaining to Social Security, housing, taxes, criminal sanctions, copyright, and veterans' benefits.

DOMA's principal effect is to identify a subset of state sanctioned marriages and make them unequal. The principal purpose is to impose inequality, not for other reasons like governmental efficiency. Responsibilities, as well as rights, enhance the dignity and integrity of the person. And DOMA contrives to deprive some couples married under the laws of their State, but not other couples, of both rights and responsibilities. By creating two contradictory marriage regimes within the same State, DOMA forces same-sex couples to live as married for the purpose of state law but unmarried for the purpose of federal law, thus diminishing the stability and predictability of basic personal relations the State has found it proper to acknowledge and protect. By this dynamic DOMA undermines both the public and private significance of state sanctioned same-sex marriages; for it tells those couples and all the world, that their otherwise valid marriages are unworthy of federal recognition. This places same-sex couples in an unstable position of being in a second-tier marriage. The differentiation demeans the couple, whose moral and sexual choices the Constitution protects, see *Lawrence*, and whose relationship the State has sought to dignify. And it humiliates tens of thousands of children now being raised by same-sex couples. The law in question makes it even more difficult for the children to understand the integrity and closeness of their own family and its concord with other families in their community and in their daily lives.

Under DOMA, same-sex married couples have their lives burdened, by reason of government decree, in visible and public ways. By its great reach, DOMA touches many aspects of married and family life, from the mundane to the profound. It prevents same-sex married couples from obtaining government healthcare benefits they would otherwise receive. See 5 U.S.C. §§ 8901(5), 8905. It deprives them of the Bankruptcy Code's special protections for domestic-support obligations. See 11 U.S.C. §§ 101(14A), 507(a)(1)(A), 523(a)(5), 523(a)(15). It forces them to follow a complicated procedure to file their state and federal taxes jointly. Technical Bulletin TB-55, 2010 Vt. Tax LEXIS 6 (Oct. 7, 2010). It prohibits them from being buried together in veterans' cemeteries. National Cemetery Administration Directive 3210/1, p. 37 (June 4, 2008). * * *

DOMA also brings financial harm to children of same sex couples. It raises the cost of health care for families by taxing health benefits provided by employers to their workers' same-sex spouses. See 26 U.S.C. § 106; Treas. Reg. § 1.106–1, 26 CFR § 1.106–1 (2012); IRS Private Letter Ruling 9850011 (Sept. 10, 1998). And it denies or reduces benefits allowed to families upon the loss of a spouse and parent, benefits that are an integral part of family security. See Social Security Administration, Social Security Survivors Benefits 5 (2012) (benefits available to a surviving spouse caring for the couple's child), online at http://www.ssa. gov/pubs/EN-05-10084.pdf.

DOMA divests married same-sex couples of the duties and responsibilities that are an essential part of married life and that they in most cases would be honored to accept were DOMA not in force. For instance, because it is expected that spouses will support each other as they pursue educational opportunities, federal law takes into consideration a spouse's income in calculating a student's federal financial aid eligibility. See 20 U.S.C. § 1087nn(b). Same-sex married couples are exempt from this requirement. The same is true with respect to federal ethics rules. Federal executive and agency officials are prohibited from "participat[ing] personally and substantially" in matters as to which they or their spouses have a financial interest. 18 U.S.C. § 208(a). A similar statute prohibits Senators, Senate employees, and their spouses from accepting high-value gifts from certain sources, see 2

U.S.C. § 31–2(a)(1), and another mandates detailed financial disclosures by numerous high-ranking officials and their spouses. See 5 U.S.C. App. §§ 102(a), (e). Under DOMA, however, these Government-integrity rules do not apply to same-sex spouses.

What has been explained to this point should more than suffice to establish that the principal purpose and the necessary effect of this law are to demean those persons who are in a lawful same-sex marriage. This requires the Court to hold, as it now does, that DOMA is unconstitutional as a deprivation of the liberty of the person protected by the Fifth Amendment of the Constitution. * * *

The class to which DOMA directs its restrictions and restraints are those persons who are joined in same-sex marriages made lawful by the State. DOMA singles out a class of persons deemed by a State entitled to recognition and protection to enhance their own liberty. It imposes a disability on the class by refusing to acknowledge a status the State finds to be dignified and proper. DOMA instructs all federal officials, and indeed all persons with whom same-sex couples interact, including their own children, that their marriage is less worthy than the marriages of others. The federal statute is invalid, for no legitimate purpose overcomes the purpose and effect to disparage and to injure those whom the State, by its marriage laws, sought to protect in personhood and dignity. By seeking to displace this protection and treating those persons as living in marriages less respected than others, the federal statute is in violation of the Fifth Amendment. This opinion and its holding are confined to those lawful marriages.

■ CHIEF JUSTICE ROBERTS, dissenting.

[The Chief Justice dissented, on the ground that neither the United States (which agreed with plaintiff Edie Windsor on the merits) nor the Bipartisan Legislative Advisory Group (which provided the primary brief supporting the constitutionality of DOMA § 3) had constitutional standing to bring this appeal to the Supreme Court. Hence, the Court had no power or authority to hear the controversy. But he also urged caution to lower courts applying the Court's analysis to state marriage exclusions.] The Court does not have before it, and the logic of its opinion does not decide, the distinct question whether the States, in the exercise of their "historic and essential authority to define the marital relation," may continue to utilize the traditional definition of marriage. * * *

* * * Thus, while "[t]he State's power in defining the marital relation is of central relevance" to the majority's decision to strike down DOMA here, that power will come into play on the other side of the board in future cases about the constitutionality of state marriage definitions. So too will the concerns for state diversity and sovereignty that weigh against DOMA's constitutionality in this case.

■ JUSTICE SCALIA, with whom JUSTICE THOMAS joins, and with whom the CHIEF JUSTICE [ROBERTS] joins as to Part I, dissenting.

[Joined by the Chief Justice and Justice Thomas, Part I of Justice Scalia's dissent objected that the petitioners lacked constitutional standing. Joined by Justice Thomas, Part II of Justice Scalia's dissent assailed the Court's opinion on the merits. He started with a number of technical criticisms. First, Justice Scalia found himself baffled that the Court would devote so much discussion to the primacy of state law in defining and regulating marriage and families: What relevance did traditional state primacy have to the Fifth Amendment issue, especially in light of the Court's concession that Congress was authorized by the Constitution to pass laws like DOMA? Second, Justice Scalia was confused as to whether the Court's treatment was a pure equal protection approach—or also entailed substantive due process analysis. Third, he wondered why the majority had failed to set forth the level of scrutiny to which it was subjecting DOMA.]

Some might conclude that this loaf could have used a while longer in the oven. But that would be wrong; it is already overcooked. The most expert care in preparation cannot redeem a bad recipe. The sum of all the Court's nonspecific hand-waving is that this law is invalid (maybe on equal-protection grounds, maybe on substantive-due process grounds, and perhaps with some amorphous federalism component playing a role) because it is motivated by a " 'bare . . . desire to harm' " couples in same-sex marriages. It is this proposition with which I will therefore engage.

* * *

* * * Bear in mind that the object of this condemnation is not the legislature of some once-Confederate Southern state * * *, but our respected coordinate branches, the Congress and Presidency of the United States. Laying such a charge against them should require the most extraordinary evidence, and I would have thought that every attempt would be made to indulge a more anodyne explanation for the statute. The majority does the opposite—affirmatively concealing from the reader the arguments that exist in justification. It makes only a passing mention of the "arguments put forward" by the Act's defenders, and does not even trouble to paraphrase or describe them. I imagine that this is because it is harder to maintain the illusion of the Act's supporters as unhinged members of a wild-eyed lynch mob when one first describes their views as *they* see them.

To choose just one of these defenders' arguments, DOMA avoids difficult choice-of-law issues that will now arise absent a uniform federal definition of marriage. See, *e.g.,* Baude, Beyond DOMA: Choice of State Law in Federal Statutes, 64 Stan. L. Rev. 1371 (2012). Imagine a pair of women who marry in Albany and then move to Alabama, which does not "recognize as valid any marriage of parties of the same sex." Ala. Code § 30–1–19(e) (2011). When the couple files their next federal tax return, may it be a joint one? Which State's law controls, for federal-law purposes: their State of celebration (which recognizes the marriage) or their State of domicile (which does not)? (Does the answer depend on whether they were just visiting in Albany?) Are these questions to be answered as a matter of federal common law, or perhaps by borrowing a State's choice-of-law rules? If so, *which* State's? And what about States where the status of an out-of-state same-sex marriage is an unsettled question under local law? DOMA avoided all of this uncertainty by specifying which marriages would be recognized for federal purposes. That is a classic purpose for a definitional provision.

Further, DOMA preserves the intended effects of prior legislation against then-unforeseen changes in circumstance. When Congress provided (for example) that a special estate-tax exemption would exist for spouses, this exemption reached only *opposite-sex* spouses—those being the only sort that were recognized in *any* State at the time of DOMA's passage. When it became clear that changes in state law might one day alter that balance, DOMA's definitional section was enacted to ensure that state-level experimentation did not automatically alter the basic operation of federal law, unless and until Congress made the further judgment to do so on its own. That is not animus—just stabilizing prudence. Congress has hardly demonstrated itself unwilling to make such further, revising judgments upon due deliberation. See, *e.g.,* Don't Ask, Don't Tell Repeal Act of 2010, 124 Stat. 3515. * * *

[Justice Scalia concluded his dissenting opinion with a prophecy about the Court's longer term strategy.] I do not mean to suggest disagreement with The Chief Justice's view that lower federal courts and state courts can distinguish today's case when the issue before them is state denial of marital status to same-sex couples—or even that this Court could *theoretically* do so. Lord, an opinion with such scatter-shot rationales as this one (federalism noises among them) can be distinguished in many ways. And deserves to be. State and lower federal courts should take the Court at its word and distinguish away.

In my opinion, however, the view that *this* Court will take of state prohibition of same-sex marriage is indicated beyond mistaking by today's opinion. As I have said, the real rationale of today's opinion, whatever disappearing trail of its legalistic argle-bargle one chooses to follow, is that DOMA is motivated by " 'bare . . . desire to harm' " couples in same-sex marriages. How easy it is, indeed how inevitable, to reach the same conclusion with regard to state laws denying same-sex couples marital status. * * *

■ [JUSTICE ALITO also dissented on the merits. In an analysis also joined by JUSTICE THOMAS, JUSTICE ALITO agreed with the CHIEF JUSTICE, that the Court's federalism analysis ought to suggest greater judicial deference to state law exclusions of same-sex couples from civil marriage. He criticized the majority for striking down DOMA as "not satisfying some form of heightened scrutiny." JUSTICE ALITO argued that the judiciary should defer to legislatures choosing between two views of marriage: the "traditional" or "conjugal" view, which requires a different-sex couple, and the "consent-based" view, which prioritizes the mutual commitment functions of marriage. Either, he argued, is a rational legislative choice.]

NOTES AND QUESTIONS

There are many doctrinal mysteries in the Court's invalidation of DOMA § 3, several of which we explicate below. To what extent do these conflicts beneath the surface of the opinion survive *Obergefell v. Hodges*, *infra*?

1.   *The Relevance of Federalism.* If DOMA § 3 had defined marriage in federal statutes and regulations, across the board, as always *including* same-sex couples, would that inclusion have been unconstitutional, or constitutionally problematic in any way? What role does the federalism discussion play in the Court's analysis striking down DOMA § 3? Put it this way: If you had read Justice Kennedy's equal protection analysis in Part IV of his opinion for the Court, does the federalism analysis in Part III add anything? Justice Scalia does not think that it does, but the Chief Justice and Justices Thomas and Alito think it might. What does it add? For an analysis of the role that federalism plays in the Court's decision, see, e.g., Courtney G. Joslin, "*Windsor*, Federalism, and Family Equality," 113 *Colum. L. Rev. Sidebar* 156 (2013). Consider this issue in light of the *values of federalism* instinct in the constitutional structure.

First, federalism provides a double layer of protection for citizens' liberty and freedom. Does the "double security" promised by the Framers for people's "liberty" find protection in state regulatory authority, and judicial deference to it? As you will see in *Obergefell*, Justice Alito is particularly attuned to the liberty interests of religious groups that do not want state validation of relationships they consider immoral. Is there a neutral principle addressing that concern?

Second, federalism leaves primary regulatory regimes with the level of government where most people are most civically engaged (i.e., local and state governments). Indeed, the marriage equality issue has engaged the voters directly in most states, through ballot initiatives and referenda. Most, such as California's Proposition 8, have barred marriage equality; others, such as four in 2012, have favored it. DOMA resolved the marriage issue in a sweeping way at the national level. The *Windsor* dissenters argued that federal courts should be more reluctant to take this issue away from the political process at the state level, and repeated many of these arguments in *Obergefell*.

Third, federalism allows diversity of policy within the country—and diversity permits different states to satisfy different groups or preferences, with the possibility that states can be laboratories of experimentation, generating experience and data from which we all might learn. Imagine that post-*Windsor*, all the Courts of Appeals concluded that state law marriage exclusions of same-sex couples were unconstitutional. Would it have been appropriate for the Supreme Court to simply deny review as the cases unfolded, allowing national disuniformity to persist? Would that have been an example of strong or weak constitutional statesmanship? Why?

2. *Animus or Rational Policy?* The key doctrinal question in *Windsor* is whether DOMA reflected a bare desire to harm a minority group, or an application of rational policy thinking to a new issue. The strongest portion of Justice Kennedy's opinion for the Court is his examination of the legislative history and background of DOMA, which are replete with derogatory references to gay people. The strongest portion of Justice Scalia's dissent is his articulation of possible "rational bases" for § 3's exclusion of same-sex marriages from 1100+ federal statutory provisions and regulations. Under the equal liberty approach, however, Justice Scalia's argument could not command a majority.

3. *The Wall Falls.* After the decision in *Windsor*, challenges to exclusionary marriage laws were filed in every state that still had one, mostly in federal court. Given its extensive discussion of federalism, what about the *Windsor* opinion made advocates so certain of success? We think that the most powerful signal to lower courts was the Court's condemnation of the traditionalist discourse used when DOMA was enacted. The extraordinary shift was that the reasons accepted by an overwhelming majority of political leaders in 1996 had become toxic 17 years later.

C. *OBERGEFELL* AND BEYOND

In the two years after the Supreme Court's decision in *Windsor* (i.e., between June 2013 and June 2015), dozens of federal and state judges, in more than 50 courts, considered marriage equality challenges under the Fourteenth Amendment and (for the state judges) under state constitutions. All but one of the federal district courts that heard the challenges during this period ruled in favor of the challengers, and the cases swiftly moved to the federal courts of appeal.

A divided Tenth Circuit required Utah to recognize marriage equality in *Kitchen v. Herbert*, 755 F. 3d 1193 (10th Cir. 2014), a precedent followed by that court in the Oklahoma appeal, *Bishop v. Smith*, 760 F. 3d 1070 (10th Cir. 2014). The Fourth and Seventh Circuits also agreed with the challengers. *Bostic v. Schaefer*, 760 F. 3d 352 (4th Cir. 2014) (Virginia); *Baskin v. Bogan*, 766 F. 3d 648 (7th Cir. 2014) (Wisconsin and Indiana). The Supreme Court denied review in the Fourth, Seventh, and Tenth Circuits on October 6. The next day, the Ninth Circuit ruled that Idaho's denial of marriage equality was unconstitutional. *Latta v. Otter*, 771 F. 3d 456 (9th Cir. 2014).

Literally overnight, the marriage equality map changed dramatically. Note that on the day *Windsor* was decided, there were 13 marriage equality states, including the District of Columbia. By October 4, there were 19 marriage equality states. On October 7, there were potentially 35 marriage equality states—adding the five states whose petitions had been denied, together with three more states in the Fourth Circuit (governed by *Bostic*), three more states in the Tenth Circuit (governed by *Kitchen*), and five more states in the Ninth Circuit (governed by *Latta*).

A split in the circuits materialized when the Sixth Circuit rejected the marriage equality claims in cases from Michigan, Ohio, Kentucky, and Tennessee. See *DeBoer v. Snyder*, 772 F. 3d 388 (6th Cir. 2014). The Supreme Court granted review for all four states, under the caption *Obergefell v. Hodges* (the Ohio cases). Before turning to the Court's disposition, consider the arguments developed within the courts of appeals.

NOTES ON POST-*WINDSOR* CASES

1. *Fundamental Right to Marry.* The Tenth Circuit (*Kitchen*) and the Fourth Circuit (*Bostic*), as well as many of the trial courts, invoked the fundamental right to marry, which is protected under both the Due Process Clause (*Loving*) and the Equal Protection Clause (*Zablocki*). Conceding that the right to marry precedents, including *Loving*, assumed different-sex and even procreative marriage, the Tenth and Fourth Circuit decisions relied on *Lawrence* and *Windsor* to insist that the general right protected lesbian and gay people and their partners as well. Finding that the same-sex couples were denied the fundamental right to marry, these courts applied strict scrutiny and found none of the state justifications narrowly tailored to advance a compelling public goal.

2. *Level of Equal Protection Scrutiny.* If lesbian and gay couples have a fundamental right to marry, that right might be protected with heightened scrutiny under either the Due Process Clause or, if denial of a fundamental right operates only as to a minority, also under the Equal Protection Clause. A second ground for heightened scrutiny under the Equal Protection Clause arises—independently of a fundamental right—when the state relies on "suspect classifications" such as race (*Loving*) or "quasi-suspect classifications" such as sex (*Craig*).

The Ninth Circuit found that sexual orientation classifications were subject to heightened equal protection scrutiny in *SmithKline Beecham Corp. v. Abbott Laboratories*, 740 F.3d 471 (9th Cir. 2014), involving the exclusion of a juror based on sexual orientation. The court adopted a "watch what they do, not what they say" approach to ascertaining the standard of review:

> * * * *Windsor* requires that when state action discriminates on the basis of sexual orientation, we must examine its actual purposes and carefully consider the resulting inequality to ensure that our

most fundamental institutions neither send nor reinforce messages of stigma or second-class status. In short, *Windsor* requires heightened scrutiny. Our earlier cases applying rational basis review to classifications based on sexual orientation cannot be reconciled with *Windsor*. Because we are bound by controlling, higher authority, we now hold that *Windsor*'s heightened scrutiny applies to classifications based on sexual orientation.

Id. at 483–84. In *Latta*, the Ninth Circuit applied heightened scrutiny to strike down the Idaho marriage ban.

Other courts, such as the Tenth Circuit in *Kitchen*, continued to skirt the issue. Judge Posner's opinion in *Baskin* gestured in favor of heightened scrutiny for state discriminations against sexual minorities but ultimately ruled that the Wisconsin and Indiana marriage exclusions did not satisfy even rational basis review. Judge Posner demanded that the state demonstrate how including lesbian and gay couples would harm the institution of marriage, or any other public interest, and was unimpressed, indeed disdainful, of the reasons advanced.

3. *The Sex Discrimination Argument for Lesbian and Gay Rights.* In the post-*Windsor* cases, not a single appellate court embraced the sex discrimination argument for gay marriage. Its high water mark came in Judge Marsha Berzon's concurring opinion in *Latta v. Otter*:

> * * * Idaho and Nevada's same-sex marriage prohibitions, as the justifications advanced for those prohibitions in this Court demonstrate, patently draw on "archaic and stereotypic notions" about gender. These prohibitions, the defendants have emphatically argued, communicate the state's view of what is both "normal" and preferable with regard to the romantic preferences, relationship roles, and parenting capacities of men and women. By doing so, the laws enforce the state's view that men and women "naturally" behave differently from one another in marriage and as parents. * * *

> * * * [T]he long line of cases since 1971 invalidating various laws and policies that categorized by sex have been part of a transformation that has altered the very institution at the heart of this case, marriage. Reviewing that transformation, including the role played by constitutional sex discrimination challenges in bringing it about, reveals that the same sex marriage prohibitions seek to preserve an outmoded, sex-role-based vision of the marriage institution, and in that sense as well raise the very concerns that gave rise to the contemporary constitutional approach to sex discrimination. * * *

> In short, a combination of constitutional sex-discrimination adjudication, legislative changes, and social and cultural transformation has, in a sense, already rendered contemporary marriage "genderless," to use the phrase favored by the defendants. For, as a result of these transformative social, legislative, and doctrinal developments, * * * in the states that currently ban same-

sex marriage, the legal norms that currently govern the institution of marriage are "genderless" in every respect *except* the requirement that would-be spouses be of different genders. With that exception, Idaho and Nevada's marriage regimes have jettisoned the rigid roles marriage as an institution once prescribed for men and women. In sum, "the sex-based classification contained in the[se] marriage laws," as the *only* gender classification that persists in some states' marriage statutes, is, at best, "a vestige of sex-role stereotyping" that long plagued marital regimes before the modern era, *see Baker* [*v. Vermont*], 744 A.2d at 906 (Johnson, J., concurring in part and dissenting in part), and, at worst, an attempt to reintroduce gender roles.

What are the strengths and weaknesses of this argument? Why the hesitancy by most judges to utilize it? Consider the reasons offered in Suzanne B. Goldberg, "Risky Arguments in Social-Justice Litigation: The Case of Sex Discrimination and Marriage Equality," 114 *Colum. L. Rev.* 2087 (2014).

James Obergefell et al. v. Richard Hodges et al.

United States Supreme Court, 2015.
___ U.S. ___, 135 S.Ct. 2584, 192 L.Ed.2d 609.

■ KENNEDY, J., delivered the opinion of the Court, in which GINSBURG, BREYER, SOTOMAYOR, and KAGAN, JJ., joined. ROBERTS, C. J., filed a dissenting opinion, in which SCALIA and THOMAS, JJ., joined. SCALIA, J., filed a dissenting opinion, in which, J., joined. THOMAS, J., filed a dissenting opinion, in which SCALIA, J., joined. ALITO, J., filed a dissenting opinion, in which SCALIA and THOMAS, JJ., joined.

■ JUSTICE KENNEDY delivered the opinion for the Court.

[Michigan, Ohio, Kentucky, and Tennessee did not allow same-sex couples to receive marriage licenses, nor did those states recognize same-sex marriages validly celebrated in another state. The petitioners were fourteen same-sex couples and two men whose male spouses were deceased. They challenged their exclusion from the state marriage recognition laws as a violation of both their due process fundamental right to marry, and their equal protection right not to be arbitrarily excluded by the state because of their sex or sexual orientation.]

[II.A]   From their beginning to their most recent page, the annals of human history reveal the transcendent importance of marriage. The lifelong union of a man and a woman always has promised nobility and dignity to all persons, without regard to their station in life. Marriage is sacred to those who live by their religions and offers unique fulfillment to those who find meaning in the secular realm. Its dynamic allows two people to find a life that could not be found alone, for a marriage becomes greater than just the two persons. Rising from the most basic human needs, marriage is essential to our most profound hopes and aspirations. The centrality of marriage to the human condition makes it unsurprising that the institution has existed for millennia and across civilizations.

[The centrality of marriage has been expressed with the understanding that marriage is a union between two persons of the opposite sex.]

That history is the beginning of these cases. The respondents say it should be the end as well. To them, it would demean a timeless institution if the concept and lawful status of marriage were extended to two persons of the same sex. Marriage, in their view, is by its nature a gender-differentiated union of man and woman. This view long has been held—and continues to be held—in good faith by reasonable and sincere people here and throughout the world.

The petitioners acknowledge this history but contend that these cases cannot end there. Were their intent to demean the revered idea and reality of marriage, the petitioners' claims would be of a different order. But that is neither their purpose nor their submission. To the contrary, it is the enduring importance of marriage that underlies the petitioners' contentions. This, they say, is their whole point. Far from seeking to devalue marriage, the petitioners seek it for themselves because of their respect—and need—for its privileges and responsibilities. And their immutable nature dictates that same-sex marriage is their only real path to this profound commitment.

Recounting the circumstances of three of these cases illustrates the urgency of the petitioners' cause from their perspective. Petitioner James Obergefell, a plaintiff in the Ohio case, met John Arthur over two decades ago. They fell in love and started a life together, establishing a lasting, committed relation. In 2011, however, Arthur was diagnosed with amyotrophic lateral sclerosis, or ALS. This debilitating disease is progressive, with no known cure. Two years ago, Obergefell and Arthur decided to commit to one another, resolving to marry before Arthur died. To fulfill their mutual promise, they traveled from Ohio to Maryland, where same-sex marriage was legal. It was difficult for Arthur to move, and so the couple were wed inside a medical transport plane as it remained on the tarmac in Baltimore. Three months later, Arthur died. Ohio law does not permit Obergefell to be listed as the surviving spouse on Arthur's death certificate. By statute, they must remain strangers even in death, a state-imposed separation Obergefell deems "hurtful for the rest of time." He brought suit to be shown as the surviving spouse on Arthur's death certificate.

April DeBoer and Jayne Rowse are co-plaintiffs in the case from Michigan. They celebrated a commitment ceremony to honor their permanent relation in 2007. They both work as nurses, DeBoer in a neonatal unit and Rowse in an emergency unit. In 2009, DeBoer and Rowse fostered and then adopted a baby boy. Later that same year, they welcomed another son into their family. The new baby, born prematurely and abandoned by his biological mother, required around-the-clock care. The next year, a baby girl with special needs joined their family. Michigan, however, permits only opposite-sex married couples or single individuals to adopt, so each child can have only one woman as his or her legal parent. If an emergency were to arise, schools and hospitals may treat the three children as if they had only one parent. And, were tragedy to befall either DeBoer or Rowse, the other would have no legal rights over the children she had not been permitted to adopt. This couple seeks relief from the continuing uncertainty their unmarried status creates in their lives.

Army Reserve Sergeant First Class Ijpe DeKoe and his partner Thomas Kostura, co-plaintiffs in the Tennessee case, fell in love. In 2011, DeKoe received orders to deploy to Afghanistan. Before leaving, he and Kostura married in New York. A week later, DeKoe began his deployment, which lasted for almost a year. When he returned, the two settled in Tennessee, where DeKoe works full-time for the Army Reserve. Their lawful marriage is stripped from them whenever they reside in Tennessee, returning and disappearing as they travel across state lines. DeKoe, who served this Nation to preserve the freedom the Constitution protects, must endure a substantial burden.

The cases now before the Court involve other petitioners as well, each with their own experiences. Their stories reveal that they seek not to denigrate marriage but rather to live their lives, or honor their spouses' memory, joined by its bond.

[II.B.]   The ancient origins of marriage confirm its centrality, but it has not stood in isolation from developments in law and society. The history of marriage is one of both continuity and change. That institution—even as confined to opposite-sex relations—has evolved over time. For example, marriage was once viewed as an arrangement by the couple's parents based on political, religious, and financial concerns; but by the time of the Nation's founding it was understood to be a voluntary contract between a man and a woman. See N. Cott, Public Vows: A History of Marriage and the Nation 9–17 (2000); S. Coontz, Marriage, A History 15–16 (2005). As the role and status of women changed, the institution further evolved. Under the centuries-old doctrine of coverture, a married man and woman were treated by the State as a single, male-dominated legal entity. See 1 W. Blackstone, Commentaries on the Laws of England 430 (1765). As women gained legal, political, and property rights, and as society began to understand that women have their own equal dignity, the law of coverture was abandoned. These and other developments in the institution of marriage over the past centuries were not mere superficial changes. Rather, they worked deep transformations in its structure, affecting aspects of marriage long viewed by many as essential. See generally N. Cott, Public Vows; S. Coontz, Marriage; H. Hartog, Man & Wife in America: A History (2000).

These new insights have strengthened, not weakened, the institution of marriage. Indeed, changed understandings of marriage are characteristic of a Nation where new dimensions of freedom become apparent to new generations, often through perspectives that begin in pleas or protests and then are considered in the political sphere and the judicial process.

This dynamic can be seen in the Nation's experiences with the rights of gays and lesbians. Until the mid-20th century, same-sex intimacy long had been condemned as immoral by the state itself in most Western nations, a belief often embodied in the criminal law. For this reason, among others, many persons did not deem homosexuals to have dignity in their own distinct identity. A truthful declaration by same-sex couples of what was in their hearts had to remain unspoken. Even when a greater awareness of the humanity and integrity of homosexual persons came in the period after World War II, the argument that gays and lesbians had a just claim to dignity was in conflict with both law and widespread social conventions. Same-sex intimacy remained a crime in many States. Gays and lesbians were prohibited from most government employment, barred from military service, excluded under immigration laws, targeted by police, and burdened in their rights to associate.

For much of the 20th century, moreover, homosexuality was treated as an illness. When the American Psychiatric Association published the first Diagnostic and Statistical Manual of Mental Disorders in 1952, homosexuality was classified as a mental disorder, a position adhered to until 1973. See Position Statement on Homosexuality and Civil Rights, 1973, in 131 Am. J. Psychiatry 497 (1974). Only in more recent years have psychiatrists and others recognized that sexual orientation is both a normal expression of human sexuality and immutable.

In the late 20th century, following substantial cultural and political developments, same-sex couples began to lead more open and public lives and to establish families. This development was followed by a quite extensive discussion of the issue in both governmental and private sectors and by a shift in public attitudes toward greater tolerance. As a result, questions about the rights of gays and lesbians soon reached the courts, where the issue could be discussed in the formal discourse of the law. * * *

[The Court's first engagement with these issues, *Bowers v. Hardwick* (1986), was not a successful engagement, and *Bowers* was overruled in *Lawrence v. Texas* (2003). The Court recounted gay and lesbian couples' litigation of marriage equality from *Baehr v. Lewin* (Haw. 1993) to *Goodridge v. Department of Social Services* (Mass. 2003) and subsequent litigation.]

[III.] Under the Due Process Clause of the Fourteenth Amendment, no State shall "deprive any person of life, liberty, or property, without due process of law." The fundamental liberties protected by this Clause include most of the rights enumerated in the Bill of Rights. See *Duncan v. Louisiana*, 391 U.S. 145, 147–149 (1968). In addition these liberties extend to certain personal choices central to individual dignity and autonomy, including intimate choices that define personal identity and beliefs. See, *e.g., Eisenstadt v. Baird*, 405 U.S. 438, 453 (1972); *Griswold v. Connecticut*, 381 U.S. 479, 484–486 (1965). * * *

Applying these established tenets, the Court has long held the right to marry is protected by the Constitution. In *Loving v. Virginia*, 388 U.S. 1, 12 (1967), which invalidated bans on interracial unions, a unanimous Court held marriage is "one of the vital personal rights essential to the orderly pursuit of happiness by free men." The Court reaffirmed that holding in *Zablocki v. Redhail*, 434 U.S. 374, 384 (1978), which held the right to marry was burdened by a law prohibiting fathers who were behind on child support from marrying. The Court again applied this principle in *Turner v. Safley*, 482 U.S. 78, 95 (1987), which held the right to marry was abridged by regulations limiting the privilege of prison inmates to marry. Over time and in other contexts, the Court has reiterated that the right to marry is fundamental under the Due Process Clause. See, *e.g., M. L. B. v. S. L. J.*, 519 U.S. 102, 116 (1996); *Cleveland Bd. of Ed. v. LaFleur*, 414 U.S. 632, 639–640 (1974); *Griswold, supra*, at 486; *Skinner v. Oklahoma ex rel. Williamson*, 316 U.S. 535, 541 (1942); *Meyer v. Nebraska*, 262 U.S. 390, 399 (1923).

It cannot be denied that this Court's cases describing the right to marry presumed a relationship involving opposite-sex partners. The Court, like many institutions, has made assumptions defined by the world and time of which it is a part. This was evident in *Baker v. Nelson*, 409 U.S. 810, a one-line summary decision issued in 1972, holding the exclusion of same-sex couples from marriage did not present a substantial federal question.

Still, there are other, more instructive precedents. This Court's cases have expressed constitutional principles of broader reach. In defining the right to marry these cases have identified essential attributes of that right based in history, tradition, and other constitutional liberties inherent in this intimate bond. See, *e.g., Lawrence*; *Turner*; *Zablocki*; *Loving*; *Griswold*. And in assessing whether the force and rationale of its cases apply to same-sex couples, the Court must respect the basic reasons why the right to marry has been long protected.

This analysis compels the conclusion that same-sex couples may exercise the right to marry. The four principles and traditions to be discussed demonstrate that the reasons marriage is fundamental under the Constitution apply with equal force to same-sex couples.

A first premise of the Court's relevant precedents is that the right to personal choice regarding marriage is inherent in the concept of individual autonomy. This abiding connection between marriage and liberty is why *Loving* invalidated interracial marriage bans under the Due Process Clause. Like choices concerning contraception, family relationships, procreation, and childrearing, all of which are protected by the Constitution, decisions concerning marriage are among the most intimate that an individual can make. Indeed, the Court has noted it would be contradictory "to recognize a right of privacy with respect to other matters of family life and not with respect to the decision to enter the relationship that is the foundation of the family in our society." *Zablocki.*

Choices about marriage shape an individual's destiny. As the Supreme Judicial Court of Massachusetts has explained, because "it fulfils yearnings for security, safe haven, and connection that express our common humanity, civil marriage is an esteemed institution, and the decision whether and whom to marry is among life's momentous acts of self-definition." *Goodridge.*

The nature of marriage is that, through its enduring bond, two persons together can find other freedoms, such as expression, intimacy, and spirituality. This is true for all persons, whatever their sexual orientation. See *Windsor.* There is dignity in the bond between two men or two women who seek to marry and in their autonomy to make such profound choices.

A second principle in this Court's jurisprudence is that the right to marry is fundamental because it supports a two-person union unlike any other in its importance to the committed individuals. This point was central to *Griswold v. Connecticut*, which held the Constitution protects the right of married couples to use contraception. Suggesting that marriage is a right "older than the Bill of Rights," *Griswold* described marriage this way:

> "Marriage is a coming together for better or for worse, hopefully enduring, and intimate to the degree of being sacred. It is an association that promotes a way of life, not causes; a harmony in living, not political faiths; a bilateral loyalty, not commercial or social projects. Yet it is an association for as noble a purpose as any involved in our prior decisions."

And in *Turner*, the Court again acknowledged the intimate association protected by this right, holding prisoners could not be denied the right to marry because their committed relationships satisfied the basic reasons why marriage is a fundamental right. The right to marry thus dignifies couples who "wish to define themselves by their commitment to each other." *Windsor.* Marriage responds to the universal fear that a lonely person might call out only to find no one there. It offers the hope of companionship and understanding and assurance that while both still live there will be someone to care for the other.

As this Court held in *Lawrence*, same-sex couples have the same right as opposite-sex couples to enjoy intimate association. *Lawrence* invalidated laws that made same-sex intimacy a criminal act. And it acknowledged that "[w]hen sexuality finds overt expression in intimate conduct with another person, the conduct can be but one element in a personal bond that is more enduring." But while *Lawrence* confirmed a dimension of freedom that allows individuals to engage in intimate association without criminal liability, it does not follow that freedom stops there. Outlaw to outcast may be a step forward, but it does not achieve the full promise of liberty.

A third basis for protecting the right to marry is that it safeguards children and families and thus draws meaning from related rights of childrearing, procreation, and education. See *Pierce v. Society of Sisters*; *Meyer*. The Court has recognized these connections by describing the varied rights as a unified whole: "[T]he right to 'marry, establish a home and bring up children' is a central part of the liberty protected by the Due Process Clause." *Zablocki* (quoting *Meyer*). Under the laws of the several States, some of marriage's protections for children and families are material. But marriage also confers more profound benefits. By giving recognition and legal structure to their parents' relationship, marriage allows children "to understand the integrity and closeness of their own family and its concord with other families in their community and in their daily lives." *Windsor*. Marriage also affords the permanency and stability important to children's best interests.

As all parties agree, many same-sex couples provide loving and nurturing homes to their children, whether biological or adopted. And hundreds of thousands of children are presently being raised by such couples. Most States have allowed gays and lesbians to adopt, either as individuals or as couples, and many adopted and foster children have same-sex parents. This provides powerful confirmation from the law itself that gays and lesbians can create loving, supportive families.

Excluding same-sex couples from marriage thus conflicts with a central premise of the right to marry. Without the recognition, stability, and predictability marriage offers, their children suffer the stigma of knowing their families are somehow lesser. They also suffer the significant material costs of being raised by unmarried parents, relegated through no fault of their own to a more difficult and uncertain family life. The marriage laws at issue here thus harm and humiliate the children of same-sex couples. See *Windsor*.

That is not to say the right to marry is less meaningful for those who do not or cannot have children. An ability, desire, or promise to procreate is not and has not been a prerequisite for a valid marriage in any State. In light of precedent protecting the right of a married couple not to procreate, it cannot be said the Court or the States have conditioned the right to marry on the capacity or commitment to procreate. The constitutional marriage right has many aspects, of which childbearing is only one.

Fourth and finally, this Court's cases and the Nation's traditions make clear that marriage is a keystone of our social order. Alexis de Tocqueville recognized this truth on his travels through the United States almost two centuries ago:

> "There is certainly no country in the world where the tie of marriage is so much respected as in America . . . [W]hen the

American retires from the turmoil of public life to the bosom of his family, he finds in it the image of order and of peace . . . [H]e afterwards carries [that image] with him into public affairs." 1 Democracy in America 309 (H. Reeve transl., rev. ed. 1990).

In *Maynard v. Hill*, 125 U.S. 190, 211 (1888), the Court echoed de Tocqueville, explaining that marriage is "the foundation of the family and of society, without which there would be neither civilization nor progress." Marriage, the *Maynard* Court said, has long been " 'a great public institution, giving character to our whole civil polity.' " This idea has been reiterated even as the institution has evolved in substantial ways over time, superseding rules related to parental consent, gender, and race once thought by many to be essential. Marriage remains a building block of our national community.

For that reason, just as a couple vows to support each other, so does society pledge to support the couple, offering symbolic recognition and material benefits to protect and nourish the union. Indeed, while the States are in general free to vary the benefits they confer on all married couples, they have throughout our history made marriage the basis for an expanding list of governmental rights, benefits, and responsibilities. These aspects of marital status include: taxation; inheritance and property rights; rules of intestate succession; spousal privilege in the law of evidence; hospital access; medical decisionmaking authority; adoption rights; the rights and benefits of survivors; birth and death certificates; professional ethics rules; campaign finance restrictions; workers' compensation benefits; health insurance; and child custody, support, and visitation rules. Valid marriage under state law is also a significant status for over a thousand provisions of federal law. See *Windsor*. The States have contributed to the fundamental character of the marriage right by placing that institution at the center of so many facets of the legal and social order.

There is no difference between same- and opposite-sex couples with respect to this principle. Yet by virtue of their exclusion from that institution, same-sex couples are denied the constellation of benefits that the States have linked to marriage. This harm results in more than just material burdens. Same-sex couples are consigned to an instability many opposite-sex couples would deem intolerable in their own lives. As the State itself makes marriage all the more precious by the significance it attaches to it, exclusion from that status has the effect of teaching that gays and lesbians are unequal in important respects. It demeans gays and lesbians for the State to lock them out of a central institution of the Nation's society. Same-sex couples, too, may aspire to the transcendent purposes of marriage and seek fulfillment in its highest meaning.

The limitation of marriage to opposite-sex couples may long have seemed natural and just, but its inconsistency with the central meaning of the fundamental right to marry is now manifest. With that knowledge must come the recognition that laws excluding same-sex couples from the marriage right impose stigma and injury of the kind prohibited by our basic charter.

Objecting that this does not reflect an appropriate framing of the issue, the respondents refer to *Washington v. Glucksberg*, which called for a " 'careful description' " of fundamental rights. They assert the petitioners do not seek to exercise the right to marry but rather a new and nonexistent "right to same-sex marriage." *Glucksberg* did insist that liberty under the Due Process Clause must be defined in a most circumscribed manner, with central reference to specific historical practices. Yet while that approach may have been appropriate for the asserted right there involved (physician-assisted suicide), it is inconsistent with the approach this Court has used in discussing other fundamental rights, including marriage and intimacy. *Loving* did not ask about a "right to interracial marriage"; *Turner* did not ask about a "right of inmates to marry"; and *Zablocki* did not ask about a "right of fathers with unpaid child support duties to marry." Rather, each case inquired about the right to marry in its comprehensive sense, asking if there was a sufficient justification for excluding the relevant class from the right. See also *Glucksberg* (Souter, J., concurring in judgment); *id.* (Breyer, J., concurring in judgments).

That principle applies here. If rights were defined by who exercised them in the past, then received practices could serve as their own continued justification and new groups could not invoke rights once denied. This Court has rejected that approach, both with respect to the right to marry and the rights of gays and lesbians. See *Loving*; *Lawrence*.
* * *

The right of same-sex couples to marry that is part of the liberty promised by the Fourteenth Amendment is derived, too, from that Amendment's guarantee of the equal protection of the laws. The Due Process Clause and the Equal Protection Clause are connected in a profound way, though they set forth independent principles. Rights implicit in liberty and rights secured by equal protection may rest on different precepts and are not always coextensive, yet in some instances each may be instructive as to the meaning and reach of the other. In any particular case one Clause may be thought to capture the essence of the right in a more accurate and comprehensive way, even as the two Clauses may converge in the identification and definition of the right. This interrelation of the two principles furthers our understanding of what freedom is and must become.

Indeed, in interpreting the Equal Protection Clause, the Court has recognized that new insights and societal understandings can reveal unjustified inequality within our most fundamental institutions that once passed unnoticed and unchallenged. To take but one period, this occurred with respect to marriage in the 1970s and 1980s. Notwithstanding the gradual erosion of the doctrine of coverture, invidious sex-based classifications in marriage remained common through the mid-20th century. See App. to Brief for Appellant in *Reed v. Reed*, O. T. 1971, No. 70–4, pp. 69–88 (an extensive reference to laws extant as of 1971 treating women as unequal to men in marriage). These classifications denied the equal dignity of men and women. One State's law, for example, provided in 1971 that "the husband is the head of the family and the wife is subject to him; her legal civil existence is merged in the husband, except so far as the law recognizes her separately, either for her own protection, or for her benefit." Ga. Code Ann. § 53–501 (1935). Responding to a new awareness, the Court invoked equal protection principles to invalidate laws imposing sex-based inequality on marriage. See, *e.g., Kirchberg v. Feenstra*, 450 U.S. 455 (1981); *Wengler v. Druggists Mut. Ins. Co.*, 446 U.S. 142 (1980); *Califano v. Westcott*, 443 U.S. 76 (1979); *Orr v. Orr*, 440 U.S. 268 (1979); *Califano v. Goldfarb*, 430 U.S. 199 (1977) (plurality opinion); *Weinberger v. Wiesenfeld*, 420 U.S. 636 (1975); *Frontiero v. Richardson*, 411 U.S. 677 (1973). Like *Loving* and *Zablocki*, these precedents show the Equal Protection Clause can help to identify and correct inequalities in the institution of marriage, vindicating precepts of liberty and equality under the Constitution. * * *

In *Lawrence* the Court acknowledged the interlocking nature of these constitutional safeguards in the context of the legal treatment of gays and lesbians. Although *Lawrence* elaborated its holding under the Due Process Clause, it acknowledged, and sought to remedy, the continuing inequality that resulted from laws making intimacy in the lives of gays and lesbians a crime against the State. *Lawrence* therefore drew upon principles of liberty and equality to define and protect the rights of gays and lesbians, holding the State "cannot demean their existence or control their destiny by making their private sexual conduct a crime."

This dynamic also applies to same-sex marriage. It is now clear that the challenged laws burden the liberty of same-sex couples, and it must be further acknowledged that they abridge central precepts of equality. Here the marriage laws enforced by the respondents are in essence unequal: same-sex couples are denied all the benefits afforded to opposite-sex couples and are barred from exercising a fundamental right. Especially against a long history of disapproval of their relationships, this denial to same-sex couples of the right to marry works a grave and continuing harm. The imposition of this disability on gays and lesbians serves to disrespect and subordinate them. And the Equal Protection Clause, like the Due Process Clause, prohibits this unjustified infringement of the fundamental right to marry. See, *e.g., Zablocki.*

These considerations lead to the conclusion that the right to marry is a fundamental right inherent in the liberty of the person, and under the Due Process and Equal Protection Clauses of the Fourteenth Amendment couples of the same-sex may not be deprived of that right and that liberty. The Court now holds that same-sex couples may exercise the fundamental right to marry. No longer may this liberty be denied to them. *Baker v. Nelson* must be and now is overruled, and the State laws challenged by Petitioners in these cases are now held invalid to the extent they exclude same-sex couples from civil marriage on the same terms and conditions as opposite-sex couples.

[In Part IV, Justice Kennedy rejected the argument that the Court should leave the issue to further deliberation in state democratic processes. But marriage equality has been discussed extensively, and private as well as public institutions have reached agreement that there are no neutral reasons to exclude lesbian and gay couples from this institution.]

This is not the first time the Court has been asked to adopt a cautious approach to recognizing and protecting fundamental rights. In *Bowers*, a bare majority upheld a law criminalizing same-sex intimacy. That approach might have been viewed as a cautious endorsement of the democratic process, which had only just begun to consider the rights of gays and lesbians. Yet, in effect, *Bowers* upheld state action that denied gays and lesbians a fundamental right and caused them pain and humiliation. As evidenced by the dissents in that case, the facts and principles necessary to a correct holding were known to the *Bowers* Court. That is why *Lawrence* held *Bowers* was "not correct when it was decided." Although *Bowers* was eventually repudiated in *Lawrence*, men and women were harmed in the interim, and the substantial effects of these injuries no doubt lingered long after *Bowers* was overruled. Dignitary wounds cannot always be healed with the stroke of a pen.

A ruling against same-sex couples would have the same effect—and, like *Bowers*, would be unjustified under the Fourteenth Amendment. The petitioners' stories make clear the urgency of the issue they present to the Court. James Obergefell now asks whether Ohio can erase his marriage to John Arthur for all time. April DeBoer and Jayne Rowse now ask whether Michigan may continue to deny them the certainty and stability all mothers desire to protect their children, and for them and their children the childhood years will pass all too soon. Ijpe DeKoe and Thomas Kostura now ask whether Tennessee can deny to one who has served this Nation the basic dignity of recognizing his New York marriage. Properly presented with the petitioners' cases, the Court has a duty to address these claims and answer these questions.

Indeed, faced with a disagreement among the Courts of Appeals—a disagreement that caused impermissible geographic variation in the meaning of federal law—the Court granted review to determine whether same-sex couples may exercise the right to marry. Were the Court to uphold the challenged laws as constitutional, it would teach the Nation that these laws are in accord with our society's most basic compact. Were the Court to stay its hand to allow slower, case-by-case determination of the required availability of specific public benefits to same-sex couples, it still would deny gays and lesbians many rights and responsibilities intertwined with marriage.

The respondents also argue allowing same-sex couples to wed will harm marriage as an institution by leading to fewer opposite-sex marriages. This may occur, the respondents contend, because licensing same-sex marriage severs the connection between natural procreation and marriage. That argument, however, rests on a counterintuitive view of opposite-sex couple's decisionmaking processes regarding marriage and parenthood. Decisions about whether to marry and raise children are based on many personal, romantic, and practical considerations; and it is unrealistic to conclude that an opposite-sex couple would choose not to marry simply because same-sex couples may do so. The respondents have not shown a foundation for the conclusion that allowing same-sex marriage will cause the harmful outcomes they describe. Indeed, with respect to this asserted basis for excluding same-sex couples from the right to marry, it is appropriate to observe these cases involve only the rights of two consenting adults whose marriages would pose no risk of harm to themselves or third parties.

Finally, it must be emphasized that religions, and those who adhere to religious doctrines, may continue to advocate with utmost, sincere conviction that, by divine precepts, same-sex marriage should not be condoned. The First Amendment ensures that religious organizations and persons are given proper protection as they seek to teach the principles that are so fulfilling and so central to their lives and faiths, and to their own deep aspirations to continue the family structure they have long revered. The same is true of those who oppose same-sex marriage for other reasons. In turn, those who believe allowing same-sex marriage is proper or indeed essential, whether as a matter of religious conviction or secular belief, may engage those who disagree with their view in an open and searching debate. The Constitution, however, does not permit the State to bar same-sex couples from marriage on the same terms as accorded to couples of the opposite sex.

[In Part VI, Justice Kennedy ruled that the Fourteenth Amendment requires states to recognize valid same-sex marriages entered in other states. His opinion for the Court then concluded with the following:]

No union is more profound than marriage, for it embodies the highest ideals of love, fidelity, devotion, sacrifice, and family. In forming a marital union, two people become something greater than once they were. As some of the petitioners in these cases demonstrate, marriage embodies a love that may endure even past death. It would misunderstand these men and women to say they disrespect the idea of marriage. Their plea is that they do respect it, respect it so deeply that they seek to find its fulfillment for themselves. Their hope is not to be condemned to live in loneliness, excluded from one of civilization's oldest institutions. They ask for equal dignity in the eyes of the law. The Constitution grants them that right.

■ CHIEF JUSTICE ROBERTS, with whom JUSTICE SCALIA and JUSTICE THOMAS join, dissenting.

Petitioners make strong arguments rooted in social policy and considerations of fairness. They contend that same-sex couples should be allowed to affirm their love and commitment through marriage, just like opposite-sex couples. That position has undeniable appeal; over the past six years, voters and legislators in eleven States and the District of Columbia have revised their laws to allow marriage between two people of the same sex.

But this Court is not a legislature. Whether same-sex marriage is a good idea should be of no concern to us. Under the Constitution, judges have power to say what the law is, not what it should be. The people who ratified the Constitution authorized courts to exercise "neither force nor will but merely judgment." The Federalist No. 78, p. 465 (C. Rossiter ed. 1961) (A. Hamilton) (capitalization altered).

Although the policy arguments for extending marriage to same-sex couples may be compelling, the legal arguments for requiring such an extension are not. The fundamental right to marry does not include a right to make a State change its definition of marriage. And a State's decision to maintain the meaning of marriage that has persisted in every culture throughout human history can hardly be called irrational. In short, our Constitution does not enact any one theory of marriage. The people of a State are free to expand marriage to include same-sex couples, or to retain the historic definition.

Today, however, the Court takes the extraordinary step of ordering every State to license and recognize same-sex marriage. Many people will rejoice at this decision, and I begrudge none their celebration. But for those who believe in a government of laws, not of men, the majority's approach is deeply disheartening. Supporters of same-sex marriage have achieved considerable success persuading their fellow citizens—through the democratic process—to adopt their view. That ends today. Five lawyers have closed the debate and enacted their own vision of marriage as a matter of constitutional law. Stealing this issue from the people will for many cast a cloud over same-sex marriage, making a dramatic social change that much more difficult to accept.

The majority's decision is an act of will, not legal judgment. The right it announces has no basis in the Constitution or this Court's precedent. The majority expressly disclaims judicial "caution" and omits even a pretense of humility, openly relying on its desire to remake society according to its own "new insight" into the "nature of injustice." *Ante*. As a result, the Court invalidates the marriage laws of more than half the States and orders the transformation of a social institution that has formed the basis of human society for millennia, for the Kalahari Bushmen and the Han Chinese, the Carthaginians and the Aztecs. Just who do we think we are?

It can be tempting for judges to confuse our own preferences with the requirements of the law. But as this Court has been reminded throughout our history, the Constitution "is made for people of fundamentally differing views." *Lochner v. New York,* 198 U.S. 45, 76 (1905) (Holmes, J., dissenting). Accordingly, "courts are not concerned with the wisdom or policy of legislation." *Id.,* at 69 (Harlan, J., dissenting). The majority today neglects that restrained conception of the judicial role. It seizes for itself a question the Constitution leaves to the people, at a time when the people are engaged in a vibrant debate on that question. And it answers that question based not on neutral principles of constitutional law, but on its own "understanding of what freedom is and must become." *Ante.* I have no choice but to dissent. [Proceeds to discuss just that]

Understand well what this dissent is about: It is not about whether, in my judgment, the institution of marriage should be changed to include same-sex couples. It is instead about whether, in our democratic republic, that decision should rest with the people acting through their elected representatives, or with five lawyers who happen to hold commissions authorizing them to resolve legal disputes according to law. The Constitution leaves no doubt about the answer.

[I.] Petitioners and their *amici* base their arguments on the "right to marry" and the imperative of "marriage equality." There is no serious dispute that, under our precedents, the Constitution protects a right to marry and requires States to apply their marriage laws equally. The real question in these cases is what constitutes "marriage," or—more precisely—*who decides* what constitutes "marriage"?

The majority largely ignores these questions, relegating ages of human experience with marriage to a paragraph or two. Even if history and precedent are not "the end" of these cases, *ante,* at 4, I would not "sweep away what has so long been settled" without showing greater respect for all that preceded us. *Town of Greece v. Galloway,* 572 U.S. ___, ___ (2014).

As the majority acknowledges, marriage "has existed for millennia and across civilizations." *Ante.* For all those millennia, across all those civilizations, "marriage" referred to only one relationship: the union of a man and a woman. See *ante*; Tr. of Oral Arg. on Question 1, p. 12 (petitioners conceding that they are not aware of any society that permitted same-sex marriage before 2001). As the Court explained two Terms ago, "until recent years, . . . marriage between a man and a woman no doubt had been thought of by most people as essential to the very definition of that term and to its role and function throughout the history of civilization." *United States v. Windsor.*

This universal definition of marriage as the union of a man and a woman is no historical coincidence. Marriage did not come about as a result of a political movement, discovery, disease, war, religious doctrine, or any other moving force of world history—and certainly not as a result of a prehistoric decision to exclude gays and lesbians. It arose in the nature of things to meet a vital need: ensuring that children are conceived by a mother and father committed to raising them in the stable conditions of a lifelong relationship. See G. Quale, A History of Marriage Systems 2 (1988); cf. M. Cicero, De Officiis 57 (W. Miller transl. 1913) ("For since the reproductive instinct is by nature's gift the common possession of all living creatures, the first bond of union is that between husband and wife; the next, that between parents and children; then we find one home, with everything in common.").

The premises supporting this concept of marriage are so fundamental that they rarely require articulation. The human race must procreate to survive. Procreation occurs through sexual relations between a man and a woman. When sexual relations result in the conception of a child, that child's prospects are generally better if the mother and father stay together rather than going their separate ways. Therefore, for the good of children and society, sexual relations that can lead to procreation should occur only between a man and a woman committed to a lasting bond.

Society has recognized that bond as marriage. And by bestowing a respected status and material benefits on married couples, society encourages men and women to conduct sexual relations within marriage rather than without. As one prominent scholar put it, "Marriage is a socially arranged solution for the problem of getting people to stay together and care for children that the mere desire for children, and the sex that makes children possible, does not solve." J.Q. Wilson, The Marriage Problem 41 (2002). * * *

The Constitution itself says nothing about marriage, and the Framers thereby entrusted the States with "[t]he whole subject of the domestic relations of husband and wife." *Windsor*. There is no dispute that every State at the founding—and every State throughout our history until a dozen years ago—defined marriage in the traditional, biologically rooted way. * * *

This Court's precedents have repeatedly described marriage in ways that are consistent only with its traditional meaning. Early cases on the subject referred to marriage as "the union for life of one man and one woman," *Murphy v. Ramsey,* 114 U.S. 15, 45 (1885), which forms "the foundation of the family and of society, without which there would be neither civilization nor progress," *Maynard v. Hill,* 125 U.S. 190, 211 (1888). We later described marriage as "fundamental to our very existence and survival," an understanding that necessarily implies a procreative component. *Loving v. Virginia*; see *Skinner v. Oklahoma ex rel. Williamson.* More recent cases have directly connected the right to marry with the "right to procreate." *Zablocki v. Redhail.*

As the majority notes, some aspects of marriage have changed over time. Arranged marriages have largely given way to pairings based on romantic love. States have replaced coverture, the doctrine by which a married man and woman became a single legal entity, with laws that respect each participant's separate status. Racial restrictions on marriage, which "arose as an incident to slavery" to promote "White Supremacy," were repealed by many States and ultimately struck down by this Court. *Loving.*

The majority observes that these developments "were not mere superficial changes" in marriage, but rather "worked deep transformations in its structure." They did not, however, work any transformation in the core structure of marriage as the union between a man and a woman. If you had asked a person on the street how marriage was defined, no one would ever have said, "Marriage is the union of a man and a woman, where the woman is subject to coverture." The majority may be right that the "history of marriage is one of both continuity and change," but the core meaning of marriage has endured. * * *

[II.] Petitioners first contend that the marriage laws of their States violate the Due Process Clause. The Solicitor General of the United States, appearing in support of petitioners, expressly disowned that position before this Court. See Tr. of Oral Arg. on Question 1, at 38–39. The majority nevertheless resolves these cases for petitioners based almost entirely on the Due Process Clause.

The majority purports to identify four "principles and traditions" in this Court's due process precedents that support a fundamental right for same-sex couples to marry. In reality, however, the majority's approach has no basis in principle or tradition, except for the unprincipled tradition of judicial policymaking that characterized discredited decisions such as *Lochner v. New York.* Stripped of its shiny rhetorical gloss, the majority's argument is that the Due Process Clause gives same-sex couples a fundamental right to marry because it will be good for them and for society. If I were a legislator, I would certainly consider that view as a matter of social policy. But as a judge, I find the majority's position indefensible as a matter of constitutional law.

[II.A.] * * * This Court has interpreted the Due Process Clause to include a "substantive" component that protects certain liberty interests against state deprivation "no matter what process is provided." *Reno v. Flores,* 507 U.S. 292, 302 (1993). The theory is that some liberties are "so rooted in the traditions and conscience of our people as to be ranked as fundamental," and therefore cannot be deprived without compelling justification. *Snyder v. Massachusetts,* 291 U.S. 97, 105 (1934).

Allowing unelected federal judges to select which unenumerated rights rank as "fundamental"—and to strike down state laws on the basis of that determination—raises obvious concerns about the judicial role. Our precedents have accordingly insisted that judges "exercise the utmost care" in identifying implied fundamental rights, "lest the liberty protected by the Due Process Clause be subtly transformed into the policy preferences of the Members of this Court." *Glucksberg*; see Kennedy, Unenumerated Rights and the Dictates of Judicial Restraint 13 (1986)

(Address at Stanford) ("One can conclude that certain essential, or fundamental, rights should exist in any just society. It does not follow that each of those essential rights is one that we as judges can enforce under the written Constitution. The Due Process Clause is not a guarantee of every right that should inhere in an ideal system.").

The need for restraint in administering the strong medicine of substantive due process is a lesson this Court has learned the hard way. The Court first applied substantive due process to strike down a statute in *Dred Scott v. Sandford*. There the Court invalidated the Missouri Compromise on the ground that legislation restricting the institution of slavery violated the implied rights of slaveholders. The Court relied on its own conception of liberty and property in doing so. * * *

Dred Scott's holding was overruled on the battlefields of the Civil War and by constitutional amendment after Appomattox, but its approach to the Due Process Clause reappeared. In a series of early 20th-century cases, most prominently *Lochner v. New York,* this Court invalidated state statutes that presented "meddlesome interferences with the rights of the individual," and "undue interference with liberty of person and freedom of contract." In *Lochner* itself, the Court struck down a New York law setting maximum hours for bakery employees, because there was "in our judgment, no reasonable foundation for holding this to be necessary or appropriate as a health law."

The dissenting Justices in *Lochner* explained that the New York law could be viewed as a reasonable response to legislative concern about the health of bakery employees, an issue on which there was at least "room for debate and for an honest difference of opinion." *Id.,* at 72 (opinion of Harlan, J.). The majority's contrary conclusion required adopting as constitutional law "an economic theory which a large part of the country does not entertain." *Id.,* at 75 (opinion of Holmes, J.). As Justice Holmes memorably put it, "The Fourteenth Amendment does not enact Mr. Herbert Spencer's Social Statics," a leading work on the philosophy of Social Darwinism. The Constitution "is not intended to embody a particular economic theory. . . . It is made for people of fundamentally differing views, and the accident of our finding certain opinions natural and familiar or novel and even shocking ought not to conclude our judgment upon the question whether statutes embodying them conflict with the Constitution." * * *

Eventually, the Court recognized its error and vowed not to repeat it. * * * Rejecting *Lochner* does not require disavowing the doctrine of implied fundamental rights, and this Court has not done so. But to avoid repeating *Lochner*'s error of converting personal preferences into constitutional mandates, our modern substantive due process cases have stressed the need for "judicial self-restraint." *Collins v. Harker Heights,* 503 U.S. 115, 125 (1992). Our precedents have required that implied fundamental rights be "objectively, deeply rooted in this Nation's history and tradition," and "implicit in the concept of ordered liberty, such that neither liberty nor justice would exist if they were sacrificed." *Glucksberg.* * * *

Proper reliance on history and tradition of course requires looking beyond the individual law being challenged, so that every restriction on liberty does not supply its own constitutional justification. The Court is right about that. But given the few "guideposts for responsible decisionmaking in this unchartered area," *Collins,* 503 U.S., at 125, "an approach grounded in history imposes limits on the judiciary that are more meaningful than any based on [an] abstract formula," *Moore,* 431 U.S., at 504, n. 12 (plurality opinion). Expanding a right suddenly and dramatically is likely to require tearing it up from its roots. Even a sincere profession of "discipline" in identifying fundamental rights, *ante,* does not provide a meaningful constraint on a judge, for "what he is really likely to be 'discovering,' whether or not he is fully aware of it, are his own values," J. Ely, Democracy and Distrust 44 (1980). The only way to ensure restraint in this delicate enterprise is "continual insistence upon respect for the teachings of history, solid recognition of the basic values that underlie our society, and wise appreciation of the great roles [of] the doctrines of federalism and separation of powers." *Griswold v. Connecticut,* 381 U.S. 479, 501 (1965) (Harlan, J., concurring in judgment).

[II.B.] The majority acknowledges none of this doctrinal background, and it is easy to see why: Its aggressive application of substantive due process breaks sharply with decades of precedent and returns the Court to the unprincipled approach of *Lochner.* The majority's driving themes are that marriage is desirable and petitioners desire it. The opinion describes the "transcendent importance" of marriage and repeatedly insists that petitioners do not seek to "demean," "devalue," "denigrate," or "disrespect" the institution. *Ante.* Nobody disputes those points. Indeed, the compelling personal accounts of petitioners and others like them are likely a primary reason why many Americans have changed their minds about whether same-sex couples should be allowed to marry. As a matter of constitutional law, however, the sincerity of petitioners' wishes is not relevant. When the majority turns to the law, it relies primarily on precedents discussing the fundamental "right to marry." These cases do not hold, of course, that anyone who wants to get married has a constitutional right to do so. They instead require a State to justify barriers to marriage as that institution has always been understood. * * *

None of the laws at issue in those cases purported to change the core definition of marriage as the union of a man and a woman. * * * Removing racial barriers to marriage therefore did not change what a marriage was any more than integrating schools changed what a school was. As the majority admits, the institution of "marriage" discussed in every one of these cases "presumed a relationship involving opposite-sex partners."

In short, the "right to marry" cases stand for the important but limited proposition that particular restrictions on access to marriage *as traditionally defined* violate due process. These precedents say nothing at all about a right to make a State change its definition of marriage, which is the right petitioners actually seek here. See *Windsor* (Alito, J., dissenting) ("What Windsor and the United States seek . . . is not the protection of a deeply rooted right but the recognition of a very new right."). Neither petitioners nor the majority cites a single case or other legal source providing any basis for such a constitutional right. None exists, and that is enough to foreclose their claim.

[II.B2.] * * * [T]he privacy cases provide no support for the majority's position, because petitioners do not seek privacy. Quite the opposite, they seek public recognition of their relationships, along with corresponding government benefits. Our cases have consistently refused to allow litigants to convert the shield provided by constitutional liberties into a sword to demand positive entitlements from the State. See *DeShaney v. Winnebago County Dept. of Social Servs.,* 489 U.S. 189, 196 (1989); *San Antonio Independent School Dist. v. Rodriguez,* 411 U.S. 1, 35–37 (1973); *post* (Thomas, J., dissenting). Thus, although the right to privacy recognized by our precedents certainly plays a role in protecting the intimate conduct of same-sex couples, it provides no affirmative right to redefine marriage and no basis for striking down the laws at issue here.

[II.B3.] Perhaps recognizing how little support it can derive from precedent, the majority goes out of its way to jettison the "careful" approach to implied fundamental rights taken by this Court in *Glucksberg.* It is revealing that the majority's position requires it to effectively overrule *Glucksberg,* the leading modern case setting the bounds of substantive due process. At least this part of the majority opinion has the virtue of candor. Nobody could rightly accuse the majority of taking a careful approach. * * *

One immediate question invited by the majority's position is whether States may retain the definition of marriage as a union of two people. Although the majority randomly inserts the adjective "two" in various places, it offers no reason at all why the two-person element of the core definition of marriage may be preserved while the man-woman element may not. Indeed, from the standpoint of history and tradition, a leap from opposite-sex marriage to same-sex marriage is much greater than one from a two-person union to plural unions, which have deep roots in some cultures around the world. If the majority is willing to take the big leap, it is hard to see how it can say no to the shorter one. * * *

I do not mean to equate marriage between same-sex couples with plural marriages in all respects. There may well be relevant differences that compel different legal analysis. But if there are, petitioners have not pointed to any. When asked about a plural marital union at oral argument, petitioners asserted that a State "doesn't have such an institution." Tr. of Oral Arg. on Question 2. But that is exactly the point: the States at issue here do not have an institution of same-sex marriage, either. * * *

[III.] In addition to their due process argument, petitioners contend that the Equal Protection Clause requires their States to license and recognize same-sex marriages. The majority does not seriously engage with this claim. Its discussion is, quite frankly, difficult to follow. The central point seems to be that there is a "synergy between" the Equal Protection Clause and the Due Process Clause, and that some precedents relying on one Clause have also relied on the other. *Ante.* Absent from this portion of the opinion, however, is anything resembling our usual framework for deciding equal protection cases. It is casebook doctrine that the "modern Supreme Court's treatment of equal protection claims has used a means-ends methodology in which judges ask whether the classification the government is using is sufficiently related to the goals it is pursuing." G. Stone, L. Seidman, C. Sunstein, M. Tushnet, & P. Karlan, Constitutional Law 453 (7th ed.2013). * * * The majority goes on to assert in conclusory fashion that the Equal Protection Clause provides an alternative basis for its holding. *Ante.* Yet the majority fails to provide even a single sentence explaining how the Equal Protection Clause supplies independent weight for its position, nor does it attempt to justify its gratuitous violation of the canon against unnecessarily resolving constitutional questions. In any event, the marriage laws at issue here do not violate the Equal Protection Clause, because distinguishing between opposite-sex and same-sex couples is rationally related to the States' "legitimate state interest" in "preserving the traditional institution of marriage." *Lawrence,* 539 U.S., at 585 (O'Connor, J., concurring in judgment).

It is important to note with precision which laws petitioners have challenged. Although they discuss some of the ancillary legal benefits that accompany marriage, such as hospital visitation rights and recognition of spousal status on official documents, petitioners' lawsuits target the laws defining marriage generally rather than those allocating benefits specifically. The equal protection analysis might be different, in my view, if we were confronted with a more focused challenge to the denial of certain tangible benefits. Of course, those more selective claims will not arise now that the Court has taken the drastic step of requiring every State to license and recognize marriages between same-sex couples.

[IV.] * * * The Court's accumulation of power does not occur in a vacuum. It comes at the expense of the people. And they know it. Here and abroad, people are in the midst of a serious and thoughtful public debate on the issue of same-sex marriage. They see voters carefully considering same-sex marriage, casting ballots in favor or opposed, and sometimes changing their minds. They see political leaders similarly reexamining their positions, and either reversing course or explaining adherence to old convictions confirmed anew. They see governments and businesses modifying policies and practices with respect to same-sex couples, and participating actively in the civic discourse. They see countries overseas democratically accepting profound social change, or declining to do so. This deliberative process is making people take seriously questions that they may not have even regarded as questions before. * * *

But today the Court puts a stop to all that. By deciding this question under the Constitution, the Court removes it from the realm of democratic decision. There will be consequences to shutting down the political process on an issue of such profound public significance. Closing debate tends to close minds. People denied a voice are less likely to accept the ruling of a court on an issue that does not seem to be the sort of thing courts usually decide. As a thoughtful commentator observed about another issue, "The political process was moving . . ., not swiftly enough for advocates of quick, complete change, but majoritarian institutions were listening and acting. Heavy-handed judicial intervention was difficult to justify and appears to have provoked, not resolved, conflict." Ginsburg, Some Thoughts on Autonomy and Equality in Relation to *Roe v. Wade,* 63 N.C.L.Rev. 375, 385–386 (1985) (footnote omitted). Indeed, however heartened the proponents of same-sex marriage might be on this day, it is worth acknowledging what they have lost, and lost forever: the opportunity to win the true acceptance that comes from persuading their fellow citizens of the justice of their cause. And they lose this just when the winds of change were freshening at their backs. * * *

If you are among the many Americans—of whatever sexual orientation—who favor expanding same-sex marriage, by all means celebrate today's decision. Celebrate the achievement of a desired goal. Celebrate the opportunity for a new expression of commitment to a partner. Celebrate the availability of new benefits. But do not celebrate the Constitution. It had nothing to do with it.

I respectfully dissent.

■ [We omit the three other dissenting opinions, authored by JUSTICES SCALIA, THOMAS, and ALITO, but incorporate their criticisms in the notes that follow.]

NOTES AND QUESTIONS

1. *The Theme of Equal Liberty Continues.* Speaking for the Court, with no concurring opinions, Justice Kennedy's opinion extends *Loving v. Virginia* to assure marriage rights for LGBT persons, but without *Loving*'s emphasis on the Equal Protection Clause. Justice Kennedy's opinion instead tracks his analysis in *Lawrence v. Texas* by recognizing that LGBT persons have liberty rights equal to those of different-sex couples. Whereas *Lawrence* eschewed the Equal Protection Clause as an independent ground for its holding, however, the *Obergefell* Court explicitly adopted both provisions, finding that the right of same-sex couples to marry was protected "under the Due Process

and Equal Protection Clauses of the Fourteenth Amendment." Where does this leave the law of equal protection as applied to sexual orientation classifications? Has the doctrine changed since *Romer v. Evans*? How would a *Loving*-like opinion been different? Do the differences matter?

More fundamentally, why has equal liberty emerged as the dominant paradigm for LGBT and reproductive issues? Some possibilities:

(a) Justice Kennedy is more of a libertarian than any of the four more consistently progressive or liberal Justices. For him, the central question revolves around how the courts should resolve the tension between individual freedom and the values of society as expressed in legislation. As he wrote in *Lawrence*, quoting the *Casey* Joint Opinion, "Our obligation is to define the liberty of all, not to impose our own moral code." Each individual is entitled to respect and to sufficient leeway to enjoy freedom as others do. In his view, sexual orientation is not volitional; therefore to deny the value of lesbian and gay lives is to demean and deny the humanity of one's fellow Americans based on a characteristic not within an individual's control or susceptible to change. Query what his reactions might be if confronted with a case involving bisexual persons who frankly acknowledge attraction to both sexes.

(b) In addition to a pull toward liberty, there may also be something of a push away from the strongest form of equal protection politics. Justice Kennedy often finds himself aligned with his more conservative colleagues on sex discrimination issues and has become the Court's center on many questions of race discrimination, with a somewhat unpredictable vote. His concern with equality separate from liberty manifests in his insistence on state respect for the dignity of all citizens. In fact, dignity has come to seem almost its own new thread of constitutional jurisprudence. In some countries (e.g., South Africa) dignity is a right protected by explicit constitutional text. In the U.S., what, if anything, does dignity add to individual rights?

(c) Sexuality exceptionalism may also play a part. Equal liberty has become the dominant theme in the Supreme Court's LGB rights jurisprudence, as imported from *Casey* and from the Stevens dissent in *Hardwick*. As noted earlier, *Skinner v. Oklahoma* presages this development; it, too, was a reproductive rights case (involving forced sterilization). Will equal liberty emerge in other doctrinal areas as well? Consider its potential as a grounding for Free Exercise Clause jurisprudence when you read Chapter 4.

2. *The Liberty-Conformity Paradox.* Justice Kennedy's opinion reflects a very high regard for marriage—as the foundation of family *and* society *and* government, "without which there would be neither civilization or progress." Reading the opinion, one feels like the Court wants everyone to get married—at least to avoid the existential loneliness that Justice Kennedy depicts for those who are unmarried. (Note that his three female colleagues are all unmarried—one a widow, one divorced, and one never married.) What is the purpose of so much marriage celebration? Was it necessary? Is it counterproductive for LGBT persons or ominous for anyone who chooses not to marry? For the concept of liberty in the realm of family life? See Nan D. Hunter, "Interpreting Liberty and Equality Through the Lens of Marriage," 6 *Calif. L. Rev. Circuit* 105 (2015).

3. *Positive and Negative Liberty.* In dissent, Justice Thomas pointed out that due process "liberty" has traditionally been freedom *from* government interference in our private lives. (This was true even in *Loving*, which involved Virginia's criminal prosecution of the inter-racial couple.) Marriage, however, is a highly regulatory institution. Its function is more disciplinary than liberatory. Even Justice Kennedy would have to admit that each spouse gives up a lot of liberties (including sexual freedoms) when he or she gets married. Recall the channeling effect of marriage that Justice Cordy's dissent in *Goodridge* sought to preserve for different-sex couples; has it simply been extended, in modified form, to same-sex couples?

It appears (to us) that the Court is presenting a modern, regulatory, and hierarchical understanding of liberty. One role of government is to provide a productive structure within which each of us makes choices, always seeking to create a distinctively flourishing life. The "liberty" in the marriage cases is a freedom to marry the partner who will make you happy and enable your joint flourishing; this is a "positive" liberty, not the "negative" liberty Justice Thomas invokes. On this view, because lesbian and gay Americans would not flourish in a different-sex marriage, their freedom is effectively circumscribed unless they have access to dignifying and reinforcing and benefit-conferring civil marriage. But should the institution of marriage be structured as such a powerful gatekeeper to flourishing?

4. *The Public-Private Border.* Although LGBT rights groups would have appreciated a Supreme Court holding that sexual orientation is a suspect classification, such a holding might have seemed premature or risky to Justice Kennedy. In particular, Justice Kennedy might have been concerned that formally elevating sexual orientation discrimination to the same level as race and sex discrimination would have spillover effects for too many realms of private association. A libertarian like Justice Kennedy might argue that change in civil society is less destabilizing when driven from the ground up, as is happening in the Boy Scouts, who have ended their ban on gay scoutmasters after having successfully defended it in the Supreme Court. *Boy Scouts v. Dale* (Chapter 1, Section 3D). (Recall that Justice Kennedy was the fifth vote for the majority in that decision.) Note the tension between sheltering the private sphere and the concept of equal dignity.

5. *Religious Liberty.* Justice Kennedy also did not want to disrespect Americans who for religious or other reasons believe that marriage ought to remain tethered to the traditional definition. In dissent, Justice Alito worried that supporters of traditional marriage were going to be "vilified" for their beliefs, just as people who believe in racial segregation today would be ostracized as bigots. Justice Alito's dissenting opinion raised a concern that had been voiced at oral argument: If sexual orientation is a suspect classification, like race, would the Internal Revenue Service not have to say that churches, schools, and other "charitable" associations with anti-gay policies were ineligible for the § 501(c)(3) federal income tax exemption? Private entities discriminating on the basis of race do not receive such exemptions. See *Bob Jones Univ. v. United States,* 461 U.S. 574 (1983). Solicitor General Donald Verelli, arguing in support of the plaintiffs, responded that he did not know whether tax exemptions could be put at risk, at some point in the future, by sexual orientation discrimination. For extensive analysis of the conflicts between equality principles and religious liberty arguments, see Chapter 4, *infra.*

6. Lochner, *Tradition and Marriage.* Chief Justice Roberts argued in dissent that the majority was resuscitating the ghost of *Lochner,* the leading substantive due process decision for economic liberty of contract. For the same reasons Justice Holmes rejected *Lochner'*s aggrandizement of judicial power untethered by constitutional text or original meaning, Chief Justice Roberts rejected what he saw as the Court's power grab in *Obergefell.* The Chief acknowledged that the right to marry is fundamental even though it is not mentioned in the text, but distinguished the right to marry cases on the ground that all of them assumed different-sex marriage. Petitioners were asking the Court to *redefine marriage*—a pretty tall order for unelected officials. "Just who do we think we are?" wondered the Chief Justice.

The Roberts-Kennedy debate over *Lochner* was, at the doctrinal level, a debate about how to read the "traditions" that inform the Court's application of substantive due process. Recall that in the leading pre-*Lawrence* analysis, Chief Justice Rehnquist's opinion for the Court (joined by Justice Kennedy) insisted on longstanding tradition at a specific level to support a fundamental liberty right. *Washington v. Glucksberg, supra.* In *Obergefell,* Justice Kennedy associated *Glucksberg* with the discredited opinion in *Bowers* and then jettisoned the historical specificity demanded by both decisions. However, there was no explicit overruling of *Glucksberg.* Will the *Glucksberg* approach return in future cases? *See* Kenji Yoshino, "A New Birth of Freedom?: *Obergefell v. Hodges,*" 129 *Harv. L. Rev.* 147 (2015).

7. *Collateral Rights.* Two years after *Obergefell,* the Court struck down an Arkansas statute under which birth certificates were required to list only the birth mother's male spouse, even when the sperm was contributed by a donor. The Court held that the statute denied to lesbian couples the same "constellation of benefits that the Stat[e] ha[s] linked to [different-sex] marriage" as required by *Obergefell. Pavan v. Smith,* 137 S.Ct. ___, 2017 WL 2722472 (2017); see Chapter 7, Section 3A. Within days, a very different view of the "constellation of [marriage] benefits" emerged from the Texas Supreme Court. *Pidgeon v. Turner,* ___ S.W.3d ___, 2017 WL 2829350 (2017), a case challenging a Houston city policy of awarding the same job benefits to its employees in same-sex as in different-sex marriages, was remanded to the trial court for consideration of whether *Obergefell* controlled. According to the Texas Supreme Court, *Obergefell* "did not hold that states must provide the same publicly funded benefits to all married persons." If the composition of the U.S. Supreme Court changes, will the broad sweep of *Obergefell* be endangered?

8. *Backlash and Next Steps.* With the winning of marriage equality, both the LGBT rights movement and the traditional values movement faced a new reality. Imagine that you are called upon by an advocacy group in each movement to offer proposals for how to take the greatest advantage of the post-*Obergefell* political and legal environment. What will you advise? Certainly one major battleground will be over whether individuals and businesses can claim exemptions based on religion from having to comply with recognition of same-sex marriages or anti-discrimination laws. See Chapter 4, *infra*. As described in the previous note, collateral benefits may also become subject to dispute. What other issues do you expect to arise?

PROBLEM 2-6
THE SCOPE OF *OBERGEFELL*

How broadly or narrowly courts will interpret the principles of *Obergefell* remains an open question. Consider the best arguments for and against the constitutionality of two possible laws:

(a) A polyamorous trio of persons in the state of Massafornia bring a challenge to the limitation of marriage to two persons. A, B, and C are raising two children together; live together; have a joint banking account; and describe their household as a "stable relationship of 12 years duration."

(b) The state of Georgiana enacts a law requiring schools in grades 7 through 12 to include in their mandatory health curriculum materials "an emphasis on the greater contribution of different-sex marriage, compared to same-sex marriage, to public and personal well-being." (See Chapter 8, Section 3.) Note that Georgiana already has a law requiring that the same curriculum include materials expressing the state's belief that "human life begins at conception."

NOTE ON THE POLITICS AND FUTURE OF MARRIAGE

Progressives seek a regime of equality that is more than formal; a truly egalitarian model would be transformative. Queer theorists have taken up this theme to interrogate the extent to which the goal of securing same-sex marriage was prioritized and whether there will be negative as well as positive results from its success. The debate originated before any nation had legalized same-sex marriage, and it continues now that marriage equality is the law of the land. (See generally, Chapter 3, Section 3 and Chapter 6, Section 2.)

Paula L. Ettelbrick, "Since When Is Marriage a Path to Liberation?"

OUT/LOOK, Autumn 1989, Pages 8–12.[*]

* * * Marriage runs contrary to two of the primary goals of the lesbian and gay movement: the affirmation of gay identity and culture and the validation of many forms of relationships. * * *

The fight for justice has as its goal the realignment of power imbalances among individuals and classes of people in society. A pure "rights" analysis often fails to incorporate a broader understanding of the underlying inequities that operate to deny justice to a fuller range of people and groups. * * * At this point in time, making legal marriage for lesbian and gay couples a priority would set an agenda of gaining rights for a few, but would do nothing to correct power imbalances between those who are married (whether gay or straight) and those who are not. Thus, justice would not be gained.

Justice for gay men and lesbians will be achieved only when we are accepted and supported in this society *despite* our difference from the dominant culture and the choices we make regarding our relationships. * * * Being queer means pushing the parameters of sex, sexuality, and family, and in the process transforming the very fabric of society. Gay liberation is inexorably linked to women's liberation. Each is essential to the other.

The moment we argue, as some amongst us insist on doing, that we should be treated as equals because we are really just like married couples and hold the same values to be true, we undermine the very purpose of our movement and begin the dangerous process of silencing our different voices. As a lesbian, I am fundamentally different from nonlesbian women. That's the point. Marriage, as it exists today, is antithetical to my liberation as a lesbian and as a woman because it mainstreams my life and voice. I do not want to be known as "Mrs. Attached-To-Somebody-Else." Nor do I want to give the state the power to regulate my primary relationship. * * *

The thought of emphasizing our sameness to married heterosexuals in order to obtain this "right" terrifies me. It rips away the very heart and soul of what I believe it is to be a lesbian in this world. It robs me of the opportunity to make a difference. We end up mimicking all that is bad about the institution of marriage in our effort to appear to be the same as straight couples.

By looking to our sameness and de-emphasizing our differences, we do not even place ourselves in a position of power that would allow us to transform marriage from an institution that emphasizes property and state regulation of relationships to an institution that recognizes one of many types of valid and respected relationships. * * * We would be

---

[*]   Reprinted by permission of the author.

perpetuating the elevation of married relationships and of "couples" in general, and further eclipsing other relationships of choice.

Ironically, gay marriage, instead of liberating gay sex and sexuality, would further outlaw all gay and lesbian sex that is not performed in a marital context. Just as sexually active nonmarried women face stigma and double standards around sex and sexual activity, so too would nonmarried gay people. * * *

Undoubtedly, whether we admit it or not, we all need to be accepted by the broader society. * * * Those closer to the norm or to power in this country are more likely to see marriage as a principle of freedom and equality. Those who are more acceptable to the mainstream because of race, gender, and economic status are more likely to want the right to marry. It is the final acceptance, the ultimate affirmation of identity.

On the other hand, more marginal members of the lesbian and gay community (women, people of color, working class and poor) are less likely to see marriage as having relevance to our struggles for survival. After all, what good is the affirmation of our relationships (that is, marital relationships) if we are rejected as women, people of color, or working class? * * *

If the laws change tomorrow and lesbians and gay men were allowed to marry, where would we find the incentive to continue the progressive movement we have started that is pushing for societal and legal recognition of all kinds of family relationships? To create other options and alternatives? * * * To get the law to acknowledge that we may have more than one relationship worthy of legal protection? * * *

Thomas Stoddard, "Why Gay People Should Seek the Right to Marry"
OUT/LOOK, Autumn 1989, Pages 8–12.*

* * * [D]espite the oppressive nature of marriage historically, and in spite of the general absence of edifying examples of modern heterosexual marriage, I believe very strongly that every lesbian and gay man should have the right to marry the same-sex partner of his or her choice, and that the gay rights movement should aggressively seek full legal recognition for same-sex marriages. To those who may not agree, I respectfully offer three explanations, one practical, one political, and one philosophical.

The legal status of marriage rewards the two individuals who travel to the altar (or its secular equivalent) with substantial economic and practical advantages. Married couples * * * are entitled to special government benefits, such as those given surviving spouses and dependents through the Social Security program. They can inherit from one another even when there is no will. They are immune from subpoenas

---

*   Reprinted by permission of the author.

requiring testimony against the other spouse. And marriage to an American citizen gives a foreigner a right to residency in the United States.

Other advantages have arisen not by law but by custom. Most employers offer health insurance to their employees, and many will include an employer's spouse in the benefits package, usually at the employer's expense. Virtually no employer will include a partner who is not married to an employee, whether of the same sex or not. * * *

In short, the law generally presumes in favor of every marital relationship, and acts to preserve and foster it, and to enhance the rights of the individuals who enter into it. It is usually possible, with enough money and the right advice, to replicate some of the benefits conferred by the legal status of marriage through the use of documents like wills and power-of-attorney forms, but that protection will inevitably, under current circumstances, be incomplete. [Stoddard notes the "suspicion" many judges cast upon documents protecting lesbian and gay families, the cost of obtaining such documents, and the inability of private contracting to affect the public advantages of marriage, such as spousal immunities.]

* * * Why devote resources to such a distant goal? Because marriage is, I believe, the political issue that most fully tests the dedication of people who are not gay to full equality for gay people, and it is also the issue most likely to lead ultimately to a world free from discrimination against lesbians and gay men.

Marriage is much more than a relationship sanctioned by law. It is the centerpiece of our entire social structure, the core of the traditional notion of "family." Even in its present tarnished state, the marital relationship inspires sentiments suggesting that it is something almost suprahuman. The Supreme Court, in striking down an anticontraception statute in 1965, called marriage "noble" and "intimate to the degree of being sacred." * * *

Lesbians and gay men are now denied entry to this "noble" and "sacred" institution. The implicit message is this: two men or two women are incapable of achieving such an exalted domestic state. Gay relationships are somehow less significant, less valuable. Such relationships may, from time to time and from couple to couple, give the appearance of a marriage, but they can never be of the same quality or importance.

I resent—indeed, I loathe—that conception of same-sex relationships. And I am convinced that ultimately the only way to overturn it is to remove the barrier to marriage that now limits the freedom of every gay man and lesbian. * * *

I confessed at the outset that I personally found marriage in its present state rather unattractive. Nonetheless, even from a philosophical perspective, I believe the right to marry should become a goal of the gay-rights movement.

First, and most basically, the issue is not the desirability of marriage, but rather the desirability of the *right* to marry. That I think two lesbians or two gay men should be entitled to a marriage license does not mean that I think all gay people should find appropriate partners and exercise the right, should it eventually exist. * * *

Furthermore, marriage may be unattractive and even oppressive as it is currently structured and practiced, but enlarging the concept to embrace same-sex couples would necessarily transform it into something new. If two women can marry, or two men, marriage—even for heterosexuals—need not be a union of a "husband" and a "wife." Extending the right to marry to gay people—that is, abolishing the traditional gender requirements of marriage—can be one of the means, perhaps the principal one, through which the institution divests itself of the sexist trappings of the past. * * *

NOTES AND QUESTIONS

As the LGBT rights movement goes forward into a future in which marriage equality is the norm, many themes raised during the Ettelbrick-Stoddard exchange remain relevant.

1.   *Assimilation and New Bases for Stratification.* Ettelbrick argued for radical transformation and faulted the same-sex marriage campaign for sacrificing the transformative features of gay liberation. Both Ettelbrick and Nancy Polikoff asserted that the primary goal instead should be for family law to abandon civil marriage as the central institution for relationship and parental recognition. See, especially, Nancy D. Polikoff, *Beyond Gay (and Straight) Marriage* (2008). Related to assimilation, Ettelbrick and Polikoff were also concerned with the normalizing features of marriage—the coercive social pressure on *everyone* to get married and the delegitimation of non-marital unions of either straight or gay couples. Stoddard's arguments can be characterized as positive toward the process of assimilation. If neither position is entirely right or wrong, how should a legal regime be structured to maximize human flourishing? For a critique of assimilationism throughout the LGBT rights movement, see Urvashi Vaid, *Virtual Equality: The Mainstreaming of Gay and Lesbian Liberation* (1995).

2.   *Selective State Regulation.* In *Wedlocked: The Perils of Marriage Equality* (2015), Katherine Franke analyzes how the advent of marriage under the law for formerly enslaved persons led to alteration, rather than elimination, of restraints on individual freedom. Recognition of slave marriages after the American Civil War was often the occasion for the state to impose its conceptions of sexual fidelity and monogamy on unions that had been more flexibly organized before the law entered the picture. She attributes the difference between that state policy and the much more positive way that society has responded to same-sex marriage to the different structures of race and homophobia: "By design or not, the gay community

has been able to leverage its social capital in whiteness to their advantage in the marriage equality movement, yet African Americans have received little benefit in any endowment they might enjoy from the stereotype that all or most black people are heterosexual." *Id.* at 198.

3. *Sexual Liberty.* One of us has embraced the possibility that same-sex marriage might contribute to the normalization of monogamy or fewer sexual partners. Eskridge, *Case for Same-Sex Marriage* ch. 1. Some fear that this position could be understood as a critique of "excessive" liberation and derogate from gay liberation's valorization of sexual pleasure. On the other hand, data indicate that gay male couples continue to have a larger number of sexual partners—including during marriage—than either heterosexual or lesbian couples. Should family law explicitly allow for open marriages?

4. *Could Same-Sex Marriage Change the Institution for the Better?* One of us has argued: "Marriage between men or between women could also destabilize the cultural meaning of marriage. It would create for the first time the possibility of marriage as a relationship between members of the same social status categories. However valiantly individuals try to build marriages grounded on genuine equality, no person can erase his or her status in the world as male or female, or create a home life apart from culture. Same-sex marriage could create the model in law for an egalitarian kind of interpersonal relation, outside the gendered terms of power, for many marriages. At the least, it would radically strengthen and dramatically illuminate the claim that marriage partners are presumptively equal." Nan D. Hunter, "Marriage, Law, and Gender: A Feminist Inquiry," *1 Law & Sexuality* 9, 11 (1991).

Nancy Polikoff responded with a prediction, based upon historical and anthropological evidence that another of us collected, that same-sex partners would tend to adopt and act out traditional gender roles. (Polikoff, "We Will Get What We Ask For," 79 Va. L. Rev. 1535, 1538 (1993); see Eskridge, *Case for Same-Sex Marriage* ch. 2.)

In **"The Future Impact of Same-Sex Marriage: More Questions Than Answers," 100** *Geo. L. J.* **1855, 1866–68 (2012),** Hunter updated data relevant to some of the 1990s debate points:

> * * * A number of studies have found, on average, that division of household labor is most egalitarian between same-sex partners, and more egalitarian in different-sex cohabiting couples than in different-sex married couples. A host of other factors may be implicated, however, and may affect how a couple divides domestic labor, such as the presence of children, the power dynamics related to being the sole biological parent in a couple, income differences between partners, the length of the relationship, women's experience of and commitment to employment outside the home, and the strength of individual desire to conform to gender expectations. For different-sex couples, division of labor tends to be accomplished in less traditional ways in couples who cohabited prior to marriage, than in those who did not, suggesting either a selection effect—individuals for whom household-work equality is

more important may be more likely to cohabit prior to marriage—or that the experience of cohabitation itself has an impact.

Another dimension of the household-labor issue is the distinction between specialization and gender normativity. The division-of-household-labor gap is decreasing between different- and same-sex couples, but versions of that pattern exist in both groups. In an ethnographic study of 52 gay and lesbian couples in the San Francisco Bay area, sociologist Christopher Carrington found that one person "specialize[d] in domesticity" in 75% of the couples, and that the tendency to specialize increased with the length of the relationship. Carrington, who did not compare his sample with different-sex couples, concluded that gay families were reacting to the broader economic pressure to maximize household income by having the partner with lower earning potential assume more of the domestic chores. Obviously, in same-sex couples, that individual's identity does not align with a sex category different from the other partner. Conversely, different-sex couples have responded to the economic pressure to have two income earners in the household (as well as to individual pressure from the female partner) by mitigating the amount of domestic labor once assumed almost entirely by the (often stay-at-home) wife. Husbands, who typically earn the higher income, now do a greater share of household work than before, although seldom an equal share. * * *

* * * [A]nother major marker of difference between gay and straight relationships pertains to children. A large majority of heterosexual couples have children, but only about one in six same-sex couples raise children. The decision to marry is often associated with the decision to become parents. At least at the moment, the percentage of same-sex couples who are raising children is dropping, probably because the pattern of raising children from the prior heterosexual marriage of one or both partners is fading, as younger lesbians and gay men are less inclined to pass through a heterosexual marriage stage before coming out. (This pattern is somewhat mitigated by same-sex couples who choose to adopt children.) If the overall trend away from child raising continues, it may signal a de-heteronormalization effect, in which individuals who felt social pressure to become parents while in a heterosexual marriage can more easily discount that pressure once they adopt a lesbian or gay social identity. * * *

In making the decision whether to have children, race appears to be a more salient factor than sexual orientation. In the population as a whole, households in which one or both adults are a racial or ethnic minority are more likely to include children. Similarly, same-sex couples in which at least one individual is a person of color are substantially more likely than white same-sex couples to be raising a child: African-Americans are 2.4 times more likely and Latinos and Latinas are 1.7 times more likely to be in parenting households. Future trends in childbearing among persons of color, rather than among gay and lesbian couples, may better predict the percentage of same-sex couples who decide to raise children. * * *

PROBLEM 2-7
NEXT GENERATION MARRIAGE LAW

Now that sexual orientation is no longer the dividing line between legal regimes governing adult relationships, consider whether the law of marriage and divorce might more logically be organized along lines of whether a couple has children. How might the rules differ for the two types of couples? See Chapters 6 and 7, *infra*.

CHAPTER 3

THEORIES OF SEXUALITY, GENDER, AND THE LAW

SECTION 1   Natural Law Theories of Sexuality, Gender, and the Law
SECTION 2   Modern or Liberal Theories of Sexuality, Gender, and the Law
SECTION 3   Post-Liberal Theories of Sexuality, Gender, and the Law

One reason that our society finds it so difficult to resolve issues related to sexuality and gender is that we disagree so fundamentally about even what it is we are talking about. Three substantially irreconcilable models form the bases for most contemporary thinking about sexuality:

- Sexuality as a *natural force* grounded in universals, which society has the moral and ethical obligation to encourage in its healthy manifestations and discourage in its "distorted" forms.

- Sexuality as a *biological force* grounded in the individual body or psyche, usually described as a "sex drive," which society, usually with great futility, seeks to constrain.

- Sexuality as a *social production*, the result of the complex interaction of the particularities of the cultural and historical eras in which we live and the patterns of socialization that we experience.

Likewise, gender is conceptualized as a natural force flowing from one's natural sex, as a biological consequence of hormones, or as a social production. Most debate in the legal arena still is limited to the first and second of these models; this chapter will open with theories of these sorts. It is the third model, however, which is producing most of the current scholarship on theories of sexuality, and it is on variants of this approach that we focus much of this chapter.

Section 1 examines *natural law* theories. The best known natural law theories are rooted in philosophy and religion, especially the doctrines developed by the Roman Catholic Church. Because they proceed from axioms or religious beliefs, they are arguably premodern forms of thinking. As articulated by current writers such as John Finnis, Robert George, and Gerard Bradley, the "new" natural law offers a non-religious model premised upon the idea that procreative marital sex is the only valid form of sexual intercourse. Theirs is a sophisticated but difficult theory for modern intellectuals, in part because it is non-instrumental and in part because it rests upon premises that are widely shared but hard to demonstrate to someone who does not already believe them (or the conclusions that derive from them).

Section 2 explores modern theories, by which we mean theories that are as a positive matter interested in sexuality and gender as biological forces and as a normative matter tend to focus on individual dignity or social utility (or both). These modern theories tend to be *liberal*. Descriptively, liberal theories assume a wide range of sexual or gender variation within the human population. Normatively, liberal theories accept that variation is presumptively benign and resist social or state standardization that suppresses or penalizes that variety. Arguments for regulation of sexuality or gender role focus on harm to third parties. British philosophers Jeremy Bentham and John Stuart Mill are the intellectual parents of this kind of thinking, and Judge Richard Posner and Nobel laureate Gary Becker are leading exemplars today.

Also in Section 2, we examine the important feminist theories of gender and sexuality, namely, those which view issues of sexuality and gender from the perspective or interests of women. Professor Catharine MacKinnon was the first legal academic to propound an ambitious theory of sexuality, gender, and the law. Hers is a theory about social and political power. It is illiberal in its argument that women's social inferiority is deeply rooted in a male-dominated "man fucks woman" understanding of sexuality, a gendered understanding accepted by many women as well as most men. It is feminist in its call for consciousness raising among women to critique their own desires and to reclaim their humanity. It is liberal in its insistence that the Hobbesian state ensure women's freedom from sexual violence, gender-based discrimination, and social denigration.

Professor MacKinnon's theory has generated reform proposals, heated disagreement, and competing theories. Gayle Rubin, for example, rejects MacKinnon's close association of sexuality and gender role and supports a pro-sex understanding of feminism. Likewise, Professor Robin West maintains that MacKinnon's "critique of desire" is mistaken; women's sexual feelings are authentic, and their gendered identity is socially valuable. Responding to both West and MacKinnon, Professors Angela Harris and Kimberlé Crenshaw argue that these feminist theorists understand problems through the perspectives of white women and that theory needs to incorporate the experiences of women of color, people at the "intersection" of race and sex.

Section 2 closes with theories focusing on the role of transgender and intersex persons in the politics of sexuality, gender, and the law. Transsex author Julia Serano offers a theory of sex and gender that is both deeply feminist and a challenge to some feminist assumptions. Mary

Dunlap explains how intersex as well as transgender persons challenge traditional understandings of sex and gender.

Section 3 introduces what we have grouped together as *post-liberal* theories, those that view sexuality and gender as social constructions rather than natural or biological categories. Recently, scholars have paid special attention to how discourse (a system consisting of texts, beliefs, and/or actions) functions both to organize social practices and to constitute our individual understandings and experiences of, for example, gender and sexuality. Note that there is some overlap with the writers in Section 2 as well, because Gayle Rubin, for example, can be characterized as a social constructionist. In general, though, the materials in Section 3 tend to differ from those in Section 2 in that they describe sexuality and gender as driven by forces more diverse and dispersed than either patriarchy (feminism) or the market or capitalism (economic theory). Michel Foucault is often viewed as the primary expositor of this school of thought. Judith Butler's work builds on Foucault's, adding a more explicitly feminist approach. Eve Kosofsky Sedgwick shows how our tropes of sexuality, prominently the homosexual/heterosexual dichotomy, reveal the complex interdependence of identities that other theories treat as disparate.

PROBLEM 3-1
APPLICATION OF THEORY TO CONSTITUTIONAL ISSUES OF SEXUALITY AND GENDER

Chapters 1 and 2—presenting the rights of sexual privacy, equal protection, and free expression—are largely doctrinal; the chapters contained legal and constitutional theory produced by law professors drawing from the overall purposes of the Due Process and Equal Protection Clauses, the First Amendment, and other legal materials. In this chapter, we shall present more conceptual theories of sexuality and gender; for the most part, these theories have been generated by intellectuals outside of law schools. But all of them have potential relevance for issues of public law, and we now challenge you to consider the implications of different theories for the cutting edge issues of privacy and equality law surveyed in the previous chapters.

Assume a federal appeals court consisting of the following: (1) natural law scholar John Finnis; (2) economics-minded thinker Richard Posner; and (3) feminist theorist Catharine MacKinnon. In constitutional cases, this Court is weakly constrained by stare decisis; its Justices can rethink precedents contrary to their theoretical commitments and can construe precedents narrowly or broadly. How would each of these Justices analyze the following cutting-edge issues:

(a) Should *Griswold*, *Eisenstadt*, and *Lawrence* be overruled? If not, should they be extended to invalidate statutes making it a crime for adult first cousins to have consensual sexual intercourse? Statutes criminalizing sexual cohabitation? Statutes requiring public school students (including transgender persons) to use bathrooms matching their birth certificates?

(b) Was the VMI Case correctly decided? Specifically, was it unconstitutional for VMI to have excluded women? If so, what remedy was appropriate? Today, would it be unconstitutional for VMI to discriminate against otherwise qualified transgender applicants? Against an intersex person, such as someone with XX chromosomes (associated with being a woman) but also testes (associated with being a man)?

(c) Does the Constitution require the state to extend the institution of civil marriage to same-sex couples? If so, under what constitutional provision? Does the Constitution require the state to recognize unions of more than two consenting adults (*i.e.*, polygamous unions)?

For each ruling by this made-up court, consider, next, what critique would be leveled against it by critical thinkers such as Michel Foucault, Judith Butler, and Dean Spade, all discussed in Section 3.

SECTION 1

NATURAL LAW THEORIES OF SEXUALITY, GENDER, AND THE LAW

We start with a theory of sexual activity and gender role as old as Plato and Aristotle—natural law. Such theory posits humans' *natural* or *universal* needs or constitution and argues for certain *basic goods* that best meet those needs or best fit that constitution. A natural law argument proceeds in this way: (1) The order of nature (human nature however conceptualized) entails a certain basic good. (2) The practice in question is inconsistent with or undermines that basic good. (3) That practice is therefore morally wrong ("unnatural"). For example, (1) human life is a basic good; (2) abortion (and, for many natural law thinkers, contraception) destroys human life; therefore, (3) abortion (contraception) is morally wrong. According to most natural law theories, other basic (or fundamental or natural) goods are *integrity of self*, the harmony of all the parts of a person which can be engaged in freely chosen action, and *marriage*, the procreative union of a husband and a wife committed to one another and to their children.

Roman Catholic theology, epitomized by St. Augustine's *De Bono Conjugali* and St. Thomas Aquinas's *Summa Theologica*, is the best known form of natural law theory. A classic restatement can be found in Joseph Cardinal Ratzinger & Angelo Amato, Congregation for the Doctrine of the Faith, "Considerations Regarding Proposals to Give Legal Recognition to Unions Between Homosexual Persons" (June 3, 2003). The "natural truth" about marriage is found in the divine "Revelation contained in the biblical accounts of creation, an expression also of the original human wisdom, in which the voice of nature itself is heard." *Id.* ¶ 3. Extrapolating from God's Word in the Book of Genesis, the document announced three principles that are foundational to the Roman Catholic Church's theory of sexuality, gender, and law:

> In the first place, man, the image of God, was created "male and female" (*Gen* 1:27). Men and women are equal as persons and complementary as male and female. Sexuality is something that pertains to the physical-biological realm and has also been raised to a new level—the personal level—where nature and spirit are united.

> Marriage is instituted by the Creator as a form of life in which a communion of persons is realized involving the use of the sexual faculty. "That is why a man leaves his father and

mother and clings to his wife and they become one flesh" (*Gen* 2:24).

> Third, God has willed to give the union of man and woman a special participation in his work of creation. Thus, he blessed the man and the woman with the words "Be fruitful and multiply" (*Gen* 1:28). Therefore, in the Creator's plan, sexual complementarity and fruitfulness belong to the very nature of marriage.

Id. As a corollary to these precepts, the document reasoned that "homosexual acts go against the natural moral law." *Id.* ¶ 4. Because state recognition of same-sex marriages would encourage people into moral fault, the document urged the devout to oppose civil recognition. *Id.* ¶ 5. "Civil laws are structuring principles of man's life in society, for good or for ill. They 'play a very important and sometimes decisive role in influencing patterns of thought and behaviour'. Lifestyles and the underlying presuppositions these express not only externally shape the life of society, but also tend to modify the younger generation's perception and evaluation of forms of behaviour. Legal recognition of homosexual unions would obscure certain basic moral values and cause a devaluation of the institution of marriage." *Id.* ¶ 6. For a recent reaffirmation of these general principles of doctrine, see Pope Francis I, Post-Synodal Exhortation, *Amoris Laetitia* (April 2016) ("On Love in the Family").

The views expressed in the Congregation's "Considerations" are not unique to Catholic theologians, however; the Protestant denominations that dominated the American colonies and the faith tradition of the early United States articulated a similar philosophy. Thus, in the nineteenth century, social norms and legal rules were organized around the biological binary of *man* and *woman*. What we would call a person's gendered traits or sexual roles, linguistically as well as culturally, were indistinguishable from the biological categories. Noah Webster's *An American Dictionary of the English Language* (1828) defined "gender" as "[a] sex, male or female" and "sexuality" to be "[t]he state of being distinguished by sex." Each sex carried with it assumed traits and roles that were considered essential features of being a man or a woman. Consistent with faith-based natural law, the traits and roles were tied to procreation within God-sanctioned marriage: a woman's highest calling was to be a wife or mother, so that her sex-based roles were private, domestic, and nurturing; a man's highest calling was to be the head of the household, so that his sex-based roles were public, economic, and civic. Figure 3-1, below, diagrams the relationship among sex, gender, and sexuality that has traditionally been the premise of natural law theory. See William N. Eskridge Jr., "Sexual and Gender Variation in American Public Law: From Malignant to Tolerable to Benign," 57 *UCLA L. Rev.* 1333 (2010).

Figure 3-1. The Natural Law Model of Sexuality and Gender

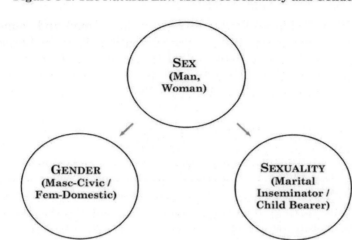

These natural law premises saturated American public law. Until the late twentieth century, American criminal law prohibited procreative intercourse outside of marriage and nonprocreative intercourse (sodomy, or anal sex) within or outside of marriage. Cross-dressing was a crime in most large cities. Property and contract law, as well as family law, cemented a gendered division of labor within the household, where inseminating husbands held legal and economic authority—a power that found a parallel in the exclusion of women from the armed forces, juries, and the voting booth. Although early feminists were successful in repealing many of the legal disabilities imposed upon wives and all women (culminating in voting rights through the Nineteenth Amendment), Congress and state legislatures adopted new legal restrictions on abortion, contraception, oral sex, excessive hours for women, sex work outside the home, etc. These new restrictions were inspired by religious natural law premises, but were justified by "scientific" experts in medicine and other fields. See William N. Eskridge Jr., *Gaylaw: Challenging the Apartheid of the Closet* (1999); Carroll Smith-Rosenberg, *Disorderly Conduct: Visions of Gender in Victorian America* (1985).

In the latter half of the twentieth century, many of the newer as well as old natural law restrictions fell by the wayside—and religion-based rules came under sustained attack. In the last generation, natural law theory has staged a comeback, however. Oxford Professor John Finnis is the leading representative of a *new natural law* theory,[a] an effort to

---

[a]   E.g., John Finnis, *Natural Law and Natural Rights* (1980); Finnis, "Marriage: A Basic and Exigent Good," 91 *Monist* 388 (2008); Finnis, "The Good of Marriage and the Morality of Sexual Relations: Some Philosophical and Historical Observations," 42 *Am. J. Juris.* 97 (1997); Other leading scholars in the new natural law tradition are Robert P. George, see George, *In Defense of Natural Law* (1999), and Gerard V. Bradley, see Bradley, *Essays on Law, Morality, and Religion* (2009). See also Patrick Lee & Robert P. George, *Body-Self Dualism in Contemporary Ethics and Politics* 179–220 (2008).

develop a systematic natural law philosophy of sexuality that is not dependent on religious authority in the way the Vatican documents are. One of the features of this kind of philosophy is its *non-consequentialism*. Whereas most modern moralists rely on utilitarian balancing or some hierarchy of values, Finnis and allied thinkers maintain that natural basic goods are incommensurable and can never validly be sacrificed; they also maintain that the primary principle of morality is to choose those actions which are consistent with "integral human fulfillment." Accordingly, a decision is judged not by its consequences, but by its consistency with integral human fulfillment.

Thus, new natural law theorists have a distinctive understanding of marriage. They agree that marital communion serves instrumental goals, such as procreation, and is a good environment for rearing those children. But marriage also serves non-instrumental ends, such as the "good of friendship," which is "promoted and realized by the propagation of the human race, and the intrinsic good of inner integration [is] promoted and realized by the remedying of the disordered desires of concupiscence." Even when the marital union does not produce children, it serves the "further good of marriage, the natural *societas* (companionship) of the two sexes." Finnis, "Law, Morality, and 'Sexual Orientation,' " 69 *Notre Dame L. Rev.* 1049, 1064 (1994).

Professor Finnis claims that the foregoing conception of the good has its roots in classical thought (Plato, Aristotle, Plutarch) and therefore represents a timeless philosophy not limited to religious theorists.[b] In *Gorgias,* for example, Plato criticizes hedonism, the notion that people should maximize their pleasure. Simply finding pleasure in sexual acts— whether solitary masturbation or sodomy or intercourse outside of marriage—is not morally worthy, for it uses and therefore degrades the body. Only marital intercourse involves the self-giving and unitive experience that distinguishes human beings from animals.

New natural law thinkers, such as Professor Robert George of Princeton, contrast this "conjugal" understanding of marriage against the "hedonic" understanding. See Sherif Girgis, Ryan T. Anderson & Robert P. George, *What Is Marriage? Man and Woman: A Defense* (2014). The conjugal understanding sees marriage as "a bodily as well as an emotional and spiritual bond, distinguished by its comprehensiveness, which is, like all love, *effusive*: flowing out into the wide sharing of family life and ahead to lifelong fidelity." *Id.* at 1. Thus, marriage is "the community formed by a man and a woman who publicly consent to share their whole lives, in a relationship oriented toward begetting, nurturing

---

[b]   The difference between the old and the new natural law theory is that the latter (represented by Finnis) relies on the consensus of secular as well as religious authorities for moral guidance. For an argument that the "new" natural law is religious dogma in secular garb, see Justin T. Wilson, "Preservationism, or The Elephant in to Room: How Opponents of Same-Sex Marriage Deceive Us into Establishing Religion," 14 *Duke J. Gender L. & Pol'y* 561 (2007), as well as Martin E. Marty, "The Foundations of Law: The Religious Foundations of Law," 54 *Emory L.J.* 291, 305 (2005).

and educating children together. This openness to procreation, as the community's natural fulfillment, distinguishes this community from other types." Robert P. George, *In Defense of Natural Law* 168 (1999). Within marriage, penile-vaginal (procreative) intercourse is the only kind that enables the participants to unite "organically"—to join their bodies in a "one-flesh union." *Id.* at 10. (Unlike other forms of intercourse, therefore, it is also consistent with integrity of self.) That such a joint human project can result in procreation unites it with the larger human community.

NOTES ON IMPLICATIONS OF THE NEW NATURAL LAW FOR STATE REGULATION

1.   *Criminal Laws Targeting Sexual Activities.* Under the premises of natural law, sex that is not procreative (masturbation, fornication, sodomy, bestiality, contraceptive intercourse, sex with prepubescent children) or that is outside marriage (fornication, adultery, bigamy) is not morally acceptable. The only sex that is not self-alienating and not illusory is penile-vaginal intercourse within marriage. Natural law advances a clear and transparent moral code for sexuality. Indeed, one virtue of the new natural law may be that it provides a coherent justification for barring sex with children, animals, multiple partners, etc. that other theories do not provide. See George, *In Defense*, 179–81.

Under this philosophy. "homosexual sodomy" is deeply and always immoral, because it is inconsistent with two basic goods, the integrity of self and marriage. Hence, natural law provides a basis for criminalizing this activity, but Professor Finnis cautions that practical reasons might counsel lawmakers not to criminalize activities that occur in private between consenting adults, and this view has prevailed all over the western world, with many faith traditions supporting it. See Finnis, "Law, Morality, and 'Sexual Orientation,' " 1051–53, 1076. Indeed, Professor Finnis (consistent with the Roman Catholic and other faith traditions) advocates a tolerant pedagogy rather than a criminal prosecution: the state has an obligation to teach the immorality of homosexual sodomy, but not necessarily to make it a crime. There is room in their natural law for the pragmatic concern that criminalization of consensual sodomy is ineffective, creates opportunities for blackmail, and visits unnecessary hardships onto sexual minorities.

Several American states still have statutes making only "homosexual sodomy" and not "heterosexual sodomy" a crime. Does natural law's condemnation support this distinction? For wives who cannot come to orgasm from coitus, is it immoral for the husband to assist her orgasm through oral stimulation? If so, is the natural law understanding of marriage not "naturally" gendered? If not, how is the husband's oral sex different in kind from that between two lesbians? *Cf.* Mary Becker, "Women, Morality, and Sexual Orientation," 8 *UCLA Women's L.J.* 165 (1998) (suggesting that it is not a coincidence that the only sexual activity natural law valorizes, penile-vaginal sex, is activity where the man is assured an orgasm and the woman typically not).

Michael Perry, "The Morality of Homosexual Conduct: A Response to John Finnis," 1 *Notre Dame J.L. Ethics & Pub. Pol'y* 41 (1995), criticizes Finnis's distinction between procreative sex (good) versus non-procreative sex (bad). St. Augustine believed that sterile couples (incapable of procreation) ought to be able to marry, because marriage involves a *unitive* as well as *procreative* good. Finnis does not disagree with St. Augustine's conclusion, but argues that the sterile couple can have moral penile-vaginal sex, a form of intercourse where the unitive goal is consistent, at least generally (even if not in their case), with the procreative goal. For the couple engaged in sodomy or contraceptive intercourse, the unitive and procreative goals can never be consistent, and so their sex is always immoral.

2.   *The Constitutional Right to Privacy.* One consequence of natural law thinking is a measured skepticism about the right to privacy. A male-female couple that deliberately thwarts the possibility of procreation by using contraception during coital intercourse would under natural law premises be engaging in immoral activity—yet *Griswold* (married couples) and *Eisenstadt* (unmarried couples) ruled that the state cannot criminalize this activity. The abortion right is, if anything, more strongly inconsistent with natural law premises, which maintain that the fetus is a human life. Natural law, therefore, would not be receptive to *Griswold* or to *Roe v. Wade* and its reaffirmation in *Casey.* Overall, new natural law thinkers would be deeply alarmed that the philosophy of *Griswold* and *Roe v. Wade* contributes to a social culture where it is harder than ever before to appreciate the intrinsic value of marriage and marital intercourse.

In *Lawrence v. Texas,* the Supreme Court extended the *Griswold-Roe-Casey* constitutional liberty to include consensual sodomy. Even though many natural law thinkers are critical of state criminalization as a public policy, they believe that the state has the discretion to express community values by making consensual sodomy a crime—and that judges, especially if unelected, ought not substitute their judgment for that of legislators in a matter where there is a serious, objective moral basis for such laws. As Professor George argued in an *amicus* brief filed in *Lawrence*, Justice Kennedy's sweeping invalidation of consensual sodomy laws was the first time the Court had held that channeling sexual activities into procreative marriage was not a sufficient basis for state regulation of adult sexual activities.

Recall the late Justice Scalia's outraged dissenting opinions in *Casey* and *Romer/Lawrence*, for they reflect the relevance of natural law thinking in the Court's deliberations. Anyone interested in the original understanding of the Constitution's Framers ought to be interested in natural law, which formed the assumptions for many Framers. See Clarence Thomas, "The Higher Law Background of the Privileges or Immunities Clause of the Fourteenth Amendment," 12 *Harv. J.L. & Pub. Pol'y* 63 (1989) (natural law thinking links the Declaration of Independence, the Constitution of 1787 and its Ninth Amendment, and the Fourteenth and other Reconstruction Amendments). On the current Court, Justices Thomas and Alito are learned in natural law and have thoughtfully contemplated its relevance to public law.

Note that natural law enables even non-adherents to think creatively about some of the privacy precedents. Indeed, the new natural law could provide support for the controversial compromise the U.S. Supreme Court has reached in this arena: The state cannot put people in jail for engaging in contraceptive coitus or sodomy, but the state does not have to pay for their contraceptives, cf. *Maher v. Roe*, 432 U.S. 464 (1977) (state welfare program not required to fund abortions even if it funds childbirth services), or recognize (i.e., "promote") so-called "immoral" relationships the same way it recognizes and promotes marriages. See *Boy Scouts of Am. v. Dale*, 533 U.S. 640 (2000).

3.   *Gender and Sexual Equality.* Natural law valorizes the male-female relationship as the foundational relationship for bearing and raising children, and the *old* natural law emphasized the husband as the ruler of the household. It is not clear how *new* natural law thinkers would conceptualize the matter today; its most closely allied religions have taken subtly different approaches. The Roman Catholic Church treats marriage as a *companionate* relationship, where the husband and the wife owe *mutual obligations* to one another. In 1994, the Roman Catholic Bishops in the United States issued a pastoral letter on family life which urged "mutual submission" of husband and wife to one another, and joint submission to their children and the family unit.

In partial contrast, the Southern Baptist Convention in 1998 amended its statement of beliefs, the Baptist Faith and Message, to include this declaration:

> The husband and wife are of equal worth before God. Both bear God's image but each in differing ways. The marriage relationship models the way God relates to His people. A husband is to love his wife as Christ loved the church [see Ephesians 5:22–33]. He has the God-given responsibility to provide for, to protect and to lead his family. A wife is to submit graciously to the servant leadership of her husband even as the church willingly submits to the headship of Christ [see *id.*]. She, being "in the image of God" as is her husband and thus equal to him, has the God-given responsibility to respect her husband and to serve as his "helper" in managing the household and nurturing the next generation.

Gustav Niebuhr, "Southern Baptists Declare Wife Should 'Submit' to Her Husband," *N.Y. Times*, June 10, 1998, at A1, A24. The Faith and Message is not binding on Baptists, and the Convention has not pursued this traditional understanding of gender role as relentlessly as it has pursued its understanding of homosexuality as a dangerous public contagion.

In our view, the new natural law is open (or perhaps neutral) to much of the Supreme Court's sex discrimination jurisprudence, but its thinkers are strongly skeptical of its cases striking down discriminations based upon homosexuality. The big constitutional punch line of the Vatican's pronouncement on "Unions Between Homosexual Persons" is that the state ought not discriminate against or persecute sexual minorities but ought to promote and encourage all citizens to engage themselves in conjugal marriage as the only institution where their sexuality can be natural and good. This stance supports what we call "no promo homo" discourse: the state should be *tolerant* of homosexuals but should *not promote homosexuality*.[c] Accordingly, the natural law position would reject policies that persecuted gay people based upon antigay stereotypes and prejudices—precisely the policy followed by federal and state governments for most of the twentieth century. But a responsible morality, says the Church, is one that recognizes the "homosexual lifestyle" as greatly inferior to one man/one woman heterosexual marriage—and state policy ought to promote the latter and not the former. If the state treated "unions between homosexual persons" the same as "conjugal [heterosexual] marriage," it would be misleading its population on the most important of moral matters.

This point of view has considerable constitutional bite. Professor Finnis gave evidence for the state of Colorado in the *Romer v. Evans* litigation. The State asserted as one of the justifications for Amendment 2 that it expressed the moral judgment of the people of the state. The plaintiffs argued that this expression of morality amounted to no more than prejudice, which was not a legitimate state interest. In response to that argument, the defendants introduced Finnis's affidavit, which asserted that discourse morally skeptical of homosexual behaviors had been part of western philosophy since the ancient Greeks. Finnis's affidavit read in part:[d]

> A political community that judges that the stability and educative generosity of family life is of fundamental importance to the community's present and future can rightly judge that it has a compelling interest in denying that homosexual conduct is a valid, humanly acceptable choice and form of life, and in doing whatever it properly can, as a community with uniquely wide but still subsidiary functions, to discourage such conduct.

The state sought to link this philosophical tradition with contemporary Colorado by citing polling data which showed that the state's residents did not view homosexuality as morally equivalent to heterosexuality. They were *tolerant* of "homosexuals" but disapproving of "homosexuality" and the "homosexual lifestyle." Amendment 2, the state argued, represented the voters' expression of those views. Notice that this argument shows up at the end of Justice Scalia's dissenting opinion. How does Justice Kennedy's opinion respond to this argument?

Among philosophers, the gay-skeptical conclusions of Professors Finnis, George, and their new natural law allies have been sharply contested. In the excerpt that follows, a Princeton University colleague of Professor George

---

[c] *See* William Eskridge Jr., "No Promo Homo: The Sedimentation of Antigay Discourse and the Channeling Effect of Judicial Review," 75 *NYU L. Rev.* 1327 (2000).

[d] Excerpts from Finnis's testimony were published in "Is Homosexual Conduct Wrong? A Philosophical Exchange," *New Republic*, Nov. 15, 1993, at 12. For an account of the trial, where Finnis and other experts battled over the proper interpretation of ancient Greek texts, see Daniel Mendelsohn, "The Stand: Expert Witnesses and Ancient Mysteries in a Colorado Courtroom," *Lingua Franca*, Sept./Oct. 1996, at 34 ff. See also Timothy Tymkovich, "A Tale of Three Theories: Reason and Prejudice in the Battle over Amendment 2," 68 *U. Colo. L. Rev.* 287, 310 (1997) (defense of Amendment 2 by counsel on appeal). (The author is now a judge on the Tenth Circuit.)

offers a competing understanding of natural law that refocuses its precepts in a way that includes lesbians, gay men, and bisexuals within the moral lives called forth by natural law philosophy. The notes suggest other directions for natural law thinking.

Stephen Macedo, "Homosexuality and the Conservative Mind," 84 *Geo. L.J.* **261, 281–87 (1995).** Professor Macedo challenges the new natural law's sharp distinction between procreative marital intercourse and all other sexual activities. In his view, the new natural law "exaggerate[s] greatly the subjective, self-centered character of all nonprocreative sexuality. The reductionism here is striking: 'whatever the generous hopes and dreams' of 'some same-sex partners' (and many heterosexuals), their sexual acts cannot express or do more than is expressed or done if two strangers engage in such activity to give each other pleasure, or a prostitute pleasures a client to give him pleasure in return for money, or (say) a man masturbates to give himself a fantasy of more human relationships after a grueling day on the assembly line.

" * * * My guess is that most committed, loving couples—whether gay or straight—are sensitive to the difference between loving sexual acts expressing a shared intimacy and mere mutual masturbation. Finnis [et al.] may not be all wrong: promiscuous, 'anonymous,' casual sex very likely tends toward the valueless character he describes. Even sexual acts within marriage may tend to become 'masturbatory' if the aim is merely to heighten and intensify one's own erotic pleasure, with no thought given to mutuality, romantic self-giving, or the proper subordination of lust to love. Having said all this, and having agreed with Finnis [et al.] that a healthy sexual life requires a measure of self-control that may be hard to achieve for many people—especially in a culture such as ours that is heavily charged with sexuality—it seems, nevertheless, strikingly simplistic and implausible to portray the essential nature of *every form* of nonprocreative sexuality as no better than the *least valuable* form.

"Many will find deeply unreasonable, as well, the judgment that pleasure is not in and of itself a good. Consider the analogy between sex and eating. We eat and have sex not only to sustain and reproduce human life, but also for their intrinsic pleasure. Eating is especially pleasurable when shared with others (most think that the same is true of sex): social dining cements friendships, expresses affection, and so on. But suppose eating and nourishment are severed? Is eating for the sake of mere pleasure unnatural or irrational? Is it permissible to chew sugarless gum, which gives pleasure but has no nutritional value, as Andrew Koppelman asks, or is doing so the gastronomic equivalent of masturbation (assuming that we are not doing it to exercise the jaw or clean the teeth)? Is it immoral? Is either sexual or gastronomic pleasure sought and achieved for its own sake immoral, or does the immorality lie in excessive or compulsive pursuit of these pleasures (as seems far more reasonable)? * * *

"The reasonable core of the conservative sexual teaching is opposition to promiscuity and sexual license. There surely is something to the observation of Plato, Aristotle, and others that the relative intensity of the 'animal pleasures' means that most people will tend toward overdoing rather than underdoing with respect to sex and food—at least absent efforts at self-control and a well-developed character. The sexual appetite, conservatives properly remind us, is tyrannical and unruly: 'a powerful, continuing motivator, not easily restrained and not naturally opposed by other emotional motives.' The self-control crucial to a healthy and happy life is a difficult and fragile achievement that benefits greatly from social support. This includes a general atmosphere of restraint and reasonable modesty, as well as the inducements to stability that flow from the institution of marriage."

Understood in this way, Professor Macedo argues that natural law actually supports gay marriage. "It seems not only unjust but irrational to deny to homosexuals access to the social institutions intended precisely to cement and stabilize sexual relationships, and thereby to foster a culture of sexual restraint." In the remainder of his essay, he addresses popular arguments against gay marriage, including the slippery slope argument that gay marriage today means polygamy tomorrow. Here again, Professor Macedo suggests, a humane natural law helps us make distinctions: polygamy typically undermines the human flourishing of the wives, while lesbian marriage has been shown to create families where every member can flourish.

Robert George & Gerard Bradley, "Marriage and the Liberal Imagination," 84 *Geo. L.J.* 301 (1995). Responding to Professor Macedo's article, Professors George and Bradley argue that canonical philosophers from Plato and Aristotle through Christ and St. Paul and into the present understand *marriage* to entail a one-flesh communion of persons consummated by acts "of the reproductive type" which unite the spouses biologically and interpersonally. The spouses are biologically united because their bodies are joined in the one *kind* of act (coitus) that can reproduce the species; the spouses are interpersonally united because their union in one flesh renews their marital commitment. Backed upon by human experience across civilizations and the wisdom of the world's greatest thinkers, this norm is one that does not accommodate gay marriage and disrespects non-marital sexuality as morally unworthy "self-gratification."

The authors recognize the formidable task of persuading neutral observers that only marriage (as they define it) is an intrinsic human good, and that lesbian and gay unions (for example) cannot be. "Intrinsic value cannot, strictly speaking, be demonstrated. * * * Hence, if the intrinsic value of marriage, knowledge or any other basic human good is to be affirmed, it must be grasped in non-inferential acts of understanding. Such acts require imaginative reflection on data provided by inclination and experience, as well as knowledge of empirical patterns, which underlie possibilities of action and achievement. The practical insight that marriage * * * as a one-flesh communion of persons is consummated and actualized in the reproductive-type acts of spouses, cannot be attained by someone who has no idea of what these terms mean; nor can it be attained, except with strenuous efforts of imagination, by people who, due to personal or cultural circumstances, have little acquaintance with actual marriages thus understood. For this reason, we believe that whatever undermines the sound understanding and practice of marriage in a culture—including ideologies that are hostile to that understanding and practice—makes it difficult to grasp the intrinsic value of marriage and marital intercourse."

NOTES ON A NEWER NATURAL LAW OPEN TO SEXUAL MINORITIES

1. *Response of the New Natural Law.* Is the response by Professors George and Bradley a sufficient answer to Professor Macedo's charge that the new natural lawyers offer an impoverished account of sexual activities as either marital or nothing more than "self-gratification"? Empirical evidence suggests that lesbian and gay unions offer the partners enduring friendships, deep interpersonal intimacies, and situses for cooperative rearing of children. If a lesbian couple is committed to one another, sexually monogamous, and successfully raising children within their home and union, can it reasonably be said that their intercourse is something nobler than "self-gratification"? See Patrick Lee & Robert P. George, *Body-Self Dualism in Contemporary Ethics and Politics* 179–220 (2008).

How should George and Bradley respond to Macedo's suggestion that pleasure and sociability can be valuable goods from the perspective of a humanist, rather than religion-inspired, natural law? Do George and Bradley have a cogent reply? See also Andrew Koppelman, *The Gay Rights Question in Contemporary American Law* 86–93 (2002).

2. *Moral Arguments for Gay Rights.* Professor Macedo argues that natural rights for gay people and lesbian and gay couples serve genuine human goods. There has long been a thriving literature making similar points.[e] Indeed, some of the same philosophers that Professors Finnis, George, and Bradley cite for making universal natural law claims can also be cited for the proposition that homosexual relationships have also enjoyed the support of "natural reason" from the time of the ancients. Plato's *Symposium* may be the first classic essay on romantic love—yet the focus of much of the conversation was romantic relationships between men. Pausanias delivers an impassioned speech praising long-term relationships between men as the romantic ideal (lines 181C–D). Likewise, Phaedrus praises unselfish love (*agape*) and cites as examples Alcestis's willingness to die for her husband Admetus and Achilles' willingness to die for his beloved Patroclus. Although Plato would have found same-sex marriage incomprehensible, neither is he a dogmatic exemplar of compulsory heterosexuality.[f]

Moreover, historians and anthropologists have documented the flourishing of intimate relationships between persons of the same sex in most cultures throughout history, and many cultures have recognized, tolerated, and even celebrated these relationships as marriages or their cultural equivalents (Eskridge, *Case for Same-Sex Marriage*, 15–42). Thus, history

---

[e]   *E.g.,* Carlos Ball, *The Morality of Gay Rights: An Exploration of Political Philosophy* (2003); William N. Eskridge Jr., *The Case for Same-Sex Marriage: From Sexual Liberty to Civilized Commitment* (1996); John Corvino, "Homosexuality and the PIB [Polygamy, Incest, and Bestiality] Argument," 115 *Ethics* 501 (2005); Chai Feldblum, "Gay Is Good: The Moral Case for Marriage Equality and More," 17 *Yale J.L. & Fem.* 139 (2005).

[f]   On Plato's ambivalence toward homoerotic attraction, see Eva Cantarella, *Bisexuality in the Ancient World* 61–63 (1992); Gregory Vlastos, *Platonic Studies* 38-44 (1981).

demonstrates that same-sex relationships, unions, and even marriages have served social purposes and have contributed to flourishing lives. Modern scholarship is accumulating evidence that lesbian and gay relationships offer strong emotional, financial, and spiritual benefits for those participating in them. *E.g.*, Mark L. Hatzenbuehler et al., "Effect of Same-Sex Marriage Laws on Health Care Use and Expenditures in Sexual Minority Men: A Quasi-Natural Experiment," 102 *Am. J. Pub. Health* 285 (2012) (recognition of gay marriages generated significant health benefits for gay men).

3. *Libertarian Natural Law.* Some natural law thinkers reject Professor Finnis's interpretation of natural law. A lawyer for the Pacific Legal Foundation, Timothy Sandefur argues that, properly speaking, *natural law* ought not be grounded in biology but in "our human nature—the quality or qualities that make us human." Arguments such as Finnis's "rel[y] on biology to explain human nature, when human nature is to be found precisely in the fact that we, unlike all other known species, are liberated from our biological nature by our unique grasp of culture. Our humanity is in our minds, not in our genes." Sandefur, "Liberal Originalism: A Past for the Future," 27 *Harv. J.L. & Pub. Pol'y* 489, 523–32 (2004).[g]

Other authors derive a libertarian natural law from the experience of nations—and indeed Justice Kennedy's opinion for the Court in *Lawrence* has been supported along these lines. Justice Kennedy not only explored American legal tradition, which had never clearly supported the criminalization of sex between consenting adults in private places, but also the ongoing traditions and lessons from other constitutional democracies. "*Lawrence*'s appeal to comparative material is comprehensible only when considered from the perspective of natural law understandings of ordered liberty," the substantive due process standard applied by the Supreme Court since the 1930s. Roger P. Alford, "In Search of a Theory for Constitutional Comparativism," 52 *UCLA L. Rev.* 639, 670 (2005).

NOTES ON A DIFFERENT KIND OF NATURAL LAW THEORY: EVOLUTIONARY PSYCHOLOGY (SOCIOBIOLOGY)

1. *Introduction to Evolutionary Psychology and Sex-Based Gender Roles.* A different kind of naturalist thinking posits that human beings tend to behave in certain predictable ways because of phenomena that are rooted in human biology or psychology that are products of Darwinian evolution. This theory is *evolutionary psychology* (EP) or, as it is more popularly known from the work of Edward O. Wilson, *sociobiology*.[h]

---

[g] Supporting the same idea from a Tomist (Roman Catholic) perspective is Patrick Glen, "Why *Plessy/Brown* and *Bowers/Lawrence* Are Correct: Thomistic Natural Law as the Content of a Moral Constitutional Interpretation," 31 *Ohio N.U.L. Rev.* 75 (2005).

[h] Leading sources for the general approach taken by and conclusions reached by EP include Jerome Barkow, Leda Cosmides & John Tooby, *The Adapted Mind: Evolutionary Psychology and the Generation of Culture* (1992); Richard Dawkins, *The Selfish Gene* (1976); Steven Pinker, *The Blank Slate: The Modern Denial of Human Nature* (2002); Edward O. Wilson, *Sociobiology: The New Synthesis* (1975); David M. Buss, "The Evolution of Human Mating," 39 *Acta Psychologica Sinica* 502 (2007); John Tooby, "The Emergence of Evolutionary Psychology," in *Emerging Syntheses in Science* (D. Pines ed. 1988). A good journalistic account

EP starts with the proposition that the human mind, emotions, and sex drive have been molded by the same kind of evolutionary process that has yielded adaptive, survival-oriented physical features such as our ability to walk upright, thumbs that face the other fingers, and our superior mental abilities. The procreative sex drive, where an eager male inserts his penis into the vagina of a woman who will responsibly bear and nurture the resulting child, is not only fundamental to the survival of the species but is also the root of individual incentives. That is, traits that contribute to biological prosperity, *i.e.*, reproduction, will proliferate in human beings; traits not so contributing ought to die out or become rare. This insight is derived from the basic theory of evolution through natural selection.

More strikingly, EP argues that different traits will be biologically selected for women, who bear the offspring, than for men, the inseminators. The male (unconsciously) desires to spread his genes by inseminating as many fertile females as possible; this activity is costless to the male, but he is concerned that offspring be capably reared. Women, who do all the work of child-bearing and usually assume main responsibility for child-rearing as well, have incentives to be more discriminating about who inseminates them; they will want a male who will help with the child-rearing and who will support the children.

This theory of sex carries with it a theory of gender role: different reproductive strategies have over the eons of natural selection endowed the typical man and the typical woman with different secondary traits. Women's primary role in child care selects in favor of females who are nurturing; men's primary role in providing for the family selects in favor of males who are aggressive. EP suggests that at least some stereotypes about aggressive men and cooperative women have deep roots in natural selection. *See* David Buss, "Sex Differences in Human Mate Preferences: Evolutionary Hypotheses Tested in 37 Cultures," 12 *Behav. & Brain Sciences* 1 (1989). That is, because men who are aggressive and not entirely faithful will tend to reproduce more prolifically than less aggressive but more trustworthy men, genes for the former traits will win against genes for the latter traits. Women who are not nurturing will have less reproductive success than nurturing women because fewer of their children will live to maturity, and so nurturant genes ought to win for women over time. Interpreting the same evidence, other EP scholars argue that culture plays a significant role in strongly bifurcated gender evolution. *See* Alice Eagly & Wendy Wood, "The Origins of Sex Differences in Human Behavior: Evolved Dispositions Versus Social Roles," 54 *Am. Psychologist* 408 (1999).

2.   *Evolution and Homosexuality?* If homosexuality is genetic, as many biologists and psychologists think it is, e.g., J.M. Bailey et al., "Sexual Orientation, Controversy, and Science," 17 *Psychology Sci. in Pub. Interest* 45–101 (2016), then why would a "gay gene" succeed in the highly competitive marketplace of human evolution? One would expect "homosexuals" not to reproduce as much as heterosexuals, and over time this gap ought to eliminate the gay gene, yes? Apparently not. Why? Some writers

---

is Robert Wright, *The Moral Animal: Why We Are the Way We Are: The New Science of Evolutionary Psychology* (1994).

say that EP has no good theory for homosexuality (Wright, *Moral Animal* 384–86).

One possible theory is that a preference or inclination to engage in homosexual behavior may be associated with another trait which increases the chance of reproductive success. *See* R.C. Kirkpatrick, "The Evolution of Human Homosexual Behavior," 41 *Current Anthropology* 385–413 (2000); Frank Muscarella, "The Evolution of Homoerotic Behavior in Humans," 40 *J. Homosexuality* 51–77 (2000).[i] Some sociobiologists have argued that homosexuality piggybacks onto a gene carrying a trait which is evolutionarily productive, namely *cooperation*: hominids who were able to cooperate most productively with their colleagues on the savannah also tended to be what we today would call "bisexual" and were able to cement their alliances with sexual relations. Such an understanding suggests that homosexual behavior is the product of reciprocal altruism. This is an improvement over earlier theories—but it will strike some critics as essentially nonfalsifiable, like much of EP theory.[j]

3. *From Description to Prescription.* EP is largely a descriptive, not a normative, theory. EP scientists are cautious in moving from their descriptions to any prescriptions about how the community ought to respond to the various evolutionary phenomena. Law professors who have read in the EP literature have not been so reluctant. For example, Professor Richard Epstein draws from EP the idea that "men and women are more comfortable in playing the roles that are congenial to their biological roles, and will find themselves uneasy with powerful social [or legal] conventions that dictate a parity in social role in courtship, marriage, and parenting." Richard Epstein, "Two Challenges for Feminist Thought," 18 *Harv. J.L. & Pub. Pol'y* 331, 336 (1995). Although he concedes that nature is not a sure guide to regulation, the general thrust of his prescriptive argument is that legal regulations cutting against the evolutionary grain bear a particularly high burden of persuasion, because they will be hard to achieve and costly. Thus, Professor Epstein believes that Supreme Court sex discrimination decisions like *Frontiero* and *Craig* (Chapter 1) were problematic, because they trumped "real" differences between the sexes with a costly equality rule: society, he argued, would have been richer if the state could have taken account of natural differences in enforcing important public policies (pensions and rules to prevent drunk driving). *See* Epstein, "The Rule of Sex-Blind Jurisprudence Isn't Always Fair," *Wall St. J.*, July 21, 1993, at A15.

Under such assumptions, the VMI decision (Chapter 1) could be criticized as requiring a wasteful integration. If men are hard-wired to be more aggressive than women, the adversarial method deployed at VMI is tailored for men; to adapt the method to accommodate the new female

---

[i]   A recent synthesis is Frank Muscarella, "Evolution of Homoerotic Behavior in Humans," in Francis J. Turner, ed., *Social Work Diagnosis in Contemporary Practice* 162–64 (2005).

[j]   Another theory is that male homosexuality enhances female fertility in the man's maternal line. See Andrea Camperio-Ciani et al., "Evidence for Maternally Inherited Factors Favouring Male Homosexuality and Promoting Female Fecundity," 271 *Procs. Biological Sciences* 2217 (2004), and Francesca Iemmola & Andrea Camperio-Ciani, "New Evidence of Genetic Factors Influencing Sexual Orientation in Men: Female Fecundity Increase in the Maternal Line," 38 *Arch. Sex. Behav.* 393 (2009).

students would not only be costly, but would alter—perhaps dramatically— the nature of the VMI experience. (Note how this kind of critique inverts Professor Katherine Franke's critique of the VMI decision: Professor Franke would criticize the Court for treating sex as natural, when it is socially constructed—like gender. Professor Epstein would criticize the Court for treating gender as socially constructed, when it is natural—like sex.)

Professor Epstein's arguments are driven, at least in part, by a normative baseline of *Lochner*-like liberty for markets to operate free from state interference. From a feminist regulatory baseline, entirely different conclusions could follow from EP's descriptive themes. Professor Mary Anne Case argues that if men are genetically wired to be super-aggressive, rape and other forms of sexual assault against women might be a consequence of evolution as well as cultural patriarchy. Mary Anne Case, "Of Richard Epstein and Other Radical Feminists," 18 *Harv. J.L. & Pub. Pol'y* 369 (1995). That rape-like conduct is natural for many men does not make it normatively acceptable. To the contrary, EP suggests that society should be investing much greater resources into enforcement of rape, sexual assault, and domestic violence laws.

Consider some other speculations about how EP theories might contribute to legal and constitutional thinking about the regulation of sexuality and gender for people thinking from feminist or humanitarian baselines:

(a) *Polygyny and Same-Sex Marriage.* EP theorists have maintained that polygyny is a good system for women, for more of them can partake of the most genetically endowed men. From a feminist point of view, this line of thinking underestimates the value many women place on the companionate feature of marriage, which would be sacrificed if the woman had to share the man with other women. (Moreover, if the well-endowed man followed EP and chose wives increasingly younger than he, the older wives and their children might be left destitute or under-supported.) We think EP provides much better support for lesbian marriages, where each partner shops for the best sperm, and then the couple raises the children together. Lesbian marriage accrues the big EP advantage of polygyny (superior sperm), without the huge disadvantage (the undependable male spouse is replaced by a more evolutionarily dependable female one).

(b) *The No-Fault Divorce Revolution.* EP posits that men are sexual wanderers, prone to cheat on their relationships and dump aging spouses for younger, more fertile women. Thus, the theory predicts that easy divorce would be bad for women, because it removes an important barrier to marital exit (Wright, *Moral Animal* 133–34). This prediction is borne out by data showing that the no-fault divorce revolution of the last generation allowed some men to walk away from their spousal and child-support obligations and impoverished some women. Citing high divorce rates, traditional moralists and religious figures bemoan the decline of marriage; EP suggests that more feminists ought to join this lament.

(c)   *Fornication and Adultery Laws.* In 1900, thousands of people were arrested each year for fornication (sex between unmarried persons) and adultery (one or both of the persons is married). By 2000, virtually no one was arrested for fornication and adultery, and most states have formally decriminalized this conduct. EP suggests an argument for fornication and adultery laws. Monogamous marriage offers advantages for women, including women who do not desire children, because of their asserted genetic predisposition in favor of relationship-building. But because men are genetically prone to cheat, marriages are hard to maintain without strong social sanction—and perhaps legal sanction as well. Fornication and adultery laws serve to reinforce that sanction, and their abandonment over the last generation has been a signal to men that cheating and promiscuity are acceptable.

MODERN OR LIBERAL THEORIES OF SEXUALITY, GENDER, AND THE LAW

In the modern era, both the normative premises and the descriptive understandings of traditional natural law have come under challenge, as western societies moved in the direction of a global consumer-driven market economy. (The world of Adam Smith replaced that of St. Thomas Aquinas.) As a normative matter, British philosophers Thomas Hobbes and Jeremy Bentham sharply challenged the premises of natural law theories. Contrary to natural law theory, Hobbes posited that the state existed to provide protection and security—but not necessarily moral perfection or even "betterment"—for its citizens. Also contrary to natural law, Bentham argued that human beings properly seek "utility," their own pleasure and happiness, rather than conformity with the natural order. The goal of the law ought to be overall social utility—namely, the greatest good for the greatest number.

Three principles of liberalism are worth highlighting from these modernist classics. The first is a normative baseline of human *equality*. Utilitarianism represented a democratizing shift in ethics: before the eyes of a utility function, each member of society is morally equal. Rejecting premodernist class preferences, the utilitarian calculus operates on the principle of "one person, one util." The second is an emphasis on individual *liberty*. Liberal theories should not offer substantive theses on what the greatest good might be—each person in society should be free to determine his or own conception of the good and to pursue it, as long as it did not interfere with the free pursuit of another. The third is the liberal vision of the *self*. Liberal thinkers assume that the human being is an autonomous, rational agent—which, in turn, grounds the first two principles. It is because of this shared nature that we are moral equals, and it is because that nature is essentially rational and self-governing that we deserve the freedom to pursue our own versions of the good life.

The role of the state is thus transformed. Its normative mandate is not to promote the natural order, but to maximize welfare across a society of agents who possess different, often conflicting aims. The state need not, and should not, regulate beyond what is necessary to promote maximal social utility. For example, in his (unpublished) essay "On Paederasty" (1785), Bentham urged that the British law against consensual sodomy be repealed, because it harmed people who enjoyed that activity and did not serve offsetting social purposes.[a] The sodomy essay illustrates the key argument for a "libertarian" (beyond merely liberal) approach to consensual sexual behavior: so long as one's personal choices do not harm third parties or invade the public sphere, the state should tolerate them. John Stuart Mill generalized this idea in his famous book, *On Liberty* (1859), which laid down this precept in chapter four:

> [E]veryone who receives the protection of a society owes a return of the benefit, and the fact of living in society renders it indispensable that each should be bound to observe a certain line of conduct toward the rest. This conduct consists, *first*, in not injuring the interests of one another; or rather certain interests, which, either by express legal provision or by tacit understanding, ought to be considered as rights; and *secondly*, in each person's bearing his share (to be fixed on some equitable principle) of the labors and sacrifices incurred for defending the society or its members from injury and molestation.

Correlatively, Mill objected to "moral police" regulations, where the polity punishes or coerces individuals based upon public judgments about the morality of those individuals or their conduct that does not harm others. Among the objects of Mill's scorn were America's persecution of the Mormons based upon their religious belief in polygamous marriages; Mill himself believed that polygamy was misguided but censured the United States for making it a crime.

On Liberty offers three different arguments in support of a libertarian presumption against state regulation of private behaviors or personal status. *First*, as Bentham had argued, such regulation violates the policy of the greatest good for the greatest number, because it imposes harm upon a minority without corresponding benefit for the majority. *Second*, such regulation is paternalistic, denying agency and opportunities for education to its citizens. *Third*, such regulation is likely to be very costly and misguided, imposing far more costs to society than can be justified by the meager benefits. Missing from Mill's defense of liberty was any kind of non-consequentialist argument such as those developed by natural law scholars or by modern non-consequentialist philosophers such as Immanuel Kant.

In the United States, Margaret Sanger's planned parenthood movement (Chapter 1, Section 1) demanded that the Hobbesian state serve the interests of women. Consistent with the teachings of Bentham and Mill, Sanger argued that the state's withholding birth control information and materials from wives was indefensible, because it imposes enormous harm on families without any corresponding social benefit, beyond worthless moral posturing. Opponents of Prohibition

---

[a] Jeremy Bentham, *Offences Against One's Self: Paederasty* (1785) (written 1785, annotated 1816), a modern edition published in two parts in 3 *J. Homosexuality* 389 (1978), and 4 *J. Homosexuality* 91–107 (1978).

invoked the libertarian presumption to argue that the state was meddling in people's private behavior without good justification. In the course of America's disastrous experiment, even advocates learned precisely the lessons Mill predicted (on this very issue) in *On Liberty*: state regulation would be very costly and would generate a huge and potentially oppressive bureaucratic apparatus as well.

Even more important than these normative critiques of traditional (religion-based) natural law baselines, were descriptive critiques. For example, Columbia University anthropologists Ruth Benedict and Margaret Mead demonstrated that Americans' obsession with the distinction between "masculine" and "feminine," and their demonization of homosexuality, were idiosyncratic to western culture and had no universal applicability, contrary to natural law thinking.[b] See Ruth Benedict, *Patterns of Culture* (1934); Margaret Mead, *Sex and Temperament in Three Primitive Societies* (1935).

Other contemporary anthropologists confirmed the Benedict and Mead reports, that different cultures, both today and through human history, have assigned different gender roles to men and women than those assumed by western culture. Indeed, contrary to western society, dozens and perhaps hundreds of nonwestern societies recognized marriages (or their social equivalent) between persons of the same sex. *E.g.*, Clellan Ford & Frank Beach, *Patterns of Sexual Behavior* (1951).

Medical experts questioned rigid attitudes about gender and sexuality as well—but it was the pioneering empirical studies of Dr. Alfred Kinsey and his colleagues that created the largest public stir. Kinsey et al., *Sexual Behaviors in the Human Male* (1948) and *Sexual Behaviors in the Human Female* (1953), documented that Americans engaged in a greater variety of sexual practices (especially homosexual activities) and gender performances than the law and public culture assumed. Descriptively, there was a great deal of sexual variation among Americans. Prescriptively, almost all of the variation is benign—not harmful to others and perfectly functional for some people. Dr. Kinsey openly argued that state regulation of consensual sexual practices was ridiculously overbroad and relentlessly lobbied for laws revoking such regulation for precisely those reasons advanced by Bentham and Mill.

Other scientists demonstrated that many people have hormonal patterns, genitals, sexual organs, and gender identities that do not fit the man-woman binary.[c] Doctors in Europe and, later, the United States developed surgical techniques for clarifying or even changing human

---

    [b]   See generally Lois Banner, *Intertwined Lives: Margaret Mead, Ruth Benedict, and Their Circle* (2004); Hilary Lapsley, *Margaret Mead and Ruth Benedict: The Kinship of Women* (2001); Lee Wallace, "Academic Recognition: Margaret Mead, Ruth Benedict, and Sexual Secrecy," 11 *Hist. & Anthropology* 417 (1999).

    [c]   Harry Benjamin, *The Transsexual Phenomenon* 21–22 (1966) (gender identity continuum); John Money, Joan G. Hampson & John L. Hampson, "An Examination of Some Basic Sexual Concepts: The Evidence of Human Hermaphroditism," 97 *Bull. Johns Hopkins Hosp.* 301 (1955).

bodies to gender or re-gender them; such techniques ultimately included surgical construction of vaginas and penises—and these medical developments fueled a growing "sex reassignment" movement within the United States. Its first public figure was Christine Jorgenson, who underwent male-to-female reassignment in Denmark and was for almost two decades (1950s–60s) a celebrity in the United States. See Joanne Meyerowitz, *How Sex Changed: A History of Transsexuality in the United States* (2002); Noa Ben-Asher, "The Necessity of Sex Change: A Struggle for Intersex and Transsex Liberties," 29 *Harv. J.L. & Gender* 51 (2006). Johns Hopkins Medical School was a pioneer in the idea that variation in chromosomes, sexual organs, and gender identity are natural and nonproblematic from a medical perspective. Elizabeth Reis, *Bodies in Doubt: An American History of Intersex* (2009); Ben-Asher, *supra.*

Figure 3-2 below diagrams a libertarian understanding of sex, sexuality, and gender reflected in these scientific documents. No longer is "sex" considered a binary relationship; like gender and sexuality, sex is a more like a continuum than a dichotomy. More important, one's gender and sexual roles are no longer dictated, either descriptively (this is natural) or prescriptively (this is best for the person), from one's sex. Thus, a biological man might be feminine as well as masculine, might be a caregiver as well as an entrepreneur, and might enjoy being the passive partner in sexual relations with either men or women (or both). See William N. Eskridge Jr., "Sexual and Gender Variation in American Public Law: From Malignant to Tolerable to Benign," 57 *UCLA L. Rev.* 1333 (2010).

Figure 3-2. The Libertarian Model of Sex, Gender, and Sexuality

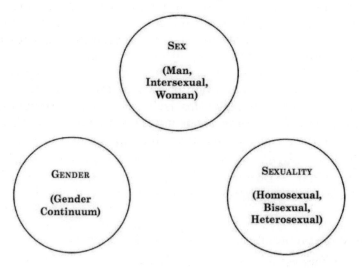

Figure 3-2 is largely descriptive, laying out the modern view that there is a great deal of naturally occurring gender and sexual variation—

and that biological sex does not "naturally" dictate specific gender traits and sexual preferences. Within the modern Benthamite (utilitarian) tradition, however, there is a great deal of debate concerning the normative issues: Should the state regulate or channel gender role and sexual activities toward particular ideal states? One's attitude toward this question is greatly influenced by whether you agree with Dr. Kinsey, that virtually all sexual and gender variation is *benign*. Or whether you think that sexual and gender variation are, at best, *tolerable* (not to be encouraged, but not positively harmful to others) and in some instances *malignant* (the variation is harmful).

Mill's *On Liberty* argued that state regulation is appropriate (1) to protect third parties against harm, (2) to prevent disruption of public order, and (3) to encourage certain conduct or relationships (such as companionate marriage) that are productive for society. Any of these three categories can be expansively applied to justify a great deal of state regulation—and a purely utilitarian (Benthamite) approach would justify state regulations whose benefits to society outweigh their costs.

Without pretending to be exhaustive, the three parts of this section lay out different normative approaches to these questions. Part A suggests the diversity among rational choice theorists who largely reason from utilitarian assumptions. We try to give a flavor of the different ways even economics can approach issues of sexuality and gender role. Carol Rose's essay links the economics-based theories in Part A with the feminist theories in Part B, for she maintains that maximization of utility for the overall community is routinely secured through a cultural process that shortchanges women.

Part B offers, in three parts, several sharply different feminist understandings of the relationship among women's needs, gender categories and role, and heterosexuality. Early feminist theorists like Wendy Williams worked with traditional liberal conceptions of equality: because we were all fundamentally the same, equality is secured when marginalized and privileged groups are treated the same. Another group of theorists postulated that marginalized genders and sexualities were importantly different from dominant groups; equal protection of the law therefore necessitated more than "neutral" treatment. These differences may be founded on gender-based subordination (Catharine MacKinnon), sexual choice (Gayle Rubin), or the content of women's distinct desires (Robin West). Yet another group of theorists criticizes these theses as essentializing "gender" by assimilating the experiences of all women into a single grand narrative of power, choice, or desire. Kimberlé Crenshaw argues that an intersectional framework that integrates multiple axes of subordination will broaden and deepen feminist theory.

Part C offers yet another perspective for modern or liberal thinking about sexuality, gender, and the law—namely, that of authors who reject the naturalized views that everyone is either a man or a woman (the assumption of the sex binary) and that one's biological sex automatically matches one's subconscious sex or gender identity. Transsex author Julia Serano offers a theory of sex and gender that is both deeply feminist and a challenge to some feminist assumptions. Mary Dunlap explains how intersex as well as transgender persons challenge traditional understandings of sex and gender.

A. ECONOMIC THEORIES

Modern rational choice or economic theories assume that human beings are rational actors; as such, they seek to satisfy their personal needs and preferences through appropriate strategies. (The assumption of most rational choice theories is a strong version of liberal individualism, and Chicago School thinkers in particular start from what they consider libertarian baselines.) They respond to economic, social, and environmental stimuli; patterns of economic and social change decisively contribute to the evolution of understandings about sex, gender, and sexuality. Standard economics applies rational actor concepts to commercial markets, but neither logic nor history suggests that this is the limit of economic analysis. Hence, economists and allied law professors have applied the methodology of economics to the operation of domestic and sexual interactions.

There are several different strands of economic theory that can help us understand and evaluate sexuality, gender, and the law. Evolutionary psychology, examined in the Note at the end of Section 1, is a species of rational actor theory. Recall that a central premise is the "selfish gene," which seeks its own perpetuation through generations of rational adaptations. That feature has made evolutionary psychology appealing to some law and economics theorists. *E.g.*, Richard Epstein, "Two Challenges for Feminist Thought," 18 *Harv. J.L. & Pub. Pol'y* 331 (1995).

Judge Posner's *Sex and Reason* (1992), excerpted at the beginning of this part, takes evolutionary psychology seriously and advances a distinctive cost-benefit approach to sexual decisionmaking. Like Professor Epstein, Judge Posner is a Chicago School theorist, skeptical of state regulation of rational actor behaviors. This part will also explore Nobel Prize laureate Gary Becker's application of these insights to the family. Throughout this part, we shall offer feminist and other criticisms of Chicago School arguments. We close with Carol Rose's game-theoretic critique of how the "market" operates for women.

Richard Posner, *Sex and Reason* **(1992).** Working under the assumption that sexual choices, gender roles, and family activities are subject to the same kind of analysis as economic markets, Judge Posner's *Sex and Reason* (1992) propounds an economic theory that combines an individual cost-benefit approach to sexual choice with a Benthamite or Millian approach to state regulation.

In Posner's calculus, people's sex, gender, and sexual appetites are treated as exogenous variables, but their actual sexual practices are driven by their personal cost-benefit calculation. Specifically, one's sexual behavior is a function of the benefits and costs of different forms of sexual activity and the possibility of substituting one sexual practice for another. According to Posner, there are three potential benefits of sex: procreative, hedonistic (pleasure), and sociable (pp. 111–12). One's various sexual activities will be determined in part by one's purposes and one's non-volitional preferences. For example, penile-vaginal intercourse between a man and a woman is the primary sexual activity meeting the goal of procreation, but it is not the only activity that can meet the goal of sociability (and indeed may be disfavored unless reliable means of contraception are available), and it may be inferior to masturbation as a means of gratification, especially if one is not predominantly heterosexual. Posner assumes that humans have different sexual preferences, generally heterosexual or weakly bisexual, with a tiny minority (2–5% men, 1% women) "real homosexual[s]" (pp. 294–95). The costs of sex also fall into three categories: various personal risks or "taxes" associated with different kinds of sex (*e.g.*, children with noncontraceptive vaginal sex, disease with promiscuous sex), social or legal disapproval, and search costs (pp. 115–26).

In Posner's calculus, the balance of benefits and costs will determine the relative frequency of different sexual practices (p. 116). The economic concept of substitution of one practice for another renders his analysis particularly dynamic: when the cost of a particular sexual activity increases, humans will tend to reduce their level of that activity but will also tend to substitute previously less desirable activities (pp. 114–19). This is a reason that homosexual behavior is common in prisons. Even heterosexual men will be likely to have intercourse with other men, because the search costs for a female partner are impossibly high. As a result of high search costs, many inmates seeking sexual gratification will tend to substitute sex with other inmates.

Like most economic analysis, Posner's calculus of sexuality is reductionist, but its idea of substitution may be useful in thinking about human sexual practices and their regulation. For instance, consider the argument (advanced by an *amicus* brief in *Bowers v. Hardwick*) that the spread of AIDS through unprotected anal intercourse is a modern justification for sodomy laws. A hard-headed cost-benefit analysis undercuts such an argument: sodomy laws are way over-inclusive for this purpose, because oral sex poses little risk of HIV transmission and anal sex little risk if condoms are used; such laws are also way under-inclusive, because they ignore penile-vaginal sex (which also transmits HIV) and focus on the type of sexual interaction rather than on the taking of precautions (condoms). Because regulation tends to drive criminal activities underground, a modern Benthamite like Posner would fear that criminal sodomy laws contribute to HIV transmission by deterring educational campaigns. Not surprisingly, therefore, *Sex and Reason* is highly skeptical of state sodomy laws—and indeed was cited by the Supreme Court in *Lawrence*.

Tomas Philipson and Richard Posner, *Private Choices and Public Health: The AIDS Epidemic in an Economic Perspective* (1993), represents a more elaborate cost-benefit model and set of policy prescriptions. Philipson and Posner posit that the decision to engage in HIV-risky sex can be modeled as a two-partner transaction. In their model, partners 1 and 2 will engage in HIV-risky sex only if the "expected utilities" of risky sex are positive values for both partners. Like most of the medical and public health literature, Philipson and Posner posit that many people will seek to minimize the costs of sex, and will alter their behavior to reduce the risk of HIV infection by substituting "safer sex" practices or abstinence. As a matter of public policy, the authors urge the state to educate its citizens about the risks of HIV transmission and ways to minimize or avoid it, to subsidize the distribution of condoms and clean needles to prevent HIV transmissions, and to consider same-sex marriage as a strategy to encourage monogamy. The argument for even more state interventions is stronger if one agrees with scholars who argue that Posner and Philipson greatly overstate the "voluntariness" (or consensual nature) of transactions transmitting the HIV virus.[d]

An explicit assumption of Judge Posner's work is that sexuality can be understood in market terms. Thinkers from Aristotle onward have disputed such an assumption, but it remains an influential one, not only from Judge Posner's books, but also from the most celebrated (and hotly disputed) Chicago School publication in this area. Excerpts from it follow.

Gary Becker, *A Treatise on the Family* (enlarged edition 1991). Professor Becker maintains that family formation follows the economic model. Individuals form family units because families increase their personal utilities. (Utility can include children and emotional gains, as well as economic gains.) Thus, person A and person B will often enjoy greater utility if they are married and living together than if they are just dating and living apart. Becker assumes a male-female marriage as the foundation of family.

Each partner in a marriage seeks to maximize the goods produced by the union. Thus, each will devote himself or herself to tasks in which he or she enjoys a *comparative advantage*. Even though person A might be absolutely better at both housework and income generation than person B, the couple will be better off if A specializes in income generation and B specializes in housework. Becker explicitly posits the comparative advantage point in gendered terms: Husbands tend to work in the market, while wives tend to specialize in household functions (pp. 14–39). To begin with, men have a comparative advantage in outside-the-home work, because longstanding workplace discrimination assures that

---

[d]   See, *e.g.*, William Eskridge Jr. & Brian Weimer, "The Economics Epidemic in an AIDS Perspective," 61 *U. Chi. L. Rev.* 733 (1994).

women will receive a lower wage for the same work and skills (pp. 14–26). If a wife can make only 60% of the husband's income in the workplace and can do as good a job as he can in housekeeping, she has a comparative advantage in the latter. (The advantage is an absolute one if she is 120% as good as the husband in household tasks.)

Professor Becker also justifies this gendered division of labor by reference to "intrinsic differences between the sexes" (p. 21), which might reveal some sociobiology-based assumptions in his theory. "Women not only have a heavy biological commitment to the production and feeding of children, but they also are biologically committed to the care of children in other, more subtle ways." (p. 21) Women, according to Becker, are also more willing to spend time on childcare. These biological differences suggest that when the couple has children, it is relatively more productive for the wife to devote her energies to nonmarket production and the husband to devote his to market activities generating income. Because specialization is per se useful for the joint production of the household, even small differences in preference or capacity would support large differences in activity. B, the woman who slightly prefers housework, will often end up doing all of it, while the man with greater career options will often be the sole breadwinner.

Professor Becker does not insist that families seeking advantages of specialization will—or ought to—follow the traditional gendered pattern, but he does maintain that such a pattern will be the norm, even as employment markets change to allow women more opportunities. Normatively, this model of the family might be read to support specialization within the household and, therefore, the traditional gendered family. Like much Chicago School work, Becker's thesis can be an apologia for the status quo or, less dramatically, a caution that legal or other efforts to reform or change the status quo—to make the family more egalitarian and less specialized—will be hard or impossible to accomplish. The behavior of many individuals behaving rationally (the market) will swallow up or negate efforts to change efficient outcomes.

The Becker thesis has other more exciting possible applications, at least one of them quite radical. That is, it might be deployed as a defense of polygamy. The husband-wife-wife family or the husband-husband-wife-wife family allows more specialization (especially in our era, when families believe they need two incomes) than the husband-wife family: the husband and one wife can work outside the home and build lucrative careers, and the second wife can maintain the home.[e] Becker's model might also be deployed to oppose same-sex marriages, if one believes that a woman-woman household would not generate as much specialization as a man-woman household. "Complementarity implies that households with men and women are more efficient than households with only one sex," he says (p. 23). If that is right (there is reason to doubt that it is),

---

[e] For an example of such a family, see Elizabeth Joseph, "My Husband's Nine Wives," *N.Y. Times*, May 23, 1991, at A31.

then the Becker thesis might be deployed to support a gay man-gay man-lesbian-lesbian family, where the women bear the men's children through artificial insemination and the men earn great incomes for the family by specializing in careers. (A problem is that a four-person family might involve too many enforcement and relationship-maintaining costs to justify the advantages.)

NOTES ON ECONOMIC THEORIES OF SEX AND THE FAMILY

1. *Can Sexuality Be Understood in Market Terms? Should It Be?* The basic assumption behind Judge Posner's argument is unsettling to many: the unique importance of sexuality seems irreducible to commercial value. Nevertheless, it seems like people frequently think of sex and sexuality in these terms. Consider some examples. Surrogacy, which separates sex from its procreative benefit, is mostly governed by private contracts. Sex work (see below) depends on the supply of and demand for sexual labor. Prison inmates engage in sexual relations to gain commissary goods or protection from prison violence.[f] A more dramatic example is when the state itself can promise some benefit in exchange for someone performing a sexual act. That is, police officers can promise to reduce or drop charges against someone on the condition that they engage in sexual activity for a sting operation. This issue came before Judge Posner in 2003, who held that a state official violated a woman's due process rights by threatening her with a forty-year sentence unless she performed oral sex on a police officer under criminal investigation. *Alexander v. DeAngelo*, 329 F.3d 912 (7th Cir. 2003). Judge Posner was careful to note that "inducing a confidential informant to engage in sex" does not in itself give rise to a due process claim. *Id.* at 918. The state's error, rather, was that it threatened a forty-year sentence when the woman's charge carried a ten-year sentence, thereby "deceiv[ing the woman] about the benefits and costs of the distasteful act." By preventing her from making an informed, "rational decision," the state deprived her of her liberty interest. *Id.*

Do these examples address the deeper concern? That is, people may in *fact* think of sexuality in economic terms, but *should* they? Natural law theorists would object that Judge Posner's explanation does not fully capture the relevant harm and leaves out something important about sexuality. The state should not exchange reduced sentences for sex acts because selling such labor is inherently wrong or damaging. Using bodies for sex is different in kind from using bodies to build a house, drive a taxi, or play a violin; only the latter kind can enter the economic market as services. For other theories on what economic models may leave out, see Margaret F. Brining, *From Contract to Covenant* (2000) (arguing that contract law applied to family relationships leave out the critical roles of love, fidelity, and trust in family life); Debra Satz, "Markets in Women's Sexual Labor," 106 *Ethics* 63 (1995) (arguing that some sales of sexual labor are wrong not because they decrease welfare or efficiency, or are inherently wrong, but because they reinforce

---

[f] Rebecca Trammell, "Symbolic Violence and Prison Wives: Gender Roles and Protective Pairings in Men's Prisons," 91 *Prison J.* 305 (2011).

gender hierarchies and sex discrimination). Even if something about sexuality is lost in these models, might the powerful flexibility of a model that can explain so many actual sexual practices justify its continued use?

2. *The Supply and Demand of Sex Work.* Contemporary debates around sex work often involve narratives of human trafficking and slavery. But for many sex workers, the choice to engage in the exchange of sex for money or other goods is a rational one in economic terms, consisting of the substitution of social capital (and positioning in the marriage market) for increased income. Income inequality in the labor market contributes to this economic calculus, which helps explain why 87% of sex workers are women. *See* Maria Laura Di Tommaso et al., "Who Is Watching? The Market for Prostitution Services," *J. of Pop. Econ.* (Feb. 2009). Consider also why a disproportionate number of transgender people, who experience lessened opportunities for education and employment, might engage in sex work. "The high rate of employment discrimination among transgender women directly impacted their economic opportunities, which consequently influenced individual-level risk factors [to begin sex work]." Lydia Sausa et al, "Perceived Risks and Benefits of Sex Work Among Transgender Women of Color in San Francisco," 36 *Archives of Sexual Behavior* 768, 775 (2007).

The availability of sex work as an economic option relies on continuing demand for sex worker services, which also can be explained in economic terms. For the (mostly) men who seek such services, the decision to acquire sex through commercial rather than personal interactions involves weighing the respective financial and time costs to achieving sex. Because of sex workers, "any desired amount or type of sexual contact can more reliably be scheduled in a given allocated time slot, more or less on demand. For many, particularly wealthy individuals, it is the time constraint rather than any budget constraint which is far more important." Alan Collins & Guy Judge, "Client Participation and the Regulatory Environment," in *Demanding Sex: Critical Reflections on the Regulation of Prostitution* 137, 137 (Vanessa E. Munro & Marina Della Giusta, eds. 2008).

3. *Critiques of the Becker Thesis?* Empirical and normative work has been highly critical of the Becker thesis about the efficiency of the gender-differentiated household. Start with critiques that the real world is starkly inconsistent with Becker's assumptions and his conclusions. For example, is it true, from a rational actor model, that strong divisions of labor within the household are always efficient? According to Sarah Fenstermaker Berk, *The Gender Factory: The Apportionment of Work in American Households* 163–64 (1985), specialization of family tasks is not presumptively efficient.[g]

Additionally, sociologists have been unable to substantiate the Becker assumptions that women are better at housework than men *or* that women

---

[g] The rule of diminishing marginal returns suggests that specialization becomes inefficient at some point: the wife's 50th hour devoted to housework and baby care will not be as effective as the husband's 1st or 10th hour. Moreover, the family will often benefit from nontraditional specialization, as where the husband does the housework and the wife works outside the home—or where both work outside the home and outsource the housework. Finally, diversification is a useful strategy: if Dr. Mom falls ill, Dad needs to be able to carry the household and childcare load for a while.

have more of a taste for housework. "Women's commitment to family is not necessarily a function of their preferences or their productivity. It is often constrained by the reluctance of other family members to help with housework and child care responsibilities." Nancy Folbre & Heidi Hartmann, "The Rhetoric of Self-Interest: Ideology of Gender in Economic Theory," in *The Consequences of Economic Rhetoric* 184, 195 (Arjo Klamer et al. eds. 1988). Moreover, if housework-loving or -hating attitudes are themselves the result of childhood socialization or gender stereotypes, then one might question Becker's assumption that the preferences are intrinsic to sex differentiation. *See* George Akerlof & Rachel Kranton, "Economics and Identity," 115 *Q.J. Econ.* 715, 745–48 (2000). One might also question whether any such preferences are universal and stable. Vicki Schultz argues in "Life's Work," 100 *Colum. L. Rev.* 1881 (2000), that the new structure of the workplace is producing changes in women's attitudes as well as the way they spend their time.

The Becker thesis suggests that lesbian and gay households will engage in less specialization and will for that reason be less efficient. Though still in preliminary stages, empirical studies suggest that gay and (especially) lesbian households do specialize a lot less than straight households. Lesbian couples, in particular, share housework much more evenly than either gay male or straight couples and are somewhat more likely to have two full-time jobs outside the home.[h] On the whole, then, lesbian and gay couples engage in some specialization, but not nearly as much as straight couples. Interestingly, lesbian couples with children—a substantial population—report continued division of labor within an egalitarian framework.[i] Given all this evidence, would the Chicago School say that lesbian families are less efficient? Do you agree?

No one disputes Becker's claim that women as a rule do not do as well in the workplace as men—but many scholars object that men's "comparative advantage" is the result of illegal discrimination, including job segregation. *E.g.*, Vicki Schultz, "Reconceptualizing Sexual Harassment," 107 *Yale L.J.* 1683 (1998). Indeed, the wage gap between women and men has eroded in the last several decades. As young women enter higher prestige occupations, spend more time in the market, and insist on equal pay for equal work (as required by state and federal law), "[t]he overall gender gap in earnings should decline considerably more." Francine Blau et al., *The Econimics of Men, Women and Work* (7th ed. 2013). The possible plasticity of the wage gap also suggests a circularity in Becker's theory: women specialize in home production because they do not make as much money as men in the

---

[h]   *See* Philip Blumstein & Pepper Schwartz, *American Couples: Money, Work, Sex* (1983) (large-scale survey of several thousand lesbian, gay, and straight couples); Lawrence Kurdek, "The Allocation of Household labor in Gay, Lesbian, and Heterosexual married Couples," 49 *J. Soc. Issues* 127 (1993), findings replicated and elaborated in Kurdek, "The Allocation of Household Labor by Partners in Gay and Lesbian Couples," 28 *J. Fam. Issues* 132 (2007) (finding that both gay and lesbian couples divide household labor tasks equally, gay men tend to specialize in different tasks, while lesbians tend to perform the same tasks equally).

[i]   Abbie E. Goldberg & Maureen Perry-Jenkins, "The Division of Labor and Perceptions of Parental Roles: Lesbian Couples Across the Transition to Parenthood," 24 *J. Soc. & Pers. Relationships* 297 (2007) (finding that the birth mother in lesbian relationships tends to specialize in child care more than the non-birth mother).

workplace, which is in part a function of women's home specialization. Is this fair to women? To society? *See* Akerlof & Kranton, "Economics and Identity," 735–37 (no).

PROBLEM 3-2
APPLICATION OF ECONOMIC THEORY TO LEGAL ISSUES INVOLVING TRANSGENDER AND INTERSEX PERSONS

(a) *Medical Procedures Performed on Sex-Ambiguous Children.* An objection raised by advocates for intersex persons is that doctors have traditionally performed procedures on infants of indeterminate or ambiguous sex to reduce the sex-ambiguity. From a Chicago School perspective, should these procedures be allowed? Should there be certain protective rules in place before they are accomplished?

(b) *Definitions of Civil Marriage.* Before 2015, American jurisdictions traditionally limited civil marriage to "one man and one woman." Would a Chicago School approach support a judicial decision striking down bars to same-sex marriage? *Compare* Richard A. Posner, "Should There Be Homosexual Marriages? And If So, Who Should Decide?," 95 *Mich. L. Rev.* 1578 (1997) (no), *with Baskin v. Bogan*, 766 F.3d 648 (7th Cir. 2014) (Posner, J.) (delivering such a ruling). See generally Richard Posner, "Eighteen Years On: A Re-Review of William Eskridge, *The Case for Same-Sex Marriage*," 125 *Yale L.J.* 533 (2015) (reflecting on his evolution regarding this issue).

(c) *Access to Gender-Reparative Treatment.* A prisoner is a male-to-female transsexual and requires regular doses of female hormones to maintain her sex of choice. From a Posnerian perspective, should the prison have an obligation to provide these hormones to the prisoner? *See Maggert v. Hanks,* 131 F.3d 670 (7th Cir. 1997) (Posner, J.).

Carol Rose, "Women and Property: Gaining and Losing Ground," 78 *Va. L. Rev.* 421 (1992). Professor Rose starts with the assumption that women are, on average, more cooperative than men. Under this assumption, "we can predict that it will be easier for Sam and Louise to arrive at a cooperative use of the grazing field than it would have been for, say, Sam and Tom. This means that Louise's taste for cooperation aids in the creation of the agreement that produces collective gains. We also can predict that Louise will be better off than she was before she and Sam decided to cooperate. But, alas, we also can predict that she will not be as much better off as Sam. She will wind up with the smaller share of the proceeds. * * *

"At the outset, Louise has to offer Sam more to induce him to cooperate. He may not even notice so readily that cooperative arrangements are beneficial. In any event, he puts his own interests before a cooperative deal and certainly will not take any risky first steps to get things started. Because a cooperative deal does not rank as high in Sam's priorities as in Louise's, he can insist that he take a disproportionate amount of the proceeds, so that, in the now-familiar example, he gets to run more cows than Louise.

"Louise, of course, is just the reverse. She is quick to see the mutual benefits of cooperation, she likes such cooperative relationships, and she is willing to take responsibility for getting such arrangements off the ground. All those traits mean, however, that she may be willing to accept a deal even though she pays a higher price for it. Sam thus has an advantage in bargaining with Louise, just as he would with anyone who is more anxious than he for the deal, or who has a 'higher discount rate' about it. When Sam knows that Louise is the more eager player, he can offer her less favorable terms right from the start. In other words, when the two of them successfully play the larger positive-sum game, Sam has an advantage in the smaller zero-sum game of splitting the proceeds."

Rose then applies the same kind of analysis to male-female relationships. She starts with the Beckerian assumption that Sam and Louise are both better off being married than living separately. "But from Sam and Louise's bargaining pattern, we can predict that Louise is going to have to do more to keep the household together. In particular, she (like wives generally) will be stuck doing the bulk of the housework. She is the one with the taste for commonality, whereas he can bide his time until he gets a favorable offer on the household work front. Moreover, he can make a more credible threat of withdrawing from the household unless she cooks the meals and keeps his shirts ironed. We may think he is a lout for doing so—indeed, he probably is a lout—but that is not the point. The point is that, because her desire or sense of responsibility for cooperative arrangements is stronger than his, he can cut a deal in which he gets the lion's share of their joint gains." For some of the same reasons that wives usually end up with less of the marital surplus than husbands, Professor Rose argues that female employees will tend to bargain for smaller portions of the employment surplus with their bosses than male employees, on average.

"It is important to notice that Louise's taste for cooperation is not a *bad* taste, from the point of view of the world at large. In fact, we are much better off if at least some people have such a taste; otherwise, it would be much harder to start and to sustain cooperative arrangements. Indeed, the taste for cooperation is not a bad taste even for those individuals who have it, so long as they are dealing with other individuals who share the taste. Nor, finally, is a taste for cooperation entirely a bad thing for those who have it even if they have to deal with others who do not share it equally. Even in this circumstance the cooperators do get something out of the deals they make. They just do not get as much as their bargaining partners, who are less eager to work collectively."

NOTES ON THE CONSEQUENCES OF WOMEN'S "TASTE FOR COOPERATION"

1. *The Assumption That Women Are More Cooperative than Men.* Professor Rose's assumption is controversial among feminists. Although cultural feminists such as Carol Gilligan and Robin West maintain that females think and behave differently from males, other feminists criticize that assumption as unproven or contingent at best and blatantly sexist at worst. Gary Becker and many of the older Chicago economists would probably agree with the Rose assumption, as would sociobiologists. But Professor Rose does not defend the assumption and, instead, maintains that her dynamics still operate (albeit at a diminished level) so long as women are *perceived* to be more cooperative than men. (That is, Sam will still be more aggressive in demanding most of the surplus so long as he *thinks* Louise is a relative pushover.) One interesting implication of the Rose model is its showing us how the perpetuation of even "benign" gender stereotypes, such as the supposedly inherent tendency of women to be more nurturing and cooperative, can tangibly undermine women's position in American society. Recall *Craig v. Boren* (Chapter 2).

2. *Efficiency Defenses for Women's Unequal Share?* Professor Becker might analogize women's "taste for cooperation" with bigots' "taste for discrimination." Becker, *The Economics of Discrimination* (2d ed. 1971). If so, he might suggest that the "inequality" which Professor Rose criticizes might actually be efficient. His point would be that a woman who has a "taste for cooperation" is willing to pay more for a relationship than the man without as much of a taste. Just as it is not unequal for a person with a taste for old cars to pay more for an old car than someone (like your Casebook editors) who value cars purely on the basis of their ability to start in the morning—so it is not unequal for women to pay more than men for stuff they value more highly. Whatever the theoretical efficiency of the apportionment of the marital and other surpluses between men and women, one might further argue that society is better off even if women are not. The existence of so many cooperators in our society facilitates the formation of more deals—and more families. If women demanded equal shares to form deals with loutish men, then there would be fewer deals, fewer families, and society as a whole would suffer losses. This would be a most unfortunate scenario! Is there any Rosean way around it?

3. *Consequences of the Rose Bargaining Model for Legal Rules.* In this article and a subsequent book, *Property and Persuasion* (1996), Professor Rose pursues the "men are louts/women are cooperative" point to argue that women would benefit from the legalization of polygamy, where men could marry more than one woman. Under such a regime, the good Sams could attract most of the good Louises, and the loutish Sams would be left without wives. This would not only increase the satisfaction of the Louises, but could provide really strong incentives for future Sams to clean up their acts. Is this a cogent case for polygamy? Are the two Louises better off married to one Sam? Is there any guarantee that the polygamous Sam will not be a lout? Or that good Sam will not turn into a lout as the number of wives increases?

Professor Rose's analytic might better support the legal approval of same-sex marriage. This twist on Rose has a normative appeal (why not just lose the louts?), but not if you are one of the louts being left out of marriage. At best, these louts would be left lonely and perhaps devastated; their pitiable condition would provide incentives for the next generation of heterosexual males to clean up their acts. At worst, however, lonely and devastated louts might become disaffected outlaws and terrorists, which would be socially terrible. One might worry that the more women are siphoned off from heterosexual marriages with male louts, the greater the danger of social unrest. Is there any game-theoretic answer to this Rose Nightmare?

B. FEMINIST THEORIES

Recall that modern liberalism emphasizes both *liberty* and *equality*. While rational choice theorists of the last section tend to emphasize the *liberty* strain of liberalism, feminist theories emphasize *equality*, asking how we best secure genuine equality for both men and women. Liberal theories of equality tend to focus on sameness: we are all equal because we share a common human nature. One way to organize modern feminist theory is to track how different theorists react to liberal understandings of equality and universality. In this part, we follow that approach.

Subpart 1 reviews feminist theories that embrace the basic liberal commitment: where it matters, men and women are the same. The law should therefore treat different genders and sexualities the same, largely by being sex-neutral. Subpart 2 reviews theories that reject the premise of equality based on sameness. For theorists like Catherine MacKinnon and Robin West, women differ from men, and the law must account for such differences to secure equal citizenship. Treating people the same based on a purportedly shared nature assimilates them into a particular standard—male—disguised as universal.

Subpart 3 reviews theories that retreat even further from the universalist liberal starting point: not only are women different from *men*, but women are different from *one other*. Just as theorizing based on "sameness of all human beings" tends to assume a male perspective as the baseline, theorizing based on "women's difference from men" tends to assume a white, heterosexual female perspective as the baseline for "woman." Kimberlé Crenshaw introduces the concept of *intersectionality* to analyze how different axes of subordination like race, gender, and sexuality, interact to subordinate different groups in different ways.

As they postulated more and more difference, feminist theories moved further from traditional liberalism and into the realm of the post-modern. See Patricia Cain, "Feminist Jurisprudence: Grounding the Theories," 4 *Berkeley Women's L.J.* 191 (1988); Clare Dalton, "Where We Stand: Observations on the Situation of Feminist Legal Thought," 3 *Berkeley Women's L.J.* 1 (1987). For many feminists, the rational choice actor of the previous section is not a necessary, universal truth, but is instead a historical construct that served the interests of the male theoreticians who created it. As more diverse perspectives were permitted to join the conversation—first white women, and then women of color and LGBTQIA advocates—feminist theory refined its generalizations to accommodate increasing claims to particularity.

Post-modern theories are examined in Section 3 of this chapter. But as you read this section, note which liberal premises feminists have kept, and which they have modified or rejected. Note also the troubles this trajectory inevitably raises: theorizing inevitably involves operating at some level of generality. Just how much particularity can theory absorb before it loses its explanatory or normative power? How much particularity and anti-generalization can *legal* theory absorb, given "the practical necessity that most legislation classifies for one purpose or another"? *Romer v. Evans*, 517 U.S. 620, 631 (1996).

1. FORMAL EQUALITY

The feminist movement came to life in its modern (second-wave) form during the 1960s and 1970s when mass mobilizations of women began to demand—and soon to win—more legal and constitutional rights. In law and policy, the National Organization for Women (NOW) played a large role in forcefully advocating women's equality. Founded in 1966, its original Statement of Purpose embodies the dominant strategy of the time: "The purpose of NOW is to take action to bring women into full participation in the mainstream of American society now, exercising all the privileges and responsibilities thereof in truly equal partnership with men." *1966 Statement of Purpose, available at* http://www.now.org.

The idea, in short, was to secure sex equality through sex neutrality. In many ways, this was the natural reaction to a long history of denying women the full privileges of "the mainstream" based on some purported deep difference between the sexes. See, *e.g., Bradwell v. Illinois*, 83 U.S. 130, 141 (1873) ("Civil law, as well as nature herself, has always recognized a wide difference in the respective spheres and destinies of man and woman"); *Muller v. Oregon*, 208 U.S. 412 (1908) (upholding a law limiting work hours for women, but not men, on account of physical and social differences); *Hoyt v. Florida*, 368 U.S. 57, 62 (1961) (upholding a law that automatically exempted women from jury duty, because as the "center of home and family life," women should not be obliged to perform civic duties outside the home). Formal equality demands the elimination of this harmful differential treatment: instead of distinguishing between male and female persons, the law should use sex-neutral categories to treat the sexes the same.

Many early victories against sex discrimination operated on this theory of sex equality, which was advanced by prominent leaders of the women's movement like Ruth Bader Ginsburg (as head of the ACLU's Women's Right Project), activist and theorist Pauli Murray (as co-founder of NOW), and Betty Friedan. See, *e.g., Frontiero v. Richardson*,

411 U.S. 677 (1973) (striking down a statute requiring different qualifications for male and female military spouse dependency); *Weinberger v. Wiesenfeld*, 420 U.S. 636 (1975) (striking down a provision in the Social Security Act granting different benefits to widows and to widowers); *Stanton v. Stanton*, 421 U.S. 7 (1975) (striking down a statute defining different ages-of-majority for males and females); *Orr v. Orr*, 440 U.S. 268 (1979) (striking down a statute that required only husbands to pay alimony). Justice Ginsburg's opinion for the Court in the VMI Case (Chapter 1) is a classic application of the formal equality approach.

An early feminist litigator and now the official biographer of Justice Ginsburg, Professor Wendy Williams wrote an early explication of equality theory.

Wendy Webster Williams, "The Equality Crisis: Some Reflections on Culture, Courts, and Feminism," 14 *Women's Rights L. Rep.* 151, 164, 170 (1992). For Professor Williams, the cases just cited were the "easy cases" of sex discrimination jurisprudence: they challenged gender roles that were obviously antiquated by the time they got to court. The "hard cases" of the 1970s and 1980s involved subtler gender norms that more profoundly challenged feminists' commitment to equality.

Some of these hard cases turned on cultural conceptions of men as inherently aggressive, and women as passive and in need of protection. *Rostker v. Goldberg*, 453 U.S. 57 (1981), for example, upheld a statute requiring only men to register for the draft. In explaining its rationale, the Court cited congressional deliberations that asserted the "fundamental principle" that women should not engage in combat. *Id.* at 77. The same year, the Court upheld a California law that made only males liable for statutory rape. *Michael M. v. Superior Court of Sonoma County*, 450 U.S. 464 (1981). In his opinion for the Court, Justice Rehnquist explained that "[b]ecause males alone can physiologically cause the result which the law properly seeks to avoid"—teenage pregnancy—the distinction was "readily justified as a means of identifying offender and victim." *Id.* at 467. In *Dothard v. Rawlinson*, 433 U.S. 321 (1977), the Court upheld an Alabama statute that barred women from being prison guards. Because of the risk of sexual assault, the "employee's very womanhood . . . directly undermine[s] her capacity" to provide security. *Id.* at 336. Underlying the cases is the belief that men and women are inherently different—the man is the aggressor in both war and sex (going so far as to "cause" pregnancy), and woman is the "victim," in need of protection from assault.

"The single-sex laws upheld in [these cases] ultimately do damage to women. For one thing, they absolve women of personal responsibility in the name of protection. There is a sense in which women have been victims of physical aggression in part because they have not been permitted to act as anything but victims. For another, do we not acquire a greater right to claim our share from society if we too share its ultimate jeopardies? To me, *Rostker* never posed the question of whether women should be forced as men now are to fight wars, but whether we, like them, must take the responsibility for deciding whether or not to fight, whether or not to bear the cost of risking our lives, on the one hand, or resisting in the name of peace, on the other. And do we not, by insisting upon our differences at these crucial junctures, promote and reinforce the us-them dichotomy that permits the Rehnquists [Justice Rehnquist authored *Rostker* and *Michael M.*] * * * to resolve matters of great importance and complexity by the simplistic, reflexive assertion that men and women 'are simply not similarly situated?' "

Professor Williams also argues that thinking of pregnancy as a special case of disability likewise perpetuates inequality. In *Geduldig v. Aiello*, 417 U.S. 484 (1974), the Court held that discriminating on the basis of pregnancy did not constitute sex-based discrimination. Insurance plans that excluded pregnancy-related disabilities were thus subject to only the rational basis standard. Two years later in *General Elec. Co. v. Gilbert*, 429 U.S. 125 (1976), Justice Rehnquist reaffirmed and expanded upon *Geduldig*, ruling that men and women received coverage for the disabilities they had in common. Pregnancy was an "extra" disability that only women got; additional compensation would give women more than men. *Id.* at 139 n7. In response, Congress passed the Pregnancy Discriminatory Act (PDA) of 1978, which required that pregnant women "shall be treated the same for all employment-related purposes . . . as other persons not so affected but similar in their ability or inability to work." 42 U.S.C. § 2000e(k). (Professor Williams and her Georgetown colleague, Professor Susan Deller Ross, headed the coalition petitioning Congress to pass the PDA.)

Some feminists argued that the PDA did not go far enough. The PDA guaranteed only that pregnancy would be treated like prostate cancer, but the special nature of pregnancy required more affirmative protections. Professor Williams, however, warns that if pregnancy is treated as a "special case," then unfavorable treatment (as in *Gilbert's* claim that pregnancy was a special "extra" disability) may follow just as well as favorable treatment. "Our history provides too many illustrations of the former to allow us to be sanguine about the wisdom of urging special treatment." Rationalizations of irreducible difference drove the Court's opinion in *Muller* and *Hoyt*: since women had a special place in preserving "the future well-being of the race," the Court reasoned that men and women could be treated differently. Feminists who advocate special protections for pregnancy "start from the same basic assumption, namely, that women have a special place in the scheme of human existence when it comes to maternity." This route would ultimately constrict women's freedom of choice by allowing the state to maintain an interest in women's procreational capacities—all while disincentivizing employers from hiring women of childbearing age at all in the name of equality.

The PDA's approach of formal equality "creates not only the desired floor under the pregnant woman's rights" but also a "ceiling" that limits the kinds of special claims women can make. For Professor Williams, this ceiling is the cost of a floor that bars claims like those in *Muller* and *Gilbert*. Where difference is grounds for disadvantage, women should embrace sex-neutrality and give up claims to special treatment, for better or for worse: "we can't have it both ways."

2. ANTI-SUBORDINATION

Law and philosophy have traditionally been written only by men, and one would expect law and philosophy to reflect men's perspectives. In a society where women are formally equal citizens and should be equal citizens normatively, this state of affairs is unacceptable. Feminist theorists argue that the perspective and interests of women must be centrally considered in any matter of social ordering or public policy. Important feminist thinkers of the late twentieth century emphasized women's differences from men and strongly objected to the ways in which society and law have exploited gendered and sexed differences to subordinate and even brutalize women.

One of the earliest feminist theoreticians of an integrated understanding of sexuality, gender, and the law was Catharine MacKinnon. Her *Sexual Harassment of Working Women* (1979), was instrumental in helping to win recognition of sexual harassment as a form of sex discrimination prohibited by Title VII. More broadly, Professor MacKinnon articulated a claim that sexuality is central, not just to women's lives, but to the feminist campaign against patriarchy and the subordination of women. As you read this excerpt, think about its implications for the standard liberal model mapping the relationship among sex, sexuality, and gender (Figure 3-2 above).

Catharine A. MacKinnon, "Feminism, Marxism, Method, and the State: An Agenda for Theory"
7 *Signs* 515, 516–17, 529, 530, 533–35, 541 (1982).*

Sexuality is to feminism what work is to marxism: that which is most one's own, yet most taken away. Marxist theory argues that society is fundamentally constructed of the relations people form as they do and make things needed to survive humanly. Work is the social process of shaping and transforming the material and social worlds, creating people as social beings as they create value. It is that activity by which people become who they are. Class is its structure, production its consequence, capital its congealed form, and control its issue.

[Professor MacKinnon argues that women's sexuality has been systematically expropriated by men in the same way that Karl Marx claimed that capital systematically expropriates the labor of workers.] Sexuality is that social process which creates, organizes, expresses, and directs desire, creating the social beings we know as women and men, as their relations create society. As work is to marxism, sexuality to feminism is socially constructed yet constructing, universal as activity yet historically specific, jointly comprised of matter and mind. As the organized expropriation of the work of some for the benefit of others defines a class—workers—the organized expropriation of the sexuality of some for the use of others defines the sex, woman. Heterosexuality is its structure, gender and family its congealed forms, sex roles its qualities generalized to social persona, reproduction a consequence, and control its issue.

Marxism and feminism are theories of power and its distribution: inequality. They provide accounts of how social arrangements of patterned disparity can be internally rational yet unjust. But their specificity is not incidental. In marxism to be deprived of one's work, in feminism of one's sexuality, defines each one's conception of lack of power per se. They do not mean to exist side by side to insure that two separate spheres of social life are not overlooked, the interests of two groups are not obscured, or the contributions of two sets of variables are not ignored. They exist to argue, respectively, that the relations in which many work and few gain, in which some fuck and others get fucked, are the prime moment of politics. * * *

* * * [C]onceiving nature, law, the family, and roles as consequences, not foundations, I think that feminism fundamentally identifies sexuality as the primary social sphere of male power. The centrality of sexuality emerges not from Freudian conceptions but from feminist practice on diverse issues, including abortion, birth control, sterilization abuse, domestic battery, rape, incest, lesbianism, sexual harassment, prostitution, female sexual slavery, and pornography. In all these areas, feminist efforts confront and change women's lives concretely and experientially. Taken together, they are producing a feminist political theory centering upon sexuality: its social determination, daily construction, birth to death expression, and ultimately male control.

Feminist inquiry into these specific issues began with a broad unmasking of the attitudes that legitimize and hide women's status, the ideational envelope that contains women's body: notions that women desire and provoke rape, that girls' experiences of incest are fantasies, that career women plot and advance by sexual parlays, that prostitutes are lustful, that wife beating expresses the intensity of love. Beneath each of these ideas was revealed bare coercion and broad connections to woman's social definition as a sex. Research on sex roles, pursuing Simone de Beauvoir's insight that "one is not born, one rather becomes a woman," disclosed an elaborate process: how and what one learns to become one. Gender, cross-culturally, was found to be a learned quality, an acquired characteristic, an assigned status, with qualities that vary

independent of biology and an ideology that attributes them to nature.
* * *

If the literature on sex roles and the investigations of particular issues are read in light of each other, each element of the female *gender* stereotype is revealed as, in fact, *sexual*. Vulnerability means the appearance/reality of easy sexual access; passivity means receptivity and disabled resistance, enforced by trained physical weakness; softness means pregnability by something hard. Incompetence seeks help as vulnerability seeks shelter, inviting the embrace that becomes the invasion, trading exclusive access for protection . . . from the same access. Domesticity nurtures the consequent progeny, proof of potency, and ideally waits at home dressed in saran wrap. Woman's infantilization evokes pedophilia * * *.

Socially, femaleness means femininity, which means attractiveness to men, which means sexual attractiveness, which means sexual authority on male terms. What defines woman as such is what turns men on. Good girls are "attractive," bad girls "provocative." Gender socialization is the process through which women come to identify themselves as sexual beings, as beings that exist for men. It is that process through which women internalize (make their own) a male image of their sexuality *as* their identity as women. * * * Sex as gender and sex as sexuality are thus defined in terms of each other, but it is sexuality that determines gender, not the other way around. * * *

Many issues that appear sexual from this standpoint have not been seen as such, nor have they been seen as defining a politics. Incest, for example, is commonly seen as a question of distinguishing the real evil, a crime against the family, from girlish seductiveness or fantasy. Contraception and abortion have been framed as matters of reproduction and fought out as proper or improper social constraints on nature. Or they are seen as private, minimizing state intervention into intimate relations. Sexual harassment was a nonissue, then became a problem of distinguishing personal relationships or affectionate flirtation from abuse of position. Lesbianism, when visible, has been either a perversion or not, to be tolerated or not. Pornography has been considered a question of freedom to speak and depict the erotic, as against the obscene or violent. Prostitution has been understood either as mutual lust and degradation or an equal exchange of sexual need for economic need. The issue in rape has been whether the intercourse was provoked/mutually desired, or whether it was forced: was it sex or violence? Across and beneath these issues, sexuality itself has been divided into parallel provinces: traditionally, religion or biology; in modern transformation, morality or psychology. Almost never politics.

In a feminist perspective, the formulation of each issue, in the terms just described, expresses ideologically the same interest that the problem it formulates expresses concretely: the interest from the male point of view. Women experience the sexual events these issues codify as a cohesive whole within which each resonates. The defining theme of that whole is the male pursuit of control over women's sexuality—men not as individuals nor as biological beings, but as a gender group characterized by maleness as socially constructed, of which this pursuit is definitive. For example, * * * women notice that sexual harassment looks a great deal like ordinary heterosexual initiation under conditions of gender inequality. Few women are in a position to refuse unwanted sexual initiatives. That consent rather than nonmutuality is the line between rape and intercourse further exposes the inequality in normal social expectations. * * * Pornography becomes difficult to distinguish from art and ads once it is clear that what is degrading to women is compelling to the consumer. Prostitutes sell the unilaterality that pornography advertises. That most of these issues codify behavior that is neither countersystematic nor exceptional is supported by women's experience as victims: these behaviors are either not illegal or are effectively permitted on a large scale. As women's experience blurs the lines between deviance and normalcy, it obliterates the distinction between abuses *of* women and the social definition of what a woman *is*. * * *

Sexuality, then, is a form of power. Gender, as socially constructed, embodies it, not the reverse. Women and men are divided by gender, made into the sexes as we know them, by the social requirements of heterosexuality, which institutionalizes male sexual dominance and female sexual submission. If this is true, sexuality is the linchpin of gender inequality. * * *

The substantive principle governing the authentic politics of women's personal lives is pervasive powerlessness to men, express and reconstituted daily *as* sexuality. To say that the personal is political means that gender as a division of power is discoverable and verifiable through women's intimate experience of sexual objectification, which is definitive of and synonymous with women's lives as gender female. * * *

* * * Sexual objectification is the primary process of the subjection of women. It unites act with word, construction with expression, perception with enforcement, myth with reality. Man fucks woman; subject verb object.

NOTES ON RADICAL FEMINISM AND THE RELATIONSHIP BETWEEN COMPULSORY HETEROSEXUALITY AND PATRIARCHY

1. *The Jurisprudential Underpinnings of Professor MacKinnon's Theory.* In the *Signs* article and her pathfinding book, *Feminism Unmodified: Discourses on Life and Law* (1987), Professor MacKinnon brilliantly grounds a bold feminism in a reconceptualized political theory. It synthesizes insights from the Marxist critique of liberal individualism, the Hobbesian theory of the state, and early feminist consciousness-raising. Thus, MacKinnon builds upon "Marx's view of the incompatibility of social, private-sphere subordination with the theory of value propounded by liberal individualism. That entailed, in turn, a firm rejection of the liberal (and libertarian) claim that the maximization of individual choices is the way to maximize well-being," a sharp rejection of reductionist Benthamite analysis such as that reflective of most economic thinkers. Robin West, "Law's Nobility," 17 *Yale J.L. & Fem.* 385, 399 (2005) (providing an excellent analysis of MacKinnon's philosophy and a friendly critique).

"MacKinnon argues that the structures of domination that so misdirect the subordinated individual's felt preferences and manifest choices also have the effect of polluting—or rendering suspect—the content of her desire." *Id.* at 399. But she invokes the Hobbesian state as a mechanism for rectifying this injustice: women's security is at risk because of private violence from husbands, fathers, boyfriends, employers, coworkers, stalkers, stepfathers, rapists, sexual harassers, teachers, fellow students, brothers, social workers, supervisors, and so on. MacKinnon goes beyond Hobbes in her insistence that women's "security" includes not just freedom from physical violence, but also freedom from "subordination" and bullying by a male-saturated sexual culture. What is particularly brilliant is her "fusion of a radical feminist claim regarding the dangerous and violative nature of heterosexuality, with a deeply familiar liberal commitment to countering private violence with state power, no less than with a deeply Marxist understanding of the impact of subordination on the objective nature and subjective life of the subordinated class." *Id.* at 402.

Linked to this synthesis, but capable of separation, is Professor MacKinnon's further claim, drawn from women's experience, that the subordination of women is so pervasive (vide widespread rape, sex trafficking, abuse of girls, sexual harassment) that it calls into question women's acceptance of sex generally and hierarchic sex in particular. (West dubs this MacKinnon's "critique of desire.") This separate claim has been especially controversial, but consider first its roots in earlier feminist and lesbian feminist theory.

2. *Compulsory Heterosexuality and Patriarchy—The Lesbian Feminist Contribution.* Professor MacKinnon brought together (hetero)sexuality, gender subordination, and the law under one powerful theoretical umbrella, but her contribution built upon the foundations laid by earlier feminists, including lesbian feminists. A landmark publication was Adrienne Rich, "Compulsory Heterosexuality and Lesbian Existence," 5 *Signs* (1980), reprinted in Rich, *Blood, Bread, and Poetry: Selected Prose, 1979–1985*, at 23–75 (1986). Just as Margaret Sanger had argued that "compulsory motherhood" (her language) is a political institution which contributes to women's subordination, so Adrienne Rich argued that "compulsory heterosexuality" is a political institution which contributes to women's subordination. Male culture, she argued, systematically coerces women into frequently unsatisfying marriages to men, by denying women access to means of production and income by which they could maintain female households, by suppressing any mention of lesbian relationships and smothering such mentions as escaped censorship with lies and deceits, by idealizing (heterosexual) romantic marriage and empowering husbands to physically and emotionally dominate their wives under shrouds of privacy and privilege. Other lesbian feminists of the 1970s and 1980s were even more specific than Rich, arguing that homophobia is an instrument of sexism, lesbian-bashing a mechanism of misogyny.

In the context of the feminist movement's ambivalence about its lesbian leaders, MacKinnon's essay was brave as well as pathbreaking. It goes well beyond Rich in interrogating heterosexuality as the situs of women's subordination and oppression. Professor MacKinnon continued this hard-hitting indictment in *Feminism Unmodified,* 6: "[O]ur rapists * * *, serial murderers * * * and child molesters * * * enjoy their acts sexually and as men, to be redundant. It is sex *for them.* * * * When acts of dominance and submission, up to and including acts of violence, are experienced as sexually arousing, as sex itself, that is what they are." Gender is "the congealed form of the sexualization of inequality between men and women."

3. *Radical Feminism, Its Critics, and Constitutional Rights.* For the sake of convenience and clarity, we focus on the debates most directly relevant to issues of sexuality, specifically, the contrast between MacKinnon's critique of desire and the "critique of the critique" rendered by other feminists, who reject the proposition that women's reported desire for sexual satisfaction, including satisfaction through hierarchic sex, must be discounted in light of oppressive sexual practices that are unwelcome to women.

As to the question of sexuality, MacKinnon's view that the male-constructed version of (hetero)sexuality forms the central core and formative engine of gender oppression is the logic underlying her normative understanding of constitutional rights, especially equality rights. Her view is that existing entitlements rest upon patriarchal foundations, and that such entitlements affect women's physical safety, as well as their status and ability to earn a living. The state has a responsibility for remedying abuses of women, for which it is directly and pervasively responsible. See Catherine MacKinnon, "Reflections on Sex Equality Under the Law," 100 *Yale L.J.* 1281 (1991). From these views flow a number of other consequences for equal protection theory and doctrine, some of which are shared with other radical feminist theorists, and some not.

(a) *Liberal Equality Is Toothless; Law Should Be Transformed Rather than Tinkered with.* Professor MacKinnon is critical of the way in which liberal (ACLU) feminist challenges to sex-based classifications have done so little to benefit women. So now male spouses can receive comparable benefits in the armed forces (*Frontiero*), 18 year-old boys can drink two per cent beer (*Craig*), men can attend state nursing schools (*Hogan*) and women can attend state paramilitary schools (the VMI Case). MacKinnon finds none of this cause for celebration. If the subordination of women fundamentally rests upon the male construction of an aggressive sexuality, none of these constitutional "victories" will help—and the VMI "victory" may set us back because under it women join a frat-boy hazing ritual that epitomizes the sexual structure of gender oppression. The point of radical feminism is that giving women the same "opportunities" as men, but without attacking the underlying subordination, does women no good. The challenges must be deeper, and the remediation more drastic.

(b) *A More Aggressive Role for the State.* In the 1980s, Professor MacKinnon and Andrea Dworkin drafted and defended ordinances providing a tort cause of action for women and men harmed by pornography. (The ordinance, the Seventh Circuit decision striking it down, and the commentary are excerpted and digested in Chapter 1.) Her argument was that the state was not providing women "the equal protection of the laws" when it was protecting harmful pornographers against lawsuits; because porn directly as well as indirectly harms women and leaves them unsafe, the state has an affirmative obligation to provide women with legal tools against that hazard. MacKinnon and Dworkin's attempt to utilize the power of the state elicited opposition by both traditional liberals and by pro-sex feminists. Liberals such as ACLU lawyers argued that such a law abridged First Amendment liberties of speech and press, to which MacKinnon responded that a neutral First Amendment should no more protect misogynistic porn harming women than it should protect cross-burners threatening men of color.

(c) *A Critique of the Public-Private Distinction; An Expansive Understanding of State Responsibility.* Other feminist scholars join Professor MacKinnon in holding the state responsible for protecting women against pervasive private violence. See Robin West, *Caring for Justice* (1997); Robin West, "Equality Theory, Marital Rape, and the Promise of the Fourteenth Amendment," 42 *Fla. L. Rev.* 45 (1990). Indeed, from a feminist perspective, the main physical threats to women are not from the state, but from private spouses, boyfriends, dates, employers, teachers, doctors, strangers, and other men acting under state allowance or acquiescence. Therefore, the state has a constitutional obligation to protect women, and statutes adopted for that purpose should be upheld (contrary to *United States v. Morrison*, 529 U.S. 598 [2000], which struck down the Violence Against Women Act) and broadly construed (contrary to *Bray v. Alexandria Women's Health Clinic*, 506 U.S. 263 [1993], which refused to protect women seeking abortions from allegedly violent interference by private conspirators).

Professor MacKinnon supports recognition of a woman's right to have an abortion, but argues that "reproductive freedom" struggles should properly emphasize the sex discrimination involved in abortion laws. Not only is privacy doctrine an incomplete understanding of the harm caused by abortion laws, but it is a misleading understanding insofar as it vests power in doctors, parents, and judges to control what is most central to any woman's (or any man's) life—her body. *Accord*, Reva Siegel, "Reasoning from the Body: A Historical Perspective on Abortion Regulation and Questions of Equal Protection," 44 *Stan. L. Rev.* 261 (1992) (making this kind of argument from a feminist-historical perspective).

MacKinnon's work on privacy aligns with the equality-based critique of the public-private distinction. Women's history reveals the dangers of legal immunity afforded by the right to privacy. The idea of privacy is too protective of traditional spaces where women have been victimized; wife-beating, for example, was long immunized from legal culpability by judges' reluctance to intrude into the "privacy" of the home and family. Professor MacKinnon takes this feminist point one step further, however, to argue that most man-on-woman sex (and a great deal of gay sex) is oppressive to women because it is hierarchic. Consider another perspective on this issue.

Gayle Rubin, "Thinking Sex: Note for a Radical Theory of the Politics of Sexuality"

In *Pleasure and Danger: Exploring Female Sexuality* 11–16, 31–34.
Carole Vance, Editor, 1984.[*]

The new scholarship on sex has brought a welcome insistence that sexual terms be restricted to their proper historical and social contexts, and a cautionary scepticism towards sweeping generalizations. But it is important to be able to indicate groupings of erotic behavior and general trends within erotic discourse. In addition to sexual essentialism, there are at least five other ideological formations whose grip on sexual thought is so strong that to fail to discuss them is to remain enmeshed within them. These are sex negativity, the fallacy of misplaced scale, the hierarchical valuation of sex acts, the domino theory of sexual peril, and the lack of a concept of benign sexual variation.

Of these five, the most important is sex negativity. Western cultures generally consider sex to be a dangerous, destructive, negative force. Most Christian tradition, following Paul, holds that sex is inherently sinful. It may be redeemed if performed within marriage for procreative purposes and if the pleasurable aspects are not enjoyed too much. In turn, this idea rests on the assumption that the genitalia are an intrinsically inferior part of the body, much lower and less holy than the mind, the "soul," the "heart," or even the upper part of the digestive system (the status of the excretory organs is close to that of the genitalia). Such notions have by now acquired a life of their own and no longer depend solely on religion for their perseverance.

This culture always treats sex with suspicion. It construes and judges almost any sexual practice in terms of its worst possible expression. Sex is presumed guilty until proven innocent. Virtually all erotic behavior is considered bad unless a specific reason to exempt it has been established. The most acceptable excuses are marriage, reproduction, and love. Sometimes scientific curiosity, aesthetic experience, or a long-term intimate relationship may serve. But the exercise of erotic capacity, intelligence, curiosity, or creativity all require pretexts that are unnecessary for other pleasures, such as the enjoyment of food, fiction, or astronomy.

What I call the fallacy of misplaced scale is a corollary of sex negativity. Susan Sontag once commented that since Christianity focused "on sexual behavior as the root of virtue, everything pertaining to sex has been a 'special case' in our culture." Sex law has incorporated the religious attitude that heretical sex is an especially heinous sin that deserves the harshest punishments. Throughout much of European and

---

American history, a single act of consensual anal penetration was grounds for execution. In some states, sodomy still carries twenty-year prison sentences. Outside the law, sex is also a marked category. Small differences in value or behavior are often experienced as cosmic threats. Although people can be intolerant, silly, or pushy about what constitutes proper diet, differences in menu rarely provoke the kinds of rage, anxiety, and sheer terror that routinely accompany differences in erotic taste. Sexual acts are burdened with an excess of significance.

Modern Western societies appraise sex acts according to a hierarchical system of sexual value. Marital, reproductive heterosexuals are alone at the top of the erotic pyramid. Clamoring below are unmarried monogamous heterosexuals in couples, followed by most other heterosexuals. Solitary sex floats ambiguously. The powerful nineteenth-century stigma on masturbation lingers in less potent, modified forms, such as the idea that masturbation is an inferior substitute for partnered encounters. Stable, long-term lesbian and gay male couples are verging on respectability, but bar dykes and promiscuous gay men are hovering just above the groups at the very bottom of the pyramid. The most despised sexual castes currently include transsexuals, transvestites, fetishists, sadomasochists, sex workers such as prostitutes and porn models, and the lowliest of all, those whose eroticism transgresses generational boundaries.

Individuals whose behavior stands high in this hierarchy are rewarded with certified mental health, respectability, legality, social and physical mobility, institutional support, and material benefits. As sexual behaviors or occupations fall lower on the scale, the individuals who practice them are subjected to a presumption of mental illness, disreputability, criminality, restricted social and physical mobility, loss of institutional support, and economic sanctions. * * *

Popular culture is permeated with ideas that erotic variety is dangerous, unhealthy, depraved, and a menace to everything from small children to national security. Popular sexual ideology is a noxious stew made up of ideas of sexual sin, concepts of psychological inferiority, anti-communism, mob hysteria, accusations of witchcraft, and xenophobia. The mass media nourish these attitudes with relentless propaganda. I would call this system of erotic stigma the last socially respectable form of prejudice if the old forms did not show such obstinate vitality, and new ones did not continually become apparent.

All these hierarchies of sexual value—religious, psychiatric, and popular—function in much the same ways as do ideological systems of racism, ethnocentrism, and religious chauvinism. They rationalize the well-being of the sexually privileged and the adversity of the sexual rabble.

The charmed circle:

Good, Normal, Natural, Blessed Sexuality

Heterosexual
Married
Monogamous
Procreative
Non-commercial
In pairs
In a relationship
Same generation
In private
No pornography
Bodies only
Vanilla

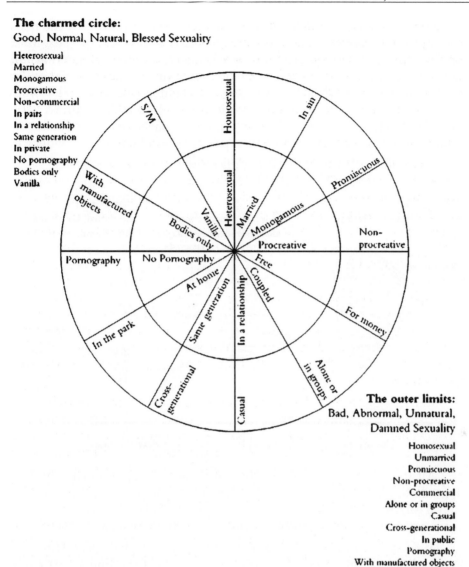

The outer limits:
Bad, Abnormal, Unnatural,
Damned Sexuality

Homosexual
Unmarried
Promiscuous
Non-procreative
Commercial
Alone or in groups
Casual
Cross-generational
In public
Pornography
With manufactured objects
Sadomasochistic

Figure 1 diagrams a general version of the sexual value system. According to this system, sexuality that is "good," "normal," and "natural" should ideally be heterosexual, marital, monogamous, reproductive, and non-commercial. It should be coupled, relational, within the same generation, and occur at home. It should not involve pornography, fetish objects, sex toys of any sort, or roles other than male and female. Any sex that violates these rules is "bad," "abnormal," or "unnatural." Bad sex may be homosexual, unmarried, promiscuous, non-procreative, or commercial. It may be masturbatory or take place at orgies, may be casual, may cross generational lines, and may take place in "public," or at least in the bushes or the baths. It may involve the use of pornography, fetish objects, sex toys, or unusual roles (see Figure 1).

Figure 2 diagrams another aspect of the sexual hierarchy: the need to draw and maintain an imaginary line between good and bad sex. Most of the discourses on sex, be they religious, psychiatric, popular, or political, delimit a very small portion of human sexual capacity as sanctifiable, safe, healthy, mature, legal, or politically correct. The "line" distinguishes these from all other erotic behaviors, which are understood to be the work of the devil, dangerous, psychopathological, infantile, or politically reprehensible. Arguments are then conducted over "where to draw the line," and to determine what other activities, if any, may be permitted to cross over into acceptability.

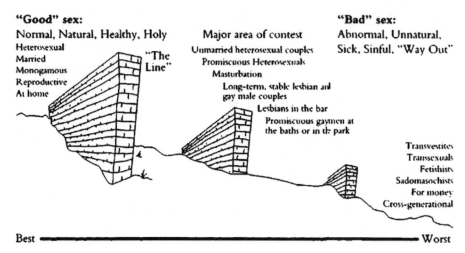

FIGURE 2.   The sex hierarchy: the struggle over where to draw the line

All these models assume a domino theory of sexual peril. The line appears to stand between sexual order and chaos. It expresses the fear that if anything is permitted to cross this erotic DMZ, the barrier against scary sex will crumble and something unspeakable will skitter across.

Most systems of sexual judgment—religious, psychological, feminist, or socialist—attempt to determine on which side of the line a particular act falls. Only sex acts on the good side of the line are accorded moral complexity. For instance, heterosexual encounters may be sublime or disgusting, free or forced, healing or destructive, romantic or mercenary. As long as it does not violate other rules, heterosexuality is acknowledged to exhibit the full range of human experience. In contrast, all sex acts on the bad side of the line are considered utterly repulsive and devoid of all emotional nuance. The further from the line a sex act is, the more it is depicted as a uniformly bad experience.

As a result of the sex conflicts of the last decade, some behavior near the border is inching across it. Unmarried couples living together, masturbation, and some forms of homosexuality are moving in the direction of respectability (see Figure 2). Most homosexuality is still on the bad side of the line. But if it is coupled and monogamous, the society is beginning to recognize that it includes the full range of human interaction. Promiscuous homosexuality, sadomasochism, fetishism, transsexuality, and cross-generational encounters are still viewed as unmodulated horrors incapable of involving affection, love, free choice, kindness, or transcendence.

This kind of sexual morality has more in common with ideologies of racism than with true ethics. It grants virtue to the dominant groups, and relegates vice to the underprivileged. A democratic morality should judge sexual acts by the way partners treat one another, the level of mutual consideration, the presence or absence of coercion, and the quantity and quality of the pleasures they provide. Whether sex acts are gay or straight, coupled or in groups, naked or in underwear, commercial or free, with or without video, should not be ethical concerns.

It is difficult to develop a pluralistic sexual ethics without a concept of benign sexual variation. Variation is a fundamental property of all life, from the simplest biological organisms to the most complex human social formations. Yet sexuality is supposed to conform to a single standard. One of the most tenacious ideas about sex is that there is one best way to do it, and that everyone should do it that way.

Most people find it difficult to grasp that whatever they like to do sexually will be thoroughly repulsive to someone else, and that whatever repels them sexually will be the most treasured delight of someone, somewhere. One need not like or perform a particular sex act in order to recognize that someone else will, and that this difference does not indicate a lack of good taste, mental health, or intelligence in either party. Most people mistake their sexual preferences for a universal system that will or should work for everyone.

This notion of a single ideal sexuality characterizes most systems of thought about sex. For religion, the ideal is procreative marriage. For psychology, it is mature heterosexuality. Although its content varies, the format of a single sexual standard is continually reconstituted within other rhetorical frameworks, including feminism and socialism. It is just as objectionable to insist that everyone should be lesbian, nonmonogamous, or kinky, as to believe that everyone should be heterosexual, married, or vanilla—though the latter set of opinions are backed by considerably more coercive power than the former.

Progressives who would be ashamed to display cultural chauvinism in other areas routinely exhibit it towards sexual differences. We have learned to cherish different cultures as unique expressions of human inventiveness rather than as the inferior or disgusting habits of savages. We need a similarly anthropological understanding of different sexual cultures. * * *

Whichever feminist position on sexuality—right, left, or center— eventually attains dominance, the existence of such a rich discussion is evidence that the feminist movement will always be a source of interesting thought about sex. Nevertheless, I want to challenge the assumption that feminism is or should be the privileged site of a theory of sexuality. Feminism is the theory of gender oppression. To assume automatically that this makes it the theory of sexual oppression is to fail to distinguish between gender, on the one hand, and erotic desire, on the other.

In the English language, the word "sex" has two very different meanings. It means gender and gender identity, as in "the female sex" or "the male sex." But sex also refers to sexual activity, lust, intercourse, and arousal, as in "to have sex." This semantic merging reflects a cultural assumption that sexuality is reducible to sexual intercourse and that it is a function of the relations between women and men. The cultural fusion of gender with sexuality has given rise to the idea that a theory of sexuality may be derived directly out of a theory of gender. * * *

Catharine MacKinnon has made the most explicit theoretical attempt to subsume sexuality under feminist thought. According to MacKinnon, "Sexuality is to feminism what work is to marxism . . . the molding, direction, and expression of sexuality organizes society into two sexes, women and men." This analytic strategy in turn rests on a decision to "use sex and gender relatively interchangeably." It is this definitional fusion that I want to challenge.

There is an instructive analogy in the history of the differentiation of contemporary feminist thought from Marxism. Marxism is probably the most supple and powerful conceptual system extant for analyzing social inequality. But attempts to make Marxism the sole explanatory system for all social inequalities have been dismal exercises. Marxism is most successful in the areas of social life for which it was originally developed—class relations under capitalism.

In the early days of the contemporary women's movement, a theoretical conflict took place over the applicability of Marxism to gender statification. Since Marxist theory is relatively powerful, it does in fact detect important and interesting aspects of gender oppression. It works best for those issues of gender most closely related to issues of class and the organization of labor. The issues more specific to the social structure of gender were not amenable to Marxist analysis.

The relationship between feminism and a radical theory of sexual oppression is similar. Feminist conceptual tools were developed to detect and analyze gender-based hierarchies. To the extent that these overlap with erotic stratifications, feminist theory has some explanatory power. But as issues become less those of gender and more those of sexuality, feminist analysis becomes misleading and often irrelevant. Feminist thought simply lacks angles of vision which can fully encompass the social organization of sexuality. The criteria of relevance in feminist thought do not allow it to see or assess critical power relations in the area of sexuality.

In the long run, feminism's critique of gender hierarchy must be incorporated into a radical theory of sex, and the critique of sexual oppression should enrich feminism. But an autonomous theory and politics specific to sexuality must be developed.

It is a mistake to substitute feminism for Marxism as the last word in social theory. Feminism is no more capable than Marxism of being the ultimate and complete account of all social inequality. Nor is feminism the residual theory which can take care of everything to which Marx did not attend. These critical tools were fashioned to handle very specific areas of social activity. Other areas of social life, their forms of power, and their characteristic modes of oppression, need their own conceptual implements. In this essay, I have argued for theoretical as well as sexual pluralism.

NOTES ON THE DEBATE BETWEEN MACKINNON'S AND RUBIN'S THEORIES OF SEXUALITY, GENDER, AND THE LAW

1.   *Pro-Sex Feminism Versus Anti-Dominance Feminism.* The major theoretical point in dispute between Catherine MacKinnon and Gayle Rubin is the nature of the relationship between sexuality and gender. In MacKinnon's view, the two are closely intertwined: the sexual dominance of (most) women by (most) men constitutes the meaning of gender. Gender inequality has a sexual dynamic which sustains it more powerfully than do economic institutions, for example. Rubin, on the other hand, argues that sexuality is analytically independent of gender. Note her important claim that feminism ought not be the *privileged* site for evaluating sexuality. See Interview of Gayle Rubin, with Judith Butler, "Sexual Traffic," *differences: A Journal of Feminist Cultural Studies* 62 (1994).

Rubin asserts the need for developing theories specifically of sexuality, comparable to our theories of the marketplace or of the state. Consistent with the work of Kinsey and his colleagues, Rubin maintains that a modern theory ought to view sexuality as a positive, joyful force rather than as a presumptively negative, disdained force and that a non-materialist women's sexuality should be celebrated. For other explorations of such a "pro-sex" critique of MacKinnon, see Kathryn Abrams, "From Autonomy to Agency: Feminist Perspectives on Self-Direction," 40 *Wm. & Mary L. Rev.* 805 (1999), and "Sex Wars Redux: Agency and Coercion in Feminist Legal Theory," 95 *Colum. L. Rev.* 304 (1995); Katherine Franke, "Theorizing Yes: An Essay on Feminism, Law and Desire," 101 *Colum. L. Rev.* 181 (2001); Robin West, "Law's Nobility," 17 *Yale J.L. & Fem.* 385 (2005) (advocating a focus on "unwelcome" sex rather than hierarchic [dominance] sex).

2.   *Feminism and Gaylaw.* Professors MacKinnon and Rubin are both gay-friendly, but from different theoretical angles. MacKinnon emphasizes the ways in which homophobia is linked to sexism; recall her debt to Rich's critique of compulsory heterosexuality. Rubin emphasizes the ways in which homophobia is linked to sex negativity. Indeed, her intervention was inspired by the strong anti-gay backlash after Anita Bryant's 1977 "Save Our Children" campaign, which Rubin links to other state and social crackdowns

on sexual and gender rebels (such as sex workers, men engaging in quasi-public sex). Rubin Interview, "Sexual Traffic," 71–73. Indeed, Rubin was also alarmed at how much feminists as well as lesbian rights advocates were romanticizing female friendships and sexual relationships in that period. *Id.* at 74.

The sex/gender/sexual orientation relationship in law is analyzed at length in Francisco Valdes, "Queers, Sissies, Dykes and Tomboys: Deconstructing the Conflation of 'Sex,' 'Gender,' and 'Sexual Orientation' in Euro-American Law and Society," 83 *Cal. L. Rev.* 1 (1995). Professor Valdes posits a triangular structure, in which the three points are sex, gender, and sexual orientation. Because they are arranged in a triangle, each point is linked to both of the other two. He argues that social thought and legal doctrine conflate, or blur, these three distinct concepts into each other and into what is often a confused stew of conventional wisdom. Accordingly, "there is no such thing as discrimination 'based' only on any single endpoint. In fact, all acts and strains of discrimination always occur, or are situated, within one (or more) of the legs linking the endpoints" of sex, gender, and sexual orientation (p.17). Each act of discrimination, therefore, always involves two or more of the three (sex, gender, sexual orientation). How does this insight cut in the Rubin-MacKinnon debate?

3. *The Role of the State.* The MacKinnon-Rubin debate has profound consequences in thinking about the role of the state in regulating sexuality, a topic explored in greater detail in our chapters on the workplace and education. Anti-dominance feminism views private sexuality-based violence as the primary threat to women, and so the state is a natural ally. (This can yield unusual alliances. As to strong regulation of rape, sexual harassment, and pornography, the principled natural law thinker ought to be, and often is, politically allied with the anti-dominance feminist.) Pro-sex feminism views sex negativity as a threat to women's sexual agency, and so the state is a frequent adversary. Even when the state is adopting valid rules protecting women against sexual harassment, for example, pro-sex feminists are concerned about the way the implementation of those rules will often be sex negative.

Many commentators argue that the state is a potential and needed ally, but only if it structures its rules in ways that are both feminist and efficacious. Vicki Schultz, "The Sanitized Workplace,"112 *Yale L.J.* 2061 (2003), supports state rules against sexual harassment in the workplace but argues that Title VII is being implemented in ways that suppress and distort healthy sexual feelings and interactions in the workplace. The Supreme Court has ruled that employers can escape liability for supervisor harassment of employees if they have in place and enforce anti-harassment rules. *See Faragher v. City of Boca Raton*, 524 U.S. 775 (1998). Encouraged by that interpretation, employers have increasingly monitored workplace sexual interactions—beyond the requirements of Title VII and, argues Schultz, beyond what is good for female as well as male workers. Under cover of sexual harassment law, employers are seeking to instantiate a sterile, sexless conception of the workplace that is bad for both female and male workers.

Professor Schultz argues for a structural solution to the dilemma of sexual harassment law. Sociologists have found that workplace structure makes a difference. When women hold subordinate positions, workplace sexuality tends to be oppressive—but not when there are a number of women in the office and they hold positions of authority and responsibility. Under conditions of gender integration, workplace sexuality, for all its complex pluses and minuses, does not tend to disadvantage or oppress women. So the best doctrinal solution is not to reward employers for having a disciplinary policy in place, but for actually integrating their workforces. (So a gender-integrated workforce would create some kind of presumption against employer liability for hostile work environments.) How would MacKinnon respond to this kind of thinking? Consider Schultz's thesis in light of the next excerpt.

Robin West, "The Difference in Women's Hedonic Lives: A Phenomenological Critique of Feminist Legal Theory," 3 *Wisconsin Women's L.J.* 81, 92, 116–17, 140 (1987). This article presents another way feminist theory analyzes sexuality and gender. Professor West starts: "Women's subjective, hedonic lives are different from men's. The quality of our suffering is different from that of men's, as is the nature of our joy." From this idea, West criticizes both liberal feminism (*e.g.*, that of Justice Ginsburg illustrated in the VMI Case; to some extent, Professor Rubin's stance as to issues of sexual choice) and radical feminism (*e.g.*, that of Professor MacKinnon and illustrated in her anti-pornography ordinances). Liberal feminists treat women's problem as a lack of choices, and urge that women be given more choices; radical feminists treat women's problem as a lack of power, and therefore urge as a solution greater power. Both kinds of theory direct women's thinking outward, to change the world, and thus neglect inwardness strategies of understanding women's needs—the robust insight of feminism's distinct methodology of consciousness-raising.

Like liberalism generally, and rational choice theories such as those explored above, liberal feminist legal theory starts with the descriptive claim that human beings consent to transactions that maximize their own welfare. But this liberal approach might be a gendered conception of rationality. "Thus it may be that women generally *don't* consent to changes *so as to* increase our own pleasure or satisfy our own desires. It may be that women consent to changes so as to increase the pleasure or satisfy the desires of *others*. The descriptive account of the phenomenology of choice that underlies the liberal's conceptual defense of the moral primacy of consent may be wildly at odds with the way women phenomenologically experience the act of consent. If it is—if women 'consent' to transactions not to increase our own welfare but to increase the welfare of others—if women are 'different' in this psychological way—then the liberal's ethic of consent, with its presumption of an essentially selfish consensual act, when evenhandedly applied to both genders, will have disastrous implications for women." Recall the game-theoretic feminist argument by Carol Rose.

A consequence of liberal legal feminism, West argues, is that law then "validates" much of the suffering women endure, because they have "chosen" it through marriage, saying yes on a date, and acceding to the advances of a professor or a job supervisor. The fear and coercion that supposedly differentiates rape from sex is so pervasive as to blur the distinction, for many women, beyond liberal recognition, West claims. See, *e.g.,* Del Martin, *Battered Wives* (1984); *Women Against Violence Against Women* (Rhodes & McNeil eds. 1985).

Professor West also criticizes Professor MacKinnon's radical feminism for placing theory ahead of women's experience and discounting women's own understanding of their preferences. Radical legal feminism assumes that equality in power relationships equates with happy and good lives and takes as its project the eradication of any kind of hierarchy, whether or not it is experienced by women as bad or painful. The major situs for this gap between theory and experience is *sexuality*. According to MacKinnon, "male dominance and female submission in sexuality *is* the evil: they express as well as *are* women's substantive inequality. But women report—with increasing frequency and as often as not in consciousness-raising sessions—that equality *in sexuality* is not what we find pleasurable or desirable. Rather, the experience of dominance and submission that go with the controlled, but fantastic, 'expropriation' of our sexuality is precisely what *is* sexually desirable, exciting, and pleasurable—in fantasy for many; in reality for some."[j] (Page 113.) West faults some radical legal feminists for ignoring these reports and insisting that theory obliterate these stories, contrary to consciousness-raising. Note that both West and MacKinnon fail to account for, or even acknowledge, the frequency of female dominance and male submission in the fantasies and experiences of both men and women.

Most deeply, Professor West questions an assumption common to both Rubin and MacKinnon—"the Kantian assumption that *to be human* is to be in some sense autonomous—meaning, minimally, to be differentiated, or individuated, from the rest of social life" (pp. 139–40).

"Underlying and underscoring the poor fit between the proxies for subjective well-being endorsed by liberals and radicals—choice and power—and women's subjective, hedonic lives is the simple fact that women's lives—*because of our biological, reproductive role*—are drastically at odds with this fundamental vision of human life. Women's lives are *not* autonomous, they are profoundly relational. * * * The experience of being human, for women differentially from men, includes the counter-autonomous experience of a shared physical identity between

---

[j]   For examples, see Pat Califia, *Sapphistry: The Book of Lesbian Sexuality* (1980); Maria Marcus, *A Taste for Pain: On Masochism and Female Sexuality* (1981). Professor West pursues this line of critique in "Law's Nobility," 17 *Yale J.L. & Fem.* 385 (2005).

woman and fetus, as well as the counter-autonomous experience of the emotional and psychological bond between mother and infant." Women's greater responsibility for children also presses women toward greater dependence on others, and relationships with others. Motherhood, and perhaps even its potential, leaves women vulnerable, unequal, and non-autonomous. To the extent that neither MacKinnon nor Rubin starts with this hedonic reality, neither creates a completely satisfying feminist theory of sexuality, gender, and the law.

Professor West argues for a reconception of what "good" sexuality is. Unlike Professor Rubin, she does not ground her theory on consent or choice; unlike Professor MacKinnon, she does not ground her theory on dominance or submission. Recalling Bentham but giving him a feminist reading, West's theory is hedonic: What conception of sexuality seems to make women's lives happier? Her conclusion: sexuality, including sexual submission, has "erotic *value* when it is an expression of *trust*; is damaging, injurious and painful when it is an expression of *fear*; and is *dangerous* because of its ambiguity; both others and we ourselves have difficulty in disentangling the two" (p. 129).

Query. Has West rightly captured women's hedonic experience? If not, have MacKinnon or Rubin? If so, do West's conclusions then follow? Has she essentialized a gendering of sexual roles? Note particularly West's emphasis on women's monopoly on pregnancy, which creates a more relational humanity. See Robin West, "Sex and Gender," 55 *U. Chi. L. Rev.* 1 (1988). This kind of thinking has some affinities to cultural feminism and even to some theories of sociobiology (see the note above). Is it subject to the charge of "false essentialism"? For example, does West adequately capture the experience of lesbians? How about the experience of male-to-female transsexuals? Are they an important part of the feminist constituency?

3. INTERSECTIONALITY

Critical theory in the 1970s questioned the determinacy or objectivity of formalist and legal process theories of law. Critical theory took a big turn in the 1980s, rethinking law from the perspectives of women and people of color. At the same time that MacKinnon, Rubin, and West were writing feminist critiques of American law, other authors were criticizing American law from race-based perspectives.[k]

Much critical race theory dovetailed with radical or progressive feminist theories. For example, progressive feminists and race theorists both criticized equal protection law for marginalizing the anti-subordination view that the central goals of the Reconstruction

---

[k] For some leading works, see, *e.g.*, Derrick Bell Jr., *Race, Racism, and American Law* (6th ed. 2008); Ian Haney-Lopez, *White by Law* (1996); Kimberlé Crenshaw, "Race, Reform, and Retrenchment: Transformation and Legitimation in Antidiscrimination Law," 93 *Harv. L. Rev.* 518 (1980); Mari Matsuda, "Public Response to Racist Speech: Considering the Victim's Story," 87 *Mich. L. Rev.* 2320 (1989).

Amendments were to overturn laws and practices unfairly subordinating social groups and to assure all persons the same protection of law that white males have traditionally enjoyed.[l] Relatedly, theorists from both camps have argued that the Equal Protection Clause imposes upon the state an obligation to *protect* women and minorities to the same effect that it protects white men.[m] Just as the Fourteenth Amendment *required* the state to reconstruct segregated public education systems after *Brown*, so it should now be construed to *require* the state to combat violence against women and prejudice-inspired hate crimes. See Tanya Kateri Hernandez, "Sexual Harassment and Racial Harassment: The Mutual Construction of Gender and Race," 4 *J. Gender, Race & Just.* 183 (2001).

On the other hand, women of color have challenged the predominant whiteness of the women's movement.[n] Critical race feminist scholars questioned the extent to which feminist theories were built on the assumption that the experiences of white women captured the ways in which patriarchy operated in the lives of women of color. In "Race and Essentialism in Feminist Legal Theory," 42 *Stan. L. Rev.* 581 (1990), Professor Angela Harris cited the writings of Professors MacKinnon and West as examples of "gender essentialism"—"the notion that there is a monolithic 'women's experience' that can be described independent of other facets of experience like race, class and sexual orientation" (p. 585). From the anti-essentialist critique grew another contribution of critical race theory: the idea that social norms and the law operate not only differently upon black women than upon black men or white women, but that the operation of intersecting prejudices and stereotypes is synergistic. The black woman is not just more subordinated than the white woman or the black man, but subordinated in different ways.

Kimberlé Crenshaw, Demarginalizing the Intersection of Race and Sex: A Black Feminist Critique of Antidiscrimination Doctrine, Feminist Theory, and Antiracist Politics

1989 *University of Chicago Legal Forum* 140, 150–152 (1989).

[Professor Crenshaw reviews three cases to illustrate how current antidiscrimination doctrine fails to account for intersectional discrimination. Such discrimination occurs when a single person may be

---

[l]   *Compare* Catharine MacKinnon, "Reflections on Sex Equality under the Law," 100 *Yale L.J.* 1281 (1991), with Kimberlé Crenshaw, "Race, Reform, and Retrenchment: Transformation and Legitimation in Antidiscrimination Law," 93 *Harv. L. Rev.* 518 (1980).

[m]   Compare Robin West, *Progressive Constitutionalism* (1994), with Mari Matsuda, "Public Response to Racist Speech: Considering the Victim's Story," 87 *Mich. L. Rev.* 2320 (1989).

[n]   Three important books were Angela Davis, *Women, Race and Class* (1981); Paula Giddings, *When and Where I Enter: The Impact of Black Women on Race and Sex in America* (1984); *This Bridge Called My Back: Writings by Radical Women of Color* (Cherie Moraga & Gloria Anzaldua, eds. 1983).

"multiply burdened" across multiple axes of subordination, like race or gender, which interact to subordinate people in novel ways. In *DeGraffenreid v. General Motors*, 413 F. Supp. 142 (E.D. Mo. 1976), five black women employees sued G.M., claiming that its seniority system perpetuated effects of past discrimination. Because black women were hired only after the Civil Rights Act of 1964, they were the first to be fired in a seniority-based layoff during a recession. The court chose to address the plaintiffs' race and sex discrimination claims independently: "this lawsuit must be examined to see if it states a cause of action for race discrimination, sex discrimination, or alternatively either, but not a combination of both." *Id.* at 143.]

The court dismissed the sex discrimination claim, concluding that since (white) women had been hired before 1964, the seniority system could not be perpetuating sex discrimination. It then consolidated the case with another race discrimination case against G.M.—despite the fact that this second case did not challenge G.M.'s seniority system.

In *Moore v. Hughes Helicopter, Inc.*, 708 F.2d 475 (9th Cir. 1983), the court refused to certify a black female plaintiff as the representative of a class alleging both race and sex discrimination. Because Moore claimed to be discriminated against as a black female, the court had "serious doubts as to Moore's ability to adequately represent white female employees." *Id.* at 480.

Finally, in *Payne v. Travenol*, 416 F. Supp. 248 (N.D. Miss 1976), two black female plaintiffs filed a class action suit alleging racial discrimination on behalf of black employees. Determining that the disparities between black male and black female employees were too great, the court allowed the plaintiffs to represent only other black female employees. Though it ultimately found evidence of general race discrimination, the court granted remedy to only the class of black female employees.]

* * *   *DeGraffenreid*, *Moore* and *Travenol* are doctrinal manifestations of a common political and theoretical approach to discrimination which operates to marginalize Black women. Unable to grasp the importance of Black women's intersectional experiences, not only courts, but feminist and civil rights thinkers as well have treated Black women in ways that deny both the unique compoundedness of their situation and the centrality of their experiences to the larger classes of women and Blacks. Black women are regarded either as too much like women or Blacks [as in *DeGraffenreid*] and the compounded nature of their experience is absorbed into the collective experiences of either group or as too different [as in *Moore* and *Travenol*], in which case Black women's Blackness or femaleness sometimes has placed their needs and perspectives at the margin of the feminist and Black liberationist agendas.

While it could be argued that this failure represents an absence of political will to include Black women, I believe that it reflects an uncritical and disturbing acceptance of dominant ways of thinking about discrimination. Consider first the definition of discrimination that seems to be operative in antidiscrimination law: Discrimination which is wrongful proceeds from the identification of a specific class or category; either a discriminator intentionally identifies this category, or a process is adopted which somehow disadvantages all members of this category. According to the dominant view, a discriminator treats all people within a race or sex category similarly. Any significant experiential or statistical variation within this group suggests either that the group is not being discriminated against [as in *DeGraffenreid*] or that conflicting interests exist which defeat any attempts to bring a common claim [as in *Moore* and *Travenol*]. Consequently, one generally cannot combine these categories. Race and sex, moreover, become significant only when they operate to explicitly *disadvantage* the victims; because the *privileging* of whiteness or maleness is implicit, it is generally not perceived at all.

Underlying this conception of discrimination is a view that the wrong which antidiscrimination law addresses is the use of race or gender factors to interfere with decisions that would otherwise be fair or neutral. This process-based definition is not grounded in a bottom-up commitment to improve the substantive conditions for those who are victimized by the interplay of numerous factors. Instead, the dominant message of antidiscrimination law is that it will regulate only the limited extent to which race or sex interferes with the process of determining outcomes. This narrow objective is facilitated by the top-down strategy of using a singular "but for" analysis to ascertain the effects of race or sex. Because the scope of antidiscrimination law is so limited, sex and race discrimination have come to be defined in terms of the experiences of those who are privileged *but for* their racial or sexual characteristics. Put differently, the paradigm of sex discrimination tends to be based on the experiences of white women; the model of race discrimination tends to be based on the experiences of the most privileged Blacks. Notions of what constitutes race and sex discrimination are, as a result, narrowly tailored to embrace only a small set of circumstances, none of which include discrimination against Black women.

NOTES ON INTERSECTIONALITY AND ITS IMPLICATIONS FOR THE CONSTITUTIONAL POLITICS OF SEXUALITY AND GENDER

1. *Intersectionality and the Difference Model.* The intersectional thesis uses moves similar to those the difference model made against formal equality, but extends them to social categories beyond gender.

Difference feminists claimed that theory must begin with the lived experiences of women, which strain and ultimately expose the limitations of male-centered constructs and laws. Likewise, intersectionality begins with the perspectives of multiply marginalized women to demonstrate the heterogeneity of the class "woman" and to broaden feminist theory beyond dominant (white) voices. For both, marginalized perspectives ultimately undermine theories that claim a universal, objective, and neutral "view from nowhere."

Both bodies of thought conceptualize a more dynamic relationship between the individual and society than traditional liberal theories. Liberal thinkers often presume that society is built up by autonomous individuals who strive to maximize welfare. The state exists to allow self-interested creatures with conflicting desires live together in community. Crenshaw rejects such a liberal ordering: society is not merely the sum of individuals who rush around maximizing pre-existing ends. The historical particularities of the time and place create people's ends and self—or in modern parlance, *construct* them. Who we are and the things we hope to maximize are molded by society, its institutions, and its laws. If the state helps shape the ends and very identities of its members, it invariably plays a larger role than mere coordination of independent utility-maximizers.

Given the social construction of the self, these theories also advocate a malleability of our social categories. Gender, sexuality, race, and class are not fixed universals, but evolve through history. For theorists like MacKinnon or Patricia Collins, the ultimate *explanation* for these fluid categories is power. Gender, sexuality, and race are all essentially systems of power and subordination, and specific hierarchical arrangements shift as groups collectively struggle to dominate or resist domination. For some theorists, attaining equality would then spell the disappearance of categories like race and gender. *E.g.,* Sally Haslanger, "Gender and Race: (What) are They? (What) Do We Want Them to Be?," 34 *Nous* 31 (2000).

Other theorists emphasize how these categories mutually constitute each other: what it *means* to be a woman is partially constituted by the experiences of women at the intersections of race, sexuality, and so on. *E.g.,* Lynn Weber, *Understanding Race, Class, Gender, and Sexuality* (2009); Nira Yuval-Davis, "Intersectionality and Feminist Politics," 13 *Eur. J. of Women's Stud.* 193 (2006). Intersectionality theorists claim that feminists must pay more attention to how these multiple axes interact in order to avoid replacing one grand Enlightenment narrative of human-as-rational-being with another grand narrative of woman-as-sexual-subordinate or woman-as-caretaker.

2. *Empirical Investigations.* Recent scholarship has put the intersectionality thesis to empirical testing. Reviewing 35 years of judicial opinions in federal employment discrimination cases, social scientists found that nonwhite women are less likely to win their cases than any other kind of plaintiff (white women, nonwhite men, and white men). Rachel Best et al., "Multiple Disadvantages: An Empirical Test of Intersectionality Theory in EEO Litigation," 45 *Law & Soc'y Rev.* 991 (2001). Moreover, plaintiffs who made "intersectional claims"—*i.e.,* claims that they were discriminated against based on more than one characteristic—were only half as likely to win their cases as other plaintiffs.

Another empirical approach investigates how advocacy organizations prioritize their resources and efforts around different constituent subgroups. In the first quantitative study of its kind, Professor Dara Strolovitch examined how nearly 300 American advocacy groups organized around policy issues that affected subgroups that were multiply marginalized. Groups were far more willing to expend a disproportionate amount of resources and political capital on issues that affected *advantaged* subgroups. For example, Asian-American organizations were more active on affirmative action (advantaged subgroup issue) than on violence against women (disadvantaged subgroup issue). Latino/Hispanic groups also focused more on affirmative action than welfare. Women's groups were more active on abortion coverage by insurance (advantaged subgroup issue) than on public funding for abortion (disadvantaged subgroup), while labor organizations focused more on white-collar unionization than job discrimination against women and minorities. Dara Strolovitch, *Affirmative Advocacy: Race, Class, and Gender in Interest Group Politics* 36, 116 (2007). Strolovitch found that the relative status of the subgroup, not the number of people affected by an issue, better explained the differences in resource allocation.

Conversely, some populations have responded to such marginalization by forming narrower interest groups. Professor Kia Caldwell traces how African-descendent women in Brazil responded to their exclusion from both the women's movements and black movements of the 1970s and 1980s by forming their own organizations. Kia Caldwell, "Black Women and Health Policy in Brazil," in *The Intersectional Approach* 118, 123–126 (Michele Berger and Kathleen Guidroz eds. 2009). These organizations coalesced to form the Network of Black Brazilian Women's Organizations, which participated in the 2001 United Nations World Conference Against Racism in 2001. Scholars trace a significant shift in official government policy following the U.N. conference, such as the development of a national health plan that made provisions to promote health issues that disproportionately affected black women. *Id.* at 128–130.

3. *Difference and the Women's March on Washington.* The January 21, 2017 Women's March on Washington drew 3 to 4.5 million participants—about 1 in every 100 Americans—for one of the largest marches in American history. See generally Jeremy Pressman & Erica Chenoweth, *Crowd Counting Consortium* (2017). The highly visible protest was a testament to how far the concept of intersectionality has permeated popular culture—and to both the promise and perils of intersectional organizing.

Women of color joined organizational leadership only after vocal push-back against an initially predominately white slating, and the final platform promoted a mission that would "reflect our multiple and intersecting identities." "Mission and Vision," *available at* http://www.womensmarch. com. The breadth of the platform likely helped mobilize such staggering numbers: while 60% reported "women's rights" as a reason for protesting, racial justice (35.1%), LGBTQ rights (34.7%), and the environment (35.5%) were tied as the second-most common reasons. Dawn Dow et al., "This is What Democracy Looks Like!" *available at* http://www.thesocietypages.org.

But the March's platform was critiqued from both sides—both for ignoring difference and for paying too much attention to difference. Transgender activists, for example, claimed that the emphasis on biological anatomy (such as in the omnipresent pink "pussy hats") excluded transgender women. Others, however, found the emphasis on difference—on black rights, immigrant status, Islamophobia, and so on—inapposite for a time that demanded unity. "This is a women's march," remarked one white woman who declined to attend the march. "We're supposed to be allies in equal pay, marriage, adoption. Why is it now about, 'White women don't understand black women'?" Farah Stockman, "Women's March on Washington Opens Contentious Dialogue About Race," *N.Y. Times*, Jan. 9, 2017.

Note that this conversation rehearses many of the points outlined in this section. Are "equal pay, marriage, and adoption" more neutral, less alienating grounds on which all women can coalesce? Or do calls for neutrality, by concealing the different experiences of the less visible and privileged, only further subjugate the multiply marginalized? And even if one believes in the importance of recognizing different experiences and claims, just how much difference can theorists and activists accommodate?

4. *Different Ways That Intersectionality Plays out.* In a subsequent article, Professor Crenshaw outlined three dimensions of intersectionality. Crenshaw, "Mapping the Margins: Intersectionality, Identity Politics, and Violence Against Women of Color," 42 *Stan. L. Rev.* 1241 (1991). *Structural intersectionality* refers to the ways that law and social institutions pose unique obstacles for women of color. *Political intersectionality* refers to how the separate politics of racism and sexism marginalize minority women. Antiracist politics are defined by men, while women's mobilization is driven by white women. When their political agendas conflict, women of color are caught in the cross-hairs of campaigns they had no hand in creating. *Representational intersectionality* refers to the cultural construction of women of color in ways that disempower them. The next two notes will illustrate each dimension.

5. *Intersectionality and Privacy.* These different articulations of intersectionality can be seen in the litigation campaigns and judicial opinions around privacy. Note how the big privacy cases involved white women and mostly white gay men and were litigated by white lawyers. (An exception: *Lawrence* involved a male couple of different races. According to the Harris County brief defending the law, its police were called to John Lawrence's apartment building upon the report of an alarmed neighbor that a black man [Tyron Garner, Lawrence's sexual partner] had been seen in the building and was thought to be a burglar.)

(a) *Structural Intersectionality.* Counsel for the complainants in the privacy cases emphasized American libertarian traditions, which preserve valuable private spaces for those Americans who have the financial resources and social position to enjoy them. The right to an abortion does little good for a poor woman of color who cannot afford an abortion, and the same Justices who decided *Roe* later ruled that the state did not have to fund abortions for the indigent, *Maher v. Roe*, 432 U.S. 464 (1977), and that the state did not even have to open its public hospitals to abortions. *Poelker v. Doe*, 432 U.S. 519 (1977) (per curiam). Women who can afford abortions have a valuable right; those who cannot, disproportionately people of color, have no meaningful right. Even contraceptives cost money that many women do not have, and state policies against meaningful pro-contraception sex education deprive women of access to information that would be valuable to them. Women who do not speak English are particularly vulnerable to information deficits.

(b) *Political Intersectionality.* Some early birth control advocates maintained that birth control was useful for eugenic reasons—it would encourage poor women of color not to reproduce. A few states in the South offered birth control information mainly to people of color. Obviously, this kind of argument deployed racist stereotypes of black women being unable to control their sexuality. Contrariwise, some black males opposed birth control because they feared race suicide. While understandable, this was unfair to black women, who bore most of the burdens of pregnancy and raising children.

(c) *Representational Intersectionality.* A consequence of the political discourse of privacy was often to depict black women as sexually loose or even promiscuous. Emphasizing the eugenics argument, supporters of birth control warned middle-class whites that immigrants and people of color could overrun the country if their birth rates were not checked. Opponents of birth control warned middle-class whites that their use of contraceptives posed the same risk. Note, however, that black women also spoke for themselves. In 1941, the National Council of Negro Women endorsed the idea of birth control by arguing for racial betterment, rather than individual freedom.

6. *Intersectionality and Sexual Orientation.* Like feminism, gaylaw has been predominantly white and (gay) male in its agenda and outlook. Consult the recent histories of the marriage equality struggle, and you will find very little (and sometimes no) discussion of the critical contributions made by African Americans, such as Presidential Adviser Valerie Jarrett, Mayor Willy Brown, Reverend Delman Coates, Assistant Attorney General Tony West, and Attorney General Eric Holder (even President Barack Obama is often neglected or treated begrudgingly); by Latinos and Latinas such as Christine Chavez, Justice Carlos Moreno, Tammy Rodrigues, Senator Rey Graulty; by transgender persons and attorneys, such as Shannon Minter, Christie Lee Littleton (whose marriage lawsuit was the first test case for DOMA), and Phyllis Frye (the parent of translaw); and even by women (a list of ignored or neglected figures too long for this space).

Significantly, there were at least four pioneering marriage lawsuits in the early 1970s. The only ones mentioned in any of the recent published histories of marriage equality are the lawsuits involving white couples. *E.g.*, Nathaniel Frank, *Awakening: How Gays and Lesbians Brought Marriage Equality to America* (2017). Yet the marriage lawsuit of Donna Burkett and Manonia Evans—two working class black women—was actually the *first federal lawsuit* challenging the exclusion of lesbian and gay couples from civil marriage. See *Burkett v. Zablocki*, 54 F.R.D. 626 (E.D. Wis. 1972). Is this not worth mentioning? Why are the accounts of early marriage equality lawsuits "whitewashed" in this way? Think about this serious question without necessarily attributing racist motives to thoughtful authors.

The dominance of white, middle-class perspectives in the LGBTQ rights movement extends well beyond marriage equality. See Darren Lenard Hutchinson, " 'Gay Rights' for 'Gay Whites': Race, Sexual Identity, and Equal Protection Discourse," 85 *Cornell L. Rev.* 1358 (2000). Professor Hutchinson broadens the concept of intersectionality into one that he calls *multidimensionality*, *i.e.,* the idea that a majority of people (the black male and the white woman, for example) share a mixture of privileging and disempowering traits, a phenomenon that ought to be figured into equal protection jurisprudence. See, *e.g.,* Tomás Almaguer, "Chicano Men: A Cartography of Homosexual Identity and Behavior," in *The Lesbian and Gay Studies Reader* 255, 264 (Henry Abelove et al. eds., 1993) (detailing the ways gay Chicanos face different cultural problems and stereotype-based difficulties than white gays).

Elisabeth Young-Bruehl, The Anatomy of Prejudices 32–35 (1996). The standard twentieth century account of prejudice, classically captured in Gordon Allport, *The Nature of Prejudice* (1954) and reflected in the NAACP's campaign against apartheid, is that prejudiced people are exceptional and dysfunctional—emotionally rigid, unconnected from their feelings, irrational. Critical race theory suggests that race-based prejudices and stereotypes are not exceptional, and some of them have lamented that racists are quite functional.

Philosopher Elisabeth Young-Bruehl builds upon this insight. "There is, in fact, no empirical evidence at all that people who are prejudiced are any more pathological than the general population, and also no evidence that particular pathologies subtend either prejudice as a 'generalized attitude' or specific prejudices. On the contrary, many people have prejudices *instead of* the conventional forms of the various pathologies, somewhat as people have perversions instead of neuroses if they act on their forbidden desires rather than repressing them. It has often been noted that many neurotics 'recover' in terrible social circumstances—in war zones, for example—where the pain of the external world distracts them from the pain of their internal worlds. Participating in a supremacist movement can have a similar effect. It gives people 'real' (to them) targets for hatreds they might otherwise expend on themselves. And it gives them a context in which their hatreds are 'normal' (which may mean, of course, that the *society* is pathological). In 1961, when the political philosopher Hannah Arendt attended the trial of Adolf Eichmann in Jerusalem and pronounced him 'terrifyingly normal,' 'banal,' she raised a storm of controversy, but I think she was quite correct in the sense that Eichmann functioned better in his [Nazi Germany genocidal] bureaucracy than he would have without it." In short, prejudice can be a rational adaptive mechanism for many human beings.

Professor Young-Bruehl also rejects the traditional idea that *prejudice* is *univocal*. Different kinds of prejudices serve different kinds of emotional needs. To take three common prejudices, anti-semitism is different from racism, and both are different from sexism. "*Obsessional prejudices* [like anti-semitism] are the prejudices toward which people who are given to fixed ideas and ritualistic acts gravitate and through which they can behave sadistically without being conscious of their victims—as though in a trance, completely 'in cold blood.' Obsessional characters are cut off from their own feelings," and their prejudices "feature conspiracies of demonic enemies everywhere, omnipresent pollutants, filthy people, which the obsessionally prejudiced feel compelled to eliminate—wash away, flush away, fumigate, demolish." The abject failure can rationalize his condition on the ground that it is not his fault—but is instead the work of people conspiring to advance themselves unscrupulously at the expense of decent people like him.

"Racism, by contrast, exemplifies *hysterical prejudice*, by which I mean a prejudice that a person uses unconsciously to appoint a group to act out in the world forbidden sexual and sexually aggressive desires that the person has repressed. Racism is a prejudice that represents or symbolizes genital power or prowess and sexual desires by bodily features like skin color, thick hair, muscularity, or big breasts; it equates strength, size, and darkness with primitivity, archaic and unrestrained sexual activity forbidden in 'civilization.' * * * Racism is a prejudice of desire for regression expressed as a charge that people who are 'other' and sexually powerful—as parents and siblings are in the eyes of children—have never progressed, are intellectually inferior, are uncivilized. The 'lower' men are imagined as brutal, the 'lower' women as either (and sometimes both) sexually lascivious or maternally bountiful, milk giving and care giving." Racist societies are, according to Young-Bruehl, typically split between a formally egalitarian, puritanical facade, and an explosively sexual underbelly constantly threatening to break the surface placidity.

"Sexists," finally, are people (usually but not always male) who cannot tolerate the idea that there exist people not like them, not—specifically—anatomically like them. "Their prejudice has a *narcissistic* foundation, that is, of the ideologies of desire, the most universal—as universal as narcissism is—even though it is most life defining and extreme in people whose narcissistic desires dominate their character. The narcissistic prejudices of boundary establishment, of genital intactness asserted and mental integrity are insisted upon. On the other side of the narcissists' boundaries there is not a 'them,' a 'not-us,' but blank, a lack—or at the most, a profound mystery. Women challenge male gender identity and represent the possibility of castration." The central mechanism of sexism is control over women's sexuality and reproduction.

Professor Young-Bruehl views homophobia as a synthesis of all three types of prejudice. Unlike many gay or feminist theorists, she refuses to see homophobia as either dysfunctional or univocally sexist. Instead, homophobia is triply functional: It can be *obsessional* for the bigot who sees his own failures as a consequence of homosexual (Jewish, Communist) cabals and conspiracies; *hysterical* for the homophobe who is projecting onto others his own disgusting and forbidden fantasies; and *narcissistic* for the person whose own gender identity (masculinity/femininity) is unstable.

Does the complexity Professor Young-Bruehl brings to an understanding of homophobia also apply to other prejudices? For example, most race theorists (and your Casebook authors) would argue that racism, like homophobia, partakes of narcissistic or obsessional as well as hysterical elements. Feminists might say the same thing about sexism. Are there other serious criticisms of this approach?

NOTES ON YOUNG-BRUEHL'S THEORY OF PREJUDICE AND IMPLICATIONS FOR CONSTITUTIONAL RIGHTS

1. *Sexual Orientation as a Suspect Classification?* Ought sexual orientation be treated as a suspect classification, like race or ethnicity, or a quasi-suspect classification, like sex? A popular argument to the contrary is that sexual orientation discrimination does not mobilize the same concerns as discrimination based on race, ethnicity, or sex discrimination. Professor Young-Bruehl suggests otherwise, that homophobia is not only irrational in the same hysterical, obsessional, and narcissistic ways as racism, antisemitism, and sexism (respectively), but is irrational in all the ways these other prejudices are. Does this strengthen the suspect classification argument? How might critics respond?

Recall the argument in Chapter 1, that many antigay discriminations are entitled to heightened scrutiny because they are sex discriminations. On the one hand, Young-Bruehl argues a close connection between the narcissistic prejudice entailed in both sexism and homophobia. On the other hand, her theory suggests that more is going on regarding homophobia, which mobilizes hysterical and obsessional anxieties as well. If sex discrimination jurisprudence polices narcissistic anxieties, primarily, then maybe it is an extension to apply it to a prejudice that entails more violent sexual anxieties. How might Andy Koppelman, a defender of the sex discrimination argument, respond to this quandary?

2. *The Colorado Amendment 2 Case and "Prejudice."* Justice Kennedy's opinion in *Romer v. Evans* (Chapter 1) opined that Amendment 2 was motivated by "animus," a term synonymous with prejudice; Justice Scalia's dissenting opinion assailed that reading of Amendment 2 and vigorously maintained that Colorado voters were motivated by a tolerant morality. Make up your own mind. Reread the Amendment 2 ballot materials (Appendix 7 to this Casebook) in light of Young-Bruehl's theory of prejudices. Be alert for materials that appeal to hysterical, obsessional, or narcissistic anxieties. Does such a reading support Justice Kennedy?

3. *If Prejudice Is Rational and Multivocal, Can It Be Tamed by Constitutional Discourse?* Two themes of Young-Bruehl's book are the rationality and multivocality of prejudice. Neurotics benefit psychologically from harboring prejudice against other people, and there are many different kinds of prejudices, each fitting emotional needs of the functioning neurotic. If this is true, can a judiciary regulate prejudice? One would expect prejudice to be *hydraulic*: Once suppressed or thwarted in one place, it will resurface elsewhere. Civil rights groups have encountered this dilemma; once de jure racial segregation (founded on open expressions of prejudice) was outlawed, segregation reemerged in de facto form (founded on unconscious or ambivalent racist attitudes). At the very least, prejudiced attitudes will not change overnight. They may never change.

Assume that the state or social forces do actually succeed in reducing the amount of racist prejudice in the United States. The economic and psychological concept of *substitution* suggests that if the neurotic loses one prejudice-based outlet to manage his emotions, he will substitute a new prejudice for the old one. So if racism actually disappeared in the United States, the hysterical needs of those neurotics might be met by heightened prejudice against gay people—or against someone else (if gay people are not available as the new scapegoats). Does this appear plausible? If it is, a core assumption of civil rights movements (all minorities benefit from reducing prejudice and discrimination against any one minority) needs to be reexamined. Keep this hydraulic theory in mind as you read later materials in this chapter, especially Professor Puar's book on "homonationalism" that concludes the chapter.

C. TRANSGENDER AND INTERSEX VOICES IN FEMINIST DEBATES

At the same time liberal feminists (such as Ruth Bader Ginsburg) and radical feminists (such as Catherine MacKinnon and Andrea Dworkin) were challenging traditional sexist exclusions of women based upon sex and subordination of women based upon (hetero)sexuality, transgender and intersex persons and their lawyers were challenging the idea, held by traditionalists and most feminists, that sex is immutable, that sex (woman) matches up with gender (feminine), and that "woman" is a stable category of person. Just as the organized women's rights movement was anxious about the role of lesbians in the movement in the 1970s, so the movement was skeptical of the claims of transgender persons. Intersex persons were virtually invisible to the gay rights and women's movements.

Led by Texas attorney (now Judge) Phyllis Frye, transgender activists in the 1990s demanded a place at the gay rights table, and a good many transgender persons came out of the closet and asserted their own right to be accepted by the gay rights movement as well as by society. By 2000, the lesbian and gay rights movement was morphing into the LGBT rights movement. Many progressive lawyers represented transgender clients suffering from discrimination or violence from state as well as private actors. *E.g.,* Phyllis Randolph Frye & Katrina Rose,

"Responsible Representation of Your First Transgendered Client," 66 *Tex. B.J.* 558 (July 2003).

Today, it is common to refer to the LGBTQIA (lesbian, gay, bisexual, transgender, queer, intersex, allies) rights movement. Transgender and intersex theorists have not only expanded the agenda of the social movement, but have advanced new claims within feminist theory itself. Consider some of the claims and some of the consequences.

Julia Serano, *Whipping Girl: A Transsexual Woman on Sexism and the Scapegoating of Femininity* (2007). Written from the perspective of a *trans woman* (a male-to-female transsexual), this manifesto advocates "the end of the scapegoating, deriding, and dehumanizing of trans women everywhere. For the purposes of this manifesto, *trans woman* is defined as any person who was assigned a male at birth, but who identifies as and/or lives as a woman" (p. 11). The author claims that no sexual or gender minority has been more "ridiculed and despised," because trans women "are uniquely positioned at the intersection of multiple binary gender-based forms of prejudice: transphobia, cissexism, and misogyny" (p. 12).

Cissexism is the belief that "transsexuals' identified genders are inferior to, or less authentic than, those of *cissexuals* (i.e., people who are not transsexual and who have only ever experienced their subconscious and physical sexes as being aligned)." Like homophobia and transphobia, cissexism is "rooted in *oppositional sexism*, which is the belief that female and male are rigid, mutually exclusive categories, each possessing a unique and nonoverlapping set of attributes, aptitudes, abilities, and desires" (p. 13). Oppositional sexism explains why LGBT persons are lumped into the same category (often just "gay") by society at large.

Unlike gay and bisexual men and many lesbians, however, trans women are also victims of "*traditional sexism*—the belief that maleness and masculinity are superior to femaleness and femininity" (p. 14). By embracing femaleness and femininity, and abandoning male privilege, trans women constitute a deep threat to the male supremacy undergirding traditional sexism. Society assails this minority by "hyperfeminizing" trans women with the most derogatory female stereotyping, by "hypersexualizing" trans women by depicting them as sex workers, and by objectifying their bodies with obsessive attention to sex reassignment surgery.

Like liberal feminists, Serano maintains that it "is no longer enough for feminism to fight solely for the rights of those born female," and the movement must "empower femininity itself" (pp. 17–18). This entails a normative movement that challenges *both* oppositional sexism *and* traditional sexism.

As suggested in Figure 3-2 above, liberal theory posits the independence of (1) biological sex, (2) gender expression, and (3) sexual attraction and conduct. Liberal feminist theory has traditionally accepted (1) sex as biological and fixed, and (2) gender expression as social and mobile. Serano challenges this assumption by introducing a new category, namely, *subconscious sex*, the intrinsic understanding our brains have regarding what sex our bodies ought to be (p. 80). In her case, Serano was born a man but had a subconscious understanding that her body ought to be that of a woman. This understanding is different from gender expression, which is social, albeit linked with biology and psychology in ways that vary from person to person.

Serano's is essentially a liberal theory, because she maintains that subconscious sex, gender expression, and sexual orientation are determined by factors largely independent of one another but that are intrinsic to each person (p. 99). Following in the tradition of the Kinsey Institute, she observes that there is a lot of naturally occurring variation in how these traits emerge in individuals—and that that sex and gender variation is benign (*i.e.,* there is no public-regarding reason to discourage or disparage the naturally-occurring variation).

Hence, Serano's primary normative agenda is simple: Because oppositional as well as traditional sexism denigrates productive people and serves no public purpose, society (and, presumably, the law) ought to reject "*cissexual privilege*—that is, the double standard that promotes the idea that transsexual genders are distinct from, and less legitimate than, cissexual genders" (p. 162).

Because cissexuals cannot easily imagine a life where one's biological and subconscious sexes are not aligned, the country generally and feminism specifically need to attend to trans voices, without obsessing about features of a trans person that the cissexual observer deems to reflect the originally assigned sex. More generally, feminist theory ought to challenge "all forms of *gender entitlement*, the privileging of one's own perceptions, interpretations, and evaluations of other's people's gender over the way those people understand themselves" (p. 359).

Serano's secondary normative agenda is to rescue femininity from social denigration. Although many feminine traits (such as fashion or even color preferences) are social, she maintains that there is a core biological source for many feminine traits, such as being in tune with one's emotions (pp. 323–24). "[W]hile most reasonable people see women and men as equals, few (if any) dare to claim that femininity is masculinity's equal. Indeed, much of what has historically been called misogyny—a hatred of women—has clearly gone underground, disguising itself as the less reprehensible derision of femininity" (p. 340).

NOTES ON TRANS THEORY: CRITIQUING OPPOSITIONAL AND TRADITIONAL SEXISM

1.   *Traditional Sexism.* Notice how Julia Serano clarifies the feminist project, in a manner that might be acceptable to many liberal feminists.

Traditional sexism is not just the separation of men and women into different categories, but it is a separation that consigns women to the less prestigious, less remunerative "feminine" jobs, roles, and duties. Notice how this articulation fits the Supreme Court's liberal sex discrimination jurisprudence, including the VMI Case (*Virginia*), the Nursing School Case (*Hogan*), and the Executrix Case (*Reed*), all examined in Chapter 1. The articulation may provide support for liberal critiques of the Supreme Court's Women and the Draft Case (*Rostker*) and the Pregnancy Cases (*Geduldig* and *Gilbert*), also noted in Chapter 1.

Many liberal feminists—notably Justice Ruth Bader Ginsburg as well as Professors Wendy Webster Williams, Susan Deller Ross, and Joan Williams—maintain that the feminist project cannot be achieved until men embrace female roles and feminine traits or values. Serano provides an extended brief in favor of the valuing of femininity—a voice that may be especially timely in light of the widespread denigration of female bodies and feminine traits during the presidential campaign of 2016.°

2. *Oppositional Sexism.* Julia Serano's approach also represents a sharp departure from some of the traditional premises of liberalism, including liberal feminism, when she criticizes oppositional sexism. The Supreme Court's sex discrimination jurisprudence relentlessly separates the world into two sexes (man and woman). The VMI Case, for example, goes so far as to "celebrate" the "inherent" differences between the two sexes—a celebration that has been called "the central mistake" of sex discrimination jurisprudence. Katherine Franke, "The Central Mistake of Sex Discrimination Law: The Disaggregation of Sex from Gender," 144 *U. Pa. L. Rev.* 1 (1995); see *id.* at 32–50 (illustrating her thesis by arguing that discrimination based upon gender identity ought to be a central example of sex discrimination).

Do the VMI Case and other precedents bar the Supreme Court from recognizing state discrimination against trans women because of their gender identity as unconstitutional sex discrimination?

3. *Trans Men?* Julia Serano's *Whipping Girl* focuses on the brutal discrimination suffered by trans women like her and targets the social denigration of femininity as the primary object of feminist politics. An increasing number of trans men present the question: Where do they fit in? Don't trans men suffer brutal discrimination as well? And might their discrimination be gendered, albeit for a different reason, namely, a woman's effort to appropriate male privilege? In any event, should a trans-inclusive LGBT rights movement make any distinction between trans women and trans men? Consider the next problem.

° For example, during the 2016 campaign presidential candidate (now President) Donald Trump mocked journalist Megyn Kelly as a "bimbo" whose questioning was accompanied by (menstrual?) bleeding, ridiculed Carly Fiorina as having a face not compatible with being President (even as he admitted he should not say "bad things" about a woman), and dismissed former Secretary of State Hillary Clinton as someone who was "not strong enough" and did not have enough "stamina" to be President.

PROBLEM 3-3
MARY DUNLAP'S PROPOSAL FOR SEX-CHOICE

A generation before Julia Serano published *Whipping Girl* (2007), and fourteen years before Phyllis Frye established the first association for trans lawyers (1992), lawyer Mary Dunlap proposed a pro-choice regime to address the discriminations suffered by transgender persons. Specifically, she proposed that the "two-sex presumption in law [be] replaced by a principle that one's sex could be determined by that person, that the choice of sex were not limited to male or female, and that the person could make different determinations as to sex identification for various purposes, such as education, marriage, living arrangements, or personal physical appearance. In such a legal system, the individual would be free, at least in theory, not only to determine, maintain, change, and control personal sexual identity, but also to avoid suffering the limitations and sanctions that [transgender persons] suffer, consciously or not, by the present coercive enforcement of the two-sex presumption through law." Mary Dunlap, "The Constitutional Rights of Sexual Minorities: A Crisis of the Male/Female Dichotomy," 30 *Hastings L.J.* 1131, 1137 (1978–1979).

Is this a good proposal? Can you foresee problems of workability or fairness that might beset Dunlap's proposal? How would you overcome those practical or dignitary problems? Consider these abstract questions also in the context of the use of public restrooms, which remain sex-segregated in most public spaces.

NOTES ON FEMINIST THEORY AND INTERSEX PERSONS

1.   *The Complexity of Biological "Sex."* Julia Serano writes from a perspective that understands transgender persons as a primary challenge to the man-woman binary. A somewhat different group, and a different challenge to the notion of sex as a binary, are "intersex" persons, "who were born with mutated, incomplete, or dual genitals; with chromosomal patterns other than XX or XY; or whose gender identity development was affected in some manner by pre-natal hormonal imbalances." Frye & Rose, "Responsible Representation of Your First Transgendered Client." Some trans as well as feminist theorists accept biological sex as a given; intersex persons expose that assumption as more complicated.

A biological *man* is conventionally understood to have XY chromosomes; the androgen hormone is the dominant one in his body; physiologically, he has testes (reproductive organs), a prostate and seminal vesicles (internal organs), and a penis/scrotum (external organs). A biological *woman* is conventionally understood to have XX chromosomes; the estrogen hormone is the dominant one in her body; physiologically, she has ovaries (reproductive organs), a vagina and a uterus (internal organs), and a clitoris/labia (external organs). As many as two percent of the human population varies from these templates. Among the variations are the following:

- *Chromosomal Variation.* Some humans are born with XXX, XXY, XXXY, XYY, XYYY, XYYYY, XO chromosomes. This often causes other characteristics to be ambiguous.

- *Hormonal Variation.* Humans usually have both androgen and estrogen; prototypical males and females have a balance strongly tipped toward the former (men) or the latter (women). Many humans have a different balance or a balance that does not match their chromosomes. Hormonal variation usually produces non-typical secondary characteristics such as breast development or facial hair.

- *Physiological Variation.* Many individuals have ambiguous reproductive organs, including one ovary and one testis, "streak gonads" that are neither ovaries nor testes, and ovotestes which combine the functions of both ovaries and testes. Others have ambiguous external organs, such as an undeveloped penis or a large clitoris that resembles a penis.

Julie Greenberg, "The Road Less Traveled: The Problem with Binary Sex Categories," in *Transgender Rights* 51, 56 (Paisley Currah et al. eds., 2006) (documenting these and other natural variations).

As a matter of biology, *sex* is not so much a binary (man/woman) as it is a continuum, with man and woman as poles and with variations falling in between. See Anne Fausto-Sterling, "The Five Sexes: Why Male and Female Are Not Enough," *The Sciences*, Apr./May 1993, at 20–24, and "Five Sexes, Revisited," 40 *Sciences* 18–23 (2000) (responding to objections). Indeed, if biological sex is some kind of continuum, it is not inevitable that man and woman are the poles; the categories might be arrayed in any number of ways.

2. *Should Feminists Be Challenging the Man-Woman Binary?* Mary Dunlap, Katherine Franke, Julia Serano, and other theorists argue that transsexuals are *central* to the feminist project, understood as one that challenges rigid gender roles. Adding to that line of thinking, Professor Julie Greenberg argues that feminists should reject the man-woman binary on the ground that it is oppressive to intersex persons, whose lives are complicated and sometimes ruined by their struggles to fit into the categories. See Greenberg, "Problem with Binary Sex Categories," 51. Professor Dean Spade makes a similar argument on the ground that such categorization is oppressive to transsexual persons. See Dean Spade, "Documenting Gender," 59 *Hastings L.J.* 731 (2008) (excerpted in Section 3 of this chapter).

Other feminists have been reluctant to include transsex and intersex persons in the movement. Why would feminists be reluctant on this score? In the 1970s, feminists were nervous that transsexuals endangered their prospects for the ERA, as Dunlap points out; these political concerns have abated but by no means disappeared. A great power of the women's rights movement is that women are a majority of the voting population, and any issue as to which women are largely united is one that even the most traditionalist politician can ignore at his peril. But many women themselves are nervous about transgender persons, and most do not understand intersex persons.

As a theoretical matter, Robin West believes that women are fundamentally different from men because of their potential pregnancies; male-to-female transsexuals and most intersexuals are not "like" biological women in this regard. On the other hand, West's individualistic focus on hedonic goods suggests that she would agree with Dunlap, Greenberg, and Spade, that social or legal categories ought not close off life opportunities for sex and gender minorities. Surely Gayle Rubin would agree with this latter point. How about Catharine MacKinnon? Does anti-dominance theory have any room for intersex persons?

3. *Should Sex Be Irrelevant? Or a Matter of Choice?* Recall, from Problem 3-3, that Mary Dunlap proposed that one's *sex* ought to be a matter of the individual's choice, a classically liberal rule. Specifically, she proposed that "the two-sex presumption in law" be replaced by "a principle that one's sex could be determined by that person, that the choice of sex were not limited to male or female, and that the person could make different determinations as to sex identification for various purposes, such as education, marriage, living arrangements, or personal physical appearance." Dunlap, "Constitutional Rights of Sexual Minorities," 30 *Hastings L.J.* at 1137.

Remarkably, in the generation since Dunlap's article was published, agencies all over the country have developed policies that allow persons to seek reclassification of their "sex" on state and federal identification documents, including birth certificates, social security cards, driver's licenses, and passports. *See* Spade, "Documenting Gender," 760–75 (documenting this development and outlining the formal procedures one must follow). But the transgender person is still faced with a bewildering array of different rules and often ends up being a man for some regulatory purposes and a woman for others (pp. 790–801).

The United Kingdom has largely followed Mary Dunlap's suggestion. Its Gender Recognition Act of 2004 created a central administrative process for sex reassignment, which then applies across the full range of sex-identifying documents. Does this solve the problem? In "Documenting Gender," Dean Spade argues not. Much of Spade's argument rests upon our sad experience with the current system. "Despite the fact that 'common sense' suggests that gender is a stable, obvious, clear indicator of human difference, rulemakers using 'common sense' definitions of gender have come up with dozens of different rules about what indicates that difference and those rules are enforced inconsistently because the 'common sense' assumptions about gender in the minds of front line workers often differ from the assumptions of the rule. Further, even within a particular agency or institution, the assumptions of the gender reclassification rules are not upheld across the whole population being classified." (Pages 802–03)

Professor Spade's suggestion is that sex and gender be *largely* eliminated as legal categories that show up on identification documents and are used for regulatory policies (such as sex-segregated facilities such as prisons). He would allow the continued use of sex or gender for health care documents and for affirmative action policies, but not for passports, birth certificates, social security documents, etc. Is this where feminist theory should lead? Consider the following problem after you have thought about your response.

PROBLEM 3-4
THE INTERSEX OLYMPIAN?

The International Association of Athletic Federations and the International Olympic Committee have had clear policies to deal with transgender athletes since 2003. Under the Stockholm Consensus, individuals that undergo sex reassignment surgery after puberty may be eligible to compete against others of their chosen gender provided that: (1) they have undergone gonadectomy and surgical modification of their external genitalia, (2) they have obtained legal recognition of their assigned sex, and (3) they have begun hormonal therapy for the assigned sex at least three years prior to competition. IOC Medical Comm'n, "Statement of the Stockholm Consensus on Sex Reassignment in Sports" (2003).

This policy did not resolve the case of Caster Semenya, the 2008 World Champion in the women's 800 meter sprint. Although raised as a woman, Semenya was physiologically ambiguous, as she had a pair of undescended testes, a physical trait that provided her with three times the testosterone generated by the body of the average female. *See* Ariel Levy, "Either/Or," *The New Yorker,* Nov. 30, 2009. Once this was uncovered, Semenya was barred from international competition and her world title stripped (and later reinstated). Should feminists be concerned about this? Jot down your answer now, and then consider the following materials.

Testes produce androgen hormones at much higher levels than those generally present in the female population. These hormones not only increase the protein component of muscle, making it stronger, they also stimulate the production of red blood cells, which allows the body to process oxygen more quickly. Some experts believe that male-to-female transsexuals (or trans women, as Serano would argue) are, as a class, systematically stronger than natural-born females because they "have been under the influence of hormones under their former gender during their puberty." Arne Ljungqvist, Explanatory Note to the Recommendation on Sex Reassignment and Sports (2004).

How that plays out for intersex persons depends on whether they produce greater-than-average levels of androgen compounds, as Caster Semenya does.

The estrogen therapy that trans women undergo increases body fat even as the drop in testosterone due to castration decreases muscle mass and oxygen uptake. Because hormone therapy does not affect bone mass, trans men must support a heavy skeletal structure and additional fat with substantially less muscle than they possessed prior to transitioning. This can put these athletes at a distinct disadvantage, even vis-à-vis genotypic females, in sports that require body mass to be supported by the limbs. This kind of argument does not apply to Semenya, however, because she has not been taking estrogen therapy. (Indeed, she did not "transition" in any way, as she believed herself to be a woman.)

Consider also Catharine MacKinnon's argument in "Women, Self-Possession, and Sport," in *Feminism Unmodified* 119, that women's participation in athletics would be a powerful force undermining stereotypes of women as weak and submissive. There is a lot of evidence that this phenomenon has been a very powerful one. Would this project be advanced by treating intersex persons such as Caster Semenya as a woman? Trans women?

Postscript. Caster Semenya won the gold medal in the women's 800 meters at the 2016 Olympics in Rio de Janeiro—but only after a court required the Olympics to allow her to participate in that event.

SECTION 3

POST-LIBERAL THEORIES OF SEXUALITY, GENDER, AND THE LAW

Liberal theories of sex, sexuality, gender, and the law have been ascendant in the last generation—but their very success has stirred not only the traditionalist responses noted above (the new natural law and modernized justifications for at least some features of the natural law model), but also progressive responses. We group the progressive critics of the liberal model *post-liberal*.[a] A critical difference between liberal and post-liberal thinkers is the extent to which they believe the "self" is prior to or independent of society. Liberals claim there are *some* fixities—like sex as a biological category—that constitute the individual separate from societal forces, while post-liberal thinkers claim that society produces all or most of the self. From this observation, we can trace three ideas that unite post-liberal thinkers (including some that have made important contributions to liberal theories, such as Professors Catharine MacKinnon and Dean Spade) and that distinguish them from liberal views.

First, the liberal model can disaggregate sex, gender, and sexuality, because only some of these features are socially produced. On this model, sex belongs to the realm of biology, gender to the realm of culture, and sexuality to something of both (Figure 3-2). In contrast, post-liberal thinkers claim that sex, gender, and sexuality are all socially produced in interdependent "performances," as diagrammed in Figure 3–3. Even if sex had some fixed, biological basis, our understanding of it is invariably translated through a social or cultural lens.

---

[a] For different surveys of the landscape of post-liberal, or "queer," theories about sexuality, gender, and the law, see, e.g., Janet Halley, *Split Decisions: How and Why to Take a Break From Feminism* (2006).

Figure 3-3. A Post-Liberal Model of Sex, Gender, and Sexuality

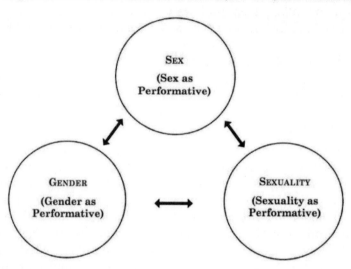

Second, different views of the self also produce different views of the state and its ideal role. For the liberal, the individual responds to external stimuli to realize personal desires. (Recall Richard Posner's cost-benefit analysis of sexual preferences.) The Hobbesian state then takes these preferences as exogenous variables along which to maximize social welfare and minimize harm. In contrast, post-liberals claim that people's preferences and identities are endogenous to law. They are not set givens to which the state then responds; laws *produce* the very preferences, behaviors, and identity categories they attempt to regulate. Post-liberal thinkers (like traditionalists who support the natural law model) thus question the notion that the liberal state can ever be neutral.

Take the example government-issued identification documents that require gender classifications. Recall Mary Dunlap's classically liberal solution to the issues these create for transgender people: let people choose their identifications. In contrast, a post-liberal approach would criticize the state for making the classification in the first place. By making salient certain distinctions over others, the state constructs a reality in which these differences are considered essential, and embeds certain social norms (*e.g.*, everyone must have a determinate gender, either male or female). A state that does not openly discriminate can just as powerfully harm minorities by contributing to pervasive normalizing discourse that marginalizes them. What, then, is the role of the state for the post-liberal? Answers vary. In our excerpt below, Dean Spade advocates deregulation—*e.g.*, get rid of state-required gender classifications altogether. Other approaches, such as the excerpt from Jasbir Puer below, advocate that the state aim for *counterhegemonic* discourse.

Third, post-liberals also diverge from liberal ideals of *liberty* and *equality*. A libertarian baseline for regulation makes sense when the state is seen as built up from individuals in social contract. Because the state exists to facilitate the flourishing of members, it owes a high degree of respect to individual liberty and preferences. The baseline makes less sense for the post-liberal, who sees facts about society creating and explaining facts about individuals (and not the other way around). The baseline concern then focuses less on individuals and more on the society that produces them: which social discourses are productive, and which are ossified and hegemonic?

The post-modern picture of equality is also more complicated. The liberal paradigm begins with a strong assumption that people are moral equals. This presumption then tends to explain away differences as irrelevant to social standing: where it counts, we are the same. When people are marginalized, reforms should aim at disrupting hierarchies to bring people on equal footing. Post-liberal thinkers imagine power, subordination, and inequality in a more dynamic fashion. Power relations do not merely subjugate and suppress, but invariably produce resistance, rebellion, and new discourses that transform the landscape of ever-shifting power dynamics.

One way to cash out these differences is through the theories' respective responses to sex, gender, and sexual variations. Beginning with strong egalitarian premises, liberal thinkers like Dr. Alfred Kinsey argued that these variations were benign: we should attach no normative significance to them because they harm neither their bearer nor third parties. Post-liberal thinkers, in contrast, emphasize these differences for their critical productivity in dislodging the baseline against which they are considered deviations.

Consider an example. Some traditionalists argue that the presence of openly gay, transgender, or intersex people in elementary and secondary schools is "disruptive" of the educational enterprise. Liberals respond that sex, gender, or sexuality differences are benign and have no relationship to the merit of a schoolteacher or guidance counselor. Post-liberals insist that the differences are not just benign, but also socially productive and transformative, precisely because microperformances[b] by gender benders and sexual minorities in educational settings disrupt notions that being gay or transgender is "weird" or "unnatural." It is *good* and not just tolerable to have gay, transgender, and intersex persons in schools, for their open presence disrupts misleading natural law notions that one man, one woman marriages are to some extent socially constructed and not inevitable as a matter of biology. (Cf. Professor

---

[b] Erving Goffman, *The Presentation of Self in Everyday Life* xi (1959); *see* Marc Poirier, "Microperformances of Identity: Visible Same-Sex Couples and the Marriage Controversy," 15 *Wash. & Lee J. C.R. & Soc. Just.* 3 (2008) (applying Goffman's insight to gay rights identity politics).

Crenshaw's argument that analyzing differences among women leads to critical insights in feminist theory.)

We could have included Professor MacKinnon's *Signs* article in this section (and you might reread the article now)—but instead we start with Michel Foucault's exciting thesis that sexuality is socially constructed and with feminist and transgender expansions of that theory (Part A). More briefly, we consider Eve Kosofsky Sedgwick's brilliant but more difficult deconstructionist understanding of the mobility of sexual and gender tropes (Part B). The concluding part takes up the role that law plays in the social construction process (Part C). For example, Professor Dean Spade argues that law's obsession with categories and classifications creates much greater misery for transgender persons. Equally alarming is the work of Jasbir Puar, who links traditional western homophobia with our newer Islamophobia in her argument that "homonationalism" helps rally the populace behind the common enemy, cast as "queer terrorists."

A. SOCIAL CONSTRUCTIONIST THEORIES

1. SEXUALITY AS A SOCIAL CONSTRUCTION (MICHEL FOUCAULT)

Interpreting the Kinsey data, Mary McIntosh, "The Homosexual Role," 16 *Soc. Prob.* 182 (1968), reprinted in *Forms of Desire: Sexual Orientation and the Homosexual Role* 25 (Edward Stein ed. 1990), asked: Why is it that "sexual orientation" is considered such an important object of study? She maintained that sexual orientation is a role created by society, and indeed created for socially regulatory purposes. Thus, there is no transhistorical phenomenon that can be called "homosexuality." For most Americans, this is an astonishing statement. What about the Greeks? Weren't they "homosexuals"? While it is true that men and women of earlier times engaged in same-sex intimacies, sodomy between two men in ancient Greece had different social and even physical meanings than it does today. A *sodomite* in the nineteenth century perceived himself much differently than the *pederast* of ancient Athens or the *homosexual* of today.

The French philosopher Michel Foucault brilliantly developed McIntosh's insight.[c] The first volume (*Introduction*) of his *History of Sexuality* (published in English 1978) maintains that "sexuality" is a consequence of an ongoing and increasingly focused attention to the body by priests, doctors, psychiatrists, and bureaucrats. Foucault explores the

---

[c] The account of Foucault draws mainly from his *Introduction*, volume one of *History of Sexuality* (Robert Hurley trans. 1978), and from his essay "Afterword: The Subject and the Power," in *Beyond Structuralism and Hermeneutics* (Hubert L. Dreyfuss & Paul Rabinow eds., 1982). Particularly useful secondary sources are Vikki Bell, *Interrogating Incest: Feminism, Foucault and the Law* (1993); Celia Kitzinger, *The Social Construction of Lesbianism* (1987); David Macey, *The Lives of Michel Foucault* (1995).

archaeology of sexuality (its genealogy as an idea) through several interrelated inquiries and critiques.

(a) *Foucault's Critique of the Repressive Hypothesis.* One of Foucault's central insights was to challenge the conventional wisdom that the relationship between power and sexuality and erotic activity is one of repression. It is a staple of popular thinking that traditionalist societies repressed sex and that, in the last several decades, sexual rebels have sought liberation from these edicts. Not so, said Foucault. He perceived a very different history.

Foucault started with the seventeenth-century Christian practice of the confessional. A conventional view understands the confessional only as a moment when the Church exercises its power over the penitent, who is required to divulge any sins against ecclesiastical proscriptions. Foucault, however, describes the confessional as the practice that "prescribed as a fundamental duty the task of passing everything having to do with sex through the endless mill of speech." (*Introduction* 21.) This method of transforming sex into discourse became "a rule for everyone" and thus a prime example of what Foucault calls "an incitement" to talk about sex. "This is the essential thing: that Western man has been drawn for three centuries to the task of telling everything concerning his sex" (p. 23). Thus, while laws and customs may have formally prohibited certain sexual behaviors and effectively limited sexual speech in many situations (between parent and child, for example), "at the level of discourses and their domains . . . the opposite phenomenon occurred[:] . . . a proliferation of discourses concerned with sex" (p. 18).

The technique of generating confessional speech or sex-talk was later reinforced and expanded by mechanisms of power other than the Church. Beginning in the eighteenth century, governments started to understand that they were dealing not just with subjects or citizens, but with a "population." At the heart of the issue of population was sex. Thus agencies of the state developed an interest in birth rates, age of marriage, illegitimacy and procreative practices. In short, sexual conduct began to be understood as having a direct relationship to the wealth and security of nations. "It was essential that the state know what was happening with its citizens' sex, and the use they made of it, but also that each individual be capable of controlling the use he made of it. Between the state and the individual, sex became an issue, and a public issue no less; a whole web of discourses, special knowledges, analyses and injunctions settled upon it" (p. 26).

Foucault cites the (French) school system of the 1700s as an example of an institutional system in which, on the surface, sex was eradicated but where, *sub rosa,* it was a driving force. "The space for classes, the shape of the tables, the planning of the recreation lessons, the distribution of the dormitories (with or without partitions, with or without curtains), the rules for monitoring bedtime and sleep periods— all this referred, in the most prolix manner, to the sexuality of children"

(*Introduction*, p. 28).[d] It was deemed of paramount importance to monitor the children (boys) for any signs of sexuality and to take all possible precautions to prevent masturbation. Because of the perceived dangers of masturbation, "devices of surveillance were installed; traps were laid for compelling admissions; inexhaustible and corrective discourses were imposed; parents and teachers were alerted, and left with the suspicion that all children were guilty, and with the fear of being themselves at fault if their suspicions were not sufficiently strong; they were kept in readiness in the face of this recurrent danger; their conduct was prescribed and their pedagogy recodified; an entire medico-sexual regime took hold of the family milieu" (p. 42).

In the nineteenth century, medical discourse became the primary arena in which sexuality was penalized and stigmatized, yet also simultaneously incited, monitored, and commented upon. In a critical development, the mode of the confessional was medicalized and, in turn, was reconceptualized as "therapeutic." Modern sexology acquired its professional status during the Victorian period. Officially, Victorians adhered to the "triple edict of taboo, nonexistence and silence" about sex (p. 3). But that era also witnessed an unprecedented explosion of detailed examination, analysis, and speculation about these supposedly taboo topics.

In sum, Foucault interpreted the history of sexuality not as a simple story of the repression of sex, but as a much more complicated process "that spreads [sex] over the surface of things and bodies, arouses it, draws it out and bids it speak, implants it in reality and enjoins it to tell the truth" (p. 72).

(b) Systems of Power. This is interesting, you may be thinking, but what about all those repressive laws? Foucault saw power systems as more complex than law and rejected the underlying assumptions of a law-centered view of the world. He critiqued the precepts of what he called "juridico-discursive power" (classically displayed in the *liberal model*) as naive. Power is not simply the state, he wrote, but resides in a multiplicity of interconnecting (and sometimes contradictory) systems. For example, Foucault maintained that the educational, religious, and medical systems exercised greater power with respect to sexuality than did the law. Where others might see a social/sexual structure dichotomized as freedom and repression or the individual versus the state, Foucault saw "a veritable 'technology' of sex" with multiple and conflicting players and effects (p. 90).

---

[d]   *Règlement de police pour les lycées* (1809) (quoted in *Introduction* 28 n. 12) sets forth a regime that Foucault maintains was primarily geared toward preventing masturbation, e.g., art. 67: "There shall always be, during class and study hours, an instructor watching the exterior, so as to prevent students who have gone out to relieve themselves from stopping and congregating."

Foucault maintained that power comes from everywhere—from the bottom up and not just from the top down. The *Introduction* to his *History of Sexuality* understood power as a complex web:

> It seems to me that power must be understood in the first instance as the multiplicity of force relations immanent in the sphere in which they operate and which constitute their own organization; as the process which, through ceaseless struggles and confrontations, transforms, strengthens, or reverses them; as the support which these force relations find in one another, thus forming a chain or a system, or on the contrary, the disjunctions and contradictions, which isolate them from one another; and lastly, as the strategies in which they take effect, whose general design or institutional crystallization is embodied in the state apparatus, in the formulation of the law, in the various social hegemonies. * * * [P]ower is not an institution, and not a structure; neither is it a certain strength we are endowed with; it is the name that one attributes to a complex strategical situation in a particular society. (Pages 92–93.)

Systems of power relations ("force relations") enable and produce specific discourses, such as the discourses on sex. Discourses, or systems of understanding and practice, implement power relations, but also create points of resistance. "Discourse transmits and produces power; it reinforces it, but also undermines and exposes it, renders it fragile and makes it possible to thwart it" (p. 101.) A hegemonic (or dominant) discourse that presents homosexuality as an illness, for example, not only propagates that idea, but also can incite reaction, rebuttal, and rebellion.

Key to Foucault's theory is the belief that the operation of power is not simply prohibitory or negative. Power systems *produce* sexuality as well as prohibit it.

(c) Sexuality as a Discursive Production. As the "discursive explosion" regarding sex continued through the nineteenth century, its subjects (and objects) began to jell. Foucault perceived a gradual organization of power-knowledge around four subjects: the "hysterization" of women's bodies (in which women's bodies were analyzed "as being thoroughly saturated with sexuality"); a "pedagogization" of children's sex; "a socialization of procreative sex"; and "a psychiatrization of perverse pleasure" (pp. 104–05). What occurred was nothing less than "the very production of sexuality. Sexuality must not be thought of as a kind of natural given which power tries to hold in check, or as an obscure domain which knowledge tries gradually to uncover. It is the name that can be given to a historical construct: not a furtive reality that is difficult to grasp, but a great surface network in which the stimulation of bodies, the intensification of pleasures, the incitement to discourse, the formation of special knowledges, the strengthening of controls and resistances, are linked to one another, in

accordance with a few major strategies of knowledge and power" (pp. 105–06). In other words, the very same regulatory discourse that is conventionally described as repressive actually *produced* what we understand as sexuality.

One specific example of this was the production of (the idea of) homosexuality. In analyzing the sexologists's study of "perverse pleasures" and what Foucault called "peripheral sexualities," he made his now famous observation dating the invention of homosexuality (as distinct from same-sex sexual practices) as a nineteenth century event:

> This new persecution of the peripheral sexualities entailed an *incorporation of perversions* and a new *specification of individuals.* As defined by the ancient civil or canonical codes, sodomy was a category of forbidden acts; their perpetrator was nothing more than the juridical subject of them. The nineteenth-century homosexual became a personage, a past, a case history, and a childhood. * * * Nothing that went into his total composition was unaffected by his sexuality. * * * The sodomite had been a temporary aberration; the homosexual was now a species. (Pages 42–43, emphasis in the original.)

Consider also that some of the arguments advocating equality for gay people are framed in terms suggestive of a view of the homosexual as a distinct type of person. We tend to think of *Bowers v. Hardwick* as the classic situs of repression, to which "gay liberation" was a response. Himself a gay man, Foucault would critique both homophobia and gay rights, as representing simply the flip sides of a coin, both equally trapped inside one discursive system.

We hope this discussion gives you some understanding of the complicated way in which sexual discourse operates, and the larger context in which Foucault comprehends this system. A further and important feature of that larger context is Foucault's tentative theory of sexuality as a dynamic system, and its implications for the future. Before *sexuality* became an important system, *alliance* was the primary system for understanding and organizing households (in rural, nonwestern societies alliance is still typically the primary organizational system). In contrast to sexuality, a new and destabilizing system, alliance was a longstanding and homeostatic system: its mechanism was to establish ties of blood and marriage, and its goal was to protect and reproduce the traditional patriarchal family (pp. 105–06). The modern era may be characterized by the eclipse of the regime of alliance and its gradual supplantation by the regime of sexuality.

The family is the situs of this transition, and now its battleground. Premodern society viewed the family as the fundamental unit of society, and individuals were formed in the shadow of family ties. One's identity was framed in relation to one's parents, one's spouse, and kinship group. Where families had earlier left children to their own devices in exploring genitals and gender, bourgeois families of the early modern era became highly attentive to children's masturbation and so forth. The attention showered on this matter not only sexualized certain body parts, but also sexualized the family itself. Thus the family, the apex of alliance, became the birthplace of sexuality, which now often overshadows alliance as the basis of individual identity.

The discourse of sexuality has hardly abated in western culture, and Foucault saw its productiveness only multiplying in the future. Traditional ties of family and kinship will be evermore overtaken by ties of pleasure and corporality. Foucault believed that the future would dissolve many of the boundaries that we cleave to insistently now (such as the significance of sexual orientation) and would multiply the categories of pleasure. In his most visionary moment, he predicted "nothing less than a transgression of laws, a lifting of prohibitions, an irruption of speech, a reinstating of pleasure within reality, and a whole new economy in the mechanisms of power will be required" (p. 5.)

PROBLEM 3-5
FOUCAULDIAN STRATEGIES FOR UNDERSTANDING LAWS REGULATING SEX, GENDER, AND SEXUALITY

Consider three different kinds of laws: (a) state regulation of contraceptives and private nonprocreative (oral and anal) intercourse; (b) state maintenance of a sex-segregated public college that provides para-military training for its students, many of whom go on to serve as officers in the armed forces; and (c) state and federal requirements that persons eligible to drive, receive social security and medicare, and travel internationally have different identification cards that include a face picture, a physical description (hair and eye color, height, weight, etc.), and specification of the person's sex (man or woman). How would Foucault's philosophy understand the discourses involved in each law? What power dynamics does each law reflect? How does each law contribute to the construction of a particular understanding of sexuality or gender? How would the invalidation affect that discourse? Jot down your thoughts, and then read the following materials.

Jed Rubenfeld, "The Right to Privacy"
102 *Harvard Law Review* 737, 783–84, 800 (1989).*

* * * The methodology heretofore universal in privacy analysis has begun with the question, "What is the state trying to forbid?" The proscribed conduct is then delineated and its significance tested through a pre-established conceptual apparatus: for its role in "the concept of ordered liberty," its status as a "fundamental" right, its importance to one's identity, or for any other criterion of fundamentality upon which a court can settle. Suppose instead we began by asking not what is being *prohibited*, but what is being *produced*. Suppose we looked not to the negative aspect of the law—the interdiction by which it formally

---

*   Copyright © Harvard Law Review Association. Reprinted by permission.

expresses itself—but at its positive aspect: the real effects that conformity with the law produces at the level of everyday lives and social practices. * * *

* * * There *is* something fundamental at stake in the privacy decisions, but it is not the proscribed conduct, nor even the freedom of decision—it is not what is being taken away.

The distinctive and singular characteristic of the laws against which the right to privacy has been applied lies in their *productive* or *affirmative* consequences. There are perhaps no legal proscriptions with more profound, more extensive, or more persistent affirmative effects on individual lives than the laws struck down as violations of the right to privacy. Anti-abortion laws, anti-miscegenation laws, and compulsory education laws all involve the forcing of lives into well-defined and highly confined institutional layers. At the simplest, most quotidian level, such laws tend to *take over* the lives of the persons involved: they occupy and preoccupy. They affirmatively and very substantially shape a person's life; they direct a life's development along a particular avenue. These laws do not simply proscribe one act or remove one liberty; they inform the totality of a person's life.

The principle of the right to privacy is not the freedom to do certain, particular acts determined to be fundamental through some ever-progressing normative lens. It is the fundamental freedom not to have one's life too totally determined by a progressively more normalizing state. * * *

The danger, then, is a particular kind of creeping totalitarianism, an unarmed *occupation* of individuals' lives. That is the danger of which Foucault as well as the right to privacy is warning us: a society standardized and normalized, in which lives are too substantially or too rigidly directed. That is the threat posed by state power in our century. * * *

Most fundamentally, the prohibition against homosexual sex channels individuals' sexual desires into *reproductive* outlets. Although the prohibition does not, like the law against abortions, produce as an imminent consequence compulsory child-bearing, it nonetheless forcibly directs individuals into the pathways of reproductive sexuality, rather than the socially "unproductive" realm of homosexuality. These pathways are further guided, in our society, into particular institutional orbits, chief among which are the nuclear family and the constellation of practices surrounding a heterosexuality that is defined in conscious contradistinction to homosexuality. Indeed, it is difficult to separate our society's inculcation of a heterosexual identity from the simultaneous inculcation of a dichotomized complementarity of roles to be borne by men and women. Homosexual couples by necessity throw into question the allocation of specific functions—whether professional, personal, or emotional—between the sexes. It is this aspect of the ban on homosexuality—its central role in the maintenance of institutionalized sexual identities and normalized reproductive relations—that have made its *affirmative* or *formative* consequences, as well as the reaction against these consequences, so powerful a force in modern society. * * *

NOTES ON FOUCAULT AND CONSTITUTIONAL DISCOURSE

1. *Implications for the Constitutional Privacy Right.* If Professor Rubenfeld is correct that law produces as well as restricts behaviors, consider this suggestion: "Rather than ask how individuals can be shielded from the exercise of state power, we should ask how state power might be invoked to restructure aspects of personal life in order to eliminate distorting factors in people's own interactions and personal decisionmaking." Stephen Schnably, "Beyond *Griswold*: Foucauldian and Republican Approaches to Privacy," 23 *Conn. L. Rev.* 861, 870 (1991). Professor Schnably argues that the state should set the proper context for abortion counseling not merely by mandating that high quality, personalized counseling be made available, but also by providing funding for abortions and for day care, so that a woman's decision can be truly uncoerced (pp. 940–41).

This analysis might suggest that the Supreme Court might have been right in *Planned Parenthood v. Casey* (1992) (Chapter 2) to uphold the state's informed consent requirements before a woman could secure an abortion. Does this analysis also support *Casey*'s holding that the state may require minors to notify or obtain the consent of one or both parents before they can secure abortions (with a bypass process where notice or consent is not practical)? The state's argument is that minors are prey to "distorting factors" and so need a more guided process. This is also an argument offered by Operation Outcry, a pro-life group: because many women regretted the procedure, the state could ban it. As you see, Foucault can come in quite handy for traditionalists to support natural law baselines; recall that the central claim of natural law theory is that it reflects the best, time-tested way to structure people's lives.

2. *Gender, Sex, and Equal Protection.* Professor Rubenfeld's Foucauldian approach to the constitutional privacy right could also support equal protection arguments for women and transgender persons denied state benefits and opportunities because of their sex, including gender stereotyping and gender identity. Rather than asking whether sex is a suspect classification, Rubenfeld might ask, instead, what life opportunities women or transsexuals were being denied and whether this was fair for the state to deny them such opportunities. An important punchline of Rubenfeld's analysis is that it might apply to positive governmental benefits, such as Medicaid (of great value to transsex people), as well as to negative governmental actions, such as allowing reparative surgery on intersex infants.

3. *Foucault and Religious Liberty?* Foucauldian theory may be postmodern, but progressives have no monopoly on its reasoning. For example, religious minorities (today, Americans who believe gay marriage violates the Word of God) have Foucauldian arguments to support their plea for religious exemptions from anti-discrimination laws? For example, a devout Southern Baptist baker now finds himself surrounded by married same-sex couples, out lesbian and gay performers, and gay pride parades and so forth. If Rubenfeld is right that the religious baker has a "fundamental freedom not to have one's life too totally determined by a progressively more normalizing state," why doesn't he have a fundamental right to pull his children from school on days that "homosexuality" or "homosexual marriages" are discussed? To be free of any duty (sometimes imposed by laws barring discrimination by public accommodations and service providers) to bake wedding cakes for lesbian or gay marriage ceremonies? How might gay rights supporters respond to this Foucauldian argument?

NOTE ON FEMINISM AND FOUCAULT

Michel Foucault's theory enjoys a complicated relationship with feminist theory.[e] Foucault's analysis of power relations simultaneously criticizes the feminist emancipation agenda, while providing fresh tools for the critical evaluation of patriarchy. For their part, feminists have cogently challenged and amended Foucault's theories. Consider the following lines of dialogue between feminists and Foucault.

There is much that Foucault and feminist theories have in common, for both lines of thought are critical of the traditional wisdom about sex and sexuality. Foucault provides feminism another vocabulary for situating and problematizing the work of the early sexologists. Most of the sexologists (including Freud) have insisted that women's sexual pleasure is tied to the male penis. Both feminists and Foucault deny that this claim flows from any "natural science" and insist that the thought is instead linked with other power relations, such as the traditional subordination of women to men in western society. For Foucault as for most feminists, there is nothing unnatural about sex between two women, and the hysteria it creates in men is related to threats those men see to their power, specifically, their monopoly on female sexuality.

For many feminists, Foucault's thought is not very helpful, however, in ignoring the *gendering aspects of sexuality*. As Professor Vikki Bell puts it,

> Foucault's central interest is with the production of the concept of sexuality and categories of sexuality ('homosexual', 'heterosexual', 'paedophiliac', etc.) through knowledge/power networks. By contrast, feminists are more interested in those knowledges which create a differential relationship between men and women, or that act against women as a group. Knowledges which suggest that women need men in order to experience sexual satisfaction, which situate lesbianism as a deviant sexual choice, which depict

---

[e] The works most helpful to us in this regard include Vikki Bell, *Interrogating Incest: Feminism, Foucault and the Law* (1993); Judith Butler, *Gender Trouble: Feminism and the Subversion of Identity* (1990), and *Undoing Gender* (2004); Janet Halley, *Split Decisions: How and Why to Take a Break From Feminism* (2006); Susan Hekman, *Gender and Knowledge: Elements of a Postmodern Feminism* (1990); Carol Smart, *Feminism and the Power of Law* (1989); Ann Snitow et al., *Powers of Desire: The Politics of Sexuality* (1984); Biddy Martin, "Feminism, Criticism and Foucault," and other essays in *Feminism and Foucault: Reflections on Resistance* (Irene Diamond & Lee Quinby eds. 1988); Nancy Hartsock, "Foucault on Power: A Theory for Women?" in *Feminism/Postmodernism* (Linda J. Nicholson ed. 1990).

masculine sexuality as inherently predatory, have been considered by feminists not simply as powerful knowledges that constrain all individuals, but as powerful knowledges that differentially constrain women. Crucially, the central concern of feminism is the way in which these ways of understanding sexuality have operated to make women subordinate to men as individuals and as a group.

The major feminist criticism of Foucault's thesis on sexuality therefore is that he fails to consider what one might term the *gendering* aspects of sexuality. * * * What he fails to do is consider how the strategies of sexuality affect the relationship *between* men and women as gendered individuals.

Bell, *Interrogating Incest*, 26–27. Foucault does not view the operation of power as so consistently oppressing one group as feminist theorists do. Recall Professor MacKinnon's argument that the social construction of male and female sexuality is the key to gender oppression.

Foucault, in turn, poses an important critique of early feminist theory, namely, its too-simple understanding of power and truth. To the extent that some feminists believe that patriarchy unifies traditional power structures and that the feminist project is to overthrow patriarchy and thereby to liberate women's own true selves, Foucault would dissent. He argues that feminists have no better access to truth than the Victorians and that the feminist emancipatory project is merely the flip side of traditional views that sex is essential and univocal. Feminist resistance to the Victorians is trapped in basically the same vocabulary.

A different strain in early feminist thought was grounded in radical challenges to the sorts of fixed identity categories that Foucault found wanting:

> [T]he real strength of the women's liberation movements is not that of having laid claim to the specificity of their sexuality and the rights pertaining to it, but that they have actually departed from the discourse conducted within the apparatuses of sexuality. Ultimately, it is a veritable movement of de-sexualisation, a displacement effected in relation to the sexual centering of the problem, formulating the demand for forms of culture, discourse, language and so on, which are no longer part of that rigid assignation and pinning-down to their sex which they had initially in some sense been politically obliged to accept in order to make themselves heard.

Michel Foucault, *Power/Knowledge: Selected Interviews and Other Writings* 219–20 (Colin Gordon ed. 1980). Note how Foucault's analysis mixes concepts of sex, sexuality, and, implicitly, gender.

Consider Professor Judith Butler's elaboration. Sex for the Victorians was univocal insofar as there was a simple identity between a person and her sex—"one is one's sex" (Butler, *Gender Trouble*, 94). The Victorians argued that sex was the "continuous cause and signification of bodily pleasures." Thus sex was biological, not social. This view produced a distorted understanding of sex, by essentializing it. For the social constructionist, sex is not a cause, but rather an effect of "an open and complex historical system of discourse and power." Sex is social, not biological; and feminism misses this by taking sex as the starting point of its analysis. By accepting sex as the root cause of female domination, some feminist theory fails to grasp that sex is merely an effect of female domination. Some feminists too quickly agree with the patriarch that sex is the reason men dominate women, for she or he should see that men dominate women through the creation of sex. By accepting this effect as a cause, feminism legitimates the regulatory strategy of patriarchy, and is thus self-defeating (pp. 94–95).

A Foucauldian approach emphasizes a more complex understanding of power. Some feminist thought, especially in the early stages, seemed to operate under traditional views about power—what Foucault calls the *juridical* (or legal) model of power: power acts in negative (prohibitory) ways, repressing the illicit; power flows from a central hierarchical source; hence power can be overthrown by the powerless. If, as Foucault imagines, power is "omnipresent," productive rather than prohibitory, and normalizing rather than repressive, the feminist target (patriarchy) becomes more elusive and the role of the state (protect women against patriarchy) more ambiguous.

Butler's expansion of Foucault might be said to undermine the feminist agenda, basically by removing its subject. However theoretically attractive such a stance might be, its effect might be politically enervating. On the other hand, as Susan Hekman has argued, "the assumption that political action, to be valid, must be founded in absolute values is precisely the assumption that Foucault is challenging" (Hekman, *Gender and Knowledge*, 180). The current situation of women is an "unstable truth" that can be the basis for political action and resistance, even if centuries from now our descendants might wonder why we became so anxious about gender as well as sexuality (recall the delphic conclusion of volume one of the *History of Sexuality*). Feminism might be viewed as a resistance discourse, which even if unstable is useful for an often silenced group to be heard (Bell, *Interrogating Incest* 55–56). As Biddy Martin puts it,

> Our task is to deconstruct, to undo our own meanings and categories, the identities and the positions from which we intervene at any given point so as not to close the question of woman and discourse around new certainties and absolutes. We cannot afford to refuse to take a political stance 'which pins us to our sex' for the sake of abstract theoretical correctness, but we can refuse to be content with fixed identities or to universalize ourselves as revolutionary subjects.

Martin, "Feminism, Criticism, and Foucault," 16.

PROBLEM 3-6
FOUCAULT, FEMINISM, RAPE, STATUTORY RAPE, AND INCEST

The criminal codes in virtually all the United States prohibit each of the following three situses of sex: rape (sexual assault), coercive sex against the will of one of the partners; statutory rape, where one of the partners is under the age of consent; and incest, where the partners are closely related. Consider the following case which involves all three of these issues, and consider further how this case illustrates the particular ways our culture has constructed sex and sexuality. Note that the defendant was charged with only one offense (incest), even though the facts also support a charge of rape.

State v. Marvin Kaiser

Washington Court of Appeals, 1983.
34 Wash.App. 559, 663 P.2d 839.

■ MUNSON, ACTING CHIEF JUDGE.

Marvin K. Kaiser appeals his incest conviction, RCW 9A.64.020.[1] He contends the trial court erred in admitting his confession, the evidence was insufficient, improper evidence was admitted at trial, and the incest statute denied him equal protection. We affirm.

Mr. Kaiser was charged with having committed incest with his 16-year-old stepdaughter. On May 13 and 14, Mr. Kaiser met with a police detective to informally discuss the accusation. On May 15, 1981, Mr. Kaiser was advised of his rights as required by *Miranda v. Arizona*, 384 U.S. 436 (1966), and progeny. He indicated he wished to speak to an attorney. The questioning stopped; the detective made immediate arrangements for Mr. Kaiser to meet with a public defender who was present at the jail. Mr. Kaiser and the public defender discussed the charge for 20 to 25 minutes. Mr. Kaiser stated the public defender told him the crime was a felony and advised him not to make a statement.

Mr. Kaiser returned to the detective and decided to make a statement. The detective gave him the *Miranda* warnings from a printed form which Mr. Kaiser initialed and signed. The detective then taped an oral confession from Mr. Kaiser which also began with a waiver of all *Miranda* rights. Mr. Kaiser stated he entered the stepdaughter's bed against her will, disrobed her, engaged in full intercourse for a brief time, realized he had erred, and left. At the end of the statement, Mr. Kaiser signified the statement was true, he understood his *Miranda* rights and waived them, and no promises had been made. [The trial judge held that the confession was voluntary and therefore admissible against Kaiser, a finding the appeals court affirmed.] * * *

At the subsequent nonjury trial, the stepdaughter testified Mr. Kaiser had engaged in sexual intercourse against her wishes. She was asked whether her stepfather put his penis into her vagina. She replied that he had and that she knew this because of the pain. On cross

---

[1] Former RCW 9A.64.020 provided as follows:

"(1) A person is guilty of incest if he engages in sexual intercourse with a person whom he knows to be related to him, either legitimately or illegitimately, as an ancestor, descendant, brother, or sister of either the whole or the half blood.

"(2) As used in this section, "descendant' includes stepchildren and adopted children under eighteen years of age."

examination, she was asked whether there was penetration. She replied, "I can't be sure."

Mr. Kaiser denied the event all together. He again explained the false statement was given to the detective to protect the family from publicity.

The stepdaughter's boyfriend testified she told him the following day that she had been raped by her stepfather. The boyfriend indicated she was distraught and cried for over an hour and a half before telling him; they later reported the incident to school officials.

The detective who received Mr. Kaiser's statement was asked by Mr. Kaiser's counsel whether he had recorded in any statement by the stepdaughter anything which showed penetration had occurred. From her statement, the detective testified she had told him Mr. Kaiser inserted his penis in her vagina. The detective testified he explained the terms to her prior to the statement and she stated she understood them.

The trial court found Mr. Kaiser guilty of incest, reasoning that where the stepdaughter's testimony was equivocal the confession was not. Because the trial court could not accept Mr. Kaiser's stated reasons for making a false statement, the court accepted the statement over the in-court testimony. The court found the stepdaughter's version to be more credible. * * *

Mr. Kaiser * * * contends the stepdaughter's answer on cross examination raised a reasonable doubt. Her testimony was not as equivocal as first appears. On direct, she gave no doubt penetration had occurred. She may not have known the meaning of the word "penetration" because there is a question of whether she knew the meaning of the word "erection". This confusion was not clarified.

Even if a doubt remained after her testimony, Mr. Kaiser's statement and the testimony of both the boyfriend and the detective bolstered her credibility. Although Mr. Kaiser's statement differed from the stepdaughter's testimony in the degree of violence, it essentially agreed on the specific act of intercourse. * * *

Mr. Kaiser finally contends the incest statute denies him equal protection of the law. His argument appears to be twofold: (1) because the "object of the statute was obviously to prevent a procreation of children which may be affected by the relationship of the parties who are closer than second cousins," the inclusion of stepchildren bears no rational relationship to a legitimate governmental objective; and (2) nonconsensual intercourse is punished until age 16 under the statutory rape statutes; equal protection is denied under the incest statute because even consensual intercourse is forbidden to age 18.

Historically, incest was prohibited by ecclesiastical canon; now, it is prohibited by statute. The statutory schemes differ; some states prevent illicit intercourse by consanguinity while others also include relation by affinity. R. Perkins, *Criminal Law*, ch. 5, § 1(c), at 383–84 (2d ed. 1969);

M. Barnes, *Clark & Marshall on Crimes* § 11.05, at 770 (7th ed. 1967); 2 C. Torcia, *Wharton on Criminal Law* § 245, at 403–04 (14th ed. 1979).

Prevention of mutated birth is only one reason for these statutes. The crime is also punished to promote and protect family harmony, to protect children from the abuse of parental authority, and because society cannot function in an orderly manner when age distinctions, generations, sentiments and roles in families are in conflict. *Clark & Marshall, supra* at 770; 2 C. Torcia, *Wharton on Criminal Law* § 242, at 400 (14th ed. 1979). Thus, the statute bears a rational relation to a legitimate governmental objective. The legislation bears a reasonable and substantial relationship to the health, safety, morals or welfare of the public. We hold the statute is therefore constitutional.

Mr. Kaiser notes consensual intercourse is not punishable after a female reaches age 16 except under the incest statute where even consensual intercourse is forbidden to age 18. He then asserts: "Had the defendant chosen merely to live with the mother of Connie, he would have incurred no penalties because of his act of intercourse with the child." Disregarding the fact that this intercourse was not consensual, and was therefore punishable as third degree rape, such a distinction would deny equal protection only if Mr. Kaiser could show the Legislature did not have a legitimate interest in discriminating between such individuals. As noted earlier, incest is a crime which affects the individuals, society, and, to a degree greater than other crimes, the family. The additional 2 years can be seen as an important protection for the family. The State has a legitimate interest in protecting children from parental abuse for an additional 2 years. Whether by consanguinity or affinity, parents have tremendous emotional and material leverage, even after a child reaches 16, which may not exist outside the home. The distinction is reasonable. [The court affirmed Kaiser's conviction.]

Notes on Foucault and Incest, Statutory Rape, and Rape

1.   *The Incest Issue.* Incest is the tension point of Foucault's overlapping systems of individual identity: it is the key taboo in the system of kinship alliance, but the system of sexuality inspires and generates it as part of the family dynamics which literally inculcate sexuality. "[Incest] is manifested as a thing that is strictly forbidden in the family insofar as the latter functions as a deployment of alliance; but it is also a thing that is continually demanded in order for the family to be a hotbed of sexual incitement." (Foucault, *Introduction*, 109.) Thus the incest taboo is not at all the old-fashioned idea moderns make it out to be—its intensity is owed to its central spot in both regimes, of sexuality and alliance. Note, for example, the centrality of the incest taboo for psychoanalysis; Freud is best known for his metaphorical statement of the relationship between family and sexuality—the Oedipus complex.

Consider the implications of Foucault's thought for *Kaiser* and for feminism. Foucault's theory of sexuality provides an interesting defense (only to incest, not to rape) and a fascinating problem with *Kaiser*. By making incest illegal, the state is announcing the convergence between the old regime of alliance and the new regime of sexuality: both are threatened by incest, and their coinciding concerns give incest prohibitions their particular power. On the other hand, criminalizing incest, and making it the occasion for the drama of a court proceeding, ought to intensify the family as a situs for sexuality.

In *Kaiser*, the incest is between a father and a (step)daughter. This is a common scenario, and its typicality has generated enormous feminist interest. Feminists have encouraged women and girls to tell their stories of family (father) abuse and have encouraged mothers and prosecutors to punish men (fathers) who have sex with daughters and stepdaughters. Foucault would question this strategy. Does it not yield the same sort of discourse that produces rather than suppresses sexuality? Is it possible that prohibitory laws make incest "sexy" for men like Marvin Kaiser? How would feminist theorists answer this charge? See Vikki Bell, *Interrogating Incest,* ch. 4, for an excellent discussion.

It has been argued by feminist writers that incest is not quite the taboo that Foucault makes it out to be. Although the taboo may be a deterrent to mother-son sex, fathers apparently have sex often with daughters and stepdaughters, albeit with great secrecy and often some degree of shame. See Judith Lewis Herman & Lisa Hirschman, *Father-Daughter Incest* (1981). Some feminist writers have conceptualized the asymmetrical incest taboo as reflecting the system by which men dominate women: the mother relinquishes her sexual feelings for the son, who enters into the father's world, while the father remains free to initiate the daughter into a sexualized world where men call the shots. See Elizabeth Ward, *Father-Daughter Rape* (1984). These feminists, therefore, understand incest differently from Foucault: incest is important to the system of alliance, not just of family and kinship ties, but of a household which is dominated by men and whose denizens are sexually available to the paterfamilias.

Professor Bell believes that "the incest prohibition functions by making people consider the reaction their behaviour would receive. The imagined reaction may be somebody's reaction in particular, people's reaction in general, or the law's response. * * * On the other hand, MacKinnon's argument that the prohibition or illegality of acts can be 'part of their excitement potential' suggests that the 'prohibition of incest' as a discursive phenomenon may also be involved in the *commission* of incest." (Bell, *Interrogating Incest,* 122.) Within this understanding, what role does *Kaiser*—the prosecution and a court decision affirming a conviction—play in the drama of the incest taboo?

2. *The Sex-with-Minors Issue.* In 1978, Foucault, Guy Hocquenghem, and Jean Danet proposed that consensual sex between adults and minors be legalized. *See* Michel Foucault, *Politics, Philosophy, Culture: Interviews and Other Writings, 1977–1984* (Lawrence Kritzman ed. 1988). Their argument was that existing laws contributed to the child's fragile sexuality by setting it off limits, and deprives the child of the chance to explore her or his desires. Conversely, by creating and focusing on a special breed of criminal, the "child molester," the law sexualizes a certain line and implicitly inviting people to cross over it—in derogation of the policy of protecting children. The three thinkers challenged the naturalness of the categories thus created ("vulnerable child," "child molester") and urged that the policy be abandoned.

Feminist theory has contributed importantly to the regulation of child abuse, and feminist discourse therefore was directly called into question by Foucault, Hocquenghem, and Danet. Feminist theory has tended to see all sex with children as akin to rape. "Adult-child sex is wrong because the fundamental conditions of consent cannot prevail in the relationship between an adult and a child." Emily Driver, "Introduction" to *Child Sexual Abuse: Feminist Perspectives* 5 (1989). If, as some feminists believe, there is a power disparity in all heterosexual relations, how much weight should be given to differences in age? Should relations between an adult woman and an underage male be treated the same or differently than relations between an adult man and an underage woman?

Professor Bell believes that the Foucault critique is much more cogent than his prescription (Bell, *Interrogating Incest*, 154–60). Once he descends into the realm of policy prescription, Foucault falls victim to all the questionable intellectual moves he criticized in *History of Sexuality*—giving too much credit to law as a directive force and ignoring the greater importance of other social forces, idealizing "freedom" as the absence of legal prohibition, and neglecting the impossible question of what "consent" even is. More important, Bell worries that the introduction of a consent defense into adult-child sex will create new and painful discursive possibilities. Testimony in ordinary abuse cases is traumatic enough for the child, and testimony by adult women (subject to vicious cross-examination to establish consent or acquiescence) is traumatic enough for women; consider the double trauma for a child pressed on issues of consent, invitation, and acquiescence. As Bell reminds the Foucauldians, sometimes lines cut off discourse.

3.   *The Rape Issue*. Foucault was no defender of coerced sex, but he found perplexing the way in which rape laws privilege specific zones of the body. If Kaiser had struck his stepdaughter and knocked her teeth loose, he would be in much less legal trouble than if he had intercourse with her. One is assault, the other is sexual assault, which carries a much higher penalty and much greater social stigma. Foucault found such disparities ridiculous, for they gave too much significance to one orifice. See Foucault, *Politics, Philosophy, Culture*, 201–02. Foucault resisted the way in which the deployment of sexuality—the way in which our sexuality is tied up with our identity—is so imperial in our laws as well as our lives.

Moreover, the higher penalty rests upon some fine distinctions. As *Kaiser* suggested, if there had been no "penetration" of the penis into the vagina, there would have been no rape (or statutory rape or incest). Apparently under Washington law, if Kaiser had forced his finger into his stepdaughter's vagina, he would not have been guilty of rape (other states do regulate this as sex, however). Foucault found this just as ridiculous as before. "Sex" is not limited to penis-in-vagina, for it includes a panoply of pleasure-seeking touches. Foucault would both narrow sexuality's imperialism and expand what we mean by sexual pleasure.

Feminists tend to be more favorably impressed with this latter point than the former. *See* especially Monique Plaza, "Our Costs and Their Benefits," 4 *m/f* 31–32 (1980). While feminists do tend to see rape as violence and not just sex, they see it as an especially harmful kind of violence, contrary to Foucault. What he missed is the political dimension of rape's violence: each rape is an assault against womanhood as well as woman, a marker for man's collective power to use and even erase woman. Like Bell, Plaza argues that Foucault neglects the insights of his own earlier work, namely, the social features of actions. A man punching another man is assault of a different nature than a man forcing his penis into a woman or even (Plaza agrees) punching a woman. The latter is more serious because of the other relations of power involved in man's hurting woman.

2. GENDER AND SEX AS SOCIAL CONSTRUCTIONS

Judith Butler, Gender Trouble: Feminism and the Subversion of Identity
Pages 6–7, 22–23, 24–25 (1990).[*]

Although the unproblematic unity of "women" is often invoked to construct a solidarity of identity, a split is introduced in the feminist subject by the distinction between sex and gender. Originally intended to dispute the biology-is-destiny formulation, the distinction between sex and gender serves the argument that whatever biological intractability sex appears to have, gender is culturally constructed: hence, gender is neither the causal result of sex nor as seemingly fixed as sex. The unity of the subject is thus already potentially contested by the distinction that permits of gender as a multiple interpretation of sex.

If gender is the cultural meanings that the sexed body assumes, then a gender cannot be said to follow from a sex in any one way. Taken to its logical limit, the sex/gender distinction suggests a radical discontinuity between sexed bodies and culturally constructed genders. Assuming for the moment the stability of binary sex, it does not follow that the construction of "men" will accrue exclusively to the bodies of males or that "women" will interpret only female bodies. Further, even if the sexes appear to be unproblematically binary in their morphology and constitution (which will become a question), there is no reason to assume that genders ought to remain as two. * * * When the constructed status of gender is theorized as radically independent of sex, gender itself becomes a free-floating artifice, with the consequence that *man* and *masculine* might just as easily signify a female body as a male one, and *woman* and *feminine* a male body as easily as a female one.

* * * And what is "sex" anyway? Is it natural, anatomical, chromosomal, or hormonal, and how is a feminist critic to assess the scientific discourses which purport to establish such "facts" for us? * * *

---

[*]   Copyright © Routledge, 1990. Reprinted by permission.

Is there a history of how the duality of sex was established, a genealogy that might expose the binary opinions as a variable construction? Are the ostensibly binary facts of sex discursively produced by various scientific discourses in the service of other political and social interests? If the immutable character of sex is contested, perhaps this construct called "sex" is as culturally constructed as gender; indeed, perhaps it was always already gender, with the consequence that the distinction between sex and gender turns out to be no distinction at all.

It would make no sense, then, to define gender as the cultural interpretation of sex, if sex itself is a gendered category. Gender ought not to be conceived merely as the cultural inscription of meaning on a pregiven sex (a juridical conception); gender must also designate the very apparatus of production whereby the sexes themselves are established. As a result, gender is not to culture as sex is to nature; gender is also the discursive/cultural means by which "sexed nature" or "a natural sex" is produced and established as "prediscursive," prior to culture, a politically neutral surface *on which* culture acts. * * *

Gender can denote a *unity* of experience, of sex, of gender, and desire, only when sex can be understood in some sense to necessitate gender—where gender is a psychic and/or cultural designation of the self—and desire—where desire is heterosexual and therefore differentiates itself through an oppositional relation to that other gender it desires. The internal coherence or unity of either gender, man or woman, thereby requires both a stable and oppositional heterosexuality. That institutional heterosexuality both requires and produces the univocity of each of the gendered terms that constitute the limit of gendered possibilities within an oppositional, binary gender system. This conception of gender presupposes not only a causal relation among sex, gender, and desire, but suggests as well that desire reflects or expresses gender and that gender reflects or expresses desire. The metaphysical unity of the three is assumed to be truly known and expressed in a differentiating desire for an oppositional gender—that is, in a form of oppositional heterosexuality. Whether as a naturalistic paradigm which establishes a causal continuity among sex, gender, and desire, or as an authentic-expressive paradigm in which some true self is said to be revealed simultaneously or successively in sex, gender, and desire, here "the old dream of symmetry," as [Luce] Irigaray has called it, is presupposed, reified, and rationalized.

This rough sketch of gender gives us a clue to understanding the political reasons for the substantializing view of gender. The institution of a compulsory and naturalized heterosexuality requires and regulates gender as a binary relation in which the masculine term is differentiated from the feminine term, and this differentiation is accomplished through the practices of heterosexual desire. The act of differentiating the two oppositional moments of the binary results in a consolidation of each term, the respective internal coherence of sex, gender, and desire. * * *

In this sense, *gender* is not a noun, but neither is it a set of free-floating attributes, for we have seen that the substantive effect of gender is performatively produced and compelled by the regulatory practices of gender coherence. Hence * * * gender proves to be performative—that is, constituting the identity it is purported to be. In this sense, gender is always a doing, though not a doing by a subject who might be said to preexist the deed. * * * There is no gender identity behind the expressions of gender; that identity is performatively constituted by the very "expressions" that are said to be its results.

Price Waterhouse v. Ann Hopkins

United States Supreme Court, 1989.
490 U.S. 228, 109 S.Ct. 1775, 104 L.Ed.2d 268.

■ BRENNAN, J., announced the judgment of the Court and delivered an opinion in which JUSTICE MARSHALL, JUSTICE BLACKMUN, and JUSTICE STEVENS join.

Ann Hopkins was a senior manager in an office of Price Waterhouse when she was proposed for partnership in 1982. She was neither offered nor denied admission to the partnership; instead, her candidacy was held for reconsideration the following year. When the partners in her office later refused to repropose her for partnership, she sued Price Waterhouse under Title VII, * * * charging that the firm had discriminated against her on the basis of sex in its decisions regarding partnership. [Of the 662 partners at the firm at that time, 7 were women. Of the 88 persons proposed for partnership that year, only 1—Hopkins—was a woman. Forty-seven of these candidates were admitted to the partnership, 21 were rejected, and 20—including Hopkins—were "held" for reconsideration the following year. Thirteen of the 32 partners who had submitted comments on Hopkins supported her bid for partnership. Three partners recommended that her candidacy be placed on hold, eight stated that they did not have an informed opinion about her, and eight recommended that she be denied partnership.]

[District Judge Gesell found, as a matter of fact, that Hopkins had "played a key role in Price Waterhouse's successful effort to win a multi-million dollar contract with the Department of State" and that "[n]one of the other partnership candidates at Price Waterhouse that year had a comparable record in terms of successfully securing major contracts for the partnership." Both clients and partners at the Washington DC office praised Hopkins as "an outstanding professional." Judge Gesell found that Hopkins "had no difficulty dealing with clients and her clients appear to have been very pleased with her work" and that she "was generally viewed as a highly competent project leader who worked long hours, pushed vigorously to meet deadlines and demanded much from the multidisciplinary staffs with which she worked." On the other hand, both "[s]upporters and opponents of her candidacy," stressed Judge

Gesell, "indicated that she was sometimes overly aggressive, unduly harsh, difficult to work with and impatient with staff."]

There were clear signs, though, that some of the partners reacted negatively to Hopkins' personality because she was a woman. One partner described her as "macho"; another suggested that she "overcompensated for being a woman"; a third advised her to take "a course at charm school." Several partners criticized her use of profanity; in response, one partner suggested that those partners objected to her swearing only "because it's a lady using foul language." Another supporter explained that Hopkins "ha[d] matured from a tough-talking somewhat masculine hard-nosed mgr to an authoritative, formidable, but much more appealing lady ptr candidate." But it was the man who, as Judge Gesell found, bore responsibility for explaining to Hopkins the reasons for the Policy Board's decision to place her candidacy on hold who delivered the *coup de grace*: in order to improve her chances for partnership, Thomas Beyer advised, Hopkins should "walk more femininely, talk more femininely, dress more femininely, wear make-up, have her hair styled, and wear jewelry."

Dr. Susan Fiske, a social psychologist and Associate Professor of Psychology at Carnegie-Mellon University, testified at trial that the partnership selection process at Price Waterhouse was likely influenced by sex stereotyping. Her testimony focused not only on the overtly sex-based comments of partners but also on gender-neutral remarks, made by partners who knew Hopkins only slightly, that were intensely critical of her. One partner, for example, baldly stated that Hopkins was "universally disliked" by staff and another described her as "consistently annoying and irritating"; yet these were people who had had very little contact with Hopkins. According to Fiske, Hopkins' uniqueness (as the only woman in the pool of candidates) and the subjectivity of the evaluations made it likely that sharply critical remarks such as these were the product of sex stereotyping—although Fiske admitted that she could not say with certainty whether any particular comment was the result of stereotyping. Fiske based her opinion on a review of the submitted comments, explaining that it was commonly accepted practice for social psychologists to reach this kind of conclusion without having met any of the people involved in the decisionmaking process.

In previous years, other female candidates for partnership also had been evaluated in sex-based terms. As a general matter, Judge Gesell concluded, "[c]andidates were viewed favorably if partners believed they maintained their femin[in]ity while becoming effective professional managers"; in this environment, "[t]o be identified as a 'women's lib[b]er' was regarded as [a] negative comment." In fact, the judge found that in previous years "[o]ne partner repeatedly commented that he could not consider any woman seriously as a partnership candidate and believed that women were not even capable of functioning as senior managers—

yet the firm took no action to discourage his comments and recorded his vote in the overall summary of the evaluations."

[Although finding that some of the partners' complaints about Hopkins were legitimate, Judge Gesell found] that some of the partners' remarks about Hopkins stemmed from an impermissibly cabined view of the proper behavior of women, and that Price Waterhouse had done nothing to disavow reliance on such comments. He held that Price Waterhouse had unlawfully discriminated against Hopkins on the basis of sex by consciously giving credence and effect to partners' comments that resulted from sex stereotyping. Noting that Price Waterhouse could avoid equitable relief by proving by clear and convincing evidence that it would have placed Hopkins' candidacy on hold even absent this discrimination, the judge decided that the firm had not carried this heavy burden. [The Court of Appeals affirmed, but cautioned that even if a plaintiff proves that discrimination played a role in an employment decision, the defendant will not be found liable if it proves, by clear and convincing evidence, that it would have made the same decision in the absence of discrimination. The Supreme Court substantially agreed with the Court of Appeals.]

[Justice Brennan rejected Price Waterhouse's assault on Judge Gesell's finding of fact, especially insofar as they relied on Dr. Fiske's expert opinion about sex stereotyping.] Indeed, we are tempted to say that Dr. Fiske's expert testimony was merely icing on Hopkins' cake. It takes no special training to discern sex stereotyping in a description of an aggressive female employee as requiring "a course at charm school." Nor, turning to Thomas Beyer's memorable advice to Hopkins, does it require expertise in psychology to know that, if an employee's flawed "interpersonal skills" can be corrected by a soft-hued suit or a new shade of lipstick, perhaps it is the employee's sex and not her interpersonal skills that has drawn the criticism.

Price Waterhouse also charges that Hopkins produced no evidence that sex stereotyping played a role in the decision to place her candidacy on hold. As we have stressed, however, Hopkins showed that the partnership solicited evaluations from all of the firm's partners; that it generally relied very heavily on such evaluations in making its decision; that some of the partners' comments were the product of stereotyping; and that the firm in no way disclaimed reliance on those particular comments, either in Hopkins' case or in the past. Certainly a plausible—and, one might say, inevitable—conclusion to draw from this set of circumstances is that the Policy Board in making its decision did in fact take into account all of the partners' comments, including the comments that were motivated by stereotypical notions about women's proper deportment.* * *

Nor is the finding that sex stereotyping played a part in the Policy Board's decision undermined by the fact that many of the suspect comments were made by supporters rather than detractors of Hopkins.

A negative comment, even when made in the context of a generally favorable review, nevertheless may influence the decisionmaker to think less highly of the candidate; the Policy Board, in fact, did not simply tally the "yeses" and "noes" regarding a candidate, but carefully reviewed the content of the submitted comments. The additional suggestion that the comments were made by "persons outside the decisionmaking chain" * * *—and therefore could not have harmed Hopkins—simply ignores the critical role that partners' comments played in the Policy Board's partnership decisions.

Price Waterhouse appears to think that we cannot affirm the factual findings of the trial court without deciding that, instead of being overbearing and aggressive and curt, Hopkins is, in fact, kind and considerate and patient. If this is indeed its impression, petitioner misunderstands the theory on which Hopkins prevailed. The District Judge acknowledged that Hopkins' conduct justified complaints about her behavior as a senior manager. But he also concluded that the reactions of at least some of the partners were reactions to her as a *woman* manager. Where an evaluation is based on a subjective assessment of a person's strengths and weaknesses, it is simply not true that each evaluator will focus on, or even mention, the same weaknesses. Thus, even if we knew that Hopkins had "personality problems," this would not tell us that the partners who cast their evaluations of Hopkins in sex-based terms would have criticized her as sharply (or criticized her at all) if she had been a man. It is not our job to review the evidence and decide that the negative reactions to Hopkins were based on reality; our perception of Hopkins' character is irrelevant. We sit not to determine whether Ms. Hopkins is nice, but to decide whether the partners reacted negatively to her personality because she is a woman.

We hold that when a plaintiff in a Title VII case proves that her gender played a motivating part in an employment decision, the defendant may avoid a finding of liability only by proving by a preponderance of the evidence that it would have made the same decision even if it had not taken the plaintiff's gender into account. Because the courts below erred by deciding that the defendant must make this proof by clear and convincing evidence, we reverse the Court of Appeals' judgment against Price Waterhouse on liability and remand the case to that court for further proceedings.

■ [JUSTICE WHITE concurred only in the judgment. *Mt. Healthy City School District Bd. of Educ. v. Doyle*, 429 U.S. 274 (1977), held that a public employee complaining of discharge in violation of his First Amendment rights had the burden of proving that constitutionally protected conduct was a "substantial factor" in the discharge decision. JUSTICE WHITE believed that the *Mt. Healthy* standard could be applied to Title VII cases without violence to the Court's precedents.]

■ [JUSTICE O'CONNOR also concurred only in the judgment. She agreed with the plurality that, "on the facts presented in this case, the burden of persuasion should shift to the employer to demonstrate by a preponderance of the evidence that it would have reached the same decision concerning Ann Hopkins' candidacy absent consideration of her gender." Like the plurality, she agreed to shift the burden of persuasion to employers once a Title VII plaintiff established that impermissible (sex) considerations were a "substantial factor" in an employment decision. JUSTICE O'CONNOR believed that Hopkins had demonstrated that "gender stereotyping" played a role in the firm's decision not to make her a partner.]

■ JUSTICE KENNEDY, with whom THE CHIEF JUSTICE [REHNQUIST] and JUSTICE SCALIA join, dissenting.* * *

The ultimate question in every individual disparate-treatment case is whether discrimination caused the particular decision at issue. Some of the plurality's comments with respect to the District Court's findings in this case, however, are potentially misleading. As the plurality notes, the District Court based its liability determination on expert evidence that some evaluations of respondent Hopkins were based on unconscious sex stereotypes,[5] and on the fact that Price Waterhouse failed to disclaim reliance on these comments when it conducted the partnership review. The District Court also based liability on Price Waterhouse's failure to "make partners sensitive to the dangers [of stereotyping], to discourage comments tainted by sexism, or to investigate comments to determine whether they were influenced by stereotypes." * * *

Although the District Court's version of Title VII liability is improper under any of today's opinions, I think it important to stress that Title VII creates no independent cause of action for sex stereotyping. Evidence of use by decisionmakers of sex stereotypes is, of course, quite relevant to the question of discriminatory intent. The ultimate question, however, is whether discrimination caused the plaintiff's harm. Our cases do not support the suggestion that failure to "disclaim reliance" on stereotypical comments itself violates Title VII. Neither do they support creation of a "duty to sensitize." As the dissenting judge in the Court of Appeals observed, acceptance of such theories would turn Title VII "from a prohibition of discriminatory conduct into an engine for rooting out sexist thoughts." * * *

---

[5] The plaintiff who engages the services of Dr. Susan Fiske should have no trouble showing that sex discrimination played a part in any decision. Price Waterhouse chose not to object to Fiske's testimony, and at this late stage we are constrained to accept it, but I think the plurality's enthusiasm for Fiske's conclusions unwarranted. Fiske purported to discern stereotyping in comments that were gender neutral—e.g., "overbearing and abrasive"—without any knowledge of the comments' basis in reality and without having met the speaker or subject. "To an expert of Dr. Fiske's qualifications, it seems plain that no woman could *be* overbearing, arrogant, or abrasive: any observations to that effect would necessarily be discounted as the product of stereotyping. If analysis like this is to prevail in federal courts, no employer can base any adverse action as to a woman on such attributes." 825 F.2d 458, 477 (1987) (Williams, J., dissenting). Today's opinions cannot be read as requiring factfinders to credit testimony based on this type of analysis.

The language of Title VII and our well-considered precedents require this plaintiff to establish that the decision to place her candidacy on hold was made "because of" sex. Here the District Court found that the "comments of the individual partners and the expert evidence of Dr. Fiske do not prove an intentional discriminatory motive or purpose," * * * and that "[b]ecause plaintiff has considerable problems dealing with staff and peers, the Court cannot say that she would have been elected to partnership if the Policy Board's decision had not been tainted by sexually based evaluations," * * * Hopkins thus failed to meet the requisite standard of proof after a full trial. I would remand the case for entry of judgment in favor of Price Waterhouse.

NOTES ON *HOPKINS* AND LAW'S INVOCATION OF GENDER

1. *Burdens of Proof in Title VII.* In law, burdens of proof are often more important than the substantive rule. A key issue in the case was the district court's finding that other factors contributed to Hopkins' denial of partnership; the majority and dissent disagree about how to treat this "mixed motive" case. If Hopkins was not just "macho" but "abrasive," should the decision to deny her partnership be overturned? (Consider this question from the point of view of the office secretaries, who probably bore the brunt of Hopkins' testiness.) This divided the Justices in 1989. Congress overrode all nine Justices in the Civil Rights Act of 1991, codified at 42 U.S.C. § 703(m), which allows a finding of discrimination if the inadmissible criterion (sex, or gender) substantially contributed to the adverse employment decision.

2. *The Relationship Between Gender and Sex in Anti-Discrimination Law.* *Hopkins* might be criticized, as the dissent seems to do, for expanding a statutory ban on sex discrimination to include gender discrimination as well. (Title VII prohibits employment decisions "because of" the employee's "sex.") Ann Hopkins may have been denied a promotion, *either* because women were considered unfit for the masculine world of accounting *or* because she was perceived as too "mannish" a woman. Her own story was that she was penalized, not because her sex did not fit the job, but (instead) because her perceived gender did not fit her sex. *See* Ann Branigar Hopkins, *So Ordered: Making Partner the Hard Way* (1996) (Hopkins' own account of her treatment by Price Waterhouse, with ample references to trial and deposition testimony). After *Hopkins*, it appears that two slightly different kinds of discrimination can be remedied by Title VII: Price Waterhouse may be liable if it passed over Hopkins *either* because some partners didn't think women were capable of doing the job *or* because some partners were offended that this woman, however qualified, wasn't feminine enough for their tastes. In some ways, the second kind of discrimination (the kind Hopkins suffered) is even more divorced from business necessity than the first. Both kinds of discrimination are aimed at "gender stereotyping," either at the general level (women cannot do this job) or the specific (this woman can do the job, but she offends my sense of what a woman is).

Does *Hopkins* solve what Professor Franke has called the "central mistake" of sex discrimination jurisprudence, namely, judges' tendency to disaggregate sex and gender? To what extent does *Hopkins* adopt Professor Butler's notion that sex and gender are mutually constitutive, and that a statute barring "discrimination because of sex" includes discrimination because of "gender stereotyping"? (Consider the idea from this angle. If Butler is right that gendered expectations are important to the coherence of "sex" understood as binary and man-woman, then discrimination because of disappointed gendered expectations is *literally* discrimination because of sex.)

If Ann Hopkins had been a trans woman, with an excellent history of case management and client relations, and Price Waterhouse denied her partnership because of her gender expression or sex reassignment, would *Hopkins* have had a valid Title VII claim? In other words, does *Hopkins* abrogate court of appeals decisions ruling that Title VII does not provide a claim for relief for discrimination because of gender identity? What if there were findings of fact that some of the partners "felt Hopkins was not a real woman" and some of the support staff complained that "Hopkins needs to go to charm school if he wants to pretend to be a woman"? Would such remarks not be sufficient to shift the burden of persuasion to the employer? Could Price Waterhouse still prevail by showing that it was denying a transgender person partnership because she made other partners, staff, and some clients "uncomfortable"?

3.   *Sex, Gender, and Sexual Orientation*. Another implication of Professor Butler's analysis is that "discrimination because of sex," including gender stereotyping, entails discrimination because of sexual orientation. Compulsory heterosexuality creates "sex" even more specifically than gender stereotyping. *See* Adrienne Rich, "Compulsory Heterosexuality and Lesbian Existence," 5 *Signs* (1980), reprinted in *Blood, Bread, and Poetry: Selected Prose, 1979–1985*, at 23–75 (1986). Does the logic of *Hopkins* take the Court that far? For an affirmative case, see *Hively v. Ivy Tech Community College*, 853 F.3d 339 (7th Cir. en banc 2017) (excerpted in Chapter 5 of this casebook).

Doesn't *Hopkins* create a claim for relief by "effeminate" men for job discrimination because they don't conform to gender stereotypes? *See* Mary Anne Case, "Disaggregating Gender from Sex and Sexual Orientation: The Effeminate Man in the Law and Feminist Jurisprudence," 105 *Yale L.J.* 1 (1995) (yes). If the mannish woman and the effeminate man can sue because the employer penalizes them for not conforming to gender stereotypes, can the lesbian or the gay man sue because she or he does not conform to the stereotypes that all women "need" men and that a man is not a proper "man" unless he has sex with women? If the plaintiff produced evidence that partners invoked a lesbian's identity to tag her as "too mannish" to fit well with "our family values firm," would *Hopkins* or the new § 703(m) require a trial judge to place the burden of persuasion on the employer to show that a legitimate business reason justified the refusal to promote? *See Hively* (Flaum, J., concurring based on § 703(m)). Would it be a "legitimate" reason that some partners, staff, and clients were uncomfortable with the lesbian's sexual orientation?

NOTE ON IDENTITY POLITICS AND SOCIAL CONSTRUCTIONIST THINKING

The classical model of identity politics and equal protection theory invokes stable identity categories like people of color, women and men, and lesbians and gay men. Butler and Foucault claim that gender, sexuality, and even sex are cultural rather than biological categories. These theories ask us to reconsider the stability of sexuality and gender categories that social activists and judges alike take for granted. Such claims are frightening for many activists and judges, because they seem to dislodge cultural foundations that we take for granted. Is the stability of identity categories necessary for a cogent identity politics?

On the other hand, social constructionist theory can usefully expose the incoherence or contingency of accepted categories and thereby liberate our culture from them. *See* Richard R. Ford, *Racial Culture: A Critique* (2005); Dean Spade, "Documenting Gender," 59 *Hastings L.J.* 731 (2008). It is much easier to be a racist if one believes there are *natural* race-based differences, than if one believes that racial differences are *artificial* social constructions. The Price Waterhouse partners who rejected Ann Hopkins because she was "mannish" probably harbored essentialist understandings that there are only two sexes, and each sex is *naturally* associated with specific gender traits and sexual behaviors (Figure 3–1 above). The Supreme Court opinion admonishing Price Waterhouse took gender as artificial rather than natural, and this was an important reason the plurality and Justice O'Connor pushed the burden of proof onto the employer.

Although Justices Brennan and O'Connor had not read Judith Butler's theory, their understanding of "discrimination because of sex" reflects a weak reading of Butler that responds to Justice Kennedy's understanding.[f] A weak reading of Butler and Foucault would accept *sex* and *sexual orientation* as stable biological categories and would posit that the meaning of those categories (and the normative behavioral patterns associated with each) varies across time and cultures. Throughout human history there are men and women, and men attracted to other men/women attracted to other women, but the social meaning and behavior appropriate for men and women have varied. Thus, even if sex were a proper biological category, its meaning today is inflected by gendered expectations—and so it makes perfect sense to interpret Price Waterhouse's *gender*-based discrimination as, literally, discrimination because of *sex*.

A moderate reading of Butler and Foucault (yet one still not going as far as either theorist does) accepts that there might be a biological component to sex, but that we will never be sure what or how important such a biological

---

[f]   For a more complex array of social constructionist theories, see Carole Vance, "Social Construction Theory: Problems in the History of Sexuality," in *Homosexuality, Which Homosexuality?* 13, 21 (Dennis Altman et al. eds. 1989), and Janet Halley, "Sexual Orientation and the Politics of Biology: A Critique of the Argument from Immutability," 46 *Stan. L. Rev.* 503 (1994).

component is, as it is inevitably refracted through culture. Likewise, there may be a biological component to what we call homosexuality, but we will probably never be sure what that component is, as we can only apprehend it through culture. As even the weak version of social constructionism maintains, the significance of one's biological sex or one's feelings for people of the same sex is completely cultural. Society is responsible for the normative valence placed on sex, gender, and sexuality—there is no escape from social responsibility for the harm resulting from discriminatory categories, and the Equal Protection Clause is a formal mechanism for monitoring those harms.

The conventional wisdom among civil rights activists that "no person is free until the last and the least of us is free," Mari Matsuda, "Beside My Sister, Facing the Enemy: Legal Theory Out of Coalition," 32 *Stan. L. Rev.* 1183, 1189 (1991), has been challenged particularly in communities of color. Colin Powell's statement that color is a "benign, nonbehavioral characteristic, while sexual orientation is perhaps the most profound of human behavioral characteristics," see Jason Riley, "Not a Civil Rights Issue," *Wall St. J.*, Aug. 13, 1998, at A14 (quoting Powell), has triggered extensive commentary by people of color distancing the civil rights movement from gay rights. The performative turn described by Butler suggests the distinction is facile: prejudice against people of color has long been justified by assertions about their sexual conduct (including cross-dressing and sodomy), just as prejudice against women and gay people have been justified by their asserted predisposition to become pregnant and commit sodomy. Moreover, the *form* of discrimination is similar for all groups: just as discrimination against LGBTQIA people is often justified by their nonconforming dress and personal behavior, so discrimination against people of color has often been justified by their nonconforming dress and appearance and accent or language, and discrimination against women is frequently justified by pregnancy or even its possibility.

The performative features of race, sex, and sexual orientation require equal protection law to consider the ways in which conformity as to behavior, attire, appearance, and language ought to be of concern. Professor Mari Matsuda has pioneered the idea that language and appearance are just as important to anti-discrimination law as skin color and racial background. *E.g.*, Matsuda, "Accent Discrimination," 100 *Yale L.J.* 1329 (1991). By her account, the black woman who is pressured by her employer to cover her race by straightening her hair and changing her language is just as much deprived of her identity, and treated unequally, as the black woman pressured by her employer to pass as white.

This same kind of analysis can apply to lesbians, gay men, bisexuals, transgender, queer, and intersex people as well. Anti-gay employers and associations often claim that they are discriminating against gay or transgender people because of their *conduct* (immoral sodomy or disruptive cross-dressing) and not because of their *status*.[g] An implication of Judith

---

[g] *See* Brief for Petitioners, at 43, *Christian Legal Society v. Martinez* (Supreme Court, Docket No. 08–1371) (arguing that it would be unlawful discrimination for a religious group to exclude people of color from leadership posts, but not to exclude unrepentant gay people);

Butler's theory is that conduct and status are not easily separated. If a dramatic example were needed, it would be the religious history of racism in the United States: fundamentalist religion justified slavery as God's punishment of Ham (the ancestor of the African race) for disrespecting his father Noah and justified apartheid by the possibility that racial integration would lead to sexual mixing of the races.

Thus, race in the slavery and then apartheid era was *performative* in the same way that homosexuality is today (for homophobes). During slavery and apartheid, the black man suffered a degraded *status* because society constructed race as a signifier of immoral *conduct* (miscegenation) and a corrupting *message* (race confusion) dangerous to the body politic. Today, for even mild homophobes, the "homosexual" suffers a degraded *status* because society constructs sexual orientation as a signifier of immoral *conduct* (sodomy) and a corrupting *message* (gay is good) dangerous to the body politic.[h]

J. Jack Halberstam, *Gaga Feminism: Sex, Gender, and the End of Normal* (2012). Working from the notion that sex, gender, and sexuality are performative, Professor Halberstam's theory is inspired by Lady Gaga, the quintessential gender-, sex-, and sexuality-bending stage and media performer. "Gaga feminism, or the feminism (pheminism?) of the phony, the unreal, and the speculative, is simultaneously a monstrous outgrowth of the unstable concept of 'woman' in feminist theory, a celebration of the joining of femininity to artifice, and a refusal of the mushy sentimentalism that has been siphoned off into the category of womanhood" (pp. xxii–xiii).Consistent with Professor Butler's theory, gaga feminism does not assume the binary and fixed division of people into males and females, and instead assumes and celebrates the fluidity as well as variety of sexes, genders, and sexual orientations. Among the basic principles of gaga feminism are these (pp. 27–29): "Wisdom lies in the unexpected and the unanticipated." Remain open to the inevitability of transformation, change, and flux." "Think counterintuitively, act accordingly. A lot of what we learn as 'common sense' actually makes no sense." Abandon religious bromides. Be outrageous.

"This feminism is not about sisterhood, motherhood, sorority, or even women. It is about shifting, changing, morphing, extemporizing political positions quickly and effectively to keep up with the multimedia environments in which we all live and to stay apace of what some have called 'the coming insurrection.' " (Page 29.)

For a concrete illustration of "going gaga" with regard to sexuality, gender, and the law, this book offers an antidote to identity politics through the evolution of the author's Gender and Sexuality class. For

---

Christian Legal Society, Oral Argument, at 9–10 (April 19, 2010) (exchange between Justices Sotomayor and Stevens and counsel for CLS).

  [h] *See* William N. Eskridge Jr., "Noah's Curse: How Religion Often Conflates Status, Belief, and Conduct to Resist Antidiscrimination Norms," 45 *Ga. L. Rev.* 657 (2011).

years Professor Halberstam followed the minority-protective approach to the class, namely, teaching the realities of the lives of LGBTQI persons, as a lever to reject the prejudice and social scorn many others unfairly heap upon these minorities. "As a queer person, and a gender-queer person whose gender was indeterminate on a good day, I became exhibit A in the freak show that the class became." (Page 11.) How intellectually liberating was this mode of instruction for a class of largely straight but tolerant students who already knew LGBTQI people as friends and relatives? Perhaps not as liberating or educational as the course might be. . . .

So Professor Halberstam altered the focus of the course, toward a focus on heterosexuality, but from the perspective of an outside observer gathering information from such cultural artifacts as *The Bachelor*, *Desperate Housewives*, and *The Sopranos*. Viewed from the outside, heterosexuality and its associated practices are quite odd. "In many ways, the 'How weird is that?' approach to heterosexuality * * * works much better than the 'Try to be tolerant of these weirdos' approach showcasing queerness. It forces the very students who are deeply invested in norms, their own and other people's, to face the music and look at their own investments, their own issues, their own struggles with what is supposed to come naturally. The focus on the strangeness of heterosexuality allowed us to think through eating disorders as a vicious side effect of adolescent misogyny; it forced men in the class to ask themselves about their own relations to masculinity, to other men, to women, and to homophobia. And it led women to notice the significant differences between the ways in which they developed peer relations with other women (friendships often focused on food, clothes, and boys), and the ways men developed peer relations with other men (friendships focused on male bonding, drinking, and sports, but rarely stemming from long discussions about girls)." (Pages 11–12.)

Notice how gaga feminism might support a different kind of politics than traditional identity politics. Traditional identity politics tends to represent the "weird" (sexual and gender minorities) as "normal," thereby creating stratifications among minorities. The truly exceptional people, the "weirdest," have little access to "normal" and are easily left behind when a reactive politics of assimilation prevails.

Professor Halberstam's main example is the campaign for marriage equality, "an issue that appeals to affluent white gays and lesbians who will benefit from it. It has far less appeal to queers living in poverty or queers actively working on social justice issues that stretch beyond securing individual benefits or tax breaks." (Pages 107–08.) Instead of seeking to expand marriage, LGBTQIA groups ought to expand rights and safety net programs that are not marriage-dependent, such as universal health insurance (such as the Affordable Care Act of 2010). "There are many ways of creating family, kinship, intimacy, and community that exceed the marriage model. Some of these may include:

shared parenting arrangements, split families, communities living together without children, and, last but certainly not least, threesomes." (Page 109.)

The foregoing ideas already have currency in progressive feminist discourse, so what does gaga feminism add to the discussion? Following the approach Professor Halberstam applied in reconfiguring the Sexuality and Gender course, one might reverse the interrogation usually applied to reform proposals. Rather than defending an alternate family arrangement, such as living alone or cohabiting with children, one might examine "marriage" as an outsider looking into this time-honored western institution. What would strike such an observer as weird about marriage?

Well, for one thing, society's relentless romanticization of marriage creates a trap for the unwary. "Laura Kipnis, in a hilarious and razor-sharp polemic, *Against Love*, reveals how love lures young and unsuspecting idealists into marriage and then traps them through a series of social set pieces that establish couples as each others' jailors (she gives the example of how couples have to tell each other everything they are doing, report back on where they are going and with whom, and check in periodically throughout the day or evening—recall the lady Gaga video *Telephone* and the recurrent lyric 'stop calling, stop calling'). Eventually one or both of the members of this 'domestic gulag' rebels and escapes through an adulterous affair that offers a brief glimpse of freedom before it becomes love . . . and then marriage . . . and then the cycle begins again." (Page 113.)

Query. Does gaga feminism offer a distinctive perspective on Marvin Kaiser's case, discussed above? Does it add anything, for example, to Michel Foucault's outside-the-box analysis of the criminal law regime that prosecuted Mr. Kaiser? To the sharp critiques of Foucault in connection with his discussions of rape, incest, and sex with minors?

3. CONSTRUCTING SEXUALITY THROUGH DISEASE AND DISABILITY

Just as Professor Kimberlé Crenshaw complicated mainstream feminist narratives by applying a racial lens to illuminate the experiences of women of color, other post-liberal theorists add nuance to discourses of sexuality through exploring the intersections between sexuality and other facets of identity. In this section, we explore how concepts of disease and disability have changed society and academia's understanding of the constructed nature of sexuality.

Perhaps no single event has changed our understanding of sexuality as much as the AIDS crisis, which emerged in the United States in the early 1980s. For three years, the cause remained unknown. In 1984, scientists at the National Cancer Institute isolated the Human Immunodeficiency Virus (HIV), and in 1985 the FDA licensed a blood test that could detect the presence of the virus. However, without a cure or even effective treatment, not to mention the specter of discrimination and stigma that a diagnosis was sure to bring, people were reluctant to get tested. During these years, more than 70% of those infected were homosexual or bisexual men; 80% of those infected lived no more than two years.

AIDS also served as the impetus for a blossoming LGBT movement. Across the country, LGBTQ people realized that, without organizing, they would die. Activists in New York founded the Gay Men's Health Crisis in 1982 to help provide support services for those living with HIV and AIDS. A small group of New York artists created a poster with the slogan Silence = Death, which became a rallying cry for AIDS activists. Groups like ACT UP (the AIDS Coalition to Unleash Power), founded in 1987, pressured Congress, the President, and federal agencies to invest in more research and to expedite the approval of AIDS-related drugs. In 1995, the FDA approved the first protease inhibitor, a treatment which dramatically reduced the mortality rate of AIDS—at least in wealthier countries like the United States. For a more complete history of the early history of AIDS, see David France, *How to Survive a Plague: The Inside Story of How Citizens and Science Tamed AIDS* (2016).

The World Health Organization estimates that more than 70 million people have been infected with HIV since the start of the epidemic, of whom approximately 35 million have died of AIDS. Today, there are approximately 37 million people living with HIV, 70% of whom live in sub-Saharan Africa.

In addition to its human toll, AIDS has had significant impacts on discourses of sex and sexuality, particularly in the LGBT community. Sex, which had worked as a radical liberating force in early queer movements, became the target of medical institutions and behavioral interventions.

Among those who died of the disease in the 1980s: Michel Foucault. Foucault wrote much of *The History of Sexuality* after he had been HIV-infected. Shortly after the completion of *History of Sexuality,* Foucault died of complications associated with AIDS. Unfortunately, because he remained closeted about his own disease, Foucault never wrote a major theoretical essay about the merging discourse of AIDS and the new ways that discourse was affecting our ideas and practices. Linda Singer's essay, which follows, considers ways in which AIDS has affected our discourse of sexuality.

Linda Singer, "Bodies—Pleasures—Powers"

differences: A Journal of Feminist Cultural Studies 45, 49–51, 53–54, 55–56 (1989).*

* * * The age of sexual epidemic demands a new sexual politics and, therefore, a rethinking of the relationship between bodies, pleasures, and powers beyond the call for liberation from repression. That is because, as Michel Foucault pointed out with a certain prescience, the power deployed in the construction and circulation of an epidemic, especially a sexual epidemic, functions primarily as a force of production and proliferation rather than as a movement of repression. The determination that a situation is epidemic is always, according to Foucault, a political determination (*The Birth of the Clinic* 15). Epidemics differ from diseases not in kind but in quantity. Hence the epidemic determination is in part a mathematical one, made by those with access to information and the authority to make and circulate such determinations. An epidemic emerges as a product of a socially authoritative discourse in light of which bodies will be mobilized, resources will be dispensed, and tactics of surveillance and regulation will appear to be justified. Foucault argues that a medicine of epidemic could only exist with supplementation by the police (*The Birth of the Clinic* 15). In this view, the construction of an epidemic situation has a strategic value in determining the configurations of what Foucault calls "bio-power," since the epidemic provides an occasion and a rationale for multiplying points of intervention into the lives of bodies and populations. For this reason, epidemics are always historically specific in a way that diseases are not, since the strategic imperatives motivating particular ways of coping with an epidemic always emerge as tactical responses to local utilities and circumstances. The construction of a sexual epidemic, as Foucault argues, provides an optimum site of intersection between individual bodies and populations. Hence sexual epidemic provides access to bodies and a series of codes for inscribing them, as well as providing a discourse of justification. When any phenomenon is represented as "epidemic," it has, by definition, reached a threshold that is quantitatively unacceptable. It is the capacity to make and circulate this determination, and to mobilize people in light of it, that constitutes the real political force of the discourse of sexual epidemic (Cindy Patton, *Sex and Germs: The Politics of AIDS* 51–66 [1985]). * * *

The history of the institutional responses to AIDS reveals how the politics of epidemics can work to solidify hegemonies. For years, gay activists and supporters lobbied for better funding for AIDS treatment and research, as the impact of the disease on their community increased. Such efforts went largely unrecognized and received little support from elected officials and health care professionals (Randy Shilts, *And the Band Played On* [1987]). It was not until the disease spread to other segments of the population and taxed health care resources that medical professionals began to speak of an epidemic. This indicates not only how power is operative in constructing epidemics but also how that construction can be used to organize attention, energy, and material support. * * *

The establishment of a connection between epidemic and transgression has allowed for the rapid transmission of the former to phenomena that are outside the sphere of disease. We are thus warned of the "epidemics" of teenage pregnancies, child molestation, abortion, pornography, and divorce. The use of this language marks all of these phenomena as targets for intervention because they have been designated as unacceptable, while at the same time reproducing the power that authorizes and justifies their deployment. According to this discourse, it is existing authority that is to be protected from the plague of transgressions. * * *

The limits of existing political discourse, as well as the urgency of the current situation, call for new forms of sexual political discourse, currency, and struggle. In this context, Foucault's work is especially helpful since his analysis of the proliferative operation of power supplements the limits of the repressive hypothesis, and offers the option of a strategic analysis which allows us to consider not only what is lost but also what is produced by the current organization of the sexual field which is itself a product of previous power deployments. This means that, counter to a logic which opposes erotic urgency and social utility or ghettoizes the sexual as some stable and invariable set of imperatives, Foucault's analysis demonstrates how the construction of each is dependent upon and made in light of the others, often, as in our age, with dire results which place our existence as a species in question. Part of the agenda for a sexual politics of epidemic will have to be a reconsideration of this "Faustian bargain," along with the generation of alternatives capable of mobilizing bodies sufficiently so as not to paralyze them in an economy of deprivation (Simon Watney, *Policing Desire* 123–35 [1987]). * * *

The underlying assumptions about the relationships among bodies, pleasures, and powers which make safe sex possible depend, at least indirectly, on Foucault's analysis and its destabilizing consequences. Safe sex presumes that pleasure and practice can be reorganized in response to overriding utilities and presumes, as well, the capacity of regimentary procedures to construct a body capable of taking pleasure in this new form of discipline. Unless bodies and pleasures are politically determined, they can not be redetermined, even in cases where that is what rational prudence would demand. The success of this strategy will thus depend not only on promulgating these techniques, but also on circulating a discourse that allows individuals to reconsider their bodies in a more liberatory and strategic way. What is new about the new sobriety is that its aesthetic of restraint is not represented in terms of a monastic economy of self-denial or obedience to some authoritative imperative, but is instead presented as a gesture of primary narcissism, a way of caring for and about oneself. Liberation, in this context, is relocated in an economy of intensification of control over one's body and one's position in sexual exchanges. * * *

Part of the change proffered by epidemic conditions is a shift in the relationship between knowledge and desire as they function in erotic situations. Specifically, knowledge of one's partner's physical condition and sexual history now becomes a prime object of concern. The erotic gaze is thus infected to some degree by the medical gaze which must learn to see sickness. The prudential aesthetic which characterizes the new sobriety creates specific forms of desire, like dating agencies, which promise matches with prescreened AIDS-free partners.

Failing such elaborate screening procedures, and given the limits of their reliability, the ideology of safe sex encourages a reorganization of the body away from the erotic priorities with which it has already been inscribed. Specifically, safe sex advocates indulgence in numerous forms of non-genital contact and the reengagement of parts of the body marginalized by an economy of genital primacy. It also entails a reconfiguration of bodies and their pleasures away from an ejaculatory teleology toward a more polymorphous decentered exchange, reviving and concretizing the critique of genital condensation begun over twenty years ago by sexual theorists like Marcuse and Firestone.

The new sobriety constructs a body well designed for the complexities of life in late capitalism, which requires a worker's body and a body of workers that are well-managed in the way a portfolio is well-managed, i.e., a body with flexible and diverse investments which maximize accumulated surplus as negotiable profits. The body constructed in the discourse of the new sobriety is inscribed with a discipline that is supposed to allow for more efficient functioning and control in both sex and work, in part, because this bodily regimen has been represented as an exercise in self-fulfillment and development which should be part of the well-managed enlightened life. * * *

NOTE ON AIDS AND PRODUCTIVE DISCOURSES

AIDS has been an occasion for law and society to create new categories of signification—categories which are restructuring the ways Americans understand their society and their own bodies. Linda Singer maintains that AIDS is an occasion for redirecting the mechanisms by which the body is deployed for pleasure. By problematizing unprotected vaginal and anal sex, public health professionals and sex educators have, one might speculate, contributed to a latex sexuality, a focus on other body parts (nipples, necks, feet, etc.) as erogenous zones for more people, and so forth.

There is another discursive consequence, however. "[M]onogamy is coming back into its own, along with abstention, the safest sex of all. The virus in itself—by whatever name—has come to represent the moment of truth for the sexual revolution: as though God has once again sent his only beloved son to save us from our high-risk behavior. Who would have thought He would take the form of a virus: a viral Terminator ready to die for our sins." Paula Treichler, "AIDS, Homophobia and Biomedical Discourse: An Epidemic of Signification," 1 *Cultural Studies* 263 (1987). Traditionalists maintained that AIDS ought to be the occasion for a new discipline of the body that puts a lid back on sex outside of marriage. By counseling gay men against "promiscuity," doctors contributed to a renewed discourse of sexual abstinence. *See* Ralph Bolton, "AIDS and Promiscuity: Muddles in the Models of HIV Prevention," 14 *Medical Anthropology* 145 (1992).

Relatedly, AIDS generated discourses that fueled gay people's demand for domestic partnership protections in the 1980s. Many AIDS patients had no health insurance because their partners could not include them, and others suffered indignities because hospitals excluded their caregivers. In Berkeley and San Francisco, activists invoked these injustices as a reason for cities to recognize their relationships as "domestic partnerships," an institution that spread to dozens of cities and hundreds of companies in the 1990s.

Larry Kramer and other AIDS activists urged monogamous marriage as a logical response, e.g., Gabriel Rotello, *Sexual Ecology: AIDS and the Destiny of Gay Men* (1997), and legal scholars argued that AIDS prevention was one argument supporting state recognition of same-sex marriages. E.g., Tomas Philpson & Richard Posner, *Private Choices and Public Health: The AIDS Epidemic in an Economic Perspective* (1993). In 1989, Tom Stoddard, Lambda's HIV-positive Executive Director, urged the gay rights movement to support same-sex marriage in his celebrated debate with Paula Ettelbrick, Lambda's Legal Director. In 1993, Stoddard married his partner, Walter Rieman, who survived him upon his death from complications associated with AIDS in 1997.

Conversely, AIDS fueled the coalescing of a "queer" reaction to what activists considered AIDSphobic responses, such as sexual restraint. *See* Caleb Train, *Pleasure Principles: Queer Theorists and Gay Journalists Wrestle Over the Politics of Sex*, Lingua franca, Oct. 1997. For example, ACT-UP activist Jim Eigo acidly criticized Rotello's *Sexual Ecology* for its advocacy of a "crabbed monogamy" and celebrated a "healthy promiscuity" as the enduring legacy of Stonewall. Advances in AIDS science have fueled the queer prosex response to monogamy advocates.

While there is still no cure for AIDS, medical treatments have advanced to the point that with proper care, HIV infection is not the death sentence it once was, reducing the sense of urgency to follow proposed behavioral modifications. Researchers, providers and activists have also become increasingly more critical of behavioral interventions, which they see as ineffective and overused. This "condom message fatigue" necessitated an alternative form for preventing HIV infection. *See* Jason Potter Burda, *When Condoms Fail: Making Room Under the ACA Blanket for PrEP HIV Prevention,* 52 San Diego L. Rev 171 (2015). Enter pharmacological prevention. In pharmacological prevention, individuals who have not contracted an illness or condition but who are identified as having specific risk factors are proscribed medication to reduce the chance of infection or transmission. Other examples of pharmacological prevention include anti-malaria pills and contraception.

Today, the most widely studied primary mode of pharmacological prevention for HIV is oral HIV pre-exposure prophylactic medication, or PrEP. An HIV-negative individual taking PrEP (a single or compound anti-retroviral) significantly reduces his risk of infection during intercourse with someone who is HIV-positive. This method of HIV prevention no longer attempts to use social pressure as a means of managing individual behavior but instead deploys medicine to manage risk across populations.

Alain Giami & Christopher Perrey, "Transformations in the Medicalization of Sex: HIV Prevention between Discipline and Biopolitics" 49 *J. Sex Research* 353 (2012). Public health researchers Alain Giami and Christopher Perrey draw on Foucault's concept of biopolitics to trace the impact that evolving HIV treatment has had on discourses of sex and sexuality. "HIV Prevention, be it behavioral or biomedical, represents one of the major forms of medicalization of sexuality in the 20th century and current changes in preventative approaches also imply changes in sexual conduct and meanings and representations of sexuality that need to be carefully understood." (Page 353.) Initial societal responses to AIDS—between 1981 and 2007—are representative of the Foucauldian concept of "discipline"—the process by which social forces and institutions like medicine and education (what Foucault identifies as biopowers) exert influence over the bodies and behaviors of individuals. (How might the law also exert influence as a biopower?) These biopowers worked to attribute new meanings and significations to certain sexual behaviors in light of AIDS. For instance, masturbation—described by some in the medical community since the 18th century as carrying significant health risks—was renegotiated to become a recommended, healthy sexual practice.

The advent of pharmacological prevention has ushered in a second phase of HIV prevention, what Giami and Perrey call "biopolitics." With pharmacological prevention, "the exposure to the risk of HIV infection becomes a medical condition in itself, which can be treated medically with these new drugs. * * * There is a shift from a situation in which behavioral modifications were the only possibility to prevent the occurrence of HIV infection toward a situation in which these behavioral medications will no longer be necessary thanks to the use of pharmacological medication." (Page 354.) The goal of biopolitical prevention strategies is not to influence individual tendencies to engage (or not engage) in particular behaviors but instead to insulate populations against risk regardless of individual behavior. Biopolitics looks at individuals in the context of their membership in an "organic body" and seeks to control the "masses and their sociodemographic equilibrium." But pharmacological prevention strategies still require individual buy-in; in the case of PrEP, people must actively take a pill every day for the regimen to be effective. Giami and Perry explain that "these new biomedical recommendations remain rooted in the principle of individual responsibility. Individual responsibility remains the unifying thread bringing together the preventive measures proposed in both stages of the history of HIV/AIDS prevention" (p. 357.)

While a new emphasis on biopolitics has not fully displaced earlier approaches rooted in discipline, it has served to simultaneously medicalize and desexualize HIV prevention. "Disciplinary prevention was based on the voluntary modification of sexual behaviors and sexual relations, grounded on a change in their social and symbolic meanings. The new biomedicalized approach represents a shift away from the monitoring of sexual behavior toward the monitor of screening, the taking of virological tests, chemoprevention for the HIV-negative individuals, the early treatment of seropositive individuals, and the practice of male circumcision." (Page 358.)

But PrEP and other forms of pharmacological prevention have not proven easy to implement. As Giami and Perry postulate, the success of these new modes of prevention in slowing (and potentially eradicating) the spread of HIVAIDS will depend on political will and financial support. Social and cultural attitudes will play a role as well. The CDC reported in 2016 that despite increasing PrEP use, white gay men were twice as likely as black gay men to use PrEP. In this next essay, Professor Russell Robinson explores some theoretical and concrete implications of being black and gay in the context of HIV/AIDS.

Russell K. Robinson, "Racing the Closet," 61 _Stan. L. Rev._ 1463 (2009). Professor Robinson questions the demonization, both from black and mainstream culture, directed against African-American men who sleep with men ("MSM") but reject gay identity and live instead on the "down low." Black men living on the down low are charged with responsibility for the spread of HIV infections among black women. "Perhaps the most inflammatory example of this discourse is an episode of The Oprah Winfrey Show from April 2004. This episode featured J.L. King, an African American man and author of On the Down Low. In case King's stories of sleeping with men while being married to and raising children with a black woman were not disturbing enough, Oprah featured two men with even more salacious tales of life on the low. Oprah began the show by stating that 'AIDS is on the rise again. Here's a shocker! It's one of the big reasons why so many women are getting AIDS. Their husbands and their boyfriends are having secret sex with other men.' Then two men whose identities were obscured provided accounts of their sex lives with women and men." (Page 1472.)

In focusing on stories like this, gay white men and straight black women mobilize traditional racist discourse, argues Professor Robinson. By demonizing "promiscuous" black MSMs, white gays idealize a form of relationship that involves open gay identity and heterosexual, monogamous relationships, while straight black women seek to reaffirm the heterosexual requirements of black men by portraying black MSMs as traitors to the women of their community. It is striking how closely this down low discourse, such as that on the Oprah Winfrey Show, tracks traditional stereotypes about black men as oversexed, irresponsible, and sexually predatory. Moreover, Professor Robinson argues that this totalizing discourse leaves out critically important features of the nation's sexual sociology, including the sociology of the ongoing AIDS epidemic:

- *Women having sex with men on the down low are usually not victims.* Many women having sex with men on the down low are perfectly well aware that the men are having sex with other men, and a lot of the women are not sexually monogamous either. A lot of white women choose to remain in what the media deem "Brokeback marriages" (with a MSM), but stories about those marriages do not tend to demonize the white man nearly as much as down low discourse demonizes black men.

- *Many black women live on the down low.* But the media ignores them, and when they are noticed such women are not treated as some kind of predatory threat that MSM on the down low were portrayed on the Oprah Winfrey Show. Robinson speculates that our culture does not view women who sleep with women as sexualized or as dangerous as it views MSMs, especially BMSMs.

- *Down low MSMs are themselves victims of a racist social scene.* The social life of a bisexual or gay black man is limited by "at least four structural constraints that do not similarly restrict white gay men: (1) his racial group is in the minority; (2) men of his race are less likely to be out; (3) there is a substantially smaller proportion of black men who are not incarcerated or otherwise under the supervision of the criminal justice system; and (4) he must navigate racialized expectations, including gendered sex-role expectations, which are likely to be particularly salient when dealing with white men" (p. 1496). Hence, MSMs on the down low are, to a certain extent, victims of circumstances that press them toward the closet and toward deceptive practices.

Professor Robinson's point is not that MSMs on the down low are blameless, but rather that such men are being scapegoated well beyond their relative culpability.

"[Down low] discourse relies on an individualistic presentation that erases the social structures that account for much of the behavior that the media demonizes. Different but related structural conditions channel the sexual decision making of black MSM and women. The interlocking pressures of heterosexism, racism, and patriarchy push black MSM to hide their interest in men and maintain public relationships only with women. Meanwhile, the requirement that a woman maintain a committed relationship with a man, no matter the personal cost, pushes women to acquiesce in unprotected sex with men and to overlook their male partner's concurrent sexual relationships, which may be with women, men, or both. At the same time, the aesthetic hierarchy that deems black women relatively undesirable limits black women's pool of potential romantic partners. Heteronormativity also bounds black women's romantic choices, ruling out for many the possibility of choosing a female partner. This examination of structural constraints shows that black MSM and women can find common ground in critiquing and challenging the structures that limit their romantic possibilities rather than simply blaming each other." (Page 1500.)

The law plays a major role in creating the pathologies of the down low. Not only does the criminal justice system target and incarcerate large numbers of black men (decimating the potential dating population for straight black women), but its HIV-targeted interventions also contribute to down low pathologies. "Because HIV continues to be viewed primarily as a problem of gay men and IV drug users, nongay-identified MSM and their female partners may not see themselves as at risk. Although public health scholars have to some extent moved away from a focus on gay identity and adopted more inclusive terms such as 'MSM,' HIV prevention and testing efforts remain highly concentrated in gay communities. Under current law, this underinclusive approach to HIV testing is paired with HIV-specific criminal laws. Criminal laws in many states impose strong penalties on people who know they are HIV positive and fail to disclose their status to a sexual partner. But * * * these laws have done little to stem HIV transmission, partly because they fail to engage the complex dynamics of many sexual relationships and reflect a simplistic perpetrator-victim dichotomy like that fostered by DL discourse. My principal proposal here is a legally mandated expansion of HIV testing beyond so-called 'risk groups,' which would reach some of the people who inadvertently transmit HIV, which appears to be a bigger problem than knowing transmission.[i] Rather than focusing on individual bad actors, I recommend a legal focus on public health interventions, which may alter the conditions in which people negotiate the risks of sexual intimacy." (Page 1516.)

NOTE ON THE RACED CLOSET AND AIDS POLICY

Professor Robinson's article is notable in its combination of a post-liberal understanding of sexuality and gender role with the insights of critical race theory **and** a positive policy recommendation, namely, universal HIV testing. Such testing would be very expensive and poses privacy issues,

---

[i]   The Center for Disease Control has long recommended that all persons between the ages of 13 and 64 be tested for HIV infection. CDC, Act Against AIDS, available at https://www.cdc.gov/actagainstaids/basics/testing.html (viewed May 1, 2017).

but Robinson supports it because most HIV-positive persons are not precisely aware of their HIV status and because it would help bring infected down low persons out of their "raced closets." He agrees that universal testing would be in tension with the criminal HIV-exposure laws, which he would prefer to see repealed (they are virtually unenforced already). Consider what observations Michel Foucault would have regarding Robinson's proposal. Is mandatory testing rooted in a discipline approach aiming at behavioral modification or a biopolitics of population control? What kind of state apparatus would universal HIV-testing entail? What kind of discourse would it create? Effect on sexuality itself? For a highly skeptical analysis of universal or compulsory AIDS testing, see Philpson & Posner, *Private Choices and Public Health* (universal testing would be very costly, with few benefits).

Much of HIV prevention focuses on transmission—that is, identifying and preventing the moments at which a person or population is at risk of becoming HIV positive. Equally important is caring for those living with HIV—something that, in the early years of the epidemic in the U.S., fell primarily on LGBT communities themselves. In 1986, 50 percent of adults surveyed indicated they would be in favor of quarantining people living with HIV/AIDS. Twelve years later, the Supreme Court ruled that HIV, at least when asymptomatic, qualifies as a disability under the ADA, adding an important anti-discrimination argument to the legal toolkit of AIDS activists fighting for access to treatment and services. *Bragdon v. Abbott*, 524 U.S. 624 (1998).

It's interesting, and certainly not inevitable, that narratives of HIV/ AIDS became enmeshed with narratives of disability—not all medical conditions are considered disabilities under the ADA. Just as HIV/AIDS forced a societal renegotiation of ideas of sex and sexuality, broader theories of disability challenge some of our most foundational concepts of sexuality. Namely, what does it mean to be sexual? Whom do we consider sexual, and whom do we not? How do theories of disability critique or contribute to theories of sexuality?

Robert McRuer, "Disabling Sex: Notes for a Crip Theory of Sexuality," 17 *GLQ: A Journal of Lesbian and Gay Studies* 107 (2011). Professor McRuer's title offers a spinoff of Gayle Rubin's "Thinking Sex," excerpted earlier in this chapter. McRuer nods to Rubin's theoretical work while also seeking to locate narratives of disability within discourses of sexuality. To achieve this goal, McRuer puts Rubin's piece into a dialectical relationship with a contemporaneous work in disability theory: Deborah Stone's *The Disabled State*. Together, these two works highlight the theoretical potential of what McRuer coins a "crip theory of sexuality."

Professor McRuer opens with the observation that "sex and disability at times seem not so much intersectional as incongruous. * * * Although stereotypes of the oversexed disabled person engaged in unspeakable acts do exist, disabled people are more commonly positioned as asexual—incapable of or uninterested in sex. Speaking to such expectations, the disability activist Anne Finger wrote more than a decade ago, in an assertion now well known in the disability rights movement, 'Sexuality is the source of our deepest oppression; it is also often the source of our deepest pain. It's easier to talk about and formulate strategies for changing discrimination in employment, education, and housing than it is to talk about our exclusion from sexuality and reproduction." (Page 107.) McRuer challenges this premise: "What if disabled people were understood to be both subjects and objects of a multiplicity of erotic desires and practices, both within and outside the parameters of heteronormative sexuality?" (Page 107.)

Professor McRuer begins his argument by noting that disability and people with disabilities are already present in much of the discourse on sexuality:

- *The distinction between able-bodied and disabled maps neatly onto Rubin's idea of the charmed circle and outer limits.* All kinds of disabled sex—sex in wheelchairs or crutches, sex while HIV positive, sex between people with cognitive disabilities—are located in the outer limits of Rubin's framework.

- *Sex panics are invariably connected to narratives of disability.* For example, historical concerns about masturbation came from its supposed link to disabilities ranging from blindness to insanity. Many of these sexual norms and practices were then renegotiated in light of the AIDS crisis in large part because the significant disability (and ultimately death) that almost always resulted from infection.

- *Benign sexual variation must include disability.* In deconstructing normative sex and sexuality to expand our ideas of what's considered "acceptable" or "good" sex, Rubin's concept of benign sexual variation must incorporate disabled bodies and disabled sexualities to truly carry theoretical weight.

Rubin and Stone's work, and sexuality and disability theories generally, both link their respective subjects to the development of the modern state and institutions of capitalism. "Rubin's project in *Thinking Sex* involved, at least partly, linking emergent forms of sexual hierarchization to the consolidation of industrial capitalism and paralleling resistance to that hierarchization to struggles around and against the bourgeois mode of production. Stone, as well, was concerned with how newly configured capitalist states were sorting bodies and behaviors into dominant and subordinated categories. At the same time that Rubin was insisting that 'like the capitalist organization of labor and its distribution of rewards and powers, the modern sexual system has been the object of political struggle since it emerged and as it has evolved,' Stone too was reflecting on distributions of rewards and powers and on how structures of inequality rigidified in and through that system of distribution." (Page 110) Both sexuality and disability, then, include state power over and categorization of bodies, behaviors and identities at least in part for the purposes of distribution and production, resulting in an "uneven biopolitical incorporation—the incorporation of some bodies (but not others) into the state." (Page 110.)

Professor McRuer closes by tracing the story of sex surrogacy in the Netherlands, in order to demonstrate the explicit ways in which a state positions itself through discourses around sexuality and disability. For at least 15 years, the Dutch government has paid for sex workers to work directly with disabled people or to facilitate their sexual interaction with a third party. This benefit covers both mentally and physically disabled citizens as well as both hetero- and homosexual interactions. State involvement in disability and sexuality, in this case, contributes to a certain national identity around sex—namely, that the Netherlands is welcoming to a variety of sexuality identities and behaviors and is even willing to provide for the sexual health of its population.

The danger of this state use of disabled bodies and nonnormative sexualities to perpetuate a discourse of inclusivity is how the state may use that identity (and by extension its minorities) to perpetuate other forms of oppression. In the case of the Netherlands, a national identity defined by sexual openness contributed to the rise in the early 2000s of xenophobia and Islamophobia. McRuer makes two final observations: first, "a crip theory of sexuality, then, would insist on thinking seriously around [a disabled person's] rights and pleasures while being wary of how those *might* get discursively positioned by and around the state. Second * * * the potential use of disability and sex to shore up who 'we' are can and will coexist with plenty of 'panic' (to invoke Rubin again), plenty of residual or even dominant discourses that still position disability and desire at odds, or put differently, disability as undesirable." (Page 114.)

NOTE ON DISABILITY AND SEXUALITY

As Professor McRuer's essay highlights, the parallels between disability and sexuality studies make them a natural pair for intersectional dialogue, particularly because of their shared critical analysis of the state and state-sponsored institutions. *Disabling Sex* also has important consequences for how we think about sexuality. What is the potential of sexuality studies if it is not able to incorporate the experiences of other marginalized groups? The year after publishing *Disabling Sex*, McRuer edited an anthology on sex and disability with disability theorist Anna Mollow. Several essays from that anthology offer further insights into how disability studies can and should complicate our discourses on sexuality.

Tobin Siebers, *A Sexual Culture for Disabled People*, in *Sex and Disability*, 38–53 (2012), argues that disability reveals the limitations of our conception of sexuality while also expanding its possibilities. "First, thinking about disabled sexuality broadens the definition of sexual behavior. Second, the sexual experiences of disabled people expose with great clarity both the fragile separation between the private and public spheres, as well as the role played by this separation in the history of regulating sex. Third, co-thinking sex and disability reveals unacknowledged assumptions about the ability to have sex and how the ideology of ability determines the value of some sexual practices and ideas over others. Finally, the sexual history of disabled people makes it possible to theorize patterns of sexual abuse and victimization faced by other sexual minorities." (Page 38).

Disability is not always solely or even primarily physical. Rachael Groner, *Sex as "Spock": Autism, Sexuality and Autobiographical Narrative*, in *Sex and Disability*, 263–81, notes the lack of sexual narratives for people with autism spectrum disorder (ASD); in their place, she sees both a presumed and imposed sexuality. Contrary to these myths, however, "people with ASD may choose relationships and sexual expressions that are unconventional, but they are definitely not asexual; in fact, the personal narratives written by and about autistic people form a complex challenge to heteronormativity and to mainstream cultural assumptions about sex and disability." (Page 264).

PROBLEM 3-7
A RIGHT TO SEX OR A RIGHT TO PRIVACY?

Recall McRuer's description of sex surrogacy in the Netherlands. In what ways does that policy position sex as something that both occurs in the public sphere and is a right? How does that conceptualization of sex differ from the U.S. interpretation seen in cases like *Lawrence v. Texas*, which frame the issue not as a right to sex but as a right to privacy? Which is the better approach? What do Foucault's ideas of discipline, biopower and biopolitics have to say about the policy? Would Professor MacKinnon, known for her staunch opposition to sex work, have anything positive to say about sex surrogacy?

B. POST-LIBERAL THEORIES OF IDENTITY AND STRATEGIES OF EMPOWERMENT

Social scientists in the middle part of the twentieth century maintained that society and the state bear responsibility for individuals injured by the effect of *prejudice*, especially race-, religion-, and ethnicity-based prejudice. When society signals that certain traits are inferior or degraded, the individual internalizes that message and spends her entire lifetime struggling with that sense of inferiority. Throughout the twentieth century, this modernist evidence was deployed by identity-based social movements to challenge traditional discriminations against minorities and women. The social science appendix to the NAACP's brief in *Brown v. Board of Education* made this precise argument, and it was key to Chief Justice Warren's opinion for the Court. Feminist and gay rights litigators in cases like *Frontiero* and *Romer* made the same kinds of arguments: cultural prejudices and stereotypes about women and gay people harmed individuals and were therefore deeply inconsistent with state obligations to afford "equal protection of the law."

In this part, we examine some post-liberal approaches to identity politics. We start with Erving Goffman's influential theory of stigma and strategies people follow to cope with their stigmatized traits. Eve Kosofsky Sedgwick's account of minoritizing and universalizing strategies helps us understand the mobility of identity categories and justifications for both discrimination and liberation. This part will close with an essay suggesting, from a post-liberal and indeed global perspective, some important advantages of a liberty-based rather than equality-based strategy for social movements.

***Erving Goffman, Stigma: Notes on the Management of a Spoiled Identity* (1963).** "Stigmas" in our society include features such as homosexuality, minority religious views, mental and physical disabilities, etc. "In all of these various instances of stigma, * * * the same sociological features are found: an individual who might have been received easily in ordinary social intercourse possesses a trait that can obtrude itself upon attention and turn those of us whom he meets away from him, breaking the claim that his other attributes have on us" (pp. 6–7). Individuals thus stigmatized internalize society's views into their own identity understandings. "[A] discrepancy may exist between an individual's virtual and actual identity. This discrepancy, when known about or apparent, spoils his social identity; it has the effect of cutting him off from society and from himself so that he stands a discredited person facing an unaccepting world" (p. 138). This is unfair to people who must manage "spoiled identities."

The classical model of identity politics—the civil rights movement and ensuing social movements for women, gay people, the disabled, and others—has maintained that certain variations (like race, skin color, now sex, and perhaps sexual orientation) from the norm are benign and ought not be the basis for social or legal stigma. As Goffman put it, identity politics rests upon the assumption that social mores or the law creates a rupture between the individual's virtual and his or her actual identity; its claim is that many of these ruptures are illegitimate. That claim has been taken up by identity-based social movements; in each case, the movement argues that its identifying trait is a benign variation from that enjoyed by the majority and should not be the basis for stigma or discrimination. See *Loving, Frontiero,* and *Romer,* for Supreme Court decisions accepting this proposition with regard to race, sex, and sexual orientation.

The state's response to traits considered socially malignant (homosexuality) or degraded (femininity) has varied widely—ranging from campaigns of expulsion to incarceration to segregation to denigration. *See* Gordon Allport, *The Nature of Prejudice* (1954). Social psychologists like Allport and philosophers like Goffman worried that these campaigns harmed minorities by the wasteful responses they triggered in those whose identities were spoiled by social prejudice. "The stigma and the effort to conceal it or remedy it become 'fixed' as part of his personal identity. * * * [W]hen his differentness is not immediately apparent, and is not known beforehand (or at least not known by him to be known to the others) * * * [t]he issue is * * * of managing information about his failing. To display or not to display; to tell or not to tell; to let on or not to let on; to lie or not to lie; and in each case, to whom, how, when, and where." (p. 138.)

In the previous passage, Goffman is describing the phenomenon of *passing*. To avoid the disadvantages of stigma, women have passed as men, people of color have passed as white, Jews have passed as gentiles, Catholics have passed as Protestants, people with disease have passed as healthy, transgender people have passed as gender-conforming, and gay people have passed as straight. Passing is often not wholly successful (the deviant's effort to pass is not persuasive or is exposed), and even when it succeeds it exacts huge psychic costs for the individual. Social constructionist theory, however read, reinforces the traditional liberal view that society is responsible for those costs. So if a trait, like race or sex or sexual orientation, is not a legitimate basis for stigma, then it is impermissible for society to pressure individuals to hide their distinctiveness. Conversely, identity-based social movements urge everyone having the stigmatized trait to "come out of the closet" as a way of disrupting the pervasive social stigma.

But even minority persons who have come out of the closet have another Goffmanian strategy available to them: "[P]ersons who are ready to admit possession of a stigma (in many cases because it is known about or immediately apparent) may nonetheless make a great effort to keep the stigma from looming large. The individual's object is to reduce tension, that is, to make it easier for himself and others to withdraw covert attention from the stigma, and to sustain spontaneous involvement in the official content of the interaction." (Page 102.) The person of color who wears her hair in corn rows, the woman who does not wear dresses, and the gay man who does—all can be disciplined by society or even the law for not *comforting* their colleagues or for not *covering* their difference and conforming to the norm accepted by traditional society.[j] The system of performances associated with passing and comforting/covering is, according to Goffman, "a form of tacit cooperation between normals and the stigmatized: the deviator can afford to remain attached to the norm because others are careful to respect his secret, pass lightly over its disclosure, or disattend evidence

---

[j]   *See* Devon W. Carbado & Mitu Gulati, "Working Identity," 85 *Cornell L. Rev.* 1259 (2000) (drawing from Goffman the notion that outsiders engage in "comforting" behavior to make insiders more accepting of their presence); Kenji Yoshino, "Covering," 111 *Yale L.J.* 769 (2002) (drawing a similar inference from Goffman, and substituting the felicitous term "covering").

which prevents a secret from being made of it; these others, in turn, can afford to extend this tactfulness because the stigmatized will voluntarily refrain from pushing claims for acceptance much past the point normals find comfortable" (p. 130).

Note on Goffmanian Strategies for Dealing with Stigma: Passing, Covering, and Microperformances

Reading Goffman's theory of stigma together with Foucault's and Butler's constructionist theories of sexuality and gender yields exciting implications for *Hopkins* and other equality cases. Thus, *woman* might be considered a performative category whose socially constructed coherence rests just as much on dress, demeanor, and the like as on chromosomes and genitalia. This helps us see how Price Waterhouse's treatment of Ann Hopkins is *sex* discrimination: Hopkins was refusing to perform as a gender-stereotypical woman, and the firm disciplined her for essentially a failure to conform to gender stereotypes (i.e., restrain her "mannish" tendencies). Goffman suggests connections among the gender stereotyping in *Hopkins,* sex reassignment in the bathroom statutes, and homosexuality in *Lawrence*: sexual and gender minorities were disciplined because they did not perform as the classic stereotypes of their assigned sex.

A normative lesson many legal scholars draw from Goffman is that law or society's demands that sexual and gender minorities engage in a masquerade to accommodate mainstream tastes are unreasonable and ought to be illegal. Title VII prohibits "discrimination because of sex" in the workplace. Does such a legal rule prohibit an employer who disciplines a trans employee for not remaining in the closet? For not covering? How much nonconformity must an employer accommodate in the workplace? Title VII allows a defense when an employer can prove that "sex" is a bona fide occupational qualification (§ 703(e)): Ought that allow an employer require a trans employee to "present" as unambiguously one sex or the other?

The Ann Hopkins Case, excerpted above, presents a normative challenge: Does Title VII protect female employees against employer demands to "cover," namely, to behave in a manner her supervisors consider appropriate gender performance? Goffman's contrast between passing and comforting/covering helps us appreciate the big conceptual advance the Supreme Court achieved in *Hopkins* (the Brennan plurality plus the O'Connor concurrence). Traditional sex discrimination cases had objected to employer use of *descriptive* stereotypes: women are too weak, not sufficiently aggressive, etc. as a matter of their nature as women. In a society committed to women's equal citizenship, descriptive stereotypes are pernicious and cannot be tolerated. In nineteenth century American society, before women won recognition of their equal citizenship, thousands of women passed as men in order to secure careers.

According to her complaint, however, Ann Hopkins was not discriminated against because Price Waterhouse thought that women could not be excellent accountants or executives. Instead, Price Waterhouse refused to promote Ann Hopkins because of *prescriptive* stereotypes:[k] she ought to act more like a lady! In other words, Price Waterhouse was asking Hopkins to comfort its partners with a more feminine performance. This is a less onerous demand upon female employees, but it is remarkable that the Supreme Court found purely prescriptive stereotyping to be a violation of Title VII.

Consider a variation on *Hopkins*: What if Ann Hopkins were a lesbian? Goffman suggests two strategies for Hopkins: passing as straight or (if she chose not to pass) covering or softening her deviation. These strategies are the most likely ones in a culture where homosexuality is severely stigmatized—but how about a culture where the normative valence of homosexuality is "in play," a subject of social and corporate debate? (Indeed, many corporate cultures have been much more pro-lesbian and gay than larger American society has been.) Passing and covering remain strategies that are available to Hopkins, but a third strategy is one that the lesbian and gay rights social movement would prefer her to follow: coming out of the closet (so not passing) and engaging the culture on a daily basis as an "out" lesbian (so not covering, at least not all the time).

In *Presentation of Self in Everyday Life* (1959), Erving Goffman explored the ways in which an individual in ordinary day-to-day *microperformances* "presents himself" and creates a frame for his identity (pp. xi, 15–16). That frame is interactive, for when "the individual projects a definition of the situation when he appears before others, we must also see that the others, however passive their role may seem to be, will themselves effectively project a definition of the situation by virtue of their response to the individual and by virtue of any lines of action they initiate to him" (p. 9). The individual's performance will evolve—as will the audience.

Professor Marc Poirier has applied these Goffmanian insights to the gay rights (or marriage equality) movement. Before May 2004, increasing numbers of gay and lesbian couples celebrated "marriages" that were "unauthorized, visible microperformances" disrupting traditional cultural understandings long held by the surrounding culture. Poirier, "Microperformances of Identity: Visible Same-Sex Couples and the Marriage Controversy," 15 *Wash. & Lee J. Civ. Rts. & Soc. Just.* 3, 29 (2008). Critical race literature has argued that "microaggressions" in daily life perpetuate and deepen racism, e.g., Peggy C. Davis, "Law as Microaggression," 98 *Yale L.J.* 1559 (1989), and Poirier flips that idea to argue that microaggressions can be deployed to destabilize prejudiced status quos as well as perpetuate them. Now that same-sex marriage is legal everywhere in the United States, these microaggressions are becoming a powerful engine of persuasion for advocates of gay marriage in other jurisdictions.

---

[k] On the difference between descriptive (or ascriptive) and prescriptive stereotyping and Title VII, see Zachery Herz, Note, "*Price*'s Progress: Sex Stereotyping and Its Potential for Antidiscrimination Law," 124 *Yale L.J.* 396 (2014).

Eve Kosofsky Sedgwick, *The Epistemology of the Closet*

Pages 67–68, 71–76, 78–90 (1990).*

* * * As D.A. Miller points out, secrecy can function as "the subjective practice in which the oppositions of private/public, inside/outside, subject/object are established, and the sanctity of their first term kept inviolate. And the phenomenon of the 'open secret' does not, as one might think, bring about the collapse of those binarisms and their ideological effects, but rather attests to their fantasmatic recovery." ["Secret Subjects, Open Secrets," in *The Novel and the Police* 207.] Even at an individual level, there are remarkably few of even the most openly gay people who are not deliberately in the closet with someone personally or economically or institutionally important to them. Furthermore, the deadly elasticity of heterosexist presumption means that, like Wendy in *Peter Pan,* people find new walls springing up around them even as they drowse: every encounter with a new classful of students, to say nothing of a new boss, social worker, loan officer, landlord, doctor, erects new closets whose fraught and characteristic laws of optics and physics exact from at least gay people new surveys, new calculations, new draughts and requisitions of secrecy or disclosure. Even an out gay person deals daily with interlocutors about whom she doesn't know whether they know or not; it is equally difficult to guess for any given interlocutor whether, if they did know, the knowledge would seem very important. Nor—at the most basic level—is it unaccountable that someone who wanted a job, custody or visiting rights, insurance, protection from violence, from "therapy," from distorting stereotype, from insulting scrutiny, from simple insult, from forcible interpretation of their bodily product, could deliberately choose to remain in or to reenter the closet in some or all segments of their life. The gay closet is not a feature only of the lives of gay people. But for many gay people it is still the fundamental feature of social life; and there can be few gay people, however courageous and forthright by habit, however fortunate in the support of their immediate communities, in whose lives the closet is not still a shaping presence. * * *

The closet is the defining structure for gay oppression in this century. [But the metaphor is not limited to homosexuality.] I recently heard someone on National Public Radio refer to the sixties as the decade when Black people came out of the closet. For that matter, I recently gave an MLA talk purporting to explain how it's possible to come out of the closet as a fat woman. The apparent floating-free from its gay origins of that phrase "coming out of the closet" in recent usage might suggest that the trope of the closet is so close to the heart of some modern preoccupations that it could be, or has been, evacuated of its historical

---

gay specificity. But I hypothesize that exactly the opposite is true. I think that a whole cluster of the most crucial sites for the contestation of meaning in twentieth-century Western culture are consequentially and quite indelibly marked with the historical specificity of homosocial/homosexual definition, notably but not exclusively male, from around the turn of the century. Among those sites are, as I have indicated, the pairings secrecy/disclosure and private/public. Along with and sometimes through these epistemologically charged pairings, condensed in the figures of "the closet" and "coming out," this very specific crisis of definition has then ineffaceably marked other pairings as basic to modern cultural organization as masculine/feminine, majority/minority, innocence/initiation, natural/artificial, new/old, growth/decadence, urbane/provincial, health/illness, same/different, cognition/paranoia, art/kitsch, sincerity/sentimentality, and voluntarity/addiction. So permeative has the suffusing stain of homo/heterosexual crisis been that to discuss any of these indices in any context, in the absence of an antihomophobic analysis, must perhaps be to perpetuate unknowingly compulsions implicit in each.

For any modern question of sexuality, knowledge/ignorance is more than merely one in a metonymic chain of such binarisms. The process, narrowly bordered at first in European culture but sharply broadened and accelerated after the late eighteenth century, by which "knowledge" and "sex" become conceptually inseparable from one another—so that knowledge means in the first place sexual knowledge; ignorance, sexual ignorance; and epistemological pressure of any sort seems a force increasingly saturated with sexual impulsion—was sketched in Volume I of Foucault's *History of Sexuality*. In a sense, this was a process, protracted almost to retardation, of exfoliating the biblical genesis by which what we now know as sexuality is fruit—apparently the only fruit—to be plucked from the tree of knowledge. Cognition itself, sexuality itself, and transgression itself have always been ready in Western culture to be magnetized into an unyielding though not an unfissured alignment with one another, and the period initiated by Romanticism accomplished this disposition through a remarkably broad confluence of different languages and institutions. * * *

* * * Vibrantly resonant as the image of the closet is for many modern oppressions, it is indicative for homophobia in a way it cannot be for other oppressions. Racism, for instance, is based on a stigma that is visible in all but exceptional cases (cases that are neither rare nor irrelevant, but that delineate the outlines rather than coloring the center of racial experience); so are the oppressions based on gender, age, size, physical handicap. Ethnic/cultural/religious oppressions such as anti-Semitism are more analogous in that the stigmatized individual has at least notionally some discretion—although, importantly, it is never to be taken for granted how much—over other people's knowledge of her or his membership in the group: one could "come out as" a Jew or Gypsy, in a

heterogeneous urbanized society, much more intelligibly than one could typically "come out as," say, female, Black, old, a wheelchair user, or fat. A (for instance) Jewish or Gypsy identity, and hence a Jewish or Gypsy secrecy or closet, would nonetheless differ again from the distinctive gay versions of these things in its clear ancestral linearity and answerability, in the roots (however tortuous and ambivalent) of cultural identification through each individual's originary culture of (at a minimum) the family.

[Sedgwick provides a powerful example from religious history, the story of Esther (as told in Racine's play). Esther concealed her Judaism from her husband, King Assuérus (Ahasuerus), who considers the Jews "unclean" and an "abomination" against nature. Egged on by his evil adviser Aman (Haman), the King decides to execute the Jews. In a brave move, Esther "comes out" to her husband the King—and that impulse dooms the genocidal plot.] Revelation of identity in the space of intimate love effortlessly overturns an entire public systematics of the natural and the unnatural, the pure and the impure. The peculiar strike that the story makes to the heart is that Esther's small, individual ability to risk losing the love and countenance of her master has the power to save not only her own space in life but her people.

[As powerful as Esther's "coming out" was, Sedgwick notes that coming out of the homosexual closet is even more fraught in modern times for a variety of reasons, including the instability of what it means to be "homosexual" and the aspersions my coming out as gay has on the sexual identity of the person I come out to. "What does your homosexuality say about my own sexuality?"] Each of these complicating possibilities stems at least partly from the plurality and the cumulative incoherence of modern ways of conceptualizing same-sex desire and, hence, gay identity; an incoherence that answers, too, to the incoherence with which *hetero*sexual desire and identity are conceptualized. * * *

For surely, if paradoxically, it is the paranoid insistence with which the definitional barriers between "the homosexual" (minority) and "the heterosexual" (majority) are fortified, in this century, by nonhomosexuals, and especially by men against men, that most saps one's ability to believe in "the homosexual" as an unproblematically discrete category of persons. Even the homophobic fifties folk wisdom of *Tea and Sympathy* detects that the man who most electrifies those barriers is the one whose own current is at most intermittently direct. It was in the period of the so-called "invention of the 'homosexual'" that Freud gave psychological texture and credibility to a countervalent, universalizing mapping of this territory, based on the supposed protean mobility of sexual desire and on the potential bisexuality of every human creature; a mapping that implies no presumption that one's sexual penchant will always incline toward persons of a single gender, and that offers, additionally, a richly denaturalizing description of the psychological motives and mechanisms of male paranoid, projective homophobic definition and enforcement. Freud's antiminoritizing account only gained, moreover, in influence by being articulated through a developmental narrative in which heterosexist and masculinist ethical sanctions found ready camouflage. If the new common wisdom that hotly overt homophobes are men who are "insecure about their masculinity" supplements the implausible, necessary illusion that there could be a *secure* version of masculinity (known, presumably, by the coolness of its homophobic enforcement) and a stable, intelligible way for men to feel about other men in modern heterosexual capitalist patriarchy, what tighter turn could there be to the screw of an already off-center, always at fault, endlessly blackmailable male identity ready to be manipulated into any labor of channeled violence?

It remained for work emerging from the later feminist and gay movements to begin to clarify why the male paranoid project had become so urgent in the maintenance of gender subordination; and it remained for a stunningly efficacious coup of feminist redefinition to transform lesbianism, in a predominant view, from a matter of female virilization to one of woman-identification [e.g., Rich's essay on "Compulsory Heterosexuality"]. * * * Most moderately to well-educated Western people in this century seem to share a similar understanding of homosexual definition.* * * [I]t is organized around a radical and irreducible incoherence. It holds the minoritizing view that there is a distinct population of persons who "really are" gay; at the same time, it holds the universalizing views that sexual desire is an unpredictably powerful solvent of stable identities; that apparently heterosexual persons and object choices are strongly marked by same-sex influences and desires, and vice versa for apparently homosexual ones; and that at least male heterosexual identity and modern masculinist culture may require for their maintenance the scapegoating crystallization of a same-sex male desire that is widespread and in the first place internal.

It has been the project of many, many writers and thinkers of many different kinds to adjudicate between the minoritizing and universalizing views of sexual definition and to resolve this conceptual incoherence. * * * A perfect example of this potent incoherence was the anomalous legal situation of gay people and acts in this country after one recent legal ruling. The Supreme Court in *Bowers v. Hardwick* [Chapter 1] notoriously left the individual states free to prohibit any *acts* they wish to define as "sodomy," by whomsoever performed, with no fear at all of impinging on any rights, and particularly privacy rights, safeguarded by the Constitution; yet only shortly thereafter a panel of the Ninth Circuit Court of Appeals ruled (in *Sergeant Perry J. Watkins v. United States Army* [Chapter 1]) that homosexual *persons,* as a particular kind of person, *are* entitled to Constitutional protections under the Equal Protection [C]lause. To be gay in this system is to come under the radically overlapping aegises of a universalizing discourse of acts and a minoritizing discourse of persons. Just at the moment, at least within the discourse of law, the former of these prohibits what the latter of them protects; but in the concurrent public-health constructions related to AIDS, for instance, it is far from clear that a minoritizing discourse of persons ("risk groups") is not even more oppressive than the competing, universalizing discourse of acts ("safer sex"). In the double binds implicit in the space overlapped by the two, at any rate, every matter of definitional control is fraught with consequence.

The energy-expensive but apparently static clinch between minoritizing and universalizing views of *homo/heterosexual definition* is not, either, the only major conceptual siege under which modern homosexual and heterosexist fates are enacted. The second one, as important as the first and intimately entangled with it, has to do with defining the relation to gender of homosexual persons and same-sex desires. (It was in this conceptual register that the radical-feminist reframing of lesbianism as woman-identification was such a powerful move.) Enduringly since at least the turn of the century, there have presided two contradictory *tropes of gender* through which same-sex desire could be understood. On the one hand there was, and there persists, differently coded (in the homophobic folklore and science surrounding those "sissy boys" and their mannish sisters, but also in the heart and guts of much living gay and lesbian culture), the trope of inversion, * * * "a woman's soul trapped in a man's body"—and vice versa. * * * [O]ne vital impulse of this trope is the preservation of an essential *heterosexuality* within desire itself, through a particular reading of the homosexuality of persons: desire, in this view, by definition subsists in the current that runs between one male self and one female self, in whatever sex of bodies these selves may be manifested. * * *

[T]he persistence of the inversion trope has been yoked, however, to that of its contradictory counterpart, the trope of gender separatism. Under this latter view, far from its being of the essence of desire to cross boundaries of gender, it is instead the most natural thing in the world that people of the same gender, people grouped together under the single most determinative diacritical mark of social organization, people whose economic, institutional, emotional, physical needs and knowledges may have so much in common, should bond together also on the axis of sexual desire. As the substitution of the phrase "woman-identified woman" for "lesbian" suggests, * * *this trope tends to reassimilate to one another identification and desire, where inversion models, by contrast, depend on their distinctness. Gender-separatist models would thus place the woman-loving woman and the man-loving man each at the "natural" defining center of their own gender, again in contrast to inversion models that locate gay people—whether biologically or culturally—at the threshold between genders (see Figure 2).

	Separatist:	Integrative:
Homo/hetero *sexual* definition:	*Minoritizing,* e.g., gay identity, essentialist, third-sex models, civil rights models	*Universalizing,* e.g., bisexual potential, "social constructionist," "sodomy" models, "lesbian continuum"
Gender definition:	*Gender separatist,* e.g., homosocial continuum, lesbian separatist, manhood-initiation models	*Inversion / liminality / transitivity,* e.g., cross-sex, androgyny, gay/lesbian solidarity models

Figure 2. Models of Gay/Straight Definition in Terms of Overlapping Sexuality and Gender

The immanence of each of these models throughout the history of modern gay definition is clear from the early split in the German homosexual rights movement between Magnus Hirschfeld, founder (in 1897) of the Scientific-Humanitarian Committee, a believer in the "third sex" who posited * * * "an exact equation ... between cross-gender behaviors and homosexual desire"; and Benedict Friedländer, co-founder (in 1902) of the Community of the Special, who concluded to the contrary "that homosexuality was the highest, most perfect evolutionary stage of gender differentiation." As James Steakley explains, "the true *typus inversus,*" according to this latter argument, "as distinct from the effeminate homosexual, was seen as the founder of patriarchal society and ranked above the heterosexual in terms of his capacity for leadership and heroism."

Like the dynamic impasse between minoritizing and universalizing views of homosexual definition, that between transitive and separatist tropes of homosexual gender has its own complicated history, an especially crucial one for any understanding of modern gender asymmetry, oppression, and resistance. One thing that does emerge with clarity from this complex and contradictory map of sexual and gender definition is that the possible grounds to be found there for alliance and cross-identification among various groups will also be plural. To take the issue of gender definition alone: under a gender-separatist topos, lesbians have looked for identifications and alliances among women in general, including straight women (as in Adrienne Rich's "lesbian continuum" model); and gay men, as in Friedländer's model—or more recent "male liberation" models—of masculinity, might look for them among men in general, including straight men. "The erotic and social presumption of women is our enemy," Friedländer wrote in his "Seven Theses on Homosexuality" (1908). Under a topos of gender inversion or liminality, in contrast, gay men have looked to identify with straight women (on the grounds that they are also "feminine" or also desire men), or with lesbians (on the grounds that they occupy a similarly liminal position);

while lesbians have analogously looked to identify with gay men or, though this latter identification has not been strong since second-wave feminism, with straight men. (Of course, the political outcomes of all these trajectories of potential identification have been radically, often violently, shaped by differential historical forces, notably homophobia and sexism.) Note, however, that this schematization over "the issue of gender definition alone" also does impinge on the issue of homo/heterosexual definition, as well, and in an unexpectedly chiasmic way. Gender-*separatist* models like Rich's or Friedländer's seem to tend toward *universalizing* understandings of homo/heterosexual potential. To the degree that gender-integrative inversion or liminality models, such as Hirschfeld's "third-sex" model, suggest an alliance or identity between lesbians and gay men, on the other hand, they tend toward gay-*separatist*, minoritizing models of specifically gay identity and politics. * * *

Like the effect of the minoritizing/universalizing impasse, in short, that of the impasse of gender definition must be seen first of all in the creation of a field of intractable, highly structured discursive incoherence at a crucial node of social organization, in this case the node at which *any* gender is discriminated. I have no optimism at all about the availability of a standpoint of thought from which either question could be intelligibly, never mind efficaciously, adjudicated, given that the same yoking of contradictions has presided over all the thought on the subject, and all its violent and pregnant modern history, that has gone to form our own thought. Instead, the more promising project would seem to be a study of the incoherent dispensation itself, the indisseverable girdle of incongruities under whose discomfiting span, for most of a century, have unfolded both the most generative and the most murderous plots of our culture.

NOTE ON BINARIES, DOUBLE BINDS, AND THE LAW

An important concept in Sedgwick's work is the *double bind*. The double bind exploits the way in which discourse about gender can always be conceived as either sharply binary or nuanced in a continuum, and discourse about sexuality or gender can always be conceived as either universalizing or minoritizing. Any underlying agenda can be achieved by one's choice of conceptual alternatives. The different ways Ann Hopkins's dilemma was conceptualized exemplifies the relationship of legal theory to feminist theory to queer theory through a series of double binds.

One double bind: Ann Hopkins was a macho woman who was making it in a macho male environment. Aggressiveness was a requisite to be successful at Price Waterhouse (integrative), but a disability if one were a woman (separatist). So Hopkins might not have had the economic push to make partner if she weren't aggressive, but her aggressiveness turned off many male partners because they thought it unfeminine. Damned if you are, damned if you aren't. The dissenting Justices felt that the law did not address this double bind, because "discrimination because of sex" only monitors employer-supported gender separatism and does not address gender inversion, however motivated.

Motivated by the record evidence of blatant sexism among the partners, the majority Justices in *Hopkins* (Brennan and O'Connor) rejected this double bind as inconsistent with Title VII's commitment to women's equal position in the workplace, and perhaps to disavowing gender stereotypes as the basis for workplace decisions. In Sedgwick's terminology, the majority viewed gender inversion (and not just gender separatism) as a problem Title VII was enacted to address. In her influential commentary, Professor Mary Anne Case interprets the majority in this way. See Case, "Effeminate Man." Does *Hopkins* therefore support the notion that Title VII bars discrimination against employees because of their being transgender? Professor Case thinks the answer to that is clearly *yes*. Would the current Supreme Court agree? (Does it make a difference if we tell you that Justice Kennedy is now the median Justice on issues of sex and gender discrimination?)

By the way, there is another conceivable explanation for Price Waterhouse's treatment of Ann Hopkins: homophobia. If the underlying reason for Price Waterhouse's action was fear of lesbians, the reason may have been legally admissible—and it was the made-up pretext (the abrasive woman) that got them into legal trouble. Hopkins was straight, but history is replete with straight women who were penalized because their assertiveness generated suspicions about their sexual orientations. If she had been a lesbian rejected by an intolerant employer, the Court's Title VII jurisprudence might place her in a different kind of double bind: if she were open about her sexual orientation, she would have been dismissed for disrupting the operation of the workplace, either because she was too odd for coworkers to deal with (a minoritizing move) or because she would sexualize the workplace and distract coworkers (a universalizing move). *See Hively v. Ivy Tech Community College*, 853 F.3d 339 (7th Cir. en banc 2017) (ruling that discrimination against gender-inverting lesbian was sex discrimination, based on *Hopkins*).

Notice how Sedgwick's notion of the double bind helps us understand Justice White's analytical moves in *Bowers v. Hardwick,* which upheld Georgia's consensual sodomy law. To reject Hardwick's claim that people have a "fundamental right" to engage in private consensual sodomy, Justice White engaged in a *universalizing* move, as he examined the lengthy history of consensual sodomy laws. The danger of universalizing anti-sodomy rules, however, was that the law might then be criminalizing (with a mandatory minimum one year jail sentence) conduct "everyone" engaged in—and so Justice White simultaneously insisted that the challenge was only to "homosexual sodomy" prosecutions, a classic *minoritizing* move. *See* Janet Halley, "Reasoning about Sodomy: Act and Identity In and After *Bowers v. Hardwick,*" 79 *Va. L. Rev.* 1721 (1993). Consider another case that classically presents Sedgwick's double bind.

Marjorie Rowland v. Mad River
Local School District

United States Court of Appeals for the Sixth Circuit, 1984.
730 F.2d 444, *cert. denied*, 470 U.S. 1009 (1985).

■ LIVELY, CHIEF JUDGE:

[Marjorie Rowland was a vocational guidance counselor at Stebbins High School in Montgomery County, Ohio. In the same time period she was counseling two gay students, Rowland "came out" to her secretary and the assistant principal that she was bisexual and had a female lover. The school principal (and other officials) asked her to resign, and when she did not they suspended her with pay for the remainder of her contract, which was not renewed. Rowland sued several officials and the school district for reinstatement and damages for violation of her federal constitutional rights to equal protection and free speech. The jury found that Rowland's private statements did not interfere with her job performance or with the operation of the school, and that her dismissal was motivated in part by these statements regarding her bisexuality. The jury further found that the school officials were motivated by Rowland's sexual orientation but acted in good faith; that the school board acted in good faith upon the officials' recommendations; and that Rowland behaved unprofessionally in revealing the names to the two gay students she was counseling.

[Based on the jury's findings, the magistrate entered an order finding in favor of the individual defendants based upon a good faith defense but against the school district for the suspension and transfer in violation of her rights to equal protection of the law and free speech and for nonrenewal of her contract in violation of her right to free speech. The Court of Appeals reversed the findings against the school district. Judge Lively ruled that Rowland had no claim as a matter of law under the First Amendment because her speech did not concern "a matter of public concern." Judge Lively then ruled that Rowland had no equal protection claim because there was evidence of unsatisfactory job performance in her disclosure that two students were homosexual and because the jury found she was fired for the combined reason of being bisexual and speaking about it, and the latter was a permissible basis for termination.]

The dissent's gratuitous statement that the majority treats this case as one involving a sick person is totally wrong. It is true that plaintiff has attempted to make homosexual rights the issue in this case. However, her personal sexual orientation is not a matter of public concern, and we have decided the First Amendment issue on the basis of the latest Supreme Court treatment of legally similar claims. And, as we have pointed out, the plaintiff sought to prevail on her equal protection claim without any showing that heterosexual school employees in situations similar to hers have been, or would be, treated differently for making their personal sexual preferences the topic of comment and discussion in the high school community. Again, this is nothing more than the required analysis of an equal protection claim.

■ GEORGE CLIFTON EDWARDS, JR., CIRCUIT JUDGE, dissenting.* * *

This school teacher has been deprived of her job solely because she let it be known to some colleagues and, through them, to her administrative superiors that her sexual preference was for another woman. * * *

This record presents a clear cut issue as to whether a citizen's mere statement of a homosexual preference may be punished by job loss by the joint decision of a school superintendent, a public school principal and assistant principal, and the school board, as a matter of institutional policy. I find no language in the Constitution of the United States which excludes citizens who are bisexual or homosexual from its protection, and particularly of the protection of the first and fourteenth amendments thereto. The Constitution protects all citizens of the United States; no language therein excludes the homosexual minority. Like all citizens, homosexuals are protected in these great rights, certainly to the extent of being homosexual and stating their sexual preference in a factual manner where there is no invasion of any other person's rights. * * *

My colleague's opinion seems to me to treat this case, *sub silento*, as if it involved only a single person and a sick one at that—in short, that plaintiff's admission of homosexual status was sufficient in itself to justify her termination. To the contrary, this record does not disclose that she is subject to mental illness; nor is she alone.

Careful studies of homosexuality have now established two facts of which the courts should be aware and should take judicial notice. The first is that homosexuality is not a mental disease, like insanity or a psychopathic personality. The second is the extent of homosexuality in the United States. [The dissent then quotes at length from the 1979 Surgeon General's opinion stating that "homosexuality per se will no longer be considered a 'mental disease or defect' " and from a summary of Kinsey's work, stating "On the basis of these various studies it is fair to conclude, conservatively, that the incidence of more or less exclusively homosexual behavior in Western culture ranges from 5 to 10 percent for adult males and from 3 to 5 percent for adult females. If bisexual behavior is included, the incidence may well be twice these figures. It is clear, therefore, that the propensity for homosexual reactivity is a widespread one even in societies such as ours which strongly discourage it."]

NOTES ON THE *MAD RIVER* CASE, THE CONSTRUCTION OF HETEROSEXUALITY, AND THE ERASURE OF BISEXUALITY

1. *Marjorie Rowland, Identity Politics, Equal Protection, and the First Amendment.* Like many other famous litigants, Rowland was not a political activist. Indeed, she was closeted about her bisexuality. So the school was

disciplining her for publicity surrounding an identity Rowland did not openly claim and as to which she believed discretion was due. By outing Rowland, the state created her as an "open bisexual" and as a political activist—and ultimately as a lawyer. (After the Mad River debacle, Rowland was unable to work as an educator in Ohio, and she went to law school. Later, she settled in the Southwest, far from Mad River.)

The lengthy and ultimately unavailing lawsuit by a reluctant activist produced the first statement of equal rights for gay people from a Supreme Court Justice. As the caption to the case indicates, the Supreme Court refused to take certiorari. Justice Brennan wrote an opinion, joined by Justice Marshall, dissenting from the denial of certiorari. His opinion argued that sexual orientation should be a suspect classification, like race. In addition, he maintained that the lower court had erred in dismissing Rowland's First Amendment argument. He wondered whether even the most confidential communication of bisexuality does not trigger the "public issue" protections of the First Amendment, because homosexuality and bisexuality were so controversial in southern Ohio. "The fact of petitioner's bisexuality, once spoken, necessarily and ineluctably involved her in that [public] debate." Justice Brennan suggested how Rowland's "First Amendment and equal protection claims may be seen to converge, because it is realistically impossible to separate her spoken statements from her status." 470 U.S. at 1016 n.11 (Brennan, J., dissenting from denial of certiorari).

2. *The Construction of Mad River as a Heterosexual Community.* Janet Halley, "The Construction of Heterosexuality," in *Fear of a Queer Planet: Queer Politics and Social Theory* 84–85 (Michael Warner ed. 1993), extends Justice Brennan's reading of Marjorie Rowland's case. "Both Rowland and the town of Mad River were engaged in a diacritical struggle—one in which the self-definition of both players was at stake. This should make visible what otherwise should remain hidden—Rowland's discursive exertions were made in interaction with a class of heterosexuals *also in the process of self-constitution*." Halley also says: "Mad River as a political entity emerges from the Rowland controversy *heterosexual*, but heterosexual only because it silences those—not only Rowland the guidance counselor but also the possibly homosexual students she was counseling—who would even quietly question orientation orthodoxy. The price of citizenship in Mad River is silence about deviant sexuality, an insistence upon unknowing, a regimen of the closet."

Although most people would read Halley's point as a critique of Mad River's actions, her point can also support the school system. Rowland claimed a constitutional right to assert her identity as a bisexual. Why doesn't the school system have a constitutionally cognizable interest in asserting its identity as heterosexual? If identity is purely performative, and if Mad River's citizens truly believe that heterosexuality is the best "lifestyle" for its adolescents on the cusp of maturity, then why shouldn't it be able to impose a philosophy of heterosexuality-only discourse within its school system? This is part of a larger discourse, which we call *no promo homo*: Rather than arguing that "homosexuals" ought to be locked up, the state takes the position that its citizens are better off being straight than gay. Is this a legitimate defense of the *Rowland* majority?

3. *Bisexual Erasure*. Marjorie Rowland considered herself bisexual, but the lower court and the court of appeals present her as a "bisexual or homosexual"; within the court of appeals, both the majority and the dissent analyze her claims as ones involving "homosexual rights." Notice how bisexuality, as a category distinct from homosexuality, slowly disappears from a case involving a bisexual person. And *Rowland* is unusual in that the judges were able to see the complainant as bisexual, even if only briefly. Compare *Boutilier v. INS*, 387 U.S. 120 (1967), where the Supreme Court lumped an apparently bisexual Canadian in with all "homosexuals and sex perverts," and thereby ruled that the Canadian bisexual was "afflicted with psychopathic personality" that public health officials associated with homosexuality. Although dissenting from the Court's brutal ruling, Justice Douglas's dissent also treated the Canadian as a "homosexual."

This phenomenon reflects the tendency not only of judges but also of litigants to view sexuality in binary terms (homosexual/heterosexual) rather than in terms of a continuum from exclusive heterosexuality through various degrees of bisexuality to exclusive homosexuality. For speculation as to why bisexuals tend to be elided with "homosexuals," see Kenji Yoshino, "The Epistemic Contract of Bisexual Erasure," 52 *Stan. L. Rev.* 353 (2000). Note that the same phenomenon occurs in matters of race, where the biracial person is considered a person of color, and sex, where the intersex person is pressed into either the male or female box as early as birth.

NOTE ON MINORITIZING VERSUS UNIVERSALIZING STRATEGIES FOR SEX, GENDER, AND SEXUAL MINORITIES

For constitutional law, one implication of Professor Sedgwick's theory is that sex, gender, and sexual minorities have different kinds of strategies for resisting their oppression. One cluster of strategies would be *minoritizing*. Under such strategies, persons sharing a common stigmatized trait would conceptualize themselves as a *minority* subject to social and legal discrimination that is unfair. Minoritizing strategies would focus on the classification of the minority's identifying trait, and the group's goal would be to persuade society or the polity that its trait-variation is not malignant or degraded. The variation is either tolerable or benign (in the latter case, there is no single norm). In constitutional law, such a strategy mobilizes equal protection arguments, especially the notion that the group's defining trait is a "suspect" or "quasi-suspect" classification like race and sex, respectively. See Justice Brennan's opinion arguing for strict scrutiny of sexual orientation classifications in *Rowland*. Even if the classification is not (quasi) suspect, minorities should not be closed out of "fundamental" state opportunities (like voting) and benefits (like privacy and marriage).

The dilemma for minoritizing strategies is to persuade the majority that it should be nice to the minority. Why should the majority do anything for "these people"? One mechanism would be pluralism, the notion that we are a nation of minorities, and each has to be accommodated lest the polity fall apart. History is rife with stories of national decline because of intolerance toward a productive minority, from Spain's expulsion of the Jews in 1492 to France's revocation of the Edict of Nantes in 1685 to the persecutions of good people by the Nazis in the 1930s and the Communists in the 1950s and 1960s. Conversely, the United States, in particular, has benefitted from being an asylum for persecuted minorities, whose energy and human resources have made the nation great.

Another way to provide incentives to the majority might be *universalizing* strategies, warning the majority that persecution and exclusion cut more broadly than its leaders realize. Under universalizing strategies, minorities would emphasize that their stigmatized trait or activities are characteristic of many more people than is commonly supposed, and so it is dangerous for society or the polity to penalize this trait or these activities. Universalizing strategies might be useful to displace majority concerns with minority behaviors and traits. Thus, a minority religion that disgusts the majority might argue that faith-based practices are universal human rights that protect both the majority and various minorities. Or the right to privacy includes sexual activities between consenting adults of various kinds (oral sex as well as penile-vaginal intercourse) in the seclusion of the bedroom. See Justice Blackmun's dissenting opinion in *Bowers*.

A danger of universalizing strategies is that they might be offensive to the majority. Justices White and Powell (the key Justices in *Bowers*) were appalled by Hardwick's argument that his one-night stand was analogous to marital intercourse within the home. (We can scarcely imagine their horrified reaction if Hardwick had taken Sedgwick to heart and argued that *everyone* has same-sex attractions and is a potential homosexual.) This risk requires the minority and its leaders to be very careful about precisely which analogies might be persuasive to some in the majority.

Of course, most minorities pursue both minoritizing and universalizing strategies at the same time—as in *Lawrence v. Texas*, which overruled *Bowers*. The challengers to the Texas Homosexual Conduct Law made the minoritizing argument that the law represented anti-gay prejudice and therefore violated the Equal Protection Clause. And they made the universalizing argument that what Lawrence and Garner were doing in their bedroom is sexual activity that everyone has a Due Process Clause liberty to pursue. The Court majority synthesized the minoritizing and universalizing moves—while Justice Scalia's dissenting opinion followed the *Bowers* approach of universalizing legal condemnations of sodomy and minoritizing the current operation of the law so that only "homosexuals" suffered its consequences (though Justice Scalia modernized his argument to claim that "homosexuals" are very popular and enjoy elite support so that they can easily seek relief in the political process).

Sonia Katyal, "Exporting Identity"

14 *Yale Journal of Law & Feminism* 97, 98–102, 114–115,
133–134, 148–149, 153–154, 168–169 (2002).[*]

Now is the ideal time to study the limitations and possibilities of a global gay rights movement. The term "gay" has been borrowed into Japanese, Portuguese, Spanish, Thai, Turkish, and other languages, signifying its increasingly perceived universality. Gay and lesbian organizations now exist in virtually every continent and in many major urban centers throughout the world. A growing number of legislators and judges have taken up the cause of gay civil rights, and have actively supported protections based on sexual orientation in a host of areas, such as adoption, employment, domestic partnership, and immigration. Throughout these global developments, American activists, scholars and media figures have played a visible role, leading at least one commentator to characterize gay pride as "America's global gay export."

Nevertheless, although the struggle for gay rights has attracted enormous global attention in the past decade, it has also encountered many challenges. A number of governments, particularly across the developing world, have mounted vocal, and often violent, attacks against nascent gay and lesbian movements within their borders. For example, in Namibia, just last year, Home Affairs Minister Jerry Ekandjo told the National Assembly that the existence of homosexuality was entirely attributable to Western influences, observing "[w]e take everything [from Western culture] lock, stock, and barrel without carefully analyzing what is good and what is harmful to us. Today it is homosexuality, tomorrow the right to walk naked, the day after it will be the right to abuse drugs. At the end the so-called rights will lead to our own extinction." In this leader's view, "so-called gay rights can never qualify as human rights" because they are "inimical to true Namibian culture, African culture, and religion." Such commentary represents the point of view shared by some political leaders that indigenous homosexuality fails to exist in non-Western countries, and that the formation of gay communities is an undesirable byproduct of foreign influence and globalization.

As we realize that the struggle for gay civil rights is becoming more global, we must necessarily also confront an uncomfortable reality: for many politicians, the identity "gay" or "lesbian" is perceived to be tantamount to a foreign threat. Yet rather than addressing the complex questions of identity, culture, and sexuality raised by the increasingly transnational posture of the gay civil rights movement, legal scholars have remained painfully silent. Their silence is vexing, particularly given the influx of recent anthropological and social constructionist scholarship that actively challenges the prevailing assumption that concepts of sexual orientation can be universally generalized across different cultures and behaviors. Even though the performance of same-sex sexual

---

conduct has occurred throughout recorded history, the emergence of a tangible gay and lesbian identity is an extremely recent development. As one author observes, in India, to commit a homosexual act is one thing; to be a homosexual is an entirely different phenomenon. As this observation suggests, this divergence between identity and conduct raises the difficult question of whether sexual orientation itself is a culturally specific concept. * * *

* * * [G]ay and lesbian activists have made a divisive mistake by singlehandedly focusing on identity-based protections in order to achieve equality for sexual minorities. When considered in a cross-cultural context, identity-based protections actually reveal their own inherently self-destructive limitations, demonstrating a central paradox of global gay rights discourse. Instead of liberating sexual minorities, the use of identity-based frameworks may paradoxically exclude them from protection. I contend, therefore, that a global gay rights movement must take into account sexualities and behaviors that fall outside of traditional categories of sexual orientation. If a constitutional framework for protection of sexual minorities is to be globally effective, it must recognize that many individuals who fall outside of neatly circumscribed categories of sexual identity are just as deserving of a model of liberation that includes them.

While this Article stops short of advocating a culturally relativistic approach to gay civil rights in general, it does argue that the changing social meanings surrounding gay or lesbian sexual identities raise deeply complex questions that are often ignored by scholars and activists in the name of globalizing gay civil rights. For laws based on sexual orientation impose—and require—a certain relationship between identity and conduct that is deeply context-specific. By exploring other permutations of the relationship between identity and same-sex sexual conduct, we can come to a better understanding of some of the complexities that accompany nascent gay civil rights movements in other cultural contexts. * * *

* * * [T]he most prominent model of gay civil rights (particularly in domestic American law) [ ] is based upon a specific relationship between sexual identity and sexual conduct that I call "substitutive." The substitutive model assumes that one's public sexual identity and private sexual conduct are interchangeable; that is, individuals who engage in same-sex sexual conduct can be legally classified by a fixed and clearly demarcable gay, lesbian, or bisexual sexual identity. Based on this equation, gay civil rights activists tend to opt between two strategies of constitutional protection: privacy-based strategies (which protect same-sex sexual conduct) or identity-based anti-discrimination strategies (which protect against discrimination based on sexual orientation). * * *

* * * By focusing on a series of examples from Thailand and India, among other places, I demonstrate how this "substitutive" model of sexual identity and conduct may be a profoundly inadequate means of

obtaining protection for the vast numbers of sexual minorities throughout the world.

In each context, I argue that the introduction of this substitutive model clashes with preexisting social meanings of same-sex sexual conduct. In Thailand, for example, although a similarly substitutive model of sexual identity is swiftly emerging, the social meaning of homosexuality has been traditionally associated with transgenderism (what I call a transformative model of the relationship between identity and conduct). In contrast, in India, public health activists claim that many individuals view the performance of same-sex sexual conduct as totally separate from, rather than representative of, their sexual identity (what I call an additive model of the relationship between identity and conduct). Yet, rather than incorporating these different variations of sexuality and sexual identity, the substitutive model actively excludes them from its purview, both simplifying and ignoring their richness and complexity. * * *

* * * [T]he predominant gay civil rights movement in the United States has displayed a yearning tendency to substitute a discernible sexual orientation and identity for same-sex sexual conduct; and then to attach a categorical imperative to "coming out." Just as gay and lesbian activists in the United States have successfully sought to transform the social meaning of homosexuality in a legal context, they have also asserted significant leadership over the global constitution of that identity, exerting enormous power in determining the manner by which individuals define their sexual identities. Gay pride parades have become a global phenomenon; and gay and lesbian activists have made their way around the globe to assist the formation of nascent movements.

Yet this monopoly power over sexual self-definition can also be deeply problematic. Categories of gay, lesbian, heterosexual, or bisexual identity, as a basis for individual and collective identity, often obscure a deeper question of whether such categories of sexual orientation can—or should—serve as universal categories for everyone. Moreover, imposing a gay, lesbian, or bisexual identity on individuals who may engage in same-sex sexual behavior, but who do not fit a substitutive paradigm between identity and conduct, can be unduly confining, exclusionary, and inappropriate. * * *

As Professor David Greenberg explains [in *The Construction of Homosexuality* 3 (1988)]:

> Homosexuality is not a conceptual category everywhere. To us, it connotes symmetry between male-male and female-female relationships ... When used to characterize individuals, it implies that erotic attraction originates in a relatively stable, more or less exclusive attribute of the individual. Usually it connotes an exclusive orientation: the homosexual is not also heterosexual; the heterosexual is not also homosexual. Most non-Western societies make few of these assumptions.

Distinctions of age, gender and social status loom larger. The sexes are not necessarily conceived symmetrically. * * *

Transgendered persons are not the only alternative configurations of identity and conduct that are excluded by the substitutive model. * * *

Ritualized homosexuality conclusively demonstrates that legal definitions of sexual orientation are extraordinarily context-specific. Contrary to the perception that one's "gay" or "lesbian" sexual orientation is defined by a predisposition towards sexual activity with members of a particular sex, some cultures may view same-sex sexual behavior as a normal part of social development rather than an identity-based phenomenon. Such differences force us to recognize, following the insights yielded by social construction, that same-sex sexual behavior does not always relate to sexual desire, sexual orientation, or sexual identity and underscores the point that a community can have different social meanings for such behavior. Yet all too often, these important examples are cast as "archaeological artifacts" or anthropological differences rather than crucial legal considerations. * * *

Age-structured models of ritualized homosexuality challenge traditional perceptions of sexual identity and desire in both culture and law. First, at its most basic level, such rituals demonstrate the possibility that other cultures may completely lack a concept of homosexuality as a sexual identity or a type of person, and yet routinely engage in same-sex sexual practices. Second, such patterns also challenge the very definition of homosexual identity as deviant or abnormal, reminding us that homosexual relations do not always take on a social meaning that is external to preexisting organizations of gender, kinship and economy. Indeed, as [Gilbert] Herdt observes [*Same Sex, Different Cultures* (1997)], in Sambia, "to be 'normal and natural' [male] is to be inseminated by another man and then to take the role of inseminator, first to a boy, and then to a woman, at a later stage following marriage." * * *

In India, in the public health field, several prominent activists have concluded that the language of "identities" and Western constructions of sexuality are markedly inappropriate in delivering culturally specific HIV/AIDS health services to some men in South Asia. Instead of the term "gay" or "homosexual," public health activists have opted to use the term "men who have sex with men" (MSM). The term MSM refers to men from all age groups, marital status, economic classes, educational backgrounds, caste and religious communities, sexual identities, and gender identities who engage in sexual activity with other men. Use of the term, they argue, is necessary for effective health interventions, because MSM do not possess a "gay" self-identity, do not see themselves as bisexual, yet are not "conventionally straight." In other words, the term is used to denote those for whom homosexuality connotes a behavior, not an identity. By examining the reduced salience of terms like "gay" and "homosexual" among MSM, we can come to a greater understanding of the culturally specific assumptions underlying them. * * *

In South Asia, public health advocates report that they have found the word "gay" to have "little meaning, political or otherwise," to many men who have sexual relations with other men. Even where it appears, the term "gay" is used to refer to a sexual behavior alone, rather than an identity in and of itself, reflecting a perception shared by many public health experts that male-to-male sexual activity is not a "widely acceptable criterion around which all MSM can define themselves as a community." In stark contrast to the United States' focus on identity as a mode of community building, for some MSM, building a demarcable community around sexual conduct is characterized as "unnecessary" and "devoid of meaning." Thus, instead of taking on a "gay" self-identity, MSM may adopt instead a variety of indigenous terms and identities to describe particular sexual behaviors; or none at all. * * *

One way to overcome the dissonance—cultural, legal, subjective—between one's conduct and one's social and sexual identity is to turn to another framework that encompasses both the expressive and private aspects of sexuality and sexual identity: sexual autonomy, or sexual self-determination. * * * [A] focus on sexual autonomy is preferable to one based on identity for three primary reasons. First, a model based on sexual autonomy is a deliberative one, thereby encompassing potential dissonance between subjectivity and external representation. Second, a sexual autonomy model focuses more squarely on the protection of sexual conduct, so that it includes protection for individuals who may engage in same-sex sexual conduct but who view themselves as heterosexual. Third, protections based on sexual autonomy are expressive, in that they protect the freedoms of individuals to express their public gender or sexual identities, and publicly voice the need for such protections. Finally, because the right to sexual autonomy encompasses aspects of both identity-based and privacy protections, it provides a much more thorough conceptual and legal framework for protection than existing models, which normally focus on either framework to the exclusion of other possibilities. * * *

C. THE ROLE OF LAW IN THE SOCIAL CONSTRUCTION PROCESS

Professors Ellen Ross and Rayna Rapp are anthropologists who start with the assumption that sexuality is socially constructed and then pose the questions: How does society shape sexuality? How do family contexts, religious ideologies, community norms, and political policies interact in the formation of sexual experience? What role does law play? Ross and Rapp resist the psychoanalytic approach which maintains that sexuality is constructed entirely within the family, and they insist that larger social and legal contexts help shape sexuality over the years. Following their account are Dean Spade's very concrete demonstration of some ways that the modern regulatory state entrenches gender binarism and creates difficulties for transgender people; Noa Ben-Asher's contrast between the law-driven politics of the transsex and intersex rights movements; and Jasbir Puar's exploration of the way the modern state creates "homonationalism" as a mechanism to mobilize citizens against "queer terrorists."

Ellen Ross and Rayna Rapp, "Sex and Society: A Research Note From Social History and Anthropology"

In *Powers of Desire: The Politics of Sexuality* 51, 62–64, 67–68.
Ann Snitow et al., editors, 1985.*

Legal systems provide a material background against which sexual relations are played out, whether they affect sexuality directly (*e.g.*, legitimacy clauses, the outlawing of abortion, and sex codes defining prostitution) or at a distance (*e.g.*, welfare and the responsibilities of fathers). Laws defining paternity, for example, are important in setting up the context in which sexuality occurs. The effect does not necessarily result from forcing fathers to support their illegitimate children. Few women in England, either before or after the 1834 Bastardy Clauses undermined putative fathers' legal obligations, seem to have applied for child support, and we know too well how few divorced fathers in contemporary America pay child support consistently over the years. Rather, as such laws become known, they help to establish an atmosphere that changes the sexual balance of power. The commissioners investigating the causes of the "Rebecca Riots" in 1844 were convinced that this is what happened in southern Wales. Traditional marriage and courtship patterns in England had condoned pre-marital pregnancies, and eighteenth-century legislation made it relatively easy for mothers of bastards to collect regular support payments. The Bastardy Clauses to the 1834 Poor Law Amendment Act assigned financial responsibility solely to the mothers (or their parishes). Now, courting men seemed to feel a new license to avoid marriage. "It is a bad time for the girls, Sir," a woman reported to a Haverfordwest Poor Law Guardian who testified before the Commission. "The boys have their own way." The Bastardy Clauses were probably among the factors that influenced a shift in popular sexual culture: an earlier tradition of lively female sexual assertiveness as traced in folk ballads and tales gave way to a more prudish, cautious image of womanhood by the 1860s. Such a transformation appears quite rational in light of the shifting legal environment. What Flandrin calls the "legal disarming of women vis-à-vis their seducers" took place earlier and more thoroughly in France. In the seventeenth century it was legally possible for a seducer, unless he

---

married the woman, to be charged with rape if the woman was under twenty-five. As the penalty for rape was death, many seducers charged in court no doubt preferred marriage. The Civil Code of 1804, however, forbade searching for putative fathers and made unmarried women solely responsible for their children.

Throughout Europe and America, the mid-to late-nineteenth century witnessed a hardening of legal definitions of sexual outcasts, as sexual behavior came under increasing state and cultural surveillance. It is from this period that many of the sex and vice codes still prevalent in Western societies can be dated. In England, a series of Contagious Disease Acts passed from 1864 on to control venereal disease in the army and navy by registering prostitutes had the effect of stigmatizing the women and isolating them from the working-class neighborhoods in which they lived and worked. Although a campaign to repeal the acts was ultimately successful, its social purity orientation led to still further sexually restrictive legislation. The Criminal Law Amendment Act, an omnibus crime bill passed in 1885, raised the age of consent for girls from thirteen to sixteen in response to a movement to "save" working-class girls from the perceived evils of "white slavery" and aristocratic male lust. The newly increased powers of the police were turned not on the wealthy buyers of sex, but on its poorer sellers. Lodging-house keepers were commonly prosecuted as brothel keepers, and prostitutes were often uprooted and cast out from their neighborhoods. Forced to find new lodging in areas of cities more specialized in vice, they became increasingly dependent on male pimps once community support, or at least toleration, of their occupation was shattered by legal prosecution.

In the Labouchere Amendment to the same 1885 act, all forms of sexual activity between men (with consent, in private as well as in public) were subject to prosecution. This represents a dramatic extension of the definition of male homosexuality (and its condemnation) beyond the "abominations of buggery" clauses promulgated under Henry VIII and remaining in force in the centuries that followed. The Labouchere Amendment was followed in 1898 by the Vagrancy Act, which turned police attention to homosexual solicitation. Anti-homosexual legislation was passed in an atmosphere of a purity campaign that viewed homosexuality as a vice of the rich visited on the poor. But the effects of the legislation were turned against working-class homosexuals, who were most likely to be tried, while wealthier men were often able to buy their way out of public notice and prosecution. * * *

* * * [C]ontemporary culture tempts us to reify sex as a thing-in-itself. The modern perception of sex is an ideological reflection of real changes that have occurred in the contexts of daily life within which sexuality is embedded. The separation, with industrial capitalism, of family life from work, of consumption from production, of leisure from labor, of personal life from political life, has completely reorganized the context in which we experience sexuality. These polarities are grossly

distorted and miscast as antimonies in modern ideological formulations, but their seeming separation creates an ideological space called "personal life," one defining characteristic of which is sexual identity. Modern consciousness permits, as earlier systems of thought did not, the positing of "sex" for perhaps the first time as having an "independent" existence. * * * [A] common American complaint is that families are losing control over their children's sexual education and behavior, challenged by public schools, the mass media, and state policies (which grant sex education and abortions to teenagers, even without parental consent). The power of families and communities to determine sexual experience has indeed sharply diminished in the past two centuries, allegedly allowing for individual sexual "liberation."

Although the movement toward self-conscious sexuality has been hailed by modernists as liberatory, it is important to remember that sexuality in contemporary times is not simply released or free-floating. It continues to be socially structured, but we would argue that the dominant power to define and regulate sexuality has been shifting toward the group of what we have labeled large-scale social and economic forces, the most salient of which is perhaps the state. States now organize many of the reproductive relations that were once embedded in smaller scale contexts. Sexuality thus enters the "social contract," connecting the individual citizen and the state. In the process, an ideological space is created that allows us to "see" sex as a defining characteristic of the individual person, "released" from the traditional restraints of family and community. The rise of the two great ethnosciences of sexual and personal liberation—sexology and psychoanalysis—have accompanied this transformation, attempting to explain and justify it.

But the ideology of sexual freedom and the right to individual self-expression have come increasingly into conflict with both state hegemony and the residual powers of more traditional contexts such as family and community control. Today, abortion, sterilization abuse, sex education, homosexual rights, and welfare and family policies are explosive political issues in the United States and much of Western Europe. For as states claim a greater and greater interest in the structuring of sexuality, sexual struggles increasingly become part of public, consciously defined politics. * * *

Dean Spade, "Documenting Gender," 59 *Hastings L.J.* 731, 733–35, 802–04 (2008). This article is an excellent example of the Ross and Rapp thesis, but applied to gender and sex rather than sexuality. Professor Spade examines the different regulatory regimes relying on the classification of people as man or woman, including identity documents (birth certificates, driver's licenses and passports, and social security and medicare cards) as well as sex segregation in public programs (such as prisons and schools). These regimes are themselves an important instrument of national state-building.[1] Thus, the modern and centralized nation state is created in large part through the utility of standard weights and measures, the coercive authority of a universal national language and state-sponsored education, and the uniformity of contracting and property ownership. By a process of classification and categorization, the state not only asserts a centralized power but also creates regularized (and regulable) identities.

As America increasingly became a *caretaker state,* the governance strategy of "regulating through freedom" grew exponentially.[m] For example, "the collection of birth data arose as a response to public health concerns and other interests related to monitoring the well-being of the population based on birth rates and infant mortality. The process of creating standardized birth registration met with consistent resistance across the country, in both overt ways, such as doctors refusing to register births because of the extra work, and passive ways, such as people neglecting to register home births (which constituted the majority of births until relatively recently) out of habit or custom. A variety of interventions from federal and state governments encouraged birth registration, but what finally pushed birth registration into ubiquity was new requirements that emerged during and after WWII that families present birth certificates to collect increased rations when a new child entered the family or to register children for school. After that, birth certificates came to be required for an ever-increasing number of activities, and took on the role of certifying identity and immigration status for important areas of civic and economic participation. This shift—from gathering standardized data in order to achieve caretaking population-level interventions related to public health, to having such data become part of identity-verification for purposes of law enforcement and other uses that can be classified as surveillance—can be seen across programs that issue identity documentation such as the SSA and DMVs."

State classification systems do more than sort things based upon natural differences. Rather, classification systems and the things they classify are *mutually constitutive.*[n] Systems of classification create reality, grouping and sorting things such that certain distinctions become essential while others are ignored. The constructed reality is more powerful when different systems converge upon one regulatory norm, for

---

[1]   On the theory and mechanics of state-building through centralized categorization regimes, see James C. Scott, *Seeing Like a State* (1998), as well as Patricia C. Cohen, *A Calculating People: The Spread of Numeracy in Early America* (1999) (the turn toward data collection represented a shift in U.S. governance from the colonial period to the modern state); Mitchell Dean, *Governmentality: Power and Rule in Modern Society* (1999); Michel Foucault, "Governmentality," in *The Foucault Effect: Studies in Governmentality* 87–104 (Graham Burchell et al. eds., 1991).

[m]   Dean, *Governmentality*, 14. Rather than the state directly forcing people to register births, governance occurs through the distribution of rights and privileges, like the right to drive or to free education for children or public benefits like rations, where people "choose" to comply with requirements like birth registration in order to claim their rights and freedoms.

[n]   *See* Geoffrey C. Bowker & Susan Leigh Star, *Sorting Things Out: Classification and Its Consequences* (1999).

then the norm is reinforced, invisibly yet inexorably. One regulatory norm that has been cemented in modern society is the idea that every person has a determinate *sex*, either *man* or *woman*. Administrative systems of classification demand categorization of every subject as either a man or a woman in three general and interconnected fields: (a) identification documents, starting with birth certificates and now including homeland security-required travel documents; (b) sex-segregated facilities, including homeless shelters, youth facilities, and jails/prisons; and (c) health-care documents and facilities.

For most Americans, the regulatory nature of these systems is invisible and painless. Neither is the case for transgender and many intersex Americans. For them, the system is visible, strongly regulatory, and oppressive. Once upon a time, it was oppressive because the state refused to treat transgender persons as falling in the sex of their identity. Today, the state is more accommodative—but in ways that have actually increased the sense of oppression for many transgender persons. Most identity document-issuing agencies have adopted policies or practices allowing individuals to change the gender marker on their documents and records from 'M' to 'F' (male to female) or 'F' to 'M' (female to male).

"The rules of gender reclassification * * * differ across jurisdictions and 'expert' agencies responsible for creating and enforcing these policies, producing bureaucratic confusion and serious consequences for those directly regulated. Figure I [on the next page] is a continuum on which some sample policies have been placed to show different approaches to gender reclassification. The continuum represents the point at which the given agency or institution will allow a person to be recognized in a gender different than the one assigned at birth. On the extreme right side, I have placed policies that refuse reclassification, explicitly indicating that for the purposes of the agency or institution, gender may never be changed. The middle range represents a variety of policies that use medical authority to assess reclassification. These policies vary extensively regarding the type of medical intervention considered sufficient to grant reclassification. On the far left reside policies that allow recognition of the new gender based solely on self-identification of the applicant, requiring no medical evidence."

This mishmash of different policies regarding sex reassignment creates terrible dilemmas for transgender persons who are *male* for some documents and regulatory purposes, but *female* for others. To make matters much worse, the recently enacted Real ID Act requires cross checks between agencies; inconsistencies in identity documents result in "no match" letters sent to employers from the Social Security Administration resulting in the outing of the transgender individual, resulting in their firing. Similar problems result in the revocation of driver's licenses, housing discrimination, health discrimination etc. Moreover, institutions housing the poor, from jails and prisons, to shelters are often sex segregated according to their birth sex, leading to harassment of transgender individuals in the facility to which they are assigned. Overall, state surveillance and state-created discipline of transgender persons is increasing—and one reason for the uptick in surveillance and discipline is the "liberalization" of sex reassignment policies (but not liberalization across the board).

FIGURE I: REQUIREMENTS FOR STATES ALLOWING GENDER RECLASSIFICATION: A CONTINUUM WITH EXAMPLES TO ILLUSTRATE

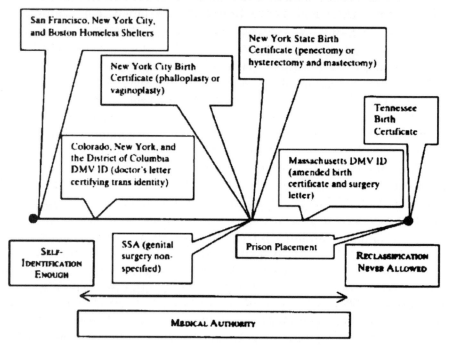

What should be done, as a matter of policy? Recalling Mary Dunlap's reform proposal in the 1970s, the United Kingdom enacted the Gender Recognition Act of 2004, which establishes a national process whereby persons can petition for a recharacterization of their sex; any sex reassignment made by the central authority is binding throughout the nation for purposes of identification documents, sex-segregated facilities, health care, and civil marriage. This solution would seem to be the classic *liberal* (pro-choice) solution—and could be substantially adopted in the United States under the auspices of the Real ID Act, which requires uniformity of state documents along certain criteria, including sex or gender. Yet this is not the recommendation Professor Spade ultimately makes.

Instead, Professor Spade recommends that sex and gender cease being a classificatory mechanism altogether. Consider his reasoning. "Under the current regime, there is no agreement amongst the hundreds of agencies and institutions that classify people according to gender about what criteria should be used for determining gender. Many individuals possess multiple identity documents, some that say 'M' and some that say 'F.' * * * Despite the fact that 'common sense' suggests that gender is a stable, obvious, clear indicator of human difference, rulemakers using 'common sense' definitions of gender have come up with dozens of different rules about what indicates that difference and those rules are enforced inconsistently because the 'common sense' assumptions about gender in the minds of front line workers often differ from the assumptions of the rule. Further, even within a particular agency or institution, the assumptions of the gender reclassification rules are not upheld across the whole population being classified. For example, in jurisdictions where it has been decided that to be reclassified from 'F' to 'M' a person must prove they have a penis (through documentation of phalloplasty), 'M' on an ID cannot really be used as evidence of a penis, because when non-trans men lose their penises their 'M'-marked IDs are not taken away. The anatomy-based gender reclassification rules, which seem to rest on the assumption that body parts correspond to gender markers, are only applied in some cases. So where the rules appear to suggest that 'M's' mean penises, in fact that is not true.

"Looking at the whole universe of people classified by these markers, there is no physical or psychological characteristic we can say are shared by people with 'Ms' or 'Fs' marked on their IDs. The rules are written based on a set of assumptions that are not only more shifting and diverse than we might expect—one jurisdiction thinks you need a penis to be reclassified as male, one jurisdiction thinks you need to remove your uterus and ovaries and breasts to be reclassified as male but you do not have to get a penis, another jurisdiction thinks you need a letter about your psychological identity to be reclassified as male—but that do not adhere to the ways the rules are enforced. Thus, the gender marker, when looked at closely, provides little or no concrete identifying information consistently across the entire population of people being classified.

"Gender, then, is not just unstable on the documents of transgender people who are directly impacted by * * * inconsistent policies * * * but is unstable and unreliable as an indicator of any particular 'truth' across the entire system."

Thus, Professor Spade concludes that social security cards, passports, driver's licenses, and the like do not need sex on the face of the document. Furthermore, the protection of individuals in sex-segregated shelters and bathrooms are obtained, not through segregation but through supervision. Spade points to institutions such as co-ed prisons to question sex segregation in prisons as well. In limited contexts, he agrees that information collection for health purposes and for use in affirmative action/diversity programs is acceptable, but notes that for some purposes, e.g. collecting information regarding uterine cancer, sex should not be used as a proxy. Rather, data should only be collected from those individuals who have uteri.

Query. Are you persuaded by Professor Spade's argument that "sex" as a regulatory or reporting category ought to be *eliminated* almost entirely? This would be an extension of the Supreme Court's heightened-but-not-fatal scrutiny for sex-based classifications. Should the U.S. Census not collect data on the population's sex? Why isn't the United Kingdom's approach (a national register of sex designations made at the choice of the individual) preferable? Finally, consider how Professor Spade's proposal would tie into concrete legal arguments made by transsex and intersex advocates, explored in our next excerpt.

Noa Ben-Asher, "The Necessity of Sex Change: A Struggle for Intersex and Transsex Liberties," 29 *Harv. J.L. & Gender* 51, 52, 54–55, 57, 61–62 (2006). "Feminist and queer theories are generally concerned with the cohesive effects that gender, as a system of normalization, has on legal subjects." Professor Ben-Asher focuses on "two such harms of gender normalization: the current state of Medicaid coverage of adult transsex surgeries, and the current management of intersex subjects. [The article] proceeds by focusing on the discursive relationships of these two social movements with medical experts and texts, and the translation of medical theories into legal narratives. 'Medical necessity,' 'cosmetic surgery,' and 'experimentation' are terms currently offered in legal narratives by both movements to achieve the two distinct goals of (1) obtaining Medicaid coverage of sex reassignment surgeries and (2) ending normalizing genital surgeries on intersex infants and young children."

Both the intersex and transsex rights movements have had fraught relationships with the medical community that offer both potential validation of their respective identity claims *and* potential threats to their different agendas for their bodies. "[T]ranssex advocacy for Medicaid coverage of sex reassignment surgeries for lower-income Americans (and support of transsex sex change surgeries in general) historically has been supported by experts like John Money and Richard Green who consider gender a social imprinting of behavioral patterns through the socialization process of the child. By contrast, intersex efforts seeking the termination of unwanted normalizing genital surgeries are ordinarily supported by medical theorists on the opposite end of the nature/nurture binary [such as Martin Diamond], who view gender identity as the result of the biologically hormonalized sexual brain. * * *

"A claim for Medicaid coverage of transsex surgery is based on the notion that sex change is a medical necessity and the main form of treatment for the transsex individual who seeks it. * * * Since Medicaid coverage for procedures requires a 'medical necessity' determination, and the statute does not provide coverage for 'optional' services, 'transsexual' is narrowly defined in Medicaid litigation as a 'very complex medical and psychological problem,' and as a severe form of 'gender identity disorder'

(GID). Courts generally have adopted this psychiatric definition of GID, and explained transsexual identities through medical terminology." Professor Dean Spade and other transsex activists have objected that lawyers must argue that their clients have a medical "disorder" to secure needed legal assistance.

States are often able to persuade judges that sex reassignment surgeries and treatments are "cosmetic" and "experimental"—precisely the claims made by intersex activists against surgical interventions upon intersexed children. Pediatric guidelines advise that newborn "boys" ought to have a "stretched penile length" of about an inch—and so medical protocols advise testosterone injections for a child with a shorter penis and, ultimately removal of the testes if hormone therapy does not "work." Conversely, newborn "girls" with clitorises longer than 3/8 inch are supposed to have clitoral reductions (and enlargement of vaginas) according to the medical protocols. "Adults who have undergone normalizing surgery as young children and their allies are often displeased with this forced medical intervention and, like transsex persons, they have set out to define and control their own futures." In 1993, Cheryl Chase founded the Intersex Society of North America (ISNA), which has opposed genital surgery on intersexed infants and children.

"ISNA's goal is the opposite of that of Medicaid litigants—to stop medical surgeries on intersex subjects. Thus, while the transsex double-edged sword described above produces a strategic legal argument for a medicalized transsex identity, ISNA attempts just the opposite—to de-medicalize intersex bodies in order to avoid early normalizing surgeries. Another way to understand these mirror claims of medical necessity (transsex) and non-necessity (intersex) of surgery and of attempts for medicalization (transsex) versus non medicalization (intersex) is that, while GID is presented as a psychological disorder, intersex is presented in medical literature as a physical condition. ISNA and other intersex alliances are focused on the de-medicalization of a physical condition in order to stop surgeries and sex reassignment, while transsex advocacy for Medicaid coverage medicalizes a psychological condition in order to pursue surgeries and sex change." In contrast to transsex advocacy relying on a federal statute to provide for the medical needs of lower-income Americans, intersex anti-surgery litigation relies on legal doctrines that regulate notions of bodily autonomy and the right to self-determination, including international human rights treaties protecting the bodies of children and the tort of battery.

NOTES ON CONSTITUTIONAL RESISTANCE TO LAW'S REGIMENTATION OF TRANSSEX AND INTERSEX PERSONS

1.   *Challenges to Legal Reifications of "Gender."* Dean Spade and other transsex activists argue that law and welfare politics, working together, help entrench the notion of two sexes. Noa Ben-Asher's article argues that law

and medicine, working together, help entrench the notion that a stable "psychological gender" is essential to a child's development into a healthy adult. Notice how the legal rights movement associated with both groups has also contributed to the reification of "gender" as an important, stable identity trait. Transsex advocates say medical "disorder" when the reified gender does not match the biological sex; intersex advocates say medical "assault" when doctors tamper with the body to impose an unwanted gender upon an infant. How does this advocacy relate to social constructionist theory? *Cf.* Judith Butler, *Undoing Gender* (2004) (even though socially constructed, gender can be the source for identity and even play (as in the case of drag)).

In 2016, a federal judge ruled that the Passport Office of the Department of State did not act rationally in enforcing a strict sex-binary passport policy to deny an intersex veteran a passport with a non-binary gender marker. Dana Zzyym, the associate director for the United States affiliate of the Organization Intersex International, applied for a passport to attend the Intersex Forum in Mexico City. But despite Zzyym's writing "intersex" on their application, informing the passport officials of their sex by letter, and submitting in two physician letters confirming their status as intersex, the agency denied the application on the grounds that "the Department of State currently requires the sex field on United States passports to be listed as 'M' or 'F'. In reviewing the agency's decision, Judge Jackson ruled that it is "undisputed that in every other respect Dana is qualified to receive a passport," and that "the administrative record contains no evidence the Department followed a rational decision-making process in deciding to implement its binary-only gender passport policy." *See Zzyym v. Kerry*, 220 F.Supp.3d 1106 (D. Colo. 2016). *See also* Christopher Mele, "Oregon Court Allows a Person to Choose Neither Sex," N.Y. Times, June 13, 2016 (noting that an Oregon Circuit Court judge granted a transgender veteran's petition to change the legal gender from female to nonbinary).

The Colorado decision reflects swiftly changing public opinion on issues of gender identity. The Williams Institute reports that 67% of Americans support gender reassignments on government identification documents, and 71% support governmental anti-discrimination protections for transgender people. Williams Institute, *Public Support for Transgender Rights: A Twenty-Three Country Survey* 13, 14 (2017). Public opinion splits on bathroom bills: as of 2016, 51% thought transgender people should be allowed to use the bathrooms of their gender identities, while 46% thought they should be required to use the bathrooms of the gender they were designated at birth. Pew Research Center, *Americans Are Divided Over Which Public Bathrooms Transgender People Should Use* (2016). As is often the case on social issues, young people (ages 18–29) are the most likely to support access to bathrooms by gender identity (67%), further suggesting shifting social mores.

2.   *Resistance to Medicalization and Allegories of Gender.* Professor Ben-Asher's article reflects a skepticism of the role doctors and biologists play in the lives of transgender and intersex persons. One modern horror story is told in John Colapinto, *As Nature Made Him* (2002), the story of "John," an intersex child who was raised as a girl ("Joan") because Dr. Money persuaded his parents that he could be socialized as a girl, regardless of hormones and other physical indications of boyness (which Dr. Money snipped away from the infant). Dr. Money trumpeted the John/Joan case as a triumph of his socialization theory—but the experience of the child (now known to be David Riemer) was disastrous. Rejecting Dr. Money, Joan reverted to John through sex reassignment procedures.

Judith Butler finds the story of John/Joan a fascinating allegory, not so much about which medical theory (gender as biological or as a product of socialization) is correct, but more about how important gender was to David Riemer's life (and his death, for he committed suicide as an adult) and how his case revealed interesting interactions between intersex and transsex. After being the victim of one medical experiment, "to return to who he is, [Riemer] requires—and wants, and gets—a subjection to hormones and surgery. He allegorizes transsexuality to achieve a sense of naturalness. And this transformation is applauded by the endocrinologists on the case, since they understand his appearance now to be in accord with an inner truth. Whereas Money's institute enlists transsexuals to instruct Joan in the ways of women, and in the name of normalization, the endocrinologists prescribe the sex change protocol of transsexuality to John for him to reassume his genetic destiny, the name of nature." Butler, "Doing Justice to Someone: Sex Reassignment and Allegories of Transsexuality," 7 *GLQ: J. Lesbian & Gay Stud.* 621, 628 (2001) (digested in *Doing Gender* as well).

3. *Constitutionalization: Liberty and Equality Claims.* Professor Ben-Asher argues that both transsex and intersex movements should de-emphasize medical-based claims and reconfigure their identity politics in terms of liberty—the "negative liberty" of intersex infants to the protection of their bodies and the "positive liberty" of transsexuals to enjoy sex reassignment therapies and surgeries. If intersex rights are conceived as "liberties," can the Constitution's right of privacy be far behind? Cf. *Cruzan v. Director, Mo. Dep't of Health*, 497 U.S. 261 (1990) (dicta extending the common law's protection against unwanted medical interventions to assure dying persons negative liberty protections). Who would assert such liberties? Surely the parents may do so—but what if they defer to the medical authorities: Who can advocate for the child when the parents will not?

Transsexuals would have a much harder time constitutionalizing, or even politicizing, claims of positive liberty; judges are notoriously reluctant to accept such arguments unless backed up by legislative authorizations. Instead, transsex activists would seem to have better equal protection arguments: state denial of Medicaid support for sex reassignment surgery is "discrimination because of sex," and so presumptively unconstitutional.

Constitutional claims and the regulatory power of sex almost collided at the Supreme Court in March 2017. High school student Gavin Grimm sued the Gloucester County School Board over a policy that prohibited transgender students like Gavin from using the bathroom consistent with their gender identity. The Fourth Circuit ruled for Gavin but grounded its opinion in a 2016 guidance document from the Obama Departments of Justice and Education stating that Title IX protections against gender discrimination encompass discrimination on the basis of gender identity. The

Supreme Court granted certiorari on August 3, 2016, but after the Trump Administration rescinded the Obama guidance letter in February 2017, the Court remanded the case back to the Fourth Circuit. Drawing from the work of Professors Spade and Ben-Asher, what are Gavin's best arguments now that the Obama-era guidance has been repealed? If you agree with Professor Spade's argument that gender and sex classifications should be done away with entirely, should Gavin be arguing for universal gender-neutral bathrooms instead of just for access to the male restroom? Can the Equal Protection Clause be enlisted for such an argument?

Jasbir Puar, Terrorist Assemblages: Homonationalism in Queer Times (2007). Professor Puar explores the striking connections between the post-9/11 war on terror and the post-*Lawrence* recognition of the constitutional rights of LGBTQI persons. Particularly exciting chapters are the ones critiquing the Abu Ghraib photographs of American service personnel posing Muslim bodies in sexually degrading positions and applying a similar critique to the Supreme Court's invalidation of homosexual sodomy laws in *Lawrence v. Texas.*

During the Cold War era, sexual and gender minorities were considered Trojan Horses, undermining America's moral fiber in support of Godless Communist subversion. The GOP's Senate leader in 1950 exclaimed that homosexuality was sure evidence of Communist sympathies. *See* David Johnson, *The Lavender Scare: The Cold War Persecution of Gays and Lesbians in the Federal Government* (2004). In the 1980s, gay and bisexual men were depicted as Trojan Horses, importing the HIV virus and AIDS into America's body politick. The question was always: "What is terrorist about the queer?"

After 9/11, Professor Puar flips the question: "What is queer about the terrorist? And what is queer about terrorist corporealities? The depictions of masculinity most rapidly disseminated and globalized at this historical juncture are terrorist masculinities: failed and perverse, these emasculated bodies always have femininity as their reference point of malfunction, and are metonymically tied to all sorts of pathologies of the mind and body—homosexuality, incest, pedophilia, madness, and disease." According to Puar's account, "queerness is already installed in the project of naming the terrorist; the terrorist does not appear as such without the concurrent entrance of perversion, deviance."

In the Abu Ghraib photographs, ordinary service personnel—women as well as men—gleefully displayed Muslim bodies in a variety of perverse poses, each illustrating the natural perversity (queerness) of the terrorist body. Recall some of the images: naked male bodies piled on top of one another, with some penises touching some buttocks; men placing their hands on their displayed penises, in mock masturbation; sodomy of a prisoner with a light bulb and possibly a broomstick; a man being led around by a leash. For other descriptions, see Seymour Hersh, "Torture at Abu Ghraib," *The New Yorker,* May 10, 2004.

At the same time the Bush-Cheney Administration was exploiting homophobia as a weapon in the war on terror, the Supreme Court was unsheathing the Constitution to assure "homosexuals" and other sexual or gender minorities rights associated with equal citizenship. (Recall *Romer v. Evans* and *Lawrence v. Texas*, both decided before Abu Ghraib [2004].) Professor Puar argues that America's normalization of some kinds of "homosexuals" has contributed to the production and demonization of the queer terrorist.

The first chapter, "The Sexuality of Terrorism," explains the ascendency of *homonationalism*, that is, "the dual movement in which certain homosexual constituencies have embraced U.S. nationalist agendas and have also been embraced by nationalist agendas." Based upon terrorist studies and field interviews, Professor Puar uncovers the pairing of our "western romance of the heteronormative family coupled with the assumed sexual pathologies of terrorists" and reports that queer and feminist discussions of terrorists "unwittingly reproduce these investments." But they do so in a manner that invests homonationalism with narrow white, well-to-do, and male-centered ideals that are presented as national values.

Homonationalism reflects a special sexual exceptionalism that entrenches the exceptionalism of America's empire. That is, the United States remains a firmly heteronormative society, but after *Lawrence* this society offers tolerance and inclusion to sexual minorities—but only *some* sexual minorities, namely, the white, the well-to-do, and the male. Likewise, the United States firmly denies that it presides over an empire, but its limited embrace of some sexual minorities and some women enables the country to represent itself as the tolerant, liberal alternative to Muslim radicalism and its open embrace of misogyny and homophobia. Gender exceptionalism, for example, operates as a "missionary discourse" to rescue Muslim women from Islamic misogyny, even as its adherents are pessimistic that such women, as a group, can be saved.

Queer groups have been particularly aggressive in demonizing Muslim populations for their alleged homophobia. Examples include the British group OutRage!, which declared a "queer fatwa" against an Islamic religious leader in Great Britain; the gay Dutch politician Pim Fortuyn, whose anti-Muslim rhetoric propelled his party to prominence after he was murdered by an animal rights activist; and gay bloggers who denounce prejudice but nevertheless maintain that the jihadist tenets of Islam foment radicalism an violence. "Islamophobia has become central to the subconscious of homonormativity."

[**Eds.** A recent example may be Milo Yiannopoulos—a flamboyantly gay white male apologist for President Donald Trump and acid critic of feminists and civil rights advocates. In September 2016, Yiannopoulos delivered a speech entitled, "Ten Things I Hate About Islam," remarks that read like a parody of Professor Puar's account of homonationalism. In the wake of the terrorist attack on Pulse, the gay bar in Orlando,

Yiannopoulos started with a series of jokes about Islam: "Anything more intentionally ironic [than] a religion that hates gays but gets its men in a room 5 times a day to stick their asses in the air." He then turned serious and described Islam as a "real rape culture" where men "think they own women to such a degree." Islam, he explained, is even more dangerous to gay people such as himself. Muslims want to stone people like him or throw them off rooftops. Similar remarks followed. In closing, Yiannopoulos tied Islamophobia to proper national security: "Hordes of homophobic Muslims are being imported to the West so they can blow up gay nightclubs—and the left says nothing." Note the irony: the flaming queer, who a generation ago, was considered the Trojan Horse destroying western civilization, became the media representative alerting the country to the new Trojan Horse, "homophobic Muslims." In 2017, another layer was added: Caught on tape seeming to advocate sex between adult men and adolescent boys, Yiannopoulos himself was decried by both conservatives and liberals.]

That Islamophobic gay groups and provocateurs are white and on the whole quite privileged is not an accident, Professor Puar maintains. This may surprise many readers: Isn't "queer" politics an exercise in rejection of conventional norms? Doesn't that include rejection of racism and anti-religious bigotry? Not necessarily. "Queerness here is the modality through which 'freedom from norms' becomes a regulatory queer ideal that demarcates the ideal queer." But not everybody can be the ideal queer. Most LGBTQI people are not positioned to be free in this way; queerness might be an opportunity available mostly to cosmopolitan elites who enjoy wealth and mobility. Hence, queerness in operation may be exclusionary along lines of race, class, and sex. Queer theory and many individual queers focus their critiques on heteronorms so intensely that they miss or submerge the related discriminations and exclusions based on race, class, and even sex.

In the chapter on Abu Ghraib, Professor Puar explores the phenomenon whereby the deaths of tens of thousands of Iraqis in the wake of the American invasion in 2003 barely penetrated the national consciousness, while the Abu Ghraib photos raised a national outcry, in large part because they depicted torture mimicking "deviant" sexual acts such as anal sex, SM, bondage, leashing, and hooding. On the other hand, Professor Puar understands Abu Ghraib to be the apotheosis of, rather than the exception to, American imperialism. The photos are an extension of war's brutality—but they also illustrate a key feature of homonationalism: the contrast between the gay-tolerant United States and the gay-hating Muslim terrorist whose display in the photos illustrates the hypocrisy of the religion's homophobia.

A central script for the American occupation of Iraq was Raphael Patai's *The Arab Mind* (1973, 2001), whose chapter on sex emphasized strong mores of sexual modesty, chaste heterosexuality, and bodily privacy. Using Patai's book as a guide, American policy in Iraq relied, in part, on the threat of disseminating these humiliating photos as a lever to secure cooperation from reluctant Iraqis (according to journalist Seymour Hersh). So the Abu Ghraib photos of Muslim prisoners in sexually perverse poses may have grown out of official policy, in a certain way. What Professor Puar finds significant is that the American torture not only exploited stereotypes about Muslim men, but produced those stereotypes. "Thus, the body informs the torture, but the torture also forms the body. That is, the performative force of torture not only produces an object but also proliferates that which it names."

When the photos went viral, the photos created a discursive space where American sexual fantasies about Muslim men could be the object of disgust, shame, and pride. The photos also brought into sharper public discourse the American practice of "rendition," where the Clinton and Bush-Cheney Administrations sent suspected terrorists to countries like Saudi Arabia and Syria, where torture is not so saturated with stereotypes but is expected to be more physically brutal and, perhaps, "effective" at inducing "confessions."

"As this space of 'illicit and dangerous sex,' the Orient is the site of carefully suppressed animalistic, preserve, homo- and hypersexual instincts. This paradox is at the heart of Orientalist notions of sexuality that are reanimated through the transnational production of the Muslim terrorist as torture object. Underneath the veils of repression sizzles an indecency waiting to be unleashed." Abu Ghraib press narratives expanded upon this imagery, as American soldiers reported their alleged observations of Muslim prisoners masturbating, "like animals," suggesting a mental process whereby religion, sexuality, and prejudice combine to reduce human beings to animal status—and therefore bringing them into a human rights exceptionalism (i.e., the human rights values touted by the United States do not apply to subhuman types, another disturbing parallel between America's anti-homosexual Kulturkampf of the 1950s and its anti-Muslim Kulturkampf of the 2000s).

Feminism must face the fact that female as well as male guards participated in this theatre of degradation. One much-discussed photo revealed Private Lynndie England leading a naked Iraqi on a leash, a practice called "pussy whipping." So an armed forces where women serve (albeit never on equal terms with men) is not a military cured of its hazing rituals; indeed, the female soldiers might intensify the humiliating theatre of Muslim bodies tortured, used, and displayed by American guards. More troubling, if one agrees that "violence is a form of sociality, then women are not only the recipients of violence, but are actually connected to and benefit from forms of violence in myriad ways, regardless of whether or not they are the perpetrators of violence themselves. That is to say, the economy of violence produces a circulatory system whereby no woman is strictly an insider or an outsider."

If feminism faces hard facts, gaylaw in the wake of *Lawrence* is exposed as apologetic for the continued biases of American society. With white gay men leading the way, the United States can pride itself on its new-found tolerance, consistent with our self-image as a liberal, open democracy, in contrast to the closed, repressed, prejudice-filled system of "radical Islam." Focus on what is oppressive and closed about some Muslim societies facilitates the process by which the "home front" closets the ways in which it remains a situs of homophobic and transphobic violence and injustice.

For example, Puar reads the universal reprehension visited by the gay press upon the Abu Ghraib guards with a critical eye that wonders how many of the guards were gay or lesbian? Isn't the humiliation of the Iraqi prisoners just as racist and misogynistic and imperialist as homophobic? Maybe more so? "To favor the gay male spectator—here, presumably white—is to negate the multiple and intersectional viewers implicated by these images, and oddly, is also to privilege as victim the identity * * * of white gay male sexuality in the west (and those closeted in the military) over the signification of acts, not to mention the bodies of the tortured Iraqi prisoners themselves."

NOTES ON ABU GHRAIB AND THEORIES OF SEXUALITY, GENDER, AND THE LAW

Seizing upon a dramatic intersection among sexuality, gender, and the law that emerged in the course of the war against terror, Jasbir Puar offers a powerful situs for theoretical discourse. *Terrorism Assemblages* incorporates theoretical insights from a wide range of post-modern thinkers surveyed above—most notably Foucault, Butler, Rubin, and Sedgwick. Consider how these and other thinkers have valuable things to educate us about Abu Ghraib, as well as American imperialism generally.

1.   *Social Construction Theories.* Michel Foucault and Judith Butler are most insightful here. Abu Ghraib is performative in the extreme—as though the prison guards had read *Gender Trouble* as well as *The Arab Mind* (and some Marquis de Sade) and then devised interrogation/propaganda techniques accordingly. That sexual and gender roles are performative does not absolve the performers of moral responsibility.

Foucault's critique of the repressive hypothesis is central to Jasbir Puar's critique of Abu Ghraib, as Foucault demonstrates how repression is more likely to be productive than suppressive of sexuality and "perversion." Abu Ghraib seems to be the "performance" of this theoretical point. Additionally, Foucault would press Puar to explore the discursive explosion about sexuality within the Arab as well as Western world as these photos circulated on the Internet.

2.   *Sex-Positive Theory and the Misplaced Scale.* Gayle Rubin's work is relevant, especially her notions of the misplaced scale and the hierarchy of sexual practices. Hers is the most cogent explanation for why the Abu Ghraib photos created the biggest backlash against the illegal Iraq policies followed

by the Bush-Cheney Administration. America's self-image as a chaste nation is exploded by these photos. They do more damage to the Administration than the revelation of so many deaths of civilian Iraqis in the wake of our invasion, because Americans are appalled not just at the lack of consent to sexual violation, but to the kinkiness of the sex forced upon these men by "all American" white guards.

3.   *Intersectionality Theories.* Jasbir Puar's account lends considerable specificity and cogency to intersectionality theories. Kimberlé Crenshaw and most other theorists have focused on the intersection of African-American and other identities—but here is a powerful example of the intersection of race, religion, sexuality, sex, and gender, as they play out in a totalistic legal context (an American-run prison). This may be Professor Puar's most distinctive theoretical contribution—to demonstrate how complicated intersectional analysis might be and how corrosive it is to simple identity politics. To see the power of Puar's analysis, consider this thought experiment:

- When you first saw the Abu Ghraib photos (probably years ago), what was your initial reaction? Did it get beyond the horror of the torture and the racism of the enterprise?

- Professor Puar draws attention to the intersection of culture, religion, and homosexuality. Does this deepen your understanding of how those poses might have been imposed and those photos might have been taken?

- Professor Puar also places Abu Ghraib within a larger theoretical context, one that involves the role of women and gay men as participants in a politics where Islamophobia becomes a discursive mechanism to reassure Americans that they are a tolerant and democratic culture and to motivate all Americans to demonize Muslims.

Are there other contributions an intersectional analysis makes to or understanding of Abu Ghraib or the war on terror?

4.   *Feminist Theories.* Jasbir Puar discusses how dispiriting Abu Ghraib is to feminists, who lament the role of Private England and other women who gleefully participated. In our view, Catherine MacKinnon would not be dispirited at all; instead, she would have a critical response to Abu Ghraib, including insightful thoughts about the participation of women. How would you articulate her response? Abu Ghraib would seem to be more dispiriting to Robin West, who seems to valorize women's distinctive normative contribution. How might she respond to this phenomenon?

5.   *Natural Law Theories.* Natural law theorists and opinion-setters were surprisingly vocal in defense of the Bush-Cheney Iraq War. When the Abu Ghraib photos emerged, natural law theorists (if they said anything) had no choice but to criticize the Bush-Cheney Administration. What could be more violative of natural law than sexualized torture? But most of the natural law apologists for the war said very little in response to Abu Ghraib, and some shifted the blame onto "homosexuals" themselves. Thus, Robert Knight of the Concerned Women of America (founded by prominent evangelicals

Beverly and Tim LeHaye) attributed Abu Ghraib to the "cultural depravity" inculcated by liberals, homosexuals, and feminists. Representing the Southern Baptist Convention, Richard Land blamed the "lost moral compass" of the participants on society's prevailing "cultural relativism." *See* Anne Norton, "On the Uses of Dogs: Abu Ghraib and the American Soul," in *Performances of Violence* 102 (Austin Sarat et al., eds., 2011) (reporting these and other reactions by natural law religious spokesmen). Is there anything to these explanations? In other words, set aside the blame-shifting features of these explanations: Do they raise concerns about relativist culture?

6. *Economic Theories.* Leading economic theorists had little to say about Abu Ghraib, but one would expect them to be highly critical, if for no other reason than standard Benthamite cost-benefit analysis: Is the pain and humiliation inflicted upon the prisoners offset by the intelligence benefits secured by this kind of torture? The question answers itself, but of course the costs and benefits need to be expanded. On the costs of torture, we should add the animosity toward the Americans in Iraq, a point made by Seymour Hersh's *New Yorker* article. On the benefits of torture, a utilitarian might include the satisfaction derived by Private England and the other guards. Even then, the balance seems to be quite lopsided: this was a bad idea, and criminally so. In the wake of Abu Ghraib, Richard Posner opined that torture should remain illegal but that anti-torture laws ought not be invoked in extreme circumstances, as when there is a ticking time bomb and torture offers the last clear chance to avoid the explosion. Richard Posner, "Torture, Terrorism, and Interrogation," in *Torture: A Collection* 298 (Sanford Levinson, ed., 2004). Can this position be conclusively defended through cost-benefit analysis? Does it reveal some of the limitations of such analysis?

CHAPTER 4

CLASHES BETWEEN RELIGIOUS LIBERTY AND SEXUAL AND GENDER EQUALITY

SECTION 1   Religious Freedom Restoration Acts
SECTION 2   Specific Religious Exemptions from Antidiscrimination Laws
SECTION 3   Religious Liberty vs. LGBT Equality Clashes in Schools

The Supreme Court's movement from *Roe* to *Casey* on abortion choice and its movement from *Bowers* to *Lawrence* on homosexual sodomy laws share one important conceptual (and doctrinal) feature: In both instances, the Court treated the individual liberty as one that had important equal protection ramifications as well. The Court's recognition of equality interests in the abortion and sodomy cases (weakly) reflected the understanding of abortion and sodomy laws that was held by women and gay people and articulated with increasing power by their social movements' leaders and lawyers. Although people in both movements believe that women and gay people do not enjoy complete equality, the Constitution and many statutes reflect formal equality for these groups (especially women) much more today than a generation ago.

We express this idea in the following way. One hundred years ago, when women, cross-dressers, and sexual "inverts" were considered degraded, second-class citizens, the state closely monitored their conduct and denied them the freedom to deploy their own bodies as they would have liked. Their accepted inequality was closely connected to limits on their liberty. During the twentieth century, when these groups formed identity-based social movements, a primary goal was to secure the liberty of their own bodies—and that goal was closely tied to their goal of reducing or eliminating discriminations and exclusions. Constitutionally, the first victories secured by each social movement were body-based liberties—women's freedom to control the size of their families (the contraception and abortion cases), transgender people's freedom to dress in the attire of the sex they chose, and gay people's freedom to have intimate relations (the sodomy cases, where there were many state victories in the generation before *Lawrence*).

In the new millennium, the constitutional full equality discourse of women, transgender persons, and sexual minorities has triggered a constitutional counter-discourse from traditionalists, especially religious traditionalists. Some traditionalists still cling to their old discourse, which demonizes the conduct of "abortionists," "sodomites," and cross-dressers as morally evil, and denies that women and gender or sexual minorities enjoy a valid "liberty" to violate fundamental precepts of public morality. This morality-based discourse has been submerged in public debate, though it retains an underground power. The public discourse has now shifted to claims that full equality, as defined by women and gender or sexual minorities, comes at the price of important, and well-recognized, *liberties* enjoyed by traditionalist citizens, including the privacy rights of parents, a fetus's right to life, religious freedom, and the freedom to associate (or not to associate).

This chapter examines the general equality-liberty clash with a focus on religious liberty. Most lawyers and judges understand religious liberty very narrowly, as freedom from government interference in religious sacraments, services, and institutional governance. Thus, the Supreme Court has protected churches against targeted persecution and against government interference in their selection and discharging of "ministerial" officials. See *Hosanna-Tabor Evangelical Lutheran Church & School v. EEOC*, 565 U.S. 171 (2012). Many religious persons and institutions view religious freedom much more broadly, as a freedom of each devout person to carry forth his or her scriptural precepts and prohibitions into daily life. Because religion is, by its nature, moralistic and discriminatory, this broad understanding would gum up the operation of government if liberally followed. For example, the Supreme Court has ruled that religious objection cannot be a legal justification for a devout citizen to refuse to pay taxes. See *United States v. Lee*, 455 U.S. 252 (1982).

Consider the Jehovah's Witnesses. During World War II, they clashed with local governments over rules compelling everyone to salute the American flag. Although loyal Americans, Witnesses believed their only allegiance was to God and that it would be heretical to salute a secular authority. In a memorable opinion, *West Virginia State Bd. of Educ. v. Barnette,* 319 U.S. 624 (1943), the Supreme Court ruled that public schools could not compel their Jehovah's Witness students to salute the flag. Remarkably, the Court did not invoke the Free Exercise Clause but, instead, protected the student under the Speech Clause. "If there is any fixed star in our constitutional constellation, it is that no official, high or petty, can prescribe what shall be orthodox in politics, nationalism, religion, or other matters of opinion or force citizens to confess by word or act their faith therein. If there are any circumstances which permit an exception, they do not now occur to us." *Id.* at 642.

The wave of antidiscrimination laws that swept America after World War II was the beginning of the modern clash between equality for racial and other minorities and liberty for religious minorities. The Civil Rights Act of 1964 enjoyed critical support from religious groups, and of course the headliner for the 1963 March on Washington was Reverend Martin Luther King Jr. But many white fundamentalist religions opposed the law as inconsistent with the Bible and their faith traditions. See William Eskridge Jr., "Noah's Curse: How Religion Often Conflates Status, Belief, and Conduct to Resist Antidiscrimination Norms," 45 *Ga. L. Rev.* 657 (2011) (documenting the racist doctrines supported by southern Protestant churches from the 1820s through the 1960s, as well as the deployment of that doctrine to oppose the 1964 Act because it would invade religious liberties).

Title VII of the 1964 Act, prohibiting workplace discrimination because of race, ethnicity, sex, and religion, contains several different exemptions for religious employers: Section 702(a) 42 U.S.C. § 2000e–1(b), exempts religion-based discrimination for positions needed to carry out the missions of religious corporations, associations, or societies; § 703(e)(2), 42 U.S.C. § 2000e–2(e)(2), exempts religion-based discrimination by educational institutions substantially controlled or managed by a religious organization. To these limited exemptions, the Supreme Court in the 1960s and 1970s expansively interpreted the Free Exercise Clause to protect religious employees against being penalized for not being willing to work on the Sabbath. See, *e.g., Sherbert v. Verner,* 374 U.S. 398 (1963) (government could not deny unemployment compensation to worker discharged because of Sabbatarian beliefs). In recent years, the Court has ruled that religious organizations enjoy a blanket exemption from antidiscrimination laws for employment decisions relating to "ministerial" officials. *Hosanna-Tabor.* In other words, the Free Exercise Clause expands the Title VII-based exemptions beyond religion: a church can discriminate because of race, sex, national origin, or religion in the hiring and firing of "ministers" or the equivalent.

Sherbert ruled that states could not impose a "substantial burden" on an individual's free exercise *unless* the state could show that the burden was narrowly tailored to serve a compelling government interest. This was a potentially powerful set of protections for religious persons and groups. In *Employment Division v. Smith,* 494 U.S. 872 (1990), however, the Supreme Court ruled that generally applicable state rules and laws that do not target religion or deploy religion-based criteria are not subject to strict scrutiny under the Free Exercise Clause simply because they are neutrally deployed in a way that restrict religion-based freedom of action. (In that case, the Court upheld a state law barring drug use as applied to religious sacramental use of peyote.) "It may fairly be said that leaving accommodation to the political process will place at a relative disadvantage those religious practices that are not widely engaged in; but that unavoidable consequence of democratic government must be preferred to a system in which each conscience is a law unto itself or in which judges weight the social importance of all laws against the centrality of all religious beliefs." *Id.* at 890.

Responding to *Smith,* Congress enacted the Religious Freedom Restoration Act of 1993 (RFRA), Pub. L. No. 103–141, 107 Stat. 1488–89, codified at 42 U.S.C. §§ 2000bb–1 through 4. Section 1 of RFRA, 42 U.S.C. § 2000bb(b)(1), criticized *Smith* by name in the statutory findings. *Id.* § 2000bb(a)(4). Section 3(b) directed that "Government may substantially burden a person's exercise of religion only if it demonstrates that application of the burden to the person—

(1) is in furtherance of a compelling governmental interest; and

(2) is the least restrictive means of furthering that compelling governmental interest.

Id. § 2000bb–1(b). "Government" was defined in RFRA § 5 to include all branches, departments, and instrumentalities of the federal and state governments (including the District of Columbia). Section 6 of RFRA provided that the law should have retroactive effect, applying to state and federal statutes adopted before 1993. Almost half the states have adopted junior-RFRAs, namely, similar statutory protections applicable to governmental policies within those particular states.

The Supreme Court in *City of Boerne v. Flores,* 521 U.S. 507 (1997), ruled that RFRA's application to state governments was beyond the authority of Congress to adopt under its Fourteenth Amendment power to "enforce" free exercise guarantees beyond the limits set by the Supreme Court in *Employment Division.* Under *Boerne,* however, RFRA could still apply to the federal government, because Congress is not relying on its limited Fourteenth Amendment authority to regulate activities of the federal government itself. In 2000, Congress reenacted and strengthened RFRA and adopted a new law, the Religious Land Use and Institutionalized Persons Act (RLUPIA).

In the wake of RLUPIA, marriage equality for LGBT people emerged as a large, divisive issue deliberated in state courts, legislatures, and executive departments. The same year Congress enacted RLUPIA, the Vermont Legislature enacted its civil unions law. Between 2009 and 2015, ten states and the District of Columbia enacted marriage equality laws. Religious groups—especially the Catholic, Baptist, and Mormon Churches—were the primary opponents of such measures, and one reason for their opposition was that they belived equal treatment of LGBT people would mean loss of liberty for traditional family values religious people and institutions. If gay marriages were valid, might fundamentalist ministers be forced or pressured to perform wedding ceremonies they believed to be apostasies? Might churches lose their tax exemptions? *Cf. Bob Jones Univ. v. United States,* 461 U.S. 574 (1983) (denying tax exemptions to religious university and high school because their admissions process discriminated because of race).

Borrowing from earlier health care laws (adopted after *Roe v. Wade*) that protected health care providers against performing services contrary to their religious consciences, legislators and their academic advisers included conscience exemptions in the new wave of marriage equality and civil union statutes. See Robin Fretwell Wilson, "Calculus of Accommodation: Contraception, Abortion, Same-Sex Marriage, and Other Clashes Between religion and the State," 53 *B.C.L. Rev.* 1417 (2012). Because of typically narrow margins for victory in one or both chambers of the legislatures passing such controversial laws, it is likely that conscience exemptions were decisive in some states.

Most states, however, recognize same-sex marriages only because of court orders, culminating in the Supreme Court's disposition in *Obergefell v. Hodges* (Chapter 2). The most acute clashes between LGBT equality and religious liberty have been in jurisdictions with broad antidiscrimination laws, having limited or no conscience exemptions, but also a sizeable population of religious traditionalists who object to any kind of activity that might be understood as "complicity" with immoral activities such as gay weddings.

In the materials that follow, we explore the reach of RFRA as to federal burdens on religious freedom and Junior-RFRAs as to state burdens (Section 1), as well as constitutional and statutory exemptions for religious persons and institutions (Section 2). Given the huge number of religiously affiliated primary and secondary schools, colleges, and universities, we devote an entire Section 3 to clashes in those venues.

PROBLEM 4-1
DEVISING A BALANCE BETWEEN RELIGIOUS LIBERTY AND LGBT EQUALITY

You are the Chair of the Senate Judiciary Committee in a "red" state, namely, a state controlled by the Republican Party. Like all other states, your state has a general antidiscrimination law, but it does not include sexual orientation or gender identity as a prohibited category. Forty percent of your state's citizens live in cities or counties with antidiscrimination ordinances that include sexual orientation and gender identity. Your state has no Junior-RFRA.

The Chamber of Commerce and other business supporters of your party want your state to add sexual orientation and gender identity to your state's antidiscrimination law, and you are personally sympathetic. Your sister and her partner have been subject to discrimination, which you consider intolerable and unChristian (you are a devout fundamentalist Christian).

Consulting with LGBT groups and church groups, you want to draft legislation that would add *both* sexual orientation and gender identity to the antidiscrimination law *and* new religious exemptions that would satisfy some of the religion-based skeptics, *but* without alienating the LGBT groups, who would also create opposition among businesses. Consider the following:

(a) What argument should you make to your conservative GOP caucus that would motivate them to *want* to pass legislation? Many of them will ask, Why do we need to do anything? Others will fear that whatever they do, they will stir up a fuss that will hurt them on primary or general election day.

(b) What conscience exemptions would you consider? For example, you might broaden the law's existing exemptions to provide that religious organizations will not lose government benefits (such as tax exemptions) because of policies excluding people because of a protected trait (race, sex, sexual orientation, gender identity).

(c) What other provisions would you consider adding to your legislation, in order to attract moderate conservatives, but without scaring off progressives?

Jot down your thoughts in the space below—and then revisit them after you have studied the materials in this chapter.

SECTION 1

RELIGIOUS FREEDOM RESTORATION ACTS

When Congress enacted the Religious Freedom Restoration Act (RFRA) in 1993, liberals as well as conservatives joined to protect religious minorities and their churches against state and federal government bullying and coercion—often based on animus against or insensitivity toward minority religions. By reaffirming *Sherbert* and overriding *Smith,* RFRA was obviously aimed at protecting Americans who followed unusual Sabbatarian (*Sherbert*) and sacramental (*Smith*) practices. But RFRA's language is much broader—and the context for applying that broad language changed radically in the next quarter century. Today, RFRA is increasingly invoked to protect current or recent religious majorities and their churches against state and federal government bullying and coercion—but in the service of the antidiscrimination norm or the right to abortions and contraceptives. The controversial Affordable Care Act of 2010 (ObamaCare) was the occasion for RFRA to show its teeth and to raise the stakes of religious liberty/gender and sexual equality clashes.

Sylvia Mathews Burwell, Secretary of Health and Human Services v. Hobby Lobby Stores, Inc., et al.

United States Supreme Court, 2014.
___ U.S. ___, 134 S.Ct. 2751, 189 L.Ed.2d 675.

■ JUSTICE ALITO delivered the opinion of the Court.

We must decide in these cases whether the Religious Freedom Restoration Act of 1993 (RFRA), 107 Stat. 1488, 42 U.S.C. § 2000bb *et seq.*, permits the United States Department of Health and Human Services (HHS) to demand that three closely held corporations provide health-insurance coverage for methods of contraception that violate the sincerely held religious beliefs of the companies' owners. We hold that the regulations that impose this obligation violate RFRA, which prohibits the Federal Government from taking any action that substantially burdens the exercise of religion unless that action constitutes the least restrictive means of serving a compelling government interest.

In holding that the HHS mandate is unlawful, we reject HHS's argument that the owners of the companies forfeited all RFRA protection when they decided to organize their businesses as corporations rather than sole proprietorships or general partnerships. The plain terms of RFRA make it perfectly clear that Congress did not discriminate in this way against men and women who wish to run their businesses as for-profit corporations in the manner required by their religious beliefs.

Since RFRA applies in these cases, we must decide whether the challenged HHS regulations substantially burden the exercise of religion, and we hold that they do. The owners of the businesses have religious objections to abortion, and according to their religious beliefs the four contraceptive methods at issue are abortifacients. If the owners comply with the HHS mandate, they believe they will be facilitating abortions, and if they do not comply, they will pay a very heavy price—as much as $1.3 million per day, or about $475 million per year, in the case of one of the companies. If these consequences do not amount to a substantial burden, it is hard to see what would.

In fact, HHS has already devised and implemented a system that seeks to respect the religious liberty of religious nonprofit corporations while ensuring that the employees of these entities have precisely the same access to all FDA-approved contraceptives as employees of companies whose owners have no religious objections to providing such coverage. The employees of these religious nonprofit corporations still have access to insurance coverage without cost sharing for all FDA-approved contraceptives; and according to HHS, this system imposes no net economic burden on the insurance companies that are required to provide or secure the coverage.

Although HHS has made this system available to religious nonprofits that have religious objections to the contraceptive mandate, HHS has provided no reason why the same system cannot be made available when the owners of for-profit corporations have similar religious objections. We therefore conclude that this system constitutes an alternative that achieves all of the Government's aims while providing greater respect for religious liberty. And under RFRA, that conclusion means that enforcement of the HHS contraceptive mandate against the objecting parties in these cases is unlawful.

As this description of our reasoning shows, our holding is very specific. We do not hold, as the principal dissent alleges, that for-profit corporations and other commercial enterprises can "opt out of any law (saving only tax laws) they judge incompatible with their sincerely held religious beliefs." Nor do we hold, as the dissent implies, that such corporations have free rein to take steps that impose "disadvantages . . . on others" or that require "the general public [to] pick up the tab." And we certainly do not hold or suggest that "RFRA demands accommodation of a for-profit corporation's religious beliefs no matter the impact that accommodation may have on . . . thousands of women employed by Hobby Lobby." The effect of the HHS-created accommodation on the women employed by Hobby Lobby and the other companies involved in these cases would be precisely zero. Under that accommodation, these women would still be entitled to all FDA-approved contraceptives without cost sharing.

[I] * * * At issue in these cases are HHS regulations promulgated under the Patient Protection and Affordable Care Act of 2010 (ACA), 124 Stat. 119. ACA generally requires employers with 50 or more full-time employees to offer "a group health plan or group health insurance coverage" that provides "minimum essential coverage." 26 U.S.C. § 5000A(f)(2); §§ 4980H(a), (c)(2). Any covered employer that does not provide such coverage must pay a substantial price. Specifically, if a covered employer provides group health insurance but its plan fails to comply with ACA's group-health-plan requirements, the employer may be required to pay $100 per day for each affected "individual." §§ 4980D(a)–(b). And if the employer decides to stop providing health insurance altogether and at least one full-time employee enrolls in a health plan and qualifies for a subsidy on one of the government-run ACA exchanges, the employer must pay $2,000 per year for each of its full-time employees. §§ 4980H(a), (c)(1).

Unless an exception applies, ACA requires an employer's group health plan or group-health-insurance coverage to furnish "preventive care and screenings" for women without "any cost sharing requirements." 42 U.S.C. § 300gg–13(a)(4). Congress itself, however, did not specify what types of preventive care must be covered. Instead, Congress authorized the Health Resources and Services Administration (HRSA), a component of HHS, to make that important and sensitive decision. The HRSA in turn consulted the Institute of Medicine, a nonprofit group of volunteer advisers, in determining which preventive services to require.

In August 2011, based on the Institute's recommendations, the HRSA promulgated the Women's Preventive Services Guidelines. The Guidelines provide that nonexempt employers are generally required to provide "coverage, without cost sharing" for "[a]ll Food and Drug Administration [(FDA)] approved contraceptive methods, sterilization procedures, and patient education and counseling." 77 Fed. Reg. 8725 (internal quotation marks omitted). Although many of the required, FDA-approved methods of contraception work by preventing the fertilization of an egg, four of those methods (those specifically at issue in these cases) may have the effect of preventing an already fertilized egg from developing any further by inhibiting its attachment to the uterus.

HHS also authorized the HRSA to establish exemptions from the contraceptive mandate for "religious employers." 45 CFR § 147.131(a). That category encompasses "churches, their integrated auxiliaries, and conventions or associations of churches," as well as "the exclusively religious activities of any religious order." In its Guidelines, HRSA exempted these organizations from the requirement to cover contraceptive services.

In addition, HHS has effectively exempted certain religious nonprofit organizations, described under HHS regulations as "eligible organizations," from the contraceptive mandate. See 45 CFR § 147.131(b); 78 Fed. Reg. 39874 (2013). An "eligible organization" means a nonprofit organization that "holds itself out as a religious organization" and "opposes providing coverage for some or all of any contraceptive services required to be covered . . . on account of religious objections." 45 CFR § 147.131(b). To qualify for this accommodation, an employer must certify that it is such an organization. § 147.131(b)(4). When a group-health-insurance issuer receives notice that one of its clients has invoked this provision, the issuer must then exclude contraceptive coverage from the employer's plan and provide separate payments for contraceptive services for plan participants without imposing any cost-sharing requirements on the eligible organization, its insurance plan, or its employee beneficiaries. § 147.131(c). Although this procedure requires the issuer to bear the cost of these services, HHS has determined that this obligation will not impose any net expense on issuers because its cost will be less than or equal to the cost savings resulting from the services. 78 Fed. Reg. 39877.

In addition to these exemptions for religious organizations, ACA exempts a great many employers from most of its coverage requirements. Employers providing "grandfathered health plans"—those that existed prior to March 23, 2010, and that have not made specified changes after that date—need not comply with many of the Act's requirements, including the contraceptive mandate. And employers with fewer than 50 employees are not required to provide health insurance at all.

* * * Over one-third of the 149 million nonelderly people in America with employer-sponsored health plans were enrolled in grandfathered plans in 2013. The count for employees working for firms that do not have to provide insurance at all because they employ fewer than 50 employees is 34 million workers. * * *

[III.A] RFRA prohibits the "Government [from] substantially burden[ing] *a person's* exercise of religion even if the burden results from a rule of general applicability" unless the Government "demonstrates that application of the burden to *the person*—(1) is in furtherance of a compelling governmental interest; and (2) is the least restrictive means of furthering that compelling governmental interest." 42 U.S.C. §§ 2000bb–1(a), (b) (emphasis added). The first question that we must address is whether this provision applies to regulations that govern the activities of for-profit corporations like Hobby Lobby, Conestoga, and Mardel. * * *

* * * RFRA was designed to provide very broad protection for religious liberty. By enacting RFRA, Congress went far beyond what this Court has held is constitutionally required. Is there any reason to think that the Congress that enacted such sweeping protection put small-business owners to the choice that HHS suggests? An examination of RFRA's text, to which we turn in the next part of this opinion, reveals that Congress did no such thing.

As we will show, Congress provided protection for people like the Hahns and Greens [owners of the plaintiff corporations] by employing a familiar legal fiction: It included corporations within RFRA's definition of "persons." But it is important to keep in mind that the purpose of this fiction is to provide protection for human beings. A corporation is simply a form of organization used by human beings to achieve desired ends. * * * Protecting corporations from government seizure of their property without just compensation protects all those who have a stake in the corporations' financial well-being. [P]rotecting the free-exercise rights of corporations like Hobby Lobby, Conestoga, and Mardel protects the religious liberty of the humans who own and control those companies. * * *

[Under the Dictionary Act, "the wor[d] 'person' . . . include[s] corporations, companies, associations, firms, partnerships, societies, and joint stock companies, as well as individuals." 1 U.S.C. § 1. The Court has followed the Dictionary Act understanding of "person" to include companies, unless Congress has negated that definition. In this case, there was no dispute that RFRA applies to at least some companies, such as religiously affiliated charities, and so the Court ruled that "person" included Hobby Lobby and the other corporations.]

* * * The principal argument advanced by HHS and the principal dissent regarding RFRA protection for Hobby Lobby, Conestoga, and Mardel focuses not on the statutory term "person," but on the phrase "exercise of religion." According to HHS and the dissent, these corporations are not protected by RFRA because they cannot exercise religion. Neither HHS nor the dissent, however, provides any persuasive explanation for this conclusion. Is it because of the corporate form? The corporate form alone cannot provide the explanation because, as we have pointed out, HHS concedes that nonprofit corporations can be protected by RFRA. The dissent suggests that nonprofit corporations are special because furthering their religious "autonomy . . . often furthers individual religious freedom as well." But this principle applies equally to for-profit corporations: Furthering their religious freedom also "furthers individual religious freedom." In these cases, for example, allowing Hobby Lobby, Conestoga, and Mardel to assert RFRA claims protects the religious liberty of the Greens and the Hahns.

If the corporate form is not enough, what about the profit-making objective? [T]he "exercise of religion" involves "not only belief and profession but the performance of (or abstention from) physical acts" that are "engaged in for religious reasons." [*Employment Division v. Smith*, 494 U.S. 872, 877 (1990)]. Business practices that are compelled or limited by the tenets of a religious doctrine fall comfortably within that definition. * * *

While it is certainly true that a central objective of for-profit corporations is to make money, modern corporate law does not require for-profit corporations to pursue profit at the expense of everything else, and many do not do so. For-profit corporations, with ownership approval, support a wide variety of charitable causes, and it is not at all uncommon for such corporations to further humanitarian and other altruistic objectives. Many examples come readily to mind. So long as its owners agree, a for-profit corporation may take costly pollution-control and energy-conservation measures that go beyond what the law requires. A for-profit corporation that operates facilities in other countries may exceed the requirements of local law regarding working conditions and benefits. If for-profit corporations may pursue such worthy objectives, there is no apparent reason why they may not further religious objectives as well.

HHS would draw a sharp line between nonprofit corporations (which, HHS concedes, are protected by RFRA) and for-profit corporations (which HHS would leave unprotected), but the actual picture is less clear-cut. Not all corporations that decline to organize as nonprofits do so in order to maximize profit. For example, organizations with religious and charitable aims might organize as for-profit corporations because of the potential advantages of that corporate form, such as the freedom to participate in lobbying for legislation or campaigning for political candidates who promote their religious or charitable goals. In fact, recognizing the inherent compatibility between establishing a for-profit corporation and pursuing nonprofit goals, States have increasingly adopted laws formally recognizing hybrid corporate forms. Over half of the States, for instance, now recognize the "benefit corporation," a dual-purpose entity that seeks to achieve both a benefit for the public and a profit for its owners. * * *

Finally, HHS contends that Congress could not have wanted RFRA to apply to for-profit corporations because it is difficult as a practical matter to ascertain the sincere "beliefs" of a corporation. HHS goes so far as to raise the specter of "divisive, polarizing proxy battles over the religious identity of large, publicly traded corporations such as IBM or General Electric."

These cases, however, do not involve publicly traded corporations, and it seems unlikely that the sort of corporate giants to which HHS refers will often assert RFRA claims. HHS has not pointed to any example of a publicly traded corporation asserting RFRA rights, and numerous practical restraints would likely prevent that from occurring. * * *

[IV] Because RFRA applies in these cases, we must next ask whether the HHS contraceptive mandate "substantially burden[s]" the exercise of religion. 42 U.S.C. § 2000bb–1(a). We have little trouble concluding that it does.

As we have noted, the Hahns and Greens have a sincere religious belief that life begins at conception. They therefore object on religious grounds to providing health insurance that covers methods of birth control that, as HHS acknowledges, may result in the destruction of an embryo. By requiring the Hahns and Greens and their companies to arrange for such coverage, the HHS mandate demands that they engage in conduct that seriously violates their religious beliefs.

If the Hahns and Greens and their companies do not yield to this demand, the economic consequences will be severe. If the companies continue to offer group health plans that do not cover the contraceptives at issue, they will be taxed $100 per day for each affected individual. 26 U.S.C. § 4980D. For Hobby Lobby, the bill could amount to $1.3 million per day or about $475 million per year; for Conestoga, the assessment could be $90,000 per day or $33 million per year; and for Mardel, it could be $40,000 per day or about $15 million per year. These sums are surely substantial. * * *

In taking the position that the HHS mandate does not impose a substantial burden on the exercise of religion, HHS's main argument (echoed by the principal dissent) is basically that the connection between what the objecting parties must do (provide health-insurance coverage for four methods of contraception that may operate after the fertilization of an egg) and the end that they find to be morally wrong (destruction of an embryo) is simply too attenuated. HHS and the dissent note that providing the coverage would not itself result in the destruction of an embryo; that would occur only if an employee chose to take advantage of the coverage and to use one of the four methods at issue.

This argument dodges the question that RFRA presents (whether the HHS mandate imposes a substantial burden on the ability of the objecting parties to conduct business in accordance with *their religious beliefs*) and instead addresses a very different question that the federal courts have no business addressing (whether the religious belief asserted in a RFRA case is reasonable). The Hahns and Greens believe that providing the coverage demanded by the HHS regulations is connected to the destruction of an embryo in a way that is sufficient to make it immoral for them to provide the coverage. This belief implicates a difficult and important question of religion and moral philosophy, namely, the circumstances under which it is wrong for a person to perform an act that is innocent in itself but that has the effect of enabling or facilitating the commission of an immoral act by another. Arrogating the authority to provide a binding national answer to this religious and philosophical question, HHS and the principal dissent in effect tell the plaintiffs that their beliefs are flawed. For good reason, we have repeatedly refused to take such a step. * * *

[O]ur "narrow function . . . in this context is to determine" whether the line drawn reflects "an honest conviction," and there is no dispute that it does.

[V] Since the HHS contraceptive mandate imposes a substantial burden on the exercise of religion, we must move on and decide whether HHS has shown that the mandate both "(1) is in furtherance of a compelling governmental interest; and (2) is the least restrictive means of furthering that compelling governmental interest." 42 U.S.C.

§ 2000bb–1(b). [The Court assumes without deciding that the mandate furthers a compelling governmental interest.]

The least-restrictive-means standard is exceptionally demanding, and it is not satisfied here. HHS has not shown that it lacks other means of achieving its desired goal without imposing a substantial burden on the exercise of religion by the objecting parties in these cases.

The most straightforward way of doing this would be for the Government to assume the cost of providing the four contraceptives at issue to any women who are unable to obtain them under their health-insurance policies due to their employers' religious objections. This would certainly be less restrictive of the plaintiffs' religious liberty, and HHS has not shown, that this is not a viable alternative. * * * According to one of the Congressional Budget Office's most recent forecasts, ACA's insurance-coverage provisions will cost the Federal Government more than $1.3 trillion through the next decade. If, as HHS tells us, providing all women with cost-free access to all FDA-approved methods of contraception is a Government interest of the highest order, it is hard to understand HHS's argument that it cannot be required under RFRA to pay *anything* in order to achieve this important goal. * * *

In the end, however, we need not rely on the option of a new, government-funded program in order to conclude that the HHS regulations fail the least-restrictive-means test. HHS itself has demonstrated that it has at its disposal an approach that is less restrictive than requiring employers to fund contraceptive methods that violate their religious beliefs. As we explained above, HHS has already established an accommodation for nonprofit organizations with religious objections. Under that accommodation, the organization can self-certify that it opposes providing coverage for particular contraceptive services. If the organization makes such a certification, the organization's insurance issuer or third-party administrator must "[e]xpressly exclude contraceptive coverage from the group health insurance coverage provided in connection with the group health plan" and "[p]rovide separate payments for any contraceptive services required to be covered" without imposing "any cost-sharing requirements . . . on the eligible organization, the group health plan, or plan participants or beneficiaries." 45 CFR § 147.131(c)(2); 26 CFR § 54.9815–2713A(c)(2).

We do not decide today whether an approach of this type complies with RFRA for purposes of all religious claims. At a minimum, however, it does not impinge on the plaintiffs' religious belief that providing insurance coverage for the contraceptives at issue here violates their religion, and it serves HHS's stated interests equally well. * * *

* * * [O]ur decision in these cases is concerned solely with the contraceptive mandate. Our decision should not be understood to hold that an insurance-coverage mandate must necessarily fall if it conflicts with an employer's religious beliefs. Other coverage requirements, such as immunizations, may be supported by different interests (for example,

the need to combat the spread of infectious diseases) and may involve different arguments about the least restrictive means of providing them.

The principal dissent raises the possibility that discrimination in hiring, for example on the basis of race, might be cloaked as religious practice to escape legal sanction. Our decision today provides no such shield. The Government has a compelling interest in providing an equal opportunity to participate in the workforce without regard to race, and prohibitions on racial discrimination are precisely tailored to achieve that critical goal.

HHS also raises for the first time in this Court the argument that applying the contraceptive mandate to for-profit employers with sincere religious objections is essential to the comprehensive health-insurance scheme that ACA establishes. HHS analogizes the contraceptive mandate to the requirement to pay Social Security taxes, which we upheld in [*United States v. Lee*, 455 U.S. 252 (1982)] despite the religious objection of an employer, but these cases are quite different. Our holding in *Lee* turned primarily on the special problems associated with a national system of taxation. We noted that "[t]he obligation to pay the social security tax initially is not fundamentally different from the obligation to pay income taxes." 455 U.S., at 260. Based on that premise, we explained that it was untenable to allow individuals to seek exemptions from taxes based on religious objections to particular Government expenditures: "If, for example, a religious adherent believes war is a sin, and if a certain percentage of the federal budget can be identified as devoted to war-related activities, such individuals would have a similarly valid claim to be exempt from paying that percentage of the income tax." *Ibid.* We observed that "[t]he tax system could not function if denominations were allowed to challenge the tax system because tax payments were spent in a manner that violates their religious belief." *Ibid.*

Lee was a free-exercise, not a RFRA, case, but if the issue in *Lee* were analyzed under the RFRA framework, the fundamental point would be that there simply is no less restrictive alternative to the categorical requirement to pay taxes. Because of the enormous variety of government expenditures funded by tax dollars, allowing taxpayers to withhold a portion of their tax obligations on religious grounds would lead to chaos. Recognizing exemptions from the contraceptive mandate is very different. ACA does not create a large national pool of tax revenue for use in purchasing healthcare coverage. Rather, individual employers like the plaintiffs purchase insurance for their own employees. And contrary to the principal dissent's characterization, the employers' contributions do not necessarily funnel into "undifferentiated funds." The accommodation established by HHS requires issuers to have a mechanism by which to "segregate premium revenue collected from the eligible organization from the monies used to provide payments for contraceptive services." 45 CFR § 147.131(c)(2)(ii). Recognizing a religious accommodation under RFRA for particular coverage requirements, therefore, does not threaten the viability of ACA's comprehensive scheme in the way that recognizing religious objections to particular expenditures from general tax revenues would. * * *

■ JUSTICE KENNEDY, concurring.

It seems to me appropriate, in joining the Court's opinion, to add these few remarks. At the outset it should be said that the Court's opinion does not have the breadth and sweep ascribed to it by the respectful and powerful dissent. The Court and the dissent disagree on the proper interpretation of the Religious Freedom and Restoration Act of 1993 (RFRA), but do agree on the purpose of that statute. It is to ensure that interests in religious freedom are protected.

In our constitutional tradition, freedom means that all persons have the right to believe or strive to believe in a divine creator and a divine law. For those who choose this course, free exercise is essential in preserving their own dignity and in striving for a self-definition shaped by their religious precepts. Free exercise in this sense implicates more than just freedom of belief. It means, too, the right to express those beliefs and to establish one's religious (or nonreligious) self-definition in the political, civic, and economic life of our larger community. But in a complex society and an era of pervasive governmental regulation, defining the proper realm for free exercise can be difficult. In these cases the plaintiffs deem it necessary to exercise their religious beliefs within the context of their own closely held, for-profit corporations. They claim protection under RFRA, the federal statute discussed with care and in detail in the Court's opinion.

As the Court notes, under our precedents, RFRA imposes a " 'stringent test.' " The Government must demonstrate that the application of a substantial burden to a person's exercise of religion "(1) is in furtherance of a compelling governmental interest; and (2) is the least restrictive means of furthering that compelling governmental interest." § 2000bb–1(b).

As to RFRA's first requirement, the Department of Health and Human Services (HHS) makes the case that the mandate serves the Government's compelling interest in providing insurance coverage that is necessary to protect the health of female employees, coverage that is significantly more costly than for a male employee. There are many medical conditions for which pregnancy is contraindicated. It is important to confirm that a premise of the Court's opinion is its assumption that the HHS regulation here at issue furthers a legitimate and compelling interest in the health of female employees.

But the Government has not made the second showing required by RFRA, that the means it uses to regulate is the least restrictive way to further its interest. As the Court's opinion explains, the record in these cases shows that there is an existing, recognized, workable, and already-implemented framework to provide coverage. That framework is one that HHS has itself devised, that the plaintiffs have not criticized with a specific objection that has been considered in detail by the courts in this litigation, and that is less restrictive than the means challenged by the plaintiffs in these cases.

The means the Government chose is the imposition of a direct mandate on the employers in these cases. But in other instances the Government has allowed the same contraception coverage in issue here to be provided to employees of nonprofit religious organizations, as an accommodation to the religious objections of those entities. The accommodation works by requiring insurance companies to cover, without cost sharing, contraception coverage for female employees who wish it. That accommodation equally furthers the Government's interest but does not impinge on the plaintiffs' religious beliefs.

On this record and as explained by the Court, the Government has not met its burden of showing that it cannot accommodate the plaintiffs' similar religious objections under this established framework. RFRA is inconsistent with the insistence of an agency such as HHS on distinguishing between different religious believers—burdening one while accommodating the other—when it may treat both equally by offering both of them the same accommodation.

The parties who were the plaintiffs in the District Courts argue that the Government could pay for the methods that are found objectionable. In discussing this alternative, the Court does not address whether the proper response to a legitimate claim for freedom in the health care arena is for the Government to create an additional program. The Court properly does not resolve whether one freedom should be protected by creating incentives for additional government constraints. In these cases, it is the Court's understanding that an accommodation may be made to the employers without imposition of a whole new program or burden on the Government. As the Court makes clear, this is not a case where it can be established that it is difficult to accommodate the government's interest, and in fact the mechanism for doing so is already in place.

* * * Among the reasons the United States is so open, so tolerant, and so free is that no person may be restricted or demeaned by government in exercising his or her religion. Yet neither may that same exercise unduly restrict other persons, such as employees, in protecting their own interests, interests the law deems compelling. In these cases the means to reconcile those two priorities are at hand in the existing accommodation the Government has designed, identified, and used for circumstances closely parallel to those presented here. RFRA requires the Government to use this less restrictive means. As the Court explains, this existing model, designed precisely for this problem, might well suffice to distinguish the instant cases from many others in which it is more difficult and expensive to accommodate a governmental program to

countless religious claims based on an alleged statutory right of free exercise. * * *

■ JUSTICE GINSBURG, with whom JUSTICE SOTOMAYOR joins, and with whom JUSTICE BREYER and JUSTICE KAGAN join as to all but Part III-C-1, dissenting.

In a decision of startling breadth, the Court holds that commercial enterprises, including corporations, along with partnerships and sole proprietorships, can opt out of any law (saving only tax laws) they judge incompatible with their sincerely held religious beliefs. Compelling governmental interests in uniform compliance with the law, and disadvantages that religion-based opt-outs impose on others, hold no sway, the Court decides, at least when there is a "less restrictive alternative." And such an alternative, the Court suggests, there always will be whenever, in lieu of tolling an enterprise claiming a religion-based exemption, the government, *i.e.,* the general public, can pick up the tab.

The Court does not pretend that the First Amendment's Free Exercise Clause demands religion-based accommodations so extreme, for our decisions leave no doubt on that score. Instead, the Court holds that Congress, in the Religious Freedom Restoration Act of 1993 (RFRA), dictated the extraordinary religion-based exemptions today's decision endorses. In the Court's view, RFRA demands accommodation of a for-profit corporation's religious beliefs no matter the impact that accommodation may have on third parties who do not share the corporation owners' religious faith—in these cases, thousands of women employed by Hobby Lobby and Conestoga or dependents of persons those corporations employ. Persuaded that Congress enacted RFRA to serve a far less radical purpose, and mindful of the havoc the Court's judgment can introduce, I dissent.

[I] "The ability of women to participate equally in the economic and social life of the Nation has been facilitated by their ability to control their reproductive lives." *Planned Parenthood of Southeastern Pa.* v. *Casey,* 505 U.S. 833, 856 (1992). Congress acted on that understanding when, as part of a nationwide insurance program intended to be comprehensive, it called for coverage of preventive care responsive to women's needs. Carrying out Congress' direction, the Department of Health and Human Services (HHS), in consultation with public health experts, promulgated regulations requiring group health plans to cover all forms of contraception approved by the Food and Drug Administration (FDA). The genesis of this coverage should enlighten the Court's resolution of these cases.

[II.A] The Affordable Care Act (ACA), in its initial form, specified three categories of preventive care that health plans must cover at no added cost to the plan participant or beneficiary. Particular services were to be recommended by the U.S. Preventive Services Task Force, an independent panel of experts. The scheme had a large gap, however; it left out preventive services that "many women's health advocates and medical professionals believe are critically important." 155 Cong. Rec. 28841 (2009) (statement of Sen. Boxer). To correct this oversight, Senator Barbara Mikulski introduced the Women's Health Amendment, which added to the ACA's minimum coverage requirements a new category of preventive services specific to women's health.

As altered by the Women's Health Amendment's passage, the ACA requires new insurance plans to include coverage without cost sharing of "such additional preventive care and screenings . . . as provided for in comprehensive guidelines supported by the Health Resources and Services Administration [(HRSA)]," a unit of HHS. 42 U.S.C. § 300gg–13(a)(4). [The HRSA developed recommendations in consultation with the Institute of Medicine (IOM), which convened a group of independent experts. The IOM experts determined that preventive coverage should include the "full range" of FDA-approved contraceptive methods. The HRSA guidelines adopted the IOM recommendations, and subsequent HHS and Department of Labor regulations followed those guidelines. These regulations comprise the contraceptive coverage requirement.]

[Justice Ginsburg described the concerns about the impact of excluding full contraceptive coverage on women's health, reflected in statements by medical experts and members of Congress. These included cost-related barriers to receiving medical tests and treatments and to filling prescriptions; contraindications to pregnancy for women with certain medical conditions; the usefulness of contraceptives in reducing risk of endometrial cancer and other serious medical conditions; and the greater risk that women with unintended pregnancies will experience depression and anxiety, and their children will face preterm birth and low birth weight.]

[II.B] While the Women's Health Amendment succeeded, a countermove proved unavailing. The Senate voted down the so-called "conscience amendment," which would have enabled any employer or insurance provider to deny coverage based on its asserted "religious beliefs or moral convictions." 158 Cong. Rec. S539 (Feb. 9, 2012); see id., at S1162–S1173 (Mar. 1, 2012) (debate and vote). That amendment, Senator Mikulski observed, would have "pu[t] the personal opinion of employers and insurers over the practice of medicine." Id., at S1127 (Feb. 29, 2012). Rejecting the "conscience amendment," Congress left health care decisions—including the choice among contraceptive methods—in the hands of women, with the aid of their health care providers.

* * * [T]he Free Exercise Clause [does] not require the exemption Hobby Lobby and Conestoga seek. Accommodations to religious beliefs or observances, the Court has clarified, must not significantly impinge on the interests of third parties. * * *

[III] Lacking a tenable claim under the Free Exercise Clause, Hobby Lobby and Conestoga rely on RFRA, a statute instructing that "[g]overnment shall not substantially burden a person's exercise of religion even if the burden results from a rule of general applicability" unless the government shows that application of the burden is "the least restrictive means" to further a "compelling governmental interest." 42 U.S.C. § 2000bb–1(a), (b)(2). * * *

[Justice Ginsburg argues that the intent of Congress in enacting RFRA was to reinstate the strict scrutiny test in Free Exercise case law that existed prior to the decision that RFRA was designed to overrule: *Employment Division v. Smith*, 494 U.S. 872 (1990). "Despite these authoritative indications, the Court sees RFRA as a bold initiative departing from, rather than restoring, pre-*Smith* jurisprudence."]

[III.C] With RFRA's restorative purpose in mind, I turn to the Act's application to the instant lawsuits. That task, in view of the positions taken by the Court, requires consideration of several questions, each potentially dispositive of Hobby Lobby's and Conestoga's claims: Do for-profit corporations rank among "person[s]" who "exercise . . . religion"? Assuming that they do, does the contraceptive coverage requirement "substantially burden" their religious exercise? If so, is the requirement "in furtherance of a compelling government interest"? And last, does the requirement represent the least restrictive means for furthering that interest?

Misguided by its errant premise that RFRA moved beyond the pre-*Smith* case law, the Court falters at each step of its analysis.

[III.C.1] RFRA's compelling interest test, as noted, applies to government actions that "substantially burden *a person's exercise of religion*." 42 U.S.C. § 2000bb–1(a) (emphasis added). This reference, the Court submits, incorporates the definition of "person" found in the Dictionary Act, 1 U.S.C. § 1, which extends to "corporations, companies, associations, firms, partnerships, societies, and joint stock companies, as well as individuals." The Dictionary Act's definition, however, controls only where "context" does not "indicat[e] otherwise." § 1. Here, context does so indicate. RFRA speaks of "a person's *exercise of religion*." 42 U.S.C. § 2000bb–1(a) (emphasis added). Whether a corporation qualifies as a "person" capable of exercising religion is an inquiry one cannot answer without reference to the "full body" of pre-*Smith* "free-exercise caselaw." There is in that case law no support for the notion that free exercise rights pertain to for-profit corporations.

Until this litigation, no decision of this Court recognized a for-profit corporation's qualification for a religious exemption from a generally applicable law, whether under the Free Exercise Clause or RFRA. The absence of such precedent is just what one would expect, for the exercise of religion is characteristic of natural persons, not artificial legal entities. As Chief Justice Marshall observed nearly two centuries ago, a corporation is "an artificial being, invisible, intangible, and existing only in contemplation of law." *Trustees of Dartmouth College* v. *Woodward*, 4 Wheat. 518, 636 (1819). Corporations, Justice Stevens more recently reminded, "have no consciences, no beliefs, no feelings, no thoughts, no desires." *Citizens United* v. *Federal Election Comm'n*, 558 U.S. 310, 466 (2010) (opinion concurring in part and dissenting in part).

The First Amendment's free exercise protections, the Court has indeed recognized, shelter churches and other nonprofit religion-based organizations. "For many individuals, religious activity derives meaning in large measure from participation in a larger religious community," and "furtherance of the autonomy of religious organizations often furthers individual religious freedom as well." *Corporation of Presiding Bishop of Church of Jesus Christ of Latter-day Saints* v. *Amos*, 483 U.S. 327, 342 (1987) (Brennan, J., concurring in judgment). The Court's "special solicitude to the rights of religious organizations," *Hosanna-Tabor Evangelical Lutheran Church and School* v. *EEOC*, 565 U.S. ___, ___ (2012), however, is just that. No such solicitude is traditional for commercial organizations. Indeed, until today, religious exemptions had never been extended to any entity operating in "the commercial, profit-making world." *Amos*, 483 U.S., at 337.

The reason why is hardly obscure. Religious organizations exist to foster the interests of persons subscribing to the same religious faith. Not so of for-profit corporations. Workers who sustain the operations of those corporations commonly are not drawn from one religious community. Indeed, by law, no religion-based criterion can restrict the work force of for-profit corporations. See 42 U.S.C. §§ 2000e(b), 2000e–1(a), 2000e–2(a). The distinction between a community made up of believers in the same religion and one embracing persons of diverse beliefs, clear as it is, constantly escapes the Court's attention. One can only wonder why the Court shuts this key difference from sight.

Reading RFRA, as the Court does, to require extension of religion-based exemptions to for-profit corporations surely is not grounded in the pre-*Smith* precedent Congress sought to preserve. Had Congress intended RFRA to initiate a change so huge, a clarion statement to that effect likely would have been made in the legislation. The text of RFRA makes no such statement and the legislative history does not so much as mention for-profit corporations.

The Court notes that for-profit corporations may support charitable causes and use their funds for religious ends, and therefore questions the distinction between such corporations and religious nonprofit organizations. Again, the Court forgets that religious organizations exist to serve a community of believers. For-profit corporations do not fit that bill. * * *

* * * [E]ven accepting, *arguendo*, the premise that unincorporated business enterprises may gain religious accommodations under the Free Exercise Clause, the Court's conclusion is unsound. In a sole proprietorship, the business and its owner are one and the same. By incorporating a business, however, an individual separates herself from the entity and escapes personal responsibility for the entity's obligations.

One might ask why the separation should hold only when it serves the interest of those who control the corporation. * * *

The Court's determination that RFRA extends to for-profit corporations is bound to have untoward effects. Although the Court attempts to cabin its language to closely held corporations, its logic extends to corporations of any size, public or private. Little doubt that RFRA claims will proliferate, for the Court's expansive notion of corporate personhood—combined with its other errors in construing RFRA—invites for-profit entities to seek religion-based exemptions from regulations they deem offensive to their faith.

[III.C.2] Even if Hobby Lobby and Conestoga were deemed RFRA "person[s]," to gain an exemption, they must demonstrate that the contraceptive coverage requirement "substantially burden[s] [their] exercise of religion." 42 U.S.C. § 2000bb–1(a). Congress no doubt meant the modifier "substantially" to carry weight. * * *

The Court barely pauses to inquire whether any burden imposed by the contraceptive coverage requirement is substantial. Instead, it rests on the Greens' and Hahns' "belie[f] that providing the coverage demanded by the HHS regulations is connected to the destruction of an embryo in a way that is sufficient to make it immoral for them to provide the coverage." I agree with the Court that the Green and Hahn families' religious convictions regarding contraception are sincerely held. But those beliefs, however deeply held, do not suffice to sustain a RFRA claim. RFRA, properly understood, distinguishes between "factual allegations that [plaintiffs'] beliefs are sincere and of a religious nature," which a court must accept as true, and the "legal conclusion . . . that [plaintiffs'] religious exercise is substantially burdened," an inquiry the court must undertake. *Kaemmerling* v. *Lappin*, 553 F. 3d 669, 679 (CADC 2008). * * *

Undertaking the inquiry that the Court forgoes, I would conclude that the connection between the families' religious objections and the contraceptive coverage requirement is too attenuated to rank as substantial. The requirement carries no command that Hobby Lobby or Conestoga purchase or provide the contraceptives they find objectionable. Instead, it calls on the companies covered by the requirement to direct money into undifferentiated funds that finance a wide variety of benefits under comprehensive health plans. Those plans, in order to comply with the ACA, must offer contraceptive coverage without cost sharing, just as they must cover an array of other preventive services.

Importantly, the decisions whether to claim benefits under the plans are made not by Hobby Lobby or Conestoga, but by the covered employees and dependents, in consultation with their health care providers. * * * It is doubtful that Congress, when it specified that burdens must be "substantia[l]," had in mind a linkage thus interrupted by independent decisionmakers (the woman and her health counselor) standing between the challenged government action and the religious exercise claimed to be infringed. Any decision to use contraceptives made by a woman covered under Hobby Lobby's or Conestoga's plan will not be propelled by the Government, it will be the woman's autonomous choice, informed by the physician she consults.

[III.C.3. Justice Ginsburg maintains that the compelling nature of the government's interests supporting the coverage requirement is not undermined by either the fact that Hobby Lobby and Conestoga resist coverage for only 4 of the 20 FDA-approved contraceptives or the existence of other exemptions.]

Notably, the corporations exclude intrauterine devices (IUDs), devices significantly more effective, and significantly more expensive than other contraceptive methods. * * * It bears note in this regard that the cost of an IUD is nearly equivalent to a month's full-time pay for workers earning the minimum wage; that almost one-third of women would change their contraceptive method if costs were not a factor; and that only one-fourth of women who request an IUD actually have one inserted after finding out how expensive it would be [citations omitted]. * * *

The ACA's grandfathering provision allows a phasing-in period for compliance with a number of the Act's requirements (not just the contraceptive coverage or other preventive services provisions). Once specified changes are made, grandfathered status ceases. * * *

[III.C.4] After assuming the existence of compelling government interests, the Court holds that the contraceptive coverage requirement fails to satisfy RFRA's least restrictive means test. But the Government has shown that there is no less restrictive, equally effective means that would both (1) satisfy the challengers' religious objections to providing insurance coverage for certain contraceptives (which they believe cause abortions); and (2) carry out the objective of the ACA's contraceptive coverage requirement, to ensure that women employees receive, at no cost to them, the preventive care needed to safeguard their health and well being. A "least restrictive means" cannot require employees to relinquish benefits accorded them by federal law in order to ensure that their commercial employers can adhere unreservedly to their religious tenets.

Then let the government pay (rather than the employees who do not share their employer's faith), the Court suggests. "The most straightforward [alternative]," the Court asserts, "would be for the Government to assume the cost of providing . . . contraceptives . . . to any women who are unable to obtain them under their health-insurance policies due to their employers' religious objections." The ACA, however, requires coverage of preventive services through the existing employer-based system of health insurance "so that [employees] face minimal logistical and administrative obstacles." 78 Fed. Reg. 39888. Impeding women's receipt of benefits "by requiring them to take steps to learn about, and to sign up for, a new [government funded and administered]

health benefit" was scarcely what Congress contemplated. Moreover, Title X of the Public Health Service Act, 42 U.S.C. § 300 *et seq.*, "is the nation's only dedicated source of federal funding for safety net family planning services. Safety net programs like Title X are not designed to absorb the unmet needs of . . . insured individuals." [citing amicus brief]
* * *

In sum, in view of what Congress sought to accomplish, *i.e.*, comprehensive preventive care for women furnished through employer-based health plans, none of the proffered alternatives would satisfactorily serve the compelling interests to which Congress responded.

[IV] Among the pathmarking pre-*Smith* decisions RFRA preserved is *United States* v. *Lee*. * * * [T]he *Lee* Court made two key points one cannot confine to tax cases. "When followers of a particular sect enter into commercial activity as a matter of choice," the Court observed, "the limits they accept on their own conduct as a matter of conscience and faith are not to be superimposed on statutory schemes which are binding on others in that activity." The statutory scheme of employer-based comprehensive health coverage involved in these cases is surely binding on others engaged in the same trade or business as the corporate challengers here, Hobby Lobby and Conestoga. Further, the Court recognized in *Lee* that allowing a religion-based exemption to a commercial employer would "operat[e] to impose the employer's religious faith on the employees." No doubt the Greens and Hahns and all who share their beliefs may decline to acquire for themselves the contraceptives in question. But that choice may not be imposed on employees who hold other beliefs. Working for Hobby Lobby or Conestoga, in other words, should not deprive employees of the preventive care available to workers at the shop next door, at least in the absence of directions from the Legislature or Administration to do so.

Why should decisions of this order be made by Congress or the regulatory authority, and not this Court? Hobby Lobby and Conestoga surely do not stand alone as commercial enterprises seeking exemptions from generally applicable laws on the basis of their religious beliefs. See, *e.g.*, *Newman* v. *Piggie Park Enterprises, Inc.*, 256 F. Supp. 941, 945 (SC 1966) (owner of restaurant chain refused to serve black patrons based on his religious beliefs opposing racial integration), aff'd in relevant part and rev'd in part on other grounds, 377 F. 2d 433 (CA4 1967), aff'd and modified on other grounds, 390 U.S. 400 (1968); *In re Minnesota ex rel. McClure*, 370 N. W. 2d 844, 847 (Minn. 1985) (born-again Christians who owned closely held, for-profit health clubs believed that the Bible proscribed hiring or retaining an "individua[l] living with but not married to a person of the opposite sex," "a young, single woman working without her father's consent or a married woman working without her husband's consent," and any person "antagonistic to the Bible," including "fornicators and homosexuals" (internal quotation marks omitted)), appeal dismissed, 478 U.S. 1015 (1986); *Elane Photography, LLC* v. *Willock*, 2013-NMSC-040, 309 P.3d 53 [N. Mex. 2014] (for-profit photography business owned by a husband and wife refused to photograph a lesbian couple's commitment ceremony based on the religious beliefs of the company's owners), cert. denied, 572 U.S. ___ (2014). Would RFRA require exemptions in cases of this ilk? And if not, how does the Court divine which religious beliefs are worthy of accommodation, and which are not? Isn't the Court disarmed from making such a judgment given its recognition that "courts must not presume to determine . . . the plausibility of a religious claim"?

Would the exemption the Court holds RFRA demands for employers with religiously grounded objections to the use of certain contraceptives extend to employers with religiously grounded objections to blood transfusions (Jehovah's Witnesses); antidepressants (Scientologists); medications derived from pigs, including anesthesia, intravenous fluids, and pills coated with gelatin (certain Muslims, Jews, and Hindus); and vaccinations (Christian Scientists, among others)? According to counsel for Hobby Lobby, "each one of these cases . . . would have to be evaluated on its own . . . apply[ing] the compelling interest-least restrictive alternative test." Not much help there for the lower courts bound by today's decision.

The Court, however, sees nothing to worry about. Today's cases, the Court concludes, are "concerned solely with the contraceptive mandate. Our decision should not be understood to hold that an insurance-coverage mandate must necessarily fall if it conflicts with an employer's religious beliefs. Other coverage requirements, such as immunizations, may be supported by different interests (for example, the need to combat the spread of infectious diseases) and may involve different arguments about the least restrictive means of providing them." But the Court has assumed, for RFRA purposes, that the interest in women's health and well being is compelling and has come up with no means adequate to serve that interest, the one motivating Congress to adopt the Women's Health Amendment.

* * * The Court, I fear, has ventured into a minefield by its immoderate reading of RFRA. I would confine religious exemptions under that Act to organizations formed "for a religious purpose," "engage[d] primarily in carrying out that religious purpose," and not "engaged . . . substantially in the exchange of goods or services for money beyond nominal amounts." [See *Spencer* v. *World Vision, Inc.*, 633 F. 3d 723 (CA9 2010) at 748 (Kleinfeld, J., concurring).] * * *

NOTES ON THE BROAD REACH OF RFRA

1.   *How Broad Will the Court's Decision Sweep?* In her dissent, Justice Ginsburg critiques the Court's opinion on doctrinal grounds as "startling" for its (too strong) interpretation of the narrowly tailored requirement in RFRA and its (too weak) understanding of the importance of the commercial versus

non-commercial line between assertedly religious entities. At the outset, the most "startling" feature of the Court's opinion is that it untethers RFRA's statutory rule from the free exercise constitutional precedents that Congress was "restoring." The text of the statute and its ample legislative history make clear that Congress was codifying the pre-*Smith* free exercise precedents and not authorizing the Supreme Court to ignore those precedents.

On a more conceptual level, Justice Ginsburg seeks to reframe the conflict as one about the welfare of women versus an "attenuated" impact on the beliefs of family-owned businesses. The dissent repeatedly emphasizes the importance and broader ramifications of women's health interests. Does the strategy of the dissent succeed? Justice Alito deftly seeks to deflect this line of attack by accepting as a given that the interests behind the regulation are compelling. Does he succeed in defanging this objection?

Much of the debate between Justices Alito and Ginsburg, and apparently an impetus for Justice Kennedy's concurrence, lies in the question of how broadly the rule announced in *Hobby Lobby* will be extended. Are there principled limits to the reach of the majority opinion beyond its facts? Will this case amount to yet more reproductive rights exceptionalism in constitutional jurisprudence? Or will a much broader religious liberty defense be extended beyond reproductive rights cases?

Note that Justice Ginsburg suggests that one additional field that could be vulnerable is anti-discrimination law, and one of the cases she cites is *Elane Photography,* excerpted below. Justice Alito's disavowal of opening the door for pretextual defenses against discrimination claims is carefully limited to the example of race discrimination. Justice Kennedy speaks of the "the right . . . to establish one's religious (and non-religious) self-definition in the political, civic, and economic life of our larger community," which suggests support for claims to equal access to commercial services, as was the case in *Elane Photography*. In light of *Hobby Lobby*, how strong are the arguments against allowing for-profit businesses to claim an exemption from public accommodations laws?

2. *Continuing Litigation over the HHS Fallback Plan.* Three days after issuing the decision in *Hobby Lobby,* stressing that the exemption system HHS had developed for religious non-profits could be applied to for-profit employers, the Court granted a religious college an injunction pending appeal to relieve it from having to comply with filing a form to obtain that exemption. *Wheaton College v. Burwell*, 136 S.Ct. 2806 (2014). Wheaton College asserted that submitting the government form claiming an exemption made it complicit in the provision of abortifacients because one use of the form was to notify its insurer that the insurer would have to bear the cost of contraceptive coverage.

A dissent by Justice Sotomayor, joined by Justices Ginsburg and Kagan, accused the majority of reneging on assurances in *Hobby Lobby*: "Those who are bound by our decisions usually believe that they can take us at our word. Not so today." *Id.* at 2808. The dissent argued that eliminating the one-page form would mean that HHS, when notified that a religious employer claimed the exemption, would have to keep track of which insurer should be notified, an administrative burden that could potentially involve hundreds of employers and insurance companies. The simple form, Justice Sotomayor argued, was the least restrictive burden on religious conscience that the government could impose and still assure that all employees received access to contraceptive coverage.

The broader question is whether the substantial burden requirement of RFRA can be satisfied by the subjective experience of the religious entity, without more. If so, then Wheaton College's assertion of complicity made sense. Justice Sotomayor disagreed:

> If a religious nonprofit chooses not to pay for contraceptive services, it is true that someone else may have a legal obligation to pay for them, just as someone may have to go to war in place of the conscientious objector. But the obligation to provide contraceptive services, like the obligation to serve in the Armed Forces, arises not from the filing of the form but from the underlying law and regulations.

> It may be that what troubles Wheaton is that it must participate in *any* process the end result of which might be the provision of contraceptives to its employees. But that is far from a substantial burden on its free exercise of religion.

Id. at 2813. Should the test for a substantial burden on religious liberty be subjective, to insulate claims of conscience from civil demands, or objective? In the Wheaton College case, the Seventh Circuit later found that the filing requirement did not constitute a substantial burden. *Wheaton College v. Burwell*, 2015 WL 3988356 (7th Cir. July 1, 2015). Other Courts of Appeals have also found the absence of a substantial burden on religious organizations in the same situation. See, *e.g.*, *Geneva College v. Secretary, U.S. Dept. of Health and Human Services*, 778 F.3d 422 (3d Cir. 2015); *Priests for Life v. U.S. Dept. of Health and Human Services*, 772 F.3d 229 (D.C. Cir. 2014).

The Supreme Court granted review in seven cases, to evaluate the sufficiency of HHS's accommodation. Operating with only eight Justices (after the death of Justice Scalia), the Court unanimously vacated the court of appeals decisions denying relief and remanded the cases back to the courts of appeals. "Given the gravity of the dispute and the substantial clarification and refinement in the positions of the parties, the parties on remand should be afforded an opportunity to arrive at an approach that accommodates the challengers' religious exercise while at the same time ensuring that the women covered by the challengers' health plans receive full and equal health coverage, including contraceptive coverage." *Little Sisters of the Poor Home for the Aged v. Burwell*, 136 S.Ct. 446 (2015) (per curiam). The parties had stipulated that the challengers' insurers were able to provide the needed coverage without any notification from the challengers.

3. *Political Fallout: The Court Strikes a Blow Against Conscience Exemptions.* The Employment Nondiscrimination Act (ENDA), which would prohibit workplace discrimination based on sexual orientation and gender identity, passed the Senate in November 2013 with a broad religious exemption. Less than a week after the *Wheaton College* dissent in 2014, most of the LGBT rights organizations withdrew their support from that version of ENDA, because they had reconsidered supporting exemptions in light of the broad sweep accorded RFRA by the Supreme Court. Essentially, the LGBT rights groups were saying that they no longer trusted the federal courts to read religious exemptions in a restrained way.

Likewise, when President Obama was considering an executive order adding sexual orientation and gender identity to the stated grounds for denying federal contracts to firms that discriminate, LGBT rights groups strongly urged the President not to include any religious exemptions. Is this a wise strategy by LGBT rights groups? Are they overreading Justice Alito's opinion for the Court?

PROBLEM 4-2
EXECUTIVE ORDER BARRING SEXUAL ORIENTATION AND GENDER IDENTITY DISCRIMINATION BY FEDERAL CONTRACTORS

On July 21, 2014, President Obama promulgated Executive Order 13672, amending earlier executive orders to prohibit discrimination in the civilian federal workforce on the basis of gender identity and to prohibit both gender identity and sexual orientation discrimination by federal contractors. Most major federal contractors already had such nondiscrimination policies, but this was considered an important initiative. With ENDA abandoned by LGBT rights groups after *Hobby Lobby* and job discrimination legislation bogged down in a gridlocked Congress, the executive order was a big move, as it would cover as much as a quarter of the nation's workforce.

On June 25, 160 religious leaders (including Leith Anderson, President of the National Association of Evangelicals) sent a letter to the President, imploring him to exempt religious organizations from the anticipated executive order, at least as generous as those in Title VII. On July 1, Reverend Rick Warren (an Evangelical who delivered the prayer at the President's first inauguration) and other prominent religious leaders reminded the President that his initial reluctance on same-sex marriage was grounded in sincere religious beliefs and urged him "to find a way to respect the diversity of opinion" on these issues. Senator Orrin Hatch, a conservative sponsor of ENDA, urged the President to include the religious exemptions included in ENDA when it passed the Senate in 2013.

In July, the LGBT groups withdrew their support for ENDA, because of the religious exemptions (and the possibility of their broad interpretation by the *Hobby Lobby* Court). On July 15, sixty-nine civil rights organizations and progressive religious groups petitioned the President to issue the anticipated executive order with *no* religious exemptions and, instead, to rescind religious protections added by President Bush's Executive Order 13,279 (2002). The earlier order protected the right of religious organizations engaged in social service activities to employ "individuals of a particular religion."

The President's July 21 executive order included no new religious exemptions but left the 2002 exemption in place. Father Larry Snyder, the

President of Catholic Charities, praised the President's restraint, and Professor Doug Laycock applauded the retention of the 2002 exemption. The Family Research Council, the Traditional Values Coalition, and other faith-based organizations condemned the order because it lacked a broad religious exemption. On December 3, 2014, the Department of Labor issued rules for enforcing the mandate by agencies; individuals discriminated against have no private cause of action to enforce the executive order.

You are the Assistant Attorney General who heads the Office of Legal Counsel in the Department of Justice. On June 26, 2014, the White House Counsel asks you for your opinion, in response to the Leith Anderson et al. letter, whether the anticipated executive order, without any new religious exemptions, would violate RFRA as applied, for example, to Hobby Lobby. That is, if Hobby Lobby were a government contractor, would it violate RFRA for a federal agency to terminate contracting with Hobby Lobby solely because, for faith-based reasons, it does not have an antidiscrimination policy to protect LGBT employees?

Postscript. On March 27, 2017, President Trump rescinded a companion order, Executive Order 13,673, issued by President Obama to require companies seeking to do business with the federal government to keep and produce documents demonstrating their compliance with applicable federal laws and executive orders (including of course Executive Order 13,672, issued to protect LGBT employees). White House rumors say there is a "religious freedom" executive order in the works. If you were Leith Anderson, how would you advise the President to proceed along these lines?

NOTES ON POST-*HOBBY LOBBY* EFFORTS TO UPDATE JUNIOR-RFRAS

After *Hobby Lobby*, religious groups have sought to update state junior-RFRAs to protect corporations as well as religious organizations and private persons. Recall that *Hobby Lobby* was decided a year after *Windsor* and the year before *Obergefell*—in other words, at the very point in time when LGBT rights organizations were on a winning streak. To the surprise of most observers, that winning streak continued in the legislatures of some of the reddest of states.

1. *Arizona.* In 1999, Arizona adopted a junior-RFRA. Ariz. Rev. Stat. Ann. § 41–1493. This law, like the federal RFRA, provides that the state government can only "substantially burden a person's exercise of religion" if the burden is "[i]n furtherance of a compelling government interest" and "[t]he least restrictive means of furthering that compelling government interest." Ariz. Rev. Stat. Ann. § 41–1493.01(C). In contrast to the broader definition in the federal RFRA, however, the Arizona law defined "person" to mean religious assemblies or institutions. Ariz. Rev. Stat. Ann. § 41–1493. After *Hobby Lobby*, in February 2014, the Arizona legislature passed Senate Bill 1062 ("S.B. 1062"), which sought to redefine "person" to mean "any individual association, partnership, corporation, church, religious assembly or institution, estate, trust, foundation or other legal entity."

Opponents expressed concern that if S.B. 1062 were signed into law, it would permit corporations to legally discriminate against gay and lesbian patrons under the guise of religious freedom. Civil rights groups, gay rights groups, the Chamber of Commerce, and many businesses joined in opposing the bill. The National Football League (NFL) issued a statement emphasizing that it supported tolerance and inclusiveness and was following the debate over S.B. 1062 in Arizona. Media outlets speculated that the NFL's statement signaled an intention to relocate future Super Bowls out of Arizona if S.B. 1062 went into effect. In the face of opposition from business leaders, Governor Jan Brewer (a conservative Republican) vetoed the legislation on February 26, 2014.

2.   *Arkansas.* One year after Governor Brewer of Arizona vetoed amendments to the state's religious freedom laws, the Arkansas Legislature began debating a similar statute. On February 10, 2015, state representative Robert Ballinger introduced the Freedom of Conscience Act (H.B. 1228). Modeled after federal law, H.B. 1228 said that a state action could not "substantially burden a person's right to exercise of religion" unless the substantial burden was the least restrictive means of furthering a compelling governmental interest. Like Arizona's vetoed S.B. 1062, Arkansas's H.B. 1228 defined "person" broadly to mean any legal entity (hence, partnerships, nonprofit companies, for-profit close corporations like Hobby Lobby, and large for-profit corporations). It also went further than federal law and other states' religious freedom laws by allowing a "person" to assert "the violation or *impending* violation" of religious freedom as a defense in a lawsuit, even if the adverse party was a private litigant. *See* H.B. 1228 (emphasis added).

H.B. 1228 passed the Arkansas Legislature on March 31, 2015. As in Arizona, there was a backlash from civil rights groups and employers—including Walmart, the largest company in the state. Opponents of the law argued that it would allow businesses the freedom to discriminate on the basis of sexual orientation. As hundreds of protestors descended on the state capitol, Governor Asa Hutchinson announced that he would not sign the bill as written. In response, the Legislature passed a compromise version of the legislation, S.B. 975. The compromise legislation tracked the federal RFRA closely and removed the most controversial elements of H.B. 1228. In particular, S.B. 975 removed the expansive definition of "persons," and was written such that a person can only invoke their religious liberty in litigation where the government is a party; the law cannot be invoked as a defense in a lawsuit between two private parties. See Ark. Code Ann. § 16–123. On April 2, 2015, Gov. Hutchinson signed the compromise bill into law.

3.   *Indiana.* At the same time Arkansas was considering H.B. 1228, the Indiana Legislature enacted a junior-RFRA. As in other states and at the federal level, the Indiana law provides that the government cannot substantially burden a "person's exercise of religion," even if the burden results from a generally applicable rule, unless the government can show that the burden (1) furthers a compelling government interest and (2) is the least restrictive means of furthering that interest. Ind. Code Ann. § 34–13–9–8(b). But as in Arizona and Arkansas, Indiana's junior-RFRA went further

than the federal RFRA. It defined "person" to include corporations and other organizations that are capable of being sued and exercising religious views. Ind. Code Ann. § 34–13–9–7. It also permits any person sued to assert a defense in any action based on a sincerely held religious belief. Though the law did not expressly refer to sexual orientation, critics charged that it would effectively provide a license to businesses to discriminate against LGBT people without fear of legal repercussions.

Indiana's junior-RFRA prompted immediate and widespread controversy, as business leaders and activists condemned the law and announced an intent to boycott the state. In response to this criticism, Indiana amended the law in April 2015 to clarify that the junior-RFRA does not "authorize a provider to refuse to offer or provide services, facilities, use of public accommodations, goods, employment, or housing . . . on the basis of . . . sexual orientation [or] gender identity." Ind. Code Ann. § 34–13–9–0.7(1). Nor does it "establish a defense" for a refusal to provide services on the basis of sexual orientation or gender identity. Ind. Code Ann. § 34–13–9–0.7(2). LGBT advocates agreed these amendments represented an improvement, though most remained critical of the law. The anti-discrimination amendments also provoked a fresh round of criticism from advocates for religious freedom who worried that the amendments undermined the law's original purpose of protecting the exercise of sincerely held religious beliefs.

Query. What do these red state episodes tell us about the federal RFRA and *Hobby Lobby*? A big lesson is that the cultural meaning of "religious freedom" has been transformed by the abortion and gay marriage debates. In 1993, when RFRA was adopted by overwhelming bipartisan majorities, religious freedom was understood in libertarian terms: protect Native American rituals (the subject of burden in *Smith*), Saturday Sabbatarians (as in *Sherbert*), traditionalist parents, and other "little guys" against Big Brother, government bullying.

By 2014–15, religious liberty meant freedom of traditionalists not to cooperate with women needing abortions (or even contraceptives) and "homosexuals" needing assistance securing marriage licenses and then celebrating their marriages. The Chamber of Commerce and the Business Roundtable did not care about the peyote ritual at issue in *Smith*, and they were not actively engaged in the *Hobby Lobby* litigation, but they were very much engaged in support of sexual orientation anti-discrimination protections and hostile to any expansion of religious exemptions. This explains the implosion of GOP support for that agenda.

SECTION 2

SPECIFIC RELIGIOUS EXEMPTIONS FROM ANTIDISCRIMINATION LAWS

The red state disarray as religious leaders sought to expand state junior-RFRAs, and the high drama over the *Hobby Lobby* decision, stand in some contrast to the red state politics in Utah in 2015. During the autumn of 2014, the leadership of the Church of Jesus Christ of the Latter-day Saints (LDS, the Mormons) decided to support an amendment adding sexual orientation and gender identity to the state laws barring discrimination in the workplace and in housing (but not public accommodation discrimination).[a] With the LDS Church in the background, the GOP leadership negotiated with Equality Utah to add sexual orientation and gender identity to the jobs and housing laws, with specific exemptions added to protect the Boy Scouts (as an employer) and BYU (its married student housing), as well as employee speech on matters of religion, sexual morals, and marriage.

Although the celebrated "Utah Compromise" has not been replicated in another red state since 2015, it does represent a "way forward," for both LGBT and religious groups. At present, LGBT groups seem to be more resistant to compromise—a stance that may change if a religious constitutional challenge to antidiscrimination laws were to be accepted by the Supreme Court.

Robin Fretwell Wilson, "When Governments Insulate Dissenters from Social Change: What *Hobby Lobby* and Abortion Conscience Clauses Teach Us About Specific Exemptions," 48 *U.C. Davis L. Rev.* 703, 717–23 (2014). The legal architect and primary drafter of the Utah Compromise, Professor Wilson contrasts the RFRA approach with the specific exemptions approach followed in the Utah statutes. "The [g]eneralized protections, like those in RFRA and RLUIPA, and specific exemptions both seek to preserve religious liberty but do so in different ways that yield quite different burdens and impacts. Legislatures enact generalized protections to protect believers of all religions from the burdens of facially neutral, generally applicable laws that adversely affect legitimate religious practice. Generalized

---

[a] LDS support for LGBT rights was a process that followed huge backlash, within and outside the Church, for the decisive role the Mormons played in passing Proposition 8 in California in 2008. Facing the loss of a generation of youth and significant embarrassment as the face of antigay discrimination, the Church opened up a dialogue with Equality Utah in 2009 and moved in fits and starts toward endorsing state legislation by late 2014. See William Eskridge Jr., "Latter-Day Constitutionalism: Sexuality, Gender, and Mormons," 2016 *Ill. L. Rev.* 1227.

protections are necessary because legislatures cannot possibly craft specific exemptions to anticipate the entire range of conflicts that might arise between the obligations of law and the obligations of faith, years in advance."

"To police the varied forms that government overreaching may take, generalized protections must necessarily be written as standards, not rules. Thus, RFRA instructs and entrusts judges to 'strik[e] sensible balances between religious liberty and competing *prior* governmental interests.' Because judges (and agency officials when writing regulations) find the facts and balance the competing interests whenever a collision arises, whether a duty under a challenged statute will apply usually cannot be known in advance.

"By contrast, specific exemptions respond to predictable, foreseeable collisions between the demands of a new social order and the demands of faith, often in the *same* legislation that effects the social change. Unlike generalized protections, specific exemptions resolve one particular social conflict or address one religious practice at a time. Thus, legislatures have enacted abortion conscience clauses, conscience clauses about dispensing emergency contraceptives, conscience protections for certain religious beliefs governing definitions of death, and sundry other matters. Most provide easily enforceable, bright-line rules to resolve certain foreseeable clashes between religious strictures and legal obligations that would otherwise flow from a new legal regime, like the right to abortion after *Roe v. Wade*. Unlike RFRA, which employs a single standard to protect all faiths, specific exemptions may be crafted by legislatures to suit individual religious practices and conflicts."

"The standard-like approach taken in RFRA and RLUIPA serves a second purpose that specific exemptions do not readily serve. The heightened scrutiny under RFRA and RLUIPA protects minority faiths too unpopular to garner the political support necessary to secure a specific exemption in the political process. * * * By contrast, specific exemptions are much more majoritarian. Sometimes they result from nearly unanimous support for permitting a particular religious group or the adherents of a particular belief to wall themselves off from social change, as the Church Amendment allowed abortion objectors to do.

"A third difference also emerges between generalized protections and specific exemptions: likelihood of enforcement. While judges applying RFRA or RLUIPA might balk at a balancing test in which they are forced to consider all the facts and circumstances, courts are generally quicker to enforce a clearly written rule. Yet, entrusting judges to protect religious freedom has advantages over the political process. Under generalized protections, judges find the facts and balance the competing interests. In contrast, with specific exemptions written as rules, legislators do. Judges sometimes stumble at this, but legislators may be prejudiced by off-the-record discussions and rarely conduct serious empirical investigations of political issues. With a generalized protection, each side marshals its evidence and presents it case before a judge who is focused (presumably) on only that case and is largely insulated from political pressure."

In light of these differences, Professor Wilson also argues that specific exemptions are not subject to the strong criticisms that have been leveled against RFRAs: lack of predictability, hardship for third parties denied important rights, and impediments to social progress. As to the third criticism, Professor Wilson documents the importance of specific religious exemptions contained in marriage equality legislation adopted by eleven states before *Windsor*: Vermont (2009), Connecticut (2009), New Hampshire (2009), New York (2011), Maryland (2012), Washington (2012), Delaware (2013), Hawaii (2013), Illinois (2013), Minnesota (2013), and Rhode Island (2013). In all but three of these jurisdictions (Connecticut, Hawaii, and Rhode Island), the vote for marriage equality was close in one or both chambers of the state legislatures, and Wilson claims that the presence of religious exemptions made the difference between victory and defeat in all of these jurisdictions. That is, without conscience clauses, key legislators (Democrats as well as Republicans) would not have voted for those laws.

"In every instance, jurisdictions that voluntarily embraced same-sex marriage built in important, if imperfect, protections for religious organizations and individuals who adhere to a heterosexual view of marriage * * *. These protections for dissenters largely exempt church-affiliated organizations from requirements to celebrate or facilitate marriages inconsistent with their religious beliefs—for example, by providing a reception hall for a wedding or opening marriage retreats to couples in marriages that the organization cannot recognize consistent with its religious tenets. Some states extend protections to religiously affiliated adoption or social services agencies, fraternal organizations, or universities that provide student housing.

"Absent such protections for non-clergy members, same-sex marriage bills uniformly fail to become law. Beginning with the earliest attempt to voluntarily enact same-sex marriage in 2004, every time state legislators introduced proposed legislation shorn of protections for anyone other than the clergy—who simply do not need protection given the First Amendment—that proposed legislation has failed. By contrast, when state legislatures began acting, as Vermont did in 2004, to 'allow[ ] [religious organizations] to keep doing the things they've always done,' the effort to voluntarily recognize same-sex marriage gathered momentum."

For example, the New Hampshire Legislature passed a marriage bill by a handful of votes in each chamber in 2009, but Governor John Lynch threatened to veto the bill if it was not amended to contain broadened protections for religious institutions and organizations. Sponsors amended the bill to allow certain religious organizations and their employees to refuse to facilitate the celebration or solemnization of any marriage, and to release them from any duty to promote marriages "through religious counseling . . . or housing designated for married individuals." Covered objectors received immunity from civil suit and insulation from government penalty.

Maryland's experience was just as dramatic. In 2008 and 2009, marriage bills with protections only for clergy (not really needed in light of constitutional protections) failed in the Maryland Legislature. The Maryland Senate added further protections in 2011, but time ran out before that bill could be considered by the House of Delegates. In 2012, Governor Martin O'Malley pressed for a bill that also shielded religious adoption agencies—and that bill was enacted, albeit by slender margins. O'Malley signed the bill into law on March 1, 2012, and it survived a referendum challenge in November 2012. Speaker of the House of Delegates Michael Busch reported that the adoption agency allowance was essential to enactment of this law. The Roman Catholic Church has its lobbying office a few houses down the hill from the state capitol building, and its lobbyists have a strong ongoing relationship with many legislators. Several devout Protestant as well as Catholic legislators said the conscience exemptions were important to their ultimate support for the law.

"As in New Hampshire and Maryland, in every jurisdiction to pass same-sex marriage legislation (except Minnesota and Delaware), successful legislation followed unsuccessful attempts to enact same-sex marriage *with* purely symbolic protections limited only to the clergy. Thus, although counter-intuitive for some, thicker protections for religious believers advanced the interests of same-sex marriage advocates."

NOTE ON STATUTORY EXEMPTIONS FOR RELIGIOUS ORGANIZATIONS

Professor Wilson's main punch line is that conscience exemptions were necessary for marriage equality statutes between 2004 and 2013—but all of the advances for marriage equality after 2013 were the result of state and federal court orders, grounded on constitutional requirements. Hence, in those states there were no legislative exemptions for religious organizations. A large majority of the court order states had no state-wide antidiscrimination law that included sexual orientation and/or gender identity. Although municipalities in those states had such laws, they were often not enforceable through private lawsuits, and so threats to religious liberty were not felt as keenly.

From an LGBT rights point of view, what are the virtues of including specific conscience allowances in the new marriage equality regimes? Would such allowances render the new regimes more legitimate? Reduce popular backlash against them? What organizations should receive exemptions, and how broad should they be?

An important limitation of the statutory exemptions is that almost all of them tend to protect religious *institutions*, but not religious *persons*. The latter are protected by RFRA and junior-RFRAs. The last Note in Section 1 revealed the difficult politics that now accompanies efforts, even in red states, to expand junior-RFRA protections.

Religious freedom groups—including powerhouse litigation groups Alliance Defending Freedom (ADF) and the American Center for Law and Justice (ACLJ)—have seized upon applications of public accommodations laws to small business to press for First Amendment protection for religious persons and businesses that do not want to be "complicit" with gay weddings and other public events celebrating LGBT people and their unions. While not ignoring the Free Exercise Clause, ADF and ACLJ have emphasized the Speech Clause in their challenges to state antidiscrimination laws as applied to religious florists, bakers, and photographers who have declined to participate in gay weddings. Before reading the cases that follow, you might want to review the "compelled speech" cases (*Hurley* and *FAIR*) excerpted in Chapter 1. The leading case, involving an owner-run photography business represented by ADF, immediately follows.

Elane Photography, LLC v. Vanessa Willock

New Mexico Supreme Court, 2013.
309 P.3d 53.

■ CHAVEZ, JUSTICE.

* * * Vanessa Willock contacted Elane Photography, LLC, by e-mail to inquire about Elane Photography's services and to determine whether it would be available to photograph her commitment ceremony to another woman. Elane Photography's co-owner and lead photographer, Elaine Huguenin, is personally opposed to same-sex marriage and will not photograph any image or event that violates her religious beliefs. Huguenin responded to Willock that Elane Photography photographed only "traditional weddings." Willock e-mailed back and asked, "Are you saying that your company does not offer your photography services to same-sex couples?" Huguenin responded, "Yes, you are correct in saying we do not photograph same-sex weddings," and thanked Willock for her interest. * * *

Willock filed a discrimination complaint against Elane Photography with the New Mexico Human Rights Commission for discriminating against her based on her sexual orientation in violation of the New Mexico Human Rights Act (NMHRA). [ADF counsel represented Elane Photography, but Willock prevailed before the Commission, the state trial court and the Court of Appeals.]

[The Statutory Issue] Elane Photography argues that it did not violate the NMHRA because it did not discriminate on the basis of sexual orientation when it refused service to Willock. Instead, Elane Photography explains that it "did not want to convey through [Huguenin]'s pictures the story of an event celebrating an understanding of marriage that conflicts with [the owners'] beliefs." Elane Photography argues that it would have taken portrait photographs and performed other services for same-sex customers, so long as they did not request photographs that involved or endorsed same-sex weddings. However, Elane Photography's owners testified that they would also have refused to take photos of same-sex couples in other contexts, including photos of a couple holding hands or showing affection for each other. * * * Therefore, Elane Photography reasons that it did not discriminate "because of . . . sexual orientation," but because it did not wish to endorse Willock's and Collinsworth's wedding.

The NMHRA prohibits discrimination in broad terms by forbidding "any person in any public accommodation to make a distinction, *directly or indirectly,* in offering or refusing to offer its services . . . because of . . . sexual orientation." Section 28–1–7(F) (emphasis added). Elane Photography is primarily a wedding photography business. It provides wedding photography services to heterosexual couples, but it refuses to work with homosexual couples under equivalent circumstances.

Elane Photography's argument is an attempt to distinguish between an individual's status of being homosexual and his or her conduct in openly committing to a person of the same sex. It was apparently Willock's e-mail request to have Elane Photography photograph Willock's commitment ceremony to another woman that signaled Willock's sexual orientation to Elane Photography, regardless of whether that assessment was real or merely perceived. The difficulty in distinguishing between status and conduct in the context of sexual orientation discrimination is that people may base their judgment about an individual's sexual orientation on the individual's conduct. To allow discrimination based on conduct so closely correlated with sexual orientation would severely undermine the purpose of the NMHRA. * * *

[W]hen a law prohibits discrimination on the basis of sexual orientation, that law similarly protects conduct that is inextricably tied to sexual orientation. Otherwise we would interpret the NMHRA as protecting same-gender couples against discriminatory treatment, but only to the extent that they do not openly display their same-gender sexual orientation.

In this case, we see no basis for distinguishing between discrimination based on sexual orientation and discrimination based on someone's conduct of publicly committing to a person of the same sex. Our role is to determine and follow the intent of the Legislature, and the NMHRA evinces a clear intent to prevent discrimination as it is broadly defined. * * *

We are not persuaded by Elane Photography's argument that it does not violate the NMHRA because it will photograph a gay person (for example, in single-person portraits) so long as the photographs do not reflect the client's sexual preferences. The NMHRA prohibits public accommodations from making any distinction in the services they offer to customers on the basis of protected classifications. For example, if a restaurant offers a full menu to male customers, it may not refuse to serve entrees to women, even if it will serve them appetizers. The NMHRA does not permit businesses to offer a "limited menu" of goods or services to customers on the basis of a status that fits within one of the protected categories. Therefore, Elane Photography's willingness to offer some services to Willock does not cure its refusal to provide other services that it offered to the general public. * * * Therefore, we hold that Elane Photography discriminated against Willock on the basis of sexual orientation in violation of the NMHRA. * *

[The Free Speech Issues] Elane Photography observes that photography is an expressive art form and that photographs can fall within the constitutional protections of free speech. Elane Photography also states that in the course of its business, it creates and edits photographs for its clients so as to tell a positive story about each wedding it photographs, and the company and its owners would prefer not to send a positive message about same-sex weddings or same-sex marriage. Elane Photography concludes that by requiring it to photograph same-sex weddings on the same basis that it photographs opposite-sex weddings, the NMHRA unconstitutionally compels it to "create and engage in expression" that sends a positive message about same-sex marriage not shared by its owner. * * *

* * * [T]he NMHRA does not require Elane Photography to recite or display any message. It does not even require Elane Photography to take photographs. The NMHRA only mandates that if Elane Photography operates a business as a public accommodation, it cannot discriminate against potential clients based on their sexual orientation. * * *

* * * The fact that compliance with the NMHRA will require Elane Photography to produce photographs for same-sex weddings to the extent that it would provide those services to a heterosexual couple does not mean that the NMHRA compels speech. * * * Elane Photography's argument here is [ ] analogous to the claims raised by the law schools in *Rumsfeld v. FAIR*. In that case, a federal law made universities' federal funding contingent on the universities allowing military recruiters access to university facilities and services on the same basis as other, non-military recruiters. A group of law schools that objected to the ban on gays in the military challenged the law on a number of constitutional grounds, including that the law in question compelled them to speak the government's message. In order to assist the military recruiters, schools had to provide services that involved speech, "such as sending e-mails and distributing flyers."

The United States Supreme Court held that this requirement did not constitute compelled speech. The Court observed that the federal law "neither limits what law schools may say nor requires them to say anything." Schools were compelled only to provide the type of speech-related services to military recruiters that they provided to non-military recruiters. "There [was] nothing ... approaching a Government-mandated pledge or motto that the school [had to] endorse."

The same situation is true in the instant case. Like the law in *Rumsfeld,* the NMHRA does not require any affirmation of belief by regulated public accommodations; instead, it requires businesses that offer services to the public at large to provide those services without regard for race, sex, sexual orientation, or other protected classifications. The fact that these services may involve speech or other expressive services does not render the NMHRA unconstitutional. Elane Photography is compelled to take photographs of same-sex weddings only to the extent that it would provide the same services to a heterosexual couple.

The second line of compelled-speech cases deals with situations in which a government entity has required a speaker to "host or accommodate another speaker's message." Elane Photography argues that a same-sex wedding or commitment ceremony is an expressive event, and that by requiring it to accept a client who is having a same-sex wedding, the NMHRA compels it to facilitate the messages inherent in that event. Elane Photography argues that there are two messages conveyed by a same-sex wedding or commitment ceremony: first, that such ceremonies exist, and second, that these occasions deserve celebration and approval. Elane Photography does not wish to convey either of these messages. * * *

The NMHRA does not, nor could it, regulate the content of the photographs that Elane Photography produces. It does not, for example, mandate that Elane Photography take posed photographs rather than candid shots, nor does it require every wedding album to contain a picture of the bride's bouquet. Indeed, the NMHRA does not mandate that Elane Photography choose to take wedding pictures; that is the exclusive choice of Elane Photography. Like all public accommodation laws, the NMHRA regulates "the act of discriminating against individuals in the provision of publicly available goods, privileges, and services on the proscribed grounds." Elane Photography argues that because the service it provides is photography, and because photography is expressive, "some of [the] images will inevitably express the messages inherent in [the] event." In essence, then, Elane Photography argues that by limiting its ability to choose its clients, the NMHRA forces it to produce photographs expressing its clients' messages even when the messages are contrary to Elane Photography's beliefs.

Elane Photography has misunderstood this issue. It believes that because it is a photography business, it cannot be subject to public accommodation laws. The reality is that because it is a public accommodation, its provision of services can be regulated, even though those services include artistic and creative work. If Elane Photography took photographs on its own time and sold them at a gallery, or if it was hired by certain clients but did not offer its services to the general public, the law would not apply to Elane Photography's choice of whom to photograph or not. The difference in the present case is that the photographs that are allegedly compelled by the NMHRA are photographs that Elane Photography produces for hire in the ordinary course of its business as a public accommodation. This determination has no relation to the artistic merit of photographs produced by Elane Photography. If Annie Leibovitz or Peter Lindbergh worked as public accommodations in New Mexico, they would be subject to the provisions of the NMHRA. * * * Elane Photography sells its expressive services to the public. It may be that Elane Photography expresses its clients' messages in its photographs, but only because it is hired to do so. The NMHRA requires that Elane Photography perform the same services for a same-sex couple as it would for an opposite-sex couple; the fact that these services require photography stems from the nature of Elane Photography's chosen line of business. * * *

* * * [T]he NMHRA applies not to Elane Photography's photographs but to its business operation, and in particular, its business decision not to offer its services to protected classes of people. While photography may be expressive, the operation of a photography business is not. By way of analogy, the NMHRA could not dictate which groups a parade organizer had to include. However, if a business sold parade-planning services, and that business operated as a public accommodation, the NMHRA would prohibit that business from refusing to offer parade-planning services to persons because of their sexual orientation. * * *

Elane Photography also argues that if it is compelled to photograph same-sex weddings, observers will believe that it and its owners approve of same-sex marriage. The United States Supreme Court incorporates the question of perceived endorsement into its analysis in cases that involve compulsion to host or accommodate third-party speech. *See, e.g., Hurley* ("Without deciding on the precise significance of the likelihood of misattribution, it nonetheless becomes clear that in the context of an expressive parade . . . the parade's overall message is distilled from the individual presentations along the way, and each unit's expression is perceived by spectators as part of the whole."). * * *

Elane Photography makes an argument very similar to one rejected by the *Rumsfeld* Court: by treating customers alike, regardless of whether they are having same-sex or opposite-sex weddings, Elane Photography is concerned that it will send the message that it sees nothing wrong with same-sex marriage. Reasonable observers are unlikely to interpret Elane Photography's photographs as an endorsement of the photographed events. It is well known to the public that wedding photographers are hired by paying customers and that a photographer may not share the happy couple's views on issues ranging from the minor (the color scheme, the hors d'oeuvres) to the decidedly major (the religious service, the choice of bride or groom). * * * Elane

Photography is free to disavow, implicitly or explicitly, any messages that it believes the photographs convey.

[Free Exercise Issues] * * * It is an open question whether Elane Photography, which is a limited liability company rather than a natural person, has First Amendment free exercise rights. * * * However, it is not necessary for this Court to address whether Elane Photography has a constitutionally protected right to exercise its religion. Assuming that Elane Photography has such rights, they are not offended by enforcement of the NMHRA.

Under established law, "the right of free exercise does not relieve an individual of the obligation to comply with a valid and neutral law of general applicability on the ground that the law proscribes (or prescribes) conduct that his religion prescribes (or proscribes)." *Emp't Div., Dep't of Human Res. of Or. v. Smith,* 494 U.S. 872, 879 (1990) (internal quotation marks and citation omitted). In order to state a valid First Amendment free exercise claim, a party must show either (a) that the law in question is not a "neutral law of general applicability," *id.,* (internal quotation marks and citation omitted) or (b) that the challenge implicates both the Free Exercise Clause and an independent constitutional protection. * * *

[The New Mexico Supreme Court concluded that the exemptions in the NMHRA were not of the kind to render the statute not generally applicable, nor would they authorize the actions taken by defendant in this case. It also concluded that the Free Speech claims asserted by defendant, rejected *supra*, did not constitute a sufficient basis upon which to find that an independent constitutional right has been violated. The Court ruled that the New Mexico Religious Freedom Act was inapplicable, because the government was not a party.]

Postscript. The Supreme Court denied certiorari. 134 S.Ct. 1787 (April 2014). *Elane Photography* was the first major appellate decision for a small but steady stream of claims brought by disgruntled gay customers against small businesses run by persons whose religious faith believed that participation in any deviation from traditional one man, one woman marriage to be deeply immoral. ADF and ACLJ attorneys have represented most of the businesses, and some of the plaintiffs are represented by Lambda Legal or the ACLU. E.g., *State v. Arlene's Flowers, Inc.,* 389 P.3d 543 (Wash. 2017) (unanimously rejecting constitutional arguments advanced by ADF, representing a florist prosecuted under the state antidiscrimination law for refusing to deliver flowers for a gay wedding, whose participants were represented by the ACLU, with *amicus* briefs from NCLR and Lambda Legal).

Charlie Craig and David Mullins v. Masterpiece Cakeshop, **373 P.3d 272 (Colo. App.).** In July 2012, Craig and Mullins visited Masterpiece Cakeshop, a bakery in Lakewood, Colorado, and requested that Phillips design and create a cake to celebrate their same-sex wedding. A Christian who believes that decorating wedding cakes is a form of art and that decorating a gay wedding cake would be displeasing to God, Phillips declined, but told Craig and Mullins that he would be happy to make and sell them any other baked goods. Craig and Mullins filed charges with the Colorado agency enforcing the law barring sexual orientation discrimination by places of public accommodation, which includes bakeries. The Commission found a violation. ADF defended the bakery before the Commission and on appeal. Several LGBT rights groups filed *amicus* briefs in support of the Commission.

The Court of Appeals affirmed the Commission, in an opinion by **Judge Taubman**. As in *Elane Photography,* the business admitted that it was a "public accommodation" as broadly defined by the statute but claimed that it was not discriminating "because of sexual orientation." Masterpiece is happy to serve gay people—but not willing to engage in expressive conduct associated with a gay wedding. Like the New Mexico Supreme Court, the Colorado Court of Appeals refused to distinguish between the couple's status as gay and their "conduct closely associated with that status," namely, marrying someone of the same sex. *Accord, Christian Legal Society v. Martinez*, 561 U.S. 661, 689 (2010) (excerpted in Section 3, below).

Like Elane Photography, Masterpiece Cakeshop claimed that the state was compelling expression (i.e., "a celebratory message about marriage"), in violation of *Hurley* and other Supreme Court precedents. "We disagree. We conclude that the Commission's order merely requires that Masterpiece not discriminate against potential customers in violation of CADA [the Colorado antidiscrimination law] and that such conduct, even if compelled by the government, is not sufficiently expressive to warrant First Amendment protections.

"We begin by identifying the compelled conduct in question. As noted, the Commission's order requires that Masterpiece 'cease and desist from discriminating against [Craig and Mullins] and other same-sex couples by refusing to sell them wedding cakes or any product [it] would sell to heterosexual couples.' Therefore, the compelled conduct is the Colorado government's mandate that Masterpiece comport with CADA by not basing its decision to serve a potential client, at least in part, on the client's sexual orientation. This includes a requirement that Masterpiece sell wedding cakes to same-sex couples, but only if it wishes to serve heterosexual couples in the same manner. * * *

"We conclude that the act of designing and selling a wedding cake to all customers free of discrimination does not convey a celebratory message about same-sex weddings likely to be understood by those who view it. We further conclude that, to the extent that the public infers from a Masterpiece wedding cake a message celebrating same-sex marriage, that message is more likely to be attributed to the customer than to Masterpiece.

"First, Masterpiece does not convey a message supporting same-sex marriages merely by abiding by the law and serving its customers equally. In *FAIR,* several law schools challenged a federal law that denied funding to institutions of higher education that either prohibit or prevent military recruiters from accessing their campuses. The law schools argued that, by forcing them to treat military and nonmilitary recruiters alike, the law compelled them to send "the message that they see nothing wrong with the military's policies [regarding gays in the military], when they do." *Id.* The Court rejected this argument, observing that students "can appreciate the difference between speech a school sponsors and speech the school permits because legally required to do so."

"As in *FAIR,* we conclude that, because CADA prohibits all places of public accommodation from discriminating against customers because of their sexual orientation, it is unlikely that the public would view Masterpiece's creation of a cake for a same-sex wedding celebration as an endorsement of that conduct. Rather, we conclude that a reasonable observer would understand that Masterpiece's compliance with the law is not a reflection of its own beliefs.

" * * * The public recognizes that, as a for-profit bakery, Masterpiece charges its customers for its goods and services. The fact that an entity charges for its goods and services reduces the likelihood that a reasonable observer will believe that it supports the message expressed in its finished product. Nothing in the record supports the conclusion that a reasonable observer would interpret Masterpiece's providing a wedding cake for a same-sex couple as an endorsement of same-sex marriage, rather than a reflection of its desire to conduct business in accordance with Colorado's public accommodations law. See *FAIR.*

"For the same reason, this case also differs from *Hurley,* on which Masterpiece relies. There, the Supreme Court concluded that Massachusetts' public accommodations statute could not require parade organizers to include among the marchers in a St. Patrick's Day parade a group imparting a message the organizers did not wish to convey. Central to the Court's conclusion was the "inherent expressiveness of marching to make a point," and its observation that a "parade's overall message is distilled from the individual presentations along the way, and each unit's expression is perceived by spectators as part of the whole." The Court concluded that spectators would likely attribute each marcher's message to the parade organizers as a whole.

"In contrast, it is unlikely that the public would understand Masterpiece's sale of wedding cakes to same-sex couples as endorsing a celebratory message about same-sex marriage. * * *

"We also find the Supreme Court's holding in [*Nevada Commission on Ethics v. Carrigan* 564 U.S. 117 (2011)] instructive. There, the Court concluded that legislators do not have a personal, First Amendment right to vote in the legislative body in which they serve, and that restrictions on legislators' voting imposed by a law requiring recusal in instances of conflicts of interest are not restrictions on their protected speech. The Court rejected the argument that the act of voting was expressive conduct subject to First Amendment protections. Although the Court recognized that voting "discloses . . . that the legislator wishes (for whatever reason) that the proposition on the floor be adopted," it "symbolizes nothing" and is not "an act of communication" because it does not convey the legislator's reasons for the vote.* * *

"Finally, CADA does not preclude Masterpiece from expressing its views on same-sex marriage—including its religious opposition to it—and the bakery remains free to disassociate itself from its customers' viewpoints. We recognize that section 24–34–601(2)(a) of CADA prohibits Masterpiece from displaying or disseminating a notice stating that it will refuse to provide its services based on a customer's desire to engage in same-sex marriage or indicating that those engaging in same-sex marriage are unwelcome at the bakery. However, CADA does not prevent Masterpiece from posting a disclaimer in the store or on the Internet indicating that the provision of its services does not constitute an endorsement or approval of conduct protected by CADA. Masterpiece could also post or otherwise disseminate a message indicating that CADA requires it not to discriminate on the basis of sexual orientation and other protected characteristics. Such a message would likely have the effect of disassociating Masterpiece from its customers' conduct."

Judge Taubman also rejected Masterpiece Cakeshop's Free Exercise Clause claim. CADA is precisely the kind of law of general application that *Smith v. Employment Division* allowed, notwithstanding an incidental effect on religious free exercise. The compelled speech claim is too weak to elevate this case into the realm of "hybrid rights" claims (free exercise plus a serious infringement on another constitutional right). Finally, the Court declined to apply the Colorado Constitution's free exercise clause more liberally than the U.S. Supreme Court applied the federal Free Exercise Clause.

Postscript. On June 26, 2017, the last day of the 2016 Term, the Supreme Court has agreed to review the Colorado decision to determine whether the application to Masterpiece Cakeship violates the First Amendment. The case will be heard during the 2017 Term of the Court.

Lexington Fayette Urban County Human Rights Commission v. Hands On Originals, Inc., No. 2015-CA-000745-MR (Kentucky Court of Appeals, May 17, 2017). The Court overruled the Commission's finding that Hands On Originals (HOO) violated the county's ordinance barring sexual orientation discrimination by a public accommodation. Hands On prints customized T-shirts, mugs, pens, and other accessories. It declined an order from the Gay and Lesbian Services Organization (GLSO) to print T-shirts decorated with the words, "Lexington Pride Festival 2012." The owner explained that such an order would violate his Christian beliefs, because it would participate in "pride" for activities he considered sinful.

Chief Judge Kramer delivered the judgment of the Court, in an opinion only he joined. He ruled that HOO had not discriminated because of the GLSO's sexual orientation and had only discriminated because of the message the customer wanted HOO to produce. The owner testified that he never inquired about the sexual orientation of the GLSO representative, and Chief Judge Kramer found that GLSO has no sexual orientation: "it is a gender-neutral organization that functions as a *support network* and *advocate* for individuals who identify as gay, lesbian, bisexual, or transgendered" (emphasis in the original).

"In other words, the 'service' HOO offers is the promotion of *messages*. The 'conduct' HOO chose not to promote was pure speech. There is no contention that HOO is a public *forum* in addition to a public *accommodation*. Nothing in the fairness ordinance prohibits HOO, a private business, from engaging in *viewpoint* or *message* censorship." Thus, there was no discrimination against gay *people*. Indeed, the president of GLSO, the only person to deal with HOO, was openly straight.

Judge Lambert concurred only in the result. Following *Hobby Lobby,* he ruled that the Kentucky Religious Freedom Statute (Kentucky's junior-RFRA) precluded the Commission's relief. Accepting, arguendo, that HOO violated the antidiscrimination ordinance, Judge Lambert found that the ordinance substantially burdened HOO's freedom of religion (the Kentucky law applied to "persons," and Judge Lambert applied *Hobby Lobby* to interpret that term broadly). The county has a compelling interest in preventing businesses from discriminating because of sexual orientation, but the process in this case was not the "least restrictive means to further that interest" (the RFRA test, as well as that of the junior-RFRA).

The owner of HOO offered to find a printer who would do the work at the same price. "Here, instead of providing an owner of a closely-held business, or the like, with an alternative means of accommodating a patron who wishes to promote a cause contrary to the owner's faith, the fairness ordinance forces the owner to either join in the requested violation of a sincere religious belief, or face a penalty."

Judge Taylor dissented. Because "GLSO serves gays and lesbians and promotes an 'alternative lifestyle' that is contrary to some religious beliefs," and because HOO's refusal to deal was based on its owner's disapproval of "same-sex relationships," this is a straightforward case of discrimination because of sexual orientation. Indeed, *Obergefell* makes legal recognition of same-sex relationships the law of the land.

Judge Taylor did not consider *Hobby Lobby* binding on Kentucky state courts and did not find the state junior-RFRA applicable here. "[T]he statute does not prohibit a governmental entity from enforcing laws or ordinances that prohibit discrimination and protect a citizen's fundamental rights. * * * See *Bob Jones Univ. v. United States*, 461 U.S. 574 (1983) (holding that the government has an overriding interest in eradicating racial discrimination in education)."

NOTES ON FIRST AMENDMENT PROTECTION FOR SMALL BUSINESSES DECLINING TO COLLABORATE WITH GAY EVENTS

1. *Natural Law and Religious Freedom.* Natural law scholars such as Princeton Professor Robert George take the position that gay pride events and same-sex marriages are bad for society generally and, hence, that religious persons, companies, and institutions ought to have virtual carte blanche to opt out of the operation of antidiscrimination laws when they clash with religious faith traditions. ADF and ACLJ interpret the First Amendment along these lines. Such scholars and advocates celebrated *Hobby Lobby* and would read RFRA (and junior-RFRAs) liberally to protect conscience even when such protection would be at the expense of rights under antidiscrimination laws, as in *Elane Photography* and *Hands On Originals*. Other natural law scholars take the gentler position that on matters of significant moral disagreement—such as same-sex marriage—a pluralist society ought to accommodate both sides and not require either the traditionalist or the gay couple to give up foundational liberties.

Freedom of religion scholars and advocates not explicitly adopting the natural law perspective offer important arguments in favor of a broad reading of RFRA as well as Supreme Court First Amendment precedents such as *Hurley* (the Boston Parade Case) and *Dale* (the Boy Scouts Case), both discussed in Chapter 1. *Hurley* and *Dale* involved broad state court applications of public accommodations statutes to cover a parade and an expressive association, respectively. One precept to emerge from these precedents is that courts should be cautious about applying public accommodations laws to groups, associations, and even businesses that are not traditional "public accommodations" (i.e., hotels, restaurants, taxis). Judge Lambert suggests another idea: junior-RFRAs protect such nontraditional public accommodations against liability when there are alternative sources of the service needed by the gay person or organization.

A staunch supporter of RFRA and religious accommodations, Professor Douglas Laycock is often the author of *amicus* briefs supporting First Amendment defenses by small businesses owned by religious skeptics of marriage equality. Nonetheless, Professor Laycock warns natural law traditionalists that their intense opposition to marriage equality and equal treatment for gay people, as well as their broad opposition to contraception, pose deep risks to religion in America. He draws a parallel to the Catholic Church's fervent opposition to the French Revolution and its support for Counter-Revolution throughout the nineteenth century: That stance destroyed religion in France. The same risk is posed to traditionalist religion in America: By opposing the Sexual Revolution and frequently demonizing sexual and gender minorities, conservative, GOP-aligned religion risks its own relevance for the generation growing up with gay teachers, lesbian neighbors, same-sex couples raising children, and "homosexual" role models.

Douglas Laycock, "Religious Liberty and the Culture Wars," 2014 *U. Ill. L. Rev.* 839, 865–69.

2. *Liberal Theory.* Most of the academic debate over cases like *Elane Photography* has been from the liberal, rights-protecting perspective. Although such scholarship typically founders when liberal rights are squarely in conflict, a variety of intensely held positions has emerged. The position embraced by most liberal academics is expressed in Douglas NeJaime, "Marriage Inequality: Same-Sex Relationships, Religious Exemptions, and the Production of Sexual Orientation Discrimination," 100 *Calif. L. Rev.* 1169 (2012). Professor NeJaime argues that conscience exemptions reflect the fallback position of religious opponents of marriage equality and should be viewed skeptically, lest they open the door to widespread discrimination against lesbian and gay couples.[b] This perspective is reflected in the *Elane Photography* majority opinion and the *Hands On Originals* dissent.

The liberal theory that undergirds the NeJaime position seems to be the idea that the state should be neutral in moral debates and should, therefore, abstain from giving special exemptions to groups whose moral message is that homosexual relations are immoral or, more gently, marriage is ideally a procreative union between man and wife. Traditional family values scholars are quick to observe, however, that gay marriage finds the state taking a strong and novel moral position, that "homosexual" relations are comparable to procreative marital ones. If gay rights supporters are confident of the justness of their victory, shouldn't they be happy to see it openly debated in the marketplace of ideas and vigorously contested in the marketplace of good. *See* Sherif Girgis, "Nervous Victors, Illiberal Measures" (YLS Substantial Paper 2016).

Like Girgis but from within the liberal tradition, Professor Andrew Koppelman starts with a pluralistic norm: Why raise the stakes of politics by penalizing traditionalist photographers, bakers, and florists? Just as gay people resented government efforts to control their identities by forcing them to hide their relationships, so religious people like Elaine Huguenin resent government efforts to control their identities by forcing them to participate in gay weddings that they consider immoral. Censorship of politically incorrect photographers, bakers, printers, and florists only creates scapegoats. Drawing from the purposes of anti-discrimination law (amelioration of economic inequality, preventing dignitary harms, signaling norms of tolerance for minorities), Koppelman argues that individual actors and small businesses (like Elane Photography and Hands On Originals) ought to be accommodated, but that businesses covered by antidiscrimination laws (usually with more than fifteen employees) should not. See Andrew Koppelman, "Gay Rights, Religious Accommodations, and

---

[b] *Accord,* Douglas NeJaime & Reva Siegel, "Conscience Wars: Complicity-Based Conscience Claims in Religion and Politics," 124 *Yale L.J.* 2516 (2015); James M. Oleske, Jr., "The Evolution of Accommodation: Comparing the Unequal Treatment of Religious Objections to Interracial and Same-Sex Marriages," 50 *Harv. C.R.-C.L. L. Rev.* 99, 104 (2015) (concluding "that if a state were to follow the advice of many academic commentators and adopt exemptions designed to allow businesses to refuse services and benefits to same-sex couples, it would run afoul of the Equal Protection Clause").

the Purposes of Antidiscrimination Law," 88 *S. Cal. L. Rev.* 619, 621–22, 630–38 (2015).[c]

3. *The First Amendment Tradition.* Writing from within the First Amendment tradition, Professor Greenawalt argues for some accommodation of religious dissenters. See Kent Greenawalt, *Exemptions: Necessary, Justified, or Misguided?* (2016). He distinguishes between expressive and nonexpressive businesses. The former, like the Boy Scouts protected in *Dale*, should be accommodated and not required to "participate" in a gay wedding of which its owners disapprove. The latter ought not have an exemption. Thus, the wedding photographer ought to receive First Amendment protection, while the wedding cake baker ought not. *Id.* at 170–71. Where would Hands On Originals fit into this analysis?

Professor Koppelman dissents from that resolution, in part because he doubts that the expressive/nonexpressive business distinction is workable in this context, as illustrated by the inability of lower courts to figure out, after *Boy Scouts v. Dale,* exactly what organizations are "expressive associations."[d] Like most legal academics, he is unimpressed with constitutional arguments requiring the gay-friendly state to accommodate religious photographers as well as bakers and florists, but he also supports constitutional tolerance for religious bakers etc. to post, in their shops and on their websites, "not welcome" messages for gay weddings. The First Amendment prohibits the state from penalizing such messages. See Andrew Koppelman, "A Free Speech Response to the Gay Rights/Religious Liberty Conflict," 110 *Nw. U. L. Rev.* 1125, 1129–30 (2016).

Consider yet another First Amendment angle. In remarks at a Yale Law School conference on religious liberty and gay rights in January 2017, Professor Michael McConnell made an important distinction. He read from a news article describing the reluctance of many couture fashion firms to provide dresses for the current First Family (the Trumps). He was fine with that: If they want to express their dismay with President Trump by refusing to apply their talents to dress the First Lady, the First Amendment guarantees that freedom. But if Yves St. Laurent has a right not to participate in the pomp and circumstance of the Trump White House, why shouldn't Elane Photography not have a right not to participate in the pomp and circumstance of a gay wedding that is strongly antithetical to its owner's religion? Likewise, a baker should not be compelled to create a wedding cake adorned with a lesbian couple. McConnell distinguishes traditional public accommodations doing traditional accommodating: a hotel cannot turn away a gay couple seeking a room for the night, but it can decline to host a gay wedding. Is this a useful distinction? If you disagree, would you allow Melania Trump to sue Yves St. Laurent? Other tony fashionistas?

---

[c] See also Alan Brownstein, "Gays, Jews, and Other Strangers in A Strange Land: The Case for Reciprocal Accommodation of Religious Liberty and the Right of Same-Sex Couples to Marry," 45 U.S.F. L. Rev. 389 (2010).

[d] See Andrew Koppelman & Tobias Barrington Wolff, *A Right to Discriminate? How the Case of* Boy Scouts of America v. James Dale *Warped the Law of Free Association* (2009) (sharply critical of *Dale*).

Queries. You have read the views of eminent scholars: How would you vote in *Elane Photography*? *Hands On Originals*? *Masterpiece Cakeshop*? Why?

Proposed Marriage Conscience Protection Act

Section _____

(a) Religious organizations protected.

No religious or denominational organization, no organization operated for charitable or educational purposes which is supervised or controlled by or in connection with a religious organization, and no individual employed by any of the foregoing organizations, while acting in the scope of that employment, shall be required to

(1)   provide services, accommodations, advantages, facilities, goods, or privileges for a purpose related to the solemnization or celebration of any marriage; or

(2)   solemnize any marriage; or

(3)   treat as valid any marriage

if such providing, solemnizing, or treating as valid would cause such organizations or individuals to violate their sincerely held religious beliefs.

(b) Individuals and small businesses protected.

(1)   Except as provided in paragraph (b)(2), no individual, sole proprietor, or small business shall be required to

(A)   provide goods or services that assist or promote the solemnization or celebration of any marriage, or provide counseling or other services that directly facilitate the perpetuation of any marriage; or

(B)   provide benefits to any spouse of an employee; or

(C)   provide housing to any married couple

if providing such goods, services, benefits, or housing would cause such individuals or sole proprietors, or owners of such small businesses, to violate their sincerely held religious beliefs.

(2)   Paragraph (b)(1) shall not apply if

(A)   a party to the marriage is unable to obtain any similar good or services, employment benefits, or housing elsewhere without substantial hardship; or

(B)   in the case of an individual who is a government employee or official, if another government employee or official is not promptly available and willing to provide the requested government service without inconvenience or delay; *provided that* no judicial officer authorized to solemnize marriages shall be required to solemnize any marriage if to do so would violate the judicial officer's sincerely held religious beliefs.

(3) A "small business" within the meaning of paragraph (b)(1) is a legal entity other than a natural person

   (A) that provides services which are primarily performed by an owner of the business; or

   (B) that has five or fewer employees; or

   (C) in the case of a legal entity that offers housing for rent, that owns five or fewer units of housing.

(c) No civil cause of action or other penalties.

No refusal to provide services, accommodations, advantages, facilities, goods, or privileges protected by this section shall

(1) result in a civil claim or cause of action challenging such refusal; or

(2) result in any action by the State or any of its subdivisions to penalize or withhold benefits from any protected entity or individual, under any laws of this State or its subdivisions, including but not limited to laws regarding employment discrimination, housing, public accommodations, educational institutions, licensing, government contracts or grants, or tax-exempt status.

PROBLEM 4-3
APPLYING THE PROPOSED EXEMPTION LAW

No state has enacted the proposed legislation, and it is doubtful that any state would enact it in precisely this form—but the proposal might be treated as a starting point for negotiation among business groups, religious groups, and LGBT rights groups. If this were the governing statutory rule, how would a judge decide the following cases:

Wedding Service Providers. How would *Elane Photography* be decided under this law? How about *Masterpiece Cakeshop*? Would the statute protect a small owner-run bakery if a lesbian couple ordered a cake to celebrate their 50th anniversary as a couple?

Gay Pride. How would *Hands On Originals* be decided under this law? Would you revise the proposed text in light of this case?

Spousal Health Care Benefits. The Boy Scouts has a local office in the jurisdiction with this exemption law. There are 25 employees in the office, and one of them asks the Boy Scouts to add his same-sex spouse to his employer-provided spousal health insurance plan. Can the Boy Scouts be sued for refusing to do this?

SECTION 3

RELIGIOUS LIBERTY VS. LGBT EQUALITY CLASHES IN SCHOOLS

The clashes between TFV religious liberty and LGBT equality is especially pronounced in the nation's schools. Both TFV and LGBT groups consider schools an important forum for their competing messages. LGBT teen suicide is a huge phenomenon, and the turmoil suffered by minority youth can be ameliorated by supportive schools. Such support is the nightmare imagined by TFV parents, who do not want their children "exposed" to pro-gay messages that undermine what they are teaching at home. As you will easily see, the First Amendment is pervasively relevant in the legal clashes centered around schools, especially public schools and religious schools.

We start this section with an examination of a surprisingly broad array of state or local laws and policies that disparage or discriminate against LGBT people (Part A). Supporters of these policies have relied on religion-based arguments as well as the preferences of traditionalist (typically religious) parents. But these policies have not been the primary focus of liberty-equality clashes. The application of sexual orientation antidiscrimination laws to religious vendors, employers, schools, colleges, and universities has been fraught with controversy. Part B will focus on clashes involving religious vendors and employers, while Part C will focus on clashes involving colleges, universities, and high schools.

A. PUBLIC SCHOOL LGBT STUDENTS BURDENED BY NO PROMO HOMO AND ANTI-TRANS POLICIES

For most of the twentieth century, the big issue for public schools was whether they could tolerate openly gay or lesbian teachers. Generally, before Stonewall, almost no teacher was "out," but occasionally witch hunts would expose "homosexual" teachers, who would be quietly purged from the system. Most Americans believed that lesbian and gay people were unacceptable as teachers, because they would prey on the students.

In the 1970s and 1980s, more teachers inched out of the closet, and some of them were fired. Courts generally allowed schools to discriminate in this way, e.g., *Rowland v. Mad River Sch. Dist.*, 730 F.2d 444 (6th Cir. 1984) (excerpted in Chapter 3, § 3A), but by the 1990s the tide had turned and courts were usually willing to protect such public employees against discharge based only on their sexual orientation. Today, there are fewer public schools that will openly discriminate against LGBT teachers.

In these earlier decades, LGBT students were largely unseen but not heard. Today, public schools are teeming with students who are gay, gender-bending, undecided, and so forth. Gay-straight alliances have blossomed in high schools all over America. Nonetheless, a lot of states and school districts still operate under policies that are unfriendly or hostile to LGBT students.

Clifford Rosky, "Anti-Gay Curriculum Laws," (forthcoming 2017). Scholars have observed that several states have "no promo homo" education laws, namely, laws requiring teachers and curricula to avoid any support for "homosexuality." Professor Rosky's article is the most thorough survey and analysis of these kinds of laws and policies.

"While scholars and advocates have claimed that 'no promo homo' laws exist in seven, eight, or nine states, a comprehensive survey shows that anti-gay curriculum laws actually exist in twenty states.[a] More than 25 million children—nearly half of all school-aged children in the United States—are attending public schools in these twenty states. In half of these states, teachers are affirmatively required to teach anti-gay curricula in all public schools. In the other half, teachers may choose between offering students an anti-gay curriculum or providing no health, sex, or HIV education at all."

Professor Rosky identifies five different kinds of anti-gay curriculum laws: (1) "don't say gay" laws that bar any mention of homosexuality; (2) "no promo homo" laws that admonish against saying anything positive about homosexuality; (3) "anti-gay" policies requiring negative treatment of homosexuality; (4) "promo hetero" laws that require instruction promoting "monogamous heterosexual marriage"; and (5) "abstinence until marriage" laws, requiring teachers to emphasize "abstinence from sexual activity until marriage," while defining the term "marriage" to exclude same-sex couples (these laws are the most common, found in seventeen states). The most prominent example of an "abstinence until marriage" law is Title V of the Social Security Act, governing the distribution of funds for "abstinence education" programs.

Professor Rosky maintains that all of these laws violate the Equal Protection Clause. "In four rulings issued over a period of twenty years, the Supreme Court has invalidated anti-gay laws under the equal

---

[a] Ala. Code § 16–40A–2; Ariz. Rev. Stat. Ann. § 15–716; Ark. Code Ann. § 6–18–703; Florida Stat. Ann. § 1003.46; 105 Ill. Comp. Stat. Ann. 5/27–9.1; Ind. Code Ann. § 20–34–3–17(a) & § 20–30–5–13; La. Rev. Stat. § 17:281; Mich. Comp. Laws Ann. § 380.1507; Miss. Code Ann. § 37–13–171; Mo. Stat. Ann. § 170.015; N.C. Gen. Stat. Ann. § 115C–81; N.D. Cent. Code Ann. § 15.1–21–24; Ohio Rev. Code Ann. § 3313.6011; 70 Okla. Stat. Ann. § 11–103.3 (2016); S.C. Code Ann. § 59–32–30(A) (2016); Tenn. Code Ann. § 49–6–1304; Tex. Health & Safety Code Ann. § 85.007 & § 163.002; Utah Code Ann. § 53A–13–101; Va. Code Ann. § 22.1–207.1; Wis. Stat. Ann. § 118.019.

protection and due process guarantees of the Fifth and Fourteenth Amendments. Based on the principles articulated in these cases, [the article explains] how anti-gay curriculum laws injure and stigmatize lesbian, gay, and bisexual students, as well as students who are the children of same-sex couples. Like anti-gay sodomy and marriage laws, anti-gay curriculum laws demean the lives of lesbian, gay, and bisexual people, inviting others to discriminate against them. In particular, these laws promote a climate of silence and shame for lesbian, gay, and bisexual students, and students who are the children of same-sex couples, by instructing them that 'homosexuality' is so shameful, immoral, or unlawful that it should not be discussed. By doing so, these laws deny this class of students an equal opportunity to learn basic information about themselves and their families—information about the social prevalence and legal status of their own feelings, relationships, identities, and family members. Finally, anti-gay curriculum laws contribute to the pervasive isolation, bullying and harassment experienced by LGBT students in our nation's schools, exposing them to increased risks of pregnancy, HIV, school dropout, unemployment, and suicide."

Professor Rosky then "explains why these laws are not rationally related to any legitimate governmental interests. In particular, he reviews and rejects four interests that state legislatures have historically invoked to justify anti-gay curriculum laws: (1) promoting moral disapproval of homosexual conduct; (2) promoting children's heterosexual development; (3) preventing sexually transmitted infections; and (4) recognizing that States have broad authority to prescribe the curriculum of public schools. "Under the principles articulated in *Romer v. Evans*, *Lawrence v. Texas*, and *United States v. Windsor*, the first and second interests do not qualify as legitimate. The third and fourth interests qualify as legitimate, but anti-gay curriculum laws are not rationally related to either of them. Although no court has ruled on the issue yet, the Supreme Court's jurisprudence leaves no doubt that anti-gay curriculum laws violate the Constitution's equal protection guarantees.

"Since the Supreme Court's invalidation of anti-gay marriage laws, scholars and advocates have begun asking 'what's next' for the LGBT movement. The article concludes by explaining why LGBT advocates have waited until now to launch a campaign against anti-gay curriculum laws—and why they should not wait any longer. As long as anti-gay sodomy and anti-gay marriage laws were enforceable, anti-gay curriculum laws could have been justified by reference to them—as the state's means of deterring public school students from engaging in criminal conduct or extramarital sex. Now that sodomy and marriage laws have been declared unconstitutional, LGBT advocates can launch a national campaign to invalidate anti-gay curriculum laws."

Postscript. In the course of writing this article, Professor Rosky worked with Equality Utah to bring a lawsuit challenging the constitutionality of Utah's anti-gay curriculum law. In response to the lawsuit and the arguments developed in the article, the Utah Legislature repealed its anti-gay curriculum law in 2017. The sponsor of the repeal was Senator Stuart Adams, who had sponsored the Utah Compromise in 2015. Utah was out in front of all the other deep red states, in part thanks to the leadership of statesmen like Senator Adams and in part because of encouragement by the LDS Church.

PROBLEM 4-4
THE NORTH CAROLINA PUBLIC SCHOOLS BATHROOM LAW

In March 2016, the North Carolina General Assembly passed, and Governor Pat McCrory signed, the Public Facilities Privacy & Security Act, also known as House Bill 2 ("H.B. 2"). H.B. 2 contained several provisions relevant to public schools in the state. First, it prohibited transgender individuals from using multiple occupancy restrooms that correspond to the gender with which the individual identifies. Specifically, the law directed local boards of education to establish "single-sex multiple occupancy bathroom and changing facilities." N.C. Gen. Stat. § 115C–47(63). Local boards were mandated to require that all single-sex bathrooms may be "used only by students based on their biological sex." N.C. Gen. Stat. § 115C–521.2(b). The law defined biological sex as "the physical condition of being a male or female, which is stated on a person's birth certificate." Gen. Stat. § 115C–521.2(a)(1).

Proponents argued that these amendments are a common sense effort to protect privacy and prevent against the risk of assault or harassment in bathrooms. Opponents countered that the law is intended to demean and ostracize, and it heightens the risk of violence against transgender people.

Second, H.B. 2 preempted local government regulations that created more expansive anti-discrimination protections. Existing state laws forbade discrimination on the basis of *inter alia*, sex. But H.B. 2 amended that law to clarify that discrimination is prohibited on the basis of "biological sex," defined to mean the sex stated on one's birth certificate. N.C. Gen. Stat 143–422.2(a). Declaring the regulation of discriminatory practices to be "an issue of general statewide concern," H.B. 2 explicitly "supersede[d] and preempt[ed] any ordinance, regulation, resolution, or policy adopted or imposed by a unit of local government * * * pertaining to the regulation of discriminatory practices in employment * * *." N.C. Gen. Stat. 143–422.2(c). The law's drafters stated that H.B. 2's provision preempting local anti-discrimination measures was necessary to ensure that employment obligations are consistent across the state.

Opponents asserted that this justification was mere pretext and H.B. 2 is motivated by animus towards LGBT individuals. They noted that H.B. 2 came after the City of Charlotte passed an ordinance extending local anti-discrimination protections to LGBT individuals on February 22, 2016. But before the ordinance could go into effect, the North Carolina legislature moved quickly to preempt Charlotte's anti-discrimination protections: H.B. 2 was introduced in a special session on March 23, and was signed into law twelve hours later. Governor McCrory and state legislators made statements indicating that H.B. 2 was indeed intended to overturn Charlotte's ordinance. Shortly after H.B. 2 went into effect, the University of North Carolina announced it would be complying with the new policy.

Civil liberties groups and the Department of Justice immediately challenged H.B. 2. In *Carcaño v. McCrory*, the ACLU alleged that H.B. 2 was unconstitutional under the Equal Protection Clause. In their challenge to the law's provisions regarding restroom usage, plaintiffs asserted that H.B. 2 facially classified and discriminated against individuals based on sex. While "non-transgender people are able to access restrooms and other single-sex facilities consistent with their gender identity * * * transgender people are banned from restrooms and other single-sex facilities consistent with their gender identity." Complaint at 34, *Carcaño v. McCrory*, No. 1:16-cv-00236 (M.D.N.C. Mar. 28, 2016). Accordingly, plaintiffs argued that the law is subject to, and fails, heightened scrutiny.

Plaintiffs in *Carcaño* also pointed to the law's preemption of local non-discrimination protections to demonstrate that H.B. 2 was motivated by animus and discriminatory intent. They said that the state's claimed interest—uniform anti-discrimination obligations throughout the state—was merely a pretext; as evidence plaintiffs pointed to the fact that H.B. 2's drafters rejected proposals to add sexual orientation and gender identity to statewide public accommodation laws. *Id.*

In May 2016, the U.S. Department of Justice also filed a complaint against North Carolina and the University of North Carolina, alleging that the implementation of H.B. 2 violated Title VII of the Civil Rights Act of 1964, Title IX of the Education Amendments of 1972, and the Violence Against Women Reauthorization Act of 2013. The Department of Justice, like the ACLU, asserted in its complaint that H.B. 2 was a "facially discriminatory policy" that "stigmatizes and singles out transgender employees, results in their isolation and exclusion, and perpetuates a sense that they are not worthy of equal treatment and respect." Complaint at 9, *United States v. North Carolina*, No. 1:16-cv-00425 (M.D.N.C May 9, 2016). In a press statement, Attorney General Loretta Lynch said H.B. 2 was "state-sponsored discrimination against transgender individuals."

Did H.B. 2's regulation of public schools and their restrooms violate the Equal Protection Clause? Specifically, did the law discriminate because of sex and, hence, trigger intermediate scrutiny (the VMI Case)? What was the best state justification for this regulation of restrooms in public schools? Should courts defer to state laws regulating high school facilities? (Another issue presented in the case was whether courts should defer to the Department of Education's interpretation of its regulations, to the effect that such bathroom policies violated Title IX's bar to sex discrimination by educational institutions receiving federal funds.)

In March 2017, after suffering an estimated $3.5 billion in lost business opportunities, the North Carolina Legislature repealed H.B. 2 but replaced it with a three-year ban on local government adoption of antidiscrimination ordinances pertaining to "private employment practices of regulating public accommodations." The new law (H.B. 142) also bars local school boards and government agencies from regulating "multiple occupancy bathrooms, showers or changing facilities."

The next month, Attorney General Jeff Sessions announced that the Department of Justice was terminating its lawsuit against North Carolina, on the ground that the new law has solved the problem. The ACLU and Lambda Legal announced that their constitutional challenge would continue, with amended Complaint adapted to the new law. What is the constitutional problem with the new law?

B. PRIVATE SCHOOLS BURDENED BY EDUCATION ANTIDISCRIMINATION LAWS

Gay Rights Coalition of Georgetown University Law Center et al. v. Georgetown University

District of Columbia Court of Appeals, *en banc*, 1987.
536 A.2d 1.

■ MACK, ASSOCIATE JUDGE.

In the District of Columbia, the Human Rights Act [Appendix 5 to this Casebook] prohibits an educational institution from discriminating against any individual on the basis of his or her sexual orientation. Two student gay rights groups contend that Georgetown University violated this statutory command by refusing to grant them "University Recognition" together with equal access to the additional facilities and services that status entails. The University, relying on the trial court's factual finding that Georgetown's grant of "University Recognition" includes a religiously guided "endorsement" of the recipient student group, responds that the Free Exercise Clause of the First Amendment protects it from official compulsion to "endorse" an organization which challenges its religious tenets. Upholding the asserted constitutional defense, the trial court entered judgment in favor of Georgetown. The student groups appeal.

Our analysis of the issues differs from that of the trial court. At the outset, we sever the artificial connection between the "endorsement" and the tangible benefits contained in Georgetown's scheme of "University Recognition." With respect to the University's refusal to grant the status of "University Recognition," we do not reach Georgetown's constitutional defense. Contrary to the trial court's understanding, the Human Rights Act does not require one private actor to "endorse" another. Thus, Georgetown's denial of "University Recognition"—in this case a status carrying an intangible "endorsement"—does not violate the statute. Although affirming the trial court's entry of judgment for the University on that point, we do so on statutory rather than constitutional grounds.

We reach a contrary conclusion with respect to the tangible benefits that accompany "University Recognition." While the Human Rights Act does not seek to compel uniformity in philosophical *attitudes* by force of law, it does require equal *treatment*. Equality of treatment in educational institutions is concretely measured by nondiscriminatory provision of access to "facilities and services." D.C. Code § 1–2520 (1987). Unlike the "endorsement," the various additional tangible benefits that accompany a grant of "University Recognition" are "facilities and services." As such, they must be made equally available, without regard to sexual orientation or to any other characteristic unrelated to individual merit. Georgetown's refusal to provide tangible benefits without regard to sexual orientation violated the Human Rights Act. To that extent only, we consider the merits of Georgetown's free exercise defense. On that issue we hold that the District of Columbia's compelling interest in the eradication of sexual orientation discrimination outweighs any burden imposed upon Georgetown's exercise of religion by the forced equal provision of tangible benefits. * * *

There are two reasons why, as a matter of statutory construction, the Human Rights Act cannot be read to compel a regulated party to express religious approval or neutrality towards any group or individual. First, the statute prohibits only a discriminatory denial of access to "facilities and services" provided by an educational institution. D.C. Code § 1–2520 (1987). An "endorsement" is neither. The Human Rights Act provides legal mechanisms to ensure equality of *treatment*, not equality of *attitudes*. Although we fervently hope that nondiscriminatory attitudes result from equal access to "facilities and services," the Human Rights Act contains nothing to suggest that the legislature intended to make a discriminatory state of mind unlawful in itself. Still less does the statute reveal any desire to force a private actor to express an idea that is not truly held. The Human Rights Act demands action, not words. It was not intended to be an instrument of mind control. * * *

Second, * * * unless the language of the statute is plainly to the contrary, we must construe it so as to uphold its constitutionality. To read into the Human Rights Act a requirement that one private actor must "endorse" another would be to render the statute unconstitutional. The First Amendment protects both free speech and the free exercise of religion. Its essence is that government is without power to intrude into the domain of the intellect or the spirit and that only conduct may be regulated. Interpreting the Human Rights Act so as to require Georgetown to "endorse" the student groups would be to thrust the statute across the constitutional boundaries set by the Free Speech Clause and also, where sincere religious objections are raised, the Free Exercise Clause. Nothing in the statute suggests, let alone requires, such a result. * * *

Freedom of expression is a right to which we all lay equal claim, irrespective of the content of our message. This is easily illustrated.

Suppose that the Gay University of America (GUA) is established as a private educational institution. Part of its mission is to win understanding and acceptance of gay and bisexual persons in an intolerant society. Although open to everyone, regardless of sexual orientation, GUA does expect its faculty, staff and students to maintain a sympathetic attitude towards gay practices and the philosophies that support them. GUA has, as the trial court finds, a system of "University Recognition" through which it expresses its approval or tolerance of various student groups desiring that status. But the GUA administration refuses to grant "University Recognition" to the Roman Catholic Sexual Ethics Association (RCSEA). In that situation, the Human Rights Act's ban on discrimination based on religion could not avail the Catholic student group, for the simple reason that the statute does not require GUA to give expressions of approval or tolerance. Insincere statements of opinion are not what the Human Rights Act requires. On the other hand, the statute would require equal distribution of any attendant tangible benefits if GUA's denial of these was based on the religion of RCSEA members. Georgetown's protection against compelled expression is no more and no less.

The trial court's construction of the Human Rights Act would transform the statute into a violation of the First Amendment. It would compel Georgetown to "endorse" the student groups despite the Supreme Court's warning that a religious actor may not be forced to "say . . . anything in conflict with [its] religious tenets." This construction of the Human Rights Act is required neither by its language nor by its purpose of ensuring equal *treatment*—treatment concretely measured by access to "facilities and services," not by the educational institution's expressed approval of the "purposes and activities" of recipient student groups. * * *

Although the student groups were not entitled to summary judgment on the ground that Georgetown's denial of "University Recognition"—including an "endorsement"—violated the Human Rights Act, the statute does require Georgetown to equally distribute, without regard to sexual orientation, the tangible benefits contained in the same package. If discrimination appears from the record, this court may sustain the statutory ruling "on a ground different from that adopted by the trial court." Our review of the record reveals no genuine dispute that the tangible benefits were denied on the basis of sexual orientation. The Human Rights Act was violated to that extent.

The Human Rights Act cannot depend for its enforcement on a regulated actor's purely subjective, albeit sincere, evaluation of its own motivations. * * * It is particularly difficult to recognize one's own acts as discriminatory. Apart from organizations that failed to meet purely technical requirements such as a minimum membership, the record shows that Georgetown never denied "University Recognition" to a student group that was not mainly composed of persons with a homosexual orientation. Where, as here, those possessing characteristics identified by the legislature as irrelevant to individual merit are treated less favorably than others, the Human Rights Act imposes a burden upon the regulated actor to demonstrate that the irrelevant characteristic played no part in its decision. Georgetown failed to present facts that could show it was uninfluenced by sexual orientation in denying the tangible benefits.

One nondiscriminatory reason asserted by Georgetown for its denial of the tangible benefits contained in "University Recognition" was that it could not give its accompanying "endorsement" to the student groups without violating its religious principles. But as the Human Rights Act, properly construed, requires no direct, intangible "endorsement," Georgetown cannot avoid a finding of discrimination on that ground. The remaining nondiscriminatory reasons asserted by Georgetown may be summarized as follows: the "purposes and activities" of the student groups fell outside the boundaries set by "Recognition Criteria," rendering them ineligible for the tangible benefits they sought and not "otherwise qualified" within the meaning of the statute, D.C. Code § 1–2520 (1987); and, in any event, the denial of tangible benefits was based on the "purposes and activities" of the student groups, not on the homosexual status of their members, so that the sexual orientation of the students involved played no part in the decisionmaking process, *id.*

In this case, the nondiscriminatory reasons asserted by Georgetown have the effect of fusing together what would normally be two separate inquiries—are the student groups "otherwise qualified" for the tangible benefits they seek, and, if so, did Georgetown deny those tangible benefits due to the sexual orientation of their members? Here, because the answer to both of those distinct questions is determined by objective reference to the "purposes and activities" of the student groups, what are normally two separate inquiries collapse into one: did the homosexual orientation of the group members cause them to be treated differently from other applicants?

We are not bound by Georgetown's subjective perception of the "purposes and activities" to which it objected. Georgetown must view the "purposes and activities" of a student group in a way which is free from impermissible reliance upon factors unrelated to individual merit. Accordingly, if the homosexual status of group members entered into Georgetown's assessment of the "purposes and activities" of the student groups, albeit unconsciously, the denial of tangible benefits was itself based on sexual orientation. Put differently, it would be irrelevant that Georgetown saw itself as doing nothing more than applying neutral guidelines established by "Recognition Criteria" if sexual orientation had in fact influenced how those standards were applied.

In denying GPGU's application for "University Recognition" Georgetown adverted to that group's expressed purpose (one of four) to "provide a forum for the development of responsible sexual ethics consonant with one's personal beliefs." That purpose is at odds with

Roman Catholic teachings. But GRC's constitution contained no comparable statement; Georgetown's stated objection was to GRC's much broader intention to "[p]rovide lesbians and gay men entering the Law Center with information about Washington's gay community, including educational, cultural, religious, social and medical services." Because GRC's purposes include an asexual commitment to serving the broad range of needs experienced by homosexual students, but no statement as to the propriety of homosexual conduct, Georgetown's objection to that organization must to some extent have been prompted by the sexual orientation of its members.

That Georgetown's treatment of the gay student groups was not exclusively influenced by a specific objection to "purposes and activities" inconsistent with Roman Catholic dogma was further evidenced by Debbie Gottfried, the University's Director of Student Activities. In clarifying GPGU's status after it had obtained "Student Body Endorsement," but had failed to obtain "University Recognition," Gottfried wrote that the University would not change its position "on what it feels would be interpreted as endorsement and official support of *the full range of issues associated with this cause.*" At no time has Georgetown defined what it meant by "the full range of issues" associated with the gay student groups, despite its insistence that Roman Catholic doctrine favors the provision of equal civil and political rights to homosexually oriented persons and that its religious objection was directed only to the promotion of homosexual conduct. Gottfried's statement was later repeated by Dean Schuerman, who wrote that the University would not lend its endorsement, support or approval to "the positions taken by the gay movement *on a full range of issues*" or "the major activities and issues which, *by definition*, are associated with a *gay organization.*" Similarly, when Dean McCarthy turned down GRC's application at the Law Center, he wrote that the University would not lend its official subsidy and support to a gay law student organization because that "would be interpreted by many as endorsement of the positions taken by the gay movement on *a full range of issues.*" Georgetown thus ascribed to the student groups not only "purposes and activities" which they may have had, but also a host of others automatically assumed to be a necessary attribute of their homosexual orientation. * * *

It is apparent from this correspondence, all of which was before Judge Braman when he granted summary judgment on the discrimination issue, that Georgetown's denial of tangible benefits was not closely tied to specific "purposes and activities" of the student groups promoting the homosexual conduct condemned by Roman Catholic doctrine. The conclusion is inescapable that the predominantly gay composition of the student groups played at least some role in their treatment by Georgetown. By objecting to the student groups' assumed connection, "by definition," to a "full range of issues" associated with the "gay movement," rather than to specific "purposes and activities" inconsistent with its Roman Catholic tradition, Georgetown engaged in the kind of stereotyping unrelated to individual merit that is forbidden by the Human Rights Act. In short, the record reveals no genuine doubt that Georgetown's asserted nondiscriminatory basis for its action was in fact tainted by preconceptions about gay persons. Georgetown did not apply "Recognition Criteria" on an equal basis to all groups without regard to the sexual orientation of their members. * * *

■ [CHIEF JUDGE PRYOR concurred in the result reached by Judge Mack. JUDGE NEWMAN wrote a concurring opinion one section of which commanded a majority of the Court. He observed that the Human Rights Act protected against race, sex, and sexual orientation discrimination (etc.) with no differentiation as to the importance of eradicating each kind of discrimination. All three goals were of equal importance.]

■ BELSON, ASSOCIATE JUDGE, with whom NEBEKER, ASSOCIATE JUDGE, Retired, joins, concurring in part and dissenting in part. * * *

The Human Rights Act, by its plain language, does not prohibit discrimination against persons or groups based upon their advocacy. Rather, it prohibits discrimination against persons based upon their "sexual orientation" which, in the words of the statute, "means male or female homosexuality, heterosexuality and bisexuality, by preference or practice." D.C.Code § 1–2502(28) (1987). It follows that Judge Braman erred if he granted summary judgment against Georgetown on the theory that it violated the Act by denying recognition because of the groups' advocacy of homosexual life-styles.

* * * [A] construction of the Act that would prohibit a private actor from differentiating among persons based on their advocacy of ideas would not only be untrue to the Act, it would also abridge the first amendment's guarantees of free speech and, in this case, the free exercise of religion. Judge Mack interprets the Act to prohibit the public and private educational institutions covered by it from engaging in certain types of conduct but, in an attempt to avoid conflict with the first amendment, she construes the Act not to reach the speech activities of a private institution. Judge Mack concludes that the Act therefore does not require one private actor to "endorse" another.

I would use a different analysis to determine whether Georgetown's denial of recognition to the student groups falls outside the scope of the Human Rights Act. I interpret the Act to prohibit adverse action taken against persons on the basis of their status as members of a protected class. The Act does not purport to prohibit actions taken against persons because of their promotion of ideas or activities (here, for example, promotion of ideas and conduct antithetical to Catholic teachings). Thus, in my view, if an entity covered by the Act fails to grant facilities and services to an individual because of his or her status as a member of a protected group, the Act is violated. In contrast, if an entity covered by the Act fails to provide facilities and services to an individual because of his or her promotion of ideas or activities, that conduct does not violate the Act. Furthermore, as developed below, a construction of the Act that would prevent a private actor from differentiating among others on the basis of the content of their speech would be unconstitutional, at least in the absence of a compelling state interest. Thus, a statutorily imposed requirement of neutrality toward the promotion of an idea, *viz.*, the morality of homosexual life-styles, would abridge first amendment rights. Similarly, an imposed duty either to endorse or to subsidize a position on that issue would also abridge those rights.

An analogy is illustrative. It could not seriously be suggested that the Human Rights Act could force a private, church-affiliated school to lend its endorsement or subsidy to a group that advocated or purposely facilitated fornication or adultery. Such a group, however, could argue that those activities reflect the group members' heterosexual orientation, an orientation that triggers the Act's protection to the same extent as does homosexual orientation. There can be no doubt that university authorities in such a case could recognize that the purposes and activities of an organization of this type would foster or promote acts that the Church deems immoral. While Catholic doctrine deems all homosexual acts immoral and only some heterosexual acts immoral, the principle is the same. Both this hypothetical group and the groups before us can properly be denied endorsement and subsidy by a religious institution because of their sponsorship and promotion of acts that the institution considers immoral, rather than on the basis of their members' status as homosexuals, heterosexuals, or bisexuals. See Tr. 541 (Georgetown would not subsidize activities of student "playboy" club); Tr. 628–30 (Georgetown would not support group that distributes information about abortion clinics to students). * * *

Even if there were a valid finding that Georgetown had violated the Human Rights Act, Georgetown should prevail in this litigation on the basis of its constitutional rights under the free speech and free exercise clauses of the first amendment. I discuss the constitutional issues here on the premise that Georgetown denied recognition to the student groups at least in large part because of the groups' sponsorship and promotion of ideas and activities. Although it has not yet been determined by a factfinder whether sexual orientation entered at all into Georgetown's motivation, it is clear from the record and from Judge Bacon's findings that Georgetown's concern over the groups' advocacy and speech activities permeated its consideration of the question of whether to grant them recognition. Therefore, Georgetown's right of free speech comes strongly into play. With respect to free exercise, Judge Bacon's findings firmly established that Georgetown denied recognition "because recognition would be inconsistent with its duties as a Catholic institution." * * *

■ FERREN, ASSOCIATE JUDGE, with whom TERRY, ASSOCIATE JUDGE, joins, concurring in part and dissenting in part.

I continue to subscribe to the views expressed in the opinion of the division vacated by the en banc court, *Gay Rights Coalition of Georgetown University v. Georgetown University*, 496 A.2d 567, 587 (D.C. 1985). Thus, I continue to believe that Georgetown University may not lawfully refuse to accord the plaintiff gay rights groups "University Recognition," which means (1) *status* equal to that of the other student groups formally recognized by the university, including permission to use the university name, and (2) the *tangible benefits* uniformly available to other recognized groups such as office space, supplies and equipment, a telephone, computer label and mailing services, student advertising privileges, financial counseling, and the opportunity to apply for lecture fund privileges and for other funding. I therefore concur, as far as it goes, in the result proposed by Judge Mack, joined by Chief Judge Pryor and Judge Newman, requiring the university to make the second category of (tangible) benefits available to the gay rights groups. But I respectfully dissent from the views of those three colleagues, as well as Judges Belson and Nebeker, who would deny the first category of (intangible) relief plaintiffs have requested. * * *

In contrast with Judge Mack, Judge Belson reads the Human Rights Act in a way that may not proscribe any of Georgetown's discriminatory conduct. He argues that the Act's reference to "sexual orientation" only forbids discrimination based on sexual "preference or practice," not discrimination based on "advocacy," meaning "promotion of ideas or activities." If Georgetown engaged only in the latter sort of discrimination, he says, it did not violate the Act. But for his disposition of the appeal on constitutional grounds, on the assumption that Georgetown has violated the Act, Judge Belson would remand for further proceedings to clarify the university's motives.

There are two problems with Judge Belson's analysis. First, given the trial court findings on which he relies—and which are supported by the record—no remand is necessary to determine the university's motives for purposes of evaluating whether Georgetown has violated the Human Rights Act. Indeed, on the basis of the findings by both trial judges in the statutory and constitutional phases of the proceeding—which Judge Belson himself suggests we can rely on for purposes of analyzing all issues in this case—the student groups are entitled to prevail on the statutory issue. Second, Judge Belson incorrectly argues that the Act can never, consistent with the Constitution, interdict discrimination directed at "speech" or "advocacy."

[The initial problem with Judge Belson's analysis is that it falls athwart findings of fact by both trial judges, Bacon and Braman, that Georgetown denied recognition and services in part because of the sexual orientation of the students. At worst, from Judge Ferren's perspective, the trial judges both found issues of fact precluding Georgetown from receiving summary judgment. At best, the trial judges firmly established summary judgment against Georgetown because part of its motivation was the prohibited one.]

There is a more general, though fundamental weakness of Judge Belson's analysis—of his unqualified proposition that the Act cannot be construed to forbid the suppression of "speech" or "advocacy." The distinction between discrimination based on advocacy and on status will not work. Part of who a person is, is what he or she says; to deny the right to speak is to deny an essential aspect of one's person. In this sense, therefore, an asserted right to discriminate against someone's advocacy of homosexuality is clearly a claimed right to discriminate against the person on the basis of one's sexual "preference" and thus "sexual orientation." D.C.Code §§ 1–2502(28)–2520(1) (1987).

Assume, however, it is true, as Judge Belson contends, that the Act does not forbid discrimination motivated solely by a desire to prevent the speech activities of a group. Two caveats are in order. First, the means chosen to discriminate against advocacy (here, non-recognition of the plaintiff groups) does not necessarily prove that the underlying motive is merely to prevent the propagation of a repugnant doctrine on campus. The university's action may be directed solely at speech activities (let us assume it is), but that action may still be illegal under the Act if motivated, even in part, by dislike for those who prefer or practice homosexuality. I believe Judge Belson agrees.

Second, even if the university were motivated solely by a desire to shut down offensive speech activities, the means chosen to counter repugnant speech might nonetheless violate the Act. Even if the Act were construed not to forbid discrimination against homosexual ideas, it unquestionably does forbid discrimination against homosexuals because of their ideas. Discrimination that goes beyond the ideas to the person violates the Act no matter what the motive. *See* D.C. Code § 1–2532 (1987) (any practice having "effect or consequence" of violating Act is unlawful). Accordingly, even if censorship in this context, when properly motivated, were lawful, an act excluding or degrading a group to accomplish censorship would not be lawful.

As indicated, I believe any effort to distinguish under the Act between legal discrimination against ideas and illegal discrimination against persons fails to take into account that ideas—and advocacy—are an essential part of the person. But even if the distinction could be made, it is not easy to draw, in part because means capable of achieving the former may amount to the latter. I believe Judge Belson has overlooked, both in his analysis and in its application, the possibility that Georgetown's refusal to recognize the plaintiff groups, if only because of an aversion to their advocacy, is likely to be—indeed, inevitably is in the context of a university—an overly broad response that effectively discriminates against persons in violation of the Act. * * *

The fundamental [constitutional] question is: whether plaintiffs' request for "University Recognition"—meaning full citizenship as student groups at Georgetown University—may be denied, even though in violation of the Human Rights Act, because of Georgetown's first amendment rights. * * * I want to emphasize again that, on this record, "University recognition" or "endorsement" of the plaintiff student groups does not mean, explicitly or implicitly, a statement of approval—or even of neutrality-toward homosexuality, gay rights, or related matters. Because of the nature of the university, the Human Rights Act in no way compels Georgetown to take a position in violation of its right to free exercise of religious beliefs.

In context—and context is critically important—the Act only requires Georgetown not to discriminate against student groups that wish to express their own views in what I believe we may call, without fear of contradiction, a typical private university marketplace of ideas, which inherently stands for freedom of expression. That marketplace is analogous, for constitutional purposes, to the shopping center in *Prune Yard* [*Shopping Center v. Robins*, 447 U.S. 74 (1980)]. There, the Supreme Court held that the first amendment rights of the shopping center owner did not justify barring pamphleteers from exercising their own free speech rights in the common areas open to the public. A legal requirement that Georgetown make its university-wide forum available on a nondiscriminatory basis to all student citizens of the university does not, in my view, imply in any way that the university corporation/administration itself can be reasonably identified with the views of any particular student organization or that the university, as such, has a position-pro, con, or neutral-on any particular message a student group happens to spread. The Human Rights Act, therefore, does not require Georgetown to espouse any view or to intimate even a neutral opinion. * * *

There is a recognized constitutional distinction between a requirement that others be permitted to express what are clearly their own ideas in your forum, when you manifestly provide a public forum (*PruneYard*), and a requirement that you must express the ideas of others (*Barnette*) or must spread, and thus implicitly affirm, those ideas in your own private forum, absent a dissociative statement. * * * I believe the *Prune Yard* analysis is controlling here. While there obviously are differences between a private university and a private shopping center, the fact that each, for entirely different reasons, has become a traditional forum for the expression of diverse, often conflicting ideas provides a context compelling a conclusion that, *by definition*, even a private university proprietor cannot *reasonably* be associated with any idea it does not affirmatively embrace. At most, therefore, "University recognition" of a gay rights group implies no more than the university's "official tolerance," of still another student organization in a pluralistic environment—a tolerance to be expected, indeed taken for granted, in any university that purports to be open to free expression of ideas, and thus a tolerance that implies no university position whatsoever about the ideas any group stands for. To tolerate another's values or speech is not to approve of them; nor is it to express indifference or neutrality. It is simply an expressed willingness to let someone else have a say without indicating what you think about it. This distinction between toleration and endorsement (or, more generally, between toleration and taking a position of some sort) lies at the heart of the first amendment's demand that government tolerate dissident beliefs and speech; it is equally essential to our civil rights statutes. Conceptually, perhaps, one could quibble about whether government-compelled toleration amounts to forced conduct or forced speech; but, for constitutional purposes, the salient point is that, in context, such "University recognition" does not suggest the university is taking a position on the group that it tolerates/recognizes. Thus, required "recognition" does not run afoul of the absolute protection against compelled utterances.* * * As I see it, therefore, only in refusing to recognize a student group expressly for ideological or theological reasons is the university making a statement about the group's ideas and thus making its own position known. * * *

Postscript. Georgetown University ultimately withdrew its petition for Supreme Court review of the foregoing decision, and settled the lawsuit. Congress had a different response: it used its power over D.C. local law to amend the D.C. Human Rights Act to exempt religious institutions from the prohibition against discrimination on the basis of sexual preference. Public Law No. 101–168, § 141, 103 Stat. 1267 (1989). Despite the amendment, the University adhered to its agreement with the students; gay student groups are a flourishing presence at both the main campus and at the law center.

NOTES ON THE GEORGETOWN CASE AND THE INTERACTION OF CONDUCT, STATUS, AND VIEWPOINT

1.   *Status, Conduct, and Viewpoint.* Notice how Georgetown and Judge Belson present the case as one involving the university's discrimination based primarily on (anti-Christian) viewpoint and secondarily on (immoral) conduct—and therefore *not* based on sexual orientation per se. (Recall Chief Judge Kramer's argument to the same effect in *Hands On Originals.*) Their viewpoint-status distinction illustrates what a difference the institutional form of the defendant makes. If the discrimination is committed by a state institution, a finding that the state discriminates against the gay group because of their "viewpoint" mobilizes the First Amendment and is almost always fatal. See *Rosenberger* v. *Rector & Visitors of Univ. of Va.*, 515 U.S. 819 (1995). But the same First Amendment may protect a private institution that says it discriminates because of a group's viewpoint, as in the Boy Scouts Case.

"Notions of identity increasingly form the basis for gay and lesbian equality claims. Those claims merge not only status and conduct, but also viewpoint, into one whole. To be openly gay, when the closet is an option, is to function as an advocate as well as a symbol. The centrality of viewpoint to gay identity explains the logic behind what has become the primary strategy of anti-gay forces: the attempted penalization of those who 'profess' homosexuality, in a series of 'no promo homo' campaigns." Nan D. Hunter, "Identity, Speech and Equality," 79 *Va. L. Rev.* 1695, 1696 (1993).

Note that the Georgetown Case was decided before *Hurley v. Irish-American Gay, Lesbian, and Bisexual Group of Boston*, 515 U.S. 557 (1995), striking down the application of a non-discrimination law requiring that a parade include a gay-affiliated marching group, and *Boy Scouts of America v. Dale*, 530 U.S. 640 (2000), striking down the application of a non-discrimination law requiring that an association include an openly gay official. (Both cases are excerpted and discussed in Chapter 1.) The Boston Parade Case relied on the compelled speech line of cases, and the Boy Scouts Case protected a right of expressive association. Georgetown pressed both First Amendment rights. Would the case be decided differently today? Ought it?

Consider the claim of William Eskridge Jr., "Noah's Curse: How Religion Often Conflates Status, Belief, and Conduct to Resist Antidiscrimination Norms," 45 *Ga. L. Rev.* 657 (2011), that racist religion in the slavery and apartheid eras demonized people of color by sexualizing them and generalizing their degraded status and sexual conduct to denigrate anti-slavery and anti-apartheid viewpoints. Eskridge finds exactly the same synthesis of degraded status, sexualized conduct, and anti-Christian belief in religions that demonize gay people. He diagrams his historical research into racist and homophobic religion in the following way:

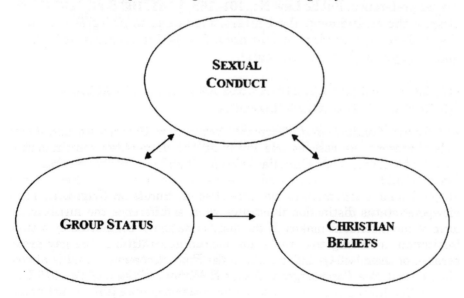

Thus, if Georgetown prevails, then so ought Bob Jones University, which until recently discriminated based upon religious teachings against persons who dated or married outside their own race. Should the First Amendment tolerate this?

Consider Georgetown's claims from another angle. Imagine that a group of lesbian, gay, and bisexual students had formed to seek and provide support for becoming heterosexual. Would Georgetown have been likely to charter the group? If so, wouldn't viewpoint (not identity) be the only explanation for its different treatment of the plaintiffs in this case? Conversely, imagine that heterosexual students seek to form a chapter of "Straight But Not Narrow." Wouldn't Georgetown have refused to recognize that group?

2. *Must One Choose Between Viewpoint and Identity?* Judge Ferren's opinion tries to tackle the foregoing dilemma. "Even if the Act were construed not to forbid discrimination against homosexual ideas, it unquestionably does forbid discrimination against homosexuals because of their ideas." Is that true? Is it illegal to discriminate against Latinos "because of their ideas"? Because of their ideas only about race or ethnicity? What *are* "homosexual ideas"?

Judge Mack's opinion tackles the issue in a creative way. Responsive to the plaintiffs' charge that they were being discriminated against because of their identity (and stereotypes based on that identity), she ruled that Georgetown had to give them equal access and services. Responsive to Georgetown's insistence that its identity as a Roman Catholic institution was tied up with its refusal to recognize an organization whose members opposed a fundamental moral teaching of that church, Judge Mack ruled that Georgetown did not have to recognize the student group. Is this a good compromise? Are Judge Ferren's criticisms of the compromise cogent?

3. *Does the Georgetown Compromise Hold up?* Georgetown withdrew its appeal to the Supreme Court, so the Court never had a chance to review Judge Mack's Solomonic disposition. Much has happened in First Amendment doctrine since 1987. To begin with, the Supreme Court in *Employment Division v. Smith* (1990) ruled that generally applicable state policies do not violate the Free Exercise Clause when neutrally applied to religious institutions such as Georgetown. Georgetown had virtually no free exercise claim after *Smith*. RFRA revived the pre-*Smith* free exercise jurisprudence. Although *Boerne* nullified that for claims against states, Washington D.C. falls within the purview of the federal government, which has plenary authority over the nation's capital. Hence, RFRA is still applicable.

As noted above, Georgetown's freedom of expression claim is stronger after *Hurley* (1995), the Boston Parade Case, and its expressive association claim much stronger after *Dale* (2000), the Boy Scouts Case. Would Georgetown prevail today? Would the current Court dissolve Judge Mack's careful compromise? Consider the next case.

C. PUBLIC SCHOOL RELIGIOUS STUDENTS (AND THEIR PARENTS) BURDENED BY NONDISCRIMINATION POLICIES

Christian Legal Society Chapter of the University of California, Hastings College of the Law v. Leo Martinez

United States Supreme Court, 2010.
561 U.S. 661, 130 S.Ct. 2971, 177 L.Ed.2d 838.

■ JUSTICE GINSBURG delivered the opinion of the Court.

In a series of decisions, this Court has emphasized that the First Amendment generally precludes public universities from denying student organizations access to school sponsored forums because of the groups' viewpoints. See *Rosenberger* v. *Rector and Visitors of Univ. of Va.*, 515 U.S. 819 (1995); *Widmar* v. *Vincent*, 454 U.S. 263 (1981); *Healy* v. *James*, 408 U.S. 169 (1972). This case concerns a novel question regarding student activities at public universities: May a public law school condition its official recognition of a student group—and the attendant use of school funds and facilities—on the organization's agreement to open eligibility for membership and leadership to all students?

In the view of petitioner Christian Legal Society (CLS), an accept-all-comers policy impairs its First Amendment rights to free speech, expressive association, and free exercise of religion by prompting it, on pain of relinquishing the advantages of recognition, to accept members who do not share the organization's core beliefs about religion and sexual orientation. From the perspective of respondent Hastings College of the Law (Hastings or the Law School), CLS seeks special dispensation from an across-the-board open-access requirement designed to further the reasonable educational purposes underpinning the school's student-organization program.

In accord with the District Court and the Court of Appeals, we reject CLS's First Amendment challenge. Compliance with Hastings' all-comers policy, we conclude, is a reasonable, viewpoint-neutral condition on access to the student-organization forum. In requiring CLS—in common with all other student organizations—to choose between welcoming all students and forgoing the benefits of official recognition, we hold, Hastings did not transgress constitutional limitations. CLS, it bears emphasis, seeks not parity with other organizations, but a preferential exemption from Hastings' policy. The First Amendment shields CLS against state prohibition of the organization's expressive activity, however exclusionary that activity may be. But CLS enjoys no constitutional right to state subvention of its selectivity. * * *

[I.   Through its "Registered Student Organization" (RSO) program, Hastings extends official recognition and several tangible benefits (such as subsidies for events) to recognized student groups. The groups also get to use the Hastings logo. In return, recognized student organizations must abide by the Law School's policies, including its Policy on Nondiscrimination (Nondiscrimination Policy), which states:

> [Hastings] is committed to a policy against legally impermissible, arbitrary or unreasonable discriminatory practices. All groups, including administration, faculty, student governments, [Hastings]-owned student residence facilities and programs sponsored by [Hastings], are governed by this policy of nondiscrimination. [Hasting's] policy on nondiscrimination is to comply fully with applicable law.

> [Hastings] shall not discriminate unlawfully on the basis of race, color, religion, national origin, ancestry, disability, age, sex or sexual orientation. This nondiscrimination policy covers admission, access and treatment in Hastings-sponsored programs and activities.

Hastings interpreted the Nondiscrimination Policy, as it relates to the RSO program, to mandate acceptance of all comers: School-approved groups must "allow any student to participate, become a member, or seek leadership positions in the organization, regardless of [her] status or beliefs." * * * Operating under mandatory national guidelines, Hastings' CLS chapter required members and officers to sign a "Statement of Faith" and to conduct their lives in accord with prescribed principles. Among those tenets is the belief that sexual activity should not occur outside of marriage between a man and a woman; CLS thus interprets its bylaws to exclude from affiliation anyone who engages in "unrepentant homosexual conduct." CLS also excludes students who hold religious convictions different from those in the Statement of Faith.]

[II. CLS urged the Court to review the Nondiscrimination Policy as written—prohibiting discrimination on several enumerated bases, including religion and sexual orientation—and not as a requirement that all RSOs accept all comers. According to its brief before the Court, CLS argued that the Nondiscrimination Policy, by its plain language, "targe[t] solely those groups whose beliefs are based on religion or that disapprove of a particular kind of sexual behavior," and leaves other associations free to limit membership and leadership to individuals committed to the group's ideology. For example, "[a] political . . . group can insist that its leaders support its purposes and beliefs," CLS alleges, but "a religious group cannot." Justice Ginsburg rejected that invitation: at the summary judgment stage in the trial court proceedings, CLS and Hastings entered into a binding stipulation that Hastings followed the all-comers policy.]

[III] In support of the argument that Hastings' all-comers policy treads on its First Amendment rights to free speech and expressive association, CLS draws on two lines of decisions. First, in a progression of cases, this Court has employed forum analysis to determine when a governmental entity, in regulating property in its charge, may place limitations on speech. Recognizing a State's right "to preserve the property under its control for the use to which it is lawfully dedicated," the Court has permitted restrictions on access to a limited public forum, like the RSO program here, with this key caveat: Any access barrier must be reasonable and viewpoint neutral, *e.g., Rosenberger.* See also, *e.g., Good News Club* v. *Milford Central School*, 533 U.S. 98, 106–107 (2001); *Lamb's Chapel* v. *Center Moriches Union Free School Dist.*, 508 U.S. 384, 392–393 (1993); *Perry Ed. Assn.* v. *Perry Local Educators' Assn.*, 460 U.S. 37, 46 (1983).

Second, as evidenced by another set of decisions, this Court has rigorously reviewed laws and regulations that constrain associational freedom. In the context of public accommodations, we have subjected restrictions on that freedom to close scrutiny; such restrictions are permitted only if they serve "compelling state interests" that are "unrelated to the suppression of ideas"—interests that cannot be advanced "through . . . significantly less restrictive [means]." *Roberts* v. *United States Jaycees*, 468 U.S. 609, 623 (1984). See also, *e.g., Boy Scouts of America* v. *Dale*, 530 U.S. 640, 648 (2000). "Freedom of association," we have recognized, "plainly presupposes a freedom not to associate." [*Roberts*] Insisting that an organization embrace unwelcome members, we have therefore concluded, "directly and immediately affects associational rights." [*Dale*]

[T]his case fits comfortably within the limited-public-forum category, for CLS, in seeking what is effectively a state subsidy, faces only indirect pressure to modify its membership policies; CLS may exclude any person for any reason if it forgoes the benefits of official recognition. The expressive-association precedents on which CLS relies, in contrast, involved regulations that *compelled* a group to include unwanted members, with no choice to opt out.

In diverse contexts, our decisions have distinguished between policies that require action and those that withhold benefits. Application of the less-restrictive limited-public-forum analysis better accounts for the fact that Hastings, through its RSO program, is dangling the carrot of subsidy, not wielding the stick of prohibition

In sum, we are persuaded that our limited-public-forum precedents adequately respect both CLS's speech and expressive-association rights, and fairly balance those rights against Hastings' interests as property owner and educational institution. We turn to the merits of the instant dispute, therefore, with the limited-public-forum decisions as our guide.

[In earlier cases, the Court had invalidated state public forum restrictions that were not viewpoint-neutral, such as the university's exclusion of the SDS in *Healy,* of religious worship in *Widmar,* and of faith-based publications in *Rosenberger.*] In all three cases, we ruled that student groups had been unconstitutionally singled out because of their points of view. "Once it has opened a limited [public] forum," we emphasized, "the State must respect the lawful boundaries it has itself set." [*Rosenberger*.] The constitutional constraints on the boundaries the State may set bear repetition here: "The State may not exclude speech where its distinction is not reasonable in light of the purpose served by the forum, . . . nor may it discriminate against speech on the basis of . . . viewpoint."

[Deferring to the law school's ground-level understanding of its needs, the majority concluded that the school's all-comers requirements was reasonable because it served several university interests: (1) it "ensures that no Hastings student is forced to fund a group that would reject her as a member"; (2) it helps the school "police the written terms of its Nondiscrimination Policy without inquiring into an RSO's motivation for membership restrictions"; (3) by bringing together students with diverse backgrounds and beliefs, it "encourages tolerance, cooperation, and learning among students"; and (4) it "conveys the Law School's decision 'to decline to subsidize with public monies and benefits conduct of which the people of California disapprove [violation of discrimination policies]."]

The Law School's policy is all the more creditworthy in view of the "substantial alternative channels that remain open for [CLS-student] communication to take place." *Perry Ed. Assn.* If restrictions on access to a limited public forum are viewpoint discriminatory, the ability of a group to exist outside the forum would not cure the constitutional shortcoming. But when access barriers are viewpoint neutral, our decisions have counted it significant that other available avenues for the group to exercise its First Amendment rights lessen the burden created by those barriers. [Justice Ginsburg noted that CLS enjoyed access to law school facilities for some of its publicity and activities and had electronic alternatives to communicate with students.]

CLS nevertheless deems Hastings' all-comers policy "frankly absurd." "There can be no diversity of viewpoints in a forum," it asserts, "if groups are not permitted to form around viewpoints." This catch phrase confuses CLS's preferred policy with constitutional limitation— the *advisability* of Hastings' policy does not control its *permissibility*. Instead, we have repeatedly stressed that a State's restriction on access to a limited public forum "need not be the most reasonable or the only reasonable limitation." *Cornelius.*

CLS also assails the reasonableness of the all-comers policy in light of the RSO forum's function by forecasting that the policy will facilitate hostile takeovers; if organizations must open their arms to all, CLS contends, saboteurs will infiltrate groups to subvert their mission and message. This supposition strikes us as more hypothetical than real. CLS points to no history or prospect of RSO hijackings at Hastings. Students tend to self-sort and presumably will not endeavor en masse to join—let alone seek leadership positions in—groups pursuing missions wholly at odds with their personal beliefs. And if a rogue student intent on sabotaging an organization's objectives nevertheless attempted a takeover, the members of that group would not likely elect her as an officer.

RSOs, moreover, in harmony with the all-comers policy, may condition eligibility for membership and leadership on attendance, the payment of dues, or other neutral requirements designed to ensure that students join because of their commitment to a group's vitality, not its demise. * * *

We next consider whether Hastings' all-comers policy is viewpoint neutral.

Although this aspect of limited-public-forum analysis has been the constitutional sticking point in our prior decisions * * * we need not dwell on it here. It is, after all, hard to imagine a more viewpoint-neutral policy than one requiring *all* student groups to accept *all* comers. In contrast to *Healy*, *Widmar*, and *Rosenberger*, in which universities singled out organizations for disfavored treatment because of their points of view, Hastings' all-comers requirement draws no distinction between groups based on their message or perspective. An all-comers condition on access to RSO status, in short, is textbook viewpoint neutral. * * *

Hastings' requirement that student groups accept all comers, we are satisfied, "is justified without reference to the content [or viewpoint] of the regulated speech." The Law School's policy aims at the *act* of rejecting would-be group members without reference to the reasons motivating that behavior: Hastings' "desire to redress th[e] perceived harms" of exclusionary membership policies "provides an adequate explanation for its [all-comers condition] over and above mere disagreement with [any student group's] beliefs or biases." CLS's conduct—not its Christian perspective—is, from Hastings' vantage point, what stands between the group and RSO status. "In the end," as Hastings observes, "CLS is simply confusing its *own* viewpoint-based objections to . . . nondiscrimination laws (which it is entitled to have and [to] voice) with viewpoint *discrimination*." * * *

[IV] In its reply brief, CLS contends that "[t]he peculiarity, incoherence, and suspect history of the all-comers policy all point to pretext." Neither the District Court nor the Ninth Circuit addressed an argument that Hastings selectively enforces its all-comers policy, and this Court is not the proper forum to air the issue in the first instance. On remand, the Ninth Circuit may consider CLS's pretext argument if, and to the extent, it is preserved. * * *

■ [JUSTICE STEVENS wrote a concurring opinion arguing that the Non-Discrimination Policy, even without the all-comers rule, posed no serious First Amendment problem. A simple non-discrimination rule is viewpoint-neutral, just as the all-comers rule is. JUSTICE STEVENS specifically rejected CLS's argument, picked up by the dissent, that CLS was itself not discriminating against a person's status but was only discriminating based upon misconduct. "A person's religion often simultaneously constitutes or informs a status, an identity, a set of beliefs and practices, and much else besides. (So does sexual orientation for that matter, notwithstanding the dissent's view that a rule excluding those who engage in "unrepentant homosexual conduct" does not discriminate on the basis of status or identity.) Our First Amendment doctrine has never required university administrators to undertake the impossible task of separating out belief-based from status-based religious discrimination."]

■ [JUSTICE KENNEDY also wrote a concurring opinion, emphasizing that this case was very different from *Rosenberger*, where the university was excluding religious publications because of their viewpoint.] An objection might be that the all-comers policy, even if not so designed or intended, in fact makes it difficult for certain groups to express their views in a manner essential to their message. A group that can limit membership to those who agree in full with its aims and purposes may be more effective in delivering its message or furthering its expressive objectives; and the Court has recognized that this interest can be protected against governmental interference or regulation. See *Dale*. By allowing like-minded students to form groups around shared identities, a school creates room for self-expression and personal development.

In the instant case, however, if the membership qualification were enforced, it would contradict a legitimate purpose for having created the limited forum in the first place. Many educational institutions, including respondent Hastings College of Law, have recognized that the process of learning occurs both formally in a classroom setting and informally outside of it. Students may be shaped as profoundly by their peers as by their teachers. Extracurricular activities, such as those in the Hastings "Registered Student Organization" program, facilitate interactions between students, enabling them to explore new points of view, to develop interests and talents, and to nurture a growing sense of self. The Hasting program is designed to allow all students to interact with their colleagues across a broad, seemingly unlimited range of ideas, views, and activities.

Law students come from many backgrounds and have but three years to meet each other and develop their skills. They do so by participating in a community that teaches them how to create arguments in a convincing, rational, and respectful manner and to express doubt and disagreement in a professional way. A law school furthers these objectives by allowing broad diversity in registered student organizations. But these objectives may be better achieved if students can act cooperatively to learn from and teach each other through interactions in social and intellectual contexts. A vibrant dialogue is not possible if students wall themselves off from opposing points of view."

■ JUSTICE ALITO, with whom THE CHIEF JUSTICE [ROBERTS], JUSTICE SCALIA, and JUSTICE THOMAS join, dissenting.

The proudest boast of our free speech jurisprudence is that we protect the freedom to express "the thought that we hate." *United States v. Schwimmer*, 279 U.S. 644, 654–655 (1929) (Holmes, J., dissenting). Today's decision rests on a very different principle: no freedom for expression that offends prevailing standards of political correctness in our country's institutions of higher learning.

[The dissenters argued that Hastings was not actually observing an "an all-comers" policy, but was actually operating under another policy that singled out discrimination based on religion or sexual orientation. The dissenters also argued that the application of Hastings' policies was pretextual, motivated by disapproval of the Christian Legal Society's viewpoint. The majority left the issue of pretext open on remand. We have excerpted only portions of the dissent relating to the constitutionality of the "all comers" policy.]

Once a state university opens a limited forum, it "must respect the lawful boundaries it has itself set." Hastings' regulations on the registration of student groups impose only two substantive limitations: A group seeking registration must have student members and must be non-commercial. Access to the forum is not limited to groups devoted to particular purposes. The regulations provide that a group applying for registration must submit an official document including "a statement of *its purpose*," but the regulations make no attempt to define the limits of acceptable purposes. The regulations do not require a group seeking registration to show that it has a certain number of members or that its program is of interest to any particular number of Hastings students. Nor do the regulations require that a group serve a need not met by existing groups.* * *

Taken as a whole, the regulations plainly contemplate the creation of a forum within which Hastings students are free to form and obtain registration of essentially the same broad range of private groups that nonstudents may form off campus. That is precisely what the parties in this case stipulated: The RSO forum "seeks to promote a diversity of viewpoints *among* registered student organizations, including viewpoints on religion and human sexuality." * * *

The accept-all-comers policy is antithetical to the design of the RSO forum for the same reason that a state-imposed accept-all-comers policy would violate the First Amendment rights of private groups if applied off campus. As explained above, a group's First Amendment right of expressive association is burdened by the "forced inclusion" of members whose presence would "affec[t] in a significant way the group's ability to advocate public or private viewpoints." The Court has therefore held that the government may not compel a group that engages in "expressive association" to admit such a member unless the government has a compelling interest, " 'unrelated to the suppression of ideas, that cannot be achieved through means significantly less restrictive of associational freedoms.' " * * *

In sum, Hastings' accept-all-comers policy is not reasonable in light of the stipulated purpose of the RSO forum: to promote a diversity of viewpoints *"among"*—not within—"registered student organizations."

* * * I do not think it is an exaggeration to say that today's decision is a serious setback for freedom of expression in this country. Our First Amendment reflects a "profound national commitment to the principle that debate on public issues should be uninhibited, robust, and wide-open." Even if the United States is the only Nation that shares this commitment to the same extent, I would not change our law to conform to the international norm. I fear that the Court's decision marks a turn in that direction. Even those who find CLS's views objectionable should be concerned about the way the group has been treated—by Hastings, the Court of Appeals, and now this Court. I can only hope that this decision will turn out to be an aberration.

NOTES ON THE CHRISTIAN LEGAL SOCIETY CASE

1. *Narrowness of the Court's Decision: What Is Left Unsaid, and Why.* In strong contrast to the opinions for the Court in both *Hurley* and *Dale*, Justice Ginsburg's opinion for the Court in *Hastings* is written very narrowly. Because the non-discrimination rule here was applied in the context of a public institution, the limited public forum cases were on point—and Justice Ginsburg was able to avoid the thorny issue (addressed by Justice Stevens) whether *Dale* or *Hurley* protected CLS's viewpoint-sensitive rules.

What are the advantages and disadvantages of taking Justice Ginsburg's, rather than Justice Stevens's, approach to deciding this case? Would Justice Kennedy, the author of *Rosenberger* as well as *Lawrence* and *Romer*, have been willing to join Justice Stevens's opinion if Justice Ginsburg's option were not available? Or would he have followed *Rosenberger* and *Dale* (where Kennedy was the fifth vote for the Boy Scouts)? How does Stevens distinguish *Rosenberger* and *Dale*?

2. *The Analogy to Race.* At oral argument, Justice Sotomayor asked whether the First Amendment protects associations that exclude students based on their race, sex, or disability. Of course not, replied Michael McConnell for CLS. "Race, any other *status* basis Hastings is able to enforce," but CLS was only excluding unrepentant gay people based upon their *conduct* and, by inference from their unrepentant conduct, their *beliefs*, the core area protected by the First Amendment. Justice Stevens then asked, "What if the *belief* is that African Americans are inferior?" McConnell answered that such an organization might have that *belief*, but they could not then exclude students of color based on their *status.*

The argument of William N. Eskridge Jr., "Noah's Curse: How Religion Often Conflates Status, Belief, and Conduct to Resist Antidiscrimination Norms," 45 *Ga. L. Rev.* 657 (2011), is that racial equality and religious liberty have been at loggerheads throughout American history. Religious fundamentalists long objected that equality rights for blacks would promote "racial mixing," impose an unwanted association upon whites, or censor white people's expression, all contrary to God's Mandates. Social conservatives today shy away from constitutional claims that religious institutions or persons can be exempted from legal obligations not to discriminate because of race. McConnell and other advocates for religious fundamentalists reject the race analogy on the ground that racial equality does not implicate sincere religious belief in the same way that sexual orientation does.

In the CLS Case, Chief Justice Roberts lectured counsel for Hastings that "[r]eligious belief, it has to be based on the fundamental notion that we are not open to everybody." But on what basis can CLS exclude the many "homosexuals" who consider themselves Christians? The answer appears to be that "unrepentant homosexuals," who continue to engage in "homosexual activities" CLS condemns, cannot be "genuine" Christians. According to Eskridge, however, the race analogy still has bite, because nineteenth century Christian theology condemned persons of African descent to slavery and then apartheid because of the immoral conduct of their ancestor Ham (whose descendants were cursed by Noah, Gen. 9: 24–27). "Miscegenation" was considered conduct abhorrent to God (e.g., Gen. 28:1; Acts 17:26), and this racialized sexuality was the basis for apartheid as well as state anti-miscegenation laws such as those struck down in *Loving v. Virginia*.

Thus, both racist religion and homophobic faith demonized minorities according to a Scripture-soaked script: the degraded *status,* immoral *conduct,* and anti-Christian *message* of "practicing homosexuals" and "integrationists" were deeply interconnected. Racist religion depended upon the mythic rape of Noah by Ham, conduct that justified God's condemnation of the descendants of Canaan to slavery and later to apartheid. In the same way, homophobic faith depends today on the mythic Biblical condemnation of "homosexual" conduct that justifies a degraded or second-class status for gay people. Accordingly, when CLS excludes "unrepentant homosexuals," it is discriminating based upon *conduct* and *message*, as McConnell said at oral argument, but it is *also* discriminating based upon *status,* the point made by Greg Garre, who represented Hastings. Religion constructs a minority person so that his *status* as an inferior or demon grows out of his sinful lusts and other *conduct*, which bespeaks a Godless *message* of hedonism and dissolution. Race like sexual orientation has been both a status and an inferred conduct, and the status/conduct carried messages that polluted the religious community if they were not excluded. Status, conduct, and message have been the holy trinity of religion-based discrimination and subordination of both citizens of color and homosexual citizens. It is notable that the American religions that were the strongest supporters of abolition and desegregation were also the first to support equal rights for gay people: Quakers, Reformed Jews, and Unitarians. The religions that were the staunchest supporters of slavery and apartheid have also been the staunchest opponents of gay rights: Southern Baptists and Mormons. The Roman Catholic Church was muted on race issues but has been outspoken against gay rights.

Do you accept Eskridge's doctrinal point, regarding the link among conduct, status, and message? Note how it draws upon the pioneering article analyzing anti-gay discourse as a conflation of status, conduct, and message, namely, Nan D. Hunter, "Identity, Speech and Equality," 79 *Va. L. Rev.* 1695 (1993). If these authors are correct, should the Supreme Court create a broader exception to the First Amendment, along the lines suggested by Justice Stevens?

3. *Strategies on Remand.* If you represent CLS in this case, you get a remand to argue that the "all comers" policy is, essentially, a pretext to discriminate on the basis of fundamentalist religion (or just to get rid of CLS perhaps). What evidence might you find to support this proposition? If you represent Hastings, do you have any advice for the law school administration that would strengthen its case on remand? *See Christian Legal Society v. Wu,* 626 F.3d 483 (9th Cir. 2010).

David Parker; Tonia Parker; Joshua Parker; Jacob Parker; Joseph Robert Wirthlin; Robin Wirthlin; Joseph Robert Wirthlin Jr. v. William Hurley et al., **514 F.3d 87 (1st Cir. 2008).** In the wake of *Goodridge,* many parents were concerned that the state was pushing gay marriage onto their families, contrary to their religious beliefs. Two sets of parents sued the Lexington, Massachusetts school district in which their children were enrolled.

In kindergarten, Jacob Parker received a picture book, *Who's in a Family?*, which depicted different families, including a family with two dads and a family with two moms. Who's in a family? The book said: "The people who love you the most!" Jacob's parents were concerned that this book was part of an effort by the public schools "to indoctrinate young children into the concept that homosexuality and homosexual relationships or marriage are moral and acceptable behavior." Such an effort might require their sons to affirm a belief inconsistent with their religion. When Jacob entered first grade that fall, his classroom's book collection included *Who's in a Family?* as well as *Molly's Family,* a picture book about a girl who is at first made to feel embarrassed by a classmate because she has both a mommy and a mama but then learns that families can come in many different varieties. As before, the Parkers requested notification of such materials, so they could keep Jacob at home on those days.

The Wirthlins, a prominent Mormon family who had relocated to Massachusetts, objected that their son Joey was exposed to *King and King* in his second grade class. This picture book tells the story of a prince, ordered by his mother to get married, who first rejects several princesses only to fall in love with another prince. The book depicts a wedding scene between the two princes and closes with a picture of the two princes kissing, albeit with a red heart superimposed over their mouths. It does not appear that the teacher discussed the book with the class. That evening, Joey told his parents about the book; his parents described him as "agitated" and remembered him calling the book "so silly."

The Parkers and Wirthlins objected that they should be given prior notice by the school and the opportunity to exempt their children from exposure to books they found "religiously repugnant." The parents claimed violations of their own and their children's rights under the Free Exercise Clause and their substantive parental and privacy rights under the U.S. Constitution. In an opinion by Judge Lynch, the First Circuit affirmed the district court's judgment dismissing the parents' federal constitutional claims.[a]

In its schools code, Massachusetts mandates that educational standards "be designed to inculcate respect for the cultural, ethnic and racial diversity of the commonwealth." Further, "[a]cademic standards shall be designed to avoid perpetuating gender, cultural, ethnic or racial stereotypes." The state health curriculum established Learning Standards for different grades. For grades 6–8, the Learning Standards address "the detrimental effect of prejudice (such as prejudice on the basis of race, gender, sexual orientation, class, or religion) on individual relationships and society as a whole." There was also a Reproduction/Sexuality component under the Physical Health Strand of the Learning Standards; that component directed that, by grade 5, students should be able to "[d]efine sexual orientation using the correct terminology (such as heterosexual, and gay and lesbian)." Also by state statute, the selection of books is the responsibility of a school's principal, with the approval of the local superintendent of schools.

The plaintiffs argued that their ability to inculcate their religious views with their young children was undermined in fundamental ways. First, they felt that their children are too young to be introduced to the topic of gay marriage. Second, they did not like the school's apparent endorsement of gay marriage. Third, they believed that the school was sending a message of intolerance toward traditionalist religious views more generally. Given what they considered the "important influence teachers have on this age group," the parents argued that this instructional curriculum threatened their religious as well as parental liberties—and their constitutional rights under the Free Exercise and Due Process Clauses of the Constitution.

As to the parents' free exercise claims, Judge Lynch observed that "a law that is neutral and of general applicability need not be justified by a compelling governmental interest even if the law has the incidental effect of burdening a particular religious practice." *Church of the Lukumi Babalu Aye, Inc. v. City of Hialeah*, 508 U.S. 520, 531 (1993). Strict

---

[a] Massachusetts requires that parents be given notice and the opportunity to exempt their children from the human sexuality curriculum. Mass. Gen. Laws ch. 71, § 32A. The school declined to apply this statutory exemption, because the materials did not "primarily involve human sexual education." The district court's opinion dismissing the parents' claims was without prejudice to a lawsuit in state court to press this state statutory claim.

scrutiny is needed only if a law "targets" religious groups or persons. In these cases, the "school was not singling out plaintiffs' particular religious beliefs or targeting its tolerance lessons to only those children from families with religious objections to gay marriage. The fact that a school promotes tolerance of different sexual orientations and gay marriage when such tolerance is anathema to some religious groups does not constitute targeting."

Judge Lynch recognized the substantive due process right of parents "to make decisions concerning the care, custody, and control of their children." *Troxel v. Granville*, 530 U.S. 57, 66 (2000) (plurality opinion). *Troxel* involved the custody of children; the Court held that parents have a privacy interest in visitation rights that the state cannot always override. Other cases, such as *Wisconsin v. Yoder*, 406 U.S. 205 (1972), involved parental decisions whether to send their children to public schools in the first place. Although the Parkers and the Wirthlins had a constitutional right to home school their children, Judge Lynch followed other courts in holding they did not have a constitutional right to "direct how a public school teaches their child." *Blau v. Fort Thomas Pub. Sch. Dist.*, 401 F.3d 381, 395 (6th Cir. 2005). "[W]e have found no federal case under the Due Process Clause which has permitted parents to demand an exemption for their children from exposure to certain books used in public schools. In *Mozert v. Hawkins County Board of Education*, 827 F.2d 1058 (6th Cir.1987), for example, the Sixth Circuit rejected parental claims for an exemption from a school district's use of an entire series of texts. The parents claimed that specified books taught values contrary to their religious beliefs and that, as a result, the school violated the parents' religious beliefs by allowing their children to read the books and violated their children's religious beliefs by requiring the children to read them. Rejecting such a claim, the Sixth Circuit ruled that exposure to ideas through the required reading of books was not a constitutionally significant burden on the plaintiffs' free exercise of religion. "[T]he evil prohibited by the Free Exercise Clause, said the court, is "governmental compulsion either to do or refrain from doing an act forbidden or required by one's religion, or to affirm or disavow a belief forbidden or required by one's religion," and reading or even discussing the books did not compel such action or affirmation."

Judge Lynch agreed. "The heart of the plaintiffs' free exercise claim is a claim of 'indoctrination': that the state has put pressure on their children to endorse an affirmative view of gay marriage and has thus undercut the parents' efforts to inculcate their children with their own opposing religious views. The Supreme Court, we believe, has never utilized an indoctrination test under the Free Exercise Clause, much less in the public school context. The closest it has come is *West Virginia Board of Educ. v. Barnette*, [319 U.S. 624 (1943), where] the Court held that the state could not coerce acquiescence through compelled statements of belief, such as the mandatory recital of the pledge of allegiance in public schools. It did not hold that the state could not attempt to inculcate values by instruction, and in fact carefully distinguished the two approaches. We do not address whether or not an indoctrination theory under the Free Exercise Clause is sound. Plaintiffs' pleadings do not establish a viable case of indoctrination, even assuming that extreme indoctrination can be a form of coercion.

"First, as to the parents' free exercise rights, the mere fact that a child is exposed on occasion in public school to a concept offensive to a parent's religious belief does not inhibit the parent from instructing the child differently. A parent whose 'child is exposed to sensitive topics or information [at school] remains free to discuss these matters and to place them in the family's moral or religious context, or to supplement the information with more appropriate materials.' *C.N. v. Ridgewood Bd. of Educ.*, 430 F.3d 159 (3d Cir. 2005). The parents here did in fact have notice, if not prior notice, of the books and of the school's overall intent to promote toleration of same-sex marriage, and they retained their ability to discuss the material and subject matter with their children. Our outcome does not turn, however, on whether the parents had notice.

"Turning to the children's free exercise rights, we cannot see how Jacob's free exercise right was burdened at all: two books were made available to him, but he was never required to read them or have them read to him. Further, these books do not endorse gay marriage or homosexuality, or even address these topics explicitly, but merely describe how other children might come from families that look different from one's own. There is no free exercise right to be free from any reference in public elementary schools to the existence of families in which the parents are of different gender combinations.

"Joey has a more significant claim, both because he was required to sit through a classroom reading of *King and King* and because that book affirmatively endorses homosexuality and gay marriage. It is a fair inference that the reading of *King and King* was precisely intended to influence the listening children toward tolerance of gay marriage. That was the point of why that book was chosen and used. Even assuming there is a continuum along which an intent to influence could become an attempt to indoctrinate, however, this case is firmly on the influence-toward-tolerance end. There is no evidence of systemic indoctrination. There is no allegation that Joey was asked to affirm gay marriage. Requiring a student to read a particular book is generally not coercive of free exercise rights.

"On the facts, there is no viable claim of 'indoctrination' here. Without suggesting that such showings would suffice to establish a claim of indoctrination, we note the plaintiffs' children were not forced to read the books on pain of suspension. Nor were they subject to a constant stream of like materials. There is no allegation here of a formalized curriculum requiring students to read many books affirming gay marriage. The reading by a teacher of one book, or even three, and even if to a young and impressionable child, does not constitute 'indoctrination.' "

Notes on the Free Exercise of Religion and Liberty-Based Objections to Marriage Equality

Would an exemption for objecting parents be good policy even if not constitutionally mandated? Dean Martha Minow, "Should Religious Groups Be Exempt from Civil Rights Law?," 48 *B.C.L. Rev.* 781 (2007), argues in favor of negotiated rather than zero-sum outcomes in disputes such as this one. Under her approach, it would have made sense for the local school system to work out an arrangement with traditionalist parents where they would receive some notice of religion-sensitive materials and an opportunity to figure out how they want to respond. From a gay-friendly point of view, what are the likely benefits as well as costs for Dean Minow's approach?

Recall that the federal judges in *Parker* did not adjudicate the applicability of the instruction-in-sexuality exemption under state law (editors' note "e" above). William N. Eskridge Jr., "A Jurisprudence of 'Coming Out': Religion, Sexuality, and Liberty/Equality Collisions in Public Law," 106 *Yale L.J.* 2411 (1997), argues that state as well as federal judges should interpret ambiguous statutes in ways that accommodate religion, to the extent that accommodation does not clearly thwart important state policies. Under Eskridge's theory, Massachusetts state judges should be open to the Parkers' interpretation of the state statutory exemption. What are the costs as well as benefits to such an approach to statutory interpretation?

Note on California's Education Anti-Discrimination Laws

In contrast to "no promo homo" jurisdictions like North Carolina and Texas, the California Legislature has restructured, by law, the tone of public, and some private, education in that state. As amended in 2011, California's Education Code provides the following mandate:

> It is the policy of the State of California to afford all persons in public schools, regardless of their disability, gender, gender identity, gender expression, nationality, race or ethnicity, religion, sexual orientation, or any other characteristic that is contained in the definition of hate crimes set forth in Section 422.55 of the Penal Code, equal rights and opportunities in the educational institutions of the state.

As an element in this policy, 2011 Cal. Stats. ch. 81 (S.B. 48) amended the Education Code to protect LGBT students and teachers against discrimination:

> No person shall be subjected to discrimination on the basis of disability, gender, gender identity, gender expression, nationality, race or ethnicity, religion, sexual orientation * * * in any program or activity conducted by an educational institution that receives, or benefits from, state financial assistance or enrolls pupils who receive state student financial aid. No person shall be subjected to

discrimination on the basis of disability, gender, gender identity, gender expression, nationality, race or ethnicity, religion, sexual orientation * * * in any program or activity conducted by an educational institution that receives, or benefits from, state financial assistance or enrolls pupils who receive state student financial aid.

Cal. Educ. Code § 220. In addition to this broad prohibition, the 2011 law imposes more particular duties: "A teacher shall not give instruction and a school district shall not sponsor any activity that promotes a discriminatory bias on the basis of race or ethnicity, gender, religion, disability, nationality, or sexual orientation, or because of a characteristic listed in Section 220." Cal. Educ. Code § 51500. Section 51501 prohibits the use of textbooks or other instructional materials that "contain any matter reflecting adversely upon persons on the basis of * * * sexual orientation."

Although the Legislature viewed these new policies as doing nothing more than creating a neutral classroom setting where LGBT students can flourish, some parents view these as policies "promoting" homosexuality, and in ways they do not like. Indeed from the perspective of some religious parents, "normalizing" homosexuality, as these laws do, is the same as "promoting" it. See *Parker v. Hurley*, 514 F.3d 87 (1st Cir. 2008), where parents unsuccessfully sought a constitutional right to withdraw their children from instruction valuing same-sex marriage. In California, although parents do not have a right to remove their children from general instruction, they do have a right to remove their children from public school "instruction in health [that] conflicts with the religious training and beliefs of a parent or guardian or a pupil." Cal. Educ. Code § 51240.

Under the foregoing legal regime, and encouraged by the inclusive constitutional culture of the state, California schools are often proactive—celebrating sexual and gender diversity as well as barring anti-LGBT bullying and discrimination. Sometimes, that celebration triggers pushbacks from religious students who oppose the celebration of conduct their faith traditions consider sinful and socially destructive.

Tyler Chase Harper v. Poway Unified School District

United States Court of Appeals for the Ninth Circuit, 2006.
445 F.3d 1166.

■ JUDGE REINHARDT delivered the opinion for the court:

[In 2003, the school permitted a student group called the Gay-Straight Alliance to hold a "Day of Silence" to "teach tolerance of others, particularly those of a different sexual orientation." Several incidents occurred at the school as a result of antihomosexual comments made by students in response; a week later, a group of students organized a "Straight-Pride Day," during which they wore T-shirts which displayed antigay slogans; some students were asked to remove the shirts and did so, while others were suspended for their actions.

[The day after the 2004 Day of Silence, Chase Harper wore a T-shirt whose front read "BE ASHAMED, OUR SCHOOL EMBRACED WHAT GOD HAS CONDEMNED"; the back read "HOMOSEXUALITY IS SHAMEFUL 'Romans 1:27.' " One of Harper's teachers reported that the T-shirt caused quite a stir among the students and sent Harper to the principal's office, where the principal explained why that particular T-shirt was inappropriate and how students of faith could express their views in a less inflammatory manner. According to the principal, Harper said that he had already been "confronted by a group of students on campus" and was "involved in a tense verbal conversation" earlier that morning. When Harper refused to remove the T-shirt, the principal confined Harper to his office for the remainder of the day; the student was not suspended, nor was a disciplinary report placed in his file. Harper brought a lawsuit seeking an injunction against future censorship of his attire.]

In [*Tinker v. Des Moines Indep. Community Sch. Dist.*, 393 U.S. 503 (1969)], the Supreme Court held that public schools may restrict student speech which "intrudes upon . . . the rights of other students" or "colli[des] with the rights of other students to be secure and to be let alone." Harper argues that *Tinker's* reference to the "rights of other students" should be construed narrowly to involve only circumstances in which a student's right to be free from direct physical confrontation is infringed. * * *

* * * Public school students who may be injured by verbal assaults on the basis of a core identifying characteristic such as race, religion, or sexual orientation, have a right to be free from such attacks while on school campuses. As *Tinker* clearly states, students have the right to "be secure and to be let alone." Being secure involves not only freedom from physical assaults but from psychological attacks that cause young people to question their self-worth and their rightful place in society. * * * Because minors are subject to mandatory attendance requirements, the Court has emphasized "the obvious concern on the part of parents, and school authorities acting *in loco parentis*, to protect children—especially in a captive audience. . . ." Although name-calling is ordinarily protected outside the school context, "students cannot hide behind the First Amendment to protect their 'right' to abuse and intimidate other students at school."

Speech that attacks high school students who are members of minority groups that have historically been oppressed, subjected to verbal and physical abuse, and made to feel inferior, serves to injure and intimidate them, as well as to damage their sense of security and interfere with their opportunity to learn. [Judge Reinhardt cited studies showing a corresponding decline in academic performance among gay students because of anti-gay harassment by other students, and cited but did not rely upon a California statute guaranteeing the right to education free of discrimination because of sexual orientation and other traits.]

* * * [T]he School had a valid and lawful basis for restricting Harper's wearing of his T-shirt on the ground that his conduct was injurious to gay and lesbian students and interfered with their right to learn.

* * * It is simply not a novel concept * * * that such attacks on young minority students can be harmful to their self-esteem and to their ability to learn. [*Brown v. Board of Education.*] If a school permitted its students to wear shirts reading, "Negroes: Go Back To Africa," no one would doubt that the message would be harmful to young black students. * * *

[Judge Reinhardt responded to the dissent's argument that Harper was merely participating in an intense debate about a "political" issue, namely, homosexuality. But disparaging remarks that "strike[ ] at a core identifying characteristic of students on the basis of their membership in a minority group" are more than just political.] T-shirts proclaiming, "Young Republicans Suck," or "Young Democrats Suck," for example, may not be very civil but they would certainly not be sufficiently damaging to the individual or the educational process to warrant a limitation on the wearer's First Amendment rights. * * *

* * * Limitations on student speech must be narrow * * *. Accordingly, we limit our holding to instances of derogatory and injurious remarks directed at students' minority status such as race, religion, and sexual orientation. * * * As young students acquire more strength and maturity, and specifically as they reach college age, they become adequately equipped emotionally and intellectually to deal with the type of verbal assaults that may be prohibited during their earlier years. Accordingly, we do not condone the use in public colleges or other public institutions of higher learning of restrictions similar to those permitted here.

[T]he School's actions here were no more than necessary to prevent the intrusion on the rights of other students. * * * Harper was not suspended from school * * *. [Judge Reinhardt ruled that the school's action was justified by *Tinker*'s indication that schools could limit expression where needed to protect the "rights of others"; the opinion had "no cause to decide whether the evidence would be sufficient to warrant denial of a preliminary injunction under the 'substantial disruption' prong" of *Tinker*. Judge Reinhardt also rejected Harper's claim that the school's action constituted impermissible viewpoint discrimination, noting that "[p]art of a school's 'basic educational mission' is the inculcation of 'fundamental values of habits and manners of civility essential to a democratic society.' [*Fraser.*]"]

■ JUDGE KOZINSKI dissenting:

[Although Judge Reinhardt did not rest his opinion on *Tinker*'s dictum that schools could limit student expression that would materially disrupt the educational process, Judge Kozinski engaged in a lengthy analysis rejecting the school's argument based upon that prong of *Tinker*.

He strongly criticized the school's argument that Harper's t-shirt would "materially disrupt[ ] classwork." Although one teacher said that several students in class were "off-task talking about [the] content of Chase's shirt," the only evidence of actual disruption, Judge Kozinski minimized that evidence on the ground that "it is not unusual in a high school classroom for students to be 'off-task.'" The authorities were also concerned about possible connections between Harper's T-shirt and disruptions the year before, but Judge Kozinski responded that the record contained no evidence demonstrating that his T-shirt was similar to past anti-gay provocations.]

[As to the court's argument that Harper's T-shirt was an "invasion of the rights of others," *Tinker*'s alternative basis for school regulation of expression, Judge Kozinski expressed skepticism that the single T-shirt violated statutory or other rights gay students might have. In response to the majority's idea that messages such as Harper's are so offensive and demeaning that they interfere with the ability of homosexual students to partake of the educational environment, Judge Kozinski suggested that there was no support in the record nor was there systematic empirical evidence to that effect.]

I find it significant, moreover, that Harper did not thrust his view of homosexuality into the school environment as part of a campaign to demean or embarrass other students. Rather, he was responding to public statements made by others with whom he disagreed. Whatever one might think are the psychological effects of unprovoked demeaning statements by one student against another, the effects may be quite different when they are part of a political give-and-take. By participating in the Day of Silence activities, homosexual students perforce acknowledge that their status is not universally admired or accepted; the whole point of the Day of Silence, as I understand it, is to dispute views like those characterized by Harper's t-shirt. Supporters of the Day of Silence may prefer to see views such as Harper's channeled into public discourse rather than officially suppressed but whispered behind backs or scribbled on bathroom walls. Confronting—and refuting—such views in a public forum may well empower homosexual students, contributing to their sense of self-esteem.

* * * The new doctrine [the majority creates] applies only to statements that demean students based on their "minority status such as race, religion, and sexual orientation." Is this a right created by state law? By federal law? By common law? And if interference with the learning process is the keystone to the new right, how come it's limited to those characteristics that are associated with minority status? Students may well have their self-esteem bruised by being demeaned for being white or Christian, or having bad acne or weight problems, or being poor or stupid or any one of the infinite number of characteristics that will not qualify them for minority status. * * *

Even the concept of minority status is not free from doubt. In defining what is a minority—and hence protected—do we look to the national community, the state, the locality or the school? In a school that has 60 percent black students and 40 percent white students, will the school be able to ban t-shirts with anti-black racist messages but not those with anti-white racist messages, or vice versa? Must a Salt Lake City high school prohibit or permit *Big Love* t-shirts?

And at what level of generality do we define a minority group? If the Pope speaks out against gay marriage, can gay students wear to school t-shirts saying "Catholics Are Bigots," or will they be demeaning the core characteristic of a religious minority? And, are Catholics part of a monolithic Christian majority, or a minority sect that has endured centuries of discrimination in America? * * *

The school's harassment policy seems to prohibit any student speech, whether it be in the classroom, elsewhere on campus, in connection with any school activity, going to and returning from school and quite possibly at all other times and places, if it is derogatory, intended to be derogatory or believed to be derogatory of other students based on certain characteristics—race, ethnicity, sexual orientation, religion, sex or disability. The prohibition extends to jokes or caricatures—based on negative stereotypes—wearing of clothing that portrays "derogatory connotations directed toward sexual identity," name-calling, anything that someone who is a member of one of the protected categories believes was directed against him on account of his status, and any statement by the speaker that exalts his own status in comparison to that of others. * * *

So interpreted, the school's harassment policy is substantially overbroad. * * * The policy here * * * is not limited to speech that is vulgar, as defined by *Fraser*, or likely to cause substantial disruption under *Tinker*. * * *

* * * Assuming, as we must, that on the next Day of Silence Harper will not be allowed to wear a t-shirt expressing his interpretation of Romans 1:27, what exactly *can* he say or wear? Would a t-shirt quoting Romans 1:27 be permissible, or is it prohibited because a homosexual student might interpret it as "motivated by bias against him/her"? * * * May Harper have a discussion at lunchtime where he says: "Homosexuality is sinful"? On his way home from school, may he tell another student a joke disparaging the movie *Brokeback Mountain*? Once he gets home, can he post criticism of the Day of Silence on his MySpace page? Given the broad language of the policy, I believe any and all of these could be punished by the school authorities as hate behavior. * * *

I also have sympathy for defendants' position that students in school are a captive audience and should not be forced to endure speech that they find offensive and demeaning. There is surely something to the notion that a Jewish student might not be able to devote his full attention to school activities if the fellow in the seat next to him is wearing a t-shirt with the message "Hitler Had the Right Idea" in front and "Let's Finish the Job!" on the back. This t-shirt may well interfere with the educational experience even if the two students never come to blows or even have words about it.

Perhaps school authorities should have greater latitude to control student speech than allowed them by Justice Fortas's Vietnam-era opinion in *Tinker*. * * * While I sympathize with my colleagues' effort to tinker with the law in this area, I am not convinced we have the authority to do so, which is why I must respectfully dissent.

NOTES ON HIGH SCHOOL CENSORSHIP IN THE "T-SHIRT WARS"

1. *Evolving Social Norms and First Amendment "Neutrality."* Notice how the First Amendment context changes between the Stonewall riots in 1969 and *Harper* in the new millennium. In the twentieth century, when "homosexuals" were stigmatized by the state as well as society, gay people relied on the First Amendment (not always successfully) to protect themselves when they "came out of the closet"; high schools students relied on the First Amendment so that they could express their gay identity. *E.g., Fricke v. Lynch,* 491 F. Supp. 381 (D.R.I. 1980). In contrast, the student in *Harper* invoked the First Amendment so that he could express his traditionalist identity. In the earlier cases, traditionalists were offended by the student's expression; in *Harper*, gay students and their friends were offended by the student's expression. In the earlier cases (like *Fricke*), courts often enjoined school censorship; in *Harper*, the court does not.

Judge Kozinski argues that *Harper* represents a departure from the First Amendment's norm of neutrality—a norm that persuaded homophobic as well as gay-friendly judges in the past to give gay rights advocates space to make their case within college and university settings, as well as high school settings in more recent cases. Why shouldn't traditionalist students like Chase Harper have the same First Amendment protections that Aaron Fricke had a generation ago?

In *Nuxoll ex rel. Nuxoll v. Indian Prairie Sch. Dist. No. 204*, 523 F.3d 668 (7th Cir. 2008), the Seventh Circuit considered a high school's censorship of a T-shirt that read "Happy, Not Gay" in response to the school's celebration of diversity. Judge Posner's opinion sustained an injunction protecting that particular message but narrowed the injunction so that school officials could regulate or ban more aggressive antigay messages. Judge Kozinski seems open to a similar idea in *Harper*. Where should they draw the line? Should administrators be able to ban a T-shirt that says "Leviticus 20:13"? How about if the T-shirt also contains this message: "God says, 'Death to Homosexuals'"?

2. *Hate Speech in Schools.* Professor Mari Matsuda argues that hate speech is not entitled to normal First Amendment protection. See Mari Matsuda, "Public Response to Racist Speech: Considering the Victim's Story," 87 *Mich. L. Rev.* 2320 (1989). This line of theory is applied to *Harper* and *Nuxoll* by Shannon Gilreath, " 'Tell Your Faggot Friend He Owes Me $500 for My Broken Hand': Thoughts on a Substantive Equality Theory of

Free Speech," 44 *Wake Forest L. Rev.* 557 (2009). Professor Gilreath makes an analogy between antigay hate speech in American public schools and anti-Semitic hate speech in Nazi public schools. Both are forms of *anti-identity speech* exploiting social prejudice and stereotypes to demonize a minority group with impressionable youth, so that prejudice and stereotypes will continue to the next generation.

"Indeed," argues Professor Gilreath, "the parallels between anti-Semitic speech [of the Nazi era] and anti-Gay speech now are overwhelming—not obvious only to those who do not wish to see. * * * Anti-identity speech labeling Gays as the maniacal 'other' abounds and finds the receptive ear of many public policymakers." One Nazi propagandist wrote: "[T]he wire-pullers behind every disaster that has overtaken the people is the eternal Jew." * * * Professor Gilreath compares these anti-Semitic utterances to the testimony before Congress of Robert Knight, leader of the Family Research Council: "Homosexuals display political control far beyond their numbers. A tiny fraction of the population (about one percent), homosexuals have one of the largest and fastest growing Political Action Committees in the country (the Human Rights Campaign) and give millions of dollars to candidates." Concludes Professor Gilreath: "Like Jews, Gays are a threat because we are supposedly better educated, have better jobs, and make more money than other people." (Recall Justice Scalia's dissenting opinion in *Romer v. Evans* [Chapter 1, Section 2B].)

Is this a persuasive analogy? Or is the social context different in a material way? How would Judges Posner and Kozinski respond to playing the "Nazi card"? For an excellent discussion of the challenges to multiculturalism presented by the religion-homosexuality clashes in schools, see Doug NeJaime, "Inclusion, Accommodation, and Recognition: Accounting for Differences Based on Religion and Sexual Orientation," 32 *Harv. J. L. & Gender* 303 (2009).

3. *The Legal Aftermath of* Harper: *Bong Hits 4 T-Shirts?* At roughly the same time the Ninth Circuit was deciding Tyler Harper's case, the Supreme Court was deciding *Morse v. Frederick,* 551 U.S. 393 (2007). In *Morse,* a divided Court upheld a high school principal's discipline of a student who displayed a sign "BONG HiTS 4 JESUS" when the Olympic torch passed through town. Chief Justice Roberts' opinion for the Court did not credit the sign as political speech and ruled that the principal had authority to regulate the sign, because the students were watching the torch pass as part of an official school field trip and because its implications were contrary to the school's antidrug philosophy. Thus, the sign was inherently "disruptive" under *Tinker.* (Justice Thomas wrote a concurring opinion indicating that *Tinker* should be overruled.)

After *Morse* was decided, the Supreme Court vacated the *Harper* decision, and remanded it with instructions to dismiss the case as moot, as Harper had graduated from Poway by this time. *Harper v. Poway Unified Sch. Dist.,* 127 S. Ct. 1484 (2007). Does the Supreme Court's decision in *Morse* result in strengthening or weakening Harper's claim? Might cases like *Harper* have motivated Justice Alito's concurring opinion, which supported school censorship of an ambiguous "BONG HiTS 4 JESUS" banner but left open the possibility that the First Amendment would protect religious identity speech, including "Homosexuality Is Shameful" and "Happy, Not Gay" slogans?

NOTE ON PROPOSITION 8 AND LIBERTY-PROTECTING ARGUMENTS AGAINST MARRIAGE EQUALITY

Parker v. Hurley, California's progay Education Code, and perhaps even the *Harper* appeal figured into the most divisive and dramatic popular initiative of the new millennium: Proposition 8, which amended the California Constitution to override the California Supreme Court's decision invalidating the state's limitation of civil marriages to one man, one woman.

The home page of the Protect Marriage website offered a pop-up cartoon that depicted a happy suburban family: Tom the Dad, Jan the Mom, Two Kids, their dog—and their neighbors, a male couple (Dan and Michael). See Appendix 8 to this Casebook.[b] The gays kept the family's pet dog when they went on vacation, and Jan brought Dan soup when he was sick. Dramatic tension comes to the cartoon when Proposition 8 is placed on the election ballot, and the family has to decide: Should we take away the matrimonial rights of our nice neighbors?

The dramatic tension eases when Jan and Tom do some research on the internet and discover that their gay buddies have *all the rights and benefits of marriage*, through the domestic partnership statute. Why do Dan and Michael need to have "marriage" when they already have all these rights? Then, Jan learns from her sister Nancy that when Massachusetts recognized same-sex marriage, one school forced children to learn that gay marriage was as good as traditional marriage; even though parents objected, the courts ruled that the school could do this without even notifying the parents. (The case, of course, was *Parker v. Hurley,* excerpted above.) Concerned by *Parker,* Jan and Tom wonder whether changing the definition of marriage would open a Pandora's Box: Would the school system teach their children that gay marriage is just as good as traditional marriage? What message would that send the children? Would their church be required to perform same-sex marriages, contrary to its teachings? The decision becomes easier and easier, the more Tom and Jan research and deliberate. They decide to support Proposition 8—and then invite the gay guys over for a barbecue.

Parker fueled a liberty-based argument against *The Marriage Cases*: If gay marriage were "forced" upon the citizenry by "activist" judges, then *Parker* meant that traditionalist parents could be forced to allow their children to be "indoctrinated" into the "homosexual agenda," violating the natural rights of parents to rear their children in their own values.[c] If gay marriage meant that parental rights would be sacrificed, it also might mean

---

[b] Appendix 8 to this Casebook reprints this cartoon and some of the other background materials developed by supporters of Proposition 8.

[c] For examinations of the Proposition 8 campaign, see William Eskridge Jr., "The California Supreme Court, 2007–2008—Foreword: The Marriage Cases, Reversing the Burden of Inertia in a Pluralist Democracy," 97 *Calif. L. Rev.* 1785, 1825–34 (2009); Melissa Murray, "Equal Rites and Equal Rights," 96 *Calif. L. Rev.* 1395 (2008); Douglas NeJaime, "Winning Through Losing," 96 *Iowa L. Rev.* 941 (2011).

that churches and other traditionalist institutions would also be forced into acquiescence in the "homosexual agenda," contrary to core religious beliefs. This argument was also made in early October 2008 by a series of television ads, including the famous "Two Princes" ad, showing a little Latina who alarms her Mother with the news that she wants to marry a Princess, based on what she learned in school. These ads were the turning point in the campaign, all but ensuring the triumph of Proposition 8.

Ironically, California law was not entirely consistent with the *Parker v. Hurley* scenario. Although California law before the *Marriage Cases* (and after Proposition 8) barred public schools from disrespecting sexual minorities, California law both before and after the *Marriage Cases* (1) did *not* require schools to teach anything about gay marriage, (2) *did* require school districts to consult with parents if they offered instruction on "controversial topics such as homosexuality," and (3) *did* provide parents rights to remove their children from "instruction that conflicts with their religious beliefs." See Eskridge, "Marriage Cases," 1832–33 (providing references to California law).

CHAPTER 5

SEXUALITY AND GENDER IN THE WORKPLACE

SECTION 1   Cultural and Legal Discourses at Work
SECTION 2   Pregnancy and Parenthood
SECTION 3   Sexual and Gender Harassment
SECTION 4   Gender Performance
SECTION 5   The Scope of "Because of Sex"

What does it mean to talk about sexuality or gender in the workplace? Possibilities include:

- Sexualized persons (unmarried pregnant women, out-of-the-closet gay men, lesbians, or bisexuals) or gender-inappropriate persons (transgender or non-binary persons, effeminate men, or masculine women) who others think do not "fit" in the workplace;

- The visible manifestation of sexual activity, such as pregnancy and photographs of partners or spouses;

- The choreographed display of gendered norm ideals, such as a waitress' wearing tight, body-revealing clothing, or their confusion, such as a man's wearing such clothing;

- Eroticized behavior, from flirting to office affairs;

- The use of sexuality to gain advantages in the workplace (*e.g.*, sleeping your way to the top);

- The use of sexuality as a mechanism of harassment, usually to dominate the space and dynamics of the workplace, and usually directed against those with traditionally less power.

Much of the law in this field implicitly seeks the purging of sexuality from the workplace. The traditional mechanism for purging sexuality from the (non-domestic) workplace was the exclusion of women, a norm that was naturalized in tandem with the idea that women's "place" was in the home. This began to slowly change after the adoption of the Fourteenth Amendment in 1868, as women brought colorable claims that state policies excluding them from the public sphere were unconstitutional.

In line with the old norms, the Illinois Supreme Court denied Myra Bradwell's application for a license to practice law solely because she was a (married) woman. The U.S. Supreme Court affirmed this judgment in

Bradwell v. Illinois, 83 U.S. (16 Wall.) 130 (1873), holding that Bradwell's exclusion did not violate the Privileges and Immunities Clause. Justice Bradley, speaking for himself and Justices Swayne and Field, concurred in the judgment on broad grounds, reflecting a widely held theory of sex and gender:

> [T]he civil law, as well as nature herself, has always recognized a wide difference in the respective spheres and destinies of man and woman. Man is, or should be, woman's protector and defender. The natural and proper timidity and delicacy which belongs to the female sex evidently unfits it for many of the occupations of civil life. The constitution of the family organization, which is founded in the divine ordinance, as well as in the nature of things, indicates the domestic sphere as that which properly belongs to the domain and functions of womanhood. The harmony, not to say identity, of interests and views which belong, or should belong, to the family institution is repugnant to the idea of a woman adopting a distinct and independent career from that of her husband. So firmly fixed was this sentiment in the founders of the common law that it became a maxim of that system of jurisprudence that a woman had no legal existence separate from her husband. * * *

After *Bradwell*, the Privileges and Immunities Clause was a dead end for challenges to state exclusions of women from the workplace, but constitutional litigation over sex discrimination issues continued under the Due Process and Equal Protection Clauses of the Fourteenth Amendment. The framing of the litigation varied with doctrine, but both lines of cases initially accepted then prevailing beliefs about the natural difference between sexes.

A century ago, the due process cases involved challenges to workplace "protections" for women. Early in the women's rights movement, Elizabeth Cady Stanton and Susan B. Anthony had advocated equal pay for equal work, eight-hour days, and better workplace conditions for women. Unions tended to fight for maximum hour laws mainly for women and children. Male workers often favored "protective" legislation as a way to channel women into "women's work" and away from competition with men. When Oregon's law setting maximum hours only for women was challenged, the main defenders of the law were the state, the National Consumers' League (founded during the Progressive era by social reformer Jane Addams), and its chief legal theoretician and advocate, Louis Brandeis. Notwithstanding its precedents at the time shielding employer-employee "liberty of contract" from regulation, the Supreme Court unanimously upheld the law, based upon the state's compelling interest in protecting women:

> That woman's physical structure and the performance of maternal functions place her at a disadvantage in the struggle for subsistence is obvious. * * * [B]y abundant testimony of the

medical fraternity continuance for a long time on her feet at work, repeating this from day to day, tends to injurious effects upon the body, and as healthy mothers are essential to vigorous offspring, the physical well-being of woman becomes an object of public interest and care in order to preserve the strength and vigor of the race. * * *

Muller v. Oregon, 208 U.S. 412, 421 (1908).

Thus, because of many factors, women constituted only about 20% of the paid labor force at the turn of the twentieth century. (Today the figure is 47%.) Because of gender segregation in the workforce, an overwhelming pattern then and a continuing problem today, they tended to be segregated into "women's work," jobs reflecting home-based values such as teaching, caretaking, or preparing and serving food.[a]

As a result, the early Equal Protection Clause cases involved statutes that "protected" women in traditional "women's" occupations, while excluding or restricting them from traditional "men's" occupations. In *Quong Wing v. Kirkendall*, 223 U.S. 59 (1912), the Court upheld a statute exempting any laundry operation of two or fewer women from a ten-dollar licensing fee. Justice Holmes wrote for the Court, finding the legislature's "ground of distinction in sex * * * not without precedent," citing *Muller*. "If Montana deems it advisable to put a lighter burden upon women than upon men with regard to an employment that our people commonly regard as more appropriate for the former, the Fourteenth Amendment does not interfere by creating a fictitious equality where there is a real difference."

In a case that resonated with the policing of women's sexuality, the Court upheld a statute allowing a woman to work as a bartender only if she were the wife or daughter of the bar owner. *Goesaert v. Cleary*, 335 U.S. 464 (1948). When, 15 years later, advocates challenged a policy requiring the firing of pregnant schoolteachers, the Court returned to the Due Process Clause as the anchor for its ruling. School districts at that time commonly had mandatory leave policies, forcing pregnant teachers to resign their position at least four to five months before the expected birth. As Justice Powell noted, "The records before us abound with proof that a principal purpose behind the adoption of the regulations was to keep visibly pregnant teachers out of the sight of schoolchildren." *Cleveland Board of Education v. LaFleur*, 414 U.S. 632, 653 (1974) (Powell, J., concurring). The Supreme Court held that the policies "employ irrebuttable presumptions that unduly penalize a female teacher for deciding to bear a child." *Id.* at 648 (opinion of the Court). Soon after *LaFleur*, the Court began analyzing exclusionary government employment policies under the Equal Protection Clause. (See Chapter 1,

---

[a] See Philip Foner, *Women and the American Labor Movement* (1979); Alice Kessler-Harris, *Out to Work: A History of Wage-Earning Women in the United States* 201–02 (1982); Julie Matthei, *An Economic History of Women in America* (1982); Elizabeth Brandeis, "Labor Legislation," in 3 *History of Labor in the United States* 462 (John Commons et al. eds. 1935).

Section 2A.) (The biggest advance during this period came not from constitutional law, but from the enactment of the Civil Rights Act of 1964.)

The story of sexual orientation discrimination in employment began with *Norton v. Macy* in 1969. (See Chapter 1, Section 2B.) It too is a story of early cases decided on due process grounds (such as *Norton*), with the courts later applying an equal protection analysis to the same issue.

Throughout, the baseline for all American employment law has been the at-will doctrine, under which employees could be fired or disciplined for any reason that was not prohibited by law. Today, civil rights laws form part of a web of statutory regulation of the workplace, the bounds of which are continuously contested.

SECTION 1

CULTURAL AND LEGAL DISCOURSES AT WORK

Until the twentieth century, when urbanization and industrialization definitively ended the reign of agrarian dominance, most Americans experienced work and family as one unitary institution. Its governance model was an idealized patriarchy. As work and family diverged, the role of public law increased, beginning in the Progressive era, continuing into the New Deal, and shaping the anti-discrimination principles enacted during the second half of the century.

Today, work and family are distinct rather than merged, but strong and overlapping connections between them remain, in life and law. Indeed, the relationship between an individual's work and other aspects of life—economic, interpersonal, psychodynamic, political—is too complex for any one theory to capture.

As you read the materials in this section, consider how the debates over the law related to sexuality and gender in the workplace have been shaped by, and how they are reshaping, some of the major intellectual and jurisprudential frameworks from the last century. For example:

- For a believer in classical law and economics, the dominant purpose of law is to maximize efficiency. The regulation of markets, including labor markets, is desirable only when the result produces greater aggregate wealth than would result from allowing private parties to negotiate.

- For those influenced by Marx and socialism, as were the Legal Realists, the workplace is a venue for a continuous power struggle between the forces of labor and capital, with law inevitably reinforcing the subordination of the former and the dominance of the latter.

- Disciples of Max Weber and Talcott Parsons would evaluate the success of an economic enterprise by the extent to which it incorporates the impersonal dynamics of bureaucracy, in which success is based on merit and workplace relations are governed by rules rather than by relationships or social status.

- Followers of the Frankfort School of Critical Theory and Critical Legal Studies scholars, skeptical that there can be objective knowledge independent of intersubjective forms of understanding, would look closely at the social, historical and ideological processes for construction of workplace law and norms.

- For liberal scholars such as John Rawls and Ronald Dworkin, the lodestar value for society is equality, and so the primary question is whether the full network of workplace relations (not just management-employee relations) is regulated in such a way as to maximize social equality.

- For feminist, queer theory and critical race scholars, the workplace provides perhaps the example par excellence of an institution in which systems of subordination can erect barriers, perpetuate privilege and shape individual self-conception. But, as Michel Foucault pointed out, institutional sites of oppression can also provide venues of resistance.

Differences in jurisprudential philosophy are embedded in the very structure of the law. For example, most of the analysis in this chapter relates to some form of anti-discrimination law. Might there be a different starting point chosen by followers of some of these schools of thought? What would those be? For example, should sexual harassment be a tort instead of a civil rights claim? When does anti-discrimination law overlap with social welfare? Consider the challenges that lie ahead as the categories of protected classifications in anti-discrimination statutes must be applied to persons with fluid sexual and gender identities.

In this first section of the chapter, we begin with a sampling of socio-legal texts in Part A, and then turn to the densely statutory field of employment law. Part B summarizes federal law, focusing on the primary statute with which we will be concerned: Title VII of the Civil Rights Act. (Title VII is also excerpted in Appendix 2) In Part C, we briefly describe state and local law. In subsequent sections, we examine a series of recurring issues that challenge both the doctrinal and theoretical components of employment law.

A. NO SEX AT WORK?

Before delving into legal doctrine, consider how different authors have analyzed the management of sexuality in the workplace. How might each form the basis for legal regulation?

Rosemary Pringle, "Sexuality at Work"
From *Secretaries Talk* (1988).*

If the boss-secretary relation is organised around sexuality and family imagery this seems to place it outside the modern bureaucratic structures that are a feature of all large organisations. The relationship is often conceptualised either as archaic or as marginal to the workings

---

* Copyright © 1988, Verso Books. Reprinted by permission.

of bureaucracy "proper". It is argued here that, on the contrary, the boss-secretary relationship is the most visible aspect of a pattern of domination based on desire and sexuality. Far from being an exception, it vividly illustrates the workings of modern bureaucracies. Gender and sexuality are central not only in the boss-secretary relation but in all workplace power relations.

Two bodies of theory are important to the development of this argument. A variety of feminist analyses, particularly of sexual harassment, indicate the ubiquity of coercive sexual encounters in the workplace; and theorists such as Marcuse and Foucault have indicated, in their different ways, the connections between sexual *pleasure* and the operations of *power*. By contrast, most organisation theory continues to treat sexuality and gender as marginal or incidental to the workplace. In doing so, however, it expresses a widely held view that while gender was central to "traditional" social relations it has become outmoded in "modern" society which is more concerned with "personhood". Since degendering is implicit in the modernist emphasis on rationality and in the development of liberal democratic institutions, it is important to start by considering the ways in which gender is suppressed in the main texts.

For [Max] Weber bureaucracy is progressive in that it breaks down the old patriarchal structures and removes the arbitrary power held by fathers and masters in traditional society. He distinguishes between traditionalism, which is patriarchal, and the rational-legal order of the modern world which promises the end of tyranny and despotism and the development of liberal democracy. All attempts to theorise bureaucracy have been carried out in the shadow of Weber's classical account. He still sets the terms of the dominant frameworks for studies of power and organisations. Although the limits of his theory have been clearly shown in more than half a century of organisation studies, Weber's version retains a powerful ideological hold. People's views of how organisations actually do work and how they "ought" to work are still filtered through Weber and the theory becomes, in some sense, a self-fulfilling prophecy.

Weber has been given a favourable reading by liberal feminists because he does appear to provide a basis for understanding breakdown of patriarchal relations. Equal Employment Opportunity and Affirmative Action plans, for example, emphasize the importance of excluding "private" considerations and insist on the impersonal application of rules. Secretaries, it is thought, should ignore or reject the sexual and familial images and focus on skills and career ladders. The implication here is that secretarial work should be "rationalized", made to fit the bureaucratic pattern. In her broadly liberal feminist analysis, *Men and Women of the Corporation* [1977], Rosabeth Moss Kanter denies that gender or sexuality have much explanatory potential. She observes that "what look like sex differences may really be power differences" and that "power wipes out sex" [pp. 201–12]. In this framework the problem for secretaries is that they lack power; they are caught up in an old-fashioned patriarchal relationship that is out of kilter with "modern" business practices. The question then becomes how can individual secretaries remove themselves from these backwaters and place themselves on the management ladder? Kanter's very lucid analysis of the power structure is designed to help individuals articulate their positions and thereby improve their own manoeuvering for power.

According to Weber the overriding concerns of bureaucratic organisations are efficiency and consistency in the application of rules. Authority established by rules stands in contrast to the "regulation of relationships through individual privilege and bestowals of favour" which characterizes patrimonialism. Traditional forms of domination are based on the household unit and are patriarchal in the direct sense that the father, as head of the family, possesses authority. In larger forms of traditional organisation authority is patrimonial, that is, it takes the form of personal allegiance to the master. In bureaucracy, by contrast, loyalty is to an office not to a particular person. Impersonality and the separation of the public and private spheres distinguish bureaucracy from traditionalism. As theorised by Weber, bureaucracy "has a 'rational' character: rules, means, ends, and matter-of-factness dominate its bearing. . . . The march of bureaucracy has destroyed structures of domination which had no rational character, in the special sense of the term."

According to Weber's "ideal type," bureaucracies are based on impersonality, functional specialisation, a hierarchy of authority and the impartial application of rules. There are well-defined duties for each specialised position and recruitment takes place on criteria of demonstrated knowledge and competence. Authority is held in the context of strict rules and regulations and graded hierarchically with the supervision of lower offices by higher ones. Authority established by rules stands in contrast to the "regulation of relationships through individual privileges and bestowals of favor" which characterised traditional structures. Above all there is a separation of the public world of rationality and efficiency from the private sphere of emotional and personal life.

The boss-secretary relationship runs against every one of these criteria. By having direct access to the powerful, secretaries are outside the hierarchy of authority. Far from being specialised, they can be called upon to do just about anything, and their work may overlap with that of their bosses. The relationship is based on personal rapport, involves a degree of intimacy, day-to-day familiarity and shared secrets unusual for any but lovers or close friends, and is capable of generating intense feelings of loyalty, dependency and personal commitment. How are we to explain this least "bureaucratic" of relationships? Is it merely an exception or does its existence suggest problems with the way bureaucracy itself has been theorised? * * *

It remains important to analyse the discourse of "bureaucratic rationality" as it affects men and women. This involves not so much a rejection of Weber as a rereading designed to bring out the underlying assumptions. It can be argued that while the rational-legal or bureaucratic form presents itself as gender-neutral, it actually constitutes a new kind of patriarchal structure. The apparent neutrality of rules and goals disguises the class and gender interests served by them. Weber's account of "rationality" can be interpreted as a commentary on the construction of a particular kind of masculinity based on the exclusion of the personal, the sexual and the feminine from any definition of "rationality". The values of instrumental rationality are strongly associated with the masculine individual, while the feminine is associated with that "other" world of chaos and disorder. This does not mean that men are in fact "rational" or that women are "emotional" but rather that they learn to recognise themselves in these conceptions.

It may be argued that "rationality" requires as a condition of its existence the simultaneous creation of a realm of the Other, be it personal, emotional, sexual or "irrational". Masculine rationality attempts to drive out the feminine but does not exist without it. "Work" and "sex" are implicitly treated as the domains of the "conscious" and the "unconscious". But far from being separate spheres the two are thoroughly intertwined. Despite the illusion of ordered rationality, workplaces do not actually manage to exclude the personal or sexual. Rather than seeing the presence of sexuality and familial relations in the workplace as an aspect of traditional, patriarchal authority, it makes more sense to treat them as part of modern organisational forms. I am concerned here not with "actual" families but with the family symbolism that structures work as well as personal relationships. The media, advertising and popular culture are saturated in such imagery, which provides a dominant set of social meanings in contemporary capitalist society. * * *

If we accept that a series of discourses on sexuality underpin bureaucratic control it is possible to see secretaries not as marginal but as paradigmatic of how that power operates. Thus the boss-secretary relation need not be seen as an anomalous piece of traditionalism or of an incursion of the private sphere, but rather as a site of strategies of power in which sexuality is an important though by no means the only dimension. Far from being marginal to the workplace, sexuality is everywhere. It is alluded to in dress and self-presentation, in jokes and gossip, looks and flirtations, secret affairs and dalliances, in fantasy, and in the range of coercive behaviours that we now call sexual harassment. Rather than being exceptional in its sexualisation, the boss-secretary relation is an important nodal point for the organisation of sexuality and pleasure. This is no less true when the boss happens to be a woman.

Sex at work is very much on display. It is undoubtedly true that for both men and women sexual fantasies and interactions are a way of killing time, of giving a sense of adventure, of livening up an otherwise boring day. As Michael Korda put it, "the amount of sexual energy circulating in any office is awe-inspiring, and given the slightest sanction and opportunity it bursts out".[a] Marcuse was one of the first to recognise the pervasiveness of sexuality in the workplace and to try to theorise it. He recognised that it was not just an instance of incomplete repression but was encouraged as a means of gratification in otherwise boring jobs. If open-plan offices are about surveillance they are also, he suggests, about controlled sex.

Marcuse introduced the concept of "repressive desublimation" to explain how people were being integrated into a system which in its sweeping rationality, which propels efficiency and growth, is itself irrational.[b] He pointed to the ways in which, without ceasing to be an instrument of labour, the body is allowed to exhibit its sexual features in the everyday work world and in work relations . . . The sexy office and sales girls, the handsome, virile junior executive and floor worker are highly marketable commodities, and the possession of suitable mistresses . . . facilitates the career of even the less exalted ranks in the business community . . . Sex is integrated into work and public relations and is thus made susceptible to (controlled) satisfaction . . . But no matter how controlled . . . it is also gratifying to the managed individuals . . . Pleasure, thus adjusted, generates submission.[c]

In Foucault's account, sexuality in the workplace is not simply repressed or sublimated or subjected to controlled expression. It is actively produced in a multiplicity of discourses and interactions. Modern Western societies have accumulated a vast network of discourses on sex and pleasure. We expect to find pleasure in self-improvement in both our work and non-work activities. Purposive activity operates not through the denial of pleasure but its promise: we will become desirable. * * *

The difficulty with both Marcuse and Foucault is that they are gender-blind. While they establish the centrality of sexuality in the workplace they pay very little attention to gender. Marcuse presumes that men and women are equally and similarly oppressed, ignoring the ways that women are required to market sexual attractiveness to men. Foucault acknowledges gender struggles but does not afford them any priority or permanence. Central to his work is the idea that there is no constant human subject or any rational course to history. If there is no human subject then for Foucault there is no gendered subject. Feminist struggles are, like any others, merely immediate responses to local and specific situations. Foucault's account of power is counterposed to any binary opposition between rulers and ruled. Though he underplays the significance of gender he does provide the basis for developing a more dynamic and fluid conception of power relations between men and

---

[a] Michael Korda, *Male Chauvinism! How It Works* 108 (1972).

[b] Herbert Marcuse, *One Dimensional Man* 12 (1968).

[c] *Id.* at 70–71.

women. "Male power" is not simply and unilaterally imposed on women—gender relations are a process involving strategies and counter-strategies of power. * * *

Vicki Schultz, "The Sanitized Workplace"

112 *Yale Law Journal* 2061, 2158–60, 2191 (2003).[*]

* * * [F]or many employees, the determination of whether certain sexual behaviors are offensive (or perhaps even "sexual") turns on who is engaging in it. Such findings are not surprising, for they confirm the general insight that workplace sexuality is given meaning within organizational context. As a result, the same sexual conduct that would be tolerated—or even welcomed—from coworkers of a similar status may well be labeled sexual harassment if it is engaged in by coworkers of a different status, particularly if they are perceived as part of a social group culturally marked as "sexual."

In a recent study of waiters in restaurants that employ equal numbers of men and women, for example, the researchers found that, as in many restaurants, their subjects worked in cultures that were highly sexualized.[400] In the restaurants where they worked:

> [S]exual joking, touching, and fondling were common, everyday occurrences. . . . For example, when asked if he and other waitpeople ever joke about sex, one waiter replied, "about 90% percent of [the jokes] are about sex." According to a waitress, "at work . . . [we're] used to patting and touching and hugging." Another waiter said, "I do not go through a shift without someone . . . pinching my nipples or poking me in the butt or grabbing my crotch. . . . It's just what we do at work."

* * * [I]n these gender-integrated workplaces, the women as well as the men said they enjoyed the sexualized interactions; they actively participated in the ritualized displays of heterosexuality with their male coworkers, and did not consider their sexual advances improper. Yet, when some of the Mexican men, who were concentrated in positions as kitchen cooks and busing staff, made identical sexual overtures, the white waitresses were quick to take offense and to label the conduct sexual harassment. When asked if she had ever experienced sexual harassment, for example, one of the waitresses, Beth, said:

> Yes, but it was not with the people . . . that I work with in the front of the house. It was with the kitchen. . . . In the kitchen, the lines are quite different. Plus, it's a Mexican staff. It's a very different attitude . . . . One guy, like, patted me on the butt

---

[*] Copyright 2003 Yale Law Journal. Reprinted by permission.

[400] Patti A. Giuffre & Christine L. Williams, Boundary Lines: Labeling Sexual Harassment in Restaurants, 8 *Gender & Soc'y* 378 (1994).

and . . . I went off on him. I said, "No. Bad. Wrong. I can't speak Spanish to you, but, you know, this is it."

Other white waitresses had similar reactions. Ann conceded that the Mexican men in the kitchen "would see the waiters hugging on us, kissing us and pinching our rears and stuff," but that she considered their attempt to take the same liberties a form of sexual harassment. Brenda complained that "[t]he kitchen can be kind of sexist. . . . They're not as bad as they used to be because they got warned. They're mostly Mexican, not even Mexican-American." She criticized relatively harmless interactions that fell far short of sexual touching; for instance, "sometimes, they will take a relleno in their hands like it's a penis"—an action she berated as "Sick!" Several of the white waitresses admitted that they felt comfortable engaging in sexual banter and touching with the other waitpeople (who were predominantly white), but not with the Mexican workers. In the racial and occupational hierarchy of the restaurant culture, the white women closed ranks against the Mexican men as sexual harassers, whom they perceived as too beneath them to be assuming sexual familiarities.

In addition to these racial/status differences, the researchers found that sexual orientation mattered to how sexual conduct was perceived. Male waiters who saw themselves as heterosexual characterized sexual horseplay and conversation as "sexual harassment" when it came from openly gay men, even though the waiters welcomed similar interactions with other straight men. One of the straight men objected to a gay coworker touching him on the rear end, for example, and another expressed discomfort about a gay baker talking about his sexual experiences and desires. Yet, these same men conceded that similar sexual conversation and horseplay from straight men didn't bother them, and bragged that they themselves initiated such interactions. In the eyes of many of the straight men, the gay men were marked as potential sexual harassers from the beginning. Thus, any expression of sexuality by gay men became a self-fulfilling prophecy—a confirmation of the misplaced sexual desire they were expected to embody and enact. * * *

These results are disheartening, but they are not surprising. As Woods and Lucas point out, "The situation is familiar to anyone whose gender, race, or background has placed them in the minority; the 'few' will always stand out against the background of the 'many.'"[416] Within many sectors of American society, members of stigmatized minority groups are stereotyped as overly—even pathologically—"sexual." African-American men have learned not to participate in the sexual banter and horseplay of predominantly white organizations, or else risk threatening organizational power relations.[417] Black women, too, must

---

[416] James D. Woods & Jay H. Lucas, *The Corporate Closet: The Professional Lives of Gay Men in America* (1993).

[417] David A. Thomas, Mentoring and Irrationality: The Role of Racial Taboos, 28 *Hum. Resource Mgmt.* 279 (1989).

downplay their sexuality—and even their sexual attractiveness—or else risk bringing unwanted attention to themselves. Gay men and lesbians often feel pressure to suppress information about their personal lives in the workplace to protect themselves from stigma, and other sexual minorities occupy an even lower place on the hierarchy of sexual propriety. Working-class men of all races are seen as crude and vulgar, especially when they engage in sexual displays toward their female "betters." Even white working-class women are often considered bad girls whose bawdy sexuality places them outside the bounds of respectability and protection. * * *

As the sexual sanitization campaign advances, some people are harmed more than others, but we all lose. In the name of preventing sexual harassment, employers increasingly ban or discourage employee romance, chilling intimacy and solidarity among employees of both a sexual and nonsexual variety. Many companies are punishing employees for behavior that does not meet the legal definition of sex harassment, costing many workers their jobs and undercutting their ability to express themselves and create their own cultures and sexual norms. Women are encouraged to translate—and perhaps even to understand—broader forms of discrimination and managerial abuse as sexual harms. * * *

B. FEDERAL LAW PROTECTION AGAINST WORKPLACE DISCRIMINATION

For employees of any government entity, modern constitutional law generally recognizes the loss of a job as the deprivation of a property interest, and as a result, accords the protections of due process and equal protection principles to government workers who suffer adverse job actions. As a practical matter, however, statutory claims provide the preferred mechanisms for litigating workplace discrimination. Compared to constitutional law, statutory law provides broader coverage (using its Commerce Clause authority, Congress can extend anti-discrimination mandates to private sector employers) and wider scope (Title VII plaintiffs can prevail by showing the disparate impact of practices without having to prove intentional discrimination, whereas intent is required under the Equal Protection Clause). As a result, constitutional law has had its strongest impact in the workplace context when litigants did not have the option of invoking a statutory claim. That is why the early employment discrimination claims for LGBT workers were litigated under the Constitution, when there were few if any applicable statutes. See Chapter 1, Section 2B. It also explains why the early pregnancy discrimination cases were brought on behalf of government workers, mostly schoolteachers, before it became clear that Title VII covered pregnancy discrimination. See Section 2, *infra*. Today, public sector workers who allege job discrimination usually plead both statutory and constitutional causes of action. For an example of a decision addressing both claims, see Judge Barkett's opinion in *Glenn v. Brumby*, Chapter 1, Section 2B.

Title VII of the Civil Rights Act of 1964, codified as amended [in 1972 and 1991] at 42 U.S.C.A. § 2000e *et seq.*, provides the primary protection against workplace discrimination because of sex. It covers both the private sector and, since 1972, state and federal employment. The prime directive of Title VII is found in § 703(a), 42 U.S.C.A. §§§ 2000e–2(a):

> It shall be an unlawful employment practice for an employer—
>
> (1) to fail or refuse to hire or to discharge any individual, or otherwise to discriminate against any individual with respect to his compensation, terms, conditions, or privileges of employment, because of such individual's race, color, religion, sex, or national origin; or
>
> (2) to limit, segregate, or classify his employees or applicants for employment in any way which would deprive or tend to deprive any individual of employment opportunities or otherwise adversely affect his status as an employee, because of such individual's race, color, religion, sex, or national origin.

Section 703(b)–(c), *id.* Section 2000e–2(b)–(c), sets forth similar prohibitions of "unlawful employment practices" by employment agencies and labor organizations (unions). Section 703(d), *id.* § 2000e–2(d), applies the anti-discrimination principle specifically to apprenticeship or training programs.

As it was introduced, the legislation that became Title VII targeted only discrimination because of race, color, religion, or national origin. There is a strange bedfellows aspect to the story of how "sex" was included. Until recently, popular accounts have repeated the story that the addition of sex was an attempt to kill the overall bill by using coverage of sex as a poison pill, but the reality was far more complex. The amendment to add sex was proposed by Representative Howard W. Smith, a southern Democrat who opposed bills for racial equality but supported an Equal Rights Amendment. Speaking in opposition was Representative Emmanuel Celler of New York, a sponsor of the bill to ban race discrimination and an opponent of the ERA. Much of the reason for this anomalous line-up of supporters and opponents was a split among feminists and other progressives about whether an ERA would hurt women more than help them by destroying certain protective labor laws then in force. Most labor unions at that time opposed an ERA, and, for the same reason, were apprehensive about the impact of including sex in Title VII.

The true moving force behind adding sex as a protected category was a group of women lawyers who had sought prohibitions of employment discrimination for years. One leader of that group—Pauli Murray, an activist in racial justice as well as women's rights efforts (and a gender rebel as well)—wrote a widely circulated memorandum arguing that inclusion of sex was the only way to protect African-American women from discrimination. The House voted to add sex as a protected class, and later efforts to delete it failed. But because sex had been added in floor debate, the committee reports for the bill as a whole did not mention it or elaborate on Congressional intent. See Serena Mayeri, *Reasoning from Race: Feminism, Law, and the Civil Rights Revolution* 20–23 (2011); Vicki Schultz, "Taking Sex Discrimination Seriously," 91 *Denv. U.L. Rev.* 995, 1014–20 (2015). This absence of legislative history has compounded the indeterminacy of "because of sex" as used in Title VII.

As the bill made its way through Congress, other changes in language accommodated the interests of employers. Congressional negotiators adopted various exemptions or defenses to any charge of unlawful employment practices. The main defenses are those that qualify the meaning of "unlawful employment practice" in § 703. For our purposes, the most important defense is one based on bona fide occupational qualifications ("BFOQ") in Section 703(e), *id.* § 2000e–2(e), which we will examine in greater detail in Section 4B, *infra*:

> Notwithstanding any other provision of this subchapter, (1) it shall not be an unlawful employment practice for an employer to hire and employ employees, for an employment agency to classify, or refer for employment any individual, for a labor organization to classify its membership or to classify or refer for employment any individual, or for an employer, labor organization, or joint labor-management committee controlling apprenticeship or other training or retraining programs to admit or employ any individual in any such program, on the basis of his religion, sex, or national origin in those certain instances where religion, sex, or national origin is a bona fide occupational qualification reasonably necessary to the normal operation of that particular business or enterprise * * *.

Other defenses include Section 703(h), *id.* § 2000e–2(h), which protects employment decisions based upon bona fide seniority or merit systems. Section 713(b)(1), *id.* § 2000e–12(b)(1) provides a defense to a person charged with violating Title VII "if he pleads and proves that the act or omission complained of was in good faith, in conformity with, and in reliance on any written interpretation or opinion of the Commission," which is charged with enforcement of Title VII.

After the enactment of Title VII, the EEOC interpreted the law to prohibit not just "disparate treatment" of employees because of their race or sex, but also the adoption or retention of employment policies that have an unjustified (not job-related) "disparate impact" on employees that is race-or sex-based. The Supreme Court ratified that EEOC view in *Griggs v. Duke Power Co.*, 401 U.S. 424 (1971). Although *Griggs*, and indeed § 703(a) generally, were not applied with full force to sex discrimination cases immediately, they proved to have significant bite over time, such as in cases invalidating minimum height restrictions that were customary but not necessary for certain jobs. In response to the Supreme Court's perceived retreat from *Griggs* in race discrimination decisions in 1989, Congress codified its understanding of disparate impact in the Civil Rights Act of 1991, Pub. L. No. 102–166, 105 Stat. 1071, which added § 703(k)(1) to Title VII, 42 U.S.C.A. § 2000e–2(k). Section 703(k)(1) recognizes a claim for relief if the plaintiff can show that the employer uses an employment practice that causes a disparate impact on the basis of race, sex, etc., and the employer "fails to demonstrate that the challenged practice is job related for the position in question and consistent with business necessity."

In recent years, courts have begun to address intersectional claims under Title VII—the allegation that an employer discriminated against an individual because of prejudice against or stereotypes about the conjunction of protected characteristics, for example, a particular gender and race combination, even if there is no proof of discrimination against all persons of the same gender or the same race as the plaintiff. See, e.g., Jeffries v. Harris Cnty. Community Action Ass'n, 615 F.2d 1025 (5th Cir. 1980); Craig v. Yale Univ. School of Medicine, 838 F.Supp.2d 4 (D.Conn. 2011); Kimble v. Wisconsin Dep't of Workforce Development, 690 F.Supp.2d 765 (E.D.Wis. 2010). Evidence of discrimination based on any component of an intersectional claim can be probative, and plaintiffs often allege each separate ground as well as the particular combination. But for the intersectional claim to prevail, the plaintiff must prove adverse treatment because of bias specifically against persons with the two (or more) fused characteristics. *See generally* Kathryn Abrams, "Title VII and the Complex Female Subject," 92 *Mich. L. Rev.* 2479 (1994); Devon Carbado & Mitu Gulati, "Working Identity," 85 *Cornell L. Rev.* 1259 (2000) and "The Fifth Black Woman," 11 *J. of Contemp. Legal Issues* 701 (2001); Kimberlé Crenshaw, "Demarginalizing the Intersection of Race and Sex," 1989 *U. Chi. Legal F.* 139.

For sexual orientation and gender identity minorities, the status of federal anti-discrimination law covering the workplace is in flux. In 1974, Representative Bella Abzug introduced the first bill in Congress to prohibit sexual orientation discrimination (not limited to employment). In the early 1990s, advocates switched strategies to promote legislation that covered only employment, called the Employment Non-Discrimination Act (ENDA), because job protections had the greatest public support. In 1998, President Clinton amended Executive Order No. 11,478, which mandates anti-discrimination protections for federal government employees, by adding sexual orientation to the list of prohibited bases for discrimination. Exec. Order No. 13,087, 63 Fed. Reg. 30097 (June 2, 1998). Recently, advocates returned to Abzug's omnibus coverage approach and dropped proposals limited to employment. These current efforts center on the proposed Equality Act. [Appendix 3] None of these approaches has yet produced a new statute.

Meanwhile, the EEOC and several courts have ruled that the ban on discrimination "because of sex" encompasses discrimination based on sexual orientation or gender identity. It appears likely that the Supreme Court will accept one of these cases for review and determine whether the existing language in Title VII protects LGBT plaintiffs. In the meantime, persons alleging employment discrimination based on sexual orientation and gender identity now routinely file Title VII charges with the EEOC (a prerequisite to initiating litigation). See Section 5, *infra.*

If an employer has a contract with the federal government and thereby is paid with federal funds, employees alleging discrimination can also seek relief by filing a claim with the Office of Federal Contract Compliance within the Department of Labor. Presidential Executive Orders provide the authorization for these claims. In 2014, President Obama signed Executive Order No. 13,672, which added anti-discrimination protections for gender identity and sexual orientation. Exec. Order No. 13,672, 79 Fed. Reg. 42971 (July 23, 2014).

The oldest federal law to ban adverse treatment of women in employment—the Equal Pay Act (EPA)—was enacted in 1963 as an amendment to the Fair Labor Standards Act. It prohibits paying employees of one sex lower wages than employees of the other sex for "for equal work on jobs the performance of which requires equal skill, effort, and responsibility, and which are performed under similar working conditions, except where such payment is made pursuant to (i) a seniority system; (ii) a merit system; (iii) a system which measures earnings by quantity or quality of production; or (iv) a differential based on any other factor other than sex." 29 U.S.C. § 206(d)(1). When a plaintiff asserts a wage discrimination claim under Title VII, courts may rely on the standards developed under the EPA.

During the early 1980s, equality advocates sought to expand the equal pay principle to incorporate a comparable worth theory of discrimination. Driven by the widespread sex segregation in the workforce, the movement's goal was to force comparisons of jobs such as secretarial staff and truck drivers, based on their comparative worth to the enterprise, rather than their similarity. The litigation campaign ended when the Ninth Circuit, in an opinion by then-Judge Anthony Kennedy, ruled that the Washington state civil service system could base its pay scales on the market rates of pay for the same positions in the private sector. "A compensation system that is responsive to supply and demand and other market forces is not the type of specific, clearly delineated employment policy" that can be challenged under anti-discrimination laws. American Federation of State, County, and Municipal Employees v. State of Washington, 770 F.2d 1401, 1406 (9th Cir. 1985).

C. STATE LAW PROTECTIONS

In some locations, LGBT persons who experience workplace discrimination can bring claims based on state or local law. Before the current EEOC interpretation of sex discrimination, state and local laws provided the only relief for employees of private companies. Local governments adopted the first anti-discrimination provisions in municipal ordinances, beginning with East Lansing, Michigan, in 1972. Wisconsin enacted the first statewide prohibition on such discrimination in 1982, by including sexual orientation in the statute's definition of sex discrimination.

As of 2017,

- In 20 states plus D.C., anti-discrimination laws protect against discrimination based on both sexual orientation and gender identity.[d] *See, e.g.,* D.C. Human Rights Law, Appendix 5.

- In an additional 2 states, the laws cover only sexual orientation.[e]

- In 10 other states, statutes or executive orders bar such discrimination solely against public sector employees.[f]

---

[d]   See CAL. LABOR CODE § 1102.1 (sexual orientation protection adopted in 1992) (replaced by CAL. GOV'T CODE §§ 12920–21, 12940; CAL. GOV'T CODE §§ 12920–21, 12940, 12949 (gender identity protection adopted 2003); COLO. REV. STAT. ANN. § 24–34–401 to –402 (sexual orientation protection adopted 1991, gender identity protection adopted in 2007); CONN. GEN. STAT. ANN. §§ 46a–60, 81c, 81h (sexual orientation protection adopted in 1991, gender identity protection adopted in 2011,); 19 DEL. CODE ANN. § 711 (sexual orientation protection adopted in 2009, gender identity protection adopted in 2013); D.C. CODE ANN. § 2–1402.11 (sexual identity protection adopted 1977, gender identity protection adopted in 2005); HAW. REV. STAT. ANN. §§ 368–1, 378–1, 378–2 (sexual orientation protection adopted in 1991, gender identity protection adopted in 2011); 775 ILL. COMP. STAT. ANN. 5/1–102, 5/1–103, 5/2–102 (sexual orientation and gender identity protections adopted in 2006); IOWA CODE ANN. §§ 216.6, 216.6A (sexual orientation and gender identity protections adopted in 2007); ME. REV. STAT. ANN. tit. 5, §§ 4553, 4571–72 (sexual orientation and gender identity protections adopted in 2005); MD. CODE ANN., STATE GOV'T § 20–606 49B § 16 (derived from MD. CODE ANN., ART. 49B, § 16; sexual orientation protection adopted in 2001, gender identity protection adopted in 2013); MASS. GEN. LAWS ANN. ch. 151B, § 4 (sexual orientation protection adopted in 1989, gender identity protection adopted in 2011); MINN. STAT. ANN. §§ 363A.02, -.03, -.08 (sexual orientation and gender identity protections adopted in 1993); NEV. REV. STAT. ANN. §§ 610.185, 613.330, 613.340, 613.405, 338.125 (sexual orientation protection adopted in 1999, gender identity protection adopted in 2011); N.J. STAT. ANN. §§ 10:5–3, –4, –5, –12 (sexual orientation protection adopted in 1991, gender identity protection adopted in 2006); N.M. STAT. ANN. § 28–1–7 (sexual orientation and gender identity protections adopted in 2003); N.Y. EXEC. LAW § 296 (sexual orientation protection adopted in 2002); N.Y. COMP. CODES R. & REGS. tit. 9, § 466.13 (gender identity protection adopted in 2016); OR. REV. STAT. ANN. §§ 659A.030, 174.100 (sexual orientation and gender identity protection adopted in 2007); R.I. GEN. LAWS ANN. § 28–5–7 (sexual orientation protection adopted in 1995, gender identity protection adopted in 2001); UTAH CODE ANN. § 34A–5–106 (sexual orientation and gender identity protections adopted in 2015); VT. STAT. ANN. tit. 3, § 961 and tit. 21 §§ 495, 1726 (sexual orientation protection adopted in 1991, gender identity protection adopted in 2007); WASH. REV. CODE ANN. §§ 49.60.180, -.40 (sexual orientation and gender identity protections adopted in 2006).

[e]   N.H. REV. STAT. ANN. § 354–A:7 (sexual orientation protection adopted in 1997) (New Hampshire also protects gender identity for public employees by Executive Order No. 2016–04 (2016)); WIS. STAT. ANN. §§ 111.31, 230.18 (sexual orientation protection adopted in 1982).

[f]   Alaska, Admin. Order No. 195 (2002); Arizona, Executive Order No. 2003–22 (2003); Ind. Governor's Affirmative Action Policy Statement (Apr. 26, 2005); Kentucky, Executive Order

These latter provisions may be enforceable only administratively, and may not provide for private rights of action. In addition, executive orders can be rescinded by subsequent governors.

- At the local level, several hundred cities and counties have ordinances prohibiting job discrimination because of sexual orientation and/or gender identity, either generally or only for municipal employment. (Some state laws prohibit or truncate the capacity of municipalities to enact anti-discrimination laws.)

The primary significance of state and local laws is that individuals may be able to secure some relief even if there is no coverage under Title VII or the Constitution. These laws are highly variable. They may be more or less plaintiff-friendly than Title VII. For example, most have more limited enforcement mechanisms than Title VII, but many cover employers with fewer than 15 employees.

No. 2008–473 (2008)); Michigan, Executive Directive No. 2003–24 (2003) (sexual orientation); Michigan, Executive Directive No. 2007–24 (2007) (gender identity); Missouri, Executive Order No. 10–24 (2010); Montana, Montana Nondiscrimination-EEO Rules, 2.21.4005 (2000); Montana, Executive Order No. 41–2008 (2008); Montana, Executive Order No. 04–2016 (2016); Ohio, Executive Order No. 2001–05K (2011); Pennsylvania, Executive Order No. 2016–04 (2016) (state employees); Pennsylvania, Executive Order No. 2016–05 (2016) (state contractors); Virginia, Executive Order No. 2014–01 (2014) (state employees); Virginia, Executive Order No. 2017–B1 (2017) (state contractors). In addition, North Carolina, Executive Order No. 2016–93 (2016) states that state employment policies will be administered "without unlawful discrimination" based on sexual orientation and gender identity. Louisiana, Executive Order No. 2016–11 (2016) has been enjoined by a state court.

SECTION 2

PREGNANCY AND PARENTHOOD

One of the earliest and most important goals for women's rights advocates was the effort to prohibit discrimination based on pregnancy. As late as the 1970s, many employers routinely laid off women who became pregnant.

PROBLEM 5-1
THE BIG PICTURE

In this section of the chapter, we will track the results as feminists embarked on a multi-decade effort to modify workplace policies and norms to incorporate women's childbearing experiences. Before reading the materials that follow, think about the problems that might arise for women workers during the cycle of reproduction. Consider each of the following hypotheticals:

(a) The delivery truck driver who cannot lift more than 20 pounds during the second half of pregnancy;

(b) The receptionist whose employer has a rule mandating that all pregnant workers must take unpaid leave from the fourth month of pregnancy until 3 months after the child is born;

(c) The waitress whose medical complications during pregnancy require 10 weeks of bed rest before childbirth;

(d) The flight attendant who needs to express breast milk twice during each workday for the first several months after childbirth; and

(e) The sales manager whose newborn infant requires special care for a year.

For each scenario, what are the roadblocks to winning relief for the client under a sex discrimination theory? Are there rational (i.e., not based on stereotype) concerns that the employers will raise? What theories of equality from Chapter 3 will apply?

A. ADDING PREGNANCY TO TITLE VII

The first pregnancy-related cases were filed primarily as Equal Protection Clause claims on behalf of public sector employees. In *Struck v. Secretary of Defense*, 460 F.2d 1372 (9th Cir. 1972), Ruth Bader Ginsburg, then head of the ACLU Women's Rights Project, challenged the military's policy requiring immediate discharge upon discovery of pregnancy. The Defense Department changed its policy during the pendency of the litigation, mooting the case before it reached the

Supreme Court. In the first pregnancy discrimination case decided by the Supreme Court, the Justices ruled on due process instead of equal protection grounds, reasoning that mandatory discharge created an irrebuttable presumption of unfitness to work, and thus was an arbitrary deprivation of property. *Cleveland Board of Education v. LaFleur*, 414 U.S. 632 (1974); see Chapter 1, Section 2A.

The first Supreme Court Equal Protection Clause decision regarding pregnancy was ***Dwight Geduldig v. Carolyn Aiello*, 417 U.S. 484, 94 S.Ct. 2485, 41 L.Ed.2d 256 (1974).** California's disability insurance program paid benefits to persons in private employment temporarily unable to work because of a physical disability not covered by worker's compensation. The program excluded disabilities associated with pregnancy from coverage (but covered some less costly conditions that occur only in men). The Court held that the exclusion did not constitute sex discrimination and was therefore constitutional. The case elicited two diametrically opposed views of how the law should define equality when addressing differences that are both related to biology and produced by the processes of social construction, the recurring conundrum of sex discrimination law.

Justice Stewart's opinion for the Court found that the program did not discriminate based on sex:

> California does not discriminate with respect to the persons or groups which are eligible for disability insurance protection under the program. The classification challenged in this case relates to the asserted underinclusiveness of the set of risks that the State has selected insure. Although California has created a program to insure most risks of employment disability, it has not chosen to insure all such risks, and this decision is reflected in the level of annual contributions exacted from participating employees. * * *

> These policies provide an objective and wholly noninvidious basis for the State's decision not to create a more comprehensive insurance program than it has. There is no evidence in the record that the selection of the risks insured by the program worked to discriminate against any definable group or class in terms of the aggregate risk protection derived by that group or class from the program. There is no risk from which men are protected and women are not. Likewise, there is no risk from which women are protected and men are not.

417 U.S. at 494–96. In a famous (or infamous) footnote, the Court added: "The program divides potential recipients into two groups—pregnant women and nonpregnant persons. While the first group is exclusively female, the second includes members of both sexes. The fiscal and actuarial benefits of the program thus accrue to members of both sexes." 417 U.S. at 496 n.20. Indeed, noted Justice Stewart, the annual claim rate and the annual claim cost were greater for women than for men.

In the absence of a classification that discriminated based on sex, the Court found that the exclusion was rationally related to the program's financial structure and cost containment goals, particularly to whether it would remain self-supporting without needing to increase the cost of premiums or rely on revenue raised by taxes.

Three dissenting Justices (Brennan, Douglas, Marshall) argued that the program did discriminate "by singling out for less favorable treatment a gender-linked disability peculiar to women," and that a more exacting scrutiny was required to justify any such discrimination under *Reed* and *Frontiero*. (See Chapter 1, Section 2A.) They would have required the benefits system to treat pregnancy the same as any other temporarily disabling condition. 417 U.S. at 504.

The Court's decision in *Geduldig* technically remains good law on the application of Equal Protection Clause doctrine to discrimination based on pregnancy. As a practical matter, however, adoption of the Pregnancy Discrimination Act, *infra*, provided a substitute avenue for workplace discrimination claims.

After *Geduldig*, the emphasis in litigation shifted to the question of whether Title VII prohibited pregnancy discrimination, even if the Constitution did not. The Supreme Court held in ***General Electric v. Gilbert*, 429 U.S. 125, 97 S. Ct. 401, 50 L.Ed.2d 343 (1976),** that the answer was the same under Title VII: pregnancy-based discrimination did not constitute sex-based discrimination. Justice Rehnquist's opinion for the Court relied on the same pregnant versus nonpregnant persons reasoning as in the earlier case. Because an Equal Protection violation requires the plaintiff to demonstrate discriminatory intent, whereas a Title VII claimant can prevail upon a showing of discriminatory effect, the Court also had to address the impact of a disability benefits plan that excluded pregnancy. Like the plan at issue in *Geduldig*, the GE plan covered men and women for the same risks. With regards to its effects, the Court reasoned:

> As there is no proof that the package [of what is covered] is in fact worth more to men than to women, it is impossible to find any gender-based discriminatory effect in this scheme simply because women disabled as a result of pregnancy do not receive benefits; that is to say, gender-based discrimination does not result simply because an employer's disability-benefits plan is less than all-inclusive. For all that appears, pregnancy-related disabilities constitute an additional risk, unique to women, and the failure to compensate them for this risk does not destroy the presumed parity of the benefits, accruing to men and women alike, which results from the facially evenhanded inclusion of risks.

429 U.S. at 138–39.

From the perspective of feminist advocates, the underlying question in both cases centered on whether coverage of pregnancy-related conditions should be treated as an essential part of the norm for insurance and leave policies or as an add-on and therefore expendable. As Justice Brennan's dissent in *Gilbert* pointed out, the resolution of the legal question turned largely on one's perspective. For the plaintiffs, the argument began by identifying a risk uniquely affecting women that was excluded from an otherwise comprehensive program, and led to the conclusion that the policy had the effect of subjecting only women to substantial loss of income from a temporary medical disability. For GE, the defense was the use of "normal actuarial techniques," which resulted in the exclusion of a costly, because frequent, condition, while providing coverage for other conditions on a gender-neutral basis.

In 1978, Congress effectively overruled the Court's decision in *Gilbert* by amending Title VII to "prohibit sex discrimination on the basis of pregnancy." The amendment, entitled the Pregnancy Discrimination Act ("PDA"), added a new § 701(k):

> The terms "because of sex" or "on the basis of sex" include, but are not limited to, because of or on the basis of pregnancy, childbirth, or related medical conditions; and women affected by pregnancy, childbirth, or related medical conditions shall be treated the same for all employment-related purposes, including receipt of benefits under fringe benefit programs, as other persons not so affected but similar in their ability or inability to work * * *.

42 U.S.C.A. § 2000e(k). In *Newport News Shipbuilding and Dry Dock Co. v. EEOC*, 462 U.S. 669 (1983), the Supreme Court held that the PDA not only reversed the *Gilbert* result, but also rejected *Gilbert*'s pregnant versus non-pregnant person approach to sex discrimination in pregnancy discrimination cases.

Feminists also pursued relief at the state level. While the PDA was pending in Congress, California enacted a law that included the specific issue of maternity leave:

> It shall be an unlawful employment practice unless based upon a bona fide occupational qualification: * * * (b) For any employer to refuse to allow a female employee affected by pregnancy, childbirth, or related medical conditions * * * (2) To take a leave on account of pregnancy for a reasonable period of time; provided, such period shall not exceed four months * * *. Reasonable period of time means that period during which the female employee is disabled on account of pregnancy, childbirth, or related medical conditions. * * *

NOTE ON THE EQUAL TREATMENT/SPECIAL TREATMENT DEBATE

Although the PDA and the California statute both sought to fix the problem created by *Gilbert*, differences between the two laws also set the stage for one of the most contentious feminist debates of the 1980s, the echoes of which still resonate. The intent behind the "shall be treated the same" language in the PDA was to equalize "up," by forcing employers to include pregnancy in their comprehensive health insurance coverage and medical leave policies. (Logically, it is also possible to equalize "down" by eliminating such benefits entirely.) The California law, on the other hand, specified that pregnant workers were entitled to medical leave; this requirement applied even if an employer did not provide leaves for any other temporarily disabling conditions.

When Lillian Garland sought to return from her pregnancy leave in 1982, her employer, California Federal Savings & Loan Association, informed her that it had not saved her position. She charged the bank with violating the California statute, and it responded by seeking a declaration that the California statute was invalid as inconsistent with, and pre-empted by, the PDA. The bank argued that it treated male and female workers identically and thus was in compliance with the PDA, and that the pregnancy leave mandated by the state statute would force it to treat pregnant workers differently, which the PDA prohibited.

Feminists filed briefs on all sides of the case, and scholars engaged in lengthy debates in the pages of law reviews. The group that became known as the "special treatment" advocates argued in support of the California statute, reasoning that its effect was to produce an outcome that put women on equal footing with men, even if it violated formal strictures of equality in doing so. Pregnancy had been excluded from coverage and leave policies because the underlying norm was the male worker, they reasoned. The California approach guaranteed that women's life experiences, including pregnancy, had to be treated also as the norm. Without the promise that they could return to their jobs after childbirth, women could never achieve equality in the workforce. Professor Christine Littleton and others authored a brief for the Coalition for Reproductive Equality in the Workplace that supported the California law.

The "equal treatment" feminists saw that approach as a trap. For decades, protectionist labor laws had been enacted with the purported goal of helping women, but had functioned only to disadvantage them. A California-style system would reinforce the old notion that women were more expensive as workers and generated bothersome special rules, ultimately hurting women. Such laws would also reinforce and perpetuate the assumption that children were women's concern and responsibility; a father who sought to spend even one day caring for an infant could be fired for doing so. Joan Bertin and others authored a brief for the American Civil Liberties Union opposing the California law and arguing that it was pre-empted. Professors Wendy Webster Williams and Susan Deller Ross, authors of the PDA, wrote a brief for the National Organization for Women and the Women's Legal Defense Fund arguing that the proper remedy was to extend the benefits of the California law to men in order to meet the requirements of the PDA.

At a more theoretical level, feminists disagreed over how special the experiences of pregnancy and childbirth are. The text of the PDA reflects the perspective that the experience of giving birth is analogous to other temporarily disabling conditions. Some special treatment feminists characterized insistence on that analogy as assimilationism. At bottom, this was a debate about the extent to which the meaning of pregnancy was a social construct, amid an intense battle over what was the best strategy to advance the interests of most women, in both the long term and the short term. It touched a nerve underlying many disputes in feminism, dating back to the early twentieth century. The debate continues today, in newer forms.

California Federal Savings and Loan Association v. Mark Guerra

United States Supreme Court, 1987.
479 U.S. 272, 107 S.Ct. 683, 93 L.Ed.2d 613.

■ JUSTICE MARSHALL delivered the opinion of the Court. * * *

In order to decide whether the California statute requires or permits employers to violate Title VII, as amended by the PDA, or is inconsistent with the purposes of the statute, we must determine whether the PDA prohibits the States from requiring employers to provide reinstatement to pregnant workers, regardless of their policy for disabled workers generally.

Petitioners argue that the language of the federal statute itself unambiguously rejects California's "special treatment" approach to pregnancy discrimination, thus rendering any resort to the legislative history unnecessary. They contend that the second clause of the PDA forbids an employer to treat pregnant employees any differently than other disabled employees. Because " '[t]he purpose of Congress is the ultimate touchstone' " of the pre-emption inquiry, however, we must examine the PDA's language against the background of its legislative history and historical context. * * *

* * * By adding pregnancy to the definition of sex discrimination prohibited by Title VII, the first clause of the PDA reflects Congress' disapproval of the reasoning in *Gilbert*. Rather than imposing a limitation on the remedial purpose of the PDA, we believe that the second clause was intended to overrule the holding in *Gilbert* and to illustrate how discrimination against pregnancy is to be remedied. * * * [W]e agree with the Court of Appeals' conclusion that Congress intended the PDA to be "a floor beneath which pregnancy disability benefits may not drop—not a ceiling above which they may not rise."

The context in which Congress considered the issue of pregnancy discrimination supports this view of the PDA. Congress had before it extensive evidence of discrimination *against* pregnancy, particularly in disability and health insurance programs like those challenged in *Gilbert* * * *. The Reports, debates, and hearings make abundantly clear that Congress intended the PDA to provide relief for working women and to end discrimination against pregnant workers. In contrast to the thorough account of discrimination against pregnant workers, the legislative history is devoid of any discussion of preferential treatment of pregnancy, beyond acknowledgments of the existence of state statutes providing for such preferential treatment. Opposition to the PDA came from those concerned with the cost of including pregnancy in health and disability-benefit plans and the application of the bill to abortion, not from those who favored special accommodation of pregnancy. * * *

[Congress was aware of state laws that required employers to give reasonable leave to pregnant workers; committee reports suggest that Congress assumed that these laws would continue in effect after enactment of the PDA.]

Title VII, as amended by the PDA, and California's pregnancy disability leave statute share a common goal. The purpose of Title VII is "to achieve equality of employment opportunities and remove barriers that have operated in the past to favor an identifiable group of . . . employees over other employees." *Griggs v. Duke Power Co.*, 401 U.S. 424, 429–430 (1971). Rather than limiting existing Title VII principles and objectives, the PDA extends them to cover pregnancy. As Senator Williams, a sponsor of the Act, stated: "The entire thrust . . . behind this legislation is to guarantee women the basic right to participate fully and equally in the workforce, without denying them the fundamental right to full participation in family life." 123 Cong. Rec. 29658 (1977).

Section 12945(b)(2) also promotes equal employment opportunity. By requiring employers to reinstate women after a reasonable pregnancy disability leave, § 12945(b)(2) ensures that they will not lose their jobs on account of pregnancy disability. * * * By "taking pregnancy into account," California's pregnancy disability-leave statute allows women, as well as men, to have families without losing their jobs.

We emphasize the limited nature of the benefits § 12945(b)(2) provides. The statute is narrowly drawn to cover only the period of *actual physical disability* on account of pregnancy, childbirth, or related medical conditions. Accordingly, unlike the protective labor legislation prevalent earlier in this century, § 12945(b)(2) does not reflect archaic or stereotypical notions about pregnancy and the abilities of pregnant workers. A statute based on such stereotypical assumptions would, of course, be inconsistent with Title VII's goal of equal employment opportunity. * * *

■ The concurring opinions of JUSTICES STEVENS and SCALIA are omitted.

■ JUSTICE WHITE, with whom The CHIEF JUSTICE [REHNQUIST] and JUSTICE POWELL join, dissenting. * * *

The second clause [of the PDA] could not be clearer: it mandates that pregnant employees "shall be treated the same for all employment-related purposes" as nonpregnant employees similarly situated with respect to their ability or inability to work. This language leaves no room for preferential treatment of pregnant workers. * * *

Contrary to the mandate of the PDA, California law requires every employer to have a disability leave policy for pregnancy even if it has none for any other disability. An employer complies with California law if it has a leave policy for pregnancy but denies it for every other disability. On its face, § 12945(b)(2) is in square conflict with the PDA and is therefore pre-empted. * * *

The majority nevertheless would save the California law on two grounds. First, it holds that the PDA does not require disability from pregnancy to be treated the same as other disabilities; instead, it forbids less favorable, but permits more favorable, benefits for pregnancy disability. The express command of the PDA is unambiguously to the contrary, and the legislative history casts no doubt on that mandate.

The legislative materials reveal Congress' plain intent not to put pregnancy in a class by itself within Title VII, as the majority does with its "floor . . . not a ceiling" approach. The Senate Report clearly stated:

> By defining sex discrimination to include discrimination against pregnant women, the bill rejects the view that employers may treat pregnancy and its incidents as *sui generis*, without regard to its functional comparability to other conditions. Under this bill, the treatment of pregnant women in covered employment must focus not on their condition alone but on the actual effects of that condition on their ability to work. Pregnant women who are able to work must be permitted to work on the same conditions as other employees; and when they are not able to work for medical reasons, they must be accorded the same rights, leave privileges and other benefits, as other workers who are disabled from working. * * *

The majority correctly reports that Congress focused on discrimination against, rather than preferential treatment of, pregnant workers. * * * Given the evidence before Congress of the widespread discrimination against pregnant workers, it is probable that most Members of Congress did not seriously consider the possibility that someone would want to afford preferential treatment to pregnant workers. The parties and their *amici* argued vigorously to this Court the policy implications of preferential treatment of pregnant workers. In favor of preferential treatment it was urged with conviction that preferential treatment merely enables women, like men, to have children without losing their jobs. In opposition to preferential treatment it was urged with equal conviction that preferential treatment represents a resurgence of the 19th-century protective legislation that perpetuated sex-role stereotypes and which impeded women in their efforts to take their rightful place in the workplace. It is not the place of this Court, however, to resolve this policy dispute. Our task is to interpret Congress' intent in enacting the PDA. Congress' silence in its consideration of the PDA with respect to preferential treatment of pregnant workers cannot fairly be interpreted to abrogate the plain statements in the legislative history, not to mention the language of the statute, that equality of treatment was to be the guiding principle of the PDA. * * *

NOTES AND QUESTIONS

1. *The PDA Clause by Clause.* One way to understand the dispute in *Cal Fed* is between an emphasis on the first clause of the PDA, prohibiting discrimination based on pregnancy, and the second clause, directing that pregnancy be treated the same as similarly disabling conditions. Justice Marshall's opinion relies on the first, in significant part because Congress was focused on eliminating workplace practices that disadvantage women. Since the majority of women become pregnant at some point in their lives, the burdens of job loss because of pregnancy affect women as a group much more than the absence of job protections for a short-term disability affects men. How does the dissent respond? How would you characterize the two ways of conceptualizing "discrimination"?

2. *Medical Leave Policies.* After *Cal Fed*, it was permissible for state law to require that employers grant medical leave to pregnant workers, thereby ensuring them a job when they returned to work. But few states had such laws, and no federal law required medical leave in any situation. Led by the "equal treatment" feminists who had wanted to "equalize up," advocates began pressing for a federal law to require employers to offer such leaves. The result was the Family and Medical Leave Act, described *infra*, which created equal access to parental leave for both new parents. The path not taken was to seek federal adoption of a California-style law that provided maternity leave only. What were the advantages and disadvantages of each approach?

3. *The Disability Paradigm.* When *Cal Fed* was decided, there was no federal statute prohibiting private sector employers from discriminating against workers on the basis of disability. In 1990, Congress enacted the Americans with Disabilities Act, 42 U.S.C. § 12101 *et seq.*, which defined disability as an impairment that substantially limits a major life activity. Some courts ruled that conditions arising because of pregnancy were not included, because of the time-limited nature of such impediments. That changed in 2008, with enactment of the Americans with Disabilities Act Amendment Act. 42 U.S.C. § 12102. The ADAAA made clear that *any* impairment which substantially limits an individual's ability to stand, walk, lift, bend or engage in other major life activities constitutes a disability. The question for courts became whether the substantial limitation standard is met, regardless of duration. A typical cold or flu, for example, would not qualify as a disability, but a temporary condition such as a broken leg or certain pregnancy-related impairments (e.g., severe back pain) would. (Pregnancy alone does not constitute a disability.) While the impairment lasts, the employer has an obligation to accommodate the worker, unless doing so would impose an undue hardship on the employer.

NOTE ON THE COMPARATOR QUESTION

Consider the situation of a woman in a physically demanding job who needs an accommodation to be able to continue working throughout her pregnancy. She might ask for temporary re-assignment to a job of similar rank but with less demanding physical requirements, such as a shift to office work from delivery of packages. The PDA does not directly require employers to provide such accommodations, but the second clause does require covered employers to treat pregnant women "the same for all employment-related purposes . . . as other persons not so affected but similar in their ability or inability to work."

After enactment of the PDA, industry policies dropped explicit exclusions targeting pregnancy and instead identified two categories of workers with temporary disabilities: those whose disabilities were caused by injuries suffered on the job and those with similar disabilities caused by injury or other condition that occurred off duty. Light duty accommodations were offered to the first group, but not the second. Employers argued that pregnant women were similarly situated to the second group and thus not entitled to accommodations. Until *Young v. UPS*, *infra*, courts accepted the argument that the second clause prohibited only policies that differentiated explicitly on pregnancy. In other words, as long as the accommodations policy was based on some pregnancy-neutral basis, it did not violate the PDA. See, e.g., *Urbano v. Cont'l Airlines, Inc.*, 138 F.3d 204, 208 (5th Cir. 1998).

In *Young*, the Supreme Court grappled with these two approaches to the meaning of the second clause of the PDA. Plaintiff argued that if the employer granted light duty to any employee temporarily disabled for any reason, it was required to offer the same accommodation to pregnant employees. Defendant argued that because it set the criteria for light duty accommodations in a pregnancy-neutral manner, based primarily on whether the injury occurred at work, there was no violation of the PDA. The result was the most important Supreme Court decision on pregnancy discrimination since the *Cal Fed* case.

Peggy Young v. United Parcel Service, Inc.

United States Supreme Court, 2015.
___ U.S. ___, 135 S.Ct. 1338, 191 L.Ed. 2d 279.

■ JUSTICE BREYER delivered the opinion of the Court.

The Pregnancy Discrimination Act makes clear that Title VII's prohibition against sex discrimination applies to discrimination based on pregnancy. It also says that employers must treat "women affected by pregnancy . . . the same for all employment-related purposes . . . as other persons not so affected but similar in their ability or inability to work." 42 U.S.C. § 2000e(k). We must decide how this latter provision applies in the context of an employer's policy that accommodates many, but not all, workers with nonpregnancy-related disabilities.

In our view, the Act requires courts to consider the extent to which an employer's policy treats pregnant workers less favorably than it treats nonpregnant workers similar in their ability or inability to work. And here—as in all cases in which an individual plaintiff seeks to show disparate treatment through indirect evidence—it requires courts to consider any legitimate, nondiscriminatory, nonpretextual justification for these differences in treatment. See *McDonnell Douglas Corp. v. Green,* 411 U.S. 792, 802 (1973). Ultimately the court must determine whether the nature of the employer's policy and the way in which it burdens pregnant women shows that the employer has engaged in intentional discrimination. The Court of Appeals here affirmed a grant of summary judgment in favor of the employer. Given our view of the law, we must vacate that court's judgment.

[I.A]   We begin with a summary of the facts. The petitioner, Peggy Young, worked as a part-time driver for the respondent, United Parcel Service (UPS). Her responsibilities included pickup and delivery of packages that had arrived by air carrier the previous night. In 2006, after suffering several miscarriages, she became pregnant. Her doctor told her that she should not lift more than 20 pounds during the first 20 weeks of her pregnancy or more than 10 pounds thereafter. UPS required drivers like Young to be able to lift parcels weighing up to 70 pounds (and up to 150 pounds with assistance). UPS told Young she could not work while under a lifting restriction. Young consequently stayed home without pay during most of the time she was pregnant and eventually lost her employee medical coverage.

Young subsequently brought this federal lawsuit. We focus here on her claim that UPS acted unlawfully in refusing to accommodate her pregnancy-related lifting restriction. Young said that her co-workers were willing to help her with heavy packages. She also said that UPS accommodated other drivers who were "similar in their . . . inability to work." She accordingly concluded that UPS must accommodate her as well.

UPS responded that the "other persons" whom it had accommodated were (1) drivers who had become disabled on the job, (2) those who had lost their Department of Transportation (DOT) certifications, and (3) those who suffered from a disability covered by the Americans with Disabilities Act of 1990 (ADA). UPS said that, since Young did not fall within any of those categories, it had not discriminated against Young on the basis of pregnancy but had treated her just as it treated all "other" relevant "persons." * * *

[I.C]   [Young filed a complaint of pregnancy discrimination in Federal District Court.]

After discovery, UPS filed a motion for summary judgment. * * * As evidence that she had made out a prima facie case under *McDonnell Douglas,* Young relied, in significant part, on evidence showing that UPS would accommodate workers injured on the job, those suffering from ADA disabilities, and those who had lost their DOT certifications. That evidence, she said, showed that UPS had a light-duty-for-injury policy with respect to numerous "other persons," but not with respect to pregnant workers. * * *

[The Fourth Circuit affirmed the District Court's grant of summary judgment to UPS.] It wrote that "UPS has crafted a pregnancy-blind policy" that is "at least facially a 'neutral and legitimate business practice,'" and not evidence of UPS's discriminatory animus toward pregnant workers." 707 F.3d 437, 446 (2013). It also agreed with the District Court that Young could not show that "similarly-situated employees outside the protected class received more favorable treatment than Young." *Id.,* at 450. Specifically, it believed that Young was different from those workers who were "disabled under the ADA" (which then protected only those with permanent disabilities) because Young was "not disabled"; her lifting limitation was only "temporary and not a significant restriction on her ability to perform major life activities." *Ibid.* Young was also different from those workers who had lost their DOT certifications because "no legal obstacle stands between her and her work" and because many with lost DOT certifications retained physical (*i.e.,* lifting) capacity that Young lacked. *Ibid.* And Young was different from those "injured on the job because, quite simply, her inability to work [did] not arise from an on-the-job injury." *Id.,* at 450–451. Rather, Young more closely resembled "an employee who injured his back while picking up his infant child or . . . an employee whose lifting limitation arose from her off-the-job work as a volunteer firefighter," neither of whom would have been eligible for accommodation under UPS' policies. *Id.,* at 448.

[II.] The parties disagree about the interpretation of the Pregnancy Discrimination Act's second clause. * * * [T]he Act's first clause specifies that discrimination " 'because of sex' " includes discrimination "because of . . . pregnancy." But the meaning of the second clause is less clear; it adds: "[W]omen affected by pregnancy, childbirth, or related medical conditions shall be treated the same for all employment-related purposes . . . as *other persons* not so affected but *similar in their ability or inability to work.*" 42 U.S.C. § 2000e(k) (emphasis added). Does this clause mean that courts must compare workers *only* in respect to the work limitations that they suffer? Does it mean that courts must ignore all other similarities or differences between pregnant and nonpregnant workers? Or does it mean that courts, when deciding who the relevant "other persons" are, may consider other similarities and differences as well? If so, which ones?

The parties propose very different answers to this question. Young and the United States believe that the second clause of the Pregnancy

Discrimination Act "requires an employer to provide the same accommodations to workplace disabilities caused by pregnancy that it provides to workplace disabilities that have other causes but have a similar effect on the ability to work." In other words, Young contends that the second clause means that whenever "an employer accommodates only a subset of workers with disabling conditions," a court should find a Title VII violation if "pregnant workers who are similar in the ability to work" do not "receive the same [accommodation] even if still other non-pregnant workers do not receive accommodations."

UPS takes an almost polar opposite view. It contends that the second clause does no more than define sex discrimination to include pregnancy discrimination. Under this view, courts would compare the accommodations an employer provides to pregnant women with the accommodations it provides to others *within* a facially neutral category (such as those with off-the-job injuries) to determine whether the employer has violated Title VII. Cf. *post* (SCALIA, J., dissenting) (hereinafter the dissent) (the clause "does not prohibit denying pregnant women accommodations . . . on the basis of an evenhanded policy").

[II.A]   We cannot accept either of these interpretations. Young asks us to interpret the second clause broadly and, in her view, literally. As just noted, she argues that, as long as "an employer accommodates only a subset of workers with disabling conditions," "pregnant workers who are similar in the ability to work [must] receive the same treatment even if still other nonpregnant workers do not receive accommodations." She adds that, because the record here contains "evidence that pregnant and nonpregnant workers were not treated the same," that is the end of the matter, she must win; there is no need to refer to *McDonnell Douglas*. The problem with Young's approach is that it proves too much. It seems to say that the statute grants pregnant workers a "most-favored-nation" status. As long as an employer provides one or two workers with an accommodation—say, those with particularly hazardous jobs, or those whose workplace presence is particularly needed, or those who have worked at the company for many years, or those who are over the age of 55—then it must provide similar accommodations to *all* pregnant workers (with comparable physical limitations), irrespective of the nature of their jobs, the employer's need to keep them working, their ages, or any other criteria. * * *

We agree with UPS to this extent: We doubt that Congress intended to grant pregnant workers an unconditional most-favored-nation status. The language of the statute does not require that unqualified reading. The second clause, when referring to nonpregnant persons with similar disabilities, uses the open-ended term "other persons." It does not say that the employer must treat pregnant employees the "same" as "*any* other persons" (who are similar in their ability or inability to work), nor does it otherwise specify *which* other persons Congress had in mind.

Moreover, disparate-treatment law normally permits an employer to implement policies that are not intended to harm members of a protected class, even if their implementation sometimes harms those members, as long as the employer has a legitimate, nondiscriminatory, nonpretextual reason for doing so. * * * There is no reason to believe Congress intended its language in the Pregnancy Discrimination Act to embody a significant deviation from this approach. Indeed, the relevant House Report specifies that the Act "reflect[s] no new legislative mandate." And the Senate Report states that the Act was designed to "reestablis[h] the law as it was understood prior to" this Court's decision in *General Electric Co. v. Gilbert.* * * *

[II.C]   We find it similarly difficult to accept the opposite interpretation of the Act's second clause. UPS says that the second clause simply defines sex discrimination to include pregnancy discrimination. But that cannot be so.

The first clause accomplishes that objective when it expressly amends Title VII's definitional provision to make clear that Title VII's words "because of sex" and "on the basis of sex" "include, but are not limited to, because of or on the basis of pregnancy, childbirth, or related medical conditions." We have long held that " 'a statute ought, upon the whole, to be so construed that, if it can be prevented, no clause' " is rendered " 'superfluous, void, or insignificant.' " * * * But that is what UPS' interpretation of the second clause would do. * * * *McDonnell Douglas* itself makes clear that courts normally consider how a plaintiff was treated relative to other "persons of [the plaintiff's] qualifications" (which here include disabilities). If the second clause of the Act did not exist, we would still say that an employer who disfavored pregnant women relative to other workers of similar ability or inability to work had engaged in pregnancy discrimination. In a word, there is no need for the "clarification" that the dissent suggests the second sentence provides.

Moreover, the interpretation espoused by UPS and the dissent would fail to carry out an important congressional objective. As we have noted, Congress' "unambiguou[s]" intent in passing the Act was to overturn "both the holding and the reasoning of the Court in the *Gilbert* decision." *Newport News Shipbuilding & Dry Dock Co. v. EEOC,* 462 U.S. 669, 678 (1983); see also *post* (recognizing that "the object of the Pregnancy Discrimination Act is to displace this Court's conclusion in [*Gilbert*]"). In *Gilbert,* the Court considered a company plan that provided "nonoccupational sickness and accident benefits to all employees" without providing "disability-benefit payments for any absence due to pregnancy." 429 U.S., at 128, 129. The Court held that the plan did not violate Title VII; it did not discriminate on the basis of sex because there was "no risk from which men are protected and women are not." *Id.,* at 138 (internal quotation marks omitted). Although pregnancy is "confined to women," the majority believed it was not "comparable in all other respects to [the] diseases or disabilities" that the plan covered. *Id.,* at 136.

Specifically, the majority explained that pregnancy "is not a 'disease' at all," nor is it necessarily a result of accident. *Ibid.* Neither did the majority see the distinction the plan drew as "a subterfuge" or a "pretext" for engaging in gender-based discrimination. *Ibid.* In short, the *Gilbert* majority reasoned in part just as the dissent reasons here. The employer did "not distinguish between pregnant women and others of similar ability or inability *because of pregnancy.*" *Post.* It distinguished between them on a neutral ground—*i.e.,* it accommodated only sicknesses and accidents, and pregnancy was neither of those.

Simply including pregnancy among Title VII's protected traits (*i.e.,* accepting UPS' interpretation) would not overturn *Gilbert* in full—in particular, it would not respond to *Gilbert* 's determination that an employer can treat pregnancy less favorably than diseases or disabilities resulting in a similar inability to work. * * *

[III.]   The statute lends itself to an interpretation other than those that the parties advocate and that the dissent sets forth. Our interpretation minimizes the problems we have discussed, responds directly to *Gilbert*, and is consistent with longstanding interpretations of Title VII.

In our view, an individual pregnant worker who seeks to show disparate treatment through indirect evidence may do so through application of the *McDonnell Douglas* framework. That framework requires a plaintiff to make out a prima facie case of discrimination. But it is "not intended to be an inflexible rule." *Furnco Constr. Corp. v. Waters,* 438 U.S. 567, 575 (1978). Rather, an individual plaintiff may establish a prima facie case by "showing actions taken by the employer from which one can infer, if such actions remain unexplained, that it is more likely than not that such actions were based on a discriminatory criterion illegal under" Title VII. *Id.,* at 576 (internal quotation marks omitted). The burden of making this showing is "not onerous." *Texas Dept. of Community Affairs v. Burdine,* 450 U.S. 248, 253 (1981). In particular, making this showing is not as burdensome as succeeding on "an ultimate finding of fact as to" a discriminatory employment action. *Furnco, supra,* at 576. Neither does it require the plaintiff to show that those whom the employer favored and those whom the employer disfavored were similar in all but the protected ways. * * * Thus, a plaintiff alleging that the denial of an accommodation constituted disparate treatment under the Pregnancy Discrimination Act's second clause may make out a prima facie case by showing, as in *McDonnell Douglas*, that she belongs to the protected class, that she sought accommodation, that the employer did not accommodate her, and that the employer did accommodate others "similar in their ability or inability to work."

The employer may then seek to justify its refusal to accommodate the plaintiff by relying on "legitimate, nondiscriminatory" reasons for denying her accommodation. *McDonnell Douglas* at 802. But, consistent with the Act's basic objective, that reason normally cannot consist simply of a claim that it is more expensive or less convenient to add pregnant women to the category of those ("similar in their ability or inability to work") whom the employer accommodates. After all, the employer in *Gilbert* could in all likelihood have made just such a claim.

If the employer offers an apparently "legitimate, non-discriminatory" reason for its actions, the plaintiff may in turn show that the employer's proffered reasons are in fact pretextual. We believe that the plaintiff may reach a jury on this issue by providing sufficient evidence that the employer's policies impose a significant burden on pregnant workers, and that the employer's "legitimate, nondiscriminatory" reasons are not sufficiently strong to justify the burden, but rather—when considered along with the burden imposed—give rise to an inference of intentional discrimination.

The plaintiff can create a genuine issue of material fact as to whether a significant burden exists by providing evidence that the employer accommodates a large percentage of nonpregnant workers while failing to accommodate a large percentage of pregnant workers. Here, for example, if the facts are as Young says they are, she can show that UPS accommodates most nonpregnant employees with lifting limitations while categorically failing to accommodate pregnant employees with lifting limitations. Young might also add that the fact that UPS has multiple policies that accommodate nonpregnant employees with lifting restrictions suggests that its reasons for failing to accommodate pregnant employees with lifting restrictions are not sufficiently strong—to the point that a jury could find that its reasons for failing to accommodate pregnant employees give rise to an inference of intentional discrimination.

This approach, though limited to the Pregnancy Discrimination Act context, is consistent with our longstanding rule that a plaintiff can use circumstantial proof to rebut an employer's apparently legitimate, nondiscriminatory reasons for treating individuals within a protected class differently than those outside the protected class. * * *

[IV.]   Under this interpretation of the Act, the judgment of the Fourth Circuit must be vacated. * * * Viewing the record in the light most favorable to Young, there is a genuine dispute as to whether UPS provided more favorable treatment to at least some employees whose situation cannot reasonably be distinguished from Young's. * * *

Young * * * introduced evidence that UPS had three separate accommodation policies (on-the-job, ADA, DOT). Taken together, Young argued, these policies significantly burdened pregnant women. See App. 504 (shop steward's testimony that "the only light duty requested [due to physical] restrictions that became an issue" at UPS "were with women who were pregnant"). The Fourth Circuit did not consider the combined effects of these policies, nor did it consider the strength of UPS' justifications for each when combined. That is, why, when the employer accommodated so many, could it not accommodate pregnant women as well?

We do not determine whether Young created a genuine issue of material fact as to whether UPS' reasons for having treated Young less favorably than it treated these other nonpregnant employees were pretextual. We leave a final determination of that question for the Fourth Circuit to make on remand, in light of the interpretation of the Pregnancy Discrimination Act that we have set out above. * * * For the reasons above, we vacate the judgment of the Fourth Circuit and remand the case for further proceedings consistent with this opinion.

■ [The concurring opinion of JUSTICE ALITO is omitted.]

■ JUSTICE SCALIA, with whom JUSTICE KENNEDY and JUSTICE THOMAS join, dissenting.

* * * The most natural way to understand the same-treatment clause is that an employer may not distinguish between pregnant women and others of similar ability or inability *because of pregnancy*. Here, that means pregnant women are entitled to accommodations *on the same terms* as other workers with disabling conditions. If a pregnant woman is denied an accommodation under a policy that does not discriminate against pregnancy, she *has* been "treated the same" as everyone else. UPS's accommodation for drivers who lose their certifications illustrates the point. A pregnant woman who loses her certification gets the benefit, just like any other worker who loses his. And a pregnant woman who keeps her certification does not get the benefit, again just like any other worker who keeps his. That certainly sounds like treating pregnant women and others the same. * * *

* * * The point of Title VII's bans on discrimination is to prohibit employers from treating one worker differently from another *because of a protected trait*. It is not to prohibit employers from treating workers differently for reasons that have nothing to do with protected traits. Against that backdrop, a requirement that pregnant women and other workers be treated the same is sensibly read to forbid distinctions that discriminate against pregnancy, not all distinctions whatsoever.

Prohibiting employers from making *any* distinctions between pregnant workers and others of similar ability would elevate pregnant workers to most favored employees. If Boeing offered chauffeurs to injured directors, it would have to offer chauffeurs to pregnant mechanics. And if Disney paid pensions to workers who can no longer work because of old age, it would have to pay pensions to workers who can no longer work because of childbirth. It is implausible that Title VII, which elsewhere creates guarantees of *equal* treatment, here alone creates a guarantee of *favored* treatment.

Let it not be overlooked, moreover, that the thrust of the Pregnancy Discrimination Act is that pregnancy discrimination is sex discrimination. Instead of creating a freestanding ban on pregnancy discrimination, the Act makes plain that the existing ban on sex discrimination reaches discrimination because of pregnancy. Reading the same-treatment clause to give pregnant women special protection unavailable to other women would clash with this central theme of the Act, because it would mean that pregnancy discrimination differs from sex discrimination after all.

All things considered, then, the right reading of the same-treatment clause prohibits practices that discriminate against pregnant women relative to workers of similar ability or inability. It does not prohibit denying pregnant women accommodations, or any other benefit for that matter, on the basis of an evenhanded policy. * * *

My disagreement with the Court is fundamental. I think our task is to choose the best possible reading of the law—that is, what text and context most strongly suggest it conveys. The Court seems to think our task is to craft a policy-driven compromise between the possible readings of the law, like a congressional conference committee reconciling House and Senate versions of a bill. * * *

■ [The dissenting opinion of JUSTICE KENNEDY is omitted.]

NOTES AND QUESTIONS

1.   *Disparate Treatment versus Disparate Impact.* After the decision in *Young*, the EEOC issued a Revised Enforcement Guidance on Pregnancy. (See https://www.eeoc.gov/laws/guidance/pregnancy_guidance.cfm.) It provides in part:

> Pregnancy discrimination may take the form of disparate treatment (pregnancy, childbirth or a related medical condition is a motivating factor in an adverse employment action) or disparate impact (a neutral policy or practice has a significant negative impact on women affected by pregnancy, childbirth or a related medical condition, and either the policy or practice is not job related and consistent with business necessity or there is a less discriminatory alternative and the employer has refused to adopt it. * * *

> Employer policies that do not facially discriminate on the basis of pregnancy may nonetheless violate [clause 2] of the PDA where they impose significant burdens on pregnant employees that cannot be supported by sufficiently strong justification.

The Department of Labor also revised its regulations on pregnancy discrimination, which apply to all federal contractors by way of Executive Order 11246. The DoL regulations specify that denying light duty assignments to pregnant workers may be challenged under both disparate treatment and disparate impact theories of discrimination. It is a *disparate treatment* violation "for a contractor to deny alternative job assignments, modified duties or other accommodations to employees who are unable to perform some of their job duties because of pregnancy, childbirth or related medical conditions where [the contractor provides them to other similarly affected employees and the employer's reason for denying them to pregnant workers does not justify the refusal]." For contractors with policies that do not offer such short-term accommodations to any workers, it is a *disparate impact* violation to deny them to pregnant employees unless the employer "ensure[s] that such policies or practices do not have an adverse impact on the basis of sex [or] unless they are shown to be job-related and consistent with business necessity." 41 C.F.R. § 60–20.5(c), 81 *Fed. Reg.* 39168 (June 15, 2016).

2. *The Burden of Proof Under Title VII.* The evidentiary obligations of the parties differ depending on whether the claim is one of disparate treatment or disparate impact. (Plaintiffs sometimes assert both types of claims.) Under a disparate treatment analysis, which is what the Court used in *Young,* plaintiff must satisfy the criteria for a prima facie case by demonstrating that she belongs to a protected class, that she met the qualifications or criteria for a job (or accommodation), that she applied for (or requested) it, and that the employer denied her the position (or accommodation) in favor of others. If there is "smoking gun" evidence of intent to discriminate, the case ends here. Young argued that the UPS itself demonstrated intentional discrimination against pregnant workers, but the Court did not agree. Why not?

Instead, had the *Young* case gone to trial upon remand (in fact, the case settled), the burden would have shifted to UPS to produce evidence of non-discriminatory reasons for its treatment of the plaintiff. Proof of greater expense or administrative burden will not suffice. If the employer does not carry this burden of production, the plaintiff must prevail as a matter of law. If the employer does carry the burden, the plaintiff has an opportunity to show that the reasons proffered by the employer were a pretext for discrimination. Here, Justice Breyer's opinion broadens the concept of pretext by holding that "evidence that the employer's policies impose a significant burden on pregnant workers, and that a finding that the employer's 'legitimate, nondiscriminatory' reasons are not sufficiently strong to justify the burden—when considered along with the burden imposed—[can] give rise to an inference of intentional discrimination." Justice Scalia objected to the vagueness of "substantial burden." How might such a burden be measured?

In disparate impact cases, the plaintiff must identify a policy or practice that has a disproportionately harmful effect on a protected class. The plaintiff usually shows the disparate impact by demonstrating a statistically significant difference in the number women employed compared to men. The plaintiff must demonstrate that the statistical disparity is caused by the employment policy or practice that she is challenging. The burden of persuasion then shifts to the employer to show that the policy or practice is "job related for the position in question and consistent with business necessity." If the employer meets this burden, the plaintiff may still prevail if she can show that an alternative employment practice has less disadvantageous impact and would also serve the employer's legitimate business interest. 42 U.S.C. § 2000e–2(k)(1)(A).

3.   *Equalizing down?* Denial of a pregnant employee's request for light duty (or a similar accommodation) will now almost certainly be pled under both Title VII and the ADA, as amended, so long as the employee has a pregnancy-related disabling condition. Assume that an employer's policy is never to grant light duty requests, for any reason. How would this situation be treated under each of the two laws? See Deborah Widiss, "The Interaction of the Pregnancy Discrimination Act and the Americans with Disabilities Act after Young v. UPS," 50 *UC Davis L. Rev.* 1423 (2017). Should pregnancy alone be considered a disabling condition? See Jeannette Cox, "Pregnancy as 'Disability' and the Amended Americans with Disabilities Act," 53 *B.C. L. Rev.* 443 (2012).

NOTE ON DISCRIMINATION AND (RE)DISTRIBUTION

One can analyze pregnancy policy from many angles, but one is surely economic. For individual women, the financial consequences can be catastrophic. To take one example, Lillian Garland, the original plaintiff in the *Cal Fed* case, *supra*, lost her apartment and custody of her child as a result of losing her job, and did not regain custody for several years. From a systemic perspective, the devaluation of pregnant workers has been a major reason for the persistence of wage inequality between men and women: employers have assumed that women workers as a class will leave their jobs to have children and not return. This stereotype perpetuates itself in a vicious circle for women who become mothers: after childbirth, they must decide whether to continue their careers in a workplace that does not afford them equal opportunity for higher pay or advancement.

There are other society-wide economic costs to pregnancy as well. Even without medical complications, childbirth temporarily disables a sizeable minority of the American workforce at some point(s) in their lives. And even the healthiest infants require sustained care and attention. How should society allocate the costs of the reproductive process? Under the traditional family wage system, the father-breadwinner assumed the financial cost and the mother-homemaker supplied the necessary labor, thereby privatizing responsibility by incorporating cost into the household economy. This model was based on a series of assumptions that no longer hold true in the majority of cases: the sufficiency of one (male) wage, the (minor) role of women in the labor market, and the (two married adult) composition of the household. And with increases in the cost of living having outpaced gains in income, the full internalization of reproductive costs is no longer financially feasible for most Americans, regardless of family make-up.

In the United States, anti-discrimination laws such as Title VII and the ADA have served allocative as well as fairness goals. To a modest extent, these laws have shifted a portion of reproductive costs from individual women and families to employers, where the costs may in turn be incorporated into and spread out through overall wage levels and/or product pricing. (The regulation of access to health insurance coverage, often through workplace plans, has also contributed to cost-sharing.) To a lesser extent (and much less than in other countries), the state has assumed some costs of the social costs of reproduction through human services programs and tax policies. See generally, Deborah Dinner, *The Costs of Reproduction: History and the Legal Construction of Sex Equality*, 46 HARV. C.R.-C.L. L. REV. 415 (2011). Traditionally, anti-discrimination laws are thought to serve two purposes: minimizing the economic inefficiencies of irrational discrimination (i.e., discrimination based on prejudice and false stereotypes) and rectifying patterns of material inequality that have burdened the classes of persons protected under such laws. Are other functions served when these laws are applied to pregnancy?

The social costs of pregnancy are but a fraction of the overall political economy of reproduction. Childcare policy raises even more consequential dollars and cents issues. We address those in Part C, *infra*.

B. PREGNANCY, MARRIAGE AND THE BFOQ

It is now settled that the Title VII prohibition against discrimination based on pregnancy applies as much to unmarried as to married women, but this principle was not established easily. Especially pernicious were widespread school board policies of firing unmarried pregnant schoolteachers on grounds of immorality, which was once common. The leading case was litigated as an intersectional claim (though the term was not then in use) of sex and race discrimination, challenging a prohibition on hiring teachers or aides who were unmarried mothers, a policy with a heavily disproportionate impact on African-American women in that rural Mississippi district. The Fifth Circuit found sex discrimination, but did not reach the race discrimination question. Andrews v. Drew Mun. Separate Sch. Dist., 507 F.2d 611 (5th Cir. 1975). When the case reached the Supreme Court, the Justices initially appeared to be almost evenly divided as to the validity of the policy, with the outcome in doubt. The matter was resolved when Title IX regulations were issued that prohibited public schools from inquiring into the marital status of job applicants. Justices leaning both ways agreed to dismiss the case on the ground that, in light of the new regulations, certiorari had been improvidently granted. Serena Mayeri, *Reasoning from Race: Feminism, the Law, and the Civil Rights Revolution* 145–65 (2011). In later cases, other Courts of Appeals followed the *Andrews* decision, and the issue is now settled . . . except in cases such as those that follow.

PROBLEM 5-2
ROLE MODEL JOBS

Emma works as guidance counselor for a statewide chapter of the Girls Honor Society (GHS). In that capacity, she travels to different high schools throughout the state and provides advice and information on the college application process. Emma, who is unmarried, learns that she is pregnant. You are the lawyer for GHS. The executive director tells you that there are no problems with Emma's job performance, but that she is distressed that the high school students with whom Emma works would interpret her continuation as a guidance counselor without getting married as implicit endorsement of pregnancy before marriage. The E.D. tells you that she asked Emma about her plans, and Emma responded that she had no desire to marry or to be secretive about her pregnancy, and that she believes that she can model the importance of having a job before becoming pregnant. The GHS motto is "honor and excellence in all things." Your research into Title VII reveals that there is an affirmative defense to sex discrimination claims called bona fide occupational qualification (BFOQ), for "those certain instances where religion, sex, or national origin is a bona fide occupational qualification reasonably necessary to the normal operation of that particular business or enterprise." How will you advise GHS? Compare, Harvey v. YWCA, 533 F.Supp. 949 (W.D.N.C.1982).

Leigh Cline v. Catholic Diocese of Toledo

United States Court of Appeals for the Sixth Circuit, 2000.
206 F.3d 651.

■ JUDGE NATHANIEL JONES.

Plaintiff-Appellant Leigh Cline ("Cline") brought a pregnancy discrimination suit against Defendants-Appellees, Catholic Diocese of Toledo, et al., ("St. Paul"), under Title VII. * * * Cline appeals the summary judgment granted by the district court in favor of St. Paul. * * *

St. Paul Elementary and High School employed Leigh Cline as a teacher from June 1994 until St. Paul decided not to renew her contract after the 1995–1996 year. St. Paul is a parish of the Roman Catholic Church located within the Catholic Diocese of Toledo. The defendants-appellees in this case include St. Paul Elementary School, the Catholic Diocese of Toledo, the Catholic Diocesan School of Toledo and Father Herbert J. Willman. Father Willman is responsible for all religious matters within the parish, including oversight of the parish schools.

After graduating from Bowling Green in 1993, Cline began teaching at St. Paul as an elementary substitute teacher. In June 1994, she was awarded a full-time eighth-grade teaching position for the 1994–1995 school year, assuming religion and math class duties, and also teaching high school math and coaching girls' basketball. After her first year, the school renewed Cline's teaching contract for the 1995–1996 school term and granted her request to teach the second grade. Cline's position as a second-grade teacher involved significant training and ministry in the Catholic faith. She provided daily religious instruction to students, took students to Mass on a regular basis, and prepared her second-grade students for the sacraments of Reconciliation and Holy Communion. Cline acknowledged that her position at St. Paul required her to "build and live Christian community," "integrate learning and faith," and "instill a sense of mission" in her students.

For each of her two years at St. Paul, Cline's employment was governed by the standard St. Paul one-year employment contract (titled the "Teacher-Minister Contract") ("Contract") as well as the

"Affirmations for Employment in the Diocese of Toledo" ("the Affirmation"), both of which she signed for each year. In addition to laying out basic terms of salary, duration and other routine aspects of the position, the Contract incorporates the provisions of the Affirmation document as part of its terms and conditions. The Affirmation outlines the ministerial responsibilities of the "teacher/minister," including the following provisions: 1) a statement that the signer "believe[s] that the work of the Catholic Church, [its agencies] and institutions has characteristics that make it different from the work of other agencies and institutions;" 2) a statement that the signer will "work[ ] diligently to maintain and strengthen the Catholic Church and its members," and that "[b]y word and example, [the signer] will reflect the values of the Catholic Church;" 3) statements that the signer believes in "mutual trust" and "open communication;" and 4) a statement by the signer that she "is more than a professional." The Contract also incorporates the Teacher Handbook, which states that the mission of the school is to "instill in our children the Gospel message of Jesus Christ." Neither the Teacher's Handbook nor the Affirmation explicitly states, nor was Leigh Cline ever expressly informed—in writing, orally or otherwise—that premarital sex comprised a violation of the terms of either the Contract or the Affirmation.

In the fall of 1995, Cline and her boyfriend (now husband) Tom Cline met with Fr. Brickner, the associate pastor of St. Paul Church, to discuss their intention to marry. The Clines married at St. Paul in February 1996. In early March, Leigh Cline informed the assistant principal, Stephen Schumm, and other St. Paul teachers that she was pregnant. Around late March or early April, Cline became visibly pregnant and began to wear maternity clothing to school. Based on his observation of Cline's pregnancy, Fr. Willman correctly concluded that she had engaged in premarital sex.

On learning that she had engaged in premarital sex, St. Paul officials did not immediately terminate Cline. Instead, Fr. Willman considered "all options," including immediate termination. Ultimately, according to Fr. Willman, he decided that the most appropriate course of action was to permit Cline to continue teaching for the remainder of the school year, without renewing her contract after the year had finished. On May 3, 1996, Fr. Willman advised Cline in a conference that "under the circumstances," the Diocese "would not renew her contract or hire her for the next school year." According to Fr. Willman's deposition, the "circumstances" he was referring to were that "Leigh [ ] became pregnant before she got married." In a formal letter explaining the decision not to renew her contract, sent May 4, Fr. Willman wrote:

> We expect our teachers to be good, strong role models for our children. . . . It is stated in your contract, working agreement that "by word and example you will reflect the values of the Catholic Church." . . . [P]arents in the community have serious

concerns about a teacher who marries and is expecting a child 5 months after the wedding date. We expect teachers and staff members at St. Paul to observe the 6 month preparation time for marriage. . . . The Church does not uphold sexual intercourse outside of marriage. We consider this a breach of contract/ working agreement.

Cline continued teaching at St. Paul through the end of the school year. Her child was born on July 10, 1996.

Cline disputes some of St. Paul's evidence about the events preceding her non-renewal. * * * Cline received a glowing Teacher Performance Evaluation on April 19, 1996—nearly two months after the school concluded that she had premarital sex. In addition to noting her "successful" performance in almost all of fifteen objective criteria, Principal Schumm praised Cline for "adjust[ing] very well" to the "busy and changing year in regard to [her] classroom reassignment and personal life." Finally, the evaluation implied that a contract renewal would be forthcoming for the following year, concluding: "Your class of 2nd grade students is well managed and respectful. I would expect continued growth for the 1996–97 school year." * * *

Title VII's prohibition on employment practices that discriminate "because of [an] individual's sex," 42 U.S.C.A. § 2000e–2(a)(1), applies with all its force to employers who discriminate on the basis of pregnancy. See 42 U.S.C.A. § 2000e(k). Thus, a claim of discrimination on the basis of pregnancy "must be analyzed in the same manner as any other sex discrimination claim brought pursuant to Title VII." * * *

The Congressional drafters of the 1964 Civil Rights Act recognized the sensitivity surrounding the status of religious groups and institutions. Thus, while Title VII exempts religious organizations for "discrimination based on religion," it does not exempt them "with respect to all discrimination. . . . [ ] Title VII still applies . . . to a religious institution charged with sex discrimination." [citations omitted] Because discrimination based on pregnancy is a clear form of discrimination based on sex, religious schools can therefore not discriminate based on pregnancy. In suits like Cline's, courts have made clear that if the school's purported "discrimination" is based on a policy of preventing nonmarital sexual activity which emanates from the religious and moral precepts of the school, and if that policy is applied equally to its male and female employees, then the school has not discriminated based on pregnancy in violation of Title VII.

The central question in this case, therefore, is whether St. Paul's nonrenewal of Cline's contract constituted discrimination based on her pregnancy as opposed to a gender-neutral enforcement of the school's premarital sex policy. While the former violates Title VII, the latter does not. This is primarily a factual battle, to be resolved on summary judgment only if Cline presented insufficient evidence to create a genuine dispute over the relevant material facts. Because we find that Cline put forth sufficient evidence to create such a dispute, we hold that summary judgment was inappropriate. * * *

* * * Cline adduced evidence that the policy was not applied equally among men and women. St. Paul officials acknowledged in their depositions that Cline's pregnancy alone had signaled them that she engaged in premarital sex, and that the school does not otherwise inquire as to whether male teachers engage in premarital sex. At oral argument, counsel for St. Paul conceded the same—that it was only Cline's pregnancy that made it evident that she had engaged in premarital sex. These admissions raise an issue of material fact as to whether St. Paul enforces its policy solely by observing the pregnancy of its female teachers, which would constitute a form of pregnancy discrimination. * * *

When faced with a similar fact situation, Judge Weinstein of the Eastern District of New York concluded:

> Plaintiff's evidence ... might lead a jury to find that the religious reason—premarital sex—for the termination is a pretext. Contrariwise, a jury might well find that [the school's decision was made] because [of] the school's religious beliefs. ... Or it might simply not believe the Plaintiff's version of the incident. ... Under such circumstances, a decision by a cross-section of the community in a jury trial is appropriate.

Ganzy v. Allen Christian School, 995 F.Supp. 340, 360–61 (E.D.N.Y.1998). The situation in this case is no different. Cline has introduced sufficient evidence to make out a prima facie case, and sufficient evidence to call into question St. Paul's proffered reason for her non-renewal. * * *

Crystal Chambers v. Omaha Girls Club, Inc.

United States Court of Appeals for the Eighth Circuit, 1987.
834 F.2d 697, *rehearing en banc denied*, 840 F.2d 583 (1988).

■ WOLLMAN, CIRCUIT JUDGE.

[The Omaha Girls Club is a private, non-profit corporation that offers self-development programs for girls. Among the Club's many activities are programs directed at pregnancy prevention. Most of the girls and staff members who participate in this and other programs in two Omaha locations are African American. One of the Club's "role model rules" is a ban of single-parent pregnancies among staff. Crystal Chambers, a black single woman, was employed as an arts and crafts instructor. The Club terminated her when she became pregnant. Chambers challenged the rule on two grounds: that it had a disparate impact based on race and that it constituted disparate treatment in violation of the PDA.]

* * * [At trial,] Chambers established the disparate impact of the role model rule. The Club then sought to justify the rule as a business necessity.

Establishing a business necessity defense presents an employer with a "heavy burden." Business necessity exists only if the challenged employment practice has "a manifest relationship to the employment in question." The employer must demonstrate that there is a "compelling need * * * to maintain that practice," and the practice cannot be justified by "routine business considerations." Moreover, the employer may be required to show that the challenged employment practice is "necessary to safe and efficient job performance," or that the employer's goals are "significantly served by" the practice.

The district court found that the role model rule is justified by business necessity because there is a manifest relationship between the Club's fundamental purpose and the rule. Specifically, the court found:

> The Girls Club has established by the evidence that its only purpose is to serve young girls between the ages of eight and eighteen and to provide these women with exposure to the greatest number of available positive options in life. The Girls Club has established that teenage pregnancy is contrary to this purpose and philosophy. The Girls Club established that it honestly believed that to permit single pregnant staff members to work with the girls would convey the impression that the Girls Club condoned pregnancy for the girls in the age group it serves. The testimony of board members * * * made clear that the policy was not based upon a morality standard, but rather, on a belief that teenage pregnancies severely limit the available opportunities for teenage girls. The Girls Club also established that the policy was just one prong of a comprehensive attack on the problem of teenage pregnancy. The Court is satisfied that a manifest relationship exists between the Girls Club's fundamental purpose and its single pregnancy policy.

The court also relied in part on expert testimony to the effect that the role model rule could be helpful in preventing teenage pregnancy. Chambers argues, however, that the district court erred in finding business necessity because the role model rule is based only on speculation by the Club and has not been validated by any studies showing that it prevents pregnancy among the Club's members. * * *

We believe that the district court's account of the evidence is plausible in light of the record viewed in its entirety. Therefore, we cannot say that the district court's finding of business necessity is clearly erroneous. The district court's conclusion on the evidence is not an impermissible one. Although validation studies can be helpful in evaluating such questions, they are not required to maintain a successful business necessity defense. Indeed, we are uncertain whether the role model rule by its nature is suited to validation by an empirical study. * * *

[The court also found that it was not feasible for the Club to hire a temporary replacement Chambers because of the training required for the position, nor were there alternative positions available for Chambers that did not involve contact with the Club's members.]

Unlike the disparate impact theory, the disparate treatment theory requires a plaintiff seeking to prove employment discrimination to show discriminatory animus. * * * No violation of Title VII exists, however, if the employer can show that the challenged employment practice is a bona fide occupational qualification (BFOQ). * * *

The BFOQ exception is "an extremely narrow exception to the general prohibition of discrimination on the basis of sex." In *Dothard v. Rawlinson*, 433 U.S. 321 (1977), the Supreme Court found that a rule that prohibited employment of women in contact positions in all-male Alabama prisons was a BFOQ under the particular circumstances of that case, which involved a prison system rife with violence. The statutory language is, of course, the best guide to the content of the BFOQ exception; however, the courts, including the Supreme Court in *Dothard*, have noted the existence of several formulations for evaluating whether an employment practice is a BFOQ. The formulations include: whether "the essence of the business operation would be undermined" without the challenged employment practice; whether safe and efficient performance of the job would be possible without the challenged employment practice; and whether the challenged employment practice has "a manifest relationship to the employment in question."

Although the district court did not clearly conclude that the role model rule qualified as a BFOQ, several of the court's other findings are persuasive on this issue. The court's findings of fact, many of which are relevant to the analysis of a potential BFOQ exception, are binding on this court unless clearly erroneous. The facts relevant to establishing a BFOQ are the same as those found by the district court in the course of its business necessity analysis. * * * This court has noted that the analysis of a BFOQ "is similar to and overlaps with the judicially created 'business necessity' test." [citation omitted] The various standards for establishing business necessity are quite similar to those for determining a BFOQ. Indeed, this court has on different occasions applied the same standard—"manifest relationship"—to both business necessity and BFOQ. Inasmuch as we already have affirmed the district court's finding of business necessity as not clearly erroneous, we feel compelled to conclude that "[i]n the particular factual circumstances of this case," the role model rule is reasonably necessary to the Club's operations. Thus, we hold that the role model rule qualifies as a bona fide occupational qualification. * * *

■ McMILLAN, CIRCUIT JUDGE, dissenting. * * *

* * * The district court, and now this court, accepts without any proof OGC's assumption that the presence of an unwed pregnant instructor is related to teenage pregnancies. OGC failed to present surveys, school statistics or any other empirical data connecting the incidence of teenage pregnancy with the pregnancy of an adult instructor. OGC also failed to present evidence that other girls clubs or similar types of organizations employed such a rule. OGC instead relied on two or three highly questionable anecdotal incidents to support the rule. * * *

Although there are no cases that have considered precisely the issue raised in this case, a few courts have considered the role model defense in school settings and all have rejected the schools' role model defenses. In *Andrews v. Drew Municipal Separate School District*, 507 F.2d 611 (5th Cir.1975), two unwed mothers challenged the school district's policy that prohibited the employment of teachers and teachers' aides who were unwed parents. Not unlike OGC, the school district defended the policy on the basis that such teachers would be poor role models for the children and that employing such teachers could lead to schoolgirl pregnancies. The Fifth Circuit struck down the rule.

> In the absence of overt, positive statements to which the children can relate, we are convinced that the likelihood of inferred learning that unwed parenthood is necessarily good or praiseworthy, is highly improbable, if not speculative. We are not at all persuaded by defendants' suggestions, quite implausible in our view, that students are apt to seek out knowledge of the personal and private life-styles of teachers or other adults within the school system (i.e. whether they are divorced, separated, happily married or single, etc.), and, when known, will approve and seek to emulate them.

[*Id.* at 617. Judge MacMillan also cites *Avery v. Homewood City Board of Education*, 674 F.2d 337 (5th Cir.1982) and *Ponton v. Newport News School Board*, 632 F.Supp. 1056 (E.D.Va.1986).]

The district court in the present case, although correctly articulating the BFOQ and business necessity tests, failed to actually apply the tests. Instead of requiring OGC to demonstrate a reasonable relationship between teenage pregnancy and the employment of single pregnant women, the district court accepted the beliefs and assumptions of OGC board members. * * *

Neither an employer's sincere belief, without more, (nor a district court's belief), that a discriminatory employment practice is related and necessary to the accomplishments of the employer's goals is sufficient to establish a BFOQ or business necessity defense. The fact that the goals are laudable and the beliefs sincerely held does not substitute for data which demonstrate a relationship between the discriminatory practice and the goals. The district court, recognizing that there was no data to support such a relationship, should have held that OGC failed to carry its burden of showing a BFOQ or business necessity. * * *

NOTES AND QUESTIONS

1. *A Critical Race Theory Analysis.* *Chambers* illustrates how issues pertaining to gender and sexuality are thoroughly "raced." The plaintiff uses race as part of her claim, asserting successfully that the role model policy has a disparate impact on African-American women, because they are more likely to be single mothers. But the fact that both she and her charges are African-American also seems to strengthen the defendant's argument about the extent to which the role model effect operates. Would such an effect be accepted if the adult and the teenagers were all white? If the adult were African American, and the girls were white?

Professor Regina Austin sees *Chambers* as a battle over racialized meanings of sexuality. Noting that most of the teenagers' own mothers were not married, Austin reads a deeper meaning into the case:

> Although Crystal Chambers' firing was publicly justified on the ground that she would have an adverse impact on the young Club members, it is likely that the Club in part sacked her because she resisted its effort to model her in conformity with white and middle-class morality. In its struggles against the culture of the girls' mothers, Crystal Chambers, employee and arts and crafts instructor, was supposed to be on the Club's side. But like a treasonous recruit, Crystal turned up unmarried and pregnant. As such, she embodied the enemy. If the Club could not succeed in shaping and restraining the workers whose economic welfare it controlled, how could it expect to win over the young members and supplant their mothers' cultural legacy? * * *

> The critique of the images of black women whites have historically promoted is relevant to the assessment of the treatment accorded contemporary role models. Role models are supposed to forgo the vices of Jezebel and exhibit the many virtues of Mammy. The case of Crystal Chambers illustrates this quite well. When Crystal Chambers refused to subordinate her interest in motherhood to the supposed welfare of the Club girls, she essentially rejected the Club's attempt to impose upon her the "positive" stereotype of the black female as a repressed, self-sacrificing, nurturing woman whose heart extends to other people's children because she cannot (or should not) have kids of her own. Instead, like a Jezebel, Crystal Chambers "flaunted" her sexuality and reproductive capacity, but, unlike her counterpart in slavery, she did so in furtherance of her own ends, in defiance of her white employers, and in disregard of a rule that forbade her from connecting with a man outside of the marriage relationship.

Regina Austin, "Sapphire Bound!" 1989 *Wis.L.Rev.* 539, 557, 571.

2. *Pregnancy as Expression.* One theme that runs through this casebook is the question of whether the mere presence of certain persons (pregnant unmarried women, openly gay men or lesbian women) communicates a message of disagreement from the institutional beliefs of an expressive entity, including some employers. Compare *Cline* and *Chambers* with *Boy Scouts of America v. Dale* (Chapter 1, Section 3D, *supra*). Which approach do you think provides the best analysis of the expressive impact of the plaintiff's sexuality? Is pregnancy a less expressive identity than homosexuality? Does it seem less expressive because it is more common? Should a court require social science evidence as to whether there is significant expressive impact, as the dissent argued in *Chambers*?

3.   *Double Standards.* Cline survived the defendant's motion for summary judgment by proffering evidence that the policy against premarital sex was applied unequally to men and to women. How should employers address that problem? Consider its application to the scenario in Problem 5-2.

C. Parenting and Work

Throughout the 1980s and early 1990s, as their next step after enactment of the PDA, women's rights advocates sought a law guaranteeing leave for both parents after the birth or adoption of a child. Several such bills passed Congress, but were killed by presidential veto. In 1993, as one of his first official acts, President Clinton signed the Family and Medical Leave Act (FMLA) into law. Under it, employers of 50 or more workers must offer eligible employees up to 12 weeks of unpaid leave, with continuation of health benefits and a right to return to the same or similar job, in order to enable the worker to engage in certain activities: caring for a newly-born or newly-adopted child; dealing with the employee's own serious health problem; or caring for a spouse, child, parent, or a child with whom the employee has an in loco parentis relationship, who has a serious health problem. 29 U.S.C. §§ 2601–2654 (2012). Note that this law covers fewer employers than does Title VII, which applies to employers with 15 or more employees, and fewer employees: to be eligible, the individual must have worked for the employer for at least a year, for at least 1,250 hours during the previous year.

In **Nevada Department of Human Resources v. William Hibbs, 538 U.S. 721, 123 S.Ct. 1972, 155 L.Ed.2d 953 (2003)**, the Supreme Court upheld the FMLA against a challenge which would have barred suits against state governments as employers, on the ground that the FMLA's scope exceeded Congress's authority to abrogate the sovereign immunity of the states. The Court found that Congress properly exercised its power under Section 5 of the Fourteenth Amendment to redress violations of the Equal Protection Clause. In so doing, **Chief Justice Rehnquist**'s opinion for the Court adopted this analysis:

> Stereotypes about women's domestic roles are reinforced by parallel stereotypes presuming a lack of domestic responsibilities for men. Because employers continued to regard the family as the woman's domain, they often denied men

similar accommodations or discouraged them from taking leave. These mutually reinforcing stereotypes created a self-fulfilling cycle of discrimination that forced women to continue to assume the role of primary family caregiver, and fostered employers' stereotypical views about women's commitment to work and their value as employees. Those perceptions, in turn, Congress reasoned, lead to subtle discrimination that may be difficult to detect on a case-by-case basis. * * *

By creating an across-the-board, routine employment benefit for all eligible employees, Congress sought to ensure that family-care leave would no longer be stigmatized as an inordinate drain on the workplace caused by female employees, and that employers could not evade leave obligations simply by hiring men. By setting a minimum standard of family leave for *all* eligible employees, irrespective of gender, the FMLA attacks the formerly state-sanctioned stereotype that only women are responsible for family caregiving, thereby reducing employers' incentives to engage in discrimination by basing hiring and promotion decisions on stereotypes. * * *

Indeed, in light of the evidence before Congress, a statute mirroring Title VII, that simply mandated gender equality in the administration of leave benefits, would not have achieved Congress' remedial object. Such a law would allow States to provide for no family leave at all. * * * [T]he FMLA is narrowly targeted at the fault line between work and family—precisely where sex-based overgeneralization has been and remains strongest * * *."

538 U.S. at 736–39.

The FMLA is an example of a law that undercuts stereotypes even though it is not an anti-discrimination statute. Its potential, however, is still not fully realized. The Court in *Hibbs* cited data stating that the overwhelming majority of workers who take leave upon the arrival of a child are women, even though men are equally entitled to do so. That is still the case.

In **Anthony Marchioli v. Garland Co., Inc., 94 Empl. Prac. Dec. P. 44,179 (N.D.N.Y. 2011),** the plaintiff was not eligible for FMLA leave because he was a new employee. Upon learning that his partner, who lived in a different city, was pregnant, he requested a Friday afternoon off to help her find a doctor. Soon afterward, he received the following message from his supervisor:

> * * * I'm not here to tell you how to live your life but the situation with your girlfriend spells big trouble to me. The distractions you are going to have over the next 10 months are going to be too much if you're constantly being pulled back to Buffalo. It's already started. I set aside October 8th and 9th for

you and let you know last month we would be working together. You guys had to make a Dr's appointment in Buffalo on Friday afternoon so you let me know you'd have to leave by lunch time! You need to decide if you want to totally commit yourself to this endeavor. If you don't want to "buy in" and put a maximum effort into developing your career, do me and Josh a favor and quit now. Don't waste our time or yours. * * * I'm not going to tolerate working with a guy who does not give it his all. * * * You need to decide what you want to do. I intend to monitor very closely your progress from here on out. If you do not want to work under that kind of scrutiny, leave now.

The court ruled that Marchioli had no viable claim under Title VII, citing *Piantanida v. Wyman Ctr., Inc.,* 116 F.3d 340, 342 (8th Cir.1997):

An employer's discrimination against an employee who has accepted [a] parental role * * * [is] not based on the gender-specific biological functions of pregnancy and child-bearing, but rather is based on a gender-neutral status potentially possessible by all employees, including men and women who will never be pregnant.

Compare Marchioli's experience with that of the plaintiff in the following case:

Elana Back v. Hastings on Hudson Union Free School District, et al.

United States Court of Appeals for the Second Circuit, 2004.
365 F.3d 107.

■ CALABRESI, CIRCUIT JUDGE.

* * * This appeal * * * asks whether stereotyping about the qualities of mothers is a form of gender discrimination, and whether this can be determined in the absence of evidence about how the employer in question treated fathers. We answer both questions in the affirmative. * * *

As the school psychologist at Hillside Elementary School, Elana Back counseled and conducted psychological evaluations of students, prepared reports for the Committee on Special Education, assisted teachers in dealing with students who acted out in class, worked with parents on issues related to their children, and chaired the "Learning Team," a group made up of specialists and teachers which conducted intensive discussions about individual students. Defendant-Appellee Marilyn Wishnie, the Principal of Hillside, and defendant-appellee Ann Brennan, the Director of Pupil Personnel Services for the District, were Back's supervisors. * * *

In the plaintiff's first two years at Hillside, Brennan and Wishnie consistently gave her excellent evaluations. In her first annual evaluation, on a scale where the highest score was "outstanding," and the second highest score was "superior," Back was deemed "outstanding" and "superior" in almost all categories, and "average" in only one. [Her marks were even higher in her second year evaluation. Plaintiff also received ratings of "superior" from the Superintendent of the School District.] In addition, according to Back, all three individual defendants repeatedly assured her throughout this time that she would receive tenure.

Back asserts that things changed dramatically as her tenure review approached. The first allegedly discriminatory comments came in spring 2000, when Back's written evaluations still indicated that she was a very strong candidate for tenure. At that time, shortly after Back had returned from maternity leave, the plaintiff claims that Brennan, (a) inquired about how she was "planning on spacing [her] offspring," (b) said " '[p]lease do not get pregnant until I retire,' " and (c) suggested that Back "wait until [her son] was in kindergarten to have another child."

[In December of Back's third year, Brennan allegedly told her that] she was expected to work until 4:30 p.m. every day, and asked " 'What's the big deal. You have a nanny. This is what you [have] to do to get tenure.' " Back replied that she did work these hours. * * * [A]ccording to Back, Brennan also indicated that Back should "maybe . . . reconsider whether [Back] could be a mother and do this job * * *," and that Brennan and Wishnie were "concerned that, if [Back] received tenure, [she] would work only until 3:15 p.m. and did not know how [she] could possibly do this job with children." * * *

[Beginning in January 2001, according to Back, Brennan and Wishnie began to raise complaints about Back's work and her hours. Both] reportedly told Back that this was perhaps not the job or the school district for her if she had "little ones," and that it was "not possible for [her] to be a good mother and have this job." The two also allegedly remarked that it would be harder to fire Back if she had tenure, and wondered "whether my apparent commitment to my job was an act. They stated that once I obtained tenure, I would not show the same level of commitment I had shown because I had little ones at home. They expressed concerns about my child care arrangements, though these had never caused me conflict with school assignments." They did not—as Back told the story—discuss with her any concerns with her performance at that time. * * *

[Brennan and Wishnie denied having made the statements alleged by Back.] * * *

* * * On May 29, 2001, Brennan and Wishnie sent a formal memo to Russell informing him that they could not recommend Back for tenure. Their reasons included * * * that there were "far too many" parents and teachers who had "serious issues" with the plaintiff and did not wish to work with her, and that she had persistent difficulties with the planning and organization of her work, and with inaccuracies in her reports, and

that she had not shown improvement in this area, despite warnings. * * * [Several parents also wrote to the Superintendent to complain about Back's demeanor and performance.] * * * In September 2001, the Board notified Back that her probationary appointment would be terminated. * * *

* * * In deciding whether Back has alleged facts that could support a finding of discrimination, we must first address the district court's suggestion, and the defendants' argument, that Back's claim is a "gender-plus" claim, and as such, not actionable. This contention is without merit. The term "sex plus" or "gender plus" is simply a heuristic. It is, in other words, a judicial convenience developed in the context of Title VII to affirm that plaintiffs can, under certain circumstances, survive summary judgment even when not all members of a disfavored class are discriminated against. Although we have never explicitly said as much, "sex plus" discrimination is certainly actionable. The Equal Protection Clause forbids sex discrimination no matter how it is labeled. The relevant issue is not whether a claim is characterized as "sex plus" or "gender plus," but rather, whether the plaintiff provides evidence of purposefully sex-discriminatory acts.

To show sex discrimination, Back relies upon a *Price Waterhouse* "stereotyping" theory. [See Part D of this section, *infra.*] Accordingly, she argues that comments made about a woman's inability to combine work and motherhood are direct evidence of such discrimination. In *Price Waterhouse,* Ann Hopkins alleged that she was denied a partnership position because the accounting firm where she worked had given credence and effect to stereotyped images of women. Hopkins had been called, among other things, " 'macho' " and " 'masculine,' " was told she needed " 'a course at charm school,' " and was instructed to " 'walk more femininely, talk more femininely, dress more femininely, wear make-up, have her hair styled, and wear jewelry' " if she wanted to make partner. * * *

It is the law, then, that "stereotyped remarks can certainly be evidence that gender played a part" in an adverse employment decision. The principle of *Price Waterhouse,* furthermore, applies as much to the supposition that a woman *will* conform to a gender stereotype (and therefore will not, for example, be dedicated to her job), as to the supposition that a woman is unqualified for a position because she does *not* conform to a gender stereotype. * * *

The instant case, however, foregrounds a crucial question: What constitutes a "gender-based stereotype"? *Price Waterhouse* suggested that this question must be answered in the particular context in which it arises, and without undue formalization. We have adopted the same approach, as have other circuits. Just as "[i]t takes no special training to discern sex stereotyping in a description of an aggressive female employee as requiring 'a course at charm school,' " *Price Waterhouse,* so it takes no special training to discern stereotyping in the view that a woman cannot "be a good mother" and have a job that requires long hours, or in the statement that a mother who received tenure "would not show the same level of commitment [she] had shown because [she] had little ones at home." These are not the kind of "innocuous words" that we have previously held to be insufficient, as a matter of law, to provide evidence of discriminatory intent.

Not surprisingly, other circuit courts have agreed that similar comments constitute evidence that a jury could use to find the presence of discrimination. *See, e.g., Santiago-Ramos v. Centennial P.R. Wireless Corp.,* 217 F.3d 46, 57 (1st Cir.2000) (evidence that a direct supervisor had "specifically questioned whether [the plaintiff] would be able to manage her work and family responsibilities" supported a finding of discriminatory animus, where plaintiff's employment was terminated shortly thereafter); *Sheehan v. Donlen Corp.,* 173 F.3d 1039, 1044–45 (7th Cir.1999) (holding, in a Pregnancy Discrimination Act case, that a reasonable jury could have concluded that "a supervisor's statement to a woman known to be pregnant that she was being fired so that she could 'spend more time at home with her children' reflected unlawful motivations because it invoked widely understood stereotypes the meaning of which is hard to mistake"); *id.* at 1044 (remarks by the head of plaintiff's department that "she would be happier at home with her children" provided direct evidence of discriminatory animus).

Moreover, the Supreme Court itself recently took judicial notice of such stereotypes. [The court quotes parts of Chief Justice Rehnquist's opinion in *Hibbs* excerpted above.]

The defendants argue that stereotypes about pregnant women or mothers are not based upon gender, but rather, "gender plus parenthood," thereby implying that such stereotypes cannot, without comparative evidence of what was said about fathers, be presumed to be "on the basis of sex." *Hibbs* makes pellucidly clear, however, that, at least where stereotypes are considered, the notions that mothers are insufficiently devoted to work, and that work and motherhood are incompatible, are properly considered to be, themselves, gender-based. *Hibbs* explicitly called the stereotype that "women's family duties trump those of the workplace" a "*gender* stereotype," and cited a number of state pregnancy and family leave acts—including laws that provided *only* pregnancy leave—as evidence of "pervasive sex-role stereotype that caring for family members is women's work."

Defendants are thus wrong in their contention that Back cannot make out a claim that survives summary judgment unless she demonstrates that the defendants treated similarly situated men differently. Back has admittedly proffered no evidence about the treatment of male administrators with young children. Although her case would be stronger had she provided or alleged the existence of such evidence, there is no requirement that such evidence be adduced. Indeed we have held that,

In determining whether an employee has been discriminated against "because of *such individual's* . . . sex," the courts have consistently emphasized that the ultimate issue is the reasons for *the individual plaintiff's* treatment, not the relative treatment of different *groups* within the workplace. As a result, discrimination against one employee cannot be cured, or disproven, solely by favorable, or equitable, treatment of other employees of the same race or sex.

Brown v. Henderson, 257 F.3d 246, 252 (2d Cir.2001) (citations omitted).

* * * Because we hold that stereotypical remarks about the incompatibility of motherhood and employment "can certainly be *evidence* that gender played a part" in an employment decision, *Price Waterhouse,* we find that *Brown* applies to this case. As a result, stereotyping of women as caregivers can by itself and without more be evidence of an impermissible, sex-based motive. * * *

NOTES AND QUESTIONS

1.   *Anti-Discrimination Versus Entitlement Laws.* Mr. Marchioli's claim fell into the gap between the elements of a Title VII claim and the eligibility requirements for leave under the FMLA. Consider this formulation by the First Circuit, in an opinion reversing summary judgment for the employer in a case similar to *Back*:

> * * * It is undoubtedly true that if the work performance of a woman (or a man, for that matter) actually suffers due to childcare responsibilities (or due to any other personal obligation or interest), an employer is free to respond accordingly, at least without incurring liability under Title VII. However, an employer is not free to assume that a woman, because she is a woman, will necessarily be a poor worker because of family responsibilities. The essence of Title VII in this context is that women have the right to prove their mettle in the work arena without the burden of stereotypes regarding whether they can fulfill their responsibilities.

> * * * Given the common stereotype about the job performance of women with children * * *, we believe that a reasonable jury could find that WellPoint would not have denied a promotion to a similarly qualified man because he had "too much on his plate" and would be "overwhelmed" by the new job, given "the kids" and his schooling. * * *

Chadwick v. Wellpoint, Inc., 561 F.3d 38, 45, 48 (1st Cir. 2009). In *Marchioli,* the employer seems to have assumed that the *male* plaintiff would "necessarily be a poor worker because of family responsibilities." How would a gender stereotyping theory be framed to accommodate those facts?

2.   *"Family Responsibilities Discrimination."* According to Professor Joan Williams at UC-Hastings School of Law, "discrimination against mothers * * * is the strongest and most open form of gender discrimination in today's workplace." 110 *Colum. L. Rev. Sidebar* 24, 25–26 (2010). Professor Williams

coined the term "family responsibilities discrimination" to describe the problem. Is it time for a law prohibiting adverse treatment based on parenting? How would such a provision be constructed, with what exceptions or baselines? Should it be an amendment to Title VII? For more data and materials on this topic, see the Center for Worklife Law, www.worklifelaw. org.

3.   *Discrimination and (Re)Distribution, Redux.* In a provocative article, Professor Julie Suk argues that the anti-discrimination model, specifically the insistence reflected in the PDA and FMLA that leave for pregnancy/childbirth be treated the same as leave for other short-term disabilities, has created a major obstacle to achieving progress for women workers. "Are Gender Stereotypes Bad for Women? Rethinking Antidiscrimination Law and Work," 110 *Colum. L. Rev.* 1 (2010). Professor Suk points out that the majority of leave time granted under the FMLA is used by employees as sick leave for their own conditions. For employers, medical/sick leave produces much more administrative cost, largely because of the unpredictability of its timing, than does childbirth-related leave. Disaggregating family leave (for childbirth or adoption) from medical leave might enable advocates to gain business support for expanding family leave, in return for making eligibility for medical leave more stringent. Under this approach, new mothers would be treated differently (and better) than workers with other health care needs. To create incentives for equal parenting, Suk suggests making paternity leave mandatory and maternity leave optional. What are the advantages and disadvantages of this approach? Should we revisit the equal treatment versus special treatment debate?

SECTION 3

SEXUAL AND GENDER HARASSMENT

The prohibition in Title VII of discrimination "because of * * * sex" includes harassment. Either speech or conduct or both may constitute harassment, and harassment may be sex-based without being sexual. Arguing that women should not be in top management positions or refusing to repair equipment operated by women, for example, may not implicate sexual conduct or crude language, but can be considered evidence of gender harassment.

In case law, two categories of sexual harassment have emerged:

- In a typical *quid pro quo* case, a plaintiff alleges that her boss or supervisor required her to engage in sexual conduct or continue a sexual relationship as a condition for not being fired, receiving satisfactory job performance evaluations, gaining choice job assignments, or earning promotions. In such a case, the plaintiff must prove that the harassment was a sexual advance tied to a tangible job benefit.

- The second form of sexual harassment is the creation or allowance of a *hostile work environment.* Proof may refer to threats or acts of physical assault, other hostile conduct (such as pouring sand into someone's gas tank), and/or verbal abuse. The harm is not necessarily tangible or economic; rather, it is the burden of being forced to work in an environment of constantly feeling under attack, whether by managers or coworkers or both.

For both types of claims, plaintiff must establish that unwelcome sexual harassment occurred and that the harassment was because of sex,

Plaintiff must also demonstrate that the employer knew or should have known of the harassment in question and failed to take proper remedial action. The Supreme Court established legislative-style rules for notice and remedy in *Faragher v. City of Boca Raton*, 524 U.S. 775 (1998), and *Burlington Indus. v. Ellerth*, 524 U.S. 742 (1998). When there has been a tangible job detriment (*e.g.*, discharge, demotion), an employer is vicariously liable for sexual harassment by a supervisor or by another person with authority over the employee. When there has not been a tangible job detriment, an employer may have an affirmative defense to vicarious liability, *viz.*, that the employer exercised reasonable care to prevent and promptly correct any sexually harassing behavior, and that plaintiff unreasonably failed to take advantage of any preventive or corrective opportunities policies.

Yet despite the elaboration of many fine points in the law of sexual harassment, fundamental questions remain.

A. CORE CONCEPTS: UNWELCOMENESS AND HARM

Under both types of sex harassment claims—quid pro quo and hostile environment—the concepts of unwelcomeness and harm play a central, if sometimes murky, role. As the Supreme Court noted in *Meritor Savings Bank v. Vinson*, "[t]he gravamen of any sexual harassment claim is that the alleged sexual advances were unwelcome." 477 U.S. 57, 68 (1986). The concept applies to "advances" or demands for sexual favors, and it also applies to whatever conduct or speech is alleged to constitute a hostile environment. Seven years later, the Court implicitly incorporated the idea of unwelcome conduct into its approach to the pervasiveness prong of a hostile environment claim:

> Conduct [must be] severe or pervasive enough to create an objectively hostile or abusive work environment—an environment that a reasonable person would find hostile or abusive... [I]f a victim does not subjectively perceive the environment to be abusive, the conduct has not actually altered the conditions of the victim's employment, and there is no Title VII violation.

Harris v. Forklift Sys., Inc., 510 U.S. 17, 21–22 (1993). Thus, for the level of hostility or abusiveness to be actionable, it must meet both a reasonable person, or objective, test and a subjective test, under which the plaintiff must prove that she or he in fact experienced the speech or conduct as unwelcome. Overall, pervasiveness or severity of hostility is the analog, in a hostile environment claim, to the material harm requirement in a *quid pro quo* claim. In assessing these factors, courts are directed to consider the totality of the circumstances.

Marcia Hocevar v. Purdue Frederick Co.

United States Court of Appeals, Eighth Circuit, 2000.
223 F.3d 721.

■ Before BEAM, LAY and JOHN R. GIBSON, CIRCUIT JUDGES.

■ BEAM, CIRCUIT JUDGE, with whom JUDGE JOHN R. GIBSON joins. * * *

The record shows that Marcia Hocevar began working at Purdue in August 1988 as a pharmaceutical sales representative. While working for Purdue in Minnesota between 1988 and 1992, Hocevar consistently out performed her then co-worker Timothy Amundsen (Amundsen) and was often ranked in the top sales percentile nationally. Hocevar was promoted three times in five years, the final promotion being to the position of sales training manager at corporate headquarters in Norwich,

Connecticut. Hocevar's bonuses reflect her good sales record, and her performance was rated at the highest possible level.

In June 1994, Hocevar transferred to Minnesota due to her impending marriage where she was placed under the supervision of Amundsen, the new district manager, and took over the sales territory previously assigned to him. Despite Hocevar's history of top-notch performance evaluations, Amundsen rated Hocevar at the lowest possible level in October and November 1994. Amundsen gave Hocevar an additional adverse rating in February 1995.

In March 1995, Amundsen accused Hocevar of lying and making false sales reports. A company investigation concluded no wrongdoing on Hocevar's part. Shortly thereafter, in July 1995, Amundsen again gave Hocevar the lowest possible performance rating despite the fact that she demonstrated a sales growth of seven percent. At some point, Purdue took away a portion of Hocevar's sales territory-an area including the world renowned Mayo Clinic and LaCrosse, Wisconsin. This action was taken by Amundsen despite the fact that Hocevar exceeded Amundsen's *own prior sales record* in the same territory and received bonuses for exceeding sales quota. These areas remained unstaffed for three months following removal from Hocevar's territory.

On August 11, 1995, Amundsen recommended Hocevar for probation based on her past year's performance. Following an automobile accident, Hocevar took disability leave from August 16, 1995, until September 15, 1995. Despite her absence, Hocevar again met her sales quota and earned a bonus. Hocevar took additional disability leave on October 21, 1995, and requested a part-time work schedule accommodation. Amundsen denied her request. As a result, Hocevar was unable to return to full-time work and remained on disability leave until her termination on June 7, 1996.

Following Hocevar's return to Minnesota in 1994, Amundsen engaged in hostile behavior in the workplace over a two-year period: he distributed sexually explicit material at business meetings; he made threats of violence towards female staff members; he constantly referred to women as "bitches," "fucking bitches," and "fat fucking bitches;" he told stories of animal violence (e.g., placing a loaded gun in the mouth of a dog that wandered into his yard); he told jokes at meetings that were derogatory towards women and contained profanity; he introduced a new employee as the "fucking new guy;" and claimed that new pharmaceutical products were so exciting a physician would be "creaming his jeans" to get them. Hocevar also testified that Amundsen exhausted a portion of a staff meeting by playing an audiotape of the Jerky Boys which contained obscene, vulgar, and sexually explicit "prank" phone calls to businesses on topics such as genital warts.

Hocevar also testified that in April 1992, Purdue Regional Manager Paul Kasprzycki (Kasprzycki) had made sexual advances toward her at a bi-regional meeting in Denver, Colorado. She testified that she was afraid to report complaints to Kasprzycki (Amundsen's supervisor) due to incidents of Kasprzycki making unwelcome sexual advances towards her, including pulling her toward him resulting in "full body contact" during what began as a consensual "fast" dance that led into a "slow" dance. She testified that Kasprzycki's made "very clear his wish to have a sexual relationship" with her and made suggestive comments about being available for a sexual relationship. Hocevar testified that Kasprzycki's advances were even more explicit when no witnesses were around. According to Hocevar, this was not an isolated incident, as Kasprzycki had previously made "unwelcome and uninvited" sexual advances toward her following a Purdue national meeting in New Orleans in January 1992. Then, in front of nearly 150 people Kasprzycki made statements at a bi-regional meeting in April 1995 implying a female manager had a sexual device in her hand and, in a separate incident, that he would be engaging in a sexual liaison in his hotel room later that day with three female sales representatives that had just performed a singing skit. Additionally, she describes an incident at a national meeting in Texas in 1993 involving two other Purdue District Managers, Dan Mackavoy and Dick Silverman. Hocevar stated that the district managers talked throughout her presentation; afterwards, she approached them about their "rude" behavior, to which Mackavoy responded: "We were talking about what great legs you have."

In yet another incident, also following a Purdue bi-regional meeting, Hocevar and six male and female co-workers were discussing Susan Faludi's book *Backlash: The Undeclared War Against American Women* (discussing public reaction to successful working women). During this conversation, a male employee called Hocevar a "bitch" and the then new district manager, Kelly Bartlett, became "very angry" and "exploded" stating: "You women, since when are women always right and men are always wrong? If your women's movement had its way, every woman would be working and our children would be being raised in communes." The incident was so upsetting that Kathy Kiekhaefer (Kiekhaefer) and a co-worker were crying and were "scared" and concerned at the prospect of working for a manager with such a feeling of hostility toward working women.

In October 1995, Hocevar complained to Dennis Merlo, a Purdue managerial employee, about Amundsen's inappropriate behavior, foul language, and stories of animal violence. On December 20, 1995, Hocevar's attorney notified Purdue of her intention to file a complaint against Purdue with the Minnesota Department of Human Rights alleging sexual harassment. The letter also voiced concerns about the "ongoing sexual harassment" of Hocevar and other women at Purdue. In January 1996, another female employee, Kiekhaefer, filed a claim of sexual harassment with Purdue, which prompted Purdue to investigate the complaints.

Danielle Nelson (Nelson), Purdue's Vice President of Equal Employment Opportunity Compliance and Human Resources Administration, conducted an investigation into the complaints of sexual harassment. Nelson found that Amundsen's extensive use of profanity and off-color jokes violated company policy and was "unprofessional behavior." Nelson concluded, however, that no sexual harassment occurred. Despite Nelson's determination that no sexual harassment occurred, Purdue directed Amundsen-under threat of termination-to take a three month unpaid leave of absence during which he would receive counseling and management training. Thereafter, Nelson and James Lang (Lang), Purdue's National Sales Manager, traveled to Amundsen's district, informed the employees that Amundsen's language was inappropriate and unacceptable, and trained employees on Purdue sexual harassment complaint procedures. After the Nelson/Lang visit, Hocevar's co-worker Mary Beck-Johnson testified that workplace conduct "absolutely changed"-"personal" matters were no longer discussed and inappropriate language was no longer used at meetings.

In mid-April 1996, Amundsen returned from the unpaid leave of absence. On May 2, 1996, Hocevar filed a charge of sexual harassment with the Equal Employment Opportunity Commission (EEOC) and Purdue terminated her a little over a month later by letter dated June 7, 1996. * * * Hocevar now appeals the district court's grant of summary judgment in favor of Purdue. * * *

Hocevar has not demonstrated that Amundsen's use of offensive language was unwelcome. A plaintiff must indicate by her conduct that the alleged harassment was unwelcome. A plaintiff cannot create a genuine issue of material fact with regard to unwelcome behavior when she engages in the conduct complained about. Hocevar's own testimony indicates that Amundsen's use of offensive language was not unwelcome because she used the offensive language herself. Hocevar admitted that she also called the new co-worker the "fucking new guy" at the business meeting. She further admitted that she used the words "bitch" and "fuck" around both Amundsen and other Purdue employees. I find that these actions on the part of Hocevar vitiate her contention that the mere use of these words was unwelcome.

Hocevar also failed to establish that the discrimination was based on sex. Harassing conduct constitutes discrimination based on sex when members of one sex are exposed to disadvantageous terms or conditions of employment to which members of the other sex are not exposed. Hocevar failed to demonstrate that the language complained about was based on sex. Offensive language was used to describe both men and women. While Amundsen described a *female* client who had treated him rudely as a "fat fucking bitch," he also referred to a new *male* employee as a "fucking new guy". Offensive language was used in front of both men and women at company meetings and the Jerky Boys tapes were played in front of both men and women. The use of foul language in front of both men and women is not discrimination based on sex.

Hocevar claims that Amundsen's use of the term "bitch" itself shows a discriminatory attitude toward females. Gender-based insults may create an inference that discrimination was based on sex. *See Carter v. Chrysler Corp.* However, mere use of the word "bitch," without other evidence of sex discrimination, is not particularly probative of a general misogynist attitude. *See Kriss v. Sprint Communications Co.*

In this case, Hocevar has presented no additional evidence demonstrating that Amundsen's use of the word "bitch" connotes a misogynist attitude. This is not a case where Amundsen used the term bitch as a synonym for female-specific characteristics of which he did not approve. *See id.* (noting that evidence where supervisor used word "bitch" as synonym for "complain" would provide stronger evidence of sex harassment because that would demonstrate that supervisor associated complaining with females). Neither is this a case where Amundsen blamed Hocevar's sexuality for his use of the word "bitch." *Carter* (holding that use of sexual epithets is evidence of sexual harassment when co-employee claims he used sexual epithets because plaintiff dressed provocatively and put "her ass up in our faces"). Nor is this a case in which Amundsen engaged in a litany of obscene name calling against Hocevar. *See Burns v. McGregor Elec. Indus. Inc.*, (finding discrimination based on sex when male co-worker called female plaintiff a "bitch," "asshole," "slut," and "cunt"). Because Hocevar has failed to present any additional evidence to bolster her contention that Amundsen's pervasive use of the term "bitch" shows his misogynist attitude, I find that Hocevar cannot demonstrate the harassment was based on sex.

Finally, Hocevar cannot show that the harassment was sufficiently severe or pervasive so as to alter a term, condition, or privilege of employment. "Conduct that is not severe or pervasive enough to create an objectively hostile or abusive environment-an environment that a reasonable person would find hostile or abusive-is beyond Title VII's purview." *Oncale v. Sundowner Offshore Services, Inc.* Factors to consider when determining whether sexual harassment is sufficiently severe or pervasive include: "the frequency of the discriminatory conduct; its severity; whether it is physically threatening or humiliating, or a mere offensive utterance; and whether it unreasonably interferes with an employee's work performance." *Harris v. Forklift Sys. Inc.* More than a few isolated instances are required. While the use of foul language may have been pervasive, I have already concluded that it was neither unwelcome nor based on sex.

This leaves Hocevar with four events that might constitute unwelcome behavior based on sex: (1) the *Backlash* incident; (2) the "great legs" incident; (3) the dancing incident; and (4) the skit incident. I will assume that all of these incidents could constitute unwelcome behavior based on sex. However, these incidents were clearly not pervasive because they occurred over at least a three-year period. In addition, a few inappropriate comments and an unwanted slow dance do not amount to particularly severe conduct that was threatening or humiliating.

I have little doubt that Amundsen's behavior was boorish and unprofessional. But, Title VII is not a general civility code. The simple fact is that the cases on which Hocevar relies involved far, far more evidence than Hocevar has presented. *See Rorie v. United Parcel Serv.,* 151 F.3d 757 (8th Cir.1998) (reversing summary judgment against plaintiff where supervisor patted female employee on back, brushed up against her, told her she "smelled good," always "came-on" to her, and asked her about co-worker's penis size); *Howard v. Burns Bros. Inc.,* 149 F.3d 835 (8th Cir.1998) (affirming jury verdict where co-employee always used sexual innuendos, told plaintiff she had nice legs, brushed her buttocks, told jokes involving lewd gestures, and touched the buttocks of and talked "nasty" to other female employees); *Hall v. Gus Const. Co.,* 842 F.2d 1010 (8th Cir.1988) (upholding judgment when plaintiffs' male co-workers made repeated requests for sex and touched plaintiffs' breasts and thighs). While I sympathize with Hocevar's having to endure Amundsen's conduct, her assertions fall far short of proof of a hostile work environment.

■ JOHN R. GIBSON, CIRCUIT JUDGE, concurring specially in affirmance of grant of summary judgment on hostile work environment claim.

I concur separately in the decision to affirm judgment against Hocevar on her hostile environment claim. I do not concur in Judge Beam's opinion, because I believe it engages in * * * an unnecessary semantic dissection of the language in question. * * * It is beyond question that the repetitive use of the word [bitch] in this case was demeaning to females, and the discipline which Purdue Frederick imposed on Amundsen, who used the word, shows that the company recognized the utterance was improper.

Even unquestionably offensive words do not necessarily make a hostile work environment, without considering the context. I have examined the whole record and conclude that the facts taken in the light most favorable to Hocevar do not add up to a hostile work environment case.

At the outset, it is necessary to focus on the key facts. I believe that the only conduct on the record that might be substantial enough to alter a term, condition, or privilege of employment, is Amundsen's use of sexual vulgarities. The other allegations about Amundsen's conduct, such as his involvement in a bar fight and his statements to employees at sales meetings that if sales did not improve, he was "going to kill you" or "kill your dog," do not appear to be gender-related. Hocevar's complaints about people other than Amundsen are based on incidents that were simply too few and far between to make a hostile environment.

Hocevar alleges that Amundsen chronically used foul language, specifically the words "fuck" and "bitch." In a letter dated December 20, 1995, Hocevar's counsel notified Purdue Frederick that Amundsen had engaged in ongoing sexual harassment against Hocevar. In January 1996 Purdue Frederick investigated the complaint. The investigation revealed that the members of the Viking District interviewed had "all participated in the use of profanity and, from time to time, off-color jokes. And the general consensus was that they carried it too far." In particular, the investigator concluded that Hocevar herself had participated in the profanity and improper jokes. Hocevar admitted at her deposition in this case that she used the same offensive language around Amundsen and other sales representatives. * * *

Hocevar complains most specifically of an incident in September 1994, at Dr. Kubics's office, in which Amundsen became enraged at being treated disrespectfully by a female doctor. Amundsen repeatedly referred to the doctor as a "fat fucking bitch," and talked about how he would like to "slam her one" and make her fear him.

In deciding when inappropriate conduct rises to the level of a hostile environment that changes a term or condition of employment, courts must look at all the circumstances. "These may include the frequency of the discriminatory conduct; its severity; whether it is physically threatening or humiliating, or *a mere offensive utterance;* and whether it unreasonably interferes with an employee's work performance." *Harris* (emphasis added). In this regard, it is important that the conduct complained of consists only of "offensive utterances" of a type Hocevar herself engaged in at work, and that to the extent the gender-based utterances were threatening or abusive, they were not aimed at Hocevar, but at the female doctor, who was not a Purdue employee.

* * * [I]n the cases in our circuit where we have considered conduct directed at others in upholding sexual harassment claims, that conduct augmented evidence of harassment directed at the plaintiff, *see, e.g., id.* (evidence of harassment of others augmented evidence of physical contact of plaintiff and chronic innuendos); *Hall v. Gus Const. Co.,* 842 F.2d 1010, 1015 (8th Cir.1988) (each plaintiff endured abuse). Abuse directed at a third party is part of the picture, but it is less significant than abuse directed at the plaintiff. *See Gleason v. Mesirow Fin., Inc.,* 118 F.3d 1134, 1144–45 (7th Cir.1997) ("Second hand harassment" not as great an invasion as harassment directed at plaintiff); *Black v. Zaring Homes, Inc.,* 104 F.3d 822, 826 (6th Cir.1997) (fact that most comments not directed at plaintiff contributes to conclusion of insufficiency of evidence). *But see Leibovitz v. New York City Transit Auth.,* 4 F Supp.2d 144, 150–53 (E.D.N.Y.1998) (upholding hostile environment verdict based entirely on harassment of others). Here, the conduct was directed at someone who was not a Purdue Frederick employee, and who was not even present to hear the hostile remarks. Therefore, even considering the evidence of Amundsen's reaction to the female doctor, Hocevar did not start out with

a strong case. The standards for establishing a hostile environment are set high so that Title VII "does not become a 'general civility code.'" *Faragher v. City of Boca Raton,* (quoting *Oncale*).

But Hocevar's claim truly struck the shoals when she admitted she used the sort of language she now complains of. In *Scusa v. Nestle U.S.A. Co.,* 181 F.3d 958, 967 (8th Cir.1999), we held that a plaintiff could not show others' workplace conduct was subjectively offensive when she did the same thing herself. "Appellant's evidence of a hostile work environment falls flat in light of the fact that she engaged in the very type of conduct about which she now complains. . ."

For these reasons, I concur in affirming the summary judgment entered against Hocevar on her hostile environment claim.

■ LAY, CIRCUIT JUDGE, dissenting. * * *

That the conduct in question is unwelcome is "[t]he gravamen of any sexual harassment claim." *Meritor Sav. Bank, FSB v. Vinson.* In determining whether conduct is "unwelcome," we should consider whether the plaintiff indicated, by her conduct, that the alleged harassment was unwelcome. This is a fact question for the jury and turns largely on credibility determinations.

The district court focused its inquiry on whether the incidents of harassment were "offensive" and concluded that they failed to constitute an offensive environment due to their infrequent use. Under review of the record, I find sufficient evidence and inference therefrom that there was an ongoing use of sexual vulgarity directed at the plaintiff as well as all women employees in general. Based on the evidence set forth below, the plaintiff has certainly met the threshold of proof of pervasiveness as a matter of law. The ultimate determination as to whether the harassment was pervasive must be made by the jury.

The record in the present case shows Amundsen's use of sexual vulgarity occurred throughout the workplace, on sales calls and during meetings. Hocevar's female co-worker, Kiekhaefer, indicates Amundsen repeatedly referred to women as "bitches," used the "F" word in virtually every other sentence, called clients "fuckers" and "assholes," and routinely referred to female nurses and female physicians as "fucking bitches." Similar testimony is in the record from another female employee of Amundsen's, Mary Beck-Johnson, indicating Amundsen "routinely" used the terms "bitch" and "fuck" in meetings. Further, Hocevar testified that sexually explicit behavior occurred at meetings chaired by Amundsen, which Amundsen either condoned or failed to stop, and that sexually suggestive comments were made by two Purdue managers, one of whom subjected Hocevar to unwelcome physical contact during a consensual dance, which made Hocevar "extremely uncomfortable." Under the record presented, these vulgar attacks cannot be simply regarded as "off-hand" or isolated incidents.

The defendant, as does Judge Beam, relies on the fact that Hocevar herself had used the words "bitch" and "fuck" on occasion in the workplace. On this basis, it is argued that the words are not unwelcome by Hocevar. Hocevar, however, qualifies her use of these words by saying that they were not used in the same context that Amundsen had used them. There is a world of difference between the use of the infrequent swear word in the workplace, not actionable when not directed to a specific gender, and direct words demeaning to women in general. While Hocevar's infrequent use of foul language may indeed, when presented to a jury, diminish her claim that the behavior of Amundsen and others was "unwelcome," it in no way bars her claim as a matter of law. I am unaware of any case that precludes a plaintiff from arguing that the employer's constant use of sexually charged language and off-color jokes is unwelcome merely because the plaintiff at times engaged in swearing. Such a reading is inconsistent with the mandate that courts consider the totality of the circumstances of a case. Further, Judge Beam's analysis utterly fails to address Amundsen's threats of violence, his dissemination of sexually explicit material at meetings, his condonation of sexually graphic behavior at meetings, and the behavior of other Purdue managers, all apparently because Hocevar admitted to the infrequent use of foul language. The record further shows that Hocevar's swearing was not directed as a demeaning word of harassment at any person or group of people. It is one thing that an employee use vulgarity in his or her general communication; it is quite another when the vulgarity is directed at a specific social group who reasonably could find it to be demeaning to their own self-being.

Even if one concedes that use of foul language by an employee can diminish a claim that the harassment was unwelcome and subjectively offensive, evidence of Hocevar's reaction could still support a finding that Amundsen's behavior was unwelcome.

Hocevar testified that she suffered fear, depression, anxiety and self-doubt as a result of Amundsen's behavior, including his degrading and demeaning criticism of her work performance. If she was not offended by this, as I think any reasonable person would be, it is difficult to explain that both she and her co-worker were under the continuing care of a psychologist and that Hocevar was treated with Prozac for anxiety and depression. Hocevar's complaint to Purdue manager Dennis Merlo is also "reaction" evidence revealing that Hocevar viewed Amundsen's sexually derogatory language unwelcome. * * * Giving her the benefit of all favorable inferences, this conduct could be found by a jury to support a finding that the harassment was unwelcome and that it was subjectively offensive. * * *

Whether harassing conduct is based on sex is determined by inquiring whether "members of one sex are exposed to disadvantageous terms or conditions of employment to which members of the other sex are not exposed." *Harris* (Ginsburg, J., concurring).

This court has recently reaffirmed that gender-based insults, such as the term "bitch," may give rise to an inference of discrimination based on sex, and has rejected the notion that an employee must be propositioned, touched offensively, or harassed by sexual innuendo in order to have been sexually harassed. Additionally, we have held that intimidation and hostility toward women in general can result from conduct other than explicit sexual advances. Moreover, it is well settled that verbal abuse, violence, or physical aggression may constitute sexual harassment, and that such need not be explicitly sexual in nature. * * *

* * * Judge Beam recognizes that the use of foul language may have been pervasive. Because he concludes that the offensive language is not based on sex, however, he sets this evidence aside, then proceeds to consider whether the remaining facts of Hocevar's case are sufficiently severe or pervasive. This approach errs because it fails to consider the totality of the circumstances and imposes a per se test requiring harassment be "directed at" plaintiff to be actionable. * * *

The allegations, if found true by a jury, are sufficient to permit a finding that the cumulative effect of Amundsen's conduct, along with that of other Purdue managers, was sufficiently severe or pervasive to create a hostile work environment based on sexual harassment. * * *

Julie Gallagher v. C.H. Robinson Worldwide, Inc.

United States Court of Appeals for the Sixth Circuit, 2009.
567 F.3d 263.

■ McKEAGUE, CIRCUIT JUDGE.

[According to the opinion below, Julie Gallagher began working as a sales representative in the defendant's Cleveland office in 2002, alongside approximately 20 sales employees and 3 support personnel. Sales employees' job duties included booking freight loads, ensuring the timely and safe arrival of loads and negotiating rates. In order to carry out those duties, the sales staff worked in cubicle work stations that were organized in pods in an open floor plan. Short dividers separated them so they could freely communicate with one another while conducting business. The divider walls between cubicles provided little privacy; co-workers' computers were visible to each other, conversations between employees as well phone conversations with customers were easily overheard. The environment at the Company was noisy; the job was high pressured and fast paced.]

* * * The district court was persuaded by C.H. Robinson's argument that most of the complained of offensive conduct in its Cleveland office was common and indiscriminate, was not targeted at Gallagher, would have taken place whether Gallagher was present or not, and therefore was not "based on" Gallagher's femaleness. This conclusion reflects a mistaken perception of what is required to find that conduct is "based on sex" in the legal sense.

There were instances in the workplace when Gallagher was repeatedly called a "bitch" by a co-worker in anger, was referred to by another as a "heifer" with "milking udders," and was taunted by a male co-worker wearing nothing but a towel around his waist when she was the only female in the office. These incidents, in which offensive conduct was directed at Gallagher, reflect sex-discriminatory animus. Yet, the record suggests that much of the other highly offensive conduct was not directed at Gallagher. Among the commonplace offensive occurrences, Gallagher complained of: co-workers' vulgar descriptions of female customers, associates and even friends as "bitches," "whores," "sluts," "dykes," and "cunts;" co-workers' joint ogling and discussions of obscene photographs and pornographic magazines; and co-workers' explicit conversations about their own sexual practices and strip club exploits. Gallagher could not avoid exposure to these offensive behaviors because they occurred in close proximity to her work station, where she was required to be. Still, the offensive conduct does not appear to have been motivated by Gallagher's presence or by the fact that she is a woman. * * *

The district court * * * concluded that because much of the offensive conduct Gallagher complained of occurred in an open forum where men and women worked together, it did not occur because she is a woman and was therefore not based on sex. * * *

Here, * * * most of the complained of harassment just summarized—both conduct directed at Gallagher and indiscriminate conduct—is explicitly sexual and patently degrading of women. The natural effect of exposure to such offensive conduct is embarrassment, humiliation and degradation, irrespective of the harasser's motivation—especially and all the more so if the captive recipient of the harassment is a woman. In connection with such evidence, it is hardly necessary for Gallagher to otherwise show that the conduct evinces anti-female animus; it is obvious. Hence, even though members of both sexes were exposed to the offensive conduct in the Cleveland office, considering the nature of the patently degrading and anti-female nature of the harassment, it stands to reason that women would suffer, as a result of the exposure, greater disadvantage in the terms and conditions of their employment than men. See Oncale v. Sundowner Offshore Servs., Inc., (observing that the critical issue, for purposes of Title VII sexual harassment, is whether members of one sex are subject to more disadvantageous terms or conditions of employment than members of the other sex).

The district court, in evaluating the "based on sex" element, focused too narrowly on the motivation for the harassers' offensive conduct rather than on the effects of the conduct on the victim-recipient. This very point was recently clarified by the Eleventh Circuit in Reeves v. C.H. Robinson Worldwide, Inc., 525 F.3d 1139 (11th Cir.2008). * * * The Reeves court [held] that "sex specific" language satisfies the "based on sex" element even when the language does not target the plaintiff. *Id.* at 1144. The court reasoned:

> The language in the CHRW office included the "sex specific" words "bitch," "whore," and "cunt" that . . . may be more degrading to women than men. The subject matter of the conversations and jokes that allegedly permeated the office on a daily basis included male and female sexual anatomy, masturbation, and female pornography, all of which was discussed in a manner that was similarly more degrading to women than men. . . . Therefore, even if such language was used indiscriminately in the office such that men and women were equally exposed to the language, the language had a discriminatory effect on Reeves because of its degrading nature.

Id. * * *

The district court also determined that the harassment was not shown to be so severe and pervasive as to interfere with Gallagher's job performance. Although the court found the evidence sufficient to create a genuine issue of fact as to whether the alleged workplace conduct was subjectively severe or pervasive to her, the court determined Gallagher could not show that it was "sufficiently objectively severe or pervasive" to withstand the motion for summary judgment. The court acknowledged its obligation to consider the totality of the circumstances, but summarized these merely as entailing "the frequent use of crude language, the occasional instances of offensive e-mails and pornographic material to which Gallagher was not intentionally exposed, and the few instances of offensive conduct directed at Gallagher." Further, the court faulted plaintiff for failing to present any evidence that the harassment interfered with her work performance. * * *

* * * The district court emphasized that most of the offensive conduct was not directed at Gallagher. This is not an irrelevant consideration, but the district court appears to have ignored the fact that, due to the configuration of the Cleveland workplace, it was practically impossible for Gallagher to avoid her co-workers' offensive conduct. Whether the offensive conduct was intentionally directed specifically at Gallagher or not, the fact remains that she had no means of escaping her co-workers' loud insulting language and degrading conversations; she was unavoidably exposed to it. Her complaints to co-workers and her supervisor were not only ignored, but actually tended to exacerbate the harassment.

Further, the district court erroneously insisted on a showing that the harassment was both subjectively and objectively severe and pervasive; whereas the [correct] standard requires a showing that the environment is objectively hostile and the harassment subjectively severe and pervasive. The district court had no trouble concluding there was a triable issue as to whether the harassment was subjectively severe and pervasive. The next question thus should have been whether a reasonable person could have found the environment objectively hostile. Considering the totality of the circumstances as described in Gallagher's deposition, the conclusion is inescapable that a reasonable person could have found the Cleveland office—permeated with vulgar language, demeaning conversations and images, and palpable anti-female animus—objectively hostile. The district court reached a contrary conclusion by erroneously limiting its consideration only to some instances of abusive conduct, instead of considering the workplace as a whole.

Moreover, the district court also erred in requiring evidence that Gallagher's work performance suffered measurably as a result of the harassment. The court placed inordinate weight on Gallagher's testimony that she was able to meet her daily and weekly quotas and that her work performance was rated average to above average. In finding that Gallagher failed to present any evidence that the harassment unreasonably interfered with her work, the court ignored her testimony that, from day one in the Cleveland office, she was "horrified" by the loudness, constant swearing and vulgar language, and that she "left there every day crying." Considering Gallagher's description of the offensive conduct to which she was exposed, her reaction can hardly be dismissed as implausible, unreasonable, exaggerated or hypersensitive. Nor is it improbable that the hostility and antagonism she experienced rendered her work more difficult. In *Williams,* the court made it clear that a plaintiff need not prove a tangible decline in her work productivity; only "that the harassment made it more difficult to do the job." Based on the instant record, a reasonable jury could certainly find that the complained of harassment made it more difficult for Gallagher to do her job.

We therefore conclude that the district court erred in its determination that Gallagher presented insufficient evidence that she was subjected to such severe and pervasive harassment as to unreasonably interfere with her work performance and create a hostile work environment. * * *

NOTES AND QUESTIONS

1.　*The Totality of Many Circumstances.* We do not envy judges who must adjudicate sex harassment claims and determine when a workplace environment has become so "boorish and unprofessional" that it has crossed the line into creating a Title VII violation. What should the baseline be for a "normal" workplace? What is the point at which Title VII's requirements would "become a general civility code"? As an exercise, draft criteria for identifying verbal abuse without creating overly intrusive word policing. Not impossible, but also not easy. It is no wonder that there are hundreds of reported decisions in this area, virtually all of which are heavily fact dependent. Can you think of institutions other than courts that might contribute significantly to combatting the underlying problem of abusiveness? From the perspective of employers that want to avoid liability, what beyond the current prevention strategies (such as training videos and procedures for reporting) could they develop?

2. *A Day in the Office.* Both of the preceding cases involved plaintiffs who worked as sale representatives. The popular impression of sex harassment claims is that they are most likely to arise in traditionally male-dominated jobs such as construction work, in which women are outnumbered. These plaintiffs, however, worked in white-collar office jobs in gender-integrated occupations. How might differences among settings and types of jobs affect proof of "because of sex" or unwelcomeness?

3. *Unwelcomeness and Consent.* Why would consent not be a defense to an allegation of quid pro quo sexual harassment as it is to a charge of sexual assault? In the criminal context of rape, there traditionally has been a requirement that the complainant was physically forced to engage in the sexual acts. How do both consent and unwelcomeness compare to the element of affirmative consent that is now being debated on campuses? See Chapter 8, Section 2. How would the different feminist theorists in Chapter 3, Section 3C analyze the trend toward the criminal law adopting a standard closer to unwelcomeness?

B. COMPETING PARADIGMS

Because the meaning or meanings of "sex" are encoded into the statutory text of Title VII, the opportunities for elaboration and re-creation of those meanings in litigation and in legal scholarship are almost endless. Recall Foucault's insight that contemporary society "spreads [sex] over the surface of things and bodies, draws it out and bids it speak, implants it in reality and enjoins it to tell the truth." *History of Sexuality.* See Chapter 3, Section C, *supra.* Sexual harassment litigation has become one site for a voluminous amount of meaning creation. Questions about how society should understand and respond to the practices that sexual harassment law seeks to define as discrimination have, in turn, produced a wealth of legal scholarship.

Catharine MacKinnon is often credited with having formulated the civil rights approach to harassment, and she published the first fully developed conceptualization of it in her 1979 book, *The Sexual Harassment of Working Women.* MacKinnon considers sexual harassment to be one example (along with pornography and sex work) of the "sexual enactment of inequality." Should sexual relations between two persons of different power or status in a workplace constitute a prima facie case of harassment? Consider how MacKinnon approaches the related issue of whether a plaintiff must show intentional discrimination in a quid pro quo case as is required in other disparate treatment claims: "[S]exual harassment law has been essentially indifferent to intent requirements as they are known elsewhere in equality law, possibly because asking whether a perpetrator meant to discriminate against a woman or only meant to impose sex on her at work looks as beside the point of her inequality injury as it is." Catharine A. MacKinnon, "The Logic of Experience: Reflections on the Development of Sexual Harassment Law," 90 *Geo. L. J.* 813, 826 (2002).

Katherine Franke would reframe the claim with gender norms as fundamental, sexualized conduct as exemplary. Franke argues that sexual harassment "is a form of sex discrimination when it reflects or perpetuates gender stereotypes in the workplace. I suggest a reconceptualization of sexual harassment as gender harassment. Understood in this way, sexual harassment is a kind of sex discrimination not because the conduct would not have been undertaken if the victim had been a different sex, not because it is sexual, and not because men do it to women, but precisely because it is a technology of sexism. That is, it perpetuates, enforces, and polices a set of gender norms that seek to feminize women and masculinize men." Franke, "What's Wrong with Sexual Harassment?," 49 *Stan. L. Rev.* 691, 696 (1997)

Vicki Schultz criticizes sexual harassment case law for both under- and over-inclusiveness. Vicki Schultz, "Reconceptualizing Sexual Harassment," 107 *Yale L.J.* 1683 (1998). As to the former, she argues that courts have conflated gender harassment and sexual abuse, by too often presuming that sexualized harassment indicated and was necessary for attempts to drive women out of certain workplaces. As a result, the law misses much of the worst harassment of women because it isn't sexual. Gender-based, non-sexual insults ("you don't look like a mechanic") undermine women's competence and authority. What they have in common with sexualized harassment, Schultz argues, is that the victim's very woman-ness is used as evidence of her inadequacy.

Sexual harassment law is also over-inclusive, Schultz says, because judges often tend to assume that all sexualized conduct or speech is discriminatory. She elaborates on this point in *The Sanitized Workplace*, *supra*. The change that she proposes is that feminists prioritize ending gender-segregated or gender-imbalanced workplaces. She cites studies showing that when women workers have achieved critical mass in a particular workplace, they exercise sufficient power to informally establish the norms of sexualized interaction that will occur there. Compare this research to the *Hocevar* and *Gallagher* cases, *supra*. Can you suggest new strategies for preventing harassment in gender-integrated workplaces?

Janet Halley takes Schultz's over-inclusiveness point further, calling it "sexuality harassment." She argues that the fatal flaw of MacKinnon's approach is the totalism of a "rigid, monolithic association of men with male gender with superordination, and of women with female gender and subordination." She aligns herself with a non-identitarian politics that recognizes that "gender and power circulate far more complexly and with far more contingency than is thought in most women's-subordination feminisms." Janet Halley, "Sexuality Harassment" in *Directions in*

Sexual Harassment Law (Catharine A. MacKinnon and Reva B. Siegel, ed. 2004).

PROBLEM 5-3
APPLYING THEORY TO PRACTICE

As a way of concretizing these various theoretical approaches, consider the following hypothetical:

> Ann Peterson is a sales clerk at a furniture store. She has a good relationship with her co-workers but a problem has arisen since a new regional manager—Robert Davis—joined the company. Peterson states that Davis asked her immediate supervisor to set up a private meeting after the end of a regional training session. The training was held in one of the large conference rooms in a local hotel. When it was over, Peterson's supervisor told her that Davis wished to speak privately with her, and directed her to Davis' hotel room. When she arrived, Davis made her a drink and briefly discussed her job. He then beckoned her to lie down on the bed and began to masturbate. Peterson said, I want to leave. Davis did not attempt to touch her or to stop her from leaving, but said only, "I hope that you'll keep this interaction just between us. After all, we will see each other again at these events." (He admits the facts as stated.)

First, outline how Peterson would frame her sexual harassment claims in doctrinal terms (e.g., type of harassment). Then draft opinions for Justices MacKinnon, Franke, Schultz and Halley. If you were counsel for the furniture company, what specific provisions would you recommend that the firm adopt to prevent harassment?

C. SAME-SEX HARASSMENT

Does being harassed "because of sex" mean something different if the person being harassed is a man? What are the social meanings of men sexually harassing men? In what situations would this most likely occur?

Joseph Oncale v. Sundowner Offshore Services, Inc., et al.

United States Supreme Court, 1998.
523 U.S. 75, 118 S.Ct. 998, 140 L.Ed.2d 201.

■ JUSTICE SCALIA delivered the opinion of the Court. This case presents the question whether workplace harassment can violate Title VII's prohibition against "discriminat[ion] . . . because of . . . sex," 42 U.S.C.A. § 2000e–2(a)(1), when the harasser and the harassed employee are of the same sex.

* * * In late October 1991, Oncale was working for respondent Sundowner Offshore Services on a Chevron U.S.A., Inc., oil platform in the Gulf of Mexico. He was employed as a roustabout on an eight-man crew which included respondents John Lyons, Danny Pippen, and Brandon Johnson. Lyons, the crane operator, and Pippen, the driller, had supervisory authority. On several occasions, Oncale was forcibly subjected to sex-related, humiliating actions against him by Lyons, Pippen and Johnson in the presence of the rest of the crew. Pippen and Lyons also physically assaulted Oncale in a sexual manner, and Lyons threatened him with rape.

Oncale's complaints to supervisory personnel produced no remedial action; in fact, the company's Safety Compliance Clerk, Valent Hohen, told Oncale that Lyons and Pippen "picked [on] him all the time too," and called him a name suggesting homosexuality. Oncale eventually quit—asking that his pink slip reflect that he "voluntarily left due to sexual harassment and verbal abuse." When asked at his deposition why he left Sundowner, Oncale stated "I felt that if I didn't leave my job, that I would be raped or forced to have sex." * * *

* * * We have held that [Title VII] not only covers "terms" and "conditions" in the narrow contractual sense, but "evinces a congressional intent to strike at the entire spectrum of disparate treatment of men and women in employment." *Meritor Savings Bank, FSB v. Vinson*, 477 U.S. 57, 64 (1986) (citations and internal quotation marks omitted). "When the workplace is permeated with discriminatory intimidation, ridicule, and insult that is sufficiently severe or pervasive to alter the conditions of the victim's employment and create an abusive working environment, Title VII is violated." *Harris v. Forklift Systems, Inc.*, 510 U.S. 17, 21 (1993) (citations and internal quotation marks omitted).

Title VII's prohibition of discrimination "because of . . . sex" protects men as well as women, and in the related context of racial discrimination in the workplace we have rejected any conclusive presumption that an employer will not discriminate against members of his own race. * * * In *Johnson v. Transportation Agency, Santa Clara Cty.*, 480 U.S. 616 (1987), a male employee claimed that his employer discriminated against him because of his sex when it preferred a female employee for promotion. Although we ultimately rejected the claim on other grounds, we did not consider it significant that the supervisor who made that decision was also a man. If our precedents leave any doubt on the question, we hold today that nothing in Title VII necessarily bars a claim of discrimination "because of . . . sex" merely because the plaintiff and the defendant (or the person charged with acting on behalf of the defendant) are of the same sex.

Courts have had little trouble with that principle in cases like *Johnson*, where an employee claims to have been passed over for a job or promotion. But when the issue arises in the context of a "hostile environment" sexual harassment claim, the state and federal courts have taken a bewildering variety of stances. Some, like the Fifth Circuit in this case, have held that same-sex sexual harassment claims are never cognizable under Title VII. Other decisions say that such claims are actionable only if the plaintiff can prove that the harasser is homosexual (and thus presumably motivated by sexual desire). Compare *McWilliams v. Fairfax County Board of Supervisors,* 72 F.3d 1191 (C.A.4 1996), with *Wrightson v. Pizza Hut of America,* 99 F.3d 138 (C.A.4 1996). Still others suggest that workplace harassment that is sexual in content is always actionable, regardless of the harasser's sex, sexual orientation, or motivations. See *Doe v. Belleville,* 119 F.3d 563 (C.A.7 1997).

We see no justification in the statutory language or our precedents for a categorical rule excluding same-sex harassment claims from the coverage of Title VII. As some courts have observed, male-on-male sexual harassment in the workplace was assuredly not the principal evil Congress was concerned with when it enacted Title VII. But statutory prohibitions often go beyond the principal evil to cover reasonably comparable evils, and it is ultimately the provisions of our laws rather than the principal concerns of our legislators by which we are governed. Title VII prohibits "discriminat[ion] . . . because of . . . sex" in the "terms" or "conditions" of employment. Our holding that this includes sexual harassment must extend to sexual harassment of any kind that meets the statutory requirements.

Respondents and their *amici* contend that recognizing liability for same-sex harassment will transform Title VII into a general civility code for the American workplace. But that risk is no greater for same-sex than for opposite-sex harassment, and is adequately met by careful attention to the requirements of the statute. Title VII does not prohibit all verbal or physical harassment in the workplace; it is directed only at "*discriminat[ion]* . . . because of . . . sex." We have never held that workplace harassment, even harassment between men and women, is automatically discrimination because of sex merely because the words used have sexual content or connotations. "The critical issue, Title VII's text indicates, is whether members of one sex are exposed to disadvantageous terms or conditions of employment to which members of the other sex are not exposed." *Harris, supra,* at 25 (Ginsburg, J., concurring).

Courts and juries have found the inference of discrimination easy to draw in most male-female sexual harassment situations, because the challenged conduct typically involves explicit or implicit proposals of sexual activity; it is reasonable to assume those proposals would not have been made to someone of the same sex. The same chain of inference would be available to a plaintiff alleging same-sex harassment, if there were credible evidence that the harasser was homosexual. But harassing conduct need not be motivated by sexual desire to support an inference of discrimination on the basis of sex. A trier of fact might reasonably find such discrimination, for example, if a female victim is harassed in such sex-specific and derogatory terms by another woman as to make it clear that the harasser is motivated by general hostility to the presence of women in the workplace. A same-sex harassment plaintiff may also, of course, offer direct comparative evidence about how the alleged harasser treated members of both sexes in a mixed-sex workplace. Whatever evidentiary route the plaintiff chooses to follow, he or she must always prove that the conduct at issue was not merely tinged with offensive sexual connotations, but actually constituted "discrimina[tion] . . . because of . . . sex."

And there is another requirement that prevents Title VII from expanding into a general civility code: As we emphasized in *Meritor* and *Harris*, the statute does not reach genuine but innocuous differences in the ways men and women routinely interact with members of the same sex and of the opposite sex. The prohibition of harassment on the basis of sex requires neither asexuality nor androgyny in the workplace; it forbids only behavior so objectively offensive as to alter the "conditions" of the victim's employment. "Conduct that is not severe or pervasive enough to create an objectively hostile or abusive work environment—an environment that a reasonable person would find hostile or abusive—is beyond Title VII's purview." *Harris,* 510 U.S., at 21, citing *Meritor*, 477 U.S., at 67. We have always regarded that requirement as crucial, and as sufficient to ensure that courts and juries do not mistake ordinary socializing in the workplace—such as male-on-male horseplay or intersexual flirtation—for discriminatory "conditions of employment."

We have emphasized, moreover, that the objective severity of harassment should be judged from the perspective of a reasonable person in the plaintiff's position, considering "all the circumstances." *Harris, supra*, at 23. In same-sex (as in all) harassment cases, that inquiry requires careful consideration of the social context in which particular behavior occurs and is experienced by its target. A professional football player's working environment is not severely or pervasively abusive, for example, if the coach smacks him on the buttocks as he heads onto the field—even if the same behavior would reasonably be experienced as abusive by the coach's secretary (male or female) back at the office. The real social impact of workplace behavior often depends on a constellation of surrounding circumstances, expectations, and relationships which are not fully captured by a simple recitation of the words used or the physical acts performed. Common sense, and an appropriate sensitivity to social context, will enable courts and juries to distinguish between simple teasing or roughhousing among members of the same sex, and conduct which a reasonable person in the plaintiff's position would find severely hostile or abusive. * * *

■ JUSTICE THOMAS, concurring.

I concur because the Court stresses that in every sexual harassment case, the plaintiff must plead and ultimately prove Title VII's statutory requirement that there be discrimination "because of . . . sex."

NOTES AND QUESTIONS

1. *Proof.* The Court rules that same-sex harassment claims are not prohibited as a matter of law. But how will a plaintiff like Oncale prove that the sexually assaultive conduct fell within the "because of . . . sex" requirement? The Court stated that one way would be to offer "credible evidence that the harasser was homosexual." How will discovery proceed in such cases, especially if the harasser denies that he or she is homosexual? See the description of "stereotypical homosexual behavior" in *Griswold v. Fresenius USA, Inc.*, 978 F. Supp. 718, 723–24 (N.D.Ohio 1997). Would bisexuality count?

2. *"Common Sense"?* The final portion of the opinion exhorts lower courts not to confuse "ordinary socializing in the workplace—such as male-on-male horseplay—with harassment." Does that suggest that the bounds of what is inoffensive horseplay are determined by gender? If so, how can a court require a showing of differential treatment? Isn't differential treatment built into the very distinction between "horseplay" and harassment?

3. *Determining Severity.* Whose sensibilities will establish the reasonable person standard for severity? Should there be a reasonable woman standard? What about when the alleged harasser is gay and the plaintiff is straight? Do you think that the Court's use of "intersexual" to modify "flirtation" was intended as a specific limit, to guard against a man being allowed to flirt with another man, or a woman with another woman? Justice Scalia used the example of a professional football coach patting a player on the buttocks to illustrate harmless behavior. What if the coach is gay? One court has stated that it "cannot rule out that the homosexual aspect of harassment could objectively contribute to a hostile environment." *Miller v. Vesta, Inc.*, 946 F.Supp. 697, 712–13 (E.D. Wis. 1996).

Medina Rene v. MGM Grand Hotel, Inc.

United States Court of Appeals for the Ninth Circuit, *en banc*, 2002.
305 F.3d 1061, *cert. denied*, 538 U.S. 922 (2003).

■ CIRCUIT JUDGE [WILLIAM] FLETCHER.

* * * Medina Rene, an openly gay man, appeals from the district court's grant of summary judgment in favor of his employer MGM Grand Hotel in his Title VII action alleging sexual harassment by his male coworkers and supervisor. The relevant facts are not in dispute. Rene worked for the hotel, located in Las Vegas, Nevada, from December 1993 until his termination in June 1996. He worked as a butler on the 29th floor, where his duties involved responding to the requests of the wealthy, high-profile and famous guests for whom that floor was reserved. All of the other butlers on the floor, as well as their supervisor, were also male.

Rene provided extensive evidence that, over the course of a two-year period, his supervisor and several of his fellow butlers subjected him to a hostile work environment on almost a daily basis. The harassers' conduct included whistling and blowing kisses at Rene, calling him "sweetheart" and "muñeca" (Spanish for "doll"), telling crude jokes and giving sexually oriented "joke" gifts, and forcing Rene to look at pictures of naked men having sex. On "more times than [Rene said he] could possibly count," the harassment involved offensive physical conduct of a sexual nature. Rene gave deposition testimony that he was caressed and hugged and that his coworkers would "touch [his] body like they would to a woman." On numerous occasions, he said, they grabbed him in the crotch and poked their fingers in his anus through his clothing. When asked what he believed was the motivation behind this harassing behavior, Rene responded that the behavior occurred because he is gay. * * *

It is clear that Rene has alleged physical conduct that was so severe and pervasive as to constitute an objectively abusive working environment. It is equally clear that the conduct was "of a sexual nature." Rene's tormentors did not grab his elbow or poke their fingers in his eye. They grabbed his crotch and poked their fingers in his anus.

Physical sexual assault has routinely been prohibited as sexual harassment under Title VII. * * * Such harassment—grabbing, poking, rubbing or mouthing areas of the body linked to sexuality—is inescapably "because of . . . sex." * * *

In granting MGM Grand's motion for summary judgment, the district court did not deny that the sexual assaults alleged by Rene were so objectively offensive that they created a hostile working environment. Rather, it appears to have held that Rene's otherwise viable cause of action was defeated because he believed he was targeted because he is gay. This is not the law. We have surveyed the many cases finding a violation of Title VII based on the offensive touching of the genitalia, buttocks, or breasts of women. In none of those cases has a court denied relief because the victim was, or might have been, a lesbian. The sexual orientation of the victim was simply irrelevant. If sexual orientation is irrelevant for a female victim, we see no reason why it is not also irrelevant for a male victim.

The premise of a sexual touching hostile work environment claim is that the conditions of the work environment have been made hostile "because of . . . sex." The physical attacks to which Rene was subjected, which targeted body parts clearly linked to his sexuality, were "because of . . . sex." Whatever else those attacks may, or may not, have been "because of" has no legal consequence. "[S]o long as the environment itself is hostile to the plaintiff because of [his] sex, why the harassment was perpetrated (sexual interest? misogyny? personal vendetta? misguided humor? boredom?) is beside the point." *Doe v. City of Belleville*, 119 F.3d 563, 578 (7th Cir. 1997), *vacated and remanded*, 523 U.S. 1001 (1998).

Our opinion today is guided by the principles established by the Supreme Court in *Oncale v. Sundowner Offshore Servs., Inc.* * * * We take two lessons from the Court's decision in *Oncale*.

First, Title VII forbids severe or pervasive same-sex offensive sexual touching. The Court made clear that a plaintiff's action for sexual harassment under Title VII cannot be defeated by a showing that the perpetrator and the victim of an alleged sexual assault are of the same gender. * * *

Second, offensive sexual touching is actionable discrimination even in a same-sex workforce. The Court in *Oncale* made clear that "discrimination" is a necessary predicate to every Title VII claim. That is, a defendant's conduct must not merely be "because of . . . sex"; it must be " '*discriminat[ion]* . . . because of . . . sex.' " (emphasis in original). The Court in *Oncale* held that "discrimina[tion] . . . because of . . . sex" can occur entirely among men, where some men are subjected to offensive sexual touching and some men are not. There were no women on Oncale's drilling rig; indeed, there were no women on any of his employer's oil rigs. Discrimination is the use of some criterion as a basis for a difference in treatment. In the context of our civil rights laws, including Title VII, discrimination is the use of a *forbidden* criterion as a basis for a *disadvantageous* difference in treatment. "Sex" is the forbidden criterion under Title VII, and discrimination is any disadvantageous difference in treatment "because of . . . sex." The *Oncale* Court's holding that offensive sexual touching in a same-sex workforce is actionable discrimination under Title VII necessarily means that discrimination can take place between members of the same sex, not merely between members of the opposite sex. Thus, Oncale did not need to show that he was treated worse than members of the opposite sex. It was enough to show that he suffered discrimination *in comparison to other men.*

* * * Rene has alleged that he was treated differently—and disadvantageously—based on sex. This is precisely what Title VII forbids: "discriminat[ion] . . . because of . . . sex."

In sum, what we have in this case is a fairly straightforward sexual harassment claim. Title VII prohibits offensive "physical conduct of a sexual nature" when that conduct is sufficiently severe or pervasive. *Meritor Savings Bank v. Vinson*, 477 U.S. 57, 65 (1986). It prohibits such conduct without regard to whether the perpetrator and the victim are of the same or different genders. And it prohibits such conduct without regard to the sexual orientation—real or perceived—of the victim.

There will be close cases on the question of what constitutes physical conduct of a sexual nature, for there are some physical assaults that are intended to inflict physical injury, but are not intended to have (and are not interpreted as having) sexual meaning. That is, there will be some cases in which a physical assault, even though directed at a sexually identifiable part of the body, does not give rise to a viable Title VII claim. But this is not such a case. Like the plaintiff in *Oncale*, Rene has alleged a physical assault of a sexual nature that is sufficient to survive a defense motion for summary judgment.

This opinion is joined by JUDGES TROTT, THOMAS, GRABER, and FISHER. JUDGE PREGERSON, in a separate opinion joined by JUDGES TROTT and BERZON, reaches the same result but under a different rationale. Taken together, these two opinions are joined by a majority of the en banc panel. * * *

■ CIRCUIT JUDGE PREGERSON, with whom CIRCUIT JUDGES TROTT and BERZON join, concurring.

I concur in the result of Judge Fletcher's opinion. I write separately to point out that in my view, this is a case of actionable gender stereotyping harassment. * * *

The conduct suffered by Rene is indistinguishable from the conduct found actionable in *Nichols v. Azteca Restaurant Enterprises, Inc.*, 256 F.3d 864 (9th Cir.2001). In that case,

> Male co-workers and a supervisor repeatedly referred to [the male gay plaintiff] in Spanish and English as "she" and "her." Male co-workers mocked [him] for walking and carrying his serving tray "like a woman," and taunted him in Spanish and English as, among other things, a "faggot" and a ". . . female whore."

We concluded in *Nichols* that "[the] rule that bars discrimination on the basis of sex stereotypes" set in *Price Waterhouse* "squarely applies to preclude the harassment here." More generally, we held that "this verbal abuse was closely related to gender," "occurred because of sex," and therefore "constituted actionable harassment under . . . Title VII."

The similarities between *Nichols* and the present case are striking. In both cases, a male gay employee was "teased" or "mocked" by his male co-workers because he walked "like a woman." And in both cases, a male gay employee was referred to by his male-co-workers in female terms— "she," "her," and "female whore" in *Nichols*; "sweetheart" and "muñeca" ("doll") in the present case—to "remind [ ] [him] that he did not conform to their gender-based stereotypes." For the same reasons that we concluded in *Nichols* that "[the] rule that bars discrimination on the basis of sex stereotypes" set in *Price Waterhouse* "squarely applie[d] to preclude the harassment" at issue there, I conclude that this rule also squarely applies to preclude the identical harassment at issue here. Accordingly, this is a case of actionable gender stereotyping harassment.

■ [Separate concurring opinions by JUDGES GRABER and FISHER are omitted.]

■ CIRCUIT JUDGE HUG, with whom CHIEF JUDGE SCHROEDER, and JUDGES FERNANDEZ and T.G. NELSON join, dissenting.

* * * The basis for Judge Fletcher's opinion is that harassment of a person in the workplace in the form of severe unwelcome physical conduct of a sexual nature is sufficient to establish a cause of action under Title VII of the Civil Rights Act, regardless of whether that

harassment constitutes discrimination *because of* race, color, religion, gender, or national origin. I disagree because this completely eliminates an essential element of that statute, that the harassment be *because of* discrimination against one of the five specified categories of persons named in the statute. * * *

* * * In this case, the parties do not dispute the existence of a hostile work environment, for there is no doubt that the harassment that Rene alleged was so objectively offensive that it created a hostile work environment. The dispute is whether he was discriminated against because of his gender.

Rene relies on *Oncale* to make his case, contending that the Supreme Court impliedly held that discrimination based on sexual orientation is actionable under Title VII. This is a misreading of *Oncale*. * * * Never has it been held "that workplace harassment, even harassment between men and women, is automatically discrimination because of sex merely because the words used have sexual content or connotations." *Oncale*. Rather, under Title VII, the plaintiff "must always prove that the conduct at issue was not merely tinged with offensive sexual connotations, but actually constituted '*discrimina [tion]* . . . because of . . . sex.'" *Id.*

* * * Thus, the Supreme Court in *Oncale* did not hold that the harassment alleged by the plaintiff in that case was actionable under Title VII. The Court, rather, simply rejected the Fifth Circuit's holding that same-sex harassment could *never* be actionable under Title VII. * * *

Judge Fletcher's opinion in effect interprets *Oncale* to mean that if the defendant's conduct was "sexual in nature" the statutory requirements of Title VII are met. The opinion then reasons that because the touching in this case was sexual in nature and was discriminatory, Rene has stated a claim under Title VII. This misinterprets *Oncale*. The *Oncale* Court did say that "[w]e see no justification in the statutory language or our precedents for a categorical rule excluding same-sex harassment claims from the coverage of Title VII." However, the Court qualified that by stating "Title VII prohibits 'discriminat[ion] . . . because of . . . sex' in the 'terms' or 'conditions' of employment. Our holding that this includes sexual harassment must extend to sexual harassment of any kind *that meets the statutory requirements*." (emphasis added). Thus, the Court stressed that the harassment type of discrimination must meet the statutory requirement of "because of sex." * * *

NOTES AND QUESTIONS

1. *What's Bad for the Goose.* In an *amicus* brief in *Oncale*, Catharine MacKinnon framed male-on-male harassment in the following terms:

> [There are] several common myths about male-on-male sexual abuse * * * : that men, acting as members of their gender, cannot and do not dominate other men as well as women; that when a man sexually abuses another man, the actions are not sexual and not

gender-based; and that male domination of some men over other men is not part of the social system whereby men dominate women. * * *

* * * The denial that interactions among men can have a sexual component, and that sexual abuse of men is gendered, are twin features of the social ideology of male dominance. * * * In this ideology, men are seen as sexually invulnerable. This image protects men from much male sexual violence and naturalizes the sexual abuse of women, making it seem that women, biologically, are sexual victims. Denying that men can be sexually abused as men thus supports the gender hierarchy of men over women in society. The illusion is preserved that men are sexually inviolable, hence naturally superior, as the sexual abuse of men by men is kept invisible.

One cannot presume that behavior that is sexual in opposite-sex contexts is not sexual in same-sex contexts. * * * Just as acts do not automatically become sexual simply because they are engaged in by members of different sexes, acts do not become nonsexual simply because they are engaged in by members of the same sex.

Brief Amici Curiae of National Organization of Male Sexual Victimization, et al., 1997 WL 471814. This argument seems directly contrary to the *Oncale* opinion's indulgence of "horse play." (Recall that it was a unanimous decision.) Can you reconcile the two positions?

2. *If the Conduct Is Sexual, It Must Be Based on Sex.* In considering whether the "because of sex" element of a Title VII claim was met by allegations that an employee's job was conditioned on whether she had sexual relations with her male supervisor, the Ninth Circuit said, "[S]exual harassment is *ordinarily* based on sex. What else could it be based on?" Nichols v. Frank, 42 F.3d 503, 511 (9th Cir. 1994) (emphasis in the original). Consider the different meanings of "sex" that one could infer from that statement. Do you agree that the statement is self-evident? If it is, should the implied conclusion be equally obvious in a situation of same-sex harassment?

3. *Comparator or Motive?* The majority opinion in *Rene* stresses that the plaintiff suffered discrimination "in comparison to other men." The opinion also asserts that the harassment was grounded in Rene's failure to conform to gender stereotypes. Both points relate to the question of whether the necessary element of "because of sex" has been satisfied. When you untangle these approaches, don't they point to discrimination based on Rene's homosexual (or perceived homosexual) orientation? If the comparison is between Rene and other men, then one must examine how gay (or perceived gay) men are treated relative to straight (or perceived straight) men. Why is this a problem under the "because of sex" doctrine developed in Title VII law? (See Section 5, *infra*.)

SECTION 4

GENDER PERFORMANCE

In this section, we examine how a rich conception of gender has developed in the case law interpreting Title VII. In the prior two sections, we have addressed the biological dimensions of pregnancy and the desire- (or hostility-) related dynamics operating in harassment cases, both inflected with gender norms. In this section, we focus on cases in which courts have explicitly analyzed the operations of socially constructed gender, often described as stereotypes. You may want to review the materials in Chapter 3, Section 3 that explicate the work of some of the leading theorists of gender and assess how their ideas apply to law. Work, along with education and kinship, is a near-universal life experience. How does the law of the workplace contribute to the broader construction of gender norms and shape how we understand our own gender identities?

A. STEREOTYPING

Discrimination based on sex stereotyping has become an increasingly important aspect of employment law. In many ways, one can argue that eliminating stereotypes, rather than formal challenges to sex-specific laws, was the primary goal of women's rights advocates going back to Ruth Bader Ginsburg's work at the ACLU in the 1970s. Although she did not frame cases such as *Reed v. Reed* or *Frontiero v. Richardson* as about stereotypes per se, the reasoning in those decisions rejects "archaic notions" and assumptions about women's capacity in multiple fields. (Chapter 1, Section 2A.) See Cary Franklin, "The Anti-Stereotyping Principle in Constitutional Sex Discrimination Law," 85 *N.Y.U. L. Rev.* 83 (2010). The big step forward in the law of gender stereotypes came in the Title VII case below. In Section 5, *infra*, we will explore the impact of stereotyping on the fundamental question of what constitutes discrimination "because of sex."

Price Waterhouse v. Ann Hopkins

United States Supreme Court, 1989.
490 U.S. 228, 109 S.Ct. 1775, 104 L.Ed.2d 268.

■ BRENNAN, J., announced the judgment of the Court and delivered an opinion in which JUSTICE MARSHALL, JUSTICE BLACKMUN, and JUSTICE STEVENS join.

Ann Hopkins was a senior manager in an office of Price Waterhouse when she was proposed for partnership in 1982. She was neither offered nor denied admission to the partnership; instead, her candidacy was held for reconsideration the following year. When the partners in her office later refused to repropose her for partnership, she sued Price Waterhouse under Title VII, * * * charging that the firm had discriminated against her on the basis of sex in its decisions regarding partnership. [Of the 662 partners at the firm at that time, 7 were women. Of the 88 persons proposed for partnership that year, only 1—Hopkins—was a woman. Forty-seven of these candidates were admitted to the partnership, 21 were rejected, and 20—including Hopkins—were "held" for reconsideration the following year. Thirteen of the 32 partners who had submitted comments on Hopkins supported her bid for partnership. Three partners recommended that her candidacy be placed on hold, eight stated that they did not have an informed opinion about her, and eight recommended that she be denied partnership.]

[District Judge Gesell found, as a matter of fact, that Hopkins had "played a key role in Price Waterhouse's successful effort to win a multi-million dollar contract with the Department of State" and that "[n]one of the other partnership candidates at Price Waterhouse that year had a comparable record in terms of successfully securing major contracts for the partnership." Both clients and partners at the Washington DC office praised Hopkins as "an outstanding professional." Judge Gesell found that Hopkins "had no difficulty dealing with clients and her clients appear to have been very pleased with her work" and that she "was generally viewed as a highly competent project leader who worked long hours, pushed vigorously to meet deadlines and demanded much from the multidisciplinary staffs with which she worked." On the other hand, both "[s]upporters and opponents of her candidacy," stressed Judge Gesell, "indicated that she was sometimes overly aggressive, unduly harsh, difficult to work with and impatient with staff."]

There were clear signs, though, that some of the partners reacted negatively to Hopkins' personality because she was a woman. One partner described her as "macho"; another suggested that she "overcompensated for being a woman"; a third advised her to take "a course at charm school." Several partners criticized her use of profanity; in response, one partner suggested that those partners objected to her swearing only "because it's a lady using foul language." Another supporter explained that Hopkins "ha[d] matured from a tough-talking somewhat masculine hard-nosed mgr to an authoritative, formidable, but much more appealing lady ptr candidate." But it was the man who, as Judge Gesell found, bore responsibility for explaining to Hopkins the reasons for the Policy Board's decision to place her candidacy on hold who delivered the *coup de grace*: in order to improve her chances for partnership, Thomas Beyer advised, Hopkins should "walk more femininely, talk more femininely, dress more femininely, wear make-up, have her hair styled, and wear jewelry."

Dr. Susan Fiske, a social psychologist and Associate Professor of Psychology at Carnegie-Mellon University, testified at trial that the partnership selection process at Price Waterhouse was likely influenced by sex stereotyping. Her testimony focused not only on the overtly sex-based comments of partners but also on gender-neutral remarks, made by partners who knew Hopkins only slightly, that were intensely critical of her. One partner, for example, baldly stated that Hopkins was "universally disliked" by staff and another described her as "consistently annoying and irritating"; yet these were people who had had very little contact with Hopkins. According to Fiske, Hopkins' uniqueness (as the only woman in the pool of candidates) and the subjectivity of the evaluations made it likely that sharply critical remarks such as these were the product of sex stereotyping—although Fiske admitted that she could not say with certainty whether any particular comment was the result of stereotyping. Fiske based her opinion on a review of the submitted comments, explaining that it was commonly accepted practice for social psychologists to reach this kind of conclusion without having met any of the people involved in the decisionmaking process.

In previous years, other female candidates for partnership also had been evaluated in sex-based terms. As a general matter, Judge Gesell concluded, "[c]andidates were viewed favorably if partners believed they maintained their femin[in]ity while becoming effective professional managers"; in this environment, "[t]o be identified as a 'women's lib[b]er' was regarded as [a] negative comment." In fact, the judge found that in previous years "[o]ne partner repeatedly commented that he could not consider any woman seriously as a partnership candidate and believed that women were not even capable of functioning as senior managers—yet the firm took no action to discourage his comments and recorded his vote in the overall summary of the evaluations." * * *

Congress' intent to forbid employers to take gender into account in making employment decisions appears on the face of the statute. * * * We take these words to mean that gender must be irrelevant to employment decisions. * * *

In saying that gender played a motivating part in an employment decision, we mean that, if we asked the employer at the moment of the decision what its reasons were and if we received a truthful response, one of those reasons would be that the applicant or employee was a woman. In the specific context of sex stereotyping, an employer who acts on the basis of a belief that a woman cannot be aggressive, or that she must not be, has acted on the basis of gender.

Although the parties do not overtly dispute this last proposition, the placement by Price Waterhouse of "sex stereotyping" in quotation marks throughout its brief seems to us an insinuation either that such stereotyping was not present in this case or that it lacks legal relevance. We reject both possibilities. As to the existence of sex stereotyping in this case, we are not inclined to quarrel with the District Court's conclusion that a number of the partners' comments showed sex stereotyping at work. As for the legal relevance of sex stereotyping, we are beyond the day when an employer could evaluate employees by assuming or insisting that they matched the stereotype associated with their group, for "'[i]n forbidding employers to discriminate against individuals because of their sex, Congress intended to strike at the entire spectrum of disparate treatment of men and women resulting from sex stereotypes.'" *Los Angeles Dept. of Water and Power v. Manhart*, 435 U.S. 702, 707, n. 13 (1978). An employer who objects to aggressiveness in women but whose positions require this trait places women in an intolerable and impermissible catch 22: out of a job if they behave aggressively and out of a job if they do not. Title VII lifts women out of this bind. * * *

[Justice Brennan rejected Price Waterhouse's attack on Judge Gesell's findings of fact, especially insofar as they relied on Dr. Fiske's expert opinion about sex stereotyping.] Indeed, we are tempted to say that Dr. Fiske's expert testimony was merely icing on Hopkins' cake. It takes no special training to discern sex stereotyping in a description of an aggressive female employee as requiring "a course at charm school." Nor, turning to Thomas Beyer's memorable advice to Hopkins, does it require expertise in psychology to know that, if an employee's flawed "interpersonal skills" can be corrected by a soft-hued suit or a new shade of lipstick, perhaps it is the employee's sex and not her interpersonal skills that has drawn the criticism.

Price Waterhouse also charges that Hopkins produced no evidence that sex stereotyping played a role in the decision to place her candidacy on hold. As we have stressed, however, Hopkins showed that the partnership solicited evaluations from all of the firm's partners; that it generally relied very heavily on such evaluations in making its decision; that some of the partners' comments were the product of stereotyping; and that the firm in no way disclaimed reliance on those particular comments, either in Hopkins' case or in the past. Certainly a plausible—and, one might say, inevitable—conclusion to draw from this set of circumstances is that the Policy Board in making its decision did in fact take into account all of the partners' comments, including the comments that were motivated by stereotypical notions about women's proper deportment. * * *

Price Waterhouse appears to think that we cannot affirm the factual findings of the trial court without deciding that, instead of being overbearing and aggressive and curt, Hopkins is, in fact, kind and considerate and patient. If this is indeed its impression, petitioner misunderstands the theory on which Hopkins prevailed. The District Judge acknowledged that Hopkins' conduct justified complaints about her behavior as a senior manager. But he also concluded that the reactions of at least some of the partners were reactions to her as a *woman* manager. Where an evaluation is based on a subjective assessment of a person's strengths and weaknesses, it is simply not true that each evaluator will focus on, or even mention, the same weaknesses. Thus, even if we knew that Hopkins had "personality problems," this would not tell us that the partners who cast their evaluations of Hopkins in sex-based terms would have criticized her as sharply (or criticized her at all) if she had been a man. It is not our job to review the evidence and decide that the negative reactions to Hopkins were based on reality; our perception of Hopkins' character is irrelevant. We sit not to determine whether Ms. Hopkins is nice, but to decide whether the partners reacted negatively to her personality because she is a woman. * * *

■ [The concurring opinions of JUSTICE WHITE and JUSTICE O'CONNOR are omitted.]

■ JUSTICE KENNEDY, with whom THE CHIEF JUSTICE [REHNQUIST] and JUSTICE SCALIA join, dissenting. * * *

* * * I think it important to stress that Title VII creates no independent cause of action for sex stereotyping. Evidence of use by decisionmakers of sex stereotypes is, of course, quite relevant to the question of discriminatory intent. The ultimate question, however, is whether discrimination caused the plaintiff's harm. Our cases do not support the suggestion that failure to "disclaim reliance" on stereotypical comments itself violates Title VII. Neither do they support creation of a "duty to sensitize." As the dissenting judge in the Court of Appeals observed, acceptance of such theories would turn Title VII "from a prohibition of discriminatory conduct into an engine for rooting out sexist thoughts." * * *

NOTES AND QUESTIONS

1. *Multiple Motivation Cases.* At the time it was decided, *Hopkins* was most significant for the debate among the Justices regarding how to allocate burdens of proof when there was evidence that an employer based adverse action on both unlawful grounds (Hopkins was not feminine enough) and lawful grounds (Hopkins' management style was a barrier to her own and others' job performance). Justice O'Connor proffered an approach to evidentiary burdens that differed from that in the Brennan opinion, and in so doing supplied the necessary fifth vote for the judgment, writing:

> * * * At this point Ann Hopkins had taken her proof as far as it could go. She had proved discriminatory input into the decisional process, and had proved that participants in the process considered her failure to conform to the stereotypes credited by a number of the decisionmakers had been a substantial factor in the decision. * * *

> * * * Particularly in the context of the professional world, where decisions are often made by collegial bodies on the basis of largely subjective criteria, requiring the plaintiff to prove that *any* one factor was the definitive cause of the decisionmakers' action may be tantamount to declaring Title VII inapplicable to such decisions. * * *

490 U.S. at 272–73 (emphasis in the original).

Congress later obviated the debate about burdens by adopting Section 703(m): "[A]n unlawful employment practice is established when the complaining party demonstrates that race, color, religion, sex, or national origin was a motivating factor for any employment practice, even though other factors also motivated the practice."

2.   *"Sex Plus."* The multiple aspects of gender represent one of the complexities of employment discrimination litigation. Women face job discrimination on grounds that are about sex, but not only about sex. In one of the earliest cases brought under Title VII, the Supreme Court rejected the employer's attempt to justify a policy of not hiring women with small children by arguing that it was not sex discrimination, but "sex plus." *Phillips v. Martin Marietta*, 400 U.S. 542 (1971). One can conceptualize many of the cases raising claims related to gender as "sex plus" cases because they involve issues deriving more from gender stereotypes than from anatomic sex differences.

3.   *Applications of Anti-Stereotyping.* After *Hopkins*, an employer can be sued for refusing to hire or promote women because they do not conform to traditional "feminine" characteristics. *Hopkins* has also been invoked to challenge adverse actions against women because of a perception that they *do* conform to stereotypes of femininity. See, *e.g.*, *Lindahl v. Air France*, 930 F.2d 1434 (9th Cir. 1991) (employer described male candidate for promotion as "aggressive and cool," females as "nervous and emotional"). Similarly, the logic of *Hopkins* requires protection of men who are penalized for not conforming to traditional "masculine" characteristics.

Professor Mary Anne Case summarized the relevant issues in the following chart:

TABLE 1. ANALYSIS OF GENDER DISCRIMINATION CLAIMS UNDER TITLE VII

	SEX OF EMPLOYEE	GENDER OF EMPLOYEE	GENDER OF JOB	EMPLOYER DEMAND	ANALYSIS & RESULT UNDER TITLE VII
1	Female	Masculine	Masculine (e.g., accountant) or none	Act more femininely[1]	Disparate treatment: *Price Waterhouse v. Hopkins*
2	Male	Feminine	Feminine (e.g., nursery school teacher) or none	Act more masculinely[2]	Disparate treatment: result governed by *Hopkins*: impermissible sex stereotyping
3	Female	Feminine	Masculine (e.g., commission salesperson) or none	Act more masculinely[2]	Disparate impact: once employee shows that requiring masculine or disfavoring feminine qualities has disparate impact on females, who are disproportionately feminine and not masculine, employer must then show that requiring masculine or disfavoring feminine characteristics is job-related and consistent with business necessity
4	Male	Feminine	Masculine	Act more masculinely[2]	*Ius tertii* claim, raising argument made by feminine woman in row 3 above
5	Male	Masculine	Feminine (e.g., Jenny Craig counselor)	Act more femininely[1]	Disparate impact: analysis is mirror image of row 3 above
6	Female	Masculine	Feminine	Act more femininely[1]	Analysis is mirror image of row 4 above

Notes:

[1] "Act more femininely" is here a shorthand for, e.g., the advice given Ann Hopkins to "walk more femininely, talk more femininely, dress more femininely, wear make-up, have [your] hair styled, . . . wear jewelry" and go to "charm school." 490 U.S. at 235 (1989).

[2] Or act less femininely. Both phrases are shorthand for the reverse of the advice given Hopkins, e.g., take off your makeup and jewelry, cut your hair short and go to assertiveness training class.

Source: Mary Anne C. Case, "Disaggregating Gender from Sex and Sexual Orientation: The Effeminate Man in the Law and Feminist Jurisprudence," 105 *Yale L.J.* 1, 5 (1995).

B. WHEN IS GENDER ITSELF A BFOQ?

A bona fide occupational qualification (BFOQ) exists when the selection of persons of one sex (or religion or national origin) is "reasonably necessary to the normal operation of that particular business or enterprise." 42 U.S.C. § 2000e–2(e). The EEOC interprets the BFOQ exception narrowly, as does the Supreme Court. *See International Union, UAW v. Johnson Controls*, 499 U.S. 187, 201 (1991) ("[t]he BFOQ defense is written narrowly, and this Court has read it narrowly."). EEOC regulations forbid basing a BFOQ on "assumptions of the comparative employment characteristics" of each sex, "stereotyped characterizations of the sexes," or customer preferences. 29 C.F.R. § 1604.2(a)(1)(i)-(iii). Few types of job have met these criteria for the applicability of a BFOQ. (We believe that the reliance on a BFOQ defense in *Chambers, supra,* was mistaken.) One example of a job position for which courts have allowed the BFOQ defense is personal care assistant, when the job involves undressing and providing bodily care assistance for persons in institutions such as nursing homes. *See, e.g., Fesel v. Masonic Home of Delaware*, 447 F. Supp. 1346 (D.Del. 1978), *summarily aff'd* 591 F.2d 1334 (3d Cir. 1979). However, the institution cannot use a blanket exclusion to bar staff of one sex unless it can demonstrate that it cannot match assistants to patients of the same sex and to patients who do not object to different-sex care assistants. *See, e.g., Little Forest Medical Center of Akron v. Ohio Civil Rights Com'n*, 575 N.E.2d 1164 (Ohio 1991).

In *Johnson Controls*, the Supreme Court struck down a fetal protection policy that forbade women, but not men, from taking jobs with high exposures to lead, even though some research showed that the reproductive capacity of both sexes could be affected by the lead. The defendant argued that its safety concerns justified the exclusion. The Court held that the safety of unborn children was not relevant to the essence of the defendant's business, which was manufacturing lead batteries, or to the ability of women workers to fulfill the requirements of the jobs that required exposure to lead. Drawing on the PDA, the Court held that Title VII required that "the decision to become pregnant or to work while being either pregnant or capable of becoming pregnant was reserved for each individual woman to make for herself." 499 U.S. at 206.

The *Johnson Controls* decision left in place an earlier case in which the Court had accepted a third-person safety rationale as satisfying the criteria for a BFOQ. In *Dothard v. Rawlinson*, 433 U.S. 321 (1977), the Court allowed the state to hire only men for certain security guard positions in prisons with male inmates. Describing the prison system as an "environment of violence and disorganization," *id.* at 335, the Court ruled that

> The likelihood that inmates would assault a woman because she was a woman would pose a real threat not only to the victim of the assault but also to the basic control of the penitentiary and

protection of its inmates and the other security personnel. The employee's very womanhood would thus directly undermine her capacity to provide the security that is the essence of a correctional counselor's responsibility.

Id. at 336.

Since *Dothard*, arguments over use of the BFOQ in prison employment have become common. Is the restriction of prison security guard positions to men about vulnerability to assault, or about a sufficient perception of strength, i.e., of masculinity, to deter assault? Is the vulnerability biological or as much a product of social construction? Did the *Dothard* court slip into stereotyping, despite its protestations that the exclusion of women was based on "real" differences between men and women and not romantic paternalism? Consider whether the following decision succeeds in escaping the trap of stereotypes. How does it differ from *Dothard*?

Teamsters Local No. 117 v. Washington Dep't of Corrections

United States Court of Appeals for the Ninth Circuit, 2015.
789 F.3d 979.

■ McKEOWN, CIRCUIT JUDGE

* * * The Department runs two women's prisons. The Washington Corrections Center for Women in Gig Harbor has a capacity of 738 inmates, although it is often overcrowded. That prison runs the gamut from minimum security facilities to housing for violent offenders and those with mental health issues. It also houses Washington's death row for female prisoners. The second facility is Mission Creek Corrections Center for Women in Belfair, a smaller minimum-security prison that houses around 300 inmates.

For decades, men dominated the ranks of prison guards, though neither party has provided precise figures. Facing a shortage of female guards in the late 1980s, state prison administrators began allowing male guards to perform random, clothed body searches—commonly known as pat searches—of the female inmates at Washington Corrections Center. Female inmates challenged these cross-gender searches as unconstitutional [and won an injunction stopping the practice. Departmental policy became that female correctional officers must perform all non-emergency pat searches of female inmates.] * * *

[Beginning in 2003, the Department conducted investigations of the abuse of female prisoners and found numerous instances of misconduct by the male guards, including harassment and exchange of contraband goods for sexual encounters. Two inmates became pregnant by guards.] * * *

Following the expert recommendations, the Department in January 2008 implemented an array of reforms to "reduce prison sexual assaults and related behavior." Those efforts included aggressive recruitment of female prison guards; pre-hiring psychological testing; training programs to enhance "gender awareness"; and the installation of privacy curtains, security cameras, and restricted access entry cards.

[In 2008, the Department sought an allowance from the state's Human Rights Commission to establish] 110 female-only guard post assignments at the two prisons. The Department submitted a tailored request for each post, explaining the job responsibilities and why the positions needed a female officer. The state told the Commission that "[i]ncreasing the number of female staff will reduce the risk of sexual misconduct, reduce allegations of sexual misconduct, and protect male staff exposed to vulnerable situations" and unfounded complaints of abuse. The state also emphasized the privacy requirements of female inmates and the operational need to have female officers on hand to perform necessary searches and other tasks. [The Commission approved the request.]

* * * In September 2011, Teamsters, which represents some 6,000 state correctional workers, filed this federal lawsuit, alleging that the sex-based staffing policy implemented in 2009 violates the civil rights of male prison guards. * * *

Under [Circuit] precedent, the BFOQ defense "may be invoked only when the *essence* of the business operation would be undermined by hiring individuals of both sexes." [citations omitted] To justify discrimination under the BFOQ exception, an employer must show, by a preponderance of the evidence, that: (1) the "job qualification justifying the discrimination is reasonably necessary to the essence of its business"; and (2) that "sex is a legitimate proxy for determining" whether a correctional officer has the necessary job qualifications. * * *

In 2009 the Department determined that designating 110 female-only guard positions at the two prisons would substantially improve prison security, protect the privacy of female inmates, and prevent sexual assaults. Teamsters challenges approximately sixty of those positions, which fall into four general categories: medium- and high-security housing units (18 positions); programs and activities supervisors (3 positions); work crew supervisors (6 positions); and relief posts to replace female guards who are on breaks or absent from work (32 positions).

The Union paints the Department staffing policy as "broad and overreaching"—a "blunderbuss approach to the issue." The record demonstrates the opposite. Instead of a blanket ban on male prison personnel, the Department crafted the staffing needs to fit each specific facility and guard post. It targeted only guard assignments that require direct, day-to-day interaction with inmates and entail sensitive job responsibilities such as conducting pat and strip searches and observing inmates while they shower and use the restroom. * * *

Although [documented reports of] sexual assaults * * * permeate this lawsuit, the state did not justify its BFOQ positions solely as a means to prevent sexual assaults. Instead, it identified several intertwined reasons for designating the female-only positions. In the initial request to the Human Rights Commission, the Department cited the need to "enhance the security of the prisons, safety of staff and offenders, and to protect the privacy and dignity of female offenders." The Commission, in turn, concluded that absent the BFOQ designations, the prison is "unable to ensure a proper balance between security considerations and privacy rights of offenders" and endorsed the female job assignments "for the explicit purpose of ensuring privacy rights of female offenders." * * * [A]ll of these interrelated objectives go to the heart of prison operations. * * *

We have little difficulty holding that the state's reasons for adopting the BFOQ designations—improving security, protecting inmate privacy, and preventing sexual assaults—are each reasonably necessary to the essence of operating Washington's women's prisons. That conclusion does not end the analysis, however. The state also must demonstrate that sex is a "legitimate proxy" to achieve one or more of these goals, meaning that there is a "high correlation between sex and ability to perform job functions." In addition, the state must show that alternatives to the sex-based classification were "reasonably considered and refuted." * * *

Teamsters argues at length that the state policy is based on an impermissible stereotype that male guards are more likely to commit sexual misconduct than their female counterparts. This stereotyping argument misses the mark. To begin, the Union acknowledged that the policy was adopted in the face of documented allegations of abuse. The Department also did not rest on assumptions; it provided objective legal and operational justifications for why only women can perform particular job functions, like observing inmates unclothed and conducting non-emergency searches. * * *

We conclude that sex is an objective, verifiable job qualification for the posts designated as female-only by the Department and that the Department appropriately considered reasonable alternatives. * * *

PROBLEM 5-4
THE TRANS PRISON GUARD

You are consulted about the situations of two individuals who work as guards in the same prison system. Person A was employed under the name Patricia; Patricia has since transitioned and is now Patrick. Person B, originally named Bert, has also transitioned and is now known as Barbara. Both have sterling work records. The Department of Corrections has been supportive of both individuals in their process of changing gender, but is unsure whether or how to alter their work assignments. Each held a front-line job (working directly with inmates) that had been classified for employees of one sex, as a BFOQ. Patrick now seeks a transfer to guarding male inmates and Barbara wishes to work with female inmates. How would you analyze their requests under a BFOQ standard?

C. SEX @ WORK

The two cases that follow arise from situations where the Weberian stricture to banish sexuality from the workplace never applied: the highly sexualized adult entertainment industry. Is the anti-discrimination principle irreconcilable with such workplaces? If not, how should it be administered?

Darlene Jespersen v. Harrah's Operating Co., Inc.

United States Court of Appeals for the Ninth Circuit, *en banc*, 2006.
444 F.3d 1104.

■ SCHROEDER, CHIEF JUDGE.

* * * The plaintiff, Darlene Jespersen, was terminated from her position as a bartender at the sports bar in Harrah's Reno casino not long after Harrah's began to enforce its comprehensive uniform, appearance and grooming standards for all bartenders. The standards required all bartenders, men and women, to wear the same uniform of black pants and white shirts, a bow tie, and comfortable black shoes. The standards also included grooming requirements that differed to some extent for men and women, requiring women to wear some facial makeup and not permitting men to wear any. Jespersen refused to comply with the makeup requirement and was effectively terminated for that reason. * * *

We [conclude] that on this record, Jespersen has failed to present evidence sufficient to survive summary judgment on her claim that the policy imposes an unequal burden on women. With respect to sex stereotyping, we hold that appearance standards, including makeup requirements, may well be the subject of a Title VII claim for sexual stereotyping, but that on this record Jespersen has failed to create any triable issue of fact that the challenged policy was part of a policy motivated by sex stereotyping. * * *

[I.] Plaintiff Darlene Jespersen worked successfully as a bartender at Harrah's for twenty years and compiled what by all accounts was an exemplary record. During Jespersen's entire tenure with Harrah's, the company maintained a policy encouraging female beverage servers to wear makeup. The parties agree, however, that the policy was not enforced until 2000. In February 2000, Harrah's implemented a "Beverage Department Image Transformation" program at twenty Harrah's locations, including its casino in Reno. Part of the program consisted of new grooming and appearance standards, called the "Personal Best" program. The program contained certain appearance standards that applied equally to both sexes, including a standard uniform of black pants, white shirt, black vest, and black bow tie.

Jespersen has never objected to any of these policies. The program also contained some sex-differentiated appearance requirements as to hair, nails, and makeup.

In April 2000, Harrah's amended that policy to require that women wear makeup. Jespersen's only objection here is to the makeup requirement. The amended policy provided in relevant part: * * * [For female employees:]

> Make up (face powder, blush and mascara) must be worn and applied neatly in complimentary colors. Lip color must be worn at all times.

Jespersen did not wear makeup on or off the job, and in her deposition stated that wearing it would conflict with her self-image. It is not disputed that she found the makeup requirement offensive, and felt so uncomfortable wearing makeup that she found it interfered with her ability to perform as a bartender. Unwilling to wear the makeup, and not qualifying for any open positions at the casino with a similar compensation scale, Jespersen left her employment with Harrah's. * * *

In her deposition testimony, * * * Jespersen described the personal indignity she felt as a result of attempting to comply with the makeup policy. Jespersen testified that when she wore the makeup she "felt very degraded and very demeaned." In addition, Jespersen testified that "it prohibited [her] from doing [her] job" because "[i]t affected [her] self-dignity . . . [and] took away [her] credibility as an individual and as a person." * * * Her response to Harrah's motion for summary judgment relied solely on her own deposition testimony regarding her subjective reaction to the makeup policy, and on favorable customer feedback and employer evaluation forms regarding her work.

The record therefore does not contain any affidavit or other evidence to establish that complying with the "Personal Best" standards caused burdens to fall unequally on men or women, and there is no evidence to suggest Harrah's motivation was to stereotype the women bartenders. * * *

[II. Unequal Burdens.] We have long recognized that companies may differentiate between men and women in appearance and grooming policies, and so have other circuits. The material issue under our settled law is not whether the policies are different, but whether the policy imposed on the plaintiff creates an "unequal burden" for the plaintiff's gender.

Not every differentiation between the sexes in a grooming and appearance policy creates a "significantly greater burden of compliance[.]" *Gerdom v. Continental Airlines, Inc.* [692 F.2d 602, 606 (9th Cir. 1982)]. * * * Under established equal burdens analysis, when an employer's grooming and appearance policy does not unreasonably burden one gender more than the other, that policy will not violate Title VII.

Jespersen asks us to take judicial notice of the fact that it costs more money and takes more time for a woman to comply with the makeup requirement than it takes for a man to comply with the requirement that he keep his hair short, but these are not matters appropriate for judicial notice. Judicial notice is reserved for matters "generally known within the territorial jurisdiction of the trial court" or "capable of accurate and ready determination by resort to sources whose accuracy cannot reasonably be questioned." Fed.R.Evid. 201. The time and cost of makeup and haircuts is in neither category. * * *

Having failed to create a record establishing that the "Personal Best" policies are more burdensome for women than for men, Jespersen did not present any triable issue of fact. The district court correctly granted summary judgment on the record before it with respect to Jespersen's claim that the makeup policy created an unequal burden for women.

[III. Sex Stereotyping.] Harrah's "Personal Best" policy is very different [from the stereotyping that occurred in *Price Waterhouse*]. The policy does not single out Jespersen. It applies to all of the bartenders, male and female. It requires all of the bartenders to wear exactly the same uniforms while interacting with the public in the context of the entertainment industry. It is for the most part unisex, from the black tie to the non-skid shoes. There is no evidence in this record to indicate that the policy was adopted to make women bartenders conform to a commonly-accepted stereotypical image of what women should wear. The record contains nothing to suggest the grooming standards would objectively inhibit a woman's ability to do the job. The only evidence in the record to support the stereotyping claim is Jespersen's own subjective reaction to the makeup requirement.

Judge Pregerson's dissent improperly divides the grooming policy into separate categories of hair, hands, and face, and then focuses exclusively on the makeup requirement to conclude that the policy constitutes sex stereotyping. This parsing, however, conflicts with established grooming standards analysis. The requirements must be viewed in the context of the overall policy. The dissent's conclusion that the unequal burdens analysis allows impermissible sex stereotyping to persist if imposed equally on both sexes is wrong because it ignores the protections of *Price Waterhouse* our decision preserves. * * *

We respect Jespersen's resolve to be true to herself and to the image that she wishes to project to the world. We cannot agree, however, that her objection to the makeup requirement, without more, can give rise to a claim of sex stereotyping under Title VII. If we were to do so, we would come perilously close to holding that every grooming, apparel, or appearance requirement that an individual finds personally offensive, or in conflict with his or her own self-image, can create a triable issue of sex discrimination.

This is not a case where the dress or appearance requirement is intended to be sexually provocative. * * * Nor is this a case of sexual harassment. * * * Harrah's actions have not condoned or subjected Jespersen to any form of alleged harassment. It is not alleged that the "Personal Best" policy created a hostile work environment. * * *

We emphasize that we do not preclude, as a matter of law, a claim of sex-stereotyping on the basis of dress or appearance codes. Others may well be filed, and any bases for such claims refined as law in this area evolves. This record, however, is devoid of any basis for permitting this particular claim to go forward, as it is limited to the subjective reaction of a single employee, and there is no evidence of a stereotypical motivation on the part of the employer. This case is essentially a challenge to one small part of what is an overall apparel, appearance, and grooming policy that applies largely the same requirements to both men and women. * * * [T]he touch-stone is reasonableness. A makeup requirement must be seen in the context of the overall standards imposed on employees in a given workplace.

■ PREGERSON, CIRCUIT JUDGE, with whom JUDGES KOZINSKI, GRABER, and W. FLETCHER join, dissenting:

* * * I part ways with the majority * * * inasmuch as I believe that the "Personal Best" program was part of a policy motivated by sex stereotyping and that Jespersen's termination for failing to comply with the program's requirements was "because of" her sex. Accordingly, I dissent from Part III of the majority opinion and from the judgment of the court.

The majority contends that it is bound to reject Jespersen's sex stereotyping claim because she presented too little evidence—only her "own subjective reaction to the makeup requirement." I disagree. Jespersen's evidence showed that Harrah's fired her because she did not comply with a grooming policy that imposed a facial uniform (full makeup) on only female bartenders. Harrah's stringent "Personal Best" policy required female beverage servers to wear foundation, blush, mascara, and lip color, and to ensure that lip color was on at all times. Jespersen and her female colleagues were required to meet with professional image consultants who in turn created a facial template for each woman. Jespersen was required not simply to wear makeup; in addition, the consultants dictated where and how the makeup had to be applied.

Quite simply, her termination for failing to comply with a grooming policy that imposed a facial uniform on only female bartenders is discrimination "because of" sex. Such discrimination is clearly and unambiguously impermissible under Title VII, which requires that "gender must be *irrelevant* to employment decisions." *Price Waterhouse.*

Notwithstanding Jespersen's failure to present additional evidence, little is required to make out a sex-stereotyping—as distinct from an undue burden—claim in this situation. * * *

* * * This policy did not, as the majority suggests, impose a "grooming, apparel, or appearance requirement that an individual finds personally offensive," but rather one that treated Jespersen differently from male bartenders "because of" her sex. I believe that the fact that Harrah's designed and promoted a policy that required women to conform to a sex stereotype by wearing full makeup is sufficient "direct evidence" of discrimination.

* * * The fact that a policy contains sex-differentiated requirements that affect people of both genders cannot excuse a particular requirement from scrutiny. By refusing to consider the makeup requirement separately, and instead stressing that the policy contained some gender-neutral requirements, such as color of clothing, as well as a variety of gender-differentiated requirements for "hair, hands, and face," the majority's approach would permit otherwise impermissible gender stereotypes to be neutralized by the presence of a stereotype or burden that affects people of the opposite gender, or by some separate non-discriminatory requirement that applies to both men and women. * * * [T]he fact that employees of both genders are subjected to gender-specific requirements does not necessarily mean that particular requirements are not motivated by gender stereotyping. * * *

* * * The inescapable message is that women's undoctored faces compare unfavorably to men's, not because of a physical difference between men's and women's faces, but because of a cultural assumption—and gender-based stereotype—that women's faces are incomplete, unattractive, or unprofessional without full makeup. We need not denounce all makeup as inherently offensive * * * to conclude that *requiring* female bartenders to wear full makeup is an impermissible sex stereotype and is evidence of discrimination because of sex. Therefore, I strongly disagree with the majority's conclusion that there "is no evidence in this record to indicate that the policy was adopted to make women bartenders conform to a commonly-accepted stereotypical image of what women should wear."

I believe that Jespersen articulated a classic case of *Price Waterhouse* discrimination and presented undisputed, material facts sufficient to avoid summary judgment. Accordingly, Jespersen should be allowed to present her case to a jury. Therefore, I respectfully dissent.

■ KOZINSKI, CIRCUIT JUDGE, with whom JUDGES GRABER and W. FLETCHER join, dissenting:

I agree with Judge Pregerson and join his dissent—subject to one caveat: I believe that Jespersen also presented a triable issue of fact on the question of disparate burden.

The majority is right that "[t]he [makeup] requirements must be viewed in the context of the overall policy." But I find it perfectly clear that Harrah's overall grooming policy is substantially more burdensome for women than for men. Every requirement that forces men to spend time or money on their appearance has a corresponding requirement that is as, or more, burdensome for women: short hair v. "teased, curled, or styled" hair; clean trimmed nails v. nail length and color requirements; black leather shoes v. black leather shoes. The requirement that women spend time and money applying full facial makeup has no corresponding requirement for men, making the "overall policy" more burdensome for the former than for the latter. The only question is how much. * * *

* * * Even those of us who don't wear makeup know how long it can take from the hundreds of hours we've spent over the years frantically tapping our toes and pointing to our wrists. It's hard to imagine that a woman could "put on her face," as they say, in the time it would take a man to shave—certainly not if she were to do the careful and thorough job Harrah's expects. * * * We could—and should—take judicial notice of these incontrovertible facts.

Alternatively, Jespersen did introduce evidence that she finds it burdensome to *wear* makeup because doing so is inconsistent with her self-image and interferes with her job performance. My colleagues dismiss this evidence, apparently on the ground that wearing makeup does not, as a matter of law, constitute a substantial burden. This presupposes that Jespersen is unreasonable or idiosyncratic in her discomfort. Why so? Whether to wear cosmetics—literally, the face one presents to the world—is an intensely personal choice. * * * If you are used to wearing makeup—as most American women are—this may seem like no big deal. But those of us not used to wearing makeup would find a requirement that we do so highly intrusive. Imagine, for example, a rule that all judges wear face powder, blush, mascara and lipstick while on the bench. Like Jespersen, I would find such a regime burdensome and demeaning; it would interfere with my job performance. I suspect many of my colleagues would feel the same way.

Everyone accepts this as a reasonable reaction from a man, but why should it be different for a woman? It is not because of anatomical differences, such as a requirement that women wear bathing suits that cover their breasts. Women's faces, just like those of men, can be perfectly presentable without makeup; it is a cultural artifact that most women raised in the United States learn to put on—and presumably enjoy wearing—cosmetics. But cultural norms change. * * *

* * * [Jesperson] quit her job—a job she performed well for two decades—rather than put on the makeup. That is a choice her male colleagues were not forced to make. To me, this states a case of disparate burden, and I would let a jury decide whether an employer can force a woman to make this choice. * * *

Jacqueline Schiavo, et al. v. Marina District Development Co.

New Jersey Superior Court, Appellate Division, 2015.
123 A.3d 272, 442 N.J. Super. 346.

■ LIHOTZ, P.J.A.D.

Plaintiffs, twenty-one women who are present or former employees of defendant Marina District Development Company, LLC, operating as the Borgata Casino Hotel & Spa, appeal from the summary judgment dismissal of their complaint alleging violations of the New Jersey Law Against Discrimination (LAD), as informed by Title VII of the Civil Rights Act of 1964 (Title VII). Plaintiffs allege defendant's adoption and application of personal appearance standards (the PAS) subjected them to illegal gender stereotyping, sexual harassment, disparate treatment, disparate impact, and as to some plaintiffs, resulted in adverse employment actions. * * *

* * * Defendant's business decision to differentiate itself from the existing Atlantic City casinos included the creation of the "BorgataBabes," a specialized group of costumed beverage servers. The BorgataBabes reflected "the fun, upscale, sensual, international image that is consistent with the Borgata brand" bringing "Las Vegas[-]style to Atlantic City." All Babes were expected to comply with the "Five Fs": "Fun, Friendly, Focused, Fresh, and Fast."

Defendant's recruiting brochure described its image of the BorgataBabes this way:

> They're beautiful. They're charming. And they're bringing drinks.

> She moves toward you like a movie star, her smile melting the ice in your bourbon and water. His ice blue eyes set the olive in your friend's martini spinning. You forget your own name. She kindly remembers it for you. You become the most important person in the room. And relax in the knowledge that there are no calories in eye candy.

> Part fashion model, part beverage server, part charming host and hostess. All impossibly lovely. The sensational BorgataBabes are the new ambassadors of hospitality representing our beautiful hotel casino and spa in Atlantic City. On a scale of 1 to 10, elevens all.

> Eyes, hair, smile, costumes as close to absolute perfection as perfection gets. BorgataBabes do look fabulous, no question. But once you can breathe again, prepare to be taken to another level by the BorgataBabe attitude. The memory of their warm, inviting, upbeat personalities will remain with you long after the vision has faded from your dreams.

> ARE YOU A BABE?

Of the more than 4000 male and female applicants for approximately 200 placements, the final candidates underwent two rigorous interviews, and a twenty-minute audition in-costume. The audition notification, sent to those who were chosen following the interviews, made clear "[p]ersonal appearance in costume" was one evaluative criteria and the audition required "performing" mock customer scenarios. Chosen candidates were also advised of the PAS requirements, which required male and female Babes be physically fit, with their weight proportionate to height, and display a clean, healthy smile. Female BorgataBabes were to have a natural hourglass shape; males were to have a natural "V" shape with broad shoulders and a slim waist. Women were to have hair that was clean and naturally styled, and tasteful, professional makeup that complimented their facial features. Men were to be either clean shaven or have neatly trimmed and sculpted facial hair. BorgataBabes were to deliver excellent customer service and create a feeling of "upscale classiness, sensuality, and confidence to build customer loyalty." Defendant maintained the PAS was designed to maximize its ability to maintain and preserve the image defendant seeks to project to the public.

The men and women chosen as BorgataBabes contractually agreed to adhere to these strict personal appearance and conduct standards. The final candidates were sent a notice, which attached the PAS, recited the terms of engagement, and stated: "During your employment, you must maintain approximately the same physical appearance in the assigned costume. You must appear to be comfortable while wearing the assigned costume for which you were fitted."

Defendant viewed the BorgataBabes as "entertainers who serve complimentary beverages to ... casino customers," "similar to performance artists," who would act as entertainers and ambassadors of the Borgata's "stylish brand of hospitality." BorgataBabes were required not only to serve drinks to customers on the casino floor, but also, on an as-needed basis, would represent the Borgata and appear at special marketing events; be photographed in advertising; perform at player promotions; make radio, television, and media appearances; attend restaurant parties, parades, and designated charity and community events. Defendant considered the BorgataBabes "high-profile entertainment positions [similar to] professional cheerleaders and models—careers which require a certain appearance to portray a certain image to the public." Starting in 2004, BorgataBabes could voluntarily participate in the "Babes of Borgata Calendar," a marketing publication containing photographs of twelve female BorgataBabes, who were provocatively clad and assumed sexually suggestive poses.

* * * Unlike other employees, BorgataBabes enjoyed the use of the "Babe Lounge," which was a "private, Hollywood-style dressing room"; an extra forty-five minutes of paid time to change into costume and complete their personal grooming; photo opportunities; gratuitous spa and fitness

center access; and reimbursement for gym memberships, nutritionists, and personal trainers.

* * * Under the modified PAS, barring medical reasons, BorgataBabes could not increase their baseline weight, as established when hired, by more than 7% (weight standard). "[Defendant] selected the 7% standard because it reasonably approximated a change of one clothing size and because it was consistent with the scientific definition of a clinically significant weight gain." * * *

* * * "Courts have recognized that the appearance of a company's employees may contribute greatly to the company's image and success with the public and thus that a reasonable dress or grooming code is a proper management prerogative." *Craft v. Metromedia, Inc.,* 766 F.2d 1205, 1215 (8th Cir.1985), *cert. denied,* 475 U.S. 1058 (1986). Moreover, there is no protected class based solely on one's weight. The LAD addresses no such category nor does Title VII "proscribe discrimination based upon an employee's excessive weight. . . ." *Taylor v. Small,* 350 F.3d 1286, 1292 (D.C.Cir.2003).

The LAD addresses appearance at *N.J.S.A.* 10:5–12(p):

> Nothing in the provisions of this section shall affect the ability of an employer to require employees to adhere to reasonable workplace appearance, grooming and dress standards not precluded by other provisions of State or federal law, except that an employer shall allow an employee to appear, groom and dress consistent with the employee's gender identity or expression.

* * *

The PAS applied to both male and female associates. Although defining different but analogous general gender appearance standards, the PAS weight standard imposed the same 7% above baseline weight increase for men as for women. The policy recognized pregnancy, a gender specific condition, in the category of bona fide medical conditions representing an exception to enforcement. We find these provisions are not facially discriminatory. * * * [T]he PAS did not impose a designated weight for associates of a certain height, or use differing standards to determine whether weight of males and females met defined limits. Rather, the PAS accepted an associate's baseline weight as of the date of adoption and mandated weight gain or loss must not exceed 7% of that baseline.

All plaintiffs individually expressed dislike for, or struggled to comply with, the weight standard. However, this does not demonstrate the facially neutral policy more adversely affects women than men. In addition to plaintiffs' subjective response, their evidence challenging the PAS appears to rely on sheer numbers: They argue because a disproportionately higher number of female BorgataBabes were disciplined, this proves the weight standard unequally affected women.

However, such simple statistical disparities are insufficient to show the weight standard was facially discriminatory.

Here, no expert evidence explained how the PAS weight standard, which was neutral on its face, posed an unequal burden on one gender over the other. Also, no proof supports the contention the PAS weight standard adversely affected female over male applicants for positions or advancement. Further, nothing reveals defendant's reliance on a 7% increase as representing a clinically significant weight gain was erroneous or disproportionately burdensome to women.

We also cannot find the use of the differentiated costumes for male and female BorgataBabes actionable. All associates, whether male or female, are required to wear costumes as a condition of employment; women were not singled out. * * *

This is not a case similar to *Equal Employment Opportunity Commission v. Sage Realty Corp.*, 507 F.Supp. 599, 602–04 (S.D.N.Y.1981), where a lobby attendant was required to wear a short, revealing outfit, resembling an American flag, to commemorate the Bicentennial. There, when the plaintiff refused to continue to wear the uniform because it provoked sexualized comments, her employment was terminated. The court rejected the employer's claim the uniform fell within reasonable appearance standards, noting the lobby attendant's job was to greet and direct those who entered the building, making the sexually provocative "uniform" inappropriate to the employment task. Here, defendant's business was to provide customers entertainment and the BorgataBabes' costumes aided the Las Vegas-style casino theme. * * *

We generally agree customer preferences cannot justify discriminatory hiring or the use of stereotyping gender roles in employment positions. However, the hiring of BorgataBabes was not gender restricted and the record contains no evidence female BorgataBabes' assignments or earning ability were compromised because of their gender.

Moreover, the entertainment nature of the casino and its associates distinguishes it from a restaurant or tavern that serves customers drinks. Notably, the casino has several restaurants and cocktail lounges. Also, plaintiffs acknowledge non-PAS positions serving drinks were available in casino areas not designated for the BorgataBabe positions. As a casino, defendant's entertainment business distinguishes this matter from other cases, as the costume may lend authenticity to the intended entertainment atmosphere.

We also reject plaintiffs' contention the discriminatory impact of the PAS was "obvious and self-evident." The facts in this record offer no evidence defendant's use of the weight standard or differentiated costumes deprived women employment, earning opportunities, or privileges of employment. Indisputably, the PAS reflects defendant's overemphasis on appearance, including weight. Nevertheless, that alone is not actionable as illegal discrimination under the LAD. While we understand plaintiffs' desire to require a unisex, gender-neutral costume, which eliminates all sex-based distinctions among BorgataBabes, we cannot conclude the LAD mandates this result.

We conclude on this record the evidence fails to present a cognizable claim of facial discrimination based on defendant's PAS weight policy. We cannot read the LAD to bar as discriminatory an employer's appearance policy requiring an associate, representing a casino business to the public, must remain fit and within a stated weight range, such as required by the PAS. * * *

[With regard to the harassment claims, the court finds for the plaintiffs.] We agree [that] material factual disputes regarding harassment experienced by some plaintiffs made summary judgment dismissal of their claims unwarranted.* * * In essence, but for the subjected plaintiffs' sex, they would not have been the object of the harassment. We recite these examples:

(1) Barrella was weighed at least nine or ten times despite presenting documentation of a medical condition explaining her weight gain.

(2) Booker became pregnant with her second child and her supervisor stated she did not know whether to congratulate her, suggesting she believed Booker made up the statement to avoid a weigh-in.

(3) Kennelly was required by her shift manager Diane Hardie to wear a maternity costume in the early stages of her pregnancy, prior to any need to do so. When she returned from maternity leave, Hardie expressed disbelief Kennelly's weight was within limits and required Kennelly to undergo a weigh-in twice during that day.

(4) B. Johnson was prescribed several medications for depression after giving birth. Without regard for the status of her medical condition, defendant informed her she would be terminated upon the one-year anniversary of her child's birth if she did not comply with the weight standard. She resigned.

(5) Lopez suffered severe asthma following her child's birth for which she was prescribed several medications that impacted her weight. Despite medical documentation, she was suspended for violating the PAS weight standard. Although she was shortly reinstated, she received only partial compensation. Later, despite Lopez's medical condition, Singe Huff, Borgata's Vice President of Talent, insisted Lopez lose one pound per week. Her physician

documented the health detriment she would suffer to accomplish such weight loss, which Huff rejected.

(6) Nelson was weighed despite being pregnant and was told by Hardie it was "just in case you're just getting fat and that's the real reason why you want to wear [the maternity costume]."

(7) Nouel recounted offensive comments by Jeffrey Rankin, in the presence of her shift manager Stephanie Brown that women who have children should not come back to work because they get fat.

(8) Rivera suffered a medical condition and despite returning to compliance with the PAS weight standard, was required to be reweighed every few weeks.

(9) Schiavo grieved a suspension for failing to comply with the PAS weight standard. Her medical documentation explaining post-surgery medication contributed to her weight gain was rejected.

(10) Taylor returned from maternity leave and was found out of compliance with the PAS weight standard. She produced medical documentation stating she was breastfeeding and it was "medically impossible" for her to lose weight. She was suspended when she failed to return to compliance within ninety days.

(11) Vaisyte returned from maternity leave and Brown suggested she pump out her breast milk to reach the weight standard. A subsequent weigh-in revealed she was out of compliance. She submitted a physician's note stating she was breastfeeding and told not to diet for medical reasons. After a few days, she was permitted to return to work, but was required to be reweighed every few months.

These instances are all inclusive of the facts presented to support this claim. Additional evidence reinforces similar hostile work environment allegations, unmitigated by defendant's management. Schiavo complained to Preston Patterson, the Beverage Manager, when another employee was snorting like a pig toward certain female associates; Patterson did not take action. Werthmann related Patterson's comment to the BorgataBabes: "Don't anybody get pregnant. I don't want to hear anything about anybody's family or kids." The record shows only women suffered such harassment. It is obvious similar comments were not directed toward men. * * *

NOTES AND QUESTIONS

1. *The Road Not Taken.* Both of the preceding cases illustrate the current legal status of gendered appearance standards, which can be summed up as: different but equal is ok, so long as reliance on stereotypes does not impose

a heavier burden on one sex than the other. Courts then proceed to the question of weighing burdens. This logic skips over the threshold question of how facially different requirements for males and females can be justified. To satisfy the BFOQ test, an employer must show that a qualification is reasonably necessary to the normal operation of the particular business or enterprise. How would the rules set for appearance by Harrah's and Borgata fare under that standard? Can stereotypes justify stereotypes?

2.   *Burdens and Norms.* Title VII recognizes two bases for a finding of unequal burden: that the practical requirements of the rule are more demanding for one sex than the other or that the rules produce hypersexualization. For the former, how should impact be measured? For the latter, what is the comparator for sexualization, i.e., what would "normal sexualization" look like? How do the two courts answer these questions?

3.   *Consent or Coercion?* The New Jersey court found that "for the individual labeled a babe to become a sex object requires that person's participation." Should the Borgata Babes be considered (sex) workers who are entitled to employee protections or did they sign up to be (sex) objects? Can anti-discrimination law be reconciled with sexualized workplaces? How would feminist legal scholars address this question? Law and economics scholars? Review the materials on sex work in Chapter 2, Section 2B.

SECTION 5

THE SCOPE OF "BECAUSE OF SEX"

Beginning in the 1970s, LGBT plaintiffs brought suits alleging that workplace discrimination against them was a form of sex discrimination and thus actionable under Title VII. Courts rejected these claims, reasoning that sexual orientation and transgender status were distinct from and not encompassed by "sex" within the meaning of Title VII; that Congress in 1964 would not have intended Title VII to encompass sexual orientation or transgender status; and that the failure of efforts to enact sexual orientation-specific protections proved that Congress has never intended to include such coverage.

Since then, debates over the definition of "sex" have changed radically. Today, the question of whether and to what extent "sex" as used in Title VII covers gender identity and sexual orientation is the single most important employment law question for LGBT plaintiffs. Because of how Title VII has been interpreted more expansively over several decades (e.g., to recognize claims for harassment, stereotyping and intersectional discrimination), the litigation landscape has shifted from one in which no courts accepted the argument that Title VII covered sexual orientation and gender identity to one in which some lower federal courts have found that there is coverage. The Supreme Court will almost certainly issue the determinative ruling on how "sex" should be interpreted.

Embedded in this issue is a critically important question for civil rights generally: whether the Roberts Court will continue interpret Title VII broadly, for remedial purposes. As you read the materials in this section, consider what arguments you would make to persuade the Court how the word "sex"—which as we know, can refer to male/female anatomy, culturally determined gender or intimate conduct—should be defined. Note the irony that both the early cases—uniformly rejecting coverage of sexual orientation or gender identity as part of sex—and the most recent decisions—reaching the opposite conclusion—base their reasoning on the "plain meaning" of the statute.

A. FROM SEX TO GENDER TO GENDER IDENTITY

As we know, the word "sex" was added to Title VII by floor amendment, so there is almost no legislative history as to its intended scope. At the time, there was great anxiety about how disruptive to workplace and family norms this provision would be. See Cary Franklin, "Inventing the 'Traditional Concept' of Sex Discrimination," 125 *Harv. L.*

Rev. 1307 (2012). The Equal Employment Opportunity Commission, the enforcement agency for Title VII, initially announced that it would not expend resources on sex discrimination cases; another early EEOC policy determined that pregnancy discrimination was not covered by Title VII. (The EEOC reversed its position before the Supreme Court's decision in *Gilbert v. GE*.) It was the EEOC's recalcitrance in enforcing Title VII that led Pauli Murray and others to form the National Organization for Women.

By the 1970s the EEOC had begun to take sex discrimination seriously and Congress had amended Title VII to encompass pregnancy. LGBT plaintiffs also began to argue that "sex" should include gender and gender norms, but courts universally rejected this interpretation of the statute through the turn of the century. For example, in *Holloway v. Arthur Andersen & Co.*, 566 F.2d 659, 663 (9th Cir. 1977), the court held that Title VII did not apply to a trans plaintiff whose employer discriminated against her for undergoing sex reassignment surgery, stating:

> Congress has not shown any intent other than to restrict the term "sex" to its traditional meaning. Therefore, this court will not expand Title VII's application in the absence of Congressional mandate. The manifest purpose of Title VII's prohibition against sex discrimination in employment is to ensure that men and women are treated equally, absent a bona fide relationship between the qualifications for the job and the person's sex.

Claims by lesbian and gay plaintiffs produced similar results. For example, in *DeSantis v. Pac. Tel. & Tel. Co.*, 608 F.2d 327 (9th Cir. 1979), several lesbian and gay employees sued their employers under Title VII. The plaintiffs made a number of arguments as to why discrimination against lesbian and gay employees should be prohibited by Title VII, all of which were rejected. As in *Holloway*, the court ruled that the term "sex" had a narrow meaning, and "should not be judicially extended to include sexual preference such as homosexuality." The plaintiffs also argued that "discrimination because of the sex of the employees' sexual partner should constitute discrimination based on sex." The court rejected this argument, *id.* at 329, stating:

> Appellants, however, have not alleged that appellees have policies of discriminating against employees because of the gender of their friends. That is, they do not claim that the appellees will terminate anyone with a male (or female) friend. They claim instead that the appellees discriminate against employees who have a certain type of relationship, i.e., homosexual relationship with certain friends. As noted earlier, that relationship is not protected by Title VII. * * * Thus, assuming that it would violate Title VII for an employer to

discriminate against employees because of the gender of their friends, appellants' claims do not fall within this purported rule.

Finally, the court held "that discrimination because of effeminacy, like discrimination because of homosexuality * * * does not fall within the purview of Title VII." *no?*

In *Ulane v. Eastern Airlines, Inc.*, 742 F.2d 1081 (7th Cir.1984), the Seventh Circuit upheld the firing of a male airline pilot who, following sex reassignment surgery, attempted to return to work as a woman. In a strong affirmation of the Ninth Circuit's result in *Holloway*, the Seventh Circuit concluded that Ulane was not protected under Title VII because Congress meant "sex" to include only "biological sex."

> The phrase in Title VII prohibiting discrimination based on sex, in its plain meaning, implies that it is unlawful to discriminate against women because they are women and against men because they are men. The words of Title VII do not outlaw discrimination against a person who has a sexual identity disorder, *i.e.,* a person born with a male body who believes himself to be a female, or a person born with a female body who believes herself to be male; a prohibition against discrimination based on an individual's sex is not synonymous with a prohibition based on an individual's sexual identity disorder or discontent with the sex into which they were born. The dearth of legislative history on section 2000e–2(a)(1) strongly reinforces the view that the section means nothing more than the plain language implies.

Id. at 1085. *Ulane* dominated judicial interpretation of Title VII for 20 years.

In other contexts during the 1980s, however, courts had begun to expand the scope of discrimination covered under Title VII. Most important for LGBT plaintiffs was the Supreme Court's decision in *Price-Waterhouse v. Hopkins* (Section 4, *supra*), which held that a claim of sex discrimination could be based on evidence of sex stereotyping. Reliance on that precedent led to the breakthrough decision for transgender plaintiffs: *Smith v. Salem,* 378 F.3d 566 (6th Cir. 2004). There, a lieutenant in a fire department informed his supervisor that he had been diagnosed as having gender identity disorder and would begin the process of transitioning to a female identity. The Sixth Circuit reversed a district court ruling that he had not stated a claim under Title VII.

> [D]iscrimination against a plaintiff who is transsexual—and therefore fails to act and/or identify with his or her gender—is no different from the discrimination directed against Ann Hopkins in *Price Waterhouse*, who, in sex-stereotypical terms, did not act like a woman. Sex stereotyping based on a person's gender nonconforming behavior is impermissible discrimination, irrespective of the cause of that behavior.

378 F.3d at 574–75; *see also Barnes v. City of Cincinnati,* 401 F.3d 729, 737 (6th Cir. 2005).

Other expansions of Title VII coverage were also important. In race discrimination cases, lower federal courts have found that discrimination against a person in an inter-racial marriage or relationship stated a claim under Title VII. See, e.g., *Parr v. Woodmen of the World Life Ins. Co.,* 791 F.2d 888 (11th Cir. 1986). Victoria Schwartz argues that the principle should apply equally in the context of same-sex relationships, to cover discrimination against an employee who has a same-sex partner or spouse. Victoria Schwartz, "Title VII: A Shift from Sex to Relationships," 35 *Harv. J. L. & Gender* 209, 249 (2012). And in *Oncale v. Sundowner,* Section 3 *supra,* the Supreme Court held that a claim of sex discrimination is not barred simply because the perpetrator is of the same sex as the victim. The Court ruled that so long as the plaintiff can prove that the discrimination was "because of sex," the claim is cognizable. While the *Oncale* opinion did not discuss harassment caused by anti-gay hostility, it did establish that situations could be covered by the plain language of Title VII even if it is unlikely that members of Congress had those situations in mind when adding coverage because of sex.

The following decision broke new ground in going beyond the *Price Waterhouse* sex stereotyping theory in a Title VII trans case. As you read the following cases, consider the different varieties of the "because of sex" argument that have been made by plaintiffs and accepted by a court or agency. Which are most persuasive? Why?

Diane Schroer v. James H. Billington, Librarian of Congress

United States District Court for the District of Columbia, 2008.
577 F.Supp.2d 293.

■ ROBERTSON, DISTRICT JUDGE.

* * * Diane Schroer is a male-to-female transsexual. Although born male, Schroer has a female gender identity—an internal, psychological sense of herself as a woman. In August 2004, before she changed her legal name or began presenting as a woman, Schroer applied for the position of Specialist in Terrorism and International Crime with the Congressional Research Service (CRS) at the Library of Congress. The terrorism specialist provides expert policy analysis to congressional committees, members of Congress and their staffs. The position requires a security clearance.

Schroer was well qualified for the job. She is a graduate of both the National War College and the Army Command and General Staff College, and she holds masters degrees in history and international relations. During Schroer's twenty-five years of service in the U.S. Armed Forces, she held important command and staff positions in the Armored

Calvary, Airborne, Special Forces and Special Operations Units, and in combat operations in Haiti and Rwanda. Before her retirement from the military in January 2004, Schroer was a Colonel assigned to the U.S. Special Operations Command, serving as the director of a 120-person classified organization that tracked and targeted high-threat international terrorist organizations. In this position, Colonel Schroer analyzed sensitive intelligence reports, planned a range of classified and conventional operations, and regularly briefed senior military and government officials, including the Vice President, the Secretary of Defense, and the Chairman of the Joint Chiefs of Staff. At the time of her military retirement, Schroer held a Top Secret, Sensitive Compartmented Information security clearance, and had done so on a continuous basis since 1987. * * *

When Schroer applied for the terrorism specialist position, she had been diagnosed with gender identity disorder and was working with a licensed clinical social worker * * * to develop a medically appropriate plan for transitioning from male to female. * * * Because she had not yet begun presenting herself as a woman on a full-time basis, however, she applied for the position as "David J. Schroer," her legal name at the time. * * * Schroer attended the [job] interview dressed in traditionally masculine attire—a sport coat and slacks with a shirt and tie.

[After being offered the job and accepting the offer but before beginning work, Schroer invited the hiring official to lunch and disclosed that she was about to begin the phase of her gender transition during which she would be dressing in traditionally feminine clothing and presenting as a woman on a full-time basis. She believed that starting work at CRS as a woman would be less disruptive than if she started as a man and later began presenting as a woman. After the lunch and during the next day, the hiring official described the situation to a number of other management personnel at CRS. The hiring official and others repeatedly expressed concern about whether Schroer could qualify for a security clearance, but they took no steps to ascertain whether Schroer would in fact lose her clearance. The job offer was withdrawn.]

The Library made no effort to determine whether Schroer's previous clearance would receive reciprocal recognition or to determine whether the agency previously holding Schroer's clearance already knew of, and had already investigated any concerns related to Schroer's gender identity disorder. * * *

[II.] Schroer contends that the Library's decision not to hire her is sex discrimination banned by Title VII, advancing two legal theories. The first is unlawful discrimination based on her failure to conform with sex stereotypes. The second is that discrimination on the basis of gender identity is literally discrimination "because of . . . sex."

[A. Sex stereotyping.] What makes Schroer's sex stereotyping theory difficult is that, when the plaintiff is transsexual, direct evidence of discrimination based on sex stereotypes may look a great deal like discrimination based on transsexuality itself, a characteristic that, in and of itself, nearly all federal courts have said is unprotected by Title VII. Take Preece's testimony regarding Schroer's credibility before Congress. As characterized by Schroer, the Library's credibility concern was that she "would not be deemed credible by Members of Congress and their staff because people would perceive her to be a woman, and would refuse to believe that she could possibly have the credentials that she had." Plaintiff argues that this is "quintessential sex stereotyping" because Diane Schroer is a woman and does have such a background. But Preece did not testify that she was concerned that Members of Congress would perceive Schroer simply to be a woman. Instead, she testified that "everyone would know that [Schroer] had transitioned from male to female because only a man could have her military experiences."

Ultimately, I do not think that it matters for purposes of Title VII liability whether the Library withdrew its offer of employment because it perceived Schroer to be an insufficiently masculine man, an insufficiently feminine woman, or an inherently gender-nonconforming transsexual. One or more of Preece's comments could be parsed in each of these three ways. While I would therefore conclude that Schroer is entitled to judgment based on a *Price Waterhouse*-type claim for sex stereotyping, I also conclude that she is entitled to judgment based on the language of the statute itself.

[B. Discrimination because of sex.] Schroer's second legal theory is that, because gender identity is a component of sex, discrimination on the basis of gender identity is sex discrimination. In support of this contention, Schroer adduced the testimony of Dr. Walter Bockting, a tenured associate professor at the University of Minnesota Medical School who specializes in gender identity disorders. Dr. Bockting testified that it has long been accepted in the relevant scientific community that there are nine factors that constitute a person's sex. One of these factors is gender identity, which Dr. Bockting defined as one's personal sense of being male or female.

The Library adduced the testimony of Dr. Chester Schmidt, a professor of psychiatry at the Johns Hopkins University School of Medicine and also an expert in gender identity disorders. Dr. Schmidt disagreed with Dr. Bockting's view of the prevailing scientific consensus and testified that he and his colleagues regard gender identity as a component of "sexuality" rather than "sex." According to Dr. Schmidt, "sex" is made up of a number of facets, each of which has a determined biologic etiology. Dr. Schmidt does not believe that gender identity has a single, fixed etiology.

The testimony of both experts—on the science of gender identity and the relationship between intersex conditions and transsexuality—was impressive. Resolving the dispute between Dr. Schmidt and Dr. Bockting as to the proper scientific definition of sex, however, is not within this Court's competence. More importantly (because courts render opinions about scientific controversies with some regularity), deciding whether Dr. Bokting or Dr. Schmidt is right turns out to be unnecessary.

The evidence establishes that the Library was enthusiastic about hiring David Schroer—until she disclosed her transsexuality. The Library revoked the offer when it learned that a man named David intended to become, legally, culturally, and physically, a woman named Diane. This was discrimination "because of . . . sex." * * *

Imagine that an employee is fired because she converts from Christianity to Judaism. Imagine too that her employer testifies that he harbors no bias toward either Christians or Jews but only "converts." That would be a clear case of discrimination "because of religion." No court would take seriously the notion that "converts" are not covered by the statute. Discrimination "because of religion" easily encompasses discrimination because of a *change* of religion. But in cases where the plaintiff has changed her sex, and faces discrimination because of the decision to stop presenting as a man and to start appearing as a woman, courts have traditionally carved such persons out of the statute by concluding that "transsexuality" is unprotected by Title VII. In other words, courts have allowed their focus on the label "transsexual" to blind them to the statutory language itself. * * *

* * * In their holdings that discrimination based on changing one's sex is not discrimination because of sex, *Ulane, Holloway*, and *Etsitty* essentially reason "that a thing may be within the letter of the statute and yet not within the statute, because not within its spirit, nor within the intention of its makers." *Church of the Holy Trinity v. United States*, 143 U.S. 457, 459 (1892). This is no longer a tenable approach to statutory construction. Supreme Court decisions subsequent to *Ulane* and *Holloway* have applied Title VII in ways Congress could not have contemplated. As Justice Scalia wrote for a unanimous court:

> Male-on-male sexual harassment in the workplace was assuredly not the principal evil Congress was concerned with when it enacted Title VII. But statutory prohibitions often go beyond the principal evil to cover reasonably comparable evils, and it is ultimately the provisions of our laws rather than the principal concerns of our legislators by which we are governed.

Oncale v. Sundowner Offshore Services, Inc., 523 U.S. 75, 79 (1998).

For Diane Schroer to prevail on the facts of her case, however, it is not necessary to draw sweeping conclusions about the reach of Title VII. Even if the decisions that define the word "sex" in Title VII as referring only to anatomical or chromosomal sex are still good law—after that approach has been eviscerated by *Price Waterhouse*—the Library's refusal to hire Schroer after being advised that she planned to change her anatomical sex by undergoing sex reassignment surgery was *literally* discrimination "because of . . . sex." * * *

Vandiver Elizabeth Glenn v. Sewell R. Brumby

United States Court of Appeals for the Eleventh Circuit, 2011.
663 F.3d 1312.

[This case is excerpted in Chapter 1, Section 2C.]

Mia Macy v. Eric Holder

Equal Employment Opportunity Commission, 2012.
Appeal No. 0120120821, 2012 WL 1435995.

[Mia Macy, the Complainant, is a transgender woman and former Arizona police detective who sought a job transfer to a Bureau of Alcohol, Tobacco, Firearms and Explosives crime laboratory in Walnut Creek, California. When she first applied for the transfer to the Walnut Creek lab, she was still presenting as male. According to the complaint, the Director of the lab told her she would be able to have the available position if there were no problems with her background check. While her background check was being processed, she notified the Director that she was transitioning from male to female and updated her name and gender on her paperwork. Shortly thereafter, she was informed the position had been eliminated. When she spoke to an EEO counselor, she learned the position had not been cut and had been given to another applicant.] * * *

Title VII states that, except as otherwise specifically provided, "[a]ll personnel actions affecting [federal] employees or applicants for employment . . . shall be made free from any discrimination *based on . . . sex* . . . ." 42 U.S.C. § 2000e–16(a) (emphasis added). * * * As used in Title VII, the term "sex" "encompasses both sex—that is, the biological differences between men and women—and gender." [citations omitted] As the Eleventh Circuit noted in *Glenn v. Brumby*, 663 F.3d 1312, 1316 (11th Cir. 2011), six members of the Supreme Court in *Price Waterhouse* agreed that Title VII barred "not just discrimination because of biological sex, but also gender stereotyping—failing to act and appear according to expectations defined by gender." As such, the terms "gender" and "sex" are often used interchangeably to describe the discrimination prohibited by Title VII. * * *

When an employer discriminates against someone because the person is transgender, the employer has engaged in disparate treatment "related to the sex of the victim." See *Schwenk*, 204 F.3d at 1202. This is true regardless of whether an employer discriminates against an employee because the individual has expressed his or her gender in a non-stereotypical fashion, because the employer is uncomfortable with the fact that the person has transitioned or is in the process of transitioning from one gender to another, or because the employer simply does not like that the person is identifying as a transgender person. In each of these circumstances, the employer is making a gender-based evaluation, thus violating the Supreme Court's admonition that "an employer may not take gender into account in making an employment decision." *Price Waterhouse*, 490 U.S. at 244. * * *

[Decisions since *Price Waterhouse* have recognized the sex stereotyping theory as a method of establishing discrimination "on the basis of sex."] [I]n *Schwenk v. Hartford*, a prison guard had sexually assaulted a pre-operative male-to-female transgender prisoner, and the prisoner sued, alleging that the guard had violated the Gender Motivated Violence Act (GMVA), 42 U.S.C. § 13981. * * * According to the court, the guard had targeted the transgender prisoner "only after he discovered that she considered herself female[,]" and the guard was "motivated, at least in part, by [her] gender"—that is, "by her assumption of a feminine rather than a typically masculine appearance or demeanor." *Id.* On these facts, the Ninth Circuit readily concluded that the guard's attack constituted discrimination because of gender within the meaning of both the GMVA and Title VII[,] * * * [and] discrimination against transgender females—i.e., "as anatomical males whose *outward behavior and inward identity* [do] not meet social definitions of masculinity"—is actionable discrimination "because of sex." *Id.* (emphasis added) * * * .

[The discussion of *Smith*, *supra* and *Brumby*, *supra*, is omitted.]

To be sure, the members of Congress that enacted Title VII in 1964 and amended it in 1972 were likely not considering the problems of discrimination that were faced by transgender individuals. But as the Supreme Court recognized in *Oncale v. Sundowner Offshore Services, Inc.*:

> [S]tatutory prohibitions often go beyond the principal evil [they were passed to combat] to cover reasonably comparable evils, and it is ultimately the provisions of our laws rather than the principal concerns of our legislators by which we are governed. Title VII prohibits "discrimination . . . because of . . . sex" in . . . employment. [This] . . . must extend to [sex-based discrimination] of any kind that meets the statutory requirements.

523 U.S. at 79–80; see also *Newport News*, 462 U.S. at 679–81 (rejecting the argument that discrimination against men does not violate Title VII despite the fact that discrimination against women was plainly the principal problem that Title VII's prohibition of sex discrimination was enacted to combat). * * *

Complainant could establish a case of sex discrimination under a theory of gender stereotyping by showing that she did not get the job as an NIBIN ballistics technician at Walnut Creek because the employer believed that biological men should consistently present as men and wear male clothing.

Alternatively, if Complainant can prove that the reason that she did not get the job at Walnut Creek is that the Director was willing to hire her when he thought she was a man, but was not willing to hire her once he found out that she was now a woman—she will have proven that the

Director discriminated on the basis of sex. Under this theory, there would actually be no need, for purposes of establishing coverage under Title VII, for Complainant to compile any evidence that the Director was engaging in gender stereotyping.

In this respect, gender is no different from religion. Assume that an employee considers herself Christian and identifies as such. But assume that an employer finds out that the employee's parents are Muslim, believes that the employee should therefore be Muslim, and terminates the employee on that basis. No one would doubt that such an employer discriminated on the basis of religion. There would be no need for the employee who experienced the adverse employment action to demonstrate that the employer acted on the basis of some religious stereotype—although, clearly, discomfort with the choice made by the employee with regard to religion would presumably be at the root of the employer's actions. But for purposes of establishing a prima facie case that Title VII has been violated, the employee simply must demonstrate that the employer impermissibly used religion in making its employment decision. * * *

Applying Title VII in this manner does not create a new "class" of people covered under Title VII[.] Rather, it would simply be the result of applying the plain language of a statute prohibiting discrimination on the basis of religion to practical situations in which such characteristics are unlawfully taken into account.

Thus, we conclude that intentional discrimination against a transgender individual because that person is transgender is, by definition, discrimination "based on . . . sex," and such discrimination therefore violates Title VII. * * *

NOTES AND QUESTIONS

1.   *Stereotypes or Per Se Discrimination.* One reason why *Schroer* was so important was that the court recognized two separate theories of a Title VII claim—stereotypes and sex discrimination per se—and found that the Library of Congress was liable under both. In *Macy*, the EEOC goes out of its way to emphasize the viability of both of these theories. By comparison, the Eleventh Circuit decided *Glenn* solely on the basis of gender stereotyping. Are both theories necessary? Why or why not?

2.   *Gender "Expression."* Some state anti-discrimination statutes use the phrase "gender identity or expression." See, e.g., Nev. Rev. Stat. 613–330 (2015). Could expression of a non-conforming gender identity be construed as a speech right? If so, state actors could be forbidden from discriminating on that ground, but the First Amendment does not apply to private entities; in fact, the private employer's own expression of an anti-trans viewpoint could constitute a defense to the First Amendment claim. See Chapter 1, Section 3D. How would you argue for the primacy of either the speech or the equality claim?

3. *Administrative Agency Precedent.* The EEOC has two types of authority: adjudicative authority with respect to federal employees and administrative enforcement authority as to private sector employers. EEOC decisions are final for federal employees but not binding on courts. In private sector cases, courts consider EEOC decisions to be formal guidance—the reasoned opinion of an expert agency (receiving deference under *Skidmore v. Swift & Co.,* 323 U.S. 134 (1944))—in the same manner as other non-adjudicative formal statements of policy. Decisions such as *Macy* set agency policy and announce the Commission's litigation posture for negotiation and litigation, subject of course to Supreme Court decisions interpreting Title VII. For a look behind the scenes at the process of EEOC's adoption of a new interpretation of "sex" that includes gender identity, see Chai Feldblum, "Law, Policies in Practice and Social Norms: Coverage of Transgender Discrimination Under Sex Discrimination Law," 14 *J. L. Society* 1 (2013).

B. FROM GENDER TO SEXUAL ORIENTATION

Does the argument that "because of sex" should be interpreted broadly extend to sexual orientation? The argument that a sex stereotyping analysis should encompass anti-gay practices has been made for many years. See Chapter 1, Sections 2B and 2C. As we saw in the introduction to this section, Title VII cases filed on that theory began in the 1970s. Until recently, however, courts ruled that discrimination based on sexual orientation was a separate practice from sex discrimination and not covered by Title VII. *See, e.g., Higgins v. New Balance Athletic Shoe, Inc.,* 194 F.3d 252, 259 (1st Cir. 1999) ("Title VII does not proscribe harassment simply because of sexual orientation."); *Vickers v. Fairfield Med. Ctr.,* 453 F.3d 757, 762 (6th Cir. 2006) ("[S]exual orientation is not a prohibited basis for discriminatory acts under Title VII."); *Williamson v. A.G. Edwards & Sons, Inc.,* 876 F.2d 69, 70 (8th Cir. 1989) ("Title VII does not prohibit discrimination against homosexuals."); *Medina v. Income Support Div.,* 413 F.3d 1131, 1135 (10th Cir. 2005) ("Title VII's protections, however, do not extend to harassment due to a person's sexuality. . . . Congress has repeatedly rejected legislation that would have extended Title VII to cover sexual orientation.") (internal quotations omitted).

In both the Third and Ninth Circuits, courts have allowed sex discrimination claims by gay plaintiffs to go forward, on the ground that gay persons should have the same opportunity to prove gender stereotyping discrimination as any other plaintiff, even though discrimination based on sexual orientation without evidence of stereotyping was not a per se violation of Title VII. See *Prowel v. Wise Business Forms, Inc.,* 579 F.3d 285 (3d Cir. 2009); *Rene v MGM Grand Hotel, supra.* Was the following case the next logical step?

David Baldwin v. Anthony Foxx, Secretary, Dept. of Transportation

Equal Employment Opportunity Commission, 2015.
Appeal No. 0120133080, 2015 WL 4397641.

[Complainant, an openly gay man, was selected as a temporary frontline manager [FLM] at the Miami facility of the Federal Aviation Administration, a component agency of the Department of Transportation. When he was not selected to fill the permanent FLM position, he filed a complaint of sex and sexual orientation discrimination, alleging that a supervisor involved in selection for the permanent position made comments that demonstrated anti-gay bias.]

Title VII's prohibition of sex discrimination means that employers may not "rel[y] upon sex-based considerations" or take gender into account when making employment decisions. *See Price Waterhouse*; *Macy*. This applies equally in claims brought by lesbian, gay, and bisexual individuals under Title VII.

When an employee raises a claim of sexual orientation discrimination as sex discrimination under Title VII, the question is not whether sexual orientation is explicitly listed in Title VII as a prohibited basis for employment actions. It is not. Rather, the question for purposes of Title VII coverage of a sexual orientation claim is the same as any other Title VII case involving allegations of sex discrimination—whether the agency has "relied on sex-based considerations" or "take[n] gender into account" when taking the challenged employment action.

In the case before us, we conclude that Complainant's claim of sexual orientation discrimination alleges that the Agency relied on sex-based considerations and took his sex into account in its employment decision regarding the permanent FLM position. The Complainant, therefore, has stated a claim of sex discrimination. Indeed, we conclude that sexual orientation is inherently a "sex-based consideration," and an allegation of discrimination based on sexual orientation is necessarily an allegation of sex discrimination under Title VII. A complainant alleging that an agency took his or her sexual orientation into account in an employment action necessarily alleges that the agency took his or her sex into account.

Discrimination on the basis of sexual orientation is premised on sex-based preferences, assumptions, expectations, stereotypes, or norms. "Sexual orientation" as a concept cannot be defined or understood without reference to sex. A man is referred to as "gay" if he is physically and/or emotionally attracted to other men. A woman is referred to as "lesbian" if she is physically and/or emotionally attracted to other women. Someone is referred to as "heterosexual" or "straight" if he or she is physically and/or emotionally attracted to someone of the opposite-sex. It follows, then, that sexual orientation is inseparable from and inescapably linked to sex and, therefore, that allegations of sexual orientation discrimination involve sex-based considerations. One can describe this inescapable link between allegations of sexual orientation discrimination and sex discrimination in a number of ways.

Sexual orientation discrimination is sex discrimination because it necessarily entails treating an employee less favorably because of the employee's sex. For example, assume that an employer suspends a lesbian employee for displaying a photo of her female spouse on her desk, but does not suspend a male employee for displaying a photo of his female spouse on his desk. The lesbian employee in that example can allege that her employer took an adverse action against her that the employer would not have taken had she been male. That is a legitimate claim under Title VII that sex was unlawfully taken into account in the adverse employment action. * * *

Sexual orientation discrimination is also sex discrimination because it is associational discrimination on the basis of sex. That is, an employee alleging discrimination on the basis of sexual orientation is alleging that his or her employer took his or her sex into account by treating him or her differently for *associating* with a person of the same sex. For example, a gay man who alleges that his employer took an adverse employment action against him because he associated with or dated men states a claim of sex discrimination under Title VII; the fact that the employee is a man instead of a woman motivated the employer's discrimination against him. Similarly, a heterosexual man who alleges a gay supervisor denied him a promotion because he dates women instead of men states an actionable Title VII claim of discrimination because of his sex.

In applying Title VII's prohibition of race discrimination, courts and the Commission have consistently concluded that the statute prohibits discrimination based on an employee's association with a person of another race, such as an interracial marriage or friendship. * * *

Sexual orientation discrimination also is sex discrimination because it necessarily involves discrimination based on gender stereotypes. In *Price Waterhouse*, the Court reaffirmed that Congress intended Title VII to "strike at the entire spectrum of disparate treatment of men and women resulting from sex stereotypes." In the wake of *Price Waterhouse*, courts and the Commission have recognized that lesbian, gay, and bisexual individuals can bring claims of gender stereotyping under Title VII if such individuals demonstrate that they were treated adversely because they were viewed—based on their appearance, mannerisms, or conduct—as insufficiently "masculine" or "feminine." But as the Commission and a number of federal courts have concluded in cases dating from 2002 onwards, discrimination against people who are lesbian, gay, or bisexual on the basis of gender stereotypes often involves far more than assumptions about overt masculine or feminine behavior.

Sexual orientation discrimination and harassment "[are] often, if not always, motivated by a desire to enforce heterosexually defined gender norms." *Centola v. Potter*, 183 F. Supp. 2d 403, 410 (D. Mass. 2002). * * *

[The EEOC rejects the implication that sexual orientation is not encompassed within the scope of sex discrimination because the statute was silent on this point and has not been amended since.] Congress may not have envisioned the application of Title VII to these situations. But as a unanimous Court stated in *Oncale v. Sundowner Offshore Services, Inc.*, "statutory prohibitions often go beyond the principal evil [they were passed to combat] to cover reasonably comparable evils, and it is ultimately the provisions of our laws rather than the principal concerns of our legislators by which we are governed." 523 U.S. 75, 79, 78–80 (1998) (holding that same-sex harassment is actionable under Title VII). Interpreting the sex discrimination prohibition of Title VII to exclude coverage of lesbian, gay or bisexual individuals who have experienced discrimination on the basis of sex inserts a limitation into the text that Congress has not included.

The idea that congressional action is required (and inaction is therefore instructive in part) rests on the notion that protection against sexual orientation discrimination under Title VII would create a new class of covered persons. But analogous case law confirms this is not true. When courts held that Title VII protected persons who were discriminated against because of their relationships with persons of another race, the courts did not thereby create a new protected class of "people in interracial relationships." [citations omitted] * * *

Our task is the same. We apply the words of the statute Congress has charged us with enforcing. We therefore conclude that Complainant's allegations of discrimination on the basis of sexual orientation state a claim of discrimination on the basis of sex. We further conclude that allegations of discrimination on the basis of sexual orientation necessarily state a claim of discrimination on the basis of sex. An employee could show that the sexual orientation discrimination he or she experienced was sex discrimination because it involved treatment that would not have occurred but for the individual's sex; because it was based on the sex of the person(s) the individual associates with; and/or because it was premised on the fundamental sex stereotype, norm or expectation that individuals should be attracted only to those of the opposite sex. * * *

Postscript. The *Baldwin* case settled in December 2016.

NOTES AND QUESTIONS

1. *Theories of the Case.* How is the EEOC's reasoning as to why sexual orientation discrimination is "inherently sex-based" different from its reasoning in *Macy*, *supra*, concerning gender identity? Can you articulate why inclusion of sexual orientation under "sex" might be a bigger lift for Title VII plaintiffs than inclusion of gender identity? Do you agree that they should be treated the same?

2. *Administrative Constitutionalism.* Although the *Baldwin* ruling did not create a direct mandate that applies to private employers (see note 3 following *Macy*, *supra*), it did set agency policy for the EEOC. Probably its greatest practical impact has been to create a new means of redress for LGBT plaintiffs during the pre-litigation stage.[a] According to EEOC data, during fiscal years 2013 to 2016, the EEOC received 5,119 charges alleging discrimination on the basis of sexual orientation or gender identity. (This includes charges in which other grounds may have also been alleged.) Through settlements and other non-litigation avenues, a total of $10.8 million was awarded to the plaintiffs in these cases. See https://www. eeoc.gov/eeoc/newsroom/wysk/enforcement_protections_lgbt_workers.cfm. These data reflect arguably the single largest extension of workplace anti-discrimination coverage for LGBT persons in U.S. history.

3. *Waiting for the Supreme Court.* Whether that extension of anti-discrimination coverage will last is a question for the Supreme Court and/or Congress. The ground is shifting rapidly on the issue of whether sex discrimination under Title VII inherently includes sexual orientation discrimination. In the first half of 2017, courts in the Second, Seventh, and Eleventh Circuits weighed in with reconsiderations of whether sexual orientation is covered. As we go to press, the Seventh Circuit has issued an *en banc* decision (*Hively*); the Eleventh Circuit has denied rehearing *en banc* of its panel decision (*Evans*), and plaintiff's counsel is seeking Supreme Court review; and the Second Circuit *en banc* has heard *Zarda v. Altitude Express*, 855 F.3d 76 (2d Cir. 2017). Meanwhile, federal agencies have split on the issue. To date, the EEOC has maintained the position that it took in *Baldwin*, but the Department of Justice now argues that sexual orientation is not covered.

Kimberly Hiveley v. Ivy Tech Community College of Indiana

United States Court of Appeals for the Seventh Circuit, *en banc*, 2017.
853 F.3d 339.

(handwritten margin note: ① Comparative ② Associated ③ Gender Stereotypes)

■ WOOD, CHIEF JUDGE.

* * * [Kimberly Hively is an openly lesbian part-time professor at Ivy Tech Community College. Between 2000 and 2014, she was denied six full-time positions for which she applied and in 2014, her contract was not renewed. She filed an EEOC charge alleging that she was discriminated against because of her sexual orientation.]

We must decide * * * what it means to discriminate on the basis of sex, and in particular, whether actions taken on the basis of sexual

---

[a] Under Title VII procedures, a person "claiming to be aggrieved" may not initially file suit herself, but must file a "charge" with the EEOC asserting violation of the substantive norms of Title VII, pursuant to § 706(a), 42 U.S.C.A. § 2000e–5(a). Once the aggrieved person has filed a timely charge, the EEOC determines whether there is "reasonable cause to believe that the charge is true," and if so it will try to eliminate the unlawful practice informally through "conference, conciliation, and persuasion" (§ 706(a), *id.* § 2000e–5(a)). If the EEOC is unable to obtain voluntary compliance with Title VII, it notifies the aggrieved person and informs her that she may bring a lawsuit in federal court within thirty days (§ 706(e), *id.* § 2000e–5(e)). To remedy an unlawful employment practice, a court may enjoin the practice and order "such affirmative action as may be appropriate, which may include reinstatement or hiring of employees, with or without back pay" (§ 706(g), *id.* § 2000e–5(g)).

orientation are a subset of actions taken on the basis of sex. This is a pure question of statutory interpretation and thus well within the judiciary's competence. * * *

[The court reviews methodologies of statutory interpretation, including the statute's plain language, its legislative history; and later actions of the legislature. Much ink has been spilled about the proper way to go about the task of statutory interpretation.]* * *

Ivy Tech sets great store on the fact that Congress has frequently considered amending Title VII to add the words "sexual orientation" to the list of prohibited characteristics, yet it has never done so. Many of our sister circuits have also noted this fact. In our view, however, it is simply too difficult to draw a reliable inference from these truncated legislative initiatives to rest our opinion on them. The goalposts have been moving over the years, as the Supreme Court has shed more light on the scope of the language that already is in the statute: no *sex* discrimination. * * *

[In *Oncale*, Section 3B *supra*, the] Court could not have been clearer: the fact that the enacting Congress may not have anticipated a particular application of the law cannot stand in the way of the provisions of the law that are on the books.

It is therefore neither here nor there that the Congress that enacted the Civil Rights Act in 1964 and chose to include sex as a prohibited basis for employment discrimination (no matter why it did so) may not have realized or understood the full scope of the words it chose. Indeed, in the years since 1964, Title VII has been understood to cover far more than the simple decision of an employer not to hire a woman for Job A, or a man for Job B. The Supreme Court has held that the prohibition against sex discrimination reaches sexual harassment in the workplace, see *Meritor Sav. Bank, FSB v. Vinson*, including same-sex workplace harassment, see *Oncale*; it reaches discrimination based on actuarial assumptions about a person's longevity, see *City of Los Angeles, Dep't of Water and Power v. Manhart*, 435 U.S. 702 (1978); and it reaches discrimination based on a person's failure to conform to a certain set of gender stereotypes, see *Hopkins*. It is quite possible that these interpretations may also have surprised some who served in the 88th Congress. Nevertheless, experience with the law has led the Supreme Court to recognize that each of these examples is a covered form of sex discrimination.

Hively offers two approaches in support of her contention that "sex discrimination" includes discrimination on the basis of sexual orientation. The first relies on the tried-and-true comparative method in which we attempt to isolate the significance of the plaintiff's sex to the employer's decision: has she described a situation in which, holding all other things constant and changing only her sex, she would have been treated the same way? The second relies on the *Loving v. Virginia* line of cases, which she argues protect her right to associate intimately with a person of the same sex. Although the analysis differs somewhat, both avenues end up in the same place: sex discrimination. * * *

Hively alleges that if she had been a man married to a woman (or living with a woman, or dating a woman) and everything else had stayed the same, Ivy Tech would not have refused to promote her and would not have fired her. This describes paradigmatic sex discrimination. * * * Ivy Tech is disadvantaging her *because she is a woman*. Nothing in the complaint hints that Ivy Tech has an anti-marriage policy that extends to heterosexual relationships, or for that matter even an anti-partnership policy that is gender-neutral.

Viewed through the lens of the gender non-conformity line of cases, Hively represents the ultimate case of failure to conform to the female stereotype (at least as understood in a place such as modern America, which views heterosexuality as the norm and other forms of sexuality as exceptional): she is not heterosexual. Our panel described the line between a gender nonconformity claim and one based on sexual orientation as gossamer-thin; we conclude that it does not exist at all. Hively's claim is no different from the claims brought by women who were rejected for jobs in traditionally male workplaces, such as fire departments, construction, and policing. The employers in those cases were policing the boundaries of what jobs or behaviors they found acceptable for a woman (or in some cases, for a man).

* * * [A] policy that discriminates on the basis of sexual orientation does not affect every woman, or every man, but it is based on assumptions about the proper behavior for someone of a given sex. The discriminatory behavior does not exist without taking the victim's biological sex (either as observed at birth or as modified, in the case of transsexuals) into account. Any discomfort, disapproval, or job decision based on the fact that the complainant—woman or man—dresses differently, speaks differently, or dates or marries a same-sex partner, is a reaction purely and simply based on sex. That means that it falls within Title VII's prohibition against sex discrimination, if it affects employment in one of the specified ways.

* * * Hively also has argued that action based on sexual orientation is sex discrimination under the associational theory. It is now accepted that a person who is discriminated against because of the protected characteristic of one with whom she associates is actually being disadvantaged because of her own traits. This line of cases began with *Loving*. * * * [Subsequent Title VII cases have held that adverse employment actions based on the race of one's partner or spouse constitute discrimination because of race.]

* * * The Court in Loving recognized that equal application of a law that prohibited conduct only between members of different races did not save it. Changing the race of one partner made a difference in determining the legality of the conduct, and so the law rested on "distinctions drawn according to race," which were unjustifiable and

racially discriminatory. So too, here. If we were to change the sex of one partner in a lesbian relationship, the outcome would be different. This reveals that the discrimination rests on distinctions drawn according to sex. * * *

It would require considerable calisthenics to remove the "sex" from "sexual orientation." The effort to do so has led to confusing and contradictory results. * * * The EEOC concluded, in its Baldwin decision, that such an effort cannot be reconciled with the straightforward language of Title VII. Many district courts have come to the same conclusion. [citations omitted] Many other courts have found that gender-identity claims are cognizable under Title VII. [citations omitted]

This is not to say that authority to the contrary does not exist. As we acknowledged at the outset of this opinion, it does. But this court sits en banc to consider what the correct rule of law is now in light of the Supreme Court's authoritative interpretations, not what someone thought it meant one, ten, or twenty years ago. The logic of the Supreme Court's decisions, as well as the common-sense reality that it is actually impossible to discriminate on the basis of sexual orientation without discriminating on the basis of sex, persuade us that the time has come to overrule our previous cases that have endeavored to find and observe that line. * * *

■ POSNER, CIRCUIT JUDGE, concurring.

* * * It is helpful to note at the outset that the interpretation of statutes comes in three flavors. The first and most conventional is the extraction of the original meaning of the statute—the meaning intended by the legislators—and corresponds to interpretation in ordinary discourse. * * * The second form of interpretation, illustrated by the commonplace local ordinance which commands "no vehicles in the park," is interpretation by unexpressed intent, where by we understand that although an ambulance is a vehicle, the ordinance was not intended to include ambulances among the "vehicles" forbidden to enter the park. * * *

Finally and most controversially, interpretation can mean giving a fresh meaning to a statement (which can be a statement found in a constitutional or statutory text)—a meaning that infuses the statement with vitality and significance today. * * *

Title VII of the Civil Rights Act of 1964, now more than half a century old, invites an interpretation that will update it to the present, a present that differs markedly from the era in which the Act was enacted. But I need to emphasize that this third form of interpretation—call it judicial interpretive updating—presupposes a lengthy interval between enactment and (re)interpretation. A statute when passed has an understood meaning; it takes years, often many years, for a shift in the political and cultural environment to change the understanding of the statute. * * *

The argument that firing a woman on account of her being a lesbian does *not* violate Title VII is that the term "sex" in the statute, when enacted in 1964, undoubtedly meant "man or woman," and so at the time people would have thought that a woman who was fired for being a lesbian was not being fired for being a woman unless her employer would not have fired on grounds of homosexuality a man he knew to be homosexual; for in that event the only difference between the two would be the gender of the one he fired. Title VII does not mention discrimination on the basis of sexual orientation, and so an explanation is needed for how 53 years later the meaning of the statute has changed and the word "sex" in it now connotes both gender *and* sexual orientation.

It is well-nigh certain that homosexuality, male or female, did not figure in the minds of the legislators who enacted Title VII. * * * A diehard "originalist" would argue that what was believed in 1964 defines the scope of the statute for as long as the statutory text remains unchanged, and therefore until changed by Congress's amending or replacing the statute. But as I noted earlier, statutory and constitutional provisions frequently are interpreted on the basis of present need and understanding rather than original meaning. Think for example of Justice Scalia's decisive fifth vote to hold that burning the American flag as a political protest is protected by the free-speech clause of the First Amendment, provided that it's your flag and is not burned in circumstances in which the fire might spread. [citations omitted] Burning a flag is not speech in the usual sense and there is no indication that the framers or ratifiers of the First Amendment thought that the word "speech" in the amendment embraced flag burning or other nonverbal methods of communicating. * * *

It's true that even today if asked what is the sex of plaintiff Hively one would answer that she is female or that she is a woman, not that she is a lesbian. Lesbianism denotes a form of sexual or romantic attraction; it is not a physical sex identifier like masculinity or femininity. A broader understanding of the word "sex" in Title VII than the original understanding is thus required in order to be able to classify the discrimination of which Hively complains as a form of sex discrimination. That broader understanding is essential. Failure to adopt it would make the statute anachronistic * * *

We now understand that homosexual men and women (and also bisexuals, defined as having both homosexual and heterosexual orientations) are normal in the ways that count, and beyond that have made many outstanding intellectual and cultural contributions to society * * *. We now understand that homosexuals, male and female, play an essential role, in this country at any rate, as adopters of children from foster homes—a point emphasized in our [same-sex marriage] decision. The compelling social interest in protecting homosexuals (male and female) from discrimination justifies an admittedly loose "interpretation" of the word "sex" in Title VII to embrace homosexuality: an interpretation that cannot be imputed to the framers of the statute but that we are entitled to adopt in light of (to quote Holmes) *"what this country has become,"* or, in Blackstonian terminology, to embrace as a sensible deviation from the literal or original meaning of the statutory language. * * *

The most tenable and straightforward ground for deciding in favor of Hively is that while in 1964 sex discrimination meant discrimination against men or women as such and not against subsets of men or women such as effeminate men or mannish women, the concept of sex discrimination has since broadened in light of the recognition, which barely existed in 1964, that there are significant numbers of both men and women who have a sexual orientation that sets them apart from the heterosexual members of their genetic sex (male or female), and that while they constitute a minority their sexual orientation is not evil and does not threaten our society. Title VII in terms forbids only sex discrimination, but we now understand discrimination against homosexual men and women to be a form of sex discrimination; and to paraphrase Holmes, *"We must consider what this country has become in deciding what that [statute] has reserved."* * * *

* * * *We* understand the words of Title VII differently not because we're smarter than the statute's framers and ratifiers but because we live in a different era, a different culture. Congress in the 1960s did not foresee the sexual revolution of the 2000s. * * *

I would prefer to see us acknowledge openly that today we, who are judges rather than members of Congress, are imposing on a half-century-old statute a meaning of "sex discrimination" that the Congress that enacted it would not have accepted. This is something courts do fairly frequently to avoid statutory obsolescence and concomitantly to avoid placing the entire burden of updating old statutes on the legislative branch. We should not leave the impression that we are merely the obedient servants of the 88th Congress (1963–1965), carrying out their wishes. We are not. We are taking advantage of what the last half century has taught.

■ FLAUM CIRCUIT JUDGE, joined by RIPPLE, CIRCUIT JUDGE, concurring.

* * * Does Title VII's text require a plaintiff to show that an employer discriminated against them *solely* "because of" an enumerated trait? [The text clearly states:]

> Except as otherwise provided in this subchapter, an unlawful employment practice is established when the complaining party demonstrates that . . . sex . . . was *a motivating factor for any employment practice, even though other factors also motivated the practice.*

42 U.S.C. § 2000e–2(m) (emphasis added). Congress added this amendment to Title VII partially in response to the Supreme Court's plurality decision in *Hopkins,* [in which the] Court made clear that "[t]he

critical inquiry . . . is whether gender was *a factor* in the employment decision" when it was made. (emphasis added). So if discriminating against an employee because she is homosexual is equivalent to discriminating against her because she is (A) a woman who is (B) sexually attracted to women, then it is motivated, in part, by an enumerated trait: the employee's sex. That is all an employee must show to successfully allege a Title VII claim. * * *

■ SYKES, CIRCUIT JUDGE, with whom BAUER and KANNE, CIRCUIT JUDGES, join, dissenting.

Any case heard by the full court is important. This one is momentous. All the more reason to pay careful attention to the limits on the court's role. The question before the en banc court is one of statutory interpretation. The majority deploys a judge-empowering, common-law decision method that leaves a great deal of room for judicial discretion. So does Judge Posner in his concurrence. Neither is faithful to the statutory text, read fairly, as a reasonable person would have understood it when it was adopted. The result is a statutory amendment courtesy of unelected judges. Judge Posner admits this; he embraces and argues for this conception of judicial power. The majority does not, preferring instead to smuggle in the statutory amendment under cover of an aggressive reading of loosely related Supreme Court precedents. Either way, the result is the same: the circumvention of the legislative process by which the people govern themselves. * * *

* * * Sexual orientation is not on the list of forbidden categories of employment discrimination [in Title VII], and we have long and consistently held that employment decisions based on a person's sexual orientation do not classify people on the basis of sex and thus are not covered by Title VII's prohibition of discrimination "because of sex." [citations omitted] This interpretation has been stable for many decades and is broadly accepted; all circuits agree that sexual-orientation discrimination is a distinct form of discrimination and is not synonymous with sex discrimination.

Today the court jettisons the prevailing interpretation and installs the polar opposite. Suddenly sexual-orientation discrimination *is* sex discrimination and thus is actionable under Title VII. What justification is offered for this radical change in a well-established, uniform interpretation of an important—indeed, transformational—statute? My colleagues take note of the Supreme Court's "absence from the debate." What debate? There is no debate, at least not in the relevant sense. Our long-standing interpretation of Title VII is not an outlier. * * * The Supreme Court has had no need to weigh in, and the unanimity among the courts of appeals strongly suggests that our long-settled interpretation is correct.

Of course there *is* a robust debate on this subject in our culture, media, and politics. * * * This striking cultural change informs a case for legislative change and might eventually persuade the people's representatives to amend the statute to implement a new public policy. But it does not bear on the sole inquiry properly before the en banc court: Is the prevailing interpretation of Title VII—that discrimination on the basis of sexual orientation is different in kind and not a form of sex discrimination—*wrong as an original matter*?

[Judge Sykes agrees with the majority "that the proposed new interpretation is not necessarily incorrect simply because no one in the 1964 Congress that adopted Title VII intended or anticipated its application to sexual-orientation discrimination. The subjective intentions of the legislators do not matter. Statutory interpretation is an objective inquiry that looks for the meaning the statutory language conveyed to a reasonable person at the time of enactment. The objective meaning of the text is not delimited by what individual lawmakers specifically had in mind when they voted for the statute."]

That is where our agreement ends. * * * [T]he analysis must begin with the statutory text; it largely ends there too. Is it even remotely plausible that in 1964, when Title VII was adopted, a reasonable person competent in the English language would have understood that a law banning employment discrimination "because of sex" also banned discrimination because of sexual orientation? The answer is no, of course not. * * *

Title VII does not define discrimination "because of sex." In common, ordinary usage in 1964—and now, for that matter—the word "sex" means biologically *male* or *female*; it does not also refer to sexual orientation. [dictionary citations omitted]

To a fluent speaker of the English language—then and now—the ordinary meaning of the word "sex" does not fairly include the concept of "sexual orientation." The two terms are never used interchangeably, and the latter is not subsumed within the former; there is no overlap in meaning. Contrary to the majority's vivid rhetorical claim, it does not take "considerable calisthenics" to separate the two. The words plainly describe different traits, and the separate and distinct meaning of each term is easily grasped. More specifically to the point here, discrimination "because of sex" is not reasonably understood to include discrimination based on sexual orientation, a different immutable characteristic. Classifying people by sexual orientation is different than classifying them by sex. The two traits are categorically distinct and widely recognized as such. There is no ambiguity or vagueness here. * * *

This commonsense understanding is confirmed by the language Congress uses when it *does* legislate against sexual-orientation discrimination. For example, the Violence Against Women Act prohibits funded programs and activities from discriminating "on the basis of actual or perceived race, color, religion, national origin, *sex*, gender identity, . . . *sexual orientation*, or disability." 42 U.S.C. § 13925(b)(13)(A) (emphases added). If sex discrimination is commonly understood to encompass sexual-orientation discrimination, then listing the two categories separately, as this statute does, is needless surplusage. The federal Hate Crimes Act is another example. [citations to additional examples omitted] * * *

My colleagues in the majority superficially acknowledge *Ulane*'s "truism" that sex discrimination is discrimination based on a person's biological sex. As they see it, however, even if sex discrimination is understood in the ordinary way, sexual-orientation discrimination *is* sex discrimination because "it is actually impossible to discriminate on the basis of sexual orientation without discriminating on the basis of sex."

Not true. An employer who refuses to hire homosexuals is not drawing a line based on the job applicant's sex. He is not excluding gay men because they are men and lesbians because they are women. His discriminatory motivation is independent of and unrelated to the applicant's sex. Sexism (misandry and misogyny) and homophobia are separate kinds of prejudice that classify people in distinct ways based on different immutable characteristics. Simply put, sexual-orientation discrimination doesn't classify people by sex; it doesn't draw male/female distinctions but instead targets homosexual men and women for harsher treatment than heterosexual men and women. * * *

The comparative method of proof is a useful technique for uncovering the employer's real motive for taking the challenged action. Comparing the plaintiff to a similarly situated employee of the opposite sex can help the fact finder determine whether the employer was actually motivated by the plaintiff's sex or acted for some other reason. It's a device for ferreting out a prohibited discriminatory motive as an actual cause of the adverse employment action; it does this by controlling for other possible motives. If a female plaintiff can point to a male employee who is identical to her in every material respect and was treated more favorably, then the fact finder can draw an inference that the unfavorable treatment was actually motivated by the plaintiff's sex. * * *

But the comparative method of proof is an evidentiary test; it is not an interpretive tool. It tells us *nothing* about the meaning or scope of Title VII. In ordinary English usage, sexual-orientation discrimination is a distinct form of discrimination and is not synonymous with sex discrimination. That's the plain meaning of Title VII's text as originally understood. An *evidentiary test* like the comparative method of proof has no work to do here and is utterly out of place. * * *

[Judge Sykes also rejects the associational theory of Title VII utilized by the majority.] *Loving* rests on the inescapable truth that miscegenation laws are inherently racist. They are premised on invidious ideas about white superiority and use racial classifications toward the end of racial purity and white supremacy. Sexual-orientation discrimination, on the other hand, is not inherently *sexist*. No one argues that sexual-orientation discrimination aims to promote or perpetuate the supremacy of one sex. In short, *Loving* neither compels nor supports the majority's decision to upend the long-settled understanding that sex discrimination and sexual-orientation discrimination are distinct.

* * * The Equal Protection Clause and Title VII's prohibition of racial discrimination in the workplace *both* operate to curtail the evil of racism inherent in antimiscegenation. That explains why *Loving* applies to Title VII racial-discrimination claims but is not a warrant for reading sexual-orientation discrimination into the statute.

[Judge Sykes disagrees with interpreting *Hopkins* to mean that a claim of sexual-orientation discrimination is indistinguishable from a claim involving sex stereotyping. Nothing in *Hopkins* casts doubt on the distinction between sex discrimination and sexual orientation discrimination.]

To put the matter plainly, heterosexuality is not a *female* stereotype; it is not a *male* stereotype; it is not a *sex-specific* stereotype at all. An employer who hires only heterosexual employees is neither assuming nor insisting that his female and male employees match a stereotype specific to their sex. He is instead insisting that his employees match the dominant sexual orientation *regardless of their sex*. Sexual-orientation discrimination does not classify people according to invidious or idiosyncratic *male* or *female* stereotypes. It does not spring from a sex-specific bias at all.

The point is easy to see if we take the question posed by the plurality opinion in *Hopkins* and map it onto this case. Hively suspects that the real reason Ivy Tech rejected her repeated applications for promotion is her sexual orientation. Assume for the moment that her suspicion is correct. If we asked Ivy Tech "at the moment of the decision what its reasons were and if we received a truthful response would it be reasonable to expect Ivy Tech to respond that it rejected her applications because she is a woman? No. If Ivy Tech responded truthfully, it would confess that its decisions were based on Hively's sexual orientation, not her sex.

So it's a serious mistake to think that *Hopkins* either supports or requires a new interpretation of Title VII that equates sexual-orientation discrimination with sex discrimination. To the contrary, *Hopkins* does not even gesture in that direction. If the lower-court decisions involving "sex stereotyping" are a confusing hodgepodge—and I agree that they are—the confusion stems from an unfortunate tendency to read *Hopkins* for more than it's worth. That's not a reason to embed the confusion in circuit law. * * *

If Kimberly Hively was denied a job because of her sexual orientation, she was treated unjustly. But Title VII does not provide a remedy for this kind of discrimination. The argument that it *should* must be addressed to Congress. * * *

Postscript. Ivy Tech College declined to seek review of this decision.

Jameka J. Evans v. Georgia Regional Hospital

United States Court of Appeals for the Eleventh Circuit, 2017.
850 F.3d 1248.

■ MARTINEZ, DISTRICT JUDGE.

[Jameka Evans worked as a security officer at the defendant hospital for approximately 14 months. During that time, she alleges that she was denied equal pay or work, harassed, and physically assaulted or battered. She was discriminated against on the basis of her sex and targeted for termination for failing to carry herself in a "traditional woman[ly] manner." She asserts that she was punished because her status as a gay female did not comport with gender stereotypes and this caused her to experience a hostile work environment. A less qualified individual was appointed to be her direct supervisor. Moreover, internal e-mails provided evidence that the chief of security was trying to terminate Evans by making her employment unbearable, because she had too much information about his wrongdoing in the security department. The district court dismissed her complaint for failure to state a viable claim.] * * *

Even though we hold, *infra*, that discrimination based on gender non-conformity is actionable, Evans's *pro se* complaint nevertheless failed to plead facts sufficient to create a plausible inference that she suffered discrimination. In other words, Evans did not provide enough factual matter to plausibly suggest that her decision to present herself in a masculine manner led to the alleged adverse employment actions. Therefore, while a dismissal of Evan's gender non-conformity claim would have been appropriate on this basis, these circumstances entitle Evans an opportunity to amend her complaint one time unless doing so would be futile. * * *

Accordingly, we vacate the portion of the district court's order dismissing Evans's gender non-conformity claim with prejudice and remand with instructions to grant Evans leave to amend such claim.

Evans next argues that she has stated a claim under Title VII by alleging that she endured workplace discrimination because of her sexual orientation. She has not. Our binding precedent forecloses such an action. *Blum v. Gulf Oil Corp.*, 597 F.2d 936, 938 (5th Cir. 1979) ("Discharge for homosexuality is not prohibited by Title VII. . . ."). "Under our prior precedent rule, we are bound to follow a binding precedent in this Circuit unless and until it is overruled by this court en banc or by the Supreme Court." [citation omitted] [The court affirms the dismissal of Evans' claim that sexual orientation discrimination is a form of sex discrimination.]* * *

■ WILLIAM PRYOR, CIRCUIT JUDGE, concurring:

I concur in the majority opinion, but I write separately to explain the error of the argument of the Equal Employment Opportunity Commission and the dissent that a person who experiences discrimination because of sexual orientation necessarily experiences discrimination for deviating from gender stereotypes. Although a person who experiences the former will sometimes also experience the latter, the two concepts are legally distinct. And the insistence otherwise by the Commission and the dissent relies on false stereotypes of gay individuals. I also write separately to explain that the dissent would create a new form of relief based on status that runs counter to binding precedent and would undermine the relationship between the doctrine of gender nonconformity and the enumerated classes protected by Title VII.

The majority opinion correctly holds that a claim of discrimination for failure to conform to a gender stereotype is not "just another way to claim discrimination based on sexual orientation." Like any other woman, Evans can state a claim that she experienced, for example, discrimination for wearing a "male haircut" if she includes enough factual allegations. But just as a woman cannot recover under Title VII when she is fired because of her heterosexuality, neither can a gay woman sue for discrimination based on her sexual orientation. Deviation from a particular gender stereotype may correlate disproportionately with a particular sexual orientation, and plaintiffs who allege discrimination on the basis of gender nonconformity will often also have experienced discrimination because of sexual orientation. *See, e.g., Prowel v. Wise Bus. Forms, Inc.* But under Title VII, we ask only whether the individual experienced discrimination for deviating from a gender stereotype.

The unsurprising reality that some individuals who have experienced discrimination because of sexual orientation will also have experienced discrimination because of gender nonconformity by no means establishes that *every* gay individual who experiences discrimination because of sexual orientation has a "triable case of gender stereotyping discrimination." *Prowel.* The [EEOC] and the dissent would have us hold that sexual orientation discrimination always constitutes discrimination for gender nonconformity. They contend, for example, that all gay individuals necessarily engage in the same behavior. But that argument stereotypes all gay individuals in the same way that the Commission and the dissent allege that the Hospital stereotyped Evans.

By assuming that all gay individuals behave the same way or have the same interests, the Commission and the dissent disregard the diversity of experiences of gay individuals. Some gay individuals adopt what various commentators have referred to as the gay "social identity" but experience a variety of sexual desires. Like some heterosexuals, some gay individuals may choose not to marry or date at all or may choose a celibate lifestyle. And other gay individuals choose to enter mixed-orientation marriages. A gay individual may establish with enough factual evidence that she experienced sex discrimination because her behavior deviated from a gender stereotype held by an employer, but our review of that claim would rest on behavior alone. * * *

The dissent misreads our precedent by framing the pertinent question in an appeal involving the doctrine of gender nonconformity as whether an employee's *status* deviated from the ideal held by an employer as to what a woman "should be." * * * But *Price Waterhouse* and *Glenn v. Brumby* concerned claims that an employee's *behavior*, not status alone, deviated from a gender stereotype held by an employer.

Because a claim of gender nonconformity is a behavior-based claim, not a status-based claim, a plaintiff still "must show that the employer actually relied on her gender in making its decision." *Price* Waterhouse. That is, the employer must additionally establish that discrimination occurred on the basis of an enumerated class in Title VII. Remarks based on gender nonconformity are only "*evidence* that gender played a part" in the employer's decision and are not always determinative. *Id.* For example, under Title VII, an employee could fire a male who wore a dress to work—even if that violated the employer's gender stereotypes—if the reason for the firing was that all employees were required to wear a uniform that included pants. The doctrine of gender nonconformity is, and always has been, behavior based. Status-based protections must stem from a separate doctrine or directly from the text of Title VII. The dissent's contrary view would undermine the evidentiary approach established by *Price Waterhouse* and the relationship of that doctrine to the text of Title VII. * * *

■ ROSENBAUM, CIRCUIT JUDGE, concurring in part and dissenting in part:

* * * [W]hen a woman alleges, as Evans has, that she has been discriminated against because she is a lesbian, she necessarily alleges that she has been discriminated against because she failed to conform to the employer's image of what women should be—specifically, that women should be sexually attracted to men only. And it is utter fiction to suggest that she was not discriminated against for failing to comport with her employer's stereotyped view of women. That is discrimination "because of . . . sex," and it clearly violates Title VII under *Price Waterhouse*. * * *

* * * Before *Price Waterhouse*, the Supreme Court had recognized only one type of discrimination rooted in stereotyping that Title VII prohibits: discrimination based on the employer's assumption that, merely by virtue of membership in a protected group, the plaintiff possesses an attribute or will act against the employer's desire, in conformity with a supposed stereotypical characteristic of the group. * * *

In these cases, the employer violated Title VII by ascribing certain characteristics to individual women—without considering whether any individual woman actually possessed the characteristics—based on the employer's stereotyping of women as a group. So the employer discriminated because it *assumed* that all members of the protected group *would conform to* an undesired characteristic of the employer's stereotyped perception of the group. At least one commentator has referred to this view of Title VII as prohibiting "ascriptive" stereotyping. Zachary R. Herz, "Price's Progress: Sex Stereotyping and Its Potential for Antidiscrimination Law," 124 *Yale L.J.* 396, 405 (2014).

But *Price Waterhouse* substantially broadened the scope of actionable discriminatory stereotyping under Title VII. In that case, the Supreme Court for the first time recognized that discrimination because of an individual plaintiff's *failure to conform* to the discriminator's desired and stereotyped perception of how members of the individual's protected group should be or act—essentially the mirror image of ascriptive stereotyping—violated Title VII. This kind of stereotyping has been called "prescriptive" stereotyping, presumably because discrimination occurs on the basis that an employee does not satisfy an employer's stereotyped prescription of what the employee of that protected group should be or how the employee should act. * * *

Price Waterhouse and *Glenn* likewise demand the conclusion that discrimination because an employee is gay violates Title VII's proscription on discrimination "because of . . . sex." By definition, a gay employee is sexually attracted to members of her own sex. So when an employer discriminates against an employee solely because she is a lesbian, the employer acts against the employee only because she is sexually attracted to women, instead of being attracted to only men, like the employer prescriptively believes women should be. This is no different than when an employer discriminates against an employee because she is an aggressive or "macho" woman or solely because she is a transgender woman. In all cases, the employer discriminates against the employee because she does not conform to the employer's prescriptive stereotype of what a person of that birth-assigned gender should be. And so the employer discriminates against the employee "because of . . . sex." * * *

* * * [D]iscrimination against an employee solely because she fails to conform to the employer's view that a woman should be sexually attracted to men only is no different than discrimination against a transsexual because she fails to conform to the employer's view that a birth-assigned male should have male anatomy. In both cases, the employer discriminates because the employee does not comport with the employer's vision of what a member of that particular gender should be. It's just as simple as that.

To avoid this obvious conclusion, the concurrence recharacterizes the discrimination that a lesbian experiences when her employer discriminates against her for failure to conform to the employer's view that women should not be sexually attracted to women; the concurrence says that this is discrimination based on sexual orientation, and sexual orientation is not a protected class under Title VII. But the fact that such discrimination may be alternatively characterized does not make the employer's discrimination any less based on the employee's failure to conform to the employer's prescriptive gender stereotype. Nor does it make the discrimination any less actionable under *Price Waterhouse*'s gender nonconformity theory. * * *

If an employer discriminates against a lesbian solely because she fails to conform to the employer's view that women should be sexually attracted to only men, the employer clearly discriminates against that woman for failure to conform to gender stereotypes as much as if the employer discriminates against a woman because she engages in the behavior of dating women.

But in the concurrence's world, only the person who acts on her feelings enjoys the protection of Title VII. This makes no sense from a practical, textual, or doctrinal point of view.

As a practical matter, this construction protects women who act or dress in ways that the employer perceives as gay, because that behavior fails to conform to the employer's view of how a woman should act. But it allows employers to freely fire women that the employer perceives to be lesbians—as long as the employer is smart enough to say only that it fired the employee because it thought that the employee was a lesbian, without identifying the basis for the employer's conclusion that she was a lesbian. It cannot possibly be the case that a lesbian who is private about her sexuality—or even a heterosexual woman who is mistakenly perceived by her employer to be a lesbian—can be discriminated against by the employer because she does not comport with the employer's view of what a woman should be, while the outwardly lesbian plaintiff enjoys Title VII protection. * * *

The concurrence's argument seems to fundamentally misunderstand what it means to be a lesbian. Lesbians are women who are sexually attracted to women. That's not a stereotype; it's a definition.

And if an employer discriminates against a woman for the reason that the employer believes the employee is sexually attracted to women, how the employee expresses—or suppresses—her feelings of sexual attraction is irrelevant to the fact that the employer has discriminated against the woman for failing to conform to the employer's stereotype that women should be sexually attracted to only men. * * *

NOTES AND QUESTIONS

1. *How Does "Plain Meaning" Change?* If we start from the premise (from *Oncale* and accepted by Judge Sykes) that statutes can cover more than the original legislators intended—i.e., that courts are bound by the text rather than the intent—then how do judges determine whether new interpretations are legitimate? Both Judge Wood's opinion for the *Hively* majority and Judge

Posner's concurrence argue that the social logic has changed, as a result of the recognition of gender non-conformity as the basis for a viable Title VII claim and of the acceptance of a lesbian and gay minority as part of the civil rights fabric of the "society that we have become." Judges Sykes and Pryor argue that these social changes do not alter the reality that sexual orientation is still distinct from sex. Of course, it does not help that "sex" has so many meanings.

We believe that Judge Wood's dynamic version of text-tied interpretation will prove most appealing to the current Supreme Court, because of its deep congruence with Title VII's equality enhancement purposes and the history of its interpretation, including the congressional updating of the law in response to its interpretation by agencies and judges. See William N. Eskridge Jr., "Dynamic Title VII: Workplace Discrimination 'Because of Sex'", 127 *Yale L. J.* (forthcoming 2017). This statutory evolution includes the initial rejection and then acceptance of coverage for pregnancy discrimination; the judicial recognition of sexual harassment as a viable claim, even though it still lacks an explicit provision in statutory text; the articulation of new affirmative defenses in Supreme Court decisions; and the Court's ruling that harassment can be actionable if it occurs between two persons of the same sex. In addition, as Judge Flaum pointed out, if adverse treatment is motivated in part by sex discrimination (even if also by sexual orientation bias), plaintiff can succeed on the mixed motivation provision in Title VII that was added after *Hopkins*. Ultimately, "rule of law and democracy norms" are not in conflict with the updating needs emphasized by Judge Posner," and in fact provide a stronger grounding for Posner's dynamism.

2. *"Difficult but not impossible"?* In her opinion for the panel in *Hively*, Judge Ilana Rovner elaborated on the incoherency of excluding sexual orientation from the definition of "sex" in Title VII while also applying the anti-stereotyping case law that is the progeny of *Hopkins*:

> * * * [F]or the last quarter century since *Price Waterhouse*, courts have been haphazardly, and with limited success, trying to figure out how to draw the line between gender norm discrimination, which can form the basis of a legal claim under *Price Waterhouse's* interpretation of Title VII, and sexual orientation discrimination, which is not cognizable under Title VII. As one scholar has stated, "The challenge facing the lower courts since *Price Waterhouse* is finding a way to protect against the entire spectrum of gender stereotyping while scrupulously not protecting against the stereotype that people should be attracted only to those of the opposite gender." Brian Soucek, *Perceived Homosexuals: Looking Gay Enough for Title VII*, 63 AM. U. L. REV. 715, 726 (2014). * * * Lesbian women and gay men upend our gender paradigms by their very status—causing us to question and casting into doubt antiquated and anachronistic ideas about what roles men and women should play in their relationships. * * * In this way the roots of sexual orientation discrimination and gender discrimination wrap around each other inextricably. * * * Whether

the line is nonexistent or merely exceedingly difficult to find, it is certainly true that the attempt to draw and observe a line between the two types of discrimination results in a jumble of inconsistent precedents.

* * * [S]ome courts attempting to differentiate between actions which constitute discrimination on the basis of sexual orientation and those which constitute discrimination on the basis of gender non-conformity essentially throw out the baby with the bathwater. For those courts, if the lines between the two are not easily discernible, the right answer is to forego any effort to tease apart the two claims and simply dismiss the claim * * * Several other courts likewise have thrown up their hands at the muddled lines between sexual orientation and gender non-conformity claims and simply have disallowed what they deem to be "bootstrapping" of sexual orientation claims onto gender stereotyping claims. * * *

Other courts address the problem of the ill-defined lines between sexual orientation and gender non-conformity claims by carefully trying to tease the two apart and looking only at those portions of the claim that appear to address cognizable gender non-conformity discrimination. * * *

Nevertheless, although disentangling gender discrimination from sexual orientation discrimination may be difficult, we cannot conclude that it is impossible. There may indeed be some aspects of a worker's sexual orientation that create a target for discrimination apart from any issues related to gender. Harassment may be based on prejudicial or stereotypical ideas about particular aspects of the gay and lesbian "lifestyle," including ideas about promiscuity, religious beliefs, spending habits, child-rearing, sexual practices, or politics. Although it seems likely that most of the causes of discrimination based on sexual orientation ultimately stem from employers' and co-workers' discomfort with a lesbian woman's or a gay man's failure to abide by gender norms, we cannot say that it must be so in all cases. Therefore we cannot conclude that the two must necessarily be coextensive unless or until either the legislature or the Supreme Court says it is so. * * *

In sum, the distinction between gender non-conformity claims and sexual orientation claims has created an odd state of affairs in the law in which Title VII protects gay, lesbian, and bisexual people, but frequently only to the extent that those plaintiffs meet society's stereotypical norms about how gay men or lesbian women look or act—i.e. that gay men tend to behave in effeminate ways and lesbian women have masculine mannerisms. By contrast, lesbian, gay or bisexual people who otherwise conform to gender stereotyped norms in dress and mannerisms mostly lose their claims for sex discrimination under Title VII, although why this should be true is not entirely clear. * * *

In short, the district courts—the laboratories on which the Supreme Court relies to work through cutting-edge legal problems—are beginning to ask whether the sexual orientation-denying emperor of Title VII has no clothes. * * *

830 F.3d 698, 705–13 (7th Cir. 2016). Despite these concerns with logic and administrability, the panel unanimously found that it was bound by prior precedent and ruled for the defendant. When the Circuit agreed to rehear the case *en banc*, it vacated the Rovner opinion.

3. *Stereotypes Thick and Thin.* In *Evans*, Judges Rosenbaum and Pryor debate the extent to which stereotyping can supply the rule of decision. The focus on stereotypes is understandable, given that *Glenn v. Brumby* established circuit precedent that gender identity discrimination is a form of stereotype-based sex discrimination (in an opinion joined by Judge Pryor). Judge Pryor seeks to distinguish his earlier view as contingent on the understanding of gender nonconformity as conduct, which falls within the rubric of the *Price Waterhouse* reasoning concerning stereotyping; whereas by contrast, sexual orientation *per se* is merely a status, one not enumerated in Title VII. Judge Rosenbaum argues for a richer understanding of how stereotypes operate, whether intentionally expressed or merely perceived. The only Justice who was on the Supreme Court at the time of *Price Waterhouse* who remains today is Justice Kennedy (who dissented). What jurisprudential underpinnings for stereotyping theory do you think that today's Court will find most appealing?

4. *"But For."* In yet another case raising the same statutory interpretation question, Chief Judge Robert Katzmann of the Second Circuit suggested using the framework of the traditional "but for" test: if the employee would have been treated differently but for his or her sex, a prima facie case of discrimination has been made. Christiansen v. Omnicom Group Inc., 852 F.3d 195, 203 (2d Cir. 2017). Judge Katzmann argued that this approach encompasses sexual orientation, quoting the EEOC decision in *Baldwin*: "sexual orientation 'cannot be defined or understood without reference to sex,' because sexual orientation is defined by whether a person is attracted to people of the same sex or opposite sex (or both, or neither)." The Trump Justice Department position also includes a "but for" argument, but to the opposite effect. The Department's brief in *Zarda* argued that the plaintiff must show that men and women are treated differently. In other words, a policy of treating gay men the same as other men but for their sexual orientation (i.e., as compared to straight men) is not prohibited by Title VII. To succeed, the gay male plaintiff would have to demonstrate that the "but for" reason was his sex (i.e., that he was treated differently as compared to women). What do you think are the strengths and weaknesses of each "but for" argument?

5. *Law and Politics.* Recall that LGBT advocates have sought federal anti-discrimination legislation since the 1970s. A Supreme Court decision holding that "because of sex" in Title VII covers discrimination based on sexual orientation and gender identity would obviate the need for new legislation as to employment, and the rationale of such an opinion presumably would be extended to other federal laws that ban discrimination based on sex, such as

Title IX (education), the Fair Housing Act, and the Equal Credit Opportunity Act. A loss, on the other hand, would set the effort back to square one, and refocus attention on the proposed Equality Act (Appendix 3) or similar legislation. In what ways do you think these two possible outcomes would affect the broader LGBT rights movement? The women's rights movement?

C. FROM GENDER IDENTITY COVERAGE TO THE BATHROOM ACCESS QUESTION

The category of cases that have proven most difficult for transgender plaintiffs to win have been those in which the defense focused on concern with a transitioning person (usually male to female) using the bathroom, locker room or showers assigned to her new gender. This has been true even when the statutory basis for the claim clearly includes gender identity as a protected characteristic, as in the next case.

Julienne Goins v. West Group
Minnesota Supreme Court, 2001.
635 N.W.2d 717.

■ JUSTICE ANDERSON.

* * * Respondent Julienne Goins was designated male at birth and given the name Justin Travis Goins, but Goins was confused about that sexual identity throughout much of childhood and adolescence. Since 1994, Goins has taken female hormones and, with the exception of one occasion, has presented publicly as female since 1995. In October 1995, a Texas court granted Goins' petition for a name change as well as a request for a gender change "from genetic male to reassigned female." Goins identifies as transgender or "trans-identified."

In May 1997, Goins began full-time work with West in its Rochester, New York, office. Goins transferred to West's Minnesota facility in Eagan in October 1997. Prior to the actual relocation, Goins visited the Eagan facility and used the employee women's restrooms. A few of West's female employees observed Goins' use of the women's restrooms and, believing Goins to be biologically male, expressed concern to West supervisors about sharing a restroom with a male. This concern was brought to the attention of West's director of human resources who, in turn, discussed the concern with other human resources personnel and legal counsel. West's director of human resources considered the female employees' restroom use complaint as a hostile work environment concern and decided to enforce the policy of restroom use according to biological gender. After considering the options, the director decided that it would be more appropriate for Goins to use either a single-occupancy restroom in the building where she worked but on a different floor or another single-occupancy restroom in another building.

The decision on restroom use was conveyed to Goins by the director of human resources in the morning of her first day of work at the Eagan facility. The director explained that West was attempting to accommodate the conflicting concerns of Goins and the female employees who expressed uneasiness about sharing their restroom with a male. Goins objected, proposing instead education and training regarding transgender individuals so as to allay female coworker concerns. She also refused to comply with the restroom use policy, in protest in part, and continued to use the employee women's restroom closest to her workstation. In November 1997, Goins was threatened with disciplinary action if she continued to disregard the restroom use policy. In January 1998, Goins tendered her resignation, declining West's offer of a promotion and substantial salary increase, and accepted a job offer elsewhere. In her letter of resignation, Goins stated that West's human resources department had treated her in a manner that had caused undue stress and hostility. * * *

The MHRA [Minnesota Human Rights Act] prohibits sexual orientation discrimination in the workplace. The definition of "sexual orientation" includes "having or being perceived as having a self-image or identity not traditionally associated with one's biological maleness or femaleness." Minn.Stat. § 363.01, subd. 41a (2000). The parties agree that Goins consistently presents herself as a woman. Her discrimination claim is predicated on her self-image as a woman that is or is perceived to be inconsistent with her biological gender. Accordingly, for purposes of Goins' discrimination claim, her self-image is inconsistent with her biological gender. * * *

Goins does not argue that an employer engages in impermissible discrimination by designating the use of restrooms according to gender. Rather, her claim is that the MHRA prohibits West's policy of designating restroom use according to biological gender, and requires instead that such designation be based on self-image of gender. Goins alleges that West engaged in impermissible discrimination by denying her access to a restroom consistent with her self-image of gender. We do not believe the MHRA can be read so broadly. As the district court observed, where financially feasible, the traditional and accepted practice in the employment setting is to provide restroom facilities that reflect the cultural preference for restroom designation based on biological gender. To conclude that the MHRA contemplates restrictions on an employer's ability to designate restroom facilities based on biological gender would likely restrain employer discretion in the gender designation of workplace shower and locker room facilities, a result not likely intended by the legislature. * * * [A]bsent more express guidance from the legislature, we conclude that an employer's designation of employee restroom use based on biological gender is not sexual orientation discrimination in violation of the MHRA. * * *

Krystal Etsitty v. Utah Transit Authority

United States Court of Appeals for the Tenth Circuit, 2007.
502 F.3d 1215.

■ MURPHY, CIRCUIT JUDGE.

* * * Etsitty is a transsexual who has been diagnosed with Adult Gender Identity Disorder. Although Etsitty was born as a biological male and given the name "Michael," she identifies herself as a woman and has always believed she was born with the wrong anatomical sex organs. Even before she was diagnosed with a gender identity disorder, Etsitty lived and dressed as a woman outside of work and used the female name of "Krystal." Eventually, Etsitty began to see an endocrinologist who prescribed her female hormones to prepare for a sex reassignment surgery in the future. Etsitty made the decision at that time to live full time as a woman. While she has begun the transition from male to female by taking female hormones, she has not yet completed the sex reassignment surgery. Thus, Etsitty describes herself as a "pre-operative transgendered individual."

Nearly four years after Etsitty had begun taking female hormones, she applied for a position as a bus operator with UTA. She was hired. * * * While on their routes, UTA employees use public restrooms.

Throughout her training period at UTA, Etsitty presented herself as a man and used male restrooms. Soon after being hired, however, she met with her supervisor, Pat Chatterton, and informed him that she was a transsexual. She explained that she would begin to appear more as a female at work and that she would eventually change her sex. Chatterton expressed support for Etsitty and stated he did not see any problem with her being a transsexual. After this meeting, Etsitty began wearing makeup, jewelry, and acrylic nails to work. She also began using female restrooms while on her route.

[Betty] Shirley, the operations manager of the UTA division where Etsitty worked, heard a rumor that there was a male operator who was wearing makeup. She spoke with Chatterton and he informed her Etsitty was a transsexual and would be going through a sex change. When Chatterton told her this, Shirley expressed concern about whether Etsitty would be using a male or female restroom. Shirley told Chatterton she would speak with Human Resources about whether Etsitty's restroom usage would raise any concerns for UTA.

Shirley then called Bruce Cardon, the human resources generalist for Shirley's division, and they decided to set up a meeting with Etsitty. At the meeting, Shirley and Cardon asked Etsitty where she was in the sex change process and whether she still had male genitalia. Etsitty explained she still had male genitalia because she did not have the money to complete the sex change operation. Shirley expressed concern about the possibility of liability for UTA if a UTA employee with male genitalia was observed using the female restroom. Shirley and Cardon also expressed concern that Etsitty would switch back and forth between using male and female restrooms.

Following their meeting with Etsitty, Shirley and Cardon placed Etsitty on administrative leave and ultimately terminated her employment. Shirley explained the reason Etsitty was terminated was the possibility of liability for UTA arising from Etsitty's restroom usage. * * *

Assuming [without deciding] Etsitty has established a prima facie case under the *Price Waterhouse* theory of gender stereotyping, the burden then shifts to UTA to articulate a legitimate, nondiscriminatory reason for Etsitty's termination. * * *

UTA has explained its decision to discharge Etsitty was based solely on her intent to use women's public restrooms while wearing a UTA uniform, despite the fact she still had male genitalia. The record also reveals UTA believed, and Etsitty has not demonstrated otherwise, that it was not possible to accommodate her bathroom usage because UTA drivers typically use public restrooms along their routes rather than restrooms at the UTA facility. UTA states it was concerned the use of women's public restrooms by a biological male could result in liability for UTA. This court agrees with the district court that such a motivation constitutes a legitimate, nondiscriminatory reason for Etsitty's termination under Title VII.

Etsitty argues UTA's concern regarding which restroom she would use cannot qualify as a facially non-discriminatory reason because the use of women's restrooms is an inherent part of Etsitty's status as a transsexual and, thus, an inherent part of her non-conforming gender behavior. Therefore, she argues, terminating her because she intended to use women's restrooms is essentially another way of stating that she was terminated for failing to conform to sex stereotypes.

Title VII's prohibition on sex discrimination, however, does not extend so far. It may be that use of the women's restroom is an inherent part of one's identity as a male-to-female transsexual and that a prohibition on such use discriminates on the basis of one's status as a transsexual. * * * [H]owever, Etsitty may not claim protection under Title VII based upon her transsexuality *per se*. Rather, Etsitty's claim must rest entirely on the *Price Waterhouse* theory of protection as a man who fails to conform to sex stereotypes. However far *Price Waterhouse* reaches, this court cannot conclude it requires employers to allow biological males to use women's restrooms. Use of a restroom designated for the opposite sex does not constitute a mere failure to conform to sex stereotypes.

* * * Because an employer's requirement that employees use restrooms matching their biological sex does not expose biological males to disadvantageous terms and does not discriminate against employees who fail to conform to gender stereotypes, UTA's proffered reason of

concern over restroom usage is not discriminatory on the basis of sex. * * *

UTA's legitimate explanation is not made implausible by any of the circumstantial evidence relied on by Etsitty in her brief. The fact UTA had not yet received complaints about Etsitty's restroom usage at the time of the termination does not mean UTA could not have been concerned about such complaints arising in the future, especially where Etsitty had only recently begun using the women's restroom. * * *

Tamara Lusardi v. John M. McHugh, Secretary, Department of the Army

United States Equal Employment Opportunity Commission, 2015.
Appeal No. 0120133395, 2015 WL 1607756.

* * * [The Complainant, a transgender woman, is a civilian employee with the U.S. Army Aviation and Missile Research Development and Engineering Center ("AMRDEC") at Redstone Arsenal in Huntsville, Alabama, where she served as a Software Quality Assurance Lead.]

* * * Although Complainant had discussed her gender identity with S [Supervisor] 1 as early as 2007, she began the process of transitioning her gender presentation/expression in 2010. In April 2010, Complainant obtained a decree from an Alabama court changing her name from one commonly associated with men to one commonly associated with women. At that time, she also requested that the government change her name and sex on all personnel records. The Office of Personnel Management ("OPM") effected those changes on October 13, 2010. This caused Complainant's work e-mail address to reflect her new name.

On October 26, 2010, at the request of S2, Complainant met with S2 and S1 to discuss the process of transitioning from presenting herself as a man to living and working, in conformance with her gender identity, as a woman. At that meeting, Complainant and her supervisors discussed how Complainant would explain her transition to colleagues and the estimated timeline for any medical procedures.

As part of that meeting, they also discussed which bathrooms Complainant would use when she began presenting as a woman. The plan, written in the form of a memorandum from Complainant to management, indicated that Complainant would use a single-user restroom referred to as the "executive restroom" or the "single shot rest room" rather man the multi-user "common women's restroom" until Complainant had undergone an undefined surgery.

S2 testified that in his recollection no one "insisted" that Complainant utilize only the executive restroom but that the plan was mutually crafted by himself, S1, and Complainant. * * * According to Complainant, "We agreed up front in order to allow people to become accustomed to me and not feel uncomfortable that I would use the front bathroom for a period of time." * * * She testified that she agreed to use the executive bathroom for the initial period "[b]ecause I have a good heart and I did believe there were people who might have issues with it and the ability for them to grow comfortable with who I was . . . would have provided it." * * * S1 expressed at the time that it was her belief, after consulting with Human Resources, that because Complainant was a woman, she was free to use whichever women's restroom she wanted. * * *

Regardless of the motivations behind the creation of the transition plan, it apparently had to be "approved" by higher level management. The Deputy Program Manager of the Program Executive Office testified that he made the final decision as to which bathroom Complainant would use. He stated:

> I made the decision based on the fact that I have a significant number of women in my building who would probably be extremely uncomfortable having an individual, despite the fact that she is conducting herself as a female, is still basically a male, physically.

> And that would cause as many problems if more problems [sic] than having the individuals use a private bathroom. I also thought that under the circumstances, a male restroom would be inappropriate. So, that was left [sic] to use the single use bathrooms.

Additionally, a Lieutenant who supervised S2 testified that Complainant's bathroom access was conditioned on a medical procedure:

> [W]e all agreed back then that there was a procedure, operation that was to take place that would essentially signify a complete transformation to a female. * * * And that procedure would be the point of where all the bathrooms would be on limits for or within limits for [the Complainant] to use for that point.

The transition plan was given final approval by the Deputy Program Manager in early November 2010. Complainant e-mailed the entire staff on November 22, 2010, explaining her situation and indicating that for an initial period, she would use the executive restroom. She began presenting as a woman at work following the Thanksgiving holiday. Complainant regularly used the executive restroom except on three occasions in early 2011. On one occasion, the executive restroom was out of order for several days. On another occasion, the executive restroom was being cleaned. In these incidents, Complainant felt that her only options were to leave the facility to locate a restroom off-site, use the common women's restroom, or use the common men's restroom. She chose to use the restroom associated with her gender. After each incident, Complainant was confronted by S2 who told her she'd been observed using the common women's restroom, that she was making people uncomfortable, and that she had to use the executive restroom until she could show proof of having undergone the "final surgery." * * *

* * * The Agency defends its actions in part by pointing out that the Complainant agreed to use the "single shot" restroom while other employees adjusted to her transition. * * * The first step, starting in mid-November, was for Complainant to start dressing consistent with her gender identity. During this time, her plan said she would "use [the] single shot restroom." The next step, set to occur about a month later, was for Complainant to undergo an undefined "Surgical Procedure" and then put in a request to use the common facility. In accordance with her plan, Complainant used the single-shot restroom in the period following her change in dress. She apparently did not undergo a surgical procedure in December and did not submit a formal request to use the common facility exclusively. On two occasions, however, she found that the single-shot restroom was out-of-order or closed and decided to use the common facility. She was confronted by S2 after each time she used the common facility. He told her that she could not use those facilities until she had undergone "final surgery." Complainant asserted in response that she was "legally female" and entitled to use the women's restroom if needed.

This case represents well the peril of conditioning access to facilities on any medical procedure. Nothing in Title VII makes any medical procedure a prerequisite for equal opportunity (for transgender individuals, or anyone else). An agency may not condition access to facilities—or to other terms, conditions, or privileges of employment—on the completion of certain medical steps that the agency itself has unilaterally determined will somehow prove the bona fides of the individual's gender identity.

On this record, there is no cause to question that Complainant—who was assigned the sex of male at birth but identifies as female—*is* female. And certainly where, as here, a transgender female has notified her employer that she has begun living and working full-time as a woman, the agency must allow her access to the women's restrooms. This "real life experience" often is crucial to a transgender employee's transition. As OPM points out:

> [C]ommencement of the real life experience [i]s often the most important stage of transition, and, for a significant number of people, the last step necessary for them to complete a healthy gender transition. As the name suggests, the real life experience is designed to allow the transgender individual to experience living full-time in the gender role to which he or she is transitioning. . . . [O]nce [a transitioning employee] has begun living and working full-time in the gender that reflects his or her gender identity, agencies should allow access to restrooms and (if provided to other employees) locker room facilities consistent with his or her gender identity. . . . [T]ransitioning employees should not be required to have undergone or to provide proof of any particular medical procedure (including

gender reassignment surgery) in order to have access to facilities designated for use by a particular gender.

* * *

[S]upervisory or co-worker confusion or anxiety cannot justify discriminatory terms and conditions of employment. Title VII prohibits discrimination based on sex whether motivated by hostility, by a desire to protect people of a certain gender, by gender stereotypes, or by the desire to accommodate other people's prejudices or discomfort. Allowing the preferences of co-workers to determine whether sex discrimination is valid reinforces the very stereotypes and prejudices that Title VII is intended to overcome.

Finally, the Agency maintains that it is unclear whether restricting Complainant from using the common restrooms is even an adverse employment action. The Commission has long held that an employee is aggrieved for purposes of Title VII if she has suffered a harm or loss with respect to a term, condition, or privilege of employment. Equal access to restrooms is a significant, basic condition of employment. See e.g., OSHA, Interpretation of 20 C.F.R. 1910.141 § (c)(1)(i): Toilet Facilities (Apr. 4, 1998) (requiring that employers provide access to toilet facilities so that all employees can use them when they need to do so). Here the Agency refused to allow the Complainant to use a restroom that other persons of her gender were freely permitted to use. That constitutes a harm or loss with respect to the terms and conditions of Complainant's employment.

But the harm to the Complainant goes beyond simply denying her access to a resource open to others. The decision to restrict Complainant to a "single shot" restroom isolated and segregated her from other persons of her gender. It perpetuated the sense that she was not worthy of equal treatment and respect. The Agency's actions deprived Complainant of equal status, respect, and dignity in the workplace, and, as a result, deprived her of equal employment opportunities. In restricting her access to the restroom consistent with her gender identity, the Agency refused to recognize Complainant's very identity. Treatment of this kind by one's employer is most certainly adverse. * * *

NOTES AND QUESTIONS ON BATHROOM ACCESS

1.   *Consistency.* If one accepts the principle that individuals should be permitted to use the restroom that is consistent with their gender identity, the question becomes how and by whom gender identity is determined. Should individuals have to produce some form of identification with a gender marker that matches the categorization of the restroom? What about individuals who cannot afford to obtain new identification? We tend to assume that an individual's gender identity will be consistent, i.e., will not fluctuate or change frequently. If consistency is a reasonable expectation, how might legal rules incorporate that requirement?

2. *Workplaces Compared to Schools.* As you probably know, the issue of bathroom access for transgender persons has also arisen in the school context. See Chapter 8, Section 2A. Do you see differences in the school context that would generate different rules than in the employment context? What about large public accommodations such as stadiums where public restroom use is common?

3. *Title VII Defenses.* For many people, the resolution of this issue seems obvious: build more separate stalls in bathrooms and more individual changing spaces for showers and locker rooms. Those changes, however, would cost money for many employers. How might employer defenses under Title VII be applied in such a situation? What criteria should guide judges in applying them?

PROBLEM 5-5
BATHROOM ACCESS

Imagine that you are staff counsel to the Senate Committee on Health, Education, Labor and Pensions, which has jurisdiction of anti-discrimination legislation. The chair has asked you to draft language that both transgender advocates and lobbyists for business can accept that will establish clear guidelines for providing restroom facilities for trans employees and, if relevant, customers and members of the public. What will you propose?

RELATIONSHIPS WE CHOOSE: PRIVATIZATION AND PLURALITY IN FAMILY LAW

SECTION 1   The Privatization of Family Law
SECTION 2   Common Law Regulation of Cohabiting Relationships
SECTION 3   The Emerging Menu of Relationship Recognition

"Family" in western civilization has traditionally meant ties created by marriage and blood, and the typical family was a husband, wife, and as many children as possible. In the early decades of the new millennium, marriage and blood remain centrally important, but have given way to "families we choose," as anthropologist Kath Weston terms it in *Families We Choose: Lesbians, Gays, Kinship* (1991). The relative ascendancy of relationships we choose is the family law parallel of Sir Henry Maine's observation that modern law consists of the ongoing transition from status relations to contractual relations. Thus it is that sexual and other close relationships today are easier to construct and can assume a greater variety of different legal forms, most of which are easier to exit.

This chapter will survey the legal (and, to some extent, social) evolution of family law, including its diversification and partial deregulation (Section 1), the rise of contract-based legal statuses for romantic partnerships (Section 2), and the plurality of forms by which various jurisdictions are now recognizing and regulating romantic partnerships and unions (Section 3). In addition to a survey of existing law, the chapter will suggest directions for the future, the most prominent of which is the emerging *menu of options* states will be offering couples, with different benefits and obligations associated with each menu option. Finally, as in the earlier chapters, there will be materials and notes suggesting theoretical inquiries tied to the theories in Chapter 3. Chapter 7, which follows, will conduct a similar survey regarding parental rights and obligations toward children in families of choice.

Before launching into our survey, we should like to present a relatively radical approach to family law. In the problem that follows Professor Fineman's proposal (which is also relevant to Chapter 7), you have an opportunity to jot down some preliminary thoughts on the larger normative question, What *should* the state be encouraging and regulating when it recognizes, subsidizes, and regulates romantic unions?

Martha Albertson Fineman, *The Neutered Mother, the Sexual Family, and Other Twentieth Century Tragedies* **(1995).** Professor Fineman proposes "the end of family law as we know it, with the suggestion that marriage be abolished as a legal category. I offer a utopian re-visioning of the family—a reconceptualization of family intimacy that redefines the legal core unit away from our current focus on sexual or horizontal intimacy." The "caretaking dyad," modeled on the Mother/Child relationship, "would replace the historic dyad of the heterosexual married couple as the core intimate family unit upon which family policy and law are constructed" (p. 8).

Professor Fineman's argument starts with a feminist critique of our liberalized family law. Formal equality can be harmful to women when it does not take account of women's different needs *or* of the structural and societal problems imposed upon women. Fineman objects to the liberal view that women and their families would be better off if women had equal opportunities "in the world" and were not distinctively tied to their family duties. "The result is that much of the reformist rhetoric directed at family law constantly reaffirms the notion that the disabilities and disadvantages of Mother must be overcome—the family refashioned so that the individual woman is left unencumbered." (P. 74.)

Liberal feminists respond that their reforms seek functional as well as formal equality—shared parenting, where the father does half the housework and the mother works outside the home. Professor Fineman is skeptical, for shared parenting in practice has meant the double shift, where the wife works outside the home *and* does almost all the child care and housework. The reason for the double shift is that men expect women to do the housework and child care; many women share that expectation, and even when they do not, the man's usually superior bargaining position within marriage assures that husbands' preferences will usually prevail. Indeed, liberalized divorce and custody law strengthens the husband's bargaining position. The husband's threat of walking away from the marriage is one that wives are less willing to make, and so the repeat-game bargaining between husband and wife will tilt toward the husband's interests, for the reasons Professor Carol Rose posited in Chapter 4, Section 2A. In the event of a divorce, "mothers may exchange a bargained-down property settlement to avoid a custody contest because they tend, in contrast to fathers, to consider custody a nonnegotiable issue" (p. 89).

From a feminist perspective, Professor Fineman suggests, the problem is deeper—it goes to the notion abundant in our culture and law that the *sexual family* of the husband and wife is the foundational unit of society. This *meta-narrative* focuses attention on the *horizontal* relationship of the husband and the wife, which is assumed to be heterosexual and procreative, while treating *vertical* relationships such as mother/child and adult/elderly parent as special exceptions to be accommodated at the margins (p.145). "While a great deal of emotionally charged rhetoric in family law is directed at children, the primary focus is still on maintaining the traditional heterosexual family model. * * * The sexually affiliated family is still the imposed ideal and, as such, it escapes sustained, serious consideration and criticism. The nuclear family is 'natural'—it is assumed. The dominance of the idealized sexual family in social and legal thought has restricted real reform and doomed us to recreate patriarchy." (Page 147.)

Previous critics of the sexual family have pointed out that it is a situs for excluding lesbians, gay men, and many bisexuals from public culture; for marginalizing and stigmatizing single people, especially single mothers of color raising children; and for maintaining patriarchy. Professor Fineman poses a deeper critique: "The ideal of the natural family—the unit to which responsibility for inevitable dependency is referred—establishes a relationship between 'public' state and 'private' family. Dependency," where a parent cares for a child or an adult cares for her aged parent, "is allocated away from the state to the private grouping. These ideas of natural and privatized dependency reinforce one another on an ideological level. They perversely interact so that the societal tasks assigned to the natural family inevitably assume the role differentiation that exists within that sexually affiliated family." (Page 161.)

"Equality rhetoric and family law reforms aside, the burdens associated with intimacy and its maintenance have always been and continue to be disproportionately allocated to women. * * * Women, wives, mothers, daughters, daughters-in-law, sisters are typically the socially and culturally assigned caretakers. As caretakers they are tied into intimate relationships with their dependents. The very process of assuming caretaking responsibilities creates dependency in the caretaker—she needs some social structure to provide the means to care for others. In a traditional family, the caretaker herself, as wife and mother, is dependent on the wage-earning husband to provide for her so she can fulfill her tasks." (Pages 162–63.) The caretaking wife, thus conceived, is completely vulnerable in a bargaining situation; the husband, if he chooses, can insist on sexual, monetary, and allocation-of-duty advantages that many dependent wives cannot decline.

The sexual family, a product of social mores as well as legal "reform," has failed women, and it has failed children. The state's many subsidies and social pressure push women into marriages that soon leave most wives working a double shift and increasingly dependent upon their husbands' good faith—a dependency that has had devastating consequences for tens of millions of women and their children. "In its historic form [the sexual family] is not adequate to handle both the demands for equality and the contemporary manifestations of inevitable and derivative dependency. It is essential that we begin to reconceptualize the relationship between law and the family in regard to these dependencies. In doing so, we should keep a few basic principles in mind. First, we must abandon the pretense that we can achieve gender equality through family-law reform. The egalitarian family myth remains largely unassisted by other ideological and structural changes in the larger society and is belied by the statistics reflecting the ways women and men live.

"We should also recognize that family policy is a form of state regulation. We must, therefore, be explicit about the norms and values motivating public and legal decisions about what should be protected or encouraged through social and economic subsidies. Furthermore, family policy must be secular, not based on a religious model. It should reference the functional aspirations we have for families in our society and be supportive of those aspirations. I therefore propose two recommendations for legal reform: the abolition of the legal supports for the sexual family and the construction of protections for the nurturing unit of caretaker and dependent exemplified by the Mother/Child dyad." (Page 228.)

Professor Fineman's first proposal, which is the more relevant to this chapter, would allow people to continue to celebrate their marriages—but would no longer attach legal rights and duties to the relationship. "Instead, the interactions of female and male sexual affiliates would be governed by the same rules that regulate other interactions in our society—specifically those of contract and property, as well as tort and criminal law." (Page 229.) Family law has already created a choice regime for marriage; the Fineman proposal would extend current trends. It would have several advantages (pp. 229–30): (1) The state would no longer have incentives to regulate voluntary sexual interactions among adults, as "there would no longer be a state-preferred model of family intimacy to protect and support." (2) Husbands would no longer have a partial immunity for spousal rape. (3) Children would no longer be stigmatized for birth outside of marriage. (4) The idea of marital property would end, as would obligations for spousal support during and after marriage. (5) Male sexual partners would no longer have as much of a bargaining advantage if they could not use easy-exit divorce and child custody as levers to pry concessions from their female partners. (6) The law could refocus its subsidies on the relationship that is most important to society—the caregiving relationship such as that provided by a parent to her or his child or by an adult to an aged parent. The law should afford caregiving relationships not just the special protections of privacy law, but also state subsidies in the form of tax breaks, child care facilities, and outright grants of money to caregivers. For a complementary argument from the perspective of queer theory, see Nancy D. Polikoff, *Beyond Gay (and Straight) Marriage: Valuing All Families Under the Law* (2008).

PROBLEM 6-1
STATE RECOGNITION OF HORIZONTAL PARTNERSHIPS?

Professor Fineman's proposal and supporting argument provide you with an opportunity to consider what it is the state *ought* to be doing in family law. Should the state do nothing more than enforce contracts arrived at between the parties? If the state does offer a regulatory form that does more than enforce contracts, what benefits (subsidies) should the state offer couples—and why should it offer much in the way of benefits (subsidies)? What obligations should the state impose on each partner—and why? If you believe, as Fineman does, that marriage should be scrapped, do you think it should be replaced with another legal form of recognition and regulation? Outline your preliminary thoughts as to these issues.

Theory is relevant. Hence, you might review the materials in Chapter 3 and your own theoretical commitments. Different theoretical commitments will press you in different directions. For example:

- *Natural law* theories such as that of the Roman Catholic Church or Professor John Finnis (Chapter 3, Section 1) support the traditional regulatory regime of marriage and so would oppose Professor Fineman's proposal. Like Fineman, however, natural law theorists would be highly critical of the liberalization that has gone on in family law, but their primary lament is that liberalization has undermined the dad-mom family and has disconnected children from their fathers.[a] Instead of abolishing civil marriage, they generally support a strengthening of the institution, even through *covenant marriage* laws, which require counseling before marriage and make it more difficult to divorce.

- *Economic* theories (Chapter 3, Section 2A) generally support a liberal, individual-choice regime in family law but otherwise press in different directions. Chicago School theories could support a contract-based approach, but could also support a traditional approach which rewarded the parties for specialization; Professor Gary Becker is the anti-Fineman in this regard, for he focuses on overall social utility and seems unconcerned with the unfairness to women within marriage that worries Professor Fineman (Chapter 3, Section 2A). Professor Margaret Brinig applies economic analysis to support covenant marriage as the most efficient mechanism for assuring the commitment needed by mothers and children.[b] Contrast Professor Carol Rose's game-theoretical approach (Chapter 3, Section 2A), which would support

---

[a] See David Blankenhorn, *Fatherless America: Confronting Our Most Urgent Social Problem* (1995); see also David Popenoe, *Life Without Father: Compelling New Evidence that Fatherhood and Marriage Are Indispensable for the Good of Children and Society* (1996) (deploying social science data to support the natural law view that husband-wife marriage-with-kids is best for all concerned, especially husbands and children).

[b] See Margaret Brinig, *From Contract to Covenant: Beyond the Law and Economics of the Family* (2000).

Fineman's critique of the liberalized but still sexual family; if marriage were retained as a state form, Rose's model could also support its extension to same-sex couples and plural relationships (polygamy).

- Other *feminist* theorists (Chapter 4, Section 2B) appreciate Professor Fineman's critique of women's dilemmas under our current liberal regime, *e.g.*, Robin West, *Marriage, Sexuality, and Gender* (2007), but many are skeptical of her proposed solution. Even liberal feminists are reluctant to rest women's interests so much on contract and property law, and are skeptical that the state would subsidize caregiving relationships without unacceptable strings attached. The primary feminist criticism of this kind of proposal is that it risks locking women into caregiving relationships and denying them other possibilities for their lives, including work outside the home.[c]

- Critical *race* theories and theories of *intersectionality* (Chapter 3, Section 2C) welcome Professor Fineman's attention to the many ways that marriage has been used to pathologize relationships among people of color and single-parent households, including the infamous "welfare mother" demonized in the 1980s.[d] But critical race theory would argue that this demonization has deeper causes than Fineman recognizes—not just patriarchy, but also racism and class biases. As Professor M.M. Slaughter argues, the stigmatization of the single welfare mother (of color) is a complicated fantasy created to obscure the inequalities wrought by a racially selective capitalism.[e] If that is correct, Fineman's proposal will do nothing to undermine the ideological conditions for the oppression of women of color, poor women, and women with children. Experience with race in America suggests there will be no panacea, but communities of color can be models for extended family options such as

---

[c] See Miriam Johnson, "Life Course: Stages and Institutions," 24 *Contemp. Soc.* 653 (1995); Judith Stacey, "Book Review," 22 *Signs* 231 (1996) (arguing that "feminists cannot afford a family reform strategy that makes men's interests in and responsibilities to children, families, or even fetuses substantially at odds with women's"). Compare Joan Williams, "Gender Wars: Selfless Mothers in the Republic of Choice," 66 *N.Y.U. L. Rev.* 1559 (1991) (resisting the idea that women "prefer" motherhood and nurturing more than men do), with Linda Lacey, "As American as Parenthood and Apple Pie: Neutered Mothers, Breadwinning Fathers, and Welfare Rhetoric," 82 *Cornell L. Rev.* 79 (1996) (book review of Fineman) (appreciative critique of both Williams and Fineman).

[d] Dorothy Roberts, "The Unrealized Power of Mother," 5 *Colum. J. Gender & L.* 141 (1995) (suggesting a "symbiotic relationship" between Fineman's critique of the patriarchy underlying social demonization of single welfare mothers and Roberts' critique of the racism underlying that demonization)

[e] M.M. Slaughter, "Fantasies: Single Mothers and Welfare Reform," 95 *Colum. L. Rev.* 2156 (1995) (book review of Fineman, *Neutered Mother*).

child-rearing by grandparents when parents have been incapacitated.[f]

- *Social constructionist* thinkers such as Michel Foucault and Judith Butler (Chapter 3, Section 3A) would consider state regulatory efforts as having important constructive features; you might consider what you are *normalizing* when you construct a regulatory regime. Even if you reject marriage because it normalizes traditional gender roles, you might be open to other forms of state recognition in order to normalize interpersonal commitment. Or you might reject those other forms if you believe the state should not be privileging lifetime commitments between any two people (for example, because such forms privatize the social costs of intimate life). In particular, social constructionists are concerned that the marriage monopoly seeks to *standardize* people's relationships, but might be open to state recognition of a variety of relationship forms.[g]

- *Deconstructive* thinkers like Professor Eve Kosofsky Sedgwick (Chapter 3, Section 3B) would consider the ways in which different regulatory forms—from marriage to contract—can be deployed to create double binds for sexual and gender minorities. For example, gay people have been demonized both because they are believed psychologically incapable of forming committed relationships (an anti-gay *minoritizing* move) *and* because their relationships if socially or even legally recognized might infect or soil straight people's children and maybe even their marriages (an anti-gay *universalizing* move). Consider the deeper lessons Sedgwick's theory might have for thinking about Fineman's critique. *Marriage* itself assumes a dynamic relationship between advancing each individual's personal happiness, on the one hand, and advancing social welfare, on the other. Fineman argues that, from women's perspectives, the latter (to the extent that it occurs) sacrifices the interests of the former. Some critics would flip Fineman's concerns and reclaim the notion, advanced by theorists as diverse as Pope Benedict XVI and Gary Becker, that marriage has social advantages that justify personal sacrifices.

---

[f]   *See* Catherine Goodman & Merril Silverstein, "Grandmothers Raising Grandchildren: Family Structure and Well-Being in Culturally Diverse Families," 42 *Gerontologist* 676 (2002).

[g]   *See* Nancy D. Polikoff, *Beyond Gay (and Straight) Marriage: Valuing All Families Under the Law* (2008).

SECTION 1

THE PRIVATIZATION OF FAMILY LAW

In the nineteenth and most of the twentieth century, family law in the United States (and most of the western world) was centered upon the institution of *marriage*. Becoming a spouse was an important legal as well as social event in the lives of most Americans because of the many marriage-based common law and statutory rules:

- **Marriage Monopoly.** Government policy itself pressured Americans to marry: sexual activities outside of marriage (fornication, adultery, sexual cohabitation) were serious crimes, and children born outside of marriage were subject to legal as well as social discriminations. Conversely, the state conferred significant benefits upon married couples, ranging from decisionmaking default rules to spousal privileges. With the rise of the administrative state, there were even more material consequences contingent on marriage. Most were positive, though some welfare programs effectively carried a marriage penalty.

- **Lifetime Commitment.** Once a husband and wife were married, it was usually for life; divorce was unavailable in some states during the nineteenth century, and when it was available "fault" (typically adultery) had to be shown. Most social scientists believe that the difficulty of divorce had tangible effects on the duration of marriages by reinforcing or even increasing the social pressure to remain married.

- **Unitive Status.** The social and legal standing of women, in particular, were driven by their marital status. Through most of the nineteenth century, wives had many fewer legal rights than unmarried women. Even after the end of "coverture" (under which wives had few legal contract or property rights independent of those exercised by their husbands) and women's securing the right to vote (1920), the law for most of the twentieth century treated married women as second-class citizens. Common law barred a married woman from creating a legal domicile separate from that of her husband, which made it difficult for her to receive government benefits, vote, run for political office, or obtain a divorce if she in fact lived apart from her husband.

America's family law "constitution" was largely a product of the foregoing common law rules relating to family formation. The last third of the twentieth century witnessed a revolution in America's constitution of the family.

Jana Singer, "The Privatization of Family Law"

1992 *Wisconsin Law Review* 1443, 1447–53, 1456–59,
1460–64, 1470–71, 1478–79.*

Over the past twenty-five years, family law has become increasingly privatized. In virtually all doctrinal areas, private norm creation and private decision making have supplanted state-imposed rules and structures for governing family-related behavior. * * *

Perhaps the most significant way the law traditionally regulated intimate behavior was by distinguishing sharply, in virtually all important contexts, between married persons and persons in nonmarital intimate relationships. Through laws criminalizing adultery, fornication and nonmarital cohabitation, the law carved out marriage as the only legitimate arena for sexual intercourse. Tort causes of action for enticement, alienation of affections and criminal conversation penalized third parties who intentionally interfered with the marriage relationship; loss of consortium claims protected husbands (and later wives) against those who negligently impaired marital relations. No similar doctrines protected nonmarital intimate relationships from deliberate or negligent third party impairment.

An elaborate network of statutes and common law doctrines also distinguished sharply between children born within marriage and those born outside of it. * * * Similarly, state and federal programs designed to compensate families for the death or disability of a wage-earner typically excluded out-of-wedlock children as eligible beneficiaries. A major justification for these sharp distinctions between marital and nonmarital children was to protect the exclusivity of the marital unit and to punish adults (particularly women) who engaged in sex outside of marriage.

A series of Supreme Court decisions between 1968 and 1983 eliminated as unconstitutional most of the categorical legal distinctions between marital and nonmarital children.[11] These decisions explicitly rejected the traditional notion that differential treatment of legitimate and illegitimate offspring was justified as a way of encouraging matrimony and of expressing society's "condemnation of irresponsible liaisons beyond the bonds of marriage." A related series of Supreme Court decisions established that unmarried fathers who develop a relationship with their children must be given the same rights with respect to adoption and custody decisions as are accorded to married fathers.[13]

---

*   Copyright Wisconsin Law Review. Reprinted with permission.

[11]   Between 1968 and 1983, the Supreme Court decided more than 20 cases involving statutory classifications based on illegitimacy. [Citing cases, starting with *Levy v. Louisiana*, 391 U.S. 68 (1968), and *Stanley v. Illinois*, 405 U.S. 645 (1972).]

[13]   See *Stanley v. Illinois*, 405 U.S. 645 (1972); *Caban v. Mohammed*, 441 U.S. 380 (1979). Unwed fathers who have not developed a parent-child relationship need not be accorded such

These judicial declarations were paralleled and reinforced by the Uniform Parentage Act, promulgated in 1973 and approved by the American Bar Association in 1974. The Act abandons the concept of legitimacy and declares that "[t]he parent and child relationship extends equally to every child and to every parent, regardless of the marital status of the parents." * * *

Another way the law traditionally privileged marriage over nonmarital intimate relationships was by denying unmarried cohabitants access to the judicial system for resolving financial disputes arising out of their relationship. In particular, contracts between unmarried cohabitants that related in any way to their sexual relationship were considered unenforceable as contrary to public policy. The rationale for this traditional rule was that the law should not "lend its aid to either party to a contract founded upon an illegal or immoral consideration."

Over the past fifteen years, this traditional rule has eroded significantly. The erosion began with the celebrated *Marvin* case [Part B of this section], in which an ex-cohabitant claimed that she had given up a promising acting career in order to become a full-time homemaker and companion; in return, she claimed, her unmarried partner had agreed to support her financially for the rest of her life. The California Supreme Court, reversing the dismissal of the plaintiff's complaint, ruled that such an agreement between unmarried cohabitants was enforceable unless it explicitly stated that the consideration for one partner's financial support was the other partner's meretricious sexual services. The mere connection between an unmarried couple's sexual relationship and their financial arrangements was no longer enough to invalidate their cohabitation agreement. The *Marvin* court also suggested that, aside from the plaintiff's contract claim, she might be entitled to a share of the property accumulated during the couple's cohabitation relationship under equitable theories such as constructive trust, quantum meruit and resulting trust.

In the decade that followed *Marvin*, courts in many states applied both express and implied contract remedies to resolve disputes about property and financial arrangements arising out of cohabitation relationships. In doing so, courts largely abandoned public policy objections to enforcing the private agreements of parties engaged in sexual relationships outside of marriage. A few courts have reached beyond contract in resolving cohabitation disputes, and have applied principles of partnership law or have reasoned by analogy to state marital property division statutes. Consistent with the modern emphasis on private ordering, however, most courts have been unwilling to grant nonagreement-based support rights to unmarried cohabitants or to

---

similar treatment. *Lehr v. Robertson*, 463 U.S. 248 (1983); *Quillin v. Walcott*, 434 U.S. 246 (1978). [**Eds.** See also *Nguyen v. INS*, 533 U.S. 53 (2001) and notes, Chapter 1.]

extend statutory divorce obligations, such as the payment of attorneys' fees.

Although courts have shown an increased willingness to enforce the private commitments made by unmarried cohabitants to each other, they have been somewhat more reluctant to expand the rights of unmarried cohabitants vis-a-vis third parties. The California Supreme Court recently refused to extend the logic of *Marvin* to support a claim for intentional infliction of emotional distress brought by an unmarried cohabitant who had witnessed the tortious injury and death of his partner. Similarly, only a few courts have extended to nonmarital partners the common-law right of a married person to recover for loss of a spouse's consortium, and each of these decisions has been brought into question by later developments.

Unmarried cohabitants have also had mixed success in qualifying for statutory benefits traditionally reserved for married couples. In some situations, unmarried cohabitants have benefitted from federal and state statutes, such as the Equal Credit Opportunity Act, which prohibit discrimination based on marital status. In addition, at least one state has explicitly amended its worker's compensation statute to provide relief for the death of a nonmarital partner, and courts in several other states have construed existing worker's compensation laws to provide statutory benefits to dependent cohabitants. Courts in other states, however, have refused to extend such benefits to nonmarital partners, relying on a strict construction of statutory terms such as "spouse" and "family." Courts have also reached inconsistent results on whether an unmarried cohabitant who quits her job to relocate with her partner qualifies for unemployment benefits that would be available to a spouse in similar circumstances. * * *

The shift from public to private control over the definition and structure of family relationships extends as well to control over the consequences of marital status. Traditionally, the law underscored the public nature of marriage by defining for all participants the salient aspects of the marriage bond, particularly the legal and economic relationship between spouses. Although marriage has often been described as a civil contract, until recently it was the state, and not the parties, that set the terms of this contract. Parties could choose whether to enter into marriage, but they could not define the terms of their union. As the Supreme Court explained in *Maynard v. Hill* [125 U.S. 190, 211 (1888)]:

[Marriage] is something more than a mere contract. The consent of the parties is of course essential to its existence, but when the contract to marry is executed by the marriage, a relation between the parties is created which they cannot change. Other contracts may be modified, restricted, or enlarged, or entirely released upon the consent of the parties. Not so with marriage. The relation once formed, the law steps in and holds the parties to various obligations and liabilities.

The state-imposed terms of the traditional marriage contract were both hierarchical and rigidly gender-based. The husband, as head of household, was responsible for the financial support of his wife and children. The wife, as the domestic partner, was responsible for providing household services, including housework, sex and childcare. This compulsory gender-based division of labor persisted well into the 1960s, as did the inability of spouses to alter in any binding way the legal and economic incidents of marriage.

* * * Courts sometimes refused to enforce agreements between husbands and wives on the ground that these agreements lacked the consideration necessary to support a binding contract. Courts also made liberal use of factual and legal presumptions to deny enforcement of agreements between husbands and wives. Although a wife's performance of services outside the scope of her usual domestic duties could, in theory, constitute valid consideration for her husband's return promise of compensation, courts often presumed that such extraordinary services by a wife were intended to be gratuitous and, hence, not in exchange for pay or other compensation. * * *

Over the past twenty-five years, the law has loosened its control over the legal and economic incidents of marriage in three related ways. First, the state-imposed marriage contract is a far less comprehensive or precise instrument than it was a generation or two ago. In particular, the reciprocal rights and obligations of spouses are both less well-defined and less extensive than they were in previous generations. Second, individual couples today have considerably more freedom than in the past to vary by private agreement what little remains of the state-imposed marriage contract. Third, the law increasingly treats marriage partners as individuals, rather than as a single merged unit, for purposes of doctrinal analysis.

The modern trend in favor of sex-based equality has eliminated many of the explicitly gender-based terms of the traditional marriage contract. A wife is no longer required to assume her husband's surname or to accede to his choice of domicile. Wives are not automatically entitled to their husbands' financial support, nor husbands to their wives' domestic services. In most community property states, laws that previously gave husbands the right to manage and control community property during marriage have been repealed or replaced by statutes providing for joint management by both spouses. * * *

Even where state-imposed marital obligations remain as the background legal regime, spouses today have considerable freedom to alter those background obligations by private contract, either before or during marriage. For example, the Uniform Premarital Agreement Act, which has been adopted by sixteen states since its promulgation in 1983, authorizes prospective spouses to contract with each other with respect to their property rights and support obligations, as well as "any other matter, including their personal rights and obligations, not in violation of public policy or a statute imposing a criminal penalty." The commentary explains that this provision is meant to cover such matters as the choice of abode, the freedom to pursue career opportunities and the upbringing of children. Similarly, while the Second Restatement of Contracts continues to disapprove of marital contracts that would change an essential incident of marriage "in a way detrimental to the public interest in the marriage relationship," the Restators' comments make clear that both the essential incidents of marriage and the public's interest in the marriage relationship are to be interpreted more narrowly than in the past. Several states have also amended their domestic relations laws to facilitate enforcement of a broad range of spousal contracts concerning the economic aspects of marriage.

While much private contracting between persons in or contemplating marriage concerns rights and obligations in the event of divorce, there are indications that the law is becoming more receptive to enforcing private agreements that relate to the structure of an ongoing marriage. Moreover, wholly apart from enforcement by courts, many scholars, marriage counselors and manuals urge couples to use contracts or contract-like structures to govern the details of their relationship. Indeed, an entire body of literature has developed around "contracting" as a tool of marriage and family counseling. These practitioners not only contract with their clients about the goals and methods of therapy; they also initiate contracting processes between spouses as part of marital counseling, reconciliation or divorce preparation. Although the "contracts" that result from these processes generally are not legally enforceable, the counselors' use of contract terminology is intentional and significant. In particular, "the contract label dramatizes the preference for private ordering over the intrusion of outside norms as the basis for choices about life-styles."

A third way in which the state has ceded control over the legal and economic incidents of marriage is by treating married persons as individuals, rather than as a merged unit, for purposes of legal analysis. Traditionally, the common law treated married persons not as individuals, but as a single legal entity. Marriage stripped a woman of her independent legal existence and merged it into that of her husband; she became a "femme couvert," literally "a woman under cover" of her husband. This notion of marital merger had far-reaching legal consequences in a wide variety of doctrinal areas. Because husbands and wives were considered one, they could neither contract with nor sue each other. Nor could spouses testify for or against each other in civil or criminal proceedings. As the legal representatives of their wives, husbands were considered responsible for any torts their wives committed. * * * More generally, the legal fiction that the husband and wife were a single entity was one of the rationales that supported the law's traditional refusal to recognize marital rape or to provide remedies for victims of spousal violence.

* * * [T]he trend in most areas of law today is to view married persons as two separate individuals, rather than as a single unit, for purposes of legal analysis. Since 1971, at least twenty-five states have abolished interspousal tort immunity, thus allowing spouses to sue each other for negligent and other tortious behavior. Judicial decisions abrogating the immunity have explicitly rejected the argument that the doctrine is justified as a means of preserving marital harmony. Even those jurisdictions that continue to recognize some aspects of interspousal immunity, disclaim reliance on the notion of marital unity. The increased ability of spouses to contract with each other is similarly grounded in the notion of married persons as separate individuals, with potentially disparate interests.

Changes in the laws of evidence and the doctrines governing criminal responsibility also reflect the legal individuation of the married couple. The common law rule that a husband and wife could not make up the two parties necessary to constitute a conspiracy has been abolished in virtually all jurisdictions. In 1980, the Supreme Court abolished a criminal defendant's privilege against adverse spousal testimony, noting that the ancient foundations for so sweeping a privilege—including the denial to women of a separate legal identity—had long since disappeared.[89] The marital rape exemption has been abolished or narrowed in many jurisdictions.[90] Virtually all states have enacted or strengthened civil and criminal statutes designed to protect victims of domestic violence.

[Professor Singer observes that entry into marriage is still restricted by the states on the basis of age (parental consent usually required for people under age 18), consanguinity (cannot marry relatives), and bigamy (one spouse at a time). Other restrictions have been repealed or even invalidated by the Supreme Court's right to marry cases. Gone are laws prohibiting marriages that involve people with mental or physical disabilities (in some states these marriages can still be annulled by the parties), interracial couples, people with a contagious disease, or paupers. Couples "have substantially more freedom than did their counterparts a generation ago to determine whether and under what circumstances they will wed, and to effectuate their choice of marriage partner." There are also fewer and simpler formal prerequisites imposed by the state; states do not require a religious ceremony anymore, for example.]

---

[89] *Trammel v. United States*, 445 U.S. 40, 52 (1980). Under *Trammel*, the privilege is vested in the witness spouse; a witness spouse may choose not to testify but a defendant can no longer prevent his spouse from voluntarily testifying against him. *Id.* at 53.

[90] See, e.g., *People v. Liberta*, 474 N.E.2d 567, 573–76 (N.Y. 1984); *Shunn v. State*, 742 P.2d 775, 778 (Wyo. 1987); *State v. Smith*, 426 A.2d 38 (N.J. 1981). For examples of legislative abolishment of the exemption, see Colo. Rev. Stat. ch. 18–3–409 (Supp. 1989); Me. Rev. Stat. Ann. tit. 17A, § 251 (1983 & Supp. 1989); id. § 252 (1983) (repealed 1989); Neb. Rev. Stat. §§ 28–319 to 320 (1985); N.J. Stat. Ann. § 2C:14–5(b) (West 1982); N.D. Cent. Code § 12.1–20–01 to 03 (1985 & Supp. 1989); Or. Rev. Stat. § 163.335 (1971) (repealed 1977); Vt. Stat. Ann. tit. 13, § 3252 (Supp.1989); Wis. Stat. Ann. § 940.225(6) (West Supp.1989).

The shift from public to private ordering of marriage has been accompanied by the privatization of divorce and its financial consequences. Until the late 1960s, American law recognized no such thing as a consensual or privately-ordered divorce. Rather, statutes in each state established specific grounds for terminating a marriage. Most of these grounds required the spouse seeking a divorce to prove to a court that her partner had committed a marital offense and that she was innocent of marital fault. Thus, divorce was not the recognition of a private decision to terminate a marriage; it was a privilege granted by the state to an innocent spouse against a guilty one. * * *

The model of divorce as a state-bestowed remedy for an innocent spouse began eroding long before the formal adoption of no-fault divorce statutes. The adoption of these statutes, however, signaled an important shift in the legal paradigm governing divorce. The state, in essence, abandoned its role as the moral arbiter of marital behavior. In particular, the state "washed its hands" of attempting to determine when the goal of providing relief to an innocent spouse outweighed the strong public interest in preserving marriage. With the adoption of no-fault divorce statutes, the state ceded to the spouses themselves—and often to one spouse acting unilaterally—the authority to make this judgment. Thus, under no-fault divorce, the decision to end a marriage generally rests on unreviewed private judgment; the state's role is diminished to one of solemnization and recording, akin to its role in marital licensing. * * *

[The advent of no-fault divorce also initiated a process by which the state reduced its supervision of the terms on which the parties parted. Not only were separation agreements routinely enforced by the courts, but so were prenuptial agreements. See the Uniform Premarital Agreement Act (1983), which provided for enforcement of such agreements unless fraudulent or unconscionable. In order to invalidate a premarital agreement on grounds of unconscionability, an objecting party must show that he or she (i) was not provided a fair and reasonable disclosure of the other party's assets or obligations; (ii) did not waive disclosure; and (iii) did not have an adequate knowledge of the other party's assets or finances. Singer observes that in Western Europe, which has also seen significant liberation of the terms of divorce, judges are much more active in reviewing the terms of separation and divorce decrees, especially to prevent hardship to a vulnerable party or to the children.]

[Professor Singer demonstrates how the privatization of family law coincides with other developments in public law. Most notable is the gender equality revolution, which has rendered problematic any formal requirements that discriminate on the basis of sex or (sometimes) that rest upon traditional gender stereotypes. See *Orr v. Orr*, 440 U.S. 268 (1979), which invalidated state laws which impose alimony payments only on husbands and not on wives. Also, the Supreme Court's right to privacy jurisprudence has focused on individuals, rather than the marriage unit, as the possessors of legal entitlements. Professor Singer also notes how economic analysis has seeped into family law; this reflects a change in perceptions, from the family as separate and alien from the market, to the family as a setting in which "exchange" like behavior is common and expected.]

William N. Eskridge Jr., "Family Law Pluralism: The Guided-Choice Regime of Menus, Default Rules, and Override Rules," 100 *Geo. L.J.* 1881, 1887–90 (2012). This article updates Professor Singer's account of family law privatization. The biggest development since the publication of Professor Singer's article has been the almost complete collapse of the traditional monopoly marriage enjoyed as a situs for sexual relations and the creation of increasingly detailed regulatory regimes to govern nonmarital couples. Since 1982, virtually all states have repealed or nullified their laws against fornication and sexual cohabitation, and most have abandoned their adultery laws as well. Not only can couples cohabit rather than marry, but a wide array of laws and judicial decisions (not just the *Marvin* line discussed in Professor Singer's article) provide a regulatory regime for cohabiting couples.

Professor Eskridge offers an economics-based framework for understanding the enormous regulatory shift that has occurred. Thus, "family law in the last century has abandoned many of its longstanding rules prohibiting specified conduct and refusing to recognize many relationships. The dramatic decline of these kinds of rules has opened up new legal choices for romantic couples. Consistent with the traditionalist account, the state continues to regulate those choices—but more gently, through off-the-rack baselines that couples may modify according to rules that inform, guide, and sometimes inhibit their decision making. To use Dan Kahan's felicitous terminology, the state has moved away from 'hard shoves' in family law, toward a 'gentle nudges' approach to regulation.[a]

"This gentle nudges approach to family law reflects a larger normative shift in this country—away from the natural law norm of procreative marriage and strongly toward the utilitarian norm that emphasizes individual flourishing and the value of family for both partners as well as children they are rearing. The natural law approach to families emphasizes the virtues of a single institution—procreative marriage—and encourages or pressures everyone to join this institution. The country long ago moved beyond this approach and has steadily moved toward a utilitarian approach that seeks to maximize overall happiness of all the participants. The utilitarian approach accommodates our social pluralism in family formation, such that the state recognizes a variety of family institutions, each tailored to different circumstances

---

[a] Dan Kahan, "Gentle Nudges vs. Hard Shoves: Solving the Sticky Norms Problem," 67 *U. Chi. L. Rev.* 607, 608 (2000); see Carl Schneider, "The Channeling Function in Family Law," 20 *Hofstra L. Rev.* 495 (1992) (modern family law recognizes private choices but also channels them into socially productive directions).

and preferences. As the marriage-equality debate reveals, the natural law understanding has not disappeared—but the triumph of the more modern perspective is revealed when natural law enthusiasts * * * make their public appeals in largely utilitarian terms.

"An important idea that has driven the transformation of family law toward expanded choices for adult relationships has been an increasing social, political, and constitutional recognition of sexual satisfaction as a human good and, for most people, a necessary component of a flourishing life. As traditional taboos against interracial and homosexual activities have eased, so has the notion that everyone must get married in lifetime commitments. Law's response to this phenomenon has been to abandon its exclusive focus on marriage and to reconsider the legal parameters of that institution. Changes in the law have been both deregulatory and regulatory. Legal reforms to marriage law have permitted more choices by sexually active Americans, while at the same time creating new nonmarital regulatory regimes for these Americans.

"Recall the clash between the traditionalist and libertarian approaches to the marriage-equality debate: the former insists on state-enforced norms to influence family choices, while the other emphasizes a prochoice contract law approach. [T]his Article shows how these different perspectives are not entirely at odds. Specifically, I shall analyze family law's expanded-choice revolution through the analytical prism of contract theory developed by Ian Ayres and others.[b] The regulatory punch line is that American law has moved toward a *guided-choice* approach to family formation: the state imposes few rules absolutely barring a person from becoming involved in a romantic (that is, sexual) relationship with the person of her choice, but the state does guide the romantic decision makers. Guidance is provided by (1) background rules that must be consciously overridden by the couple's affirmative choice, (2) rules and procedures that require deliberation before the couple make particular choices, and (3) state-provided incentives—as well as by rules that protect the interests of vulnerable persons, especially children.

"In the argot of contract theory, family law has always been a mixture of *mandatory rules* and *default rules*. Mandatory rules are those that cannot be contracted around by private persons and corporations. In 1911, for example, states' mandatory rules criminalizing sexual activities outside of marriage (fornication and sexual cohabitation) created a marriage monopoly for procreative sexual activities. Default rules are those that romantic couples can contract around; starting in the mid-twentieth century, for example, some states decriminalized fornication and, to a lesser extent, adultery. The default in those states was still no sexual activities, but that default was easily overridden if both adult participants consented. Today, almost all states have repealed their laws

---

[b] See Ian Ayres, "Regulating Opt Out: An Economic Theory of Altering Rules," 121 *Yale L.J.* (2012); Ian Ayres & Robert Gertner, "Filling Gaps in Incomplete Contracts: An Economic Theory of Default Rules," 99 Yale L.J. 87 (1989).

criminalizing fornication and nonmarital sexual cohabitation. In effect, a mandatory rule has been replaced by a default rule. In contrast, there are still mandatory rules barring public sexual activities or sex with minors; consent of both persons who engaged in sex does not override these mandatory rules.

"Family law's default rules have been accompanied by what I call *override rules*. Override rules * * * are the legal steps or requirements that the parties must follow or meet to override a legal default. After the state decriminalization of fornication and sexual cohabitation, the override rule allowing sexual activities was very lenient. Unless one of the participants was a minor or mentally disabled, the formal override rule was consent by both participants. In the last generation, the override rule has become more stringent because of feminist complaints that the traditional rule frequently allowed intercourse that a woman did not meaningfully agree to. So today, the default is often not overridden if one participant is in a position of authority over the other, even though the other participant formally agrees to sexual activities. This illustrates how override rules are often the primary mode of regulation in the modern regulatory state.

"Contract law offers another regulatory concept that helps us understand the guided-choice approach and the evolution of family law in the last century: *menus*. Just as the state offers contracting parties different menus of off-the-rack rules that they can easily opt into, so the state might offer romantic couples varying menus, each consisting of different mandatory, default, and override rules. The concept of a menu is, in fact, the most powerful regulatory concept for understanding the guided-choice approach and for seeing how it is both strongly prochoice yet at the same time may be strongly regulatory.

"To be specific, American family law in the last century has moved *away from* a monopolistic regime where marriage—with its hundreds of legal entitlements, requirements, and defaults—was the only item on the menu, and it has moved *toward* a pluralist regime where each state offers a larger menu of options for romantic couples, including those with children. Among the regimes offered by the expanding menu, American family law in the last century has moved *away from* regimes dominated by mandatory rules, such as rules against sex outside of marriage, and it has moved *toward* regimes dominated by default rules with override requirements, some of which are quite stringent.

"The menu-default-override analysis of family law has the great virtue of making sense of the legal revolution in the last generation and tying together in a useful way the deregulatory and new regulatory features of family law. It also provides a framework for the normative questions that will be important for the future of family law: What relationships ought to be included in the topic of 'family law'? What regulatory menus should be offered to relationship partners? In each menu, what ought to be the default rules and what ought to be the override rules available to partners opting into those menus? Should there be mandatory rules as well?"

NOTES ON THE DEINSTITUTIONALIZATION OF MARRIAGE: CAUSE FOR CONCERN? WHAT CAN BE DONE?

The law described by Professors Singer and Eskridge both reflects and may have contributed to the changing face of American families. The big news is that the marriage rate has steadily declined in the last two generations. A Pew Research Center study of 2010 Census data found the percent of married households had declined from 72% in 1960 to 58.5% in 1990 to 50.5% in 2010. The marriage rate has declined even in this millennium: the marriage rate has dropped from 8.2 marriages per 1,000 people in 2000 to 6.9 in 2014. This trend has disproportionately been driven in recent years by non-college-educated adults: although adults with and without college degrees married at similar rates in 1960, in 2010 64% of adults with college degrees were married while fewer than half of adults without college degrees were married. See D'vera Cohn et al., "Barely Half of U.S. Adults Are Married—A Record Low," *Pew Research Center*, Dec. 14, 2011.

Marriage is no longer the universal norm in the United States; there are almost as many nonmarital relationships as marital unions. This trend is what sociologists call the *deinstitutionalization* of marriage. Along the lines of Ross and Rapp (Chapter 3, Section 3C), consider ways that the privatization of family law may interact with people's sex lives and their thinking about sexuality in ways that produce a diversification in the forms and norms of intimate adult relationships.

1.   *The Decline of Marriage and an Erosion in Human Happiness?* Several legal developments outlined in the previous excerpts might contribute to the decline of marriage as a monopoly institution. By decriminalizing sex outside of marriage and eliminating most penalties against nonmarital children, legal reform has removed some of the important incentives for people to get married. Arguably, this has contributed to declining rates of marriage. By making divorce available without proof of fault and, often, at the behest of just one of the partners, the no-fault divorce revolution of the 1960s and 1970s may have contributed to the higher divorce rate the country has seen since 1969. *See, e.g.*, Allen Parkman, *Good Intentions Gone Awry: No-Fault Divorce and the American Family* (2000); Jonathan Gruber, "Is Making Divorce Easier Bad for Children? The Long-Run Implications of Unilateral Divorce," 22 *J. Lab. Econ.* 799 (2004). But see Justin Wolfers, "Did Unilateral No-Fault Divorce Raise Divorce Rates? A Reconciliation and New Results," 96 *Am. Econ. Rev.* 1802 (2006) (raising methodological questions about studies finding a significant effect).

Critics of marriage liberalization emphasize the personal, health, and economic advantages they maintain accrue uniquely to married people and their children. See David Popenoe, *Life Without Father: Compelling New Evidence that Fatherhood and Marriage Are Indispensable for the Good of Children and Society* (1996); Linda Waite & Maggie Gallagher, *The Case for*

Marriage: Why Married People Are Happier, Healthier, and Better Off Financially (2000). The authors of these studies may overstate the causal claims supported by their evidence; because of *selection bias*, their empirical showing of correlation between the happiness or well-being of people and the fact that they are married does not establish causation (i.e., these people would have been less happy or well-off if they had remained unmarried).[c] But they make a point that most Americans want to believe: Marriage is not only what God wants for us, but it is good for our health, too. Further, a recent study controlled for pre-marital well-being and found that married couples did tend to be happier, indicating a possible causal relationship. John Helliwell & Shawn Grover, "How's Life at Home? New Evidence on Marriage and the Set Points for Happiness," *NBER*, Dec. 2014.

The new privatized family law also contributes to the delinking of sex and procreation. With surrogacy and artificial insemination, pregnancy is now possible without sex. With contraception (*Griswold*) and abortion (*Roe*), sex is now possible without serious risk of having children. These developments might contribute to an ever greater focus on the pleasurable or sociable qualities of sex. (This is a far cry from the eighteenth century, when public discourse about sex focused overwhelmingly on its procreative purpose.) Like other pleasurable things, sex might then be viewed as a luxury good, obtainable whenever and wherever the mood strikes. Is this good? For a critique of the law's tendency to "commodify" intangibles and thereby degrade social goods, see Margaret Jane Radin, "Market-Inalienability," 100 *Harv. L. Rev.* 1849 (1987). For a defense of hedonic flourishing as more than a luxury, see Carole S. Vance, "Towards a Politics of Sexuality," in *Pleasure and Danger: Exploring Female Sexuality* (1984).

2. *The Consequences of Non-Marital Families for Children.* The phenomena noted above have created an unprecedented number of families where children are raised in what once were considered atypical households. With more sex outside of marriage and the removal of stigmas for children born outside of wedlock, more children are born out of wedlock and there is less social pressure for the parents to marry. According to a Pew Research Center analysis of 2014 American Community Survey data, 46% of children now live with two parents in their first marriage—down from 61% in 1980. And 62% of children live with married parents (including those in a

---

[c]   Here is the selection bias problem with the studies cited in the text: married men might earn more money or be healthier because men with higher earning potential and better health are more attractive mates and therefore more likely to get married—rather than because marriage turns the ordinary schlump into an economic dynamo. *See* Paula England, "Three Reviews on Marriage," 30 *Contemp. Soc.* 564 (2001); *see also* Scott Coltrane, "Scientific Half-Truths and Postmodern Parody in the Family Values Debate," 26 *Contemp. Soc.* 7 (1997) (the new family values literature presents a disturbingly unscientific approach to evidence). James Q. Wilson responds to the selection-bias charge: "But the evidence strongly suggests that self-selection is not the key factor. No matter how men become unmarried—by being bachelors, becoming separated or divorced, or becoming widowers—they lose ground in terms of health." Wilson, "The Case for Marriage," *Nat'l Rev.*, Oct. 9, 2000, at 49. Even if these facts were true (which remains unsettled), one would expect selection to account for the first (bachelors) and the terrible effects of separation, divorce, and death to account for the latter three. On the uncertain state of the empirical evidence, see Clare Huntington, *Failure to Flourish: How Law Undermines Family Relationships* 30–43 (2014).

remarriage); in 1980, 77% of children did. Finally, 7% now live with parents who are cohabiting.

Many lesbian and gay couples raise children and are a growing feature of the family landscape. According to the 2013 American Community Survey, more than 25% of married same-sex couples and 19% of unmarried same-sex couples are raising children under age 18—more than 120,000 households. See Gary Gates, "Demographics of Married and Unmarried Same-sex Couples," *Williams Institute*, 2015.

Even if married when children are born, American parents often do not stay together, and their children are usually then raised by one parent. The high divorce rate means that even children born within marriage are often raised outside of it, usually by one parent (unless she or he remarries). Today, single parents (usually mothers) constitute about one-third of the households with children. Put simply, "fewer than half (46%) of U.S. kids younger than 18 . . . are living in a home with two married heterosexual parents in their first marriage"—the "traditional" household. Gretchen Livingston, "Fewer than half of U.S. kids today live in a 'traditional' family," *Pew Research Center*, Dec. 2014.

What is the effect on children? Most experts believe that divorce usually has a bad effect on children. The leading study is Judith Wallerstein, Julia Lewis & Sandra Blakeslee, *The Unexpected Legacy of Divorce: The 25 Year Landmark Study* (2000), who report that when parents divorce the world of their children is altered in deleterious and sometimes devastating ways; the children of divorced parents, they found, tend to have much more difficulty establishing adult relationships.

Some commentators make a more general claim, that children raised by single mothers and nontraditional families are systematically more troubled and less achieving than children raised in nuclear families. *E.g.*, David Blankenhorn, *The Future of Marriage* (2007); Popenoe, *Life Without Father*. There is ample support for the notion that single parents face much greater difficulties rearing children than two parents working together. But, thus far, the evidence fails to support the broader assertion that traditional nuclear families are better situses for child-rearing than blended step-families, *Stepfamilies: Who Benefits? Who Does Not?* (Alan Booth & Judy Dunn eds., 1994), or lesbian families. Judith Stacey, *Brave New Families: Stories of Domestic Upheaval in Late-Twentieth-Century America* (1990). A useful source of information about children in nontraditional families is the Fragile Families Project, run by Sarah McLanahan at Princeton: http://www.fragilefamilies.princeton.edu. What many of the studies produced by the project report is that family stability (for both marital and nonmarital children) is a key factor to child outcomes.

Indeed, a recent overview concludes that children raised in "nontraditional" families (including by same-sex parents or solo mothers) fare no worse than those living with two-parent, heterosexual married parents. Susan Golumbuk, *Modern Families: Parents and Children in New Family Forms* (2015). See also Michael Rosenfeld, "Nontraditional Families and Childhood Progress Through School," *Demography*, August 2010 (noting that possible advantages of children in traditional family structures are "mostly due to their higher socioeconomic status"). Although the conventional wisdom among social scientists is that lesbian and gay couples do just as good a job rearing children as straight couples, the matter is far from settled empirically. The reason is that there is no empirical study (so far) that was able to draw a large number of families from a random sample. As in studies suggesting ill effects of divorce on children or the beneficent effects of marriage, selection effects preclude dogmatic judgments.

Nonetheless, the Supreme Court has embraced the notion that marriage protects and supports children: "Without the recognition, stability, and predictability marriage offers, children suffer the stigma of knowing their families are somehow lesser. They also suffer the significant material costs of being raised by unmarried parents, relegated to a more difficult and uncertain family life." *Obergefell v. Hodges*, 135 S. Ct. 2584, 2590 (2015). The Court in this marriage equality case also seemed to assume that lesbian and gay couples are good parents—and they would be "better" parents if they could get married.

3. *Legal Reforms Addressing the Decline of Marriage?* The evidence suggests that when parents divorce, there can be bad effects for children who suffer from the change. Although the evidence is more equivocal, there is a case to be made for the proposition that children flourish more in marital households, and a very good case for households that offer children a stable environment of two engaged parents (whether married or not). Are there legal reforms that could address negative consequences of divorce on children? Consider some very different proposals.

(A) Covenant Marriage. There is demand for good old-fashioned marriage till death do us part, where individuals give up much of their freedom and altruistically commit themselves to the good of their partners, their children, and their families. See John Witte, Jr., "Propter Honoris Respectum: The Goods and Goals of Marriage," 76 *Notre Dame L. Rev.* 1019 (2001). This advocacy is not limited to traditionalists. See, *e.g.*, Milton Regan, Jr., *Family Law and the Pursuit of Intimacy* (1993) (supporting marriage from a postmodern perspective: in an era where everything seems up for grabs, humans need stable, ongoing commitments just as much as before).

Valuing the altruistic interpersonal commitment of traditional marriage may have fueled interest in the new natural law philosophy surveyed in Chapter 3, Section 1. John Finnis and allied thinkers emphasize the non-instrumentalist virtues of marriage—the qualities that render us distinctly human (or, from a religious point of view, most in the *imago Dei* [image of God]). Natural law thinking is the primary basis for statutes in Arizona (1998), Arkansas (2001), and Louisiana (1997) that recognize *covenant marriages*. This option, which couples can choose instead of regular marriage, reflects a traditionalist rejection of marriages that can be easily entered and easily exited. See Joel Nichols, Comment, "Louisiana's Covenant Marriage Law: A First Step Toward a More Robust Pluralism in Marriage and Divorce Law?," 47 *Emory L.J.* 929 (1998). If couples opt for covenant marriage pursuant to the Arkansas Covenant Marriage Act, 2001 Ark. Acts 1486, they must participate in marriage counseling before they tie the knot, cannot divorce except for strong cause, and must accept a long waiting period before they can divorce. See also Ariz. Rev. Stat. § 25–901 et seq.; La. Ann. Code §§ 272–:275, :307–:309. Although pressed mainly by traditionalists, covenant marriage has also attracted support from utilitarian defenders such as Margaret Brinig, *From Contract to Covenant: Beyond the Law and Economics of the Family* 29–34, 110–39 (2000).

Most significantly, covenant marriage statutes have been unimpressive in practice. For one thing, they are not really a return to "traditional marriage," as they only slow down the process of divorce and do not revert to the fault regime of the pre-1969 era. Almost no one enters into covenant marriages in the jurisdictions that have adopted these statutes.

(B) Encouraging Pre-Marital Education or Pre-Divorce Counseling. Other proposals build the counseling and cooling-off requirements characteristic of covenant marriages into requirements for all marriages. Thus, state legislatures have adopted laws that explicitly encourage pre-marital education. In 1998, Florida became the first state to reduce its licensing fees (by more than 50%) after four hours of a course with a registered provider. Comparable programs (including a full license fee waiver in Georgia) have popped up in Oklahoma, Georgia, and West Virginia, among other states. In Minnesota, for instance, the fee for a marriage license drops from $115 to $40 for couples that complete twelve or more hours of premarital education classes. See Francine Russo, "Can the Government Prevent Divorce?," *The Atlantic*, Oct. 1997; see also Leslie A. Mark, "Legislative Efforts to Strengthen Marriage," Public Law Research Institute at University of California Hastings College of the Law, 2004.

Though diverse in their specific designs, these programs are motivated by evidence that premarital counseling can strengthen marriages and reduce divorce. In one effort at "community marriage," which mandated training in communication and conflict resolution for couples in certain churches, the divorce rate dropped nearly 40% in a ten-year period. Larry B. Stammer, "A Crusade to Save Marriages," *Los Angeles Times*, March 17, 1997. On the other hand, this kind of training might produce another outcome: preventing marriages in the first place. Social scientist David Olson designed a 165-part written survey to facilitate marriage counseling called PREPARE. But "10 to 15 percent of those who take PREPARE break their engagements." Russo, "Can the Government Prevent Divorce?"

A similar proposal encourages pre-divorce requirements. Dubbed the "Second Chances Act," the recommendations include a one-year waiting period before divorce and high-quality education about reconciliation. See William Doherty & Leah Ward Sears, "Second Chances: A Proposal to Reduce Unnecessary Divorce," Institute for American Values, 2011; Matthew J. Astle, "An Ounce of Prevention: Marital Counseling Laws As an Anti-Divorce Measure," 38 *Fam. L.Q.* 733, 743 (2004).

(C) Redesigning Financial and Work-Centered Social Support. A range of scholars have targeted economic incentives—some built into the tax code—that make marriage financially unattractive. "Married couples with the same joint income pay the same tax under our current system regardless of

the earnings distribution between the spouses." Mitchell L. Engler & Edward D. Stein, "Not Too Separate or Unequal: Marriage Penalty Relief After *Obergefell*," 91 *Wash. L. Rev.* 1073 (2016). The system imposes costs on low-income couples that, in relative terms, are much greater than those experienced by couples with higher incomes. Many have suggested simple tax remedies, including "an option for married couples to calculate their tax on their separate earnings." Engler & Stein, 1073; see Melissa Murray & Dennis Ventry, "Eliminate the Marriage Penalty," *New York Times*, Jan. 23, 2015. Professor Eskridge has urged traditional marriage supporters to use the state tax code proactively, in a manner that would render covenant marriage more popular: reward married couples who opt into harder-to-exit marriages (such as covenant marriages) with tax credits for the children they are rearing. See Eskridge, "Family Law Pluralism."

More broadly, however, economic uncertainty and shifting employment trends may contribute to falling marriage rates and high divorce rates. Harvard sociologist Alexandra Killwald found that "[f]or marriages formed after 1975, husbands' lack of full-time employment is associated with higher risk of divorce"—a phenomenon that is, she suggests, evidence that "the husband breadwinner norm persists." Professors Cahn and Carbone have documented that marriage is holding steady for professionals, but is disappearing for working class Americans and is in peril for the middle class. With uncertain economic prospects for blue collar or unemployed males in particular, marriage does not make economic sense. June Carbone & Naomi Cahn, *Marriage Markets: How Inequality is Remaking the American Family* (2014). Like David Blankenhorn's Institute for American Values, Carbone and Cahn believe there is no solution to the deinstitutionalization of marriage without more jobs and a more equitable distribution of income in this country. *Accord,* Institute for American Values, *Marriage Opportunity: The Moment for National Action* (n.d.) (open letter diagnosing similar themes as Carbone and Cahn).

(D) Embrace Early-Marriage Separation or Divorce. In 2011, a number of Mexico City legislators suggested a civil code reform that would allow couples to decide on the length of their marriage contract, with the option to renew beginning at two years. Most of the city's divorces were happening within two years, prompting Council Member Leon Luna to push a proposal that allowed a painless separation after a trial run—but before childrearing. Apparently, the Council did not adopt the law, perhaps because the Catholic Church strongly opposed it. Would the idea of a two-year or a five-year trial marriage be a good one? Many family law experts are open to this proposal. Dr. Stephanie Coontz, Director of Research and Public Education for the Council on Contemporary Families, suggests "a reup every five years, or before every major transition in life, with a new set of vows that reflect what the couple has learned." Matt Richtel, "Till Death, or 20 Years, Do Us Part," *N.Y. Times*, September 28, 2012.

(E) Providing Birth Control Information and Contraceptives. Professors Naomi Cahn and June Carbone argue in *Red Families v. Blue Families: Legal Polarization and the Creation of Culture* (2010) that "red states" espousing traditional family values in their laws also have super-high

rates of divorce and of teenage pregnancy. These data are some indication that public law does not necessarily drive private sexual practices and family forms. Carbone and Cahn provide the following advice to red states: if you really want to encourage the formation of stable families *and* responsible childbearing, you must provide pragmatic sex education to your young people and make contraceptives available to them. The more educated and contraception-aware the state's young people are, the more likely it is that they will not have unanticipated babies when they are too young and that they will form more stable, lasting marriages when they are more mature and capable of making long-term decisions. (The elephant in the room for red states is that a liberal abortion policy would be a logical corollary of such a plan, and abortion is the *big* issue that divides red from blue states.)

(F) Plural Marriage. In a 2015 Gallup survey, 16% of Americans reported considering polygamy "morally acceptable"—up from 7% in 2001. The state of California recently ratified legislation allowing children to have more than two legal parents. 4 Cal. Fam. Code § 3040 (West 2014). Justice Scalia suggested in the *Obergefell* oral argument that the constitutional case for same-sex marriage could be reasonably extended to polygamous adults.

Plural marriage does give rise to significant concerns; it has traditionally been linked to the oppression of women and to unequal partnerships. A recent Canadian study noted "normative monogamy reduces crime rates, including rape, murder, assault, robbery and fraud, as well as decreasing personal abuses." Joseph Henrich et al., "The puzzle of monogamous marriage," 367 *Phil. Trans. R. Soc. B.* 657–69 (2012).

But "gender inequality is a contingent, not a conceptual, feature of polygamy." Cheshire Calhoun, "Who's Afraid of Polygamous Marriage? Lessons for Same-Sex Marriage Advocacy from the History of Polygamy," 42 *San Diego L. Rev.* 1023, 1039 (2005). Cornell economist Robert Frank has argued that polygamous marriage would increase competition among men and, ultimately, that "the terms of exchange would shift in favor of women. Wives would change fewer diapers, and their parents might escape paying for weddings." Robert H. Frank, "Polygamy and the Marriage Market: Who Would Have the Upper Hand?," *N.Y. Times*, Mar. 16, 2006. Other advocates note that outright bans deny both women and men the freedom to choose their ideal marital situation.

Polygyny could, in theory, benefit children and adults. Political scientist Ronald Otter notes that "[t]hree or more parental figures could be advantageous in most situations. Adolescents may benefit from having more than two adults to talk to about their lives and from whom they can receive advice." Ronald C. Den Otter, "Three May Not Be A Crowd: The Case for A Constitutional Right to Plural Marriage," 64 *Emory L.J.* 1977, 1996 (2015). And, building on the work of economist Gary Becker, additional partners could further facilitate the maximization of comparative advantage among married adults and, in turn, strengthens the partnerships.

There are many other legal fixes proposed to address the changes in marriage noted above—including explicitly feminist proposals, such as

Professor Fineman's proposal that opened this chapter. Consider some other feminist thinking on this important topic.

NOTE ON FEMINIST THINKING ABOUT PRIVATIZATION

Although initiated with substantial feminist support, experience with privatization has been mixed; many feminists are now critical of no-fault divorce as it has been implemented in the United States. Lenore Weitzman estimated that during the 1970s (when no-fault divorce was becoming the rule) the standard of living for divorced mothers fell 73%, while that of their divorced husbands increased 42%.[d] The reasons for this are apparent. Unlike a real contract regime, no-fault divorce does not realistically compensate the non-breaching party for her (or his) economic losses.[e] Women's and men's contributions to the joint marital enterprise tend to be asymmetric—women's have traditionally been frontloaded, as when the wife sacrifices her career to support the husband while in school and to raise children. So long as this traditional scenario persists, no-fault divorce will be unfair to the wife unless it realistically values her contribution to the husband's increased earning power (which usually does not happen). It also discourages partners' investment in "marriage-specific capital," like a spouse's education, as compared to individual capital (one's own work or education). See Betsey Stevenson, "The Impact of Divorce Laws on Marriage-Specific Capital," *Journal of Labor Economics*, 2007. Moreover, to the extent that wives tend to be less restless in marriage than husbands, no-fault divorce is bad because its allowance of unilateral termination empowers the husband to escape marriage without the wife's consent or, in a bargaining game, the necessity of paying her off to obtain consent.

Despite this bargaining equilibrium, no-fault divorce laws may provide benefits to some women. According to a recent study, states with no-fault divorce laws saw a 30% decline in domestic violence. Women in these states were also less likely to commit suicide under no-fault legal regimes. See Betsey Stevenson, "Is New York Ready for No-Fault Divorce?," *N.Y. Times*, June 15, 2010. Further, most divorces are initiated by wives, who are thus emboldened by no-fault divorce if and when they are the party who is ready to leave the marriage. See, *e.g.*, Liana Sayer et al., "She Left, He Left: How Employment and Satisfaction Affect Men's and Women's Decisions to Leave Marriages," *Am. J. Soc.*, 2011.

As a general matter, the parties who start off the bargaining process with fewer entitlements (often, women) will not do as well in the process of no-fault divorcing. Without highly skilled and usually expensive lawyers, they will not do as well in the courts, either. Recall Professor Carol Rose's suggestion that in a bargaining situation women will tend to fall further behind men if it is true or widely assumed that women are more cooperative

---

[d]   Leonore Weitzman, *The Divorce Revolution: The Unexpected Social and Economic Consequences for Women and Children in America* (1985); Eleanor Maccoby & Robert Mnookin, *Dividing the Child: Social and Legal Dilemmas of Custody* 260–61 (1997) (revising Weitzman's estimates downward).

[e]   *E.g.*, Jana Singer, "Alimony and Efficiency: The Gendered Costs and Benefits of the Economic Justification for Alimony," 82 *Geo. L.J.* 2423 (1994).

than men (Chapter 3, Section 2A). In either event, men will exact higher prices for their initial and continuing cooperation. In the new no-fault regime, men can unilaterally get out of marriages when they get tired, and the ease of exit fatally undermines the wife's bargaining position during the marriage if it is the case that she is more "invested" in the marriage and any children than the husband is. Notice that some and perhaps most of these problems will beset women under Professor Fineman's proposal that marriage be eliminated as a legal category; if women must rely solely on contract law as the source for their protection in sexual relationships, the Rose analysis suggests that they will be bargaining losers.

Professor Carole Pateman maintains that marriage, even as it is being reconfigured, is still gendered. What is most distinct about marriage is that it is a sexual contract, with *sexual* taking on the meaning that men have traditionally given it—"to possess and to have access to sexual property. * * * In modern patriarchy, masculinity provides the paradigm of sexuality; and masculinity means sexual mastery. The 'individual' [who enters into the 'marriage contract'] is a man who makes use of a woman's body (sexual property); the converse is much harder to imagine." Carole Pateman, *The Sexual Contract* 184–85 (1988). Pateman acknowledges that the decline of a pure status regime, where a wife was essentially the husband's property, was necessary for women's rights and, further, that feminists themselves supported no-fault divorce and other reforms that treat marriage more like a contract. But the defects of a pure status regime do not make out a case for a regime of private contracting. "For marriage to become merely a contract of sexual use—or, more accurately, for sexual relations to take the form of universal prostitution—would mark the political defeat of women *as women*," and "the patriarchal construction of sexual difference as mastery and subjection remains intact but repressed" (p. 187).

Not least important, many feminist critics follow Fineman in maintaining that liberalization has third-party effects on children. Writing from the perspectives of both difference feminism and economics, Professor Margaret Brinig argues in *From Contract to Covenant* (2000) that no-fault divorce and other mechanisms that have facilitated the break-up of horizontal relationships have had devastating effects on children. While Brinig's concerns parallel those of Fineman, her proposed solution does not, for she would strengthen rather than abolish civil marriage—not only enforcing realistic alimony obligations but also treating marriages like *covenants* accepting mutual responsibilities to the relationship and to children, rather than like contracts. She endorses *covenant marriages*, which seek to improve partners' investments in their marriages by requiring counseling before marriage and by making it harder to divorce (with a longer separation period and a requirement of fault).

PROBLEM 6-2
CONSTITUTIONAL PROTECTION FOR POLYAMOROUS RELATIONSHIPS?

Do individuals whose relationships exist outside of marriage have a constitutional right to decriminalization (if necessary) and the formal recognition of some alternative legal status? Revisit the materials in Chapters 1 and 2, especially the right to privacy cases, culminating in *Lawrence v. Texas*. After *Lawrence*, can the state continue to make sexual cohabitation outside of marriage a crime? Only a handful of states still criminalize fornication, or cohabitation outside of marriage; for the future, the issue may be more likely to materialize for polyamorous or polygamous relationships.

Sketch an argument that criminalization laws are now unconstitutional—and then the best argument the state might make in defense. In his *Lawrence* dissent, Justice Scalia warned that "[s]tate laws against bigamy, same-sex marriage, adult incest, masturbation, adultery, fornication, bestiality, and obscenity" were all "called into question" by the Court's decision. *Lawrence,* 539 U.S. at 590. The Court's later ruling in *Obergefell* proved Justice Scalia's argument regarding same-sex marriage prophetic. Was he similarly correct that anti-bigamy laws are constitutionally suspect?

The Court and commentators have tended to treat this as a nuisance argument, in light of the perception that there is not a great social demand for polygamy. That might be changing, as some faith traditions are inching out of the closet with examples of plural households and as secular polyamorous relationships emerge from a nearby closet. A constitutional right to polygamy might rest on *Obergefell*, and a constitutional objection to state persecution of polygamists might rest upon religious free exercise in those cases. Construct a constitutional argument along these lines—and then read the next case.

Kody Brown et al. v. Jeffrey R. Buhman, **947 F. Supp. 2d 1170 (D. Utah 2013), vacated as moot, 2016 WL 1399358 (10th Cir. April 11, 2016).** A plural family (the Browns) sued County Attorney Buhman and various state officials for a declaratory judgment that the Utah anti-bigamy statute, Utah Code § 76–7–101, violates the Fourteenth Amendment. Kody and Keri Brown were legally married in Utah. Their faith tradition teaches that God approves of plural marriages, and adherents to their faith are encouraged to celebrate more than one marriage. Although Kody Brown had not legally married anyone other than Keri Brown, he had celebrated religious celebrations of marriages with additional adult, consenting women. The Brown family—Kody, Keri, and the nonlegal wives—lived together in one house.

Law enforcement officials took an interest in the Browns after a reality television program, "The Sister Wives," publicized the lives of wives in a plural family. In the wake of publicity and interest about plural households, some officials took a public position that the Browns violated Utah's law regulating sexual cohabitation and bigamy. The statute, § 76–7–101, provided as follows:

> (1) A person is guilty of bigamy when, knowing he has a husband or wife or knowing the other person has a husband or

wife, the person purports to marry another person or cohabits with another person.

(2) Bigamy is a felony of the third degree.

(3) It shall be a defense to bigamy that the accused reasonably believed he and the other person were legally eligible to remarry.

In the course of the litigation, the County Attorney represented that his office has adopted a formal policy against bigamy prosecutions unless they are connected to another crime or unless one of the participants is under the age of eighteen.

Judge Waddoups upheld most of the statute against constitutional attack but struck down the anti-cohabitation language in § 76–7–101(1), which had been construed by the Utah Supreme Court to make it a crime to marry one person and then to cohabit with a second person. He also overrode a state court construction of the "purports to marry" language, and limited that language to situations involving legal second marriages.

The District Court started with the Supreme Court's declaration that Mormon-supported polygamy in nineteenth-century Utah Territory constituted "a return to barbarism" and was "contrary to the spirit of Christianity." *Late Corp. of The Church of Jesus Christ of Latter-Day Saints v. United States*, 136 U.S. 1, 49 (1890). Based upon its approval of legislation designed to protect sound morals, the Supreme Court earlier had held that a prosecution of a Mormon husband for bigamy did not violate the Free Exercise Clause. *Reynolds v. United States,* 98 U.S. 145, 164–65 (1879). Judge Waddoups wondered how much of *Reynolds* survived the Supreme Court's decision in *Lawrence*, but he conceded that the Supreme Court itself relied on *Reynolds* when it held that the Free Exercise Clause strict scrutiny is not triggered by laws that inly "incidentally" burden religion and do not target religious minorities. *Employment Division, Department of Human Resources of Oregon v. Smith*, 494 U.S. 872, 879 (1990). *Smith* also recognized strict scrutiny for "hybrid rights" cases, where a law burdened religious practice or belief and *also* infringed upon another constitutionally protected interest.

Not a Mormon but a member of a faith tradition supporting plural marriages, Kody Brown had only entered into a legal marriage to one woman, Keri Brown. The other "wives" were not his legal spouses—and so any prosecution under the Utah polygamy law would have been for unlawful *cohabitation* or for *purporting to marry* these other women whom he and his faith community considered his "wives." See *State v. Holm,* 137 P.3d 726 (Utah 2006) (holding that the "purporting to marry" prong of the statute includes nonlegal as well as legal marriages).

In light of the factual posture of the case, "despite any applicability of *Reynolds* to actual polygamy (multiple purportedly legal unions), the cohabitation prong of the statute is not operationally neutral or of general applicability because of its targeted effect on specifically religious cohabitation. It is therefore subject to strict scrutiny under the Free Exercise Clause and fails under that standard. Also, in these circumstances, *Smith*'s hybrid rights exception requires the court to apply a form of heightened scrutiny to Plaintiffs' constitutional claims, including their Due Process claim, since each of those constitutional claims are 'reinforced by Free Exercise Clause concerns,' in light of the specifically religious nature of Plaintiffs' cohabitation. Alternatively, following *Lawrence* and based on the arguments presented by Defendant in both his filings and at oral argument, the State of Utah has no rational basis under the Due Process Clause on which to prohibit the type of religious cohabitation at issue here; thus, the cohabitation prong of the Statute is facially unconstitutional, though the broader statute survives in prohibiting bigamy." The District Court also overrode *Holm*'s interpretation of "purports to marry" and (for reasons of constitutional avoidance) limited that phrase to engaging in legal marriages.

Consider, briefly, the primary constitutional claims recognized by Judge Waddoups:

1. *Substantive Due Process.* Do the Browns have a "fundamental right" to engage in polygamy? The first question is whether the governing precedent is *Washington v. Glucksberg*, 521 U.S. 702 (1997), where the Supreme Court restricted fundamental due process rights to those "deeply rooted in the Nation's history and tradition," a test "assisted suicide" (the right claimed in the earlier case) did not meet, or whether the governing precedent is *Lawrence*. (Recall from Chapter 2, Sections 2 and 3, that there is debate as to whether the *Glucksberg* approach is still good law.)

If *Glucksberg* controls, the state can argue that, like centuries-old Anglo-American bars to assisted suicide, even older traditions rejected plural marriage, and rejected it emphatically. English law prohibited bigamy, a prohibition followed religiously in the American colonies and by the states after Independence.

The Browns, however, had a more "careful description" (*Glucksberg*) of their purported right—namely, "a fundamental liberty interest in choosing to cohabit and maintain romantic and spiritual relationships, even if those relationships are termed 'plural marriage'." They relied on *Lawrence* to argue for "a fundamental liberty interest in intimate sexual conduct," thus prohibiting the state "from imposing criminal sanctions for intimate sexual conduct in the home." According to the Browns, "Lawrence was the latest iteration in a long series of constitutional decisions amplifying a core principle: the Due Process Clause circumscribes and in some cases virtually forbids state intervention in private relationships and conduct."

The District Court found the invocation of *Lawrence* analytically attractive. The Court invoked "the Fourteenth Amendment's commitment to a concept of liberty that 'protects the person from unwarranted government intrusions into a dwelling or other private places' because it 'presumes an autonomy of self that includes . . . certain intimate conduct,' and therefore 'gives substantial protection to adult persons in deciding how to conduct their lives in matters pertaining to sex.' " That is a broader understanding of due process liberty than the *Glucksberg* understanding. But Judge Waddoups ultimately rejected such a broad reading of due process liberty, because he was bound by the Tenth Circuit's decision in *Segmiller v. Laverkin City,* 528 F.3d 762 (10th Cir. 2008), which held that *Lawrence* did not recognize a fundamental right in sexual privacy and was only applying rational basis review. Only a ruling by the Tenth Circuit en banc or the Supreme Court can lift the binding nature of *Segmiller.*

2.   *Free Exercise Clause.* In *Church of the Lukumi Babalu Aye, Inc. v. City of Hialeah,* 508 U.S. 520 (1993), the Supreme Court further examined the *Smith* rule that a neutral law of general applicability need not be justified by a compelling governmental interest but that a law actually targeting religion would receive heightened scrutiny. The *Hialeah* Court found that although city ordinances against sacrificial or ritual animal killings were indeed facially neutral in their artful drafting, they nevertheless unconstitutionally targeted the practices of the Santeria religion for elimination, and thus were not neutral or of general applicability, because when "their operation is considered," their "design . . . accomplishes a 'religious gerrymander'." *Id.* at 535.

Judge Waddroups found that the cohabitation bar in the Utah bigamy statute was facially neutral but not operationally neutral as regards religion. "[A]s with the ordinances at issue in Hialeah, in the operational application of the Statute, 'few if any [cohabitations] are prohibited other than [religious cohabitations].' *Id.* at 536. That is, 'although [religious cohabitation] is prohibited,' virtually any other cohabitation is 'unpunished.' " To support this finding, the judge quoted several exchanges with the Assistant Attorney General representing Utah at oral argument:

> THE COURT: Let's assume your situation, that a man is legally by law recognized as married to one woman and then he has intimate sexual relationships continuing with two other women, but he doesn't make any professions of any commitment to these women, he just engages in adulterous conduct. Does the statute come into play in those circumstances?

> MR. JENSEN: I don't think it does. The cohabitation would apply if they were living in one household and cohabiting as a man and plural wives. . . . The situation you presented is no different than someone having an affair. * * *

> THE COURT: Now, let's—to understand your position, let's assume the same scenario, legal marriage to one woman, intimate relationships with two additional women, but as to one of those women he makes a public pronouncement that says I'm

committed to this woman, I'm going to take care of her for the rest of her life, does that change the analysis?

MR. JENSEN: Well, I don't know that it changes the analysis. The polygamy aspect of this requires that there be a marriage of some sort, a second or third or fourth marriage.

THE COURT: But that's the problem is deciding what constitutes a marriage for purposes of this act. Does the public pronouncement that I intend to be committed to this woman, I will take care of her and her children for as long as she lives, is that enough to make a marriage?

MR. JENSEN: I'm not sure that's enough to make a marriage, no. * * *

THE COURT: Okay. Let's suppose that he says the same thing, but he says it to his Jewish rabbi, does that now become a polygamist marriage? And the rabbi says I bless you and recognize you as husband and wife.

MR. JENSEN: Well, if they are holding themselves out as husband and wife, I would recognize that as marriage.

THE COURT: So is it the recognition by a religious organization that it believes that they are living together in a recognized relationship by the religion sufficient?

MR. JENSEN: No, no, no. . . . I think it's the representation that they make to the world as to what is their relationship. If they make it as husband and wife, then that constitutes marriage under the statute.

THE COURT: If they say we're not husband and wife, we just live together, then it's not under the statute.

MR. JENSEN: Then it's not governed under the statute.

Although the State insisted that not *all* the prosecuted cases involved religion, the District Court found that the enforcement against a person who had only one civil marriage license but believed himself to be married to more than one wife, had the operational effect of targeting religious minorities for prosecution and, hence, triggering heightened scrutiny under *Hialeah*. The District Court found that the criminalization of religious cohabitation was not narrowly tailored to serve a compelling public interest. (The State's interests in supporting marriage, preventing marriage fraud, and protecting vulnerable individuals were not well-served by criminalizing adult consensual committed relationships such as those of Kody Brown and his plural wives.)

3. Due Process Rational Basis. Under *Segmiller* and certainly under *Lawrence*, a statutory limitation on people's consensual sexual activities must rest upon a rational basis, perhaps independent of public morality (a ground rejected in *Lawrence*). Judge Waddoups found the

State's position ultimately irrational, for this reason: "Adultery, including adulterous cohabitation, is not prosecuted. Religious cohabitation, however, is subject to prosecution at the limitless discretion of local and State prosecutors, despite a general policy *not* to prosecute religiously motivated polygamy. The Court finds no rational basis to distinguish between the two." On top of that analysis, the District Court also held that the bar to cohabitation is void for vagueness, because its command is too vague and potentially broad to satisfy due process.

NOTES ON BIGAMY/POLYGAMY AND THE CONSTITUTION

1. *The Difficulty of Finding Test Cases.* As the caption to the case reveals, the Tenth Circuit vacated Judge Waddoups's decision and judgment, on the ground that the Browns' case or controversy was moot and therefore nonjusticiable. As both majority and dissenting Utah Supreme Court Justices had observed in *Holm*, that traditionalist state did not prosecute consensual fornication or adultery or sexual cohabitation at all. And the case was rendered moot by the District Attorney's affidavit describing a formal policy against prosecuting cohabitation of adults engaged in plural marriages, so long as there was just one state-sanctioned marriage. (The Tenth Circuit pointed out that the formal policy simply codified what the District Attorney described as his office's prior practice.)

Recall that one reason it took seventeen years to overrule *Bowers v. Hardwick* was that it took many years to find an appropriate case, where there was an arrest and prosecution for sodomy between consenting adults in a private place. Criminal sodomy laws were rarely enforced against purely private and consensual activities. The same phenomenon seems to be occurring for fornication, cohabitation, and even adultery laws (the latter have tangible third-party effects). Ought such a pattern of nonenforcement have some significance for the constitutionality of these criminal regulations of intimate sexual activities?

2. *Constitutionality of Criminal Bigamy and Cohabitation Laws?* In addition to Utah, only two states maintain laws clearly prohibiting sexual cohabitation: Michigan and Mississippi. See Mich. Comp. Laws Ann. § 750.335; Miss. Code Ann. § 97–29–1. In recent years, similar laws in other states have been amended, repealed, or held unconstitutional.[f] Judge Waddoups's decision in the Utah case fits into this account of *Lawrence*. When North Carolina's anti-cohabitation law was challenged in 2006, the state superior court summarily concluded in a two-paragraph decision that the answer was "unconstitutional." See *Hobbs v. Smith*, No. 05 CVS 267, 2006 WL 3103008, at *1 (Super. Ct. Pender Cnty., Aug. 25, 2006) (citing *Lawrence* to invalidate a law prohibiting lewd cohabitation).

---

[f] *See* Fla. Stat. Ann. § 798.02 (amended in 2016 to prohibit only "open and gross lewdness and lascivious behavior" without regard to marital status); N.C. Gen. Stat § 14–184 (held unconstitutional in *Hobbs v. Smith*, No. 05 CVS 267, 2006 WL 3103008 (N.C. Super. Aug. 25, 2006)); Va. Code Ann. § 18.2–345 (repealed in 2013); W. Va. Code Ann. § 61–8–4 (repealed in 2010). In early 2016, the Michigan Legislature considered a bill to eliminate the statutory cohabitation ban. 2015 Michigan Senate Bill No.896, Michigan Ninety-Eighth Legislature—Regular Session of 2015.

Some scholars argue that *Lawrence*'s logic does not undermine longstanding prohibitions against bigamy. They contend that states have stronger interests in prohibiting polygamy than in prohibiting intimate sexual activities between consenting adults, and *Lawrence* did nothing to weaken those interests. One typical argument is that polygamy is an unequal arrangement that elevates the role of men and denigrates the women. "Polygamy is inherently patriarchal, misogynistic, and degrading to women if following the restrictive/traditional definition of polygamy (one man and two women). * * * [W]omen in polygamous societies fail to become the moral and legal individuals that women in monogamous societies can become because polygamy fundamentally denies a woman the status as a full equal partner in the relationship." Elizabeth Larcano, Note, "A 'Pink' Herring: The Prospect of Polygamy Following the Legalization of Same-Sex Marriage," 38 *Conn. L. Rev.* 1065, 1104 (2006); *accord,* Susan Deller Ross, "Should Polygamy Be Permitted In The United States?," 38 *Hum. Rts.* 20 (2011). If polygamy promotes or perpetuates inequality between the sexes, states can and should take action to eliminate it.

Some scholars also argue that polygamous relationships impose burdens on the state that monogamous relationships—whether straight or gay—do not. They contend that entire bodies of property law, family law, and probate rely on the conception of marriage as an arrangement between two people. Legalized polygamy would deeply complicate these areas of the law. For instance, if a husband with multiple wives died intestate, the legal system would be ill-equipped to adjudicate the resulting litigation. Larcano, "Prospect of Polygamy," 1109. The state therefore has an interest in preventing relationships that would badly impair judicial economy.

Other commentators assert that the privacy and liberty interests that underpin *Lawrence* require invalidating criminal bigamy statutes. In particular, scholars note that opposition to polygamy has long been framed in moralistic terms. In *Reynolds v. United States*, 98 U.S. 145, 164 (1878), for instance, the Supreme Court called the practice "odious." But in light of *Lawrence*'s emphasis on liberty over a mandated moral code, such moralistic opposition to polygamy can no longer be supported. See, *e.g.*, Peter Nash Swisher, " 'I Now Pronounce You Husband and Wives': The Case for Polygamous Marriage After *United States v. Windsor* and *Burwell v. Hobby Lobby Stores*," 29 *BYU J. Pub. L.* 299, 325 (2015).

Yet other scholars dispute the oft-argued point that plural marriages are inherently unequal. This argument, they suggest, is paternalistic and fails to appreciate that adults can truly consent to enter into polygamous marriages. "If homosexuals have a liberty interest under the Due Process Clause in not being criminally prosecuted for their sexual conduct, it would seem that consenting adults desiring to engage in religious polygamy also should be entitled to such a liberty interest." Elijah L. Milne, "Blaine Amendments and Polygamy Laws: The Constitutionality of Anti-Polygamy Laws Targeting Religion," 28 *W. New Eng. L. Rev.* 257, 284 (2009).

3. *Regulation Under Civil Law?* Before *Lawrence*, the only normative regime that the Supreme Court had ever recognized for adult sexual relations was traditional, man-woman marriage. Even in *Eisenstadt,* where the Court struck down a contraception law as applied to unmarried adults, the majority opinion repeatedly emphasized that the state was not invoking the rationale that it was trying to discourage sex outside of marriage (Chapter 1, Section 1). After *Lawrence*, it appears that the Constitution protects a hedonic choice regime, where the state can and sometimes ought to allow romantic couples civil status outside of traditional one man, one woman marriage. Upon this reading, *Obergefell* flows naturally from *Lawrence*. What kinds of lawful status might states offer for relationships involving more than two persons? What legitimate state interests would they serve? What constraints would administrative workability impose?

NOTE ON THE AMERICAN LAW INSTITUTE'S PRINCIPLES OF THE LAW OF FAMILY DISSOLUTION (2002)

In 2002, the American Law Institute promulgated its much-anticipated *Principles of the Law of Family Dissolution*, a set of policy proposals suggested for legislative adoption. Its principles were largely informed by practical experience and the better-reasoned case law and academic commentary, including feminist critiques of no-fault divorce. Consider some examples.

When spouses separate or divorce, a primary concern of both the spouses and the state is protections for children being raised within the now-separated family. Chapter 2 of the *Principles* deals with the allocation of custodial and decisionmaking responsibilities for children. To protect the "best interests of the child," specified in § 2.02, the *Principles* call for the development of a "parenting plan." § 2.05. The presumption is that the spouses will agree on a plan, but if they do not the *Principles* recommend that "the proportion of custodial time the child spends with each parent approximates the proportion of time each parent spent performing caretaking functions for the child prior to the parents' separation." See § 2.08(1) (starting with this presumption and listing factors that would justify departures from the approximation rule). The *Principles* prohibit the court's taking into consideration the extramarital sexual conduct of a parent unless there is a showing of harm to an individual child. § 2.12(1)(d). The *Principles* flatly bar consideration of the sexual orientation of a parent. § 2.12(1)(e).

The *Principles* take into account the feminist complaint that many family break-ups involve abuse of the wife, children, or both. Thus, the court is required to screen for domestic abuse, § 2.05(3), and in cases of abuse must carefully review the parenting agreement. § 2.06(2). The court is directed to limit access to a child by a parent who has engaged in domestic abuse or has demonstrated drug or alcohol abuse that "interferes with the parent's ability to perform caretaking functions." § 2.11, 2.13.

Chapters 3–5 of the *Principles* deal with (3) calculation of child support by the nonresidential parent, (4) the division of property upon family dissolution, and (5) compensatory spousal payments. Without going into the great detail (and thought) invested in these chapters of the *Principles*, we make the limited observation that they are responsive to feminist criticisms of the tendency of divorce to pauperize wives, especially those who work inside the home in support of the husband's career. Where the wife's contribution to the family has been homebound or front-loaded, alimony courts in some jurisdictions are willing to distribute the value of commercial "goodwill" in the husband's business, *Dugan v. Dugan*, 92 N.J. 423, 457 A.2d 1 (1983), or even the income stream flowing from the husband's professional degree or license. *O'Brien v. O'Brien*, 66 N.Y.2d 576, 489 N.E.2d 712 (1985).[g]

The *Principles* presume that marital property should be divided evenly between the spouses, § 4.09, and follow the majority common law rule treating business and professional "goodwill" but not "earning capacity" as marital property, § 4.07. For long-term marriages, the spouses' "separate property" tends to be absorbed into their "marital property" in the *Principles*. § 4.12. In addition, the *Principles* respond to feminist complaints by requiring compensatory payments in situations where the marriage has been a long one, § 5.04, or where the lower-earning spouse gave up opportunities to develop her or his earning capacity in order to serve as the primary caregiver for the children, § 5.05. For both child support and compensatory payment awards, the *Principles* seek to introduce more predictability in judicial calculations, for greater predictability in legal entitlements would facilitate bargaining between the spouses without the need for judicial intervention. See Robert Mnookin & Lewis Kornhauser, "Bargaining in the Shadow of the Law: The Case of Divorce," 88 *Yale L.J.* 950 (1979).

Chapter 6 of the ALI's *Principles* (digested below) would create statewide statutory recognition of *domestic partnerships* as a structure for treating dissolution claims of cohabiting but not married couples.

---

[g] *See* June Carbone & Margaret Brinig, "Rethinking Marriage: Feminist Ideology, Economic Change, and Divorce Reform," 65 *Tul. L. Rev.* 953 (1991); Ira Ellman, "The Theory of Alimony," 77 *Calif. L. Rev.* 1 (1989); Milton Regan, Jr., "Spouses and Strangers: Divorce Obligations and Property Rhetoric," 82 *Geo. L.J.* 2303 (1994); Jana Singer, "Alimony and Efficiency: The Gendered Costs and Benefits of the Economic Justification for Alimony," 82 *Geo. L.J.* 2423 (1994). *See also* Allison Anna Tait, "Divorce Equality," 90 *Wash. L. Rev.* 1245 (2015) (noting that courts "generally have been willing to allow professional goodwill to be characterized as marital property"); Christopher A. Tiso, "Present Positions on Professional Goodwill: More Focus or Simply More Hocus Pocus?," 20 *J. Am. Acad. Matrim. Law.* 51 (2006).

COMMON LAW REGULATION OF COHABITATING RELATIONSHIPS

Privatization valorizes individual choice in configuring the choice of sexual and romantic partners and the terms under which such partnerships will operate. There are several different regulatory strategies for privatizing American family law. First, the state might *liberalize marriage* by making it easier for couples desiring to marry to gain state recognition, allowing the couples to contract out of at least some of the duties of marriage, and making it easier to exit the institution. Professor Singer's article summarizes these developments, which move in the direction of a contract-based regulatory regime. On the law's enforcement of prenuptial and other agreements that contract out of some of the benefits and obligations of marriage or that contract for more obligations, see Martha Ertman, *Love's Promises: How Formal and Informal Contracts Shape All Kinds of Families* 173–94 (2015).

Second, the state might *abolish marriage* altogether, thereby leaving romantic couples entirely to the law of contract, property, and tort in structuring their relationships. Radical feminists in the 1960s and 1970s urged that marriage's patriarchal heritage rendered it unacceptable today. In the book excerpted at the beginning of this chapter, Professor Fineman has updated this argument: the liberalization of marriage has not only failed to help women, but it has harmed their interests and impaired their lives—so it must go. *Accord*, Nancy D. Polikoff, *Beyond Gay (and Straight) Marriage: Valuing All Families Under the Law* 83–88 (2008) (similar argument from a lesbian feminist perspective).

Queer theorists object to marriage's rule of sexual fidelity to one person. Like Gayle Rubin and Michel Foucault (Chapter 3, Sections 2A and 3A, respectively), they object that western society views sex as guilty unless proven innocent, with the only defense being procreative sex within a monogamous marriage. From a sexual liberationist perspective, this is not only a confining norm, but it creates sexual neurotics. For them, too, marriage is an institution whose time is long gone. Drawing from Hayekian economics, the Cato Institute has made the same argument as queer and feminist theorists: the many regulations associated with marriage are inefficient, for they do not match the best interests of romantic couples, and the state would do better simply to enforce contractual expectations. See David Boaz [President, Cato Institute], "Privatize Marriage: A Simple Solution to the Gay-Marriage Debate," *Slate*, Apr. 25, 1997.

Third, the state might *extend (some) duties and benefits of marriage* to couples who are not married (either by choice or by law). Canada and most European countries have adopted statute-based regimes imposing specific rules upon couples deemed to be cohabiting, and the American Law Institute has proposed legislation to similar effect in its *Principles of the Law of Family Dissolution* (2002). In the United States, unlike Europe, most of the law relating to cohabiting couples has come from courts rather than legislatures. This section excerpts or digests the leading American cases; Section 3 will survey the kinds of statutes adopted in North America and Europe.

Read as a collection, the materials in this section address three different kinds of issues: (1) Should the state ever extend marital benefits or duties to unmarried but cohabiting couples? Or should civil marriage be the only venue for these special benefits and duties? Indeed, should the policy favoring marriage be a reason for the state *not* to extend ordinary contract and tort remedies to aggrieved spouses? (2) If the state adopts a regime of partial incorporation, which marital duties and benefits should the state extend to cohabiting couples? Among the most important duties of marriage are obligations of economic and emotional support, sexual fidelity, and sharing of property. Among the most important benefits of marriage are health and life insurance (provided by employers based upon marital status), capacity to act as the legal representative of one's spouse, and presumptive inheritance rights. Which of these should be extended to cohabiting partners? (3) What kind of cohabiting partners should be entitled to the array of incorporated duties and benefits? Should they be limited to the people who can marry? Or should eligibility include people related by blood or marriage or minors, none of whom can marry? Should they be limited to people who cannot marry?

Michelle Marvin v. Lee Marvin

California Supreme Court, 1976.
18 Cal.3d 660, 134 Cal.Rptr. 815, 557 P.2d 106.

■ TOBRINER, JUSTICE. * * *

In the instant case plaintiff [Michelle Marvin] and defendant [Oscar-winning actor Lee Marvin] lived together for seven years without marrying; all property acquired during this period was taken in defendant's name. When plaintiff sued to enforce a contract under which she was entitled to half the property and to support payments, the trial court granted judgment on the pleadings for defendant, thus leaving him with all property accumulated by the couple during their relationship. Since the trial court denied plaintiff a trial on the merits of her claim, its decision * * * must be reversed. * * *

In *Trutalli v. Meraviglia* (1932) 12 P.2d 430 we established the principle that nonmarital partners may lawfully contract concerning the ownership of property acquired during the relationship. We reaffirmed this principle in *Vallera v. Vallera* (1943) 134 P.2d 761, 763, stating that "If a man and a woman [who are not married] live together as husband and wife under an agreement to pool their earnings and share equally in their joint accumulations, equity will protect the interests of each in such property." * * *

Defendant [responds] that the alleged contract is so closely related to the supposed "immoral" character of the relationship between plaintiff and himself that the enforcement of the contract would violate public policy.[4] He points to cases asserting that a contract between nonmarital partners is unenforceable if it is "involved in" an illicit relationship, or made in "contemplation" of such a relationship. A review of the numerous California decisions concerning contracts between nonmarital partners, however, reveals that the courts have not employed such broad and uncertain standards to strike down contracts. The decisions instead disclose a narrower and more precise standard: a contract between nonmarital partners is unenforceable only *to the extent* that it *explicitly* rests upon the immoral and illicit consideration of meretricious sexual services. * * *

* * * [A]dults who voluntarily live together and engage in sexual relations are nonetheless as competent as any other persons to contract respecting their earnings and property rights. Of course, they cannot lawfully contract to pay for the performance of sexual services, for such a contract is, in essence, an agreement for prostitution and unlawful for that reason. But they may agree to pool their earnings and to hold all property acquired during the relationship in accord with the law governing community property; conversely, they may agree that each partner's earnings and the property acquired from those earnings remains the separate property of the earning partner. So long as the agreement does not rest upon illicit meretricious consideration, the parties may order their economic affairs as they choose, and no policy precludes the courts from enforcing such agreements.

[Justice Tobriner ruled that Michelle Marvin had made out a proper claim of express contract, based on her allegations that she and Lee Marvin had entered into an oral agreement in 1964 to live together, to hold themselves out as husband and wife, and to pool their incomes. In return for her services as "companion, homemaker, housekeeper and cook," Michelle would be supported financially by Lee Marvin. Justice Tobriner also ruled that Michelle Marvin could amend her complaint to add further causes of action founded upon theories of "implied contract" and "equitable relief."]

---

[4] Defendant also contends that the contract was illegal because it contemplated a violation of former Penal Code section 269a, which prohibited living "in a state of cohabitation and adultery." (§ 269a was repealed by Stats.1975, ch. 71, eff. Jan. 1, 1976.) Defendant's standing to raise the issue is questionable because he alone was married and thus guilty of violating section 269a. Plaintiff, being unmarried could neither be convicted of adulterous cohabitation nor of aiding and abetting defendant's violation. * * *

[*Vallera* and other early decisions allowing actions founded upon express contracts refused to allow nonmarital partners to assert claims for relief based upon contracts implied from the conduct of the parties. The court of appeals decision *In re Marriage of Cary*, 34 Cal. App. 3d 345 (1973) held that these earlier decisions were inconsistent with the Family Law Act of 1969, which eliminated fault as a basis for dividing marital property and which gave "putative spouses" (people who believed they were spouses but whose marriage was invalid) half the "quasi marital property." Justice Tobriner was not persuaded that the Act overrode *Vallera* and the earlier decisions but held that those decisions were no longer viable on the merits.]

We conclude that the judicial barriers that may stand in the way of a policy based upon the fulfillment of the reasonable expectations of the parties to a nonmarital relationship should be removed. As we have explained, the courts now hold that express agreements will be enforced unless they rest on an unlawful meretricious consideration. We add that in the absence of an express agreement, the couples may look to a variety of other remedies in order to protect the parties' lawful expectations.

The courts may inquire into the conduct of the parties to determine whether the conduct demonstrates an implied contract or implied agreement of partnership or joint venture, or some other tacit understanding between the parties. The courts may, when appropriate, employ principles of constructive trust or resulting trust. Finally, a nonmarital partner may recover in quantum meruit for the reasonable value of household services rendered less the reasonable value of support received if he can show he has rendered services with the expectation of monetary reward.[25] * * *

■ [The concurring and dissenting opinion of JUSTICE CLARK is omitted.]

Postscript. On remand, the trial court was not persuaded of Michelle Marvin's various contractual or quasi-contractual claims, and she received no recovery from her pioneering lawsuit. The Court of Appeals affirmed the lower court's judgment. *Marvin v. Marvin*, 176 Cal. Rptr. 555 (Cal. App. 1981).

NOTES ON *MARVIN* AND JUDICIAL TREATMENT OF CONTRACTUAL CLAIMS BY COHABITING PARTNERS

In a small number of states, courts have refused to follow *Marvin* and have declined to provide contractual or quasi-contractual (equitable) remedies for cohabiting partners. The reasoning has been that extending legal entitlements to cohabiting partners would be inconsistent with the special status marriage has in that jurisdiction or with the legislature's repudiation of common-law marriage. See *Hewitt v. Hewitt*, 77 Ill.2d 49, 394

---

[25] Our opinion does not preclude the evolution of additional equitable remedies to protect the expectations of the parties to a nonmarital relationship in cases where existing remedies prove inadequate; the suitability of such remedies may be determined in later cases in light of the factual setting in which they arise.

N.E.2d 1204 (1979) (leading case); *Spafford v. Coats*, 455 N.E.2d 241 (Ill. 1983) (establishing a limited exception to *Hewitt*); *Schwegmann v. Schwegmann*, 441 So.2d 316 (La. App. 1983). Minnesota courts followed *Marvin*, see *Carlson v. Olson*, 256 N.W.2d 249 (Minn. 1977), but the legislature in 1980 overrode the decision with a rule requiring an express written contract with two witnesses, Minn. Stat. § 513.075, a requirement the courts have not always strictly enforced. *See In re Estate of Eriksen*, 337 N.W.2d 671 (Minn. 1983) (interpreting the 1980 statute to allow a lawsuit for a property claim); *Gfrerer v. Lemcke*, 2009 WL 749584 (Minn. Ct. App. Mar. 24, 2009) (enforcing an implied contract where one cohabitant helped remodel his partner's home).

A handful of states enforce express written or oral contracts but refuse to do so where the contract is implied (inferred from the parties' conduct). Three rationales undergird this refusal: (1) Recognition of implied contracts would practically reinstate common law marriage and thereby thwart the will of the legislature that abolished the institution, see *Featherston v. Steinhoff*, 575 N.W.2d 6 (Mich. App.), *appeal denied*, 589 N.W.2d 774 (Mich. 1998); *Merrill v. Davis*, 100 N.M. 552, 673 P.2d 1285 (1983). (2) People who provide services in the context of a relationship generally do so for emotional reasons, without expecting compensation, see *Morone v. Morone*, 50 N.Y.2d 481, 413 N.E.2d 1154 (1980). (3) The judicial system does not have the capacity to parse private conduct and discern the existence of an implied contract, see *id.*

In a large majority of states, however, courts have followed *Marvin* to recognize express and implied contractual claims by cohabiting partners.[a] Most of the cases cited in the margin have required that the consideration for the asserted promise was not sexual services. This requirement is typically easy to satisfy. New Jersey courts, for instance, will enforce an express or implied agreement founded on "the undertaking of a way of life in which two people commit to each other, foregoing other liaisons and opportunities, doing for each other whatever each is capable of doing, providing companionship, and fulfilling each other's needs, financial, emotional, physical, and social, as best as they are able" so long as the contract does not contain an explicit obligation to provide sexual services which is inseparable from the rest of the agreement. See *In re Estate of Roccamonte*, 174 N.J. 381, 808 A.2d 838 (2002); *Kozlowski v. Kozlowski*, 80 N.J. 378, 403 A.2d 902 (1979).

---

[a]   Cases following *Marvin* include *Cook v. Cook*, 142 Ariz. 573, 691 P.2d 664 (1984); *Salzman v. Bachrach*, 996 P.2d 1263 (Colo. 2000); *Boland v. Catalano*, 202 Conn. 333, 521 A.2d 142 (1987); *Mason v. Rostad*, 476 A.2d 662 (D.C. 1984); *Poe v. Levy's Estate*, 411 So.2d 253 (Fla. Dist. Ct. App. 1982); *Glasgo v. Glasgo*, 410 N.E.2d 1325 (Ind. Ct. App. 1980); *Miller v. Ratner*, 114 Md.App. 18, 688 A.2d 976, 991 (1997) (dictum); *Margolies v. Hopkins*, 401 Mass. 88, 514 N.E.2d 1079 (1987); *Hudson v. DeLonjay*, 732 S.W.2d 922 (Mo. Ct. App. 1987); *Kinkenon v. Hue*, 207 Neb. 698, 301 N.W.2d 77 (1981); *Hay v. Hay*, 100 Nev. 196, 678 P.2d 672 (1984); *Joan S. v. John S.*, 121 N.H. 96, 427 A.2d 498 (1981) (dictum); *Kozlowski v. Kozlowski*, 80 N.J. 378, 403 A.2d 902 (1979); *Dominguez v. Cruz*, 95 N.M. 1, 617 P.2d 1322 (1980); *Collins v. Davis*, 68 N.C.App. 588, 315 S.E.2d 759 (1984); *Latham v. Latham*, 281 Or. 303, 574 P.2d 644 (1978); *Knauer v. Knauer*, 323 Pa.Super. 206, 470 A.2d 553 (1983); *Doe v. Burkland*, 808 A.2d 1090 (R.I. 2002); *Small v. Harper*, 638 S.W.2d 24 (Tex. App. 1982); *Layton v. Layton*, 777 P.2d 504 (Utah App. 1989); *Belcher v. Kirkwood*, 238 Va. 430, 383 S.E.2d 729 (1989); *Lawlis v. Thompson*, 137 Wis.2d 490, 405 N.W.2d 317 (1987); *Kinnison v. Kinnison*, 627 P.2d 594 (Wyo. 1981).

Most of the express and implied contract cases have been *palimony* (financial support) cases. Unlike Michelle Marvin's lawsuit, many of the reported palimony cases have been successful, with cohabitants either winning a trial judgment or an out-of-court settlement. For example, when celebrity lawyer Johnnie Cochran ended his 27-year relationship with Patty Sikora Cochran, she successfully sued him to enforce his written contractual obligations to her and their son and to enforce unwritten promises as well, even though Johnnie Cochran was married to other women during most of their time together. Ertman, *Love's Promises,* 137. For excellent, informative analysis of *Marvin*'s impact on American law, see Cynthia Grant Bowman, *Unmarried Couples, Law, and Public Policy* (2010), and Bowman, "Legal Treatment of Cohabitation in the United States," 26 *L. & Pol'y* 119 (2004).

Marvin has also led many states to provide equitable, or quasi-contractual, remedies to cohabiting partners. State courts have mandated a range of equitable remedies, including partition or conveyance of property, distribution of assets, constructive trusts, and resulting trusts. Many times these remedies serve as restitution for one party's unjust enrichment at the expense of the other. Theories of unjust enrichment often only succeed where the cohabitant can point to specific contributions to his or her partner's property or assets. For example, Minnesota courts have refused to reimburse a cohabitant for providing household services throughout the relationship but have allowed an unjust enrichment claim to move forward where the cohabitant donated her money and labor to the construction of a log cabin on her partner's property. See *In re Estate of Palmen,* 588 N.W.2d 493 (Minn. 1999); *In re Estate of Boyer,* No. A03–1688, 2004 WL 1557803 (Minn. Ct. App. July 13, 2004).

1. *Quasi-Contract or Contract as a Basis for Gender Equity?* The *Marvin* cause of action in quasi-or implied contract can operate in feminist ways, as illustrated by *Alderson v. Alderson,* 180 Cal.App.3d 450, 225 Cal.Rptr. 610 (1986). The courts there applied *Marvin* to create an implied contract for community property division of assets in favor of Jonne Alderson, based on the following facts. She and Steve Alderson held themselves out as husband and wife for twelve years; Jonne and their three children took Steve's name; Jonne participated in Steve's business and property dealings, including both money and management. The Aldersons' arrangement bore traces of traditional bargaining where women get less than men: Jonne acquiesced in the decision to live together after the couple originally planned to marry; Steve depended on Jonne's support and expertise and then expected to walk away with most of the tangible assets; Jonne not only kept house and took care of the children, but also had a job outside the home and contributed to purchase of the properties, yet Steve believed she was not entitled to an equal division. Not only did the court impose an equitable division of property to protect the interests of Jonne, but it also invalidated a quitclaim deed signed by Jonne that renounced her interest in the acquired properties, on the ground that she signed under duress (physical assaults and threats by Steve). This looks like a legal feminist success story.

Are there disadvantages to *Marvinizing*, from a feminist perspective? For feminist critiques that *Marvin* is the law's imposition of bourgeois ideals on unconventional families and "repressive benevolence" on women like Jonne Alderson, see Michael Freeman & Christina Lyon, *Cohabitation Without Marriage* (1983); Ruth Deech, "The Case Against Legal Recognition of Cohabitation," 29 *Int'l & Comp. L.Q.* 480 (1980). Compare Grace Ganz Blumberg, "Cohabitation Without Marriage: A Different Perspective," 28 *UCLA L. Rev.* 1125 (1981).

2. *Application of Contract Principles to Same-Sex Relationships.* According to 2017 Gallup-Williams Institute data, approximately 10% of LGBT Americans are married to someone of the same sex. This figure compares to roughly 55% of the entire adult population, indicating that the take-up rate for marriage among same-sex couples remains considerably below the overall average. (This rate may increase in the future, but assume for purposes of argument that it does not.) Although there is no basis post-*Obergefell* for courts to treat couples who choose not to marry differently based on sexual orientation, the history of adverse treatment for same-sex couples is long. And it may be that a significant number of the unmarried couples seeking *Marvin*-like adjudications will continue to be either gay or lesbian.

Do such couples enjoy *Marvin* rights? Although California courts said that same-sex relationships are protected by *Marvin*, courts in the 1980s were more likely to sexualize those relationships than different-sex ones. *E.g., Jones v. Daly*, 122 Cal.App.3d 500, 176 Cal.Rptr. 130 (1981). A case that resisted this temptation was *Whorton v. Dillingham*, 202 Cal.App.3d 447, 248 Cal.Rptr. 405 (1988), a precedent which represents the trend in California and other gay-neutral or gay-friendly states. See Ertman, *Love's Promises,* 134–37, discussing *Posik v. Layton*, 695 So. 2d 759 (Fla. Dist. Ct. App. 1997) (holding that a cohabitation agreement between two gay men was enforceable); *accord, Silver v. Starrett*, 176 Misc. 2d 511, 520, 674 N.Y.S.2d 915, 921 (Sup. Ct. 1998) (holding a contract between two "self-described lesbian[s]" to be valid and enforceable).[b]

For most of American history, courts failed to enforce wills and other contracts sealing "homosexual" relationships. See Jeffrey Sherman, "Undue Influence and the Homosexual Testator," 42 *U. Pitt. L. Rev.* 225 (1981) (surveying the case law). Even before *Lawrence v. Texas* swept away the formal stigma imposed upon "homosexuals" by consensual sodomy laws, courts all over the country were increasingly willing to enforce contractual and sometimes quasi-contractual agreements between cohabiting gay and lesbian partners. See Ertman, *Love's Promises*, 134–37. As Professor Ertman argues, most of the benefits and duties of marriage can be created by contract, and she urges cohabiting couples to consider entering into "cohabitation contracts" that set forth the expectations of the partners in as much detail as they see fit.

3. *Reluctance to* Marvinize *When There Are Third-Party Interests.* Should *Marvin* be extended to create marriage-like benefits enforceable against

---

[b]   For other cases applying contract principles to gay or lesbian couples, see *Crooke v. Gilden*, 262 Ga. 122, 414 S.E.2d 645 (1992); *Cytron v. Malinowitz*, 13 Misc.3d 1218(A), 2006 WL 2851622 (N.Y. Sup. Ct. Oct. 5, 2006); *Ireland v. Flanagan*, 51 Or.App. 837, 627 P.2d 496 (1981); *Doe v. Burkland*, 808 A.2d 1090 (R.I. 2002); *Gormley v. Robertson*, 120 Wash.App. 31, 83 P.3d 1042 (2004)

third parties? For example, should a cohabiting partner be entitled to sue for loss of consortium and other marital injuries when his or her partner is injured? The California Supreme Court ruled in *Elden v. Sheldon*, 46 Cal.3d 267, 758 P.2d 582 (1988), that a stable and intimate gay relationship does not establish the "close relationship" required in California for a third party to sue for infliction of emotional distress after witnessing an intentional tort to his or her loved one, or for loss of consortium. California courts have held that close relationships entitling one to sue include parent-child and husband-wife, but not cohabiting partners. The court emphasized the need for limits to the third-party cause of action for infliction of emotional distress and believed that social policy rendered marriage and parenthood the best place to draw the line. (In 2001, the California Legislature partially overrode *Elden* by providing that registered domestic partners could sue for the deprivation of consortium.)

Although *Elden* represents the rule followed by a majority of states,[c] some states reject *Elden*. Most of these states rely on the framework created by the New Jersey Supreme Court in *Dunphy v. Gregor*, 136 N.J. 99, 642 A.2d 372 (1994). *Dunphy* allowed cohabitants in an "intimate familial relationship" to recover for negligent infliction of emotional distress in the event of a cohabitant's death or grievous bodily injury. "The harm precipitating emotional distress must be so severe that it destroys the emotional security derived from a relationship that is deep, enduring, and intimate. The quality of the relationship creates the severity of the loss." *Id.* at 377–78. To determine whether a relationship is intimate and familial (and hence whether a tortfeasor could have foreseen the emotional harm), New Jersey courts look at "the duration of the relationship, the degree of mutual dependence, the extent of common contributions to a life together, the extent and quality of shared experience, and * * * whether the plaintiff and the injured person were members of the same household, their emotional reliance on each other, the particulars of their day to day relationship, and the manner in which they related to each other in attending to life's mundane requirements." *Id.* at 378.[d]

---

[c]   *E.g., Milberger v. KBHL, L.L.C.*, 486 F. Supp. 2d 1156 (D. Hawai'i 2007); *Beswick v. City Of Philadelphia*, 185 F. Supp. 2d 418 (E.D. Pa. 2001); *Lindsey v. Visitec, Inc.*, 804 F.Supp. 1340 (W.D. Wash. 1992); *Trombley v. Starr-Wood Cardiac Group, P.C.*, 3 P.3d 916 (Alaska 2000); *Tremblay v. Carter*, 390 So.2d 816 (Fla. App. 1980); *Sostock v. Reiss*, 92 Ill.App.3d 200, 415 N.E.2d 1094 (1980); *Smith v. Toney*, 862 N.E.2d 656 (Ind. 2007); *Laws v. Griep*, 332 N.W.2d 339 (Iowa 1983); *Sawyer v. Bailey*, 413 A.2d 165 (Me. 1980); *Gillespie-Linton v. Miles*, 58 Md.App. 484, 473 A.2d 947 (1984); *Feliciano v. Rosemar Silver Co.*, 401 Mass. 141, 514 N.E.2d 1095 (1987); *Nugent v. Bauermeister*, 195 Mich.App. 158, 489 N.W.2d 148 (1992); *Grotts v. Zahner*, 115 Nev. 339, 989 P.2d 415 (1999); *Trombetta v. Conkling*, 187 A.D.2d 213, 593 N.Y.S.2d 670 (1993); *Haas v. Lewis*, 8 Ohio App.3d 136, 456 N.E.2d 512 (1982); *Hastie v. Rodriguez*, 716 S.W.2d 675 (Tex. Ct. App. 1986).

[d]   See also *Hislop v. Salt River Project Agric. Improvement & Power Dist.*, 197 Ariz. 553, 5 P.3d 267 (Ct. App. 2000); *Yovino v. Big Bubba's BBQ, L.L.C.*, 49 Conn.Supp. 555, 896 A.2d 161 (Super. Ct. 2006); *James v. Lieb*, 221 Neb. 47, 375 N.W.2d 109 (1985); *Graves v. Estabrook*, 149 N.H. 202, 818 A.2d 1255, 1262 (2003); *Binns v. Fredendall*, 32 Ohio St.3d 244, 513 N.E.2d 278 (1987); *Thurmon v. Sellers,* 62 S.W.3d 145 (Tenn. Ct. App. 2001); and *Heldreth v. Marrs,* 188 W.Va. 481, 425 S.E.2d 157 (1992).

***Blumenthal v. Brewer*, 2016 IL 118781, 69 N.E.3d 834 (Ill. 2016).**
Eileen Brewer, a circuit judge, resided with her domestic partner, Jane
Blumenthal, for more than 25 years. The couple acquired property and had
children. When the relationship ended, Brewer remained in their co-owned
residence. Blumenthal, a physician, sued to partition their home and assets,
and Brewer brought common law counterclaims, aimed at equalizing her
share of the property and business. The trial court held that *Hewitt* barred
the counterclaims: unmarried cohabitants cannot bring quasi-contract or
equitable property claims against one another. The Court of Appeals
reversed—and the Illinois Supreme Court reversed and reinstated the trial
court's judgment.

In an opinion by **Justice Karmeier**, the divided Illinois Supreme Court
rejected the invitation to overrule *Hewitt* and held that it remains good law.
Justice Karmeier highlighted three core points: Illinois had banned common
law marriage by statute a century prior; *Hewitt* remained correct in its
reasoning that property sharing by cohabitants approached common law
marriage; and the legislature clearly intended to reserve marriage as a
uniquely protected relationship, which would require judges to be reluctant
to expand marriage-like duties onto unmarried couples (through the law of
contracts or equity).

The Court was not persuaded that *Hewitt*'s logic unfairly discriminates
against unmarried domestic partners. "Rather, it acknowledges the
legislative intent to provide certain rights and benefits to those who
participate in the institution of marriage." Because all individuals may opt
to marry and because the state has an interest in encouraging marriage, it
is not irrational for Illinois to deny contract-based rights to persons who
choose cohabitation over marriage.

In response to the argument that circumstances had changed since
Hewitt, Justice Karmeier responded that such policy arguments are best left
to the Illinois General Assembly. Indeed, the legislature had enacted,
repealed, and amended a variety of family-centered statutes since *Hewitt*—
and had not "evinc[ed] an intention . . . to change the public policy concerning
the situation presently before this court. To the contrary, the claim that our
legislature is moving toward granting additional property rights to
unmarried cohabitants in derogation of the prohibition against common-law
marriage is flatly contradicted by the undeniable fact that for almost four
decades since *Hewitt*, and despite all of these numerous changes to other
family-related statutes, the statutory prohibition against common-law
marriage set forth in section 214 of the Marriage and Dissolution Act has
remained completely untouched and unqualified." Moreover, "now that the
centrality of the marriage has been recognized as a fundamental right for all,
it is perhaps more imperative than before that we leave it to the legislative
branch to determine whether and under what circumstances a change in the
public policy governing the rights of parties in nonmarital relationships is
necessary."

In a partial dissent, **Justice Theis** wrote that *Hewitt* is "clouded by an
inappropriate and moralistic view of domestic partners who cohabit and
founded upon legal principles that have changed significantly." Indeed,

Hewitt codified "the arcane view that domestic partners who choose to cohabit, but not marry, are engaged in 'illicit' or 'meretricious' behavior. . . ." In contrast, Justice Theis noted, "the legal landscape that formed the background for our decision has changed significantly. The *Hewitt* court was puzzled by the impact that recognizing claims arising from the relationships of unmarried cohabitants would have on society."

Consider some of the challenges raised by *Blumenthal*'s affirmance of *Hewitt*, particularly in light of *Obergefell*. Professor Franke has long expressed a concern that the *right* to marry could quickly become a requirement: "Winning the right to marry is one thing; being forced to marry is quite another." Katherine Franke, "Marriage Is a Mixed Blessing," *N.Y. Times*, June 23, 2011. Does *Blumenthal* suggest that this obligation has indeed emerged? Was the plaintiff punished for the decision not to marry?[e]

Is Professor Murray correct in suggesting that "*Blumenthal* makes clear *Obergefell*'s threat to nonmarital relationship recognition"? Melissa Murray, "*Obergefell v. Hodges* and Nonmarriage Inequality," 104 *Calif. L. Rev.* 1207, 1247 (2016).

Finally, "courts in a vast majority of states, as well as the District of Columbia, have chosen to recognize claims between former domestic partners like Blumenthal and Brewer." *Id.* at 1258. As Justice Theis noted, "Illinois is a clear outlier on this issue." More American adults are living without spouses—either with partners or alone—than ever before. How can the Illinois Supreme Court's assertion that a broad national norm *encouraging* marriage be reconciled with a continued social recognition of non-marital living arrangements?

American Law Institute, Principles of the Law of Family Dissolution

(2002).

Chapter 6: Domestic Partners

§ 6.01   Scope

(1)   This Chapter governs the financial claims of domestic partners against one another at the termination of their relationship. For the purpose of defining relationships to which this Chapter applies, domestic partners are two persons of the same or opposite sex, not married to one another, who for a significant period of time share a primary residence and a life together as a couple, as determined by § 6.03. * * *

---

[e]   This obligation was referenced in and then removed from the court's decision. According to the National Center for Lesbian Rights, the Illinois Supreme Court "initially addressed the constitutionality of applying its rule to former same-sex partners in a paragraph that was subsequently removed from the decision." In the deleted passage, the Court suggested that "Brewer should have tried to marry in another state or brought a lawsuit challenging Illinois's marriage ban."

§ 6.03   Determination That Persons Are Domestic Partners

(1)   For the purpose of defining relationships to which this Chapter applies, domestic partners are two persons of the same or opposite sex, not married to one another, who for a significant period of time share a primary residence and a life together as a couple.

(2)   Persons are domestic partners when they have maintained a common household, as defined in Paragraph (4), with their common child, as defined in Paragraph (5), for a continuous period that equals or exceeds a duration, called the *cohabitation parenting period*, set in a rule of statewide application.

(3)   Persons not related by blood or adoption are presumed to be domestic partners when they have maintained a common household, as defined in Paragraph (4), for a continuous period that equals or exceeds a duration, called the *cohabitation period*, set in a rule of statewide application. The presumption is rebuttable by evidence that the parties did not share life together as a couple, as defined by Paragraph (7).

(4)   Persons *maintain a common household* when they share a primary residence only with each other and family members; or when, if they share a household with other unrelated persons, they act jointly, rather than as individuals, with respect to management of the household.

(5)   Persons have a *common child* when each is either the child's legal parent or parent by estoppel * * *.

(6)   When the requirements of Paragraph (2) or (3) are not satisfied, a person asserting a claim under this Chapter bears the burden of proving that for a significant period of time the parties shared a primary residence and a life together as a couple, as defined in Paragraph (7). * * *

(7)   Whether persons share a life together as a couple is determined by reference to all the circumstances [including (a) oral or written promises, (b) intermingling of finances, (c) economic interdependence, (d) life collaborations, (f) formal acknowledgments in wills etc., (h) emotional or physical intimacy, (i) community reputation as a couple, (j) the couple's participation in a marriage ceremony or registration as domestic partners, (*l*) the couple's adoption etc. of a child, and (m) the maintenance of a common household].

§ 6.05   Allocation of Domestic-Partnership Property [defined in § 6.04]

Domestic-partnership property should be divided according to the principles set forth for the division of marital property in [Chapter 4 of the *Principles*].

§ 6.06   Compensatory Payments

(1)   Except as otherwise provided in this section,

(a)   a domestic partner is entitled to compensatory payments on the same basis as a spouse under Chapter 5, and

(b)   wherever a rule implementing a Chapter 5 principle makes the duration of the marriage a relevant factor, the application of that principle in this Chapter should instead employ the duration of the domestic-partnership period, as defined in § 6.04(2).

(2)   No claim arises under this section against a domestic partner who is neither a legal parent nor a parent by estoppel * * * of a child whose care provides the basis of the claim.

NOTE ON THE ALI'S PROPOSED "DOMESTIC PARTNERSHIP" STATUS

The same social and intellectual developments that have given rise to the *Marvin* litigation inspired scholars to call for the creation of new legal categories for family law purposes. Some have favored revival and extension of common law marriage to long-term couples, including same-sex couples.[f] Although few states recognize common law marriages, some states have created parallel institutions. The Washington Supreme Court, for example, will apply equitable principles of property division upon the breakup of partners in a "committed intimate relationship" (previously labeled "meretricious" relationships). To qualify, the relationship must be long-term and involve commingling of assets and an intent to form a committed relationship. See *Pennington v. Pennington*, 14 P.3d 764 (Wash. 2000).

The difficulty with common law marriage and the committed intimate relationship doctrine is that it is often hard to figure out whether the cohabiting couple qualifies. Courts such as the Washington Supreme Court follow an all-factors balancing approach. For reasons of notice to couples and easier administration (litigation is expensive), scholars and policymakers have advocated bright-line rules that define such a status. Professor Cynthia Grant Bowman, for example, proposes that the law should treat a cohabiting couple as married if they have either lived together for two years or have had a child within their relationship. Bowman, *Unmarried Couples,* 224.

Professor Bowman's bright-line rule would be relatively easy to administer, but might be unfair to the reasonable expectations of cohabiting partners. Professor Martha Ertman argues that cohabitation is a different relationship choice than marriage and, hence, ought not be subject to all the rules and regulations of marriage. Deals and contracts are a better approach, enabling the partners to customize their relationships. Ertman, *Love's Promise,* 147–48. A limitation of this approach is that most cohabiting

---

[f]   *See* David Chambers, "The 'Legalization' of the Family: Toward a Policy of Supportive Neutrality," 18 *U. Mich. J.L. Reform* 805 (1985); Ellen Kandoian, "Cohabitation, Common Law Marriage, and the Possibility of a Shared Moral Life," 75 *Geo. L.J.* 1829 (1987).

partners do not negotiate cohabitation agreements, and unwritten promises are often in the eyes of the beholder and hard to prove.

To solve problems of notice and proof, other scholars advocate legislative recognition of new legal statuses. Following the practice of parliaments in Europe and Canada, William Reppy, Jr., "Property and Support Rights of Unmarried Cohabitants: A Proposal for Creating a New Legal Status," 44 *La. L. Rev.* 1677 (1984), proposed a new status of *lawful cohabitation*, applicable to parties who expressly declare their partnership status *or* have attained its functional equivalent in terms of interdependence and sharing their lives, and bestowing on these parties some of the benefits and obligations of marriage. Chapter 6 of the ALI's *Principles* substantially adopted Professor Reppy's proposal.

By shifting the inquiry from *contract* back to *status*, the Reppy-ALI idea seeks to introduce greater consistency in the treatment of the break-ups of cohabiting couples, especially long-term couples where one partner has made sacrifices for the relationship and for children. Unfortunately, perhaps, American legislatures have not shown much interest in this idea, which has been popular in Europe and Canada. Indeed, the very term "domestic partnership" has been appropriated for a somewhat different strategy, described in the next section. For an array of critical approaches to the ALI's *Principles* along these lines, see Robin Fretwell Wilson, editor, *Reconceiving the Family: A Critique of the American Law Institute's Principles of Family Disolution* (2006).

NOTE ON RIGHTS OF COHABITING PARTNERS AFTER *OBERGEFELL*

As we saw in Chapter 2, Section 3, the LGBT campaign for recognition of marriage equality was marked by internal division pitting feminists such as Paula Ettelbrick and Nancy Polikoff and queer theorists such as Michael Warner, who did not want to strengthen the (patriarchal, misogynist) institution of marriage, *against* the liberal feminists and gay activists such as Tom Stoddard and Mary Bonauto, who wanted to secure equal rights for LGBT families. Nan Hunter argued that both sides erroneously treated marriage as a kind of monolithic, unchanging institution. Why not consider the possibility that the liberalization of marriage would press the institution toward greater gender equality, as sought by radical feminists? See Nan Hunter, "Marriage, Law, and Gender: A Feminist Inquiry," 1 *Law & Sexuality* 9 (1991).

With the Supreme Court's opinion in *Obergefell v. Hodges*, 135 S. Ct. 2484 (2015)—which begins by noting that "[f]rom their beginning to their most recent page, the annals of human history reveal the transcendent importance of marriage," *id.* at 2593—renewed concerns have arisen about the state of constitutional protections for relationships and families that exist outside of the institution of marriage. The soaring rhetoric about the noble, dignity-conferring, sacred, and unique institution of marriage has the potential to reinforce cultural stigma against those who decide not to marry or who are unable to do so. By holding that same-sex couples have a right to marry because of the institution of marriage's historical and fundamental place in society, does *Obergefell* undermine efforts to ensure greater protections for more recent institutions, such as domestic partnerships and other forms of nonmarital cohabitation?

Melissa Murray, "*Obergefell v. Hodges* and Nonmarriage Inequality," 104 *Calif. L. Rev.* 1207, 1242-44 (2016). Professor Murray warns that *Obergefell* will actively contribute to the erosion of the limited number of rights that the Court has granted to individuals engaging in alternative forms of relationships. She situates *Obergefell* not as the triumphant end to a series of gay rights cases but instead in the crosshairs of two distinct jurisprudential trends: cases about the right to marry and a category of cases she refers to the "jurisprudence of non-marriage." Professor Murray identifies three major cases on the right to marry that the Court relied upon in *Obergefell*: *Loving v. Virginia* (striking down prohibitions of interracial marriage), *Zablocki v. Redhail* (striking down restrictions on 'dead-beat dads" access to marriage), and *Turner v. Safley* (striking down prohibitions on prisoner marriages). In contrast, she points out that *Eisenstadt v. Baird* and *Lawrence v. Texas*, which the Court also relied upon in *Obergefell*, dealt explicitly with nonmarriage by recognizing that rights once extended only to married couples (the rights to contraception and the right to engage in consensual sex respectively), in fact applied to individuals rather than inhering in the institution of marriage. To these, Murray also adds cases dealing with nonmarital parentage and non-nuclear family households. The major contribution of this line of cases to constitutional jurisprudence is that it clarified that departures from the marital family are entitled to constitutional protection.

Professor Murray concedes that nonmarriage constitutional protections are limited in that they appear to depend on the proximity of the relationship at issue to a marital one. In *Lawrence*, the majority opinion depicted the relationship of the petitioners as marriage-like (despite a lack of evidence to that effect); in the cases dealing with nonmarital families, the closer that the family structure in question was to a nuclear family, the stronger the Court found the liberty interest of the family to be. By basing the liberty interest of the individuals involved on the special status of marriage, *Obergefell* has the potential to foreclose the jurisprudence of nonmarriage. Murray points out that *Obergefell* leaves domestic partnerships and civil unions, which were "derided as second-rate proxies to marriage" in the course of marriage equality litigation, in a precarious position: Vermont eliminated civil unions when it provided for same-sex marriage; and the Connecticut, Delaware, New Hampshire and Rhode Island marriage equality statutes all required the conversion of existing civil unions into marriages. She worries that by constitutionalizing marriage equality, *Obergefell* will "provide a firm basis for states to refuse legal recognition of alternative statuses and other nonmarital arrangements." As a legal and a normative matter, she argues that *Obergefell* entrenches the supremacy of marriage over nonmarriage.

But is the post-*Obergefell* landscape necessarily as bleak as Professor Murray predicts? Consider another perspective in the excerpt that follows.

Courtney Joslin, "The Gay Rights Canon and the Right to Nonmarriage," 97 *B.U.L. Rev.* **101, 156–62 (2017).** Professor Joslin identifies three underlying principles of the gay rights canon, all of which are prominent in *Obergefell*: (1) an appreciation for the connection or synergy between the principles of liberty and equality; (2) support for the equal dignity of all persons and opposition to stigma upon a disfavored group; and (3) an understanding of constitutional law as a dynamic doctrine that evolves to reflect legal, cultural, and social change.

Understanding liberty and equality as interdependent helps the Court to more clearly distinguish unfair stigma in the law, which a doctrine of dynamic constitutionalism allows them to remedy. The stigma that attaches to cohabitation and other forms of nonmarital relationships cannot be remedied merely through access to the institution of marriage, partly because many people decide not to marry for political, spiritual, and/or religious reasons, and partly because "race and class now significantly affect the likelihood that one will marry and stay married," meaning that "lower income individuals and people of color disproportionately feel the effects of marriage-based rules." The race and class dimensions of marriage as an institution heighten the constitutional concerns involved in a legal order that systematically privileges marriage over nonmarriage.

"One type of rule that raises significant constitutional concerns under this theory is that which denies any meaningful property-related claims to unmarried partners upon the dissolution of their relationship. In the absence of a valid premarital agreement, all fifty states divide the available marital or community property equally or equitably upon divorce. Generally speaking, these sharing rules do not apply to unmarried cohabitants. Some states go much further. In a few states, unmarried cohabitants are not only excluded from the property division rules that apply to married spouses, but they are also precluded from asserting even common law or contract claims that any other person— married or unmarried—could assert. The Illinois Supreme Court, for example, recently reaffirmed such a rule in *Blumenthal v. Brewer*."

Although there are plausible arguments in favor of applying different property division rules to married and nonmarital couples, such as evidence that cohabitants are less likely to be financially interdependent than spouses, Professor Joslin argues that "the *complete denial of protection* to nonmarital partners nonetheless raises a serious constitutional claim." The Illinois rule violates a substantive due process right to nonmarriage. "Individuals have a constitutionally protected right to form and live in nonmarital relationships. Denying a person a legal claim that he or she would otherwise have *because* he or she has chosen to live in a nonmarital, marriage-like relationship penalizes the exercise of this liberty interest. Moreover, because those living in nonmarriage are disproportionately likely to be nonwhite and to have a lower socioeconomic status, this rule raises significant equality concerns."

Marriage-only benefit rules impose significant costs on cohabiting couples denied their benefit. "Take, for example, laws that limit wrongful death claims to legally married spouses. Many nonmarital partners are financially interdependent. If one partner was relying solely on the other for financial support, the inability to sue for the breadwinner's wrongful death could lead to financial ruin. It could inhibit the ability of the survivor to adequately care for him or herself and for any children they were raising together. To the extent that the survivor was dependent on the decedent, denying benefits is inconsistent with the purpose of the statute.

"Of course, if one abandoned the bright line rule of marriage, one would need some criteria to determine who should be entitled to sue for wrongful death. There are existing models from which to draw. Some states permit individuals who are named as beneficiaries in the decedent's will to sue for wrongful death. Such a rule is broader than a marriage-only rule, but it likely would have class-based effects because individuals with greater resources are more likely to have a will. Another possible approach is the function-based test used by two states in the context of negligent infliction of emotional distress claims. In *Graves v. Estabrook*, the New Hampshire Supreme Court rejected the bright line marriage rule in favor of a more holistic test that looks to the nature of the relationship between the individuals. Among other things, the test looks to the 'extent and quality of shared experience,' whether the parties 'were members of the same household,' and the 'particulars of their day to day relationship.' "

PROBLEM 6-3
CONSTITUTIONALIZING THE RIGHTS OF UNMARRIED COUPLES?

If Professor Joslin is correct, the Illinois Supreme Court's decision in *Blumenthal v. Brewer* might violate the Fourteenth Amendment of the U.S. Constitution. If that were the case, the U.S. Supreme Court would have jurisdiction to review the *Hewitt* rule that the Illinois court reaffirmed. What precise constitutional arguments might be made to persuade the U.S. Supreme Court to reverse or abrogate *Blumenthal v. Brewer*? Might *Romer v. Evans* be relevant to such an argument? The Illinois Attorney General might file a brief with the Supreme Court to defend its state rule: What arguments should the state make? Would the *Obergefell* Court agree with the state? Or with Professor Joslin?

Miguel Braschi v. Stahl Associates Company, **74 N.Y.2d 201, 544 N.Y.S.2d 784, 543 N.E.2d 49 (1989).** Miguel Braschi was the surviving partner of a man who lived in a New York City rent-controlled apartment until his death. Stahl Associates, the landlord, sued to remove Braschi from the apartment pursuant to New York City rent and eviction regulation 9 NYCRR 2204.6(d), which provides that upon the death of a rent-control tenant, the landlord may repossess the apartment (and rent it for a higher rate), unless the apartment is inhabited by "the surviving spouse of the deceased tenant or some other member of the deceased tenant's family who has been living with the tenant." Braschi claimed that he was a member of the decedent's "family" due to their stable partnership, and Stahl responded that "family" should be limited to relatives by blood or marriage, such as those given inheritance rights under New York's intestate decedent rules.

In an opinion by **Judge Titone**, a plurality of the New York Court of Appeals ruled that "the term family, as used in 9 NYCRR 2204.6(d), should not be rigidly restricted to those people who have formalized their relationship by obtaining, for instance, a marriage certificate or an adoption order. The intended protection against sudden eviction should not rest on fictitious legal distinctions or genetic history, but instead should find its foundation in the reality of family life. In the context of eviction, a more realistic, and certainly equally valid, view of a family includes two adult lifetime partners whose relationship is long term and characterized by an emotional and financial commitment and interdependence. This view comports both with our society's traditional concept of 'family' and with the expectations of individuals who live in such nuclear units."

Judge Titone then considered what partners should be considered "family" for purposes of the statute: "The determination as to whether an individual is entitled to noneviction protection should be based upon an objective examination of the relationship of the parties. In making this assessment, the lower courts of this State have looked to a number of factors, including the exclusivity and longevity of the relationship, the level of emotional and financial commitment, the manner in which the parties have conducted their everyday lives and held themselves out to society, and the reliance placed upon one another for daily family services. These factors are most helpful, although it should be emphasized that the presence or absence of one or more of them is not dispositive since it is the totality of the relationship as evidenced by the dedication, caring and self-sacrifice of the parties which should, in the final analysis, control." Because Braschi and the decedent had lived together as "permanent life partners" for more than 10 years, held themselves out and socialized as a couple, pooled their assets, and established the rent-controlled apartment as their joint home, Judge Titone found Braschi to fit the idea of family.

Three judges joined this plurality opinion, and **Judge Bellacosa** agreed with its holding and with its general analysis. Two judges dissented. They believed that the objectives of the rent control law "require a weighing of the interests of certain individuals living with the tenant of record at his or her death and the interests of the landlord in regaining possession of its property and re-renting it under the less onerous rent-stabilization laws. The interests are properly balanced if the regulation's exception is applied by using objectively verifiable relationships based on blood, marriage and adoption, as the State has historically done in the estate succession laws, family court acts and similar legislation. The distinction is warranted because members of families, so defined, assume certain legal obligations to each other and to third persons, such as creditors, which are not imposed on unrelated individuals and this legal interdependency is worthy of consideration in determining which individuals are entitled to succeed to the interest of the statutory tenant in rent-controlled premises. Moreover, such an interpretation promotes certainty and consistency in the law and obviates the need for drawn out hearings and litigation focusing on such intangibles as the strength and duration of the relationship and the extent of the emotional and financial interdependency. So limited, the regulation may be viewed as a tempered response, balancing the rights of landlords with those of the tenant. To come within that protected class, individuals must comply with State laws relating to marriage or adoption. Plaintiff cannot avail himself of these institutions, of course, but that only points up the need for a legislative solution, not a judicial one."

Postscript. New York's Division of Housing and Community Renewal codified *Braschi* in its regulations and extended it to rent-stabilized as well as rent-controlled apartments. N.Y. Compiled Codes, Rules & Regulations tit. 9, § 2204.6(d)(3)(i). On the other hand, New York courts have enforced lease provisions for unregulated apartments that limit occupancy to persons related by blood or marriage. *E.g., Hudson View Props. v. Weiss*, 59 N.Y.2d 733, 450 N.E.2d 234 (1983). Nor have New York courts treated *Braschi*-like partners as a surviving "spouse" for purposes of state trusts and estates law. See *In re Cooper*, 187 A.D.2d 128, 592 N.Y.S.2d 797 (1993). The New York Court of Appeals declined to constitutionalize same-sex marriage recognition in *Hernandez v. Robles*, 7 N.Y.3d 338, 855 N.E.2d 1 (2006), but the New York Legislature did so in 2011. In light of marriage equality for LGBT couples, should the Court of Appeals revisit *Braschi*?

SECTION 3

THE EMERGING MENU OF RELATIONSHIP RECOGNITION

By the twenty-first century, one could understand American family law to offer two primary regulatory regimes: statutory civil marriage and common law (*Marvin*) cohabitation rights. See William Eskridge Jr., "Family Law Pluralism: The Guided-Choice Regime of Menus, Default Rules, and Override Rules," 100 *Geo. L.J.* 1881, 1928–35 (2012) (surveying the increasing array of rights and duties imposed upon at least some cohabiting couples). Ironically, the marriage equality movement in the United States was the occasion for local and state legislatures to create new forms of family recognition, often including different-sex as well as same-sex couples. In Canada and Europe, legislatures have created a more pluralistic set of statutory regimes outside of marriage. See *Legal Recognition of Same-Sex Partnerships: A Study of National, European and International Law* (Robert Wintemute & Mads Andenaes eds., 2001) (similar legislative responses in Europe and Canada).

When state legislatures recognized marriage for same-sex couples, they sometimes revoked or preempted the new institutions, but where those institutions included different-sex couples they usually survived marriage equality laws. Most states came to marriage equality through court order, and these states generally did not repeal whatever new institutions had been created in those jurisdictions. In some states (but not most), the menu of choices for romantic and other couples now includes at least one institution apart from civil marriage and common law and administrative cohabitation.

A. DOMESTIC PARTNERSHIPS

Tom Brougham was a gay activist instrumental in Berkeley's 1978 adoption of a sexual orientation anti-discrimination ordinance—but that effort brought a new realization to Brougham: "[W]hen I went to work for the City of Berkeley in early 1979 we noticed that everybody signs up for benefits, and I realized than my partner [Barry Warren] could not be a beneficiary. It got me thinking along the lines of what it really meant to have equal opportunity and equal benefits. The City of Berkeley had very recently adopted a gay rights ordinance that basically proposed equal rights in the city, and yet here was an example in which it simply didn't function properly. So Barry and I talked about this a great deal."

"[I]n the early days, when we tried to talk about this with people within the gay movement, there was very little interest, very little expectation that anybody could do anything about it. People would just kind of shrug and say, 'Well, they're married and we're not.' And that was pretty much the end of it. But, we persisted and began to write up something which we then took to the University of California [Barry's employer] and the City of Berkeley [Brougham's employer]; both in 1979. Both of those kind of fizzled out. We sort of persisted and developed the idea, but there wasn't very much in the way of serious consideration. We took it to the university and they just pretty much went through a charade and turned it all down." OUT History Interview with Tom Brougham, 1987, available at http://outhistory.org/exhibits/show/out-and-elected/late-1980s/tom-brougham (viewed June 24, 2016); see Leland Traiman, "A Brief History of Domestic Partnerships," *Gay & Lesbian Review Worldwide*, July-Aug. 2008, at 23.

In Brougham's petition to the City, he first used the term *domestic partner*. "We were looking for something quasi-legal sounding and that was nonsexual. We wanted to emphasize the everyday living and sharing of people. What was important was that we were a household. We were taking care of each other every day, doing all the normal family things together—that's where 'domestic' comes in." Judith Scherr, "Berkeley, Activists Set Milestone for Domestic Partnership in 1984," *East Bay Times*, June 28, 2013 (quoting Brougham). But Brougham was unable to sell the domestic partnership idea in Berkeley.

The idea resurfaced at the behest of San Francisco Supervisor Harry Britt. Britt's aide, Bill Kraus, telephoned his attorney-ally Matt Coles: Gay employees are not receiving health care benefits for their partners—What can we do about this? Coles discovered that it was quite a complicated thing, politically, because the Board of Supervisors did not have control over health insurance and because there was no exact legal precedent. So in 1981 and early 1982, they had a series of meetings with stakeholders. In one early meeting at a conference room in City Hall, Coles, Kraus, Brougham, representatives of the Harvey Milk and Alice Toklas Clubs, and representatives of the primary unions pondered what term to use. Brougham, of course, suggested "domestic partnership," a term that everyone else disliked. "It sounded like a home cleaning service," cracked Coles, but no one had a better idea, and so domestic partnership it was. Eskridge Telephone Interview with Matthew Coles, August 1, 2016.

Drafted by Coles for Kraus and Britt, the first major domestic partnership was passed by the San Francisco Board of Supervisors in 1982, but the move provoked a firestorm of protest, led by the Roman Catholic Archdiocese of San Francisco, objecting that anything that even faintly "mimics a marriage license" was unacceptable. As Coles later put it, "the core religious opposition understood the ordinance, in some ways, better than some of the supporters. This was not about health insurance, not about giving benefits, it was about getting society to see gay people and heterosexual couples differently. It was about showing the public that there were couples with important intimate, supportive relationships that didn't see themselves through marriage." The measure was also important to refute society's view that "gay people * * * are incapable of any kind of emotional depth." For this reason, Mayor Diane Feinstein (whose own Rabbi opposed the measure) vetoed it in December 1982.

The idea would not die, however. Many LGBT persons were in relationships and felt they needed some of the rights conferred by marriage. The AIDS epidemic, spiraling out of control at precisely the same time, fueled this movement. Not only did AIDS bring thousands of gay men and their relationships out of the closet, but it highlighted the need for legal protections. An early AIDS discrimination lawsuit was brought by Matt Coles and the ACLU on behalf of an employee of the Southern Pacific Railroad, which refused him bereavement leave after his partner died of AIDS in March 1981. Thousands of gay and bisexual men suffered painful discrimination when medical care was denied their AIDS partners because they had no health insurance, hospitals denied them time with their loved ones, and employers refused them time to grieve.

Advocates kept pushing, and domestic partnership became a focus of AIDS and gay rights activism in California during the Reagan-Bush Administrations. In 1984, the Berkeley City Council adopted the first operative municipal domestic partnership policy. The Berkeley ordinance gave all couples (MF FF MM) rights to hospital visitation and, for city employees, sickness and bereavement leaves as well as health and dental insurance benefits for domestic partners. Similar domestic partnership benefit ordinances were adopted in West Hollywood (1985); Santa Cruz (1986); Laguna Beach, Alameda County, San Matteo County, and San Francisco (1990); Los Angeles (1991); Sacramento (1992); Oakland and Marin County (1993); San Diego (1994); Santa Monica (1995); Long Beach and Santa Barbara (1997).

Most of the California ordinances followed the AIDS model, creating a registry for domestic partners and extended health insurance and other benefits to the named partners of municipal employees; most of the laws also extended a few other legal benefits, usually the right to visit one's partner in the hospital and/or in jail. Often adopted piece by piece, this model spread to other gay-friendly cities all over the country, including New York City (1989, expanded in 1993 and 1997); Ann Arbor and Minneapolis (1991); Washington, D.C. (1992); Atlanta, Baltimore, Boston, Hartford, New Orleans, and Rochester (1993); New Orleans and Seattle (1994); St. Louis (1997); Philadelphia (1998); Denver and Milwaukee (1999); Portland, Oregon (2000); Detroit and Portland, Maine (2001). Most of these cities had significant populations of people with AIDS and their caregivers.

In 1991, Lotus Development Corp., a software company, became the first Fortune 1000 company to offer health, dental, and medical care insurance to the "spousal equivalents" of its lesbian and gay employees. This decision was greeted with major media fanfare. Before Lotus, almost all the DP employment programs were governmental (usually municipal) or nonprofit employers (like Lambda and the ACLU), but after Lotus the large majority were private companies. Between 1991 and 1999, 82 Fortune 1000 companies joined Lotus, as well as dozens of smaller firms. By March 2004, equitable benefits were provided to domestic partners of lesbian and gay (and sometimes straight) employees by 211 Fortune 500 companies, 6863 other private companies and unions, 198 colleges and universities, 10 states, 130 local governments, and the District of Columbia. See Nicole Raeburn, *Changing Corporate America from Inside Out*, at 2–3, 47–48 (2004). A major factor in the spread of these programs was the adoption by large cities and states (most significantly, California), beginning in the 1990s, of requirements that any company having a contract to provide goods or services to government agencies must offer equitable benefits.

Domestic partnership recognition by municipalities raised a number of legal and constitutional issues. Traditionalist opponents of domestic partnership ordinances have successfully challenged some of them as inconsistent with state "home rule" laws that provide limited allowances for municipal legislation. Each challenge is somewhat *sui generis*, as it is governed by the precise terms of a state's home-rule statute; municipal governments are like the federal government—they can take regulatory action only if specifically authorized to do so. Perhaps the most interesting case involved Atlanta's 1993 domestic partnership registry that entitled partners to visitation of their partners in jail and to health care benefits if they were city employees. (Like most but not all domestic partner registries, the Atlanta one included different-sex as well as same-sex couples.) Traditionalists challenged the Atlanta ordinance (and a previous one barring sexual orientation discrimination) as inconsistent with the Georgia Municipal Home Rule Act, which grants any city authority to adopt ordinances "relating to its property, affairs, and local government for which no provision has been made by general law."

The Georgia Supreme Court in *City of Atlanta v. McKinney,* 265 Ga. 161, 454 S.E.2d 517 (1995), ruled that Atlanta had the authority to create a registry and extend jail visitation to domestic partners. But the court ruled that Atlanta did not have the authority to enact ordinances "defining family relationships," as the state's general family law comprehensively covers that topic. Justice Sears and two other Justices dissented from this part of the ruling; the benefits ordinance was, in her view, merely elaborating on what persons might be "dependents" of city employees and therefore fell within the enumerated powers of the city. Justice Carley agreed with this part of the ruling but dissented from the court's upholding the creation of a registry, as that was also preempted by state law, in his view. In *City of Atlanta v. Morgan*, 268 Ga. 586, 492 S.E.2d 193 (1997), the Georgia Supreme Court followed Justice Sears' advice and upheld Atlanta's amended ordinance extending insurance benefits to domestic partners of municipal employees as "dependents" under state law.

These jurisdictional home rule problems are obviated if the state itself adopts a domestic partnership registry and defines the benefits and duties that attach to the new institution. Massachusetts and Vermont were the first states to offer domestic partnership benefits to their employees; many other states now offer such benefits as a matter of statute or executive interpretation. The first American statewide registries for same-sex partners were created by Hawaii's reciprocal benefits law in 1997 and California's domestic partnership law in 1999 (expanded significantly in 2003 and in minor ways after 2003).

The California law covered same-sex couples and different-sex couples over the age of 62 years. Subsequent state laws were usually limited to same-sex couples, but Nevada extended its domestic partnership option to all couples. Most of the municipal domestic partnership laws applied to different-sex as well as same-sex couples. Now that all states allow same-sex couples to marry, state, municipal, and corporate domestic partnership policies limited to same-sex couples have usually been terminated. In contrast, domestic partnership policies that have included different-sex couples (including policies like California's that include only some such couples) have survived marriage equality. Are there constitutional reasons to include different-sex couples? Consider the following decision.

Milagros Irizarry v. Board of Education of City of Chicago

United States Court of Appeals for the Seventh Circuit, 2001.
251 F.3d 604.

■ CIRCUIT JUDGE POSNER.

Although Milagros Irizarry has lived with the same man for more than two decades and they have two (now adult) children, they have never married. As an employee of the Chicago public school system, she receives health benefits but he does not, even though he is her "domestic partner" (the term for persons who are cohabiting with each other in a relationship similar to marriage), though he would if he were her husband. In July 1999, the Chicago Board of Education extended spousal health benefits to domestic partners—but only if the domestic partner was of the same sex as the employee, which excluded Irizarry's domestic partner, an exclusion that she contends is unconstitutional.

Besides being of the same sex, applicants for domestic-partner status must be unmarried, unrelated, at least 18 years old, and "each other's sole domestic partner, responsible for each other's common welfare." They must satisfy two of the following four additional conditions as well: that they have been living together for a year; that they jointly own their home; that they jointly own other property of specified kinds; that the domestic partner is the primary beneficiary named in the employee's will. Although the board's purpose in entitling domestic partners so defined to spousal benefits was to extend such benefits to homosexual employees, homosexual marriage not being recognized by Illinois, entitlement to the benefits does not require proof of sexual orientation.

The board of education makes two arguments for treating homosexual couples differently from unmarried heterosexual couples. First, since homosexual marriage is not possible in Illinois (or anywhere else in the United States, though it is now possible in the Netherlands), and heterosexual marriage of course is, the recognition of a domestic-partnership surrogate is more important for homosexual than for heterosexual couples, who can obtain the benefits simply by marrying. Second, the board wants to attract homosexual teachers in order to provide support for homosexual students. According to its brief, the board "believes that lesbian and gay male school personnel who have a healthy acceptance of their own sexuality can act as role models and provide emotional support for lesbian and gay students. . . . They can support students who are questioning their sexual identities or who are feeling alienated due to their minority sexual orientation. They can also encourage all students to be tolerant and accepting of lesbians and gay males, and discourage violence directed at these groups."

This line of argument will shock many people even today; it was not that long ago when homosexual teachers were almost universally considered a public menace likely to seduce or recruit their students into homosexuality, then regarded with unmitigated horror. The plaintiff does not argue, however, that the Chicago Board of Education is irrational in having turned the traditional attitude toward homosexual teachers upside down. It is not for a federal court to decide whether a local government agency's policy of tolerating or even endorsing homosexuality is sound. Even if the judges consider such a policy morally repugnant—even dangerous—they may not interfere with it unless convinced that it lacks even minimum rationality, which is a permissive standard. It is a fact that some school children are homosexual, and the responsibility for dealing with that fact is lodged in the school authorities, and (if they are public schools) ultimately in the taxpaying public, rather than in the federal courts.

The efficacy of the policy may be doubted. Although it had been in effect for a year and a half when the appeal was argued, only nine employees out of some 45,000 had signed up for domestic-partner benefits and none of the nine indicated whether he or she was homosexual; they may not all have been, as we shall see—perhaps none were. Nor is there any indication that any of the nine are new employees attracted to teach in the Chicago public schools by the availability of health benefits for same sex domestic partners. Maybe it's too early, though, to assess the efficacy of the policy. No matter; limited efficacy does not make the policy irrational—not even if we think limited efficacy evidence that the policy is more in the nature of a political gesture than a serious effort to improve the lot of homosexual students—if only because with limited efficacy comes limited cost. Because homosexuals are a small fraction of the population, because the continuing stigma of homosexuality discourages many of them from revealing their sexual orientation, and because nowadays a significant number of heterosexuals substitute cohabitation for marriage in response to the diminishing stigma of cohabitation, extending domestic-partner benefits to mixed-sex couples would greatly increase the expense of the program.

Irizarry argues that the child of an unmarried couple ought equally to be entitled to the mentoring and role-model benefits of having teachers who live in the same way the student's parents do. Cost considerations to one side, the argument collides with a nationwide policy in favor of marriage. True, it is no longer widely popular to try to pressure homosexuals to marry persons of the opposite sex. But so far as heterosexuals are concerned, the evidence that on average married couples live longer, are healthier, earn more, have lower rates of substance abuse and mental illness, are less likely to commit suicide, and report higher levels of happiness—that marriage civilizes young males, confers economies of scale and of joint consumption, minimizes sexually transmitted disease, and provides a stable and nourishing framework for child rearing—see, e.g., Linda J. Waite & Maggie Gallagher, *The Case for Marriage: Why Married People Are Happier, Healthier, and Better Off Financially* (2000); David Popenoe, *Life Without Father: Compelling New Evidence That Fatherhood and Marriage Are Indispensable for the Good of Children and Society* (1996). George W. Dent, Jr., "The Defense of Traditional Marriage," 15 *J.L. & Pol.* 581 (1999), refutes any claim that policies designed to promote marriage are irrational. The Chicago Board of Education cannot be faulted, therefore, for not wishing to encourage heterosexual cohabitation; and, though we need not decide the point, the refusal to extend domestic-partner benefits to heterosexual cohabitators could be justified on the basis of the policy favoring marriage for heterosexuals quite apart from the reasons for wanting to extend the spousal fringe benefits to homosexual couples.

Of course, self-selection is important; people are more likely to marry who believe they have characteristics favorable to a long-term relationship. But the Chicago Board of Education would not be irrational (though it might be incorrect) in assigning some causal role to the relationship itself. Linda J. Waite, "Does Marriage Matter?" 32 *Demography* 483, 498–99 (1995), finds that cohabitants are much less likely than married couples to pool financial resources, more likely to assume that each partner is responsible for supporting himself or herself financially, more likely to spend free time separately, and less likely to agree on the future of the relationship. This makes both investment in the relationship and specialization with this partner much riskier than in marriage, and so reduces them. Whereas marriage connects individuals to other important social institutions, such as organized religion, cohabitation seems to distance them from these institutions.

Irizarry and her domestic partner may, given the unusual duration of their relationship, be an exception to generalizations about the benefits of marriage. We are not aware of an extensive scholarly literature comparing marriage to long-term cohabitation. This may be due to the fact that long-term cohabitation is rare—only ten percent of such relationships last for five years or more, Pamela J. Smock, "Cohabitation in the United States: An Appraisal of Research Themes, Findings, and Implications," 26 *Ann. Rev. Sociology* 1 (2000). But there is evidence that the widespread substitution of cohabitation for marriage in Sweden has given that country the highest rate of family dissolution and single parenting in the developed world. David Popenoe, *Disturbing the Nest: Family Change and Decline in Modern Societies* 173–74 (1988). It is well known that divorce is harmful to children, and presumably the same is true for the dissolution of a cohabitation—and a cohabitation is more likely to dissolve than a marriage. True, Irizarry's cohabitation has not dissolved; but law and policy are based on the general rather than the idiosyncratic * * *. Nor is it entirely clear that this couple ought to be considered an exception to the general concern with heterosexuals who choose to have a family outside of marriage. For when asked at argument why the couple had never married, Irizarry's counsel replied that he had asked his client that question and she had told him that "it just never came up." There may be good reasons why a particular couple would not marry even after producing children, but that the thought of marriage would not even occur to them is disquieting.

The Lambda Legal Defense and Education Fund has filed an *amicus curiae* brief surprisingly urging reversal—surprisingly because Lambda is an organization for the promotion of homosexual rights, and if it is the law that domestic-partnership benefits must be extended to heterosexual couples, the benefits are quite likely to be terminated for everyone lest the extension to heterosexual cohabitors impose excessive costs and invite criticism as encouraging heterosexual cohabitation and illegitimate births and discouraging marriage and legitimacy. But Lambda is concerned with the fact that state and national policy encourages (heterosexual) marriage in all sorts of ways that domestic-partner health benefits cannot begin to equalize. Lambda wants to knock marriage off its perch by requiring the board of education to treat unmarried heterosexual couples as well as it treats married ones, so that marriage will lose some of its luster.

This is further evidence of the essentially symbolic or political rather than practical significance of the board's policy. Lambda is not jeopardizing a substantial benefit for homosexuals because very few of them want or will seek the benefit. In any event, it would not be proper for judges to use the vague concept of "equal protection" to undermine marriage just because it is a heterosexual institution. The desire of the board of education to increase the employment of homosexual teachers is admittedly a striking manifestation of the sexual revolution that has characterized, some would say convulsed, the United States in the last forty years. The courts did not try to stop the revolution. On the contrary, they spurred it on, most pertinently to this case by their decisions removing legal disabilities of birth out of wedlock, disabilities that if they still existed might have induced Ms. Irizarry and the father of her children to marry in order to remove those disabilities from their children. Likewise relevant are cases such as *Stanley v. Illinois*, that confer constitutional rights on unwed fathers. But no court has gone so far as to deem marriage a suspect classification because government provides benefits to married persons that it withholds from cohabiting couples. That would be a bizarre extension of case law already criticized as having carried the courts well beyond the point at which the Constitution might be thought to provide guidance to social policy.* * *

The least rational feature of the board's policy, though not emphasized by the plaintiff, is that although domestic-partner benefits are confined to persons of the same sex, the partners need not be homosexual. They could be roommates who have lived together for a year and own some property jointly and for want of relatives are each other's "sole domestic-partner," and if so they would be entitled to domestic-partner benefits under the board of education's policy. To distinguish between roommates of the same and of different sexes, as the policy implicitly does, cannot be justified on the ground that the latter but not the former could marry each other!

So the policy does not make a very close fit between end and means. But it doesn't have to, provided there is a rational basis for the loose fit. This follows from our earlier point that cost is a rational basis for treating people differently. Economy is one of the principal reasons for using rules rather than standards to govern conduct. Rules single out one or a few facts from the welter of possibly relevant considerations and make that one or those few facts legally determinative, thus dispensing with inquiry into the other considerations. A standard that takes account of all relevant considerations will produce fewer arbitrary differences in outcome, but at a cost in uncertainty, administrative burden, and sometimes even—as here—in invading people's privacy. It is easy to see why the board of education does not want to put applicants to the proof of their sexual preference. That would be resented. The price of avoiding an inquiry that would be costly because it would be obnoxious is that a few roommates may end up with windfall benefits. We cannot say that the board is being irrational in deciding to pay that price rather than snoop into people's sex lives.

If the result is, as it may be, that none of the nine employees who have opted for domestic-partner benefits is homosexual (or at least that none is willing to acknowledge his homosexuality publicly, for that is not required by the board's policy though it would seem implicit in the board's desire to attract homosexuals who have "a healthy acceptance of their own sexuality"), this would lend a note of irony to the board's policy and would reinforce our earlier conjecture that the purpose is to make a statement rather than to confer actual monetary benefits. But "making a statement" is a common purpose of legislation and does not condemn it as irrational. * * *

NOTE ON DOMESTIC PARTNERSHIPS DISCRIMINATING AGAINST STRAIGHT COUPLES

Judge Posner agrees with the plaintiff that the school board policy recognizing only same-sex domestic partners discriminates against different-sex cohabiting couples but upholds the discrimination under the lenient version of the rational basis test. As a formal matter, however, the discrimination is on the basis of Milagros Irigarry's sex: if she had been a male cohabiting with her male partner, she would have been entitled to the benefit. Sex discrimination cannot be justified by merely a rational basis, as *Craig v. Boren* (Chapter 1, Section 2) held. So did Judge Posner get the level of scrutiny wrong? See *Hively v. Ivy Tech Community College*, 853 F.3d 339 (7th Cir. en banc 2017) (Posner concurred in the majority opinion, holding that employer discrimination against lesbians is discrimination "because of * * * sex" made illegal by Title VII).

The policies Judge Posner invokes might not satisfactorily justify the discrimination under a rational basis approach which has the kind of bite the Supreme Court gave it in *Romer v. Evans* (Chapter 1, Section 2): (a) The school board wanted to remedy discrimination against gay people, whose unmarried partners were excluded from health insurance coverage; and the board wanted to attract lesbian and gay role models. But the policy's discrimination is way underinclusive because you don't have to be gay or lesbian to register as domestic partners, and there is no evidence that the nine registered couples are "homosexual." As the Lambda brief suggested, most gay people do not support discrimination against different-sex couples in domestic partnership policies and laws. (b) The policy is a symbolic gesture to gay people. *Romer* and *Lawrence v. Texas* (Chapter 2) ruled that symbolic statutes discriminating against gay people are not rational. Are symbolic statutes discriminating in favor of gays more rational? Even if gays oppose the discrimination against straights? (c) It would cost a lot more for the policy to cover straight cohabiting couples, and the line-drawing would be harder. Under Justice O'Connor's concurring opinion in *Lawrence*, cost would seem insufficient when personal rights are involved. Should some of Judge Posner's justifications be rethought after *Lawrence*? Why does he not consider *Romer* relevant?

Perhaps the rational basis for the school board's discrimination was the "nationwide policy in favor of marriage," which in 2001 was limited to straight couples in all 50 states. There is some analytical slippage here, too. Judge Posner does not cite evidence for the proposition that refusing to recognize different-sex domestic partnerships will encourage people to marry; this hypothesis reflects a stronger belief in legal causation than Posner ordinarily follows. Instead, Posner cites evidence that married people are happier etc. These claims are controversial among social scientists. The main criticism is selection bias in the samples: people having the traits associated with happiness etc. (good health, attractiveness, good incomes, mentally stable, etc.) are more likely to get married. *E.g.*, Lee Lillard et al., "Premarital Cohabitation and Subsequent Dissolution: A Matter of Self-Selection?," 32 *Demography* 437 (1995). There is ample evidence that marriage and good health etc. are correlated, but the causal connection remains hard to pin down.

A study by social scientist Lawrence Kurdek found a different pattern. He studied 239 straight married couples, 79 gay male unmarried couples, and 51 lesbian unmarried couples over a five-year period. Contrary to Judge Posner, Professor Kurdek found that the quality of the relationship and partner happiness was about the same for the married straight and the unmarried gay male couples—and significantly higher for the unmarried lesbian couples after five years. See Kurdek, "Relationship Outcomes and Their Predictors: Longitudinal Evidence from Heterosexual Married, Gay Cohabiting, and Lesbian Cohabiting Couples," 60 *J. Marriage & Fam.* 553 (1998). Would this study have made a difference in Posner's analysis?

In finding that a state policy designed to promote marriage over nonmarital relationships for heterosexuals passes rational basis review, Judge Posner accepts that such a policy is not based on stigma or unpopularity. Because opposite-sex couples had the opportunity to marry, both the Chicago Board of Education and Judge Posner seem to be asking: Why not? But there are many reasons that an opposite-sex couple might choose not to marry, including religious, political, and any number of personal or philosophical reasons. Judge Posner cites a number of studies to support the contention that the policy is rational, while conceding that there may be a self-selection bias—that happy, healthy people are more likely to get married rather than marriage causing people to become happy and healthy. But what if married people are happier, healthier, and wealthier than their nonmarriage counterparts precisely because of all the benefits, both practical such as health coverage, and intangible such as social capital, that come with being married? Is a political preference for marriage over nonmarriage not a form of stigma? If Judge Posner knew that access to marriage is increasingly determined along class and racial lines, with rich whites being the main beneficiaries of marriage, would he have been more likely to understand the Board of Education's policy as a form of stigma?

In the following decision, the Ninth Circuit reviewed the constitutionality of an Arizona law that limited state employee healthcare benefits to spouses, thereby eliminating coverage for domestic partners whether same- or opposite-sex. Consider the role that stigma played in this decision. If this case had occurred after *Obergefell*, would it have come out the same way?

Joseph R. Diaz v. Janice K. Brewer, Governor of the State of Arizona

United States Court of Appeals for the Ninth Circuit, 2011.
656 F.3d 1008, *rehearing denied*, 676 F.3d 823 (9th Cir. *en banc*, 2012),
cert. denied, 133 S.Ct. 2884 (2013).

■ CIRCUIT JUDGE SCHROEDER. * * *

[In April 2008, Arizona administratively adopted amendments to its Administrative Code, in order to offer access to health-care benefits for qualified opposite-sex and same-sex domestic partners of state employees. Prior to 2008, when state employees chose to participate in the State's health insurance program, they only had the option to include their spouses and children within the defined parameters of the term "dependent." In 2008, the amendments expanded the definition of "dependent" to include qualified "domestic partners," who could be of either sex. See 14 Ariz. Admin. Reg. 1420–34 (Apr. 25, 2008).

[In November 2008, Arizona voters approved Proposition 102, also known as the *Marriage Protection Amendment,* which amended the Arizona Constitution to define marriage as between one man and one woman: "Only a union of one man and one woman shall be valid or recognized as a marriage in this state." Ariz. Const. art. 30, § 1. On September 4, 2009, the Governor of Arizona signed House Bill 2013, which included a statutory provision, Ariz. Rev. Stat. § 38–651(O) that redefined "dependents" as "spouses," and thereby eliminated coverage for domestic partners. The District Court issued a preliminary injunction against the 2009 statute, and the Ninth Circuit affirmed.]

The state is correct in asserting that state employees and their families are not constitutionally entitled to health benefits. But when a state chooses to provide such benefits, it may not do so in an arbitrary or discriminatory manner that adversely affects particular groups that may be unpopular. The most instructive Supreme Court case involving arbitrary restriction of benefits for a particular group perceived as unpopular is *U.S. Department of Agriculture v. Moreno,* 413 U.S. 528 (1973). In that case, Plaintiffs challenged the constitutionality of an amendment to the Food Stamp Act of 1964, which redefined the term "household" to limit the program's eligible recipients to groups of related individuals. While noting the "little legislative history" available on the amendment, the Court concluded that the legislation was aimed at groups that were unpopular. The "amendment was intended to prevent so-called 'hippies' and 'hippie communes' from participating in the food stamp program."

In defending the amendment under rational basis review, the government contended that Congress might rationally have thought that the amendment would prevent fraud given the relative instability of households with unrelated individuals. The Court rejected both justifications. The Court held that the "practical operation" of the amendment would allow the hippies, with means, who were allegedly abusing the program, to rearrange their housing status to retain eligibility, while excluding those who were financially unable to do so, i.e., "only those persons who are so desperately in need of aid that they cannot even afford to alter their living arrangements so as to retain their eligibility." Those excluded were like the same-sex partners in this case who, because they cannot marry, are unable to alter their living arrangements to retain eligibility. The Court concluded that the "hippie" amendment's classification was "wholly without any rational basis." We must reach the same conclusion.

Here, as in *Moreno*, the legislature amended a benefits program in order to limit eligibility. Since in this case eligibility was limited to married couples, different-sex couples wishing to retain their current family health benefits could alter their status—marry—to do so. The Arizona Constitution, however, prohibits same-sex couples from doing so. Thus, this case may present a more compelling scenario, since the plaintiffs in *Moreno* were prevented by financial circumstances from adjusting their status to gain eligibility, while same-sex couples in Arizona are prevented by operation of law.

Defendants nevertheless contend on appeal that this law is rationally related to the state's interests in cost savings and reducing administrative burdens. As the district court observed, however, the savings depend upon distinguishing between homosexual and heterosexual employees, similarly situated, and such a distinction cannot survive rational basis review. The Supreme Court in *Eisenstadt v. Baird*, 405 U.S. 438 (1972), was well aware of this principle when it quoted the eloquent words of Justice Robert H. Jackson, decrying the selective application of legislation to a small group:

> The framers of the Constitution knew, and we should not forget today, that there is no more effective practical guaranty against arbitrary and unreasonable government than to require that the principles of law which officials would impose upon a minority must be imposed generally. Conversely, nothing opens the door to arbitrary action so effectively as to allow those officials to pick and choose only a few to whom they will apply legislation and thus to escape the political retribution that might be visited upon them if larger numbers were affected. Courts can take no better measure to assure that laws will be just than to require that laws be equal in operation. * * *

The state has also argued that the statute promotes marriage by eliminating benefits for domestic partners, but the plaintiffs negated that as a justification. The district court properly concluded that the denial of benefits to same-sex domestic partners cannot promote marriage, since such partners are ineligible to marry. On appeal, the state has not seriously advanced this justification.

In sum, the district court correctly recognized that barring the state of Arizona from discriminating against same-sex couples in its distribution of employee health benefits does not constitute the recognition of a new constitutional right to such benefits. Rather, it is consistent with long standing equal protection jurisprudence holding that "some objectives, such as 'a bare . . . desire to harm a politically unpopular group,' are not legitimate state interests." *Lawrence,* 539 U.S. at 580. Moreover, the district court properly rejected the state's claimed legislative justification because the record established that the statute was not rationally related to furthering such interests. Contrary to the state' assertions, the court did not place the burden on the state to prove a legitimate interest. After concluding that neither the law nor the record could sustain any of the interests the state suggested, the district court considered whether it could conceive of any additional interests Section 38–651(O) might further and concluded it could not. On appeal, the state does not suggest any interests it or the district court may have overlooked. The court ruled the plaintiffs had established a likelihood of success in showing the statute furthered no legitimate interest.

NOTE ON THE ARIZONA DOMESTIC PARTNERSHIP CASE

The Ninth Circuit denied en banc review of the panel decision, but over the dissent of Judges O'Scannlain and Bea. These judges maintained that the panel opinion was inconsistent with governing Supreme Court precedent, starting with the foundational precedent for evaluating laws that do not discriminate on their face. For nearly fifty years, Judge O'Scannlain noted, the Supreme Court has made clear that its cases "have not embraced the proposition that a law or other official act, without regard to whether it reflects a . . . discriminatory purpose, is unconstitutional *solely* because it has a . . . disproportionate impact." *Washington v. Davis*, 426 U.S. 229, 239 (1976).

The Supreme Court in *Moreno* found a discriminatory purpose, but "[t]here is no such evidence that Section 38–651(O) was motivated by animus. Section O's context and history bear out that it rests entirely on budgetary considerations. Until 2008, Arizona limited state-employee dependent-partner health benefit coverage to spouses. In 2008 it briefly relaxed that limitation. The very next year, in the face of its budget crisis, Arizona decided to return to its previous policy. That decision does not show animus, actual or implied. Nor does Section O's supposed disparate impact on gays and lesbians. Indeed, Section O most likely would burden many more opposite-sex than same-sex couples because many more opposite-sex partners would stand to lose their benefits. To conclude that the law will disproportionately affect same-sex couples would require one to assume that the vast majority of affected opposite-sex domestic partners would marry just to preserve their benefits. Though the panel seemed to credit that assumption, the Arizona legislature was entitled to presume that Section O would not spur a mass rush into matrimony."

Just as alarming to Judges O'Scannlain and Bea, "the panel decision threatens to dismantle constitutional, statutory, and administrative provisions in those states that wish to promote traditional marriage. The panel concluded—in a way that is veiled but unmistakable—that rules benefitting only traditional marriage serve no conceivable rational purpose. That conclusion broadsides Arizona voters, smothers their efforts (and the efforts of other voters in this circuit) to protect traditional marriage, and clashes with decisions of other courts."

These are potentially devastating arguments—yet no one else joined Judge O'Scannlain's dissenting opinion, and the Supreme Court itself denied review the day after it handed down *Windsor*. Two years later, the Court decided *Obergefell*. In 2014, even earlier, Arizona had started issuing marriage licenses to same-sex couples. In light of that development, the Arizona Department of Administration announced an intention to lift the federal injunction against enforcement of the 2009 statute limiting employment benefits to spouses and revoking domestic partnership benefits. Ought the District Court now lift the injunction? Does this new development take away the Ninth Circuit's chief rationale, that straight but not gay domestic partners can still receive employment benefits by marrying? That is, now that lesbian, gay, and straight state employees can marry the partners of their choice, does the 2009 Arizona law escape the doctrinal clutches of *Moreno*? See *Diaz v. Brewer*, 2015 WL 3555282 (D. Ariz. 2015).

NOTE ON FEDERAL BENEFITS FOR DOMESTIC PARTNERS

Professors Deborah Widiss and Andrew Koppelman have argued that federal law should recognize domestic partners who have registered with their state of residence and that the federal government should defer to state law policy in the same way that *Windsor* required it to defer to same-sex marriages recognized under state law. See Deborah Widiss & Andrew Koppelman, "A Marriage By Any Other Name: Why Civil Unions Should Receive Federal Recognition," *Ind. J.L. & Soc. Inequality,* vol. 3, Iss. 1, Art. 3 (2015). Do you agree? Consider the steps taken at the national level during the pre-*Obergefell* period, when same-sex couples became a prominent social phenomenon but their marriages were not recognized in most states.

Congress has enacted a number of statutes that include same-sex couples as unmarried beneficiaries. For example, the Interstate Domestic Violence Act of 1994 provides federal criminal penalties for abusing a spouse or "intimate partner" and requires that full faith and credit be granted to orders of protection that meet its requirements. 18 U.S.C.A. §§ 2261–2266. "Spouse or intimate partner" includes:

> a spouse or former spouse of the abuser, a person who shares a child in common with the abuser, and a person who cohabits or has cohabited as a spouse with the abuser; or a person who is or has been in a social relationship of a romantic or intimate nature with the abuser, as determined by the length of the relationship, the type of relationship, and the frequency of interaction between the persons involved in the relationship; and . . . any other person

similarly situated to a spouse who is protected by the domestic or family violence laws of the State or tribal jurisdiction in which the injury occurred or where the victim resides.

18 U.S.C.A. § 2266. In 2010, the Office of Legal Counsel released a memorandum stating that the criminal provisions of the Act apply to abusers when victims are the same sex. Memorandum Opinion for the Acting Deputy Attorney General, "Whether the Criminal Provisions of the Violence Against Women Act Apply to Otherwise Covered Conduct When the Offender and Victim Are the Same Sex" (Apr. 27, 2010).

The Air Transportation Safety and System Stabilization Act of 2001, Pub. L. No. 107–42, set up a Victim Compensation Fund for the survivors of those who died as a result of the 9/11 terrorist attack. The law offered monetary recoveries to the *personal representatives* of victims of 9/11 but did not define that term; Kenneth Feinberg, the Administrator of the 9/11 Fund, interpreted it to apply to same-sex partners recognized as beneficiaries under state law. Likewise, the Mychal Judge Act of 2002, Pub. L. No. 107–196, another response to 9/11, extends eligibility for the $250,000 federal benefit (for the survivors of public safety officers killed in the line of duty) to include people "designated by such officer as beneficiary under such officer's most recently executed life insurance policy." *Id.* § 2(b)(3), 116 Stat. 719. (Prior law had limited beneficiaries to the "spouse, child, or parent of the decedent.")

Taking office in 2009, the Obama Administration was for four years constrained by the Defense of Marriage Act (DOMA) to deny marital benefits to same-sex married couples. Because the Administration believed that such couples should receive federal benefits (and within two years came to believe that DOMA was unconstitutional), the White House and executive agencies worked to extend benefits to the same-sex domestic partners of federal employees. In most cases, the Administration devised its own definition of domestic partners.

On June 17, 2009, President Barack Obama issued a memorandum requiring the Secretary of State and the Director of the Office of Personnel Management to extend benefits to same-sex partners of federal employees where doing so was consistent with federal law—i.e., not in violation of DOMA (which remained enforceable federal law until 2013, when the Supreme Court invalidated it in *Windsor*). Memorandum from President Barack Obama to Heads of Executive Departments and Agencies, "Federal Benefits and Non-Discrimination" (June 17, 2009). The following day, Secretary of State Clinton stated that domestic partners of Foreign Service employees would be newly eligible for a series of benefits including use of medical facilities at posts abroad, training at the Foreign Service Institute, and inclusion in computations of overseas allowance payments. *See* Memorandum from Secretary of State Hillary Clinton, "Benefits for Same-Sex Domestic Partners of Foreign Service Employees" (June 18, 2009).

In June 2010, President Obama announced that domestic partners of all eligible federal employees would have access to employee assistance programs, child care, payments for travel, relocation, subsistence, and, in certain situations, retirement benefits. *See* Memorandum from President Barack Obama to Heads of Executive Departments and Agencies, "Extension of Benefits to Same-Sex Domestic Partners of Federal Employees" (June 2, 2010). Simultaneously, the Director of the Office of Personnel Management asked all agencies to offer the domestic partners of federal employees access to medical services, accidental death insurance, family assistance services, and other benefits. He also asked the smaller group of non-Title 5 agencies to provide more expansive benefits such as health insurance and relocation assistance to federal employees' domestic partners. Memorandum from John Berry, Director, U.S. Office of Personnel Mgmt., to Heads of Executive Departments and Agencies, "Implementation of the President's Memorandum Regarding Extension of Benefits to Same-Sex Domestic Partners of Federal Employees" (June 2, 2010).

Executive branch officials also began issuing guidance to entities other than federal agencies. The Department of Labor, in June 2010, clarified that an employee can use his FMLA leave to care for the child of his domestic partner, regardless of the employee's biological or legal relationship to the child. Nancy J. Leppink, Deputy Administrator, U.S. Dep't of Labor, Administrator's Interpretation No. 2010–3 (June 22, 2010). In November 2010, the Department of Health and Human Services issued a regulation requiring hospitals participating in Medicare and Medicaid to create written policies and procedures regarding the visitation rights of patients and to inform patients of their right to be visited by the people whom they designate, including same-sex partners. Medicare and Medicaid Programs: Changes to the Hospital and Critical Access Hospital Conditions of Participation To Ensure Visitation Rights for All Patients, 75 Fed. Reg. 70831–01 (Nov. 19, 2010) (to be codified at 42 CFR pts. 482 and 485).

PROBLEM 6-4
DEFINING ELIGIBILITY FOR PARTNER BENEFITS

One issue that recurs in any discussion of extending benefits to non-marital couples (same- or different-sex) is how to define the criteria for eligibility. Following are three different definitions currently in effect or under consideration. What are the strengths and weaknesses of each?

(a) Absence and Leave regulation for federal employees:

Domestic partner means an adult in a committed relationship with another adult, including both same-sex and opposite-sex relationships.

Committed relationship means one in which the employee, and the domestic partner of the employee, are each other's sole domestic partner (and are not married to or domestic partners with anyone else); and share responsibility for a significant measure of each other's common welfare and financial obligations. This includes, but is not limited to, any relationship between two individuals of the same or opposite sex that is granted legal recognition by a State or by the District of Columbia as a marriage or analogous relationship (including, but not limited to, a civil union).

3 C.F.R. § 630 (2010).

(b) Uniting American Families Act:

The term 'permanent partner' means an individual 18 years of age or older who is in a committed, intimate relationship with another individual 18 years of age or older in which both parties intend a lifelong commitment; is financially interdependent with that other individual; is not married to or in a permanent partnership with anyone other than that other individual; is unable to contract with that other individual a marriage cognizable under this Act; and is not a first, second, or third degree blood relation of that other individual.

H.R. 1024, 111th Cong. (2009).

(c) Proposed Domestic Partner Benefits and Obligations Act of 2009:

In order to obtain benefits and assume obligations under this Act, an employee shall file an affidavit . . . certifying that the employee and the domestic partner of the employee—(1) are each other's sole domestic partner and intend to remain so indefinitely; (2) have a common residence, and intend to continue the arrangement; (3) are at least 18 years of age and mentally competent to consent to contract; (4) share responsibility for a significant measure of each other's common welfare and financial obligations; (5) are not married to or domestic partners with anyone else; (6) are same sex domestic partners, and not related in a way that, if the 2 were of opposite sex, would prohibit legal marriage in the State in which they reside. . . .

S. 1102, 111th Cong. (2009).

Which option is the most workable? Should different statutory schemes have a unified definition—or should different definitions be used for different statutes?

Recall, too, Professor Fineman's point that the meta-narrative for American family law has been marriage. Even when the government recognizes new family forms, marriage remains the template. How does this idea affect your thinking about the foregoing definitions of domestic partnership? Consider the following article, which provides historical context for your thoughts.

Douglas NeJaime, "Before Marriage: The Unexplored History of Nonmarital Recognition and Its Relationship to Marriage," 102 *Calif. L. Rev.* 87, 87–88, 113–15 (2012). Focusing on California, Professor NeJaime explores the relationship of the domestic partnership movement of the 1980s and 1990s to the LGBT community's campaign for marriage equality in the new millennium. "[B]efore the movement began to make explicit claims to marriage in the 1990s, leading advocates engaged in a vigorous debate about whether to seek marriage. This debate went beyond mere strategic disagreement and instead focused on ideological differences regarding the role of marriage and its relationship to LGBT rights, family diversity, and sexual freedom. Those opposing the turn to marriage urged the movement to continue pursuing nonmarital rights and recognition, including domestic partnership, as a way to decenter marriage for everyone. Critics of today's marriage equality advocacy point to this history as a lost alternative past worthy of reclamation. Today's marriage-centered movement, they argue, channels relationships into traditional forms and marginalizes those who fail to fit the marital mold. Instead of continuing down this road, these critics contend, movement advocates should recover their earlier roots and embrace pluralistic models of family and intimacy outside of marriage."

Although participants in the campaigns for nonmarital/domestic partnership recognition may have seen the efforts as marriage alternatives, Professor NeJaime reveals the centrality of marriage as the meta-narrative for at least most movement leaders even during the time when LGBT advocates worked entirely on municipal, corporate, and state domestic partnership regimes (described above).

Thus, the earliest draft of the 1982 Coles-Britt bill for the San Francisco Board of Supervisors (described above) defined domestic partners as "two individuals" who "reside together," "share the common necessaries of life," and "declare that they are each other's sole domestic partners." "The language explicitly invoked the California common-law duty making spouses responsible for the 'common necessaries of life.' This language was particularly important to insurance carriers, who resisted adding domestic partnership coverage without assurances that this new relationship status would be characterized by a marriage-like level of commitment.

"The draft ordinance also included rights subject to municipal authority: hospital and jail visitation, sick and bereavement leave, and public housing eligibility. In a separate section aimed at securing health coverage for city employees' domestic partners, the drafters provided that a 'City employee who has enrolled a domestic partner may not enroll a different domestic partner until six months after notifying the Health Service System that the first domestic partner is no longer to be enrolled.' This length of time deliberately tracked the time between an interlocutory and final decree of divorce in the marriage context." As passed by the Board of Supervisors in November 1982, the ordinance defined domestic partners as two individuals, unrelated by blood, who are not married but share the "common necessaries of life" and "declare that they are each other's principal domestic partner."

Although the new institution looked like marriage-lite, Matt Coles carefully distinguished it from marriage, because of the scant number of benefits and duties and the ease of exit. Conversely, opponents of the ordinance (notably Catholic Archbishop John Quinn) framed it as an effort to mimic marriage by couples naturally excluded from the institution because they cannot procreate. Archbishop Quinn and his allies prevailed, as they persuaded Mayor Dianne Feinstein to veto the bill.

In 1984, Coles worked with LGBT and human rights activists to craft an ordinance for Berkeley that would equalize workplace benefits for committed same-sex couples. As in San Francisco, the goal was to "approximate the marriage criterion." The Council passed the ordinance, creating a registry for domestic partners, defined as two people "not related by blood closer than would bar marriage" who "reside[ ] together and share the common necessities of life" and are "responsible for [each other's] common welfare." Activists persuaded West Hollywood to create a domestic partnership registry in 1985. After family diversity task force reports and extensive public hearings, San Francisco and Los Angeles—the big prizes—followed this script in 1991 and 1992–93.

LGBT and AIDS activists followed a similar process in these and other California jurisdictions: (a) document the incidence of same-sex couples who were "like married" couples in that they were committed to one another and economically interdependent; (b) invoke the equal protection principle that "like things need to be treated the same"; and (c) reassure municipal budget hawks and health insurance carriers that domestic partnership would be narrowly defined to approximate marriage. (In each of the early cities creating domestic partnerships, there was a further process by which health insurance companies were persuaded to offer spousal insurance for domestic partners.)

From this historical process, Professor NeJaime concludes that "the relationship between nonmarital advocacy and marriage was dialogical. Marriage shaped LGBT advocacy for nonmarital recognition, and that advocacy in turn shaped marriage. To gain support for nonmarital rights and benefits, advocates cast same-sex relationships as marriage-like and built domestic partnership in reference to marriage, thus reinscribing—rather than resisting—the centrality of marriage. Yet, at the same time, this nonmarital advocacy contributed to an ascendant model of marriage characterized by adult romantic affiliation, mutual emotional support, and economic interdependence—a model of marriage capable of including same-sex couples."

B. RECIPROCAL BENEFICIARIES, DESIGNATED BENEFICIARIES, AND CIVIL UNIONS

Once LGBT couples had a taste of domestic partnership recognition at the local and company level in the 1980s and 1990s, they were encouraged to seek statewide recognition for their relationships—and many more rights associated with state law. After most of its major cities had created domestic partnership registries, the California Legislature in 1999 created a statewide registry, limited to same-sex couples and different-sex couples over the age of 62. The most tangible benefit for the

1999 law was the right to visit one's partner in the hospital, but in 2001 the Legislature expanded the benefits to include conservatorship rights, step-parent adoption rights, the right to sue for the wrongful death of a partner, and other rights. In 2003, the Legislature expanded domestic partnership to include almost all of the rights and duties of marriage (except that domestic partnership was easier to enter and exit than marriage). In 2005 and 2007, the Legislature passed bills recognizing same-sex marriages, but the Governor successfully vetoed them. For several months in 2008 and after June 2013, California recognized same-sex marriages. After marriage recognition, domestic partnership survives as a parallel institution.

Nevada, Oregon, Washington, and the District of Columbia followed the California pattern, where legislatures adopted limited domestic partnership statutes that were expanded and ultimately helped prepare the polity to accept marriage equality for lesbian and gay couples. (Nevada, for example, offered the same domestic partnership rights to different-sex as well as same-sex couples.) In Maine, Maryland, Massachusetts, New Jersey, and Wisconsin, legislatures in the first decade of the new millennium afforded limited domestic partnership protections (employee health insurance and bereavement leaves, sometimes more) that were not significantly expanded. Marriage equality in the second decade of the millennium has meant termination of many corporate, municipal, and some state domestic partnership policies—but most have survived and represent one regime for government recognition and regulation of romantic partnerships. Other institutions were also generated during the marriage equality debates, some for at least a subset of different-sex couples as well.

1. RECIPROCAL AND DESIGNATED BENEFICIARIES

After the Hawaii Supreme Court's decision requiring the state to defend its exclusion of same-sex couples from marriage under strict scrutiny, see *Baehr v. Lewin*, 852 P.2d 44 (Haw. 1993), the Hawaii Legislature considered proposals to put a constitutional amendment on the ballot that would enable voters to override *Baehr* and any trial court judgment invalidating the marriage bar. Because the governing Democratic Party enjoyed the support of the LGBT community, such an amendment could not be expeditiously passed without giving some kind of recognition to lesbian and gay unions. Even the Church of Jesus Christ of the Latter-day Saints, which was secretly funding and organizing the effort to forestall same-sex marriage in Hawaii, came to the conclusion that it would have to swallow some kind of statutory regime for partner benefits, in return for access to the ballot for its proposed constitutional amendment.

This kind of statutory regime was novel in the 1990s, but not unprecedented. After years of study in a series of expert commissions, Sweden's Parliament in 1987 adopted a nationwide law providing many legal benefits (fewer than marriage, more than American domestic partnership ordinances in that period) for cohabiting same-sex couples. This was the first national legislation legally recognizing same-sex unions in modern western history. (Canada and many European countries had laws granting some legal benefits and duties to cohabiting straight couples; the Swedish law was the first to extend this regime to gay and lesbian couples.)

More proposals along the lines of the Swedish model were debated in the 1990s. In France, for example, bills were introduced in Parliament to create *Contrats de partenariat civil* in 1990 and *Contrats d'union civile* in 1992. Both proposals were open to different-sex as well as same-sex couples, and to nonromantic as well as romantic couples. In 1993, Parliament adopted one part of the latter proposal, when it made social welfare benefits available to dependent cohabitees, regardless of sex. Simultaneously, couples were litigating (unsuccessfully) for the benefits of *concubinage*, French statutory rights of cohabiting couples. In 1998, the Socialist government secured parliamentary enactment of a law creating *Pactes civils de solidarité* (PaCS), allowing different-sex as well as same-sex couples to assume mutual responsibilities for one another, similar to the 1992 proposal. The new law added same-sex couples to the established institution of concubinage and created a new institution, the PaCS.[a]

In 1996–97, the Hawaii Legislature considered proposals similar to those debated in France. The final legislative compromise was to place on the November 1998 ballot a proposal to amend the state constitution "to clarify that the legislature has the power to reserve marriage to opposite-sex couples," 1997 Haw. Sess. Laws 2883 (H.B. 117), and to adopt a statute extending "certain rights and benefits . . . to couples composed of two individuals who are legally prohibited from marrying under state law (same-sex couples and blood relatives)." 1997 Haw. Sess. Laws 2786, Act 383 (H.B. 118).[b]

The latter statute was titled the Reciprocal Beneficiaries Act. Adults who were excluded from the marriage law either because they were too closely related or because they were considered to be of the same sex could choose to form a mutually beneficial partnership by filing a form with the state whereby the two parties affirmed that they wanted to be treated as *reciprocal beneficiaries*. Reciprocal beneficiaries enjoyed about

---

[a] Our account of the background of the French PaCS law is taken from Daniel Borrillo, "The 'Pacte Civil de Solidarité' in France: Midway Between Marriage and Cohabitation," in *Legal Recognition of Same-Sex Partnerships* 475–92 (Robert Wintemute & Mads Andenaes eds., 2001). For a more in-depth examination of this new institution, see *Au delá du PaCS: l'expertise familiale a l'épreuve de l'homosexualité* (Daniel Borrillo et al. eds. 1999); Sylvie Dibos-Lacroux, *PACS: Le guide pratique* (2000). On the great popularity of PaCS for straight couples, see Scott Sayare & Maia de la Baume, "In France, Civil Unions Gain Favor Over Marriage," *N.Y. Times*, Dec. 15, 2010.

[b] For an in-depth treatment of the Hawaii Legislature's deliberations that resulted in the 1997 compromise, see David Orgon Coolidge, "The Hawai'i Marriage Amendment: Its Origins, Meaning and Fate," 22 *U. Haw. L. Rev.* 19 (2000).

50 of the more than 200 rights and benefits enjoyed by married couples, including health care benefits for the beneficiaries/partners of state and municipal employees, workers' compensation benefits, family leave to care for a reciprocal beneficiary, hospital visitation rights, the right to own property as tenants in the entirety where the parties each enjoy complete ownership just as married spouses do, probate and life insurance benefits, the right to bring a wrongful death action for loss of care etc. from one's reciprocal beneficiary, the same protection under the state's victim's rights and domestic abuse laws as is accorded spouses, and a few tax benefits.

The reciprocal beneficiary law offered many more benefits and rights than domestic partnership ordinances did—but because lesbian and gay couples were so disappointed when the voters in 1998 ratified the amendment allowing their exclusion from marriage, few couples have taken advantage of the law. In 2011, the Hawaii Legislature enacted a civil unions law, giving all the legal benefits and duties of marriage to couples deciding to enter into a civil union. The 2011 law left the reciprocal beneficiaries measure in place, as did a 2013 statute that brought marriage equality to Hawaii.

Hawaii's reciprocal beneficiaries law was a model for a similar law adopted by the Vermont Legislature in 2000. "The purpose of this chapter is to provide two persons who are blood relatives or related by adoption the opportunity to establish a consensual reciprocal beneficiaries relationship so that they may receive the benefits and protections and be subject to the responsibilities that are granted to spouses in [specific] areas." 15 Vt. Stat. Ann. § 1301(a). In Vermont, two people can be reciprocal beneficiaries if they (1) are both at least 18 years old, are competent to contract, and agree to form this relationship; (2) are not parties to another reciprocal beneficiaries relationship, a civil union, or a marriage; and (3) are related by blood or by adoption and prohibited from establishing a civil union or marriage with the other party to the proposed reciprocal beneficiaries relationship. § 1303. The couple can be different-sex or same-sex but must be related in such a way that they cannot form a civil union or a marriage under Vermont law. Your reciprocal beneficiary is someone who has legal capacity to make decisions for you, and vice-versa. Specifically included are decisions relating to hospital visitation and medical care, anatomical gifts, disposition of remains, and nursing home care. One's reciprocal beneficiary has durable power of attorney for purposes of health care and terminal care and is entitled to the same rights vis-a-vis health providers as one's spouse would be. § 1301(a)(4). Persons form a reciprocal beneficiary relationship by submitting a signed, notarized declaration to the state, § 1304, and the relationship can be terminated by either party's submitting a sworn declaration. § 1305.

The Hawaii law was also a model, of sorts, for the state domestic partnership laws, discussed in Part A, that gave a small basket of rights and duties to couples registering their partnerships. Domestic partnership laws passed by New Jersey in 2003, Maine in 2004, and Wisconsin in 2009 offered fewer rights and duties than the Hawaii and Vermont laws did. By including older different-sex as well as same-sex couples, California's 1999 domestic partnership law also bore a family resemblance to the Hawaii law.

Colorado in 2009 adopted an even closer analogue, again, as a compromise between LGBT rights advocates and traditionalists strongly opposed to marriage-like institutions for non-procreating same-sex couples.

Colorado Designated Beneficiary Agreements Act of 2009

New Title 15, Article 22 of the Colorado Code.

15–22–102. Legislative declaration.

(1) THE GENERAL ASSEMBLY FINDS AND DETERMINES THAT:

(a) NOT ALL COLORADANS ARE ADEQUATELY PROTECTED BY THE PROVISIONS OF THE "COLORADO PROBATE CODE" * * * AND OTHER PROVISIONS OF COLORADO LAW. * * *

(b) BEYOND LEGAL IMPEDIMENTS, PEOPLE OFTEN FAIL TO PLAN FOR THEIR OWN MORTALITY. STUDIES HAVE FOUND THAT SIGNIFICANT NUMBERS OF AMERICANS DO NOT HAVE A VALID WILL, AND EVEN FEWER HAVE EXECUTED POWERS OF ATTORNEY OR OTHER ESTATE PLANNING DOCUMENTS.

(c) A BODY OF LAW HAS BEEN ENACTED TO OPERATE BY DEFAULT IN SITUATIONS IN WHICH INDIVIDUALS DO NOT PREPARE ESTATE PLANS. HOWEVER, FAILURE TO PLAN FOR DISABILITY, INCAPACITY, OR DEATH PLACES PEOPLE AT THE MERCY OF STATE LAWS THAT MAY VEST THE POWER TO ACT IN SUCH SITUATIONS IN PERSONS OTHER THAN THOSE THEY WOULD WISH TO HAVE EXERCISE THOSE POWERS. MANY LACK ACCESS TO LEGAL SERVICES DUE TO THE EXPENSE OF DRAFTING LEGAL INSTRUMENTS AND THE NECESSITY TO KEEP THESE DOCUMENTS CURRENT.

(d) THE POWER OF INDIVIDUALS TO CARE FOR ONE ANOTHER AND TAKE ACTION TO BE PERSONALLY RESPONSIBLE FOR THEMSELVES AND THEIR LOVED ONES IS OF TREMENDOUS SOCIETAL BENEFIT, ENABLING SELF-DETERMINATION AND REDUCING RELIANCE ON PUBLIC PROGRAMS AND SERVICES.

(2) THEREFORE, THE GENERAL ASSEMBLY DECLARES THAT:

(a) THE PUBLIC POLICY OF THE STATE SHOULD ENCOURAGE RESIDENTS TO EXECUTE APPROPRIATE LEGAL DOCUMENTS TO EFFECTUATE THEIR WISHES;

(b) THE PURPOSES OF THIS ARTICLE ARE TO:

(I) MAKE EXISTING LAWS RELATING TO HEALTH CARE, MEDICAL EMERGENCIES, INCAPACITY, DEATH, AND ADMINISTRATION OF DECEDENT'S ESTATES AVAILABLE TO MORE PERSONS THROUGH A PROCESS OF DOCUMENTING DESIGNATED BENEFICIARY AGREEMENTS; AND

(II) ALLOW INDIVIDUALS TO ELECT TO HAVE CERTAIN DEFAULT PROVISIONS IN STATE STATUTES PROVIDE RIGHTS, BENEFITS, AND PROTECTIONS TO A DESIGNATED BENEFICIARY IN SITUATIONS IN WHICH NO VALID AND ENFORCEABLE ESTATE PLANNING DOCUMENTS EXIST. * * *

15–22–104. Requirements for a valid designated beneficiary agreement.

(1) A DESIGNATED BENEFICIARY AGREEMENT SHALL BE LEGALLY RECOGNIZED IF:

(a) THE PARTIES TO THE DESIGNATED BENEFICIARY AGREEMENT SATISFY ALL OF THE FOLLOWING CRITERIA:

(I)   BOTH ARE AT LEAST EIGHTEEN YEARS OF AGE;

(II) BOTH ARE COMPETENT TO ENTER INTO A CONTRACT;

(III) NEITHER PARTY IS MARRIED TO ANOTHER PERSON;

(IV) NEITHER PARTY IS A PARTY TO ANOTHER DESIGNATED BENEFICIARY AGREEMENT; AND

(V) BOTH PARTIES ENTER INTO THE DESIGNATED BENEFICIARY AGREEMENT WITHOUT FORCE, FRAUD, OR DURESS; AND

(b) THE AGREEMENT IS IN SUBSTANTIAL COMPLIANCE WITH THE REQUIREMENTS SET FORTH IN THIS ARTICLE. * * *

15–22–105. Effects and applicability of a designated beneficiary agreement.

(1) A PERSON NAMED AS A DESIGNATED BENEFICIARY IN A DESIGNATED BENEFICIARY AGREEMENT SHALL BE ENTITLED TO EXERCISE THE RIGHTS AND PROTECTIONS SPECIFIED IN THE AGREEMENT BY VIRTUE OF HAVING BEEN SO NAMED.

(2) A DESIGNATED BENEFICIARY AGREEMENT THAT IS PROPERLY EXECUTED AND RECORDED * * * SHALL BE VALID AND LEGALLY ENFORCEABLE IN THE ABSENCE OF A SUPERSEDING LEGAL DOCUMENT THAT CONFLICTS WITH THE

PROVISIONS SPECIFIED IN THE DESIGNATED BENEFICIARY AGREEMENT.

(3) A DESIGNATED BENEFICIARY AGREEMENT SHALL ENTITLE THE PARTIES TO EXERCISE THE FOLLOWING RIGHTS AND ENJOY THE FOLLOWING PROTECTIONS, UNLESS SPECIFICALLY EXCLUDED FROM THE DESIGNATED BENEFICIARY AGREEMENT:

(a) THE RIGHT TO ACQUIRE, HOLD TITLE TO, OWN JOINTLY, OR TRANSFER INTER VIVOS OR AT DEATH REAL OR PERSONAL PROPERTY AS JOINT TENANTS WITH RIGHT OF SURVIVORSHIP OR AS TENANTS IN COMMON;

(b) THE RIGHT TO BE DESIGNATED AS A BENEFICIARY, PAYEE, OR OWNER AS A TRUSTEE NAMED IN AN INTER VIVOS OR TESTAMENTARY TRUST FOR THE PURPOSES OF A NONPROBATE TRANSFER ON DEATH;

(c) FOR PURPOSES OF THE FOLLOWING BENEFITS, THE RIGHT TO BE DESIGNATED AS A BENEFICIARY AND RECOGNIZED AS A DEPENDENT SO LONG AS NOTICE IS GIVEN IN ACCORDANCE WITH ANY APPLICABLE STATUTE, RULE, CONTRACT, POLICY, PROCEDURE, OR OTHER GOVERNMENT DOCUMENT OF THE FOLLOWING BENEFITS:

(I) PUBLIC EMPLOYEES' RETIREMENT SYSTEMS * * *;

(II) LOCAL GOVERNMENT FIREFIGHTER AND POLICE PENSIONS;

(III) INSURANCE POLICIES FOR LIFE INSURANCE COVERAGE; AND

(IV) HEALTH INSURANCE POLICIES OR HEALTH COVERAGE IF THE EMPLOYER OF THE DESIGNATED BENEFICIARY ELECTS TO PROVIDE COVERAGE FOR DESIGNATED BENEFICIARIES AS DEPENDENTS;

(d) THE RIGHT TO PETITION FOR AND HAVE PRIORITY FOR APPOINTMENT AS A CONSERVATOR, GUARDIAN, OR PERSONAL REPRESENTATIVE FOR THE OTHER DESIGNATED BENEFICIARY;

(e) THE RIGHT TO VISITATION BY THE OTHER DESIGNATED BENEFICIARY IN A HOSPITAL, NURSING HOME, HOSPICE, OR SIMILAR HEALTH CARE FACILITY IN WHICH A PARTY TO A DESIGNATED BENEFICIARY RESIDES OR IS RECEIVING CARE * * *;

(f) THE RIGHT TO ACT AS A PROXY DECISION-MAKER OR SURROGATE DECISION-MAKER TO MAKE MEDICAL TREATMENT DECISIONS FOR THE OTHER DESIGNATED BENEFICIARY * * *;

(g)   THE RIGHT TO RECEIVE NOTICE OF THE WITHHOLDING OR WITHDRAWAL OF LIFE-SUSTAINING PROCEDURES FOR THE OTHER DESIGNATED BENEFICIARY * * * AND THE RIGHT TO CHALLENGE THE VALIDITY OF A DECLARATION AS TO MEDICAL OR SURGICAL TREATMENT OF THE OTHER DESIGNATED BENEFICIARY * * *;

(h) THE RIGHT, WITH RESPECT TO THE OTHER DESIGNATED BENEFICIARY, TO ACT AS AN AGENT AND TO MAKE, REVOKE, OR OBJECT TO ANATOMICAL GIFTS * * *;

(i)   THE RIGHT TO INHERIT REAL OR PERSONAL PROPERTY FROM THE OTHER DESIGNATED BENEFICIARY THROUGH INTESTATE SUCCESSION;

(j)   THE RIGHT TO HAVE STANDING TO RECEIVE BENEFITS PURSUANT TO THE "WORKERS' COMPENSATION ACT OF COLORADO" * * * MADE ON BEHALF OF THE OTHER DESIGNATED BENEFICIARY;

(k) THE RIGHT TO HAVE STANDING TO SUE FOR WRONGFUL DEATH ON BEHALF OF THE OTHER DESIGNATED BENEFICIARY; AND

(l)   THE RIGHT TO DIRECT THE DISPOSITION OF THE OTHER DESIGNATED BENEFICIARY'S LAST REMAINS * * *.

15–22–106. Statutory form of a designated beneficiary agreement.

[This provision provides a template for a designated beneficiary agreement, with a list of reciprocal rights and an opportunity for each party to accept or decline the operation of each reciprocal right.]

15–22–111. Revocation of a designated beneficiary agreement.

(1)   A DESIGNATED BENEFICIARY AGREEMENT THAT HAS BEEN RECORDED WITH A COUNTY CLERK AND RECORDER MAY BE UNILATERALLY REVOKED BY EITHER PARTY TO THE AGREEMENT BY RECORDING A REVOCATION WITH THE CLERK AND RECORDER OF THE COUNTY IN WHICH THE AGREEMENT WAS RECORDED. * * * THE REVOCATION SHALL BE EFFECTIVE ON THE DATE AND TIME THE REVOCATION IS RECEIVED FOR RECORDING BY THE COUNTY CLERK AND RECORDER. THE CLERK AND RECORDER SHALL ISSUE A CERTIFIED COPY TO THE PARTY RECORDING THE REVOCATION AND SHALL MAIL A CERTIFIED COPY OF THE REVOCATION TO THE LAST-KNOWN ADDRESS OF THE OTHER PARTY TO THE DESIGNATED BENEFICIARY AGREEMENT. * * *

[Most of the other provisions of the statute are conforming amendments to various substantive statutory schemes, to which designated beneficiaries may after July 1, 2009 be entitled to participate.]

NOTES ON THE COLORADO DESIGNATED BENEFICIARIES LAW

1. *A New Form of Relationship Recognition?* The designated beneficiaries statute does not pretend to replicate the legal rights and duties of marriage and has not been the object of expansion (the way California's domestic partnership law was). The "relationships" recognized in this law include those of trust and caregiving and do not purport to be limited to (or even presumptively) romantic relationships—although persons who cannot marry or who are joined in marriage cannot become designated beneficiaries. More than any other family form explored in this chapter, this law departs from the marriage meta-narrative outlined by Professor Fineman.

The 2009 Colorado law is in many respects similar to the 1997 Hawaii reciprocal beneficiaries law, but with three important differences. Unlike the Hawaii law, the Colorado law (i) includes different-sex beneficiaries on the same terms as same-sex beneficiaries, (ii) offers each beneficiary the opportunity to opt out of any right and entails fewer benefits (focusing on default rules for decisionmaking when things go bad for one of the beneficiaries), and (iii) overlaps considerably with the population covered by the state marriage law (the Hawaii law *only* covers couples who can never be married under state law). Thus, the 2009 Colorado law was not nearly so much a "consolation prize" for marriage equality advocates as the widely disliked 1997 Hawaii law was.

2. *Advantages and Disadvantages for Romantic Cohabiting Couples.* For cohabiting couples of any sexual orientation, the 2009 law provides them with some of the decisionmaking default rules of state marriage law—but without the burdens of mutual support and sexual fidelity obligations or expensive divorce procedures. Like the French PaCs law, the 2009 Colorado designated beneficiaries law allows an easy path to dissolution.

On the other hand, the 2009 law provides no property or support protections for partners who are exploited in the relationship, such as the partner who works while the other partner completes her law school education and then moves on. Does the exploited partner have a *Marvin* lawsuit to enforce an implied contract? The Colorado Supreme Court has recognized unjust enrichment claims, under specified circumstances, for members of cohabiting couples after separation, see *Salzman v. Bachrach*, 996 P.2d 1263 (Colo. 2000). Has the 2009 law overridden *Salzman* for purposes of unjust enrichment claims?

3. *The Future of Designated Beneficiary Laws?* Some critics of the marriage equality movement fear that once marriage equality is achieved, states will repeal or phase out alternative relationships statuses, such as civil unions and designated beneficiaries. The experience so far has been mixed. A number of states have retained their alternative statuses even as they have moved towards equality for same-sex couples. For example, when Colorado adopted a civil union law in 2013, the Legislature preserved the 2009 Designated Beneficiary Agreements Act. And both statuses remain in effect even though the state began marrying same-sex couples in October 2014.

Similarly, when Hawaii's Legislature adopted a marriage equality law in 2013, it left in place the state reciprocal beneficiaries law and the state civil union law. A number of other states, including California, Illinois, Maine, Maryland, Nevada, Oregon, and the District of Columbia, have maintained their alternative relationship statuses after marriage equality. By contrast, however, a number of states, including Connecticut, Delaware, New Hampshire, Rhode Island, Vermont, and Washington phased out their alternative statuses after marriage equality was achieved. See National Center for Lesbian Rights, Marriage, Domestic Partners, and Civil Unions: Same-Sex Couples Within the United States, available at http://www.nclrights.org/wp-content/uploads/2013/07/Relationship_Recognition.pdf (viewed October 1, 2017). States were more likely to retain their alternative statuses if they were open to both same-sex and different-sex couples.

The even bigger question is whether any additional state legislatures will adopt alternative relationship statuses, now that the Supreme Court has required marriage equality for all fifty states. Canada and most European countries have statutes formalizing rights and duties of unmarried, cohabiting couples, and one wonders why the United States does not have *more* laws such as the 2009 Colorado law. Is there a concern by religious groups that such laws will undermine marriage? By the way, the decline of marriage owes nothing to the marriage equality movement for lesbian and gay couples—but might owe something to the rise of cohabitation in this country as well as elsewhere in the world. For more information about the rise of cohabitation and the legal treatment of cohabitation in other countries, see Lawrence W. Waggoner, "With Marriage on the Decline and Cohabitation on the Rise, What about Marital Rights for Unmarried Partners?," 41 *ACTEC L.J.* (2016).

2. MARRIAGE EQUIVALENT STATUSES

After a long period of official study (beginning in the 1970s), Denmark's Parliament adopted the Registered Partnership Act on May 26, 1989, and it went into effect on October 1, 1989. The Act applies only to same-sex couples (§ 1), and at least one partner must have his or her permanent residence in Denmark and be a Danish citizen (§ 2[2]). To obtain the benefits of the Act, the partners must register according to rules laid down by the Minister of Justice (§§ 1, 2[3]). Once registered, the partners have most of the rights, benefits, and obligations of married spouses (§ 3). The main exception was that registered partners did not enjoy the same rights of adoption that married couples enjoyed (§ 4[1]). Danish divorce law generally governs the terms by which a registered partnership is dissolved (§ 5).[c]

Similar registered partnership laws were then adopted in Norway (1993), Sweden (1994), Greenland (1996), Iceland (1996), and Finland (1999), making a clean sweep of Scandinavia. In 1998, The Netherlands

---

[c] The discussion of the Scandinavian registered partnership laws is taken from William Eskridge Jr. & Darren Spedale, *Gay Marriage: For Better or For Worse? What We've Learned from the Evidence* (2006).

adopted a law offering registered partnerships to different-sex as well as same-sex couples; most of the registered partners in The Netherlands have been different-sex couples. In 1999, Denmark repealed its bar to adoption by same-sex registered partners—the main legal disparity between different-sex marriage and same-sex partnerships in that country.

In *Baker v. State,* 744 A.2d 864 (Vt. 1999), the Vermont Supreme Court invalidated that state's exclusion of same-sex couples from the state's marriage law but left the remedy with the Vermont Legislature. After intense and often highly personalized debate, the Legislature responded with An Act Relating to Civil Unions, 2000 Vt. Laws No. 91 (H. 847). Following the Danish model, the main innovation was the creation of a new form for legal recognition of same-sex partnerships— the *civil union.*[d] Without recognizing same-sex unions as *marriages,* the Vermont civil union confers on the couples the same benefits and obligations as marriage; "[p]arties to a civil union shall have *all*," not almost all, "the same benefits, protections and responsibilities under law, whether they derive from statute, administrative or court rule, policy, common law or any other source of civil law, as are granted to spouses in a marriage." 15 Vt. Stat. Ann. § 1204(a) (emphasis added); see § 1204(e) (listing benefits accorded persons joined in civil union); *id.* § 39(a) of the statute (liberal rule of construction). "Parties to a civil union shall be responsible for the support of one another to the same degree and in the same manner as prescribed under law for married persons." § 1204(c). The same procedures for separation and divorce to terminate marriages are applicable to terminate civil unions. §§ 1204(d), 1206.

The civil union (or registered partnership) approach—all the legal rights and duties of marriage but not the name—proved to be a very popular approach in the new millennium. Adopting the Vermont approach, but without an action-forcing judicial decision, Connecticut created similar *civil unions* for same-sex couples through legislation in 2005. In the next decade, state legislatures adopted civil union laws in New Jersey (2006); New Hampshire (2007); Illinois, Delaware, and Hawaii (2011); and Colorado (2012). In the West, state legislatures created the functional equivalent of civil unions under the domestic partnership label, by adding all or almost all the rights and benefits of marriage to the earlier-created institution. This was the approach followed in California (1999, expanded 2003), Oregon (2007), Washington (2007, expanded 2008), and Nevada (2009).

---

[d]   In the primary legislative hearings, Representative Tom Little's Judiciary Committee deliberated over the terminology. Lesbian and gay witnesses were cool toward the west coast term "domestic partnership," as too sterile, and for that and other reasons no one proposed the Danish term, "registered partnerships." Perhaps inspired by the French proposals of the 1990s, one witness suggested "civil union," a term that appealed to Representative Little and other members of his committee. On the Vermont Civil Unions Law of 2000, see William Eskridge Jr., *Equality Practice: Civil Unions and the Future of Gay Rights* 57–82 (2002), and Michael Mello, "For Today, I'm Gay: The Unfinished Battle for Same-Sex Marriage in Vermont," 25 *Vt. L. Rev.* 149 (2000).

Some of the states whose legislatures created civil unions (or their domestic partnership equivalents) ultimately replaced civil unions for same-sex couples with legislation including those couples in state civil marriage law. This was the approach followed by 2009 legislation in Vermont, Connecticut, and New Hampshire, as well as 2013 legislation in Delaware. On the other hand, civil unions survived marriage equality legislation or court decrees in Hawaii, Illinois, Nevada, and New Jersey.

PROBLEM 6-5
THE FUTURE OF CIVIL UNIONS?

As with designated beneficiaries, the future of civil unions is uncertain. Will this institution eventually replace civil marriage, with its deep association with religious faith? *See* Robin West, *Marriage, Sexuality, and Gender* (2007) (advocating that everyone be offered civil unions, and revoking marriage as a civil institution). Or will civil unions be displaced by designated beneficiary laws as the primary alternative to civil marriage? In the U.K., Professor Robert Wintemute advised a campaign (so far unsuccessful) to open non-marriage alternative statuses to different-sex couples, as well as to open marriage to same-sex couples (successful).

3.   INTERSTATE AND FEDERAL RECOGNITION OF NEW FAMILY LAW INSTITUTIONS?

Before the 2010s, most American states did not issue marriage licenses to same-sex couples, but a few non-issuing states would recognize out-of-state marriage licenses that had been validly issued to qualified same-sex couples. Office of the Maryland Attorney General, "Whether Out-of-State Same-Sex Marriage That Is Valid in the State of Celebration May Be Recognized in Maryland," 95 Md. Op. Atty. Gen. 3, 2010 WL 886002 (2010) (surveying the variety of approaches taken in other states and opining, correctly, that Maryland courts would recognize valid same-sex marriages validly entered in another state); see Andrew Koppelman, *Same Sex, Different States: When Same-Sex Marriages Cross State Lines* (2006).

Within the United States, these marriage recognition debates ended with *Obergefell*. Justice Kennedy's opinion not only ruled that the Equal Protection Clause requires all states to issue marriage licenses to qualified same-sex couples, but also ruled (in a brief statement at the end) that all states must recognize same-sex marriages validly entered in another state. (Most of the *Obergefell* plaintiff couples were, in fact, validly married in their states of celebration, and were seeking recognition of their valid marriages in their domicile states, namely, Ohio, Kentucky, and Tennessee.)

But choice of law and recognition issues did not end with *Obergefell*. An important cluster of states offer couples a choice between getting married and entering into some other institution—namely, civil unions or its equivalent (California, Colorado, Hawaii, Illinois), reciprocal or designated beneficiaries (Colorado, Hawaii, Vermont), or municipal or statewide domestic partnerships (Maine, New Jersey, Wisconsin, and many municipalities). Will those partnerships be recognized in other states or by the federal government?

In states that do not themselves join couples in civil unions or something similar, judges are reluctant to recognize civil unions or reciprocal beneficiary relationships formalized in other jurisdictions. In *Burns v. Burns*, 253 Ga.App. 600, 560 S.E.2d 47 (2002), a divorced father successfully gained custody of his child on the ground that his former wife had violated the portion of their separation agreement stating that neither would live with an adult to whom they were not married. The mother had entered into a civil union with her new partner. The court held that Vermont law was clear that civil unions were distinct from marriages, so that she was in violation. See also *Rosengarten v. Downes*, 71 Conn.App. 372, 802 A.2d 170 (2002) (finding family court lacked jurisdiction to dissolve a civil union because its authority only covered marriages); *Langan v. St. Vincent's Hosp.*, 802 N.Y.S.2d 476 (N.Y. App. 2005) (refusing to apply a wrongful death statute to benefit a surviving civil union partner).

Recently, however, the New York Court of Appeals ruled that its courts would recognize the parent-child relationship created by a couple joined in a Vermont civil union. *Debra H. v. Janice R.*, 14 N.Y.3d 576, 30 A.2d 184 (2010). Other courts will probably follow this approach for cases involving parent-child relationships—but would they (or the New York Court of Appeals) apply *Debra H.* to other marriage-like rights and duties?

In *Neyman v. Buckley*, 153 A.3d 1010 (Pa. 2016), a same-sex couple sought to have their Vermont civil union dissolved in Philadelphia. The trial court dismissed the divorce action for lack of jurisdiction in Pennsylvania, which never instituted any form of civil union or domestic partnership, Family Court is only empowered to dissolve *marriages*. The Pennsylvania Supreme Court reversed, holding that the principle of comity required recognizing out-of-state civil unions *as marriages* for the purposes of divorce. There are anecdotal reports of trial courts that have used their equitable authority to enter decrees dissolving civil unions; absent an appeal, such orders may occur with little public notice.

Some states have provided for recognition by statute. Connecticut, Delaware, New Hampshire, and Rhode Island gradually phased out civil unions after their legislatures passed marriage equality legislation (in 2009 in Connecticut and New Hampshire; in 2013 in Delaware and Rhode Island). But the new marriage statutes in all four states provide that civil unions and comprehensive domestic partnerships entered in other jurisdictions will be recognized in Delaware, Connecticut, New Hampshire, and Rhode Island—but recognized as *marriages* and not as civil unions. Conn. Gen. Stat. § 46b–28a; Del. Code tit. 13, § 101; N.H. Rev. Stat. § 457:45; R.I. Gen. Laws § 15–1–8. Is this a rule that judges ought to follow in states like Washington, states where legislated marriage equality laws phased out their civil union and comprehensive domestic partnership laws but did not provide a choice of law rule?

States that have civil unions or a reciprocal/designated beneficiaries law generally will recognize similar statuses celebrated in other states. For example, New Jersey's Civil Union Act of 2006 authorized couples to enter into civil unions, with all the state benefits and duties of marriage. The 2006 statute provided for recognition of civil unions validly entered in other states. A 2007 Opinion of the Attorney General clarified that New Jersey would also recognize out-of-state same-sex marriages as civil unions in New Jersey. NJ. Att'y Gen. Op. 3–2007 (Feb. 16, 2007). In 2013, New Jersey courts struck down the marriage exclusion, but the civil union law remains on the statute books.

Like New Jersey's law, the civil union laws in Hawaii (2011), Illinois (2010), and Colorado (2013) explicitly recognize civil unions and comprehensive domestic partnerships from other states as Hawaii, Illinois, and Colorado civil unions. Haw. Rev. Stat. § 572B–10; 750 Ill. Comp. Stat. 75/60; C.R.S.A § 14–15–116. Likewise, states with comprehensive domestic partnership laws will usually recognize similar regimes from other states. Thus, the Nevada domestic partnerships law honors civil unions and comprehensive domestic partnerships validly recognized in other states. Nev. Rev. Stat. § 122A.500. Washington has an unusual statutory rule, recognizing out-of-state civil unions and comprehensive domestic partnerships as marriages if one or both partners are over the age of 62 and recognizing all civil unions and comprehensive domestic partnerships as marriages for the first year of a couple's residence in the state. RCWA 26.60.100

Even when state legislation assures recognition of out-of-state civil unions, there is still probably nonrecognition of beneficiary or partnership relationships that have no analogue in the state of residence. Lambda, for example, tells couples in Illinois that the state will recognize their out-of-state civil unions, but not regimes that carry fewer rights and duties. Given the statutory language, it is doubtful that New Jersey would recognize Wisconsin domestic partners or Hawaii reciprocal beneficiaries as persons joined in a civil union in New Jersey.

PROBLEM 6-6
INTERSTATE RECOGNITION OF DESIGNATED BENEFICIARIES

Jane Roe and Kristen Kim enter into a designated beneficiary agreement in Colorado in 2011. The next year they move to New York. A reckless taxi cab driver runs over Kim in a Manhattan crosswalk, and Kim is rushed to the closest hospital, one operated by the Roman Catholic Church. Because she is unconscious, she cannot make life and death decisions. Roe produces evidence that she is Kim's designated beneficiary, which authorizes her to make medical decisions for her partner under Colo. Code § 15–22–105(3)(f) (reprinted above). For religious reasons, the hospital administrator refuses to honor that designation, and Roe seeks a temporary restraining order (TRO) in state court. Assume that New York law would require the administrator to honor the designation if Kim were Roe's married spouse. Will a state judge grant the TRO?

Assume that Kim dies of her injuries and that Roe sues the taxi driver and her company for wrongful death. As designated beneficiary, Colorado law would allow her to do that. Colo. Code § 15–22–105(3)(k) (reprinted above). Notice that this lawsuit would involve the very issue decided in *Langan*. What arguments might Roe have to support her claim? As you ponder this question, consider the distinction between rights that only affect the partners themselves (such as surrogate decisionmaking and default inheritance rules) and those that impose costs on third parties, as well as the purposes of the state wrongful death law and the possible splitting of two different issues, i.e., standing to sue on the part of the plaintiff and conduct giving rise to liability on the part of the defendant. Should it make a difference if Kim and Roe were still domiciled in Colorado and were only visiting New York?

NOTE ON FEDERAL RECOGNITION OF NONMARITAL FAMILIES

Most federal government recognition of nonmarital families flows from broadly written statutes or administrative regulations implementing the President's or the agency's general powers. Agencies might borrow ideas and policies from state or municipal law. For example, the Air Transportation Safety and System Stabilization Act of 2001, Pub. L. No. 107–42, set up a Victim Compensation Fund for the survivors of those who died as a result of the 9/11 terrorist attack. The law offered monetary recoveries to the *personal representatives* of victims of 9/11 but did not define that term; Kenneth Feinberg, the Administrator of the 9/11 Fund, interpreted it to apply to same-sex partners recognized as beneficiaries under state or municipal law.

Under DOMA, the executive branch was hamstrung in many respects; the statute required agencies to avoid any construction that presented lesbian and gay couples as possibly "married," and that admonition often discouraged liberal constructions of federal statutes that applied to any kind of coupled or family relationship. After DOMA was invalidated in *Windsor*, the Obama Administration (led by Assistant Attorney General Stuart Delery) engaged in a massive project to integrate same-sex married couples into hundreds of statutory and regulatory schemes administered by dozens of departments, agencies, and commissions. Here is an early, and highly representative, example of the Administration's rethinking.

Revenue Ruling 2013–17

Internal Revenue Service, Sept. 16, 2013.
http://www.irs.gov/irb/2013-38_IRB/ar07.html.

[After the Supreme Court's decision in *Windsor,* the Internal Revenue Service expanded its analysis of what couples are "married" for purposes of the Internal Revenue Code. One issue the Service addressed in this revenue ruling was whether a marriage of same-sex individuals validly entered into in a state whose laws authorize the marriage of two individuals of the same sex even if the state in which they are domiciled does not recognize the validity of same-sex marriages. Another issue is whether the terms "spouse," "husband and wife," "husband," and "wife" include individuals (whether of the opposite sex or same sex) who have entered into a registered domestic partnership, civil union, or other similar formal relationship recognized under state law that is not denominated as a marriage under the laws of that state, and whether, for those same purposes, the term "marriage" includes such relationships.]

In Revenue Ruling 58–66, 1958–1 C.B. 60, the Service determined the marital status for Federal income tax purposes of individuals who have entered into a common-law marriage in a state that recognizes common-law marriages. The Service acknowledged that it recognizes the marital status of individuals as determined under state law in the administration of the Federal income tax laws. In Revenue Ruling 58–66, the Service stated that a couple would be treated as married for purposes of Federal income tax filing status and personal exemptions if the couple entered into a common-law marriage in a state that recognizes that relationship as a valid marriage.

The Service further concluded in Revenue Ruling 58–66 that its position with respect to a common-law marriage also applies to a couple who entered into a common-law marriage in a state that recognized such relationships and who later moved to a state in which a ceremony is required to establish the marital relationship.

The Service therefore held that a taxpayer who enters into a common-law marriage in a state that recognizes such marriages shall, for purposes of Federal income tax filing status and personal exemptions, be considered married notwithstanding that the taxpayer and the taxpayer's spouse are currently domiciled in a state that requires a ceremony to establish the marital relationship. Accordingly, the Service held in Revenue Ruling 58–66 that such individuals can file joint income tax returns under section 6013 of the Internal Revenue Code (Code).

The Service has applied this rule with respect to common-law marriages for over 50 years, despite the refusal of some states to give full faith and credit to common-law-marriages established in other states. Although states have different rules of marriage recognition, uniform nationwide rules are essential for efficient and fair tax administration. A rule under which a couple's marital status could change simply by moving from one state to another state would be prohibitively difficult and costly for the Service to administer, and for many taxpayers to apply.
* * *

There are more than two hundred Code provisions and Treasury regulations relating to the internal revenue laws that include the terms "spouse," "marriage" (and derivatives thereof, such as "marries" and "married"), "husband and wife," "husband," and "wife." The Service concludes that gender-neutral terms in the Code that refer to marital status, such as "spouse" and "marriage," include, respectively, (1) an individual married to a person of the same sex if the couple is lawfully married under state law, and (2) such a marriage between individuals of the same sex. This is the most natural reading of those terms; it is consistent with *Windsor*, in which the plaintiff was seeking tax benefits under a statute that used the term "spouse"; and a narrower interpretation would not further the purposes of efficient tax administration.

[Interpreting "Husband and Wife" in the Code.] In light of the *Windsor* decision and for the reasons discussed below, the Service also concludes that the terms "husband and wife," "husband," and "wife" should be interpreted to include same-sex spouses. This interpretation is consistent with the Supreme Court's statements about the Code in *Windsor*, avoids the serious constitutional questions that an alternate reading would create, and is permitted by the text and purposes of the Code.

First, the Supreme Court's opinion in *Windsor* suggests that it understood that its decision striking down section 3 of DOMA would affect tax administration in ways that extended beyond the estate tax refund at issue. The Court observed in particular that section 3 burdened same-sex couples by forcing "them to follow a complicated procedure to file their Federal and state taxes jointly" and that section 3 "raise[d] the cost of health care for families by taxing health benefits provided by employers to their workers' same-sex spouses."

Second, an interpretation of the gender-specific terms in the Code to exclude same-sex spouses would raise serious constitutional questions. A well-established principle of statutory interpretation holds that, "where an otherwise acceptable construction of a statute would raise serious constitutional problems," a court should "construe the statute to avoid such problems unless such construction is plainly contrary to the intent of Congress." Edward J. DeBartolo Corp. v. Fla. Gulf Coast Bldg. & Constr. Trades Council, 485 U.S. 568, 575 (1988). "This canon is followed out of respect for Congress, which [presumably] legislates in light of constitutional limitations," Rust v. Sullivan, 500 U.S. 173, 191 (1991), and instructs courts, where possible, to avoid interpretations that "would raise serious constitutional doubts," United States v. X-Citement Video, Inc., 513 U.S. 64, 78 (1994).

The Fifth Amendment analysis in *Windsor* raises serious doubts about the constitutionality of Federal laws that confer marriage benefits and burdens only on opposite-sex married couples. In *Windsor*, the Court stated that, "[b]y creating two contradictory marriage regimes within the same State, DOMA forces same-sex couples to live as married for the purpose of state law but unmarried for the purpose of Federal law, thus diminishing the stability and predictability of basic personal relations the State has found it proper to acknowledge and protect." Interpreting the gender-specific terms in the Code to categorically exclude same-sex couples arguably would have the same effect of diminishing the stability and predictability of legally recognized same-sex marriages. Thus, the canon of constitutional avoidance counsels in favor of interpreting the gender-specific terms in the Code to refer to same-sex spouses and couples.

Third, the text of the Code permits a gender-neutral construction of the gender-specific terms. Section 7701 of the Code provides definitions of certain terms generally applicable for purposes of the Code when the terms are not defined otherwise in a specific Code provision and the definition in section 7701 is not manifestly incompatible with the intent of the specific Code provision. The terms "husband and wife," "husband," and "wife" are not specifically defined other than in section 7701(a)(17), which provides, for purposes of sections 682 and 2516, that the terms "husband" and "wife" shall be read to include a former husband or a former wife, respectively, and that "husband" shall be read as "wife" and "wife" as "husband" in certain circumstances. Although Congress's specific instruction to read "husband" and "wife" interchangeably in those specific provisions could be taken as an indication that Congress did not intend the terms to be read interchangeably in other provisions, the Service believes that the better understanding is that the interpretive rule set forth in section 7701(a)(17) makes it reasonable to adopt, in the circumstances presented here and in light of *Windsor* and the principle of constitutional avoidance, a more general rule that does not foreclose a gender-neutral reading of gender-specific terms elsewhere in the Code.

Section 7701(p) provides a specific cross-reference to the Dictionary Act, 1 U.S.C. § 1, which provides, in part, that when "determining the meaning of any Act of Congress, unless the context indicates otherwise, . . . words importing the masculine gender include the feminine as well." The purpose of this provision was to avoid having to "specify males and females by using a great deal of unnecessary language when one word would express the whole." Cong. Globe, 41st Cong., 3d Sess. 777 (1871) (statement of Sen. Trumbull, sponsor of Dictionary Act). This provision has been read to require construction of the phrase "husband and wife" to include same-sex married couples. See Pedersen v. Office of Personnel Mgmt., 881 F. Supp. 2d 294, 306–07 (D. Conn. 2012) (construing section 6013 of the Code).

The Dictionary Act thus supports interpreting the gender-specific terms in the Code in a gender-neutral manner "unless the context indicates otherwise." 1 U.S.C. § 1. "'Context'" for purposes of the Dictionary Act "means the text of the Act of Congress surrounding the word at issue, or the texts of other related congressional Acts." Rowland v. Cal. Men's Colony, Unit II Men's Advisory Council, 506 U.S. 194, 199 (1993). Here, nothing in the surrounding text forecloses a gender-neutral reading of the gender-specific terms. Rather, the provisions of the Code that use the terms "husband and wife," "husband," and "wife" are inextricably interwoven with provisions that use gender-neutral terms like "spouse" and "marriage," indicating that Congress viewed them to be equivalent. For example, section 1(a) sets forth the tax imposed on "every married individual (as defined in section 7703) who makes a single return jointly with his spouse under section 6013," even though section 6013 provides that a "husband and wife" make a single return jointly of income. Similarly, section 2513 of the Code is entitled "Gifts by Husband or Wife to Third Party," but uses no gender-specific terms in its text. See also, e.g., §§ 62(b)(3), 1361(c)(1).

This interpretation is also consistent with the legislative history. The legislative history of section 6013, for example, uses the term "married taxpayers" interchangeably with the terms "husband" and "wife" to describe those individuals who may elect to file a joint return, and there is no indication that Congress intended those terms to refer only to a subset of individuals who are legally married. See, e.g., S. Rep. No. 82–781, Finance, Part 1, p. 48 (Sept. 18, 1951). Accordingly, the most logical reading is that the terms "husband and wife" were used because they were viewed, at the time of enactment, as equivalent to the term "persons married to each other." There is nothing in the Code to suggest that Congress intended to exclude from the meaning of these terms any couple otherwise legally married under state law.

Fourth, other considerations also strongly support this interpretation. A gender-neutral reading of the Code fosters fairness by ensuring that the Service treats same-sex couples in the same manner as similarly situated opposite-sex couples. A gender-neutral reading of the Code also fosters administrative efficiency because the Service does not collect or maintain information on the gender of taxpayers and would have great difficulty administering a scheme that differentiated between same-sex and opposite-sex married couples.

Therefore, consistent with the statutory context, the Supreme Court's decision in *Windsor*, Revenue Ruling 58–66, and effective tax administration generally, the Service concludes that, for Federal tax purposes, the terms "husband and wife," "husband," and "wife" include an individual married to a person of the same sex if they were lawfully married in a state whose laws authorize the marriage of two individuals of the same sex, and the term "marriage" includes such marriages of individuals of the same sex.

[The Service next concluded that its determination whether the same-sex couples were "married" or were "spouses" for purposes of the Code would be determined by the law of the state where their marriage was celebrated. Thus, couples validly married in Massachusetts but who lived in Michigan, which did not recognize their marriage in 2013, would be treated as married for federal tax purposes.]

[Marriages Recognized, Not Domestic Partnerships, Civil Unions.] For Federal tax purposes, the term "marriage" does not include registered domestic partnerships, civil unions, or other similar formal relationships recognized under state law that are not denominated as a marriage under that state's law, and the terms "spouse," "husband and wife," "husband," and "wife" do not include individuals who have entered into such a formal relationship. This conclusion applies regardless of whether individuals who have entered into such relationships are of the opposite sex or the same sex.

PROBLEM 6-7
CIVIL UNIONS UNDER THE INTERNAL REVENUE CODE AND OTHER FEDERAL STATUTES

You are the White House Counsel in the wake of *Windsor*. President Obama has asked you for your legal advice regarding the IRS's Revenue Ruling and other rulings and guidances contemplated by other agencies. The President's position is that he wants to recognize lesbian and gay unions as much as the law and established rules of legal interpretation permit; hence, he is not willing to recognize such unions where a statute constitutionally bars them. What advice do you give the President, in response to the following scenarios?

(a) *Internal Revenue Code.* At the request of the White House, the Treasury Department provides you with a preview of Revenue Ruling 2013–17. LGBT groups have also procured a copy of the proposed revenue ruling, and they have asked the White House why valid civil unions cannot be recognized as well. The IRS takes the position that couples in civil unions or domestic partnerships are not "spouses" or "married" for purposes of the Internal Revenue Code.

LGBT groups point to the Nevada domestic partnership statute, which says that "Domestic partners have the same rights, protections and benefits, and are subject to the same responsibilities, obligations and duties under law, whether derived from statutes, administrative regulations, court rules, government policies, common law or any other provisions or sources of law, as are granted to and imposed upon spouses." Nev. Rev. Stats. § 122A.200(1)(a). In Nevada, therefore, domestic partners have all the legal rights and duties as "spouses" and, hence, are similarly situated to Massachusetts married couples who have the legal rights and duties as "spouses."

What is the LGBT groups' best argument for inclusion of Nevada (and perhaps other) domestic partners in the revenue ruling? Under his directive, how should you advise the President? If you disagree with the IRS, what process would you recommend to the President? See generally Deborah Widiss & Andrew Koppelman, "A Marriage by Any Other Name: Why Civil Unions Should Receive Federal Recognition," *Ind. J.L. & Soc. Inequality,* vol. 3, Iss. 1, Art. 3 (2015).

(b) *Veterans' Benefits.* Veterans' benefits flow to a "spouse" or a "surviving spouse" of a person who served in the armed forces. Title 38 defines both terms as "a person of the 'opposite sex' who is a wife or a husband." 38 U.S.C. § 101(31) ("spouse"); *id.* § 101(3) ("surviving spouse"). These definitions exclude lesbian and gay spouses from the veterans' benefits law, and so the question is whether these definitions are unconstitutional in the wake of *Windsor*. How do you advise the President? See Dep't of Justice, Office of the Att'y Gen., Letter from Att'y Gen. Eric Holder to The Honorable John Boehner (Sept. 4, 2013) (offering the Justice Department's opinion on the constitutional issue).

Assume that White House Counsel or the Department of Justice concludes that the veterans' benefits definition of "spouse" is inconsistent with *Windsor* and, hence, must be expanded. Would you advise the Veterans Administration to include at least some couples joined in civil union or comprehensive domestic partnership, such as those under the Nevada law quoted above?

(c) *Social Security Benefits.* Consider now whether a lesbian couple joined in a Nevada domestic partnership should be treated as "married" under the Social Security Act of 1935. The governing statutory provision is 42 U.S.C. § 416(h), "Determination of Family Status":

(h)(1)(A)(i)   An applicant is the wife, husband, widow, or widower of a fully or currently insured individual for purposes of this subchapter if the courts of the State in which such insured individual is domiciled at the time such applicant files an application, or, if such insured individual is dead, the courts of the State in which he was domiciled at the time of death, or, if such insured individual is or was not so domiciled in any State, the courts of the District of Columbia, would find that such applicant and such insured individual were validly married at the time such applicant files such application or, if such insured individual is dead, at the time he died.

(ii)   If such courts would not find that such applicant and such insured individual were validly married at such time, such applicant shall, nevertheless be deemed to be the wife, husband, widow, or widower, as the case may be, of such insured individual if such applicant would, under the laws applied by such courts in determining the devolution of intestate personal property, have the same status with respect to the taking of such property as a wife, husband, widow, or widower of such insured individual.

Is there a statutory basis for the Social Security Administration to provide survivors' benefits to the surviving spouse of the Nevada couple? Cf. Social Security Administration, GN 00210.400 Same-Sex Marriage—Benefits for Surviving Spouses (Dec. 16, 2013).

Is there a statutory basis for the Social Security Administration to provide survivors' benefits to the surviving beneficiary of a Colorado couple (such as Roe and Kim, above) who have registered as designated beneficiaries under Colorado law? Reread the 2009 statute, excerpted above, before you answer this question.

C. THE EMERGING REGIME: A MENU OF STATE-RECOGNIZED FAMILY FORMS

William N. Eskridge Jr., *Equality Practice: Civil Unions and the Future of Gay Rights* **121–26 (2002).** "Each step toward same-sex marriage is typically (but not always) sedimentary: rather than displacing earlier reforms, the new reform simply adds another legal rule or institution on top of the earlier one. In this way, the same-sex marriage movement has contributed to a transformation in the options the state offers to different-sex as well as same-sex couples. Thus, when Sweden enacted its registered partnership law, it did not revoke the legal rights of cohabiting same-sex couples. The French PaCS law included cohabitation rights for same-sex couples as part of the elaborate process by which the law emerged. * * * The [2001] Dutch same-sex marriage law leaves intact the 1998 law creating registered partnerships for same-sex as well as different-sex couples. These examples suggest that the experimentation in social policy triggered by the same-sex marriage movement can, and perhaps should be expected to, create new institutions and tinker with existing institutions. Sometimes the new institutions will be available to all couples, as the French PaCS and Dutch registered partnerships are.

"The same-sex marriage movement is part of a larger evolution in the way the state regulates human coupling. Today in the Netherlands and France, and tomorrow in many other jurisdictions, couples of all kinds will have a menu of options. One way to conceptualize part of that menu is around the degree of unitive commitment expected or entailed in the partners' relationship. Drawing from legal regimes already created in the United States and Europe, the menu looks something like the following. I have arrayed the items on this particular menu from lowest to highest level of commitment, and from least to most like our romantic fantasy vision of traditional marriage.

"1. Domestic Partnership (Employment Benefits Without Necessarily Much Commitment). Municipal ordinances in the United States and the 1999 statewide law in California [before its amendment in 2003 and afterward] have provided a useful model that is being followed by many business enterprises: any employee who is willing to sign a form identifying a significant other (of any sex) ought to be able to add that person to the health care, life insurance, and other benefits provided by the employer to married employees. Being someone's domestic partner may reflect romantic as well as nonerotic love, but it reflects a level of commitment only slightly greater than being a friend. The emphasis is on employment benefits, but there is some symbolic recognition that the relationship is consequential to both parties and ought to be rewarded with a few benefits. At this level, there is no legal obligation imposed on the partners, however. They might be highly committed to one another, but that is neither a premise nor an expected effect of state recognition.

"2. Cohabitation (Economic Obligations as well as More Benefits). Canada and most European countries impose support obligations on and offer some state benefits to couples who have cohabited for a substantial period of time. Two people can be domestic partners without living together and with no expectation of a long-term relationship; cohabitation usually suggests both the reality of some legs on the relationship and the expectation for more. The assumption of greater commitment entails greater interdependence, which the state both rewards and obligates. The cohabiting household is treated by the state as a unit for purposes of economic security for each partner. Thus, a cohabitation regime will generally impose duties of support on the couple, especially if there is specialization within the household, where one partner works outside the home and builds up her outside earning capacity, while the other partner sacrifices some of hers so that the household can run smoothly and children can be cared for properly. [In the United States, this is represented by Marvin and the ALI's proposed domestic partnership institution.] European and Canadian laws also provide legal presumptions of joint property ownership and tenancy, family and bereavement leave, and sometimes wrongful death claims as well for cohabiting partners.

"3. Cohabitation-Plus (Unitive Rights as well as Economic Obligations and Benefits). The arrangement in the previous paragraph is the old version of cohabitation rules. The last ten years have seen them expand, and the compromises entailed in legislative wrangling over same-sex marriage have simulated further innovations. France's PaCS, the German life partnership, and Hawaii's reciprocal beneficiaries illustrate a new kind of cohabitation regime; because the terminology varies so much from state to state, we can call this cohabitation-plus. The regime created by these laws both assumes and creates a greater level of commitment than do domestic partnership or cohabitation. As with domestic partnership, the couple must register but, unlike domestic partnership, usually must go through a more formal process of dissolution. As with cohabitation, the state not only imposes duties of mutual support, but also provides benefits to encourage the partners' economic unity. What the French, German, and Hawaiian regimes most distinctively add is unitive rights—namely, rules treating the partners as coupled and granting them financial and other benefits that reflect their unity as to matters like health care decisions when one partner is incapacitated, organ donations after death, and mandated bereavement or sick leave for one's partner. In an ideal system, cohabitation-plus would also entail rights to enter the host country to be with one's partner. Obviously, this regime signals as well as entails a higher degree of mutual commitment than the first two.

"4. Civil Unions (Family Rights and Obligations as well as Unitive Rights, Economic Obligations, and Benefits). After or instead of cohabiting, many couples decide to commit to a longer-term

relationship. Some of those couples want full-fledged state recognition, like that accorded marriage. The Netherlands [and] the Scandinavian countries * * * allow these couples to become registered partners or join in civil unions. The state will encourage this long-term commitment with employment and other benefits, will help the couple carry out their purposes with the unitive rights and interdependence benefits, will underline the commitment's seriousness with obligations of mutual support and fidelity and with the added difficulty of legal divorce proceedings in the event of a breakup, and will reinforce family ties by giving the partners mutual rights over their adopted or biological children. What the state does not give in these civil union or registered partnership laws is the name marriage and its interstate and international portability. That is, Alabama will recognize a French marriage but probably not a French PaCS [or a Danish registered partnership].

"*5. Marriage (The Name as well as Intangible Obligations, Unitive Rights, Economic Obligations, and Benefits).* The traditional way couples in western culture commit to a long-term relationship, of course, has been marriage. Under the sedimentary precept, the state will continue to support as well as recognize marriage, with all the rights and duties entailed in civil unions as well as the trademarked name and the international portability. The progressivity principle explained above suggests that marriage will be extended to same-sex couples who choose it, but many of them (as well as some different-sex couples) will choose civil unions, cohabitation (plus), or some other form for ideological or personal reasons. Marriage will continue to be the focal point of family formation, because of its deep history and religious overtones. But the commitment it signals will continue to be diluted by the possibility of divorce without a showing of fault.

"*6. Covenant Marriage (All the Above, plus It's Harder to Exit).* Even though I strenuously disagree with traditionalists' opposition to same-sex marriage, I agree with them that no-fault divorce has rendered marriage a less reliable pre-commitment device. If the state is going to experiment with institutions exacting less commitment from couples than marriage does, why not create (or reestablish) an institution with greater commitment? This is the idea entailed in covenant marriage: the state provides all the same rights and benefits of ordinary marriage, plus all the obligations and duties, but makes it harder for couples to enter or dissolve the relationship. For example, Louisiana's pathbreaking statute requires a couple desiring to enter into a covenant marriage to receive extensive counseling and to swear an oath of mutual love and fidelity for life. A couple joined in a Louisiana covenant marriage can divorce only on grounds of serious fault (such as adultery or abuse) or after two years of separation. Covenant marriage both assumes and includes a higher level of commitment from the couple than easy-entry, easy-exit marriage does.

" * * * [T]his is only a partial menu, assuming both a romantic tie between the partners and a level of presumed commitment. Other kinds of state-sanctioned institutions are possible—such as Vermont's [2000] reciprocal beneficiary law, whose focus is intergenerational dependence. It was aimed to help the niece caring for her elderly aunt or the son giving care to his mother. As Professor Martha Fineman has argued, the law ought to support vertical (caregiving) relationships, not just horizontal (romantic) ones. Additionally, the partners themselves can edit the state's menu and create their own legal regime as long as they have access to legal services. Domestic partners or cohabitants can create some of the obligations and benefits of marriage by contracts, wills, joint tenancies, while married partners can opt out of or tailor some of the obligations through prenuptial agreements. The items arrayed in [the table immediately below] are off-the-rack rules automatically available to the couple simply by their registration for one of the different categories. Most couples, especially working-and middle-class couples, have neither the resources nor the foresight to create their own legal regime.

"Finally, there is nothing about the options laid out here that precludes the state from creating new institutions of family formation. For example, couples could mix and match the existing institutions: persons A and B could be domestic partners sharing a variety of economic benefits, but the surrogate decision-maker in the event of person B's incapacity could be person C, her niece, whom she has designated as her reciprocal beneficiary. The state could also create new institutions or (more radically) could delink existing institutions such as marriage from the many benefits associated with it. These ideas are not mere speculations. One effect of the politics of recognition associated with the same-sex marriage movement, and of the politics of preservation resisting the same, is that legislatures as well as courts all over the world are experimenting with family law and creating new legal forms. Just as domestic partnerships were unknown thirty years ago, and civil unions were unheard of until [2000], so the institutions in 2020 will include some terms that would surprise us today."

NOTES ON THE EXPANDING MENU OF STATE-RECOGNIZED FAMILY FORMS

The foregoing account is somewhat stylized, and quite speculative. No country now offers all the forms on the menu, and only a handful of states offer most of the options. Colorado is perhaps the most comprehensive state. Companies and some cities in Colorado offer domestic partnership benefits to employees, and the state offers couples a choice among the following regimes: cohabitation (common law regulation), designated beneficiaries (2009 statute), civil unions (2013 statute), and civil marriage (extended to same-sex couples through litigation settled when the Supreme Court in October 2014 denied review to a Tenth Circuit decision requiring marriage equality). California, Hawaii, and New Jersey offer a rich array of options as well. The menu is only a rough roadmap for where developments are heading.

If Professor Eskridge is right, the trend is not in the direction of Martha Fineman's proposal with which we opened the chapter. Rather than eliminating marriage as a regulatory form, the state is giving couples more options in addition to marriage. In his book, Eskridge does not mount a normative defense of the menu, beyond the implicit suggestion that the array of choices will satisfy a greater range of couples than the old marriage-or-nothing approach. But the form-of-family menu ought to be interrogated. Liberals, ranging from Richard Posner to Ruth Bader Ginsburg, would probably find some virtue in the menu approach, as it allows couples to tailor their legal regime to their own preferences for commitment and other relationship features. Consider some other perspectives:

1. *Natural Law.* Natural law thinkers (Chapter 3, Section 1) favor covenant marriage but are skeptical of the rest of the options. In practice, these theorists and their allies have been most opposed to the extension of state-recognized family forms to lesbian and gay couples—yet it is that opposition that has driven western political systems into compromises that generated new forms such as domestic partnerships, civil unions, reciprocal beneficiaries, registered partnerships, PaCS, and life partnerships. Natural law thinkers should be just as adamantly opposed to making these new forms open to different-sex couples, because the new forms will then drain some of them away from marriage into institutions that do not valorize interpersonal commitment as much. But demand from straight cohabiters in states like France, The Netherlands, and Nevada has been hard to resist once the political process commences negotiations over how to accommodate same-sex couples. Think more broadly, from a natural law point of view. What would some of these thinkers imagine to be the consequences of adopting something like this menu? Certainly, the marriage rate would fall—but what else would ensue?

2. *Feminism.* Different feminists would have a variety of different reactions to the menu of family options. The range of choices would appeal to some feminists, and the shift away from marriage might have some appeal to feminist critics of marriage. Consider how, if at all, the menu of family options would play into the core concerns of feminists we have studied, including (a) Carol Rose, who worries that women's weak bargaining position is creating dynamics of gender inequality in relationships (Chapter 3, Section 2); (b) Catharine MacKinnon, who worries that male-created sexuality is an engine of gender subordination (Chapter 3, Section 2); and (c) Martha Fineman (this chapter), who worries that existing legal forms are not giving women a legal structure within which their needs and preferences are satisfied. Assume that you do not go as far as Professor Fineman, who would abolish all legal forms for horizontal relationships. If you were designing a new institution for romantic relationships, but from a feminist

perspective, what would it look like? Is it similar to any of the forms on the Eskridge menu?

Robin West, in *Marriage, Sexuality, and Gender* (2007), argues from a feminist perspective that marriage is too much tied to religious and other patriarchal traditions and, hence, that progressives ought to abolish civil marriage and support *civil unions* for everyone. Her stance would be friendly to a menu approach that eliminated marriage and covenant marriage, though she might be open to some variety in the exit options for civil unions.

3.   *Queer Theory.* Postmodern queer theorists (Chapter 3, Section 3) would for the most part be hostile to the menu approach, especially given their objections to marriage. For the most thoughtful critique, Nancy D. Polikoff's *Beyond (Straight and Gay) Marriage: Valuing All Families Under the Law* (2008) argues that marriage has a normatively loaded history that inevitably creates dividing lines, arbitrarily excluding some kinds of couples while just as arbitrarily elevating other kinds of couples. She strongly rejects a policy whereby marriage is the entry gate to so many state benefits and rights. Professor Polikoff does not address the emerging menu, but the book's argument suggests that a menu offering a serious cohabitation-plus regime would be an improvement on the status quo but that a menu offering marriage would still be objectionable.

Consider, however, the menu's advantages from a queer point of view. For example, the menu would de-normalize marriage as the central institution it is today, and might normalize homosexuality. The experimentation entailed in the menu could also be expected to produce feedback from couples themselves as to which of the new institutions work, and which should be scrapped because they do not work. If Michel Foucault were designing a legal system for horizontal relationships, what would it look like? (Is this a question that can conceivably have an answer?)

PROBLEM 6-8
CREATE A LEGAL REGIME FOR PARTNERED RELATIONSHIPS

Having read the materials in this chapter, propose what you think is the best legal regime for regulating partnered relationships. You are not limited to the proposals we have surveyed, nor to the items on the menu above. Think about what norms or policies you think the state should be advancing and the best legal regime for accomplishing that. Take account of theory if you can. Compare your answer with what you jotted down in response to Problem 6-1.

CHAPTER 7

Parents and Children

SECTION 1   Custody and Visitation
SECTION 2   Adoption and Foster Care
SECTION 3   Establishing Parentage
SECTION 4   Polyparenting

_____

Chapter 6 explores the rights and obligations of adults in a range of family relationships. Chapter 7 turns to the parent-child relationship. As was true of the regulation of adult-adult relationship, the questions explored in this chapter are hotly contested cultural ones.

Historically, almost all families were marital ones, consisting of a husband and a wife and children. These marital families rarely ended by divorce, which was very difficult to obtain. Much has changed in the life and law of families in the last fifty or so years. In 2009, households consisting of married different-sex couples and their children constituted just a little over one-fifth (21.4%) of all American households, a dramatic decline since 1970 (40.3%). 2009 American Community Survey, http://factfinder.census.gov/servlet/ADPTable? _ bm=y&-geo _ id=01000US&-ds _ name=ACS _ 2009 _ 5YR _ G00 _ &-_ lang=en&-_ caller=geoselect&-format=; 2000 Census, www.census.gov/population/www/cen2000/briefs.html. Of this declining share of families that consist of married parents and their children, many of them will experience divorce, and some of them form blended new families. At the same time that marital families are declining, nonmarital families are on the rise. Approximately forty percent of all children in the U.S. today are born to unmarried women. Unmarried Childbearing, CDC, https://www.cdc.gov/nchs/fastats/unmarried-childbearing.htm. This is up from 5% in 1960. In addition to these changes in family form, there are also new ways of bringing children into families—of whatever type. More and more families, including LGBT families, are having children through assisted reproductive technology.

This chapter begins to explore how has the law adapted (or not) to these changes in the lives and structures of families. Many of these rules have been deeply rooted in stereotyped notions of sex, sexuality, and gender. As you go through the reading, consider the extent to which these notions continue to shape the rules governing the parent-child relationship.

Section 1 begins by considering how the law allocates rights and responsibilities between parents when the family breaks down. Historically, divorce was very rare. When divorces did happen, the rules governing custody actions between husbands and wives were deeply gendered. Under the doctrine of coverture, husbands were the masters of their wives and their children. As a result, husbands were exclusively entitled to custody of any children upon divorce.

In the mid-nineteenth century, this rule shifted to what was known as the "tender years presumption," under which custody was granted to a mother of a young child unless she was found to be unfit. *See, e.g.*, D. Kelly Weisberg & Susan Frelich Appleton, *Modern Family Law* 670 (5th ed. 2013). The tender years presumption was premised on the belief that mothers are inherently better suited "to care for and nurture young children." *Devine v. Devine*, 398 So.3d 686 (Ala. 1981) (holding "that the tender years presumption represents an unconstitutional gender-based classification which discriminates between fathers and mothers in child custody proceedings solely on the basis of sex").

By the late twentieth century, the tender years presumption had given way to the facially gender-neutral "best interests of the child" standard, which is now utilized throughout the country. Despite the facial neutrality of the best interest test, however, stereotypes about gender, sexuality, and sexual orientation continue to play a role in custody proceedings. Section 1 explores whether and to what extent these factors are or should be relevant in a child custody proceeding. Section 2 considers a related question—whether and how these considerations should be relevant in placing a child for adoption or foster care.

Section 3 then steps back and asks a much more preliminary question—how does the law determine who a child's parents are? Historically marriage was the primary basis for establishing a legal relationship between children and their fathers. Under the common law, a husband was presumed to be the parent of a child born to his wife and this presumption was extremely difficult to rebut. As Justice Scalia explained, an important rationale for the marital presumption was to protect the marital family from outside interference. *Michael H. v. Gerald D.*, 491 U.S. 110, 124–25 (1989) (noting that a core purpose of the presumption was to "promot[e] the 'peace and tranquility of States and families'"). Moreover, by hiding "situations in which the husband was not in fact the biological father," Douglas NeJaime explains, the marital presumption protected the child from being labeled "illegitimate." Douglas NeJaime, "The Nature of Parenthood," 126 *Yale L.J.* 2260, 2272 (2017).

Protecting children from this label was important because the law treated such children very harshly. Under the common law, children born outside of marriage were considered *filius nullis*, literally the child of no one. *See, e.g.*, Martha F. Davis, "Male Coverture: Law and the Illegitimate Family," 56 *Rutgers L. Rev.* 73, 81–82 (2003). In the U.S., states were quicker to recognize a relationship between mothers and their nonmarital children. *Id.* at 81. But for most of our history, "non-marital fathers remained free of the legal burdens and benefits of parenthood." *Id.* at 82. Typically, the relationship between a nonmarital father and his child was recognized only if he undertook some voluntary conduct to "legitimize" the child, which, most commonly, was done by marrying the child's mother. In this way, "the doctrine of coverture cluster[ed] parental rights and responsibilities for out-of-wedlock children with the mother." *Id.*

In the wake of a series of Supreme Court decisions in the 1960s and 1970s regarding the rights and status of children born outside of marriage, all states updated their laws governing the parentage of nonmarital children. These rules governing the parentage of nonmarital children "made biological connection an explicit basis for paternal rights in ways that did not merely supplement, but in some circumstances rivaled, marriage." Douglas NeJaime, "The Nature of Parenthood," 126 *Yale L.J.* 2260, 2275 (2017).

As Professor NeJaime explains, at the same time that biology became a more important basis for establishing the parentage of nonmarital children, states began to adopt new rules assigning parentage to husbands in the absence of biological connection. Starting in the 1970s, states began to treat husbands who consented to their wives' use of assisted reproduction as legal parents, even if everyone knew he was not a genetic parent. Until recently, however, most of these consent-based parentage rules were limited to children born to married couples through assisted reproduction. *See, e.g.,* Courtney G. Joslin, "Protecting Children(?): Marriage, Gender, and Assisted Reproductive Technology," 83 *S. Cal. L. Rev.* 1177 (2010).

Given that same-sex couples were barred from marriage until recently, and given that in most cases both members of a same-sex couple are not biologically related to their children, this section ponders how these rules map on to the estimated 220,000 children being raised by these families. Gary J. Gates, Williams Institute, UCLA, LGBT Parenting in the United States (Feb. 2013), http://williamsinstitute.law. ucla.edu/wp-content/uploads/LGBT-Parenting.pdf. This section also presses readers to ponder what the rules should be.

Finally, Section 4 considers a new frontier in parentage law— whether to expand the status of parent beyond the model of two.

SECTION 1

CUSTODY AND VISITATION

A. CHILD CUSTODY AS A FORM OF MORALS REGULATION

Historically, custody and visitation rules were deeply rooted in and reinforced gender norms. Under the common law doctrine of coverture, custody went to husbands, who were the masters of their children. (Under common law, nonmarital fathers were not consideredparents of their children.)

In the mid-19th century, this paternal custody rule gave way to the so-called "tender years" presumption, under which custody of young children was presumptively awarded to mothers. *See, e.g.*, Michael Grossberg, *Governing the Hearth: Law and the Family in Nineteenth-Century America* 248–50 (1985).

But this strong presumption of maternal custody could be rebutted if the mother did not live up to maternal standards established by the courts—especially when she had engaged in sexual infidelity or, especially in the South, a romantic relationship with someone of another race. These norms reflected not only traditional gender stereotypes (the mother must be desexualized and nurturing), but also represented one of the ways that morality entered state rulemaking. The morality involved fears of interracial sex and of sexualizing the child's household environment. Is either of these moral factors a legitimate consideration in child custody determinations?

In the current era, courts are not allowed to entertain a presumption favoring maternal custody. *See Devine v. Devine*, 398 So.2d 686 (Ala. 1981). Instead, all fifty states now apply the "best interests of the child" standard when allocating custody between two legal parents. But even though courts are no longer supposed to make assumptions about parents based on their gender, question of morality continue to loom. Is it ever proper for the state to consider the morality of the parent in determining the "best interests of the child"?

The states have been moving away from such morality-based requirements. In *Whaley v. Whaley,* 61 Ohio App.2d 111, 399 N.E.2d 1270 (1978), for a pioneering example, the Ohio Court of Appeals overturned a trial court decree revoking child custody from a former wife because she was romantically involved with a married man (who was separated from his own wife). Judge Grey relied on a statutory regime presuming against unconsented changes in custody decrees unless "[t]he child's present environment endangers significantly his physical health or his mental, moral, or emotional development and the harm likely to be caused by a change of environment is outweighed by the advantages of such change to the child." A best-interests-of-the-child standard is inconsistent with the trial judge's view that the "adulterous" parent should be punished. Judge Grey ruled: "A child must not be used to punish or reward conduct a particular judge might condemn or condone." If there were a nexus (connection) between the mother's relationship and harm to the child, only then could it be a factor. This standard is often referred to as the "nexus test."

Linda Sidoti Palmore v. Anthony Sidoti, **466 U.S. 429, 104 S.Ct. 1879, 80 L.Ed.2d 421 (1984).** When Linda and Anthony Sidoti (both European American) were divorced in 1980, Linda was awarded custody of their three-year-old daughter. In 1981, Anthony moved for an order changing custody, on the ground that Linda was living with a person of color, Clarence Palmore, Jr., whom she married two months later. The Florida judge agreed:

The father's evident resentment of the mother's choice of a black partner is not sufficient to wrest custody from the mother. It is of some significance, however, that the mother did see fit to bring a man into her home and carry on a sexual relationship with him without being married to him. Such action tended to place gratification of her own desires ahead of her concern for the child's future welfare. This Court feels that despite the strides that have been made in bettering relations between the races in this country, it is inevitable that Melanie will * * * suffer from the social stigmatization that is sure to come.

A unanimous Supreme Court reversed. **Chief Justice Burger**'s opinion ruled that such a race-based decision violates the Equal Protection Clause. "The question * * * is whether the reality of private biases and the possible injury they might inflict are permissible considerations for removal of an infant child from the custody of its natural mother. We have little difficulty concluding that they are not. The Constitution cannot control prejudices but neither can it tolerate them. Private biases may be outside the reach of the law, but the law cannot, directly or indirectly, give them effect."

NOTES ON THE IMPLICATIONS OF *PALMORE V. SIDOTI*

1. *Race.* Does *Palmore* stand for the proposition that race can *never* be considered in child custody determinations? What if there were studies showing that children of color would be deprived of their intangible but psychologically important cultural or ethnic heritage if they were raised by white families? What if there were psychiatric evidence that, for a particular child, the trauma of living in a mixed-race household would be substantial?

2. *Sexuality.* Note that the *Whaley* approach allows more judicial discretion in considering sexual relations outside of marriage than *Palmore* seems to permit for interracial relationships. Would there be a constitutional problem if the Florida judge in *Palmore* had changed custody simply based on Linda Sidoti's extramarital relationship with Clarence Palmore, without mentioning the race element? When would it be unconstitutional for the state to deprive Linda Sidoti Palmore of custody of her child?

3. *Sexual Orientation.* Would it be constitutional for Ohio to follow the approach of *Whaley* when the extramarital affair is different-sex, but follow a stricter approach when it is same-sex? Would that be sex discrimination similar to the race discrimination in *Palmore*? Would the sexual orientation discrimination be invalid under existing constitutional doctrine?

B. SEXUAL ORIENTATION AND CUSTODY

During the first wave of lesbian and gay custody disputes, many courts categorically discriminated against the lesbian or gay parents. During this period, some states applied a *per se* rule that homosexuality disqualified a parent from custody. *See, e.g., Bennett v. Clemens*, 230 Ga. 317, 196 S.E.2d 842 (1973); *Immerman v. Immerman*, 176 Cal.App.2d 122, 1 Cal.Rptr. 298 (1959); *Commonwealth v. Bradley*, 171 Pa.Super. 587, 91 A.2d 379 (1952).

The proposition that an LGB parent's "lifestyle" was per se immoral and disqualifying came under fire in the 1970s. A key case was *Schuster v. Schuster*, 90 Wash.2d 626, 585 P.2d 130 (1978), where a lesbian couple, Sandy Schuster and Madeleine Isaacson, presented expert psychiatric evidence that parental sexual orientation is irrelevant to the child's development and that their children were healthy and normal. The courts left custody with the mothers, but with conditions. The trial court admonished the mothers not to "use" the children as a showcase for "homosexuality," and the appeals court refused to allow the mothers to live together. *See* Rhonda Rivera, "Our Straight-Laced Judges: The Legal Position Of Homosexual Persons In The United States," 30 *Hastings L.J.* 799, 898–900 (1979) (discussing *Schuster*, as well as other pre-1979 cases, including unreported cases).

Over time, more and more judges adopted the (at least facially) more neutral nexus test. A leading case is *Bezio v. Patenaude*, 381 Mass. 563, 410 N.E.2d 1207 (1980), where the Massachusetts Supreme Judicial Court held that the best interests of the child standard required that there must be a specific showing of harm to the child to justify depriving a lesbian or gay parent of custody. Stated another way, the court required a *nexus* between the parent's sexual orientation and harm to the child for the orientation to be relevant in a child custody case. For an early explication of the nexus argument, see Nan Hunter & Nancy Polikoff, "Custody Rights of Lesbian Mothers: Legal Theory and Litigation Strategy," 25 *Buff. L. Rev.* 691 (1976). *See also Conkel v. Conkel*, 31 Ohio App.3d 169, 509 N.E.2d 983 (1987), where Judge Grey applied the nexus standard of *Whaley* to a case where the allegedly "immoral" conduct was the husband's homosexuality.

Today, courts in almost all jurisdictions at least purport to utilize the nexus approach of *Bezio v. Patenaude*. But even in jurisdictions that follow the nexus approach, there are a number of challenges that can arise. One issue that has not gotten much traction is the charge, sometimes but decreasingly made by straight spouses, that the LGB parent might abuse the child sexually. That would be bad for the child, but the charge is empirically unlikely. Straight males are the group most likely to molest children; the groups least likely to abuse them are lesbians and straight women; gay men fall somewhere in between, but openly gay men are also lowest-risk in this regard. See generally Carole Jenny et al., "Are Children at Risk for Sexual Abuse by Homosexuals?," 94 *Pediatrics* 41 (1994).

Another claim is that a child being raised by a lesbian or gay parent will suffer taunts, teasing, and maybe even violence from homophobic children or discrimination from teachers and other adults. This claim has some factual basis but is normatively questionable; it was disapproved in different-race cases by *Palmore v. Sidoti*. Should *Palmore*'s reasoning be applied to prevent this skewed application of the nexus approach? Finally, there is the role model argument—that exposure to a gay or lesbian parent and her same-sex partner will undermine the child's development of her own gender role and sexuality. It is unclear whether this argument has a factual basis; some studies have found no correlation to sexual orientation, while others have found a correlation to a child's conformity with traditional gender stereotypes. Assume that it does: Can it survive *VMI* (state cannot enforce traditional gender roles) and *Lawrence v. Texas* (state cannot enforce sexual conformity)?

NOTES ON THE NEXUS APPROACH IN OPERATION: THE PERSEVERANCE OF ANTI-HOMOSEXUAL TROPES

1. *Heteronormativity and the Nexus Calculus.* Even today, the nexus approach does not assure that lesbian and gay parents will be treated the same as straight parents. The operational neutrality of the nexus approach depends on what considerations will be weighed by the trier of fact, who has the burden of proof, and how high the burden is. *Conkel* exemplifies a relatively neutral approach: Judge Grey found the parent's sexuality irrelevant as a formal matter; the only relevant evidence was the best interests of the child; and social attitudes about the parent's sexuality were not relevant to determine that. An historical note may help explain this: Judge Grey sought out the assistance of Professor Rhonda Rivera of Ohio State University School of Law, and author of the first important legal scholarship in the area of gay rights.

Contrast *Stroman v. Williams*, 291 S.C. 376, 353 S.E.2d 704 (App. 1987). The trial judge rejected a husband's effort to change the custody decree because his former wife was raising the child with her lesbian partner, and the South Carolina Supreme Court affirmed. This is quite remarkable, but the highest court's opinion reveals a less-than-complete victory for gay rights. The justices emphasized that the husband had known about his wife's homosexuality when he agreed to the custody decree, that the lesbian couple was raising another daughter who was avowedly heterosexual, and that the lesbian household was quite prosperous (with a private swimming pool!). *Stromen* leaves plenty of room for anti-gay discrimination. For a comprehensive overview of custody and visitation cases involving LGBT parents, see Clifford J. Rosky, "Like Father, Like Son: Homosexuality, Parenthood, and the Gender of Homophobia," 20 *Yale J.L. & Feminism*, 257 (2009) (analyzing almost 200 custody and visitation cases involving gay and lesbian parents and concluding that "gender influences the expression of homophobic and heterosexist stereotypes about gay and lesbian parents). *See also* Suzanne A. Kim, "The Neutered Parent," 24 *Yale J.L. & Feminism* 1, 4 (2012) (arguing that, "outside of traditional marriage and its presumed heterosexuality, the identities and lives of nonconforming parents—those who resist the gendered sexual archetype of mothers having sex with husbands—register as threateningly "sexually salient").

Finally, it does appear that judges are increasingly sensitive to the charge that they are slanting their nexus analysis in anti-gay directions. For example, the North Dakota Supreme Court in *Damron v. Damron,* 670 N.W.2d 871 (N.D. 2003), overruled an earlier precedent that some lawyers had read to create a presumption that lesbian households were not healthy places for a child to be reared. And the Virginia Court of Appeals in *A.O.V. v. J.R.V.* 2007 WL 581871 (Va. App. Feb. 27, 2007), applied that state's often-slanted nexus analysis to affirm the trial judge's finding that a gay father should continue to have parental rights.

2. *Discrimination in Conditions on Parental Custody and Visitation.* Even a relatively neutral application of the nexus approach as to custody often allows discrimination to sneak in through the back door of conditions on visitation. By affirming the trial court, the appeals court in *Conkel* left in place the restriction that Charles Conkel could not have the children overnight if there were an unrelated male present, such as his same-sex partner. Would such a condition have been constitutional in *Palmore* if Linda Sidoti had not married Clarence Palmore? Note that there was no such condition in *Whaley.* Under a truly neutral nexus approach, is there any defense for treating Charles Conkel differently from Virginia Whaley?

Other appellate courts have been more skeptical of such conditions. The California Court of Appeals in *Birdsall v. Birdsall*, 197 Cal.App.3d 1024, 243 Cal.Rptr. 287 (1988), vacated a prohibition of a gay father's overnight visitation in the presence of another gay man, based upon the nexus test. "The unconventional life style of one parent, or the opposing moral positions of the parties, or the outright condemnation of one parent's beliefs by the other parent's religion, which may result in confusion for the child, do not provide an adequate basis for restricting visitation rights. Evidence of one parent's homosexuality, without a link to detriment to the child, is insufficient to constitute harm," the court held. In *Boswell v. Boswell,* 352 Md. 204, 721 A.2d 662 (1998), the Maryland Court of Appeals adopted the *Birdsall* approach to vacate conditions on a gay father's visitation with his children. "The only relevance that a parent's sexual conduct or lifestyle has in the context of a visitation proceeding of this type is where that conduct or lifestyle is shown to be detrimental to the children's emotional and/or physical well-being," the court ruled. Because there was no evidence that the presence of the father's partner had a negative effect on the children, the court found no nexus. "The reality is that their father is a homosexual who shares his home and life with [his partner]."

The majority approach today is that visitation restrictions cannot be imposed merely because of a parent's homosexuality, and that the burden of proving a nexus between sexual orientation and harm to children is on the challenging spouse. In light of these decisions, should Ohio reconsider the *Conkel* conditions in future cases? Must it do so after *Romer* and *Lawrence*?

3. *States Following More Traditional Approaches to LGBT Parental Custody.* A declining number of states still allow a court to consider a parent's sexual orientation as a negative factor weighing against the parent, even in the absence of any harm to the child. Mississippi law, for example, requires the court to consider the "moral fitness" of the parents. *Albright v. Albright*, 437 So.2d 1003, 1005 (Miss. 1983). Judges applying that statutory criterion have deployed that factor to the disadvantage of lesbian, gay, and bisexual parents. *See, e.g., Fulk v. Fulk*, 827 So.2d 736 (Miss. Ct. App. 2002).

4. *Discretion.* It is important to remember, however, that because the best interests of the child standard is so vague and discretionary, it leaves ample room for courts to cite sexual orientation-neutral reasons for ruling against the LGBT parent (in addition to our in the absence of sexual orientation-specific ones). Consider the following case.

Ex parte D.W.W., **717 So.2d 793 (Ala. 1998).** R.W. and D.W.W. were divorced in 1996. The trial court awarded custody of the two minor children to the father, D.W.W., and restricted the mother's, R.W.'s, visitation to every other weekend and to the maternal grandparents' home under their supervision, with a further restriction that "in no event shall the children be around [N.L., the mother's same-sex partner] during any visitation period. * * * Neither party shall have overnight adult guests (family excluded) while [the] children are in their home and under their custody unless they are married thereto." The Alabama Court of Civil Appeals affirmed the custody order but reversed the quoted visitation conditions. *R.W. v. D.W.W.*, 717 So.2d 790 (Ala. Civ. App. 1997). The Alabama Supreme Court reversed and reinstated the trial judge's conditions on visitation.

Chief Justice Hooper's opinion for a plurality of the court emphasized the deference appeals courts should pay to trial judges' findings in such cases and the evidence that R.W. "displayed poor parenting skills." There was evidence that she hit her daughter with a belt buckle and shook her son to control his hyperactivity. "The grandparents' presence will act as a buffer between the children and R.W.'s occasionally temperamental style of parenting as a support for R.W. as she continues to develop her parenting skills."

The prohibition of any contact with N.L. was justified on the ground that N.L. disciplined the children in "inappropriate" ways. The only example was that she "threatened to deprive R.W.'s daughter of visitation with her father, as a form of punishment." Moreover, the trial court properly considered "the effects on the children of their mother's ongoing lesbian relationship." Both women were, according to the trial court, "active in the homosexual community," went to gay bars and a "homosexual church," and "openly display affection in the children's presence." Evidence was presented suggesting that after moving in with R.W. and N.L. the children "began using inappropriate and vulgar language and required psychiatric counseling." The daughter started to lie and manipulate others.

"Even without this evidence that the children have been adversely affected by their mother's relationship, the trial court would have been justified in restricting R.W.'s visitation, in order to limit the children's exposure to their mother's lesbian lifestyle. * * * Restrictions such as those at issue here are common tools used to shield a child from the harmful effects of a parent's illicit sexual relationships—heterosexual or homosexual. Moreover, the conduct inherent in lesbianism is illegal in Alabama. R.W., therefore, is continually engaging in conduct that violates the criminal law of this state. Exposing the children to such a lifestyle, one that is illegal under the laws of the state and immoral in the eyes of most of its citizens, could greatly traumatize them."

Two other Justices concurred in the Chief Justice's opinion. Two Justices only concurred in its result. Two Justices dissented. In his dissent, **Justice Kennedy** said: "While I am not attempting to condone R.W.'s lifestyle, I cannot ignore the fact that the trial court's decision appears to be founded primarily on prejudice." He compared the isolated and minor parenting problems of R.W., which were emphasized by the trial judge and by the Chief Justice, with the "serious alcohol abuse and violence of the father." Among other escapades, the father totaled his car while driving drunk and with his daughter in the car unrestrained by a safety belt, was charged on several occasions with domestic abuse, once closed his infant son in a clothes dryer, threatened to kill R.W. and the children, and was in financial default for some obligations toward his children. Moreover, not only have the children's difficulties arisen during the period of their parents' marriage, but "the children had excelled in school over the year and a half they were in their mother's custody, and * * * N.L., who is a child guidance counselor, had spent many hours working with the parties' daughter to improve her spelling and her motor skills."

Justice Kennedy objected to the "presumptuous nature" of the plurality's characterization of R.W. as someone who "continually" violates the state sodomy law, which actually applies to heterosexual as well as homosexual sodomy. The plurality's fixation on sodomy and the mother's "lifestyle" blinded them to the best interests of the child. "In reality, the children are far more likely to be traumatized and injured by their father's illegal activities than they are by any potential violation of [the sodomy law]." **Justice Cook** dissented in a separate opinion.

NOTE ON *D.W.W.* AND THE MODERNIZATION AND SEDIMENTATION OF ANTIGAY DISCOURSE

This case might be an example of what Professor Reva Siegel calls the *modernization of justification.* Siegel, " 'The Rule of Love': Wife Beating as Prerogative and Privacy," 105 *Yale L.J.* 2117 (1996). Focusing on legal reform, Siegel argues that even when reform has been accomplished for women, oppressive practices and attitudes have been reaffirmed through a modernization of justification. By defending practices in terms that are more persuasive to a new generation, modernized justifications, Siegel argues, can actually strengthen oppressive practices (like wife-beating) and status subordination (of wives to husbands). The majority's justification emphasizes *neither* Biblical and natural law arguments against sodomites *nor* medical arguments against diseased or predatory "homosexuals." Instead, the argumentation largely rests upon social utilitarian judgments about the "best interests of the child." In other words, antigay reasoning grounded on premodern religious tropes (Sodom and Gomorrah) and pseudo-science (homosexuality as a mental illness) has been superseded by social harms imposed by gay parents.

D.W.W. also illustrates Professor William Eskridge's response to Siegel, that the discourse is not modernized so much as it is *sedimented.* That is, the new social utilitarian tropes rest on top of older medical and natural law tropes; the natural law arguments retain their power for a diminishing audience and can be mobilized by cloaked references in the modernized discourse. *See* William Eskridge Jr., "No Promo Homo: The Sedimentation of Antigay Discourse and the Channeling Effect of Judicial Review," 75 *NYU L. Rev.* 1327 (2000). The Court signals its loyalty to the old tropes: R.W., we are reminded, is a *criminal* because she is a presumptive *sodomite* (the old natural law discourse)—but she is also a *bad mother* to boot (the new best interests of the child discourse). Somehow her lack of maternal traits seems to be related to the fact that she is a *lesbian* and her presumed violation of sodomy laws. So the discourse is not just modernized, it is layered. The updating is a layer on top of the old ways of thinking.

D.W.W. was decided prior to the Supreme Court's decision in *Lawrence.* Because *Lawrence* invalidated Alabama's consensual sodomy laws, R.W. is no longer a presumptive criminal. Many predicted that, after *Lawrence,* straight parents would soon find that they no longer prevailed in cases like *D.W.W.* It turns out, however, that *Lawrence* has been less revolutionary in this area of law than some initially predicted. *See, e.g.,* Nancy D. Polikoff, "Custody Rights of lesbian and Gay Parents Redux: The Irrelevance of Constitutional Principles," 60 *UCLA L. Rev. Discourse* 226 (2013).

A newly emerging package for this disapproval of LGBT parents comes in the form of religious beliefs and practices. Consider the next case.

In re the Marriage of: Rachelle K. Black and Charles W. Black

Washington Supreme Court, 2017.
188 Wash.2d 114, 392 P.3d 1041.

■ CHIEF JUSTICE FAIRHURST.

Rachelle and Charles Black were married for nearly 20 years and have three sons [ages 17, 14, and 9. For most of their marriage, Rachelle was the primary caretaker of the children, and Charles was the primary wage earner.] They raised their children in a conservative Christian church and sent them to private, Christian schools. In 2011, Rachelle told Charles that she is a lesbian. In the order of dissolution, the trial court designated Charles as the primary residential parent. The final parenting plan also awarded Charles sole decision-making authority regarding the children's education and religious upbringing. But the record shows that the trial court considered Rachelle's sexual orientation as a factor when it fashioned the final parenting plan. Further, improper bias influenced the proceedings. * * * Accordingly, we reverse.

* * * [**I. Facts and Procedural History**.] Rachelle, Charles, and the children attended a "conservative Christian" church * * * "where the teachings are that homosexuality is a sin." Consistent with their beliefs, Rachelle and Charles agreed to send their three children to small, private, Christian schools in the Tacoma area. * * * In December 2011, Rachelle told Charles that she believed she might be " 'gay.' " * * *

Rachelle's recognition of her sexual orientation altered the status quo at the Black household * * * . Rachelle stopped attending the family church, while Charles and the children continued to attend. Around the same time, Rachelle began a romantic relationship with a woman and began spending more time away from home. * * * Charles took on more parenting responsibilities than he had in the past. * * *

In addition to Rachelle and Charles, the main witnesses at trial were Knight (the children's therapist) and Leblanc (the guardian ad litem, or "GAL").

* * * Knight described the children as "very sheltered" * * *. Knight believed that from a therapeutic perspective, "the less change that these children have to deal with[,] the better." * * * Knight testified that she believed Charles was the more stable parent. Knight noted that Rachelle was unemployed, did not have a plan for future housing, and relied on her partner for support[.] * * * On the other hand, Knight stated that Charles "has a history of employment and being a good provider, so obviously he is a stable parent." She testified that the children "have reported that over the last couple of years they've seen [Rachelle] a lot less and that they have spent more time with their father." * * *

Leblanc, the GAL, shared many of Knight's concerns. Leblanc testified that several "collateral sources" indicated Rachelle had been "absent from the home for long periods of time on a fairly frequent basis for the last two to . . . three years." This was the main reason Leblanc recommended that the trial court designate Charles as the residential parent[.]

* * * But Leblanc's recommendation was also based on Rachelle's sexual orientation, at least insofar as she believed it conflicted with the children's religious beliefs. In a preliminary report, Leblanc wrote that Rachelle's "lifestyle choice" might cause controversy given the children's background[.] * * * However, in her final report, Leblanc claimed her use of the word " 'choice' " in the preliminary report did not relate to Rachelle's sexual orientation.

* * * Leblanc's final report notes that Charles believed Rachelle "is now on a campaign to re-indoctrinate the children" and that "concepts and ideals the children have been taught throughout their lives are being eviscerated." * * * Leblanc also suggested the children might experience "bullying" as a result of Rachelle's decision to leave the marriage and begin a relationship with her partner[.] * * *

Ultimately, * * * Leblanc recommended that Charles serve as the primary residential parent. She also recommended that Knight have the discretion to determine when the children may have contact with Rachelle's partner. Leblanc further recommended broad prohibitions on Rachelle's ability to discuss religion and sexual orientation with her children[.] * * *

The trial court largely adopted Leblanc's recommendations. * * * Like Leblanc, the trial court concluded that Charles was the more stable parent. The trial court specifically noted the children's religious upbringing and the potential disruption Rachelle's sexual orientation posed to that upbringing:

> * * * These children have been taught from the Bible since age 4. I believe it will be very challenging for them to reconcile their religious upbringing with the changes occurring within their family over issues involving marriage and dissolution, as well as homosexuality.

The trial court designated Charles as the primary residential parent. * * * The Court of Appeals, Division Two, affirmed most of these provisions in an unpublished opinion. * * * We accepted Rachelle's petition for review.

[**II. Analysis.** Washington follows the nexus approach: a trial court may not consider a parent's sexual orientation as a factor for custody decisions absent a showing of harm to the children.]

* * * Charles concedes that custody decisions cannot be based on a parent's sexual orientation absent a showing of harm but nevertheless claims that * * * the trial court did not base its ruling on Rachelle's sexual orientation and that the trial court's references to Rachelle's sexual orientation were intended merely to provide context for the separation.

Charles correctly notes that the Court of Appeals upheld a parenting plan under similar circumstances in [*In re Marriage of*]Wicklund[, 932 P.2d 652 (Wash. Ct. App. 1996)]. There, the father separated from the mother after learning that he was gay. The family were active members in the Jehovah's Witnesses faith, which includes a belief that the " 'practice of homosexuality is an abomination.' " Evidence in the case included testimony addressing how the children would handle the father's sexual orientation in light of their religious upbringing. The trial court designated the mother as the primary residential parent * * * .

[On appeal,] the court concluded that the record did not demonstrate that the trial court based its decision on the father's sexual orientation[.] * * * Charles contends the same reasoning applies here. * * *

But since Wicklund was decided, courts have recognized that members of the LGBT community are vulnerable to discrimination. [*See, e.g., Obergefell*].

To guard against discriminatory impulses in custody proceedings, many jurisdictions prohibit consideration of a parent's sexual orientation unless there is an express showing of harm to the children. * * * This approach promotes fairness by fostering an attitude of neutrality. * * *

The record here shows the trial court did not remain neutral when it considered Rachelle's sexual orientation as a factor for determining provisions in the parenting plan. Although the trial court concluded that Charles is the more stable parent for a number of potentially legitimate reasons, including his availability to the children and the parenting duties he performed in the years preceding the dissolution, the record indicates that Rachelle's sexual orientation influenced the trial court's written ruling and final parenting plan.

* * * [E]ven though the trial court here did not explicitly suggest that Rachelle's sexual orientation made her an unfit parent, its reasoning is nevertheless clear: the children are allegedly uncomfortable with homosexuality due to their religious upbringing, Charles—a heterosexual who shares those same beliefs—is better suited to maintain that religious upbringing, therefore, he is the more stable parent. Leblanc advocated this same reasoning in her final recommendation and in her testimony, which the trial court relied on and largely adopted in its final ruling. Absent any other evidence, such reasoning unfairly punishes a parent in a custody proceeding on the basis of her sexual orientation.

The trial court also adopted a restriction on Rachelle's conduct that prohibited her from discussing "alternative lifestyles" with her children[.] * * * These references indicate the trial court based its ruling, at least in part, on Rachelle's sexual orientation. The prohibitions assume that a parent's discussion of sexual orientation or her own life and beliefs would have a negative impact on the children. The trial court's unnecessary references to "homosexuality" and "alternative lifestyle concepts" cast doubt on its ruling. * * *First, Leblanc repeatedly referred to Rachelle's sexual orientation as a "lifestyle choice." * * * This is contrary to our current understanding of sexual orientation. *See Obergefell*, 135 S.Ct. at 2596 ("Only in more recent years have psychiatrists and others recognized that sexual orientation is both a normal expression of human sexuality and immutable.").

Second, Leblanc suggested that the controversy surrounding Rachelle's sexual orientation could harm the children by inviting bullying. Other courts have expressly rejected this reasoning in custody disputes. [Citing *Palmore v. Sidoti*, 466 U.S. 429, 433 (1984) ("Private biases may be outside the reach of the law, but the law cannot, directly or indirectly, give them effect.")].

Third, Leblanc recommended an unconstitutional restriction of Rachelle's conduct that prohibited her from discussing religion, homosexuality, and "other alternative lifestyle concepts" with her children. * * *

Finally, Leblanc's opinion that Charles is the more stable parent seems to stem from a belief that Rachelle caused the separation[.] * * * But "custody and visitation privileges are not to be used to penalize or reward parents for their conduct." * * *The trial court here failed to remain neutral regarding Rachelle's sexual orientation and impermissibly favored Charles' religious beliefs. Further, evidence of bias permeated the proceedings. We reverse.

■ [The concurring opinion of JUSTICE WIGGINS is omitted.]

PROBLEM 7-1
THE *BLACK* CASE ON REMAND

You are the trial judge that is considering the remand in the *Black* case. Which parent should be designated the primary residential parent and why?

If the children testified that they are uncomfortable with and are experiencing anxiety related to their mother's sexual orientation due to their religious upbringing, would it be permissible for the court to take into account their mother's sexual orientation when making the custody allocation? Why or why not?

C. GENDER IDENTITY AND CUSTODY

What if the parent was a male-to-female transsexual? Could the court deny that parent custody simply because the person is transsexual? Could the court condition the parent's custody or visitation upon a requirement that the parent not dress in women's attire during custodial time? Jot down your thoughts, and then read the next case and notes.

Suzanne Lindley Daly, formerly known as Tim Daly v. Nan Toews Daly, 102 Nev. 66, 715 P.2d 56 (1986). Nan and Tim Daly were husband and wife and the biological parents of Mary Toews Daly, born in 1973. The Dalys divorced in 1981; Nan had primary custody, and Tim liberal visitation rights. During one visit, Tim confided to his daughter that he was a transsexual and intended to transition from male to female. When Mary told her mother of her father's plans, Nan took Mary to a psychologist, who advised Nan that it was "very dangerous" to allow Mary to be in the company of her father again. According to Nan, Mary became sluggish, incontinent, and inattentive in the years after this knowledge.

In May 1982, Nan asked the court to terminate Tim's parental rights; the court granted the request in April 1983, after Tim had changed his name to Suzanne and as he was transitioning to being a woman. **Justice Steffan**'s opinion for the Nevada Supreme Court affirmed the trial judge's order, based upon the following evidence and reasoning.

At trial, the mother's expert witness who examined Mary, testified that "there is a serious risk of emotional or mental injury to the child if she were allowed to be in her father's presence. In addition, the doctor testified that Mary would not be injured if she did not see her father again. The doctor also considered alternatives, such as consultation with psychologists and psychiatrists and testified there was no guarantee it would work and that there would be a serious risk of emotional injury. It is precisely this risk that the lower court was asked to eliminate. It must be remembered that in termination proceedings, the interests of the child are paramount and a child should not be forced to undergo psychological adjustments, especially in view of the risk involved, solely to avoid termination of a parent's rights. Certainly a parent's rights should be preserved if at all possible, but not at the expense of the child." In a footnote, Justice Steffan rejected the option, sometimes followed by courts in transgender parent cases, of restricting visitation rather than terminating Suzanne's parental rights entirely.

The expert "also provided support for [the mother's] position by testifying that there are children who are not able to accept a parent as a transsexual. This witness also stated this was a new area and concluded there is a risk that there would be harm done in either direction. [The expert], however, had the opportunity to observe and interview Mary and determined the risk to Mary would exist only if visitation were forced upon Mary." Moreover, Mary told the expert and the trial judge that "she did not want to see her father. Mary also said it would be disturbing to visit with her father and made it graphically clear that she didn't want to see him again."

Based on this evidence, the trial judge found that it had jurisdiction to consider termination of parental rights—and then decided that the "best interests of the child" standard required such termination. "At trial, it was undisputed that Mary's mother, Nan, is a very loving and conscientious mother who provides a desirable environment for her daughter. Nan always keeps Mary well fed and clothed and is absolutely dedicated to her child. At the present time, Mary is happy and well adjusted. Nevertheless, if visitation were permitted, there would be a risk of serious maladjustment, mental or emotional injury. Hence, recognizing Mary's present situation, her attitude and feelings, and the substantial risk of emotional or mental injury were she forced to visit with her father, it appears clear that termination of appellant's parental rights is in Mary's best interest."

"It was shown that Mary is at the tender age when she is very much concerned about the impression of her peers and doesn't want to have any sort of uncomfortable fears. Mary would prefer to have her personal life remain a private event. By terminating Suzanne's parental rights, Mary will finally have the assurance and comfort of knowing the visitation matter is settled. Also, Mary's emotional state is preserved, thereby providing her the forum to mature and resolve the situation in her own way. There is nothing to prevent Mary from rekindling the relationship with her father in later years if she so desires, but that choice should be hers, made at a time when the risk of emotional or mental injury is eliminated."

Justice Gunderson dissented, largely upon the ground that "Mary and her father currently are totally separated, for he is willing to forego visitation rights at present, in order to maintain his legal status as Mary's parent. This separation protects Mary from all of the concerns, imagined or real, which underlay the district court's termination of parental rights." Thus, "the majority opinion is premised, not upon fact, but upon suppositions which are contrary to the facts and which ignore the appellant father's basic legal position."

"In psychological distress, the father has consulted legitimate and respected medical authorities. The advice given by those medical authorities may offend the religious precepts of many. In the ultimate judgment of history, such advice may well yet be condemned as quackery. Still, I respectfully submit that a court of law should not stigmatize an emotionally distressed person for following the advice of highly trained and licensed physicians, who are practicing medicine under government authority, and who possess the most exalted credentials their profession can bestow. Nor should any parent be stigmatized for attempting to forewarn a child concerning medical procedures the parent is about to undergo pursuant to such advice.

"Recognizing that the medical procedures he has undergone currently occasion distress to her child, the father does not contend he should now be allowed visitation rights. Rather, he contends merely that he has done nothing to warrant severing his formal legal parental tie to Mary Daly, apparently hoping that the passage of time will restore in Mary a desire to know him. In the meantime, the father recognizes, he would have to accept the duty of contributing to Mary's support, while foregoing visitation with the child.

"As I assess the record, the fact that the appellant father has suffered emotional problems which are foreign to the experience of this court's members, and has followed the possibly poor advice of eminent medical authorities in his attempt to relieve them, does not justify a total and irrevocable severance of [the father's] formal legal tie to a child he obviously cares about and desires to help nurture. By holding that such a severance is justified in these facts, it seems to me, we are being unnecessarily and impermissibly punitive to the exercise of a medical option we personally find offensive, thereby depriving a child of a legal relationship which might well be to the child's advantage in the future."

NOTE ON *DALY* AND DISCRIMINATION AGAINST TRANSGENDER PARENTS

Is there any significant evidence that knowing about a parent's transgender status or his/her cross-dressing causes trauma to offspring? None whatsoever, says Kari Carter, Note, "The Best Interest Test and Child Custody: Why Transgender Should Not Be a Factor in Child Custody Determinations," 16 *Health Matrix* 209 (2006). A note in the next subpart will examine the few studies that have been done. Moreover, even if there were such evidence, would it be sufficient to deprive Suzanne Daly of her entire set of parental rights, rights protected as the core of the right to privacy? *See Meyer v. Nebraska*, 262 U.S. 390, 399, 401 (1923). If there were evidence that having an unemployed parent was traumatic to a child, would the state be justified in terminating the parental rights of unemployed persons?

Although there are few appellate decisions, the traditional approach has been that reflected in *Daly*: judges tend to separate transsexual parents from their children if the non-trans parent seeks full custody, restricted visitation, or even (as in *Daly*) permanent termination of any parental relationship. *See* Annotation, "Parent's Transsexuality as Factor in Award of Custody of Children, Visitation Rights, or Termination of Parental Rights," 59 *A.L.R.*4th 1170 (1988).

And the situation for transgender parents has not improved much in recent decades. As Professor Nancy D. Polikoff explains: "The unequivocal win for the transgender parent—indeed the *only* unequivocal win for a transgender parent in any reported appellate decision to date—came in Colorado, in 1973, in *Christian v. Randall*." Nancy D. Polikoff, *Transgender Parents—Then, Now, and the Future*, available at http://beyondstraight andgaymarriage.blogspot.com/2013/02/transgender-parents-then-now-and-future.html. After *Randall*, "[t]he backlash began." *Id*. "[L]esbian and gay parents [by and large] raise children in a more supportive legal and cultural environment than that which existed in previous decades." *Id*. By contrast, "[f]or transgender parents, there is overwhelming resistance. The *Magnuson* [*v. Magnuson*, 141 Wash. App. 347 (2007)] decision, from generally LGBT-friendly Washington state, is an example of that." *Id*.

In *Magnuson*, one of the most recently published custody cases involving a transgender parent, the Washington appellate court affirmed an award of primary custody to the non-transgender parent, concluding that the trial court had appropriate "focused on the children's need for 'environmental and parental stability.'" *Magnuson*, 141 Wash. App. at 350. What the evidence presented at trial showed, however, was that the parents had largely shared parenting responsibilities in the past, and that transgender parent was the more nurturing parent. The trial court merely speculated that placement with the transgender parent would not be in the children's best interest: "[The transgender parent] has indicated she will be undergoing sexual reassignment surgery sometime in the very near future. [The] surgery may be everything she has hoped for, or it may be disastrous. No one knows what is ahead, and the impact of gender reassignment surgery on the children is unknown." *Id.*

D. LGBT PARENTING: WHAT DO WE KNOW ABOUT IT?

Now that it is less permissible to base court opinions on expressly anti-LGBT (or at least anti-LGB) sentiments, courts making custody determinations are more likely to provide some "neutral" justification related to the child's well-being. That being the case, it is helpful to consider what the research says about how children reared in LGBT-parent households compare to children reared in comparable non-LGBT parent households. In short, among professional social scientists, all of the studies have found no "detrimental" effect on children reared in LGB-parent households. *See, e.g.*, Brief of Amici Curiae American Psychological Association et al. in support of Petitioners, *Obergefell v. Hodges*, 2015 WL 1004713 ("Scientific evidence strongly supports the conclusion that homosexuality is a normal expression of human sexuality; that gay men and lesbians form stable, committed relationships that are equivalent to heterosexual relationships in essential respects; that same-sex couples are no less fit than heterosexual parents to raise children, and their children are no less psychologically healthy and well-adjusted."). *See also* Carlos A. Ball, "Social Science Studies and the Children of Lesbians and Gay Men: The Rational Basis Perspective," 21 *Wm. & Mary Bill Rts. J.* 691 (2013). There are fewer studies examining children raised by transgender parents. The limited research, however, suggests that the same is true in that context—children are not harmed by being raised by transgender parents.

In the past, some critics attacked these studies for their use of samples that were both small and nonrandom. These criticisms are made, for example, in Lynn Wardle, "The Potential Impact of Homosexual Parenting on Children," 1997 *U. Ill. L. Rev.* 833. This persuasiveness of this piece, however, is undercut by its reliance on discredited social scientist Paul Cameron, whose studies purporting to show "harm" to children in lesbian and gay households have been savaged by experts and justified his expulsion from the American Psychological Association; the American Sociological Association censured him for willfully misrepresenting research. *See* Carlos Ball & Janice Pea, "Warring with Wardle: Morality, Social Science, and Gay and

Lesbian Parents," 1998 *U. Ill. L. Rev.* 253. For an updated review of the social science literature, see, e.g., Carlos A. Ball, "Social Science Studies and the Children of Lesbians and Gay Men: The Rational Basis Perspective," 21 *Wm. & Mary Bill Rts. J.* 691 (2013).

More recent studies, however, have utilized larger samples and are less prone to this line of attack. These more recent studies generally confirm what the older studies found—that children are not harmed by being raised by LGB parents.

Abbie E. Goldberg, Nanette K. Gartrell & Gary Gates, "Research Report on LGB-Parent Families," **Williams Institute (2014).** Professors Abbie E. Goldberg, Nanette Gartrell, and Gary Gates recently reviewed the existing research on LGB-parenting focusing "particular attention to theoretical and empirical advances [in the research], controversies, and gaps in this area." As stated in their executive summary, their findings included the following:

"LGB Parents: Functioning and Experiences

- Studies comparing LG and heterosexual parents in regard to mental health, parenting stress, and parenting competence have found few differences based on family structure.

- Conditions linked to poorer well-being for LG parents include: living in less supportive legal contexts, perceiving less support from family or supervisors, having higher levels of internalized homophobia, and encountering more child behavior problems. * * *

Impact on Children of Having LGB Parents

- Researchers have found few differences between children raised by lesbian and heterosexual parents in terms of self-esteem, quality of life, psychological adjustment, or social functioning (research on the psychosocial outcomes of children with gay male parents is limited).

- Several studies, some of which have utilized nationally representative datasets, provide no evidence that children with same-sex parents demonstrate problems with respect to their academic and educational outcomes.

- According to self-, peer-, and parent-reports, children and adolescents with same- and different-sex parents do not differ in social competence or relationships with peers.

- There is some evidence that the play behavior of girls and boys in same-sex parent families may be less gender-stereotyped than the play behavior of girls and boys in different-sex-parent families.

- Research on adolescents reared since birth by lesbian mothers found that youth with male role models were similar is psychological adjustment to adolescents without male role models.

- Although adolescents and young adults reared by LGB parents are not more likely to self-identify as exclusively lesbian/gay than those reared by heterosexual parents, having a lesbian mother was associated with a greater likelihood of considering or having a same-sex relationship, and more expansive, less categorical notions of sexuality.

- Adolescents and adults point to potential strengths associated with growing up in LGB-parent households, including resilience and empathy toward diverse and marginalized groups.

Bullying and Harassment

- Studies that compare the teasing/bullying experiences of children with LGB and heterosexual parents are conflicting, with some suggesting higher rates of reported bullying among children with LGB parents and others finding no differences in these rates, according to self- and parent-report. However, homophobic slurs were reported only by children with same-sex parents.

- Whereas perceived stigmatization by peers has been linked to compromised well-being in children of LGB parents, both the broader school context and families' processes may offset some of the negative impact of bullying."

NOTE ON STUDIES OF CHILDREN RAISED BY TRANSGENDER PARENTS

There have been few studies exploring the outcomes for children with transgender parents, and none has involved a large sample. That said, the existing studies "in this area have found no evidence that having a transgender parent affects a child's gender identity or sexual orientation development, or has an impact on any other developmental milestone." Rebecca L. Stotzer, Jody L. Herman & Amira Hasenbush, The Williams Institute, *Transgender Parenting: A Review of Existing Research* (Oct. 2014).

One of the main scholars in this area has been Dr. Richard Green. In 1998, Dr. Green published a similar study which concluded that children of transgender parents are "more likely to be hurt by a traumatic separation from their parent than because of that parent's gender identity." Green, "Transsexuals' Children," 2 *Int'l J. Transgenderism* 4 (1998).

Studies have reached conflicting conclusions about the likelihood that the children of transgender parents will face teasing and bullying. Some studies found that the likelihood was infrequent. While another study "found a substantial rate of bullying from peers." Rebecca L. Stotzer, Jody L. Herman & Amira Hasenbush, The Williams Institute, *Transgender Parenting: A Review of Existing Research* (Oct. 2014). A 2014 study found that "many transgender parents preemptively prepared themselves and their families for the possibility of experiencing stigma." *Id.*

How should the foregoing studies be weighed in judicial determinations of custody, visitation, or parental rights termination proceedings such as that in *Daly*, above? Would it be constitutional for legislatures to invoke these studies to create a statutory presumption against custody by transsexual parents in custody cases?

SECTION 2

ADOPTION AND FOSTER CARE

Section 1 considers whether the state can or should consider the sexual orientation or the gender identity of a legal parent when making custody and visitation decisions about the parent's child.

This section surveys some of the ways the state regulates efforts by LGBT people to form legally recognized relationships with children with whom they have no biological connection.

Lesbian, gay, bisexual, and transgender persons who would like to form legally recognized parental relationships have long faced significant hurdles. While some of these hurdles have been mitigated over time, they have not disappeared.

A. SEXUAL ORIENTATION AND ADOPTION

LGBT people form families in many different ways. Many of the children being raised in LGBT parent-headed households were born in the context of different-sex relationships. Increasingly, LGBT people are creating planned families. Some LGBT people adopt or foster children. For a detailed look at LGBT parenting in the United States, see Gary J. Gates, Williams Institute, *LGBT Parenting in the United States*, http://williamsinstitute.law.ucla.edu/research/census-lgbt-demographics-studies/lgbt-parenting-in-the-united-states/.

In the past, a small number of states expressly prohibited lesbian and gay people from adopting. For example, in 1977, the Florida legislature enacted Fla. Stat. § 63.042(3): "No person eligible to adopt under this statute may adopt if that person is a homosexual." This ban remained in place until 2011. During that period, both state and federal courts upheld Florida's adoption ban. *See, e.g., Lofton v. Sec'y of Dep't of Children & Family Servs.*, 358 F.3d 804 (11th Cir. 2004) (upholding Florida's then-applicable ban on adoption by "practicing homosexuals"). Today, however, no state expressly prohibits lesbian or gay individuals from adopting.

Nonetheless, some LGBT people continue to face formal and informal hurdles in the adoption and foster care processes. Mississippi, for example, has a law that prohibits adoptions by "couples of the same gender." Miss. Code Ann. § 93–17–3(5). After the Supreme Court decided *Obergefell*, a challenge to the statute was brought on behalf of two advocacy groups and four married lesbian couples who sought to adopt in Mississippi. The federal district court granted the plaintiff's request for a preliminary injunction, concluding: "It also seems highly unlikely that the same court that held a state cannot ban gay marriage because it would deny benefits—expressly including the right to adopt—would then conclude that married gay couples can be denied that very same benefit." *Campaign for S. Equal. v. Mississippi Dep't of Human Servs.*, 175 F. Supp. 3d 691, 710 (S.D. Miss. 2016).

Can the statute constitutionally be applied to unmarried same-sex couples?

NOTES ON LGBT PEOPLE AND ADOPTION

Adoption proceedings do not yield as much appellate litigation as custody proceedings; most adoptions are quietly resolved at the agency or department of social services level. Nonetheless, several themes have appeared over time:

1. *The Immoral Sodomites Argument.* In the past, even in the absence of an express ban, some courts denied adoptions by lesbian or gay individuals on the ground that the person was immoral or a criminal simply because he or she was homosexual. For example, an Arizona appellate court denied a bisexual man's petition to adopt, stating: "It would be anomalous for the state on the one hand to declare homosexual conduct unlawful and on the other create a parent after that proscribed model, in effect approving that standard, inimical to the natural family, as head of a state-created family." *In re Appeal in Pima County Juvenile Action B-10489*, 151 Ariz. 335, 727 P.2d 830, 835 (App.1986). Can this kind of reasoning survive *Romer* and *Lawrence*? Probably not—but other arguments might.

2. *The Diseased "Homosexuals" Argument.* As we saw in the context of custody, some courts moved away from expressly anti-gay decisions to ones that focused on the best interests of the child. These decisions sometimes relied on inaccurate stereotypes about lesbian and gay people. For example, in a case in which a gay man sought to adopt a child, the dissent relied on a variation of the "sick homosexuals" argument—the possibility of the parent's passing on the HIV virus to the adoptive child. *In re Adoption of Charles B.*, 552 N.E.2d 884, 891 (Ohio 1990) (Resnick, J., dissenting) (noting that while the prospective adoptive father had tested negative for HIV, "adoption is not just for today but forever. Mr. B falls within a high-risk population for AIDS. Why place a child whose immune system has already been altered in such an environment?"). On its face, this argument is breathtaking: the prospective adoptive father—Mr. B.—was not infected with the virus and he was living in a monogamous relationship. The dissent implicitly suggested that there is a good chance that Mr. B.'s bonding with the child was sexual in nature, and that presumptively "promiscuous" Mr. B. would "prey" on the child.

3. *The Role Model (Best Environment for Children) Argument.* The kinder, gentler (modern) argument for excluding lesbians, gay men, and bisexuals from adoption is the role model argument that the State of Florida relied upon in defending their ban:

> Florida argues that the statute is rationally related to Florida's interest in furthering the best interests of adopted children by placing them in families with married mothers and fathers. Such homes, Florida asserts, provide the stability that

marriage affords and the presence of both male and female authority figures, which it considers critical to optimal childhood development and socialization. In particular, Florida emphasizes a vital role that dual-gender parenting plays in shaping sexual and gender identity and in providing heterosexual role modeling. Florida argues that disallowing adoption into homosexual households, which are necessarily motherless or fatherless and lack the stability that comes with marriage, is a rational means of furthering Florida's interest in promoting adoption by marital families.

Lofton v. Sec'y of Dep't of Children & Family Servs., 358 F.3d 804, 818–19 (11th Cir. 2004).

Does such a role-model argument survive *Lawrence? VMI?*

Steven Lofton et al. v. Secretary of the Department of Children and Social Services et al.

United States Court of Appeals for the Eleventh Circuit, 2004.
358 F.3d 804, *petition for en banc review denied,* 377 F.3d 1275.

■ [JUDGE BIRCH's opinion for the court is excerpted in Chapter 2, Section 2. JUDGE BIRCH ruled that Florida's statutory ban on adoptions by "homosexual" persons did not warrant strict scrutiny: there was no "fundamental" right being denied to "homosexuals," and sexual orientation is not a suspect classification. Evaluating the discrimination under the rational basis approach, JUDGE BIRCH found the discrimination a reasonable determination of the state as to the preferred environment for rearing children. Reread JUDGE BIRCH's opinion, as well as JUDGE BARKETT's critique in her opinion dissenting from the full court's refusal to rehear the case en banc. The following portion of the opinion was omitted from the excerpt in Chapter 2.]

[*The Family Integrity Argument.*] Although the text of the Constitution contains no reference to familial or parental rights, Supreme Court precedent has long recognized that "the Due Process Clause of the Fourteenth Amendment protects the fundamental right of parents to make decisions concerning the care, custody, and control of their children." [*Troxel.*] A corollary to this right is the "private realm of family life which the state cannot enter that has been afforded both substantive and procedural protection." *Smith v. Org. of Foster Families for Equal. & Reform,* 431 U.S. 816, 842 (1977). Historically, the Court's family-and parental-rights holdings have involved biological families. [*Troxel; Meyer; Pierce.*] * * * Appellants, however, seize on a few lines of dicta from *Smith,* in which the Court acknowledged that "biological relationships are not [the] exclusive determination of the existence of a family," and noted that "adoption, for instance, is recognized as the legal equivalent of biological parenthood." Extrapolating from *Smith,* appellants argue that parental and familial rights should be extended to individuals such as foster parents and legal guardians and that the touchstone of this liberty interest is not biological ties or official legal recognition, but the emotional bond that develops between and among individuals as a result of shared daily life.

We do not read *Smith* so broadly. In *Smith*, the Court considered whether the appellee foster families possessed a constitutional liberty interest in "the integrity of their family unit" such that the state could not disrupt the families without procedural due process. Although the Court found it unnecessary to resolve that question, Justice Brennan, writing for the majority, did note that the importance of familial relationships stems not merely from blood relationships, but also from "the emotional attachments that derive from the intimacy of daily association." The *Smith* Court went on, however, to discuss the "important distinctions between the foster family and the natural family," particularly the fact that foster families have their genesis in state law. The Court stressed that the parameters of whatever potential liberty interest such families might possess would be defined by state law and the justifiable expectations it created. * * *

* * * Here, we find that under Florida law neither a foster parent nor a legal guardian could have a justifiable expectation of a permanent relationship with his or her child free from state oversight or intervention. Under Florida law, foster care is designed to be a short-term arrangement while the state attempts to find a permanent adoptive home. * * * Similarly, legal guardians in Florida are subject to ongoing judicial oversight, including the duty to file annual guardianship reports and annual review by the appointing court, and can be removed for a wide variety of reasons. In both cases, the state is not interfering with natural family units that exist independent of its power, but is regulating ones created by it. Lofton and Houghton entered into relationships to be a foster parent and legal guardian, respectively, with an implicit understanding that these relationships would not be immune from state oversight and would be permitted to continue only upon state approval. The emotional connections between Lofton and his foster child and between Houghton and his ward originate in arrangements that have been subject to state oversight from the outset. We conclude that Lofton, Doe, Houghton, and Roe could have no justifiable expectation of permanency in their relationships. Nor could Lofton and Houghton have developed expectations that they would be allowed to adopt, in light of the adoption provision itself. * * *

In re: Matter of Adoption of X.X.G. and N.R.G., No. 3D08–3044 **(Third District Court of Appeal, Florida, Sept. 22, 2010).** F.G., an openly gay man, petitioned to adopt two children for whom he had since 2004 been a foster parent in Dade County, Florida. Although an independent agency monitoring the care of the children (who had been neglected by their biological parents) found that the children had "flourished" in F.G.'s home, the Florida Department of Children and

Families denied the petition, because of the 1977 statutory ban. F.G. challenged that determination in court, and Circuit **Judge Lederman** granted the adoption, notwithstanding the statutory ban, which she ruled to be in violation of the Florida Constitution. (Shortly before that, Circuit Judge Audlin in Monroe County ruled that the law violated the Florida Constitution's protections against special laws relating to adoption, against bills of attainder, and ensuring the separation of powers. *In re Adoption of Doe*, 2008 WL 5070056 (Fla. Cir. Ct., Aug. 29, 2008).)

On appeal, **Judge Cope** affirmed Judge Lederman's judgment of adoption and agreed with her constitutional ruling. The parties had stipulated that only the state equal protection guarantee was in play, that the rational basis test rather than strict scrutiny was applicable, and that the adoption was in the best interests of the children. The state also agreed with F.G. that "gay people and heterosexuals make equally good parents."

The state's asserted rational basis for the discrimination was that "children will have better role models, and face less discrimination, if they are placed in non-homosexual households, preferably with a husband and a wife as the parents." Judge Cope found this to be a mystifying basis for the discrimination, because Florida allowed single straight persons to adopt (and one-third of the adoptions are to single parents) and allowed gay persons like F.G. to be foster parents and guardians of children.

The state attempted to rely on social science evidence to supply its rational basis, but Judge Lederman took extensive expert testimony that belied the state's evidence and supported her conclusion that "there are no differences in the parenting of homosexuals or the adjustment of their children." Indeed, she found the "issue so far beyond dispute that it would be irrational to hold otherwise." One of the state's experts, Dr. George Rekers of the University of South Carolina, testified to the contrary, but the lower court found that his testimony rested upon professionally disreputable studies and was overwhelmed by tangible evidence to the contrary, including evidence by another one of the state's own expert witnesses.

The state also claimed that there is reason to believe that "the homes of homosexuals may be less stable and more prone to domestic violence." The undisputed evidence in the case, however, supported the opposite conclusion—that women in heterosexual relationships were more likely to suffer domestic violence than women in lesbian relationships. The court also credited the undisputed testimony of Dr. Letitia Peplau, who found rates of household break-up unrelated to the sexual orientation of the partners.

Finally, the state argued that "placement of children with homosexuals presents a risk of discrimination and societal stigma." Judge Cope rejected this argument: "Florida already allows placement of children in foster care and guardianships with homosexual persons. This factor does not provide an argument for allowing such placements while prohibiting adoption. We reject the * * * argument for the same reason: they do not provide a reasonable basis for allowing homosexual foster parenting or guardianships while imposing a prohibition on adoption."

Postscript. Florida Attorney General Bill McCullom declined to appeal this ruling. Instead, the day after the ruling, the Department of Children and Families discontinued any questions about prospective adoptive parents' sexual orientation and instructed personnel to focus on the care and provision of the children rather than sexual orientation of the adults. *See* Memorandum from Alan Abramowitz, State Director, Office of Family Safety, to Regional Directors, Florida Department of Children and Families, "Third District Court of Appeal ruling on the state's ban on adoption by homosexuals as unconstitutional" (Sept. 23, 2010). In 2015, Governor Rick Scott signed into law a bill to formally repeal the gay adoption ban.

Another postscript involved Dr. Rekers, who was reportedly paid $120,000 by the state for his "expert" testimony in the adoption case. In May 2010, Dr. Rekers admitted that he took a ten-day vacation with a male sex worker who advertises on rentboy.com, a popular site for male prostitution. Joshua Schwartz, "Rekers Scandal Raises Legal Questions in Anti-Gay Cases," *N.Y. Times*, May 15, 2010, *available at* http://www.nytimes.com/2010/05/19/us/19rekers.html (viewed Jan. 3, 2011).

PROBLEM 7-2
INDIRECT WAYS TO HEAD OFF LESBIAN AND GAY ADOPTIONS

On March 14, 2000, Utah amended its child welfare law to add a new § 78–30–9, relating to "Decree of adoption—Best interest of child." The law then states:

(3)(a)   The Legislature specifically finds that it is not in a child's best interest to be adopted by a person or persons who are cohabiting in a relationship that is not a legally valid and binding marriage under the laws of this state. Nothing in this section limits or prohibits the court's placement of a child with a single adult who is not cohabiting as defined in Subsection (3)(b).

(b)   For purposes of this section, "cohabiting" means residing with another person and being involved in a sexual relationship with that person.

The primary purpose of this legislation, according to news reports, was to forbid adoptions by LGB people who were living with a sexual partner, although by its gender-neutral terms it also forbid adoptions by non-gay cohabiting couples as well. At the time it was enacted, of course, LGB people could not marry their same-sex partners. The result was that any LGB person living with a same-sex partner was precluded from adopting or serving as a foster parent.

What constitutional arguments could be mustered against this law? What are the odds of prevailing? Do you think the challenge would have been stronger before *Obergefell*? Or it is stronger post-*Obergefell*? Why? Consider the following case.

Arkansas Department of Human Services v. Sheila Cole et al.

Arkansas Supreme Court, 2011.
380 S.W.3d 429, 2011 Ark. 145.

■ The opinion of the Court was delivered by BROWN, J.

On November 4, 2008, a ballot initiative entitled "An Act Providing That an Individual Who is Cohabiting Outside of a Valid Marriage May Not Adopt or Be a Foster Parent of a Child Less Than Eighteen Years Old" was approved by fifty-seven percent of Arkansas voters. The ballot initiative is known as the Arkansas Adoption and Foster Care Act of 2008 or "Act 1." Act 1 went into effect on January 1, 2009, and is now codified at Arkansas Code Annotated sections 9–8–301 to –305. Under Act 1, an individual is prohibited from adopting or serving as a foster parent if that individual is "cohabiting with a sexual partner outside of a marriage that is valid under the Arkansas Constitution and the laws of this state." Ark. Code Ann. § 9–8–304(a) (Repl. 2009). This prohibition on adoption and foster parenting "applies equally to cohabiting opposite-sex and same-sex individuals." [However, the initiative had a distinctive impact on same-sex couples, which were unable to marry in the state.]

[The Arkansas Supreme Court affirmed the circuit court's ruling that Act 1 was unconstitutional under the Arkansas Constitution because of its fundamental violation of citizens' privacy rights.]

[T]he circuit court found that Act 1 "significantly burdens non-marital relationships and acts of sexual intimacy between adults because it forces them to choose between becoming a parent and having any meaningful type of intimate relationship outside of marriage. This infringes upon the fundamental right to privacy guaranteed to all citizens of Arkansas." The circuit court further determined that because Act 1 burdens the fundamental right to privacy implicit in the Arkansas Constitution, as recognized by Jegley v. Picado, 349 Ark. 600, 80 S.W.3d 332 (2002), the constitutionality of Act 1 must be analyzed under strict or heightened scrutiny, which means it cannot pass constitutional muster unless it provides the least restrictive method available that is narrowly tailored to accomplish a compelling state interest.

In considering the [plaintiff-]appellees' assertion in *Jegley* that the sodomy statute violated their right to privacy under the Arkansas Constitution, this court explored the rights granted to the citizens of Arkansas. We specifically found that no right to privacy is enumerated in the Arkansas Constitution. Nevertheless, we recognized that article 2, section 2 of the Arkansas Constitution does guarantee citizens certain inherent and inalienable rights, including the enjoyment of life and liberty and the pursuit of happiness, and section 15 guarantees the right of citizens to be secure in their own homes. *Jegley;* Ark. Const. art. 2, §§ 2, 15. We further noted that privacy is mentioned in more than eighty statutes enacted by the Arkansas General Assembly, thereby establishing "a public policy of the General Assembly supporting a right to privacy."

In light of the language contained in the Arkansas Constitution, our statutes and rules, and our jurisprudence, this court concluded "that Arkansas has a rich and compelling tradition of protecting individual privacy and that a fundamental right to privacy is implicit in the Arkansas Constitution." [*Jegley.*] We went on to hold that "the fundamental right to privacy implicit in our law protects all private, consensual, noncommercial acts of sexual intimacy between adults." Accordingly, because the sodomy statute burdened certain sexual conduct between members of the same sex, this court found that it impinged on the fundamental right to privacy guaranteed to all citizens of Arkansas. Furthermore, because the sodomy statute burdened a fundamental right, this court concluded that the constitutionality of the statute must be analyzed under strict or heightened scrutiny. The State conceded that it could offer no compelling State interest sufficient to justify criminalizing acts of sodomy. We held that the sodomy statute was unconstitutional as applied to private, consensual, noncommercial, same-sex sodomy.

The State and [Family Council Action Committee] now contend in the case at hand that, unlike in *Jegley,* a fundamental right is not at issue in the instant case because Act 1 only proscribes cohabitation. That argument, however, is not altogether correct. The express language of Act 1 reads that "[a] minor may not be adopted or placed in a foster home if the individual seeking to adopt or to serve as a foster parent is *cohabiting with a sexual partner* outside of a marriage that is valid under the Arkansas Constitution and the laws of this state." Ark. Code Ann. § 9–8–304(a) (emphasis added). Those words clearly make the ability to become an adoptive or foster parent conditioned on the would-be parent's sexual relationship. Hence, Act 1 does not merely prohibit cohabitation. Instead, the act expressly prohibits those persons who cohabit *with a sexual partner* from becoming adoptive or foster parents. * * * The problem with the argument mounted by the State and FCAC is that under Act 1 the exercise of one's fundamental right to engage in private, consensual sexual activity is conditioned on foregoing the privilege of adopting or fostering children. The choice imposed on cohabiting sexual partners, whether heterosexual or homosexual, is dramatic. They must chose [sic] either to lead a life of private, sexual intimacy with a partner without the opportunity to adopt or foster children or forego sexual cohabitation and, thereby, attain eligibility to adopt or foster.

[Reasoning by analogy from United States Supreme Court precedent denouncing infringement on constitutional liberties under the U.S. Constitution, the Arkansas Supreme Court rejected the petitioner's argument that establishing such conditions under Act 1 is permissible because adopting a child is a privilege rather than a right. For example, in Sherbert v. Verner, 374 U.S. 398 (1963), the Supreme Court invalidated a policy conditioning state benefits on a person's foregoing her free exercise of religious beliefs.]

Act 1 exerts significant pressure on Cole to choose between exercising her fundamental right to engage in an intimate sexual relationship in the privacy of her home without being eligible to adopt or foster children, on the one hand, or refraining from exercising this fundamental right in order to be eligible to adopt or foster children, on the other. Similar to conditioning compensation benefits in *Sherbert* on foregoing religious rights, the condition placed on the privilege to foster or adopt thwarts the exercise of a fundamental right to sexual intimacy in the home free from government intrusion under the Arkansas Constitution.

[The Arkansas Supreme Court concluded that in order to serve the best interests of children, courts and state agencies must examine all of the factors involved in a foster care determination and make a decision on a case-by-case basis.] Act 1's blanket ban provides for no such individualized consideration or case-by-case analysis in adoption or foster-care cases and makes the bald assumption that in *all* cases where adoption or foster care is the issue it is always against the best interest of the child to be placed in a home where an individual is cohabiting with a sexual partner outside of marriage. * * *

NOTE ON DISCRIMINATORY ADOPTION AND FOSTER CARE POLICIES

The Arkansas Supreme Court rested its decision on the Arkansas Constitution's sodomy jurisprudence, especially the court's precedent in *Jegley,* which was an important antecedent for *Lawrence v. Texas* (and is cited in Justice Kennedy's opinion). Does this represent a broader trend? Specifically, would the Utah Supreme Court be inclined to follow this reasoning if it addressed a challenge to its cohabitation-discriminating law?

Would the U.S. Supreme Court reach the same result under the U.S. Constitution? Would the following case be an easier one for the U.S. Supreme Court?

In *Johnston v. Missouri Department of Social Services*, 2006 WL 6903173 (Mo. Cir. Ct. Jackson Cnty. 2006), Lisa Johnston was denied an application for a Missouri foster care license because she was not deemed to be "a person of reputable character," one of the necessary qualities for individuals to hold a foster care license. The Children's Division of the Missouri Department of Social Services (DDS) conceded that she would have been considered exceptionally qualified to be foster parents "but for her sexual orientation," which suggested that she was a violator of the state sodomy law. Johnston appealed to the DDS director and then went to court. The Circuit Court deemed unsupportable the agency's finding that the petitioner lacked the "reputable character" necessary to obtain a foster parent license. The Court reasoned that the department's justification based on violation of the state sodomy law was invalid under *Lawrence v. Texas* and noted that all the evidence at trial supported Johnston's contention that she and her partner would be great parents.

At trial, DDS also relied on policy arguments, that "lesbian parenting" would be bad for children, who would suffer social stigma, and would make birth parents more reluctant to give up their offspring for adoption. Judge Midkiff found that none of these arguments rested upon any evidence whatsoever (much less the "substantial evidence" needed to affirm the agency). Additionally, the Court relied on *Palmore v. Sidoti* (Section 1A), where similar arguments had been used to support state discrimination against child custody by a different-race couple.

In recent years, a number of states—including Alabama, Michigan, Mississippi, North Dakota, South Dakota, Texas, and Virginia—enacted statutes that permit adoption and foster care organizations to refuse to place children with prospective parents if doing so would violate their moral or religious beliefs.[a] The provision in Virginia provides that private adoption and foster care agencies may refuse a child placement that "would violate the agency's written or moral convictions or policies." Va. Code Ann. § 63.2–1709.3(A).

On what grounds could this statute be challenged? Do you think the challenge would be successful? Why or why not? *See, e.g., Barber v. Bryant,*

---

[a]   Ala. Code § 38–7C–5(a) ("The state may not refuse to license or otherwise discriminate or take an adverse action against any child placing agency that is licensed by or required to be licensed by the state for child placing services on the basis that the child placing agency declines to make, provide, facilitate, or refer for a placement in a manner that conflicts with, or under circumstances that conflict with, the sincerely held religious beliefs of the child placing agency . . ."); Mich. Comp. Laws Ann. § 722.124e(3) (permitting "child placing agency" to "decline . . . to provide any services that conflict with, or provide any services under circumstances that conflict with, the child placing agency's sincerely held religious beliefs contained in a written policy, statement of faith, or other document adhered to by the child placing agency"); Miss. Code. Ann. § 11–62–5 (permitting a "religious organization that advertises, provides or facilitates adoption or foster care" to "decline[ ] to provide any adoption or foster care service, or related service, based upon or in a manner consistent with a sincerely held religious belief or moral conviction" that "(a) Marriage is or should be recognized as the union of one man and one woman; (b) Sexual relations are properly reserved to such a marriage; [or] (c) Male (man) or female (woman) refer to an individual's immutable biological sex as objectively determined by anatomy and genetics at time of birth"), enjoined by Barber v. Bryant, Case No. 3:16-cv-00417 (S.D. Miss. 2016), appeal pending; N.D. Cent. Code § 50–12–07.1 (providing that child-placing agencies may refuse to place a child in a placement that "violates the agency's written religious or moral convictions or policies"); S.D. Legis. 114 (2017), 2017 S.D. Laws Ch. 114 (S.B. 149) § 3 ("No child-placement agency may be required to provide any service that conflicts with, or provide any service under circumstances that conflict with any sincerely-held religious belief or moral conviction of the child-placement agency that shall be contained in a written policy, statement of faith, or other document adhered to by a child-placement agency."); Tex. Hum. Res. Code Ann. § 45.004 (prohibiting the government or government contractor from "discriminat[ing]" against a child welfare agency on the ground that the agency declined to provide services based on the "provider's sincerely held religious beliefs"); Va. Code Ann. § 63.2–1709.3(A) (providing that private adoption and foster care agencies may refuse a child placement that "would violate the agency's written religious or moral convictions or policies").

Case No. 3:16-cv-00417 (S.D. Miss. 2016), appeal pending (enjoining Miss. Code. Ann. § 11–62–5 (permitting a "religious organization that advertises, provides or facilitates adoption or foster care" to "decline[ ] to provide any adoption or foster care service, or related service, based upon or in a manner consistent with a sincerely held religious belief or moral conviction" that "(a) Marriage is or should be recognized as the union of one man and one woman; (b) Sexual relations are properly reserved to such a marriage; [or] (c) Male (man) or female (woman) refer to an individual's immutable biological sex as objectively determined by anatomy and genetics at time of birth")).

NOTE ON RACE AND ADOPTION

Consider the relevance of *Palmore v. Sidoti* (Section 1A) to issues of adoption: even if it is the case (as *Lofton* holds) that prospective parents have no fundamental liberty interest in adopting a particular child, adoption-based discrimination will be scrutinized very carefully if it relies on a suspect classification. So, can a state adoption agency prefer couples of the same race as the children they adopt? Can the agency prefer different-race couples when placing children born of different-race couples? There is a debate within critical scholarship as to whether or not it is good ever to place African-American babies in non-African-American households, as such babies would be deprived of their racial heritage. *See, e.g.,* Elizabeth Bartholet, "Where Do Black Children Belong? The Policies of Race-Matching in Adoption," 139 *U. Penn. L. Rev.* 1163 (1991). Could a stringent policy of not placing such children outside their race survive *Palmore*?

The Multiethnic Placement Act of 1994, Pub. L. No. 103–382, 108 Stat. 3518 (1994), codified at 42 U.S.C.A. § 5115a, provides that an adoption agency or service that is run or subsidized by the state cannot categorically discriminate on the basis of race in its child placement policies. The law also provides that such an agency "may consider the cultural, ethnic, or racial background of the child and the capacity of the prospective foster or adoptive parents to meet the needs of a child of this background as one of a number of factors used to determine the best interests of the child." 42 U.S.C.A. § 5115a(a)(2). Are there constitutional problems with this provision? *See also* Indian Child Welfare Act of 1978, 25 U.S.C.A. § 1901 et seq.

B. SECOND-PARENT ADOPTIONS

Section 2A considers adoption and foster care by LGBT people where the child previously had not been a member of the LGBT person's household. This part considers adoptions when the child is already in the household—when a person wants to adopt his or her partner's child.

In the past, when LGBT couples had children together, the law only recognized one partner, usually the genetic parent, as a legal parent of the child, even if more than one person was parenting the child. *See, e.g.,* Courtney G. Joslin, "Leaving No (Nonmarital) Child Behind," 48 *Fam. L.Q.* 495 (2014). A child can be very vulnerable if a person he or she views as a parent is not recognized in law as a parent. Such a person may not have the right to maintain a relationship with the child over the objection of the child's legal parent(s) or to make medical decisions for the child. In addition, the person may not have a legal obligation to support the child. Courtney G. Joslin, "Protecting Children(?): Marriage, Gender, and Assisted Reproductive Technology," 83 *S. Cal. L. Rev.* 1177 (2010).

In the past, the most common way for both members of a same-sex couple to establish legal parent-child relationships with their child was through what is known as a "second parent adoption." *See, e.g.,* Jane S. Schacter, "Constructing Families in a Democracy: Court, Legislatures, and Second-Parent Adoption," 75 *Chi.-Kent L. Rev.* 933 (2000). A second-parent adoption is like a step-parent adoption, but it involves a nonmarital partner rather than a spouse. A "joint adoption" is a process by which both members of a couple can simultaneously adopt a child.

The statutes in most states do not explicitly provide for the possibility of a second-parent adoption by an unmarried partner or for joint adoptions by unmarried partners. But, most statutes also don't expressly preclude such adoptions either. Instead, there are two primary procedural hurdles that unmarried couples face in this context. First, the adoption statutes in some states provide that, except in cases of step-parent adoptions by a spouse, an adoption terminates all existing legal parent-child relationships. Courtney G. Joslin, Shannon Minter & Catherine Sakimura, *Lesbian, Gay, Bisexual, and Transgender Family Law* § 5:3. These termination provisions make sense when a child is moving from one family to another, but they typically defeat the parties' intentions if applied strictly in cases where the child will remain with the existing legal parent. Second, and relatedly, in some states, again with the exception of step-parent adoptions by a spouse, a child is not considered "available for adoption" unless all legal parent-child relationships have been terminated. *Id.*

Most courts have applied principles of statutory construction to conclude that these types of provisions do not need to be applied strictly where doing so would be inconsistent with the best interests of the child. *See, e.g., In re Adoption of K.S.P.*, 804 N.E.2d 1253, 1257 (Ind. Ct. App. 2004) (holding that the purpose of the termination provision is "to shield the adoptive family from unnecessary instability and uncertainty from unwanted intrusions by the child's biological family" and that it would be "absurd" to apply the termination provision in a case involving a second-parent adoption); *Matter of Jacob*, 86 N.Y.2d 651, 660 (1995). *See also* Courtney G. Joslin, Shannon Minter & Catherine Sakimura, *Lesbian, Gay, Bisexual, and Transgender Family Law* §§ 5:3–5:10 (2017). *But see, e.g., Boseman v. Jarrell*, 704 S.e.2d 494, 500 (N.C. 2010); *In Interest of Angel Lace M.*, 516 N.W.2d 678 (Wis. 1994).

Unmarried couples seeking to adopt simultaneously—that is to complete a "joint adoption"—faced a slightly different procedural hurdle. Professor Nancy Polikoff, the author of the leading article on second parent adoptions, "This Child Does Have Two Mothers: Redefining Parenthood to Meet the Needs of Children in Lesbian-Mother and Other

Nontraditional Families," 78 *Geo. L.J.* 459 (1990), was counsel for a gay couple seeking to form a legally recognized family through joint adoption. The following case is the result of Polikoff's efforts.

In the past, state adoption laws rested on a model that families consist of different-sex married couples. Consider the statutory scheme in place for the District of Columbia. D.C.Code § 16–302 ("Persons who may adopt") provides:

> Any person may petition the court for a decree of adoption. A petition may not be considered by the court unless petitioner's spouse, if he [or she] has one, joins in the petition, except that if either the husband or wife is a natural parent of the prospective adoptee, the natural parent need not join in the petition with the adopting parent, but need only give his or her consent to the adoption. If the marital status of the petitioner changes after the time of filing the petition and before the time the decree of adoption is final, the petition must be amended accordingly.

Section 16–312 ("Legal effects of adoption") provides in paragraph (a):

> A final decree of adoption establishes the relationship of natural parent and natural child between adopter and adoptee for all purposes, including mutual rights of inheritance and succession as if adoptee were born to adopter. The adoptee takes from, through, and as a representative of his [or her] adoptive parent or parents in the same manner as a child by birth, and upon the death of an adoptee intestate, his [or her] property shall pass and be distributed in the same manner as if the adoptee had been born to the adopting parent or parents in lawful wedlock. All rights and duties including those of inheritance and succession between the adoptee, his [or her] natural parents, their issue, collateral relatives, and so forth, are cut off, except that when one of the natural parents is the spouse of the adopter, the rights and relations as between adoptee, that natural parent, and his [or her] parents and collateral relatives, including mutual rights of inheritance and succession, are in no wise altered.

In re M.M.D. & B.H.M.

District of Columbia Court of Appeals, 1995.
662 A.2d 837.

■ FERREN, ASSOCIATE JUDGE. * * *

Hillary is a healthy, happy, and delightful 2-1/2 year-old Black/Hispanic child who was born on August 15, 1991 in the District of Columbia. Hillary's biological mother is a young, attractive Black woman who met Bruce and Mark after reading an advertisement that they had placed in a local newspaper. The ad identified the petitioners as a gay couple who were seeking to adopt a child. Bruce and Mark are adult, white, homosexual males who have shared an intimate relationship for almost five years.

At the time she read the newspaper advertisement, the birth mother was several months pregnant and was not on good terms with her mother with whom she then lived. The birth mother, therefore, not only answered the ad, but shortly after meeting the petitioners, she began living with them. Eventually, she delivered Hillary on August 15, 1991. All went as planned when Hillary's mother signed her consent to an adoption of Hillary on September 9, 1991. Bruce filed the first petition to adopt the child on the following day.

The baby's natural mother and Bruce reached an agreement that the mother would continue to have visitation privileges with Hillary, even after the adoption was finalized. These visitation arrangements, however, did not proceed smoothly. Rather, the mother accused Bruce of denying her access to Hillary, and eventually she filed a motion to vacate her consent to the adoption. This motion was submitted to this court and was scheduled for a hearing.

After much discussion and several preliminary hearings, the parties reached an accord which they reduced to writing. Essentially, Hillary's mother and Bruce agreed again to permit the mother to visit with Hillary even after a final decree of adoption was issued. [The court was satisfied that the mother consented to the adoption, understood and knowingly waived her parenthood rights, and believed Bruce M. was a suitable person to adopt Hillary. The court granted the adoption. In March 1993, both Bruce M. and Mark D. petitioned to adopt Hillary. They are a committed couple with white collar jobs.]

Hillary appears to be bonded equally well to both Bruce and Mark. She calls Bruce "Daddy" and Mark "Poppy." Bruce cooks most of the meals, while Mark often reads the bedtime stories. They both take Hillary on outings. The Department of Human Services has recommended in favor of their joint petition.

[The lower court held that the adoption law did not permit the joint petition, even though it satisfied the best interests of Hillary. Writing for the court majority (himself and Judge Mack), Judge Ferren reversed. The following is his summary of the grounds for interpreting the adoption statutes to permit this joint adoption.]

1.   D.C. Code § 16–302 (1989 Repl.) expressly authorizes adoptions by "[a]ny person," without limitation. It then imposes a restriction on adoption by a spouse of the natural parent (that parent must "consent"), as well as a restriction on adoption by every other married petitioner (the petitioner's spouse must "join[ ]in the petition"). There is no mention of adoptions by unmarried couples. A later provision, D.C. Code § 16–305, refers generally to adoptions by "more than one petitioner," and D.C. Code § 16–312(a) acknowledges the "adopting parent or parents." Finally, D.C. Code § 49–202 (1990 Repl.), which antedates the adoption

statute, provides that "[w]ords importing the singular . . . shall be held to include the plural" unless that "construction would be unreasonable." These provisions, taken together, neither assuredly authorize adoptions by unmarried couples nor conclusively preclude them. The court, therefore, must consider this ambiguous statutory language in light of other interpretive criteria.

2.   The legislative histories of the 1954 (present) adoption statute and of its 1937 predecessor add little to our understanding of legislative intent except for a significant, unexplained omission: beginning with the 1937 statute, Congress withheld language found in the first (1895) District of Columbia adoption statute limiting adoptions by couples to "husband and wife." After 1895, no committee report or comment from the House or Senate floor addressed "who may adopt." And nothing in the legislative history can be said to exclude adoptions by unmarried couples.

3.   Because the statutory language and legislative history of the 1954 statute do not indicate that Congress paid attention to unmarried couples, one way or another, the language in D.C. Code § 16–302 specifying restrictions that apply "if" a petitioner has a "spouse" does not provide a basis for inferring that Congress consciously decided to exclude unmarried couples from eligibility to adopt. According to applicable case law, the *expressio unius* canon of construction (expression of one thing excludes another) only applies when the legislature is aware of the matter excluded.

4.   In contrast, the doctrine of "strict construction" would limit adoptions to couples who are married, regardless of whether Congress thought about the matter, simply because the statute refers to married couples and no others. This court, however, has rejected strict construction of the adoption statute in favor of "liberal construction" in other adoption contexts. Moreover, courts in other states have employed liberal construction to allow adoptions by unmarried couples under statutes similar to the District of Columbia statute, in order to further the statute's beneficial purposes. The trial court's adherence to strict construction, therefore, is not easily justified.

5.   The traditional interpretive criteria cautioning against statutory construction that leads to "absurd results" or "obvious injustice," while marginally relevant (if relevant at all), cut in favor of a liberal construction that includes unmarried couples as eligible adopters.

6.   Under the circumstances, where the statutory language, legislative history, and other applicable criteria are not dispositive, the controlling interpretive criterion, according to applicable case law, is the court's obligation to effectuate the legislative purpose of the adoption statute. There is no proper way of discerning legislative intent based on how Congress in 1954 would have answered the question whether unmarried couples should be eligible to adopt. This court, therefore, must focus on the general purpose or policy that motivated Congress to pass

the adoption statute. There is considerable case law emphasizing that the "paramount concern" of the adoption statute—its central beneficial purpose—is the "best interests of the prospective adoptee." We conclude that this purpose is better served by applying a liberal, inclusionary reading of the statute to the facts presented here, for which there is persuasive decisional precedent; this case and others demonstrate that adoption by an unmarried couple can be in a child's best interests—especially when the alternative would be a child's living in a family with two unmarried parents, only one of whom would be allowed to establish a formal parental relationship.

7.   As indicated earlier, the statutory rule of construction in D.C.Code § 49–202 would convert § 16–302 to say "any persons," not merely "any person," may petition for an adoption if that construction would not be "unreasonable." Because we have concluded that liberal construction of the statute is appropriate here, and because this case and others show that adoptions by unmarried couples can be in the best interests of children, there is no basis for concluding that adoptions by unmarried couples would, categorically, be "unreasonable." We therefore are satisfied that § 49–202 supports the analysis here and that § 16–302 should be construed accordingly.

8.   We conclude, finally, that the so-called "stepparent exception" in D.C. Code § 16–312(a) would apply, under the circumstances, to prevent termination of the relationship between Hillary and her unmarried natural parent (Bruce by adoption) if his life partner (Mark) is allowed to adopt the child and live as a family with Bruce and Hillary.

9.   The trial court's order is reversed and the case remanded for further proceedings to determine whether it will be in Hillary's best interest for Mark, as well as Bruce, to adopt her. * * *

■ [We omit the concurring opinion of JUDGE MACK and the dissenting opinion of JUDGE STEADMAN.]

Postscript. On remand, the trial court granted Bruce and Mark's adoption petition.

NOTES ON RACE, SEXUAL ORIENTATION, AND SECOND-PARENT ADOPTIONS

Second-parent adoptions provide critical protections and security for children. Once an adoption has been completed, that adoptive parent has all the rights and obligations of any other legal parent, including legal rights against third parties. Thus, if the biological parent or, as in the D.C. case, the first adoptive parent was to die, the second parent would automatically retain custody over the child. In the absence of such legal relationship, other legal relatives sometimes take the child away from the second parent, usually to the detriment of the child. For a heart-rending example of a child who was torn from her surviving parent by the biological grandparents, see

Laura Benkov, *Reinventing the Family: The Emerging Story of Lesbian and Gay Parents* (1994).

1. *The Submerged Race Issue.* Note the race issue in the case: a European-American couple is adopting a Latino/African-American child. Black social workers in the 1970s maintained that such adoptions are wrong, because they displace the African-American child from her or his racial heritage. This view retains a vigorous constituency. *See* Twila L. Perry, "The Transracial Adoption Controversy: An Analysis of Discourse and Subordination," 21 *N.Y.U. Rev. L. & Soc. Change* 33 (1993–94); Twila L. Perry, "Race, Color, and the Adoption of Biracial Children," 17 *J. Gender & Just.* 73, 73 (2014) (noting that "transracial adoption remains a subject of recurring public debate").

The department of social services in *M.M.D.* favored the adoption of Hillary by Mark and Bruce, but what if the department had opposed the adoption for reasons of racial heritage? How should that affect the court's exercise of its discretion? Would consideration of such factors be inconsistent with *Palmore v. Sidoti*? For examples of adoptions by white lesbian couples of children of color, over the objections of blood kin, see *In re Adoption of Jessica N.*, 202 A.D.2d 320, 609 N.Y.S.2d 209 (1994); *In re Commitment of J.N.*, 158 Misc.2d 97, 601 N.Y.S.2d 215 (Fam.Ct.1993).

2. *Dynamic Statutory Interpretation.* Judge Ferren's opinion was a highly dynamic interpretation of the District's adoption laws. Judge Steadman's dissent relied on the *expressio unius* canon to argue that adoption should be confined to the cases clearly contemplated by the legislature. Judge Ferren responded that (1) the adoption law should be liberally and not strictly interpreted; (2) the legislature was not thinking about unmarried couples generally; and (3) the D.C. Code states that singular words should also be read to be plural unless unreasonable. Are these persuasive responses? Is it plausible to think that the legislature would have acquiesced in a gay male couple's adopting a child? Note that Judge Ferren rejected almost identical arguments when he ruled that the District's Marriage Law did not include lesbian and gay couples. *See Dean v. District of Columbia*, 653 A.2d 307 (D.C. App.1995). How can you explain the different results?

The leading case to the contrary is *In re Adoption of Baby Z.*, 247 Conn. 474, 724 A.2d 1035 (Ct. 1999), which involved a request for a second-parent adoption. Interpreting a statutory scheme very similar to that found in the District and New York, the Court said this: "We recognize that all of the child care experts involved in this case have concluded that the proposed adoption would be in Baby Z.'s best interest. Because of the statutory nature of our adoption system, however, policy determinations as to what jurisdictional limitations apply are for *the legislature, not the judiciary,* to make." Dissenting justices would have followed Judge Ferren and Chief Judge Kaye's purposive, best-interests-of-the-child approach. After *Baby Z.*, the Connecticut Legislature abrogated the decision by enacting a statute allowing such adoptions.

As the *M.M.D.* dissents and the *Baby Z.* majority strenuously argued, judges ought to be reluctant to construe statutes in a manner wholly inconsistent with the "plain meaning" of the statutory text. As the *M.M.D.*

majority and *Baby Z.* dissent argued, however, adoption statutes are supposed to be "liberally" construed to serve the best interests of the child, which in these cases is aligned with allowing the adoption. These cases, therefore, present a dilemma for courts: either result is going to sacrifice some important rule of law value—either the transparency of law fostered by applying plain meanings or the policy of law fostered by adapting laws to fulfill their goals and purposes.

Note a tiebreaker idea invoked by the dissenters in *Baby Z.*: construe the statute to avoid constitutional problems. Should the child be deprived of the most desirable second parent simply because that parent is not married to the child's biological parent? Is it constitutional for the second parent to lose an important right for the same reason?

Advocacy groups report that about 14 jurisdictions have either statutes or appellate court decisions authorizing second-parent adoptions by nonmarital partners. National Center for Lesbian Rights, Adoption by LGBT Parents, available at http://www.nclrights.org/wp-content/uploads/2013/07/2PA_state_list.pdf. Second-parent adoptions may be available in some additional states, including some southern states, such as Texas and Georgia. This might astound you. Issues related to same-sex marriage would usually send any southern state, and many a state outside the South, into political frenzy—yet the government officials often facilitated second parent and joint adoptions for LGBT couples without much notice in most states of the South and Midwest. What explains this bipolar response? For consideration of this question, see Cynthia Godsoe, "Adopting the Gay Family," 90 *Tul. L. Rev.* 311 (2015). Second-parent and joint adoptions, however, remain unavailable in some states, including Kansas, Michigan, North Carolina, and Wisconsin.

Now that same-sex couples can marry in all fifty states, same-sex couples who are married or in a civil union or a registered domestic partnership can complete stepparent adoptions nationwide. Will the availability of stepparent adoptions for married same-sex couples slow the tide of unmarried LGBT couples who apply for second parent adoptions? Do you think courts in states without statutes or appellate case law permitting second-parent adoptions will be less likely to conclude they are permissible? Should they be less likely to do so? Why or why not?

3. *Second-Parent Adoptions and Sexuality/Gender Theory.* Consider the issues raised in these cases from the perspectives of various thinkers explored in Chapter 3. For example, a constitutional understanding of the rights of unmarried straight partners would be anathema to natural law thinkers like John Finnis (Chapter 3, Section 1), in large part because it affords state "recognition" to nonmarital families—not just lesbian and gay couples, but also different-sex couples who choose not to marry. Normatively, natural law thinkers would object that state recognition of second-parent adoptions is ultimately not in the child's best interests, because commitment between the partners is an essential part of their joint commitment to their children, and because marriage is an essential feature of partner commitment. Most natural law thinkers would add that the partners must be different-sex, but a gay-friendly natural law could stress the interpersonal commitment that same-sex couples could enjoy from marriage.

Law and economics utilitarians can agree with a sexual orientation-neutral natural law philosophy if it is empirically good for children. *E.g.*, Margaret Brinig, *From Contract to Covenant: Beyond the Law and Economics of the Family* (2000). But Gary Becker argues that different-sex households are more efficient because they result in divisions of labor (Chapter 3, Section 2A). (Note the implied naturalization of division of labor for mom-dad households and implied non-existence of it in same-sex households.) Does that reasoning carry over into child care?

Feminists like Catharine MacKinnon (Chapter 3, Section 2B) could defend decisions like *Jacob* on the ground that second-parent adoptions facilitate the ability of women to form their own families of choice, families that may be independent of men and less patriarchal. Would Professor MacKinnon be equally friendly to *M.M.D.*, where a gay couple was adopting a child? A cultural feminist criticism of second-parent adoptions might be along the following lines: The decline of marriage has hurt women, for they value the long-term commitment features of marriage, while men like the freedom of cohabitation; because second-parent adoptions as in *Jacob* (one plaintiff couple was different-sex) make it easier for men to avoid the commitment of marriage, they contribute to the pauperization of women who are dumped by their wandering boyfriends. On the other hand, second-parent adoption might make it easier for the dumped women to procure child support from those same men.

Social constructionists like Foucault would de-emphasize the importance of legal recognition, beyond the ways that it or legal campaigns for legal recognition contribute to the social normalization of nonmarital families. Foucault would ponder the ways in which the law is a perhaps small part of the larger phenomenon by which people seek and secure public recognition of their "interest" in children. There is a *discourse of children* that perpetuates their infantilization and that constructs a particular identity, *parent*, with complicated but perhaps far-reaching consequences for people's attitudes about lesbians on the one hand and parents on the other.

NOTE ON INTERSTATE RECOGNITION OF ADOPTIONS AND OTHER PARENTAGE JUDGMENTS

When the court of one state properly issues a final judgment, the Full Faith and Credit Clause of the U.S. Constitution requires that all other states to recognized and give exacting respect to that judgment. *Baker by Thomas v. General Motors Corp.*, 522 U.S. 222, 233 (1998) ("Regarding judgments . . . , the full faith and credit obligation is exacting. A final judgment in one State, if rendered by a court with adjudicatory authority of the subject matter and persons governed by the judgment, qualified for recognition throughout the land . . . [O]ur decisions support no roving 'public policy exception' to the full faith and credit due judgments.").

In 2016, the U.S. Supreme Court clarified that these principles apply with equal force to adoption judgments. *V.L. v. E.L.*, 136 S. Ct. 1017 (2016).

In the case, *V.L. v. E.L.*, a same-sex couple had completed second-parent adoptions in Georgia. Years later, the couple ended their relationship while residing in Alabama, and the biological mother argued that Alabama did not have to recognize and respect the Georgia second-parent adoptions. The Supreme Court disagreed and held that Alabama was required under the Full Faith and Credit Clause to give full effect to the judgments. This is true, the Court explained, even if the Alabama court "disagree[d] with the reasoning underlying the judgment or deem[ed] it to be wrong on the merits." *V.L. v. E.L.*, 136 S. Ct. 1017, 1020 (2016). *See also, e.g., Finstuen v. Crutcher*, 496 F.3d 1139 (10th Cir. 2007) ("We hold today that final adoption orders and decrees are judgments that are entitled to recognition by all other states under the Full Faith and Credit Clause. Therefore, Oklahoma's adoption amendment is unconstitutional in its refusal to recognize final adoption orders of other states that permit adoption by same-sex couples."); *Embry v. Ryan*, 11 So.3d 408, 410 (Fla. 2d DCA 2009); *Giancaspro v. Congleton*, 2009 WL 416301 (Mich. Ct. App. 2009).

These principles should also apply to other types of parentage judgments. For further discussion of these issues, see Courtney G. Joslin, "Interstate Recognition of Parentage in a Time of Disharmony: Same-Sex Parent Families and Beyond," 70 *Ohio St. L.J.* 563 (2009).

SECTION 3

ESTABLISHING PARENTAGE

In the past, in the absence of a second-parent adoption, the law recognized only one member of a same-sex couple as the parent of a child born to and raised by the couple. If the adult is not considered a legal parent, they may not have a right to maintain contact with the child, and may have no legal obligation to support the child. In the absence of a legally recognized parent-child relationship, the child may not be entitled to important benefits through the adult, like child's social security benefits or the right to sue for the wrongful death of the adult. *See, e.g.,* Courtney G. Joslin, "Protecting Children(?): Marriage, Gender, and Assisted Reproductive Technology," 83 *S. Cal. L. Rev.* 1177 (2010). Today, there are a growing number of circumstances under which both members of a same-sex couple may be recognized as the legal parents of their child as a matter of law, without an adoption.

If the adult is not recognized as legal parents, they may be accorded some, usually more limited parental rights under various equitable doctrines. Different states use different terms to describe these equitable theories, including de facto parentage, in loco parentis, or psychological parent. For an early and very influential scholarly article urging the adoption of these equitable theories, see Nancy D. Polikoff, "This Child Does Have Two Mothers: Redefining Parenthood to Meet the Needs of Children in Lesbian-Mother and other Non-Traditional Families," 78 *Geo. L.J.* 459 (1990). *See also, e.g.,* Courtney G. Joslin, "Leaving No (Nonmarital) Child Behind," 48 *Fam. L.Q.* 495 (2014) (describing current state of the law). For a critique of or a caution against the wide-spread adoption of equitable parenting theories, see Robin Fretwell Wilson, "Undeserved Trust: Reflections on the ALI's Treatment of De Facto Parents," in *Reconceiving the Family: Critique on the American Law Institute's Principles of the Law of Family Dissolution* (Robin Fretwell Wilson, ed., 2006).

The wide-spread adoption of these equitable parentage doctrines reflects a consensus among child psychologists that infants form significant relationships with caregivers and that disruption of those relationships can be traumatic for those children. The germinal body of scholarship is called *attachment theory. See, e.g.,* Linda D. Elrod, "A Child's Perspective of Defining A Parent: The Case for Intended Parenthood," 25 *BYU J. Pub. L.* 245, 249 (2011) (reviewing literature on attachment theory). Attachment theory posits that a child is open to becoming strongly attached to an adult caregiver through the first year of life; after that, the child may be open to such attachment, depending on circumstances. Separation of the child from an attached caregiver will be an occasion for distress, and will be potentially traumatic if the attached caregiver becomes completely unavailable.

PROBLEM 7-3
POLICY: BEST RULE FOR DETERMINING PARENTAGE?

You are a policy aide to a state legislator. Your legislator has asked you to draft the best rules for determining who is a parent. You are directed to think creatively, unfettered by the rules of the past. What criteria should be used? Biology? Intent? Parenting conduct? Why? Which criteria should be given the most weight? Why? Draft the rules.

For explorations of what the rules have been and what they should be, *see, e.g.*, Douglas NeJaime, "The Nature of Parenthood," 126 *Yale L.J.* 2260 (2017) (exploring developments); Katharine K. Baker, "Bionormativity and the Construction of Parenthood," 42 *Ga. L. Rev.* 649 (2008); David D. Meyer, "Parenthood in A Time of Transition: Tensions Between Legal, Biological, and Social Conceptions of Parenthood," 54 *Am. J. Comp. L.* 125, 126–27 (2006); Katharine K. Baker, "Bargaining or Biology? The History and Future of Paternity Law and Parental Status," 14 *Cornell J.L. & Pub. Pol'y* 1 (2004).

A. PARENTAGE AND MARRIED LGBT COUPLES

INTRODUCTORY NOTES ON PARENTING

1.   *Assisted Reproductive Technology Statutes.* If a same-sex couple has a child during their marriage through assisted reproduction, both spouses may be considered legal parents of a child born to one of them under the state's assisted reproductive technology (ART) statute. Many states have statutes providing that a husband who consents to his wife's insemination is the legal parent of the resulting child even if he is not genetically related to that resulting child. For example, Utah Code Ann. § 78B–15–703 provides: "If a *husband* provides sperm for, or consents to, assisted reproduction by his wife [as required by law], he is the father of a resulting child born to his wife." (Emphasis added).

Although Utah's ART statute refers only to husbands, after *Obergefell*, refusing to apply such a statute equally to a female spouse is likely unconstitutional. *See, e.g., Roe v. Patton*, 2015 WL 4476743, at *3 (D. Utah 2015) ("May Defendants extend the benefits of the assisted-reproduction statutes to male spouses in opposite-sex couples but not for female spouses in same-sex couples? As discussed below, the court concludes that Plaintiffs are highly likely to succeed in their claim that such differential treatment is unconstitutional."). The Supreme Court's decision in *Pavan* (see below) suggests that the *Roe* court is correct; refusal to apply an assisted reproduction statute equally to female spouses violates *Obergefell*.

Can you think of any persuasive argument *against* an equal application of a gender-specific ART statute?

In recent years, a number of state legislatures have amended their ART statutes to clarify that they apply equally without regard to the sex of the second intended parent. Maine's statute, for example, provides: "A *person* who provides gametes for and consents to or a person who consents to assisted reproduction by a woman [as provided in other provisions] with the intent to be the parent of a resulting child is a parent of the resulting child." Me. Stat., tit., § 1923 (emphasis added). *See also* Cal. Fam. Code § 7613(a); Nev. Rev. Stat. § 126.670; N.H. Stat. § 168–B:2(II); N.M. Stat. § 40–11A–703; Wash. Rev. Code § 26.26.710.

The relevant Uniform law—the Uniform Parentage Act (UPA)—has recently been revised. A core goal of the new Act—the UPA (2017)—is to ensure that the Act applies equally and fairly to same-sex couples. Among other changes, UPA (2017) revises the assisted reproduction provisions so that they apply equally, without regard to the sex (or marital status) of the second intended parent. Under Section 703: "An *individual* who consents [consistent with the statute] to assisted reproduction by a woman with the intent to be a parent of a child conceived by assisted reproduction is a parent of the child." UPA (2017), § 703 (emphasis added). For more information about the UPA (2017), see http://www.uniformlaws.org/Act.aspx ?title=Parentage Act (2017).

Even if it is clear that the relevant ART statute applies equally to same-sex couples, there may other hurdles. For example, the ART statutes in many states require the parties to consent in writing. For example, Utah's statutes states that "consent to assisted reproduction by a married woman must be in a record signed by the woman and her husband." Utah Code Ann. § 78B–15–704(1). Other statutes, like New York's, require not only the written consent of both intended parents, but also an acknowledgment or certification of the signatures by a doctor. N.Y. Dom. Rel. Law § 73. Often neither the parties nor the doctors are aware of these requirements.

What if the spouses don't comply with the relevant requirements, like a written consent requirement? Should the statute still apply if other evidence makes clear that the spouse consented in fact to the assisted reproduction? Why or why not? Court decisions are mixed. *See, e.g.*, *Lane v. Lane*, 121 N.M. 414, 416 (N.M. Ct. App. 1996) (holding that the statute applied even in the absence of written consent because the evidence demonstrated that the parties "substantially complied with the statute" where there was "knowing consent by both Husband and Wife"). *But see In the Interest of A.E.*, No. 09-16-00019-CV, 2017 WL 1535101, at *8 (Tex. App. Apr. 27, 2017) (holding that a female spouse was not a parent under the assisted reproduction statute because the statute required written consent and the spouse "failed to produce a record signed by M.N. and C.W. and kept by a licensed physician").

2. *Marital Presumption.* Some same-sex spouses have argued that even if they are not protected under the state's ART law (because, for example, they didn't comply with the written consent requirement), they nonetheless should be considered legal parents under the state's "marital presumption." All fifty states have statutes and/or common law rules that create a presumption that a husband is the legal parent of a child born to his wife. Leslie Harris, Lee E. Teitelbaum, June R. Carbone, *Family Law* 865 (Aspen Publishers, 5th ed. 2014). For example, the Texas Family Code provides: "(a) A man is presumed to be the father of a child if: (1) he is married to the mother of the child and the child is born during the marriage[.]" Tex. Fam. Code Ann. § 160.204 (West).

As Professor Jana Singer explains,

> The marital presumption of paternity traditionally served a number of overlapping goals. First, because biological paternity was difficult to establish, the marital presumption provided legal certainty for purposes such as inheritance and succession. Second, the presumption preserved the integrity of marriage, at least where both parties to the marriage so desired. Third, the strong version of the presumption promoted the welfare of children, because, if the marital presumption were rebutted, the consequences for the child were devastating: The child was declared a bastard, or fillius nullius—literally the "son of nobody"—and was no longer entitled to support or inheritance from either parent. The social consequences were devastating as well, for both the child and the mother.

Jana Singer, "Marriage, Biology, and Paternity: The Case for Revitalizing the Marital Presumption," 65 *Md. L. Rev.* 246, 248–49 (2006) (footnotes omitted).

As noted above, the marital presumption continues to exist in all fifty states. Most states have codified the marital presumption. Historically, the marital presumption was very difficult, if not impossible, to rebut. *See, e.g.*, Theresa Glennon, "Somebody's Child: Evaluating the Erosion of the Marital Presumption of Paternity," 102 *W. Va. L. Rev.* 547, 562–63 (2000). Today, some states place more weight on the importance of biological parentage. But many states continue to protect established parent-child relationships, even when they are not based on biology. For example, in Texas, the marital presumption becomes conclusive—that it cannot be overcome—after the child's fourth birthday. Tex. Fam. Code Ann. § 160.607 (West). And even within the first four years of the child's life, a Texas court can deny a request for genetic testing based on consideration of equitable factors, including the husband's relationship with the child. Tex. Fam. Code Ann. § 160.608(a) (West) (providing that the court may deny the request for genetic testing if (1) the conduct of the mother or the presumed father estops that party from denying parentage; and (2) it would be inequitable to disprove the father-child relationship between the child and the presumed father."). Thus, the marital presumption applies to husbands even when they are not genetic parents and, in many states, the law limits a husband's ability to rebut the presumption with genetic testing.

A question that has arisen in a post-marriage equality world is: Must states apply their marital presumptions equally to female spouses of the woman who gave birth?

As you ponder that question, consider the *Pavan* case included below which involves a related question—who should be listed on the birth certificate of a child born to same-sex couples?

3. *Birth Certificates for Children Born to Married Same-Sex Couples.* In addition to having rules for determining a child's legal parentage, states also have statutes directing who should be listed as parents on a child's birth certificate. Being listed on a child's birth certificate does not conclusively establish that the individual is a legal parent. To the contrary, typically, a birth certificate is only "prima facie" evidence of the information stated on the form. *See, e.g.*, 410 Ill. Comp. Stat. Ann. 535/25(6) (providing that a certified birth certificate "shall be considered as prima facie evidence of the facts therein stated").

That said, because birth certificates are some commonly relied upon as evidence of parenthood, being listed as a parent on one's child's birth certificate can be very helpful as a practical matter. For example, "[p]arents rely on birth certificates to prove to hospitals and health-care providers that they have the right to make health-care decisions for their children, to enroll their children in school and childcare, and to travel internationally with them. Birth certificates are important in a host of other extraordinary, as well as ordinary moments in life." Amici Curiae Brief of Professors of Family Law in support of Petitioners at 2–3, *Pavan v. Smith*, https://www.glad.org/wp-content/uploads/2017/03/pavan-v-smith-amicus-brief-of-family-law-professors.pdf. Conversely, when a child's legal parent is omitted from the birth certificate, it can create many practical problems for the family. Taking care of many mundane but important things like enrolling one's child for school and making medical decisions for one's child can be much more difficult if one is not listed on the birth certificate.

In the wake of marriage equality for same-sex couples, court decisions had been split on whether states were required to list both members of a same-sex married couple on the birth certificate of a child born to one of the spouses during the marriage. Some courts said that state officials were required to do so. *See, e.g., Carson v. Heigel*, 2017 WL 624803 (D.S.C. 2017); *Henderson v. Adams*, 209 F. Supp. 3d 1059, 1079–80 (S.D. Ind. 2016), *order clarified*, No. 115CV00220TWPMJD, 2016 WL 7492478 (S.D. Ind. Dec. 30, 2016), *appeal filed*, 2016 WL 7492478 (7th Cir. Jan 23, 2017) (No. 17-1141) (ordering state officials to "recognize the Plaintiff Spouses in this matter as a parent to their respective Plaintiff Child and to identify both Plaintiff Spouses as parents on their respective Plaintiff Child's birth certificate"); *Waters v. Ricketts*, 2016 WL 447837, *4 (D. Neb. 2016) (order in marriage equality case post-*Obergefell* providing: "Further, as an example of continuing issues, the plaintiffs contend that recently the Department of Health and Human Services has refused to issue birth certificates to same-sex couples, and are instead listing the woman who has the baby as the only parent." (footnotes omitted)); *Roe v. Patton*, 2015 WL 4476734 (D. Utah 2015); *Gartner v. Dep't of Public Health*, 830 N.W.2d 335, 341 (Iowa 2013) (holding that the state's refusal to list the birth mother's female spouse on their child's birth certificate was unconstitutional).

Other courts, including the Arkansas Supreme Court, disagreed. *Smith v. Pavan*, 2016 Ark. 437, 505 S.W.3d 169 (Ark. 2016), *rev'd, Pavan v. Smith*, 582 U.S. ___, 137 S.Ct. 2075 (2017). The relevant Arkansas statute—Arkansas Code § 20–18–401—states: "[I]f the mother was married at the time of either conception or birth or between conception and birth the name of the husband shall be entered on the birth certificate as the father of the child." Arkansas Code § 20–18–401(f)(1).

There are two narrow exceptions to this rule; proof of the husband's lack of biological parentage alone is not sufficient to remove or exclude him from the birth certificate. Rather, the husband can be removed from the birth certificate only if:

> (A) Paternity has been determined otherwise by a court of competent jurisdiction; or

> (B) The mother executes an affidavit attesting that the husband is not the father and that the putative father is the father, and the putative father executes an affidavit attesting that he is the father and the husband executes an affidavit attesting that he is not the father. * * *

Arkansas Code § 20–18–401(f)(1).

What do you think? Can this statute be applied equally to a female spouse? Must the statute be applied equally to a female spouse? Here is what the Supreme Court had to say about the matter.

Marisa N. Pavan, et al. v. Nathaniel Smith

United States Supreme Court, 2017.
___ U.S. ___, 137 S. Ct. 2075, 198 L.Ed.2d 636.

■ PER CURIAM.

As this Court explained in *Obergefell v. Hodges*, 576 U.S. ___, 135 S.Ct. 2584, 192 L.Ed.2d 609 (2015), the Constitution entitles same-sex couples to civil marriage "on the same terms and conditions as opposite-sex couples." *Id.*, at ___, 135 S.Ct., at 2605. In the decision below, the Arkansas Supreme Court considered the effect of that holding on the State's rules governing the issuance of birth certificates. When a married woman gives birth in Arkansas, state law generally requires the name of the mother's male spouse to appear on the child's birth certificate— regardless of his biological relationship to the child. According to the court below, however, Arkansas need not extend that rule to similarly situated same-sex couples: The State need not, in other words, issue birth certificates including the female spouses of women who give birth in the State. Because that differential treatment infringes *Obergefell*'s commitment to provide same-sex couples "the constellation of benefits that the States have linked to marriage," *id.*, at ___, 135 S.Ct., at 2601, we reverse the state court's judgment.

The petitioners here are two married same-sex couples[—Leigh and Jana Jacobs and Terrah and Marisa Pavan—]who conceived children through anonymous sperm donation. * * * When it came time to secure birth certificates for the newborns, each couple filled out paperwork listing both spouses as parents * * * . Both times, however, the Arkansas Department of Health issued certificates bearing only the birth mother's name.

The department's decision rested on a provision of Arkansas law, Ark.Code § 20–18–401 (2014), that specifies which individuals will appear as parents on a child's state-issued birth certificate. * * * "[I]f the mother was married at the time of either conception or birth," the statute instructs that "the name of [her] husband shall be entered on the certificate as the father of the child." § 20–18–401(f)(1). There are some limited exceptions to the latter rule—for example, another man may appear on the birth certificate if the "mother" and "husband" and "putative father" all file affidavits vouching for the putative father's paternity. *Ibid.* But as all parties agree, the requirement that a married woman's husband appear on her child's birth certificate applies in cases where the couple conceived by means of artificial insemination with the help of an anonymous sperm donor. * * *

The Jacobses and Pavans brought this suit in Arkansas state court against the director of the Arkansas Department of Health—seeking, among other things, a declaration that the State's birth-certificate law violates the Constitution. The trial court agreed, holding that the relevant portions of § 20–18–401 are inconsistent with *Obergefell* because they "categorically prohibi[t] every same-sex married couple . . . from enjoying the same spousal benefits which are available to every opposite-sex married couple." * * * But a divided Arkansas Supreme Court reversed that judgment, concluding that the statute "pass[es] constitutional muster." * * * In that court's view, "the statute centers on the relationship of the biological mother and the biological father to the child, not on the marital relationship of husband and wife," and so it "does not run afoul of *Obergefell*." * * *

The Arkansas Supreme Court's decision, we conclude, denied married same-sex couples access to the "constellation of benefits that the Stat[e] ha[s] linked to marriage." *Obergefell*, 576 U.S., at ___, 135 S.Ct., at 2601. As already explained, when a married woman in Arkansas conceives a child by means of artificial insemination, the State will—indeed, *must*—list the name of her male spouse on the child's birth certificate. See § 20–18–401(f)(1); see also § 9–10–201; *supra,* at ___. And yet state law, as interpreted by the court below, allows Arkansas officials in those very same circumstances to omit a married woman's female spouse from her child's birth certificate. * * * As a result, same-sex parents in Arkansas lack the same right as opposite-sex parents to be listed on a child's birth certificate, a document often used for important transactions like making medical decisions for a child or enrolling a child in school. * * *

Obergefell proscribes such disparate treatment. * * *

Echoing the court below, the State defends its birth-certificate law on the ground that being named on a child's birth certificate is not a benefit that attends marriage. Instead, the State insists, a birth certificate is simply a device for recording biological parentage—regardless of whether the child's parents are married. But Arkansas law makes birth certificates about more than just genetics. As already discussed, when an opposite-sex couple conceives a child by way of anonymous sperm donation—just as the petitioners did here—state law requires the placement of the birth mother's husband on the child's birth certificate. * * * And that is so even though (as the State concedes) the husband "is definitively not the biological father" in those circumstances. * * * Arkansas has thus chosen to make its birth certificates more than a mere marker of biological relationships: The State uses those certificates to give married parents a form of legal recognition that is not available to unmarried parents. Having made that choice, Arkansas may not, consistent with *Obergefell,* deny married same-sex couples that recognition.

* * * The judgment of the Arkansas Supreme Court is reversed, and the case is remanded for further proceedings not inconsistent with this opinion.

It is so ordered.

■ GORSUCH, J., with whom JUSTICE THOMAS and ALITO join, dissenting.

* * * To be sure, *Obergefell* addressed the question whether a State must recognize same-sex marriages. But nothing in *Obergefell* spoke (let alone clearly) to the question whether § 20–18–401 of the Arkansas Code, or a state supreme court decision upholding it, must go. The statute in question establishes a set of rules designed to ensure that the biological parents of a child are listed on the child's birth certificate. Before the state supreme court, the State argued that rational reasons exist for a biology based birth registration regime, reasons that in no way offend *Obergefell*—like ensuring government officials can identify public health trends and helping individuals determine their biological lineage, citizenship, or susceptibility to genetic disorders. In an opinion that did not in any way seek to defy but rather earnestly engage *Obergefell,* the state supreme court agreed. And it is very hard to see what is wrong with this conclusion for, just as the state court recognized, nothing in *Obergefell* indicates that a birth registration regime based on biology, one no doubt with many analogues across the country and throughout history, offends the Constitution. To the contrary, to the extent they speak to the question, at all, this Court's precedents suggest just the opposition conclusion. [Citing *Michael H. v. Gerald D.*] * * *

What, then, is at work here? If there isn't a problem with a biology based birth registration regime, perhaps the concern lies in this particular regime's exceptions. * * * Most importantly for our purposes, the State acknowledges that § 9–10–201 of the Arkansas Code controls how birth certificates are completed in cases of artificial insemination like the one before us. The State acknowledges, too, that this provision, written some time ago, indicates that the mother's husband generally shall be treated as the father—and in this way seemingly anticipates only opposite-sex marital unions.

But if the artificial insemination statute is the concern, it's still hard to see how summary reversal should follow for at least a few reasons. First, petitioners didn't actually challenge § 9–10–201[, the assisted reproduction statute,] in their lawsuit. * * * Second, though petitioners' lawsuit didn't challenge § 9–10–201, the State has repeatedly conceded that the benefits afforded nonbiological parents under § 9–10–201 must be afforded equally to both same-sex and opposite-sex couples. So that in this particular case and all others of its kind, the State agrees, the female spouse of the birth mother must be listed on birth certificates too. Third, further proof still of the state of the law in Arkansas today is the fact that, when it comes to adoption (a situation not present in this case but another one in which Arkansas departs from biology based registration), the State tells us that adopting parents are eligible for placement on birth certificates without respect to sexual orientation.

* * * I respectfully dissent.

NOTES ON *PAVAN*

1. *Who Was Right?* The dissent argues that the birth certificate statute is premised on biology and, therefore, refusal to list a same-sex spouse is permissible. As the majority explains, however, the basic rule set forth in the birth certificate statute—A.R.S. § 20–18–401—is not based on biology; it is based on *marriage*: "If the mother was married at the time of either conception or birth or between conception and birth the name of the husband shall be entered on the certificate as the father of the child."

Under the statute, the woman's husband *must be* listed on the child's birth certificate even if he is not the child's biological parent unless, essentially, someone else has been determined to be the child's second legal parent. This rule can and must be applied equally to female spouses, the per curiam opinion declared.

2. Pavan *and the Marital Presumption Question?* As noted above, in addition to the cases about how to complete birth certificates for children born to same-sex couples, courts around the country are grappling with a related by distinct question—whether the presumption that husbands are the legal parents of children born to their wives—can and must be applied equally to female spouses. Court decisions on the question, at least pre-*Pavan*, are split.

McLaughlin v. Jones, 240 Ariz. 560, 382 P.3d 118 (Ariz. Ct. App. 2016), *affirmed*, 401 P.3d 492 (Ariz. 2017). Some courts have reasoned, much like the *Pavan* majority, that if the marital presumption applies to husbands even if they are not genetic parents, then the presumption can and must be applied equally to female spouses. This is what one Arizona Court of Appeals concluded:

> Under § 25–814(A)(1)[, Arizona's marital presumption], the male spouse of a woman who delivers a child is the presumptive parent, and, therefore, a "legal parent" for purposes of § 25–401(4). If the female spouse of the birth mother of a child born to a same-

sex couple is not afforded the same presumption of parenthood as a husband in a heterosexual marriage, then the same-sex couple is effectively deprived of "civil marriage on the same terms and conditions as opposite-sex couples," particularly in terms of "safeguard[ing] children and families." *Obergefell*, ___ U.S. ___, 135 S.Ct. at 2600, 2605. * * * Mindful of our obligation to find statutes constitutional if possible, and given the language and purpose of § 25–814, we find it accommodates a gender-neutral application and *Obergefell* requires us to apply it in this manner.

Notwithstanding the use of male-specific terms such as "man," "paternity" and "father," a man's paternity under the statute and, therefore, his status as a legal parent under § 25–401(4) is not necessarily biologically based. Indeed, of the four circumstances specified in § 25–814(A) that give rise to the presumption of paternity, only subsection (A)(2) is based on the establishment of a biological connection between the man and the child through scientific testing. Section 25–814(A)(1) presumes paternity if the child is born during the marriage or within ten months thereafter. It does not require a biological connection between the father and child. The mere fact that the child was born during the marriage or shortly thereafter gives rise to the presumption of the husband's paternity, without regard to whether the husband is the biological parent. Similarly, neither subsection (A)(3), the father's signature on the birth certificate, nor (A)(4), acknowledgment of paternity, requires a biological link with the child. Both are based, instead, on the presumed father's declared intent to be the child's parent and thereby assume the responsibility of supporting the child.

The word "paternity" therefore signifies more than biologically established paternity. It encompasses the notion of parenthood, including parenthood voluntarily established without regard to biology. * * * The marital presumption is intended to assure that two parents will be required to provide support for a child born during the marriage. * * * The marital presumption of paternity serves the additional purpose of preserving the family unit. * * * These purposes and policies are equally served whether the child is born during the marriage of a heterosexual couple or to a couple of the same sex. *See Obergefell*, ___U.S. ___, 135 S.Ct. at 2600 (safeguarding children and families, which is among bases for protecting right to marriage, applies equally to same-sex as opposite-sex couples).

McLaughlin v. Jones, 240 Ariz. 560, 382 P.3d 118 (Ariz. Ct. App. 2016), *affirmed*, 401 P.3d 492 (Ariz. 2017). A number of other courts have agreed. *See, e.g., Barse v. Pasternek*, 2015 WL 600973 (Conn. Super. Ct. 2015).

***Turner v. Steiner*, 398 P.3d 110 (Ariz. Ct. App. 2017).** After the decision excerpted above was issued, a different Arizona Court of Appeals reached the opposite conclusion:

Here, * * * language [of the marital presumption, A.R.S. § 25–814,] clearly and unambiguously provides that it applies solely to men. The statute creates a presumption of "paternity." "Paternity" means "the fact or condition of being a father." Webster's II New College Dictionary 805 (2011). The statute further provides that a "man is presumed to be the father of a child" if one of the enumerated circumstances exists. Given their ordinary meanings, "man" means "an adult male human being," *id.* at 664, and "father" means "the male parent of a child," *id.* at 408. Each of these words is gender-specific to males and not applicable to females. * * *Notwithstanding the ordinary meaning of the statute's plain language, * * * Oakley argues that *Obergefell* nevertheless requires that the presumption statute be read gender-neutrally because it invalidates state laws "to the extent they exclude same-sex couples from civil marriage on the same terms and conditions as opposite-sex couples." 135 S. Ct. at 2605. But [this argument is flawed because] the purpose of the presumption statute is to assist in determining whether a man is a child's biological father, * * * not to broadly establish a term or condition associated with marriage. Thus, *Obergefell* does not mean that the presumption statute is unconstitutional unless its language is judicially interpreted gender-neutrally.The second flaw is that Oakley and the *McLaughlin* court misunderstand the role of biology in determining parentage in Arizona and in serving as the basis of the presumption statute. The *McLaughlin* court believed it could interpret the statute's obviously "male-specific terms" in a gender-neutral fashion because the presumptions were "not necessarily biologically based." * * * According to *McLaughlin*, the statute addresses more than mere paternity, and broadly encompasses "the notion of parenthood" "without regard to biology." *Id.* But this conclusion fails to recognize that—with the exception of adoption, which is not involved in this case—parentage in Arizona *is* determined by biology. * * *Moreover, biology—the biological difference between men and women—*is* the very reason the presumption statute exists. A child's mother is usually readily determined by a woman's biological act of giving birth. * * * Thus, Arizona does not need, and does not have, a "presumption of maternity" statute. But the act of birth reveals nothing about the identity of the child's biological father. *See Tuan Anh Nguyen v. I.N.S.*, 533 U.S. 53, 63 (2001) (noting that "fathers and mothers are not similarly situated with regard to proof of biological parenthood"). Consequently, to help determine whether a particular man is a child's father, the Legislature enacted the presumption of paternity statute. Given the statute's purpose, its limited application to men is not remarkable or constitutionally infirm. * * *

Other courts have agreed with this approach. *See, e.g., In the Interest of A.E.*, No. 09-16-00019-CV, 2017 WL 1535101, at *8 (Tex. App. Apr. 27, 2017)

("*Obergefell* did not hold that every state law related to the marital relationship or the parent-child relationship must be 'gender neutral.' ").

Which court is right? Why? Is this question about the application of the marital presumption to female spouses necessarily resolved by *Pavan*? Why or why not? On September 19, 2017, the Arizona Supreme Court affirmed the intermediate appellate court's decision in *McLaughlin*, holding that the "marital paternity presumption is a benefit of marriage, and following *Pavan* and *Obergefell*, the state cannot deny same-sex spouses the same benefits afforded opposite-sex spouses." *McLaughlin v. Jones*, 401 P.3d 492, at *5 (Ariz. 2017).

For excellent discussions of LGBT parentage issues in the post-*Obergefell* world, see Douglas NeJaime, "Marriage Equality and the New Parenthood," 129 *Harv. L. Rev.* 1185 (2016); June Carbone & Naomi Cahn, "Marriage and the Marital Presumption Post-*Obergefell*," 84 *UMKC L. Rev.* 663 (2016); Joanna L. Grossman, "Parentage Without Gender," 17 *Cardozo J. Conflict Resol.* 717 (2016); Leslie Joan Harris, "*Obergefell*'s Ambiguous Impact on Legal Parentage," 92 *Chi.-Kent L. Rev.* 55 (2017).

4. *Rebuttal of the Marital Presumption.* Typically, the marital presumption is "rebuttable," at least in some circumstances. That is, even if the husband is initially presumed to be a parent of a child born to his wife, under some circumstances a court can later determine that he is not a parent. In some states, the circumstances under which rebuttal is permitted are circumscribed by time and facts. In other states, rebuttal is more broadly permitted.

Assuming the marital presumption applies to a female spouse, under what circumstances should she be permitted to rebut the presumption?

In *McLaughlin*, the Arizona Supreme Court held that under the circumstances of that case, the female spouse was "estopped from rebutting the presumption":

> Here, Kimberly and Suzan agree that they intended for Kimberly to be artificially inseminated with an anonymous sperm donor and that Kimberly gave birth to E. during the marriage. During the pregnancy, they signed a joint parenting agreement declaring Suzan a "co-parent" of the child and their intent that the parenting relationship between Suzan McLaughlin and the child would continue if Suzan and Kimberly's relationship ended. After E.'s birth, Suzan stayed home to care for him during the first two years of his life. Thus, the undisputed facts unequivocally demonstrate that Kimberly intended for Suzan to be E.'s parent, that Kimberly conceived and gave birth to E. while married to Suzan, and that Suzan relied on this agreement when she formed a mother-son bond with E. and parented him from birth.

> * * * [B]ased on the facts of this case, we conclude that Kimberly is estopped from rebutting Suzan's presumptive parentage of E. * * * [T]o do otherwise would be patently unfair.

McLaughlin v. Jones, 401 P.3d 492, 2017 WL 4126939, at *8 (Ariz. Sept. 19, 2017).

In contrast, the *Turner* court held that even if the marital presumption applied, it would necessarily be rebutted by evidence that the female spouse was not a genetic parent:

> Because Oakley and other similarly-situated spouses are never biologically related to the children involved in the dissolution proceedings, even if the statute is read gender-neutrally, the other spouse will always defeat the presumption by proving that the former spouse is not biologically the child's parent.

> * * * Oakley [argued that] * * * A.R.S. § 25–814(C) should be interpreted in cases involving same-sex spouses to limit rebuttal evidence only to evidence that the biological mother had not consented to share parental rights with her spouse. But nothing in the language of that subsection indicates that rebuttal evidence should be so limited. Moreover, such an interpretation would mean that the statute would apply differently depending on whether the disputing parties are a same-sex or an opposite-sex couple. An opposite-sex spouse, for example, could defeat a presumption of paternity by presenting clear and convincing evidence that the presumed father is not the child's biological father. A same-sex spouse, in contrast, could rebut the presumption only by showing he or she did not consent to being a co-parent with the presumed parent. Nothing in A.R.S. § 25–814's language allows such an outcome, and such an interpretation of the statute would raise its own questions of equal protection of the laws.

Turner v. Steiner, 393 P.3d 110 (Ariz. Ct. App. 2017).

Should same-sex spouses be permitted to rebut the marital presumption? What evidence should rebut the presumption? Should evidence that the spouse is not a genetic parent necessarily rebut the presumption? Should it matter how long the spouse has parented the child? Under the UPA (2017), the marital presumption is conclusive after the child's second birthday. Is that a good rule?

5. *Legislative Developments.* In recent years, some states have amended their marital presumptions to clarify that they apply equally to all spouses— regardless of sex—of the woman who gave birth. For example, California Family Code Section 7611(a) provides:

> A person is presumed to be the natural parent of a child if * * *:
> (a) The presumed parent and the child's natural mother are or have been married to each other and the child is born during the marriage, or within 300 days after the marriage is terminated by death, annulment, declaration of invalidity, or divorce, or after a judgment of separation is entered by a court.

The relevant Uniform law—the Uniform Parentage Act (UPA)—was recently revised. Professor Courtney Joslin was the Reporter for the UPA (2017). One of the primary goals of the revision process is to update the Act so that it applies equally to same-sex couples and their children. The UPA (2017) follows the California approach. *See, e.g.*, UPA (2017), § 204(a)(1)(A) (providing that "[a]n individual is presumed to be a parent of a child if * * * the individual and the woman who gave birth to the child are married to each other and the child is born during the marriage * * * ").

One state has gone farther. Washington State amended its marital presumption so that it applies to a spouse (male or female) of a father. Wash. Rev. Code Ann. § 26.26.116 ("[A] person is presumed to be the parent of a child if: The person and the mother or father of the child are married to each other or in a domestic partnership with each other and the child is born during the marriage or domestic partnership.").

Professor Douglas NeJaime urges the adoption of a hybrid model. Professor NeJaime's model includes a "two-tiered system of marital presumptions":

> [F]irst, the person married to the woman giving birth at the time of the child's birth would be presumed the child's legal parent; second, the person married to the genetic parent at the time of the child's birth would be presumed to be the child's legal parent, if that person accepts the child into his or her home and openly holds the child out as his or her child. This approach would respect the gestational bonds of women, but at the same time account for the parental bonds of women who separate motherhood from biological connection.

Douglas NeJaime, "The Nature of Parenthood," 126 *Yale L.J.* 2260, 2347 (2017).

PROBLEM 7-4
POLICY: BEST RULE FOR THE MARITAL PRESUMPTION

You are a state legislator. The statutory marital presumption in your state refers only to the husband of the woman who gave birth. Would you support amending the presumption so that it applies to all spouses—male and female—of the woman who gave birth? Why or why not? Is the current statute unconstitutional? Why or why not?

Would you supporting amending the presumption so that it applies to the spouses of husbands like the provision in Washington State? Why or why not? What about Professor NeJaime's two-tiered marital presumption?

As you work through this problem, consider the following scenario: Bob has an affair with Carol. Carol becomes pregnant through sexual intercourse with Bob and gives birth to a child. After the birth of the child, the child primarily lives with Carol, but Bob has regular visitation in his house several days a week and the baby spends the night at his house once a week. Bob's wife, Ann, is present during the visitation and fully participates in caring for the baby.

Who should be considered the legal parents of the child? Bob and Carol, the genetic parents? Bob and his spouse? Why?

B. SURROGACY

Another way for LGBT people to bring children into their families is through surrogacy. Surrogacy is the process by which a woman agrees to gestate a fetus to term with the intention that she will relinquish the resulting child to the intended parent or parents after the child is born. Traditional or genetic surrogacy refers to an arrangement where the surrogate uses her own ova, and is therefore connected to the child through both gestation and genetics. Gestational surrogate refers to an arrangement where the ova are provided by an intended mother or a third-party provider. It is widely reported that most surrogacy arrangements in the U.S. are gestational surrogacy arrangements. Although there are no accurate statistics, some sources suggest that "as many as half [of children born through surrogacy] may be born to gay male couples." June Carbone & Naomi Cahn, "Marriage and the Marital Presumption Post-*Obergefell*," 84 *UMKC L. Rev.* 663, 670 (2016).

Determining the legal parentage of children born through surrogacy can be complicated, as states have staked out a wide range of positions on surrogacy. Some states not only ban surrogacy, but they impose criminal sanctions on parties involved in surrogacy arrangements. *See, e.g.*, Courtney G. Joslin, Shannon P. Minter, & Catherine Sakimura, *Lesbian, Gay, Bisexual, and Transgender Family Law* § 4:1. Other states permit some forms of surrogacy so long as the parties comply with an often long list of requirements. *Id.* And about half the states simply have no statutes clearly addressing the permissibility of surrogacy, or the parentage of children born through surrogacy. *Id.*

If the state permits married different-sex couples to enter into enforceable surrogacy arrangements, these rules must be applied equally to same-sex married couples. As a result, in some states, if the parties comply with all of the relevant rules, both gay male spouses may be recognized as legal parents to the resulting child. *See, e.g.*, Courtney G. Joslin, Shannon P. Minter, & Catherine Sakimura, Lesbian, Gay, *Bisexual, and Transgender Family Law* § 4:18 (2017). But, again, not all states permit surrogacy, even by married couples.

What happens if the parties participate in a surrogacy arrangement in a state that does not have any relevant statutes? Should the parties' agreement be enforceable? What if the surrogate changes her mind? Does she have a right to refuse to relinquish the child to the intended parent or parents?

Consider the still-leading case on the complicated legal and moral issues surrounding surrogacy.

In the Matter of Baby M.

New Jersey Supreme Court, 1988.
109 N.J. 396, 537 A.2d 1227.

■ The opinion of the Court was delivered by WILENTZ, J.

In this matter the Court is asked to determine the validity of a contract that purports to provide a new way of bringing children into a family. For a fee of $10,000, a woman agrees to be artificially inseminated with the semen of another woman's husband; she is to conceive a child, carry it to term, and after its birth surrender it to the natural father and his wife. The intent of the contract is that the child's natural mother will thereafter be forever separated from her child. The wife is to adopt the child, and she and the natural father are to be regarded as its parents for all purposes. The contract providing for this is called a "surrogacy contract," the natural mother inappropriately called the "surrogate mother." We invalidate the surrogacy contract because it conflicts with the law and public policy of this State. While we recognize the depth of the yearning of infertile couples to have their own children, we find the payment of money to a "surrogate" mother illegal, perhaps criminal, and potentially degrading to women. Although in this case we grant custody to the natural father, the evidence having clearly proved such custody to be in the best interests of the infant, we void both the termination of the surrogate mother's parental rights and the adoption of the child by the wife/stepparent. We thus restore the "surrogate" as the mother of the child. We remand the issue of the natural mother's visitation rights to the trial court, since that issue was not reached below and the record before us is not sufficient to permit us to decide it de novo.

[Richard Stern and Mary Beth Whitehead entered into a contract for Whitehead to bear a child using Stern's sperm and then to relinquish the child to Stern and his wife, Elizabeth Stern, in return for $10,000. Whitehead was successfully inseminated at a fertility center and gave birth to the child, a girl the Sterns named Melissa. Whitehead, however, became disconsolate when she relinquished the child to the Sterns. Fearing suicide, the Sterns allowed Whitehead to have custody of the child for five days. Whitehead and her husband fled with the child to Florida, where the Sterns found them and obtained the baby, through police intervention. The Sterns initiated a lawsuit to enforce the surrogacy contract, which the trial court granted. The trial court terminated Whitehead's parental rights.]

We have concluded that this surrogacy contract is invalid. Our conclusion has two bases: direct conflict with existing statutes and conflict with the public policies of this State, as expressed in its statutory and decisional law.

One of the surrogacy contract's basic purposes, to achieve the adoption of a child through private placement, though permitted in New Jersey "is very much disfavored." *Sees v. Baber*, 377 A.2d 628 (1977). Its use of money for this purpose—and we have no doubt whatsoever that the money is being paid to obtain an adoption and not, as the Sterns argue, for the personal services of Mary Beth Whitehead—is illegal and perhaps criminal. N.J.S.A. 9:3–54. In addition to the inducement of money, there is the coercion of contract: the natural mother's irrevocable agreement, prior to birth, even prior to conception, to surrender the child to the adoptive couple. Such an agreement is totally unenforceable in private placement adoption. *Sees.* Even where the adoption is through an approved agency, the formal agreement to surrender occurs only after birth (as we read N.J.S.A. 9:2–16 and –17, and similar statutes), and then, by regulation, only after the birth mother has been offered counseling. N.J.A.C. 10:121A–5.4(c). Integral to these invalid provisions of the surrogacy contract is the related agreement, equally invalid, on the part of the natural mother to cooperate with, and not to contest, proceedings to terminate her parental rights, as well as her contractual concession, in aid of the adoption, that the child's best interests would be served by awarding custody to the natural father and his wife—all of this before she has even conceived, and, in some cases, before she has the slightest idea of what the natural father and adoptive mother are like. * * *

The surrogacy contract's invalidity, resulting from its direct conflict with the above statutory provisions, is further underlined when its goals and means are measured against New Jersey's public policy. The contract's basic premise, that the natural parents can decide in advance of birth which one is to have custody of the child, bears no relationship to the settled law that the child's best interests shall determine custody. * * *

The surrogacy contract guarantees permanent separation of the child from one of its natural parents. Our policy, however, has long been that to the extent possible, children should remain with and be brought up by both of their natural parents. That was the first stated purpose of the previous adoption act. While not so stated in the present adoption law, this purpose remains part of the public policy of this State. This is not simply some theoretical ideal that in practice has no meaning. The impact of failure to follow that policy is nowhere better shown than in the results of this surrogacy contract. A child, instead of starting off its life with as much peace and security as possible, finds itself immediately in a tug-of-war between contending mother and father.

The surrogacy contract violates the policy of this State that the rights of natural parents are equal concerning their child, the father's right no greater than the mother's. "The parent and child relationship extends equally to every child and to every parent, regardless of the marital status of the parents." N.J.S.A. 9:17–40. As the Assembly Judiciary Committee noted in its statement to the bill, this section establishes "the principle that regardless of the marital status of the parents, all children *and all parents* have equal rights with respect to each other." Statement to Senate No. 888, Assembly Judiciary, Law, Public Safety and Defense Committee (1983) (emphasis supplied). The whole purpose and effect of the surrogacy contract was to give the father the exclusive right to the child by destroying the rights of the mother. * * *

The point is made that Mrs. Whitehead agreed to the surrogacy arrangement, supposedly fully understanding the consequences. Putting aside the issue of how compelling her need for money may have been, and how significant her understanding of the consequences, we suggest that her consent is irrelevant. There are, in a civilized society, some things that money cannot buy. In America, we decided long ago that merely because conduct purchased by money was "voluntary" did not mean that it was good or beyond regulation and prohibition. Employers can no longer buy labor at the lowest price they can bargain for, even though that labor is "voluntary," 29 U.S.C.A. § 206 (1982), or buy women's labor for less money than paid to men for the same job, 29 U.S.C.A. § 206(d), or purchase the agreement of children to perform oppressive labor, 29 U.S.C.A. § 212, or purchase the agreement of workers to subject themselves to unsafe or unhealthful working conditions, 29 U.S.C.A. §§ 651 to 678 (Occupational Safety and Health Act of 1970). There are, in short, values that society deems more important than granting to wealth whatever it can buy, be it labor, love, or life. Whether this principle recommends prohibition of surrogacy, which presumably sometimes results in great satisfaction to all of the parties, is not for us to say. We note here only that, under existing law, the fact that Mrs. Whitehead "agreed" to the arrangement is not dispositive.

The long-term effects of surrogacy contracts are not known, but feared—the impact on the child who learns her life was bought, that she is the offspring of someone who gave birth to her only to obtain money; the impact on the natural mother as the full weight of her isolation is felt along with the full reality of the sale of her body and her child; the impact on the natural father and adoptive mother once they realize the consequences of their conduct. Literature in related areas suggests these are substantial considerations, although, given the newness of surrogacy, there is little information.

The surrogacy contract is based on principles that are directly contrary to the objectives of our laws. It guarantees the separation of a child from its mother; it looks to adoption regardless of suitability; it totally ignores the child; it takes the child from the mother regardless of her wishes and her maternal fitness; and it does all of this, it accomplishes all of its goals, through the use of money.

Beyond that is the potential degradation of some women that may result from this arrangement. In many cases, of course, surrogacy may bring satisfaction, not only to the infertile couple, but to the surrogate mother herself. The fact, however, that many women may not perceive surrogacy negatively but rather see it as an opportunity does not diminish its potential for devastation to other women.

* * * [T]he proper bases for termination are found in the statute relating to proceedings by approved agencies for a termination of parental rights, N.J.S.A. 9:2–18, the statute allowing for termination leading to a private placement adoption, N.J.S.A. 9:3–48c(1), and the statute authorizing a termination pursuant to an action by DYFS, N.J.S.A. 30:4C–20. The statutory descriptions of the conditions required to terminate parental rights differ; their interpretation in case law, however, tends to equate them.

Nothing in this record justifies a finding that would allow a court to terminate Mary Beth Whitehead's parental rights under the statutory standard. It is not simply that obviously there was no "intentional abandonment or very substantial neglect of parental duties without a reasonable expectation of reversal of that conduct in the future," N.J.S.A. 9:3–48c(1), quite the contrary, but furthermore that the trial court never found Mrs. Whitehead an unfit mother and indeed affirmatively stated that Mary Beth Whitehead had been a good mother to her other children.

[Unlike the termination of parental rights issue, the custody issue turned entirely on the best interests of the child. Considering all the evidence, including the stability of the parents and the family unit and the ability to provide for the child, Justice Wilentz found that custody with the Sterns would best serve baby Melissa's interests.]

Postscript. On remand, the trial judge awarded custody of Melissa to the Sterns and gave Mary Beth Whitehead visitation rights. When she turned 18, in March 2004, Melissa terminated Mary Beth Whitehead's parental rights and formalized her maternal relationship with Elizabeth Stern through adoption proceedings. When she was in college, Melissa expressed great affection and loyalty to the Sterns and publicly distanced herself from the Whiteheads.

A.G.R. v. D.R.H. & S.H., No. FD–09–001838–07 (N.J. Super. Ct., Dec. 23, 2009). (Available at http://graphics8.nytimes.com/packages/pdf/national/20091231_SURROGATE.pdf.) *Baby M.* involved traditional or genetic surrogacy. But in *A.G.R.*, a New Jersey trial court held that the same principles apply to a gestational surrogacy arrangement.

The case involved a gay male couple—D.R. and S.H.—who had legally married in California and were registered domestic partners in New Jersey. D.R.'s sister, A.G.R., agreed to serve as a gestational carrier for the couple. S.H. provided the sperm and the eggs were provided by an anonymous woman. Before the embryo transfers occurred, A.G.R. signed a document entitled "Information Summary and Consent Form—Gestational Surrogacy," and all three parties signed a document entitled "Contract between a Genetic Father, and Intended Father, and a Gestational Carrier."

On October 4, 2006, A.G.R. gave birth to twin girls. On October 15, 2006, A.G.R. signed a "Consent to Judgment of Adoption." Eventually the situation broke down between the couple and A.G.R., and A.G.R. filed a lawsuit challenging the validity and enforceability of the parties' surrogacy arrangement. The men argued that *Baby M.* was distinguishable because here, the carrier had no genetic link to the resulting children. The court rejected this argument, concluding that just as was true in *Baby M.* the surrogacy contract was "directly contrary to the objectives of our laws." That being the case, the court held that the carrier "possesses parental rights under New Jersey law" and that "the gestational carrier agreement . . . is void and serves as no basis for termination of parental rights . . . and the consent to judgment of adoption is void."

NOTES ON CRITIQUES AND DEFENSES OF SURROGACY

1.   *Should Gestation Be Marketable?* In "The Regulation of the Market in Adoption," 67 *B.U. L. Rev.* 59 (1987), Richard Posner argued that laws prohibiting baby-selling and surrogacy are questionable, because they obstructed and drove underground a market in babies. *See also* Richard A. Posner, *Sex and Reason* 409–29 (1992). This line of argument is criticized from a libertarian point of view in Martha Field, *Surrogate Motherhood* (1990).

While such a market involves a much more precious good, human beings themselves, the truths of market dynamics are just as applicable: people's needs and preferences will be satisfied better through the market than through state regulation, and if the state prohibits something entirely a "black" market will emerge that is not only more costly but more abusive than the "free" market would be.

Even under the assumptions of Chicago School economics, however, the first part of Posner's argument holds only if the "free" market is a well-functioning one. Is the market for babies a well-functioning market? For example, do women who agree to serve as surrogate carriers properly value ex ante any loss she may feel upon relinquishing the resulting child? Mary Beth Whitehead said the answer to that question was no. Empirical studies, however, have "repeatedly demonstrated that the vast majority of surrogacy arrangements are successfully executed and consented to by women who are financially and psychologically stable." Lina Peng, "Surrogate Mothers: An Exploration of the Empirical and the Normative," 21 *Am. U.J. Gender Soc. Pol'y & L.* 555, 559–60 (2013). *See also id.* at 563 ("Out of 25,000 surrogacy arrangements estimated to have taken place since the 1970s, less than one percent of surrogate mothers have changed their minds. . . . The majority of surrogates have reported high satisfaction with the process and report no psychological problems as a result of relinquishment.").

Others argued that the intrinsic nature of bearing children is so different from other labor that it should be "market inalienable." *See* Margaret Radin, "Market Inalienability," 100 *Harv. L. Rev.* 1849 (1987). What might be called "reproductive labor" is different along several dimensions, such as the genetic connection between the "laborer" and the "product" and the duration of the "enterprise." This argument is also the cornerstone of the natural law philosophy we surveyed in Chapter 3, Section 1: whatever the costs and the benefits of a market in babies, commodifying the most deeply human of acts is profoundly immoral and must be resisted by the state. (From a natural law point of view, should the state prohibit or regulate artificial insemination more generally?)

In the early years of surrogacy practice, some feminists such as Professor Radin agreed with the natural law conclusion, but for modern philosophical reasons. Carole Pateman, *The Sexual Contract* 206–18 (1988) and Elizabeth Anderson, "Is Women's Labor a Commodity?," *Phil. & Pub. Affs.*, Winter 1990, at 71–92, maintained the key difference is that reproductive labor is more integral to a woman's identity than other labor; hence, selling this capacity sacrifices a woman's dignity. *See also* Judith Areen, "Baby M Reconsidered," 76 *Geo. L.J.* 1741 (1988). But how is selling the use of one's reproductive system more undignified than selling the temporary use of other intimate body parts, as women do when they pose for magazines such as *Playboy* or *Hustler*? Are a woman's ideas not integral to her identity as well—yet we would not regulate her ability to market them, or even change them for monetary consideration, right? Like religious and most natural law philosophers, Anderson and Pateman treat sexuality as unique, to be guarded by the state if not by the woman. Is this too close to old-fashioned (male) attitudes about women's sexuality to be considered feminist? Even more controversial is the idea that the body is sacred and to be regulated much more than the mind.

Over time, however, feminist opposition to surrogacy waned. Many feminists came to the conclusion that "support for restrictions on surrogacy undermined pro-choice advocacy." Elizabeth S. Scott, "Surrogacy and the Politics of Commodification," 72 *Law & Contemp. Probs.* 109, 144 (2009).

2. *Is Compensated Surrogacy Baby Selling?* New Jersey, like all other states, prohibits "baby-selling" in the context of adoption. The *Baby M.* court concluded that compensated surrogacy is a form of prohibited baby selling. Not all courts have agreed. In *Johnson v. Calvert*, the California Supreme Court wrote the following:

> Gestational surrogacy differs in crucial respects from adoption. . . . The parties voluntarily agreed to participate in in vitro fertilization and related medical procedures before the child was conceived; at the time when Anna entered into the contract, therefore, she was not vulnerable to financial inducements to part with her own expected offspring. . . . Anna was not the genetic mother of the child. The payments to Anna under the contract were meant to compensate her for her services in gestating the fetus and undergoing labor, rather than for giving up 'parental' rights to the child. Payments were made both during pregnancy and after the child's birth. We are, accordingly, unpersuaded that the contract

used in this case violates the public policies embodied in the [baby selling statute] and the adoption statutes.

Johnson v. Calvert, 851 P.2d 776, 784 (1993). Which court got it right? Why?

California now permits gestational surrogacy by statute. Cal. Fam. Code § 7692.

3.   *Exploitation of Women?* In the early years of surrogacy, many scholars raised concerns about the possibility that wealthy white families would utilize poor women of color to serve as their surrogate carriers. For example, Anita Allen, "The Black Surrogate Mother," 8 *Harv. Blackletter J.* 17, 30 (1991), predicted that "[m]inority women increasingly will be sought to serve as 'mother machines' for embryos of middle and upper-class clients. It's a new virulent form of racial and class discrimination. Within a decade, thousands of poor and minority women will likely be used as a 'breeder class' for those who can afford $30,000 to $40,000 to avoid the inconvenience and danger of pregnancy." Scholars were concerned not only about the potential exploitation of poor women, but also about the "commodification of bodies of color for white benefit." Khiara M. Bridges, "*Windsor*, Surrogacy, and Race," 89 *Wash. L. Rev.* 1125, 1134 (2016).

Fears that surrogacy would "result in a class of indigent black women being used for the benefit of wealth white people were not realized." *Id.* at 1139. Instead, in the U.S., surrogate carriers "tend to be fairly well educated, financially stable, white women who choose to become surrogates for a plethora of reasons; very rarely do those reasons involve financial imperatives." *Id.*

In responses to arguments against surrogacy based on concerns of financial exploitation, others, including Carmel Shalev, *Birthpower* (1989), and Lori Andrews, *Between Strangers: Surrogate Mothers, Expectant Fathers, and Brave New Babies* (1989), develop a liberal feminist case in favor of surrogacy. Shalev and Andrews reject the idea that the state should protect women from using any of their natural endowments for economic gain. (One can recall that earlier "protective" legislation, such as special maximum hour laws for women, operated to deny women economic opportunities.) They argue that the market should be neutral as between competing conceptions of human relationships, as it should be for abortion, to take a primary example. Surrogacy is a potentially large source of wealth for women, and women who choose ought to be able to take advantage of it. Recall, however, Carol Rose's model of bargaining relations between men and women, in which women systematically fail to achieve equitable deals (Chapter 4, Section 2A). One might be more pessimistic than Andrews and Shalev about how much of an economic bonanza contract pregnancy would be for women. These authors might respond that women's bargaining strategies—the key assumption in Rose's model—might themselves change over time.

Relatedly, some have argued that refusing to respect the choices that women make about their bodies "carries overtones of the reasoning that for centuries prevented women from attaining equal economic rights and professional status under the law." *Johnson v. Calvert*, 851 P.3d 776 (Cal.

1993) (finding that the legal parents of a child born through gestational surrogacy were the intended parents).

4. *Surrogacy and Conceptions of Families and Parenthood?* As noted above, today the most common form of surrogacy is gestational surrogacy. Gestational surrogacy separates not only gestation from parenthood, but it also separates genetics from gestation. In so doing, gestational surrogacy makes "reproductive biology less central to legal parenthood." Douglas NeJaime, "The Nature of Parenthood," 126 *Yale L.J.* 2260 (2017). Normatively, is this a positive or a negative development?

5. *Genetic Surrogacy.* What about genetic (also referred to as "traditional") surrogacy? Should the same rules apply to both genetic and gestational surrogacy arrangements? Why or why not? Very few states statutorily permit genetic surrogacy and in the few states that do, they generally apply different, more stringent rules to such arrangements. Should genetic and gestational surrogacy be treated differently? Why or why not?

PROBLEM 7-5
THE CONSTITUTIONALITY OF CRIMINAL SURROGACY LAWS

Michigan criminalizes some uncompensated surrogacy agreements, and all compensated surrogacy agreements. Any non-surrogate party who enters into or helps form a surrogacy agreement—uncompensated or compensated—in which the surrogate is an unemancipated minor or has been diagnosed as mentally retarded, mentally ill, or developmentally disabled, commits a felony and is subject to a maximum fine of $50,000 and/or imprisonment of up to five years. Mich. Comp. Laws § 722.857. A party to a compensated surrogacy contract is guilty of a misdemeanor and subject to a maximum fine of $10,000 and/or imprisonment of up to one year. *Id.* § 722.859. A non-party who "induces, arranges, procures, or otherwise assists in the formation" of a compensated surrogacy agreement is guilty of a felony and subject to a maximum fine of $50,000 and/or imprisonment of up to five years. *Id.*

Celia and Nick Lopez are a married couple who would like to have biological children, but carrying a fetus to term would, according to her doctors, pose a threat to Celia's life. Celia's sister agrees to carry an embryo consisting of Celia's egg fertilized by Nick's sperm but needs $3000 to compensate her for probable lost time from her job; Celia and Nick are delighted to pay her—but they worry that such payment might fall athwart Michigan's criminal laws, so they bring a declaratory judgment action seeking judicial guidance.

Would a judge construe Michigan's statutes to criminalize this plan? Would such application be constitutional as applied to the Lopezes? *See Doe v. Attorney General*, 194 Mich.App. 432, 487 N.W.2d 484, 486–87 (1992).

C. PARENTAGE AND UN-MARRIED LGBT PEOPLE

Unmarried partners who participate in assisted reproduction are even more legally vulnerable. As discussed above, in some states, an unmarried LGBT partner can establish his or her legal parentage through a second-parent adoption. But adoptions often are expensive, and they can't be completed until after the child's birth, and they are not available in all states. Are there ever circumstances under which both members of an unmarried same-sex couple will be recognized as legal parents, even in the absence of a second-parent adoption?

In most states, the laws governing the parentage of children born through assisted reproduction expressly address only married couples. *See, e.g.*, Or. Rev. Stat. Ann. § 109.243 ("The relationship, rights and obligation between a child born as a result of artificial insemination and the mother's husband shall be the same to all legal intents and purposes as if the child had been naturally and legitimately conceived by the mother and the mother's husband if the husband consented to the performance of artificial insemination.").

While there are few decisions on a point, some courts have expressly refused to apply such provisions equally to unmarried partners. For example, in a recent case, an Oregon intermediate appellate court held that Oregon's provision (cited above) can be applied to an unmarried partner only if that person can demonstrate that, at the time of the consent, the person was precluded from marrying her partner and the partners "would have chosen to marry before the child's birth had they been permitted to." *In re Madrone*, 350 P.3d 495, 501 (Or. App. Ct. 2015).

It is this right? Is it permissible to refuse to apply ART provisions equally to unmarried couples? What arguments could a party raise to challenge such an interpretation of an ART statute?

A small but growing number of states now have ART statutes that apply equally to married and unmarried couples. The District of Columbia now provides for this possibility. For an in-depth discussion of the D.C. law, see Nancy D. Polikoff, "A Mother Should Not Have to Adopt Her Own Child Parentage Laws for Children of Lesbian Couples in the Twenty-First Century," 5 *Stan. J. Civ. Rts. & Civ. Libs.* 201 (2009).

Under D.C. law, a child born to a woman is by operation of law also the legal child of a second female parent if (1) the second parent is married to the biological mother; (2) the second parent is the domestic partner of the biological mother; or (3) the biological mother and the second parent agree that both women are to be parents for the child. D.C. Code § 16–909. The agreement may be in writing or evidenced by the couple rearing the child in a common household and holding themselves to be the parents of the child.

Nevada recently enacted a similar law. Under the Nevada law: "A person who provides gametes for, or consents to, assisted reproduction by a woman . . . , with the intent to be a parent of her child is a parent of the resulting child." Nev. Rev. Stat. Ann. § 126.670 (West). *See also* Cal. Fam. Code § 7613(a); N.M. Stat. Ann. § 45–2–120(F); Wash. Rev. Code Ann. § 26.26.710.

Are there other ways by which a person might be recognized as the legal parent of a child born to or adopted by his or her unmarried same-sex partner? Consider the following case.

Bani Chatterjee v. Taya King

New Mexico Supreme Court, 2012.
280 P.3d 283.

■ CHÁVEZ, JUSTICE.

Bani Chatterjee (Chatterjee) and Taya King (King) are two women who were in a committed, long-term domestic relationship when they agreed to bring a child into their relationship. * * * [D]uring the course of their relationship, and with Chatterjee's active participation, King adopted a child (Child) from Russia. Chatterjee supported King and Child financially, lived in the family home, and co-parented Child for a number of years before * * * they dissolved their relationship. Chatterjee never adopted Child. After they ended their relationship, King moved to Colorado and sought to prevent Chatterjee from having any contact with Child.

Chatterjee filed a petition in the district court to establish parentage and determine custody and timesharing (Petition). Chatterjee alleged that she was a presumed natural parent under the former codification of the New Mexico Uniform Parentage Act. * * * [In response,] King * * * argued that Chatterjee was a third party * * * and that [New Mexico statutes] * * * prohibit[ ] a third party from receiving custody rights absent a showing of unfitness of the natural or adoptive parent. * * *

We conclude, based on the facts and circumstances of this case, that the facts pleaded by Chatterjee are sufficient to confer standing on her as a natural mother because (1) the plain language of the UPA instructs courts to apply Section 40–11–5(A)(4), which specifies criteria for establishing a presumption that a man is a natural parent, to women because it is practicable for a woman to hold a child out as her own by, among other things, providing full-time emotional and financial support for the child; (2) commentary by the drafters of the UPA supports application of the provisions related to determining paternity to the determination of maternity; (3) the approach in this opinion is consistent with how courts in other jurisdictions have interpreted their UPAs, which contain language similar to the New Mexico UPA; and (4) New Mexico's public policy is to encourage the support of children, financial and otherwise, by providers willing and able to care for the child.* * *

[**II.**] * * * Chatterjee argues that the Court of Appeals erred in holding that none of the UPA provisions relating to the father and child relationship may be applied to women. She claims that this holding directly contradicts the plain language of Section 40–11–21 [which provides that "Insofar as practicable, the provisions of the Uniform Parentage Act applicable to the father and child relationship apply [to the existence or nonexistence of a mother and child relationship].") King responds that the UPA provisions establishing paternity should not be applied to women because the UPA expressly provides the ways in which maternity can be established. We agree with Chatterjee. * * *

The Court of Appeals held that reading Section 40–11–21 to allow Chatterjee to establish parentage through Section 40–11–5(A)(4) was impracticable. * * * We disagree.

* * * Section 40–11–5(A)(4), which establishes a parental presumption, is reasonably capable of being accomplished by either a man or a woman. Section 40–11–5(A)(4) provides, in relevant part, that "[a] man is presumed to be the natural father of a child if . . . while the child is under the age of majority, he openly holds out the child as his natural child and has established a personal, financial or custodial relationship with the child." Because the presumption is based on a person's conduct, not a biological connection, a woman is capable of holding out a child as her natural child and establishing a personal, financial, or custodial relationship with that child. This is particularly true when, as is alleged in this case, the relationship between the child and both the presumptive and the adoptive parent occurred simultaneously. * * *

Moreover, we seek to avoid an interpretation of a statute that would raise constitutional concerns. * * * In this case, the Court of Appeals' reading would yield different results for a man than for a woman in precisely the same situation. If this Court interpreted Section 40–11–5(A)(4) as applying only to males, then a man in a same-sex relationship claiming to be a natural parent because he held out a child as his own would have standing simply by virtue of his gender, while a woman in the same position would not. * * * We avoid this disparate treatment, giving effect to the Legislature's intent, with a plain and simple application of Section 40–11–5(A)(4) to both men and women under Section 40–11–21.

* * * The authors of the Uniform Parentage Act of 1973 (the original UPA), anticipating situations such as this case, provided in a comment that masculine terminology was used for the sake of simplicity and not to limit application of its provisions to males. * * *.

Because Section 40–11–21 instructs courts to apply provisions relating to the father and child relationship to mother and child relationships, then Section 40–11–5(A)(4) must also be applied to women.

* * * In *Elisa B. v. Superior Court*, 37 Cal.4th 108, 33 Cal.Rptr.3d 46, 117 P.3d 660, 666–67 (2005), the California Supreme Court held that it is practicable to apply the hold out provision of the California UPA— equivalent to the provision at issue in this case—to women. * * * Since *Elisa B.* was decided, California has applied the hold out provision to women in varying factual situations [including to situations w]ith a fact pattern similar to the case before us[.] * * *

As [other courts have explained] * * * the state has a strong interest in ensuring that a child will be cared for, financially and otherwise, by two parents. *Id.* at 1039, 1042. * * * This is one of the primary reasons that the original UPA was created, and it makes little sense to read the statute without keeping this overarching legislative goal in mind. * * *

The original UPA was also written to address the interest that children have in their own support. The rationale underlying the original UPA is that every child should be treated equally, regardless of the marital status of the child's parents. *See* Unif. Parentage Act § 2, § 2 cmt. (1973). In deciding illegitimacy cases, the United States Supreme Court recognized that it is "illogical and unjust" for a state to deny a child's essential right to be supported by two parents simply because the child's parents are not married. *Gomez v. Perez*, 409 U.S. 535, 538, 93 S.Ct. 872, 35 L.Ed.2d 56 (1973) * * *.

Consistent with the underlying policy-based rationale of the New Mexico UPA that equality in child welfare requires laws that achieve equality in parentage, Child's need for love and support is no less critical simply because her second parent * * * [is not her biological parent]. * * *

Indeed, New Mexico courts have long recognized that children may form parent-child bonds with persons other than their [biological] parents. This Court has previously recognized that a grandfather could be awarded custody over a biological father's objections. We have also held that a trial court had the power to award custody to an uncle with whom a child had bonded over the biological mother's objection, even absent the mother's unfitness.

Additionally, the New Mexico Court of Appeals has already embraced the idea of a child having two mothers in appropriate situations [citing *A.C. v. C.B.*, 113 N.M. 581, 585, 829 P.2d 660, 664 (Ct.App.1992), and *Barnae v. Barnae*, 1997-NMCA-077, ¶ 10, 123 N.M. 583, 943 P.2d 1036]. As such, Chatterjee should not be disqualified from being a presumed parent simply because she is a woman.

It is inappropriate to deny Chatterjee the opportunity to establish parentage, when denying Chatterjee this opportunity would only serve to harm both Child and the state. In our view, it is against public policy to deny parental rights and responsibilities based solely on the sex of either or both of the parents. The better view is to recognize that the child's best interests are served when intending parents physically, emotionally, and financially support the child from the time the child comes into their lives. This is especially true when both parents are able and willing to care for the child. Therefore, we hold that the Legislature intended that Section 40–11–5(A)(4) be applied to a woman who is seeking to establish a natural parent and child relationship with a child whom she has held out as her natural child from the moment the child came into the lives of both the adoptive mother and the presumptive mother.

* * * [III.] We recognize that presumptions under Section 40–11–5 may be rebutted by clear and convincing evidence. *See* § 40–11–5(C). However, the presumption of parentage should only be rebutted *in an appropriate action. See* § 40–11–5(C).

Our Legislature has not defined "appropriate action," but sister jurisdictions with similar UPA provisions are instructive. In *In re Nicholas H.*, 28 Cal.4th 56, 120 Cal.Rptr.2d 146, 46 P.3d 932 (2002), the California Supreme Court held that a presumed father's admission that he was not the child's biological father did not necessarily rebut the presumption of fatherhood that arose by receiving the child into his home and openly holding out the child as his own. *Id.* at 937, 941. * * *

The California Supreme Court also considered the appropriateness of rebutting the presumption of parenthood in *Elisa B.*, 33 Cal.Rptr.3d 46, 117 P.3d at 669[, in which two women had children together through assisted reproduction]. The court upheld the presumption, despite clear and convincing evidence that the petitioner was not the biological mother of the children, for three reasons. First, the court concluded that this was not an appropriate action in which to rebut the presumption "because she actively participated in causing the children to be conceived with the understanding that she would raise the children as her own together with the birth mother." *Id.* at 670. Second, the petitioner voluntarily expressed an intention to accept the responsibilities and enjoy the benefits of parenthood together with her partner from before the children were conceived through the first years of the children's lives. *Id.* Finally, there was no competition from any other person claiming to be the children's second parent. *Id.* Allowing rebuttal of the presumption in that case would have left the children without the support of a second parent, and that responsibility would ultimately fall to the county if the petitioner did not assume it. *Id.* [Courts in Colorado and Washington also] consider[ ] the appropriateness of the action before allowing an action rebutting a presumption to move forward. * * *

Likewise in New Mexico, biology does not exclusively determine who is a "natural parent," whether that person is male or female, under the New Mexico UPA. * * *

Because we do not reach the merits of this case, we do not decide whether the district court action in which Chatterjee would seek to establish parentage would be an appropriate court proceeding in which to rebut her presumption of parentage, if indeed she is able to establish the presumption. We do, however, find persuasive the factors considered by courts in California, Colorado, and Washington. * * *

We reverse the Court of Appeals and remand this case to the district court for further proceedings consistent with this opinion.

NOTES ON THE "HOLDING OUT" PROVISION

1. *Case Law Developments.* In 2005, the California Supreme Court became the first state high court in the country to hold that the so-called "holding out" provision could be applied to a same-sex partner. *Elisa B. v. Superior Court*, 37 Cal.4th 108 (Cal. 2005). For a fascinating history of the evolution of parentage law in California, see Douglas NeJaime, "Marriage Equality and the New Parenthood," 129 *Harv. L. Rev.* 1185 (2016).

Since then, courts in a number of other states (in addition to New Mexico) have applied their state's version of the "holding out" provision to same-sex functional, but nonbiological parents. *See, e.g.*, *In re Guardianship of Madelyn B.*, 166 N.H. 453, 459, 98 A.3d 494, 499 (2014); *In re Parental Responsibilities of A.R.L.*, 318 P.3d 581 (Colo. Ct. App. 2013).

Many scholars support the development and expansion of this line of cases. *See, e.g.*, Nancy D. Polikoff, "From Third Parties to Parents: The Case of Lesbian Couples and their Children," 77 *Law & Contemp. Probs.* 195, 220 (2014) (arguing that "the importance of stability and continuity is precisely the principle that demands that the law recognize the reality of the child's perspective on his or her family"). *But see* Katherine K. Baker, "Quacking Like a Duck? Functional Parenthood Doctrine and Same-Sex Parents," 92 *Chi.-Kent L. Rev.* 135, 135 (2017) (arguing that "a functional approach to determining legal parentage is inherently problematic, especially for those concerned with expanding legal recognition of non-traditional family forms").

2. *Legislative Developments. Chatterjee* and the other cases cited above all applied the holding out provision based on the 1973 version of the Uniform Parentage Act (UPA). Section 4 of the 1973 UPA provides that "[a] man is presumed to be the natural father of a child if . . . (4) while the child is under the age of majority, he receives the child into his home and openly holds the child out as his natural child." UPA (1973), § 4(a)(4). Approximately 19 states adopted the UPA (1973).

The UPA was revised in 2002, and again in 2017. The UPA (2002) continued to include a holding out provision, but it added a two-year time requirement. UPA (2002), § 204(a)(5) ("A man is presumed to be the father of a child if . . . for the first two years of the child's life, he resided in the same household with the child and openly held out the child as his own.").

Should states adopt a "holding out" provision? Why or why not? If so, which one?

3. *Gender.* The *Chatterjee* court concludes that the holding out provision must be applied equally to women, even though if refers only to men and fathers. Is this the correct conclusion as a matter of statutory construction? Would it be constitutional to apply the holding out provision only to men?

The UPA (2017) carries over the holding out provision with the two-year requirement, but makes the provision apply equally, without regard to gender. UPA (2017), § 204(a)(2) ("the *individual* resided in the same household with the child for the first two years of the life of the child, including any period of temporary absence, and openly held out the child as the individual's child." (emphasis added)).

D. GAMETE PROVIDERS

When people have children using assisted reproduction, there may be questions about the legal parental status of any third-party gamete providers (that is, the people who provided the semen or ova). Under what circumstances is the gamete provider considered a legal parent of the child? The answer varies from state to state, and may depend upon the circumstances of the conception and/or the parties' conduct.

In some states, a known sperm provider may be considered a legal parent even if all the parties, including the gamete provider, wish otherwise. For example, this may be the result in New York under some circumstances. New York has no statute addressing the legal status of gamete providers. *See, e.g.*, Courtney G. Joslin, Shannon P. Minter & Catherine Sakimura, *Lesbian, Gay, Bisexual, and Transgender Family Law* § 3:22 (2017).

Even in jurisdictions that have statutes addressing the legal status of gamete providers, the gamete provider may be considered a legal parent—possibly against his, and maybe everyone's wishes—if the parties do not comply with the statutory requirements. For example, many states have statutes providing that a sperm provider is not considered a parent of the resulting child if the sperm is provided to a licensed doctor. *See, e.g.*, N.J. Stat. Ann. § 9:17–44(b) ("Unless the donor of semen and the woman have entered into a written contract to the contrary, the donor of semen provided to a licensed physician for use in artificial insemination of a woman other than the donor's wife is treated in law as if he were not the father of a child thereby conceived and shall have no rights or duties stemming from the conception of a child."). In jurisdictions with similar rules, if the sperm is not first provided to a licensed doctor, then the donor may be considered a legal parent of the resulting child, even if that is contrary to the wishes of the parties, and, possibly, even if they entered into a written agreement to the contrary. *See, e.g., Jhordan C. v. Mary K.*, 179 Cal. App. 3d 386, 389 (Ct. App. 1986) (holding that a man who provided sperm to a lesbian couple could be determined to be a legal parent to the resulting child where the sperm was not provided to a licensed physician, as required by the law then in effect).

Because this rule—protecting the donor only when the sperm was provided to a doctor—sometimes produces results that are inconsistent with the parties' intentions, some states have now done away with the physician involvement requirement. In these states, the sperm or ova provider will not be considered a legal parent if he or she did not intend to be a parent of the resulting child. *See, e.g.*, Nev. Rev. Stat. Ann. § 126.660 (West) ("A donor is not a parent of a child conceived by means of assisted reproduction.").

What should the rule be? Should the same rule apply to both semen and ova providers?

The following case considers the parental status of a sperm provider in a state with no relevant statutory law. (That was the case in 1994, and it remains so today.)

In re Thomas S. v. Robin Y.

New York Supreme Court, Appellate Division, First Department, 1994.
209 A.D.2d 298, 618 N.Y.S.2d 356.

■ Memorandum Decision. * * *

The child, Ry R.-Y., now 12 years old, lives with her mother, respondent Robin Y., the mother's lifetime companion, Sandra R., and Sandra's child, Cade, now 14, who was also conceived through artificial insemination by a donor known to her mother. Petitioner, who is also gay, was sought out by Robin Y. as a known donor and, after several attempts in both New York and California, Robin Y. successfully inseminated herself with petitioner's semen in February 1981 at the home of a mutual friend.

Ry was born on November 16, 1981 in San Francisco, where the household temporarily relocated in connection with Sandra R.'s employment. Like Cade, Ry was given the last names of R. and Y. Petitioner [Thomas] is not listed on Ry's birth certificate, and R. and Y. paid all expenses associated with the pregnancy and delivery. Petitioner was, however, informed of the birth and brought congratulatory flowers to R. and Y.'s home. Later that year, the household moved back to New York where they currently occupy an apartment located in a building owned by Sandra R.

For the first three years of her life, petitioner saw Ry only once or twice while in New York on business. In accordance with an oral agreement with R. and Y., he did not call, support or give presents to her during this period. When Cade, at the age of approximately five years, started asking questions about her father, R. and Y., as they had agreed between themselves, made arrangements for Ry and Cade to meet their biological fathers.

Petitioner testified that there were approximately 26 visits with the R. and Y. family over the following six-year period, ranging in duration from a few days to two weeks. Robin Y. estimates that appellant spent a total of sixty days with the R.-Y. family over the course of those six years, and petitioner estimates 148 days. Whatever the figure, it appears that all parties concerned developed a comfortable relationship with one another. Photographs included in the exhibits depict a warm and amicable relationship between petitioner and Ry, and there are numerous cards and letters from Ry to petitioner in which she expressed her love for him.

In July 1990, petitioner asked Robin Y. for permission to take Ry and Cade to see his parents and stay at a beach house with some of his siblings and their children. It seems that petitioner felt awkward about introducing R. and Y. to his parents. R. and Y., however, were not willing to allow petitioner to take the girls unless the mothers accompanied them.

It was apparently during the course of these negotiations that petitioner revealed his desire to establish a paternal relationship with Ry. Y. and R. regarded this as a breach of their oral agreement, insisting that visitation continue on the same terms as over the past six years, viz., with their supervision. They also rejected petitioner's suggestion to consult a family counselor or mediator. Unable to resolve his differences with R. and Y. and unable to see his daughter for a period of several months, petitioner moved, by order to show cause, for an order of filiation and for visitation.

During the course of the proceedings, Family Court ordered blood tests and a psychiatric evaluation of Ry. Petitioner, Robin Y. and Ry all submitted to blood genetic marker tests pursuant to Family Court Act § 532. The tests indicated a 99.9% probability of petitioner's paternity. Psychiatric evaluation revealed a belief on Ry's part that any relationship with petitioner would necessarily disrupt her relationship with Robin Y. and Sandra R. and might therefore undermine the legitimacy of her perception of the family unit. It also revealed that, since these proceedings were instituted, Ry has expressed a desire to end all contact with petitioner.

Family Court found by clear and convincing evidence, based upon the blood tests, that petitioner is the biological father of Ry. Nevertheless, citing the doctrine of equitable estoppel, the court refused to enter an order of filiation and dismissed the proceeding. The court characterized petitioner as an "outsider attacking her [Ry's] family and refusing to give it respect," concluding that "a declaration of paternity would be a statement that her family is other than what she knows it to be and needs it to be" and, therefore, "would not be in her best interests." The court added, "Even were there an adjudication of paternity, I would deny [petitioner's] application for visitation."

It is appropriate to begin with the observation that the effect of Family Court's order is to cut off the parental rights of a man who is conceded by all concerned—the child, her mother and the court—to be the biological father. The legal question that confronts us is not, as Family Court framed it, whether an established family unit is to be broken up. Custody of the child is not now, and is unlikely ever to be, an issue between the parties. Rather the question is whether the rights of a biological parent are to be terminated. Absent strict adherence to statutory provisions, termination of those rights is in violation of well established standards of due process and cannot stand.

The asserted sanctity of the family unit is an uncompelling ground for the drastic step of depriving petitioner of procedural due process. Whatever concerns and misgivings Family Court and the dissenters may entertain about visitation, custody and the child's best interests, it is clear that they are appropriately reserved for a later stage of the proceedings. * * *

The reasoning advanced by the dissent to obviate further proceedings involves the predetermination of the very issues that would normally be resolved by hearings on visitation and, if warranted, termination of parental rights. Without the order of filiation to which the law entitles him, petitioner lacks standing to seek visitation (Family Ct. Act § 549) or challenge respondent's (and the dissent's) concept of what may or may not be in the child's best interests (Social Services Law § 384–b). * * *

Even more disturbing is the suggestion that the judicial process will pose "severe traumatic consequences" to the child whose interests it is designed to protect. Petitioner is portrayed by the dissent as the villain of this case for having the temerity to request that Ry and her sister accompany him on an unsupervised visit to meet his parents, causing a "rift" and precipitating this litigation. The record, however, indicates that it was Robin Y. and Sandra S. who opposed this visit and does not reflect any initial resistance on the part of Ry. It was only some period of time after Robin Y. and Sandra S. refused petitioner any further visitation with his daughter that Ry developed overt animosity towards the man she had called "Dad" and regarded with great affection. As the Court of Appeals has noted, "The desires of young children, capable of distortive manipulation by a bitter, or perhaps even well-meaning, parent, do not always reflect the long-term best interest of the children" (*Matter of Nehra v. Uhlar*, 43 N.Y.2d 242, 249). * * *

* * * [T]he extent of petitioner's involvement in Ry's life is at once characterized by the dissent as both inadequate and overly intrusive. He is vilified for failing to sufficiently undertake his parental responsibility to provide ongoing support for the child and her education, without any consideration for whether support was necessary, solicited or even deemed desirable by her mother and Sandra R. He is criticized for having only a limited experience with the day-to-day events in his child's life, without regard for the three-thousand-mile distance between residences or the degree to which access to the child was limited by respondent and Sandra R. At the same time, petitioner's desire to communicate and visit with his daughter is portrayed as a threat to the stability and legitimacy of the family unit constituted by Ry, respondent and Sandra R. It is distressing that petitioner, who seems to have exhibited sensitivity and respect for the relationship between respondent and her domestic partner, is proposed to be compensated for his understanding by judicial extinguishment of his rights as a father. Such a result is offensive to the Court's sense of equity. Moreover, such an injustice hardly serves to promote tolerance and restraint among persons who may confront similar circumstances. It discourages resolution of disputes involving novel and complex familial relationships without resort to litigation which, ideally, should only be pursued as a last resort. * * *

Family Court's disposition is no more compelled by the equities of this matter than by the law. The notion that a lesbian mother should enjoy a parental relationship with her daughter but a gay father should not is so innately discriminatory as to be unworthy of comment. Merely because petitioner does not have custody of his daughter does not compel the conclusion, embraced by the dissent, that he may not assert any right to maintain a parental relationship with her. While much is made by Family Court of the alleged oral understanding between the parties that petitioner would not assume a parental role towards Ry, any such agreement is unenforceable for failure to comply with explicit statutory requirements for surrender of parental rights (Social Services Law § 384; Family Ct. Act § 516), as the dissent concedes. * * *

Family Court presumed to apply the doctrine of equitable estoppel to foreclose any attempt by petitioner to obtain judicial consideration of his rights as a parent. However, the doctrine is more appropriately applied against the mother than against petitioner. If respondent now finds petitioner's involvement in his daughter's life to be inconvenient, she cannot deny that her predicament is the result of her own action. Not content with the knowledge of the identity of the biological father that her chosen method of conception afforded, Robin Y. initiated and fostered a relationship between petitioner and Ry. * * *

Having initiated and encouraged, over a substantial period of time, the relationship between petitioner and his daughter, respondent is estopped to deny his right to legal recognition of that relationship. The provisions of Family Ct. Act § 542(a) are clear and unambiguous and, therefore, there is no room for judicial interpretation. Having found that petitioner is the father of Ry R.-Y., Family Court was commanded by statutory direction to enter an order of filiation. [The majority remanded the case to Family Court for further proceedings on the issue of visitation.]

■ ELLERIN, JUSTICE [joined by ROSENBERGER, PRESIDING JUSTICE] (dissenting).

* * * The complexity of the human relationships that permeate this case and the contemporary reality of millions of households that maintain alternative family life styles strongly militate against the rigid, abstract application of legal principles, not designed for situations such as this, in a way that will grievously impact upon an innocent child, now twelve years of age. This case also demonstrates, as do most emotionally charged situations, the inadequacy of current law and litigation as instruments capable of satisfactorily accommodating the competing desires and interests of each of the parties involved. Since, however, I believe that the overriding factor which must guide us is the best interests of this child, I dissent and would affirm the trial court's sensitive and well founded decision which denied a declaration of paternity to petitioner sperm donor on the basis of equitable estoppel. * * *

The record clearly establishes that for Ry's first 9 and half years of life the appellant at no time sought to establish a true parental relationship with her either by way of seeking to legally establish his paternity and assuming the responsibilities and obligations which that status entailed or by any involvement in her upbringing or schooling or by attempting to provide any support for her. He was not there when she cut her baby teeth, started to walk, was sick or in need of parental comfort or guidance, nor did he seek to involve himself in the every day decisions which are peculiarly the domain of parents—decisions as to what schools she should attend, what camps, what doctors should be consulted, the extent of her after school and social activities, the need for tutors and the like. Perhaps Ry herself best stated it when she said that to her a parent is a person who a child depends on to care for her needs. * * *

The trial court, sensitive to the issues involved, appointed a law guardian for the child and obtained the agreement of all parties to submit the child to a psychiatric evaluation. Both the law guardian and the psychiatrist strongly recommended against the declaration of paternity and further recommended that there be no court-ordered visitation. Their intensive examination of Ry's progress while raised with the family unit that she has known since birth showed that she, and Cade, in addition to having a very close and warm sisterly relationship and a warm and loving relationship with both their mothers have also functioned well in the private school which they attend and that they have strong peer relationships. Ry is a well adjusted child, who, despite experiencing some external incidents of intolerance and insensitivity to her family lifestyle, views that family as a warm, loving, supportive environment. Most significantly, Ry views this proceeding as a threat to her sense of family security. She is angry at petitioner and feels betrayed by him because she and her family had counted on him as a supporter of their unconventional family unit. The thought of visiting appellant, and her deep-seated fear that he might seek custody of her, have caused Ry anxiety and nightmares and the psychiatrist opined that forced visitation with appellant would exacerbate that anxiety and have untoward consequences. The law guardian in a lengthy and well-documented brief details the specifics of the relationships involved and the completely nonparental role occupied by appellant until the instant proceeding was commenced when Ry was almost 10 years old. Both the law guardian and the court appointed psychiatrist make clear that the best interests of Ry, now 12 years old, will be served by an affirmance of the denial of filiation, which will also eliminate Ry's custody concerns. * * *

The threshold issue that must first be determined is what rights, if any, arise from the fact that petitioner was the sperm donor and paternal biological progenitor of the child Ry. The Court of Appeals has made clear that absent "a full commitment to the responsibilities of parenthood" the mere existence of a biological link does not merit constitutional protection (*Matter of Robert O. v. Russell K.*, 604 N.E.2d 99, quoting *Lehr v. Robertson*, 463 U.S. at 261). Thus, an unwed biological father does not automatically have parental rights which must be recognized by the state independent of the child's best interests * * *.

While providing support for the child, and the child's education, would appear to be a minimal requirement for the manifestation of parenthood (see, Family Ct. Act § 513), the criteria which are particularly relevant in determining whether an unwed biological father has sufficiently undertaken his parental responsibilities to give him a protected parental interest may be garnered by reference to Domestic Relations Law § 111 which governs adoptions and delineates the various criteria which must be met before an unwed father has any protected right vis-à-vis the child. That statute provides that when the child is more than six months old, the father has a protected parental right to the extent of requiring his consent to the child's adoption, *only* if he has

> maintained substantial and continuous or repeated contact with the child as manifested by: (i) the payment by the father toward the support of the child of a fair and reasonable sum, according to the father's means, and either (ii) the father's visiting the child at least monthly when physically and financially able to do so and not prevented from doing so by the person or authorized agency having lawful custody of the child, or (iii) the father's regular communication with the child or with the person or agency having the care or custody of the child, when physically and financially unable to visit the child or prevented from doing so by the person or authorized agency having lawful custody of the child. (Domestic Relations Law § 111[1][d].)

In this case there is no question that petitioner has never sought to contribute to the ongoing support of the child, or to see to her educational or other needs despite the fact that he is a professional of substantial means. On the contrary, all of the child's economic and educational needs have been provided for through her mothers and she has enjoyed a comfortable standard of living. Nor, after not seeing the child at all for the first 3 years of her life, has petitioner ever sought to visit the child on anything close to a monthly basis. His failure to do so cannot be attributed to respondent since, until very recently, the pattern of occasional visits was one with which he was in full agreement. Whether viewed within the framework of the statutory criteria or the common understanding of what parenthood entails vis-à-vis the multiple daily facets of a child's life, petitioner's conduct until the commencement of this proceeding fell far short of manifesting the willingness to take on the parental responsibilities necessary to invest him with any constitutionally recognized parental "rights" which could be terminated subject to the provisions of Social Services Law § 384–b.

[The dissenting judges believed that the plain language of Family Law § 542, which would appear to require petitioner's parentage to be established, is subject to an implied exception based upon the principle of equitable estoppel. In the context of this case, equitable estoppel is grounded in the same considerations as the best interests of the child: the father's failure to contribute to the child's support, his infrequent contact with the child during her formative years, and the disruption threatened by his intervention in her life.]

Furthermore, and perhaps most important, a declaration of paternity in this case would be counter to this child's interests because it clearly would be only the first step in ongoing litigation which will inevitably cause severe traumatic consequences to the child and her family. Indeed, the majority's decision has already provided for further litigation in its remand for a decision on visitation. A declaration of paternity creates a platform for petitioner, as well as his parents and other members of his family, who will, by means of the order, become the child's legal relations, to seek changes in visitation and, of course, to seek custody. Indeed, even were visitation never to be granted and further litigation never to succeed, the constant, frightening potential for it is a burden that this child, who is already aware that her family is vulnerable to attack on a number of fronts, should not have to bear. It is clear that this specific fear has already taken its toll. According to the psychiatric testimony, the child believes that the order of filiation would mean that "anytime [petitioner] didn't like something he could sue." In particular, the psychiatric testimony emphasized Ry's haunting fear of the consequences should her birth mother die or become unable to care for her and the resulting ambiguous status of the woman whom she has consistently thought of as her second parent. * * *

Postscript. For an account and analysis of the *Robin Y.* litigation, *see* Katharine Arnup & Susan Boyd, "Familial Disputes? Sperm Donors, Lesbian Mothers, and Legal Parenthood," in *Legal Inversions: Lesbians, Gay Men, and the Politics of Law* 77 (Didi Herman & Carl Stychin eds., 1995). In 2004, the New York Times Magazine published a follow-up story about the child at the center of the *Thomas S.* case. Susan Dominus, *Growing Up With Mom and Mom*, N.Y. Times Magazine (Oct. 24, 2004), http://www.nytimes.com/2004/10/24/magazine/growing-up-with-mom-and-mom.html?_r=0.

NOTES ON *THOMAS S.* AND SPERM DONORS

1.   *Legal Developments.* Today, some view the rule adopted in *Thomas S.*—under which a male sperm provider may be considered the legal parent of the child, even if that is contrary to what the parties initially intended—as being out of touch with the reality of family formation today.

More recently, courts in other states that also lack relevant sperm donor statutes on point arrived at more nuanced rules. For example, the Pennsylvania Supreme Court rejected a rule that a known sperm donor always has a claim to legal parentage in ***Ferguson v. McKiernan*, 596 Pa. 78, 96–97, 940 A.2d 1236, 1247–48 (2007).** Such a rule, the court explained, would mean that:

> a woman who wishes to have a baby but is unable to conceive through intercourse could not seek sperm from a man she knows and admires, while assuring him that he will never be subject to a support order and being herself assured that he will never be able to seek custody of the child. Accordingly, to protect herself and the sperm donor, that would-be mother would have no choice but to resort to anonymous donation or abandon her desire to be a biological mother, notwithstanding her considered personal preference to conceive using the sperm of someone familiar, whose background, traits, and medical history are not shrouded in mystery. To much the same end, where a would-be donor cannot trust that he is safe from a future support action, he will be considerably less likely to provide his sperm to a friend or acquaintance who asks, significantly limiting a would-be mother's reproductive prerogatives. There is simply no basis in law or policy to impose such an unpleasant choice[.]

Ferguson v. McKiernan, 596 Pa. 78, 96–97, 940 A.2d 1236, 1247–48 (2007). Instead, the *Ferguson* court concluded that whether a known donor has a claim to legal parentage based on his genetic connection to the resulting child depends on the circumstances:

> The facts of this case, as found by the trial court and supported by the record, reveal the parties' mutual intention to preserve all of the trappings of a conventional sperm donation, including formation of a binding agreement. Indeed, the parties could have done little more than they did to imbue the transaction with the hallmarks of institutional, non-sexual conception by sperm donation and IVF. They negotiated an agreement outside the context of a romantic relationship; they agreed to terms; they sought clinical assistance to effectuate IVF and implantation of the consequent embryos, taking sexual intercourse out of the equation; they attempted to hide Sperm Donor's paternity from medical personnel, friends, and family; and for approximately five years following the birth of the twins both parties behaved in every regard consistently with the intentions they expressed at the outset of their arrangement, Sperm Donor not seeking to serve as a father to the twins, and Mother not demanding his support, financial or otherwise. That Mother knew Sperm Donor's identity, the parties failed to preserve Sperm Donor's anonymity from a handful of family members who were well acquainted with Sperm Donor and Mother alike, and Mother acted on her preference to know the identity of her sperm donor by voluntarily declining to avail herself of the services of a company that matches anonymous donors with willing mothers, reveal no obvious basis for analyzing this case any differently than we would a case involving an institutionally arranged sperm donation.

Ferguson v. McKiernan, 596 Pa. 78, 94–95, 940 A.2d 1236, 1246–47 (2007). Under those particular circumstances, where the parties "agreed to an arrangement that to all appearances was to resemble—and in large part did resemble for approximately five years—a single-parent arrangement effectuated through the use of donor sperm secured from a sperm bank," the court held, the agreement between the parties was "enforceable." *Id.* at 98.

An Indiana intermediate court reached a similar conclusion in *In re Paternity of M.F.*, **938 N.E.2d 1256, 1261 (Ind. Ct. App. 2010).** Like Pennsylvania and New York, Indiana has no statutes directly on point. The court concluded that an agreement between the parties would be enforceable if two conditions are met:

> First, as stated above, we hold today that a physician must be involved in the process of artificial insemination. At a minimum, this involvement includes the requirement that the semen first be provided to the physician. This goes a long way toward preventing last-minute decisions to attempt the endeavor without the involvement of a medical professional. In fact, in our view, it obviates the possibility altogether.

> Second, we do not mean to sanction the view that a writing consisting of a few lines scribbled on the back of a scrap of paper found lying about will suffice in this kind of case. To the contrary, the instrument in question must reflect the parties' careful consideration of the implications of such an agreement and a thorough understanding of its meaning and import.

Id. at 1261.

Are these fact-based rules a positive or a negative development?

2. *Single Women and Assisted Reproduction.* Should the rules regarding the parental status of the donor vary depending on whether there is one or two (or more) intended parents? That is, if the intended parent is a single woman, should the law treat the donor as a parent, whether he likes it or not? Professor Marsha Garrison argues that the law should insist on two. First, "outside the [ART] context, our legal system grants no parent, male or female, the right to be a sole parent." Marsha Garrison, "Law Making for Baby Making: An Interpretive Approach to the Determination of Legal Parentage," 113 *Harv. L. Rev.* 835, 906–07 (2000). Moreover, she continues, "the policy derives from the view that children are typically better off when they have the opportunity to know and experience care from both of their parents, a view that most Americans maintain and that finds support in the available evidence." Marsha Garrison, "Law Making for Baby Making: An Interpretive Approach to the Determination of Legal Parentage," 113 *Harv. L. Rev.* 835, 907 (2000).

Other scholars push back and argue that procreation through sex and procreation through assisted reproduction are different in important ways and, therefore, different parentage rules are appropriate. *See, e.g.*, Marjorie Maguire Shultz, "Reproductive Technology and Intent-Based Parenthood: An Opportunity for Gender Neutrality," 1990 *Wis. L. Rev.* 297. Just because the law insists (usually) on two parents in the context of children born through sex does not mean that the law must insist on two parents in the context of children born through assisted reproduction.

Professor Courtney Cahill takes a different approach to the question. She challenges the notion that parentage rules should be any different depending on the method of conception. That said, instead of arguing in favor of a rule of two in both contexts, she urges a rule that permits a total of one in both contexts. Courtney Megan Cahill, "Reproduction Reconceived," 101 *Minn. L. Rev.* 617, 685 (2016) (proposing "a unitary model of reproductive regulation grounded in intent and argu[ing] that that model ought to guide the regulation of sexual and alternative reproduction alike").

What is the right rule as a matter of policy? Would the rule proposed by Professor Garrison, requiring a total of two parents in the context of assisted reproduction be constitutionally permissible? Would such a rule impermissibly infringe women's reproductive autonomy rights? Or is any infringement of the woman's autonomy rights justified by the state's obligation to protect the well-being of children?

NOTE ON OVA SHARING

While it remains uncommon, some lesbian couples utilize "ova sharing" by which one woman has ova extracted; the ova are then fertilized *in vitro*. The resulting pre-embryo is transferred to the other woman, who gestates the fetus. In such cases, both women are biologically related to the resulting child—one through genetics and one through gestation. In such cases, who is the parent? A few courts have sought to answer that question.

***K.M. v. E.G.*, 37 Cal.4th 130, 117 P.3d 673 (2005).** K.M. and E.G. were a committed lesbian couple, registered as domestic partners in San Francisco. In 1995, the parties agreed that E.G. would get pregnant through in vitro fertilization using K.M.'s ova. In a form contract provided by the fertility provider K.M. "relinquish[ed]" rights to any resulting child. In the form, K.M. also agreed that she would never "attempt to discover the identity of the recipient thereof" (even though the parties lived together).

Twins were born in December 1995, and the couple celebrated a (non-legal) marriage ceremony shortly thereafter. The women's relationship ended in 2001, and K.M. sued to establish a parental relationship with the twins. The California Supreme Court, in an opinion by **Justice Moreno**, ruled that both women were the children's legal parents.

Parental rights are governed by California's enactment of the Uniform Parentage Act, Family Code § 7600 et seq. The UPA defines the "[p]arent and child relationship, [which] extends equally to every child and to every parent, regardless of the marital status of the parents." *Id.*, § 7602. Just as the Court had previously ruled that the husband in *Johnson v. Calvert* (1979) was the presumptive parent of a child conceived through gestational surrogacy, so the Court ruled in K.M.'s case that the ovum-donor was a presumptive parent. *Johnson* "concluded that 'genetic consanguinity' could be the basis for a finding of maternity just as it is for paternity. Under this authority, K.M.'s genetic relationship to the children in the present case constitutes 'evidence of a mother and child relationship as contemplated by the Act.' "

Section 7613(b) states: "The donor of semen provided to a licensed physician and surgeon for use in artificial insemination of a woman other than the donor's wife is treated in law as if he were not the natural father of a child thereby conceived." The Court declined to extend this provision to the ovum donor. Dissenting **Justice Kennard** would have extended § 7613(b) to include ovum donors as well as sperm donors. Why should ovum donors have *more* rights than sperm donors? (One answer: the statutory language only denies rights to sperm donors. Is this an unconstitutional sex discrimination?)

In a separate dissent, **Justice Werdegar** would have followed *Johnson* to inquire as to the intent of the parties. In *Johnson*, the married couple and the ovum donor intended to create a family for the couple. In this case, even K.M. agreed that her donation was to enable E.G. to have children. The majority responded that an "intent of the parties" approach would create uncertainty in the law. (Also, K.M. disputed that she "intended" to renounce all rights to the twins when she was presented with the form in 1995.) Justice Werdegar responded that her approach was more predictable than the open-ended approach of the majority, which left many questions unanswered. For example, would the Court have recognized K.M. as a parent if she and E.G. had not raised the children within a domestic partnership? A committed relationship?

Because the Court neither overruled nor questioned *Johnson*, its rule did not apply to donors providing ova to different-sex couples. By creating a new rule applicable only to lesbian couples, the Court, argued Justice Werdegar, "confers rights and imposes disabilities on persons because of their sexual orientation. * * * I see no rational basis—and the majority articulates none—for permitting the enforceability of an ovum donation agreement to depend on the sexual orientation of the parties. Indeed, lacking a rational basis, the rule may well violate equal protection. (See *Romer v. Evans* (1996); *Gay Law Students Assn. v. Pacific Tel. & Tel. Co.* (1979).) Why should a lesbian not have the same right as other women to donate ova without becoming a mother, or to accept a donation of ova without accepting the donor as a coparent, even if the donor and recipient live together and both plan to help raise the child?"

There are still only a few published decisions addressing the legal parentage of children born through ova sharing, but they seem to agree with the conclusion of the California Supreme Court. *See, e.g., D.M.T. v. T.M.H.*, 129 So. 3d 320 (Fla. 2013) (holding that both women were legal parents of the resulting child); *St. Mary v. Damon*, 309 P.3d 1027 (Nev.

2013) (overruling trial court decision holding that the gestational mother was merely a "surrogate" and remanding for further consideration), *after remand*, 385 P.3d 595 (Nev. 2016) ("[W]e conclude that the district court properly found [the gestational mother] to be the child's parent" along with the genetic parent).

E. EQUITABLE PARENTHOOD

As noted above, it is now possible for both members of an LGBT couple to be recognized as legal parents of their child automatically, from the moment of birth. But this is not always the result. The couple may have been unmarried and the state's assisted reproduction statutes may be limited to married couples. Or the couple may not have complied with the requirements of the assisted reproduction statutes. Is there any way for such a person to obtain at least some parental rights and obligations based on their post-birth parental conduct?

Historically, the law was dismissive of parentage claims by cohabiting lesbian and gay partners with respect to children born to or adopted by the person's former same-sex partner. *See, e.g., In re Alison D. v. Virginia M.*, 77 N.Y.2d 651, 572 N.E.2d 27 (1991) (rejecting the nonbiological mother's claims to visitation or joint custody based upon de facto or psychological parenting doctrines). (In 2016, the New York high court overruled *Alison D. Brooke S.B. v. Elizabeth A.C.C.*, 61 N.E.3d 488, 490 (N.Y. 2016) ("We agree that, in light of more recently delineated legal principles, the definition of "parent" established by this Court 25 years ago in *Alison D.* has become unworkable when applied to increasingly varied familial relationships. Accordingly, today, we overrule *Alison D.* and hold that where a partner shows by clear and convincing evidence that the parties agreed to conceive a child and to raise the child together, the non-biological, non-adoptive partner has standing to seek visitation and custody under Domestic Relations Law § 70.")). Some courts followed and continue to follow *Alison D. See, e.g., Jones v. Barlow,* 154 P.3d 808 (Utah 2007); *Music v. Rachford,* 654 So.2d 1234 (Fla. App.1995). Many more jurisdictions, however, protect established parent-child relationships, even if those relationships are not biological ones. *See, e.g.,* Courtney G. Joslin, Shannon P. Minter, & Catherine Sakimura, *Lesbian, Gay, Bisexual, and Transgender Family Law* §§ 7:4–7:14 (2017).

The Wisconsin Supreme Court initially followed *Alison D.* in *In re Z.J.H.*, 162 Wis.2d 1002, 471 N.W.2d 202 (1991), but reversed itself in *In re Custody of H.S.H.-K.*, 193 Wis.2d 649, 533 N.W.2d 419 (1995). In the latter case, the court held that a former cohabiting lesbian partner could not sue for custody or visitation under the state's marriage dissolution statute, but that she could petition for visitation rights under the courts' equitable authority to protect the best interests of the child. *H.S.H.-K.* has been a normative success and is gathering support from other state judiciaries, as well as the American Law Institute (ALI). The ALI's *Principles of the Law of Family Dissolution* § 2.03(1) (2002), has endorsed the concept of a *de facto parent*, namely, someone "who has lived with the child and functioned as a parent, for at least two years, regularly performing a majority of the caretaking functions for the child, with the consent or acquiescence of the legal parent." Consider a leading case adopting the Wisconsin approach to de facto parenthood.

V.C. v. M.J.B.

New Jersey Supreme Court, 2000.
163 N.J. 200, 748 A.2d 539.

■ The opinion of the court was delivered by LONG, J. * * *

[V.C. and M.J.B. were lesbian partners, with joint bank accounts, as well as wills and powers of attorney naming one another as beneficiaries. During their relationship, M.J.B. became pregnant through artificial insemination. V.C. took M.J.B. to the hospital and was present in the delivery room at the birth of the children. At the hospital, the nurses and staff treated V.C. as if she were a mother. After the children were born, M.J.B. took a three-month maternity leave and V.C. took a three-week vacation. Both women and the children considered V.C. to be a "mother" of the children, and they functioned as a family unit.

[In 1995, the couple purchased a home in 1995, and V.C. asked M.J.B. to marry her, and M.J.B. accepted. In July 1995, the parties held a commitment ceremony where they were "married." At the ceremony, V.C., M.J.B. and the twins were blessed as a "family." Nonetheless, in August 1996, M.J.B. ended the relationship. V.C. ultimately moved out of the shared family home but still visited the children and contributed financially to the household. In 1997, M.J.B. sought to discontinue V.C.'s visitation with the children and stopped accepting V.C.'s money. M.J.B. asserted that she did not want to continue the children's contact with V.C. because she believed that V.C. was not properly caring for the children, and that the children were suffering distress from continued contact with V.C. Both parties became involved with new partners after the dissolution of their relationship. Eventually, V.C. filed a complaint for joint legal custody.]

At trial, expert witnesses appeared for both parties. Dr. Allwyn J. Levine testified on behalf of V.C., and Dr. David Brodzinsky testified on behalf of M.J.B. Both experts arrived at similar conclusions after having examined the women individually and with the children, and after examining the children separately.

Dr. Levine concluded that both children view V.C. as a maternal figure and that V.C. regards herself as one of the children's mothers. "Because the children were basically parented from birth" by V.C. and M.J.B. "until they physically separated," Dr. Levine concluded that the children view the parties "as inter-changeable maternal mothering objects" and "have established a maternal bond with both of the women."

Dr. Levine likened the parties' relationship to a heterosexual marriage. Consequently, the children would be affected by the loss of V.C. just as if they had been denied contact with their father after a divorce. Dr. Levine explained that the children would benefit from continued contact with V.C. because they had a bonded relationship with her. Dr. Levine further noted that if the children felt abandoned by V.C., they might also feel unnecessary guilt and assume that they made V.C. angry or somehow caused the parties' separation. Although the doctor believed that the children could adapt to the loss of V.C., he indicated that the long-term effects were unknown. Furthermore, Dr. Levine indicated that the animosity between V.C. and M.J.B. could harm the children, but surmised that counseling could lessen the parties' animosity.

Likewise, Dr. Brodzinsky concluded that V.C. and the children enjoyed a bonded relationship that benefitted both children. Dr. Brodzinsky determined that the children regarded V.C. as a member of their family. The doctor believed that it was normal for young children to feel that way about a person with whom they have spent considerable time. However, Dr. Brodzinsky noted that as children "get older, family becomes more specifically tied . . . to biological connections." The doctor's report indicated that, when asked who their mother was, the children did not immediately point to V.C., but upon further inquiry agreed that V.C. was their mother. The doctor further noted that the children viewed M.J.B's new partner as a current member of their family. Dr. Brodzinsky expressed concern that, if visitation were permitted, the parties' animosity would negatively impact the children. The doctor, however, acknowledged that counseling would reduce the level of animosity between the parties. Dr. Brodzinsky further recognized that the children would suffer some short-term stress from the loss of V.C. but would likely recover in time.

In contrast to Dr. Levine's opinion, Dr. Brodzinsky believed that the loss of V.C. was not akin to the loss of a parent in a heterosexual divorce. The doctor explained that societal views foster the expectation that a child and a parent will continue their relationship after a divorce, but that no similar expectation would exist for the children's relationship with V.C. Still, Dr. Brodzinsky testified that "the ideal situation is that [M.J.B.] is allowed to get on with her life as she wants, but to the extent possible that . . . these children be able at times to have some contact with [V.C.] who's important to them." Assuming that the parties could maintain a reasonably amicable relationship, Dr. Brodzinsky felt that the children "would probably benefit from ongoing contact [with V.C.] as they would with any person with whom they have a good solid relationship that can nurture them."

The trial court denied V.C.'s applications for joint legal custody and visitation because it concluded that she failed to establish that the bonded relationship she enjoyed with the children had risen to the level of psychological or *de facto* parenthood. In so doing, the court gave significant weight to the fact that the decision to have children was M.J.B.'s, and not a joint decision between M.J.B. and V.C. [The court also denied V.C. visitation rights, because it was not in the children's best interests.]

There are no statutes explicitly addressing whether a former unmarried domestic partner has standing to seek custody and visitation with her former partner's biological children. That is not to say, however, that the current statutory scheme dealing with issues of custody and visitation does not provide some guiding principles. N.J.S.A. 9:2–3 prescribes:

> When the parents of a minor child live separately, or are about to do so, the Superior Court, in an action brought by either parent, shall have the same power to make judgments or orders concerning care, custody, education and maintenance as concerning a child whose parents are divorced. . . .

Further, N.J.S.A. 9:2–4 provides, in part, that

> the Legislature finds and declares that it is in the public policy of this State to assure minor children of frequent and continuing contact with both parents after the parents have separated or dissolved their marriage and that it is in the public interest to encourage parents to share the rights and responsibilities of child rearing in order to effect this policy. In any proceeding involving the custody of a minor child, the rights of both parents shall be equal. . . .

By that scheme, the Legislature has expressed the view that children should not generally be denied continuing contact with parents after the relationship between the parties ends.

N.J.S.A. 9:2–13(f) provides that "the word 'parent,' when not otherwise described by the context, means a natural parent or parent by previous adoption." M.J.B. argues that because V.C. is not a natural or adoptive parent, we lack jurisdiction to consider her claims. That is an incomplete interpretation of the Act. Although the statutory definition of parent focuses on natural and adoptive parents, it also includes the phrase, "when not otherwise described by the context." That language evinces a legislative intent to leave open the possibility that individuals other than natural or adoptive parents may qualify as "parents," depending on the circumstances. * * *

By including the words "when not otherwise described by the context" in the statute, the Legislature obviously envisioned a case where the specific relationship between a child and a person not specifically denominated by the statute would qualify as "parental" under the scheme of Title 9. Although the Legislature may not have considered the precise case before us, it is hard to imagine what it could have had in mind in adding the "context" language other than a situation such as this, in which a person not related to a child by blood or adoption has stood in a parental role vis-a-vis the child. It is that contention by V.C. that brings this case before the court and affords us jurisdiction over V.C.'s complaint.

Separate and apart from the statute, M.J.B. contends that there is no legal precedent for this action by V.C. She asserts, correctly, that a legal parent has a fundamental right to the care, custody and nurturance of his or her child. Various constitutional provisions have been cited as the source of that right, which is deeply imbedded in our collective consciousness and traditions. *Stanley; Griswold* (Goldberg, J., concurring) (privacy guarantees). In general, however, the right of a legal parent to the care and custody of his or her child derives from the notion of privacy. According to M.J.B., that right entitles her to absolute preference over V.C. in connection with custody and visitation of the twins. She argues that V.C., a stranger, has no standing to bring this action. We disagree.

The right of parents to the care and custody of their children is not absolute. For example, a legal parent's fundamental right to custody and control of a child may be infringed upon by the state if the parent endangers the health or safety of the child. Likewise, if there is a showing of unfitness, abandonment or gross misconduct, a parent's right to custody of her child may be usurped.

[Although V.C. did not allege that M.L.B. was an unfit parent, the cases also recognize an "exceptional circumstances" category for courts to exercise their *parens patriae* authority to protect children.] Subsumed within that category is the subset known as the psychological parent cases in which a third party has stepped in to assume the role of the legal parent who has been unable or unwilling to undertake the obligations of parenthood. [Citing *H.S.H.-K.* and five other state supreme court decisions, the court observed that other jurisdictions had also recognized the "psychological parent doctrine."]

At the heart of the psychological parent cases is a recognition that children have a strong interest in maintaining the ties that connect them to adults who love and provide for them. That interest, for constitutional as well as social purposes, lies in the emotional bonds that develop between family members as a result of shared daily life. That point was emphasized in *Lehr v. Robertson*, 463 U.S. 248, 261 (1983), where the Supreme Court held that a stepfather's *actual* relationship with a child was the determining factor when considering the degree of protection that the parent-child link must be afforded. The Court stressed that "the importance of the familial relationship, to the individuals involved and to the society, stems from the emotional attachments that derive from the intimacy of daily association, and from the role it plays in 'promot[ing] a way of life' through the instruction of children as well as from the fact of blood relationship." [Hence, the court ruled that V.C. had standing to maintain this action separate and apart from the statute.]

The next issue we confront is how a party may establish that he or she has, in fact, become a psychological parent to the child of a fit and involved legal parent. That is a question which many of our sister states have attempted to answer. Some have enacted statutes to address the subject by deconstructing psychological parenthood to its fundamental elements, including: the substantial nature of the relationship between the third party and the child, see, e.g., Ariz. Rev. Stat. Ann. § 25–415(G)(1); whether or not the third party and the child actually lived together, see, e.g., Minn. Stat. Ann. § 257.022(2b); Tex. Fam. Code Ann. § 102.003(a)(9); and whether the unrelated third party had previously provided financial support for the child, see, e.g. 1999 Nev. Stat. 125A.330(3)(I). * * *

The most thoughtful and inclusive definition of *de facto* parenthood is the test enunciated in *Custody of H.S.H.-K.* and adopted by the Appellate Division majority here. It addresses the main fears and concerns both legislatures and courts have advanced when addressing the notion of psychological parenthood. Under that test,

> to demonstrate the existence of the petitioner's parent-like relationship with the child, the petitioner must prove four elements: (1) that the biological or adoptive parent consented to, and fostered, the petitioner's formation and establishment of a parent-like relationship with the child; (2) that the petitioner and the child lived together in the same household; (3) that the petitioner assumed the obligations of parenthood by taking significant responsibility for the child's care, education and development, including contributing towards the child's support, without expectation of financial compensation [a petitioner's contribution to a child's support need not be monetary]; and (4) that the petitioner has been in a parental role for a length of time sufficient to have established with the child a bonded, dependent relationship parental in nature.

[The court adopted this as the legal test in New Jersey as well.]

Prong one is critical because it makes the biological or adoptive parent a participant in the creation of the psychological parent's relationship with the child. Without such a requirement, a paid nanny or babysitter could theoretically qualify for parental status. To avoid that result, in order for a third party to be deemed a psychological parent, the legal parent must have fostered the formation of the parental relationship between the third party and the child. By fostered is meant that the legal parent ceded over to the third party a measure of parental authority and autonomy and granted to that third party rights and duties vis-a-vis the child that the third party's status would not otherwise warrant. Ordinarily, a relationship based on payment by the legal parent to the third party will not qualify.

The requirement of cooperation by the legal parent is critical because it places control within his or her hands. That parent has the absolute ability to maintain a zone of autonomous privacy for herself and her child. However, if she wishes to maintain that zone of privacy she cannot invite a third party to function as a parent to her child and cannot cede over to that third party parental authority the exercise of which may create a profound bond with the child. * * *

Concerning the remaining prongs of the *H.S.H.-K.* test, we accept Wisconsin's formulation with these additional comments. The third prong, a finding that a third party assumed the obligations of parenthood, is not contingent on financial contributions made by the third party. Financial contribution may be considered but should not be given inordinate weight when determining whether a third party has assumed the obligations of parenthood. Obviously, as we have indicated, the assumption of a parental role is much more complex than mere financial support. It is determined by the nature, quality, and extent of the functions undertaken by the third party and the response of the child to that nurturance.

Indeed, we can conceive of a case in which the third party is the stay-at-home mother or father who undertakes all of the daily domestic and child care activities in a household with preschool children while the legal parent is the breadwinner engaged in her occupation or profession. Although it is always possible to put a price on the contributions of the stay-at-home parent, see Martha M. Ertman, Commercializing Marriage: A Proposal for Valuing Women's Work Through Premarital Security Agreements, 77 Tex. L. Rev. 17, 43 (1998) (outlining different economic models for placing value on homemaker's contribution), our point is that such an analysis is not necessary because it is the nature of what is done that will determine whether a parent-child bond has developed, not how much it is worth in dollars.

It bears repeating that the fourth prong is most important because it requires the existence of a parent-child bond. A necessary corollary is that the third party must have functioned as a parent for a long enough time that such a bond has developed. What is crucial here is not the amount of time but the nature of the relationship. How much time is necessary will turn on the facts of each case including an assessment of exactly what functions the putative parent performed, as well as at what period and stage of the child's life and development such actions were taken. Most importantly, a determination will have to be made about the actuality and strength of the parent-child bond. Generally, that will require expert testimony. * * *

Once a third party has been determined to be a psychological parent to a child, under the previously described standards, he or she stands in parity with the legal parent. Custody and visitation issues between them are to be determined on a best interests standard giving weight to the factors set forth in N.J.S.A. 9:2–4:

> the parents' ability to agree, communicate and cooperate in matters relating to the child; the parents' willingness to accept

custody and any history of unwillingness to allow parenting time not based on substantiated abuse; the interaction and relationship of the child with its parents and siblings; the history of domestic violence, if any; the safety of the child and the safety of either parent from physical abuse by the other parent; the preference of the child when of sufficient age and capacity to reason so as to form an intelligent decision; the needs of the child; the stability of the home environment offered; the quality and continuity of the child's education; the fitness of the parents; the geographical proximity of the parents' homes; the extent and quality of time spent with the child prior to or subsequent to the separation; the parents' employment responsibilities; and the age and number of the children.

That is not to suggest that a person's status as a legal parent does not play a part in custody or visitation proceedings in those circumstances.

* * * The legal parent's status is a significant weight in the best interests balance because eventually, in the search for self-knowledge, the child's interest in his or her roots will emerge. Thus, under ordinary circumstances when the evidence concerning the child's best interests (as between a legal parent and psychological parent) is in equipoise, custody will be awarded to the legal parent.

Visitation, however, will be the presumptive rule, subject to the considerations set forth in N.J.S.A. 9:2–4, as would be the case if two natural parents were in conflict. As we said in *Beck v. Beck*, 86 N.J. 480, 495, 432 A.2d 63 (1981), visitation rights are almost "invariably" granted to the non-custodial parent. * * * Once the parent-child bond is forged, the rights and duties of the parties should be crafted to reflect that reality.

[The court applied its approach to the dispute between M.J.B. and V.C. The court ruled that V.C. was indeed a psychological parent and granted her the visitation rights presumptively allowed for such parents. The joint custody issue was a closer one. V.C. was not seeking physical custody, but only joint decisionmaking responsibilities. The court rejected that claim, largely because V.C. had not been participating in those decisions for several years.]

■ [We omit the concurring opinion of O'HERN, J.]

In custody cases between a legal parent and an equitable parent, some legal parents have argued that ordering custody or visitation over their objection violates their constitutionally protected right to control the upbringing of their children, identified in *Meyer* and *Pierce*. The Supreme Court revisited the constitutional rights of parents in the following case.

***Jenifer Troxel et vir. v. Tommie Granville*, 530 U.S. 57 (2000).** Section 26.10.160(3) of the Revised Code of Washington permitted "[a]ny person" to petition a superior court for visitation rights "at any time," and authorizes that court to grant such visitation rights whenever "visitation may serve the best interest of the child." Jenifer and Gary Troxel petitioned for the right to visit Isabelle and Natalie Troxel, the children of their deceased son and Tommie Granville. The trial court ordered visitations of one weekend per month, one week during the summer, and four hours on the birthdays of each grandparent. Granville appealed; she wanted to limit visitation to one day per month, with no overnight stays. The state supreme court overturned the visitation order, on the ground that the statute was, on its face, unconstitutional under the Due Process Clause. The U.S. Supreme Court affirmed the decision invalidating the decree, but there was no opinion for the Court.

Justice O'Connor wrote a plurality opinion joined by the Chief Justice and Justices Ginsburg and Breyer. "The demographic changes of the past century make it difficult to speak of an average American family. The composition of families varies greatly from household to household. While many children may have two married parents and grandparents who visit regularly, many other children are raised in single-parent households. In 1996, children living with only one parent accounted for 28 percent of all children under age 18 in the United States. U.S. Dept. of Commerce, Bureau of Census, Current Population Reports, 1997 Population Profile of the United States 27 (1998). * * *

"The nationwide enactment of nonparental visitation statutes is assuredly due, in some part, to the States' recognition of these changing realities of the American family. Because grandparents and other relatives undertake duties of a parental nature in many households, States have sought to ensure the welfare of the children therein by protecting the relationships those children form with such third parties. The States' nonparental visitation statutes are further supported by a recognition, which varies from State to State, that children should have the opportunity to benefit from relationships with statutorily specified persons—for example, their grandparents. The extension of statutory rights in this area to persons other than a child's parents, however, comes with an obvious cost. For example, the State's recognition of an independent third-party interest in a child can place a substantial burden on the traditional parent-child relationship."

The "interest of parents in the care, custody, and control of their children" is "perhaps the oldest of the fundamental [due process] liberty interests recognized by this Court," observed Justice O'Connor, citing *Meyer* and *Stanley* v. *Illinois*, *supra*. The state law abrogated those rights, for it "effectively permits any third party seeking visitation to subject any decision by a parent concerning visitation of the parent's children to state-court review. Once the visitation petition has been filed in court and the matter is placed before a judge, a parent's decision that visitation would not be in the child's best interest is accorded no deference. * * * Thus, in practical effect, in the State of Washington a court can disregard and overturn *any* decision by a fit custodial parent concerning visitation whenever a third party affected by the decision files a visitation petition, based solely on the judge's determination of the child's best interests." The trial court's decree exemplified this kind of unbounded discretion to trump parental decisions with judicial ones.

Justice O'Connor emphasized that there were no "special factors that might justify the State's interference with Granville's fundamental right to make decisions concerning the rearing of her two daughters." "First, the Troxels did not allege, and no court has found, that Granville was an unfit parent. That aspect of the case is important, for there is a presumption that fit parents act in the best interests of their children." Tellingly, Justice O'Connor contrasted the statute and ruling in this case with other state laws (through a "cf" signal): Cal. Fam. Code § 3104(e) (West 1994) (rebuttable presumption that grandparent visitation is not in child's best interest if parents agree that visitation rights should not be granted); Me. Rev. Stat. Ann., Tit. 19A, § 1803(3) (1998) (court may award grandparent visitation if in best interest of child and "would not significantly interfere with any parent-child relationship or with the parent's rightful authority over the child"); Neb. Rev. Stat. § 43–1802(2) (1998) (court must find "by clear and convincing evidence" that grandparent visitation "will not adversely interfere with the parent-child relationship"). "In an ideal world, parents might always seek to cultivate the bonds between grandparents and their grandchildren. Needless to say, however, our world is far from perfect, and in it the decision whether such an intergenerational relationship would be beneficial in any specific case is for the parent to make in the first instance. And, if a fit parent's decision of the kind at issue here becomes subject to judicial review, the court must accord at least some special weight to the parent's own determination." Justice O'Connor also emphasized "there is no allegation that Granville ever sought to cut off visitation entirely."

Justice Souter concurred in the judgment, agreeing with the state supreme court that the law was unconstitutional on its face and not just as applied. He joined Justice O'Connor's judgment that the Due Process Clause protects a parent's "interests in the nurture, upbringing, companionship, care, and custody of children" and reasoned that a state law allowing "any party" at "any time" to have access to a parent's children is a violation of that due process right. "The strength of a parent's interest in controlling a child's associates is as obvious as the influence of personal associations on the development of the child's social and moral character. Whether for good or for ill, adults not only influence but may indoctrinate children, and a choice about a child's social companions is not essentially different from the designation of the adults who will influence the child in school. Even a State's considered judgment about the preferable political and religious character of schoolteachers is not entitled to prevail over a parent's choice of private school. *Pierce v. Society of Sisters*, 268 U.S. 510 (1925) (following *Meyer* to strike down a law requiring parents to send their children to public school). It would be anomalous, then, to subject a parent to any individual judge's choice of a child's associates from out of the general population merely because the judge might think himself more enlightened than the child's parent. To say the least (and as the Court implied in *Pierce*), parental choice in such matters is not merely a default rule in the absence of either governmental choice or the government's designation of an official with the power to choose for whatever reason and in whatever circumstances."

Justice Thomas also concurred in the Court's judgment on the basis of *Pierce* but suggested that the resolution of this case did not preclude the Court from reconsidering *Pierce* and the other substantive due process cases at some future time. Additionally, he suggested that strict scrutiny should govern judicial inquiry as to whether a particular state interference with a parent's rights is constitutional. (Justice O'Connor did not explicitly apply strict scrutiny.)

Justice Stevens dissented, on the ground that the state law, although broad, had a "plainly legitimate sweep" and so was constitutional on its face. He also found the "as applied" question harder than the majority, because of the "child's liberty interests in preserving established familial or family-like bonds. * * * At a minimum, our prior cases recognizing that children are, generally speaking, constitutionally protected actors require that this Court reject any suggestion that when it comes to parental rights, children are so much chattel." Although he agreed that the state may not disregard a parent's rights as the presumptively best decisionmaker, Justice Stevens declined to address the "as applied" challenge on the ground that it was not properly presented.

Justice Scalia also dissented. "In my view, a right of parents to direct the upbringing of their children is among the 'unalienable Rights' with which the Declaration of Independence proclaims 'all Men . . . are endowed by their Creator.' And in my view that right is also among the 'othe[r] [rights] retained by the people' which the Ninth Amendment says the Constitution's enumeration of rights 'shall not be construed to deny or disparage.' The Declaration of Independence, however, is not a legal prescription conferring powers upon the courts; and the Constitution's refusal to 'deny or disparage' other rights is far removed from affirming any one of them, and even further removed from authorizing judges to identify what they might be, and to enforce the judges' list against laws duly enacted by the people. Consequently, while I would think it entirely compatible with the commitment to representative democracy set forth in the founding documents to argue, in legislative chambers or in electoral campaigns, that the State has *no power* to interfere with parents' authority over the rearing of their children, I do not believe that the power which the Constitution confers upon me *as a judge* entitles me to deny legal effect to laws that (in my view) infringe upon what is (in my view) that unenumerated right."

Justice Kennedy also dissented. Contrary to Justice O'Connor, he believed that visitation may be ordered in the best interests of the child, and without a showing of harm to the child if visitation were denied. Like Justice Stevens, he felt the statute was not unconstitutional on its face. Unlike Justice Stevens, he urged a remand to the state courts to rethink their evaluation of the as-applied challenge.

NOTES ON EQUITABLE PARENTAGE

1.   *Is There a Constitutional Problem?* As noted above, many legal parents have argued that granting custody or visitation rights to an equitable or functional parent over the legal parent's objection is unconstitutional? Does application of these doctrines violate *Troxel*? Why or why not? What did the *V.C.* court say about this argument?

Professor Nancy Polikoff reports that in the "[m]ore than a decade after *Troxel*, most courts have found that [*Troxel*] does not bar claims by nonbiological lesbian mothers." Nancy D. Polikoff, "From Third Parties to Parents: The Case of Lesbian Couples and Their Children," 77 *Law & Contemp. Probs.* 195, 207 (2014).

2.   *The Nuclear Family, Still the Meta-Narrative?* Like the Wisconsin Supreme Court in *H.S.H.-K.*, the New Jersey Supreme Court in *V.C.* reasons by analogy to the traditional different-sex married couple: If a child is not being raised by her different-sex, married biological parents, the child may still be protected if her family looks enough like that model. In that respect, the nuclear family remains the normative ideal. In recent years, a number of scholars who support LGBT equality have raised concerns about the limits of this "assimilationist" approach. *See, e.g.*, Melissa Murray, "What's So New About the The New Illegitimacy?," 20 *Am. U. J. Gender Soc. Pol'y & L.*, 387, 434 (2012) (arguing that the push for marriage equality "requires positioning those outside of marriage and the traditional marital family as deviant and unworthy").

In another respect, however, these equitable parentage cases radically transform the traditional model. Because the parents in these cases are mom and mom rather than mom and dad, the nuclear family has been relocated from its heterosexual base into a feminist or lesbian terrain. This is quite remarkable. Such a rule would be viewed as "promotion of homosexuality" by natural law and religious traditionalists; even though they can no longer punish people for being gay or lesbian, traditionalists maintain that the gay-tolerant state can and must promote the family structure that best serves children's overall best interests, which they say is the old-fashioned mom/dad/kids nuclear family.

These cases also challenge beliefs about the importance of biology to questions of parentage. Sociobiologists and economists influenced by them would be especially critical, we think, of this development. From a Gary Becker/Edward O. Wilson point of view, the most efficient household is one where a husband and wife specializing in outside employment and domestic work, respectively, rear their biological children. The biological connection gives each parent strong incentives to rear the children effectively, and the specialization of labor enable the parents to work together to produce a household with maximum income and domestic harmony. These thinkers would consider a mom/mom household suboptimal (although some same-sex couples also specialize their labor), and sociobiologists would be skeptical that the "second mother" would invest as much in the children as a biological mother would. Within the assumptions of sociobiology, are these arguments persuasive?

For a discussion of how these decisions can "affirm the status quo" and, simultaneously "disrupt the status quo, transform dominant institutions, and convert distinctive features of the excluded group into more widely shared norms," see Douglas NeJaime, "Differentiating Assimilation," *Studies in Law, Politics, and Society* (forthcoming 2018).

3. *How Far Can Equitable Parentage Reach?* Some earlier cases had defined the idea of psychological or equitable parenthood very broadly. The Pennsylvania appellate court in *J.A.L. v. E.P.H.*, 453 Pa.Super. 78, 682 A.2d 1314 (1996), for example, ruled that parents must give some rights to anyone with whom "the child has established strong psychological bonds" and who "has lived with the child and provided care, nurture, and affection, assuming in the child's eye a stature like that of a parent." This broad a standard could include a babysitter, a nanny, an aunt or uncle with whom the child has bonded. The Wisconsin approach excludes people like babysitters and nannies who received money for their services. Is this fair? Should a live-in nanny who has devoted her life to a child have no rights?

4. *Allocating Custody and Visitation Between Legal Parents and Equitable Parents.* The New Jersey Supreme Court suggested that in the normal run of cases, only visitation rights should be granted to the equitable parent, although the court also suggested that, in appropriate cases, a court might use its equitable powers to transfer custody from the biological parent to the psychological or equitable parent. Other courts have disagreed, and have concluded that once the person establishes that he or she is an equitable parent, that person stands in parity with the legal parent. *See, e.g., Ramey v. Sutton*, 362 P.3d 217 (Okla. 2015); *In re Parentage of L.B.*, 122 P.3d 161 (Wash. 2005). Should there be a thumb on the scale in favor of the legal parent over the equitable parent? Why or why not?

PROBLEM 7-6
WHO IS A PARENT?

Consider each of the following three scenarios and decide whether the adult is a psychological parent under the criteria of *V.C. v. M.J.B.*

(A) Person **A** is the girlfriend of Jack, who drops his son at **A**'s house every day. **A** cares for the child every day between 8 a.m. and 6 p.m., and the child often stays at **A**'s house overnight, either because Jack stays over or because Jack is out of town for business purposes.

(B) Person **B** is a nanny who has an agreement with a child's lesbian parents to live in their house and care for their child between 8 a.m. and 6 p.m. every weekday and every other weekend. **B** is compensated for his work and lives rent-free in the house.

(C) Person **C** is Jill's retired father. Since the birth of her daughter, Jill and the child have lived in **C**'s house, and **C** has taken care of the daughter when Jill is working (40 hours per week) and often on weekends.

Would any of these people be parents under a holding out provision? Why or why not?

NOTES ON CRITIQUES OF EQUITABLE PARENTAGE

1. *Is Biological Parentage Better?* Professors Emily Buss and John DeWitt Gregory are leading commentators criticizing state courts for recognizing "parental" rights in persons who have neither biological nor marital ties to children. *See* Emily Buss, " 'Parental' Rights," 88 *Va. L. Rev.* 635 (2002); John DeWitt Gregory, "Redefining the Family, Undermining the Family," 2004 *U. Chi. Legal Forum* 381; John DeWitt Gregory, "Family Privacy and the Custody and Visitation Rights of Adult Outsiders," 36 *Fam. L.Q.* 163 (2002).

Their argument is that those adults related to the child as a matter of biology, marriage, or adoption have a privileged relationship to the child that ought not be disrupted by third-party rights. Professor Buss argues mainly from a best-interests-of-the-child perspective, but Professor Gregory also suggests that extending rights to such persons violates the constitutionally protected rights of parents to direct the upbringing of their children, first recognized in *Meyer* and *Pierce*. The Supreme Court reaffirmed this right in *Troxel.*

Other scholars have noted, however, that the constitutional protections for parents are not limited to biological parents. For example, in *Prince v. Massachusetts,* 321 U.S. 158 (1944), the Court respected the state's decision to confer "parental" rights upon a child's aunt—and then upheld a state restriction upon the parent's willingness to deploy the child to distribute religious tracts on a public street corner. Cases like *Prince* illustrate the Court's willingness to defer to state law defining who is a "parent." Indeed, in *Parentage of L.B.*, the Washington Supreme Court held that equitable parents have constitutionally protected interests in her relationship with her child. *In re Parentage of L.B.*, 155 Wash. 2d 679, 710 (2005) ("Thus, if, on remand, Carvin can establish standing as a *de facto* parent, Britain and Carvin would *both* have a 'fundamental liberty interest[ ]' in the 'care, custody, and control' of L.B." (citing *Troxel*) (emphasis in original)). What about Professor Buss' suggestion that biological parenting is best for children? Is that a good default or starting point for the law? Some scholars disagree. For example, Professor Katharine Baker argues:

> The DNA default * * * elevates genetic contributions over other biological and physical contributions to children. It makes a man's singular contribution to the reproductive process the sine qua non of parenthood, thus erasing the legal significance of

women's reproductive labor. A genetic regime also necessarily reifies a heteronormative vision of parenting. It treats as inevitable a paradigm of two and only two parents, one male and one female. In short, the DNA default embodies a vision of parenting that should be viewed with skepticism by most of those calling on the law to alter its paradigms for determining parentage.

Katharine K. Baker, "The DNA Default and Its Discontents: Establishing Modern Parenthood," 96 *B.U. L. Rev.* 2037, 2039 (2016).

Claims about the alleged superiority of biological parents featured prominently in the same-sex marriage litigation. *See, e.g.*, Courtney G. Joslin, "Marriage, Biology, and Federal Benefits," 98 *Iowa L. Rev.* 1467, 1476 (2013) (exploring such arguments).

2.   *Uncertainty?* Another critique that has been lodged against equitable parentage doctrines is the claim that it will be difficult to administer. Equitable parentage doctrines require judges, and therefore adults seeking to understand their status, to consider many factors. Because such balancing tests are less determinate, they threaten to "trap single biological and adoptive parents and their children in a limbo of doubt. These parents could not possibly know for sure when another adult's level of involvement in family life might reach the tipping point and jeopardize their right to bring up their children without the unwanted participation of a third party." *Debra H. v. Janice R.*, 930 N.E.2d 184, 193 (N.Y. 2010).

In response, Carlos Ball argues "that concerns regarding uncertainty in the application of equitable parenthood doctrines are greatly overblown and that whatever gains in certainty may accompany a narrow understanding of parenthood that is linked exclusively to (1) biology or (2) adoption or (3) the entering into a legally recognized relationship do not outweigh the harm to children that follow a categorical refusal to recognize the parentage status of individuals who have helped to raise them with the consent and encouragement of their legal parents." Carlos A. Ball, "Rendering Children Illegitimate in Former Partner Parenting Cases: Hiding Behind the Façade of Certainty," 20 *Am. U. J. Gender Soc. Pol'y & L.* 623 (2012)

How should courts best balance these concerns?

PROBLEM 7-7
EQUITABLE PARENTAGE IN A POST-*OBERGEFELL* WORLD

Note how two lines of cases have proceeded independently but sometimes intersect. As discussed above, numerous courts have recognized the idea of *equitable parentage,* whereby a person who has parented a child for a significant period of time may be entitled to some parental rights (and maybe some obligations), even though they are not legal parents. This section also explores the circumstances under which children born to married same-sex couples may be considered the legal children of both spouses.

What happens when a person claims to be an equitable parent of a child born to or adopted by her former same-sex partner, but where the parties could have, but did not marry prior to the birth or adoption of the child? Does their "choice" not to marry—and thereby obtain the protections marriage affords—preempt the court's ability to apply equitable doctrines? Some scholars have worried this result may come to pass. *See, e.g.*, Courtney G. Joslin, "Leaving No (Nonmarital) Child Behind," 48 *Fam. L.Q.* 495 (2014); Nancy D. Polikoff, "The New Illegitimacy: Winning Backward in the Protection of Children of Lesbian Couples," 20 *Am. U.J. Gender Soc. Pol'y & L.* 721 (2012); Joanna Grossman, "The New Illegitimacy: Tying Parentage to Marital Status for Lesbian Co-Parents," 20 *Am. U.J. Gender Soc. Pol'y & L.* 671 (2012); Carlos A. Ball, "Rendering Children Illegitimate in Former Partner Parenting Cases: Hiding Behind the Façade of Certainty," 20 *Am. U.J. Gender Soc. Pol'y & L.* (2012). Would such an outcome be fair? Constitutional?

Some courts seem to be resisting this temptation to cut back on equitable protections. Post-*Obergefell*, two state high courts overruled prior precedent refusing to apply equitable parenting doctrines to lesbian co-parents. *See, e.g.*, *Brooke S.B. v. Elizabeth A.C.C.*, 28 N.Y.3d 1 (N.Y. 2016) (overruling *Alison D. v. Virginia M.*); *Conover v. Conover*, 146 A.3d 433 (Md. 2016) (overruling *Janice M. v. Margaret K.*, 948 A.2d 73 (Md. 2008)).

Douglas NeJaime, "The Nature of Parenthood"
126 *Yale L.J.* 2260, 2264–70 (2017).*

Today, many courts and legislatures seek to promote gender and sexual-orientation equality in the family. Judges and lawmakers have repudiated gender-based distinctions in both spousal and parental regulation, including gendered presumptions in child custody. More recently, courts and legislatures have acknowledged same-sex couples' interest in family recognition. In extending marriage to same-sex couples in *Obergefell v. Hodges*, the United States Supreme Court sought to protect not only romantic bonds, but also parent-child relationships, formed by gays and lesbians.

Courts and legislatures claim in principle to have repudiated the privileging of men over women and different-sex over same-sex couples in the legal regulation of the family. But in parentage law, such privileging remains. * * *

[Consider just a few examples. In Connecticut, a married different-sex couple had a child through surrogacy and raised the child together for fourteen years. When they divorced, the court deemed the mother, who had neither a gestational nor genetic connection to the child, a legal stranger to her child. In Florida, an unmarried same-sex couple used the same donor sperm to have four children, with each woman giving birth to two children. They raised the children together until their relationship ended several years later, at which point the court left each woman with parental rights only to her two biological children. In New Jersey, a male same-sex couple used a donor egg to have a child through a gestational surrogate. The court recognized the gestational surrogate, rather than the biological father's husband (and the child's primary caretaker), as the second parent.]

As the examples above suggest, those who break from traditional norms of gender and sexuality—women who separate motherhood from biological ties (for instance, through surrogacy), and women and men who form families with a same-sex partner—often find their parent-child relationships discounted. * * *

Biological and social factors have long shaped the law of parental recognition. The common law tied parenthood to marriage and thus made parentage a legal, rather than biological, determination. Pursuant to the marital presumption (also known as the presumption of legitimacy), when a married woman gave birth to a child, the law recognized her husband as the child's father. This presumption channeled intuitions about biological paternity, but it could also conceal deviations from biological facts—allowing men to avoid questions of paternity and ensuring the child's legitimacy. In contrast to the marital child, the "illegitimate" child traditionally existed outside a legal family. The common law's organization of parentage through marriage reflected and enforced a gender-hierarchical, heterosexual order—giving men authority over women and children inside marriage and insulating men's property from claims to inheritance by children born outside marriage.

Slowly, American law departed from the harshest aspects of its common-law origins. Legislatures and courts began to recognize a legal relationship between a mother and her "illegitimate" child—granting the mother custody and bestowing on the child rights to support and eventually inheritance. In contrast, fathers of "illegitimate" children had financial obligations imposed on them less as a consequence of a legal family relationship and more as an effort to privatize support. Even as American law came to mitigate some of the effects of "illegitimacy," the government continued to place substantial legal impediments on nonmarital parents and children well into the twentieth century.

By the late 1960s and early 1970s, in the wake of increasing efforts to hold unmarried fathers financially accountable and to protect the rights of nonmarital children, the Court intervened by recognizing nonmarital parent-child relationships on constitutional grounds. Biological connection served as an explicit basis for constitutional protection, for both mother-child and father-child relationships. Yet even as the Court renounced "illegitimacy" and dismantled legally enforced gender hierarchy within marriage, it produced a new form of gender differentiation in parenthood—which it justified by resort to reproductive biology. At the moment of birth, the nonmarital child—unlike the marital child—had one legal parent: the mother. Gestation and birth evidenced the biological fact of maternity and furnished a relationship to the child that justified legal recognition. An unmarried man, in contrast, needed to demonstrate commitment to the parent-child relationship, in addition to his genetic connection. Of course, gestation provides a unique relationship to the child that is not only biological but functional. But in a series of cases, the logic of reproductive biology authorized more far-reaching social and legal differences between mothers and fathers— situating women, but not men, as naturally responsible for nonmarital children. Judges and lawmakers liberalized a parentage regime that had been deliberately organized around the gender-hierarchical, heterosexual status of marriage, yet continued to approach parentage within a gender-differentiated, heterosexual paradigm.

Against this legal backdrop, courts and legislatures in the late twentieth and early twenty-first centuries began to address parent-child relationships formed through a range of reproductive technologies. They determined parentage in ways that turned increasingly on social, and not simply biological, grounds—not only for men but for women, and not only for different-sex but for same-sex couples. Concepts of intentional and functional parenthood gained traction in both judicial and statutory reasoning addressing a range of family configurations.

Yet even as courts and legislatures have acted to conform parentage law to more recent egalitarian commitments, their attempts have been partial and incomplete. * * * [C]ourts and legislatures [continue to] draw distinctions between motherhood and fatherhood, different-sex and same-sex couples, biological and nonbiological parents, and marital and nonmarital families * * * [in ways that] reflect[ ] and perpetuate[ ] inequality based on gender and sexual orientation. With biological connection continuing to anchor nonmarital parenthood, unmarried gays and lesbians struggle for parental recognition. With the gender-differentiated, heterosexual family continuing to structure marital parenthood, the law assumes the presence of a biological mother in ways that burden nonbiological mothers in different-sex couples, as well as nonbiological fathers in same-sex couples.

To vindicate the parental interests of women and of gays and lesbians, [Professor NeJaime] urges greater emphasis on parenthood's social dimensions. * * * An approach that simply provides for equal treatment based on biological criteria would continue to marginalize those who parent with a same-sex partner, as well as women who defy conventional gender norms by separating the biological fact of maternity from the social role of motherhood. * * *

PROBLEM 7-8
POLICY: BEST RULES FOR DETERMINING PARENTAGE

Assume you are an aide for a legislator who agrees with Professor NeJaime's conclusion that existing parentage laws "reflect[ ] and perpetuate[ ] inequality based on gender and sexual orientation" and his policy proposal that the law should place "greater emphasis on parenthood's social dimensions."

Draft a memo to your legislator explaining how the law should be amended.

SECTION 4

POLYPARENTING

It is not only possible but common in the United States for more than two adults to play important caregiving roles for any given child. In a variety of circumstances, states already recognize this reality in more limited ways.

- **Grandparents.** As Justice O'Connor noted in her *Troxel* plurality opinion, every state in the United States has a statute that assures grandparents and other close relatives the right to petition for visitation with children related to them. *See* "Developments in the Law—The Law of Marriage and Family," 116 *Harv. L. Rev.* 1996, 2054–56 (2003).

- **Stepparents.** A number of states have statutes that allow stepparents to seek visitation and/or custody of their stepchildren after divorce. *See, e.g.*, Cal. Fam. Code § 3101(a); Tenn. Code Ann. § 36–6–303(a); Va. Code Ann. § 20–124.1; Wis. Stat. Ann. § 767.43(a).

These statutes recognize the reality that many children have more than two people who play important parenting roles in their lives.

As June Carbone and Naomi Cahn put it: "[T]he three-parent family is here. Once states accept that parenthood does not depend on either biology or marriage, then three parents are inevitable unless the states go out of their way to rule that adults who otherwise meet their definitions of parenthood will not be recognized." June Carbone & Naomi Cahn, "Parents, Babies, and More Parents," 92 *Chi.-Kent L. Rev.* 9, 13 (2017). Thus, Carbone and Cahn contend, the question is not *whether* to recognize families with more than two parents; the only question is *how* these families should be recognized.

A. EQUITABLE PARENTAGE AND NUMEROSITY

In recent years, courts in some states have begun to move even further towards recognizing the possibility of more than two parents. As noted above, the majority of states now recognize and apply equitable parentage doctrines. Much of the equitable parentage case law either ignores the issue or seems to assume that a finding of equitable parenthood does not strip other legal parents of their status (unless there is independent evidence of their unfitness). And a few cases expressly conclude that a child can have two legal parents plus an equitable parent. *See, e.g.*, *D.G. v. K.S.*, 133 A.3d 703 (N.J. Super. Ct. 2015) (concluding that biological father, his same-sex spouse, and biological mother were all entitled to joint legal and joint physical custody); *Frank G. v. P.F.*, 37 N.Y.S.3d 155 (2016) (holding that a same-sex domestic partner had standing to seek custody in a case where the surrogate carrier and the genetic father were considered legal parents); *McAllister v. McAllister*, 7779 N.W.2d 652 (N.D. 2010) (holding that a stepparent, who had assumed the role of a psychological parent, was entitled to seek visitation in a case in which the child had two legal parents); *Jacob v. Shultz-Jacob*, 923 A.2d 473 (Pa. Super. Ct. 2007) (awarding a 3-way custody and support award between the legal mother, the in loco parent mother, and the known sperm donor who had parented the child); *LaChapelle v. Denise Mitten*, 607 N.W.2d 151 (Minn. Ct. App. 2000) (affirming a three-way custody and visitation order based on a broad third-party visitation statute).

Consider the following case.

K.A.F. v. D.L.M.

New Jersey Superior Court, Appellate Division, 2014.
437 N.J. Super. 123, 96 A.3d 975.

■ The opinion of the court was delivered by KENNEDY, J. * * *

[I] K.A.F. and F.D. had been romantically involved since 1998, and in 1999 began living together. In 2000, the two women bought a house and thereafter decided to have a child. They made arrangements with an entity to obtain a sperm donor, and they agreed that K.A.F. would carry the child. All went as planned, and Arthur was born in December 2002.

Although their relationship became strained thereafter, causing them to begin living separately in June 2004, K.A.F. and F.D. apparently harbored hope for a reconciliation at some time and agreed to share equal time with Arthur and make joint decisions as to his care and welfare. On March 3, 2005, F.D. formally adopted Arthur with the consent of K.A.F., and in November of that year Arthur's birth certificate was issued listing both K.A.F. and F.D. as his parents.

In the meantime, D.M., a friend of both F.D. and K.A.F., became romantically involved with K.A.F. and they moved in together in the Fall of 2004. They subsequently bought a home and formalized their domestic partnership in May 2006.

According to D.M., she and K.A.F. "equally shared parental responsibility" for Arthur when he resided in their home. K.A.F. concedes that D.M. "participated in aspects of [Arthur's] care," but disputes the extent of the role D.M. actually undertook. F.D. also concedes that she has no direct knowledge about the extent of D.M.'s role with Arthur when he lived with K.A.F. and D.M., but claims "[a]t all times I have adamantly and wholeheartedly opposed [D.M.'s] attempts to parent" Arthur.

In any event, strains developed over time in the relationship between K.A.F. and D.M., resulting in D.M. leaving their home in March 2010. From that date through May 2011, D.M. had more or less regular visitation with Arthur, including weekly overnight stays. However, this arrangement began to end in June 2011, and ceased altogether in November 2011, amidst an angry confrontation between D.M. and K.A.F. In January 2012, K.A.F. advised D.M. in writing that she would no longer allow her to have any contact with Arthur.

On October 12, 2011, the court entered judgment dissolving the domestic relationship between K.A.F. and D.M. In February 2012, D.M. filed a complaint in the Family Part seeking "joint custody" of Arthur and a "reasonable visitation schedule," as well as other relief. K.A.F. and F.D. opposed the complaint, and, as we have explained, the Family Part judge dismissed the complaint on a motion for summary judgment. This appeal followed.

[II] * * * [T]he judge made two rulings which we are asked to review: the first ruling is that there is no genuine issue of material fact suggesting that F.D. ever consented to the creation of a psychological parent relationship between D.M. and Arthur; and the second is that where there are two fit and involved parents, both must have consented to the creation of a psychological parent relationship before a third party can maintain an action for visitation and custody based on the existence of that relationship. Although these two issues are intertwined, we shall examine them separately for purposes of clarity. Because the question of consent is a matter of first impression, we shall begin there.

[II.A]   * * * K.A.F. and F.D. argue that D.M. cannot attain the legal status of a psychological parent because F.D. did not consent to D.M. forming a parent-child relationship with Arthur. Their argument, which was adopted by the Family Part judge, is that where there are two fit and active parents, both legal parents must have consented to the development of a psychological parent relationship between a third party and their child in order for the third party to have standing to advance that claim in the first instance. They argue that the consent of only one custodial parent is not enough. We fail to perceive any basis for this argument either in the law or the policies underlying the concept of a psychological parent. * * *

While a natural parent's right to the care, custody, and control of his or her child is a "fundamental right to parental autonomy," and is recognized as "a fundamental liberty interest protected by the Due Process Clause of the Fourteenth Amendment to the United States Constitution [,]" * * *, that right * * * is not absolute. The presumption in favor of the parent will be overcome by "a showing of gross misconduct, unfitness, neglect, or 'exceptional circumstances' affecting the welfare of the child[.]" * * *

In *V.C.*, our Supreme Court explained that "[s]ubsumed within" the category of "exceptional circumstances" is the "subset known as the psychological parent cases in which a third party has stepped in to assume the role of the legal parent. . . ." *V.C., supra*, 163 N.J. at 219, 748 A.2d 539. The "exceptional circumstances" exception does not require proof that a parent is unfit. * * * * " '[E]xceptional circumstances' based on the probability of serious psychological harm to the child may deprive a parent of custody." * * *

Psychological parent cases, as noted, constitute a subset of "exceptional circumstances" cases, in recognition of children's "strong interest in maintaining the ties that connect them to adults who love and provide for them." *V.C.*, *supra*, 163 N.J. at 219, 221, 748 A.2d 539. A third party may become a psychological parent as a result of "the volitional choice of a legal parent to cede a measure of parental authority to a third party[.]" *Id.* at 227, 748 A.2d 539. Once a third party becomes a psychological parent, he or she "steps into [the] shoes" of a natural parent, *id.* at 223–24 n. 6, 748 A.2d 539, and determinations between the natural and psychological parent are made pursuant to a best interests analysis. *Id.* at 227–28, 748 A.2d 539.

Four essential requirements must be satisfied for one to become a psychological parent:

> [T]he legal parent must consent to and foster the relationship between the third party and the child; the third party must have lived with the child; the third party must perform parental functions for the child to a significant degree; and most important, a parent-child bond must be forged.

[*Id.* at 223, 748 A.2d 539.]

* * * As the Supreme Court explained in *V.C.,*

> [a]t the heart of the psychological parent cases is a recognition that children have a strong interest in maintaining the ties that connect them to adults who love and provide for them. That interest, for constitutional as well as social purposes, lies in the emotional bonds that develop between family members as a result of shared daily life. * * *

[*V.C.*, *supra*, 163 N.J. at 221, 748 A.2d 539.]

* * * With this background, we turn to the question of whether both legal parents must consent, or whether the consent of only one "fit and involved" legal parent is sufficient to support a claim by a third party of psychological parenthood. From the perspective of simple logic, it would be difficult to ignore the "psychological harm" a child might suffer because he is deprived of the care of a psychological parent simply because only one of his "legal parents" consented to the relationship.

The clear policy underlying the [New Jersey Supreme] Court's rulings * * * is that "exceptional circumstances" may require recognition of custodial or visitation rights of a third party with respect to a child where the third party has performed parental duties at home for the child, with the consent of a legal parent, however expressed, for such a length of time that a parent-child bond has developed, and terminating that bond may cause serious psychological harm to the child. It is fatuous to suggest that this fundamental policy may be subverted, and that a court may not even examine the issue at a plenary hearing, where one of the child's legal parents colorably claims lack of consent, in circumstances where the other legal parent has consented. If we were to accept the arguments of K.A.F. and F.D., a court would be powerless to avert harm to a child through the severance of the child's parental bond with a third party. That result is not supported by the Court's carefully crafted policy governing such cases.

The Family Part judge suggested in his ruling that if both fit and involved parents do not consent, a child might then in the future have "three legal parents, four legal parents[,]" depending on the romantic vagaries of the original legal parents. To this argument, we observe that the Court in *V.C.* stated that establishing psychological parenthood is "not an easy task[.]" *V.C.*, *supra*, 163 N.J. at 230, 748 A.2d 539. Moreover, we have confidence that our Family Part judges have the expertise and discretion to appropriately address such issues as they arise.

* * * Nothing in the historical development of the psychological parent policy, in the policy itself, or in the language of the Court * * * suggests that both legal parents must consent before a court may consider a claim of psychological parenthood by a third party. Rather, it is sufficient if only one of the legal custodial parents has consented to the parental role of the third party. In that circumstance, a legal custodial parent has voluntarily created the relationship and thus has permitted the third party to enter the zone of privacy between her and her child.

By so holding, we do not discount the importance of F.D.'s "consent", or lack thereof, in the case before us. * * *

It may be used by a trial court, in an appropriate context, as one factor among many in determining whether a third party has established that he or she is a psychological parent of a child, and, if so, whether the "best interests" of the child warrant some form of custody or visitation. * * * We would expect, however, that in most cases, the longer and more established the parental role of a third party has become, the lack of consent by one legal parent would diminish in analytical significance.

Once the court has determined that the role of psychological parent exists, the question of what relief is warranted entails consideration of the best interests of the child. * * *

[III] We reverse the order of the Family Part which dismissed D.M.'s complaint and we remand for a plenary hearing on whether D.M. is a psychological parent of Arthur and, if so, whether the best interests of Arthur require accommodation through a sharing of custody, visitation, or other relief. * * *

Did the court reach the right answer? That a person can become a psychological or equitable parent even where one of the child's legal parent objects? Is that fair? Is it constitutional?

B. MORE THAN TWO LEGAL PARENTS

In *K.A.F.*, the biological mother's subsequent same-sex partner was held to be a psychological parent with standing to seek visitation, or possibly custody, with the child. She was not, however, recognized as a legal parent to the child. Thus, the child, Arthur, had two legal parents and an equitable parent who had some but not all of the rights and responsibilities of parenthood.

As Carbone and Cahn note, there are now a few states that expressly permit a court to declare that a child has *more than two legal parents*. In 2013, California adopted a statute that makes this possibility explicit. California Family Code § 7612(c) permits a court to "find that more than two persons with a claim to parentage under this division are parents if the court finds that recognizing only two parents would be detrimental to the child."

Delaware, Maine, and the District of Columbia also have statutory provisions that permit a court to find that a child has more than two legal parents. Del. Code Ann. Tit. 13, §§ 8–201(a)(4); (b)(6), (c); Me. Rev. Stat. tit. 19–A § 1853(2) ("Consistent with the establishment of parentage under this chapter, a court may determine that a child has more than 2 parents."); D.C. Code Ann. § 16–909(e).

The UPA (2017) contains two approaches for states to choose from. A state could chose to include language in the statute limiting a child's parents to a total of two. Alternatively, a state could chose to include a provision permitting a court to find that a child has more than two legal parents. UPA (2017) § 613. The later option is modeled on the California statute.

Are these developments permitting courts to find that children have more than two parents positive ones? Why or why not? What are the benefits of a system that allows a court to find that a child has more than two parents? What are some of the drawbacks or challenges of such a system? Are there ways to reform the rules to mitigate some of the challenges?

Some scholars argue that having more potential caretakers and child support providers is generally a positive development. *See, e.g.*, Laura N. Althouse, "Three's Company? How American Law Can Recognize a Third Social Parent in Same-Sex Headed Families," 19 *Hastings Women's L.J.* 171 (2008); Nancy E. Dowd, "Multiple Parents/Multiple Fathers," 9 *J.L. & Fam. Stud.* 231 (2007); Melanie B. Jacobs, "Why Just Two? Disaggregating Traditional Parental Rights and Responsibilities to Recognize Multiple Parents," 9 *J.L. & Fam. Stud.* 309 (2007).

Other scholars are more wary, noting that more parents often means more disputes and, in turn, a greater likelihood of court involvement (that is, oversight) in the family. *See, e.g.*, Susan F. Appleton, "Parents by the Numbers," 37 *Hofstra L. Rev.* 11, 41 (2009) ("As the parental community expands,   * * *   the responsibilities for such disputes increase"); Katharine Baker, "Bionormativity and the Construction of Parenthood," 42 *Ga. L. Rev.* 649, 675 (2008) (noting that "[t]he more parents there are with competing claims to a child, the higher the likelihood that the state will become involved in the day-to-day business of parenting"). Still other scholars argue that question is not whether to recognize multiple parents, but how to do so. *See, e.g.*, June Carbone & Naomi Cahn, "Parents, Babies, and More Parents," 92 *Chi.-Kent L. Rev.* 9, 13 (2017) (arguing in favor of a system of multiple parent recognition but one that does not accord all parties equal status).

Consider the next case, arising out of California. Who among the three potential candidates should be deemed the child's legal parents?

S.M. v. E.C.

California Court of Appeal, 2014.
2014 WL 2921905, unpublished, uncitable.

■ SARKISIAN, J.

Appellant S.M. appeals from a trial court order finding that E.C. and Y.M. are the two parents of P.C.-M. (the minor). E.C. is the minor's biological mother, Y.M. was E.C.'s registered domestic partner when E.C. conceived and gave birth to the minor, and S.M. is the minor's biological father. After determining that Y.M. and S.M. each met a statutory presumption of parentage, the trial court found that considerations of policy and logic weighed in favor of Y.M.'s parentage claim over S.M.'s parentage claim under Family Code section 7612, subdivision (b). [Ed. note: Cal. Fam. Code § 7612(b) provides that if "two or more [parentage] presumptions arise under Section 7610 or 7611 * * * the presumption which on the facts is founded on the weightier considerations of policy and logic controls.]

On appeal, S.M. contends the court erred in resolving the competing claims for parental status under section 7612. * * *

[**Facts and Procedural History**] Y.M. and E.C. entered into a domestic partnership registered with the State of California in October 2006. [Ed. note: all of the state-conferred rights of marriage, including any marriage-based parenting rules and presumptions apply equally to registered domestic partners.] They decided to have a child together. According to Y.M., they spent "two years off and on planning and trying to conceive [a] child." They asked S.M. to be their sperm donor. Y.M. and E.C. found a sample sperm donor contract on the Internet, made some edits and deletions, and printed two copies of their edited contract. Y.M., E.C., and S.M. signed both copies of the contract. According to S.M., Y.M. and E.C. paid him $300 for his semen samples.

Y.M. assisted E.C. in artificial insemination on two occasions in October 2008, and Y.M. believed this was how E.C. became pregnant. During the time period Y.M. and E.C. were trying to conceive, however, E.C. and S.M. were in a secret romantic relationship. E.C. began having sex with S.M. in June 2008, and she believed she had conceived prior to the two artificial insemination attempts. At the time E.C. became pregnant, S.M. did not intend to be the father of the minor.

The minor was born in June 2009. Her birth certificate lists the parents as Y.M. and E.C. The minor's last name is hyphenated, combining the last names of E.C. and Y.M.

Y.M. and E.C. separated about six months after the minor was born. S.M. moved in with E.C. in July 2010, and he began holding out the minor as his child. S.M. and E.C. originally met at work; he was a sales associate and she was a loss-prevention manager at the same store. According to S.M., he and E.C. began a serious relationship in March 2010. They did not tell anyone that the minor was S.M.'s child until E.C. transferred to a different store in the summer of 2010 because there was a rule against coworkers dating and they could have lost their jobs.

In September 2010, Y.M. initiated [an action in which she named] E.C. as the respondent and the minor as the subject of the action. Y.M. alleged that she and E.C. were both mothers of the minor, and Y.M. sought joint legal and physical custody and proposed a visitation schedule.

A month later, E.C. filed a petition for dissolution of domestic partnership. She named the minor as a child of the relationship. E.C. also filed with the court a handwritten declaration by S.M. In the declaration, S.M. * * * wrote:

> "Although I donated my sperm to [E.C. and Y.M.] in [October] 2008 to [conceive] a child, I believe that [E.C.] was pregnant a month prior because we engaged in sexual relations. [E.C. and I] have been in a serious relationship since March 2010 and we [are pursuing] our relationship further in hopes of being married by next year. I have [actively] been in [the minor's] life since March and I am determined in having my parental rights established. I love both [E.C.] and [the minor] and we both want to give [the minor] a normal and healthy [*sic*] with both [the minor's] biological parents."

* * * [I]n February 2011, S.M. initiated a separate action * * * for child custody, visitation, and an injunctive order (paternity action). * * * [Judge Shirk consolidated the dissolution action and the paternity action and assigned both cases to her.] * * *

In January 2012, the court heard testimony from the parties regarding Y.M. and E.C.'s efforts at artificial insemination, E.C.'s sexual relationship with S.M. in 2008, and the sperm donor agreement. The parties agreed that they all signed an agreement regarding the sperm donation, but they were unable to locate a copy of the document. Y.M. recalled that the agreement stated S.M. would have no parental rights, he would not be asked for child support, and he could not seek parental rights after the child was born. S.M. acknowledged that he signed an agreement that he would provide semen samples to E.C. until she became pregnant, and he would provide her semen again for up to two more children. He believed the agreement provided that E.C. and Y.M. would raise the child and they would not request child support from him. E.C. remembered that the agreement provided she would not collect child support from S.M. She did not remember a paragraph stating that S.M. would not be part of the child's life.

* * * [T]he court issued a tentative ruling on March 20, 2012. * * *

The court found that Y.M. and S.M. each qualified as a presumed parent, but only one of them could be the minor's second parent. * * * In the tentative ruling, the court reasoned:

> "Both [S.M.] and [Y.M.] are adequate parents. None of the parties have raised claims of unfitness. Both have an established relationship with [the minor]. [S.M.] is a biological parent, but was not present at birth and did not assert his parental interest until some months after [the minor] was born. [Y.M.] is not a biological parent, but assisted [E.C.] during pregnancy and was [E.C.'s] Domestic Partner when [the minor] was born.

> "To this level, the legal positions between [Y.M.] and [S.M.] are nearly evenly matched. The determining factor in this matter is the ongoing stability of the family unit. [S.M.] and [E.C.] currently reside together. They intend to marry as soon as issues regarding [E.C.'s] Domestic Partnership are resolved. [E.C.] is pregnant with [S.M.'s] child and they intend to raise the new baby and [the minor] as their children. This ongoing familial relationship would best support [the minor's] needs in the future. The Court has not determined that [S.M.] is a superior parent than [Y.M.] or that [Y.M.] is, or would be, a lesser parent to [the minor]. In considering all of the factors set forth in the Family Code, based on the facts unique to this matter, the Court finds that permitting [the minor] to be raised in a family unit is determinative of parental rights."

The court believed it would be in the minor's best interest to maintain a parental relationship with all three parties, but this was not possible under [the law at the time]. * * *

[The court then held a contested hearing on] all issues, which occurred on May 22 and 23, 2012.

At the contested hearing, Y.M.'s counsel elicited testimony from S.M. that * * * [d]uring E.C.'s pregnancy, S.M. did not participate in any preparation for the minor's arrival, he was not present at her birth, * * * and he did not offer any financial support to E.C. or Y.M. for either the pregnancy or the birth. He learned that E.C. gave birth at the same time other coworkers at the store where they both worked learned the news. * * * [H]e did not acknowledge her as his child until the minor was one year old. * * * He was aware that Y.M. paid child support to E.C. for the minor.

S.M. believed that the sperm donor agreement he signed meant that he was relieved of financial responsibility. He also believed he was giving up custodial rights. Asked whether it was his intention at the time the minor was conceived to give up custodial rights, he responded: "Yes. We were both in a relationship. I didn't want to complicate [E.C.'s] life." This remained his intent until a couple months after the minor was born. At that point, he and E.C. "got heavier in [their] relationship."

S.M. agreed that the minor did not have any problem going back and forth between E.C.'s and Y.M.'s houses. He agreed that the minor had a strong attachment to Y.M. and viewed her as one of her mothers. He believed the minor loved Y.M. very much, but the minor was young enough to overcome being cut off from Y.M.

E.C. and S.M. have had a daughter since they moved in together. S.M. was present when the child was born, and he provided financial and emotional support for E.C. during the pregnancy.

E.C. testified that, at the time she became pregnant with the minor, it was her intention that she and Y.M. would raise the child together. She agreed that the minor seemed happy when Y.M. would pick her up for visits, and the minor had a bond with Y.M. and liked to spend time with her. E.C. believed it was in the minor's best interest that "she should be around [Y.M.]" because the minor had "grown to enjoy her time with her."

E.C. also believed there was a bond between S.M. and the minor. S.M. had participated in the minor's upbringing since he moved in with E.C. in July 2010. He changed her diapers, fed her, and helped with potty training. E.C. testified that S.M. plays with the minor and "does the daddy thing."

Y.M. testified she was present at the minor's birth and immediately held the minor out to the world as her child. Y.M. insured the minor through her health insurance and named the minor as her beneficiary for life insurance and work-related benefits. At the time of conception, it was Y.M.'s intent that the minor would be raised in a family unit consisting of Y.M., E.C., and the minor. E.C. told Y.M. that was her intent too. After the minor was born, the three of them lived together for about eight months. Y.M. began paying child support voluntarily after she and E.C. separated. E.C. first told Y.M. that she had changed her mind about raising the minor with Y.M. as the other parent when the minor was just over one year old.

S.M.'s counsel argued, among other things, that over the previous two years, S.M. had spent a significant amount of time with the minor on a daily basis interacting with her as a family member. S.M.'s counsel pointed out that if Y.M. prevailed and E.C. were to die, then S.M. would have no right to his child and the minor would have no legal relationship to her siblings. E.C.'s counsel joined in S.M.'s argument.

Y.M.'s counsel asserted that Y.M. had demonstrated a greater commitment to the minor than S.M. had. For example, Y.M. had accepted financial responsibility for the minor since conception, while S.M. originally "consciously wanted nothing to do with financial responsibility." * * *

On July 6, 2012, the court issued its ruling * * * [finding that] Y.M. and E.C. are the minor's legal parents. The court explained:

"[Y.M., S.M. and E.C.] are each a presumed parent and each have established a parental relationship with the child. Each seeks to maintain that relationship in these proceedings. Under existing legal authority [citations], [the minor] is limited to two parents and the Court is required to resolve the conflict between presumed parents under Family Code Section 7612(b).

* * * In its tentative ruling dated March 20, 2012, the Court struggled to find a factor which tipped those scales revealing the weightier factor. At that time, the Court settled on the fact that [S.M.] was in a committed relationship with [E.C.] and that it would be in the child's best interest to be raised in an intact family.

"However, the testimony of the parties at trial refutes the Court's impression. The Court is still convinced that [S.M., E.C. and Y.M.] are good parents and that [the minor] is fortunate to have them in her life. However, the Court was struck by [S.M.'s] lack of commitment to the mother of his pre-school-age son, during his initial relationship with [E.C.], describing the relationship as 'on again off again.' * * *

"There is no doubt that [S.M.] loves [the minor] and that he has been supporting her financially since [E.C.] moved in with him. There is also no doubt that he will always play a role in her life and will always be her father. However, the Court is limited to choosing between [S.M. and Y.M.] in determining who [the minor's] other legal parent will be. Being a parent is a joy, but it is also a tremendous commitment and responsibility. [Y.M.] has demonstrated that since conception she was completely committed to this child, not just when her relationship with [E.C.] was good, and not just when it was convenient in terms of personal or employment pressures. While commitment remains the weightier consideration, the evidence demonstrates that [Y.M.'s] commitment from day one exceeds [S.M.'s] current commitment."

DISCUSSION

* * * Section 7611 provides various statutory presumptions of parentage. Under subdivision (a) of section 7611, a person is presumed to be the natural parent of a child if the person and the child's natural mother were married to each other and the child is born during marriage. Although Y.M. and E.C. were not married at the time the minor was born, they were in a registered domestic partnership, and domestic partners are entitled to all the rights, benefits, responsibilities, and obligations granted to and imposed upon spouses by statute or any other source of

law. (§ 297.5, subds. (a).) S.M. does not dispute that Y.M. is a presumed parent under this subdivision.

Under subdivision (d) of section 7611, a person is a presumed parent if he receives the child into his home and openly holds out the child as his child. The trial court found S.M. to be a presumed parent under this subdivision * * *.

In his appellate briefing, S.M. asserts the trial court erred in determining that Y.M. rather than S.M. is the minor's second parent under section 7612, subdivision (b), which provides:

> "If two or more presumptions arise under Section . . . 7611 that conflict with each other, . . . the presumption which on the facts is founded on the weightier considerations of policy and logic controls." (§ 7612, subd. (b).)

No statutory presumption of parentage is given categorical preference over any other. * * * For example, * * * the fact that one presumed parent is also the biological father [does not] automatically defeat another presumed parent's claim for parental status. Rather, "the trial court must make its determination under section 7612 on a case-by-case basis." "In resolving such a conflict, the trial court must at all times be guided by the principle that the goal of our [parentage] statutes is 'the protection of the child's well being.'"

We review for an abuse of discretion a trial court's determination of parental status where there are competing presumed parents. * * *

We now turn to the trial court's ruling that Y.M., not S.M., is the minor's second parent. As we have described, the trial court's task was to determine, between Y.M.'s and S.M.'s claims of presumed parentage, which was "founded on the weightier considerations of policy and logic" on the facts of the case. (§ 7612, subd. (b).) * * *

After hearing two days of testimony, the court * * * determined that commitment to the child was the weightier consideration, and this consideration weighed in favor of Y.M. because she demonstrated complete commitment to the minor since conception. S.M., in contrast, began his sexual relationship with E.C. and then provided sperm for artificial insemination without any intent to be a father to the resulting child. We see no abuse of discretion in the trial court's determination. * * *

S.M. also refers to his constitutional rights, suggesting that his biological connection to the minor, together with his contact with her, establish "his constitutional right to be declared her father and second parent under the law." Yet, he recognizes that biology is not determinative of legal parentage. Curiously, he even cites *Miller v. Miller* (1998) 64 Cal.App.4th 111, a case in which we affirmed a trial court's ruling against an appellant who, like S.M., was the biological father of a child born during the mother's marriage to a different person and who subsequently married the mother. Our court specifically rejected the appellant's argument that he had a substantive due process right to establish he was the child's biological father.

* * * At most, [prior decisions] may be read to suggest that a biological father who also has a relationship with the child has a due process right to *standing* to pursue a parentage claim. Here, the trial court held that S.M. had standing to bring his paternity action as it denied Y.M.'s motion to quash and found S.M. met the statutory presumption of parentage. * * * Accordingly, we reject S.M.'s suggestion that he has a constitutional right to a determination that he is the second parent of the minor.

Finally, we consider the possibility of remand in this case. [The trial court believed that it was precluded in finding all three parties to be parents] * * * Effective January 1, 2014, however, section 7612 was amended to allow a court, in an appropriate action, to "find that more than two persons with a claim to parentage under this division are parents if the court finds that recognizing only two parents would be detrimental to the child." (§ 7612, subd. (c).)

[The court concluded that the new law could be applied to the instant action.] * * * [W]hile we have no grounds for reversing the trial court's decision that Y.M. and E.C. are the child's parents, because the new law expands the court's discretion to "find that more than two persons with a claim to parentage under this division are parents if the court finds that recognizing only two parents would be detrimental to the child" (§ 7612, subd. (c)), we believe a limited remand is appropriate in this case * * * to allow the court to consider whether S.M. may be the child's third parent under current section 7612, subdivision (c), is appropriate. Nothing in this opinion is intended to suggest how the court should rule on this limited remand. * * *

■ [The concurring and dissenting opinion of JUDGE POOCHIGIAN is omitted. According to JUDGE POOCHIGIAN, S.M. is a " 'parent' under any reasonable definition of that word."].

NOTES ON *S.M. V. E.C.*

1.   *S.M. or Y.M.?* If you were limited to a total of two parents, which two would you have chosen and why? Which factor or factors are the most important? Genetic connection? Intention? Function?

2.   *More than Two?* Is California correct? Should the law permit courts to find that a child has more than two legal parents? Why or why not? As you think about this question, you might find it interesting to note that it is now possible for a child to have three genetic parents. In September 2016, a child was born using this technique, which involves "taking the nucleus from [an egg] * * * and implanting it into a donor egg that had its nucleus removed but retained the donor's healthy mitochondrial DNA." This ovum is then fertilized with semen. Lucy Clarke-Billings, "World's First Baby Born with Three Biological Parents," *Newsweek* (Sept. 27, 2016). Does that development affect your answer to the question? Why or why not?

3. *A Detriment Standard?* Under current California law, a court can find that a child has more than two legal parents, but only in rare cases. To reach such a conclusion, the court must find that not recognizing more than two would be "detrimental" to the child. Detriment is a high bar to meet. In this case, would recognizing only two parents be detrimental? Why or why not?

4. *Is "Detriment" the Right Standard?* Assume you work for a state legislator that wants to draft a law permitting a court to find that a child has more than two legal parents, would you advise the legislator to follow California's model? Why or why not? If you don't support using the California standard, which standard would you use?

CHAPTER 8

SEXUALITY, GENDER, AND EDUCATION

SECTION 1   Regulating Expressions of Sexuality and Gender
SECTION 2   Sexuality and Gender-Based Harassment and Discrimination
SECTION 3   Sex and Sexuality Education

This chapter addresses three related issues involving sexuality and gender that can arise in the context of public schools. Section 1 introduces and grapples with questions related to student speech in schools. Resolution of these free speech questions often requires courts to consider whether public schools should primarily seek to *inculcate* good ideas and useful facts in the students, or whether schools should seek to foster *critical thinking* by students. An inculcation approach is more prone to prescribe, or censor, student comments and pedagogic materials. By contrast, a critical thinking approach permits and, indeed, encourages more speech. Historically, a critical thinking approach brought about important victories for LGBT students who wanted to speak about LGBT issues in schools.

But, of course, the additional speech may not always be pro-LGBT. In that way, a critical thinking approach may, at times, be in tension with the issues discussed in Section 2—schools' obligations to protect LGBT students from harassment and discrimination. That is, schools are sometimes called upon to balance the first amendment rights of some students against the rights of other students to have a safe and effective place to learn. It is now clear that public schools must take reasonable steps to respond to known incidents of harassment and discrimination, including sex-based harassment and discrimination. While federal law does not expressly prohibit discrimination on the basis of sexual orientation or gender identity, courts have held that the Equal Protection Clause and Title IX prohibit discrimination on the basis of sex stereotypes, and that this protection extends equally to LGBT students. Schools also have a responsibility to respond to known incidents of sexual violence. Policy makers and schools continue to grapple with how to define the line between consensual sexual intimacy and sexual violence.

Finally, Section 3 delves into what schools are teaching and what information students have and should have access to. If a school's goal is at least in part inculcative, what views about gender and sexuality should it be inculcating? A traditionalist perspective might urge that sexuality and gender roles are best not discussed in schools at all; these topics should be left to parents. This was the prevailing approach in America for most of the twentieth century. However, after the Kinsey Institute reports on men's (1948) and women's (1953) sexuality and sexual experiences galvanized national public discourse about sexuality, the openness of sexual activity among adolescents galvanized local and state public discourses about sexuality. Pregnancy and AIDS are now recognized as critical issues for adolescents in this country, and the school system has become an important forum for addressing those issues. While public schools generally are more open to the notion that school should teach sexuality education, the scope of that education remains hotly contested. Many, indeed maybe most, public schools teach that young people should abstain from sexual activities until marriage, and some schools continue to emphasize that that "proper" sexuality involves procreative intercourse between one man and one woman in a companionate marriage. On the other end of the spectrum, other schools insist that sexuality be discussed in schools and that it be discussed without emphasis on traditional gender roles, heterosexual norms, or abstinence.

SECTION 1

REGULATING EXPRESSIONS OF SEXUALITY AND GENDER

A. INCULCATION, CRITICAL THINKING, AND THE FIRST AMENDMENT

John Tinker et al. v. Des Moines Independent Community School District, 393 U.S. 503 (1969). To protest the war in Vietnam, Des Moines public school students wore black armbands to classes in December 1965. Principals at several Des Moines junior high and high schools suspended students for wearing these armbands. The case turned on whether the First Amendment's protection of core political expression should apply and, if so, whether it should apply with full force in the school setting. The Supreme Court, in an opinion by **Justice Fortas**, held that the suspensions unconstitutionally penalized students for expression protected by the First Amendment.

"First Amendment rights, applied in light of the special characteristics of the school environment, are available to teachers and students. It can hardly be argued that either students or teachers shed their constitutional rights to freedom of speech or expression at the schoolhouse gate. * * * A student's rights * * * do not embrace merely the classroom hours. When he is in the cafeteria, or on the playing field, or on the campus during the authorized hours, he may express his opinions, even on controversial subjects like the conflict in Vietnam, if he does so without 'materially and substantially interfer[ing]' with the requirements of appropriate discipline in the operation of the school and without colliding with the rights of others. But conduct by the student, in class or out of it, which for any reason whether it stems from time, place, or type of behavior-materially disrupts classwork or involves substantial disorder or invasion of the rights of others is, of course, not immunized by the constitutional guarantee of freedom of speech. * * *

"The school officials [sought] to punish [the students] for a silent, passive expression of opinion, unaccompanied by any disorder or disturbance on the part of [the students]. There is no evidence whatever of [the students'] interference, actual or nascent, with the schools' work or of collision with the rights of other students to be secure and to be let alone. * * * There is no indication that the work of the schools or any class was disrupted. Outside the classrooms, a few students made hostile remarks to the children wearing armbands, but there were no threats or acts of violence on school premises.

"The [trial judge] concluded that the action of the school authorities was reasonable because it was based upon their fear of a disturbance from the wearing of the armbands. But, in our system, undifferentiated fear or apprehension of disturbance is not enough to overcome the right to freedom of expression. * * * In order for the State in the person of school officials to justify prohibition of a particular expression of opinion, it must be able to show that its action was caused by something more than a mere desire to avoid the discomfort and unpleasantness that always accompany an unpopular viewpoint."

Dissenting, **Justice Black** referred to events in the record where other students made fun of the armbands, and one armband student threatened the hecklers. Also, a math teacher complained that his lesson plan was wrecked by the protest. According to Justice Black, the "armbands did exactly what the [officials] foresaw they would, that is, took the students' minds off their classwork and diverted them to thoughts about the highly emotional subject of the Vietnam war."

Aaron Fricke v. Richard B. Lynch, 491 F.Supp. 381 (D.R.I. 1980). Aaron Fricke, a senior at Cumberland High School in Cumberland, Rhode Island, proposed to bring another man, Paul Guilbert, as his date to the high school prom. The high school principal, Richard Lynch, denied Fricke's request because of the "real and present threat of physical harm to you, your male escort and to others," as well as the "adverse effect among your classmates" and the difficulty of providing police protection to prevent violence. Lynch testified about student hostility expressed the year before when Guilbert had made a similar request, and about Fricke's being shoved and punched by other students after his request.

Notwithstanding these arguments, **Chief Judge Pettine** granted Fricke's request for a preliminary injunction. Because Fricke's request was, essentially, a "political statement," the judge ruled that it was "expressive conduct" protected by the First Amendment. "Accordingly, the school's action must be judged by the standards articulated in *United States v. O'Brien*, 391 U.S. 367 (1968): (1) was the regulation within the constitutional power of the government; (2) did it further an important or substantial governmental interest; (3) was the governmental interest unrelated to the suppression of free expression; and (4) was the incidental restriction on alleged First Amendment freedoms no greater than essential to the furtherance of that interest?"

Chief Judge Pettine ruled that "the school's action fails to meet the last criterion set out in *O'Brien*, the requirement that the government employ the 'least restrictive alternative' before curtailing speech. The plaintiff argues, and I agree, that the school can take appropriate security measures to control the risk of harm. Lynch testified that he did not know if adequate security could be provided, and that he would still need to sit down and make the necessary arrangements. In fact he has not made any effort to determine the need for and logistics of additional security. Although Lynch did not say that any additional security measures would be adequate, from the testimony I find that significant measures could be taken and would in all probability critically reduce the likelihood of any disturbance. As Lynch's own testimony indicates, police officers and teachers will be present at the dance, and have been quite successful in the past in controlling whatever problems arise, including unauthorized drinking. Despite the ever-present possibility of violence at sports events, adequate discipline has been maintained."

Chief Judge Pettine acknowledged that the case was difficult for him because it arose in the high school setting, where judges have been deferential to policies adopted by professional educators and school boards, especially when they act to prevent disruption of the educational mission. But "*Tinker* makes clear that high school students do not 'shed their constitutional rights to freedom of speech or expression at the schoolhouse gate.'" The chief judge then quoted *Tinker*'s allowance for regulation of student speech that is disruptive.

"It seems to me that here, not unlike in *Tinker*, the school administrators were acting on 'an undifferentiated fear or apprehension of disturbance.' True, Aaron was punched and then security measures were taken, but since that incident he has not been threatened with violence nor has he been attacked. There has been no disruption at the school; classes have not been cancelled, suspended, or interrupted. In short, while the defendants have perhaps shown more of a basis for fear of harm than in *Tinker*, they have failed to make a 'showing' that Aaron's conduct would 'materially and substantially interfere' with school discipline. However, even if the Court assumes that there is justifiable fear and that Aaron's peaceful speech leads, or may lead, to a violent reaction from others, the question remains: may the school prohibit the speech, or must it protect the speaker? * * * "

"After considerable thought and research, I have concluded that even a legitimate interest in school discipline does not outweigh a student's right to peacefully express his views in an appropriate time, place, and manner. To rule otherwise would completely subvert free speech in the schools by granting other students a 'heckler's veto,' allowing them to decide through prohibited and violent methods what speech will be heard. The First Amendment does not tolerate mob rule by unruly school children. This conclusion is bolstered by the fact that any disturbance here, however great, would not interfere with the main business of school education. No classes or school work would be affected; at the very worst an optional social event, conducted by the students for their own enjoyment, would be marred. In such a context, the school does have an obligation to take reasonable measures to protect and foster free speech, not to stand helpless before unauthorized student violence."

Postscript. The world did not end after Chief Judge Pettine's decision, and the prom went ahead as scheduled on May 30, 1980. Principal Lynch isolated Aaron and Paul at a side table, and the evening started off miserably. Finally, Aaron and Paul came together on the dance floor to slow-dance to Bob Seger's *We've Got the Night*. As Aaron

Fricke tells the story in his book, *Reflections of a Rock Lobster: A Story About Growing Up Gay* (1981), "[t]he crowd receded. As I laid my head on Paul's shoulder, I saw a few students start to stare at us. I closed my eyes and listened to the music, my thoughts wandering over the events of that evening. When the song ended, I opened my eyes. A large crowd of students had formed a ring around us. Probably most of them had never before seen two happy men embracing in a slow dance. For a moment I was uncomfortable. Then I heard the sound that I knew so well as a B-52's fan. One of my favorite songs was coming up: 'Rock Lobster.'

"Paul and I began dancing free-style. Everyone else was still staring at us, but by the end of the first stanza, several couples had also begun dancing. The song has a contagious enthusiasm to it, and with each bar, more dancers came onto the floor. * * * A quarter of the way into the song, thirty people were on the dance floor. 'Down, Down, Down,' commanded the lyrics. Everyone on the dance floor sank to their knees and crouched on the ground. [More than 100 students were dancing by then.]

" 'Let's Rock!!!' bellowed the speakers, and to my surprise, when I looked up, I saw that Paul had disappeared. I looked around; several other guys were dancing with each other, and girls were dancing with girls. Everybody was rockin'. Everybody was fruggin'. Who cared why? * * * I danced with girls, I danced with guys, I danced with the entire group."

This may be an idealized story; we do not know exactly how Cumberland High changed (if at all) after this particular prom night. But the implication is that the lives of a number of students were transformed by the fact that a boy brought another boy to the prom, and danced with him. Consider the ways this plays out theoretically. For example, how would Michel Foucault or Judith Butler (Chapter 4, Section 3) analyze the dynamics of the Aaron Fricke case? What consequences might there be for the next student who wanted to bring a same-sex partner to the prom?

Tinker and *Fricke* represent the high points for those who support a critical-thinking model of student first amendment rights. Under *Tinker*, are there any limits to the type of student speech that is protected? Do schools have more leeway with regard to speech that occurs in the context of a school-sponsored event? Or speech that some might perceive as being endorsed or supported by the school? Does your analysis of the *Fricke* case change in light of the Supreme Court's subsequent decisions applying the First Amendment in the context of public secondary schools? Consider the next case.

Bethel School District No. 403 v. Matthew Fraser, a Minor, and E.L. Fraser, Guardian Ad Litem

United States Supreme Court, 1986.
478 U.S. 675, 106 S.Ct. 3159, 92 L.Ed.2d 549.

■ CHIEF JUSTICE BURGER delivered the opinion of the Court. * * *

On April 26, 1983, respondent Matthew N. Fraser, a student at Bethel High School in Pierce County, Washington, delivered a speech nominating a fellow student for student elective office. Approximately 600 high school students, many of whom were 14-year-olds, attended the assembly. Students were required to attend the assembly or to report to the study hall. The assembly was part of a school-sponsored educational program in self-government. * * * During the entire speech, Fraser referred to his candidate in terms of an elaborate, graphic, and explicit sexual metaphor. * * *

During Fraser's delivery of the speech, a school counselor observed the reaction of students to the speech. Some students hooted and yelled; some by gestures graphically simulated the sexual activities pointedly alluded to in respondent's speech. Other students appeared to be bewildered and embarrassed by the speech. One teacher reported that on the day following the speech, she found it necessary to forgo a portion of the scheduled class lesson in order to discuss the speech with the class.

[Relying on a school rule barring "the use of obscene, profane language or gestures" that "materially and substantially interferes with the educational process," the Assistant Principal called Fraser into her office for a chance to explain his speech. The student admitted to having given the speech described and that he deliberately used sexual innuendo in the speech—and the Assistant Principal suspended Fraser for three days and informed him that his name would be removed from the list of candidates for graduation speaker at the school's commencement exercises. Fraser successfully sought an injunction, which lower court granted under *Tinker*. The Supreme Court reversed.]

The role and purpose of the American public school system were well described by two historians, who stated: "[P]ublic education must prepare pupils for citizenship in the Republic. . . . It must inculcate the habits and manners of civility as values in themselves conducive to happiness and as indispensable to the practice of self-government in the community and the nation." C. Beard & M. Beard, *New Basic History of the United States* 228 (1968). In *Ambach v. Norwick*, 441 U.S. 68, 76–77 (1979), we echoed the essence of this statement of the objectives of public education as the "inculcat[ion of] fundamental values necessary to the maintenance of a democratic political system."

These fundamental values of "habits and manners of civility" essential to a democratic society must, of course, include tolerance of divergent political and religious views, even when the views expressed may be unpopular. But these "fundamental values" must also take into account consideration of the sensibilities of others, and, in the case of a school, the sensibilities of fellow students. The undoubted freedom to advocate unpopular and controversial views in schools and classrooms must be balanced against the society's countervailing interest in teaching students the boundaries of socially appropriate behavior. Even the most heated political discourse in a democratic society requires consideration for the personal sensibilities of the other participants and audiences.

In our Nation's legislative halls, where some of the most vigorous political debates in our society are carried on, there are rules prohibiting the use of expressions offensive to other participants in the debate. The Manual of Parliamentary Practice, drafted by Thomas Jefferson and adopted by the House of Representatives to govern the proceedings in that body, prohibits the use of "impertinent" speech during debate and likewise provides that "[n]o person is to use indecent language against the proceedings of the House." *Jefferson's Manual of Parliamentary Practice* §§ 359, 360, reprinted in *Manual and Rules of House of Representatives*, H.R. Doc. No. 97–271, pp. 158–59 (1982). The Rules of Debate applicable in the Senate likewise provide that a Senator may be called to order for imputing improper motives to another Senator or for referring offensively to any state. See Senate Procedure, S.Doc. No. 97–2, Rule XIX (1981). Senators have been censured for abusive language directed at other Senators. Can it be that what is proscribed in the halls of Congress is beyond the reach of school officials to regulate?

The First Amendment guarantees wide freedom in matters of adult public discourse. A sharply divided Court upheld the right to express an anti-draft viewpoint in a public place, albeit in terms highly offensive to most citizens. See *Cohen v. California*, 403 U.S. 15 (1971). It does not follow, however, that simply because the use of an offensive form of expression may not be prohibited to adults making what the speaker considers a political point, the same latitude must be permitted to children in a public school. * * * As cogently expressed by Judge Newman, "the First Amendment gives a high school student the classroom right to wear Tinker's armband, but not Cohen's jacket." *Thomas v. Board of Education, Granville Central School Dist.*, 607 F.2d 1043, 1057 (C.A.2 1979) (opinion concurring in result).

Surely it is a highly appropriate function of public school education to prohibit the use of vulgar and offensive terms in public discourse. Indeed, the "fundamental values necessary to the maintenance of a democratic political system" disfavor the use of terms of debate highly offensive or highly threatening to others. Nothing in the Constitution prohibits the states from insisting that certain modes of expression are inappropriate and subject to sanctions. The inculcation of these values is truly the "work of the schools." *Tinker*. The determination of what manner of speech in the classroom or in school assembly is inappropriate properly rests with the school board.

The process of educating our youth for citizenship in public schools is not confined to books, the curriculum, and the civics class; schools must teach by example the shared values of a civilized social order. Consciously or otherwise, teachers—and indeed the older students—demonstrate the appropriate form of civil discourse and political expression by their conduct and deportment in and out of class. Inescapably, like parents, they are role models. The schools, as instruments of the state, may determine that the essential lessons of civil, mature conduct cannot be conveyed in a school that tolerates lewd, indecent, or offensive speech and conduct such as that indulged in by this confused boy.

The pervasive sexual innuendo in Fraser's speech was plainly offensive to both teachers and students—indeed to any mature person. By glorifying male sexuality, and in its verbal content, the speech was acutely insulting to teenage girl students. The speech could well be seriously damaging to its less mature audience, many of whom were only 14 years old and on the threshold of awareness of human sexuality. Some students were reported as bewildered by the speech and the reaction of mimicry it provoked.

This Court's First Amendment jurisprudence has acknowledged limitations on the otherwise absolute interest of the speaker in reaching an unlimited audience where the speech is sexually explicit and the audience may include children. In *Ginsberg v. New York*, 390 U.S. 629 (1968), this Court upheld a New York statute banning the sale of sexually oriented material to minors, even though the material in question was entitled to First Amendment protection with respect to adults. And in addressing the question whether the First Amendment places any limit on the authority of public schools to remove books from a public school library, all Members of the Court, otherwise sharply divided, acknowledged that the school board has the authority to remove books that are vulgar. *Board of Education v. Pico* [excerpted below]. These cases recognize the obvious concern on the part of parents, and school authorities acting *in loco parentis*, to protect children—especially in a captive audience—from exposure to sexually explicit, indecent, or lewd speech.

We have also recognized an interest in protecting minors from exposure to vulgar and offensive spoken language. In *FCC v. Pacifica Foundation*, 438 U.S. 726 (1978), we dealt with the power of the Federal Communications Commission to regulate a radio broadcast described as "indecent but not obscene." There the Court reviewed an administrative condemnation of the radio broadcast of a self-styled "humorist" who described his own performance as being in "the words you couldn't say on the public, ah, airwaves, um, the ones you definitely wouldn't say ever." The Commission concluded that "certain words depicted sexual and excretory activities in a patently offensive manner, [and] noted that they 'were broadcast at a time when children were undoubtedly in the audience.'" [The Supreme Court upheld this order.]

We hold that petitioner School District acted entirely within its permissible authority in imposing sanctions upon Fraser in response to his offensively lewd and indecent speech. Unlike the sanctions imposed on the students wearing armbands in *Tinker*, the penalties imposed in this case were unrelated to any political viewpoint. The First Amendment does not prevent the school officials from determining that to permit a vulgar and lewd speech such as respondent's would undermine the school's basic educational mission. A high school assembly or classroom is no place for a sexually explicit monologue directed towards an unsuspecting audience of teenage students. Accordingly, it was perfectly appropriate for the school to disassociate itself to make the point to the pupils that vulgar speech and lewd conduct is wholly inconsistent with the "fundamental values" of public school education. * * *

■ JUSTICE BRENNAN concurring in the judgment.

Respondent gave the following speech at a high school assembly in support of a candidate for student government office:

> " 'I know a man who is firm—he's firm in his pants, he's firm in his shirt, his character is firm—but most . . . of all, his belief in you, the students of Bethel, is firm.

> " 'Jeff Kuhlman is a man who takes his point and pounds it in. If necessary, he'll take an issue and nail it to the wall. He doesn't attack things in spurts—he drives hard, pushing and pushing until finally—he succeeds.

> " 'Jeff is a man who will go to the very end—even the climax, for each and every one of you.

> " 'So vote for Jeff for A.S.B. vice-president—he'll never come between you and the best our high school can be.' "

The Court, referring to these remarks as "obscene," "vulgar," "lewd," and "offensively lewd," concludes that school officials properly punished respondent for uttering the speech. Having read the full text of respondent's remarks, I find it difficult to believe that it is the same speech the Court describes. To my mind, the most that can be said about respondent's speech—and all that need be said—is that in light of the discretion school officials have to teach high school students how to conduct civil and effective public discourse, and to prevent disruption of school educational activities, it was not unconstitutional for school officials to conclude, under the circumstances of this case, that respondent's remarks exceeded permissible limits. * * *

■ [JUSTICE BLACKMUN also concurred in the Court's result. JUSTICE MARSHALL dissented on the ground that the official reaction was too extreme in light of the trivial nature of the student's action. JUSTICE STEVENS dissented on the ground that the school's regulation was too vague to give Fraser sufficient notice that use of sexual metaphors in a speech would trigger such an extreme official reaction.]

NOTES ON *TINKER, FRICKE,* AND *FRASER*

1. *Theories of Education: Inculcation Versus Independent Thinking. Tinker* was criticized by some scholars for applying standard First Amendment doctrine (the free marketplace of ideas) to what those scholars considered to be an inappropriate setting, secondary schools. *See, e.g.,* Kevin W. Saunders, *Saving Our Children from the First Amendment* (2003); John H. Garvey, "Children and the First Amendment," 57 *Tex. L. Rev.* 321, 344 (1979) ("Except in the case of the most exceptional prodigy, it is undeniable that children's debates about adult issues serve no immediate social purpose."). *Contra* Catherine J. Ross, *Lessons in Censorship: How Schools and Courts Subvert Students' First Amendment Rights* (2015).

If a public school's mission is, at least in part, to convey to students at least some standard social and political norms (*e.g.,* that democracy is good) and some standard factual material (*e.g.,* the United States is a representative rather than direct democracy), should schools allow or even encourage students to object, resist, or even protest some of these norms? On the other hand, if the school system wants to avoid conveyor-belt approaches to learning and wants to stimulate independent individual thought by students, should public school officials *ever* be able to censor student speech? This is the "First Amendment paradox of public education." Stanley Ingber, "Socialization, Indoctrination, or the 'Pall of Orthodoxy': Value Training in the Public Schools," 1987 *U. Ill. L. Rev.* 15, 15–20.

Tinker seems to value the independent thinking model over the inculcation model (espoused in Justice Black's dissent), while *Fraser* seems to value the inculcation model over the independent thinking model (espoused in Justice Brennan's concurring opinion and Justice Marshall's dissent). For a strong endorsement of a critical-thinking model of student first amendment rights, see Catherine J. Ross, *Lessons in Censorship: How Schools and Courts Subvert Students' First Amendment Rights* (2015).

As noted above, *Tinker* may represent the zenith of student free speech rights. Two years after *Fraser*, in **Hazelwood School District v. Kuhlmeier, 484 U.S. 260 (1988)**, the Court upheld a high school's censorship of school newspaper articles describing students' experiences with pregnancy and the effect of divorce on students. Writing for a six-Justice majority, **Justice White** said:

A school must be able to set high standards for the student speech that is disseminated under its auspices—standards that may be higher than those demanded by some newspaper publishers or theatrical producers in the "real" world—and may refuse to disseminate student speech that does not meet those standards.

The Court held that "[e]ducators do not offend the First Amendment by exercising editorial control over the style and content of student speech in school-sponsored expressive activities so long as their actions are reasonably related to legitimate pedagogical concerns." Justice White reconciled *Hazelwood* with *Tinker*:

The question whether the First Amendment requires a school to tolerate particular student speech—the question that we addressed in *Tinker*—is different from the question whether the First Amendment requires a school affirmatively to promote particular student speech [the question addressed in *Fraser* and in this case, *Hazelwood*]. The former question addresses educators' ability to silence a student's personal expression that happens to occur on the school's premises. The latter question concerns educators' authority over school-sponsored publications, theatrical productions, and other expressive activities that students, parents, and members of the public might reasonably perceive to bear the imprimatur of the school. * * * Educators are entitled to exercise greater control over this second form of student expression to assure that participants learn whatever lessons the activity is designed to teach, that readers or listeners are not exposed to material that may be inappropriate for their level of maturity, and that the views of the individual speaker are not erroneously attributed to the school.

Is this a satisfactory reconciliation?

2. *The Relevance of Sex.* Another way to understand, and perhaps reconcile, the cases focuses on the content of the expression. *Tinker* was a classic "political" speech case. *Fraser* and *Hazelwood* lie somewhere in between "political" speech and "sexual" speech. Note Chief Justice Burger's skittishness about Matthew Fraser's speech, which Burger refused to quote. (Justice Brennan playfully provides the text for the reader.) Is the Court embarrassed talking about sexuality? *See* Richard A. Posner, *Sex and Reason* (1992) (yep).

Justice White's opinion in *Hazelwood* suggests other reasons why a school might have greater latitude regulating sexual speech:

[A] school must be able to take into account the emotional maturity of the intended audience in determining whether to disseminate student speech on potentially sensitive topics, which might range from the existence of Santa Claus in an elementary school setting to the particulars of teenage sexual activity in a high school setting. A school must also retain the authority to refuse to sponsor student speech that might reasonably be perceived to advocate drug or alcohol use, irresponsible sex, or conduct otherwise inconsistent with "the shared values of a civilized social order," *Fraser*, or to associate the school with any position other than neutrality on matters of political controversy. Otherwise, the schools would be unduly constrained from fulfilling their role as "a principal instrument in awakening the child to cultural values, in preparing him for later professional training, and in helping him to adjust normally to his environment." *Brown v. Board of Education*, 347 U.S. 483 (1954).

Consider also Chief Justice Burger's suggestion in *Fraser* that female students might be particularly chilled by raunchy sexual speech. As discussed in Section 2, public schools have a legal obligation to reasonably respond to (which, to be clear, often means that the school suppresses or censors) expression that creates a "hostile environment" based on prohibited categories, including sex. In your opinion, was this a substantial risk in *Fraser*? *Hazelwood*?

If the Justices were skittish about Matthew Fraser's phallic allusions, would they respond even more strongly to Aaron Fricke's same-sex date to the prom? Do *Fraser* and *Hazelwood* nullify *Fricke*? Or is there a persuasive way to defend Chief Judge Pettine's decision under current doctrine? Consider also *Morse v. Frederick,* 551 U.S. 393 (2007), where a divided Court upheld a high school principal's discipline of a student who displayed a sign "BONG HiTS 4 JESUS" when the Olympic torch passed through town. Chief Justice Roberts' opinion for the Court did not credit the sign as political speech and ruled that the principal had authority to regulate the sign, because the students were watching the torch pass as part of an official school field trip and because its implications were contrary to the school's antidrug philosophy. Thus, the sign was inherently "disruptive" under *Tinker.* (Justice Thomas wrote a concurring opinion indicating that *Tinker* was wrongly decided.)

3. *Problems with the Court's Tilt Toward Deference and Inculcation.* Certainly, the post-*Tinker* Supreme Court cases are more deferential to school authorities and more receptive to inculcation as the primary goal of public schools. Richard L. Roe, "Valuing Student Speech: The Work of the Schools as Conceptual Development," 79 *Cal. L. Rev.* 1269 (1991), argues that allowing schools to suppress student speech in cases like *Fraser* and *Hazelwood* undermines the more important goal of education at the high school level, namely, cognitive development. Indeed, American public schools themselves declare that their goal is conceptual development, rather than just inculcation. The problem, Roe maintains, is that educators are constantly tempted to fall back on an inculcative approach (*e.g.*, as a better way of keeping order in the classroom), and school boards will tend to deploy it to satisfy concerned parents who do not like current educational philosophies.

In *Morse,* Justice Alito (joined by Justice Kennedy) wrote a concurring opinion emphasizing that the Court *rejected* the Solicitor General's suggestion that the First Amendment permits public school officials to censor any student speech that interferes with a school's educational mission:

> During the *Tinker* era, a public school could have defined its educational mission to include solidarity with our soldiers and their families and thus could have attempted to outlaw the wearing of black armbands on the ground that they undermined this mission. * * * The 'educational mission' argument would give public school authorities a license to suppress speech on political and social issues based on disagreement with the viewpoint expressed. The argument, therefore, strikes at the very heart of the First Amendment. * * * For these reasons, any argument for altering the usual free speech rules in the public schools cannot rest on a theory

of delegation but must instead be based on some special characteristic of the school setting.

According to Justice Alito, the special characteristic that was relevant in *Morse* was the threat to the physical safety of students," namely the supposition that the student's sign advocated drug use.

(Writing for four dissenters, Justice Stevens disputed that implication and argued that the First Amendment should have trumped the school's disciplinary decision.)

Under the Alito approach, would *Fricke* be decided the same way today? How about the next case?

Pat Doe, By Her Next Friend [Grandmother], Jane Doe v. John Yunits, 2000 WL 33162199 (Mass. Super. Ct. 2000). The Superior Court granted an injunction requiring the South Junior High School to allow fifteen-year-old Pat Doe, a transgender student, to wear female attire. The court granted relief under the Massachusetts Declaration of Rights based upon both free speech and sex discrimination claims. As to the free speech claim, **Judge Giles** ruled that Doe's attire was expressive conduct entitled to constitutional protection. "Plaintiff in this case is likely to establish that, by dressing in clothing and accessories traditionally associated with the female gender, she is expressing her identification with that gender. In addition, plaintiff's ability to express herself and her gender identity through dress is important to her health and well-being, as attested to by her treating therapist. Therefore, plaintiff's expression is not merely a personal preference but a necessary symbol of her very identity. * * *

"This court also must consider if the plaintiff's speech 'materially and substantially interferes with the work of the school.' *Tinker.* Defendants argue that they are merely preventing disruptive conduct on the part of the plaintiff by restricting her attire at school. Their argument is unpersuasive. Given the state of the record thus far, the plaintiff has demonstrated a likelihood of proving that defendants, rather than attempting to restrict plaintiff's wearing of distracting items of clothing, are seeking to ban her from donning apparel that can be labeled 'girls' clothes' and to encourage more conventional, male-oriented attire. Defendants argue that any other student who came to school dressed in distracting clothing would be disciplined as the plaintiff was. However, defendants overlook the fact that, if a female student came to school in a frilly dress or blouse, make-up, or padded bra, she would go, and presumably has gone, unnoticed by school officials. Defendants do not find plaintiff's clothing distracting *per se,* but, essentially, distracting simply because plaintiff is a biological male." Judge Giles invoked *Fricke* for the proposition that the reactions of other students to a gender nonconformist should not be permitted as a heckler's veto of Doe's expressive conduct.

"Plaintiff has framed this issue narrowly as a question of whether or not it is appropriate for defendants to restrict the manner in which she can dress. Defendants, on the other hand, appear unable to distinguish between instances of conduct connected to plaintiff's expression of her female gender identity, such as the wearing of a wig or padded bra, and separate from it, such as grabbing a male student's buttocks or blowing kisses to a male student. The line between expression and flagrant behavior can blur, thereby rendering this case difficult for the court. It seems, however, that expression of gender identity through dress can be divorced from conduct in school that warrants punishment, regardless of the gender or gender identity of the offender. Therefore, a school should not be allowed to bar or discipline a student because of gender-identified dress but should be permitted to ban clothing that would be inappropriate if worn by any student, such as a theatrical costume, and to punish conduct that would be deemed offensive if committed by any student, such as harassing, threatening, or obscene behavior. See *Fraser*."

Invoking *Price Waterhouse v. Hopkins* (Chapter 4, Section 3B), Judge Giles also ruled that the school was discriminating against Doe because of her "failure to conform with the norms of [her] biological gender." That portion of the opinion is omitted here.

PROBLEM 8-1
GENDER IDENTITY AND THE FIRST AMENDMENT

Judge Giles treated the state constitutional claim under the same standards as those developed by the U.S. Supreme Court for First Amendment claims. Is the judge's disposition in *Yunits* consistent with the Supreme Court's deferential attitude in *Fraser*, *Hazelwood*, and *Morse*? If so, how do you distinguish those Supreme Court cases, where important student expression was censored, yet the Court rejected First Amendment challenges? Alternatively, of course, the Massachusetts courts can construe their own state constitution to protect speech and expression more strongly than the First Amendment does. Return to first principles: What goals does a constitutional free speech provision protect? Does protecting Doe's expressive conduct advance those goals? At what cost? *See* David Cole & William N. Eskridge Jr., "From Hand-Holding to Sodomy: First Amendment Protection of Homosexual (Expressive) Conduct," 29 *Harv. C.R.-C.L. L. Rev.* 319 (1994).

Under the principles balancing free speech (*Tinker*) and institutional needs (*Fraser*), where should the line be drawn? Pat Doe, a biologically male student who self-identifies as a female:

(1)   wears lipstick and mascara, which triggers giggles from other students for a day;

(2)   wears traditionally feminine clothing to school, which triggers catcalls from other students every time Pat appears this way;

(3)   wears a wig that makes her look more "girlish," with similar student reactions;

(4)   flirts with some of the male students, who do not welcome the flirting;

(5)   uses the girls' restroom, which triggers objections from two female students in her class;

(6) pinches some of the male students, without their permission or acquiescence.

At what point, if any, does the school have the authority, under the First Amendment, to discipline Doe? Would you draw the line higher up (*e.g.*, at [1] rather than [5] or [6]) if there were evidence that Doe's expression triggered assaults against her by some other students? For more consideration of the extent to which the First Amendment protects students' rights to express their gender and sexual orientation, see, e.g., Jeffrey Kosbie, "(No) State Interests in Regulating Gender: How Suppression of Gender Nonconformity Violates Freedom of Speech," 19 *Wm. & Mary J. Women & L.* 187, passim (2013); Clifford J. Rosky, "No Promo Hetero: Children's Right to Be Queer," 35 *Cardozo L. Rev.* 425, 465–69 (2013).

B. PROTECTING ANTI-GAY SPEECH

In the past, when courts were reluctant to extend protection to LGBT people under other sources of law, the First Amendment was an important source of protection for LGBT students and their allies. The First Amendment was often relied upon to protect their right to assemble and to engage in pro-LGBT speech. *See, e.g., Gay Lesbian Bisexual Alliance v. Sessions*, 917 F. Supp. 1548 (M.D. Ala. 1996) (holding Alabama state statute that prohibited any college or university from recognizing or supporting any group that "promotes a lifestyle or actions prohibited by the sodomy and sexual misconduct laws" violated the First Amendment), *aff'd sub nom. Gay Lesbian Bisexual All. v. Pryor*, 110 F.3d 1543 (11th Cir. 1997). During this period, anti-gay speech was not only common, but was also implicitly or explicitly endorsed by the government. LGBT people and their allies invoked the First Amendment to protect their right to oppose this anti-gay speech.

But the landscape began to change after *Romer* and *Lawrence*. Not only are lesbian, gay, bisexual, and transgender students and teachers no longer criminals, they are considered citizens entitled to equally dignified treatment against discrimination and harassment. Thus, many Americans now accept the notion that sexual variation can be entirely benign and that the state should accord the same respect to lesbian and gay students and teachers that is accorded to straight students and teachers. *See, e.g., Weaver v. Nebo School District*, 29 F. Supp. 2d 1279 (D. Utah 1998) (Chapter 5, Section 1A). The notion of benign sexual variation is embedded in an increasing array of local and state laws protecting against anti-gay discrimination and harassment in public schools. And school boards as well as administrators are taking responsibility for *inculcating* the new idea of benign sexual variation in student bodies.

Greater public acceptance of LGBT people has led to new kinds of clashes between school policy and dissent. Today, it is often religious teachers and students who are relying on the First Amendment to protect their right to disrupt school programs that say "Gay is OK." Is this speech—*speech that condemns homosexuality*—entitled to first amendment protection? Chapter 3, Section 3 closed with the leading Supreme Court case dealing with university anti-discrimination policies as applied to anti-gay students and groups, namely, *Christian Legal Society v. Martinez*. Consider the following case, arising out of the secondary school context and presenting different First Amendment issues than either *CLS* (limited public forum) and *Boring* (*Pickering* issues).

Tyler Chase Harper v. Poway Unified School District

United States Court of Appeals for the Ninth Circuit, 2006.
445 F.3d 1166.

[This case is excerpted in Chapter 4, Section 3C.]

NOTES ON THE HIGH SCHOOL T-SHIRT WARS

1. *Evolving Social Norms and First Amendment "Neutrality."* Notice how the First Amendment context changes between *Fricke* and *Harper*. In the former case, a student invoked the First Amendment so that he could express his gay identity; in the latter case, a student invoked the First Amendment so that he could express his traditionalist identity. In the first case, the court enjoins the school's censorship; in the latter case, the court does not. Why shouldn't traditionalist students like Chase Harper have the same First Amendment protections that Aaron Fricke had a generation ago?

In *Nuxoll ex rel. Nuxoll v. Indian Prairie Sch. Dist. No. 204*, 523 F.3d 668 (7th Cir. 2008), the Seventh Circuit considered a high school's censorship of a T-shirt that read "Happy, Not Gay" in response to the school's celebration of diversity. Judge Posner's opinion sustained an injunction protecting that particular message but narrowed the injunction so that school officials could regulate or ban more aggressive anti-gay messages. Judge Kozinski seems open to a similar idea in *Harper*. Where should they draw the line? Should administrators be able to ban a T-shirt that says "Leviticus 20:13"? How about if the T-shirt also contains this message: "God says, 'Death to Homosexuals' "?

2. *Hate Speech in Schools.* When the *Nuxoll* students returned to the Seventh Circuit on the school's (unsuccessful) appeal of summary judgment against it, Judge Posner opined that a T-shirt saying "homosexuals go to Hell" could be regulated by the school, because those are "fighting words" exempt from protection under *Chaplinsky v. New Hampshire*, 315 U.S. 568 (1942). *See Zamecnik v. Indian Prairie School Dist. No. 204*, 2011 WL 692059 (7th Cir. 2011). Would Judge Kozinski agree?

3. *The Legal Aftermath of* Harper: *Bong Hits 4 T-Shirts?* After *Morse* was decided, the Supreme Court vacated the *Harper* decision, and remanded it with instructions to dismiss the case as moot, as Harper had graduated from Poway by this time. *Harper v. Poway Unified Sch. Dist.*, 549 U.S. 1262, 127 S.Ct. 1484 (2007). Does the Supreme Court's decision in *Morse* result in strengthening or weakening Harper's claim? Might *Harper* have motivated Justice Alito's concurring opinion, which supported school censorship of an ambiguous "BONG HiTS 4 JESUS" banner but left open the possibility that the First Amendment would protect religious identity speech, including "Homosexuality Is Shameful" and "Happy, Not Gay" slogans?

NOTES ON STUDENT CLUBS IN PUBLIC HIGH SCHOOLS

High schools typically allow groups to meet during non-curricular student time. There are a number of sources of law that may limit a school's ability to deny recognition and equal treatment to such groups.

1.   *First Amendment.* Once a school has allowed some groups to meet, the First Amendment limits a public school's authority to exclude other clubs based on the content of their speech. *See, e.g., Good News Club v. Milford Cent. Sch.*, 533 U.S. 98 (2001). In *Good News Club*, the school district opened up its facilities after school to any district residents who wanted to use the school for "instruction in any branch of education, learning or the arts," or for "social, civic and recreational meetings and entertainment events, and other uses pertaining to the welfare of the community, provided that such uses shall be nonexclusive and shall be opened to the general public." *Id.* at 102. Two district residents, Stephen and Darleen Fournier, applied to use the school facilities to hold meetings of the local Good News Club, "a private Christian organization for children ages 6 to 12." *Id.* The school board denied the request on the ground that the content of the meetings would be "the equivalent of religious instruction." *Id.* at 104.

In a decision written by Justice Thomas, the Supreme Court held that "[w]hen Milford [School District] denied the Good News Club access to the school's limited public forum on the ground that the Club was religious in nature, it discriminated against the Club because of its religious viewpoint in violation of the Free Speech Clause of the First Amendment." *Id.* at 120. This First Amendment protection can be used to protect the rights of groups that support LGBT rights as well as those that oppose LGBT rights.

2.   *Equal Access Act.* In addition to the First Amendment, there is a federal statute that protects the right of student groups to meet—the Equal Access Act, 98 Stat. 1302, 20 U.S.C.A. §§ 4071–4074. The Equal Access Act applies to secondary schools that receive federal financial assistance. Under the Equal Access Act, a covered school creates a "limited public forum" when it "grants an offering to or opportunity for one or more noncurriculum related student groups to meet on school premises during noninstructional time." *Id.* at § 4071(b); *see also Board of Education v. Mergens,* 496 U.S. 226 (1990) (limited public forum triggered by school's recognition of scuba, chess, and service clubs as "noncurriculum related"). To be protected under the Act, the group's meeting must be "voluntary and student-initiated," the school cannot "sponsor[ ] . . . the meeting," and "non-school persons may not direct, conduct, control, or regularly attend activities of student groups." 20 U.S.C. § 4071(c).

If a covered school creates a limited public forum, it is unlawful for the school "to deny equal access or a fair opportunity to, or discriminate against, any students who wish to conduct a meeting within the limited open forum on the basis of the religious, philosophical, or other content of the speech at such meetings." *Id.* at § 4071(a).

The Equal Access Act was originally enacted to "counteract perceived discrimination against content-based religious speech in public high schools." *Boyd County High School Gay Straight Alliance v. Bd. of Educ. Of Boyd, Cty, Ky.*, 258 F. Supp. 2d 667, 680 (E.D. Ky. 2003). In recent years, the Act has been frequently invoked (often successfully) by Gay/Straight Alliance clubs or GSAs. *See, e.g., Gay-Straight Alliance of Yulee High School v. School Board of Nassau*, 602 F. Supp. 2d 1233 (M.D. Fla. 2009) (granting students' request for a preliminary injunction requiring school board to grant the GSA "official recognition and grant all privileges given to other student organizations"); *Boyd County High School Gay Straight Alliance v. Board of Education of Boyd County, KY*, 258 F. Supp. 2d 667 (E.D. Ky. 2003) (holding that members of GSA established a substantial likelihood of prevailing on the merits of their claim that the school violated the EAA by denying them equal access to school facilities).

Despite the law, some schools sought to deny recognition to GSAs. Among other arguments, some schools invoked an exception in the Equal Access Act that allows schools to deny recognition to student-initiated clubs that "materially and substantially interfere with the orderly conduct of educational activities within the school . . ." 20 U.S.C. § 4071(c)(4).

Assume a significant portion of the student body protests against the formation of the GSA, and assume that these protests continue for several weeks. Under such circumstances, would it be permissible for the school to deny recognition to the GSA? Consider the relevance of *Tinker, Friske, Fraser* and *Hazelwood* to the proper construction of the statute. *Compare Colin v. Orange Unified Sch. Dist. Bd. of Educ.*, 83 F. Supp. 2d 1135 (C.D. Cal. 2000) (granting preliminary injunction requiring school district to recognize GSA); *Boyd County High School Gay Straight Alliance v. Board of Education of Boyd County, KY*, 258 F. Supp. 2d 667 (E.D. Ky. 2003) (same); *with Caudillo ex rel. Lubbock Indep. Sch. Dist.*, 311 F. Supp. 2d 550 (N.D. Tex. 2004) (holding that school district's refusal to recognize GSA did not violate EAA).

In the alternative, the school might adopt a policy making all school clubs open-membership: they must accept that any student can become a club member and thus be eligible for a club officer position, whether or not the student agrees with the philosophy or mission of the club. This was the approach followed by the School of Law at Hastings College and upheld by the Supreme Court in *Christian Legal Society v. Martinez*, 561 U.S. 661 (2011) (Chapter 3, Section 3).

SECTION 2

SEXUALITY AND GENDER-BASED HARASSMENT AND DISCRIMINATION

Section 1 explores the rights of students to express their views, including views on controversial topics. Sometimes, these free speech rights come into tension with schools' obligation to ensure that students are protected from harassment and discrimination.

One important law prohibiting discrimination on the basis of sex is Title IX of the Education Amendments of 1972. Title IX provides in part: "No person in the United States shall, on the basis of sex, be excluded from participation in, be denied the benefits of, or be subjected to discrimination under any education program or activity receiving Federal financial assistance * * *." 20 U.S.C. § 1681(a).[a] Virtually all public schools and most private schools receive federal financial assistance as defined by the statute. The Supreme Court in *Cannon v. University of Chicago*, 441 U.S. 677 (1979), held that Title IX's intended beneficiaries have a private cause of action against institutions violating this directive. Thus if a school told girls they could not take advanced calculus, a course open to boys, female students could obtain an injunction requiring the school to offer the course without sex-based limits.

Title IX has been much more revolutionary than even its sponsors imagined. For example, administrators and courts have interpreted its anti-discrimination mandate to incorporate the norm against sexual harassment pioneered by the EEOC Guidelines interpreting Title VII (Chapter 5). Because Title IX applies only to schools receiving federal funds, and not as a direct regulation (like Title VII), there has been a great deal of doctrinal debate whether such an aggressive application of the statute is justified. As shown in Section 2A, the Supreme Court has, perhaps tentatively, accepted a moderately expansive application of Title IX to police a great deal of harassment in the classroom (and in the locker-room), as well as sexual violence. Lower courts and, at least until recently, the Department of Education have taken the position that these protections extend to LGBT people as well. Section 2B considers the

---

[a]   The general prohibition against sex discrimination included in § 1681(a) is followed by nine exceptions. 20 U.S.C. § 1681(a)(1)–(9). The statutory exceptions include: (1) primary and secondary school admissions policies ((a)(1)); (2) educational institutions controlled by religious organizations and discriminating for religious reasons ((a)(3)); (3) educational institutions training individuals for U.S. military service ((a)(4)); (4) public colleges which from their establishment have only admitted students of one sex ((a)(5)); and (5) social fraternities and sororities ((a)(6)).

interaction (or clash) between schools' obligation to respond to harassment, including sexual harassment, and the First Amendment. A particular type of sexual harassment—sexual violence—is explored in Section 2C.

With little Supreme Court guidance, lower courts and, again, at least until recently, the Department of Education have applied Title IX aggressively to require more equal funding of women's athletic programs in high schools and colleges and universities (Section 2D). Feminists intensely debate whether focusing on achieving *more equal funding* of separate sex-segregated programs is the best approach, as opposed to seeking more sex-integration in scholastic athletics. Nonetheless, almost everyone agrees that there has been a revolution: many more female students participate in scholastic athletics every decade, and the effect has been tremendous. As Professor Deborah Brake argues, the most radical feminist-inspired changes in America are those resulting from the normalization of the idea that women are strong, athletic, and competitive.

Section 2E addresses a larger issue under both Title IX and the Equal Protection Clause: Can sex segregation in academics advance women's interests? Many feminist advocates think that sex segregation can advance women's interests in the context of athletics. What about in the context of academics? Is sex segregation in that context a good idea from a feminist perspective? Does it violate Title IX or the Equal Protection Clause (as interpreted in *VMI*, Chapter 1, Section 3)?

A. SEX-BASED HARASSMENT IN SCHOOLS

NOTES ON TITLE IX AND SEX-BASED HARASSMENT

Studies have found great incidence of sex-based harassment of female and LGBT students at all levels of education. As many as two-thirds of female and LGBT college students report some form of sex-based harassment from their professors or fellow students. Educational Foundation of the American Association of University Women, *Drawing the Line: Sexual Harassment on Campus* (2005). The numbers are probably higher for secondary schools, as the leading survey found that four out of five students in grades 8 through 11 had experienced some form of sexual harassment, most often from their peers. Educational Foundation of the American Association of University Women, *Hostile Hallways: The AAUW Survey on Sexual Harassment in America's Schools* (2001). This survey included male as well as female students, but the latter were significantly more likely to have been traumatized by the harassment.

LGBT students report particularly high incidence of harassment, discrimination, and violence. According to the 2015 National School Climate Survey conducted by GLSEN, 85% of surveyed students reported that experienced verbal harassment based on a personal characteristic, and 66% reported that they experienced LGBTQ-related discrimination at school.

GLSEN, 2015 National School Climate Survey, The full 2015 National School Climate Survey report is available at https://www.glsen.org/article/ 2015-national-school-climate-survey. Almost a third of respondents reported that they had missed at least one day of school in the prior month because they felt unsafe or uncomfortable at school.

In short, the evidence indicates that sex-based harassment in educational settings is a major phenomenon, and one that disproportionately disadvantages female and LGBT students. Does Title IX provide a legal remedy for this conduct?

1.   *Teacher-Student Harassment.* The Supreme Court first addressed this question in the context of harassment and discrimination perpetrated *by a teacher against a student.* In *Franklin v. Gwinnett County Public Schools,* 503 U.S. 60 (1992), the Supreme Court held that Christine Franklin (a tenth grader) had a cause of action for damages against her high school because she was sexually harassed by Andrew Hill, a teacher-coach at the school. Franklin alleged that Hill quizzed Franklin about her personal sex life, pressed her about having sex with an older man, kissed her on the mouth, and called her at home with social invitations. The school never disciplined Hill, and Franklin sued. In an opinion written by Justice White, the Supreme Court held:

> Title IX placed on the Gwinnett County Schools the duty not to discriminate on the basis of sex, and "when a supervisor sexually harasses a subordinate because of the subordinate's sex that supervisor 'discriminate[s]' on the basis of sex." *Meritor Savings Bank, FSB v. Vinson* [a Title VII sexual harassment case]. We believe the same rule should apply when a teacher sexually harasses and abuses a student. Congress did not intend for federal monies to be expended to support the intentional actions it sought by statute to proscribe. * * *

Six years later, in *Gebser v. Lago Vista Indep. Sch. Dist.,* 524 U.S. 274 (1998), the Court provided additional guidance on the standard of liability. Justice O'Connor, writing for the Court, explained:

> The question in this case is when a school district may be held liable in damages in an implied right of action under Title IX of the Education Amendments of 1972 * * * for the sexual harassment of a student by one of the district's teachers. We conclude that damages may not be recovered in those circumstances unless an official of the school district who at a minimum has authority to institute corrective measures on the district's behalf has actual notice of, and is deliberately indifferent to, the teacher's misconduct.

Id. at 277. After *Franklin* and *Gebser,* it was clear that schools could be held liable for monetary damages under Title IX for their failure to respond to known incidents of harassment of students by teachers.

2.   *What About Peer-Peer Harassment?* One year after *Gebser,* the Court considered that question: "whether the misconduct identified in *Gebser*— deliberate indifferent to known acts of harassment—amounts to an

intentional violation of Title IX, capable of supporting a private damages action, when the harasser is a student rather than a teacher." *Davis v. Monroe Cty. Bd. of Educ.*, 526 U.S. 629, 643 (1999).

The *Davis* Court answered that question in the affirmative, at least where the "misconduct occurs during school hours and on school grounds." *Id.* at 646. The *Davis* Court reiterated that to support a claim for monetary damages, peer-peer harassment must be "so severe, pervasive, and objectively offensive that it can be said to deprive the victims of access to the educational opportunities or benefits provided by the School." *Id.* at 650. When making this assessment, the reviewing court must consider the "constellation of surrounding circumstances," including the fact that "children may regularly interact in a manner that would be unacceptable among adults."

In its Guidance (described below), the Office of Civil Rights for the Department of Education provides a more detailed account of factors that should inform a determination whether a "hostile environment" exists: "the type, duration and frequency of the [sexual] conduct"; the extent to which the conduct affected the education of more than one student; the relationship between the alleged harasser(s) and the object(s) of the harassment, as well as the ages of each; the number of individuals involved; previous incidents of a similar disturbing nature at the school; and incidents of gender-based but non-sexual harassment, which may not, standing alone, create a claim for sexual harassment but may reinforce a potential claim.

On March 10, 1997, the Office of Civil Rights of the Department of Education promulgated *Sexual Harassment Guidance: Harassment of Students by School Employees, Other Students, or Third Parties*, 62 Fed. Reg. 12034–50 (Mar. 13, 1997). On January 19, 2001, the Department issued a Revised Sexual Harassment Guidance, available at http://www2.ed.gov/about/offices/list/ocr/docs/shguide.html (viewed Aug. 15, 2010) to reflect and incorporate *Gebser* and *Davis*.

Both the original Guidance and Revised Guidance take the position that schools have an obligation under Title IX to take appropriate responsive actions to both teacher-student harassment (such as *Franklin*) and peer-peer harassment (such as *Davis*). Both documents also make clear that this obligation applies to both *sexual* and *gender-based* harassment, and that it applies to both same-sex and different-sex sex-based harassment.

The 2001 Revised Guidance acknowledges school districts are liable *in private damages lawsuits* only if a school district official who has authority to institute corrective measures on the district's behalf has actual notice of, and is deliberately indifferent to sexual harassment.

The Revised Guidance continues to take the position, however, that a lower standard applies with respect to the department's authority *to cut off federal funds*. The Revised Guidance asserts that federal funds can be cut off if a covered institution knew *or should have known* about the sex-based harassment and failed to take reasonable corrective action.

3. *Because of Sex.* Assuming the harassment was "bad enough" to be actionable, how does a court determine whether the harassment was "because of sex"?

In *Davis*, the harassment was perpetrated by a boy against a girl. According to the plaintiff's complaint, the harassment included "attempt[s] to touch [the girl's] breasts and genital area," as well as "vulgar comments such as 'I want to get in bed with you,' and 'I want to feel your boobs.'" *Id.* at 633. Justice O'Connor, writing for the Court, pretty much assumed that the harassment Davis experienced was based on sex.

The OCR Guidance likewise seems to assume that even verbal comments about a person's (or at least a girl's) "private part" renders the harassment "sex based." The Guidance explains: "For instance, if a young woman is taunted by one or more young men about her breasts or genital area or both, OCR may find that a hostile environment has been created, particularly if the conduct has gone on for some time, takes place throughout the school, or if the taunts are made by a number of students." Why is touching of or comments about "private parts" necessarily sex-based? Is it because such harassment is necessarily sexual in nature? Is it necessarily "sex based" regardless of the respective sexes of the individuals involved? Or only if it is by a boy on a girl?

4. *Same-Sex Sexual Harassment.* Under what circumstances can same-sex harassment be deemed "based on sex" for purposes of Title IX? In the Title VII employment context, the Supreme Court unanimously ruled that same-sex sex-based harassment could violate Title VII *if* the plaintiff could prove that the harassment was "because of * * * sex." *Oncale v. Sundowner Offshore Servs., Inc.*, 523 U.S. 75 (1998). But, unlike in *Davis*, where the Court assumed that boy-on-girl sexual overtures were based on sex, the Court in *Oncale* required an independent showing that the conduct was "because of sex" and remanded the case for a trial as to that issue. This is also (more or less) the stance taken by the Department of Education in its 1997 Guidance, noted above.

5. *Title IX and LGB Students.* Title IX only prohibits sex discrimination. But since 2001, OCR has taken the position that "[a]lthough Title IX does not prohibit discrimination on the basis of sexual orientation, sexual harassment directed at gay or lesbian students may constitute sexual harassment prohibited by Title IX." The 2001 Guidance continues:

> For example, if students heckle another student with comments based on the student's sexual orientation (e.g., 'gay students are not welcome at this table in the cafeteria'), but their actions or language do not involve sexual conduct, their actions would not be sexual harassment covered by Title IX. On the other hand, harassing conduct of a sexual nature directed toward gay or lesbian students (e.g., if a male student or a group of male students target a lesbian student for physical sexual advances) may create a sexually hostile environment and, therefore, may be prohibited by Title IX.

Revised Guidance, http://www2.ed.gov/about/offices/list/ocr/docs/shguide. html. (Of course, even if harassment directed towards an LGB person is based on sex, the student would still have to meet the Guidance's suggestions for hostile environment harassment, which is created "if conduct of a sexual nature is sufficiently severe, persistent, or pervasive to limit a student's ability to participate in or benefit from the education program or to create a hostile or abusive educational environment." *Id.* at 12041.)

How does a court determine whether the harassment against an LGBT person is actionable sex-based harassment? Consider the following decision.

Montgomery v. Independent Sch. Dist. No. 709

United States District Court, Minnesota.
109 F.Supp.2d 1081 (D. Minn. 2000).

■ TUNHEIM, DISTRICT JUDGE.

Plaintiff Jesse Montgomery brings this action against Independent School District Number 709 (the "School District") based on its failure to prevent harassment by other students that he experienced during approximately eleven years of education in defendant's schools. Plaintiff asserts that the other students harassed him both because of his gender and his perceived sexual orientation. He brings [multiple claims under federal and state law, including a claim under] Title IX of the Education Amendments of 1972, 20 U.S.C. § 1681 ("Title IX"). * * *

BACKGROUND

Plaintiff attended three of defendant's schools from kindergarten through the tenth grade, including Lakewood Elementary School, Ordean Middle School, and East High School. Plaintiff alleges, and defendant does not dispute, that while he was a student in defendant's schools he experienced frequent and continual teasing by other students beginning in kindergarten and recurring on an almost daily basis until the end of the tenth grade, when he transferred to another school district. While some of these taunts were more general in nature, many of them appear to have been directed at plaintiff because of his perceived sexual orientation, including, "faggott," "fag," "gay," "Jessica," "girl," "princess," "fairy," "homo," "freak," "lesbian," "femme boy," "gay boy," "bitch," "queer," "pansy," and "queen." A review of plaintiff's allegations, assuming them to be true for purposes of these motions, reveals that the verbal abuse to which his peers subjected him was severe and unrelenting throughout his entire tenure in defendant's school system.

According to plaintiff, the students' misconduct escalated to the point of physical violence beginning in the sixth grade, when several students punched him, kicked him, and knocked him down on the playground. Another student later super-glued him to his seat. Plaintiff claims that as he entered middle school and progressed on to high school, the harassment became noticeably worse. While the verbal taunts continued unabated, the physical threats and assaults intensified.

Students threatened to beat him up on several occasions. A group of students pushed him down in the hallway in front of his family when they were at the school to attend a choir concert. Another student unzipped his backpack, threw his books to the floor and smashed his calculator. Plaintiff also states that during a gym exercise one of the students charged him and sent him flying several feet through the air, and that during hockey drills the offending students deliberately tripped him or knocked him down on several occasions, causing bruises. Plaintiff further alleges that students frequently kicked or tripped him on the school bus, and that while he was riding the bus or in art class students would throw objects at him such as crayons, paper, popcorn, water, chunks of clay, paint brushes, pencils, pen caps, trash, and other small things.

In addition to these incidents, plaintiff claims that on some occasions the physical threats and assaults he experienced were of a more sexual nature. He specifically contends that a student in his middle school choir class grabbed his legs, inner thighs, chest and crotch. He states that the same student grabbed his buttocks on at least five or six occasions. Later another student approached him and asked to see him naked after gym class. Plaintiff states that he experienced similar incidents when he was in high school. According to plaintiff, students in his ninth and tenth grade choir classes sometimes put their arms around him or grabbed his inner thighs and buttocks while calling him names targeted at his perceived sexual orientation. Plaintiff states that one of the students grabbed his own genitals while squeezing plaintiff's buttocks, and on other occasions would stand behind plaintiff and grind his penis into plaintiff's backside. The same student once threw him to the ground and pretended to rape him anally, and on another occasion sat on plaintiff's lap and bounced while pretending to have intercourse with him. Other students watched and laughed during these incidents.

Plaintiff alleges that the harassment he experienced deprived him of the ability to access significant portions of the educational environment. During his tenure in defendant's schools, plaintiff generally achieved average to above average grades. Nonetheless, plaintiff states that he stayed home from school on approximately five or six occasions while he was in middle school in order to avoid the harassment. He further states that he did not participate or try to participate in intramural sports because his harassers were participants, that he avoided going to the school cafeteria unless absolutely necessary, and that he avoided using the school bathroom except in emergency situations. When plaintiff was in high school he stopped using the school bus in order to circumvent the continuous harassment he experienced there, requiring his parents and other family members to drive him to school.

Plaintiff states that he reported the students' misconduct to a variety of School District officials, including teachers, bus drivers, principals, assistant principals, playground and cafeteria monitors, locker room attendants, and school counselors. Plaintiff further states that on several occasions when he was in middle school, he and his parents reported the incidents of misconduct to the office of the School District's superintendent.

The officials to whom plaintiff reported the misconduct responded with a variety of measures. Defendant gave plaintiff access to school counselors, and he made appointments with them on a regular basis. Moreover, when plaintiff was in middle school defendant required him to attend a number of group sessions with other boys to discuss strategies for responding to harassment. According to plaintiff, defendant removed him from some of his favorite classes and required him to attend these sessions involuntarily.

Defendant also implemented several disciplinary measures against the offending students, although it appears that School District officials applied such discipline inconsistently. Plaintiff's teachers responded to many of his complaints by verbally reprimanding students or sending them to the principal's office. When students harassed plaintiff on the school bus, the driver sometimes stopped the bus and reprimanded the students. Defendant asserts that it assigned special seats to students on the bus at least temporarily in an attempt to circumvent the misconduct, although plaintiff claims that these seating assignments were not adequately enforced. On some occasions the cafeteria monitor responded to plaintiff's lunchtime complaints by requiring the offending students to stand in a designated area. On two occasions plaintiff's middle school counselor and principal required the offending students to meet with plaintiff and apologize to him. Plaintiff asserts that these sessions were unhelpful and ultimately resulted in a significant amount of retaliatory harassment.

In connection with the incidents of sexual touching he experienced, plaintiff alleges that he made multiple complaints to his choir teacher about the student who repeatedly grabbed his thigh, buttocks, and crotch and pretended to have intercourse with him. The teacher responded to plaintiff's complaints by verbally reprimanding the student, sending him out into the hallway, or sending him to the principal's office. There is no evidence in the record as to whether or how School District officials ultimately disciplined this student once he arrived in the principal's office.

With the exception of one occasion, defendant has not shown that any of the students whom teachers sent to the principal's office in response to plaintiff's reports ever received discipline stronger than a verbal reprimand. The disciplinary measures that defendant took on that occasion were precipitated by a formal complaint that plaintiff's mother filed with the School District in March 1995. At that time plaintiff had been experiencing almost daily harassment on the school bus and in his art class by a particular group of students who called him names, kicked him, or threw objects at him. The principal eventually referred plaintiff's complaint to Terri Kronzer ("Kronzer") with the School District's Human Resources Department. Kronzer conducted an investigation and determined that plaintiff had been sexually harassed. Based on her recommendations, defendant suspended one of the harassers for five days and another for one day. Other harassers received lectures on the School District's sexual harassment policy. Defendant also revoked the bus privileges of two of the students, who were brothers, and transferred the most egregious offender out of plaintiff's art class. Defendant further instructed the hall monitor to "keep an eye" on plaintiff.

Within one week after defendant implemented these measures, the students whose bus privileges had been revoked returned to the school bus. According to defendant, the students lived in a rural area, and their father complained to the principal that driving them to school each day would be a significant hardship. Defendant states that it permitted the students to return to the school bus on the condition that they sit directly behind the bus driver each day.

Plaintiff thereafter ceased riding the school bus altogether in order to avoid his harassers, but did not notify defendant that he had done so. Plaintiff and his parents were unhappy with defendant's decision to permit the students to ride the bus again. * * * Eventually, after plaintiff finished the tenth grade, he transferred to another school district altogether for his last two years of secondary education.

ANALYSIS

* * * D. Title IX claims

Defendant * * * argues that plaintiff's Title IX claims must be dismissed because Title IX does not protect individuals from discrimination based on sexual orientation or perceived sexual orientation. Title IX provides in relevant part that "[n]o person in the United States shall, *on the basis of sex,* be excluded from participation in, be denied the benefits of, or be subjected to discrimination under" federally-funded educational programs or activities. 20 U.S.C. § 1681(a) (emphasis added). * * * [T]o the extent that plaintiff asserts Title IX claims based on discrimination due to his sexual orientation or perceived sexual orientation, these claims are not actionable and must be dismissed. * * *

Plaintiff nevertheless contends that he has been a victim of harassment based upon sex or gender as well as harassment based upon his sexual orientation or perceived sexual orientation. In *Davis* * * *, the Supreme Court recognized that student-against-student sexual harassment may give rise to a cognizable claim under Title IX in appropriate circumstances. No federal court appears to have addressed, however, whether the kind of conduct to which plaintiff was subjected constitutes discrimination "on the basis of sex" within the meaning of Title IX. In contrast with the claims recognized as viable in *Davis,* this case primarily involves same-sex harassment by students who, through name-calling and other forms of verbal abuse, repeatedly indicated that they perceived plaintiff to be homosexual. Thus, plaintiff's harassers do not appear to have been motivated by any sexual desire towards plaintiff, but rather, by hostility based upon his perceived sexual orientation.

Plaintiff contends that the students engaged in the offensive conduct at issue not only because they believed him to be gay, but also because he did not meet their stereotyped expectations of masculinity. The facts alleged in plaintiff's complaint support this characterization of the students' misconduct. He specifically alleges that some of the students called him "Jessica," a girl's name, indicating a belief that he exhibited feminine characteristics. Moreover, the Court finds important the fact that plaintiff's peers began harassing him as early as kindergarten. It is highly unlikely that at that tender age plaintiff would have developed any solidified sexual preference, or for that matter, that he even understood what it meant to be "homosexual" or "heterosexual." The likelihood that he openly identified himself as gay or that he engaged in any homosexual conduct at that age is quite low. It is much more plausible that the students began tormenting him based on feminine personality traits that he exhibited and the perception that he did not engage in behaviors befitting a boy. Plaintiff thus appears to plead facts that would support a claim of harassment based on the perception that he did not fit his peers' stereotypes of masculinity.

* * * [S]everal courts have considered whether same-sex harassment targeting the claimant's failure to meet expected gender stereotypes is actionable under Title VII. The Court looks to these precedents in analyzing plaintiff's Title IX claim[.] * * *

In *Oncale,* the Supreme Court recognized for the first time that claims based on same-sex harassment are cognizable under Title VII. * * * The Court emphasized, however, that in order to prevail on such a claim, an employee must be able to prove that he or she was harassed "because of . . . sex." * * * The Court further suggested that a claimant could satisfy this requirement by demonstrating that the challenged conduct was motivated by sexual desire, that he or she was harassed in such sex-specific terms as to raise an inference of hostility towards his or her sex, or that employees of one sex were treated less favorably than those of the other sex. * * * Regardless of the kinds of proof offered, the decisive issue in any sexual harassment claim is "whether members of one sex are exposed to disadvantageous terms or conditions of employment to which members of the other sex are not exposed." Id. at 80.

The Court in *Oncale* did not specifically reach the issue of whether employees may prove harassment "because of sex" by demonstrating that the challenged conduct was motivated by a failure to meet expected gender stereotypes. Nevertheless, a number of federal courts have suggested that they can. *See Higgins v. New Balance Athletic Shoe, Inc.,* 194 F.3d 252, 261 n. 4 (1st Cir.1999)[.] * * *

Importantly, the *Higgins* court cited *Price Waterhouse v. Hopkins* * * * for the proposition that discrimination based on a failure to meet stereotyped gender expectations is actionable under Title VII. In *Price Waterhouse,* the Supreme Court upheld a Title VII claim raised by an employee who asserted that sex stereotyping played a role in her employer's decision not to promote her. In so doing, the Court explicitly addressed the legal relevance of sex stereotypes, holding that "we are beyond the day when an employer could evaluate employees by assuming or insisting that they matched the stereotype associated with their group, for '[i]n forbidding employers to discriminate against individuals because of their sex, Congress intended to strike at the entire spectrum of disparate treatment of men and women resulting from sex stereotypes.' " * * *. Thus, the *Higgins* opinion reminds courts that the Supreme Court has already determined that discrimination based on a claimant's failure to satisfy the stereotypes associated with his or her sex constitutes discrimination "because of sex" within the meaning of Title VII. Under *Oncale* the principles established in *Price Waterhouse* apply with equal force when the individual engaging in discriminatory conduct is of the same sex as the claimant.

* * * In this case, plaintiff alleges that his harassers called him names targeted at homosexuals and spread rumors about his sexual orientation, as well as subjecting him to more severe forms of misconduct such as asking him for sexual favors, grabbing his buttocks and inner thighs, and subjecting him to acts of pretended anal rape. The Court finds these alleged acts to be * * * indicative of harassment based on sex * * * . The Court accordingly denies defendant's motion for judgment on the pleadings against plaintiff's Title IX claim. * * *

PROBLEM 8-2
PROTECTION FOR LGB STUDENTS UNDER TITLE IX

Do you agree with the Judge Tunheim that the Jesse Montgomery experienced sex-based discrimination? Why or why not?

Now assume that the facts were the same *except that* harassment did not begin until Jesse Montgomery was in middle school, and the perpetrators did *not* use the following words "Jessica," "girl," "princess," "fairy," "lesbian," "pansy," or "queen"? Based on those facts, do you think Jesse Montgomery experienced sex-based discrimination? Why or why not? Do those changes in the facts change the outcome? If so, why?

NOTES ABOUT TRANSGENDER STUDENTS AND TITLE IX

1. *Harassment and Discrimination.* Does Title IX protect transgender students from harassment and discrimination based on their transgender status? Does it ensure their right to use the restroom consistent with their gender identity?

As of September 2017, the answer to the former question seems to be yes, and the answer to the latter question is unclear. In a number of different documents, Obama Administration officials had taken the position that Title IX protects transgender students from harassment and discrimination on the basis of their transgender status.

For example, in an October 26, 2010 Dear Colleague Letter, OCR officials stated:

> Although Title IX does not prohibit discrimination based solely on sexual orientation, Title IX does protect all students, including lesbian, gay, bisexual, and transgender (LGBT) students, from sex discrimination. When students are subjected to harassment on the basis of their LGBT status, they may also * * * be subjected to forms of sex discrimination prohibited under Title IX.

Dear Colleague Letter, OCR (Oct. 26, 2010), https://www2.ed.gov/about/offices/list/ocr/letters/colleague-201010.html.

2. *What About Those Bathrooms?* Obama Administration officials had also taken the position that, under Title IX, schools must allow transgender students to use the restroom consistent with their gender identity. For example, on May 13, 2016, the Civil Rights Division of U.S. the Department of Justice (DOJ) and the Office of Civil Rights of the U.S. Department of Education (ED) under the Obama Administration issued a joint Dear Colleague Letter (DCL). May 13, 2016, Dear Colleague Letter, https://www2. ed.gov/about/offices/list/ocr/letters/colleague-201605-title-ix-transgender.pdf. In the May 13, 2016 DCL, the DOJ and ED stated that Title IX's prohibition against sex discrimination "encompasses discrimination based on a student's gender identity, including discrimination based on a student's transgender status." This meant, the May 13, 2016 DCL continued, that schools had an obligation to respond to harassment based on gender identity, transgender status, or gender transition, all of which are "harassment based on sex." The May 13, 2016 DCL also stated that "[u]nder Title IX, a school must treat students consistent with their gender identity even if their education records or identification documents indicate a different sex."

With respect to restroom access specifically, the May 13, 2016 DCL stated, schools were also required under Title IX to allow transgender students to participate in sex-segregated activities and facilities "consistent with their gender identity." Thus, "[a] school may not require transgender students to use facilities inconsistent with their gender identity or to use individual-user facilities when other students are not required to."

OCR's position regarding transgender students and bathroom access sparked litigation around the country. Some of the lawsuits were filed by state and local officials, school district officials, parents, and community members seeking to enjoin enforcement of the DCL. *See, e.g., Students v. United States Department of Education*, No. 16-CV-4945, 2016 WL 6134121, at *1–2 (N.D. Ill. 2016) (denying request of organization and current and prospective high school students for, among other things, a preliminary injunction enjoining enforcement of the May 13, 2016 DCL); *Bd. of Educ. of the Highland Local Sch. Dist. v. United States Dep't of Educ.*, No. 2:16-CV-524, 2016 WL 5372349 (S.D. Ohio Sept. 26, 2016) (denying school district's motion for a preliminary injunction enjoining the Department of Education's finding that the school district's policy of not permitting a transgender girl to use the girls' restroom impermissibly discriminated against her on the basis of sex and granting transgender girl's request for an injunction requiring the school district to permit her to use the girls' restroom); *Texas v. United States*, 201 F. Supp. 3d 810 (N.D. Tex. 2016), *order clarified*, No. 7:16-CV-00054-O, 2016 WL 7852331 (N.D. Tex. Oct. 18, 2016) (holding that deference was not due the May 13, 2016 DCL and issuing a nationwide injunction barring its enforcement). Other lawsuits were filed by transgender students seeking to protect their rights under Title IX. *Evancho v. Pine-Richland Sch. Dist.*, No. CV 2:16-01537, 2017 WL 770619, at *1–2 (W.D. Pa. Feb. 27, 2017) (holding that transgender students had a reasonable likelihood of success on their Equal Protection challenge but not on the their Title IX challenge to the school district's policy requiring the plaintiffs to use either single-user bathrooms, or bathrooms "matching their assigned sexes").

3. *Bathrooms and Agency Deference.* A number of the cases specifically grappled whether the May 13, 2016 DCL and other agency guidance documents were entitled to agency deference. For example, in the Texas litigation, the district court accepted the challengers' argument that the May 13, 2016 DCL (and other documents) was effectively legislative rulemaking and, therefore, should have gone through the notice-and-comment process required by the Administrative Procedure Act (5 U.S.C. § 553) for such rulemaking. *See Texas v. United States*, 2016 WL 4426495, at *12 (N.D. Tex. 2016) ("The Guidelines are, in practice, legislative rules—not just interpretations or policy statements because they set clear legal standards. . . . As such, Defendants should have complied with the APA's notice and comment requirement."). Other courts, including the Fourth Circuit, disagreed. *G.G. ex rel. Grimm v. Gloucester County Sch. Bd.*, 822 F.3d 709 (4th Cir. 2016) (holding that the May 13, 2016 DCL was entitled to *Auer* deference), *vacated and remanded*, 2017 WL 855755 (March 6, 2017).

That specific question about bathroom access and agency deference, however, became moot when the Department of Education and the Department of Justice under the Trump Administration issued a new Dear Colleague Letter on February 22, 2017 rescinding the May 13, 2016 DCL. https://www2.ed.gov/about/offices/list/ocr/lgbt.html. *See also Gloucester County School Bd. v. G.G. ex rel. Grimm*, 2017 WL 855755 (March 6, 2017) (vacating the prior judgment of the Fourth Circuit granting deference to the May 13, 2016 DCL and "remand[ing] to the United States Court of Appeals for the Fourth Circuit for further consideration in light of the guidance document issued by the Department of Education and the Department of Justice on February 22, 2017"). The February 22, 2017 DCL "withdraw[s] and rescind[s] the [May 13, 2016 DCL] in order to further and more completely consider the legal issues involved."

The February 22, 2017 DCL resolves the agency deference question by essentially eliminating agency guidance on the issue. The February 22, 2017 DCL does not, however, resolve the question on the merits—whether Title IX requires school districts to permit transgender students to use restrooms consistent with their gender identity. Thus, going forward, courts will have to grapple with that question about the meaning and application of Title IX directly.

It is also important to note that the February 22, 2017 DCL did *not* rescind other guidance documents that had taken the position that Title IX requires schools to protect transgender students from harassment and discrimination.

PROBLEM 8-3
PROTECTION FOR TRANSGENDER STUDENTS UNDER TITLE IX

Chris is transgender girl. After Chris begins using the girls' restrooms at her high school, several of the other female students complain to the principal stating that having Chris in the restroom with them makes them uncomfortable. If the high school continues to permit Chris to use the girls' restroom, has it violated Title IX?

Assume that school officials continue to let Chris use the girls' restroom, and other high school students take matters into their own hands. Six female students surround Chris in the bathroom one day, overpower Chris, and push Chris's head into one of the toilets. They taunt Chris as a "fake girl" and "sissy boy." School officials apologize to Chris for this incident but do not discipline the other students, because the principal says "they were provoked" by Chris herself. Traumatized by this incident, Chris withdraws from school, and her parents sue the school under Title IX. Does Chris have a valid claim for relief? Why or why not?

Does Title IX require schools to permit students to use the restroom consistent with their gender identity? Consider the next decision.

Whitaker v. Kenosha Unified School District No. 1

United States Court of Appeals for the Seventh Circuit, 2017.
858 F.3d 1034.

■ WILLIAMS, CIRCUIT JUDGE.

Ashton ("Ash") Whitaker is a 17-year-old high school senior who has what would seem like a simple request: to use the boys' restroom while at school. However, the Defendants, the Kenosha Unified School District and its superintendent, Sue Savaglio, (the "School District") believe that the request is not so simple because Ash is a transgender boy. The School District did not permit Ash to enter the boys' restroom because, it believed, that his mere presence would invade the privacy rights of his male classmates. Ash brought suit, alleging that the School District's unwritten bathroom policy violates Title IX of the Education Amendments Act of 1972 and the Fourteenth Amendment's Equal Protection Clause. [Ed. note: The discussion of Ash's Equal Protection Clause is omitted from this excerpt.]

* * * The district court denied the [the defendant's] motion to dismiss and granted Ash's preliminary injunction motion. * * * The School District * * * argues that we should reverse the district court's decision

to grant the preliminary injunction[.] * * * [For the foregoing reasons,] we affirm the grant of preliminary injunctive relief.

I. BACKGROUND

Ash Whitaker is a 17-year-old who lives in Kenosha, Wisconsin with his mother, who brought this suit as his "next friend." * * * He entered his senior year ranked within the top five percent of his class and is involved in a number of extracurricular activities including the orchestra, theater, tennis, the National Honor Society, and the Astronomical Society. When not in school or participating in these activities, Ash works part-time as an accounting assistant in a medical office.

While Ash's birth certificate designates him as "female," he does not identify as one. Rather, in the spring of 2013, when Ash was in eighth grade, he told his parents that he is transgender and a boy. * * * In the fall of 2014, the beginning of his sophomore year, he told his teachers and his classmates that he is a boy and asked them to refer to him as Ashton or Ash and to use male pronouns.

In addition to publicly transitioning, Ash began to see a therapist, who diagnosed him with Gender Dysphoria * * * . In July 2016, under the supervision of an endocrinologist at Children's Hospital of Wisconsin, Ash began hormone replacement therapy. A month later, he filed a petition to legally change his name to Ashton Whitaker, which was granted in September 2016.

For the most part, Ash's transition has been met without hostility and has been accepted by much of the Tremper community. * * * Unfortunately, the School District has not been as accepting of Ash's requests to use the boys' restrooms.

In the spring of his sophomore year, Ash and his mother * * * request[ed] that Ash be permitted to use the boys' restrooms while at school and at school-sponsored events. Ash was later notified that the administration had decided that he could only use the girls' restrooms or a gender-neutral restroom that was in the school's main office, which was quite a distance from his classrooms. Because Ash had publicly transitioned, he believed that using the girls' restrooms would undermine his transition. Additionally, since Ash was the only student who was permitted to use the gender-neutral bathroom in the school's office, he feared that using it would draw further attention to his transition and status as a transgender student at Tremper. As a high schooler, Ash also worried that he might be disciplined if he tried to use the boys' restrooms and that such discipline might hurt his chances of getting into college. For these reasons, Ash restricted his water intake and attempted to avoid using any restroom at school for the rest of the school year.

Restricting his water intake was problematic for Ash, who has been diagnosed with vasovagal syncope. This condition renders Ash more susceptible to fainting and/or seizures if dehydrated. * * * Because Ash restricted his water intake to ensure that he did not have to utilize the restroom at school, he suffered from symptoms of his vasovagal syncope, including fainting and dizziness. He also suffered from stress-related migraines, depression, and anxiety because of the policy's impact on his transition and what he perceived to be the impossible choice between living as a boy or using the restroom. He even began to contemplate suicide.

In the fall of 2015, Ash began his junior year at Tremper. For six months, he exclusively used the boys' restrooms at school without incident. But, in February 2016, a teacher saw him washing his hands at a sink in the boys' restroom and reported it to the school's administration. In response, Ash's guidance counselor, Debra Tronvig, again told Ash's mother that he was permitted to only use the girls' restrooms or the gender-neutral bathroom in the school's main office. The next month, Ash and his mother met with Assistant Principal Holly Graf to discuss the school's policy. Like before, Ms. Graf stated that Ash was not permitted to use the boys' restrooms. However, the reason she gave this time was that he was listed as a female in the school's official records and to change those records, the school needed unspecified "legal or medical documentation."

Two letters submitted by Ash's pediatrician, identifying him as a transgender boy and recommending that he be allowed to use male-designated facilities at school were deemed not sufficient to change his designation. Rather, the school maintained that Ash would have to complete a surgical transition * * * a procedure that is prohibited for someone under 18 years of age * * * to be permitted access to the boys' restroom. * * *

Fearing that using the one gender-neutral restroom would single him out and subject him to scrutiny from his classmates and knowing that using the girls' restroom would be in contradiction to his transition, Ash continued to use the boys' restroom for the remainder of his junior year.

This decision was not without a cost. Ash experienced feelings of anxiousness and depression. He once more began to contemplate suicide. Nonetheless, the school's security guards were instructed to monitor's Ash's restroom use to ensure that he used the proper facilities. * * *

In April 2016, the School District provided Ash with the additional option of using two single-user, gender-neutral restrooms. These locked restrooms were on the opposite side of campus from where his classes were held. The School District provided only one student with the key: Ash. Since the restrooms were not near his classrooms, which caused Ash to miss class time, and because using them further stigmatized him, Ash again avoided using the bathrooms while at school. This only exacerbated his syncope and migraines. In addition, Ash began to fear for his safety

as more attention was drawn to his restroom use and transgender status.
* * *

A. Proceedings Below

* * * [T]he district court * * * enjoined the School District from: (1) denying Ash access to the boys' restroom; (2) enforcing any written or unwritten policy against Ash that would prevent him from using the boys' restroom while on school property or attending school-sponsored events; (3) disciplining Ash for using the boys' restroom while on school property or attending school-sponsored events; and (4) monitoring or surveilling Ash's restroom use in any way. This appeal followed. * * *

II. ANALYSIS * * *

B. Preliminary Injunctive Relief Was Proper

* * * A two-step inquiry applies when determining whether such [a preliminary injunction] is required. * * * First, the party seeking the preliminary injunction has the burden of making a threshold showing: (1) that he will suffer irreparable harm absent preliminary injunctive relief during the pendency of his action; (2) inadequate remedies at law exist; and (3) he has a reasonable likelihood of success on the merits. If the movant successfully makes this showing, the court must engage in a balancing analysis, to determine whether the balance of harm favors the moving party or whether the harm to other parties or the public sufficiently outweighs the movant's interests. * * *

[The court held that the trial court did not err "when it concluded that Ash would suffer irreparable harm absent preliminary injunctive relief" or when it concluded that "Ash adequately established that there was no adequate remedy of law available"].

3. Likelihood of Success on Merits

* * * i. Title IX Claim

Title IX provides that no person "shall, on the basis of sex, be excluded from participation in, be denied the benefits of, or be subjected to discrimination under any educational program or activity receiving Federal financial assistance. . . ." 20 U.S.C. § 1681(a). * * * Pursuant to the statute's regulations, an institution may provide separate, but comparable, bathroom, shower, and locker facilities. [34 C.F.R.] § 106.33. * * *

* * * Neither the statute nor the regulations define the term "sex." * * * Therefore, we turn to the Supreme Court and our case law for guidance.

* * * [T]his court has looked to Title VII when construing Title IX. * * * The School District contends that we should do so here, and relies on our reasoning in *Ulane v. Eastern Airlines, Inc.*, 742 F.2d 1081 (7th Cir. 1984), to conclude that Ash cannot state a claim under Title IX as a matter of law. * * * We disagree.

In *Ulane*, we noted in dicta that Title VII's prohibition on sex discrimination "implies that it is unlawful to discriminate against women because they are women and against men because they are men." 742 F.2d at 1085. We then looked to the lack of legislative history regarding the meaning of the term "sex" in Title VII and concluded that this prohibition should be "given a narrow, traditional interpretation, which would also exclude transsexuals." Id. at 1085–86. This reasoning, however, cannot and does not foreclose Ash and other transgender students from bringing sex-discrimination claims based upon a theory of sex-stereotyping as articulated four years later by the Supreme Court in *Price Waterhouse v. Hopkins*, 490 U.S. 228, 109 S.Ct. 1775, 104 L.Ed.2d 268 (1989).

In *Price Waterhouse*, a plurality of the Supreme Court and two justices concurring in the judgment, found that the plaintiff had adequately alleged that her employer, in violation of Title VII, had discriminated against her for being too masculine. * * *

The Supreme Court further embraced an expansive view of Title VII in *Oncale v. Sundowner Offshore Services, Inc.*, 523 U.S. 75, 118 S.Ct. 998, 140 L.Ed.2d 201 (1998), where Justice Scalia, writing for a unanimous Court, declared that "statutory prohibitions often go beyond the principal evil to cover reasonably comparable evils, and it is ultimately the provisions of our laws rather than the principal concerns of our legislators by which we are governed." Id. at 79, 118 S.Ct. 998.

Following Price Waterhouse, this court and others have recognized a cause of action under Title VII when an adverse action is taken because of an employee's failure to conform to sex stereotypes. Our most recent application occurred when, sitting *en banc*, we held that a homosexual plaintiff can state a Title VII claim of sex discrimination based upon a theory of sex-stereotyping. *Hively v. Ivy Tech Cmty. Coll. of Ind.*, 853 F.3d 339, 351–52 (7th Cir. 2017) (holding that a homosexual plaintiff may state a claim for sex-based discrimination under Title VII under either a sex stereotyping theory or under the associational theory).

The School District argues that even under a sex-stereotyping theory, Ash cannot demonstrate a likelihood of success on his Title IX claim because its policy is not based on whether the student behaves, walks, talks, or dresses in a manner that is inconsistent with any preconceived notions of sex stereotypes. Instead, it contends that as a matter of law, requiring a biological female to use the women's bathroom is not sex-stereotyping. However, this view is too narrow.

By definition, a transgender individual does not conform to the sex-based stereotypes of the sex that he or she was assigned at birth. * * *

[Accordingly, t]he Sixth Circuit [along with other circuit courts and district courts] has * * * recognized a transgender plaintiff's ability to bring a sex-stereotyping claim. [*See, e.g., Smith v. City of Salem*, 378 F.3d 566 (6th Cir. 2004).] * * *

Here, however, the School District argues that this reasoning flies in the face of Title IX, as Congress has not explicitly added transgender status as a protected characteristic to either Title VII or Title IX, despite having opportunities to do so. *See e.g.*, Student Non-Discrimination Act of 2015 S. 439 114th Cong. (2015). The Supreme Court has rejected this argument, stating that congressional inaction "lacks persuasive significance because several equally tenable inferences may be drawn from such inaction, including the inference that the existing legislation already incorporated the offered change." Therefore, Congressional inaction is not determinative.

Rather, Ash can demonstrate a likelihood of success on the merits of his claim because he has alleged that the School District has denied him access to the boys' restroom because he is transgender. A policy that requires an individual to use a bathroom that does not conform with his or her gender identity punishes that individual for his or her gender non-conformance, which in turn violates Title IX. The School District's policy also subjects Ash, as a transgender student, to different rules, sanctions, and treatment than non-transgender students, in violation of Title IX. Providing a gender-neutral alternative is not sufficient to relieve the School District from liability, as it is the policy itself which violates the Act. Further, based on the record here, these gender-neutral alternatives were not true alternatives because of their distant location to Ash's classrooms and the increased stigmatization they caused Ash. * * *

And, while the School District repeatedly asserts that Ash may not "unilaterally declare" his gender, this argument misrepresents Ash's claims and dismisses his transgender status. This is not a case where a student has merely announced that he is a different gender. Rather, Ash has a medically diagnosed and documented condition. Since his diagnosis, he has consistently lived in accordance with his gender identity. This law suit demonstrates that the decision to do so was not without cost or pain. Therefore, we find that Ash has sufficiently established a probability of success on the merits of his Title IX claim. * * *

4. Balance of Harms Favors Ash

Having already determined that the district court did not err in finding that Ash will suffer irreparable harm absent preliminary injunctive relief, we now must look at whether granting preliminary injunctive relief will harm the School District and the public as a whole. * * * This is done on a "sliding scale" measuring the balance of harms against the moving party's likelihood of success. The more likely he is to succeed on the merits, the less the scale must tip in his favor. The converse, however, also is true: the less likely he is to win, the more the balance of harms must weigh in his favor for an injunction to issue. Substantial deference is given to the district court's analysis of the balancing of harms.

The School District argues that the district court erred in determining that the balance of the harms weighed in favor of granting the injunction because it ignored the fact that the harm extends to 22,160 students in the School District whose privacy rights are at risk by allowing a transgender student to utilize a bathroom that does not correspond with his biological sex. Granting the injunction, the School District continues, also irreparably harmed these students' parents, who are now denied the right to direct the education and upbringing of their children. Additionally, the School District asserts that the injunction harms the public as a whole, since it forces other school districts nationwide to contemplate whether they must change their policies and alter their facilities or risk being found out of compliance with Title IX. Noncompliance places their federal funding at risk. Based upon this record, however, we find the School District's arguments unpersuasive.

The School District has not demonstrated that it will suffer any harm from having to comply with the district court's preliminary injunction order. Nor has it established that the public as a whole will suffer harm. As noted above, before seeking injunctive relief, Ash used the bathroom for nearly six months *without incident*. The School District has not produced any evidence that any students have ever complained about Ash's presence in the boys' restroom. Nor have they demonstrated that Ash's presence has actually caused an invasion of any other student's privacy. And while the School District claims that preliminary injunctive relief infringes upon parents' ability to direct the education of their children, it offers no evidence that a parent has ever asserted this right. These claims are all speculative.

We are further convinced that the district court did not err in finding that this balance weighed in favor of granting the injunction when considering the statements made by *amici*, who are school administrators from twenty-one states and the District of Columbia. Together, these administrators are responsible for educating approximately 1.4 million students. Each administrator has experience implementing inclusive bathroom policies in their respective schools, and each has grappled with the same privacy concerns that the School District raises here. These administrators uniformly agree that the frequently-raised and hypothetical concerns about a policy that permits a student to utilize a bathroom consistent with his or her gender identity have simply not materialized. Rather, in their combined experience, all students' needs are best served when students are treated equally.

Although the School District argues that implementing an inclusive policy will result in the demise of gender-segregated facilities in schools, the *amici* note that this has not been the case. In fact, these administrators have found that allowing transgender students to use facilities that align with their gender identity has actually reinforced the concept of separate facilities for boys and girls. When considering the experience of this group in light of the record here, which is virtually devoid of any complaints or harm caused to the School District, its students, or the public as a whole, it is clear that the district court did not err in balancing the harms.

III. CONCLUSION

Appellants' motion to have this court assert pendent appellant jurisdiction over the district court's denial of Appellants' Motion to Dismiss is DENIED. The district court's order granting the Appellee's motion for a preliminary injunction is AFFIRMED.

PROBLEM 8-4
BATHROOM ACCESS AND SEX DISCRIMINATION

Recall the discussion regarding the recently enacted North Carolina law—H.B. 2.[b] (In late March 2017, this law was amended to strip the provisions regarding bathrooms. The law continues, however, local governments and "political subdivisions of the state" from prohibiting discrimination on the basis of sexual orientation or gender identity. For purposes of this problem, consider the originally enacted version of H.B. 2.)

As originally enacted, H.B. 2 required all multiple occupancy bathrooms or changing rooms at public schools: "to be designated for and used only by students based on their biological sex." N.C. Gen. Stat. § 115C–521.2(b). "Biological sex" was defined in the statute to mean "[t]he physical condition of being male or female, which is stated on a person's birth certificate." N.C. Gen. Stat. § 115C–521.2(a)(1). The law allowed school boards to provide single-occupancy bathrooms, id. § 115C–521.2(c), and contained exceptions for custodial, maintenance, medical, and other exceptional purposes. Id. § 115C–521.2(d).

Did that bathroom-access rule, as expressed in the originally enacted version of H.B. 2, violate Title IX to the extent it applied to schools that received federal funding? What about the Equal Protection Clause?

Consider the following materials.

NOTE ON LGBT STUDENTS AND THE EQUAL PROTECTION CLAUSE

Many courts have concluded that discrimination against LGBT students may violate Title IX. What about the Equal Protection Clause? Do public schools have an obligation to protect LGBT students from harassment and discrimination under the Equal Protection Clause? Consider the *Nabozny* case excerpted below.

James Nabozny v. Mary Podlesny et al., 92 F.3d 446 (7th Cir. 1996). In 1996, the Seventh Circuit became the first federal appellate court in the country to answer that question in the affirmative. In *Nabozny*, the Seventh Circuit ruled that a gay student's constitutional (equal protection) rights were violated when his school did not protect him from anti-gay

---

[b] The original version of H.B. is available here: www.ncleg.net/sessions/2015e2/bills/house/pdf/h2v4.pdf. The amendments to H.B. 2 are available here: http://www.ncleg.net/Sessions/2017/Bills/House/HTML/H142v5.html.

harassment and violence, including a "mock rape" by two other boys in front of twenty other students, an assault in the boys' bathroom during which Jamie's head was pushed into a urinal, and an aggravated assault by eight boys in the school hallway which later caused the victim to collapse from internal bleeding. After the school bathroom assault, Mary Podlesny (who was responsible for school discipline) told James and his parents that "boys will be boys" and that such acts should be expected because James was openly gay. Although they promised to take action, school officials did nothing to prevent the harassment against James. Toward the end of the school year a district attorney purportedly suggested that James take time off from school. When James returned after one and a half weeks off, the harassment continued and James attempted suicide. The harassment of James continued throughout his high school years.

Writing for the three-judge panel, **Judge Eschbach** held that Nabozny could maintain claims for unconstitutional discrimination on the basis of both sex and sexual orientation. As to the sex discrimination claim, the court found it "impossible to believe that a female lodging a similar complaint would have received the same response. More important, the defendants do not deny that they aggressively punished male-on-female battery and harassment." The court concluded its sex discrimination discussion: "The question is not whether they are required to treat every harassment complaint the same way; as we have noted, they are not. The question is whether they are required to give male and female students equivalent levels of protection; they are, absent an important governmental objective, and the law clearly said so prior to Nabozny's years in middle school."

"Nabozny introduced sufficient evidence to show that the discriminatory treatment was motivated by the defendants' disapproval of Nabozny's sexual orientation, including statements by the defendants that Nabozny should expect to be harassed because he is gay." As to whether such discrimination is constitutionally actionable, the court said yes: "Our discussion of equal protection analysis thus far has revealed a well established principle: the Constitution prohibits intentional invidious discrimination between otherwise similarly situated persons based on one's membership in a definable minority, absent at least a rational basis for the discrimination. There can be little doubt that homosexuals are an identifiable minority subjected to discrimination in our society. * * * We are unable to garner any rational basis for permitting one student to assault another based on the victim's sexual orientation, and the defendants do not offer us one."

Other courts likewise have concluded that a school district's knowing failure to protect LGB students from harassment or discrimination may violate the Equal Protection Clause. *See, e.g., Seiwert v. Spencer-Owen Cmty. Sch. Corp.*, 497 F. Supp., 2d 942, 952 (S.D. Ind. 2007); *Flores v. Morgan Hill Unified Sch. Dist.*, 324 F.3d 1130, 1138 (9th Cir. 2003); *Schroeder ex rel. Schroeder v. Maumee Bd. of Educ.*, 296 F. Supp. 2d 869, 875 (N.D. Ohio 2003); *Massey v. Banning Unified Sch. Dist.*, 256 F. Supp. 2d 1090, 1096 (C.D. Cal. 2003).

Would the above fact pattern involving Jamie Nabozny support a claim for relief under Title IX? Would it support a claim for relief under Title IX if Nabozny had been female?

Consider the following statement: "Harassment that targets gay or lesbian students and involves explicit sexual propositions by persons of the other sex (such as threats by male students to rape a lesbian) is more likely to receive Title IX protection, even though it is not necessarily any more connected to the target's sex than same-sex sexual harassment (such as threats by male students to rape a gay male student) or nonsexual, anti-gay harassment (such as physical assaults of gay or lesbian students) against students perceived to be gay or lesbian. Yet, under current law, courts are likely to treat the former as based on sex, while treating the latter two situations as not based on sex." Deborah Brake, "Cruelest of the Gender Police: Student-to-Student Sexual Harassment and Anti-Gay Peer Harassment Under Title IX," 1 *Geo. J. Gender & L.* 37, 68 (1999).

Is this an accurate statement of the law? If this is an accurate statement of the law, how can it be criticized?

What about transgender students? Does a school district's knowing failure to protect transgender students from harassment and discrimination violate the Equal Protection Clause? Why or why not? *Cf. Glenn v. Brumby*, 663 F.3d 1312, 1320 (11th Cir. 2011) ("We conclude that a government agent violates the Equal Protection Clause's prohibition of sex-based discrimination when he or she fires a transgender or transsexual employee because of his or her gender non-conformity.").

What about bathroom access? Do public schools have an obligation under the Equal Protection Clause to allow transgender students to use the restroom consistent with their gender identity? *See, e.g., Evancho v. Pine-Richland Sch. Dist.*, No. CV 2:16-01537, 2017 WL 770619, at *1–2 (W.D. Pa. Feb. 27, 2017) (concluding that the answer may be "yes").

The *Whitaker* decision, excerpted above, also concluded that the answer may be yes. As noted above, the school district in Whitaker refused to let Ash, a transgender male, use the boys' restroom. Instead, Ash was required to use either the girls' restroom or a gender-neutral restroom. The Seventh Circuit affirmed the district court's conclusion that the student was likely to prevail on his Equal Protection Clause claim (in addition to his Title IX claim).

The school district defended its bathroom policy "by claiming it need[ed] to protect the privacy rights of all [of its] 22,160 students." The court rejected this argument. First, the court explained that the district's "privacy argument is based upon sheer conjecture and abstraction." The court noted that "[f]or nearly six moths, Ash used the boys' bathroom while at school and school-sponsored events without incident or complaint from another student." Later in the opinion, the court also noted that school administrators from 21 states filed an amici brief in which they "uniformly agree[d] that the frequently raised and hypothetical concerns about a policy that permits a student to utilize a bathroom consistent with his or her gender identity have simply not materialized."

The court also responded to the school district's assertion at oral argument that "the only way that Ash would be permitted to use the boys' restroom would be if he were to present the school with a birth certificate that designated his sex as male." The court rejected a bathroom-access rule based on sex designations on birth certificates. The court pointed out that some individuals are born with external genitalia of two sexes or genitalia that is ambiguous in nature. "In those cases," the court continued, "it is clear that the marker on the birth certificate would not adequately account for or reflect one's biological sex, which would have to be determined by considering more than what was listed on the paper."

Moreover, the court continued, different states have different standards for changing gender markers on birth certificates. In Wisconsin, an individual must undergo some form of transition-related surgery. By contrast, "in Minnesota, an individual may amend his or her birth certificate to reflect his or her gender identity without surgical reassignment." For these and other reasons, the court concluded, "the School District's reliance upon a birth certificate's sex-marker demonstrates the arbitrary nature of the policy."

B. CLASH OF FREE SPEECH AND ANTI-DISCRIMINATION

As explained above, public schools are legally obligated under the Equal Protection Clause, Title IX, and other federal and state law provisions to respond to known incidents of harassment and discrimination. But what if the school disciplines a student for their verbal harassment (that is, their speech)? Does that discipline impermissibly infringe the student's first amendment rights?

David Warren Saxe et al. v. State College Area School District (SCASD) et al.

United States Court of Appeals for the Third Circuit, 2001.
240 F.3d 200.

■ ALITO, CIRCUIT JUDGE.

The plaintiffs in this case challenge the constitutionality of a public school district's "anti-harassment" policy, arguing that it violates the First Amendment's guarantee of freedom of speech. The District Court, concluding that the policy prohibited no more speech than was already unlawful under federal and state anti-discrimination laws, held that the policy is constitutional and entered judgment for the school district. We reverse. * * *

There is of course no question that non-expressive, physically harassing *conduct* is entirely outside the ambit of the free speech clause. But there is also no question that the free speech clause protects a wide variety of speech that listeners may consider deeply offensive, including statements that impugn another's race or national origin or that denigrate religious beliefs. When laws against harassment attempt to regulate oral or written expression on such topics, however detestable the views expressed may be, we cannot turn a blind eye to the First Amendment implications. "Where pure expression is involved," anti-discrimination law "steers into the territory of the First Amendment." *DeAngelis v. El Paso Mun. Police Officers Ass'n,* 51 F.3d 591, 596 (5th Cir. 1995).

This is especially true because, as the Fifth Circuit has noted, when anti-discrimination laws are "applied to . . . harassment claims founded solely on verbal insults, pictorial or literary matter, the statutes impose[ ] content-based, viewpoint-discriminatory restrictions on speech." *DeAngelis.* Indeed, a disparaging comment directed at an individual's sex, race, or some other personal characteristic has the potential to create an "hostile environment"—and thus come within the ambit of anti-discrimination laws—precisely because of its sensitive subject matter and because of the odious viewpoint it expresses.

This sort of content-or viewpoint-based restriction is ordinarily subject to the most exacting First Amendment scrutiny. This point was dramatically illustrated in *R.A.V. v. City of St. Paul* [Chapter 1, Section 3], in which the Supreme Court struck down a municipal hate-speech ordinance prohibiting "fighting words" that aroused "anger, alarm or resentment on the basis of race, color, creed, religion or gender." While recognizing that fighting words generally are unprotected by the First Amendment, the Court nevertheless found that the ordinance unconstitutionally discriminated on the basis of content and viewpoint:

Displays containing some words—odious racial epithets, for example—would be prohibited to proponents of all views. But "fighting words" that do not themselves invoke race, color, creed, religion, or gender—aspersions upon a person's mother, for example—would seemingly be usable ad libitum in the placards of those arguing in favor of racial, color, etc. tolerance and equality, but could not be used by that speaker's opponents.

Striking down the law, the Court concluded that "the point of the First Amendment is that majority preferences must be expressed in some fashion other than silencing speech on the basis of content."

Loosely worded anti-harassment laws may pose some of the same problems as the St. Paul hate speech ordinance: they may regulate deeply offensive and potentially disruptive categories of speech based, at least in part, on subject matter and viewpoint. * * *

[Judge Alito conceded that state anti-harassment rules expressing a "discriminatory idea" can sometimes pass muster.] *R.A.V.* did acknowledge that content-discriminatory speech restrictions may be permissible when the content classification merely "happens to be associated with particular 'secondary effects' of the speech, so that the regulation is 'justified without reference to the content of the . . . speech.'" The Supreme Court has made it clear, however, that the government may not prohibit speech under a "secondary effects" rationale based solely on the emotive impact that its offensive content may have on a listener: "Listeners' reactions to speech are not the type of 'secondary effects' we referred to in *Renton*. . . . The emotive impact of speech on its audience is not a 'secondary effect.'" *Boos v. Barry,* 485 U.S. 312, 321 (1988). Nor do we believe that the restriction of expressive speech on the basis of its content may be characterized as a mere "time, place and manner" regulation.

[For the foregoing reasons, the court rejected the district court's categorical rule against First Amendment challenges to sexual harassment codes. The court then maintained that the school's challenged Policy reached much further into protected expression than analogous federal anti-harassment regulations, such as those recognized by the Department of Education and the Supreme Court under Title IX.]

For one thing, the Policy prohibits harassment based on personal characteristics that are not protected under federal law. Titles VI and IX, taken together with the other relevant federal statutes, cover only harassment based on sex, race, color, national origin, age and disability. The Policy, in contrast, is much broader, reaching, at the extreme, a catch-all category of "other personal characteristics" (which, the Policy states, includes things like "clothing," "appearance," "hobbies and values," and "social skills"). Insofar as the Policy attempts to prevent students from making negative comments about each others' "appearance," "clothing," and "social skills," it may be brave, futile, or merely silly. But attempting to proscribe negative comments about "values," as that term is commonly used today, is something else altogether. By prohibiting disparaging speech directed at a person's "values," the Policy strikes at the heart of moral and political discourse—the lifeblood of constitutional self government (and democratic education) and the core concern of the First Amendment. * * *

Moreover, the Policy's prohibition extends beyond harassment that objectively denies a student equal access to a school's education resources. Even on a narrow reading, the Policy unequivocally prohibits any verbal or physical conduct that is based on an enumerated personal characteristic and that "has the *purpose or effect* of substantially interfering with a student's educational performance or creating an intimidating, hostile or offensive environment." (emphasis added). Unlike federal anti-harassment law, which imposes liability only when harassment has "a systemic *effect* on educational programs and activities," *Davis*, the Policy extends to speech that merely has the "purpose" of harassing another. This formulation, by focusing on the speaker's motive rather than the effect of speech on the learning environment, appears to sweep in those "simple acts of teasing and name-calling" that the *Davis* Court explicitly held were insufficient for liability.

[The court ruled that the Policy was substantially overbroad under *Broadrick v. Oklahoma,* 413 U.S. 601, 615 (1973), and therefore invalidated the Policy on its face. The judges focused on the Policy's statement that harassment "can include any unwelcome verbal, written or physical conduct which offends, denigrates or belittles an individual because of any of the characteristics described above," including sexual orientation, other personal characteristics, and "values." The court considered whether the Policy could not be given a narrowing construction, to limit the Policy to speech which, as another paragraph in the Policy says, either "substantially interfere[s] with a student's educational performance or create[s] an intimidating, hostile or offensive environment."] So narrowed, the Policy would require the following elements before speech could be deemed harassing: (1) verbal or physical conduct (2) that is based on one's actual or perceived personal characteristics and (3) that has the purpose or effect of either (3a) substantially interfering with a student's educational performance or (3b) creating an intimidating hostile, or offensive environment.

It is apparent from these elements that SCASD cannot take solace in the relatively more permissive *Fraser* or *Hazelwood* standards [Section 1 of this chapter]. First, the Policy does not confine itself merely to vulgar or lewd speech; rather, it reaches any speech that interferes or is intended to interfere with educational performance or that creates or is intended to create a hostile environment. While some *Fraser*-type speech may fall within this definition, the Policy's scope is clearly broader. Second, the Policy does not contain any geographical or contextual limitations; rather, it purports to cover "any harassment of a student by a member of the school community." Thus, its strictures presumably apply whether the harassment occurs in a school sponsored assembly, in the classroom, in the hall between classes, or in a playground or athletic facility. Obviously, the Policy covers far more than just *Hazelwood*-type school-sponsored speech; it also sweeps in private student speech that merely "happens to occur on the school premises." *Hazelwood.* As a result, SCASD cannot rely on *Hazelwood*'s more lenient "legitimate pedagogical concern" test in defending the Policy from facial attack.

In short, the Policy, even narrowly read, prohibits a substantial amount of non-vulgar, non-sponsored student speech. SCASD must therefore satisfy the *Tinker* test by showing that the Policy's restrictions are necessary to prevent substantial disruption or interference with the work of the school or the rights of other students. Applying this test, we conclude that the Policy is substantially overbroad.

As an initial matter, the Policy punishes not only speech that actually causes disruption, but also speech that merely intends to do so: by its terms, it covers speech "which has the purpose or effect of" interfering with educational performance or creating a hostile environment. This ignores *Tinker*'s requirement that a school must reasonably believe that speech will cause actual, material disruption before prohibiting it.

In addition, even if the "purpose" component is ignored, we do not believe that prohibited "harassment," as defined by the Policy, necessarily rises to the level of a substantial disruption under *Tinker*. We agree that the Policy's first prong, which prohibits speech that would "substantially interfere with a student's educational performance," may satisfy the *Tinker* standard. The primary function of a public school is to educate its students; conduct that substantially interferes with the mission is, almost by definition, disruptive to the school environment.

The Policy's second criterion, however—which prohibits speech that "creates an intimidating, hostile or offensive environment"—poses a more difficult problem. There are several possible grounds on which SCASD could attempt to justify this prohibition. * * * SCASD could argue that speech creating a "hostile environment" may be banned because it "intrudes upon . . . the rights of other students." *Tinker*. The precise scope of *Tinker*'s "interference with the rights of others" language is unclear; at least one court has opined that it covers only independently tortious speech like libel, slander or intentional infliction of emotional distress. In any case, it is certainly not enough that the speech is merely offensive to some listener. Because the Policy's "hostile environment" prong does not, on its face, require any threshold showing of severity or pervasiveness, it could conceivably be applied to cover any speech about some enumerated personal characteristics the content of which offends someone. This could include much "core" political and religious speech: the Policy's "Definitions" section lists as examples of covered harassment "negative" or "derogatory" speech about such contentious issues as "racial customs," "religious tradition," "language," "sexual orientation," and "values." Such speech, when it does not pose a realistic threat of substantial disruption, is within a student's First Amendment rights.

Finally, SCASD might argue that the "hostile environment" prohibition is required to maintain an orderly and non-disruptive educational environment. However, as *Tinker* made clear, the "undifferentiated fear or apprehension of disturbance" is not enough to justify a restriction on student speech. Although SCASD correctly asserts that it has a compelling interest in promoting an educational environment that is safe and conducive to learning, it fails to provide any particularized reason as to why it anticipates substantial disruption from the broad swath of student speech prohibited under the Policy.

The Policy, then, appears to cover substantially more speech than could be prohibited under *Tinker*'s substantial disruption test. Accordingly, we hold that the Policy is unconstitutionally overbroad.

■ [We omit JUDGE RENDELL's concurring opinion, which objected to the majority's suggestion that a policy hewing to the guidelines created by federal anti-harassment law would not pass First Amendment scrutiny.]

PROBLEM 8-5
SEXUAL HARASSMENT AS A LIMIT ON ACADEMIC FREEDOM?

Professor Shock teaches English composition using a confrontational teaching style designed to command the attention and interest of his students and make them think and write about controversial subjects. He discusses subjects such as obscenity, cannibalism, and consensual sex with children. Sometimes, he uses vulgarities and profanity in the classroom. One male and a few female students find this mode of instruction unhelpful and complain to the chair of the department when Professor Shock regales the class with detailed descriptions of articles in *Hustler* and other degrading magazines, and with pointed references to the anatomy of several female students. Shock requires the students to write essays discussing the "values of pornography"; when several female students hand in papers criticizing pornography, Shock requires them to rewrite their papers to discuss the "values" rather than "problems" presented by porn.

Consider the following scenarios:

1.   Several female students complain to the Dean of Students that the materials and related classroom discussion, as well as the paper assignment and Shock's response to the papers have created a sexually hostile environment for women in the class. The dean does nothing. Is the college in violation of Title IX? First, would this be considered sexual harassment under the Department of Education's Sexual Harassment Guidance? Second, if so, should a court defer to the department's Guidance on this matter? Third, would application of the Guidance here be unconstitutional? See DOE, "Sexual Harassment Guidance," Example 1.

2.   Now assume that based upon the student complaints and discussions with Professor Shock (who confirmed the practices reported by the students), the department, backed by the university's Dean of Students, prohibits Shock from (a) reading from *Hustler* or other pornographic magazines, (b) forcing students to defend pornography, and (c) making "sexualized references" to the body or physical appearance of any female student. Although the department does not suspend the professor, it does require him to attend a two-week feminist sensitivity training session.

Professor Shock objects to this discipline. Because the university is state-supported, he sues in federal court for an injunction protecting his First Amendment rights to speak freely on matters of public concern (*Pickering*), to academic freedom in deciding how to structure his classes (*Keyishian*), and to be free of overbroad restrictions on expression (*Doe v. University of Michigan*, 721 F.Supp. 852 (E.D. Mich.1989), invalidating a hate speech code). The University denies that it has infringed on the professor's constitutional rights. Is that correct?

The University also argues that any restriction on speech or academic freedom is justified by Title IX's requirement that the University maintain an educational environment that is not "hostile" toward female students. Would the complaining students have had a valid Title IX claim against the University? *See Cohen v. San Bernardino Valley College*, 883 F.Supp. 1407 (C.D. Cal. 1995), *rev'd,* 92 F.3d 968 (9th Cir. 1996).

C. SEXUAL VIOLENCE

NOTES ON SEXUAL VIOLENCE

1. *Sexual Violence: What Is It?* As discussed above, public schools have an obligation under Title IX to respond to sex-based harassment. Sex-based harassment may, but does not need to, include sexual violence. What constitutes "sexual violence" has been a matter of dispute. Sexual violence had previously been defined by OCR as follows:

> Sexual violence * * * refers to physical sexual acts perpetrated against a person's will or where a person is incapable of giving consent (e.g., due to the student's age or use of drugs or alcohol, or because an intellectual or other disability prevents the student from having the capacity to give consent). A number of different acts fall into the category of sexual violence, including rape, sexual assault, sexual battery, sexual abuse, and sexual coercion. Sexual violence can be carried out by school employees, other students, or third parties.

OCR, *Questions and Answers on Title IX and Sexual Violence* 1 (Apr. 29, 2014), available at https://ed.gov/about/offices/list/ocr/docs/qa-201404-title-ix.pdf (last visited Jan. 31, 2017).

On September 22, 2017, however, the U.S. Department of Education issued a Dear Colleague letter withdrawing the April 29, 2014 Question and Answer guide. https://www2.ed.gov/about/offices/list/ocr/letters/colleague-title-ix-201709.pdf. Although the old definition has been withdrawn, the newly released documents do not provide a new definition of "sexual violence."

2. *What Do Schools Need to Do About It?* How schools should respond to complaints of sexual violence has also been a matter of dispute. According to the now-withdrawn April 29, 2014 Question and Answer Guide, "[w]hen a school knows or reasonably should know of possible sexual violence, it must take immediate and appropriate steps to investigate or otherwise determine what occurred[.] * * * If an investigation reveals that sexual violence created a hostile environment, the school must then take prompt and effective steps reasonably calculated to end the sexual violence, eliminate the hostile environment, prevent its recurrence, and, as appropriate, remedy its effects." April 29, 2014 Question and Answers on Title IX and Sexual Violence, at 2–3.

The now-withdrawn April 29, 2014 Question and Answer Guide had also included a list of specific elements that had to be contained in a school's policies and procedures regarding sexual violence. Among other things, the April 29, 2014 guide stated that policies had to: (1) provide notice of the grievance procedures; (2) provide for adequate, reliable, and impartial investigation of complaints; (3) provide notice "of a student's right to file a criminal complaint and a Title IX complaint simultaneously;" and (4) use a preponderance of the evidence standard. April 29, 2014 Question and Answers on Title IX and Sexual Violence at 12–13. The same, now-withdrawn document also provided guidance about cases involving alcohol and/or drug use. Specifically, the April 29, 2014 document stated that "sexual violence" included "physical sexual acts perpetrated against a person's will or where a person is incapable of giving consent (e.g., due to * * * use of drugs or alcohol * * *)."

During the Obama Administration, there was an increase in the number of schools—particularly colleges and universities—subject to federal investigation into how the schools handled complaints of sexual violence. According to a letter from OCR to then-Senator Barbara Boxer, in 2009, OCR received 20 complaints alleging sexual violence. In 2014, OCR received 123 complaints regarding sexual violence. https://www2.ed.gov/about/offices/list/ocr/correspondence/congress/20150428-t9-sexual-violence-college-campuses.pdf. The number of active investigations of sexual violence by OCR has also increased. In mid-October 2014, there were 89 investigations pending at 85 colleges and universities.

Some of the OCR investigations resulted in findings requiring schools to revise their policies. For example, in December 2014, OCR issued a letter of findings to Harvard Law School concluding that the law school violated Title IX. Available at https://www2.ed.gov/documents/press-releases/harvard-law-letter.pdf. The letter states that the Law School "failed to comply with the Title IX requirements for the prompt and equitable response to complaints of sexual harassment and sexual assault." *Id.* at 2. The letter also faulted the law school for using a "clear and convincing" standard of proof in sexual assault cases. *Id.* at 3.

3. *Backlash?* These OCR investigations and findings of violations prompted backlash at some institutions. During the pendency of the investigation of the Law School, Harvard University announced the promulgation of a new, university-wide policy on sexual harassment and sexual violence. After the adoption of the revised policy, however, twenty-eight members of the Harvard Law School faculty issued a public letter "voic[ing] their strong objections" to the new policy. https://www.bostonglobe.com/opinion/2014/10/14/rethink-harvard-sexual-harassment-policy/HFDDiZN7nU2UwuUuWMnqbM/story.html.

Among other things, the letter raises concerns about due process protections for the accused, as well as concerns about the affirmative consent rule. Specifically, the letter criticizes the new policy for:

- "The failure to ensure adequate representation for the accused, particularly for students unable to afford representation. * * *

- Adopting a definition of sexual harassment that goes significantly beyond Title IX and Title VII law.

- Adopting rules governing sexual conduct between students both of whom are impaired or incapacitated, rules which are starkly one-sided as between complainants and respondents, and entirely inadequate to address the complex issues in these unfortunate situations involving extreme use and abuse of alcohol or drugs by our students."

https://www.bostonglobe.com/opinion/2014/10/14/rethink-harvard-sexual-harassment-policy/HFDDiZN7nU2UwuUuWMnqbM/story.html.

4.   *A Response to the Backlash.* Other scholars, however, pushed back. Dean Michelle Anderson, for example, recently wrote:

> Due Process is crucial to the fairness of any adjudicatory system. Enhanced due process rights for respondents in sexual misconduct cases on campus sounds like a good idea until it is placed in historical context. It harkens back to the unequal part treatment of rape in the criminal law, as a special class of crime that required exceptional protection for those accused of it, primarily due to 'the unchaste (let us call it) mentality' of females * * *.

Michelle Anderson, "Campus Sexual Assault Adjudication and Resistance to Reform," 125 *Yale L.J.* 1940, 2005 (2016).

Anderson defends an affirmative consent rule. (Affirmative consent is discussed more in the next note.) Anderson argues that affirmative consent rules are in line with the law in many jurisdictions. *Id.* at 1979 (noting that "[a] plurality of U.S. jurisdictions that define consent use the word 'agreement' or something stronger"). Moreover, she argues, affirmative consent is the right rule as a matter of policy:

> Affirmative consent derives from the notion that bodies are not generally available for sexual penetration. If people's bodies are generally available to be sexually penetrated, then one should be able to penetrate someone else at any time, unless that person communicates an objection to being penetrated. If, by contrast, people's bodies are not generally available to be sexually penetrated, one should not be able to penetrate someone else without that person's affirmative permission. Affirmative consent thus * * * is a mechanism to maximize sexual autonomy.

Id. at 1979.

Anderson does, however, warn against the push for increased penalties for perpetrators of sexual assault. Advocates, she argues, "should oppose any moves to increase the penalties for campus sexual assault across the board or to impose mandatory minimum penalties upon those found responsible for sexual assault." Harsh penalties, she argues "will deter reporting of routine sexual assaults, deter pursuit of such claims by administrators responsible for deciding when to pursue or close cases, and deter finding respondents responsible." *Id.* at 2000–01.

5.   *Affirmative Consent.* Changes are also taking place at the state level. In 2014, California enacted a law, applicable to colleges and universities receiving state funding, establishing a new consent standard for sexual assault on campus. Among other things, the new law requires covered schools to use "[a]n affirmative consent standard" in determining whether consent was given. "Affirmative consent" is defined to mean "affirmative, conscious, and voluntary agreement to engage in sexual activity. * * * Lack of protest or resistance does not mean consent, nor does silence mean consent." Cal. Educ. Code § 67386(a)(1). New York enacted a similar law in 2015. N.Y. Educ. Law § 6441.

Is this the right rule? For an analysis of the arguments for and against affirmative consent rules, see Aya Gruber, "Consent Confusion," 38 *Cardozo L. Rev.* 415 (2016).

6. *Federal Reversal.* On September 22, 2017, the U.S. Department of Education issued a Dear Colleague letter (DCL) stating that the April 29, 2014 Questions and Answers on Title IX and Sexual Violence guide had been withdrawn. The September 22, 2017 DCL listed a number of concerns about the prior guidance documents including that: the earlier guidance "required schools to adopt a minimal standard of proof—the preponderance-of-the evidence standard—in administering student discipline," and that the earlier guidance "provided that any due-process protections afforded to accused students should not 'unnecessarily delay' resolving the charges against them." Sept. 22, 2017 DCL, available at https://www2.ed.gov/about/offices/list/ocr/letters/colleague-title-ix-201709.pdf.

Many advocates and policymakers were quick to decry this change in policy. For example, Fatima Goss Graves, president of the National Women's Law Center, stated that the change in policy would have a "devastating" impact. Stephanie Saul & Kate Taylor, "Betsy DeVos Reverses Obama-era Policy on Campus Sexual Assault Investigations," *N.Y. Times* (Sept. 22, 2017).

In October 2017, a national women's rights organization and three individual filed a lawsuit challenging the Department of Education's new interim guidance on sexual violence. *See, e.g.,* Collin Binkley, "Lawsuit Challenges DeVos' Guidance on Campus Sexual Assault," *Seattle Times* (Oct. 19, 2017).

PROBLEM 8-6
SEXUAL MISCONDUCT ON CAMPUS

Look up the policy on sexual assault issued by your university pursuant to Title IX. How does it compare to the following "Interpretative Guidance" portion of the Georgetown University Policy?

The willingness to participate must be clearly indicated prior to any sexual act or sexual contact.

If at any time during the sexual act or sexual contact any confusion or ambiguity should arise on the issue of consent, it is incumbent upon the individual to stop the activity and clarify, verbally, the other's willingness to continue.

A verbal "no," even if it may sound indecisive or insincere, constitutes lack of consent.

The absence of an overt action or an explicit verbal response to a verbal request for consent constitutes lack of consent.

It is expected that, once consent has been established, a person who changes his/her mind during the sexual act or sexual contact will communicate through words or overt actions his/her decision to no longer proceed. * * *

A person's use of alcohol and/or other drugs shall not diminish such person's responsibility to obtain consent. * * *

A person is considered incapable of giving consent if he/she is asleep, unconscious, and/or losing and regaining consciousness, or clearly mentally or physically incapacitated, for example, by alcohol and/or other drugs * * *

Available at https://georgetown.app.box.com/s/fem8xwhcozsn38awxqur.

Assume you are counsel for your university. How would you recommend that it proceed in the following situations:

1.   John and Lindsay had been dating for three months. They had been physically intimate on several occasions, but within limits set by Lindsay, who opposed having intercourse so early in their relationship. One night after both had had several drinks and while "petting," John attempted to cross their agreed boundaries. Lindsay said, "we really shouldn't do this," but continued to touch John in an intimate way. Lindsay remembers saying "I think we should just sleep," but she also remembers continuing to embrace John. Eventually they had sex. Lindsay filed a complaint of sexual assault against John.

2.   Paula, a lesbian tenured professor, attended a party for students in her chemistry class. Gayatri, a graduate student and teaching assistant for the class, and Sam, a junior chemistry major, also attended. Gayatri became inebriated and began aggressively flirting with Sam. He attempted to deflect her attentions, but she continued to ask him to dance, rubbing her body against his while dancing, and teasing him about not understanding "how certain elements interact." Paula observed this set of interactions and forcefully suggested to Gayatri that she take her home. Once in Paula's car, Gayatri kept falling asleep. Unsure where Gayatri lived, Paula took Gayatri to her own home, where she lived alone. She maneuvered Gayatri into her bed and slept beside her. No sexual conduct ensured. Sam and Gayatri both filed sexual assault complaints.

D. THE REVOLUTIONARY EXPANSION OF ATHLETIC PROGRAMS FOR FEMALE STUDENTS

One of the areas in which Title IX has had a particularly profound impact is with regard to opportunity and inclusion of women in sports. As Deborah Brake, "The Struggle for Sex Equality in Sport and the Theory Behind Title IX," 34 *U. Mich. J.L. Reform* 13 (2001), explains: "Since the enactment of Title IX, female participation in competitive sports has soared to unprecedented heights. Fewer than 300,000 female students participated in interscholastic athletics in 1971. By 1998–99, that number exceeded 2.6 million, with significant increases in each intervening year."

But despite these incredible gains, some, including Brake, contend that Title IX has not brought an end to sex discrimination in athletics. "Educational institutions continue to provide many more, and qualitatively distinct, opportunities for male than female athletes at every level of education. Although female athletic participation in high school is at an unprecedented 2.6 million, it still lags far behind the 3.8 million high school males who participate in school sports." Deborah Brake, "The Struggle for Sex Equality in Sport and the Theory Behind Title IX," 34 *U. Mich. J.L. Reform* 13 (2001).

So what does Title IX require with regard to sex equality in the area of athletics? The Javits Amendment to the Education Amendments of 1974, Pub. L. No. 93–380, § 844, 88 Stat. 484, 612 (Aug. 21, 1974) (codified as amended at 20 U.S.C. § 1681), directed the Department of Health, Education, and Welfare (HEW) to issue "reasonable provisions considering the nature of particular sports" to implement Title IX "with respect to intercollegiate activities." HEW's "A Policy Interpretation: Title IX and Intercollegiate Athletics," 44 Fed. Reg. 71,418 (Dec. 11, 1979), stated that an educational institution can comply with Title IX by meeting any of three standards:

(1) Providing intercollegiate-level participation for female and male students "in numbers substantially proportionate to their respective enrollments."

(2) Demonstrating a "history and continuing practice of program expansion which is demonstrably responsive to the developing interest and abilities" of the under-represented sex, usually women.

(3) Demonstrating that the "interests and abilities" of the under-represented sex "have been fully and effectively accommodated by the present program."

Although directly applicable to intercollegiate athletics (the precise delegation by Congress), the 1979 HEW Policy also asserts that it "may be used for guidance" in evaluating the competitive and recreational sports programs of elementary and secondary schools subject to Title IX. *Id.* at 71,413–14. Should federal courts follow the HEW Policy? Consider the leading case.

Amy Cohen et al. v. Brown University et al.

United States Court of Appeals for the First Circuit, 1996.
101 F.3d 155.

■ BOWNES, SENIOR CIRCUIT JUDGE:

This is a class action lawsuit charging Brown University ["Brown"] with discrimination against women in the operation of its intercollegiate athletics program, in violation of Title IX of the Education Amendments of 1972, 20 U.S.C. §§ 1681–1688 ("Title IX"). * * * This suit was initiated in response to the demotion in May 1991 of Brown's women's gymnastics and volleyball teams from university-funded varsity status to donor-funded varsity status. Contemporaneously, Brown demoted two men's teams, water polo and golf, from university-funded to donor-funded varsity status. As a consequence of these demotions, all four teams lost not only their university funding, but most of the support and privileges that accompany university-funded varsity status at Brown.

[During the first *Cohen* appeal, 991 F.2d 888 (1st Cir.1993), the court explained that such privileges include "salaried coaches, access to prime facilities, preferred practice time, medical trainers, clerical assistance, office support, admission preferences, and the like." The court also included specific statistics about gender distribution in athletics: "[b]efore the cuts, Brown athletics offered an aggregate of 328 varsity slots for female athletes and 566 varsity slots for male athletes. Thus women had 36.7% of the opportunities and men 63.3%. At that time * * * Brown's student body comprised approximately 52% men and 48% women."]

As a Division I institution within the National Collegiate Athletic Association ("NCAA") with respect to all sports but football, Brown participates at the highest level of NCAA competition. Brown operates a two-tiered intercollegiate athletics program with respect to funding: although Brown provides the financial resources required to maintain its university-funded varsity teams, donor-funded varsity athletes must themselves raise the funds necessary to support their teams through private donations. The district court noted that the four demoted teams were eligible for NCAA competition, provided that they were able to raise the funds necessary to maintain a sufficient level of competitiveness, and provided that they continued to comply with NCAA requirements. The court found, however, that it is difficult for donor-funded varsity athletes to maintain a level of competitiveness commensurate with their abilities and that these athletes operate at a competitive disadvantage in comparison to university-funded varsity athletes. For example, the district court found that some schools are reluctant to include donor-funded teams in their varsity schedules and that donor-funded teams are unable to obtain varsity-level coaching, recruits, and funds for travel, equipment, and post-season competition. * * *

At issue in this appeal is the proper interpretation of the first [prong of the HEW three-part test] * * * "whether intercollegiate level participation opportunities for male and female students are provided in numbers substantially proportionate to their respective enrollments." * * * [The earlier opinion had clarified how to "measure effective accommodation" under the HEW three-part test: "The first benchmark furnishes a safe harbor for those institutions that have distributed athletic opportunities in numbers 'substantially proportionate' to the gender composition of their student bodies. Thus, a university * * * may stay on the sunny side of Title IX simply by maintaining gender parity between its student body and its athletic lineup. The second and third parts of the accommodation test recognize that there are circumstances under which, as a practical matter, something short of this proportionality is a satisfactory proxy for gender balance. For example, so long as a university is continually expanding athletic opportunities in an ongoing effort to meet the needs of the underrepresented gender, and persists in this approach as interest and ability levels in its student body * * * rise, benchmark two is satisfied. * * * Or, if a school has a student body in which one sex is demonstrably less interested in athletics, Title IX does not require that the school create teams for, * * * otherwise disinterested students; rather, the third benchmark is satisfied if the underrepresented sex's discernible interests are fully and effectively accommodated."]

[Brown's original constitutional challenge to the statutory scheme had brought out two issues: equal protection and affirmative action. With respect to equal protection, Brown argued that to fully and effectively accommodate female athletes, the school disadvantaged male athletes. This argument was then remolded into an affirmative action argument, where Brown maintained that to provide intercollegiate level participation opportunities for female athletes in numbers substantially proportionate to their respective enrollments amounted to "affirmative action" for women that victimized male athletes.]

Brown's talismanic incantation of "affirmative action" has no legal application to this case and is not helpful to Brown's cause. While "affirmative action" may have different connotations as a matter of politics, as a matter of law, its meaning is more circumscribed. True affirmative action cases have historically involved a voluntary undertaking to remedy discrimination (as in a program implemented by a governmental body, or by a private employer or institution), by means of specific group-based preferences or numerical goals, and a specific timetable for achieving those goals. [E.g., *Regents of the Univ. of Cal. v. Bakke*, 438 U.S. 265 (1978).]

Title IX is not an affirmative action statute; it is an anti-discrimination statute, modeled explicitly after another anti-discrimination statute, Title VI. No aspect of the Title IX regime at issue in this case-inclusive of the statute, the relevant regulation, and the pertinent agency documents-mandates gender-based preferences or quotas, or specific timetables for implementing numerical goals. [The court specifically noted that Title IX permits affirmative action and like other anti-discrimination schemes, permits an inference that a significant gender-based statistical disparity may indicate the existence of discrimination. But, stressed that the substantial proportionality test is the starting point of analysis and one aspect of inquiry to determine if an institution's athletics program complies with Title IX. The court then emphasized that "the substantial proportionality test of prong one is applied under the Title IX framework, not mechanically, but case-by-case, in a fact specific manner."]

Brown has contended throughout this litigation that the significant disparity in athletics opportunities for men and women at Brown is the result of a gender-based differential in the level of interest in sports and that the district court's application of the three-part test requires universities to provide athletics opportunities for women to an extent that exceeds their relative interests and abilities in sports. Thus, at the heart of this litigation is the question whether Title IX permits Brown to deny its female students equal opportunity to participate in sports, based upon its unproven assertion that the * * * significant disparity in athletics opportunities for male and female students reflects, not discrimination * * * but a lack of interest on the part of its female students that is unrelated to a lack of opportunities.

We view Brown's argument that women are less interested than men in participating in intercollegiate athletics, as well as its conclusion that institutions should be required to accommodate the interests and abilities of its female students only to the extent that it accommodates the interests and abilities of its male students, with great suspicion. To assert that Title IX permits institutions to provide fewer athletics participation opportunities for women than for men, based upon the premise that women are less interested in sports than are men, is (among other things) to ignore the fact that Title IX was enacted in order to remedy discrimination that results from stereotyped notions of women's interests and abilities.

Interest and ability rarely develop in a vacuum; they evolve as a function of opportunity and experience. The Policy Interpretation recognizes that women's lower rate of participation in athletics reflects women's historical lack of opportunities to participate in sports.

Moreover, the Supreme Court has repeatedly condemned gender-based discrimination based upon "archaic and overbroad generalizations" about women. *Schlesinger v. Ballard,* 419 U.S. 498, 508 (1975). The Court has been especially critical of the use of statistical evidence offered to prove generalized, stereotypical notions about men and women. For example, in holding that Oklahoma's 3.2% beer statute invidiously discriminated against males 18–20 years of age, the Court in *Craig v. Boren,* 429 U.S. 190, 208–209 (1976), stressed that "the principles embodied in the Equal Protection Clause are not to be rendered inapplicable by statistically measured but loose-fitting generalities." * * * Thus, there exists the danger that, rather than providing a true measure of women's interest in sports, statistical evidence purporting to reflect women's interest instead provides only a measure of the very discrimination that is and has been the basis for women's lack of opportunity to participate in sports. * * * We conclude that * * * such evidence, standing alone, cannot justify providing fewer athletic opportunities for women than for men. * * * On these facts, Brown's failure to accommodate fully and effectively the interests and abilities of the underrepresented gender is clearly established.

Finally, the tremendous growth in women's participation in sports since Title IX was enacted disproves Brown's argument that women are less interested in sports for reasons unrelated to lack of opportunity.

Brown's relative interests approach is not a reasonable interpretation of the three-part test. This approach contravenes the purpose of the statute and the regulation because it does not permit an institution or a district court to remedy a gender-based disparity in athletics participation opportunities. Instead, this approach freezes that disparity by law, thereby disadvantaging further the underrepresented gender. Had Congress intended to entrench, rather than change, the status quo-with its historical emphasis on men's participation opportunities to the detriment of women's opportunities-it need not have gone to all the trouble of enacting Title IX. * * *

There can be no doubt that Title IX has changed the face of women's sports as well as our society's interest in and attitude toward women athletes and women's sports. In addition, there is ample evidence that increased athletics participation opportunities for women and young girls, available as a result of Title IX enforcement, have had salutary effects in other areas of societal concern.

One need look no further than the impressive performances of our country's women athletes in the 1996 Olympic Summer Games to see that Title IX has had a dramatic and positive impact on the capabilities of our women athletes, particularly in team sports. * * * What stimulated this remarkable change in the quality of women's athletic competition was not a sudden, anomalous upsurge in women's interest in sports, but the enforcement of Title IX's mandate of gender equity in sports.

Postscript. Brown settled the case, agreeing not to cut the women's gymnastics, fencing, skiing, and water polo teams and to maintain the percentage of female athletes within 3.5% of men's percentage participation. Lynette Labinger, "Title IX and Athletics: A Discussion of *Brown University v. Cohen* by Plaintiff's Counsel," 20 *Women's Rights L. Rep.* 85, 94 (1998). According to Joan Taylor, Brown's current Senior Associate Athletics Director who was employed in Brown's athletic department during the *Cohen* litigation, Title IX has had an ongoing impact on women's participation in sports at Brown and all over the Ivy League. Not only is the Ivy League "more equitable than other [athletic] conferences" and "at the forefront in creating varsity programming for women" but it also "involves women a lot more in the decision making process than other conferences." Telephone Interview by Eva Rigamoti, Yale Law School Class of 2012, with Joan Taylor, Senior Associate Athletics Director, Brown University (Oct. 12, 2010).

NOTE ON *COHEN*

Amy Cohen's litigation pitted a purely formalist approach to equality (Brown) against what feminist theorists call a "structural" approach, one that considers the ways in which institutional structures and practices inculcate sexist attitudes and mold women's as well as men's preferences. *See* Vicki Schultz, "Telling Stories About Women and Work: Judicial Interpretations of Sex Segregation in the Workplace in Title VII Cases Raising the Lack of Interest Argument," 103 *Harv. L. Rev.* 1749 (1990); Deborah Brake, "The Struggle for Sex Equality in Sport and the Theory Behind Title IX," 34 *U. Mich. J.L. Reform* 13, 69–82 (2000–01) (applying structural feminist theory to support the 1979 HEW Policy). The First Circuit rejected Brown's argument that because females were not as interested in sports as males, it did not have to provide equal opportunities. Although the Supreme Court ducked the Brown University case by denying review and has never addressed the 1979 HEW Policy, *Cohen* has been followed by all the courts of appeals that have addressed the issue. *See, e.g., Neal v. Board of Trustees of the Calif. State Univs.*, 198 F.3d 763 (9th Cir. 1999). The HEW Policy's results-oriented approach *plus* the interest it has stimulated in a generation of female students has revolutionized athletics in America. In 1971, fewer than 300,000 female students participated in high school athletic teams; today more than three million participate. In 1971, fewer than 32,000 women played intercollegiate sports, today more than 200,000 compete.

The significance of these numbers is hard to overstate. Athletic competition has changed the bodies and lives of millions of women in America—a matter of great consequence given studies showing that participation in sports is correlated to better physical condition, better mental health, and greater confidence for female (as well as male) participants. As the next excerpt suggests, the consequences extend to feminist theory itself.

***Deborah L. Brake, Getting in the Game: Title IX and the Women's Sports Revolution* 3–11 (2010).** Western philosophy has long marginalized the body as the antithesis of reason—and has gendered that dichotomy so that male is associated with reason and female with body. "Given the aspersions Western thought casts on the body and the role of gender in creating a mind/body hierarchy, it is not surprising that feminist theorists have sought to downplay the importance of the body in feminist projects. A major focus of the feminist movement has been to bring women into the life of the mind as full equals." When feminists have focused on the body, as with abortion bans and pregnancy discrimination, it has been to place women in the role of victims.

"In a similarly guarded stance, feminist theory downplays the significance of the body in explaining gender inequality in economic and political life. Apologists for women's subordination have pointed to 'natural' and biologically based differences rooted in men's and women's bodies. In response, much feminist legal scholarship has a social constructionist bent, minimizing the significance of the body and exposing the many ways in which society and institutions create and maintain gender inequality. Instead of regarding the female body as a source of strength, empowerment, and identity, feminist theory has kept more of an arm's-length relationship to the body, minimizing its significance in larger gender equality struggles."

Professor Brake joins other feminist scholars who insist that a positive politics of the athletic body is needed for sex equality in real life. *See also* Shirley Castelnuovo & Sharon Ruth Guthrie, *Feminism and the Female Body: Liberating the Amazon Within* (1998). Citing social scientists, Brake argues that athletics and a positive body politics "help[ ] women reconnect with their bodies and as a source of empowerment. Women who develop athletic competence as girls are better prepared both psychologically and physically to counter the cultural forces that turn women's bodies into objects that exist for the use and pleasure of others." At its best, sport helps women by improving their health and strength, teaching life and leadership skills, strengthening bonds with other women.

There are also collective benefits, as "playing sports disrupts traditional understandings of gender. Strong, athletic women expose the myth that women's bodies are 'naturally' weak. They show that there is a range of body types and abilities and that these are not neatly categorized in a gender hierarchy that associates men with physical strength and women with physical weakness. * * * As more and more women succeed in sport, the very meaning of gender and the understanding of what it means to be male and female is transformed." Consider the evolving public understanding of Martina Navratilova, arguably the greatest women's tennis champion of all time. In the 1970s, Navratilova was considered too mannish, almost freakishly strong, and the public adored her rival, the more feminine Chris Evert. But in the 1980s, women in tennis (including Evert) bulked up their strength, and the success of strong female athletes transformed Navratilova into an admired role model.

Professor Brake also applies feminist theory to understand the 1979 HEW Policy, which draws strength from its eclecticism. The baseline rule of the Policy owes much to *anti-subordination* feminist theory: deploying the law, women must assert their own power and insist upon a fair share of public resources. Thus, the Policy pushes schools toward parity in athletic participation. *See* Catherine A. MacKinnon, "Women, Self-Possession, and Sport," in *Feminism Unmodified: Discourses on Life and Law* (1987). This is the sort of policy that is reviled as a "quota policy," but even conservative judges and administrators have bit their tongues on this score. The baseline also reflects *cultural feminism*, because it contemplates sex-segregated teams as the baseline. Yet the *liberal feminist* project epitomized by Ruth Bader Ginsburg is not entirely missing, as the Policy contemplates and courts have held that women sometimes have a right to try out for men's teams. (The reverse has not been the case: judges and administrators almost never force women's teams to allow men to try out.)

On the other hand, feminist scholars and sports activists maintain that Title IX remains under-enforced. Among other things, they argue that Title XI left in place gross inequalities in the funding and staffing of women's athletic programs. Thus, women in college still have many fewer opportunities to participate in sports that might interest them than men have, and many of the opportunities are either token ones or, ironically, ones run by male rather than female coaches and staff. Indeed, women's share of coaching jobs actually "plummeted" after Title IX. For example, the NCAA's *Race and Gender Demographics Report for 2008–2009*, (http://www.ncaa publications.com/productdownloads/RGDMEMB10.pdf) shows that in all divisions (I, II, III) of women's soccer, 660 of the head coaches of women's soccer teams were men and only 302 were women. Finally, Title IX has not policed sexual harassment of female athletes very effectively.

NOTES ON PROPOSALS TO CHANGE THE DEPARTMENT OF EDUCATION'S RULES ON INTERCOLLEGIATE ATHLETICS

Consider the continuing evolution of Title IX. From the perspective of formalist understandings of equality, including those held by some Justices who joined the Court's opinion in the VMI Case, the 1979 HEW Policy should be relaxed, because it pushes colleges and universities to give more resources to female sports than is justified by current levels of interest by female students—and at the expense of male sports. Law and economics thinkers who accord normative priority to existing preferences would find the current policy inefficient, because it sometimes forces schools to fund teams for which there is not sufficient pre-existing demand. From that point of view, how should the 1979 HEW Policy be changed? Now consider the policy from the perspective of feminist structural theory such as that espoused by Professors Schultz and Brake. Such theory would press Title IX even more aggressively than the Department of Education has thus far done. Consider the soundness of the following proposals:

1. *Equal Funding. Period.* The large majority of colleges and universities provide hugely greater resources to male than to female athletic programs through scholarships, staff salaries, facilities, and so forth. And the regulations allow this: "Unequal aggregate expenditures for members of each sex or unequal expenditures for male and female teams if a recipient [school] operates or sponsors separate teams will not constitute noncompliance" with Title IX, but can be considered as one of several factors suggesting noncompliance. 34 C.F.R. § 106.41(c). Most feminist authors favor roughly equal funding and (especially) equal salaries for coaches of women's and men's teams. Given the huge expenses involved in football (the main example of a male sport [and one that is lavishly funded and generates its own revenues at most schools] with no female equivalent), this would be a radical proposal. Do you think it should be adopted? If it could only be adopted with a "football exception," would you go along? (See the third proposal below.)

2. *Sex-Integration of Athletic Teams.* Title IX regulations allow separate teams. 34 C.F.R. § 106.41(b). Some feminist scholars and sports activists argue that sex-segregated teams reinforce the connection between athletics and masculinity and relegate "women's" teams to permanent second-class status. *See, e.g.*, Mariah Burton Nelson, *Are We Winning Yet? How Women Are Changing Sports and Sports Are Changing Women* (1991). On the other hand, sex-integrated teams would probably reduce women's opportunities in many sports and reduce their participation to token numbers, a point made in Professor Brake's book. Are there other arguments that should be considered? What should the rule be?

3. *Repeal the Contact Sport Exception.* Title IX now requires that where a school has only one team for a particular sport, "members of the excluded sex must be allowed to try-out for the team offered unless the sport involved is a contact sport." 34 C.F.R. § 106.41(b). Contact sports include boxing, wrestling, rugby, ice hockey, football, and basketball. The contact-sport exception has been criticized for reinforcing the articulation of particular sports as *male/masculine* and *female/feminine*, with the suggestion that the former are the real sports and the latter are special concessions to women. Moreover, this exception for public schools would appear vulnerable to equal protection challenge, especially after the VMI Case (Chapter 2, Section 1). Professor Deborah Brake, "Theory Behind Title IX," 140, proposes that schools ought to offer a women's team in any contact sport once requested by a female student and then see whether there is sufficient interest to sustain that sport over time. Is this a cost-justifiable proposal? Is there another way to tackle the contact sports exception?

NOTE ON TRANSGENDER STUDENTS AND SEX-SEGREGATED ATHLETIC TEAMS

What does all of this mean for transgender student athletes? And, in particular, for those many instances when school sports teams are segregated by sex, on which team does a transgender student play? At the middle and high school level, the answer is often unclear. A few states have addressed the issue clearly either in legislation or policy. These states have staked out a variety of positions. In California, for example, students must be "permitted to participate in sex-segregated school programs and activities, including athletic teams and competitions * * * consistent with his or her gender identity, irrespective of the gender listed on the pupil's records." Cal. Educ. Code § 221.5(f).

In contrast, the default rule in Nebraska is that "a student's gender for purposes of eligibility for * * * athletic activities shall be determined by the sex noted on the student's birth certificate." Nebraska School Activities Association—Gender Participation Policy 2, https://nsaahome.org/about/gp policy.pdf. The policy does, however, allow transgender students to file an application with the "Gender Identity Eligibility Committee" requesting to play on a team consistent with the student's gender identity. *Id.* at 3. The policy provides guidelines regarding not only the composition of the committee, but also the standards for evaluating the application. But in many states, there simply is no clear policy.

If a school district refuses to permit a transgender student to participate on an athletic team consistent with their gender identity, does that refusal violate Title IX? The Equal Protection Clause?

For collegiate student athletes, there may be more guidance. Many colleges and universities participate in the National Collegiate Athletic Association (NCAA). The NCAA adopted the following policy in 2011:

NCAA Policy on Transgender Student-Athlete Participation

The following policies clarify participation of transgender student-athletes **undergoing hormonal treatment for gender transition:**

1.   A trans male (FTM) student-athlete who has received a medical exception for treatment with testosterone for diagnosed Gender Identity Disorder or gender dysphoria and/or Transsexualism, for purposes of NCAA competition may compete on a men's team, but is no longer eligible to compete on a women's team without changing that team status to a mixed team.

2.   A trans female (MTF) student-athlete being treated with testosterone suppression medication for Gender Identity Disorder or gender dysphoria and/or Transsexualism, for the purposes of NCAA competition may continue to compete on a men's team but may not compete on a women's team without changing it to a mixed team status until completing one calendar year of testosterone suppression treatment.

Any transgender student-athlete who is **not taking hormone treatment** related to gender transition may participate in sex-separated sports activities in accordance with his or her assigned birth gender.

- A trans male (FTM) student-athlete who is not taking testosterone related to gender transition may participate on a men's or women's team.

- A trans female (MTF) transgender student-athlete who is not taking hormone treatments related to gender transition may not compete on a women's team.

The NCAA has different rules for MTF transgender athletes and FTM transgender athletes. Is this a sex-based classification? Does it violate Title IX?

For more information about transgender student athletes, see, e.g., Erin E. Buzuvis, "Transgender Student-Athletes and Sex-Segregated Sport: Developing Policies of Inclusion for Interco0llegiate and Interscholastic Athletics," 21 *Seton Hall J. Sports & Ent. L.* 1 (2011).

E.   STRUCTURAL REFORM: SAME-SEX OR ALL-LGBT SCHOOLS?

On the whole, American schools treat female and LGBT students less favorably than male students. Whether intentionally or not, teachers discriminate against females in the manner in which they encourage students to participate in the learning experience. According to an early study of the issue, teachers have a tendency to convey curricula in a manner "that will appeal to boys' interests and to select presentation formats in which boys excel or are encouraged more than girls." American Association of University Women, *How Schools Shortchange Girls* 71 (1992) (1992 AAUW Report); see *Achieving Gender Equity in the Classroom and on the Campus: The Next Steps* (1995 AAUW

Symposium). For example, the study found that male students were asked academically related questions 80% more often than female students in lecture classes. Even today, curricula tend to focus on the achievements of men—or, at least, don't focus (as much) on the accomplishments of women—and the materials used in most schools do not even mention or acknowledge LGBT people. *See, e.g.,* GLSEN, 2015 National School Climate Survey 54 (reporting that 63.0% of respondents stated that they had not been "exposed to representations of LGBT people, history, or events in lessons at school"), https://www.glsen.org/ article/2015-national-school-climate-survey. *See also* Teemu Ruskola, "Minor Disregard: The Legal Construction of the Fantasy That Gay and Lesbian Youth Do Not Exist," 8 *Yale J.L. & Fem.* 269 (1996).

Such lack of emphasis on women's and LGBT people's achievements in school curricula, athletics, and other programs conveys a message that their accomplishments in society are not as important as those of men and non-LGBT people. It is not surprising that the self-esteem of female students tends to drop as they go through adolescence, when they are constantly taught, in essence, that they are not as valuable to society as their male peers.

The self-esteem issues are often worse for LGBT teens. A national study of youth in grades 7–12 found that LGB youth "were more twice as likely to have attempted suicide as their heterosexual peers." Centers for Disease Control, LGBT Youth, https://www.cdc.gov/lgbthealth/youth.htm (last visited Apr. 13, 2017). And while there is less data regarding transgender youth, a study of "55 transgender youth found that about 25% reported suicide attempts." *Id.* The increased risk of suicide and suicide attempts may be the result of negative attitudes and social disapproval of LGBT youth. *Id.*

Despite gains for girls and LGBT students, there are still many hurdles. In schools that provide vocational education for students who plan not to attend college, women and girls are "overwhelmingly directed into training programs for historically female—and traditionally low-wage—jobs. AAUW, *Separated by Sex: Title IX and Single-Sex Education* 2 (2013), http://www.aauw.org/files/2013/02/position-on-single-sex-education-112.pdf. Although female students tend to get better grades and score higher on standardized tests in high school and in college, scholarships awarded on the basis of grades and standardized test scores are twice as likely to be awarded to male students.

Should American law be concerned with equity for female and LGBT students in education? Most formalists are not strongly concerned, because they believe that female and LGBT students are receiving equal opportunities under existing law. *See, e.g.,* Earl C. Dudley, Jr. & George Rutherglen, "Ironies, Inconsistencies, and Intercollegiate Athletics: Title IX, Title VII, and Statistical Evidence of Discrimination," 1 *Va. J. Sports & Law* 177 (1999). This group probably includes most judges; the dissenters in *Davis,* for example, reflect a strongly formalist approach.

Most feminists, advocates for LGBT teens, social psychologists, and many parents do not agree with this perception, and they believe that equity for female and LGBT students is an important public problem. Not only have American schools long been breeding grounds for sexist and homophobic attitudes, but the structure of American education (*e.g.*, its obsession with high school male-only football) significantly contributes to those attitudes.

But if the problem is unconscious sexism and homophobia, then another anti-discrimination law may not be the most effective solution. Instead, the solution may need to be structural. As we saw with the 1979 HEW Policy for intercollegiate athletics, a structural approach, demanding progress for the group, can produce dramatic results. Can that (relative) success be replicated here?

One proposed solution is single-sex education. Proponents of single-sex schools argue that they would parallel the success of sex-segregated athletics where female teams receive a fairer share of school resources. But how does "segregated" education work? Does it reduce sexist and homophobic attitudes? Or does it increase them? Does it violate Title IX? Or the Equal Protection Clause, as construed in the *VMI* Case (Chapter 1)?

NOTES ON PROPOSALS FOR FEMALE- OR LGBT-ONLY CLASSES AND SCHOOLS

1. *Do Female-Only Schools Ameliorate Gender Equity Problems?* Some scholars and policymakers argue that female students benefit from single-sex education. *See, e.g.*, Ilana DeBare, *Where Girls Come First: The Rise, Fall and Surprising Revival of Girls' Schools* (2004); Deborah L. Rhode, "Association and Assimilation," 81 *Nw. U.L. Rev.* 106 (1986); Kristin S. Caplice, "The Case for Public Single-Sex Education," 18 *Harv. J.L. & Pub. Pol'y* 227 (1994). These scholars and policymakers often cite the studies that were assembled and analyzed by the Department of Education in a 2005 report, *Single-Sex Versus Coeducational Schooling: A Systematic Review* (2005) (cautiously defending single-sex education), and by the National Coalition of Girls' Schools (NCGS), see Linda J. Sax et al., *Women Graduates of Single-Sex and Coeducational High Schools: Differences in Their Characteristics and Transition to College* (2009) (stronger endorsement of single-sex education).

Supporter of all-female environments argue that in such a setting, female students cannot be passed over for attention by the teacher, and there is no class of people to whom female students can be made to feel inferior. Female students have greater access to athletic programs, including those tailored to their own interests. In such an environment, female students receive all of the attention and encouragement that the teachers can give. And there is a lot less competition for male attention among the female students.

Some studies have found that some young women feel safer in same-sex educational formats—safer from sexual harassment by other students, safer in their interaction with teachers, and safer in feeling they have space to express their opinions. *See, e.g.*, Ed Cairns, "The Relationship Between Adolescent Perceived Self-Competence and Attendance at Single-Sex Secondary School," 60 *Brit. J. Educ. Psychology* 210 (1990) (higher self-esteem); Bonnie Wood & Lorrie Brown, "Participation in an All Female Algebra Class: Effects on High School Math and Science Course Selection," 3 *Women & Minorities in Science & Engineering* 265–78 (1997) (better attitude toward math and science).

Other studies, however, have raised some concerns, or at least reservations about pushing for single-sex schools. For example an article published in 1999 reviewed the studies on single-sex education and found "no significant differences between the impact of coeducational and of single-sex schools on student performance and achievement." Nancy Levit, "Separating Equals: Education Research and the Long Term Consequences of Sex Segregation," 67 *Geo. Wash. L. Rev.* 451, 489 (1999). A number of more recent studies have reached similar conclusions. For example, with respect to "long-term academic achievement . . . 75% of the studies [considered in a review by the American Institutes for Research (AIR)] resulted in no differences in 'postsecondary test scores, college graduation rates, or graduate school attendance rates." David S. Cohen & Nancy Levit, "Still Unconstitutional: Our Nation's Experiment with State-Sponsored Sex Segregation in Education," 44 *Seton Hall L. Rev.* 339, 371 (2014).

Moreover, to the extent that there are some differences in achievement levels, there is a problem of selection bias: students opting (or whose parents opt) for single-sex education might start with attitudes or abilities that set them apart in the first place.

Separate and apart from claims about academic achievement, supporters of single-sex schools often claim that they will counter negative stereotypes. For example, Leonard Sax, a strong supporter of single-sex schools, has said: "Here's the paradox: coed schools tend to reinforce gender stereotypes, whereas single-sex schools can break down gender stereotypes." Leonard Sax, *Why Gender Maters: What Parents and Teachers Need to Know About the Emerging Science of Sex Differences* 243 (2005).

The evidence suggests, however, that this intuition may be inaccurate. To the contrary, "numerous researchers found that single-sex education reinforced gender stereotypes and fostered traditional and sexist attitudes." Cohen & Levit, "Still Unconstitutional," 44 *Seton Hall L. Rev.* at 370. *See also* Preliminary Findings of ACLU, "Teach Kids, Not Stereotypes Campaign, Prepared for the U.S. Dept. of Educ., OCR (Aug. 20, 2012), https://www.aclu.org/files/assets/doe_ocr_report2_0.pdf. After studying a number of single-sex programs in a variety of states, the ACLU concluded that there was "strong evidence from the documents produced and from news reports that teachers in the single-sex classes incorporated into their teaching stereotypes attitudes about boys' and girls' purportedly different interests, talents, and capacities." "Teach Kids, Not Stereotypes Campaign, Prepared for the U.S. Dept. of Educ., OCR 3–4 (Aug. 20, 2012), https://www.aclu.org/

files/assets/doe_ocr_report2_0.pdf. *See also* Diane F. Halpern et al., "The Pseudoscience of Single-Sex Schools, 333 *Science* 1706–1707 (2011) (arguing that "there is no well-designed research showing that single-sex (SS) education improves students' academic performance, but there is evidence that sex segregation increases gender stereotyping and legitimizes institutional sexism.").

Some advocates find these conclusions unsurprising, given the theories espoused by some strong supporters of single sex education. For example, Leonard Sex—a strong supporter of single-sex education—has argued that boys should only be required to read books with "strong male characters who take dramatic action to change their world," and that teachers should avoid assigning books with "weak, disabled male characters [who] are helpless to change their miserable destiny." Leonard Sax, *Why Gender Matters: What Parents and Teachers Need to Know about the Emerging Science of Sex Differences* 108–112 (2006). Teaching styles should also differ, he argues. In boys' classrooms, teachers should "speak loudly and in short, direct sentences." By contrast, in girls' classrooms, teachers should "speak much more softly, using more first names with more terms of endearment and fewer direct commands: 'Lisa, sweetie, it's time to open your book.'" Leonard Sax, *Six Degrees of Separation: What Teachers Need to Know about the Emerging Science of Sex Difference*, 190, 195 (2006).

There has been little experience (and no systematic empirical research) with schools limited to LGBT students.

2. *Statutory Limits on Single-Sex Schools or Classrooms?* Title IX only prohibits discrimination in admissions at "institutions of vocational education, professional education, and graduate higher education, and to public institutions of undergraduate higher education." 20 U.S.C. § 1681(a)(1). Thus public primary and secondary schools seem free to establish single-sex schools under Title IX, and the legislative history indicates that Congress exempted admission to elementary and secondary schools from Title IX because of the purported potential benefits of single-sex education.

In 2002, Secretary of Education Rod Paige endorsed this reading of Title IX. Although DOE regulations prohibit sex segregation in vocational schools and colleges or universities receiving federal aid, Secretary Paige opined that single-sex schools established for "remedial or affirmative action" reasons were permissible under Title IX.

But, once students are admitted to the school, Title IX generally prohibits sex discrimination. Due in part to this prohibition, at least in the past, few co-ed schools had single-sex classrooms. In 2004, for example, only "about a dozen public schools in the United States offered single-sex classrooms." Cohen & Levit, "Still Unconstitutional," 44 *Seton Hall L. Rev.* at 341.

But in 2006, the Department of Education promulgated new Title IX implementing regulations that provided more leeway for schools receiving federal funding to establish single-sex classrooms. *See* Office of Civil Rights, Department of Education, "Nondiscrimination on the Basis of Sex in

Education Programs or Activities Receiving Federal Financial Assistance," 71 Fed. Reg. 62530–43 (Oct. 25, 2006). Specifically, the Department added a new exception to the general prohibition against single-sex classes and extracurricular activities in 34 C.F.R. § 106.34. The exception applies to nonvocational classes and extracurricular activities in elementary and secondary coeducational schools that are not vocational schools.

Under the new exception, a school is permitted to offer a single-sex class or extracurricular activity if: (1) the purpose of the class or extracurricular activity is achievement of an important governmental or educational objective; (2) the single-sex nature of the class or extracurricular activity is substantially related to achievement of that objective; and (3) there are separate classes or activities that offer the same opportunities to students not eligible for the single-sex class or activity. 24 C.F.R. § 106.34(b)(1). The Department also amended § 106.34(c) to allow single-sex schools under similar circumstances.

Since these changes were made, the number of single-sex schools, and single-sex classrooms has increased dramatically. Cohen & Levit, "Still Unconstitutional," 44 *Seton Hall L. Rev.* at 341–42.

Will federal judges (and ultimately the Supreme Court) go along with the Department's new tolerance for separate single-sex instruction?

Another statute that may be invoked to challenge single-sex schools or classes is the Equal Educational Opportunity Act (EEOA) of 1974. While the goal of the EEOA was to limit the use of busing to achieve racially diverse school systems, it includes a congressional finding that "dual school systems" where students' assignation is based solely upon "race, color, *sex*, or national origin denies to those students equal protection of the laws guaranteed by the fourteenth amendment." 20 U.S.C. § 1701(a)(2) (emphasis added). The little relevant case law is mixed. *See, e.g., Vorchheimer v. School Dist.*, 532 F.2d 880, 884–85 (3d Cir. 1976), *aff'd by an equally divided Court*, 430 U.S. 703 (1977) (rejecting challenge to single-sex school on the ground that the statute only prohibits sex segregation for the purpose of preventing interracial mixing (and, one can infer, different-race dating)); *contra United States v. Hinds County School Board*, 560 F.2d 619 (5th Cir. 1977) (holding that the EEOA bans single-sex schools).

3. *Constitutional Equal Protection Questions.* Single-sex education, if accomplished in public schools, might also violate the Equal Protection Clause of the Fourteenth Amendment. Recall that sex-based classifications are subject to heightened scrutiny (Chapter 2, Section 1). Two of the leading sex discrimination precedents involve single-sex colleges. One was *Mississippi University for Women v. Hogan*, 458 U.S. 718 (1982), where the Court struck down a women's-only admission policy at a nursing school. Justice O'Connor's opinion for the Court held that the state had made no sufficient showing that a single-sex school was necessary in the field of nursing, where women's opportunities have long been substantial. If anything, limiting a nursing school to women smacked of gender stereotyping (men = doctors, women = nurses), precisely the sort of historical pattern equal protection jurisprudence was supposed to overturn. Citing the little empirical work then supporting the value of sex-segregated education, Chief Justice Burger's dissenting opinion worried that *Hogan* problematized educational experiments that could be truly useful to women in particular. Consider the Court's next word on the subject.

United States v. Virginia
United States Supreme Court, 1996.
518 U.S. 515, 116 S.Ct. 2264, 135 L.Ed.2d 735.

[■ JUSTICE RUTH BADER GINSBURG delivered the opinion for the Court, holding that Virginia's maintenance of Virginia Military Institute (VMI) as a same-sex school excluding women was sex discrimination that was not justified by the state's post-hoc rationalization that it contributed to educational diversity. Reread JUSTICE GINSBURG's opinion, excerpted in Chapter 1, Section 2. We reproduce here a portion of the dissenting opinion that we edited out of the excerpt in Chapter 1.]

■ JUSTICE SCALIA, dissenting. * * *

Under the constitutional principles announced and applied today, single-sex public education is unconstitutional. By going through the motions of applying a balancing test—asking whether the State has adduced an "exceedingly persuasive justification" for its sex-based classification—the Court creates the illusion that government officials in some future case will have a clear shot at justifying some sort of single-sex public education. Indeed, the Court seeks to create even a greater illusion than that: It purports to have said nothing of relevance to other public schools at all. "We address specifically and only an educational opportunity recognized . . . as 'unique'. . . ."

The Supreme Court of the United States does not sit to announce "unique" dispositions. Its principal function is to establish precedent— that is, to set forth principles of law that every court in America must follow. As we said only this Term, we expect both ourselves and lower courts to adhere to the "*rationale* upon which the Court based the results of its earlier decisions." *Seminole Tribe of Fla. v. Florida*, 517 U.S. 44, 66–67 (1996) (emphasis added). That is the principal reason we publish our opinions.

And the rationale of today's decision is sweeping: for sex-based classifications, a redefinition of intermediate scrutiny that makes it indistinguishable from strict scrutiny. Indeed, the Court indicates that if any program restricted to one sex is "uniqu[e]," it must be opened to members of the opposite sex "who have the will and capacity" to participate in it. I suggest that the single-sex program that will not be capable of being characterized as "unique" is not only unique but nonexistent.

In any event, regardless of whether the Court's rationale leaves some small amount of room for lawyers to argue, it ensures that single-sex public education is functionally dead. The costs of litigating the constitutionality of a single-sex education program, and the risks of ultimately losing that litigation, are simply too high to be embraced by public officials. Any person with standing to challenge any sex-based classification can haul the State into federal court and compel it to establish by evidence (presumably in the form of expert testimony) that there is an "exceedingly persuasive justification" for the classification. Should the courts happen to interpret that vacuous phrase as establishing a standard that is not utterly impossible of achievement, there is considerable risk that whether the standard has been met will not be determined on the basis of the record evidence—indeed, that will necessarily be the approach of any court that seeks to walk the path the Court has trod today. No state official in his right mind will buy such a high-cost, high-risk lawsuit by commencing a single-sex program. The enemies of single-sex education have won; by persuading only seven Justices (five would have been enough) that their view of the world is enshrined in the Constitution, they have effectively imposed that view on all 50 States.

This is especially regrettable because, as the District Court here determined, educational experts in recent years have increasingly come to "suppor[t] [the] view that substantial educational benefits flow from a single-gender environment, be it male or female, *that cannot be replicated in a coeducational setting*." (emphasis added). "The evidence in th[is] case," for example, "is virtually uncontradicted" to that effect. Until quite recently, some public officials have attempted to institute new single-sex programs, at least as experiments. In 1991, for example, the Detroit Board of Education announced a program to establish three boys-only schools for inner-city youth; it was met with a lawsuit, a preliminary injunction was swiftly entered by a District Court that purported to rely on *Hogan*, and the Detroit Board of Education voted to abandon the litigation and thus abandon the plan. Today's opinion assures that no such experiment will be tried again.

There are few extant single-sex public educational programs. The potential of today's decision for widespread disruption of existing institutions lies in its application to private single-sex education. Government support is immensely important to private educational institutions. Mary Baldwin College—which designed and runs VWIL— notes that private institutions of higher education in the 1990–1991 school year derived approximately 19 percent of their budgets from federal, state, and local government funds, not including financial aid to students. Charitable status under the tax laws is also highly significant for private educational institutions, and it is certainly not beyond the Court that rendered today's decision to hold that a donation to a single-sex college should be deemed contrary to public policy and therefore not deductible if the college discriminates on the basis of sex. See also *Bob Jones Univ. v. United States*, 461 U.S. 574 (1983). * * *

NOTES ON THE IMPACT OF THE *VMI* CASE ON THE LEGALITY OF SAME-SEX EDUCATIONAL INSTITUTIONS

1. *Are Public All-Male Educational Institutions Unconstitutional?* The only public college restricted to men, apart from VMI, was The Citadel, in South Carolina. Ironically, The Citadel litigated the sex discrimination issue throughout the 1990s and was ordered to admit Shannon Faulkner in 1995; after the exacting regimen of the first week, and the pressure caused by intense publicity, Faulkner withdrew and another plaintiff came forth. Days after the *VMI* decision, The Citadel announced that it would follow the law of the land and open its admissions to women; women enrolled during the fall of 1996. (VMI fell into line several months later.) Two women dropped out after the first semester, however; they alleged severe sexual harassment by male students, including setting their clothing on fire, and timid regulatory efforts by The Citadel to control this unusually violent "hazing."

Both VMI and The Citadel were freighted with nineteenth century origins for their men-only admissions policies, and the six Justices who joined Justice Ginsburg's opinion relied heavily on that background in traditional sex stereotypes. Was Justice Scalia right that the state is precluded now from establishing new colleges that are limited to the same sex? What if Virginia set up two new colleges—one for women and one for men—and gave them equal endowments and other state support? Are you as confident as Justice Scalia that such a set-up would be unconstitutional?

Consider also the Michigan decision striking down public secondary schools for inner-city boys. In 1991, the Board of Education of the City of Detroit planned to open three male academies to address the problems facing male inner-city youths—specifically high unemployment, high drop-out, and high homicide rates among urban males. These academies were to have, among other things, a specialized curriculum including a class called "Rites of Passage," an Afrocentric (pluralistic) curriculum, an emphasis on male responsibility, mentor programs, Saturday classes, individualized counseling, and extended classroom hours. Shawn Garrett, the father of a four year old daughter, Crystal, sued on her behalf on the grounds that the all-male schools violated Title IX, the Equal Educational Opportunity Act (EEOA) of 1974, and the Equal Protection Clause.

In *Garrett v. Board of Education*, 775 F. Supp. 1004, 1006 (E.D. Mich. 1991), the court granted a preliminary injunction against the opening of the academies. Although the state's objective of helping to improve chances for economic and literal survival of inner-city males was a valid state interest, the court found that the district failed to prove, or demonstrate in any way at all, that the problems faced by young inner-city males was at all related to the coeducational environment, or how women's absence from the classroom would improve their lot. Furthermore, the Court found that "the gender specific data presented * * * ignores the fact that all children in the Detroit public schools face significant obstacles to success." Even the school board acknowledged an "equally urgent and unique crisis facing" female students.

2. *Are Public All-Female Educational Institutions Unconstitutional?* Recall the gender equity discussion above. If the state shows that girls are disadvantaged by required coeducation and can learn more productively in single-sex schools, with equal schools for boys, can the state justify girls-only schools? In other words, is addressing gender equity the sort of "extremely persuasive" justification Justice Ginsburg would accept under the *VMI* decision? Would it matter that such schools were not compulsory (*i.e.,* parents would have to apply to send their daughters to them)? For an early (pre-*Hogan*) decision, see *Williams v. McNair*, 316 F.Supp. 134 (D.S.C. 1970). After the *VMI* decision, New York City announced that it was opening a female-only school. The school did open in the fall of 1996. Was Justice Scalia right that Justice Ginsburg's opinion "assure[d] that no such experiment [in public same-sex education] will be tried again"? Is the New York experiment likely to be upheld? What would the city have to show to meet the *VMI* standard?

3. *Are Private Single-Sex Educational Institutions Doomed?* Assume that Justice Scalia was right in *VMI* that public same-sex educational institutions are unconstitutional. If so, would he also be right in saying that private same-sex schools are also doomed, because such colleges ought to lose various federal entitlements, including their income tax exemption as charitable or educational institutions (Internal Revenue Code § 501[c]). The Court ignored this charge, and the United States denied that this would happen, but private schools discriminating on the basis of race cannot claim § 501(c) tax exemptions. If elimination of sex discrimination now has an importance similar to the elimination of race discrimination, is Justice Scalia right? There is a distinguishing factor. Private schools discriminating on the basis of race are violating federal law, 42 U.S.C. § 1981, which is a powerful reason to deny them federal tax exemptions as "charitable"; private primary and secondary schools discriminating on the basis of sex probably do not violate federal law. Recall that Title IX does not apply to admissions policies of primary and secondary schools, 20 U.S.C § 1681(a)(1).

PROBLEM 8-7
DEFENDING A SINGLE-SEX PUBLIC SCHOOL

The Tony School District (TSD) and its administrators are persuaded by the evidence indicating that female students learn better in all-female primary and secondary schools. In that spirit, the TSD starts a pilot program, whereby four of the TSD's 1000 grade schools and two of its 300 middle schools become all-female in the next school year. (All the high schools will remain mixed-sex, as will the remainder of the primary and middle schools.) Admission will be through parental application; if too many parents apply, a complicated formula will allocate seats in the new schools. There will be no all-male schools; male students and most female students will continue to be educated in the remainder of the schools. Because there are more female students than male students, the remainder of the schools will have 50–50 sex division.

Would the U.S. Supreme Court uphold this plan against statutory and constitutional challenge? How would Justices Ginsburg and Scalia vote? How would you vote if you were a Justice?

SECTION 3

SEX AND SEXUALITY EDUCATION

A generation ago, the big debate (and often a ferocious one) was whether it was appropriate for public schools to teach sex education. An ancillary issue was whether disapproving parents could get their children excused from a sex education program. Although cases held that the state could require sex education for children over their parents' objections, school districts tended to allow parents to opt out, *e.g.*, *Citizens for Parental Rights v. San Mateo County Bd. of Educ.*, 51 Cal.App.3d 1, 124 Cal.Rptr. 68 (1975), *appeal dismissed*, 425 U.S. 908 (1976), and sex education courses tended to be euphemistic "health and anatomy" courses, with little explicit instruction about sex.

The situation has changed dramatically, in large part because most teenagers are now sexually active and because the dangers of sexual experimentation are higher than before due to HIV/AIDS. According to the Guttmacher Institute, as of March 2017, 22 states and the District of Columbia require schools to provide both sex and HIV education. An additional 12 states require schools to provide HIV education.

In the schools that are teaching sex education, a key inquiry then becomes: What are the schools teaching? This has been a focus of state law, and the Guttmacher Report provides this overview. Guttmacher Institute, *Sex and HIV Education*, https://www.guttmacher.org/state-policy/explore/sex-and-hiv-education (as of April 1, 2017). When sex education is taught: 26 states require schools' sex education programs to emphasize the importance of abstinence; 19 states require that instruction emphasize the importance of limiting sexual activity to marriage; while only 13 states require that sex education and HIV instruction be medically accurate.

With regard to sexual orientation and sex or HIV education, as of April 2017, five states (Alabama, Arizona, Oklahoma, South Carolina, and Texas) require or recommend schools to teach that homosexuality is not an acceptable "lifestyle" or that homosexual conduct is an offense under state law. At least three states (Florida, Illinois, and North Carolina) officially require or recommend that schools promote monogamous "heterosexual" marriage or relationships. For a detailed and comprehensive review of state anti-LGBT curriculum laws, see Clifford Rosky, "Anti-Gay Curriculum Laws," ___ *Colum. L. Rev.*___ (forthcoming).

As the Guttmacher data suggest, the contest today is over *what* sex education courses will teach students, rather than *whether* there will be sex education. Roughly speaking, the extremes are: an approach that anchors the student on sexual abstinence until heterosexual marriage, on the one hand, and an approach that provides medically accurate information about sexuality and STDs, including neutral or sympathetic information about contraception, abortion, and homosexuality, on the other.

Is constitutional or statutory law relevant to these essentially political choices? Surprisingly, the law is mighty relevant. Consider these issues: students' right not to be exposed to inaccurate material (Section 3A); teachers' right to control what they teach (Section 3B); parental rights to control what their students learn and are exposed to (Section 3C); and state and local policies against promoting or even normalizing homosexuality in educational materials and instruction (Section 3D).

To the extent that one is opposed to what is being taught regarding sex and sexuality education, there are a number of claims one could assert.

- *Students' Right to Know.* If the information being taught excludes a particular subject matter or viewpoint, a student might assert that this instruction violates the student's right to knowledge.

- *Teachers' Academic Freedom.* What about teachers? Do they have any right to teach the material that they want? Even if it conflicts with what state law requires?

- *Parental Rights.* Another issue that sometimes arises in the context of sex education instruction is whether parents have a fundamental right to control what information about sexuality is imparted to their children. A large majority of the state sex education statutes permits parents either to opt into or opt out of sex education instruction. If there is no opt-out or opt-in, however, some parents believe that their privacy and religious freedom rights are infringed by mandatory sex education.

- *Discriminatory Instruction?* Another issue involves discrimination. As noted in the above, some states require that sex education (and sometimes other topics) be presented in a way that disapproves of homosexuality or preclude educators from presenting homosexuality in a positive light. Is it constitutional for the state to express and indeed require such a viewpoint in the classroom?

A. STUDENTS' RIGHT TO FACTUALLY ACCURATE INSTRUCTION?

Sex education has been and continues to be a source of controversy. Courts have grappled with a number of legal questions related to the content and procedures related to sex education.

One question that courts have grappled with is whether students have a constitutionally protected right to access accurate information about sex and sexuality?

Board of Education, Island Trees Union Free School District No. 26 et al. v. Steven A. Pico, 457 U.S. 853 (1982). Concerned parents persuaded the school district to remove nine books from the libraries of the high school and the junior high school.[a] The school board's examination of the books persuaded its members that the books were "anti-American, anti-Christian, anti-Sem[i]tic, and just plain filthy. * * * It is our duty, our moral obligation, to protect the children in our schools from this moral danger as surely as from physical and medical dangers." The school board reconsidered its decision in light of a report from a parent-teacher committee appointed by the board, but ultimately the board rejected the committee's recommendation that most of the banned books be returned to the school libraries.

Justice Brennan wrote for a *plurality* (Justices Marshall, Stevens, and, for most of his opinion, Blackmun) and delivered the Court's judgment striking down the school board's censorship and directing that the books be returned to the libraries. Although the Court had ruled in *Epperson v. Arkansas*, 393 U.S. 97, 104 (1968), that "public education in our Nation is committed to the control of state and local authorities," and that federal courts should not ordinarily "intervene in the resolution of conflicts which arise in the daily operation of school systems," Justice Brennan insisted that local boards exercise that authority consistent with the First Amendment as interpreted in *Tinker* and various precedents recognizing a public interest in the availability of books and information.

"[T]he First Amendment rights of students may be directly and sharply implicated by the removal of books from the shelves of a school library. Our precedents have focused 'not only on the role of the First Amendment in fostering individual self-expression but also on its role in affording the public access to discussion, debate, and the dissemination of information and ideas.' *First National Bank of Boston v. Bellotti*, 435 U.S. 765, 783 (1978). And we have recognized that 'the State may not, consistently with the spirit of the First Amendment, contract the spectrum of available knowledge.' *Griswold v. Connecticut* [Chapter 1, Section 1A]. In keeping with this principle, we have held that in a variety of contexts 'the Constitution protects the right to receive information and ideas.' *Stanley v. Georgia*, 394 U.S. 557, 564 (1969) [excerpted in Chapter

---

[a]   The nine books in the High School library were: *Slaughter House Five*, by Kurt Vonnegut, Jr.; *The Naked Ape*, by Desmond Morris; *Down These Mean Streets*, by Piri Thomas; *The Best Short Stories of Negro Writers*, edited by Langston Hughes; *Go Ask Alice*, of anonymous authorship; *Laughing Boy*, by Oliver LaFarge; *Black Boy*, by Richard Wright; *A Hero Ain't Nothin' But A Sandwich*, by Alice Childress; and *Soul On Ice*, by Eldridge Cleaver. The book in the Junior High School library was *A Reader for Writers*, edited by Jerome Archer. Still another listed book, *The Fixer*, by Bernard Malamud, was found to be included in the curriculum of a twelfth-grade literature course.

1, Section 1B]. This right is an inherent corollary of the rights of free speech and press that are explicitly guaranteed by the Constitution, in two senses. First, the right to receive ideas follows ineluctably from the *sender's* First Amendment right to send them: 'The right of freedom of speech and press ... embraces the right to distribute literature, and necessarily protects the right to receive it.' *Martin v. Struthers*, 319 U.S. 141, 143 (1943). 'The dissemination of ideas can accomplish nothing if otherwise willing addressees are not free to receive and consider them. It would be a barren marketplace of ideas that had only sellers and no buyers.' *Lamont v. Postmaster General*, 381 U.S. 301, 308 (1965) (Brennan, J., concurring).

"More importantly, the right to receive ideas is a necessary predicate to the recipient's meaningful exercise of his own rights of speech, press, and political freedom. Madison admonished us:

'A popular Government, without popular information, or the means of acquiring it, is but a Prologue to a Farce or a Tragedy; or, perhaps both. Knowledge will forever govern ignorance: And a people who mean to be their own Governors, must arm themselves with the power which knowledge gives.' 9 *Writings of James Madison* 103 (G. Hunt ed. 1910).

"As we recognized in *Tinker*, students too are beneficiaries of this principle:

'In our system, students may not be regarded as closed-circuit recipients of only that which the State chooses to communicate.... [S]chool officials cannot suppress "expressions of feeling with which they do not wish to contend." '

"In sum, just as access to ideas makes it possible for citizens generally to exercise their rights of free speech and press in a meaningful manner, such access prepares students for active and effective participation in the pluralistic, often contentious society in which they will soon be adult members. Of course all First Amendment rights accorded to students must be construed 'in light of the special characteristics of the school environment.' *Tinker*. But the special characteristics of the school *library* make that environment especially appropriate for the recognition of the First Amendment rights of students."

Justice Brennan dismissed the school board's invocation of the inculcative purpose of public education: both the theory and the practice of libraries are choice-based; "libraries afford [students] an opportunity at self-education and individual enrichment that is wholly optional. Petitioners might well defend their claim of absolute discretion in matters of curriculum by reliance upon their duty to inculcate community values. But we think that petitioners' reliance upon that duty is misplaced where, as here, they attempt to extend their claim of absolute discretion beyond the compulsory environment of the classroom, into the school library and the regime of voluntary inquiry that there holds sway."

In a portion of his opinion joined only by Justices Marshall and Stevens, Justice Brennan maintained that the legality of the school board's removal of books turned on the board's motivation. "If petitioners *intended* by their removal decision to deny respondents access to ideas with which petitioners disagreed, and if this intent was the decisive factor in petitioners' decision, then petitioners have exercised their discretion in violation of the Constitution. * * * On the other hand, respondents implicitly concede that an unconstitutional motivation would *not* be demonstrated if it were shown that petitioners had decided to remove the books at issue because those books were pervasively vulgar. And again, respondents concede that if it were demonstrated that the removal decision was based solely upon the 'educational suitability' of the books in question, then their removal would be 'perfectly permissible.' "

Justice Brennan quoted an example of impermissible motivation: "When asked to give an example of 'anti-Americanism' in the removed books, petitioners Ahrens and Martin both adverted to [Alice Childress'] *A Hero Ain't Nothin' But A Sandwich*, which notes at one point that George Washington was a slaveholder. Petitioner Martin stated: 'I believe it is anti-American to present one of the nation's heroes, the first President, . . . in such a negative and obviously one-sided life [sic]. That is one example of what I would consider anti-American.' "

Justice Blackmun concurred in all but the last part of Justice Brennan's opinion and agreed with Justice Brennan that "the State may not suppress exposure to ideas—for the sole *purpose* of suppressing exposure to those ideas—absent sufficiently compelling reasons." **Justice White** concurred only in the judgment of reversal, on the ground that there were legitimate factual issues going to the school board's motivation; those issues precluded the summary judgment granted by the district court.

Writing for four Justices, **Chief Justice Burger** dissented. "It is true that where there is a willing distributor of materials, the government may not impose unreasonable obstacles to dissemination by the third party. And where the speaker desires to express certain ideas, the government may not impose unreasonable restraints. *Tinker.* It does not follow, however, that a school board must affirmatively aid the speaker in his communication with the recipient. In short the plurality suggests today that if a writer has something to say, the government through its schools must be the courier." His fundamental objection was that a *public library* has no obligation to provide a fair and balanced array of books to the public; the First Amendment bars the government from censoring private expression and does not impose obligations on government to make information available.

"If, as we have held, schools may legitimately be used as vehicles for 'inculcating fundamental values necessary to the maintenance of a democratic political system,' *Ambach v. Norwick*, 441 U.S. 68, 77 (1979), school authorities must have broad discretion to fulfill that obligation. * * * The plurality fails to recognize the fact that local control of education involves democracy in a microcosm. In most public schools in the United States the *parents* have a large voice in running the school. Through participation in the election of school board members, the parents influence, if not control, the direction of their children's education. A school board is not a giant bureaucracy far removed from accountability for its actions; it is truly 'of the people and by the people.' A school board reflects its constituency in a very real sense and thus could not long exercise unchecked discretion in its choice to acquire or remove books. If the parents disagree with the educational decisions of the school board, they can take steps to remove the board members from office. Finally, even if parents and students cannot convince the school board that book removal is inappropriate, they have alternative sources to the same end. Books may be acquired from bookstores, public libraries, or other alternative sources unconnected with the unique environment of the local public schools."

Chief Justice Burger criticized the plurality opinion for inviting judges to usurp or second-guess the educational decisions of school boards. The standards of review announced by the plurality—courts can overturn "partisan" censorship but should allow censorship of materials that are "pervasively vulgar"—are too vague to be constraining on trial judges. They will, therefore, be free to impose their own standards and to displace those adopted by the local boards. **Justice Powell** and **Justice Rehnquist** wrote separate dissenting opinions.

NOTES ON *PICO* AND STUDENTS' RIGHT TO KNOW

1.   *A General Right to Know?* Justice Powell's *Pico* dissent contained excerpts from the censored books, including the following passage from Eldridge Cleaver's *Soul on Ice* (pp. 157–58):

> There are white men who will pay you to fuck their wives. They approach you and say, 'How would you like to fuck a white woman?' 'What is this?' you ask. 'On the up-and-up,' he assures you. 'It's all right. She's my wife. She needs black rod, is all. She has to have it. It's like a medicine or drug to her. She has to have it. I'll pay you. It's all on the level, no trick involved. Interested?' You go with him and he drives you to their home. The three of you go into the bedroom. There is a certain type who will leave you and his wife alone and tell you to pile her real good. After it is all over, he will pay you and drive you to wherever you want to go. Then there are some who like to peep at you through a keyhole and watch you have his woman, or peep at you through a window, or lie under the bed and listen to the creaking of the bed as you work out. There is another type who likes to masturbate while he stands beside the

bed and watches you pile her. There is the type who likes to eat his woman up after you get through piling her. And there is the type who only wants you to pile her for a little while, just long enough to thaw her out and kick her motor over and arouse her to heat, then he wants you to jump off real quick and he will jump onto her and together they can make it from there by themselves.

Similar sexually explicit excerpts were from Langston Hughes, editor, *The Best Short Stories by Negro Writers*, and Richard Wright, *Black Boy*. Should depictions such as this be a sufficient ground for removing the book from the library? Should Justice Powell have included these excerpts in a Supreme Court opinion that is accessible to members of the public, including children? Is the fact that most of the excerpts were authored by authors of color relevant?

Three Justices in *Pico* agreed that high school students have a constitutional right to know, which entails access to important intellectual materials; one Justice (Blackmun) agreed with a negative right, not to withhold ideas from students. Four Justices rejected a right to know and, perhaps, even Justice Blackmun's negative right. Justice White took no firm position. So *Pico* does not resolve this issue. Should high school students have some kind of right to know? *See Case v. Unified School District No. 233*, 908 F. Supp. 864 (D. Kan. 1995), applying *Pico* to overturn a school board's censorship of *Annie on My Mind*, an award-winning book about a romantic relationship between two teenage girls, and *All American Boys*, a similar story involving teenage boys.

2. *A Right to Know About Sex and Sexuality*? If the Brennan plurality opinion were right, students might have a constitutional "right to know" accurate information about sexuality. Does a teenage girl have the right to know about the risks of pregnancy and how to prevent it? Does a teenage boy have a similar need? Does he need to know how to use a condom? Does a gay teenager have a right to know that homosexuality is not a mental or physical disease, according to the medical experts and associations? Do teenagers of all genders and sexualities have a right to know about how HIV is transmitted?

Even if the Burger dissenting opinion correctly stated the law, schools might have a constitutional obligation to present accurate information about sexuality if they undertake sex education. This is the approach taken by some, but certainly not all, state laws. Approximately 13 of the 27 states that require sex and HIV education programs require the information to be medically accurate. Guttmacher Institute, *Sex and HIV Education*, https://www.guttmacher.org/state-policy/explore/sex-and-hiv-education (as of April 1, 2017).

The consequences of receiving incomplete and/or medically inaccurate sex education can be quite serious. Receiving incomplete and/or incorrect information about conception and contraception can result in unwanted pregnancies. Currently, the majority of states that require sex education require that the education stress abstinence. Indeed in some states, educators are required to "emphasize abstinence as the only sure method for avoiding pregnancy." Matthew Lashof-Sullivan, "Sex Education in Schools," 16 *Geo. J. Gender & L.* 263, 272 (2015). Often such states do not require educators to include information about contraception.

One stated goal of abstinence-focused sex education is to reduce the incidence of teen pregnancy. A number of recent studies have found, however, that "emphasis on abstinence education is positively correlated with teenage pregnancy and birth rates." Kathrin F. Stanger-Hall & David W. Hall, "Abstinence-Only Education and Teen Pregnancy Rates: Why We Need Comprehensive Sex Education in the U.S.," *PloS ONE* 6(10) (2011). By contrast, "[s]tates that taught comprehensive sex and/or HIV education and covered abstinence along with contraception and condom use * * * tended to have the lowest teen pregnancy rates." Kathrin F. Stanger-Hall & David W. Hall, *Abstinence-Only Education and Teen Pregnancy Rates: Why We Need Comprehensive Sex Education in the U.S.*, PloS ONE 6(10) (2011).

Inaccurate and/or incomplete sex education programs can also place students at greater risk of contracting HIV and other STDs. In the early 1980s, HIV spread rapidly in urban areas because of public ignorance about the means of transmission and preventive techniques. Surgeon General Everett Koop insisted upon a media campaign to educate adolescents, and more than 30 states passed statutes requiring HIV education in their school systems; this effort at education paid off with greater teenager knowledge about the means of HIV transmission and its consequences. *See* Ralph Hingson & Lee Strunin, "Monitoring Adolescents' Response to the AIDS Epidemic: Changes in Knowledge, Attitudes, Beliefs and Behaviors," in *Adolescents and AIDS: A Generation in Jeopardy* 17, 18–21 (Ralph J. DiClemente ed., 1992).

Unfortunately, three decades later, adolescents remain at greater risk for HIV infection because they frequently underestimate the possibility of HIV transmission in sexual and drug-related activities. Kaiser Family Foundation and Ford Foundation, *Fact Sheet: The HIV/AIDS Epidemic in the United States* (2001). African-American and Latino adolescents are disproportionately at risk, compared to their non-Hispanic white peers.

Some health education theorists believe that a successful AIDS education program for adolescents, especially for those most likely to engage in risky behaviors, must provide information to young people, teach them how to successfully negotiate risk-prone situations through role-playing and the like, and set in motion ideas and practices that affect youth culture generally. Thus researchers have found that programs that do nothing but supply information to adolescents are not very effective in reducing risk-taking adolescent behavior. *See generally Preventing AIDS: Theories and Methods of Behavioral Interventions* (Ralph J. DiClemente & John L. Peterson eds., 1994).

Little of this educational theory is reflected in state statutes that have authorized or (usually) required public schools to develop sex education materials focused on AIDS and ways to avoid HIV infection, and, as noted above, a number of states require the education to teach students that abstinence is the *only* sure-fire way to avoid HIV infection.

Medical experts generally do not believe that a focus on abstinence is an effective strategy in reducing HIV transmission among adolescents. Teen sexual activity is at high levels. Although most teenagers have not engaged in either penile-vaginal sex or anal sex, the two main mechanisms for sexual transmission of HIV, most have engaged in oral sex, which can also transmit the virus. To the extent that teens consider oral activities "not sex" (which seems to be the case), "abstinence" education might even be counterproductive.

B. TEACHERS' RIGHT TO TEACH?

NOTE ON ACADEMIC FREEDOM

Section 3A considers the first amendment rights of *students*. What about the first amendment rights of *teachers* in public schools, including public colleges and universities? Academic freedom serves both substantive and procedural values, according to its adherents. Substantively, defenders of academic freedom maintain that teachers and educational institutions need to be left alone, so that the "marketplace of ideas" can work freely. Procedurally, the polity should defer to educational choices made by educators. When the educational institution is run by the state, the academic freedom of educators is protected by the First Amendment. *See, e.g., Sweezy v. New Hampshire*, 354 U.S. 234, 250 (1957); *Keyishian v. Board of Regents*, 385 U.S. 589 (1967). In the college and university setting, especially, the government "acts against a background and tradition of thought and experiment that is at the center of our intellectual and philosophic tradition." *Rosenberger v. Rector and Visitors of the University of Virginia*, 515 U.S. 819, 835 (1995).

In *Regents of Univ. of Michigan v. Ewing*, 474 U.S. 214, 226 & n.12 (1985), the Court wrote that academic freedom "thrives not only on the independent and uninhibited exchange of ideas among teachers and students, but also, and somewhat inconsistently, on autonomous decision-making by the academy itself." *Accord University of Pennsylvania v. EEOC*, 493 U.S. 182, 199 (1990) ("judges * * * asked to review the substance of a genuinely academic decision * * * should show great respect for the faculty's professional judgment").

While it generally accepted that professors at public colleges and universities are entitled to some degree of academic freedom, whether this protection applies to elementary and secondary teachers is much less clear.

One of the Court's first forays into this question was its decision in *Pickering v. Board of Education*, 391 U.S. 563 (1968). In *Pickering*, a high school teacher criticized the Board of Education (his employer) in a public letter for the manner in which the district allocated funds between academic and athletic activities, and the teacher was fired for so doing. The Supreme Court held that the teacher had a right to speak out on matters of public interest without fear of reprisal by his employer, as long as the teacher's speech didn't affect his performance in the classroom, or "interfere with the regular operation of the schools."

Left unanswered in *Pickering* was the question of what happens when a teacher's speech is part of classroom or school-based activities. In *Pickering*, the speech in question occurred out of the classroom, the letter in question was drafted outside of class time, and it did not directly affect the teacher's students. By contrast, in cases in which the speech in question is part of class instruction, arguably, academic freedom cuts both ways: if the teacher's speech has been censored or if the teacher has been disciplined for the speech, failure of courts to intervene undermines the academic freedom of the teacher, but, on the other hand, intervention undermines the academic freedom of the institution. And, in another case decided the same year, *Epperson v. Arkansas*, 393 U.S. 97, 104 (1968), the Court explained that "public education * * * is committed to the control of state and local authorities [school boards]," and that federal courts should be loathe to "intervene in the resolution of conflicts which arise in the daily operation of school systems."

Section 1 explained that school officials may censor or otherwise regulate *student speech* "so long as their actions are reasonably related to legitimate pedagogical concerns." *Hazelwood*, 484 U.S. at 273 (emphasis added). But, again, what standard applies to the regulation of *teacher speech* in a school-sponsored activity?

Most recently, in a case called *Garcetti v. Ceballos*, 547 U.S. 410 (2006), the Supreme Court appeared to cut back on first amendment protection for public employees, including, possibly, secondary school teachers. In *Garcetti*, a deputy district attorney (Ceballos) felt that an affidavit used to obtain a search warrant included a number of misrepresentations. Ceballos wrote a memo outlining his concerns. After meeting with Ceballos, the prosecutor decided to proceed with the case anyway. Ceballos then informed counsel for the defendant about his concerns. Ceballos was eventually dropped from the prosecutors' team. Thereafter, Ceballos filed suit, alleging a violation of his First Amendment rights, among other claims.

In an opinion written by Justice Kennedy, the Supreme Court rejected Ceballos' First Amendment claim, stating: "We hold that when public employees make statements pursuant to their official duties, the employees are not speaking as citizens for First Amendment purposes, and the constitution does not insulate their communications from employer discipline." *Id.* at 421. Justice Kennedy noted the expressed concern that this standard may be inappropriate in the context of teacher speech, but declined to expressly state whether or not the same standard should be applied in that context:

> There is some argument that expression related to academic scholarship or classroom instruction implicates additional constitutional interests that are not fully accounted for by this Court's customary employee-speech jurisprudence. We need not, and for that reason do not, decide whether the analysis we conduct today would apply in the same matter to a case involving speech related to scholarship or teaching.

Id. at 425.

Since *Garcetti*, lower court decisions on whether this standard applies to teachers has been mixed. The Ninth Circuit recently answered this question in the negative, in a case involving a college professor, stating:

We conclude that *Garcetti* does not—indeed, consistent with the First Amendment, cannot—apply to teaching and academic writing that are performed "pursuant to the official duties" of a teacher and professor. We hold that academic employee speech not covered by *Garcetti* is protected under the First Amendment, using the analysis established in *Pickering*. The *Pickering* test has two parts. First, the employee must show that his or her speech addressed "matters of public concern." Second, the employee's interest "in commenting upon matters of public concern" must outweigh "the interest of the State, as an employer, in promoting the efficiency of the public services it performs through its employees."

Demers v. Austin, 746 F.3d 402, 412 (9th Cir. 2014).

But other circuits, including the Sixth and Seventh Circuits, reached the opposition conclusion, at least in the context of secondary school teachers. *See, e.g., Evans-Marshall v. Bd. of Educ. of Tipp City Exempted Vill. Sch. Dist.*, 624 F.3d 332 (6th Cir. 2010); *Brown v. Chicago Bd. of Educ.*, 824 F.3d 713 (7th Cir. 2016). In *Evans-Marshall*, a school decided not to renew the contract of a probationary high school teacher. During her probationary period, the teacher had the students do an assignment related to government censorship. After being divided into groups, the students were told to pick a book from the American Library Association's "100 Most Frequently Challenged Books" list, research why the book was challenged, and lead a debate about the book. Two groups choose "Heather Has Two Mommies," by Lesléa Newman. After receiving a parent complaint, the principal told the teacher that the students had to choose a different book. The teacher complied. Parents continued to complain about this and other assignments given by the teacher.

The teacher sued after her contract was not renewed claiming, among other things, a violation of her First Amendment rights. In its decision, the Sixth Circuit held that *Garcetti* applied to the dispute at hand:

In the light cast by *Garcetti*, it is clear that the First Amendment does not generally "insulate" [the teacher] "from employer discipline," . . . even discipline prompted by her curricular and pedagogical choices and even if it otherwise appears (at least on summary judgment) that the school administrators treated her shabbily. When a teacher teaches, "the school system does not 'regulate' [that] speech as much as it hires that speech. Expression is a teacher's stock in trade, the commodity she sells to her employer in exchange for a salary." And if it is the school board that hires that speech, it can surely "regulate the context of what is or is not expressed," . . . what is expressed in other words on its behalf. Only the school board has ultimate responsibility for what goes on in the classroom, legitimately giving it a say over what teachers may (or may not) teach in the classroom.

The Sixth Circuit continued:

How at any rate would a contrary approach work? If one teacher, Evans-Marshall, has a First Amendment right "to select books and methods of instruction for use in the classroom," R.1 ¶ 32, so presumably do other teachers. Evans-Marshall may wish to teach *Siddhartha* in the first unit of the school year in a certain way, but the chair of the English department may wish to use the limited time in a school year to teach *A Tale of Two Cities* at that stage of the year. Maybe the head of the upper school has something else in mind. When educators disagree over what should be assigned, as is surely bound to happen if each of them has a First Amendment right to influence the curriculum, whose free-speech rights win? Why indeed doesn't the principal, Wray, have a right to defend the discharge on the ground that he was merely exercising *his* First Amendment rights in rejecting Evans-Marshall's curricular choices and methods of teaching? Placing the First Amendment's stamp of approval on these kinds of debates not only would "demand permanent judicial intervention in the conduct of governmental operations," *Garcetti,* 547 U.S. at 423, 126 S.Ct. 1951, but it also would transform run-of-the-mine curricular disputes into constitutional stalemates.

That is not the only problem. What employer discipline arising from an employee's manner of teaching—choices of books and the methods of teaching them—does not implicate speech? Could a teacher respond to a principal's insistence that she discuss certain materials by claiming that it improperly *compels* speech? Could a teacher continue to assign materials that members of the community perceive as racially insensitive even after the principal tells her not to? Could a teacher raise a controversial topic (say, the virtues of one theory of government over another or the virtues of intelligent design) after a principal has told her not to? Could a teacher introduce mature sexual themes to fifteen year olds when discussing a work of literature after a principal has told her not to? And "[d]oes a music teacher retain veto power over that most controversial of school productions—the Holiday Concert?" *Evans-Marshall I,* 428 F.3d at 237–38 (Sutton, J., concurring).

Because "one man's vulgarity is another's lyric," *Cohen v. California,* 403 U.S. 15, 25, 91 S.Ct. 1780, 29 L.Ed.2d 284 (1971), or, as one school board member put the point at the November 2001 meeting, "what you might find offensive, I might not," R.46 at 1:41:40, parents long have demanded that school boards control the curriculum and the ways of teaching it to their impressionable children. Permitting federal courts to distinguish classroom vulgarities from lyrics or to pick sides on how to teach *Siddhartha* not only is a recipe for disenfranchising the 9,000 or so members of the Tipp City community but also tests judicial competence. "If even the most happily married parents cannot agree on what and how their own children should be taught, as [we] suspect is not infrequently the case, what leads anyone to think the federal judiciary can answer these questions?" *Evans-Marshall I,* 428 F.3d at 237–38 (Sutton, J., concurring).

The key insight of *Garcetti* is that the First Amendment has nothing to say about these kinds of decisions. An employee does not lose "any liberties the employee might have enjoyed as a private citizen" by signing on to work for the government, but by the same token, the government, just like a private employer, retains "control over what the employer itself has commissioned or created": the employee's job. *Garcetti,* 547 U.S. at 422, 126 S.Ct. 1951. And that insight has particular resonance in the context of public education. Every child in Ohio must attend school, providing public school teachers with a captive audience for their in-class speech, and providing a compelling reason for putting curricular choices in the hands of "someone [they] can vote out of office," *id.* at 479–80, or who is otherwise democratically accountable.

Evans-Marshall v. Bd. of Educ. of Tipp City Exempted Vill. Sch. Dist., 624 F.3d 332, 341–42 (6th Cir. 2010).

Which court is right? The Ninth Circuit, or the Sixth Circuit? Why? Should public school teachers have any right to control the content of their teaching without fear of reprisal? What about professors at colleges and universities? Do they have greater academic freedom rights?

To be clear, even pre-*Garcetti,* courts seemed very willing to support administration claims that censure was based on the "vulgar" content of the speech involved, and the need to protect students from "offensive" material. For example, *O'Connor v. Sobol,* 173 A.D.2d 74, 577 N.Y.S.2d 716 (1991) upheld, against First Amendment attack, the reprimand of a New York teacher for distributing a sexually explicit article to high school seniors. Similarly, an Illinois federal district court held that a school board's decision not to renew the contract of a teacher because he showed a high school class the R-rated film "About Last Night" as a modern version of Thornton Wilder's *Our Town* was justifiable under *Hazelwood. See Krizek v. Board of Education of Cicero-Stickney Township High School District No. 201,* 713 F. Supp. 1131 (N.D. Ill. 1989). *See also Miles v. Denver Public Schools,* 944 F.2d 773, 777 (10th Cir. 1991) (upholding the discipline of a teacher who while complaining about the declining quality of the school in his classroom referenced as an example two students that rumor had "making out on the tennis courts").

PROBLEM 8-8
ACCESS TO INFORMATION ABOUT SEX AND SEXUALITY IN SCHOOLS

Consider the following Alabama statute both from the perspective of a student, and from the perspective of the teacher. Do either of them have a strong basis for challenging the statute?

Alabama Statutes § 16–40A–2, Minimum Contents to be Included in Sex Education Program or Curriculum

(Added 1992; unamended as of April 2017).

(a) Any program or curriculum in the public schools in Alabama that includes sex education or the human reproductive process shall, as a minimum, include and emphasize the following:

(1) Abstinence from sexual intercourse is the only completely effective protection against unwanted pregnancy, sexually transmitted diseases, and acquired immune deficiency syndrome (AIDS) when transmitted sexually.

(2) Abstinence from sexual intercourse outside of lawful marriage is the expected social standard for unmarried school-age persons.

(b) Course materials and instruction that relate to sexual education or sexually transmitted diseases should be age-appropriate.

(c) Course materials and instruction that relate to sexual education or sexually transmitted diseases should include all of the following elements:

(1) An emphasis on sexual abstinence as the only completely reliable method of avoiding unwanted teenage pregnancy and sexually transmitted diseases.

(2) An emphasis on the importance of self-control and ethical conduct pertaining to sexual behavior.

(3) Statistics based on the latest medical information that indicate the degree of reliability and unreliability of various forms of contraception, while also emphasizing the increase in protection against pregnancy and protection against sexually transmitted diseases, including HIV and AIDS infection, which is afforded by the use of various contraceptive measures.

(4) Information concerning the laws relating to the financial responsibilities associated with pregnancy, childbirth, and child rearing.

(5) Information concerning the laws prohibiting sexual abuse, the need to report such abuse, and the legal options available to victims of sexual abuse.

(6) Information on how to cope with and rebuff unwanted physical and verbal sexual exploitation by other persons.

(7) Psychologically sound methods of resisting unwanted peer pressure.

(8) An emphasis, in a factual manner and from a public health perspective, that homosexuality is not a lifestyle

acceptable to the general public and that homosexual conduct is a criminal offense under the laws of the state.

(9) Comprehensive instruction in parenting skills and responsibilities, including the responsibility to pay child support by non-custodial parents, the penalties for non-payment of child support, and the legal and ethical responsibilities of child care and child rearing.

The Alabama Department of Education is charged with implementing the foregoing law. Its Health Education Bulletin No. 25 provides a grade-by-grade review of what schools have to do under the statute. In sixth and seventh grades, for example, schools must teach basic facts about physical and psychological changes in adolescents as they pass through puberty, the ways HIV/AIDS and other sexually transmitted diseases are spread and modes of prevention, and the need for family planning and the usefulness of resisting peer pressure to have sex too early. High school health instruction is supposed to provide detailed information about sexually transmitted diseases, individual responsibility for setting limits during dates, and the superiority of family and love to pornography and promiscuity in the development of an individual's sexuality. (See NARAL Review 2–3.)

Consider the following hypothetical applications of the Alabama statute and the Board's guidelines. You are the state lawyer advising the Board as to its legal obligation.

1. *Abortion.* The Board is asked to develop guidelines for teachers to respond to student questions about abortion. The Board is inclined to forbid teachers from talking about abortion altogether. Is that legal? *Cf. Rust v. Sullivan*, 500 U.S. 173 (1991).

2. *Contraceptives.* Some legislators have learned that contraceptives are being distributed by school health officials in some high schools; those legislators want the Board to adopt a rule prohibiting school personnel from distributing contraceptives and to require mandatory dismissal of personnel who violate such a rule. The Board asks you whether it has authority to adopt such a rule. How would you advise them? Why?

3. *The Immorality of Premarital Sex.* At one high school, the sex education class had a one-hour session in which the teacher brought in a woman who told the class that she had sex and an abortion before she was married and that these experiences "almost ruined my life." The woman witnessed before the students about the spiritual value of sex within marriage and the "sinfulness" of sex outside of marriage. The teacher assigned *Sex Respect* as the text for the class; those materials emphasize the "guilt" and psychological as well as physical harm that come from having premarital sex. The school district is uncertain whether this teacher's conduct of the sex education class is consistent with Alabama law and asks the Board for its opinion. How would you advise?

C. PARENTAL RIGHTS

NOTES ABOUT PARENTAL RIGHTS AND SCHOOL CURRICULUM

As noted above, some parents have sued school districts after their children received information about sex or sexuality that they did not want their children to receive. Should schools be permitted to impart this information to students even if the parents do not want their children to receive this information?

1. *First Amendment and Religion.* Where the sex education is rooted in a religious or moral perspective, parents who want a more scientifically-based curriculum may argue that the instruction impermissibly establishes a religious viewpoint. The Establishment Clause bars the state from "establishing" religion. In *Lemon v. Kurtzman*, 403 U.S. 602 (1971), the Court ruled that a statute seeming to advance a religious point of view is valid so long as it also has "a secular legislative purpose," a "primary effect ** * that neither advances nor inhibits religions," and does * * * "not foster 'an excessive government entanglement with religion.'" It is not clear that the Court still follows the *Lemon* test, e.g., *Good News Club v. Milford Central School*, 533 U.S. 98 (2001), but almost all (perhaps all) of the Court's decisions can be defended along *Lemon* lines.

Under *Lemon*, the state can adopt policies and views that enjoy strong support from religion, but usually cannot adopt policies or views that do not also enjoy strong support from secular sources. Some sex education materials founder on this requirement of nonentanglement. *See, e.g., Coleman v. Caddo Parish School Board*, 635 So.3d 1238 (La. Ct. App. 1994), *writ denied*, 639 So. 2d 1171 (La. 1994) (concluding that some statements from the Sex Respect curriculum, including the statement that "[s]exual intercourse is designed . . . to renew marriage vows and bind a couple that is united for life" violated this principle).

2. *Parental Right to Control the Care and Upbringing of Their Children.* More commonly, however, parental challenges to sex education are raised by parents who do not want their children to be exposed to more scientifically-based comprehensive sex education. These parents may claim that exposing their children to these materials over their objection violates their constitutionally protected right to control the upbringing of their children. The constitutional rights of parents are founded on two early substantive due process precedents, *see Meyer v. Nebraska*, 262 U.S. 390 (1923); *Pierce v. Society of Sisters*, 268 U.S. 510 (1925), reflecting the principle that "the custody, care and nurture of the child reside first in the parents." *Prince v. Massachusetts*, 321 U.S. 158, 166 (1944). The Supreme Court reaffirmed that right in *Troxel v. Granville*, 530 U.S. 57 (2000) (Chapter 7, Section 2B). Justice O'Connor's plurality opinion characterized the "right of parents to the care, custody,

and control of their children" as "perhaps the oldest of the fundamental liberty interests recognized by this Court."

This right, however, is not absolute. *See, e.g., Meyer v. Nebraska*, 262 U.S. 390, 399–400 (1923). The state can override a parent's wishes when it is necessary to protect the welfare and well-being of children. Moreover, some courts have held that while parents have the right to control the upbringing of their children, once they make a decision to send their children to a public school, they do not have the right to control what their children are taught. *See, e.g., Leebaert v. Harrington*, 332 F.3d 134, 142 (2d Cir. 2003) ("But there is nothing in *Troxel* that would lead us to conclude from the Court's recognition of a parental right in what the plurality called 'the care, custody, and control' of a child with respect to visitation rights that parents have a *fundamental* right to the upbringing and education of the child that includes the right to tell public schools what to teach or what not to teach him or her."); *C.N. v. Ridgewood Bd. of Educ.*, 430 F.3d 159, 185 (3d Cir. 2005) ("While the Supreme Court has extended constitutional protection to parental decisions regarding certain matters (see *Troxel* * * * (visitation); *Pierce* * * * (decision to enroll child in private, religious school rather than public school)), our review of these cases prompts us to conclude that the decision whether to permit a middle or high school student to participate in a survey of this type is not a matter of comparable gravity.").

Consider the next case.

Ignacia Alfonso et al. v. Joseph Fernandez et al.

New York Supreme Court, Appellate Division, Second Department, 1993.
195 A.D.2d 46, 606 N.Y.S.2d 259.

■ PIZZUTO, JUSTICE. * * *

In September 1987 the New York State Commission of Education directed all elementary and secondary schools to include, as part of health education programs, instruction concerning the Human Immunodeficiency Virus (HIV) which causes Acquired Immune Deficiency Syndrome (AIDS) (see, 8 NYCRR 135.3[b][2]; [c][2]). In late 1990, Joseph Fernandez, then Chancellor of the New York City Board of Education, suggested enlarging the existing HIV/AIDS curriculum to impart additional education about the transmission and prevention of HIV/AIDS. The former Chancellor also suggested that condoms be made available to high school students upon request. On February 27, 1991, the New York City Board of Education voted to establish an expanded HIV/AIDS Education Program in New York City's public high schools, consisting of two components. * * *

[The first component calls for classroom instructions on various aspects of HIV/AIDS; although mandatory for the students, this component allows a parent to opt his or her minor unemancipated child out of the classroom instruction upon the assurance that the child will receive such instruction at home. The second component of the program calls for the high schools to make condoms available to students who request them; this component is not mandatory for students but also does not have a parental opt-out provision. The School Board considered an opt-out provision but rejected it because they believed it would deny condoms to students most in need of them. The parent-plaintiffs challenged this second component for its lack of parental opt out.]

At common law it was for parents to consent or withhold their consent to the rendition of health services to their children. The general incapacity of minors to consent to health services derives from this common-law rule that treated a minor's "normal condition [as] that of incompetency". As legal incompetents, minors could no more consent to medical treatment than they could enter into binding contracts and they continued to be incompetent in many circumstances to give effective consent to health care. The courts identified exceptions to the common-law rule regarding the incapacity of minors. For example, children were regarded as emancipated and competent to consent when they were married; or supported themselves; or were inducted into military service; or when their parents abandoned them or failed to support them. In addition, a physician could render health services to a minor in an emergency without first consulting his or her parents.

Public Health Law § 2504, which was enacted in 1972 * * * reads as follows:

"1. Any person who is eighteen years of age or older, or is the parent of a child or has married, may give effective consent for medical, dental, *health* and hospital *services* for himself or herself, and the consent of no other person shall be necessary.

"2. Any person who has been married or who has borne a child may give effective consent for medical, dental, *health* and hospital *services* for his or her child.

"3. Any person who is pregnant may give effective consent for medical, dental, *health* and hospital *services* relating to prenatal care.

"4. Medical, dental, *health* and hospital *services* may be rendered to persons of any age without the consent of a parent or legal guardian when, in the physician's judgment an emergency exists and the person is in immediate need of medical attention and an attempt to secure consent would result in delay of treatment which would increase the risk to the person's life or health.

"5. Anyone who acts in good faith based on the representation by a person that he is eligible to consent pursuant to the terms of this section shall be deemed to have received effective consent" (emphasis supplied). * * *

[The court first determined that condom distribution is a "health service," as the parents argued, and not an "educational" service, as the school maintained.] The distribution of condoms is not * * * an aspect of education in disease prevention, but rather is a means of disease prevention. Supplying condoms to students upon request has absolutely nothing to do with education, but rather is a health service occurring after the educational phase has ceased. Although the program is not intended to promote promiscuity, it is intended to encourage and enable students to use condoms if and when they engage in sexual activity. This is clearly a health service for the prevention of disease which requires parental consent. * * *

Requiring parental consent or opt-out for the condom availability component of the respondents' program would not violate State and Federal statutory and constitutional law as urged by the *amici*, nor would it stymie every health care provider, compelling parental consent whenever an unemancipated minor seeks contraceptive services.

Under the sections of the Social Security Act governing Aid to Families with Dependent Children and Medicaid, family planning services and supplies must be provided to all eligible recipients, including sexually active minors (*see*, 42 U.S.C.A. §§ 602[a][15]; 1396d[a][4][C]). The State laws governing these programs also require that contraception be made available to "eligible persons of childbearing age, including children who can be considered sexually active" (Social Services Law § 350[1][e]; *see*, Social Services Law § 365–a[3][c]; *see also*, 18 NYCRR 431.7, 463.2[b][1]; [b][2]; 463.6 [requiring provision of family planning services to minors eligible for public assistance, Medicaid, or supplemental security income, and to foster children]). These laws entitle eligible minors to confidential services from any provider who treats them under the auspices of one of the public assistance programs previously mentioned.

In addition, title X of the Public Health Service Act, the largest source of Federal funding for family planning programs throughout the nation, mandates that minors receive confidential services (*see*, 42 U.S.C.A. § 300[a]; 42 CFR 59.5[a][4], 59.15). Interpreting these statutes as requiring that adolescents be treated confidentially, on the basis of their own consent, the Federal courts have invalidated both state laws and Federal and state regulations that imposed parental consent or notification requirements on teenagers entitled to family planning services under these programs (*see*, *Jones v. T.H.*, 425 U.S. 986 [invalidating state regulations that mandated parental consent for family planning services to otherwise eligible minors]).

These statutes are merely legislatively-enacted exceptions to requirements of parental consent (*see also*, Public Health Law § 2781[1] [providing that HIV-related tests may be administered upon the written, informed consent of anyone, including a minor if the person has an ability to understand and the capacity to consent]; Public Health Law § 2305[2] [which dispenses with consent or knowledge of a parent in the diagnosis or treatment of a sexually transmissible disease]). It is for the Congress or the Legislature, not the courts—and certainly not the State Commissioner of Education or a Board of Education—to provide the exceptions to parental consent requirements. Neither Congress nor the New York State Legislature has enacted an exception for the health service at issue here. The distribution of condoms in our public high schools, where attendance is compulsory, even though condoms are nonmedicinal and require no prescription, is quite different from making them available at clinics, where attendance is wholly voluntary, or as part of public assistance programs. There is no specific authority for the condom availability component of the respondents' program, no matter how commendable its purpose may be. * * *

The petitioner parents are being compelled by State authority to send their children into an environment where they will be permitted, even encouraged, to obtain a contraceptive device, which the parents disfavor as a matter of private belief. Because the Constitution gives parents the right to regulate their children's sexual behavior as best they can, not only must a compelling State interest be found supporting the need for the policy at issue, but that policy must be essential to serving that interest as well. We do not find that the policy is essential. No matter how laudable its purpose, by excluding parental involvement, the condom availability component of the program impermissibly trespasses on the petitioners' parental rights by substituting the respondents in loco parentis, without a compelling necessity therefor [sic]. * * *

This is not a case in which parents are complaining solely about having their children exposed to ideas or a point of view with which they disagree or find offensive. We would agree that, standing alone, such opposition would falter in the face of the public school's role in preparing students for participation in a world replete with complex and controversial issues. However, the condom availability component of the respondents' distribution program creates an entirely different situation. Students are not just exposed to talk or literature on the subject of sexual behavior; the school offers the means for students to engage in sexual activity at a lower risk of pregnancy and contracting sexually transmitted diseases. The extent to which individual minors would be affected by the availability of contraceptives in the public school system if the distribution of condoms on the scale envisioned by the respondents were to become commonplace, cannot presently be ascertained. * * *

■ EIBER, JUSTICE (dissenting).* * *

[Justice Eiber disagreed with the majority's holding that the health law required parental consent for condom distribution as a health service. In a footnote, Justice Eiber noted, "While the majority seems to suggest that the dictates of the common-law rule could be satisfied by allowing parents to opt their children out of the voluntary program, this position is inconsistent. If the condom distribution program is indeed a health service as contemplated by Public Health Law § 2504 and the common law, students under the age of 18 may participate in the program only with parental consent. A parent or guardian's failure to 'opt-out' is not the equivalent of consent." Additionally, the 1972 health law on which the majority relied was a contraction of the common-law rights of parents and in no way addressed the novel threats posed by AIDS.]

Moreover, * * * to engraft a parental consent requirement onto the condom distribution program would run counter to the United States Supreme Court's holding in *Carey v. Population Services Intl.*, 431 U.S. 678. At issue in *Carey* was the constitutionality of a New York statute which made it a crime for any person to sell or distribute a contraceptive device to a minor under the age of 16. In concluding that the statute was invalid, the plurality opinion noted that minors, as well as adults, are protected by the Constitution and possess constitutional rights, including the right to privacy in connection with decisions affecting procreation. The plurality opinion further reasoned that:

> "Since the State may not impose a blanket prohibition, or even a blanket requirement of parental consent, on the choice of a minor to terminate her pregnancy, the constitutionality of a blanket prohibition of the distribution of contraceptives is a fortiori foreclosed. The State's interests in protection of the mental and physical health of the pregnant minor, and in protection of potential life are clearly more implicated by the abortion decision than by the decision to use a nonhazardous contraceptive."

Furthermore, the majority's conclusion that the distribution of condoms is encompassed by the common-law prohibition against providing medical treatment without consent, is at odds with the fact that minors in this State are permitted to obtain abortions and treatment for sexually transmitted diseases without parental consent or notification (*see*, Public Health Law § 2305). Surely, if minors are permitted to obtain treatment for the consequences of unprotected sexual intercourse without parental consent or notification, it is inconsistent to restrict their access to the means by which they can prevent an unwanted pregnancy or protect themselves from sexually transmitted diseases, including the deadly HIV virus.

In addition, while the majority turns a blind eye to the potential ramifications of its interpretation of the common-law rule, the fact remains that if the distribution of condoms is a "health service" which cannot be undertaken without parental consent, then the many family planning clinics throughout this State which distribute condoms and other contraceptive devices to minors must also be deemed in violation of the common law and statute. Similarly, if condoms cannot be provided to minors in the absence of parental consent, then it logically follows that the commercial sale of condoms to minors violates the Public Health Law and is illegal. Thus, a broad interpretation of the term "health services" to preclude distribution of condoms to minors without parental consent would have a significant impact upon the ability of minors to obtain condoms, and thus violate their constitutionally-recognized right to make such decisions privately.

* * * If an opt-out feature is adopted * * * students will no longer be able to request condoms anonymously. The respondents have reasonably concluded that this loss of confidentiality would deter student participation in the condom distribution program, thus reducing its effectiveness. In the years following the Supreme Court's decision in *Carey*, the spread of AIDS has reached alarming proportions giving rise to a compelling state interest to halt the growth of the epidemic. Clearly, many parents, such as the petitioners, are seeking to provide guidance to their children and to protect their health and morality. The majority overlooks the unfortunate reality that many children lack such interested parents. Many children have no parents to provide guidance and discipline or who are even available to consent to the child's participation in the program should an "opt-out" be mandated. Since the consequence of contracting AIDS is death, providing practical protection against the spread of the virus which causes it, to a high-risk population, in my view, outweighs the minimal intrusion into the parent/child relationship of the more protected, more fortunate portion of the adolescent population of New York City.* * *

■ [JUSTICE MILLER's separate dissenting opinion, agreeing with that of JUSTICE EIBER, is omitted.]

NOTES ON THE LEGALITY OF CONDOM DISTRIBUTION PROGRAMS AND PARENTS' CONSTITUTIONAL RIGHTS IN THEIR CHILDREN'S UPBRINGING

In *Doe v. Irwin*, 615 F.2d 1162 (6th Cir.), *cert. denied*, 449 U.S. 829 (1980), the Sixth Circuit rejected parents' substantive due process challenge to the practice of a publicly operated family planning center distributing contraceptives (including condoms) upon request to minors without notice to or consent by parents. Is *Irwin* distinguishable from *Alfonso*? If so, how? If not, which is correctly decided? Consider analytical issues common to the cases:

1. *Parental Rights.* The majority in *Alfonso* relied on both the common law and constitutional rights of parents. Does the majority have any answer to the dissent's charge that, if parents have a common law or constitutional right to control their children's health materials or education, an actual waiver and not just a failure to opt out is required to provide condoms or other useful information to minors? If the majority is right that parents have a constitutional right to determine what sex education their children are receiving, is the dissent correct that this right cannot be taken away by an opt-out procedure?

The *Alfonso* dissent distinguished earlier cases on the ground that the condom distribution program was not mandatory and therefore did not invade parents' rights to direct their children's upbringing. Persuasive?

2.   *The Rights of Minors.* Like the *Alfonso* dissent, *Irwin* relied on *Carey*, which recognized the rights of minors to obtain contraceptives without the knowledge or consent of their parents. In both contexts the underlying tension is between parents' desire to know and perhaps control their adolescents' sexual behavior, and the adolescents' desire that their parents not know. While *Carey* seems to decide the tension in favor of the rights of minors, the case may be distinguishable from *Alfonso*, which combined compulsory public schooling with condom distribution. Also, *Carey* may be weakened by the Supreme Court's decision in *Hodgson v. Minnesota* [Chapter 3, Section 1], which held that states can require parental notification of a female minor's attempt to obtain an abortion. The minor's rights to obtain an abortion and to obtain contraceptives both derive from the right of privacy now ensconced in the due process clause, and requiring parental consent in both cases serves parents' interests in knowing that their children are sexually active, at the expense of the children's sexual freedom. Is there a persuasive argument that *Carey* survives *Hodgson* and *Troxel*?

3.   *The Public Interest.* The *Alfonso* dissent relies on the strong public interest in fighting AIDS to tip the balance in favor of condom distribution. The school board believed that adolescents were going to be sexually active, whether they had condoms or not, and that making condoms available would prevent some kids from being infected by the HIV virus. For every person whose life is saved in this way there is a multiplier effect, because also saved would be the people he might infect in turn. Public health professionals are in overwhelming agreement with this logic, and the school board agreed— but the New York Appellate Division was underwhelmed. Should the judges have been cautious about sacrificing what it considered common law or constitutional rights in the face of a public health emergency? *Cf. Jacobson v. Massachusetts*, 197 U.S. 11 (1905) (upholding state law requiring vaccination; even though law invaded fundamental liberty interest in the control of one's body, it was justified by public health concerns). If the AIDS emergency justifies sacrificing parental rights, might it not also be held to override other privacy rights, to justify mandatory HIV testing or even quarantines of people who test positive for this virus?

NOTE ON HIV/AIDS INSTRUCTION AS POSSIBLY CREATING A HOSTILE SCHOOL ENVIRONMENT FOR SOME STUDENTS

On April 8, 1992, Jason Mesiti and Shannon Silva attended a mandatory, school-wide assembly at Chelmsford High School. Both students were fifteen years old at the time. The assembly consisted of a ninety-minute presentation characterized by the school as an AIDS awareness program. The Program was staged by Suzi Landolphi and her corporation, Hot, Sexy, and Safer, Inc. Landolphi gave sexually explicit monologues and participated in sexually suggestive skits with several minors chosen from the audience.

Specifically, she allegedly (a) told the students that they were going to have a "group sexual experience, with audience participation"; (b) used profane, lewd, and lascivious language to describe body parts and excretory functions; (c) advocated and approved oral sex, masturbation, homosexual sexual activity, and condom use during promiscuous premarital sex; (d) simulated masturbation; (e) referred to being in "deep sh—" after anal sex; (f) had a male minor lick an oversized condom with her, after which she had a female minor pull it over the male minor's entire head and blow it up; (g) encouraged a male minor to display his "orgasm face" with her for the camera; (h) closely inspected a minor and told him he had a "nice butt"; and (i) made eighteen references to orgasms, six references to male genitals, and eight references to female genitals.

Mesiti and Silva were raised in very traditional homes and adhere to conservative views about human sexuality; both feel that people's sexuality is one of the most intimate things about them and should not be publicly displayed or made sport of. They were embarrassed by Landolphi's speech and its fallout among students. Many students copied Landolphi's routines and generally displayed overtly sexual behavior in the weeks following the program. They expressed their feelings to the school administration, complaining that they could not concentrate on their schoolwork because of the embarrassment they felt and the "unsettled" atmosphere created by the program.

The administration refused to change the program or otherwise be responsive to these complaints, and Mesiti's and Silva's parents complained to the Office of Civil Rights of the Department of Education that such mandatory programs constituted sexual harassment under Title IX. Should the OCR agree and pressure the school? The First Circuit in *Brown v. Hot, Sexy and Safer Productions, Inc.*, 68 F.3d 525 (1st Cir.1995), *cert. denied*, 516 U.S. 1159 (1996), ruled that the program did not create a hostile environment. Is that consistent with Chief Justice Burger's opinion for the Court in *Fraser* (Section 1 of this chapter)?

COMPARATIVE LAW NOTE: AMERICAN VERSUS EUROPEAN SEX EDUCATION POLICIES[b]

Glancing at a pair of American and German advertisements promoting safe sex, the American fear-based sex "dramatization" approach stands in stark contrast to the humorous German sex "normalization" approach, which is common elsewhere in Western Europe. *See* Amy Schalet, "Must We Fear Adolescent Sexuality?" *6(4) Medscape General Medicine* (2004), *available at* http://www.medscape.com. These visuals are perhaps the first step to understanding the difference in American and Western European teenage sex statistics: even though most teenagers in Western Europe and America first engage in sexual intercourse at age 17, there is little similarity among other teenage sexuality related statistics. *See* Jacqueline Darroch et al. "Differences in Teenage Pregnancy Rates Among Five Developed Countries: The Roles of Sexual Activity and Contraceptive Use," *33 Fam. Plan. Persp.*

---

[b]   Eva Rigamonti, Yale Law School Class of 2012, developed this Note.

244, 281 (2001); Facts on American Teen's Sexual and Reproductive Health (Jan. 2010), http://www.guttmacher.org/pubs/FB–ATSRH.html (last visited Dec. 2, 2010). In the U.S., not only is the teen pregnancy rate three to six times higher than in Western European countries, American teenagers also experience higher rates of sexually transmitted diseases. For example, the annual gonorrhea rate for U.S. adolescents is 10 or more times higher than the level in Sweden, England, and France and rates of U.S. teenage HIV are six times higher than in Germany. Darroch, "Teenage Pregnancy Rates," 244.

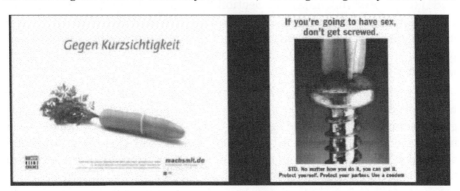

Translated as "Prevent Shortsightedness," the German ad uses humor to encourage responsible sexual behavior. (See Rachael Phelps, "Dream Team: The European Approach to Teens, Sex, and Love, in Pictures." http://www.slate.com/id/2272631?obref=obinsite (last visited Dec. 2, 2010).) In contrast the American ad is a scare tactic, exemplifying the U.S. approach to sex as a gendered conflict or inherent "battle of the sexes" where "boys want sex and girls want love." Schalet, "Adolescent Sexuality." The American approach is, apparently, less successful than that followed in Europe, as the data in the table below suggest.

Pregnancies, Abortions, & Births per 1000 American and Dutch Women, Ages 15–19

	Birth Rate US	Birth Rate NL	Abortion US	Abortion NL	Pregnancy US	Pregnancy NL
1970	68.3	22.6	19.1	6.6	95.1	U
1980	53.2	9.2	42.8	5.3	110.0	14.5
1990	60.3	6.4	40.5	4.0	116.9	10.4
2000 (all)	47.7	5.5	24.0	8.6	83.6	14.1
2000 (white)	32.2	4.1	14.6	4.9	54.7	9.0

Source: Schalet, "Adolescent Sexuality"

D. LGBT ISSUES IN THE CLASSROOM

For most of the twentieth century, the big issue for public schools was whether they could tolerate openly gay or lesbian teachers. Generally, before Stonewall, almost no teacher was "out," but occasionally witch hunts would expose "homosexual" teachers, who would be quietly purged from the system. Most Americans believed that lesbian and gay people were unacceptable as teachers, because they would prey on the students.

In the 1970s and 1980s, more teachers inched out of the closet, and some of them were fired. Courts generally allowed schools to discriminate in this way, e.g., *Rowland v. Mad River Sch. Dist.*, 730 F.2d 444 (6th Cir. 1984) (excerpted in Chapter 3, Section 3A), but by the 1990s the tide had turned and courts were usually willing to protect such public employees against discharge based only on their sexual orientation. Today, there are fewer public schools that will openly discriminate against LGBT teachers.

In these earlier decades, LGBT students were largely unseen but not heard. Today, public schools are teeming with students who are gay, gender-bending, undecided, and so forth. Gay-straight alliances have blossomed in high schools all over America. Nonetheless, a lot of states and school districts still operate under policies that are unfriendly or hostile to LGBT students.

NOTES ON THE EVOLUTION OF DISCOURSE RELATING TO LGBT ISSUES IN SECONDARY SCHOOLS

Since 1987, when Senator Jesse Helms started introducing "no promotion of homosexuality" language into federal spending bills, a big issue of education policy has been what schools can or should say about homosexuality. A handful of states, including Alabama, Arizona, Oklahoma, Texas, and Utah have statewide policies that requires public schools to talk about homosexuality in a negative light. A few states have gone in the opposite direction and have prohibited the use of curriculum that presents LGBT people in a negative light. More commonly, however, there is no official state-wide policy and the battles is fought at the school board level.

Regardless of what level of government makes the decision, there are three basic approaches with regard to teaching about LGBT issues in public schools:

1.   *Anti-LGBT Instruction.* As noted above, one approach is to send only negative messages about homosexuality. An extreme example of this approach was the requirement in Oregon's 1992 Ballot Measure 9 that would have required public schools to "recognize[ ] homosexuality, pedophilia, sadism and masochism as abnormal, wrong, unnatural and perverse and * * * to be discouraged and avoided."

More typical is the Alabama statute quoted at the beginning of this section, and the Arizona statute quoted just below. The rationale of these anti-homosexual policies is to inculcate a respect for heterosexuality among adolescents, so as to influence their sexual development in ways the society deems productive.

Teemu Ruskola, "Minor Disregard: The Legal Construction of the Fantasy That Gay and Lesbian Youth Do Not Exist," *8 Yale J.L. & Fem.* 269

(1996), disputes this approach on the ground that state signals reinforcing anti-gay social norms are extremely destructive to lesbian and gay youth and contribute to at least some of the many gay teen suicides each year. Professor Ruskola also ties these anti-gay educational policies to the double bind described by Eve Sedgwick (Chapter 4, Section 3). He considers this a decisive normative argument against such policies, but the layers of possible argument are complex. Traditionalists can respond with both the minoritizing and universalizing moves Sedgwick describes: from their point of view, homosexuality is an unspeakable aberration (minoritizing)—but it can happen to any adolescent wavering on the precipice of sexual maturity (universalizing). This mental construct has dramatic consequences for the regulatory parent or state, as they fear that the drama of sexual development can be derailed or highjacked at any point and by any number of factors and no one really is sure of all the "bad things" that can do this. Because the consequences of homosexuality for the wavering adolescent are, allegedly, so horrible and the causes of derailment so diverse and mysterious, under this scenario, the homo-anxious parent desiring to err on the side of caution will cast a beady eye on anything that seems to normalize homosexuality for the adolescent.

2.   *Don't Ask, Don't Tell.* A second approach is to try to avoid the issue altogether. In 1991, New York City School District 24 mandated that "any reference to * * * homosexuality * * * be eliminated from the curriculum." Nancy Tenney, Note, "The Constitutional Imperative of Reality in Public School Curricula: Untruths About Homosexuality as a Violation of the First Amendment," 60 *Brooklyn L. Rev.* 1599, 1603 n.16 (1995) (quoting the letter); Sexuality, Information, and Education Council of the United States, "SexEd Library," *available at* http://www.sexedlibrary.org/ (viewed Nov. 4, 2010) (providing 100 lessons that schools, including home schools, can use to provide fact-based, less normative sex education to minors).

This approach has the supposed advantage of neutrality: the state neither condemns nor endorses this controversial sexual orientation. Also, it is a policy many parents are most comfortable with.

Some argue, however, that in practice this approach is not neutral, given the negative messages about LGBT people that permeate our culture. Ruskola, for example, argues that this is almost as bad a policy as the first, for it erases homosexuality from school culture in ways that leave LGBT teens just as vulnerable, confused, and potentially suicidal. Teemu Ruskola, "Minor Disregard: The Legal Construction of the Fantasy That Gay and Lesbian Youth Do Not Exist," *8 Yale J.L. & Fem.* 269 (1996). Moreover, supportive teachers and school officials may feel as though they are precluded under such a policy from intervening when they hear or witness anti-LGBT harassment and discrimination.

3.   *LGBT-Tolerant or Pro-LGBT Instruction.* Another approach provides students with inclusive and positive information about LGBT people and issues. This approach responds to recent findings that being in a safe and supportive school environment can help students manage and even counteract the documented traumas many LGBT adolescents suffer in high school. For example, GLSEN's 2015 National School Climate Survey found that "students who feel safe and affirmed have better educational outcomes." (finding, among other things, that 57.6% of "LGBTQ students felt unsafe at school because of their sexual orientation"). This approach—to require the positive inclusion of LGBTQ issues—is consistent with or even mandated by the policies in about half the states prohibiting discrimination on the basis of sexual orientation and gender identity.

Clifford Rosky, "Anti-Gay Curriculum Laws," ___ *Colum. L. Rev.* ___ (forthcoming). Scholars have observed that several states have "no promo homo" education laws, namely, laws requiring teachers and curricula to avoid any support for "homosexuality." Professor Rosky's article is the most thorough survey and analysis of these kinds of laws and policies.

"While scholars and advocates have claimed that 'no promo homo' laws exist in seven, eight, or nine states, a comprehensive survey shows that anti-gay curriculum laws actually exist in twenty states.[24] More than 25 million children—nearly half of all school-aged children in the United States—are attending public schools in these twenty states. In half of these states, teachers are affirmatively required to teach anti-gay curricula in all public schools. In the other half, teachers may choose between offering students an anti-gay curriculum or providing no health, sex, or HIV education at all."

Professor Rosky identifies five different kinds of anti-gay curriculum laws: (1) "don't say gay" laws that bar any mention of homosexuality; (2) "no promo homo" laws that admonish against saying anything positive about homosexuality; (3) "anti-gay" policies requiring negative treatment of homosexuality; (4) "promo hetero" laws that require instruction promoting "monogamous heterosexual marriage"; and (5) "abstinence until marriage" laws, requiring teachers to emphasize "abstinence from sexual activity until marriage," while defining the term "marriage" to exclude same-sex couples (these laws are the most common, found in seventeen states). The most prominent example of an "abstinence until marriage" law is Title V of the Social Security Act, governing the distribution of funds for "abstinence education" programs.

Professor Rosky maintains that all of these laws violate the Equal Protection Clause. "In four rulings issued over a period of twenty years, the Supreme Court has invalidated anti-gay laws under the equal protection and due process guarantees of the Fifth and Fourteenth Amendments. Based on the principles articulated in these cases, [the

---

[24] ALA. CODE § 16–40A–2; ARIZ. REV. STAT. ANN. § 15–716; ARK. CODE ANN. § 6–18–703; FLORIDA STAT. ANN. § 1003.46; 105 ILL. COMP. STAT. ANN. 5/27–9.1; IND. CODE ANN. § 20–34–3–17(A) & § 20–30–5–13; LA. REV. STAT. § 17:281; MICH. COMP. LAWS ANN. § 380.1507; MISS. CODE ANN. § 37–13–171; MO. STAT. ANN. § 170.015; N.C. GEN. STAT. ANN. § 115C–81; N.D. CENT. CODE ANN. § 15.1–21–24; OHIO REV. CODE ANN. § 3313.6011; 70 OKLA. STAT. ANN. § 11–103.3 (2016); S.C. CODE ANN. § 59–32–30(A) (2016); TENN. CODE ANN. § 49–6–1304; TEX. HEALTH & SAFETY CODE ANN. § 85.007 & § 163.002; UTAH CODE ANN. § 53A–13–101; VA. CODE ANN. § 22.1–207.1; WIS. STAT. ANN. § 118.019.

article explains] how anti-gay curriculum laws injure and stigmatize lesbian, gay, and bisexual students, as well as students who are the children of same-sex couples. Like anti-gay sodomy and marriage laws, anti-gay curriculum laws demean the lives of lesbian, gay, and bisexual people, inviting others to discriminate against them. In particular, these laws promote a climate of silence and shame for lesbian, gay, bisexual students, and students who are the children of same-sex couples, by instructing them that 'homosexuality' is so shameful, immoral, or unlawful that it should not be discussed. By doing so, these laws deny this class of students an equal opportunity to learn basic information about themselves and their families—information about the social prevalence and legal status of their own feelings, relationships, identities, and family members. Finally, anti-gay curriculum laws contribute to the pervasive isolation, bullying and harassment experienced by LGBT students in our nation's schools, exposing them to increased risks of pregnancy, HIV, school dropout, unemployment, and suicide."

Professor Rosky then "explains why these laws are not rationally related to any legitimate governmental interests. In particular, [he] reviews and rejects four interests that state legislatures have historically invoked to justify anti-gay curriculum laws: (1) promoting moral disapproval of homosexual conduct; (2) promoting children's heterosexual development; (3) preventing sexually transmitted infections; and (4) recognizing that States have broad authority to prescribe the curriculum of public schools. Under the principles articulated in *Romer v. Evans*, *Lawrence v. Texas*, and *United States v. Windsor*, the first and second interests do not qualify as legitimate. The third and fourth interests qualify as legitimate, but anti-gay curriculum laws are not rationally related to either of them. Although no court has ruled on the issue yet, the Supreme Court's jurisprudence leaves no doubt that anti-gay curriculum laws violate the Constitution's equal protection guarantees.

"Since the Supreme Court's invalidation of anti-gay marriage laws, scholars and advocates have begun asking 'what's next' for the LGBT movement. The article concludes by explaining why LGBT advocates have waited until now to launch a campaign against anti-gay curriculum laws—and why they should not wait any longer. As long as anti-gay sodomy and anti-gay marriage laws were enforceable, anti-gay curriculum laws could have been justified by reference to them—as the state's means of deterring public school students from engaging in criminal conduct or extramarital sex. Now that sodomy and marriage laws have been declared unconstitutional, LGBT advocates can launch a national campaign to invalidate anti-gay curriculum laws."

Postscript. In the course of writing this article, Professor Rosky worked with Equality Utah to bring a lawsuit challenging the constitutionality of Utah's anti-gay curriculum law. In response to the lawsuit and the arguments developed in the article, the Utah Legislature repealed its anti-gay curriculum law in 2017. The sponsor of the repeal was Senator Stuart Adams, who had sponsored the Utah Compromise in 2015.

———————————

For an example of the "no promo homo" approach, consider the following Arizona statute.

Arizona Revised Statutes § 15–716, Instruction on Acquired Immune Deficiency Syndrome

(Added 1991, amended 1995; no further amendments as of April 2017).

A.   Each common, high and unified school district may provide instruction to kindergarten programs through the twelfth grade on acquired immune deficiency syndrome and the human immunodeficiency virus.

B.   Each district is free to develop its own course of study for each grade. At a minimum, instruction shall:

1.   Be appropriate to the grade level in which it is offered.

2.   Be medically accurate.

3.   Promote abstinence.

4.   Discourage drug abuse.

5.   Dispel myths regarding transmission of the human immunodeficiency virus.

C.   No district shall include in its course of study instruction which:

1.   Promotes a homosexual life-style.

2.   Portrays homosexuality as a positive alternative life-style.

3.   Suggests that some methods of sex are safe methods of homosexual sex.

D.   At the request of a school district, the department of health services or the department of education shall review instruction materials to determine their medical accuracy.

E.   At the request of a school district, the department of education shall provide the following assistance:

1.   A suggested course of study.

2.   Teacher training.

3.   A list of available films and other teaching aids.

F.   At the request of a parent, a pupil shall be excused from instruction on the acquired immune deficiency syndrome and the human immunodeficiency virus as provided in subsection A of this section. The school district shall notify all parents of their ability to withdraw their child from the instruction.

PROBLEM 8-9
STATE HIV/AIDS EDUCATION AND THE POLICY AGAINST PROMOTING HOMOSEXUALITY

You are the general counsel to Arizona's department of education. School districts describe their proposed AIDS awareness programs to you, and you counsel them on whether their proposals violate the statute. Consider the following three programs:

1. *Hot, Sexy and Safer.* Recall the program described in our Note on HIV/AIDS Instruction and Hostile School Environments, and assume that it does not constitute illegal sexual harassment. What modifications would have to be made in the program to make it acceptable under the Arizona statute?

2. *Safe Lesbian Sex.* One high school wants to teach a class on "Sexuality and Disease" (including HIV/AIDS). The school submits materials, which include a detailed description of safer sex techniques, including explicit statements that oral sex with a condom or dental dam is 99.99% safe. Also the materials note that the rate of HIV infection is lower for lesbians than it is for straight women, straight or bisexual men, and gay men. You notify the school that these portions of the instruction seem to violate § 15–716(C)(3), as they suggest that homosexual oral sex and sex between women are relatively safe. The school rejoins that § 15–716(C)(3) is unconstitutional on its face or as applied. What do you have to say to that?

3. *The Homosexual Life Style.* Another high school submits a program which contains an entire segment on gay youth. According to the compiled materials, the segment teaches that adolescents generally do not choose their sexual orientation, that this is a neutral feature of someone's personhood, and that straight as well as gay youth should consult with a health professional to learn about safer sex before they become sexually active. The segment includes stories by gay, bisexual, and straight adolescents who have been infected with HIV by their different-sex and same-sex partners; the stories warn of the ease with which inexperienced youth can lapse into unsafe sex. Throughout the materials, homosexual attraction is treated as normal but is not singled out for special attention. Do these materials pass muster under the statute?

Gay Men's Health Crisis et al. v. Dr. Louis Sullivan
United States District Court for the Southern District of New York, 1992.
792 F.Supp. 278.

■ KRAM, DISTRICT JUDGE. * * *

Subsequent to [*GMHC v. Sullivan*, 733 F. Supp. 619 (S.D.N.Y.1989) ("*GMHC I*")], the CDC [Center for Disease Control] published a notice of revised grant terms and requested public comment on the proposed changes. See 55 Fed. Reg. 10667 (March 22, 1990). Parts (a) and (b) of the proposed revised Basic Principles read as follows:

> a. Language used in written materials . . . , audiovisual materials . . . , and pictorials . . . to describe dangerous behaviors and explain less risky practices concerning HIV transmission should use terms, descriptors, or displays necessary for the intended audience to understand the messages.

> b. Written materials, audiovisual materials, and pictorials should not include terms, descriptors, or displays which will be offensive to a majority of the intended audience or to a majority of persons outside the intended audience.

The CDC received 133 comments on the proposed revised grant terms. 55 Fed. Reg. 23414 (June 7, 1990). [Although none objected to the requirement that materials not be offensive to a majority of the intended audience, 86 objected to the requirement that materials not be offensive "to a majority of persons outside the intended audience." (Five concurred with this requirement). The CDC's Revised Grant Terms revised Part (b) as follows:

> b. Written materials, audiovisual materials, and pictorials should not include terms, descriptors, or displays which will be offensive to a majority of the intended audience or to a majority of adults outside the intended audience unless, in the judgment of the Program Review Panel [PRP], the potential offensiveness of such materials is outweighed by the potential effectiveness in communicating an important HIV prevention message. 55 Fed. Reg. 23414 (June 7, 1990).

The CDC's Revision of Requirements for Content of HIV/AIDS-Related Written materials, Pictorials, Audiovisuals, Questionnaires, Survey Instruments, and Educational Sessions in Centers for Disease Control Assistance Programs eliminated the requirements of the Kennedy-Cranston Amendment from its grant terms. The Kennedy-Cranston Amendment, first incorporated into the fiscal year 1989 appropriations act, P.L. 100–436 (1988), provided that AIDS education programs funded by CDC "shall not be designed to promote or encourage, directly, intravenous drug abuse or sexual activity, homosexual or heterosexual." This language was incorporated into funding statutes for fiscal years 1989–91. But the CDC opined that the underlying standards remain unchanged, as "any material which would have failed to meet the Kennedy-Cranston standard * * * would also fail to meet the 'offensiveness' standard that continues as part of the Basic Principles to be applied by Program Review Panels."]

The Court * * * finds that in using the "offensiveness" criterion, the CDC has contravened its statutory authority which bars funding only of obscene, not offensive material. 42 U.S.C. § 300ee(d). Defendants' argument that Congress intended only to set a floor in enacting subsection (d) is untenable in light of the legislative history of the statute. In fact, the legislative history makes clear that Congress intended the language of 42 U.S.C. § 300ee(d) to be a ceiling on the conditions that can be placed on AIDS education materials. The legislative history makes reference to the "necessity of reaching the highest risk groups *by whatever means will catch their attention.*" S.Rep. No. 100–133 at 6–7 (emphasis added). Moreover, Senator Cranston explained that the language that became 42 U.S.C. § 300ee was added to the legislation to allow "an aggressive education and prevention campaign." Further, a letter by Senator Cranston, which was incorporated into his remarks, noted that through repeated votes, Congress "has made clear its intent: The federal government *must not interfere with or hamstring public health efforts to educate* all Americans, including gay and bisexual men, about AIDS. . . ." 134 Cong.Rec. S15693 (Oct. 13, 1988) (emphasis added). * * *

[The Court found that the CDC's offensiveness standard was contrary to the statute. In the next part of its opinion, the Court found the standards unconstitutional in any event, because they provided vague and standardless criteria for decision-makers and therefore opened the door for censorship of information about AIDS.]

[T]he "offensiveness" standard remains essentially undefined. To date, the CDC has made no affirmative statement as to what constitutes "offensive" materials, nor has it set forth a method by which to determine what materials will be deemed "offensive" under the Revised Grant Terms. As such, plaintiffs are correct when they assert that the Revised Grant Terms provide no way of answering questions such as: Can educational material be offensive simply because it mentions homosexuality? Because it depicts an interracial couple? Can a proposed AIDS education project be offensive because it traps a captive audience, such as subway riders, and forces them to look at a condom? Does offensive apply to all descriptions of sexual behavior, graphic depictions of sexual behavior, or descriptions of unusual sexual behavior? * * *

This lack of guidance is especially troubling given that the Revised Grant Terms require PRP members to gauge the reactions of members of the public, see *Big Mama Rag, Inc. v. United States*, 631 F.2d 1030, 1037 (D.C. Cir.1980) (the regulation's vagueness is especially apparent in that portion of the test expressly based on an individualistic—and therefore necessarily varying and unascertainable—standard: the reactions of members of the public), as well as engage in two levels of subjective analysis, *i.e.*, PRP members have to form their own subjective opinions about the subjective opinions of a majority of other adults. Specifically, PRP members have to make a subjective determination as to what a majority of other adults will think offensive. * * *

Defendants contend that the core meaning of the "offensiveness" standard has been defined not only by examples contained in the Revised

Grant Terms themselves, but by reference to the obscenity standard. According to the defendants, since the "offensiveness" standard clearly encompasses legally "obscene" materials, the Revised Grant Terms contain a core meaning. The Court disagrees.

As the plaintiffs assert, a restriction that prohibited the funding of all "rude," "unpopular," "erotic," "annoying," "controversial," or "upsetting" materials would also likely encompass legally obscene materials. However, the fact that a broad, undefined, and vague term overlaps with a more specific, well-defined and constitutional prohibition, does not make the broader language constitutional. Because the obscenity standard is inherently narrower than the offensiveness criterion, there is a vast amount of material that could be developed that would be deemed offensive, but not obscene. As such, the Court finds that reference to the obscenity standard offers no real guidance or clarification to either AIDS educators or PRP members.

Moreover, the Court will not permit the defendants to rely on the judicially defined obscenity standard to provide the grant terms with core meaning, when they have chosen instead to impose a nebulous and undefined "offensiveness" standard. If defendants seek to rely on the constitutional obscenity standard, they should adopt it, as the plaintiffs have urged. * * *

* * * [T]he results of various PRP decisions indicate the arbitrariness of the Revised Grant Terms. In one instance, the National Association of Black and White Men Together ("BWMT") received a $1 million, five-year grant from the CDC to educate minority men who have sex with men. As part of its application, the organization included information about and a sample advertising poster for "Hot, Horny, and Healthy Playshops." The CDC approved the application without comment. The San Francisco PRP also approved the advertising poster as well as a second poster that depicted a white man and black man sitting on the floor together. In the District of Columbia and in Los Angeles, however, local affiliates of BWMT suffered disapprovals of proposals to hold such workshops with locally-distributed CDC money because the workshops were perceived as offensive and contrary to the grant terms. They also suffered disapprovals of the two advertising posters. * * *

Second, documents regarding the panels' deliberations as to the Original Grant Terms provide additional evidence of the unpredictable application of the grant terms. A review of the documents indicates that PRP members were unable to recognize any core meaning in the "offensiveness" criterion. For example, all of the following were given by PRP members as reasons for disapproving materials as "offensive":

(a) "I don't think cartoon figures are necessary to get the facts of AIDS across."

(b) "The patriotic connection with protection in the case of AIDS demeans Uncle Sam and all of us."

(c) "Tacky use of a respected symbol [Uncle Sam]"

(d) "Poor Taste"

(e) "Information on detailed safe sex practices should not be included in a general informational brochure on AIDS."

(f) "I have major concerns about using the image of a noted, deceased public figure, especially a Black leader [Dr. Martin Luther King]. While a poster for alcohol and drug abuse may be acceptable, there are certain implications regarding AIDS."

Since there has been no effective clarification of the "offensiveness" criterion, there is no reason to believe that the Revised Grant Terms are being applied in a less arbitrary fashion. In fact, those that have attended PRP meetings under the Revised Grant Terms "cannot say for sure the precise test that [the panel] is applying."

Evidence of self-censorship by AIDS education groups also provides evidence of the vagueness of the Revised Grant Terms. Because the grant terms are subjective and imprecise, AIDS educators cannot predict with any certainty what materials will be approved. Thus, they are forced to censor themselves and concentrate on proposals that will pass the "offensiveness" test with room to spare. * * *

As evidence of this chilling effect, plaintiff Horizons, as well as the American Red Cross, the Reimer Foundation, and the Tucson AIDS Project, have provided the Court with specific examples of projects that have been abandoned or toned down because of anticipated problems with PRP approval. [Some examples were Trowbridge Dec., ¶ 9 ("We determined that to avoid PRP rejection we would have to use" "semen," "feces," and "urine" [instead of "cum," "shit," and "piss"]); Comment letter from the American Red Cross, included in Exhibit B to Harlow Dec. I ("In developing brochures jointly with the CDC intended for adult women and men, we had to remove the colloquialism 'cum.' ").]

Moreover, all of the declarations from AIDS educators submitted in support of plaintiffs' motion describe the need to speculate ahead of time about what might happen under the indiscernible standard of the grant terms.

Further, for some organizations the deterrent effect of the grant terms is so strong, they avoid seeking CDC funding. Plaintiff Hetrick Martin Institute, for example, focuses its services on the gay and lesbian youth population. To reach this population, the Institute has determined that comic books, other materials that use vernacular language, and a gay-positive approach are essential. Under the Revised Grant Terms, however, Hetrick Martin believes that "we probably would be unable to secure approval of our educational materials by a Program Review Panel. Thus, it does not make practical sense for us to apply for CDC funding, although we could put additional funding for HIV prevention to good use in serving lesbian and gay youth." * * *

NOTES ON CONSTITUTIONAL CHALLENGES TO ANTI-LGBT CURRICULUM POLICIES

Gay Men's Health Crisis suggests three different kinds of legal problems with no promo homo health education policies. Because the decision is that of a federal district court, its precepts must be tested against those announced by the Supreme Court, of course. (The Department of Justice did not appeal Judge Kram's decision.)

1.   *Suppression of Expression.* A policy that prohibits officials from speaking about homosexuality, or that directs their speech in one direction, might violate the core command of the First Amendment: speech about an important public topic can almost never be censored. Recall *National Gay Task Force v. Oklahoma City* (Chapter 1, Section 5), where the appeals court invalidated a state statute prohibiting teachers from talking about homosexuality. That decision might be distinguished from cases where the school system is censoring what teachers can say in the classroom. If challenged by a teacher, would the Arizona statute referenced in Problem 8-9 pass constitutional muster?

2.   *Vagueness.* When the state or the school system establishes directives abridging speech, especially speech about important public topics, the courts require that the directives provide precise guidelines for those administering the directives, lest the administrators be left to act as censors at large. This was Judge Kram's big problem with the CDC's offensiveness regulation, which would probably have been constitutional in any arena but the free speech one. Does the Arizona statute referenced in Problem 8-9 satisfy this kind of stringent vagueness test? Recall, again, that none of these decisions was delivered by the Supreme Court and that the Supreme Court has been much more deferential to school districts and public health agencies than the Ninth Circuit has been.

3.   *Equal Protection.* Is Professor Rosky correct in arguing that laws that require schools to teach about sexual orientation in a negative light violate the Equal Protection Clause? Even if sexual orientation classifications trigger only rational basis review, what is the legitimate state interest that is furthered by such statutes? Can these statutes be reconciled with the Supreme Court's decision in *Obergefell*, which struck down state marriage laws that banned same-sex marriage? Although the Court's decision in *Obergefell* largely sounded in Due Process principles, the Court also declared that the challenged statutes "abridge[d] central precepts of equality" because the laws, especially against a long history of discrimination, served to "disrespect and subordinate" LGB people. *Obergefell v. Hodges*, 135 S. Ct. 2584, 2604 (2015). Can't the same thing be said about these anti-gay curriculum laws? Is there some way to distinguish them from the anti-LGB marriage laws before the Court in *Obergefell*?

NOTE ON CALIFORNIA'S EDUCATION ANTIDISCRIMINATION LAWS

In contrast to "no promo homo" jurisdictions like Alabama and Arizona, the California Legislature has restructured, by law, the tone of public, and some private, education in that state. California law expressly prohibits discrimination on the bases of gender identity, gender expression, and sexual orientation in school:

> No person shall be subjected to discrimination on the basis of disability, gender, gender identity, gender expression, nationality, race or ethnicity, religion, sexual orientation, * * * in any program or activity conducted by an educational institution that receives, or benefits from, state financial assistance or enrolls pupils who receive state student financial aid.

Cal. Educ. Code § 220.

California also actively promotes LGBT tolerance through its instructional and material curriculum requirements. For example, all schools are required to teach comprehensive sex education, and all sexual health education requires "[i]nstruction and materials [to] affirmatively recognize that people have different sexual orientations and, when discussing or providing examples of relationships and couples, [to] be inclusive of same-sex relationships." California law also provides that sex education "[i]nstruction and materials shall not reflect or promote bias against any person on the basis of any category protected by Section 220." Cal. Educ. Code §§ 51933(d)(5), 51933(d)(4).

In California, inclusive, affirming instruction is not limited to the context of sex education. As of January 1, 2012, instruction in social sciences must include a study of the contributions of LGBT Americans. Cal. Educ. Code § 51204.5. Public school teachers in California are precluded from giving instruction or sponsoring an activity that "promotes a discriminatory bias on the basis of" gender identity, gender expression, or sexual orientation. Cal. Educ. Code § 51500.

Moreover, case law makes clear that California school districts are prohibited from ignoring or being indifferent to issues and harassment regarding sexual orientation and require school districts to actively address discrimination. *See, e.g., Donovan v. Poway Unified Sch. Dist.*, 167 Cal. App.4th 567 (2008) (finding deliberate indifference to two students, who claimed sexual orientation discrimination by the school, supporting liability).

CHAPTER 9

MILITARY, PRISONS, AND THE CONSTRUCTION OF MANHOOD

SECTION 1   Exclusions and Segregation in the U.S. Armed Forces
SECTION 2   Sexual Harassment, Sexual Violence, and Sexual Conduct in the
             U.S. Armed Forces
SECTION 3   Due Process and Equal Protection in Prison
SECTION 4   Sexual Harassment, Sexual Violence, and Sexual Conduct in Prison
SECTION 5   Access to Health Care in Prison

The military and prisons are two government-run institutions that regulate almost all aspects of the lives of individuals under their control. Through their express policies and their culture, the military and prisons are environments in which notions of manhood and masculinity are created and reproduced. As a result, both institutions play important roles in shaping attitudes about sex, gender, and sexuality.

One way in which the military has shaped conceptions of sex and sexuality is through its exclusions. Initially, the military excluded people of color. This policy later morphed into a policy of segregation, which was officially ended in the 1950s. Women, likewise were traditionally excluded from service altogether. After the blanket ban was lifted, women were still precluded from serving in combat positions until very recently. The military long banned lesbians, gay men, and bisexuals from serving. Although the ban on openly LGB servicemembers was finally ended in September 2011, the military still bans openly transgender people from enlisting and, starting in March 2018, the military will again preclude transgender people from serving openly in the armed forces. Although each exclusion has its own history, one function they all share is policing the social understanding of "manhood."

The military's exclusions have focused on three classic discriminatory classifications: race, sex, and sexual orientation. Building on the constitutional principles introduced in Chapters 1–3, Section 1 considers whether the military should be permitted to classify and exclude along these lines. Does traditional equal protection doctrine apply with equal force to the military? Why or why not? In any event, how does each exclusion fare under an equal protection challenge? Section 2 then explores other ways in which the military regulates sex and sexuality, including through the military's treatment of sex-based harassment and discrimination, and its regulation of pregnancy and sexual activity within the military.

Prison is another government-run institution that has played and continues to play an important role in shaping conceptions of sex and sexuality. While express sex-based distinctions have been largely eliminated in most other government-run programs, sex-based classifications are a core aspect of prisons, which are almost always separated (or, some may say segregated) by sex. Section 3 begins the exploration of prisons by examining the extent to which the constitutional principles of due process and equal protection apply in prison. Under what circumstances, for example, can prisons restrict prisoners' right to marry? Their right to procreate? Their right to terminate a pregnancy?

Section 4 grapples with issues related to sexual conduct and sexual violence in prison. Although formally banned, sexual conduct is common in prison. Violent or coercive sexual conduct is also common. What obligations do prisons have to respond to this reality? Is it permissible to place vulnerable individuals, including LGBT people, in isolation as a means of protecting them?

Section 5 explores the obligation of prison officials to provide health care to those in their custody, including transition-related and reproductive health care.

SECTION 1

EXCLUSIONS AND SEGREGATION IN THE U.S. ARMED FORCES

A. RACIAL EXCLUSIONS AND SEGREGATION

Military service and citizenship are and have been deeply linked throughout our history. In *Dred Scott v. Sandford*, 60 U.S. 393 (1856), the primary evidence Chief Justice Roger Taney invoked to support the proposition that an African-American could not be a *citizen* for diversity purposes was the fact that, since the 1790s, Congress had excluded men of African descent from the United States armed forces.[a] Section 1 of the Fourteenth Amendment overrode this part of the *Dred Scott* holding, but African-Americans and other men of color continued to be excluded from or segregated in the armed services for several generations after Reconstruction. A central feature of the civil rights movement's politics of recognition for black Americans was an insistence that they be permitted to serve in the military on the same terms and under the same conditions as white Americans.

We start with Professor Kenneth Karst's article, which not only presents a rich history of that struggle, but also demonstrates the linkage between citizenship and military service also involves conceptions of what it has traditionally meant in the United States "to be a man."

Kenneth L. Karst, "The Pursuit of Manhood and the Desegregation of the Armed Forces"

38 *UCLA Law Review* 499–501, 502–08, 510–20 (1991).[*]

The statue of the Minuteman stands at the edge of the Lexington Battle Green as a reminder of the American tradition of the citizen soldier. From the Revolution onward, a great many Americans have believed that a citizen has the responsibility, in time of need, to serve in

---

[a] To support his ruling that an African American could not be a "citizen" for purposes of Article III's diversity jurisdiction, Taney invoked a 1792 statute (adopted by a Congress filled with constitutional framers) requiring every "free able-bodied white male citizen" to be enrolled in the militia. This was evidence that "the African race" owes allegiance to the United States, "but it is repudiated, and rejected from the duties and obligations of citizenship in marked language." *Dred Scott*, 60 U.S. at 420. Taney therefore created as a baseline presumption "the line of division which the Constitution has drawn between the citizen race, who formed and held the Government, and the African race, which they held in subjection and slavery, and governed at their own pleasure." *Id.*

[*] Originally published in the *UCLA Law Review*. Copyright © 1991, The Regents of the University of California. All Rights Reserved. Reprinted by permission.

the armed forces. The same association of ideas also works in the other direction: when we amended the Constitution to lower the voting age to eighteen, one prominent slogan was, "If they're old enough to fight, they're old enough to vote." In the United States, as in Europe, citizenship and eligibility for military service have gone hand in hand. [Karst argues that the exclusions of African Americans, women, and LGBT people from full and equal military service share a unifying theme.]

That unifying theme is the pursuit of manhood. Manhood, of course, has no existence except as it is expressed and perceived. The pursuit of manhood is an expressive undertaking, a series of dramatic performances. Masculinity is traditionally defined around the idea of power; the armed forces are the nation's preeminent symbol of power; and, not incidentally, "the Marines are looking for a few good men." The symbolism is not a side effect; it is the main point. From the colonial era to the middle of this century, our armed forces have alternately excluded and segregated blacks in the pursuit of manhood, and today's forms of exclusion and segregation are similarly grounded in the symbolism of masculine power. * * *

[The Problem of Manhood and the Ideology of Masculinity.] The connections between military service and citizenship were well understood during the Civil War. Immediately after the first shots at Fort Sumter, black citizens began to volunteer for service in the Union Army and the militia. At first these efforts were rebuffed. By law Congress had limited membership in the militia to whites, and the Lincoln administration, still wooing the border states, feared that admitting blacks to the Army would send the signal that the Union's aim was not merely the preservation of the Union, but the abolition of slavery. Furthermore, some generals "feared that the presence of black soldiers in the army would create disharmony and drive away white volunteers." * * *

The issue of full citizenship for black people was never far below the surface of the question of black participation in the Army and the militia. Both slavery and lesser forms of racial discrimination were premised on an assumption, sometimes explicit and sometimes unspoken, that denied manhood—in the full sense of competence to be citizens—to black men. Then, as now, a citizen was a respected and responsible participant in society, and especially in society's decisions. "Manhood suffrage," a term commonly used in the era of Andrew Jackson, was not a slogan of universality; it excluded women and tribal Indians, and even in the North it typically excluded black men. * * *

In fact there was, and still is, an ideal of manhood. Historically the ideal, like the word itself, has embraced at least two meanings: masculinity and eligibility for equal citizenship. For most of our national history these meanings have been intertwined; a competence identified with masculinity has seemed a condition of full citizenship, and active participation in the community's public life has offered men reassurance of their masculinity. Because it is an abstract ideal, a construct of the mind, manhood in the sense of masculinity is in some measure unattainable; it can be pursued, but never wholly achieved. Yet, the achievement of manhood is seen by most men as essential to their identities. In combination, these elements are a recipe for anxiety. So, manhood is not just an ideal; it is also a problem. The problem begins early, when a little boy must seek his gender identity by separating himself from his mother and from the softness, domesticity, and nurturing she represents. I use the term "represents" advisedly; gender, unlike sex, is not found in nature, but created and understood through representation, the playing of roles labeled "masculine" or "feminine."

Thus, masculinity begins in escape—the perceived need to separate from a feminine identity. The main demands for positive achievement of masculinity arise outside the home, and those demands reinforce the boy's need to be what his mother is not. In the hierarchical and rigorously competitive society of other boys, one categorical imperative outranks all the others: don't be a girl. Femininity is a "negative identity," a part of the self that must be repressed. The manhood pursued through male rivalry is more than maturity, more than adulthood; it also includes a set of qualities customarily defined as masculine. Although masculinity is defined against its polar opposite, the identification with competence and power in a male-dominated world has made it seem to be society's norm for being fully human. Femininity is seen, not merely as deviance from the norm, but as a fundamental flaw—a failure, at the deepest level, to qualify.

* * * The heart of the ideology of masculinity is the belief that power rightfully belongs to the masculine—that is, to those who display the traits traditionally called masculine. This belief has two corollaries. The first is that the gender line must be clearly drawn, and the second is that power is rightfully distributed among the masculine in proportion to their masculinity, as determined not merely by their physical stature or aggressiveness, but more generally by their ability to dominate and to avoid being dominated. Both parts of the ideology contribute to the subordination of groups. This function is easy to see in efforts to express the gender line in sharp definition; the ideology of masculinity will be effective in assigning power only if those who are masculine are clearly identified. The second corollary of the ideology highlights the centrality of male rivalry. By making anxiety into an everyday fact of life, it leads nervous men to seek reassurances of their masculinity through group rituals that express domination over other groups. In combination these two beliefs purport to justify power by tautology, to ground the legitimacy of domination in domination itself.

In our country's history, the male-rivalry strand of the ideology of masculinity is repeatedly visible in the readiness of white men, and especially poor white men, to exclude black men from equal citizenship.

During the Civil War the white men in the Northeast who were most visibly offended by the sight of blacks in uniform were recent immigrants from Ireland. Because they occupied the bottom of the employment ladder, they had little in the way of traditional masculine achievement to bolster their sense of self-worth. For the same reason they had much to fear from the competition of black laborers. * * * The Northern whites most bent on denying black men a traditional way of expressing manhood were those most in need of affirming their own.

* * * One standard mode of repression of our negative identities is to project them onto other people, and especially onto members of groups that have been subordinated. The process works so well that it becomes second nature to see those people not as persons, but as the abstractions we have projected upon them. Each abstraction is a mask, and it bears a label: blackness, for example, or femininity, or homosexuality. To a great many white heterosexual men these masks of the Other are frightening; when we police the color line and the gender line in the world around us, we are policing the same line in our own minds, defending our senses of self. The fear of members of subordinated groups is more than a fear of competition, or even retaliation. No spectre is more terrifying than our own negative identity. * * *

[Male Rivalry and the Double Battle of Black Soldiers.] Frederick Douglass saw black men in the Civil War as fighting a "double battle": for the Union but also for equality, against the slave power but also against racism. Black soldiers—and sailors and airmen and marines—have always had to fight the same double battle, in war as in peacetime. Today's Army is rightly called a success story, and yet even there muted forms of racial discrimination persist; the other services have considerably farther to go in eliminating racism's effects. Like every story focused on black Americans as a group, this one begins with slavery. The story's persistent themes, from the earliest beginnings, are the associations linking race and sex and violence. All these associations are grounded in the ideology of masculinity, and many of them have been engraved in law.

[*Race, Sex, and the Roots of White Male Anxiety*] In the eyes of Englishmen in the era of colonization, slavery implied something less than humanity, a status akin to that of a beast. This assumption was part of a logic that was circular; to complete the circle of justification, the defenders of black slavery argued that blacks were not fully human. Beneath the surface of these apologies lay both male rivalry and anxieties about self-definition. African men were thought by Europeans to be especially libidinous; it was easy for white men to project their own desires onto blacks, and to connect the need for control over blacks with the need to control themselves. This association was intensified in the American colonies as many white slaveholders came to exercise sexual privileges over female slaves; if white men's fears of slave revolts came to be associated with fears of black men's supposed sexual aggressiveness, no doubt one reason was the fear of retaliation.

Even in the North, the perception of black men as threatening had roots in the fears of violent slave insurrections that had gripped the white South ever since Nat Turner's revolt in 1831. Those southern fears found a military expression. [In *The Militant South, 1800–1861* (1956)], John Hope Franklin has written of "the militant South," an amalgam of martial spirit and gentlemanly chivalry that lives even today. In the slave states the militia was composed of all adult white males. It served as a focal point for local social life in white communities, but its main function was to enforce the rigid discipline of slavery's caste system. Typically it was organized into "the patrol," a nightly sweep of the streets and highways by groups of mounted militiamen. By their actions the patrol showed that whites were whistling in the dark when they assured each other that black men were docile, even cowardly. The patrol routinely searched slaves' houses and persons for weapons or stolen property. They arrested any black person outside his or her plantation without a pass, and dispersed meetings of blacks. They dispensed summary justice, punishing transgressions as they found them, then and there. The patrol's main mission, of course, was not punishment but intimidation. Being called "Cap'n" and riding the "beat" at night also promoted the riders' masculine self-images, and surely that result was not just a by-product of the enterprise. The patrol publicly symbolized both white male power and the social gulf between citizens and slaves.

Given this historical example, it was no wonder that the black men who volunteered to serve the Union in 1861 associated manhood and citizenship. Understandably, they believed that military service would allow them to be seen as men, as citizens. Once Northern blacks put on the uniform, they believed, it would be hard to deny them the vote. If Southern blacks were freed to serve as Union soldiers, the war would become a war to end slavery. Developments like these were just the recognitions of black manhood that many white men (especially working class whites) feared and that Frederick Douglass and other black leaders hoped for. As it happened, these recognitions came to pass—but only for a season.

By the end of 1862 the enlistment of black soldiers could be seen to serve a clear military need, even if President Lincoln and Secretary of War Stanton did insist on placing white officers in command of black regiments, and Congress did peg the pay of black soldiers below that of whites. The Union had suffered some important losses in the field, white enlistments had fallen, and large numbers of slaves had begun to cross the lines seeking freedom. The Emancipation Proclamation of 1863 not only provided a legal foundation for a social upheaval already begun, but converted a war to save the Union into a crusade for liberation. By war's end almost 200,000 black men had served in the federal services, including about a quarter of the entire Navy; counting blacks who served in other capacities—cooks and carpenters, laborers and laundresses, servants and spies—one estimate places the total number of blacks who served the Union armed forces at nearly 390,000. At first these troops were used almost entirely in support functions that mainly involved manual labor. Eventually, however, black soldiers were employed in combat, and some 37,000 were killed. In 1863 black regiments showed particular heroism at Port Hudson, at Milliken's Bend, and, as the movie *Glory* dramatized, at Fort Wagner.

The moment was ripe for a triumphant ending in which the wartime sacrifices of black men vindicated the claims of black people to full citizenship. Seventy years later, W. E. B. DuBois [in *Black Reconstruction in America* 104 (1935)] said it was the fact that the black man "rose and fought and killed" that enabled whites to proclaim him "a man and a brother. . . . Nothing else made Negro citizenship conceivable, but the record of the Negro soldier as a fighter." After the war three constitutional amendments and a package of Reconstruction civil rights acts not only abolished slavery, but promised black Americans equal citizenship, including the equal right to vote. Yet, formal citizenship was one thing, brotherhood quite another. * * * Black war veterans and black people generally learned that formal equality before the law could exist alongside the gravest sort of inequalities in fact. By the end of the century, racial discrimination remained a routine part of black people's experience in the North and West while the South had descended into the systematic racial subordination called Jim Crow.

A major motivating factor behind the Jim Crow segregation laws and the myriad social practices they reinforced was the pursuit of manhood among white men. As in the days of slavery, this pursuit translated into a need to deny and repress the manhood of black men. For "the militant South"—that is, for southern white men as a group—the humiliation of military defeat was compounded during twelve years of occupation by the Union army. By the late 1880s a sharp economic decline threatened the "family provider" function of large numbers of lower class white men, many of whom responded violently, removing black tenants from competition by driving them off desirable farm land. As economic recession deepened into depression, white violence against blacks intensified, taking new and more murderous forms. In the ensuing decades southern white lynch mobs and rioters would take thousands of black lives.

The problem of manhood was central in generating this violence. In the South, white men were supposed to be not only the providers for but also the protectors of women. Then as now, the fears of losing, of not measuring up to the manly ideal, could turn men toward group action aimed at group domination. The rivalry of black men was seen in terms that were not just economic; it threatened a social status that had previously been awarded for whiteness alone. And if the day-to-day demonstrations of competence by liberated black men posed a problem for white male self-esteem, the abstraction of black manhood was frightening. This objectification originated in fear and grew on fear.

The political and social arrangements during the Reconstruction years and in the succeeding decade also threatened white Southern manhood by subjecting male-female relations to considerable strain. For the upper classes, the old chivalry was in tatters. But Southern white men of all stations in life shared a deeper anxiety about their ability to protect the women around them. At all levels of white society men had long exaggerated the sense that they were sexual aggressors. Not uncommonly they had been taught to believe that their sexuality was an animal urge that must be kept under strict control. Such a belief was heightened by the prevailing view of white women as symbols of purity who were anything but sexual beings. In this abstract, dehumanizing construction of womanhood, sex was at once a duty and a violation. For white men these beliefs were the seedbed for tension and guilt; they also translated readily into a nightmare of male rivalry.

When the anxiety about man-as-provider fused together with anxieties centered on sexuality, the combination was explosive. The abstract image of pure Southern womanhood became identified with a vision of white supremacy. The white woman, as the "perpetuator of [white] superiority's legitimate line," had to be kept remote from any sexual approach of the black man. The abstraction of black manhood was transformed into "the specific image of the black beast rapist." Anxious in the pursuit of manhood, a white man who joined a lynch mob could find three kinds of reassurance. He symbolically repressed the beast in himself; he found a sense of power in a ritual that expressed group domination; and he satisfied himself, in the safety of the crowd, that he was man enough to protect the women. Although only about one-third of all the lynchings of black men grew out of charges of rape, it was black-white rape that most whites specified as a justification of lynching in general. The explanation is plain: The image of black-white rape symbolized white men's self-doubt at the most primitive level.

[The Double Battle in the 20th Century.] Even before World War I began, black leaders were calling for the Army to establish new black regiments and to train blacks to serve as officers. At the close of the Civil War, Congress for the first time had made four black regiments part of the Regular Army. Although they saw combat in the Indian wars and the Spanish-American War, black soldiers continued to be subjected to discrimination by the civilian populations near their garrisons. When the United States entered the war in 1917, W.E.B. DuBois, like Frederick Douglass before him, argued that blacks should not "bargain with our loyalty," but should close ranks with their fellow citizens, all the while asserting their rightful claims to equal citizenship: the vote; equal educational opportunity; an end to lynchings and segregation. For the cause of racial equality, he argued, "We want victory . . . but it must not be cheap bargaining, it must be clean and glorious, won by our manliness. . . ."

The experience of black soldiers in Europe fell far short of these high hopes. All of them served in segregated units that quickly became a "dumping ground" for ineffective officers. Most black draftees were assigned to labor units. Once in Europe, most blacks were placed under French command—perhaps because the officer corps of the United States Army largely shared the racial attitudes of the white South. When some black combat units performed unsatisfactorily, as some white units also had done, a few generals reacted by pronouncing black soldiers unfit for combat—despite contrary evidence from other black units. When they returned home, black veterans encountered the same old racial discrimination in a new and virulent form. In the South, their very presence, as living symbols of black manhood, challenged the Jim Crow system at its psychic foundations. The result was a new wave of racial violence, including the lynching of black veterans in their Army uniforms.

After the war the Navy stopped enlisting blacks for general service, relegating black enlisted men to work as stewards. The Army explicitly reaffirmed its policy of racial segregation, and kept blacks ineligible for service as airplane pilots or radio signalmen. As another world war approached, black leaders had good reason for announcing that they would resist efforts to restrict black troops to labor units. * * *

More than 1,000,000 black men and about 4,000 black women served in the [armed] forces during [World War II]. Some 900,000 of the men served in the Army, about three-quarters of them in menial jobs such as "road building, stevedoring, laundry, and fumigating." Even the training of blacks for combat was exceptional; and in 1942, when someone suggested to General George Marshall, the Army Chief of Staff, that black troops be sent to fight in North Africa, he responded that the commanders there would object. As in the Civil War and World War I, blacks had to "fight for the right to fight." On this front, despite a steady drumbeat of criticism from black newspapers and black leaders, the services mostly resisted change.

Occasionally, however, those who were agitating for a racially inclusive military force could win a small victory. In 1942 the Navy announced that it would no longer limit black enlistees to messmen's duties, but would allow blacks to volunteer for general service—which, in this case, meant other support duties. By the end of the war, black enlistees constituted about four percent of the Navy and two and a half percent of the Marine Corps. Segregation remained the rule, however; given the problems of separation on shipboard, in 1944 the Navy established two ships with all-black crews. Soon thereafter a new Secretary of the Navy ordered integration of the crews on twenty-five auxiliary ships.

Around the same time the Army, which had not placed black combat troops in the line, was ordered to do so by a War Department that was reacting to political criticism. In Europe, when infantrymen became scarce, the Army inserted some black platoons into larger combat units. In the Army Air Force the black pilots of the segregated ninety-ninth Pursuit Squadron performed well. Even so, Army officials sought to minimize publicity about the achievements of black soldiers, to avoid blurring the Army's public image.

As the Navy's preposterous deployment of separate-but-equal vessels illustrated, the services' segregation policy was costly. New and separate units had to be organized and staffed, and separate training facilities had to be built; given the disparity in educational opportunities for blacks and whites before they entered the service, segregation prevented the most effective training and assignment of black soldiers and sailors. The main costs of segregation, however, lay in another dimension of human experience, one in which the problem of manhood was central. In 1941, before the attack on Pearl Harbor, William H. Hastie, an aide to Secretary of War Henry L. Stimson (and later the first black judge of the United States Court of Appeals), had written to his boss, criticizing the segregation of the Army in the strongest terms:

The traditional mores of the South have been widely accepted and adopted by the Army as the basis of policy and practice affecting the Negro soldier. . . . This philosophy is not working. . . . In tactical units of the Army, the Negro is taught to be a fighting man[,] . . . a soldier. It is impossible to create a dual personality which will be on the one hand a fighting man toward the foreign enemy, and on the other, a craven who will accept treatment as less than a man at home. One hears with increasing frequency from colored soldiers the sentiment that since they have been called to fight they might just as well do their fighting here and now.

General Marshall, asked to respond, had said that segregation was an established American custom, that "the level of intelligence and occupational skill of the Negro population is considerably below that of the white," and that "experiments within the Army in the solution of social problems are fraught with danger to efficiency, discipline, and morale."

The connection between this assessment and the historic anxieties of white men about the rivalry of black males is not hard to see. Marshall's unstated assumption was that white soldiers would lack confidence in blacks and be hostile to them, for they defined black men in general as incompetent and cowardly. Furthermore, integrating the Army would eventually result in placing black men in some positions of leadership; white soldiers would not accept this inversion of the historic racial definition of authority. Like all the Army's top leaders, Marshall had served in World War I and remembered the old accusations against black troops. But his assumption about the effect of integration on white attitudes proved mistaken. At the end of the war the Army took a survey of white soldiers who had served in combat alongside black platoons. At first, they said, they were resentful. But three-quarters of them said "their regard for the Negro had risen" as a result of the experience. By doing their jobs well, black soldiers expressed their competence and so, in this limited way, performed functions of education and persuasion. * * *

NOTES ON RACIAL SEGREGATION IN THE U.S. ARMED FORCES (1940S)

1.   *The Uniform Resistance of the Top Brass to Desegregation.* Virtually all the nation's military leaders in the 1940s were opposed to the racial integration of the armed forces. The military's top brass during World War II not only refused to integrate their armed forces, but were also reluctant to assign important duties to black units because of their "general consensus of opinion that colored units [we]re inferior to the performance of white troops, except for service duties, * * * due to the inherent psychology of the colored race and their need for leadership." Memo from General R.W. Crawford to General Eisenhower, Apr. 2, 1942, quoted in Richard Dalfiume, *Desegregation of the U.S. Armed Forces* 60 (1969). All the branches of the armed services in the 1940s concentrated African-Americans in service branches because of the "general assumption within the armed forces that Negroes could perform only unskilled jobs and that they were particularly suited for labor units." Dalfiume, *Desegregation* 61. Recall General George Marshall's comment, quoted in the Karst article. Integration, military leaders believed, would weaken the efficiency of the armed forces. Morris MacGregor, Jr., *Integration of the Armed Forces, 1940–1965* 441 (1981). Many service members, especially white soldiers, also opposed integration of the forces. A 1942 poll of Army service members found that more than 90% of the white soldiers supported segregated units, as did 30–40% of the black soldiers. *Id.* at 40.

2.   *The Attitudes of Black and White Soldiers During World War II.* Why were attitudes so sour? Theoreticians such as Professor Karst maintain that a large and perhaps preponderant part of the tension between the races was sexual in nature. *See also* Herbert Hovenkamp, "Social Science and Segregation Before *Brown*," 1985 *Duke L.J.* 624.[b] In a 1942 survey, for example, the Army surveyed its members. The report, based on the survey, reprinted some of the most extreme statements, including the following:

> [One survey response:] Negro troops have the girls come down to camp and call for them. If anything will make a Southern's Blood run hot it is to see this happen. Things around this camp is getting pretty hot about these negro troops and white [English] girls. If it

---

[b]   The documents quoted in text can all be found in the National Archives (Suitland, Maryland), Record Group 338, Records of U.S. Army Commands, 1942 ff, European Theatre, Adjutant General's Section, Administrative Branch, Classified General Correspondence, 1942–44, 1945, Decimal File 250.1.

keeps on going as it is we will have a nice negro lynching down here and then things will be better.

G-1 Section, European Theatre of Operations, "Survey of Soldier Opinion, European Theatre of Operations, Sept. 14–26, 1942."

It was reported, also in 1942, that white officers in charge of a black unit stationed in Pennsylvania issued the following order: "any association between the colored soldiers and white women, whether voluntary or not, would be considered rape." The punishment for this offense was the death penalty. Dalfiume 69.

3. *Executive Order 9981.* Although all top military officials opposed integration, others disagreed. In 1947, the President's Committee on Civil Rights condemned racial segregation in the military. "Prejudice in any area is an ugly, undemocratic phenomenon," the Committee wrote, but the Committee continued, "in the armed services where all men run the risk of death, it is particularly repugnant." *To Secure These Rights: The Report of the President's Committee on Civil Rights* 41 (1947).

On July 26, 1948, President Truman signed Executive Order 9981, which ordered the branches of the military to ensure "equality of treatment and opportunity for all persons in the armed services without regard to race, color, religion, or national origin." The order also created a "President's Committee on Equality of Treatment and Opportunity" which was tasked with determining how the "rules, procedures and practices [of the armed forces] may be altered or improved with a view to carrying out the policy" of the Executive Order.

4. *Desegregating the Armed Forces.* Chaired by former Solicitor General (later Judge) Charles Fahy, the President's Committee on Equality of Treatment and Opportunity in the Armed Services believed the Executive Order required the integration of the armed services and the Committee carried on negotiations with each branch to that effect. The Air Force had developed its own plan for integration earlier in 1948, and that plan was immediately acceptable to the Fahy Committee; substantial integration was achieved in 1949. At the same time, the Navy was committed to a policy of gradual integration, and the Fahy Committee was able to work out problems it had with the Navy's plans, yielding tangible policy commitments to integration in the Navy by mid-1949. The Fahy Committee struggled with the Army through 1949 and into 1950. Fahy and the Army reached agreement on a new gradual integration policy on January 16, 1950. The Korean War speeded up the process of integration, and on October 30, 1954, the Secretary of Defense announced that the last racially segregated unit in the armed forces had been abolished.

Although there was intense opposition to integration of the armed forces, the process went relatively smoothly. For example, a 1951 study by the Army reported that integration of black soldiers into white combat units in Korea had been accomplished generally "without undue friction and with better utilization of manpower." Under the code name Project CLEAR, outside consultants reported in 1951 that integration had not lowered white morale and had greatly increased black morale; virtually all black soldiers supported integration, while white soldiers were not overtly hostile or were supportive; and in most instances white attitudes toward integration became more favorable with firsthand experience. Morris MacGregor, Jr., *Integration of the Armed Forces, 1940–1965* 442 (1981).

The experience in the other services was similar. For example, reporter Lee Nichols interviewed members of all services in 1953 and wrote a book from what they told him, *Breakthrough on the Color Front* (1954). Nichols found that blacks and whites were amazed at how smoothly integration actually proceeded once the armed services decided to do it, but that blacks and whites continued to have different attitudes about military policy and practice. Whites tended to expect blacks to "prove themselves" in their assignments, while blacks were often skeptical that equal opportunities were really available to them. Tensions between blacks and whites proved to be even more problematic during the Vietnam War, but on the whole observers of all stripes believed that racial integration of the armed forces had been generally successful from the perspectives of whites, African-Americans, and other people of color.

B. THE EXCLUSION OF WOMEN

1. WOMEN IN THE MILITARY, 1861–1971[c]

Women, like African-Americans, were formally excluded from the armed services for most of our history. After the formal exclusion was ended, women were segregated.

It is important to note that despite the long-standing formal exclusion of women, a surprising number of passing women served in the American military (and in combat roles) during the nineteenth century. During the Civil War, Private Frank Fuller (née Frances Hook) of the Nineteenth Illinois Regiment served with distinction until she was wounded and captured in the Battle of Chattanooga. Mary Livermore, a nurse, estimated that more than 400 women "passed" as men and served in the Union Army. Most of these women were never detected. Sarah Emma Edmonds Seelye, alias Franklin Thomson, fled from home at age fifteen to escape an unwanted marriage. She donned male garb and supported herself selling Bibles; she enlisted in the Union Army and served for two years, retiring because of illness. Like hundreds, maybe thousands, of other women, her biological sex was never revealed during her service. We know about it today because Seelye published her memoirs, *Nurse and Spy*, in 1864.

Women were officially welcomed as nurses during the Civil War, an experience replicated in the Spanish-American War, but in both cases

---

c   The account that follows draws from Major General Jeanne Holm, USAF, *Women in the Military: An Unfinished Revolution* (1982), as well as Linda Bird Francke, *Ground Zero: The Gender Wars in the Military* (1997); Judith Hicks Stiehm, *Arms and the Enlisted Woman* (1989); Jill Laurie Goodman, "Women, War, and Equality: An Examination of Sex Discrimination in the Military," 5 *Women's Rights L. Rptr.* 243 (1979); Lori Kornblum, "Women Warriors in a Men's World: The Combat Exclusion," 2 *L. & Inequality* 351 (1984).

the women were viewed as civilian auxiliaries rather than as military personnel. The Army Nurse Corps was recognized as an official auxiliary in 1901 (by an act of Congress), and the Navy recognized its separate Nurse Corps in 1908. During World War I, 34,000 women served in the Nurse Corps of the various branches of service. More important, on the eve of war, Secretary of the Navy Josephus Daniels directed that women be enrolled in the naval reserves as "yeomen" who could perform clerical and other duties that would free up men for combat. The Marines followed suit immediately, but the Army refused. Congress in 1925 prohibited the Navy from enlisting women in the future.

The issue of women in the armed services went no further until General George Marshall became Army Chief of Staff in 1939. Believing that the U.S. would be hard put to staff a war machine, Marshall insisted that women be considered for service. The War Department dragged its feet—but that ended with the attack on Pearl Harbor. Congress created Women's Army Auxiliary Corps (WAAC, later WAC when the Auxiliary dropped out) in May 1942, Public Law No. 77–554, and a similar bill for the Navy and Marines was enacted in July, Public Law No. 77–689 (creating the Navy Women's Reserve, later called WAVES, and the Marine Corps Women's Reserve). The Army's Air Force also acquired a female auxiliary, called SPAR (for "Semper Paratus [sic]—Always Ready").

World War II created an insatiable demand for personnel performing all sorts of functions, which transformed the women's auxiliaries. By 1943, women (in addition to those serving as nurses) were also deployed overseas. By 1944, women were performing as control tower operators, radio repair people and operators, air navigators, parachute riggers, gunner instructors, engine mechanics, aerophotographers. Highly classified projects included women workers. Still, the majority of women served in clerical jobs.

General Eisenhower opposed women in the armed forces until he saw how valuable they were in defending Britain, and after that he supported their presence in North Africa and later Europe. By the end of World War II, there were nearly 100,000 WACs, 86,000 WAVES, 18,000 Women Marines, and 11,000 SPARs, as well as more than 18,000 nurses, serving in the U.S. armed forces. Although most women (and men) were discharged after the war, General Eisenhower insisted that the WACs continue as a permanent part of the Army.

The post-war period was one of some consolidation and much retrenchment. On the one hand, the federal government established a permanent role for women when it enacted the Women's Armed Services Act of 1948, Public Law No. 80–625, the so-called "Integration Act." But, while it established a role for women in the services, the Integration Act also required segregation and marginalization of women in significant ways. Among other things, the Act imposed a 2% cap on the number of women who could serve in each branch, restricted the number of female officers and established a separate promotion list for women, set higher minimum ages for women wanting to enlist than were required for men, and allowed women to claim husbands or children as dependents only upon a showing of actual dependency (it was automatically assumed for the dependents of military men). Most important, the Act provided that women could not be assigned flight or ship duties when the crafts were "engaged in combat missions." This was a strange integration—separate but deliberately unequal.

During the Korean War, women played less of a role than they did in World War II. Serving in smaller numbers, women were consigned to clerical and nursing jobs and became "typewriter soldiers." The training of military women sought to maintain their ladylike image. The top brass grew obsessed with apparel, for example. "Hair styles had to be fashionable but 'conservative' and 'appropriate' to the uniform. Elaborate beehives and large bouffant were frowned upon but were preferable to very short 'mannish' styles (there must be no appearance of lesbianism). According to Navy regulation, 'Hair shall be arranged and shaped to present a conservative, feminine appearance.'" Major General Jeanne Holm, USAF, *Women in the Military: An Unfinished Revolution* 181–82 (1982). The military's fetishism about appearance led to elaborate debates and regulations about skirt length (below the knee), pumps (in) versus boots (out), and hats and gloves (mandatory for most occasions).

The war in Vietnam transformed the experience of women in the military yet again. It created a substantial demand for women in a full range of military jobs, and the contemporaneous women's liberation movement problematized women's unequal treatment. The first tangible legal ramification of these circumstances was the enactment of Public Law No. 90–130 (1967), which removed the formal restrictions on promotion of women. This law addressed a practical problem: women who had entered the armed services during and after World War II had run into a glass ceiling because of the promotion restrictions of the Integration Act; in the Navy, such women were being discharged after their thirteenth year and were thereby losing pension benefits that would vest after year twenty. The 1967 law allowed these successful officers to be promoted and, without anyone much noticing, removed the 2% ceiling on women in the armed services (a ceiling that had never been reached). The law did not, however, endorse equality of women's role in the armed services. In 1970, the Army promoted two women to the rank of brigadier general, the first in Army history.

The military's policy of separate but unequal imploded after 1972, and a series of interconnected policies were terminated—segregation in procurement and training, gender quotas for promotions (stealthily continued after 1967), unequal family policies, and some of the paternalism. Some of these changes were made in anticipation of adoption of the ERA, which supporters and opponents agreed would require the armed services to end their formal discrimination against women in the draft and even in combat duty. This was the congressional testimony of Assistant Attorney General William Rehnquist, for example. Other changes resulted from aggressive congressional pressure or litigation. As we saw in Chapter 1, Section 4, the Supreme Court's Equal Protection jurisprudence was evolving rather rapidly in the early 1970s.

2. PARTIAL INTEGRATION OF WOMEN IN THE ARMED FORCES, 1971–81

Before 1971, the U.S. Supreme Court had never invalidated a statute because it discriminated against women or relied on a sex-based classification. The first decision to do so, *Reed v. Reed*, 404 U.S. 71 (1971), invalidated an Idaho statute preferring men over women as executors of estates. The next major case involved one of the policies established in the Integration Act of 1948. (See Chapter 1, Section 4 for more background.)

Sharron Frontiero and Joseph Frontiero v. Elliott Richardson

United States Supreme Court, 1973.
411 U.S. 677, 93 S.Ct. 1764, 36 L.Ed.2d 583.

[This case is excerpted in Chapter 1, Section 2A.]

CONSTITUTIONAL ISSUES FOR WOMEN IN THE MILITARY AFTER *FRONTIERO*

1. *All-Male Service Academies.* West Point, the Naval Academy, and the Air Force Academy had always been exclusively male. At 1972 congressional hearings, Captain Robin Quigley explained: "The Academy exists for one viable reason, to train seagoing naval officers. * * * There is no room, no need, for a woman to be trained in this mode, since by law and by sociological practicalities, we would not have women in these seagoing or warfare specialties." Deputy Secretary of Defense William Clements, Jr. categorically rejected the proposition: "Training cadets at the Academies is expensive, and it is imperative that these opportunities be reserved for those with potential for combat roles." At 1974 hearings, Navy Secretary J. William Middendorf II said: "Simply stated, unless the American people reverse their position on women in combat roles, it would be economically unwise and not in the national interest to utilize the expensive education and facilities of the Naval Academy to develop women officers." A woman sues the Naval Academy after *Frontiero*. The Academy makes the arguments above. What arguments should the plaintiff make? How would a court rule? *See Waldie v. Schlesinger*, 509 F.2d 508 (D.C.Cir.1974).

2. *The Combat Exclusions.* In 1977, 10 U.S.C. § 6015 (subsequently amended) provided that "women may not be assigned to duty in aircraft that are engaged in combat missions nor may they be assigned to vessels of the

Navy other than hospital ships and transports." This was a statutory exclusion applicable to the Navy and Air Force; the Army by its own regulations excluded women from combat in 1972. *See* 10 U.S.C. § 3012(e) (authorizing the Army to determine assignment policies).

In 1976, a Supreme Court majority held that sex-based classifications are subjected to an intermediate version of heightened scrutiny. See *Craig v. Boren*, 429 U.S. 190 (1976) (Chapter 1, Section 2). Under *Craig*, a sex-based classification is invalid unless it is substantially related to the achievement of an important government objective. The "administrative convenience" argument in *Frontiero* would have failed this test, for example. Moreover, Justice Brennan's opinion for a six-Justice Court held that the state's reliance on traditional gender stereotypes (girls are responsible, boys are wild) not only failed to justify the statutory classification, but also confirmed its invalidity under a regime where sex equality is the goal.

3. *Registration for the Draft.* In response to Soviet aggression in Afghanistan, President Carter acted on his own authority in January 1980 to reinstitute draft registration for men. With 150,000 women serving in the military, President Carter decided in February 1980 to request congressional authority to register women as well as men for the draft. Congress was thrown into turmoil on the issue, with military hard-liners strongly supporting the President on registration but opposing him on registering women. Their stated reasons were: (1) the limited number of noncombat jobs available to women; (2) the strain on training resources if equal numbers of women were introduced; and (3) the many ancillary issues that needed to be addressed (*e.g.*, the draft status of mothers). Most of the women in Congress—from liberal Representatives Patricia Schroeder (D-Colo.) and Barbara Mikulski (D-Md.) to conservative Senator Nancy Kassebaum (R-Kan.)—favored registration of women even if they were ambivalent about the draft. After extensive hearings, however, both the House and Senate rejected the proposal by large margins.

4. *Challenge to Women's Exclusion from the Draft.* In 1981, the Supreme Court was faced with deciding whether the male-only draft registration requirement was constitutional. In a decision written by Justice Rehnquist, the Court upheld the law by a 6–3 vote in ***Rostker v. Goldberg*, 453 U.S. 57 (1981).**

Writing for the Court in *Rostker*, **Justice Rehnquist** began by noting the history of deference to the military: "perhaps in no other area has the Court accorded Congress greater deference. * * * This Court has consistently recognized Congress' "broad constitutional power" to raise and regulate armies and navies, *Schlesinger v. Ballard*, 419 U.S. 498, 510 (1975)."

After stressing this point, the Court then relied heavily on the fact that, at that time, women were excluded from combat positions:

> Women as a group, however, unlike men as a group, are not eligible for combat. The restrictions on the participation of women in combat in the Navy and Air Force are statutory. Under 10 U.S.C. § 6015, 'women may not be assigned to duty on vessels or in aircraft that are engaged in combat missions,' and under 10 U.S.C. § 8549

female members of the Air Force 'may not be assigned to duty in aircraft engaged in combat missions.' The Army and Marine Corps preclude the use of women in combat as a matter of established policy. Congress specifically recognized and endorsed the exclusion of women from combat in exempting women from registration. In the words of the Senate Report:

'The principle that women should not intentionally and routinely engage in combat is fundamental, and enjoys wide support among our people. It is universally supported by military leaders who have testified before the Committee. . . . Current law and policy exclude women from being assigned to combat in our military forces, and the Committee reaffirms this policy.'

The Senate Report specifically found that '[w]omen should not be intentionally or routinely placed in combat positions in our military services.' The President expressed his intent to continue the current military policy precluding women from combat, and appellees present their argument concerning registration against the background of such restrictions on the use of women in combat. * * *

Thus, the Court reasoned:

This is not a case of Congress arbitrarily choosing to burden one of two similarly situated groups, such as would be the case with an all-black or all-white, or an all-Catholic or all-Lutheran, or an all-Republican or all-Democratic registration. Men and women, because of the combat restrictions on women, are simply not similarly situated for purposes of a draft or registration for a draft.

Congress' decision to authorize the registration of only men, therefore, does not violate the [Equal Protection component of the Fifth Amendment's] Due Process Clause. The exemption of women from registration is not only sufficiently but also closely related to Congress' purpose in authorizing registration. The fact that Congress and the Executive have decided that women should not serve in combat fully justifies Congress in not authorizing their registration, since the purpose of registration is to develop a pool of potential combat troops. * * *

5. *Criticism of* Rostker. Academic commentators have been critical of *Rostker. See, e.g.*, Lori Kornblum, "Women Warriors in Men's World: The Combat Exclusion," 2 *L. & Inequality* 351 (1984); Wendy Webster Williams, "The Equality Crisis: Some Reflections on Culture, Courts, and Feminism," 7 *Women's Rights L. Rep.* 175, 182–85 (1982). An issue the Court did not resolve (because plaintiffs did not raise or contest it) in *Rostker* was whether the exclusion of women from combat positions in the armed services was valid or whether such exclusion violated notions of equal protection. Judge John Sirica had struck down 10 U.S.C. § 6015, as applied to prevent Navy women from serving at sea in *Owens v. Brown*, 455 F.Supp. 291 (D.D.C.1978). Should groups critical of the military's policies have first attacked the exclusion from combat, and then the registration requirements? Does *Rostker* abrogate *Owens*?

A broader critique of *Rostker* is made by Diane H. Mazur, *A More Perfect Military: How the Constitution Can Make Our Military Stronger* (2010). Professor Mazur argues that Justice Rehnquist's opinion is an example of super-deference, where the Court goes along with a political decision supported by no military or other policy justification. (Indeed, the Joint Chiefs *favored* registration of women at the time, in order to assure a large number of potential recruits.) More important, judicial deference to political decisions about the military has had devastating consequences for civilian-military relations. The Rehnquist approach has fueled the volunteer army's increasing tendency to see its culture as "separate" from, and superior to, civilian values—and that is dangerous in a democracy. Moreover, super-deference induced the Bush-Cheney Administration to offload its most controversial policies—detention without charges, extralegal tribunals, and human torture—onto military officials, in the hope that super-deference would insulate those policies from serious judicial scrutiny. Although this gambit was not successful, critics such as Professor Mazur maintain that it exercises a corrupting influence on our armed forces.

When, if ever, should the Court defer to military judgments?

3.   ELIMINATION OF WOMEN'S COMBAT EXCLUSION

Although submerged as an issue in *Rostker*, the exclusion of women from combat-related positions in the military was already on the national agenda when the Court delivered its much-criticized opinion. While a recurring theme of the history of women in uniform had been the belief that women should not serve in combat positions,[d] military spokesmen were not called upon to defend the exclusion until the 1970s.

Early defenders of the exclusion emphasized "real differences" between women and men in terms of strength (especially lifting and throwing ability) and aggressiveness. *See, e.g., Hearings Before Subcomm. No. 2 of the House Comm. on Armed Services*, 93d Congress, 2d Session, part 5 (May 29, 1974) (hearings on gender integration of the service academies). In hand-to-hand combat, units with women would be at a disadvantage. These arguments seem like pink herrings. If strength is the key factor, then make combat roles turn on strength tests that women as well as men can take to qualify for combat duties. (Many women are stronger than many men.) Moreover, in the technologically

---

[d]   Note that even before the combat exclusion was removed, many women served in combat. Military experts agree that there can be no sharp demarcation between combat and noncombat positions; the latter are often subject to attack and are trained to defend themselves. Female nurses and doctors have served in combat zones since World War II, and women passing as men have served in combat since the Revolution. Women were also part of the World War II anti-aircraft artillery unit that was poised to defend Washington, D.C. against enemy attack. And women were integrated into the Office of Strategic Services (OSS), which performed dangerous espionage activities during World War II. *See* George Quester, "The Problem," in *Female Soldiers—Combatants or Noncombatants? Historical and Contemporary Perspectives* 217, 226–28 (Nancy Loring Goldman ed. 1982); John Lafflin, *Women in Battle* (1967).

sophisticated armed services, hand-to-hand combat is no longer the norm. Many women possess the physical skills for flying airplanes and deploying equipment that men do, and women as a group may have a comparative advantage in some physical skills (possibly stamina). Defenders of the exclusion never produced evidence demonstrating that women are less "aggressive" than men. Again, in the modern armed forces, is aggressiveness the character trait our country wants to emphasize? For practical reasons such as these, the armed forces have been moving toward more gender-neutral classifications that are based upon actual strength needs rather than stereotypes.

These arguments (especially the aggressiveness objection) were surrogates for deeper concerns, indeed concerns similar to those voiced against racial integration in the 1940s. The Superintendent of the Air Force Academy explained that opening combat or even leadership roles to women "offends the dignity of womanhood and ignores the harsh realities of war. * * * Fighting is a man's job and should remain so." *1974 Hearings* 135 (testimony of Lt. Gen. A.P. Clark, Superintendent, Air Force Academy). General Robert H. Barrow, former Commandant of the Marine Corps, had this to say:

> War is man's work. Biological convergence on the battlefield would not only be dissatisfying in terms of what women could do, but it would be an enormous psychological distraction for the male who wants to think that he's fighting for that woman somewhere behind, not up there in the same foxhole with him. It tramples the male ego. When you get right down to it, you have to protect the manliness of war.

Kenneth L. Karst, "The Pursuit of Manhood and the Desegregation of the Armed Forces," 38 *UCLA L. Rev.* 499, 534 (1991). Consistent with his overall thesis, Professor Karst argues that the exclusion of women from combat subserves the symbolism of Victorian masculinity: men protect women and the family from the outside enemy, a trope that would be disrupted by women fighting for their own protection; war is the greatest test as well as crucible of manhood, a bit of male bonding that would be undermined by women in the foxhole; men are by nature aggressive fighters, in contrast to nurturing passive women. These images are increasingly recognized as stereotypes, and after *Frontiero* it is perilous to ground military policy on such obvious stereotypes.

NOTE ON CONGRESSIONAL AND ADMINISTRATIVE DELIBERATION OVER THE WOMEN-IN-COMBAT ISSUE

In 1988, hearings held by the Subcommittee on Military Personnel and Compensation of the House Committee on Armed Services motivated the Defense Department to establish a task force on women. The result was that additional noncombat positions were opened to women, and procedures to deal with sexual harassment were strengthened.

In 1991, Congress repealed the statutory limitation on assignment of women to combat aircraft (part of § 6015). Public Law No. 102–190, § 531, 105 Stat. 1365. Congress also established a commission to assess the laws and policies restricting women from combat in general. *Id.* § 541. The commission appointed pursuant to the 1991 law recommended against participation of women in ground combat, but favored a more flexible policy in other contexts.

After further hearings, Congress repealed § 6015, the statutory restriction on the assignment of women in the Navy and Marine Corps. Public Law No. 103–160, § 541, 107 Stat. 1659 (1993). The Act also authorized the Secretary of Defense to change military personnel policies in order to make available to female members of the armed forces assignment to any type of combat unit, class of combat vessel, or type of combat platform that is not open to such assignments.

In January 1994, Secretary of Defense Les Aspin lifted the "risk rule" that had blocked women from serving in units which had a high probability of engaging in combat and codified a narrower version of the combat exclusion, excluding women from "assignment to units below the brigade level whose primary mission is to engage in direct combat on the ground." Memorandum from Sec'y of Defense Les Aspin, for the Sec'y of the Army, Sec'y of the Navy, Sec'y of the Air Force, Chairman, Joint Chiefs of Staff, Assistant Sec'y of Def. (Pers. and Readiness), Assistant Sec'y of Def. (Reserve Affairs) 1 (Jan. 13, 1994). Although narrowed, however, the combat exclusion continued to preclude women from a wide array of positions.

The wars in Iraq (2003–10) and Afghanistan (2002 through the present) introduced new variables. In those conflicts, the lines between combat and non-combat have been severely blurred and have at times disappeared. Although they were not officially allowed to serve in ground combat positions, hundreds of thousands of women have served in Iraq and Afghanistan since 2002, and they served in support units as truck drivers, gunners, medics, military police, helicopter pilots, etc. Military experts explained that even though women were not assigned to direct combat roles, the unpredictable nature of the attacks blurred the distinction between front-line and rear areas. Hence, many women who were assigned to support units found themselves in the thick of the battle. Despite this, women were still precluded from holding combat positions. This bar often impeded the ability of these women to advance in the military.

Finally, on January 24, 2013, the Joint Chiefs of Staff and the Secretary of Defense announced the rescission of the rule barring women from being assigned to combat units. *See* Memorandum from Secretary of Defense Leon E. Panetta and Chairman of the Joint Chiefs of Staff Martin E. Dempsey for Secretaries of the Military Departments: Elimination of the 1994 Direct Ground Combat Definition and Assignment Rule (Jan. 24, 2013), available at http://www.defense.gov/news/WISRJointMemo.pdf.

The impetus behind the change of policy, apparently, was the documented reality that women were already serving in combat assignments, with no sacrifice in military objectives or unit cohesion, and so it was blinking reality to continue the traditional policy. General Dempsey admitted that his mind changed when he arrived in Baghdad in 2003 and discovered that his humvee's turret gunner, the soldier assigned to protect the lives of him and the other passengers, was "Amanda." See Elisabeth Bumiller & Thom Shanker, *Military Chiefs' Personal Encounters Influenced Lifting Women's Combat Ban*, N.Y. Times, Jan. 24, 2013.

The change in policy was also justified by an official Department of Defense analysis promulgated in 2012. *See* Department of Defense, "Report to Congress on the Review of Laws, Policies and Regulations Restricting the Service of Female Members in the U.S. Armed Forces" (Feb. 2012). The Department reported that 14.5% of the 1.4 million military service personnel are female, that the combat exclusion rule denied the armed forces of needed personnel (including officers), and that the rule did not serve valid military purposes.

In January 2013, Chairman of the Joint Chiefs of Staff, Martin Dempsey, issued a memorandum stating that it was the view of the Chiefs of Staff that they should "move forward with the full intent to integrate women into occupational fields to the maximum extent possible." The memorandum required all service branches to submit plans for implementation of gender-neutral assignment rules by May 2013 and to implement such plans by January 2016.

Consistent with this timeline, in December 2015, the Defense Secretary Ashton B. Carter announced that all combat positions would be open to women. According to the N.Y. Times as a result of that decision, an additional 220,000 military jobs became open to women. Matthew Rosenberg & Dave Phillips, "All Combat Roles Now Open to Women, Defense Secretary Says," *N.Y. Times* (Dec. 3, 2015).

PROBLEM 9-1
RECONSIDERATION OF *ROSTKER*?

Now that the combat exclusion has been repealed, is the exclusion of women from registration still constitutional? Should *Rostker* be overruled? Or treated as no longer valid by Congress and the President?

C. THE MILITARY'S EXCLUSIONS OF LGBT PEOPLE

1. THE EXCLUSION OF "SODOMITES" AND SEXUAL "DEVIATES"[e]

In 1778, the Continental Army was fortunate to receive Baron Frederich Wilhelm Ludolf Gerhard Augustin von Steuben of Prussia, the

---

[e] Our discussion in text draws from Allan Bérubé, *Coming Out Under Fire: The History of Gay Men and Women in World War Two* (1990); William Eskridge Jr., *Gaylaw: Challenging the Apartheid of the Closet* chs. 1–2 (1999); Leisa Meyer, *Creating G.I Jane: Sexuality and Power in the Women's Army Corps during World War II* (1996); Lawrence Murphy, *Perverts by Official Order: The Campaign Against Homosexuals by the United States Navy* (1988); Major Jeffrey Davis, "Military Policy Toward Homosexuals: Scientific, Historical, and Legal Perspectives," 131 *Mil. L. Rev.* 55 (1991).

drillmaster who retrained General Washington's Army at Valley Forge and literally rewrote the Americans' manual on discipline and order. Historians consider his contribution to the Continental cause—and to eventual American independence—incalculable. Ironically, von Steuben was available for American service because in late 1777 he had been accused of "having taken familiarities with young boys which the law forbids and punishes severely" in Prussia, and was in danger of being prosecuted. At the very moment von Steuben rescued the struggling American cause, the Continental Army had set a precedent for excluding such men from service. Lieutenant General Frederick Enslin was discovered in bed with Private John Monhart. Lieutenant Colonel Aaron Burr presided at Enslin's court martial trial for sodomy and perjury and found him guilty. In 1778, Enslin was drummed out of the Continental Army, the first casualty of the U.S. military's efforts to police the same-sex intimacy of its soldiers. Such episodes, however, were rare until World War I.

The Articles of War of 1916 were the first complete revision of military law since 1806. Article 93 ("miscellaneous crimes and offenses") prohibited assault to commit a felony, apparently including assault to commit sodomy (defined in the Manual for Courts-Martial, 1917, ¶ 443, to be limited to anal sex). The Articles of War adopted by Congress in 1920, 41 Stat. 787, enumerated sodomy as a separate offense under Article 93, and the 1920 Manual expanded sodomy to include oral sex. Various other wartime statutes prohibited lewd practices in or near U.S. military bases. These newly specified regulations coincided with popular and medical perceptions that a new species of human—"sex perverts" or "degenerates"—could be defined by their desire to engage in sodomy with people of their own sex (usually men).

The first celebrated event in this new era of military regulation was the Newport Naval Training Station scandals of 1919–20. Lawrence Murphy, *Perverts by Official Order: The Campaign Against Homosexuals by the United States Navy* (1988). In early 1919, Lieutenant Erastus Hudson authorized Chief Machinists Mate Ervin Arnold (a former vice cop in Connecticut) to organize undercover operatives to ferret out "sex perverts" among the hospital and other military personnel at Newport, as well as among the townsfolk. Newport was the first homosexual witch-hunt in the U.S. armed forces.

Equally fascinating was the backlash against Arnold and his operatives. After starting the process by which the naval "degenerates" would be court-martialed, the military went after civilians as well, under a 1917 statute prohibiting lewd conduct with military personnel. Arnold had compiled a huge file on the Reverend Samuel Kent, an Episcopal chaplain associated with the training center and a member of the YMCA crowd. Operative after operative slept over with Kent and wrote up their experiences in reports of kissing, hugging, and oral sex. Kent denied the charges of half a dozen sworn operatives and introduced one prominent witness after another testifying to his character and probity. The jury acquitted, perhaps based upon his lawyers' outrage that military operatives would seek to entrap a man of the cloth.

The Kent acquittal initiated yet a third inquisition, in which the investigators themselves came under fire. Newport clergy pestered the Navy Department into convening a new court of inquiry in January 1920. The main charge of the new court was that the investigators themselves had violated the law by committing lewd and sodomitic practices with their targets. The poor operatives perjured themselves right and left as they tried to explain what it was they were instructed to do and what they thought they were doing when they went along repeatedly with the targets' desire to have oral sex. What is most remarkable was the operatives' nonchalance about oral sex. For the most part they would not consent to anal sex, didn't like kissing the targets, would tolerate some hugging and fondling, but repeatedly erected themselves at the hint of oral sex and allowed themselves to be fellated over and over and over again.

The Newport backlash gave homosexual witch-hunts a bad name for a while. The whole process of court-martialing for consensual sodomy was problematic: evidence was hard to come by because the activity was usually in private and there was no complaining witness, and undercover tactics carried their own risks of embarrassment. After 1922, Section VIII of the separation regulations ("inaptness or undesirable habits or traits of character") was the mechanism by which homosexuals were quietly drummed out of the service, albeit in very small numbers.

The experience of Newport and World War I generally revealed the importance of pre-induction screening. If it was so hard to kick "perverts" out, why not prevent their getting in? In 1921, Army Regulation 40–105 announced that Army recruits could be rejected for evidence of medical defects or diseases, including physical or moral "degeneration." The "degenerate" individual could be identified by stigmata such as *indecency* and *sexual perversion*. The regulation also excluded recruits who showed signs of "constitutional psychopathic state," including "sexual psychopathy," which made them "incapable of attaining a satisfactory adjustment to the average environment of civilized society."

The creation of homosexuality as a legal and medical, rather than just moral, phenomenon came to have great significance during World War II. As revised in 1941, Medical Circular No. 1 issued by the Selective Service, included "homosexual proclivities" in the list of disqualifying "deviations."

In 1941, the Selective Service started to train doctors and psychiatrists to apply the new guidelines for screening inductees. Allan Bérubé, *Coming Out Under Fire: The History of Gay Men and Women in World War Two* 14–15 (1990). The discourse of the lecturers was distinctly modern, as of 1941: "homosexuals" were described exclusively through the argot of "mental illness" and pseudo-Freudian determinism (such as sexual "latency"). They were considered psychopaths who were unable to control their sexual desires and hence would be troublemakers. They were paranoid personalities too introverted or repressed to adjust to the give-and-take of military life and the stress of combat situations. They were too effete or sissy to become good soldiers or to be accepted by their comrades. Some clues to an inductee's homosexuality were his discomfort with displaying his nude body, his curiosity or embarrassment about masturbation, or possible admissions of awkwardness around women. Such men, the lecturers insisted, were subject to "homosexual panic" and could be excluded.

A new Selective Service Director, Major General Lewis Hershey, distrusted this new science and eliminated separate psychiatric examinations at the local boards, but anti-homosexual discourse continued to be churned out. The 1942 revisions of the Army's mobilization regulations (Bérubé 19) included these precepts: "Persons habitually or occasionally engaged in homosexual or other perverse sexual practices" were "unsuitable for military service" as was anyone having "a record as a pervert." "Homosexuals" could be recognized by "feminine body characteristics" or "effeminacy in dress and manner" or "patulous [expanded] rectum." In addition, the regulations rejected physically normal but personally "effeminate" men because they "would become subject to ridicule and 'joshing' which will harm the general morale and will incapacitate the individuals."

This medicalization of the anti-homosexual exclusion combined with the draft brought millions of men under scrutiny. The military labeled every potential inductee and imposed severe informal sanctions on discovered homosexuals, who were later discharged.

The military's decision to define homosexuality as a medical problem failed to rid the service of homosexuals, contributed to the stigmatization of homosexuality, and may have helped create a "gay" consciousness. According to Allan Bérubé, a boatload of homosexual activity was unleashed by the war—yet the only big scandal was the investigation of lesbian activity at the WAC training center at Fort Oglethorpe, Georgia. Leisa Meyer, *Creating G.I. Jane: Sexuality and Power in the Women's Army Corps during World War II* (1996). The investigation was initiated by a May 1944 letter from a shocked mother who had discovered love letters between her WAC trainee daughter and an older WAC. The mother charged that her "little girl [age 20] who I know was clean of heart and mind" was corrupted by this predatory older woman, and the mother demanded an investigation. The Inspector General took this letter seriously and dispatched a team immediately. The team conducted a professional but not inquisitorial investigation and uncovered mountains of letters and testimony involving explicit same-sex intimacy at Fort Oglethorpe. Still, only a couple of women were discharged, and the investigators invoked a series of War Department medical circulars to justify retention of most involved. In a harbinger of things to come, the investigators targeted women who not only engaged in sexual relations with other women, but who also transgressed gender roles through cross-dressing and the like.

But the leniency shown by the military during World War II ended soon after the war did. The period 1947–53 saw thousands of lesbian and gay soldiers hounded from their units, and thousands of others terrorized by the prospect of being discovered in the McCarthy-era witch-hunts. President Eisenhower's 1953 executive order denying federal employment to a range of political nonconformists lumped "sex perverts" with Communists as enemies of the state. The Army's post-war policy had some flexibility to retain people with "homosexual tendencies," but generally operated under a simple principle: "True, confirmed, or habitual homosexual personnel, irrespective of sex, will not be permitted to serve in the Army in any capacity and prompt separation of known homosexuals from the Army is mandatory." AR 600–443, § I, ¶ 2 (April 10, 1953). From 1953 into the 1970s more than a thousand people were discharged from the armed forces each year on grounds of homosexuality. Many more were negotiated out quietly and do not appear on the record books.

The main concern voiced about homosexuals by the military in the 1950s was their presumed disloyalty, although the discourse of sick homosexuals remained robust and shed most of its rehabilitative medical gloss. A standard script was that homosexuals would be particularly susceptible to blackmail: their status was so repugnant that Communists would be able to extract secret information out of them by threat of exposure. A 600-page internal Navy report compiled by Admiral Crittenden debunked the security and blackmail argument in 1957, but the Navy merely suppressed the Crittenden Report and maintained its public stance.

Before 1969, expulsions of homosexuals from the armed forces were the result of military investigations and dragnets, where people were hunted down, interrogated, and expelled. The witch-hunts continued after 1969, but a new breed of soldier came to the fore—the person who openly conceded her or his homosexuality and sued the armed forces to stay in. Several of the lawsuits were successful. The most notable successes were those of Copy Berg and Leonard Matlovich, whose cases set an important precedent. *Matlovich v. Secretary of the Air Force*, 591 F.2d 852 (D.C.Cir.1978); *Berg v. Claytor*, 591 F.2d 849 (D.C.Cir.1978). The D.C. Circuit declined to hold the military's gay exclusions unconstitutional but held instead that the military vested illegal discretion with officials enforcing the exclusionary policy. Specifically, the services allowed for retention of homosexuals where appropriate but did not define when retention would be appropriate. Because Matlovich and Berg had exemplary service records and no evidence of misconduct, it was not clear why they should not have fallen under the exception.

Ironically, these successful lawsuits led to a hardening of the military's policy. The Department of Defense in the waning days of the Carter Administration decided not to compromise the gay exclusion and instead issued a new series of directives that were carried over by the new Reagan Administration. Directive 1332.14.1.H (Jan. 28, 1982) dealt with separations of enlisted personnel, 1332.30.1.H with separations of officers. The basic rule was as follows (Directive 1332.14.1.H.1(a)):

> Homosexuality is incompatible with military service. The presence in the military environment of persons who engage in homosexual conduct or who, by their statements, demonstrate a propensity to engage in homosexual conduct, seriously impairs the accomplishment of the military mission. The presence of such members adversely affects the ability of the Military Services to maintain discipline, good order, and morale; to foster mutual trust and confidence among servicemembers; to ensure the integrity of the system of rank and command; to facilitate assignment and worldwide deployment of servicemembers who frequently must live and work under close conditions affording minimal privacy; to recruit and retain members of the Military Services; to maintain the public acceptability of military service; and to prevent breaches of security.

Under Directive 1332.14.1.H.1(c), a member of the armed forces was to be separated if he or she:

> (1) "engaged in, attempted to engage in, or solicited another to engage in a homosexual act or acts" *unless* it was established that the homosexual act was "a departure from the member's usual and customary behavior" and was not coercive, the homosexual behavior was unlikely to recur, "the member's continued presence in the Service is consistent with the interest of the Service in proper discipline, good order, and morale," and the member "does not desire to engage in or intend to engage in homosexual acts"; **or**

> (2) "has stated that he or she is a homosexual or bisexual unless there is a further finding that the member is not a homosexual or bisexual"; **or**

> (3) "has married or attempted to marry a person known to be of the same biological sex (as evidenced by the external anatomy of the persons involved) unless there are further findings that the member is not a homosexual or bisexual and that the purpose of the marriage or attempt was the avoidance or termination of military service."

Would Directive 1332.14.1.H allow for the discharge of a member of the armed forces who simply said, "I am a lesbian"? Would this be constitutional?

As noted above, some challenges to individual discharges were successful, but court after court refused to find that the policy itself was unconstitutional. *See, e.g.,* *Steffan v. Perry*, 41 F.3d 677 (D.C. Cir. 1994) (en banc).

2. DON'T ASK, DON'T TELL, 1993–2011

In January 1993, President Bill Clinton announced his intention to end the armed forces exclusion of bisexuals, lesbians, and gay men by executive order. Facing a firestorm of protest from various quarters and blindsided by his own Joint Chiefs of Staff, the President agreed with Senator Sam Nunn, the Chair of the Senate Armed Services Committee, and with General Colin Powell, the Chair of the Joint Chiefs of Staff, to postpone any executive order until after Congress had studied the matter in a series of House and Senate hearings.

Policy Concerning Homosexuality in the Armed Forces: Hearings Before the Senate Committee on Armed Services

103d Congress, 2d Session. 595–97, 599–602, 606–09, 618–19 (May 11, 1993).

[Retired General H. Norman] Schwarzkopf: * * * Let me first state that my position on this matter is not based on any kind of moral outrage over what many consider immoral conduct. Also, I would like to state I am a very strong advocate of our Constitution's provisions for individual rights, and therefore my position is not a condemnation of anyone's right to choose their sexual orientation.

That said, I must say that I am opposed to an executive order lifting the ban on homosexuals in the military service, and my opposition grows out of honest concern for the impact that such a measure would have on the men and women of our Armed Forces and the resultant reduction in our Nation's ability to protect our vital interest.

The Armed Forces' principal mission is not to be instruments of social experimentation. The first, foremost, and all eclipsing mission of our military is to be ready to fight our Nation's wars and when called upon to do so to win those wars. * * *

* * * [I]n my 40 years of army service in three different wars I have become convinced that [unit cohesion] is the single most important factor in a unit's ability to succeed on the battlefield. Anyone who disputes this fact may have been to war, but certainly never led troops into battle.

Whether we like it or not, in my years of military service I have experienced the fact that the introduction of an open homosexual into a small unit immediately polarizes that unit and destroys the very bonding that is so important for the unit's survival in time of war.

For whatever reason, the organization is divided into a majority who oppose, a small minority who approve, and other groups who either do not care or just wish the problem would go away, and I do not find this surprising, given the divisiveness that I have encountered in our Nation in the past year. The attitudes of our servicemen and women simply reflect, in my opinion, the attitudes that I have encountered in the American people.

Do not get me wrong, please. I am not saying that homosexuals have not served honorably in our Armed Forces in the past. Of course they have, and I am quite sure that they will in the future, although I candidly must say that I completely reject the grossly overinflated numbers quoted by some organizations.

However, in every case that I am familiar with, and there are many, whenever it became known in a unit that someone was openly homosexual, polarization occurred, violence sometimes followed, morale broke down and unit effectiveness suffered. Plain and simply, that has been my experience.

I am also concerned from another standpoint. * * *

For the first time in anyone's memory, the pool of high quality men and women wanting to join the military greatly exceeded the number of people we needed to recruit. * * *

Will this same pool of high quality young men and women be available to us if the ban on homosexuals in the military is lifted? If what I am told by young men and women who talked to me is indicative, the answer is no. If what I am told by countless parents is indicative, the answer is clearly no.

What about those men and women already serving? Are they going to stick with us like they have in the past? There is little doubt that we will lose quite a few of them. The result of this decrease in quality of enlistees and reenlistees can only result in a decrease in the quality of our armed forces. * * *

[Marine Colonel Frederick C.] Peck: * * * [The witness describes his tour of duty with the Marines' "Hollywood Liaison Office."] I worked with a lot of people in Hollywood whose sexual orientations and a lot of other things about their personal lifestyles were much, much different than my own. I think I was successful there. * * * And I am saying this to tell you that I am not a homophobe, I am not the kind of person who has led some cloistered, sheltered military life, who has never had to deal with the homosexuals before. I have worked with them all the time. I can work with homosexuals, shoulder to shoulder.

But I do not think I can live with them and coexist with them in a military environment. It is one thing to share an office with someone, it is quite another thing to share a lifestyle; and that is what the military is: It is a way of life. * * *

[The witness discloses that his] son, Scott, is a homosexual; and I do not think there is any place for him in the military. I love him; I love him as much as I do any of my sons. I respect him, I think he is a fine person; but he should not serve in the military. And that is the strongest testimonial I think I can give. I am the father of a homosexual boy, a young man, and I do not think he should serve in the military.

I spent 27 years of my life in the military, and I know what it would be like for him if he went in. And it would be hell. And if we went into combat, which as the General said is the whole purpose for us being here, he would be at grave risk if he were to follow in my footsteps as a infantry platoon leader or a company commander. I would be very fearful that his life would be in jeopardy from his own troops.

And I am not saying that that is right, or wrong, or whatever. I am telling you that is the way it is. You get into war, the first casualty is truth; the second is the value of human life. And fraggings, let me tell you, did not begin or end in Vietnam. Fratricide is something that exists out there, and there are people who would put my son's life at risk in our own Armed Forces. * * *

Chairman [Samuel] Nunn: * * * [L]et me ask each of you this question. There are some who see this as a civil rights issue, or as an issue that is comparable to the debate about women and their role in the military, and certainly we hear over and over again that the same arguments are used against admitting openly gays and lesbians in the military as were used back in the 1940s and 1950s about the admission of blacks into integrated units in the military.

How would each of you respond to the general question as to whether you see an analogy between this debate and the debate that occurred in the civil rights era back in the forties and fifties, and also the question of women? * * *

Colonel Peck:* * * I think if someone declares their homosexuality that that is a statement that defines a behavior. It certainly connotes a behavior. If I say I am black or I am white or Jewish or Protestant or Catholic, it does not necessarily indicate how I am going to behave. But it does indicate a behavior if I say I am homosexual.

When I think of the analogy of race, I find that somewhat offensive. If I could use another analogy, it would be much akin to someone in the military saying I am a racist. Making that statement and then following up with, but I will not let my racial attitudes interfere with my behavior. You certainly would not expect the troops that had to follow that person to respect them or trust them. If the person says they are a racist, anyone of color or of the wrong ethnicity or religion working for him or her would be immediately suspect.

And it is the same analogy that I would have about someone who comes out and declares openly that they are gay or lesbian in the military. Once they do that, I think they compromise their position and it certainly has limited their effectiveness. * * *

General Schwarzkopf: There is certainly an analogy, but I do not agree that it is applicable here.

First of all, I do not think it is any secret that Colin Powell and my deputy, Cal Waller, have both said that there is no analogy, and they are certainly capable of speaking, since they entered the Armed Forces during that time and lived through a great deal of it. And I value their judgment greatly in this matter.

Second, we have a distinction between something that a person is born with and a chosen conduct. I know of no medical study anywhere that has validly proved that people are born homosexual. It is a question of choice of conduct in their case. An African American is born black and they are black, and they are going to continue to be black. And they are going to continue to be African Americans, and they have no choice in the matter whatsoever.

I think there is a very important point that we ought to remember, though. In 1953, I believe the statistic was that at the time the orders were issued to integrate our armed services, 30 percent of the people within the military were against the integration. Today, we have 78 or 80 percent of the people in the military against bringing homosexuals in. There is a rather considerable difference in the opinions of the people within our Armed Forces with regard to that issue.

I would also say that at that time I think there was a majority of the American people that were very much in favor of integration of African Americans into our Armed Forces and, indeed, into our society. And my experience has been that it is just the opposite today. The majority of the American people are not in favor of the integration of homosexuals—a lifting of the ban on open homosexuality.

So there is a rather considerable difference on that point also that I do not think we can ignore. * * *

Major [Kathleen] Bergeron: * * * I do not see an analogy to either the race issue or the women's issue. I think color and gender are benign physical characteristics, as [Colin Powell] has said, that someone is born with. They do not have a behavior that has the potential to affect other people and the people around them. And I personally resent the analogy to the females or to gender * * *. * * *

Senator Levin: * * * Now let me get to the question that is the heart of the matter. Whether or not if someone is in the military, * * * and they say I am a homosexual, that that person should be removed. They do not say that they have engaged in homosexual activity. They simply say I am a homosexual. That would be enough, for you, to remove that person from the military.

General Schwarzkopf: Right, because that would polarize the organization. * * *

Senator Levin: * * * You said that the statement I am a homosexual, that is conduct in your book.

General Schwarzkopf: Of course. It also happens to be the DOD test today.

NOTE ON THE AFTERMATH OF THE GAYS IN THE MILITARY HEARINGS: THE DON'T ASK, DON'T TELL STATUTE AND REGULATIONS

The Senate hearings yielded tons of testimony about unit cohesion, troop morale, shower facilities, close quarters on a ship, and popular views inside and outside the military. Much of it boiled down to this proposition: straight soldiers would not stand for gay soldiers to serve openly. The House hearings, chaired by Representative Ronald Dellums, were evenly balanced between witnesses supporting and those opposing the ban; the supporters of the ban made the same points they did in the Senate.

On July 17, 1993, President Clinton endorsed Senator Nunn's "don't ask, don't tell" approach. Senator Nunn's Armed Services Committee called Secretary of Defense Leslie Aspin and the entire Joint Chiefs of Staff in his immediate hearing on the new policy. The most dramatic point was when Senator Dan Coats (R-Ind.) polled the Joint Chiefs with the inquiry, "Is homosexuality incompatible with military service?" The response of the Joint Chiefs was split: General Colin Powell (the Chair of the Joint Chiefs), Admiral David Jeremiah (Navy), and General Merrill McPeak (Air Force) responded, *Open homosexuality* in a unit setting is incompatible with military service. Three other Joint Chiefs—General Carl Mundy (Marines), General Gordon Sullivan (Army), and Admiral Frank Kelso II (Naval Operations)—responded, *Homosexuality* is incompatible.

With the support of the President, Congress in Public Law No. 103–160, § 571(a)(1), 107 Stat. 1670, enacted what became known as "Don't Ask, Don't Tell," codified at 10 U.S.C. § 654. The law declared that: "The presence in the armed forces of persons who demonstrate a propensity or intent to engage in homosexual acts would create an unacceptable risk to the high standards of morale, good order and discipline, and unit cohesion that are the essence of military capability." 10 U.S.C. § 654(a)(15). The law then provided the following bases for discharge from the U.S. Armed Forces:

> (b) Policy.—A member of the armed forces shall be separated from the armed forces under regulations prescribed by the Secretary of Defense if one or more of the following findings is made and approved in accordance with procedures set forth in such regulations:
>
> > (1) That the member has engaged in, attempted to engage in, or solicited another to engage in a homosexual act or acts unless there are further findings, made and approved in accordance with procedures set forth in such regulations, that the member has demonstrated that—

(A) such conduct is a departure from the member's usual and customary behavior;

(B) such conduct, under all the circumstances, is unlikely to recur;

(C) such conduct was not accomplished by use of force, coercion, or intimidation;

(D) under the particular circumstances of the case, the member's continued presence in the armed forces is consistent with the interests of the armed forces in proper discipline, good order, and morale; and

(E) the member does not have a propensity or intent to engage in homosexual acts.

(2) That the member has stated that he or she is a homosexual or bisexual, or words to that effect, unless there is a further finding, made and approved in accordance with procedures set forth in the regulations, that the member has demonstrated that he or she is not a person who engages in, attempts to engage in, has a propensity to engage in, or intends to engage in homosexual acts.

(3) That the member has married or attempted to marry a person known to be of the same biological sex. * * *

The Act defined the term "homosexual act" to mean: "(A) any bodily contact, actively undertaken or passively permitted, between members of the same sex for the purpose of satisfying sexual desires; and (B) any bodily contact which a reasonable person would understand to demonstrate a propensity or intent to engage in an act described in subparagraph (A)." 10 U.S.C § 654(e)(3).

Although more detailed, the statute closely followed the prohibitory language and definitions of the 1982 Directive (quoted and analyzed above).

The law laid out the "Don't Tell" Rules. The implementing directives laid out the "Don't Ask" part of the equation. A Memorandum from Secretary Aspin to the Secretaries of the Military Departments et al. (Dec. 21, 1993), provided that an applicant was not be asked about his or her sexual orientation.

NOTES ON DISCHARGES UNDER THE DON'T ASK, DON'T TELL REGIME

Discharges increased during the early Reagan Administration, from 1,754 in 1980, to 1,998 in 1982—and then *steadily declined* between 1982 and 1994 (617 discharges), which was mostly a time of peace. After President Bill Clinton signed Don't Ask, Don't Tell (DADT) into law, discharges *shot up*, from 617 in 1994, to 870 in 1996, to 1,163 in 1998, to 1,212 in 2000 and 1,273 in 2001. The Clinton era also was mostly a time of peace, but the trend in DADT discharges reversed direction. After 9/11 and the initiation of two protracted wars, discharges *plummeted* to 906 in 2002; 787 in 2003; 668 in

2004; 742 in 2005; 623 in 2006; 627 in 2007; 619 in 2008; and to 428 in 2009, the lowest level in more than a generation. (The size of the national armed forces is a bit more than half what it was in 1980, so the percentage decline is not as striking as the absolute numbers.)

Note that the rate of discharge spiked up after the implementation of DADT. Ironically, a policy that was billed as a liberalization saw a doubling of the number of discharges between 1994 and 2001, a trend that is more remarkable in light of the fact that the total number of women and men in the armed forces declined sharply in that period. The first big decline in gay-related discharges in almost a decade came during a period in which the military's need for troops became acute. Consider the ways that theories of sexuality, gender, and the law help us understand the odd history of gay-related discharge numbers.

Michel Foucault and Judith Butler suggest an explanation for the high discharge rates of the 1990s: the highly visible debate about gays in the military itself creates a discourse of silent-but-intense super-scrutiny that is more harmful for closeted lesbian and gay personnel than the old policy was. Some people who opposed DADT believed that the Perry Watkins case and the 1993 debate among the White House, Congress, and the Defense Department created a false picture of the armed forces as pervasively sexualized. *See, e.g.*, Jennifer Egan, "Uniforms in the Closet," *N.Y. Times Mag.*, June 28, 1998, at 26–31, 40, 48, 56; Diane Mazur, "The Unknown Soldier: A Critique of 'Gays in the Military' Scholarship and Litigation," 29 *UC Davis L. Rev.* 223 (1996). This perception created pressure for the military to purge itself of any behavior that might be read as gay.

It is important to note that the *rate of discharge for women* from the armed forces because of homosexual acts was *higher* (as a percentage of their overall numbers in the armed forces) than it was for men. Although women have constituted between 10% and 15% of military personnel for the period 1980–2010, the share of DADT discharges for women personnel rose from 22% in 1997 to 39% in 2009. The Williams Institute, *Discharges under the Don't Ask/Don't Tell Policy: Women and Racial/Ethnic Minorities* 2 (2010).

The following excerpt provides one explanation for this pattern. Are there other possible reasons? If the Benecke and Dodge account provided were the only reason, would this disproportionate treatment of female soldiers be unconstitutional?

Michelle Benecke and Kristin Dodge, "Military Women in Nontraditional Fields: Casualties of the Armed Forces' War on Homosexuals"

13 *Harvard Women's Law Journal* 215, 219, 220–24, 226–28, 238–41 (1990).[*]

The belief that military women were particularly prone to lesbianism is apparent in the investigation and training procedures advocated by the services for ferreting out lesbians. A 1952 speech given

---

to Navy Auxiliary (WAVE) recruits combined the topics of maintenance of femininity and avoidance of homosexuality, suggesting the degree to which suspicions of lesbianism were tied to popular stereotypes that lesbians were unfeminine in appearance and actions. Officers reminded recruits that they were "supplementing and complementing" the men, not competing with them and urged them to "be sure that we retain as much of our basic femininity as possible." * * *

* * * [A] combination of [various] factors resulted in women and lesbians becoming special targets for discharge. The 1980s were characterized by a wave of investigations and discharges for alleged lesbian activities, including the following: the investigation of women on the USS Norton Sound in 1980, which resulted in the discharge of eight women sailors; investigations on the hospital ship Sanctuary and on the USS Dixon; the Army's ouster of eight female military police officers from the United States Military Academy at West Point in 1986; the 1988 investigation of thirty women, including every African-American woman, on board the destroyer-tender USS Yellowstone, which resulted in the discharge of eight women; the 1988 investigation of five of the thirteen female crewmembers on board the USS Grapple; and the now infamous Parris Island investigation.

The Marine Corps' investigation of women drill instructors from 1986 to 1988 at the Marine Corps Recruit Training Depot at Parris Island, South Carolina, is one of the most extensive investigations to come to public knowledge. Almost half of the post's 246 women were questioned about alleged lesbian activities, and sixty-five women eventually left the Marine Corps as a direct result of the investigation. At least twenty-seven of these women were administratively discharged. Three women Marines stationed at Parris Island were jailed as the result of criminal convictions for homosexual activity. Many women have chosen to resign or accept voluntary discharges rather than face extensive investigations and the possibility of criminal charges.

While the DOD policy on homosexuality does not distinguish between male and female servicemembers, recent reports indicate that women are discharged from the military services at a rate ten times that of men. The different investigative methods used to target women and men may account for this disparity. Men are typically investigated on a case-by-case basis, and allegations of male homosexuality tend to be handled quietly with efforts made to usher servicemen out of the service as quickly as possible. In sharp contrast, women are often targeted and discharged as the result of mass investigations, aptly referred to as witch-hunts.

Witch-hunts are often initiated by military authorities on the basis of rumors started by male servicemembers about women who refuse the servicemen's sexual advances. The most frequent targets of witch-hunts are competent, assertive, and athletic women. Witch-hunts flourish when women under investigation are coerced by agents into naming other military women who are rumored to be lesbians. The 1988 investigation of women sailors on the USS Grapple is one example.

The USS Grapple investigation began when a male crew member started rumors about the close friendship between a woman who rebuffed his sexual advances and another sailor, Petty Officer Mary Beth Harrison. The rumors were followed by an incident in which this male sailor, in front of the ship's crew and at least one of its officers, shouted profanities and accusations that the women were lesbians. On a subsequent deployment, flyers bearing the sign "no dykes" appeared around the ship.

A woman who files complaints about such harassment often finds that her chain-of-command either is unresponsive or responds by initiating an investigation against the woman herself, presuming incorrectly that only lesbians are lesbian-baited. The experience of the women on the USS Grapple was no exception. Harrison's superiors actually advised her not to file a complaint and appeared to have dropped the matter until, in November 1988, she and three other women were questioned by the Naval Investigative Service (NIS) about alleged homosexual activities. Like many women targeted in witch-hunts, the accused sailors were outstanding performers in nontraditional job assignments. According to Harrison, the fairness of these proceedings was dubious. "We were not asked if we were Gay—we were automatically presumed guilty."

Many women who have been investigated in witch-hunts have reported that they were subjected to lengthy and harsh interrogations. Investigative techniques used during the USS Grapple witch-hunt fit this pattern. Harrison's requests for an attorney were denied until after she had endured two and a half hours of "good guy, bad guy" questioning during her initial interrogation, and another woman was interrogated for six hours without a break.

One of the most common tactics used by investigators is to pressure women to name others who might be gay in order to save themselves. During the USS Grapple investigation, NIS agents told the sailors they would be "protected" if they turned the other women in, that the others had already confessed to being lesbians, and that the NIS had obtained "conclusive evidence" of their guilt. NIS agents have also threatened women with jail sentences and the loss of custody of their children if the women did not name others rumored to be lesbians or admit to participating in homosexual activities themselves. [One example of this tactic was the case built against Corporal Barbara Baum in 1988. Although her conviction for engaging in consensual oral sex was overturned for procedural reasons, she served almost a year in prison and of course lost her military career because a former lover had given her name to military investigators.]

A disturbing constant in the picture of harassment is the frequency with which lesbian-baiting is triggered by a servicewoman's refusal of sexual advances. For example, one officer interviewed by the authors told of sexual advances made by a male peer toward her and two colleagues. All three made it clear that they were not interested in pursuing a sexual relationship. Soon after, they learned that the spurned officer was suggesting to other men in the unit that the three were lesbians and were engaging in sexual acts together. In some respects, this follows the typical pattern of sexual harassment. The difference in the military is the degree of pressure which can be brought to bear against a woman not only by her superiors, but by her peers, and in the case of a woman officer or noncommissioned officer, by her subordinates. The legitimization of lesbian-baiting arms all men with a tool for sexual harassment because any time a woman is called a "dyke," her reputation, her career, and even her liberty are on the line. * * *

Recourse for women faced with lesbian-baiting or sexual harassment is limited. A woman who reports abuse is likely to be "labeled as . . . not being a team player," an extremely degrading pronouncement in the military. As Harrison of the USS Grapple protested, "[t]hose times when I did move to make official reports I met hostility and reluctance to believe that incidents like these could happen aboard such a fine vessel." In addition, because of the military's anti-homosexual policy, a woman who reports lesbian-baiting harassment risks focusing increased scrutiny upon herself, which may lead to full-blown investigation. As a result, many women are reluctant to report incidents, and many accede to sexual demands.

Andrea Dworkin argues that sexual intercourse is a crucial means by which men prove their masculinity to themselves and to other men. Considered from the perspective of the gender identity theory explored above, it appears that sexual access to women servicemembers may help compensate men for the breakdown of gender boundaries in nontraditional job fields by providing an alternative means of proving masculinity. * * *

This sexual accessibility analysis appears to apply to the Parris Island investigation and may help to explain why investigations of drill instructors have taken place repeatedly at the installation. At Parris Island, Marine Corps policy segregates women recruits into their own units with women drill instructors and strictly separates male and female recruits during basic training. Servicemen on Parris Island find a host of psychological and social messages in this arrangement: they see a group of women sexually inaccessible to themselves or other men, grouped together under the instruction of assertive, competent female drill instructors who have sole access to the female recruits. The mixture is a potential powder keg of sexism, homophobia, and gender identity conflict to men who may be insecure in their masculinity.

NOTES ON CHALLENGES TO DADT AND THE DEFERENCE ISSUE

In the 1990s, every federal court of appeals upheld DADT against constitutional attack, in the face of forceful dissenting opinions. *See Thomasson v. Perry*, 80 F.3d 915 (4th Cir. 1996) (en banc); *Able v. United States*, 88 F.3d 1280 (2d Cir. 1996), on remand, 968 F.Supp. 850 (E.D.N.Y. 1997), *rev'd*, 155 F.3d 628 (2d Cir. 1998); *Richenberg v. Perry*, 97 F.3d 256 (8th Cir. 1996); *Holmes v. California Army Nat'l Guard*, 124 F.3d 1126 (9th Cir. 1997).

The Second, Fourth, Eighth, and Ninth Circuits basically agreed with the analysis of the D.C. Circuit in *Steffan v. Perry*, 41 F.3d 677 (D.C. Cir. 1994) (en banc) (upholding pre-DADT Navy regulation), for disposing of the First Amendment and Equal Protection Clause claims: by penalizing a soldier because she says she is gay, the policy was not penalizing status; rather the statement was only being used as evidence that the declarant presumptively committed "homosexual acts" (sodomy) which was a crime under the Uniform Code of Military Justice.

Dissenting opinions by Judges K.K. Hall (*Thomasson*), Richard Arnold (*Richenberg*), and Stephen Reinhardt (*Holmes*; compare his dissent in *Watkins*) followed Judge Patricia Wald's *Steffan* dissent in arguing that there is no rational basis for believing that the openly lesbian soldier is *more likely* to engage in illegal behavior than her openly straight male colleague, who is more likely to have engaged in illegal sexual harassment, illegal rape, illegal anal sex and is almost as likely to have engaged in illegal oral sex as well. The dissenters' arguments received a constitutional boost from the Supreme Court's decisions in *Romer* and *Lawrence*.

The circuit court majorities responded with the deference argument: the armed forces have to make broad categorical judgments, excluding sight-impaired people as well as gays, for example, and courts should not interfere with those judgments, especially those that go to the unit cohesion and morale features central to the military mission. Recall that the Supreme Court bent over backwards to defer to political and military judgments on an issue of blatant sex discrimination in *Rostker*. Does the deference argument survive *Lawrence*? Let us explore the deference issue in greater detail.

1. *Issues of Fact Versus Issues of Law.* Perhaps deference is most appropriate as to issues of fact, such as the Administration's idea that statements of homosexuality are evidence of sodomy, which is illegal under the Uniform Code of Military Justice. This is actually quite true, but recall that the statement "I am a heterosexual" is just as probative evidence that one has and will commit sodomy in violation of the Code. Laumann et al., *Sexual Practices in the United States* 98–99. The issue of deference, therefore, does not relate to a matter of fact (homosexuals are prone to commit illegal sodomy), but relates to a matter of discrimination law (why does the military treat presumptive heterosexual sodomites differently?).

2. *Does a Historical Pattern of "Crying Wolf" Matter? What About Evidence from Experts Within the Military?* As to military judgments that LGB people would disrupt unit cohesion, the military used a similar rationale to justify racial segregation and exclusion of women from a broad range of military positions. The available evidence, recounted in this chapter, suggests that the military was crying "wolf" both times. Is the LGB exclusion the third "wolf"? Return to Professor Karst's article on military service and the construction of manhood. His overall argument seems to be that the race, sex, and sexual orientation exclusions have been inspired by similar prejudices and were long justified by the same kinds of inaccurate stereotypes and institutionalist logic. The logic of his article is that the gay exclusion should follow the path of the race and sex ones—revocation.

A number of expert studies by executive branch consultants lend support to Professor Karst's argument. The RAND Institute conducted a study for the Department of Defense in 1993. Consistent with prior findings by the Government Accounting Office and the Defense Personnel Security Research and Education Center, RAND concluded: "concerns about the potential effect of permitting [open] homosexuals to serve in the military are not groundless, but the problems do not appear insurmountable, and there is ample reason to believe that heterosexual and homosexual personnel can work together effectively." RAND, National Defense Research Institute, Report to the Office of the Secretary of Defense, *Sexual Orientation and U.S. Military Personnel Policy: Options and Assessment* 329–30 (1993). An excellent book documenting the high costs and low benefits of don't ask, don't tell is Nathaniel Frank, *Unfriendly Fire: How the Gay Ban Undermines the Military and Weakens America* (2009).

3. *Experience in Other Countries.* Almost all of our NATO and North American allies revoked their exclusions of LGB people from their armed forces much earlier than the U.S. did. The Center for the Study of Sexual Minorities in the Military at the University of California, Santa Barbara studied the transitions from gay-exclusionary to gay-inclusionary armed forces in a wide range of countries. The Center's studies concluded that the transitions went much more smoothly than anticipated. *See, e.g.,* Aaron Belkin & Jason McNichol, *The Effects of the 1992 Lifting of Restrictions on Gay and Lesbian Service in the Canadian Forces: Appraising the Evidence* (April 2000); Aaron Belkin & Melissa Levitt, *The Effects of Lifting of Restrictions on Gay and Lesbian Service in the Israeli Forces: Appraising the Evidence* (June 2000).

Although most of the international reforms came from the political branches, Great Britain's abandonment came as a result of a (nonbinding) decision by the European Court of Human Rights that a complete exclusion of gays from the armed forces violated Article 8 (right to respect for private and family life) and Article 14 (nondiscrimination obligations) of the European Convention on Human Rights. *See Lustig-Prean v. United Kingdom,* 29 EHRR 548 (ECHR Sept. 27, 1999). The government implemented the policy with virtually no friction within its armed forces. *See* Aaron Belkin & R.L. Evans, *The Effects of Including Gay and Lesbian Soldiers in the British Armed Forces: Appraising the Evidence* (Center for the Study of Sexual Minorities in the Military Nov. 2000).

NOTE ON HARASSMENT OF LGB PEOPLE IN THE ARMED FORCES

The constitutional and policy debate over the official exclusion of (openly) lesbian, gay, and bisexual persons from the armed forces overshadowed an equally important phenomenon, namely, harassment and violence against service personnel perceived to be lesbian, gay, or bisexual. These phenomena are potentially related, as the federal exclusion encouraged soldiers to pry into one another's sexuality, and this prying not only created problems for unit cohesion, but also threatened the don't ask feature of the federal policy.

The case of Private Barry Winchell brought significant media attention to this issue. On July 5, 1999, Winchell was murdered in his sleep by two soldiers who had been among those who regularly harassed him as a suspected "fag." Investigations in the wake of his murder found that antigay "banter" was routine in Fort Campbell, where Winchell was posted, and that repeated harassment of the private went unpunished by superior officers who were aware of it.

In the wake of unfavorable publicity surrounding the Winchell murder, the Defense Department's Inspector General conducted a survey of 75,000 service personnel; its report, issued in March 2000, revealed that 80% had heard antigay remarks within the last year, 37% had witnessed or experienced antigay harassment, and 5% had witnessed or experienced antigay assaults. 85% of the respondents reported that the officers in charge took no action to stop the harassment. In July 2000, a DOD working group published an *Anti-Harassment Action Plan*, with thirteen recommendations. The Department approved the findings and drafted a Directive on the matter of harassment. Each of the service branches (Army, Navy, Air Force, Marine Corps) then developed and implemented its own regulations and directives. Probably in response to better training and less tolerance of harassment, reported incidents have steadily declined from 1998 to 1999 to 2000 to 2001.

The Army, the branch in which Private Winchell served, took the lead in developing rules against harassment. In a Directive entitled "Dignity and Respect for All," ALARACT008/00 (Jan. 2000), the Army took the position that, "Harassment of soldiers for any reason, to include perceived sexual orientation, will not be tolerated." According to the Servicemembers Legal Defense Network (SLDN), the decline in antigay harassment in 2000 was most pronounced in the Army and was due in part to the new intolerant policy toward antigay harassment. Nonetheless, there were still plenty of anti-gay incidents.

3. THE DEMISE OF DADT AND ITS AFTERMATH

After 9/11, the exclusion of gay men, lesbians, and bisexuals from the armed forces went into free-fall: academics feasted upon its inconsistencies and factual assumptions like famished dieters; according to the large majority of polls, public opinion supported service by LGB people, usually by large margins; and both Republican and Democratic administrations abandoned enforcement of the policy, with the result that thousands of open or quasi-open LGB people were serving in the armed forces. Because DADT was premised on the illegality of consensual sodomy by military personnel, the Supreme Court's decision in *Lawrence* triggered a fresh round of lawsuits challenging the law.

In a number of cases, courts carefully probed the constitutionality validity of the policy and judges increasingly concluded that the policy was unconstitutional.

Thomas Cook v. Robert M. Gates, 528 F.3d 42 (1st Cir. 2008). In the wake of *Lawrence v. Texas* (2003), twelve service personnel challenged the 1993 Don't Ask, Don't Tell statute on three constitutional grounds: (1) substantive due process; (2) equal protection, and (3) freedom of expression. Although dismissing plaintiffs' constitutional claims, **Judge Howard**'s opinion for the court engaged in an interesting discussion of current law.

(1) Substantive Due Process. Rejecting the government's position, the First Circuit accepted the plaintiffs' view that *Lawrence* recognized a constitutionally protected liberty interest in "consensual sexual intimacy in the home." Some of the conduct justifying exclusion from the armed forces fell within this protected liberty interest. Although *Lawrence* did not apply strict scrutiny, it seemed to apply a level of scrutiny somewhere between rational basis and strict scrutiny. But the court also observed that its scrutiny should be deferential because the matter fell within Congress's plenary authority over military affairs, citing *Rostker*. After extensive hearings, public debate, and deliberation (including rejection of more moderate policies), Congress decided that a total exclusion was needed to preserve the military's effectiveness as a fighting force. Citing *Rostker*, Judge Howard concluded that "where Congress has articulated a substantial government interest for a law, and where the challenges in question implicate that interest, judicial intrusion is simply not warranted."

(2) Equal Protection. Judge Howard applied rational basis review for sexual orientation classifications and summarily upheld the law. "Congress has put forward a non-animus based explanation for its decision to pass the Act. Given the substantial deference owed Congress' assessment of the need for the legislation, the Act survives rational basis review."

(3) Freedom of Expression. Plaintiffs argued that the statute directly censored identity speech, as the statement "I am a lesbian" triggers automatic discharge under the 1993 law. Under *Hurley*, that statement was protected by the First Amendment, "to some degree." Following and quoting the Supreme Court's opinion in *Goldman v. Weinberger*, 475 U.S. 503 (1986) (upholding military rule barring a rabbi from wearing a yarmulke), Judge Howard cautioned that "our review of military regulations challenged on First Amendment grounds is far more deferential than constitutional review of similar laws or regulations designed for civilian society." This limitation was rooted in the recognition that free expression can sometimes conflict with the

military's compelling need to "foster instinctive obedience, unity, commitment, and espirit [sic] de corps" and that "the essence of military service is the subordination of the desires and interests of the individual to the needs of service."

Moreover, "the Act's purpose is not to restrict this kind of speech. Its purpose is to identify those who have engaged or are likely to engage in a homosexual act as defined by the statute. The law is thus aimed at eliminating certain conduct or the possibility of certain conduct from occurring in the military environment, not at restricting speech. The Act relies on a member's speech only because a member's statement that he or she is homosexual will often correlate with a member who has a propensity to engage in a homosexual act." The Supreme Court has repeatedly upheld the use of statements otherwise protected by the First Amendment to be used as evidence that someone has committed an illegal act. E.g., *Wisconsin v. Mitchell*, 508 U.S. 476 (1993) (hate speech).

Judge Saris joined the majority's discussion of the due process and equal protection claims but dissented from its disposition of the First Amendment claim. Under the test of *Wayte v. United States*, 470 U.S. 598, 611 (1985), applicable to content-neutral speech restrictions, the government must show that the restriction is "substantially related" to an "important" state interest and that the restriction on speech is no greater than is "essential" to meet such an interest. Judge Saris found that the statute applied to service personnel who made statements about their sexual orientation but were willing to forego "homosexual sodomy" during their military service.

As such, the statute as written amounted to an exclusion based upon mere status and not conduct, for at least some "homosexuals." The government claimed that there were cases where personnel had "rebutted" the case against them under the statute, but Judge Saris noted that its examples were all over 12 years old and that plaintiffs' as-applied challenge alleged that the presumption was in practice not rebuttable. (This allegation must be taken as true on motion to dismiss, as this appeal arose.)

In the context of a motion to dismiss, where plaintiffs' allegations must be treated as correct, Judge Saris also credited plaintiffs' argument that the policy had a chilling effect on protected speech. The statute apparently applies to statements made outside military settings and in private circumstances (such as doctor-patient contexts). *See* Tobias Barrington Wolff, "Political Representation and Accountability Under Don't Ask, Don't Tell," 89 *Iowa L. Rev.* 1633, 1644–50 (2004) (examples where the presumption was applied to conversations with family members, sessions with chaplains and psychotherapists, and public statements outside military confines). It is not clear from Judge Saris's opinion whether this was an independent basis for finding a First Amendment violation; it strikes us as more likely that this buttressed the conclusion that Don't Ask, Don't Tell's restriction on protected speech was potentially greater than the government's "essential" interest in preserving an efficient armed forces.

In *Cook v. Gates*, although suggesting that the issues presented in the case were serious ones, the court ultimately ruled in favor of the government and declined to invalidate the law.

Margaret Witt v. Department of the Air Force, 527 F.3d 806 (9th Cir. 2008). Contrary to the First Circuit's conclusion in *Cook v. Gates*, in *Witt v. Dep't of the Air Force*, 527 F.3d 806 (9th Cir.), rehearing en banc denied, 548 F.3d 1264 (2008), the Ninth Circuit reversed the district court's dismissal of the plaintiff's Due Process claim and remanded the case for further proceedings. **Judge Gould** first held that because DADT constituted an "[attempt] to intrude upon the personal and private lives of homosexuals," it must be subjected to "heightened scrutiny" under *Lawrence*. While Judge Gould found that the interests asserted by the government, including "unit cohesion," were important ones, he concluded that it was not clear that the policy significantly furthered those interests or whether there was a less intrusive means to achieve those ends. *Id.* at 821. The panel remanded the case to the district court to allow the parties to develop the record on those issues. However, Judge Gould dismissed Major Witt's claim that the law violated the Equal Protection clause, concluding that Lawrence did not disturb the established law that the law passed muster under rational basis review.

In a separate opinion, concurring in part and dissenting in part, **Judge Canby** argued that strict scrutiny should be applied to both of Major Witt's claims—her due process claim and her equal protection claim.

Log Cabin Republicans v. United States, 716 F. Supp. 2d 884 (C.D. Cal. 2010). Two years later, in *Log Cabin Republicans v. United States*, 716 F. Supp. 2d 884 (C.D. Cal. 2010), *vacated as moot*, 658 F.3d 1162 (9th Cir. 2011), **Judge Phillips** held that DADT was unconstitutional. Applying *Witt*, the governing precedent in the circuit, Judge Phillips ruled that DADT violated the fundamental privacy right recognized in *Lawrence*. Judge Phillips also concluded that by excluding persons who said that they were homosexual, or "words to that effect," DADT violated the First Amendment by unconstitutionally penalizing speech regarding activities that cannot be crimes after *Lawrence* **and** because it was a content-based restriction on speech. As the court explained:

> The Act does not prohibit servicemembers from discussing their sexuality in general, nor does it prohibit all servicemembers from disclosing their sexual orientation. Heterosexual members are free to state their sexual orientation, "or words to that effect," while gay and lesbian members of the military are not. Thus, on its face, the Act discriminates based on the content of the speech being regulated. It distinguishes

between speech regarding sexual orientation, and inevitably, family relationships and daily activities, by and about gay and lesbian servicemembers, which is banned, and speech on those subjects by and about heterosexual servicemembers, which is permitted.

Id. at 926. Although Judge Phillips acknowledged that "courts apply a more deferential level of review of military restrictions on speech," regulations of speech in a military context nonetheless will survive Constitutional scrutiny only if they "'restrict speech no more than is reasonably necessary to protect the substantial government interest.'" *Id.* at 926–27 (quoting *Brown v. Glines,* 444 U.S. 348, 348 (1980)). The Act, Judge Phillips concluded, "fail[ed] this test of constitutional validity. Unlike the regulations on speech upheld in *Brown* and *Spock,* for example, the sweeping reach of the restrictions on speech in the Don't Ask, Don't Tell Act [wa]s far broader than is reasonably necessary to protect the substantial government interest at stake here." *Id.* at 927.

Finally, on July 22, 2011, President Obama conveyed to the congressional defense committees the certification required to bring an end to Don't Ask, Don't Tell. On September 20, 2011, 60 days after the certification, the Don't Ask, Don't Tell law was formally repealed. Notice the parallel between the Obama Administration's rescission of the exclusion of women from combat in 2012 and its repeal of the exclusion of openly gay, lesbian, and bisexual personnel in 2011. Both were landmark administrative actions, carried out under explicit delegations from Congress, that provoked virtually no big public controversy when they were actually announced.

NOTES ON FIRST AMENDMENT ATTACKS ON DADT

1. *Was DADT's Restriction on Speech Content Neutral?* Statutes restricting speech based on content are subject to strict scrutiny in civilian cases and some form of heightened scrutiny even in the military context. The First Circuit unanimously (Judge Saris agreeing on this point) ruled that the regulation of speech in the DADT statute was content neutral. In the Log Cabin Republicans case, Judge Phillips rejected that position. Which court was correct? *See* Tobias Barrington Wolff, "Political Representation and Accountability Under Don't Ask, Don't Tell," 89 *Iowa L. Rev.* 1633, 1644–50 (2004).

Was this free speech issue intertwined with the privacy issue, namely, whether the armed forces can make it a crime for soldiers to engage in private homosexual activities with consenting adults (*Marcum*)? Consider this objection. The statement "I am a gay man" is evidence that the man has a propensity to commit sodomy—but so is the statement "I am a straight man." *See* Edward O. Laumann, John H. Gagnon, Robert T. Michael & Stuart Michaels, *The Social Organization of Sexuality: Sexual Practices in the United States* 98–99 (1994) (79% of straight men have engaged in oral sex, which is illegal "sodomy" under the Uniform Code of Military Justice).

Yet the statute censored only the former statement. The court's apparent assumption was that Congress could make "homosexual sodomy" a crime and hunt down offenders, but not "heterosexual sodomy." But Congress in fact made *both* kinds of sodomy crimes. And Justice O'Connor's opinion in *Lawrence* suggests that criminalizing *only* homosexual sodomy might violate *Romer*. In short, the law did not appear to be content neutral. Under the Supreme Court's jurisprudence, the government must demonstrate that the censorship is narrowly tailored to serve a compelling government purpose other than suppressing its message. *R.A.V. v. City of St. Paul*, 505 U.S. 377 (1992). Could DADT satisfy such a test? (Hint: the majority would say yes. What would its reasoning be?)

2.   *Did DADT Violate the* O'Brien *Test? Was It Overbroad?* Judge Saris's objection was that DADT covered more protected expression than is needed to serve the important government interest. By going along with the majority on the due process and equal protection claims, however, Judge Saris seemed to be agreeing that the exclusion of probable "homosexual sodomites" was rationally related to the efficient operation of the armed forces. A lot of the evidence Congress heard was to the effect that openly gay soldiers would disrupt military efficiency. If that was the case, the statute seemed to fit the goal better than Judge Saris admitted. Why care about chilling effect if what you are trying to chill is disruptive speech?

Judge Saris flirted with the argument that the statute was "overbroad." The Supreme Court has applied the overbreadth doctrine cautiously. In *Broadrick v. Oklahoma*, 413 U.S. 601 (1973), the Court upheld a state law restricting political activities by public employees. Although the law seemed to reach core First Amendment activities that posed no danger to state policies (e.g., display of campaign buttons or bumper stickers), the Court declined to strike down the law. Justice White's opinion required that overbreadth "must not only be real, but substantial as well," to justify invalidation. Judge Saris's opinion did not discuss *Broadrick*, perhaps because it involved a facial challenge to the Oklahoma law; *Cook* involved an as-applied challenge as well. Still, *Broadrick* might be cited for the proposition that First Amendment chilling effect arguments must meet a high threshold.

NOTE ON TRANSGENDER AND INTERSEX PERSONS IN THE U.S. ARMED FORCES

It has been estimated that there are between 2,150 and 15,500 transgender soldiers serving in the U.S. armed forces. RAND Review, Aaron Belkin, et al., "Discharging Transgender Troops Would Cost $960 Million," Palm Center (Aug. 2017), http://www.palmcenter.org/publication/discharging-transgender-troops-cost-960-million/. Until 2016, however, all of the service branches had policies barring indivudals who are transgender and intersex from enlisting or serving. *See* Army Recruiting Regulation 601–204 (2004); Marine Corps Military Personnel Manual (2004) and Order P-1100.72c; Tarynn M. Witten, *Gender Identity and the Military—Transgender, Transsexual, and Intersex-Identified Individuals in the U.S. Armed Forces* 6–7 (Palm Center Feb. 2007) (survey of other branches).

There were a number of provisions under which a transgender or intersex person could be discharged from the U.S. Armed Forces. For example, Department of Defense Instruction 6130.03 provided that a "[h]istory major abnormalities or defects of the genitalia" was a ground for disqualification. The provision further explained that these "abnormalities or defects" included "change of sex, hermaphroditism, pseudo-hermaphroditism, or pure gonadal dysgenesis." DoDI 6130.03 (as of 2010). Transgender people who had had some form of genital surgery could be discharged under this instruction.

The Department of Defense Instructions also listed "[c]urrent or history of psychosexual conditions, including but not limited to transsexualism, exhibitionism, transvestism, voyeurism, and other paraphilias" as grounds for discharge. DoDI 6130.03 (as of 2010). For a more comprehensive discussion of other provisions under which a transgender or intersex person could be discharged, see Gabriel Arkles, "No One is Disposable: Going Beyond the Trans Military Inclusion Debate," 13 *Seattle J. for Soc. Just.* 459, 486–89 (2014). Consistent with the service ban, the military previously did not provide transition-related medical care to active service members or to veterans. *Id.* at 489.

In July 2015, however, Secretary of Defense Ashton Carter directed a working group to update military policy "starting with the presumption that transgender persons can serve openly without adverse impact on military effectiveness and readiness, unless and except where objective, practical impediments are identified." *See* http://www.defense.gov/Releases/Release. aspx?ReleaseID=17378.

Thereafter, the military studied the issue by, among other things, consulting medical experts and considering the experiences of other countries that permitted openly transgender people to serve in their armed forces. Based on this study, the Department of Defense concluded that the armed forces would end its exclusion of transgender persons from military service. *See* Dep't of Defense, Press Release No. NR-246-16 (June 30, 2016), available at http://www.defense.gov/News/News-Releases/News-Release-View/Article/821675/secretary-of-defense-ash-carter-announces-policy-for-transgender-service-members (viewed July 30, 2016).

Beginning on July 1, 2016, transgender individuals who were already servicemembers were permitted to serve openly. Shortly thereafter, the military also lifted its long-standing ban on the provision of transition-related medical care.

On July 1, 2017, the military services were supposed to begin permitting openly transgender individuals to be admitted into the U.S. Armed Forces. *See, e.g.*, DoDI 1300.28, https://www.defense.gov/Portals/1/features/2016/0616_policy/DoD-Instruction-1300.28.pdf. On June 30, 2017, however, one day before this requirement was set to go into effect, the Pentagon announced that the services would "defer accessing transgender applicants into the military until Jan. 1, 2018." Matt Stevens, "Pentagon Delays Accepting Transgender Recruits for 6 Months," *N.Y. Times* (June 30, 2017).

Several weeks later, on July 26, 2017, President Donald Trump issued the following three tweets:

"After consultation with my Generals and military experts, please be advised that the United States Government will not accept or allow......"

"....Transgender individuals to serve in any capacity in the U.S. Military. Our military must be focused on decisive and overwhelming....."

"....victory and cannot be burdened with the tremendous medical costs and disruption that transgender [sic] in the military would entail. Thank you"

The next day, July 27, 2017, CNN reported "three US defense officials told CNN" that "[t]he Joint Chiefs of Staff, including chairman General Joseph Dunford, were not aware President Donald Trump planned to tweet a ban on transgender service members." Barbara Staff, Zachary Cohen & Jim Sciutto, "US Joint Chiefs Blindsided by Trump's Transgender Ban," CNN, July 27, 2017, http://www.cnn.com/2017/07/27/politics/trump-military-transgender-ban-joint-chiefs/index.html.

On August 1, 2017, fifty-six retired General and Flag Officers issued a statement which stated the following: "President Trump seeks to ban transgender service members because of the financial cost and disruption associated with transgender military service. We respectfully disagree, and consider these claims to be without merit."

In terms of the allegations of financial costs, prior studies had found that the financial cost of providing health care to transgender servicemembers would be approximately $8.4 million per year. *Id.* "This [projected cost] amounts to one one-hundredth of one percent of the military's annual health care budget." *Id.* In contrast, another study by the Palm Center found that the *cost of the ban* will be 100 times that amount – the ban will cost approximately $960 million. Aaron Belkin, et al., "Discharging Transgender Troops Would Cost $960 Million," Palm Center (Aug. 2017), http://www.palmcenter.org/publication/discharging-transgender-troops-cost-960-million/.

The statement from the fifty-six retired Generals and Flag Officers also rejected the President's suggestion that the inclusion of transgender servicemembers would cause disruption. The statement noted that "transgender troops have been serving honorably and openly for the past year, and have been widely praised by commanders." It is the ban, advocates contend, that will create more disruption, by forcing the removal of trained and experienced members of the U.S. armed forces

On August 25, 2017, President Trump issued a Presidential Memorandum for the Secretary of Defense and the Secretary of Homeland Security. The Memorandum directs the military to "return to [its former] policy and practice on military service by transgender individuals." It indefinitely extends the current ban on "accession of transgender individuals into military service." § 2(a). The Memorandum also directs the end of "all use of DoD or DHS resources to fund sex reassignment surgical procedures[

for military personnel, except to the extent necessary to protect the health of an individual who has already begun a course of treatment to reassign his or her sex." § 2(b). The directive with regard to existing servicemembers will go into effect on March 23, 2018. § 3. While it remains unclear, it is possible (indeed it is likely) that unless the ban is revoked or limited, transgender people who are openly serving in the U.S. military will be discharged or otherwise removed from the armed forces by that date.

As of September 2017, at least four lawsuits had been filed challenging the new directive regarding the ability of transgender individuals to serve in the U.S. armed forces. The first filed lawsuit, *Jane Doe, et al. v. Donald Trump*, was filed even before the Presidential Memorandum was issued. This lawsuit was filed on August 9, 2017 by GLBTQ Legal Advocates and Defenders and the National Center for Lesbian Rights. The complaint is available at http://www.nclrights.org/wp-content/uploads/2017/08/AS-FILED-COMPLAINT_Doe.v.Trump_-1.pdf. Other lawsuits were subsequently filed by Lambda Legal and the ACLU.

In terms of the thousands of transgender veterans, the Veterans Affairs department had recently considered a proposal to end its long-standing ban on the provision of gender-affirming surgery for veterans (which has been in place since the early 1990s). Samantha Michaels, "The VA Just Dealt a Big Blow to Transgender Veterans," *Mother Jones* (Nov. 15, 2016). But, in November 2016, "officials said the proposal had been scrapped by the Office of Management and Budget because it was not clear how the department would pay for it." *Id.* Of course, there are other forms of medical care for veterans that are also expensive.

Is it permissible to single out this one type of medically necessary care that is needed only by one subgroup and refuse to cover it?

PROBLEM 9-2
OPENLY TRANSGENDER SERVICEMEMBERS

Some of the plaintiffs challenging the August 25, 2017 Presidential Memorandum are current servicemembers who came out as transgender after the earlier July 1, 2016 policy change permitting existing servicemembers to serve openly. These servicemembers have raised a number of challenges to the new policy directive, including that the policy violates the Equal Protection Clause by discriminating on the bases of sex, gender, and/or gender identity; that the policy violates the Due Process clause because it is arbitrary and capricious and lacks any rational basis; and that because these individuals had come out in reliance on the July 2016 policy any subsequent discharge is impermissible.

How would a court rule on these claims and why? How much deference should be granted to the military's position in ruling on the constitutionality of the policy?

What about challenges by transgender individuals who are not yet members of the military, but who would like to enlist? Does the indefinite continuation of the accession ban violate the Constitution? Why or why not?

For consideration of these questions, see Noah Feldman, "Ban on Transgender Troops Is Doomed in the Courts," Bloomberg View, July 26, 2017, https://www.bloomberg.com/view/articles/2017-07-26/a-ban-on-trans gender-troops-is-doomed-in-the-courts; Shannon Minter, "Trump's tweets on trans soldiers won't hold up in court," CNN, July 27, 2017, http://www.cnn. com/2017/07/27/opinions/trans-military-ban-opinion-minter/.

SECTION 2

SEXUAL HARASSMENT, SEXUAL VIOLENCE, AND SEXUAL CONDUCT IN THE U.S. ARMED FORCES

A. SEXUAL HARASSMENT IN THE MILITARY

INTRODUCTORY NOTES ON SEXUAL HARASSMENT IN THE ARMED FORCES

1. *Sexual Harassment Scandals in the U.S. Armed Forces: "Gender Panic"?* Sexual harassment is a pervasive problem in the armed forces. A 2012 survey conducted by the Pentagon found that approximately 26,000 women and men had been sexually assaulted. Female servicemembers are disproportionately likely to experience sexual assault in the military. "Estimates of sexual assaults that occur during military service range from 9.5% to 43% among women and 1–12% among men." Carl Andrew Castro, et al., Sexual Assault in the Military, Curr. Psychiatry Rep. 17:54 (2015). Indeed, as Rep. Jane Harman (D-CA) puts it, sexual assault is so prevalent in the armed forces that "A woman who signs up to protect her country is more likely to be raped by a fellow soldier than killed by enemy fire."

Numerous theories have been offered to explain the high rates of sexual harassment in the military. Some scholars argue that the high rate of sexual harassment in the military is the result of "the rigid hierarchy and power differentials in its organization structure, which make it difficult for subordinates to defend themselves against harassment." Nathan Seppa, "Sexual Harassment in the Military Lingers On," *Am. Psychol. Assn. Monitor*, at 40 (May 1997). Others contend that sexual harassment is prevalent because the "macho tradition of military life may simply attract more traditional men." *Id.*

Despite the high levels of sexual harassment, many female servicemembers do not report the harassment, often due to fear. Servicemembers fear negative consequences as the result of reporting, and the evidence suggests that these fears are not unfounded. "According to a 2014 Department of Defense survey conducted by RAND Corporation, 62 percent of active service members who reported sexual assault to a military authority in the past year indicated they experienced retaliation as a result of reporting." "Embattled: Retaliation Against Sexual Assault Survivors in the US Military," *Human Rights Watch* (May 18, 2015). Moreover, in many cases, no action is taken against perpetrators. "Of the more than 59000 reports of sexual assault in the military in fiscal year 2014, less than one third of the perpetrators received any kind of legal or administrative action for substantiated charges." Carl Andrew Castro, et al., "Sexual Assault in the Military," Curr. Psychiatry Rep. 17:54 (2015).

As Benecke and Dodge explain, when DADT was still in effect, one form of retaliation that was common was lesbian baiting. After being accused by a female servicemember of engaging in inappropriate conduct, some perpetrators would accuse the victim of being a lesbian. As a result, the woman herself then often became the target of the investigation (under DADT, deflecting the focus away from the perpetrator of the assault). Even if she was not labeled a lesbian, a woman who reported sexual harassment might be "labeled as . . . not being a team player," Benecke and Dodge explain, which would often hinder the woman's advancement in the military.

Even though only a small percent of sexual assaults and other incidents of sexual harassment are reported, that has not stopped the scandals from making it into the headlines. *See* Martha Chamallas, "The New Gender Panic: Reflections on Sex Scandals and the Military," 83 *Minn. L. Rev.* 305 (1998).

On November 7, 1996, the U.S. Army announced that three soldiers at the Aberdeen Proving Ground in Maryland faced court-martial charges stemming from alleged sexual misconduct with female recruits. Among those accused of harassing conduct was Staff Sergeant Delmar Simpson. He was charged with nine counts of rape, three counts of forcible sodomy, and other serious offenses. The rape charges were based on accusations that Simpson abused his authority by requiring sex from female soldiers under his charge. Found guilty by a military jury, he was sentenced to 25 years in prison. This case and complaints from female personnel triggered an eight-month investigation by the Army. A task force suggested adding a week to basic training to teach values; instigating tougher selection, training, and supervision of drill sergeants; and exerting more pressure on the chain of command to respond to discrimination and harassment against women.

The Army's heightened sensitivity to sexual discrimination and harassment provoked various concerns and even backlashes. At Aberdeen itself, some male soldiers reacted to the scandal by adopting informal rules against any unmonitored interaction with female soldiers, thereby marginalizing women even more than before. *See* Diane Mazur, "The Beginning of the End for Women in the Military," 48 *Fla. L. Rev.* 461 (1996). Additionally, the fact that all of the Aberdeen defendants ultimately accused were black men and most of the accusers were white women provoked concern from civil rights groups that the prosecutions were racially selective.

Feminists worried that the publicity surrounding the mushrooming Aberdeen scandal created a "gender panic." Chamallas, "New Gender Panic," 316–19, cites the prosecution of Lieutenant Kelly Flinn for adultery. Flinn's memoir concluded: "[M]aybe * * * this was a way of saying, without having to say it, that women have no place in the military: let them in and all hell breaks loose." Kelly Flinn, *Proud to Be* 206 (1997). There is some evidence that the scandal made many male soldiers restive. Many enlisted personnel believed that regulations governing fraternization, sexual harassment, and adultery were applied in a discriminatory manner, where women were not penalized in circumstances where men were (the Flinn case notwithstanding).

Other military sexual harassment scandals include the Tailhook scandal in 1991, the 2003 U.S. Air Force Academy Scandal, the sexual abuse of trainees at Lackland Airforce Base between 2009 and 2012, and the 2017 scandal among Marine Corp members who shared nude photos of service women.

2.   *Proposals to Resegregate Military Training.* These scandals have also ignited a fierce debate over the future of training male and female recruits together—a practice largely adopted by all branches of the armed services except the Marine Corps. In the wake of the Aberdeen scandal, Senator Rick Santorum and others demanded that the Department of Defense reevaluate sex-integrated training. (This proposal was ultimately rejected).

Critics charged that, if adopted, the Committee's proposal would have represented a significant regression in military policy. Professor Chamallas maintains that proposals for sex resegregation would not only set back women's integration into the armed forces, but would also fuel the fires of sexual harassment. Professor Vicki Schultz, "Reconceptualizing Sexual Harassment," 107 *Yale L.J.* 1683 (1998), argues that the structure and ideology of the workplace drive sexual harassment. A workplace with a few token women working in marginalized (and sex-stereotyped) positions is a workplace that is *most* likely to have sexual harassment, while a workplace with a fair number of women, working in a variety of positions (including positions of power), is one that likely will have less sexual harassment. *See also* Kathryn Abrams, "The New Jurisprudence of Sexual Harassment," 83 *Cornell L. Rev.* 1169 (1998); Anita Bernstein, "Treating Sexual Harassment with Respect," 111 *Harv. L. Rev.* 445 (1997); Martha Chamallas, "Structuralist and Cultural Domination Theories Meet Title VII: Some Contemporary Influences," 92 *Mich. L. Rev.* 2370 (1994).

Chamallas, "New Gender Panic," 324–32, draws from Professor Schultz and other theorists the conclusion that women will inevitably be harassed and denigrated within the armed forces unless structural changes are made—especially increasing the numbers of women beyond token amounts and increasing women's access to power positions. Indeed, the Defense Department's own data supported that proposition. The Marine Corps had the lowest percentage of women and was in the 1990s the only branch to have sex-segregated basic training—yet it had the highest level of reported sexual harassment. The Navy had the most sex-integrated basic training—yet was most successful in reducing the reported levels of harassment. *Gender-Integrated Training and Related Matters: Hearing Before the Subcomm. on Personnel of the Senate Comm. on Armed Servs.*, 105th Cong., 1st Sess. 40 ff. (1997) (statement of Nancy Duff Campbell, Co-President of the National Women's Law Center on Gender-Integrated Training).

Resegregation would not only fail to address these structural concerns but would, Chamallas worries, represent a symbolic and probably practical backwards step. It would be a signal to the armed forces to de-emphasize the recruitment of women. More deeply, sex-segregated training would further undermine women's abilities to achieve leadership positions within the armed services. It is hard to doubt the feminist wisdom that fair and equal treatment of women in the workforce—including military ones—is harder if not impossible if women are not in supervisory and leadership positions, including positions where they exercise leadership over men. Chamallas, "New Gender Panic," 328–30. Under tokenism theory, "more thorough integration of women into all aspects of military life, including positions designated as combat positions, would appear to be the best response to Aberdeen" (p. 332).

3. *Congressional Responses and Possible Progress?* Since 2001, congressional focus has shifted away from sex resegregation and toward more effective bars to sexual harassment. In the Bob Stump National Defense Authorization Act for FY 2003, § 8, Congress required the DoD to collect and report annual data on sexual harassment complaints and their rate of substantiation.

Recent annual reports find that that while there has been a decrease in "military sexual assaults and increased reporting of such crimes," "rates of retaliations against victims remain stubbornly high." Daniel Costa-Roberts, "Pentagon Sexual Assault Report Shows High Rates of Perceived Retaliation Persist," PBS Newshour (May 3, 2015 2:29 PM EDT).

Military EO Policy, Department of Defense, Directive 1350.2, "The Defense Military Equal Opportunity Program"

http://www.dtic.mil/whs/directives/corres/pdf/135002p.pdf (as of April 20, 2017).

This Directive creates a "Department of Defense Military Equal Opportunity (MEO) Program," which carries out a policy against discrimination based on "race, color, religion, sex or national origin." *Id.* ¶ 4.2. The anti-discrimination policy includes a rule against sexual harassment. Paragraph E2.1.15 defines "sexual harassment" as "[a] form of sex discrimination that involves unwelcome sexual advances, requests for sexual favors, and other verbal or physical conduct of a sexual nature when:

> E2.1.15.1. Submission to such conduct is made explicitly or implicitly a term or condition of a person's job, pay, or career, or

> E2.1.15.2. Submission to or rejection of such conduct by a person is used as a basis for career or employment decisions affecting that person, or

> E2.1.15.3. Such conduct has the purpose or effect of unreasonably interfering with an individual's work performance or creates an intimidating, hostile, or offensive working environment."

NOTES ON THE ARMED FORCES' EO POLICY

1. *Definition of Sexual Harassment.* This definition of sexual harassment above is taken from the EEOC's 1980 Guidelines regulating sexual harassment in the civilian workplace, pursuant to Title VII of the Civil Rights Act of 1964. Is it appropriate to use the same definition in this context? Why or why not? *See, e.g.,* Michael Noone, "Chimera or Jackalope? Department of Defense Efforts to Apply Civilian Sexual Harassment Criteria to the Military," 6 *Duke J. Gender L. & Pol'y* 151 (1999) (critical of this borrowing); Dana Michael Hollywood, "Creating a True Army of One: Four Proposals to Combat Sexual Harassment in Today's Army," 30 *Harv. J. L. & Gender* 151 (2007) (arguing that the use of the EEOC's definition of sexual harassment "is inherently problematic, for when civilian terms are applied to the military, they lose their meaning because they have different purposes, remedies, and penalties").

2. *Enforcement Process.* One recurrent criticism that has been raised with respect to the military's sexual harassment and sexual assault policies relates to the enforcement procedures. Specifically, complaints are handled through the "chain of command." Department of Defense, Directive 1350.2, at 4.3 ("The chain of command is the primary and preferred channel for identifying and correcting discriminatory practices. This includes the processing and resolving of complaints of unlawful discrimination and sexual harassment * * *.").

Critics contend this process is "inherently unfair" and inappropriate. Jenna McLaughlin, "Reporting Sexual Abuse in the Military is 'Inherently Unfair.' Here's Why," *Mother Jones* (Mar. 3, 2015). Among other things, the commander has a "vested interest" in the resolution of the complaint; if the investigation reveals that harassment occurred, the commander (who receives the initial complaint and investigates it) "will likely be labeled a poor leader." Dana Michael Hollywood, "Creating a True Army of One: Four Proposals to Combat Sexual Harassment in Today's Army," 30 *Harv. J. L. & Gender* 151, 195 (2007). As a result, some contend, the "system is designed so that doing the right thing is often detrimental to one's career." *Id.*

Numerous bills have been introduced that would or could shift the process away from the chain of command. For example, in 2013, Senator Kristen Gillibrand (D-NY) proposed the Military Justice Improvement Act (MJIA). S. 967, 113th Cong. (2013). Among other things, the MJIA would "decreas[e] the amount of discretion the chain of command has in deciding whether to investigate and prosecute claims." Alexandra Lohman, Note and Comment, "Silence of the Lambs: Giving Voice to the Problem of Rape and Sexual Assault in the United Sates Armed Forces," 10 *N.W. J.L. & Soc. Pol'y* 230, 253 (2015). Senator Claire McCaskill proposed a different bill that would amend the U.S. personnel policy guidelines so that "the victim could decide whether to prosecute his or her case in a civilian or military jurisdiction." *Id.* So far, however, none of these proposals has been enacted.

B. THE REGULATION OF SEXUAL CONDUCT IN THE U.S. ARMED SERVICES

1. PREGNANCY AND ABORTION FOR MILITARY PERSONNEL[a]

By executive order, President Truman directed that the armed forces should discharge any female soldiers who became pregnant during their military service. *See* H.R. 5447, 2d Session, 107th Congress, Sept. 24, 2002 (apologizing for this policy, which was in effect until 1976). In *Struck v. Secretary of Defense*, Ruth Bader Ginsburg challenged this policy before it was revoked. The Air Force told the plaintiff, Captain Susan Struck, that she should could maintain her position in the Air Force if she had an abortion. Cary Franklin, "The Anti-Stereotyping Principle in Constitutional Sex Discrimination Law," 85 *N.Y.U. L. Rev.* 83, 126 (2010). Struck chose to continue her pregnancy and the Air Force discharged her after she gave birth. *Id.* In her brief on behalf of Struck, Ginsburg argued that the policy "reinforce[d] societal pressure to relinquish career aspirations for a hearth-centered existence." Brief for the Petitioner at 37, Struck v. Sec'y of Def., 409 U.S. 1071 (1972) (No. 72–178). The Court never had the chance to decide whether or not that was the case, as the Air Force granted a waiver to Struck during the pendency of the litigation. Franklin, *supra*, at 126–27.

Although the strict policy is no longer in effect, the Department of Defense discourages female personnel from becoming pregnant, *see* Maj. Leslie Christopher & Leslie Miller, "Women in War: Operational Issues of Menstruation and Unintended Pregnancy," 172 *Mil. Med.* 9–16 (January 2007), and will typically remove pregnant soldiers from theatres of war (such as Afghanistan in 2010). If pregnancy is so expensive and potentially disruptive of unit cohesion, should the armed forces facilitate abortions, especially for unplanned pregnancies?

In 1970, the first formal policy on abortion was issued by the Department of Defense (DoD), requiring "that military hospitals perform abortions when it is medically necessary or when the mental health of the mother is threatened."[b] Soon thereafter, President Nixon revised this policy to make policies at each military base "correspond with the laws of the States where the bases are located." After *Roe v. Wade* (1973), DoD began funding abortions for all women eligible for DoD health care, but this was also limited by state law. In 1975, in order to help resolve some of the conflicts between state law and *Roe*, DoD issued a memorandum requiring military medical facilities to follow the *Roe* standard in certain cases. Approximately 26,000 abortions were performed from August 1976

---

[a]   Deborah Megdal (Yale Law School, Class of 2012) did the primary research for this Note.

[b]   The history of federal policy regarding abortions for military personnel (both female servicemembers and the female spouses of male servicemembers) has been comprehensively reviewed by Congressional Research Service, *Abortion Services and Military Medical Facilities*, Updated Apr. 24, 2002, *available at* http://www.policyarchive.org/handle/10207/bitstreams/266.pdf (viewed July 1, 2010).

to August 1977, in military medical facilities or as part of the program providing medical care to dependents of service people through local health care providers. During the 1970s, pro-life activists and legislators made it an increasing priority to halt federal payments for abortions under any circumstances.

In 1978, Congress banned the use of DoD funds for abortions, unless the pregnant woman's life "would be endangered if the fetus were carried to term," if there would be "severe and long-lasting physical health damage" if the pregnancy continued, and in cases of rape or incest. Pub. L. No. 95–457, § 863, 92 Stat. 1231 (1978). The 1979 DoD appropriations act removed the exception for "long-lasting physical health damage." But even with the ban in place, there were approximately 1,300 privately funded abortions performed in FY1979 at military hospitals. The 1981, 1982, and 1983 appropriation acts removed more of the exceptions, giving the ban a wider reach, but privately funded abortions were still permitted. In 1988, Assistant Secretary of Defense William Mayer banned abortion in military medical facilities abroad. (This policy was reversed by executive order in 1993, but the reversal probably did not significantly increase access to abortions for military personnel: only 37 abortions were performed in military facilities in 1993–94.)

Public Law Nos. 104–61, §§ 8119–8119A, 109 Stat. 636 (1995), and 104–106, § 738(b), 110 Stat. 186 (1996), prohibit the use of military medical facilities to perform abortions except in cases of rape, incest, or when the pregnant woman's life is endangered; the 1996 law added a new statutory restriction on facilities. The U.S. Code now (2017) provides as follows:

10 U.S.C. § 1093.
Performance of abortions: restrictions

(a) Restriction on use of funds.—Funds available to the Department of Defense may not be used to perform abortions except where the life of the mother would be endangered if the fetus were carried to term or in a case in which the pregnancy is the result of an act of rape or incest.

(b) Restriction on use of facilities.—No medical treatment facility or other facility of the Department of Defense may be used to perform an abortion except where the life of the mother would be endangered if the fetus were carried to term or in a case in which the pregnancy is the result of an act of rape or incest.

The requirement that even victims of rape or incest must use private funding to pay for the abortion is a particular burden for military servicewomen given the high rate of rape and sexual assault on military bases.

PROBLEM 9-3
FAMILY CHOICE RIGHTS FOR MILITARY PERSONNEL

Private Kim Wo is a pregnant servicemember serving in northern Iraq. Her military doctors tell her that her fetus has a rare and fatal condition (anencephaly) that would lead to certain death before birth or shortly thereafter. Wo requests that her abortion be covered by the military health insurance policy because it is medically necessary. Invoking 10 U.S.C. § 1093(a), DoD denies her request for coverage; invoking § 1093(b), DoD also tells Wo that military doctors and the American military hospital in northern Iraq cannot assist in the abortion. Wo's doctors tell her that she should not fly at this stage in her pregnancy. Reluctant to seek treatment in Iraqi hospitals because of documented problems with the available facilities, Wo seeks a preliminary injunction requiring DoD to provide for her medically necessary abortion in Iraq.

DoD's position is that its hands are tied by § 1093 and that the statute is constitutional under *Harris v. McRae,* 448 U.S. 297 (1980). In *Harris,* the Supreme Court ruled that states do not infringe a woman's fundamental right to an abortion by refusing to pay for such procedures in public welfare or safety net programs. Wo responds that she prevails under the rational basis approach followed in *Harris*: the government has no rational basis to deny abortions under circumstances that are "medically necessary" such as this one.

Entering the case as an *amicus,* the Center for Reproductive Rights explains that "the ban's impact is particularly devastating for service members, spouses and dependents stationed overseas," because "these women are forced either to attempt to obtain an abortion in a local medical facility in the country in which they are stationed, or to travel to a medical facility in the United States or in another country to obtain the abortion." Relying on local medical providers can be problematic because they are often inadequate, unsafe, below the standards of U.S. medical facilities, or lack trained medical personnel, and because U.S. military personnel may be serving in countries where animosity toward the United States runs high, their safety may be jeopardized if they were to use local health facilities. *See* CRR, "Penalized for Serving Their Country: The Ban on Abortion for Women in the Military" (June 1, 2003), available at http://reproductiverights.org/en/document/penalized-for-serving-their-country-the-ban-on-abortion-for-women-in-the-military (visited July 6, 2010).

How would a federal judge rule in Private Wo's case? *See Britell v. United States,* 372 F.3d 1370 (Fed. Cir. 2004); Amy E. Crawford, Comment, "Under Siege: Freedom of Choice and the Statutory Ban on Abortions on Military Bases," 71 *U. Chi. L. Rev.* 1549 (2004).

Change the facts of Private Wo's case. Married and serving in northern Iraq, she is pregnant, and there is no medical problem with her pregnancy. But there is, in 2010, a legal problem with it. In November 2009, Major General Anthony Cucolo III, the commanding general in northern Iraq, issued a directive that becoming pregnant or impregnating a service member would be a violation of military policy that could be punished by court martial or jail time. NBC News, *Army General in Iraq Issues Pregnancy Ban* (Dec. 18, 2009), http://www.msnbc.msn.com/id/34483943/ns/us _ news-military/ (viewed Aug. 15, 2010). The order was " 'applicable to all United States military personnel, and to all civilians, serving with, employed by, or accompanying' the military in northern Iraq, with few exceptions"—*and also applied to married couples who were both serving* and that both would be punished for a pregnancy. In justifying the policy, army spokesman Major Lee Peters explained that "[w]hen a soldier becomes pregnant, or causes a soldier to become pregnant through consensual activity . . . the redeployment of the pregnant soldier creates a void in the unit and has a negative impact on the unit's ability to accomplish its mission. Another soldier must assume the pregnant soldier's responsibilities."

Assume that General Cucolo is authorized, as a matter of statutory authority, to issue such an order. Is it constitutional? Would the Supreme Court defer to military officials pursuant to *Rostker*? For the subsequent history of General Cucolo's directive, see Lolita Baldor, Associated Press, "Military Eases Pregnancy Rule," *Military Eases Pregnancy Rule* (Dec. 25, 2009), http://www.spokesman.com/stories/2009/dec/25/military-eases-pregnancy-rule/ (viewed Aug. 15, 2010).

2. CRIMINALIZATION OF SEXUAL CONDUCT IN THE U.S. ARMED FORCES

Until 2011, the military criminalized non-forcible sodomy. The provision, Article 125 of the Uniform Code of Military Justice (UCMJ), previously provided that it was illegal to engage in "unnatural carnal copulation with another person of the same or opposite sex." Former 10 U.S.C. § 925(a). In 2011, the provision was amended such that it now only criminalizes forcible sodomy. Was the pre-2011 version constitutional? Consider the following case.

United States v. Eric P. Marcum, 60 M.J. 198 (App. Armed Forces 2004). Air Force Sergeant Eric P. Marcum, a cryptologic linguist and the supervising noncommissioned officer in a flight of Persian-Farsi speaking intelligence analysts, was accused of engaging in oral sex with male airmen under his supervision at his off-base home. According to the testimony of multiple members of his unit, airmen "often" spent the night at his off-base home following these parties.

One of the charges was that Marcum had forcibly sodomized Senior Airman Robert Harrison, who testified that while sleeping on the couch in Marcum's apartment Marcum orally sodomized him. In his own testimony, Marcum denied performing oral sex on Harrison but did say that he "kissed" Harrison's penis two times, with the consent of Harrison. Harrison testified that he confronted Marcum and asked that this behavior not recur—yet he remained friends with Marcum, as a kind of "father-son" relationship. (A rather close one, as Harrison also testified that they danced together and publicly kissed "in the European style."

And on at least one other occasion, Harrison slept with Marcum and woke up to find Marcum's erect penis against his backside.)

Based upon this evidence, a panel of officers and enlisted members found Marcum "not guilty of forcible sodomy but guilty of non-forcible sodomy" in violation of Article 125, which the Court of Military Appeals has interpreted to prohibit "every kind of unnatural carnal intercourse, whether accomplished by force or fraud, or with consent. Similarly, the article does not distinguish between an act committed in the privacy of one's home, with no person present other than the sexual partner, and the same act committed in a public place in front of a group of strangers, who fully apprehend in the nature of the act." *United States v. Scoby*, 5 M.J. 160, 163 (C.M.A. 1978).

Marcum challenged his conviction as contrary to *Lawrence*. The government responded that *Lawrence* was not applicable to military service personnel and that the court should defer to the determination of Congress and the President that homosexual sodomy is destructive to armed forces morale.

Judge Baker wrote the opinion for the court, rejecting the government's argument that *Lawrence* had no bearing for military personnel. Because Marcum was convicted for activities that were in his home and consensual, according to the finders of fact, the Court found *Lawrence* to be a proper starting point and that Marcum had a liberty interest in engaging in the charged activities. But Judge Baker also inquired whether Marcum's conduct "encompassed any of the behavior or factors that were identified by the Supreme Court as not involved in *Lawrence*." An Air Force instruction directed officers such as Marcum:

> Unduly familiar relationships between members in which one member exercises supervisory or command authority over the other can easily be or become unprofessional. Similarly, as differences in grade increase, even in the absence of a command or supervisory relationship, there may be more risk that the relationship will be, or be perceived to be unprofessional because senior members in military organizations normally exercise authority or some direct or indirect organizational influence over more junior members.

> Relationships are unprofessional, whether pursued on- or off-duty, when they detract from the authority of superiors or result in, or reasonably create the appearance of, favoritism, misuse of office or position, or the abandonment of organizational goals for personal interests.

Dep't. of the Air Force Instruction, 36–2909 Professional and Unprofessional Relationships, ¶¶ 2.2, 3.1 (May 1, 1996).

For these reasons, Judge Baker continued:

"the military has consistently regulated relationships between servicemembers based on certain differences in grade in an effort to avoid partiality, preferential treatment, and the improper use of one's rank. Indeed, Dep't of the Air Force Instruction 36–2909 is subject to criminal sanction through operation of Article 92, UCMJ. As both the Supreme Court and this Court have recognized elsewhere, 'The fundamental necessity for obedience and the consequent necessity for imposition of discipline, may render permissible within the military that which would be constitutionally impermissible outside it.' *Parker.* While servicemembers clearly retain a liberty interest to engage in certain intimate sexual conduct, "this right must be tempered in a military setting based on the mission of the military, the need for obedience of orders, and civilian supremacy.' *United States v. Brown,* 45 M.J. 389, 397 (C.A.A.F. 1996).

"In light of Air Force Instructions at the time, [Marcum] might have been charged with a violation of Article 92 for failure to follow a lawful order. However, the Government chose to proceed under Article 125. Nonetheless, the fact that Appellant's conduct might have violated Article 92 informs our analysis as to whether [Marcum]'s conduct fell within the *Lawrence* zone of liberty. As the supervising noncommissioned officer, Appellant was in a position of responsibility and command within his unit with respect to his fellow airmen. He supervised and rated SrA Harrison. [Marcum] also testified that he knew he should not engage in a sexual relationship with someone he supervised. Under such circumstances, which Appellant acknowledged was prohibited by Air Force policy, SrA Harrison, a subordinate airman within [Marcum]'s chain of command, was a person 'who might be coerced' or who was 'situated in [a] relationship[ ] where consent might not easily be refused.' *Lawrence.* Thus, based on this factor, [Marcum]'s conduct fell outside the liberty interest identified by the Supreme Court."

Judge Baker agreed with Marcum's challenge to the sentence he received, namely, that it was tainted by a statement that defense counsel released without Marcum's authorization. The statement was an account, taken from defense counsel's notes of interviews with Marcum, of the many other homosexual liaisons Marcum had with other service personnel. (Marcum was absent without leave (AWOL) at the time of sentencing, so he had waived his right to be present and heard at sentencing, but the Court found he had not waived his attorney-client privilege.) This statement was not only unauthorized, but was prejudicial, for the prosecuting attorney used it to argue for a higher sentence, on the ground that Marcum was a predatory homosexual corrupting the entire unit, man by man.

Chief Judge Crawford dissented from this relief but concurred with Judge Baker's rejection of Marcum's *Lawrence* challenge. The Chief Judge would have found *Lawrence* completely inapplicable, because the intimate relationship with Harrison was "a far cry from the consensual adult relationship" protected by *Lawrence.*

Was the court correct that the military could constitutionally criminalize non-forcible sodomy?

NOTES ON *MARCUM* AND SEX CRIMES BY MILITARY PERSONNEL

1. *Does* Lawrence *Reach the Military?* *Marcum* does not resolve the matter. None of the judges in *Marcum* concluded that *Lawrence* is inapplicable to personnel in the armed forces, but all of them found that *Lawrence*'s articulation of the privacy right did not extend to Sergeant Marcum's conduct with Senior Airman Harrison. Sergeant Marcum's case illustrates the difficulty of finding a case where *Lawrence* clearly governs. Most of the military prosecutions involve charges of forcible sodomy, men sodomizing women as well as men without consent. Many of the cases involve sex between service personnel, and these cases often raise fraternization concerns not present in civilian cases. Finally, although not present in Marcum's case, some of the cases involve sexual activities on government property—barracks, storerooms, public toilets, etc. These, too, may not easily fall within *Lawrence*. There may never be a suitable test case.

2. *What Is "Consensual" in the Military Setting?* In *Marcum,* the Chief Judge objected that the conduct was not consensual because Airman Harrison was too frightened to protest. Although Marcum was not actually convicted of forcible sodomy (under the criminal standard of proof), the Chief Judge felt that it was more likely than not that Harrison had been orally raped (under a civil standard of proof). The civil standard rendered *Lawrence* inapplicable in his view.

Judge Baker did not accept this argument but reasoned that *Lawrence* was inapplicable because Air Force regulations prohibited sexual fraternization between officers and those under his or her command. Hence, all the activities with Airman Harrison were off-limits and constitutionally unprotected by *Lawrence*. There is some ambiguity as to the basis of Judge Baker's judgment: Is he inferring lack of "consent" on the part of Harrison? Or is this a case of "constructive non-consent" for policy reasons? Perhaps it is both: Harrison's failure to object may be a product of the officer-subordinate relationship *and* may be an example of why the Air Force needs an anti-fraternization policy.

Note the relevance of feminist theory to the *Marcum* opinions. Feminists have claimed that lack of consent can be deduced from the exercise of sexual authority by a superior (a boss as well as a commanding officer). Most states now make some of these situations a sexual assault. More controversial have been claims that sexual assault can occur when the victim is too afraid to protest. When the fear is the result of a knife to the throat or an implicit physical threat, it is easy to conclude that sexual assault has occurred. But Marcum's oral sex upon Harrison cannot be confidently characterized as physical assault, unless sexual assault is defined to include any "unwelcome" sexual contact, as some reformers have argued. Absent that understanding of "assault," Chief Judge Crawford's point has less cogency. Should it make a difference that the activities occurred between persons of the same sex?

3. *What About Adultery?* Although the Uniform Code of Military Justice (UCMJ) does not expressly criminalize adultery, the Manual for Courts Marshall (MCM) provides that a servicemember can be prosecuted for adultery under Article 134 of the UCMJ. MCM at IV-103–04.[c] Members who engage in adultery can also be punished under Article 133 of the UCMJ, which prohibits "conduct unbecoming an officer and a gentleman." 10 U.S.C. § 933. And, to be clear, "the military still regularly pursues adultery prosecutions, evidenced by the 900 men and women court-martialed in the 1990s alone for charges that included adultery." Katherine Annuschat, Comment, "An Affair to Remember: The State of the Crime of Adultery in the Military," 47 *San Diego L. Rev.* 1161, 1164–65 (2010). The potential punishments for adultery are serious; they include "[d]ishonorable discharge, forfeiture of all pay and allowances, and confinement for [one] year." MCM, pt. IV, P 62(e).

It is true that some states still have criminal adultery statutes on the books. That said, it is likely that it would be unconstitutional under *Lawrence* to apply those state statutes to consensual, private, adult sexual activity. Joanne Sweeny, "Undead Statutes: The Rise, Fall, and Continuing Uses of Adultery and Fornication Criminal Laws," 46 *Loy. U. Chi. L.J.* 127, 129–30 (2014) ("Although they are probably unconstitutional violations of privacy under *Lawrence v. Texas,* adultery and fornication laws exist. Almost twenty states currently have statutes criminalizing adultery, fornication, or both." (footnotes omitted)).

Can the military nonetheless criminally prohibit adultery? Why or why not?

---

[c]   Article 134 of the UCMJ provides: "Though not specifically mentioned in this chapter, all disorders and neglects to the prejudice of good order and discipline in the armed forces, all conduct of a nature to bring discredit upon the armed forces, and crimes and offenses not capital, of which persons subject to this chapter may be guilty, shall be taken cognizance of by a general, special, or summary court-martial, according to the nature and degree of the offense, and shall be punished at the discretion of that court." 10 U.S.C. § 934.

SECTION 3

DUE PROCESS AND EQUAL PROTECTION IN PRISON

Prison, like the military, is an institution that deeply shapes concepts of gender and sexuality. Incarceration affects an increasing large slice of the U.S. population. "In less than thirty years, the U.S. penal population exploded from around 300,000 to more than 2 million." Michelle Alexander, *The New Jim Crow: Mass Incarceration in the Age of Colorblindness* (2010). As a result, the U.S. is now the "world's largest jailer." James Forman, Jr., "Racial Critiques of Mass Incarceration: Beyond the New Jim Crow," 87 *N.Y.U. L. Rev.* 21, 22 (2012).

People of color make up a disproportionate share of this population. *See, e.g.*, Forman, *supra*, at 22 (noting that black men are imprisoned at 6.5 times the rate of white men). Many scholars, including Professors Alexander and Forman, argue that conscious and unconscious racial bias explains much of this disparity. *See, e.g.*, Forman, *supra*, at 46 ("There is overwhelming evidence that discriminatory practices in drug law enforcement contribute to racial disparities in arrests and prosecutions, and even for violent offenses there remain unexplained disparities between arrest rates and incarceration rates."). Professor Alexander notes that a 2000 report "observed that among youth who have never been sent to a juvenile prison before, African Americans were more than six times as likely as whites to be sentenced to prison for *identical* crimes." Alexander, *supra*. "In at least fifteen state, blacks are admitted to prison on drug charges at a rate from twenty to fifty-seven times greater than that of white men." *Id.* This is true even though most of the individuals who use and sell drugs are white. *Id.*

The effects of conviction are felt well beyond the period of incarceration. A person who has been convicted of a crime may be denied the right to vote, and they may be ineligible (for the rest of their lives) for a range of public benefits including subsidized housing, food stamps, and student loans. Individuals who have been convicted of a crime often find it very difficult to find employment and housing because of their past convictions. As Professor Forman puts its, "These restrictions exact a terrible toll. Given that most offenders already come from backgrounds of tremendous disadvantage, we heap additional disabilities upon existing disadvantage." Forman, *supra*, at 31.

LGBT people, particularly lesbian and bisexual women, are disproportionately represented in jails and prisons. According to the Williams Institute, "[l]esbians, gay men, and bisexuals make up about 3.5 percent of the U.S. general population but 5.5 percent of men in prisons are gay or bisexual and 33.3 percent of women in prison are lesbian or bisexual." Why are LGBT people disproportionately represented in U.S. jails and prisons? The authors of a recent Williams Institute study offer the following observations:

> [R]esearch shows that prejudice may be to blame. Growing up, sexual minorities are more likely to experience family rejection and community marginalization, which can create pathways to substance abuse, homelessness, and detention. Criminal justice profiling of sexual minorities as more likely to engage in sex work or to commit sex crimes can lead to overpolicing. For women, powerful gender stereotypes are likely at play. To the extent that sexual minority women defy norms and are labeled as aggressive or masculine, individuals or institutions may unfairly find them more deserving of punishment.

Commentary, "The Unspoken Horror of Incarcerated LGBT People," *The Advocate* (Feb. 23, 2017). And, following up on the last point, research also indicates that LGBT people, particularly lesbian and bisexual women, are sentenced to "longer periods than were straight women." Ilan H. Meyer, et al., "Incarceration Rates and Traits of Sexual Minorities in the United States, Inmate Survey, 2011–2012," 107(2) AJPH 234, 237 (Feb. 2017)

While incarcerated, LGBT people, especially gay men and transgender women, are especially vulnerable to harassment and sexual violence. The remaining three sections of this chapter explore issues related to sex, gender, and sexual orientation that may arise in prison. This section begins by exploring the extent to which inmates are entitled to the core constitutional protections of due process and equal protection.

A. PRISONS AND FUNDAMENTAL RIGHTS

The Supreme Court has identified a number of so-called "fundamental rights" that are entitled to special, more careful protection from government interference. Under the Due Process Clause, the Court has held that "our laws and tradition afford constitutional protection to personal decisions related to marriage, procreation, contraception, family relationships, child rearing, and education." *Lawrence v. Texas*, 539 U.S. 558, 573–74 (2003). And, of course, the First Amendment protects speech and religious exercise. Do inmates retain these rights while incarcerated? And, if so, are prison regulations subjected to the same standard of scrutiny that applies to regulations outside the prison context? Consider the next decision.

William R. Turner v. Leonard Safley, et al.

United States Supreme Court, 1987.
482 U.S. 78, 107 S.Ct. 2254, 96 L.Ed.2d 64.

■ O'CONNOR, J., delivered the opinion of the Court.

This case requires us to determine the constitutionality of regulations promulgated by the Missouri Division of Corrections relating to inmate marriages and inmate-to-inmate correspondence. The Court of Appeals for the Eighth Circuit, applying a strict scrutiny analysis, concluded that the regulations violate respondents' constitutional rights. We hold that a lesser standard of scrutiny is appropriate in determining the constitutionality of the prison rules. Applying that standard, we uphold the validity of the correspondence regulation, but we conclude that the marriage restriction cannot be sustained.

* * * [I.] Two regulations are at issue here. The first of the challenged regulations relates to correspondence between inmates at different institutions. It permits such correspondence "with immediate family members who are inmates in other correctional institutions," and it permits correspondence between inmates "concerning legal matters." Other correspondence between inmates, however, is permitted only if "the classification/treatment team of each inmate deems it in the best interest of the parties involved." * * * At Renz, the District Court found that the rule "as practiced is that inmates may not write non-family inmates."

The challenged marriage regulation, which was promulgated while this litigation was pending, permits an inmate to marry only with the permission of the superintendent of the prison, and provides that such approval should be given only "when there are compelling reasons to do so." The term "compelling" is not defined, but prison officials testified at trial that generally only a pregnancy or the birth of an illegitimate child would be considered a compelling reason. * * *

The District Court issued a memorandum opinion and order finding both the correspondence and marriage regulations unconstitutional. * * * The Court of Appeals for the Eighth Circuit affirmed. The Court of Appeals held that the District Court properly used strict scrutiny in evaluating the constitutionality of the Missouri correspondence and marriage regulations. * * *

We granted certiorari * * * .

[II.] We begin * * * with our decision in *Procunier v. Martinez*, [416 U.S. 396 (1974),] which described the principles that necessarily frame our analysis of prisoners' constitutional claims. The first of these principles is that federal courts must take cognizance of the valid constitutional claims of prison inmates. Id., at 405, 94 S.Ct. at 1807. Prison walls do not form a barrier separating prison inmates from the protections of the Constitution. * * *

A second principle identified in *Martinez,* however, is the recognition that "courts are ill equipped to deal with the increasingly urgent problems of prison administration and reform." Id., at 405, 94 S.Ct., at 1807. * * * Where a state penal system is involved, federal courts have, as we indicated in *Martinez,* additional reason to accord deference to the appropriate prison authorities. See id., at 405, 94 S.Ct., at 1807.

Our task, then, as we stated in *Martinez,* is to formulate a standard of review for prisoners' constitutional claims that is responsive both to the "policy of judicial restraint regarding prisoner complaints and [to] the need to protect constitutional rights." Id., at 406. As the Court of Appeals acknowledged, *Martinez* did not itself resolve the question that it framed. * * *

* * * In none of these four "prisoners' rights" cases [that followed *Martinez*—*Pell v. Procunier,* 417 U.S. 817 (1974); *Jones v. North Carolina Prisoners' Union,* 433 U.S. 119 (1977); *Bell v. Wolfish,* 441 U.S. 520 (1979); and *Block v. Rutherford,* 468 U.S. 576 (1984)] did the Court apply a standard of heightened scrutiny, but instead inquired whether a prison regulation that burdens fundamental rights is "reasonably related" to legitimate penological objectives, or whether it represents an "exaggerated response" to those concerns. * * *

If *Pell, Jones,* and *Bell* have not already resolved the question posed in *Martinez,* we resolve it now: when a prison regulation impinges on inmates' constitutional rights, the regulation is valid if it is reasonably related to legitimate penological interests. In our view, such a standard is necessary if "prison administrators . . . , and not the courts, [are] to make the difficult judgments concerning institutional operations." * * * Subjecting the day-to-day judgments of prison officials to an inflexible strict scrutiny analysis would seriously hamper their ability to anticipate security problems and to adopt innovative solutions to the intractable problems of prison administration. * * *

As our opinions in *Pell, Bell,* and *Jones* show, several factors are relevant in determining the reasonableness of the regulation at issue. First, there must be a "valid, rational connection" between the prison regulation and the legitimate governmental interest put forward to justify it. * * * Thus, a regulation cannot be sustained where the logical connection between the regulation and the asserted goal is so remote as to render the policy arbitrary or irrational. Moreover, the governmental objective must be a legitimate and neutral one. * * *

A second factor relevant in determining the reasonableness of a prison restriction, as *Pell* shows, is whether there are alternative means of exercising the right that remain open to prison inmates. * * *

A third consideration is the impact accommodation of the asserted constitutional right will have on guards and other inmates, and on the allocation of prison resources generally. * * *

Finally, the absence of ready alternatives is evidence of the reasonableness of a prison regulation. * * * By the same token, the existence of obvious, easy alternatives may be evidence that the regulation is not reasonable, but is an "exaggerated response" to prison concerns. This is not a "least restrictive alternative" test: prison officials do not have to set up and then shoot down every conceivable alternative method of accommodating the claimant's constitutional complaint. But if an inmate claimant can point to an alternative that fully accommodates the prisoner's rights at *de minimis* cost to valid penological interests, a court may consider that as evidence that the regulation does not satisfy the reasonable relationship standard.

[III.]   Applying our analysis to the Missouri rule barring inmate-to-inmate correspondence, we conclude that the record clearly demonstrates that the regulation was reasonably related to legitimate security interests. We find that the marriage restriction, however, does not satisfy the reasonable relationship standard, but rather constitutes an exaggerated response to petitioners' rehabilitation and security concerns.

[A.] According to the testimony at trial, the Missouri correspondence provision was promulgated primarily for security reasons. Prison officials testified that mail between institutions can be used to communicate escape plans and to arrange assaults and other violent acts. Witnesses stated that the Missouri Division of Corrections had a growing problem with prison gangs, and that restricting communications among gang members, both by transferring gang members to different institutions and by restricting their correspondence, was an important element in combating this problem. * * *

The prohibition on correspondence between institutions is logically connected to these legitimate security concerns. Undoubtedly, communication with other felons is a potential spur to criminal behavior: this sort of contact frequently is prohibited even after an inmate has been released on parole. See, *e.g.,* 28 CFR § 2.40(a)(10) (1986) (federal parole conditioned on nonassociation with known criminals, unless permission is granted by the parole officer). * * * Moreover, the correspondence regulation does not deprive prisoners of all means of expression. Rather, it bars communication only with a limited class of other people with whom prison officials have particular cause to be concerned—inmates at other institutions within the Missouri prison system.

We also think that the Court of Appeals' analysis overlooks the impact of respondents' asserted right on other inmates and prison personnel. Prison officials have stated that in their expert opinion, correspondence between prison institutions facilitates the development of informal organizations that threaten the core functions of prison administration, maintaining safety and internal security. * * * Where exercise of a right requires this kind of tradeoff, we think that the choice made by corrections officials—which is, after all, a judgment "peculiarly within [their] province and professional expertise," *Pell v. Procunier*, 417 U.S., at 827, 94 S.Ct., at 2806—should not be lightly set aside by the courts.

Finally, there are no obvious, easy alternatives to the policy adopted by petitioners. Other well-run prison systems, including the Federal Bureau of Prisons, have concluded that substantially similar restrictions on inmate correspondence were necessary to protect institutional order and security. See, *e.g.,* 28 CFR § 540.17 (1986). As petitioners have shown, the only alternative proffered by the claimant prisoners, the monitoring of inmate correspondence, clearly would impose more than a *de minimis* cost on the pursuit of legitimate corrections goals. * * * The risk of missing dangerous communications, taken together with the sheer burden on staff resources required to conduct item-by-item censorship, supports the judgment of prison officials that this alternative is not an adequate alternative to restricting correspondence.

The prohibition on correspondence is reasonably related to valid corrections goals. The rule is content neutral, it logically advances the goals of institutional security and safety identified by Missouri prison officials, and it is not an exaggerated response to those objectives. On that basis, we conclude that the regulation does not unconstitutionally abridge the First Amendment rights of prison inmates.

[B.] In support of the marriage regulation, petitioners first suggest that the rule does not deprive prisoners of a constitutionally protected right. They concede that the decision to marry is a fundamental right under *Zablocki v. Redhail*, 434 U.S. 374 (1978), and *Loving v. Virginia*, 388 U.S. 1 (1967), but they imply that a different rule should obtain "in . . . a prison forum." Petitioners then argue that even if the regulation burdens inmates' constitutional rights, the restriction should be tested under a reasonableness standard. They urge that the restriction is reasonably related to legitimate security and rehabilitation concerns.

We disagree with petitioners that *Zablocki* does not apply to prison inmates. It is settled that a prison inmate "retains those [constitutional] rights that are not inconsistent with his status as a prisoner or with the legitimate penological objectives of the corrections system." *Pell v. Procunier, supra*, 417 U.S., at 822. The right to marry, like many other rights, is subject to substantial restrictions as a result of incarceration. Many important attributes of marriage remain, however, after taking into account the limitations imposed by prison life. First, inmate marriages, like others, are expressions of emotional support and public commitment. These elements are an important and significant aspect of the marital relationship. In addition, many religions recognize marriage as having spiritual significance; for some inmates and their spouses, therefore, the commitment of marriage may be an exercise of religious faith as well as an expression of personal dedication. Third, most inmates eventually will be released by parole or commutation, and therefore most inmate marriages are formed in the expectation that they ultimately will be fully consummated. Finally, marital status often is a precondition to the receipt of government benefits (*e.g.,* Social Security benefits), property rights (*e.g.,* tenancy by the entirety, inheritance rights), and other, less tangible benefits (*e.g.,* legitimation of children born out of wedlock). These incidents of marriage, like the religious and personal aspects of the marriage commitment, are unaffected by the fact of confinement or the pursuit of legitimate corrections goals.

Taken together, we conclude that these remaining elements are sufficient to form a constitutionally protected marital relationship in the prison context. * * *

The Missouri marriage regulation prohibits inmates from marrying unless the prison superintendent has approved the marriage after finding that there are compelling reasons for doing so. As noted previously, generally only pregnancy or birth of a child is considered a "compelling reason" to approve a marriage. In determining whether this regulation impermissibly burdens the right to marry, we note initially that the regulation prohibits marriages between inmates and civilians, as well as marriages between inmates. * * *

Petitioners have identified both security and rehabilitation concerns in support of the marriage prohibition. The security concern emphasized by petitioners is that "love triangles" might lead to violent confrontations between inmates. With respect to rehabilitation, prison officials testified that female prisoners often were subject to abuse at home or were overly dependent on male figures, and that this dependence or abuse was connected to the crimes they had committed. * * *

We conclude that on this record, the Missouri prison regulation, as written, is not reasonably related to these penological interests. No doubt legitimate security concerns may require placing reasonable restrictions upon an inmate's right to marry, and may justify requiring approval of the superintendent. The Missouri regulation, however, represents an exaggerated response to such security objectives. There are obvious, easy alternatives to the Missouri regulation that accommodate the right to marry while imposing a *de minimis* burden on the pursuit of security objectives. See, *e.g.,* 28 CFR § 551.10 (1986) (marriage by inmates in federal prison generally permitted, but not if warden finds that it presents a threat to security or order of institution, or to public safety). * * * Moreover, with respect to the security concern emphasized in petitioners' brief—the creation of "love triangles"—petitioners have pointed to nothing in the record suggesting that the marriage regulation was viewed as preventing such entanglements. Common sense likewise suggests that there is no logical connection between the marriage restriction and the formation of love triangles: surely in prisons housing both male and female prisoners, inmate rivalries are as likely to develop without a formal marriage ceremony as with one. Finally, this is not an instance where the "ripple effect" on the security of fellow inmates and prison staff justifies a broad restriction on inmates' rights—indeed, where the inmate wishes to marry a civilian, the decision to marry (apart from the logistics of the wedding ceremony) is a completely private one.

Nor, on this record, is the marriage restriction reasonably related to the articulated rehabilitation goal. First, in requiring refusal of permission absent a finding of a compelling reason to allow the marriage, the rule sweeps much more broadly than can be explained by petitioners' penological objectives. Missouri prison officials testified that generally they had experienced no problem with the marriage of male inmates * * * . The proffered justification thus does not explain the adoption of a rule banning marriages by these inmates. Nor does it account for the prohibition on inmate marriages to civilians. * * *

Moreover, although not necessary to the disposition of this case, we note that on this record the rehabilitative objective asserted to support the regulation itself is suspect. * * * The District Court found that the Missouri prison system operated on the basis of excessive paternalism in that the proposed marriages of *all* female inmates were scrutinized carefully even before adoption of the current regulation * * * whereas the marriages of male inmates during the same period were routinely approved. That kind of lopsided rehabilitation concern cannot provide a justification for the broad Missouri marriage rule.

* * * We conclude, therefore, that the Missouri marriage regulation is facially invalid. * * *

It is so ordered.

■ [The opinion of JUSTICE STEVENS concurring in part and dissenting in part is omitted.]

NOTES ON PRISONS AND FUNDAMENTAL RIGHTS

1.   *General Rule.* According to *Turner,* at least some fundamental rights are retained during periods of incarceration. However, prison regulations that limit these fundamental rights are subjected to the lower "legitimate penological interest" standard.

2.   *What About the Right to Procreate?* The *Turner* Court concluded that the right to marry survives incarceration. Marriage, Justice O'Connor declared, was not inconsistent with the legitimate penological objectives of the facility. This is so because "[m]any important attributes of marriage" survive during incarceration.

What about procreation? Do inmates retain a constitutional right to procreate? The Ninth Circuit considered this question in ***Gerber v. Hickman*, 291 F.3d 617, 619 (9th Cir. 2002) (en banc)**. A 41 year-old inmate, William Gerber, who was serving a sentence of 100 years to life plus eleven years, filed suit in federal court alleging that the state prison officials violated his constitutional rights by "not allowing him to provide his wife with a sperm specimen that she may use to be artificially inseminated. Gerber sought an order of the court directing the institution to permit him to provide 'a sample of sperm to artificially inseminate his wife.'" *Gerber v.*

Hickman, 291 F.3d 617, 619 (9th Cir. 2002) (en banc). Gerber "request[ed] that (1) a laboratory be permitted to mail him a plastic collection container at the prison along with a prepaid return mailer, (2) he be permitted to ejaculate into the container, and (3) the filled container be returned to the laboratory in the prepaid mailer by overnight mail. Alternatively, plaintiff requested that his counsel be permitted to personally pick up the container for transfer to the laboratory or health care provider." *Id.* The relevant state prison system had a policy of prohibiting family conjugal visits for inmates "sentenced to life without the possibility of parole [or] sentenced to life, without a parole date established by the Board of Prison Terms." *Id.* (citing Cal. Code Regs. Tit. 15 § 3174(e)(2)).

To support his claim, Gerber "argue[d] that the right to be free from forced surgical sterilization [citing *Skinner v. Oklahoma*], combined with the right to marry while in prison [citing *Turner v. Safley*] inevitably le[d] to the conclusion that inmates have a constitutional right to procreate while in prison." *Id.* at 622. What do you think? Should the prison be required to facilitate his desire to utilize assisted reproduction with his wife?

Although the first three-judge panel agreed with Gerber, an en banc panel of the Ninth Circuit rejected his logic. **Judge Silverman** first concluded that forced sterilization is "intrusive, permanent, and irreparable" and, therefore, is not comparable to refusing to assist with assisted reproduction. Next, Judge Silverman explained that while the right to marry survives incarceration, many "physical aspects do not." *Id.* at 623. " '[I]ncarceration, by its very nature, deprives a convicted individual of the fundamental right to be free from physical restraint,' and this 'in turn encompasses and restricts other fundamental rights, such as the right to procreate.' " *Id.* at 621 (quoting *State v. Oakley*, 245 Wis. 3d 447 (2001)). For example, Judge Silverman continued, "it is well-settled that prisoners have no constitutional right while incarcerated to contact visits or conjugal visits." *Id.* (citing cases).

Judge Tashima, joined by Judges Kozinski, Hawkins, Paez, and Berzon, dissented. The dissent first pointed out that "[t]he majority assumes that there is a fundamental right to procreation." *Id.* at 624. Next, the dissent reasoned that "[i]t is settled that a prison inmate retains those constitutional rights that are not inconsistent with his status as a prisoner or with the legitimate penological objectives of the corrections system." (quoting *Turner*). While the dissent agreed with the majority that incarceration "necessarily involves the curtailment of certain rights," they reasoned that "[p]rocreation through artificial insemination * * * implicates none of the restrictions on privacy and association that are necessary attributes of incarceration." *Id.* at 625. The dissent also noted that for prisoners like Gerber who are serving a life sentence, the "denial of Gerber's request does mean that Gerber is forever deprived of a basic liberty," and thus, the case is not distinguishable from *Skinner*.

What do you think?

3. *What About the Right to Sexual Intimacy?* In *Lawrence v. Texas*, the Supreme Court held that individuals have a protected liberty interest in adult, consensual, non-commercial sexual intimacy. *Lawrence v. Texas*, 539 U.S. 558 (2003). It remains unsettled whether this liberty interest is in the nature of a "fundamental" right. *See, e.g.*, Laurence H. Tribe, "*Lawrence v. Texas*: The "Fundamental Right" that Dare Not Speak its Name," 117 *Harv. L. Rev.* 1893 (2004) (arguing that it is a fundamental right), *contra Lofton v. Sec'y of Dep't of Children & Family Servs.*, 358 F.3d 804, 817 (11th Cir. 2004) ("We conclude that it is a strained and ultimately incorrect reading of *Lawrence* to interpret it to announce a new fundamental right.").

Regardless of how it is characterized, does this "liberty" interest that the Court recognized in *Lawrence* survive incarceration? Courts typically have answered this question in the negative. *See, e.g., In re Anderson*, 296 F. App'x 347, 348 (4th Cir. 2008) ("The Constitution does not guarantee conjugal visitation privileges to incarcerated persons. *Turner v. Safley,* 482 U.S. 78, 95–96 (1987)."); *Hernandez v. Coughlin*, 18 F.3d 133, 137 (2d Cir. 1994) ("The Constitution, however, does not create any protected guarantee to conjugal visitation privileges while incarcerated. *See Turner,* 482 U.S. at 95–96. The Supreme Court in *Turner* held that the right of marriage survives incarceration, but the Court also noted that the consummation of marriage would take place after release from confinement. *Id.* Accordingly, even though the right to marriage is constitutionally protected for inmates, the right to marital privacy and conjugal visits while incarcerated is not."); *cf. Morales v. Pallito*, No. 2:13 CV 271, 2014 WL 1758163, at *8 (D. Vt. 2014) ("If inmates have no constitutional right to conjugal visitation with individuals from outside the prison walls, then it is difficult to see how they might enjoy a constitutional right to similar visitation with other inmates.").

Although the programs used to be more widely available, today only four states—California, Connecticut, New York, and Washington—have conjugal visit programs. "Conjugal Visits: Rules and History," Dopplr (Apr. 15, 2016), http://www.dopplr.com/social-atlas/. New Mexico and Mississippi recently ended their conjugal visit programs. Dana Goldstein, "Conjugal Visits," *The Lowdown* (Feb. 11, 2015). Conjugal visits are not available to inmates in federal facilities. Inmate Legal Matters, Federal Bureau of Prisons, https://www.bop.gov/inmates/custody_and_care/legal_matters.jsp.

B. PRISONS AND EQUAL PROTECTION

As described above, the Supreme Court has held that at least some fundamental rights survive incarceration. The Court has also held, however, that even these fundamental rights are entitled to a lower standard of protection—the *Turner* standard—inside the prison walls.

And, indeed, the Court has suggested that this new lower *Turner* standard may not be limited to the fundamental rights context. In *Washington v. Harper*, the Court stated that the *Turner* standard would "appl[y] to all circumstances in which the needs of prison administration implicate constitutional rights." 494 U.S. 210, 224 (1990).

More recently, however, the Court held that there is at least one exception to the *Turner* standard—race discrimination.

Garrison S. Johnson v. California, et al.

United States Supreme Court, 2005.
543 U.S. 499 125 S.Ct. 1141, 160 L.Ed.2d 949.

■ O'CONNOR, J., delivered the opinion of the Court.

The California Department of Corrections (CDC) has an unwritten policy of racially segregating prisoners in double cells in reception centers for up to 60 days each time they enter a new correctional facility. We consider whether strict scrutiny is the proper standard of review for an equal protection challenge to that policy.

[I.A]   CDC institutions house all new male inmates and all male inmates transferred from other state facilities in reception centers for up to 60 days upon their arrival. During that time, prison officials evaluate the inmates to determine their ultimate placement. Double-cell assignments in the reception centers are based on a number of factors, predominantly race. In fact, the CDC has admitted that the chances of an inmate being assigned a cellmate of another race are " '[p]retty close' " to zero percent. * * * The CDC further subdivides prisoners within each racial group. Thus, Japanese-Americans are housed separately from Chinese-Americans, and northern California Hispanics are separated from southern California Hispanics.

The CDC's asserted rationale for this practice is that it is necessary to prevent violence caused by racial gangs. * * * It cites numerous incidents of racial violence in CDC facilities and identifies five major prison gangs in the State: Mexican Mafia, Nuestra Familia, Black Guerilla Family, Aryan Brotherhood, and Nazi Low Riders. * * * The CDC also notes that prison-gang culture is violent and murderous. * * * [P]rison officials * * * expressed their belief that violence and conflict would result if prisoners were not segregated. * * * The CDC claims that it must therefore segregate all inmates while it determines whether they pose a danger to others. * * *

With the exception of the double cells in reception areas, the rest of the state prison facilities-dining areas, yards, and cells-are fully integrated. After the initial 60-day period, prisoners are allowed to choose their own cellmates. The CDC usually grants inmate requests to be housed together, unless there are security reasons for denying them.

[I.B]   Garrison Johnson is an African-American inmate in the custody of the CDC. * * * Johnson filed a complaint *pro se* * * * alleging that the CDC's reception-center housing policy violated his right to equal protection under the Fourteenth Amendment by assigning him cellmates on the basis of his race. * * *

The Court of Appeals for the Ninth Circuit affirmed [the district court's grant of summary judgment to the defendants]. 321 F.3d 791 (2003). It held that the constitutionality of the CDC's policy should be reviewed under the deferential standard we articulated in *Turner v. Safley*—not strict scrutiny. * * * Applying Turner, it held that Johnson had the burden of refuting the "common-sense connection" between the policy and prison violence. * * * Though it believed this was a "close case," * * * the Court of Appeals concluded that the policy survived Turner's deferential standard[ ]. * * *

We granted certiorari to decide which standard of review applies.

[II.A]   We have held that "*all* racial classifications [imposed by government] . . . must be analyzed by a reviewing court under strict scrutiny." *Adarand Constructors, Inc. v. Peña*, 515 U.S. 200, 227 (1995) (emphasis added). Under strict scrutiny, the government has the burden of proving that racial classifications "are narrowly tailored measures that further compelling governmental interests." Ibid. We have insisted on strict scrutiny in every context, even for so-called "benign" racial classifications, such as race-conscious university admissions policies, see *Grutter v. Bollinger*, 539 U.S. 306, 326 (2003), race-based preferences in government contracts, see Adarand, *supra*, at 226, and race-based districting intended to improve minority representation, see *Shaw v. Reno*, 509 U.S. 630, 650 (1993).

The reasons for strict scrutiny are familiar. Racial classifications raise special fears that they are motivated by an invidious purpose. * * * We therefore apply strict scrutiny to *all* racial classifications to " 'smoke out' illegitimate uses of race by assuring that [government] is pursuing a goal important enough to warrant use of a highly suspect tool."

The CDC claims that its policy should be exempt from our categorical rule because it is "neutral"-that is, it "neither benefits nor burdens one group or individual more than any other group or individual." In other words, strict scrutiny should not apply because all prisoners are "equally" segregated. The CDC's argument ignores our repeated command that "racial classifications receive close scrutiny even when they may be said to burden or benefit the races equally." Shaw, *supra*, at 651, 113 S.Ct. 2816. Indeed, we rejected the notion that separate can ever be equal-or "neutral"—50 years ago in *Brown v. Board of Education*, 347 U.S. 483 (1954), and we refuse to resurrect it today. * * *

We have previously applied a heightened standard of review in evaluating racial segregation in prisons. [Citing *Lee v. Washington*, 390 U.S. 333 (1968) *(per curiam).*] * * *

The need for strict scrutiny is no less important here, where prison officials cite racial violence as the reason for their policy. As we have recognized in the past, racial classifications "threaten to stigmatize individuals by reason of their membership in a racial group and to *incite racial hostility*." Shaw, *supra*, at 643 (citing *J.A. Croson Co., supra*, at 493 (plurality opinion); emphasis added). Indeed, by insisting that inmates be housed only with other inmates of the same race, it is possible that prison officials will breed further hostility among prisoners and reinforce racial and ethnic divisions. * * *

Virtually all other States and the Federal Government manage their prison systems without reliance on racial segregation. Federal regulations governing the Federal Bureau of Prisons (BOP) expressly prohibit racial segregation. 28 CFR § 551.90 (2004) ("[BOP] staff shall not discriminate against inmates on the basis of race, religion, national origin, sex, disability, or political belief. This includes the making of administrative decisions and providing access to work, housing and programs"). * * *

Because the CDC's policy is an express racial classification, it is "immediately suspect." *Shaw*, 509 U.S., at 642; see also *Washington v. Seattle School Dist. No. 1*, 458 U.S. 457, 485 (1982). We therefore hold that the Court of Appeals erred when it failed to apply strict scrutiny to the CDC's policy and to require the CDC to demonstrate that its policy is narrowly tailored to serve a compelling state interest.

[II.B]   The CDC invites us to make an exception to the rule that strict scrutiny applies to all racial classifications, and instead to apply the deferential standard of review articulated in *Turner v. Safley*, 482 U.S. 78 (1987), because its segregation policy applies only in the prison context. We decline the invitation. In *Turner*, we considered a claim by Missouri prisoners that regulations restricting inmate marriages and inmate-to-inmate correspondence were unconstitutional. Id., at 81. We rejected the prisoners' argument that the regulations should be subject to strict scrutiny, asking instead whether the regulation that burdened the prisoners' fundamental rights was "reasonably related" to "legitimate penological interests." Id., at 89.

We have never applied *Turner* to racial classifications. *Turner* itself did not involve any racial classification, and it cast no doubt on *Lee*. We think this unsurprising, as we have applied *Turner*'s reasonable-relationship test *only* to rights that are "inconsistent with proper incarceration." * * * Thus, for example, we have relied on Turner in addressing First Amendment challenges to prison regulations, including restrictions on freedom of association, *Overton, supra*; limits on inmate correspondence, *Shaw v. Murphy*, 532 U.S. 223 (2001); restrictions on inmates' access to courts, *Lewis v. Casey*, 518 U.S. 343 (1996); restrictions on receipt of subscription publications, *Thornburgh v. Abbott*, 490 U.S. 401 (1989); and work rules limiting prisoners' attendance at religious services, *Shabazz, supra*. We have also applied Turner to some due process claims, such as involuntary medication of mentally ill prisoners, *Washington v. Harper*, 494 U.S. 210 (1990); and restrictions on the right to marry, *Turner, supra*.

The right not to be discriminated against based on one's race is not susceptible to the logic of *Turner*. It is not a right that need necessarily be compromised for the sake of proper prison administration. On the contrary, compliance with the Fourteenth Amendment's ban on racial discrimination is not only consistent with proper prison administration, but also bolsters the legitimacy of the entire criminal justice system. * * *

And public respect for our system of justice is undermined when the system discriminates based on race. * * * For similar reasons, we have not used *Turner* to evaluate Eighth Amendment claims of cruel and unusual punishment in prison. We judge violations of that Amendment under the "deliberate indifference" standard, rather than *Turner*'s "reasonably related" standard. * * * This is because the integrity of the criminal justice system depends on full compliance with the Eighth Amendment. * * *

In the prison context, when the government's power is at its apex, we think that searching judicial review of racial classifications is necessary to guard against invidious discrimination. * * *

The CDC protests that strict scrutiny will handcuff prison administrators and render them unable to address legitimate problems of race-based violence in prisons. * * * Not so. Strict scrutiny is not "strict in theory, but fatal in fact." * * * Strict scrutiny does not preclude the ability of prison officials to address the compelling interest in prison safety. Prison administrators, however, will have to demonstrate that any race-based policies are narrowly tailored to that end. * * *

On remand, the CDC will have the burden of demonstrating that its policy is narrowly tailored with regard to new inmates as well as transferees. Prisons are dangerous places, and the special circumstances they present may justify racial classifications in some contexts. Such circumstances can be considered in applying strict scrutiny, which is designed to take relevant differences into account.

■ [The concurring opinion of JUSTICE GINSBURG and the dissenting opinions of JUSTICES STEVENS and THOMAS are omitted]

NOTES ON PRISONS AND EQUAL PROTECTION

1. *Prisons and Race Discrimination.* In *Johnson*, the Supreme Court held that the lower *Turner* standard does not apply to Equal Protection race discrimination claims arising out of the prison context. Instead, as is true outside the prison context, government uses of race in prison must be subjected to strict scrutiny. This is so because "compliance with the Fourteenth Amendment's ban on racial discrimination is not only consistent with proper prison administration, but also bolsters the legitimacy of the entire criminal justice system."

Justice Thomas, joined by Justice Scalia, dissented. The case, Justice Thomas explained:

> require[s] us to resolve two conflicting lines of precedent. On the one hand, as the Court stresses, this Court has said that '*all* racial classifications reviewable under the Equal Protection Clause must be strictly scrutinized.' * * * On the other, this Court has no less categorically said that 'the [relaxed] standard of review we adopted in *Turner* [*v. Safley*, 482 U.S. 78, 107 S.Ct. 2254, 96 L.Ed.2d 64 (1987),] applies to *all* circumstances in which the needs

of prison administration implicate constitutional rights.' *Washington v. Harper,* 494 U.S. 210, 224, 110 S.Ct. 1028, 108 L.Ed.2d 178 (1990) (emphasis added).

Emphasizing the former line of cases, the majority resolves the conflict in favor of strict scrutiny. I disagree. The Constitution has always demanded less within the prison walls. Time and again, even when faced with constitutional rights no less "fundamental" than the right to be free from state-sponsored racial discrimination, we have deferred to the reasonable judgments of officials experienced in running this Nation's prisons. There is good reason for such deference in this case. California oversees roughly 160,000 inmates in prisons that have been a breeding ground for some of the most violent prison gangs in America-all of them organized along racial lines. In that atmosphere, California racially segregates a portion of its inmates, in a part of its prisons, for brief periods of up to 60 days, until the State can arrange permanent housing. The majority is concerned with sparing inmates the indignity and stigma of racial discrimination. *Ante,* at 1147–1148. California is concerned with their safety and saving their lives. I respectfully dissent.

Who is right? Justice O'Connor or Justice Thomas? Why?

2. *What About Prisons and Sex Discrimination? Johnson* makes clear that the lower *Turner* standard does not apply to equal protection *race discrimination* claims. What about equal protection *sex discrimination* claims?

Currently, the case law is mixed. Grace DiLaura, Student Comment, " 'Not Susceptible to the Logic of *Turner*': *Johnson v. California* and the Future of Gender Equal Protection Claims From Prisons," 60 *UCLA L. Rev.* 506, 509 (2012). A number of courts refused to apply the lower *Turner* standard to Equal Protection gender claims arising in the prison context and instead held that intermediate scrutiny must be applied. *See, e.g., Pitts v. Thornburg,* 866 F.2d 1450, 1453 (D.C. Cir. 1989) (applying intermediate scrutiny and concluding that "after careful reflection, we believe that neither [*Turner*'s] concerns, nor *Turner* itself, suggests the appropriateness of a reasonableness standard in this particular case"); *McCoy v. Nev. Dep't of Prisons,* 776 F. Supp. 521, 523 (D. Nev. 1991) (applying intermediate scrutiny rather than rational basis review). *But see Yates v. Stalder,* 217 F.3d 332 (5th Cir. 2000). And in a number of circuits, there is still no clear rule about what standard of scrutiny applies to sex discrimination claims in the prison context. *See, e.g.,* Grace DiLaura, Student Comment, " 'Not Susceptible to the Logic of *Turner*': *Johnson v. California* and the Future of Gender Equal Protection Claims From Prisons," 60 *UCLA L. Rev.* 506, 518 (2012) (noting that there is no clear rule in the Fourth, Sixth, and Ninth Circuits). What should the rule be? Why?

To be sure, gender discrimination arises in all kinds of ways in the prison context. With regard to the inmates themselves, there, of course, is the express sex segregation that occurs with regard to the placement of prisoners into separate men's and women's facilities. Moreover, as between the men's and women's facilities, it has long been the case that conditions at men's and women's facilities differ. "Female prisoners generally experience a lower quality of programs, facilities, and basic conditions of confinement than male prisoners." Sandy de Sauvage & Kelly Head, "Correctional Facilities," 17 *Geo J. Gender & L.* 175, 176–66 (2016). Female inmates typically do not have access to the same services and programs, including educational and vocational programs, as do male inmates. *Id.* Moreover, any vocational opportunities available to female inmates tend to be in "traditionally" feminine occupations, and the schooling in female facilities is often limited to high school educational programs. *Id.* If a prisoner sued, challenging the unequal quality of the programming at a women's facility, what standard of scrutiny should the court apply and why?

3. *What About Prisons and Sexual Orientation or Gender Identity Discrimination?* What about discrimination on the basis of sexual orientation or gender identity in prison? Should the *Turner* standard apply to Equal Protection challenges alleging sexual orientation or gender identity discrimination? Or should a more careful level of scrutiny apply? If so, what level of scrutiny should be applied and why?

SEXUAL HARASSMENT, SEXUAL VIOLENCE, AND SEXUAL CONDUCT IN PRISON

A. WHAT'S HAPPENING AND WHAT DO PRISON OFFICIALS HAVE TO DO ABOUT IT?

NOTES ON SEXUAL VICTIMIZATION IN PRISON

1. *The Situation—Generally.* Harassment and violence in prison, including sexual violence, is commonplace. It has been reported that "19% of all male inmates in US prisons say they've been physically assaulted by other inmates [and] 21% say they've been assaulted by prison staff." Dave Gilson, "What We Know About Violence in America's Prisons," *Mother Jones* (July/Aug. 2016), http://www.motherjones.com/politics/2016/06/attacks-and-assaults-behind-bars-cca-private-prisons.

Inmates are also more likely than non-inmates to experience sexual assault. A recent study of California prisons found that more than 4% of respondents reported being sexually assaulted while in prison. Valerie Jenness et al., "Violence in California Correctional Facilities: An Empirical Examination of Sexual Assault," 2 *The Bulletin* 1, 2 (2007). A recent study by the U.S. Department of Justice recently reported similar findings. Bureau of Justice Statistics, Sexual Victimization in Prisons and Jails Reported by Inmates, 2011–12 (2013).

Although sex in prison is very common, most jails and prisons technically ban sexual activity of any kind. Russell Robinson, "Masculinity as Prison: Sexual Identity, Race, and Incarceration," 99 *Cal. L. Rev.* 1309, 1316 (2011). "Such bans may deter inmates from reporting sexual assault because prison officials can recharacterize a claim of rape as consensual activity, which is forbidden." *Id.* Because sex is prohibited, prisons typically do not distribute condoms or pre-exposure prophylaxis to prevent HIV infection. As a result, rates of HIV and other sexually transmitted infections (STIs) are high among inmates.

In addition, there is also "[m]uch prison sex [that] may be voluntary yet coerced, either through extortion or as a weaker prisoner's exchange of sex with one powerful prisoner for 'protection' against violence by others." Kim Shayo Buchanan, "Our Prisons, Ourselves: Race, Gender and the Rule of Law," 29 *Yale L. & Pol'y Rev.* 1, 16 (2010).

This pervasive culture of sex (as in sexual conduct) in jails and prisons functions to create and reproduce gender. As Professor Sharon Dolovich explains:

To outside observers, prison life can seem like a dog-eat-dog state of nature. Yet the sexual victimization of weaker prisoners by more powerful ones in fact takes place within a highly organized social system, in which power is allocated and exercised along surprisingly conventional lines. As with intimate relationships in society in general, the defining scripts are gendered: in men's prisons, as in the free world, men dominate women.

Sharon Dolovich, "Strategic Segregation in the Modern Prison," 48 *Am. Crim. Law Rev.* 1, 14 (2011). This gendered social system, some have argued, is fueled by the gender-segregation that is a core feature of prisons. "A society composed exclusively of men tends to generate anxieties in its members concerning their masculinity." Gresham Sykes, Society of Captives: A Study of a Maximum Security Prison 71 (2007). Professor Dolovich argues: "Desperate not to be victimized themselves, male prisoners do all they can to avoid any behaviors that might suggest qualities associated with femininity: passivity, expressing emotion, sensitivity, kindness, etc. In short, fear of rape motivates displays of hypermasculinity among prisoners wishing to avoid being 'turned out' themselves." Sharon Dolovich, "Strategic Segregation in the Modern Prison," 48 *Am. Crim. Law Rev.* 1, 17 (2011).

2. *LGBT Prisoners.* LGBT people, and especially gay men and trans women in male prisons, are disproportionately the target of this harassment and violence. "A prisoner's conformity to conventional norms of manliness greatly decreases the likelihood that he will be targeted for sexual assault. Nonstraight sexual orientation and prior sexual abuse are the two characteristics most predictive of sexual abuse by either inmates or staff." Kim Shayo Buchanan, "Our Prisons, Ourselves: Race, Gender and the Rule of Law," 29 *Yale L. & Pol'y Rev.* 1, 15 (2010).

A recent study by the U.S. Department of Justice found that "[i]nmates who reported their sexual orientation as gay, lesbian, bisexual, or other were among those with the highest rates of sexual victimization in 2011–12." Bureau of Justice Statistics, Sexual Victimization in Prisons and Jails Reported by Inmates, 2011–12 (2013). "Among heterosexual state and federal prisoners, an estimated 1.2% reported being sexually victimized by another inmate, and 2.1% reported being victimized by staff. In comparison, among non-heterosexual prison inmates (including gay, lesbian, bisexual, and other sexual orientations), 12.2% reported being sexually victimized by another inmate, and 5.4% reported being sexually victimized by staff." *Id.* at 18.

Transgender inmates, especially transgender women, are especially vulnerable to sexual violence and assault. The study of California inmates found "sexual assault is 13 times more prevalent among transgender inmates, with 59% reporting being sexually assaulted while in a California correctional facility." Valerie Jenness, et al., "Violence in California Correctional Facilities: An Empirical Examination of Sexual Assault," 2 Bulletin 1 (2007).

3. *Other Forms of Abuses.* In addition to being at increased risk of physical and sexual assault, LGBT prisoners may experience other types of harassment and victimization. For example, "[t]ransgender prisoners are frequently targeted for excessive, harassing, or public strip searches." ACLU & NCLR, Know Your Rights: Laws, Court Decisions, and Advocacy Tips to Protect Transgender Prisoners 12 (2014).

4. *Female Inmates.* Female inmates are disproportionately at risk of experiencing sexual assault by a staff member. "The 2009–2011 statistical report for prison rape revealed that in state and federal prisons, where women constitute seven percent of sentenced inmates, thirty-three percent of victims of staff-on-inmate sexual victimization were women." Sandy de Sauvage & Kelly Head, "Correctional Facilities," 17 *Geo J. Gender & L.* 175, 186 (2016).

5. *What Laws and Constitutional Provisions Protect Inmates from These Conditions?* There are a number of sources of law under which prison officials have an obligation to protect prisoners from harassment, violence, and other abuses. In 2003, Congress passed the Prison Rape Elimination Act (PREA). 42 U.S.C. § 15601 et seq. While inmates do not have a private right of action for violations of the statute, prisons are required to comply with PREA, including the requirement that covered facilities engage in regular audits or reviews. 28 C.F.R. § 115.401.

Inmates may also bring Equal Protection claims if they believe were targeted based on their gender or their perceived failure to conform to sex stereotypes. *Cf. Schwenk v. Hartford*, 204 F.3d 1187 (9th Cir. 2000) (holding that inmate had claim under Gender Motivated Violence Act).

Another potential source of protection is the Eighth Amendment, which prohibits cruel and unusual punishment. The Supreme Court has held that "[a] prison official's 'deliberate indifference' to a substantial risk of serious harm to an inmate violates the Eighth Amendment." *Farmer v. Brennan*, 511 U.S. 825, 828 (1994). In that very case, the Court made clear that the Eighth Amendment may be violated if prison officials are deliberately indifferent to physical and sexual violence experienced by transgender inmates. *See, e.g., Farmer v. Brennan*, 511 U.S. 825 (1994) (remanding case brought by a transsexual inmate for further proceedings).

Given what we know about the treatment of transgender women in male prisons, when is a prison official on notice that a particular transgender woman faces "a substantial risk of serious harm"? Consider the next case.

Ashley A. Diamond v. Brian Owens, et al.

United States District Court for the Middle District of Georgia, 2015.
131 F. Supp. 3d 1346.

■ TREADWELL, J.,

Plaintiff Ashley Diamond alleges she is a transgender woman with gender dysphoria. She alleges the Defendants, in various ways, violated her constitutional rights while she was an inmate in various Georgia prisons by failing to provide her with medical treatment and by failing to protect her from sexual assault. Some of the Defendants have moved to dismiss some of Diamond's claims. For the reasons discussed in detail below, the motions are **DENIED.**

[I] When she filed her complaint, Ashley Diamond was a "nonviolent" Georgia prison inmate who had been incarcerated after violating probation imposed after a theft conviction. In her 163 paragraph, 38 page verified complaint, Diamond alleges that officials in four different prisons repeatedly violated her constitutional rights by failing to provide her with medical treatment for her gender dysphoria and by failing to protect her from sexual assaults. As a result, she alleges that on many different occasions she attempted suicide, attempted to castrate herself, was raped, and was otherwise sexually assaulted by inmates at the maximum security prisons in which she was housed. * * *

[Diamond alleged that prison officials failed to provide her with medically necessary treatment under the prison's "freeze frame policies." Shortly after the U.S. Department of Justice filed a statement of interest supporting the plaintiff's position that the freeze frame policies were impermissible, defense counsel announced that the freeze-frame policy had been rescinded. The court's analysis of the plaintiff's claims regarding the prison's failure to provide her with necessary medical care have been omitted from this excerpt.]

[II.C] Since childhood, Diamond has "strongly identified" as female rather than her "assigned [male] gender." After attempting suicide at the age of 15, Diamond was diagnosed with gender dysphoria. Since then, she has lived and expressed herself as female. At 17, she began hormone treatments, and that treatment continued for over 17 years. As a result, she has developed female secondary sex characteristics, including "full breasts, a feminine shape, soft skin, and . . . a reduction in male attributes."

On March 27, 2012, Diamond's hormone therapy and "female expression" were terminated after she was placed in GDOC's [Georgia Department of Correction] custody for a non-violent offense. At intake, despite her female characteristics and GDOC's knowledge that she was a transgender woman on hormone therapy, "Diamond was not evaluated for gender dysphoria, referred for treatment, or given a reasonably safe or appropriate housing placement." Despite her non-violent offender status, GDOC housed Diamond at Macon State Prison—a "closed-security facility for adult male felons" with frequent gang activity and assaults. Within a month, Diamond was "brutally sexually assaulted" by six gang members. GDOC then transferred her to Baldwin State Prison, which is also a closed-security facility. There, inmates again sexually assaulted Diamond. Diamond reported these assaults, but personnel were slow to respond, lost her complaints and physical evidence of the assaults, failed to investigate, and told her she "brought her assaults upon herself" because she was transgender. Pursuant to GDOC policies, [Sharon] Lewis[, the Statewide Medical Director,] was notified after each assault but "took no action."

GDOC mental health professionals diagnosed Diamond with post-traumatic stress disorder ("PTSD") and recommended a transfer to a medium-security facility because her transgender status made her more vulnerable to sexual assaults at a closed-security facility. * * *

[II.E]   On December 31, 2013, Diamond was transferred to Valdosta State Prison, a closed-security facility. * * * GDOC personnel at Valdosta State Prison failed to provide Diamond with "safety accommodations." Rather, she was simply told at intake that the prison "lacked the means to safely house transgender persons" and that she should "guard [her] booty" because she "stood a high likelihood of being sexually assaulted based on the inmate population, which included many gang members."

The day after her transfer to Valdosta State Prison, Diamond was sexually assaulted by her cellmate. Still, no action was taken, and she remained housed with the perpetrator who continued to sexually harass and coerce her. Diamond was sexually assaulted again on February 9, 2014, and she was twice sexually assaulted in April 2014.

Lewis, [Warden Marty] Allen, and [David] McCracken[, the Director of Mental Health Services and PREA coordinator at the prison,] were notified after each report of sexual assault pursuant to GDOC's policy, but they did not adjust Diamond's placement or take other safeguarding measures. Specifically, Dr. Harrison told Allen and McCracken that Diamond should be transferred because she stood a high risk of sexual assault given Valdosta's inmate population. Diamond also personally contacted Allen and McCracken about her safety. In April 2014, Diamond told Allen of the assaults, but he "refused to act." In February, May, and June of 2014, Diamond told McCracken about the assaults and requested a transfer. But McCracken "deferred and delayed any action," resulting in further "sexual harassment and coercion." Diamond also contacted the Commissioner twice about her repeated sexual assaults at closed-security prisons and requested a transfer to a medium-security facility, but Diamond remained at Valdosta State Prison. After filing a pro se lawsuit against Allen and McCracken, Diamond was transferred back to Baldwin, where she had previously been sexually assaulted.

[III.4]   Diamond alleges Lewis, Allen, and McCracken were deliberately indifferent to a substantial risk of serious harm Diamond faced in closed-security facilities. Lewis and McCracken argue Diamond failed to state a claim against them. Lewis also contends she is entitled to qualified immunity.

[III.4.1] * * * "A prison official violates the Eighth Amendment 'when a substantial risk of serious harm, *of which the official is subjectively aware,* exists[,] the official does not respond reasonably to the risk,'" and the official's actions or inaction causes the injury. * * * The prison official must be both aware of the risk and draw the inference.

* * * In her complaint, Diamond has covered the waterfront with her allegations tending to prove subjective awareness. She has alleged that a transgender inmate's vulnerability to assault at a closed-security male facility was obvious to Lewis and McCracken and that PREA and GDOC policies made clear transgender inmates are highly vulnerable to sexual assault. Further, she alleges Lewis and McCracken spoke with her directly about her transgender status and were aware from notifications and records she was repeatedly sexually assaulted at three different closed-security facilities. Diamond met with McCracken at least three times about her sexual assaults, and Dr. Harrison contacted him directly about Diamond's vulnerability to assault at Valdosta State Prison given its population of violent offenders.

Diamond's allegations paint a picture dramatically different than the typical failure-to-protect claim asserted by inmates. The usual failure-to-protect claim involves a single assault. * * * But here Diamond alleges a series of assaults. While she does not concede that Lewis and McCracken did not have subjective awareness of the risk of harm before the first assault that occurred on their respective watches, she alleges that after they received notice of that assault, and then the next, and the next, and so on, they clearly had subjective awareness of the risk of harm she faced as a transgender inmate housed with violent offenders. Repeatedly, she alleges, they continued to receive notice of her sexual assaults. Clearly, at this stage of the litigation, these facts are sufficient to establish that Lewis and McCracken were subjectively aware of the risk of harm Diamond faced. * * *

In sum, these allegations are not threadbare recitations of the subjective awareness element. * * * Yet, despite being aware of the risk of sexual assault and despite having the authority and obligation to take reasonable safety measures after each incident, Lewis and McCracken, according to Diamond, failed to take any action. As a result, the substantial risk of harm remained unabated, and Diamond suffered further sexual assaults. Clearly, Diamond has sufficiently alleged a plausible failure-to-protect claim against Lewis and McCracken.

[III.4.b] Lewis is not entitled to qualified immunity if clearly established law gave her fair warning her conduct violated Diamond's Eighth Amendment right to be protected from assault by other inmates. "A prisoner has a right, secured by the eighth . . . amendment[ ], to be reasonably protected from constant threat of violence and sexual assault by his fellow inmates[.]" * * * Diamond argues Farmer gave Lewis fair warning that her failure to take any action to protect Diamond from the substantial risk of sexual assault she faced violated her Eighth Amendment right to be reasonably protected from sexual assault. * * * [In Farmer, t]he Supreme Court ultimately held that "a prison official may be held liable under the Eighth Amendment . . . if he knows that inmates face a substantial risk of serious harm and disregards that risk by failing to take reasonable measures to abate it." Id. at 847, 114 S.Ct. 1970.

Again, Diamond alleges Lewis was aware Diamond was a transgender female, knew she had been repeatedly sexually assaulted at closed-security male facilities, and knew she continued to be repeatedly sexually assaulted at Valdosta State Prison. Still, Lewis took no action. Therefore, Lewis, being aware of the substantial risk of sexual assault, had fair warning that her failure to take reasonable measures to abate that risk violated Diamond's clearly established right to be protected from sexual assault. Id. at 833–34, 837, 114 S.Ct. 1970. Accordingly, Lewis is not entitled to qualified immunity from Diamond's failure-to-protect claim. * * *

PROBLEM 9-4
CONDOM ACCESS AND THE EIGHTH AMENDMENT

Inmates in state and local prisons are five times more likely than those who are not incarcerated to be diagnosed with HIV. CDC, "HIV Among Incarcerated Populations." Studies have also reported high rights of sexual assault and sexual coercion among inmates. Nancy Wolff, et al., "Sexual Violence Insider Prisons: Rates of Victimization," 83 *J. Urban Health* 835– 848 (2006). Non-heterosexual inmates are particularly vulnerable to sexual assault. *See, e.g.*, Bureau of Justice Statistics, Sexual Victimization in Prisons and Jails Reported by Inmates, 2011–12 (reporting that the "inmates with the highest rates of sexual victimization are those who reported their sexual orientation as gay, lesbian, bisexual, or other"). As noted above, transgender women report particularly high rates of sexual violence. One study of inmates in California found that 59% of transgender women housed in male prisons experienced sexual assault as compared to 4% of non-transgender men in male prisons. Valerie Jenness, et al., "Violence in California Correctional Facilities: An Empirical Examination of Sexual Assault," 2 *Bulletin* 1 (2007).

Very few facilities, however, provide inmates with condoms. Only three state systems (California, Mississippi, and Vermont) distribute condoms to inmates in their facilities. Joe Watson, "Condoms Now Available to Prisoners in Three States," *Prison Legal News* (Sept. 2, 2016). In contrast, most facilities in Europe and all prisons and jails in Canada make condoms available to inmates. Kari Larsen, "Deliberately Indifferent: Government Response to HIV in U.S. Prisons," 24 *J. Contemp. Health L. & Pol'y* 251, 265 (2008).

Assume that a transgender woman contracts HIV while incarcerated. What is the likelihood that she would prevail on an Eighth Amendment claim? *See, e.g.,* *Randles v. Hester*, 2001 WL 1667821 (M.D. Fla. 2001) (holding that plaintiff adequately alleged an Eighth Amendment violation where he contracted HIV after being required on three occasions to clean up large amounts of blood without being provided with adequate protective clothing and equipment). What if prison officials were made aware that she had been sexually assaulted, but failed to change her placement or to take other steps to ensure her safety?

B. SEGREGATION AND SEXUAL VIOLENCE

NOTES ON THE USE OF ISOLATION

1. *"Protecting" LGBT Inmates by Placing Them in Isolation.* As described above, under the Eighth Amendment, prison officials have an obligation to respond when they know that an inmate is at substantial risk of experiencing serious harm. One way in which many prison officials have sought to fulfill this obligation is by placing the inmate in so-called "protective custody." Others would call this solitary confinement, because that is usually what it means. *See, e.g.*, Gabriel Arkles, "Safety and Solidarity Across Gender Lines: Rethinking Segregation of Transgender People in Detention," 18 *Temp. Pol. & Civ. Rts. L. Rev.* 515, 517 (2009). And, indeed, transgender and other gender nonconforming inmates "are far more likely than others to be put in isolating placements such as protective custody or punitive segregation." *Id.* at 544. Some facilities automatically place transgender inmates in protective custody. *Id.* at 545.

According to Professor Gabriel Arkles, "placement in solitary confinement can at times reduce certain forms of violence from other people in prison * * * . However, in many cases the opposite is true; not only are these placements almost always worse than general population in many other ways, but also they often lead to greater, not lesser, violence." *Id.* at 537.

First, placement in solitary confinement is itself harmful and damaging. "The documented psychological effects of isolation, even for short periods of time, include intense anxiety, confusion, lethargy, panic, impaired memory, psychotic behavior, hallucinations and perceptual distortions, difficulty eating, inability to communicate, hypersensitivity to external stimuli, violent fantasies, and reduced impulse control." *Id.* at 538–39. *See also, e.g.*, Stuart Grassian, "Psychiatric Effects of Solitary Confinement," 22 *Wash. U. J.L. & Pol'y* 325, 327 (2006) (noting that research confirms that isolation "can cause severe psychiatric harm").

Second, Professor Arkles argues that inmates who are placed in isolation are "more likely to be attacked in protective custody or other forms of segregation because it is easier for abusive correctional staff to access them alone and out of the sight of other prisoners or video surveillance." Arkles, "Safety and Solidarity Across Gender Lines," 18 *Temp. Pol. & Civ. Rts. L. Rev.* at 540. Finally, Arkles argues, placement in isolation inhibits the ability of the inmate to develop networks and communities, networks that may assist the inmate in times of need.

Inmates who are HIV positive are also sometimes placed in "segregation" or isolation. In addition to legal bases discussed below, individuals who are HIV positive, may also challenge their placement in segregation under the Americans with Disabilities Act (ADA), 42 U.S.C. § 12101 et seq., and under the Rehabilitation Act of 1973, 29 U.S.C. § 701 et seq. The ADA and the Rehabilitation Act both prohibit discrimination against individuals with disabilities. Even asymptomatic people with HIV are considered people with disabilities under these statutes. *Bragdon v. Abbott*, 524 U.S. 624 (1998). Notwithstanding that protection, however, most lawsuits challenging the placement of HIV-positive inmates in segregation have been unsuccessful. *See, e.g., Moore v. Mabus*, 976 F.2d 268 (5th Cir. 1992); *Harris v. Thispen*, 941 F.3d 1495 (11th Cir. 1991); *Muhammad v. Carlson*, 845 F.2d 175 (8th Cir. 1988); *Cordero v. Coughlin*, 607 F. Supp. 9 (S.D.N.Y. 1984).

2. *Bases for Challenging Placement in Isolation.* Some inmates have challenged their placement in "protective custody," but most challenges have been unsuccessful. One potential ground for challenging placement in isolation or segregation is the Eighth Amendment. The Eighth Amendment prohibits "cruel and unusual punishment." There are some decisions holding that *the particular circumstances* of an individual inmate's placement in solitary confinement violated the Eighth Amendment. *See, e.g.,* Daniel E. Manville & John Boston, *Prisoners' Self-Help Litigation Manual* 141 (3d ed. 1995) (noting that courts have found Eighth Amendment violations when the conditions of the solitary confinement were "unsanitary, degrading or unhealthful"). But generally courts have held that solitary confinement in and of itself, even for lengthy periods of time, is not a per se violation of the Eighth Amendment. *See, e.g., Madrid v. Gomez*, 889 F. Supp. 1146, 1261 (N.D. Cal. 1995) ("There is nothing per se improper about segregating inmates, even for lengthy or indefinite terms."). As the Seventh Circuit put it: "[i]nactivity, lack of companionship, and a low level of intellectual stimulation do not constitute cruel and unusual punishment." *Bono v. Saxbe*, 620 F.2d 609, 614 (7th Cir. 1980).

Inmates have also argued that placement in solitary confinement deprives them of "liberty" in violation of the Due Process Clause. The Supreme Court has explained that prison officials may violate the Due Process Clause if the prisoner is subjected to an "atypical and significant hardship * * * in relation to the ordinary incidents of prison life." *Sandin v. Conner*, 515 U.S. 472, 484 (1995). Where the inmate is subjected to such "atypical and significant hardships," prison officials have an obligation to provide the inmate with sufficient procedural protections enabling the inmate to challenge the conditions of confinement.

Here again, some plaintiffs have prevailed in cases where the conditions were particularly harsh. *See, e.g., Romero v. Bd. of Cty. Commissioners for the Cty. Of Curry*, 202 F. Supp.3d 1223, 1257 (D.N.M. 2016) (holding that plaintiff adequately alleged the elements of a Due Process violation where the inmate was forced to sleep on a "steel bed frame with no mattress," where the cell "smelled 'foul' and was repeated covered in feces and urine," and where the inmate "was not given adequate mental or physical healthcare"). But challenges that are based primarily on the placement in isolation itself generally have been unsuccessful. Consider the next case.

Estate of Miki Ann DiMarco v. Wyoming Department of Corrections, Division of Prisons, et al.

United States Court of Appeal for the Tenth Circuit, 2007.
473 F.3d 1334.

■ TYMKOVICH, J.,

Miki Ann DiMarco lived her life as a woman even though she was anatomically male. In 2000, * * * she violated the terms of her probation [for testing positive for drug use and failing to carry verifiable identification. DiMarco was on probation after pleading guilty to check fraud. A] Wyoming state court [then] sentenced her to prison. Not realizing DiMarco's medical condition and believing her to be a woman, the court placed her in Wyoming's women's correctional facility in Laramie. It was only during a routine prison intake examination that prison officials learned DiMarco was [anatomically male. A prison doctor examined her and concluded that she suffered from gender identity disorder]. Because the officials believed that she presented a safety risk, DiMarco was placed in administrative segregation apart from the rest of the prison population. After an initial evaluation period, officials decided to continue her administrative segregation because they concluded she should not be placed with the general female prison population. Her confinement was reviewed every ninety days, but she remained segregated until her release from prison 14 months later.

DiMarco does not contest her segregation on appeal. Rather, the issue is whether Wyoming had a constitutional duty to provide her an opportunity to challenge the placement and conditions of confinement under the Fourteenth Amendment's Due Process Clause. * * * The district court agreed and held that the Wyoming Department of Corrections and the individual defendants violated her procedural due process rights. * * * Because we conclude DiMarco does not have a liberty interest in her placement and the conditions of confinement, we reverse.

[I]   The [Wyoming Women's Center (WCC)] consists of two wings, the East and the West. The general prison population resides in the West wing. The East wing, where higher risk inmates are housed, consists of housing Pods 1, 2 and 3. New prisoners are routinely housed separately from the general prison population for about one month in Pod 2 while prison officials determine appropriate housing assignments. At intake, DiMarco was housed in Pod 3, the most restrictive and isolated housing pod used for inmates confined to administrative or protective custody.

Pod 3 consists of four cells, which are accessed through a small "day room." Each cell consists of a bed, a steel sink and a steel toilet. The cells are painted cement blocks with grey solid steel doors. The day room consists of a small steel table with a steel bench, both bolted to the floor, and a television, which is mounted high on the wall and controlled by correctional officers. * * *

Conditions in the West wing, by contrast, are more pleasant. The halls have brick facing, the floors are carpeted, and the cell doors are wooden. The West wing cells have cupboards for personal effects and space for hanging clothing. The day rooms in the West wing have furniture, tables, televisions, pictures and other accessories.

As part of their review of DiMarco's initial placement, prison officials determined that she was a low security risk. Placement officials nonetheless recommended that she be kept apart from the general population for three reasons: (1) DiMarco's safety and that of the general female inmate population, (2) her physical condition, and (3) the need to tailor programs for her condition. * * * After DiMarco's initial placement, prison officials reviewed her status every 90 days until her release. Each review yielded a decision to maintain DiMarco's confinement in Pod 3, relying on the initial reasons for the placement. * * *

* * * [While DiMarco was given clothing, food, and personal hygiene items, she] was denied other prison amenities. For instance, she was not allowed day-to-day contact with the other inmates. Nor did she have access to some of the educational programs that would have put her in contact with other inmates. Even though DiMarco was not allowed routine contact with other inmates, she did have access to prison staff and medical personnel. * * * Shortly after beginning her sentence, DiMarco was included in two small treatment groups, which met for one hour counseling sessions each week. These sessions included other WWC inmates.

[III.A] [DiMarco's main claim was that the state denied her procedural due process when it denied her access to challenge the conditions of her detention. Did she have a "liberty" interest protected by the Due Process Clause?] State policies or regulations will not create the basis for a liberty interest in the conditions of confinement so long as they do not "impose[] atypical and significant hardship on the inmate in relation to the ordinary incidents of prison life." *Sandin v. Conner*, 515 U.S. 472, 484, 115 S.Ct. 2293, 132 L.Ed.2d 418 (1995).

DiMarco argues that her conditions of confinement violate the rule established in *Sandin*. In particular, while conceding that segregation itself was appropriate, DiMarco contends that prison officials confined her in the most severe classification and did not give her the opportunity to obtain better amenities and more humane treatment. Moreover, although DiMarco received a review every 90 days, she argues that the prison gave her no meaningful right to appeal her living conditions throughout her confinement.

[III.A.1] The Supreme Court has held that a protected liberty interest may arise from prison placement decisions and conditions of confinement. Most recently, in *Wilkinson* [*v. Austin*, 545 U.S. 209 (2005)], the Court examined Ohio's decision to place a prisoner in the state's "supermax" maximum security prison. In applying *Sandin*, the Court emphasized that the touchstone of the due process inquiry is not the precise language of a state's regulations regarding "restrictive conditions of confinement" but "the nature of those conditions themselves 'in relation to the ordinary incidents of prison life.'" 545 U.S. at 223, 125 S.Ct. 2384 (quoting *Sandin*). The Court concluded that the inquiry requires "identifying the baseline from which to measure what is atypical and significant in any particular prison system." *Id.*

Avoiding a discussion of the contours of a baseline analysis, the Court found that Ohio's supermax placement would impose an "atypical and significant hardship under any plausible baseline." *Id.* In particular, the Court found that the supermax placement implicated a prisoner's liberty interests for two reasons: (1) it was for an indefinite duration reviewed only annually; and (2) it disqualified an otherwise eligible inmate from parole consideration. According to the Court, "[w]hile any of these conditions standing alone might not be sufficient to create a liberty interest, *taken together* they impose an atypical and significant hardship within the correctional context." Id at 224, 125 S.Ct. 2384 (emphasis added).

* * * [This Circuit, in *Jordan v. Fed. Bureau of Prisons*, 191 Fed.Appx. 639, 2006 WL 2135513 (10th Cir.2006)] concluded that a 1,825-day stay in administrative detention did not create a liberty interest because (1) the detention was reasonably related to legitimate penological interests, namely, investigating the inmate's role in a murder; (2) the detention was reasonable in light of the legitimate security concerns of the institution; and (3) the conditions were not significantly different than generally confined inmates (noting fewer social calls and less recreation time as not significant). *Jordan.* * * *

[III.A.2] The question that must be answered in this appeal, then, is two-fold. First, what is the appropriate baseline comparison? Second, how significant must the conditions of confinement deviate from the baseline to create a liberty interest in additional procedural protections?

Here the baseline comparison question lends itself to several possible solutions. One option is to compare administrative segregation with conditions in the general population. A second option is to compare it with other, typical protective custodies. And a third option is, to compare it with that experienced by other uniquely placed or difficult to place prisoners-i.e., ill inmates, elderly inmates, or inmates with disabilities or under supervision because of mental illness or dependency.

In our view, the answer lies somewhere between these choices. It is simplistic to understand the *Sandin* formulation as suggesting a rigid either/or assessment. Rather, it makes sense to look at a few key factors, none dispositive, as the Supreme Court did in *Wilkinson*. But any assessment must be mindful of the primary management role of prison officials who should be free from second-guessing or micro-management from the federal courts. *See Sandin*, 515 U.S. at 482–84, 115 S.Ct. 2293 (concluding *Sandin* test would reduce involvement of federal courts in management of prison conditions).

Relevant factors might include whether (1) the segregation relates to and furthers a legitimate penological interest, such as safety or rehabilitation; (2) the conditions of placement are extreme; (3) the placement increases the duration of confinement, as it did in *Wilkinson;* and (4) the placement is indeterminate (in *Wilkinson* the placement was reviewed only annually).

In light of these considerations, we turn to see whether DiMarco's confinement in administrative segregation violated a liberty interest.

[III.B]   In applying the above factors to DiMarco, it is helpful to keep a few background facts in mind. DiMarco was an admittedly unique prisoner, with a physiological and psychological condition never before encountered by Wyoming prison officials. No one suggests the initial segregation for evaluative purposes was inappropriate or excessive. Prison officials consulted medical professionals in evaluating DiMarco's condition and relied, in part, on those opinions in their placement decision. DiMarco had access to prison staff and doctors throughout her confinement. Her placement was evaluated every ninety days, and she was given an opportunity to be heard at each evaluation. While her confinement was isolating, it provided the ordinary essentials of prison life. Finally, the prison had to consider the needs of the general prison population, including rehabilitative goals and programs designed for them. Perhaps most importantly, DiMarco does not contend that segregation itself was unreasonable.

In this context, we examine the factors set forth above.

Purpose of Segregation

Wyoming established several reasons for its placement of DiMarco in administrative segregation. First and foremost was safety. It determined that DiMarco might be a risk if introduced to the general population of the prison. Many of the women confined in the prison were victims of sexual assault. Some might be fearful of DiMarco, even though she functioned as a woman; others might threaten DiMarco for different reasons. While DiMarco was not deemed a particularly high risk, we cannot discount the prison's concerns about placing her in what it perceived as a potential security problem. * * *

Second, Wyoming concluded that it did not have adequate facilities for inmates such as DiMarco. Wyoming is a small state with a relatively small prison population. Large states with larger urban populations have begun to establish facilities for transsexual inmates, but most states have yet to develop specific facilities or programs directed to this population. * * * Prudence dictates that sending her to Wyoming's men's prison was not a plausible alternative.

Conditions of Confinement

DiMarco's conditions of confinement were admittedly spartan, but not atypical of protective custody. She had access to the basic essentials of life, although her access to certain amenities was more limited than the general population. She had adequate clean clothing; ate the same meals as the general population; had access to library, recreational, and religious facilities; participated in out-of-cell time of at least five-and-one-half hours a day; and was given personal hygiene items. She was denied interaction with other inmates, and certain amenities such as nail clippers and mirrors in her cell that were not allowed in her pod. The prison has no constitutional duty to equalize these type[s] of amenities in every detail. Nor does a prisoner have a right to access every type of program available to other inmates, ranging from work to recreation. The district court found as much in rejecting DiMarco's equal protection and cruel and unusual punishment claims.

DiMarco was also provided access to a number of prison programs. She was part of small group counseling sessions with other inmates, she had weekly individual psychiatric sessions, and monthly visits from a psychiatric specialist. Her caseworker met regularly to discuss her concerns about her conditions and placement. * * *

Duration of Confinement

Wyoming's placement decision did not extend DiMarco's confinement. In fact, she was released after serving 14 months of a two-to four-year sentence. Given the fact that DiMarco only attacks the conditions of her segregation and not her placement in segregated housing, this factor does not weigh in her favor.

Indefiniteness of Confinement

DiMarco's placement was reviewed every ninety days. And unlike the inmate in *Wilkinson,* whose placement in supermax was subject only to an annual review and disqualified the inmate from parole consideration, DiMarco had regular reevaluations throughout her confinement. * * * Importantly, she was interviewed as a part of the review, and allowed to present her views. While the management team concluded administrative segregation was the proper assignment, DiMarco was not isolated from prison staff nor was she denied the opportunity to object to the conditions of her confinement. As noted above, DiMarco has conceded that segregation was a reasonable placement decision.

Taken together, these factors do not weigh in favor of finding that DiMarco has an enforceable liberty interest. While we are sympathetic with her complaints about the petty deprivations resulting from her confinement, and are confident prison officials could have done better, we cannot conclude that the prison imposed such an atypical and significant hardship on her as to meet the *Sandin* standard.

[III.C]   Even if we did find a protected liberty interest, DiMarco's claim would still not succeed. Wyoming provided adequate procedural protections to justify its placement decisions.

The question of "what process is due" was recently examined by the Supreme Court in *Wilkinson v. Austin, supra.* Applying the traditional framework governing procedural due process, *Mathews v. Eldridge*, 424 U.S. 319 (1976), the Court found that a relaxed set of procedures satisfied an inmate's challenge to a placement decision or conditions of confinement. Due process was satisfied as long as a state allowed (1) a sufficient initial level of process, i.e., a reasoned examination of the assignment; (2) the opportunity for the inmate to receive notice and respond to the decision; and (3) safety and security concerns to be weighed as part of the placement decision. *Wilkinson*, 545 U.S. at 226–27, 125 S.Ct. 2384. Moreover, the Court emphasized that where a decision "draws more on the experience of prison administrators, and where the State's interest implicates the safety of other inmates and prison personnel, [ ] informal, nonadversary procedures" that allow notice and the opportunity to be heard are sufficient. Id. at 228–29, 125 S.Ct. 2384 * * *.

Wyoming has met these factors. First, its initial placement decision was appropriate given DiMarco's unique background. Her confinement was the same as other female prisoners assigned to WWC, and prisoners are not entitled to notice and hearing upon intake. She was aware of and agreed to her subsequent assignment to administrative segregation. After that, the prison provided periodic and meaningful reviews of her status, including meetings that DiMarco could attend. DiMarco's objections were noted in subsequent reviews. She signed the classification form generated by the prison indicating that she had reviewed the form and the reasons for the custody level had been explained to her. While she was not allowed to present witness testimony, nor were there other trappings of the adversarial process, these are not required to satisfy due process. Her placement decision was reviewed by several decision makers, including the warden. Each concluded her placement and conditions were appropriate. Moreover, prison officials consulted and relied on psychiatric professionals in making the placement and treatment decisions.

In sum, the totality of the process DiMarco enjoyed satisfies due process.

NOTE ON LGBT INMATES AND ISOLATION

As the *DiMarco* case and the above commentary explains, LGBT inmates are often placed in isolation allegedly for their own "protection." While this placement sometimes results in increased safety (although this is not always the case), even when this is true, there are serious drawbacks for the inmate.

Another approach that has been utilized by some facilities is to place LGBT inmates in a separate facility or unit. There are a number of important potential benefits of this approach. Arguably the inmates are safer, they are not being housed in extremely isolating conditions, and they are not cut off from services. Are there any drawbacks to this approach?

In his article "Masculinity as Prison: Sexual Identity, Race, and Incarceration," 99 *Cal. L. Rev.* 1309 (2011), Professor Russell Robinson argues that, at least as implemented in Los Angeles, there are significant drawbacks to this approach. The Los Angeles jail system, which is the world's largest jail, has a separate unit for gay and trans inmates called K6G. While Professor Robinson supports the notion of extending special protection to more vulnerable inmates, Professor Robinson argues that the rules for identifying the population of K6G are problematic. As a result, he continues, its existence may cause more harm than good.

First, Professor Robinson argues that "the Jail's screening policy constructs gay and transgender identity in a narrow, stereotypical fashion and excludes some of the most vulnerable inmates." *Id.* at 1313. The standard for eligibility is based on "a test from mainstream gay culture, which affluent whites primarily shaped, and then applies it to a mostly black, brown, and poor population." *Id.* at 1399. Moreover, to be eligible for inclusion, one must come out as gay or transgender. This, he continues, has the "long-lasting ramification[ ] of coercing inmates to 'come out' as gay." *Id.* at 1313. Moreover, there are also harms for those inmates who are not placed in K6G and instead remain in the general population. "[B]y removing gay and transgender inmates—but not attending to hegemonic masculine norms in [the general population (GP)]—the Jail simply shifts victimization, making it more likely that heterosexual and bisexual inmates in GP will assume the subordinated roles that otherwise would have been occupied by K6G inmates." *Id.* at 1314.

What would you do if you were in charge of a jail or prison system? Would you create a separate unit for LGBT inmates? For inmates who are particularly vulnerable for a range of reasons, including, but not limited to their sexual orientation or gender identity?

C. THE PLACEMENT OF TRANS PRISONERS

For transgender inmates, there is another, more preliminary placement question: In which facility they should be placed—a male or a female facility? Commonly, prison officials answer that question based "on a prisoner's external genital characteristics or assigned sex at birth, regardless of their gender identity or presentation." ACLU & NCLR, "Know Your Rights: Laws, Court Decisions, and Advocacy Tips to Protect Transgender Prisoners" (2014). This is true even though the federal Prison Rape Elimination Act (PREA) standards require officials to make individualized decisions regarding the housing and placement of transgender prisoners. 28 C.F.R. § 115.42(c) ("In deciding whether to assign a transgender or intersex inmate to a facility for male or female inmates, and in making other housing and programming assignments, the agency shall consider on a case-by-case basis whether a placement would ensure the inmate's health and safety, and whether the placement would present management or security problems.").

Some transgender inmates have sued prison officials challenging their placement in a facility that is not consistent with their gender identity, on the ground that the placement violates principles of Due Process. Under this theory, inmates must demonstrate that the placement "imposes atypical and significant hardship . . . in relation to the ordinary incidents of prison life," *Sandin v. Conner*, 515 U.S. 472, 484 (1995), and that prison officials failed to provide adequate procedural safeguards or practices. *See, e.g.*, Yvette K. W. Bourcicot & Daniel Hirotsu Woofter, "Prudent Policy: Accommodating Prisoners with Gender Dysphoria," 12 *Stan. J. Civ. Rts. & Civ. Liberties* 283, 317 (2016).

Earlier challenges were uniformly unsuccessful. A representative decision is *Lamb v. Maschner*, 633 F. Supp. 351 (D. Kan. 1986). In *Lamb*, the plaintiff filed suit seeking a transfer to a women's facility, as well as access to cosmetics, women's clothing, and transition-related medical care, and relief from being placed in administrative segregation. The court rejected her transfer request, stating summarily: "A male prisoner cannot be housed in a women's prison. Even though a transfer may relieve plaintiff's anxieties, clearly a violation of the women's rights would be at issue." *Lamb*, 633 F. Supp. at 353.

More recent decisions have taken such requests more seriously, but, even so, plaintiffs typically have been unsuccessful. Yvette K. W. Bourcicot & Daniel Hirotsu Woofter, "Prudent Policy: Accommodating Prisoners with Gender Dysphoria," 12 *Stan. J. Civ. Rts. & Civ. Liberties* 283, 317–18 (2016) ("A transsexual inmate who is dissatisfied with his or her housing classification may bring a constitutional challenge, but has a low likelihood of success."). The following decision is one of the few exceptions to this statement.

Patti Hammond Shaw v. District of Columbia, et al.

United States District Court for the District of Columbia, 2013.
944 F. Supp. 2d 43.

■ HUVELLE, J.,

Plaintiff Patti Hammond Shaw ("Shaw"), a transgender woman who has undergone sex reassignment surgery and had her sex legally changed to female, alleges that on three separate occasions she has been arrested in the District of Columbia and subjected to treatment by the Metropolitan Police Department ("MPD") and the United States Marshals Service ("USMS") in violation of the Fourth and Fifth Amendments to the United States Constitution, the Federal Tort Claims Act, the D.C. Human Rights Act, and D.C. tort law. * * *

Before the Court are [defendants'] motions to dismiss * * * . [Defendants' sought to dismiss a number of the plaintiff's claims including her claim that the strip searches by male officials violated the Fourth Amendment and that her placement with male prisoners violated the Due Process Clause. The discussion of the claim regarding the cross-gender strip searches has been omitted].

[**Background**] The following factual recitation is based on the allegations in plaintiff's complaint and must, for purposes of these motions, be accepted as true. Plaintiff is now, and was at all times relevant to this case, a female whose legal name is Patti Hammond Shaw. * * * Plaintiff is also a "transgender woman," who has "undergone sex reassignment surgery," and "had her sex legally changed [from male] to female."[4] * * *

Since changing her sex to female, plaintiff has been arrested by the MPD on three occasions: June 18, 2009, December 10, 2009, and June 6, 2012. * * * In the District, the first time a person is arrested, he/she is assigned a unique Police Department identification number ("PDID"), which is recorded in the MPD's computerized record system. * * * When plaintiff was first arrested by the MPD she was male, and neither the name nor sex associated with her PDID number has ever been changed. * * *

After each of the three arrests that are the subject of plaintiff's complaint, the MPD held her with the male detainees * * * . At both locations, the male detainees verbally and physically harassed her, as did one MPD officer.[7] * * *

Essentially, the MPD treated plaintiff as if she were a male, despite knowing that she was a transgender female, and in apparent violation of its own policy, which provides that "[w]hen male and female prisoners are detained in the holding facility for adults . . . the male and female prisoners shall be separated by sight and sound." The MPD's General Order for "Handling Interactions with Transgender Individuals" was also in effect at the time of plaintiff's arrests. * * * It provides, in the section headed "Processing and Housing of Transgender Arrestees," that

---

[4] District law provides that "Upon receipt of a certified copy of an order of the Court indicating that the sex of an individual born in the District has changed by surgical procedure and that such individual's name has been changed, the certificate of birth of such individual shall be amended as prescribed by regulation." D.C. Code § 7–217(d); *see* In re Taylor, 2003 WL 22382512 (D.C.Super.Ct. Mar. 17, 2003) (§ 7–217(d) gives a transsexual person the legal right to change sex on birth certificate after having sex changed by surgical procedure).

[7] * * * [F]or example, in June 2009, plaintiff "was verbally assaulted by male detainees who asked to see her vagina, breasts, and buttocks" and "while MPD officers were taking [her] out of her cell, they were simultaneously bringing in a male detainee who touched [her] on her buttocks." (Compl. ¶ 19.) In December 2009, she "was repeatedly harassed by the men in the other cell. One man threatened that if [she] did not show him her breasts, he would hit her in the face when they would later be together in the bullpen. Feeling scared, [she] showed the man her breasts and many of the men masturbated in front of her." (*Id.* ¶ 48.) And in June 2012, when she used the bathroom "male detainees in the station made noise and said 'that's a girl' and began masturbating." (*Id.* ¶ 76.) After that incident, plaintiff told an MPD officer that "she wanted to be in the women's area, but he said he wouldn't move her." (*Id.* ¶ 76.) On this occasion she was also searched by three male MPD officers, who "made her pull down her bra, shirt, and pants, and bend over." (*Id.* ¶ 78.)

At the Central Cellblock, in December 2009, "[t]he men in the cell near [her] harassed her and masturbated in front of her" * * * and an MPD officer "exposed his genitalia to [her] and urinated in front of her." * * * Plaintiff's experience in June 2012 was similar. The "male detainees made sexual comments such as asking [plaintiff] to shake her buttocks" and "[w]hen she used the bathroom in her cell, the male detainees saw that she had female anatomy" and one of them "began masturbating and later threw some kind of thick liquid towards [her] which landed in her cell." * * *

"[w]henever practical, transgender arrestees shall be placed in a cell by him/herself, even when more than one transgender person is in custody at the same MPD facility at the same time." It also provides that "[m]embers shall bring conflicting gender information to the attention of the U.S. Marshal's Service when the arrestee is remanded to their custody." When the MPD Transgender Order was adopted in 2007, Conboy was the U.S. Marshal for the Superior Court.

From MPD custody, plaintiff was transferred to the USMS cellblock at Superior Court and to USMS custody. * * * The USMS also knew that plaintiff was legally a female, but treated her as if she were a male. Each time she was transferred to the USMS cellblock, she was searched by male USMS employees * * *, even when female USMS employees were available. * * *

As alleged, the searches of plaintiff did not comply with the USMS search policy for "in-custody" or "strip searches" as they were conducted by male USMS employees, in view of male detainees. In addition, during the searches, male USMS employees verbally harassed her * * * and intimately and inappropriately touched her. * * *

Plaintiff was also held in a bullpen with male detainees * * *, even after requesting to be moved. While there, she was harassed by the male detainees * * * and subjected to other indignities. * * * The USMS employees who were present did nothing to help stop the harassment, even when plaintiff complained. * * *

[Plaintiff alleges that relevant officials were aware of the policies regarding female transgender detainees and the relevant officials "failed to train, supervise or discipline USMS employees in the proper treatment of female transgender detainees."]

[**Analysis: Fifth Amendment Claims**] Plaintiff claims that her Fifth Amendment right to due process was violated by the conditions of confinement while she was in USMS custody and in MPD custody. * * * Specifically, she objects to the USMS's decision to hold her in a bullpen with male detainees, have her urinate in a cup in front of male detainees, transport her while chained to male detainees, and have her searched by male USMS employees and the MPD's decision to hold her in a single cell in the male area of the Central Cellblock. * * * [The defendants] argue that they are entitled to qualified immunity because none of these actions violated a clearly established constitutional right. * * *

The Due Process Clause, rather than the proscriptions of the Eighth Amendment against cruel and unusual punishment, governs the validity of the conditions and restrictions of confinement for detainees charged with crimes but not yet convicted. * * * However, because the due process rights of a pretrial detainee "are at least as great as the Eighth Amendment protections available to a convicted prisoner," * * * a pretrial detainee's rights are violated if she is "incarcerated under conditions posing a substantial risk of serious harm" and the detaining official's "state of mind is one of 'deliberate indifference' to inmate health or safety." *Farmer v. Brennan*, 511 U.S. 825, 834 (1994). To show deliberate indifference, "it is enough that the official acted or failed to act despite his knowledge of a substantial risk of serious harm." Id. at 842. * * *

Plaintiff claims that the conditions of her confinement while in USMS and MPD custody exposed her to a substantial risk of serious harm, that USMS and MPD employees "knew that such harm was likely to occur based on a report from the D.C. Office of the Inspector General, an MPD General Order [the MPD Transgender Order], MPD Standard Operating Procedure [the MPD Transgender Order], and complaints or reports from previous detainees and advocacy groups" * * *, and that the employees "intentionally, deliberately, or recklessly disregarded that risk." * * * She concludes that these actions reflected a "deliberate indifference to [her] safety and dignity" in violation of her Fifth Amendment right to due process. * * *

Defendants argue that they are entitled to qualified immunity because plaintiff's due process right not to be held in the alleged conditions of confinement is not clearly established. Specifically, defendants rely on the absence of any cases specifically holding that a female transgender detainee has the right not to be held with male detainees or otherwise treated as if she were male. They also point to the conclusion by a district court in Arizona that a transgender immigration detainee "does not have a clearly established constitutional right to be housed in a women's detention facility or in a single-occupancy cell in a men's detention facility or to be released from detention based solely on her status as a transgender woman." *See Guzman-Martinez v. Corrections Corp. of America*, 2012 WL 2873835, at *9 (D.Ariz. July 13, 2012).

Defendants' arguments again miss the significance of the fact that plaintiff is legally a female and that defendants are alleged to have known that. Thus, the absence of transgender cases is not itself dispositive. Nor is the decision in *Guzman-Martinez* controlling, because the transgender detainee plaintiff in that case was not legally female. * * * Rather, as with the Fourth Amendment claim, plaintiff's "clearly established" rights include the same rights as any other female detainee.

Accordingly, the cases involving the sexual harassment of female prisoners are not, as defendants suggest, "irrelevant." And those cases establish that a female detainee has the right not to be sexually harassed, verbally or physically, by other detainees or guards. * * * Moreover, at least in this Circuit, "the threshold for establishing a constitutional violation is clearly lower for the pretrial detainees." * * * Considering the allegations in the complaint, applicable MPD policies, and existing caselaw, the Court concludes that a reasonable officer would know that treating a female detainee as plaintiff was treated (*i.e.* holding her with male detainees and otherwise treating her as if she were male) exposed her to a substantial risk of serious harm, and, therefore, would know that those actions violated her constitutional rights. * * *

Accordingly, the Court concludes that plaintiff has alleged a violation of clearly established Fifth Amendment rights based on the conditions of her confinement while in USMS and MPD custody * * * .

PROBLEM 9-5
TRANGENDER DETAINEES AND PLACEMENT DECISIONS

Assume the basic facts are the same as those presented in *Shaw v. Hammond*, except assume that the plaintiff had not had any form of "sex reassignment surgery" and that she had not changed her gender marker on her birth certificate or driver's license, but she had obtained a legal name change changing her name from a traditionally masculine one to a traditionally feminine one. Assume also that the plaintiff had been taking female hormones for many years, and, as a result, she had female secondary-sex characteristics, including breasts. After her first interaction with the officials, assume that the plaintiff consistent represented herself as female, she identified herself with her female name, and she asked to be placed with female inmates. Under those circumstances, would the repeated placement with men, and the repeated strip searches by male officers violate the Constitution? Why or why not?

Now assume that the plaintiff had not had any form of "sex reassignment surgery" but that she had legally changed the gender marker designation on her birth certificate from male to female? Does that change your analysis? Why or why not?

SECTION 5

ACCESS TO HEALTH CARE IN PRISON

Prison officials are legally obligated to provide inmates with medically necessary treatment. One source of law for this obligation is the Eighth Amendment of the U.S. Constitution. As the Supreme Court has explained, "[a]n inmate must rely on prison authorities to treat his medical needs; if the authorities fail to do so, those needs will not be met. In the worst cases, such a failure may actually produce physical 'torture or a lingering death[.]' * * * In less serious cases, denial of medical care may result in pain and suffering which no one suggests would serve any penological purpose." *Estelle v. Gamble*, 429 U.S. 97, 103 (1976). "The infliction of unnecessary suffering" is inconsistent with principles of the Eighth Amendment, which prohibits "cruel and unusual punishment." Thus, in *Estelle*, the Supreme Court established the following principle: prison officials cannot be "deliberately indifferent to [a prisoner's] serious medical needs." *Id.* at 106.

Even when inmates are able to meet this substantive standard, however, they often face additional hurdles when seeking to access adequate medical care. First, as a result of the Prison Litigation Reform Act (PLRA), inmates must contend with a number of procedural hurdles before they are entitled to bring an Eighth Amendment claim in court. PLRA provides that "no action shall be brought by a prisoner in response to prison conditions until such administrative remedies as are available are exhausted." 42 U.S.C. § 1997(e)(a). As a result of this requirement, prior to filing a lawsuit in court, a prisoner must first file a written complaint with prison officials. Not only is the prisoner required to file a grievance complaint, but the inmate must also exhaust all administrative remedies.

In addition, even where the plaintiff complies with this administrative exhaustion requirement, PLRA also appears to bar any federal civil action "by a prisoner confined in a jail, prison, or other correctional facility, for mental or emotional injury suffered while in custody, without a prior showing of physical injury." 42 U.S.C. § 1997e(e). Court decisions are mixed as to whether this provision bars claims of constitutional violations that do not involve physical injuries, such as denials of mental health treatment or particularly egregious incidents involving the treatment of pregnant women that do not result in obvious physical injuries to the inmate.

The sections below consider a number of issues involving denials of medical treatment related to sex, sexuality, and gender.

A. ACCESS TO TRANSITION-RELATED CARE

One issue that has been frequently litigated is whether transgender inmates are entitled to medically necessary transition-related medical care and, if so, whether they are entitled to any specific type of transition-related care. The case law on this question has evolved over time.

Below is one of the more recent decisions to consider this question. The case challenges a Wisconsin statute that prohibited the provision of hormone therapy or gender-confirming surgery without regard to whether the inmate had previously been on hormone therapy or whether either form of treatment was medically necessary for a particular inmate.

Andrea Fields v. Judy P. Smith

United States Court of Appeals for the Seventh of Circuit, 2011.
653 F.3d 550.

■ GOTTSCHALL, J.,

In this appeal, we are asked to review the decision of the district court invalidating a Wisconsin state statute which prohibits the Wisconsin Department of Corrections ("DOC") from providing transgender inmates with certain medical treatments. The Inmate Sex Change Prevention Act ("Act 105") provides in relevant part:

> . . .
>
> (a)   In this subsection:
>
> 1.   "Hormonal therapy" means the use of hormones to stimulate the development or alteration of a person's sexual characteristics in order to alter the person's physical appearance so that the person appears more like the opposite gender.
>
> 2.   "Sexual reassignment surgery" means surgical procedures to alter a person's physical appearance so that the person appears more like the opposite gender.
>
> (b)   The [Wisconsin Department of Corrections] may not authorize the payment of any funds or the use of any resources of this state or the payment of any federal funds passing through the state treasury to provide or to facilitate the provision of hormonal therapy or sexual reassignment surgery. . . .

2005 Wis. Act 105, codified at Wis. Stat. § 302.386(5m) (2010). The district court concluded that this provision violates the Eighth Amendment's ban on cruel and unusual punishment and the Fourteenth Amendment's Equal Protection Clause. Defendants, various DOC officials, now appeal.

[I]   * * * The three plaintiffs—Andrea Fields, Matthew Davison (also known as Jessica Davison), and Vankemah Moaton—are male-to-female transsexuals. According to stipulated facts, each has been diagnosed with Gender Identity Disorder ("GID"). * * * Prior to the passage of Act 105, each of the plaintiffs had been diagnosed by DOC physicians with GID and had been prescribed hormones.

* * * The district court credited much of the testimony from plaintiffs' witnesses, including three experts in the treatment of GID. * * * [The plaintiffs'] experts explained that GID can cause an acute sense that a person's body does not match his or her gender identity. Even before seeking treatment and from an early age, patients will experience this dysphoria and may attempt to conform their appearance and behavior to the gender with which they identify.

The feelings of dysphoria can vary in intensity. Some patients are able to manage the discomfort, while others become unable to function without taking steps to correct the disorder. A person with GID often experiences severe anxiety, depression, and other psychological disorders. Those with GID may attempt to commit suicide or to mutilate their own genitals.

The accepted standards of care dictate a gradual approach to treatment beginning with psychotherapy and real life experience living as the opposite gender. For some number of patients, this treatment will be effective in controlling feelings of dysphoria. When the condition is more severe, a doctor can prescribe hormones, which have the effect of relieving the psychological distress. Hormones also have physical effects on the body. For example, males may experience breast development, relocation of body fat, and softening of the skin. In the most severe cases, sexual reassignment surgery may be appropriate. But often the use of hormones will be sufficient to control the disorder.

When hormones are withdrawn from a patient who has been receiving hormone treatment, severe complications may arise. The dysphoria and associated psychological symptoms may resurface in more acute form. In addition, there may be severe physical effects such as muscle wasting, high blood pressure, and neurological complications. All three plaintiffs in this case experienced some of these effects when DOC doctors discontinued their treatment following the passage of Act 105. * * *

Plaintiffs also called Dr. David Burnett, the DOC's Medical Director, and Dr. Kevin Kallas, the DOC Mental Health Director, to testify at trial. These officials explained that, prior to the enactment of Act 105, hormone therapy had been prescribed to some DOC inmates, including plaintiffs. DOC policies did not permit inmates to receive sex reassignment surgery. Drs. Kallas and Burnett served on a committee of DOC officials that evaluated whether hormone therapy was medically necessary for any particular inmate. Inmates are not permitted to seek any medical treatment outside the prison, regardless of their ability to pay. The doctors testified that they could think of no other state law or policy, besides Act 105, that prohibits prison doctors from providing inmates with medically necessary treatment.

[II] We evaluate both the district court's grant of injunctive relief and the scope of that relief for abuse of discretion. * * * The court's factual findings are reviewed for clear error, and any legal determinations are reviewed de novo. *Knapp*[*v. Northwestern Univ.*], 101 F.3d [473,] 478 [(7th Cir. 1996)].

"Prison officials violate the Eighth Amendment's proscription against cruel and unusual punishment when they display 'deliberate indifference to serious medical needs of prisoners.' " * * * In this case, the district court held that plaintiffs suffered from a serious medical need, namely GID, and that defendants acted with deliberate indifference in that defendants knew of the serious medical need but refused to provide hormone therapy because of Act 105. Defendants do not challenge the district court's holding that GID is a serious medical condition. They contend that Act 105 is constitutional because the state legislature has the power to prohibit certain medical treatments when other treatment options are available. And defendants argue that Act 105 is justified by a legitimate need to ensure security in state prisons.

Defendants rely primarily on two Seventh Circuit decisions which addressed constitutional challenges to refusals to provide treatment for gender dysphoria or transsexualism. Over twenty-four years ago, in *Meriwether v. Faulkner*, 821 F.2d 408 (7th Cir.1987), this court reversed the dismissal of a complaint which alleged that the plaintiff, who had previously been taking hormones, was denied all treatment for her gender dysphoria upon entering prison. The court held that the plaintiff stated a claim that transsexualism was a serious medical need and that prison officials acted with deliberate indifference in refusing all treatment. The court noted in dicta that "[i]t is important to emphasize, however, that she does not have a right to any particular type of treatment, such as estrogen therapy which appears to be the focus of her complaint." Id. at 413.

Ten years later, in *Maggert v. Hanks*, 131 F.3d 670 (7th Cir.1997), this court, in two brief paragraphs, upheld a decision granting summary judgment on a similar deliberate indifference claim where the plaintiff did not come forward with any evidence to rebut defendants' expert witness, who testified that plaintiff did not suffer from gender dysphoria. The court's opinion proceeded to address "a broader issue, having to do with the significance of gender dysphoria in prisoners' civil rights litigation." Id. at 671. The court commented, again in dicta, that the Eighth Amendment does not require the provision of "esoteric" treatments like hormone therapy and sexual reassignment surgery which are "protracted and expensive" and not generally available to those who are not affluent. Id. at 671–72. A prison would be required to provide some treatment for gender dysphoria, but not necessarily "curative" treatment because the Eighth Amendment requires only minimum health care for prison inmates. Id. at 672.

The court's discussion of hormone therapy and sex reassignment surgery in these two cases was based on certain empirical assumptions— that the cost of these treatments is high and that adequate alternatives exist. More than a decade after this court's decision in Maggert, the district court in this case held a trial in which these empirical assumptions were put to the test. At trial, defendants stipulated that the cost of providing hormone therapy is between $300 and $1,000 per inmate per year. The district court compared this cost to the cost of a common antipsychotic drug used to treat many DOC inmates. In 2004, DOC paid a total of $2,300 for hormones for two inmates. That same year, DOC paid $2.5 million to provide inmates with quetiapine, an antipsychotic drug which costs more than $2,500 per inmate per year. Sex reassignment surgery is significantly more expensive, costing approximately $20,000. However, other significant surgeries may be more expensive. In 2005, DOC paid $37,244 for one coronary bypass surgery and $32,897 for one kidney transplant surgery. The district court concluded that DOC might actually incur greater costs by refusing to provide hormones, since inmates with GID might require other expensive treatments or enhanced monitoring by prison security. *Fields*, 712 F.Supp.2d at 863. In fact, at oral argument before this court, counsel for defendants disclaimed any argument that Act 105 is justified by cost savings. * * *

More importantly here, defendants did not produce any evidence that another treatment could be an adequate replacement for hormone therapy. Plaintiffs' witnesses repeatedly made the point that, for certain patients with GID, hormone therapy is the only treatment that reduces dysphoria and can prevent the severe emotional and physical harms associated with it. Although DOC can provide psychotherapy as well as antipsychotics and antidepressants, defendants failed to present evidence rebutting the testimony that these treatments do nothing to treat the underlying disorder. * * *

It is well established that the Constitution's ban on cruel and unusual punishment does not permit a state to deny effective treatment for the serious medical needs of prisoners. The Supreme Court articulated this principle in *Estelle v. Gamble*:

> An inmate must rely on prison authorities to treat his medical needs; if the authorities fail to do so, those needs will not be met. In the worst cases, such a failure may actually produce physical "torture or a lingering death," the evils of most immediate concern to the drafters of the Amendment. In less serious cases, denial of medical care may result in pain and suffering which no one suggests would serve any penological purpose. . . . We therefore conclude that deliberate indifference to serious medical needs of prisoners constitutes the "unnecessary and wanton infliction of pain," proscribed by the Eighth Amendment.

429 U.S. at 103–04 (citations omitted). Surely, had the Wisconsin legislature passed a law that DOC inmates with cancer must be treated only with therapy and pain killers, this court would have no trouble concluding that the law was unconstitutional. Refusing to provide effective treatment for a serious medical condition serves no valid penological purpose and amounts to torture. * * * Although Act 105 permits DOC to provide plaintiffs with *some* treatment, the evidence at trial indicated that plaintiffs could not be effectively treated without hormones.

Defendants point to the Supreme Court's decision in *Gonzales v. Carhart*, 550 U.S. 124 (2007), for the proposition that a legislature may constitutionally limit the discretion of physicians by outlawing a particular medical procedure. In *Carhart*, the Court upheld the constitutionality of the Partial-Birth Abortion Ban Act of 2003 which outlawed a particular procedure used to perform late-term abortions. The Court noted the existence of "medical uncertainty" regarding whether the banned procedure was more dangerous than alternative procedures. Id. at 163–64. Because safe abortion alternatives to the prohibited procedure appeared to exist, the court turned away the facial challenge to the law. Id. at 164.

Carhart is not helpful to defendants in this case because they did not present any medical evidence that alternative treatments for GID are effective. As defendants point out, some medical uncertainty remains as to the causes of GID, but there was no evidence of uncertainty about the efficacy of hormone therapy as a treatment. Just as the legislature cannot outlaw all effective cancer treatments for prison inmates, it cannot outlaw the only effective treatment for a serious condition like GID. * * *

Defendants have also argued that Act 105 is justified by the state's interest in preserving prison security. Defendants' security expert, Eugene Atherton, testified that more feminine male inmates become targets for sexual assault in prisons. Because hormone therapy alters a person's secondary sex characteristics such as breast size and body hair, defendants argue that hormones feminize inmates and make them more susceptible to inciting prison violence. But the district court rejected this argument, noting that the evidence showed transgender inmates may be targets for violence even without hormones. Atherton himself, in his deposition, testified that it would be "an incredible stretch" to conclude that banning the use of hormones could prevent sexual assaults. Id. at 868. In the Colorado Department of Corrections, where Atherton worked for many years, the state had a policy of providing necessary hormones to inmates with GID. Atherton testified that this policy was reasonable and had been implemented effectively in Colorado.

Defendants cite *Whitley v. Albers* for the proposition that " '[p]rison administrators . . . should be accorded wide-ranging deference in the adoption and execution of policies and practices that in their judgment are needed to preserve internal order and discipline and to maintain institutional security.' " * * * But deference does not extend to "actions taken in bad faith and for no legitimate purpose." Id. at 322. * * *

Having determined that the district court properly held that Act 105 violates the Eighth Amendment, both on its face and as applied to plaintiffs, we need not address the district court's alternate holding that the law violates the Equal Protection Clause. * * *

NOTES ON TRANSITION-RELATED MEDICAL CARE IN PRISONS

1. *Access to Some Transition-Related Care?* As explained in *Fields*, initially, most courts concluded that the denial of hormone therapy to a transsexual prisoner did not violate the Eighth Amendment *if* prison officials were providing the inmate with some kind of transition-related care, such as psychotherapy.

Meriwether v. Faulkner, 821 F.3d 408 (7th Cir. 1987), cited in *Fields*, is a representative decision. The plaintiff in *Meriweather* had been presenting as female since she was fourteen. Prior to incarceration, she had been diagnosed with gender dysphoria. As part of her treatment, Meriweather had been receiving hormone therapy, and had had multiple gender-confirming surgeries to alter her body to enhance her traditionally feminine appearance. At some point after being sentenced, she was transferred to a different facility. Although the medical examinations after transfer "supported a diagnosis of gender dysphoria, the consensus of the staff was to treat her as [an] * * * anatomical male." *Id.* at 410. "She was therefore assigned * * * for commitment without a prescription or authorization for the use of hormone supplements." Indeed, from the beginning of her "incarceration, the plaintiff has been denied all medical treatment-chemical, psychiatric, or otherwise-for her gender dysphoria and related medical needs." *Id.* She suffered negative consequences as a result of abrupt cessation of hormone therapy and was placed in segregated protective custody for long periods. She eventually filed suit alleging, among other things, that the denial of transition-related medical care violated the Eighth Amendment's ban on cruel and unusual punishment.

Although the Seventh Circuit reversed the trial court's dismissal of her Eighth Amendment claim, the court took pains to emphasize that there was no particular type of treatment that she was entitled to; the prison was just precluded under the Eighth Amendment from denying her *any* treatment for her condition:

> We therefore conclude that plaintiff has stated a valid claim under the Eighth Amendment which, if proven, would entitle her to some kind of medical treatment. It is important to emphasize, however, that she does not have a right to any particular type of treatment, such as estrogen therapy which appears to be the focus of her complaint. The only two federal courts to have considered the issue have refused to recognize a constitutional right under the Eighth Amendment to estrogen therapy provided that some other treatment option is made available. *See Supre v. Ricketts,* 792 F.2d 958 (10th Cir. 1986); *Lamb v. Maschner,* 633 F.Supp. 351 (D.

Kansas 1986). Both of these courts nevertheless agreed that a transsexual inmate is constitutionally entitled to some type of medical treatment.

Meriwether v. Faulkner, 821 F.2d 408, 413 (7th Cir. 1987). *See also Lamb v. Maschner*, 633 F. Supp. 351 (D. Kansas 1986) (granting defendant's motion for summary judgment where the defendant was providing the transgender inmate with psychological treatment).

2.   *Access to Medically Necessary Hormone Therapy?* Later, a number of courts concluded that if the inmate had been receiving medically prescribed hormones prior to incarceration, abrupt cessation of hormones may violate the Eighth Amendment. For example, in *Phillips v. Michigan Dep't of Corr.*, 731 F. Supp. 792 (W.D. Mich. 1990), the court ordered the prison to "provide plaintiff with the same standard of care she was receiving prior to incarceration * * *—2.5 mg per day of [female hormones]." *Id.* at 801. The court reviewed the earlier case law, but concluded that where the inmate had been on hormones prior to incarceration, the refusal to provide hormones "actually reverse[d] the therapeutic effects of previous treatment." *Id.* at 800. This, the court held, was "measurably worse [than not providing hormones to someone who had not previously been on them], making the cruel and unusual determination much easier." *Id. See also Kothmann v. Rosario*, 2014 WL 889638 (11th Cir. 2014) (providing that "the state of the law was sufficiently clear to put [state prison officials] on notice that refusing to provide [a transgender inmate] with what she knew to be medically necessary hormone treatments was a violation of the Eighth Amendment"); *South v. Gomez*, 211 F.3d 1275 (9th Cir. 2000) (distinguishing cases where inmate had been receiving doctor-prescribed hormones prior to incarceration from those cases where the plaintiff had not been).

Fields, of course, goes even farther, concluding that prison officials might be required to provide hormone therapy to inmates who had not previously been on physician-prescribed hormones prior to incarceration.

This holding is consistent with the current policy of the Federal Bureau of Prisons (FBP). Until 2011, the FBP followed what was called a "freeze frame" policy "whereby the treatment level that transgender inmates could receive was frozen at the level it was when they entered prison." Esinam Agbemenu, "Medical Transgressions in America's Prisons: Defending Transgender Prisoners' Access to Transition-Related Care," 30 *Colum. J. Gender & L.* 1, 13 (2015). In May 2011, the FBP agreed to abandon its prior freeze frame policy, in favor of a policy that bases access to hormone therapy on an individualized assessment of the inmate, utilizing the accepted standards of care. U.S. Dep't of Just., Fed. Bureau of Prisons, Memorandum Re: Gender Identity Disorder Evaluation and Treatment (2011). *See also* Program Statement, Federal Bureau of Prisons, 5200.04, at 8 (Jan. 18, 2017), https://www.bop.gov/policy/progstat/5200.04.pdf.

While inmates in federal prison now have the right to seek hormone therapy treatment even if they had not previously been prescribed such therapy, many state and local prisons continue to follow a "freeze frame" approach. *Cf. Diamond v. Owens*, 131 F. Supp. 3d 1346, 1353 (M.D. Ga. 2015) (noting that the Georgia Department of Corrections had maintained "proscriptive freeze-frame policies" until it abruptly rescinded them shortly before a hearing on plaintiff's motion for a temporary restraining order).

3. *Access to Medically Necessary Gender-Confirming Surgery?* Do prison officials have an obligation under the Eighth Amendment to provide inmates with medically necessary gender-confirming surgery? Until recently, every court that considered the question concluded that prison officials had no obligation under the Eighth Amendment to provide an inmate with medically necessary gender-confirming surgery. That was, however, until the panel decision in *Kosilek v. Spencer* (*Kosilek III*), 740 F.3d 733 (1st Cir. 2014), *rev'd*, *Kosilek v. Spencer* (*Kosilek IV*), 744 F.3d 63 (1st Cir. 2014), *cert. denied*, 135 S. Ct. 2059 (2015) (mem.).

Soon after arriving at the prison, the plaintiff, Michelle Kosilek, sued seeking access to appropriate transition-related care. In 2003, after a preliminary victory in the district court, prison officials began providing her with hormone therapy, among other forms of treatment. Her treating physician, Dr. David Seil, also recommended that she be considered for gender-confirming surgery. *Kosilek II*, 889 F. Supp. 3d at 218. Thereafter, two outside consultant specialists also recommended gender-confirming surgery. Prison officials then retained two other physicians to review that recommendation. These two physicians disagreed, concluding that gender-confirming surgery was not medically necessary. After prison officials refused to provide her with access to surgery, Kosilek sued again.

On September 4, 2012, the district court agreed with the plaintiff and ordered the prison to provide her with gender-confirming surgery. This decision was initially affirmed by a three-judge panel of the First Circuit. *Kosilek III*, 740 F.3d at 772–73. But an en banc panel of the court later vacated the district court's decision. *Kosilek v. Spencer* (*Kosilek IV*), 774 F.3d 63, 68 (1st Cir. 2014), *cert. denied*, 135 S. Ct. 2059 (2015) (mem.).

More recently, a federal district court in California held that California state prison officials violated the Eighth Amendment by denying the inmate's request for gender-confirming surgery. *Norsworthy v. Beard*, 87 F. Supp. 3d 1104 (N.D. Cal. 2015). The inmate, however, was released on parole while the appeal in the case was pending and the appeal was dismissed as moot. *Norsworthy v. Beard*, No. 15-15712 D.C., No. 3:14-cv-00695-JST, https://cdn.ca9.uscourts.gov/datastore/opinions/2015/10/05/15-15712.pdf.

Although Norsworthy did not receive gender-confirming surgery while incarcerated, her case did lead to policy changes in California. In January 2017, Shiloh Heavenly Quine, an inmate in California State prison, became "the first person in the U.S. to receive state-funded sex reassignment surgery while incarcerated." Corinne Segal, "California Inmate Receives State-Funded Sex-Reassignment Surgery," *PBS News Hour* (Jan. 7, 2017 2:59 PM EDT), http://www.pbs.org/newshour/rundown/california-inmate-gender-reassign ment/.

NOTE ON MEDICAL CARE FOR HIV-POSITIVE INMATES

According to the Centers for Disease Control and Prevention (CDC), at any given moment, more than 2 million people in the U.S. are incarcerated in federal, state, and local prisons and jails. These individuals are much more likely than non-incarcerated individuals to be HIV positive and if they are HIV positive, they are more likely to die from the infection as compared to non-incarcerated individuals. Laura M. Maruschak, Bureau of Justice Statistics, *HIV in Prisons, 2001* (Jan. 2004). According to the CDC, in 2010, "the rate of diagnosed HIV infection among inmates in state and federal prisons was more than five times greater than the rate among people who were not incarcerated." CDC, "HIV Among Incarcerated Populations," https://www.cdc.gov/hiv/group/correctional.html. And the rates are even higher for men of color. "Among jail populations, African American men are 5 times as likely as white men, and twice as likely as Hispanic/Latino men, to be diagnosed with HIV." *Id.*

If inmates are or become infected with HIV, they often experience difficulties obtaining adequate medication and other medical treatment. According to advocates, "[t]hese problems include inadequacies in the distribution of medications, prescription of sub-optimal retroviral therapy, lack of choice of anti-HIV therapy, inadequate monitoring of antiretroviral treatment regimes, lack of access to HIV/AIDS specialists, and lack of monitoring for opportunistic infections." "Prisoners' Rights," AIDS Legal Referral Panel, at 18.

Some courts have granted injunctions requiring facilities "to follow the federal guidelines for HIV care published by the National Institute for Health (NIH)." "Prisoners' Rights," AIDS Legal Referral Panel, at 19. That said, it remains unsettled whether inmates have a right to any particular course of treatment or medication. So, for example, in *Perkins v. Kansas Department of Corrections*, 165 F.3d 803 (8th Cir. 1999), the Eighth Circuit dismissed a case brought by an inmate who challenged the facility's refusal to provide him with access to a particular type of medication—a protease inhibitor. *But see Sullivan v. County of Pierce*, 216 F.3d 1084 (9th Cir. 2000) (holding that denying an HIV-positive inmate access to his retroviral "cocktail" for two to three days might be an Eighth Amendment violation).

B. ACCESS TO REPRODUCTIVE HEALTH CARE IN PRISON

Getting access to appropriate and necessary medical treatment in prison is a challenge that any inmate may face. Many female inmates face a challenge that male inmates typically do not face—obtaining appropriate care related to their reproductive health. "A safe estimate is that at any given time, more than 10,000 pregnant women are in prison or jail: The population of adult women detained in prison or jail is more than 200,000, and 6–10% of women entering prison or jail are pregnant." Diana Kasdan, "Abortion Access for Incarcerated Women: Are Correctional Health Practices in Conflict with Constitutional

Standards," 41 *Viewpoint* 59, 59 (2009). *See also* Rachel Roth, "Obstructing Justice: Prisons as Barriers to Medical Care for Pregnant Women," 18 *UCLA Women's L.J.* 79, 81–82 (2010).

Women in prison face difficulties caring for their pregnancies, and obtaining adequate and appropriate reproductive health services more generally. "Prisons do not perform routine gynecological exams, often fail to ask appropriate initial screening questions, and typically do not have on-site physicians trained in obstetrics and gynecology." Sandy de Sauvage & Kelly Head, "Correctional Facilities," 17 *Geo. J. Gender & L.* 175, 191 (2016). Moreover, "[m]any incarcerated women's pregnancies are classified as high risk due to drug addition, sexually transmitted disease, or pelvic inflammatory disease." *Id.* at 192. Recent news reports highlight that even getting access to basic feminine hygiene products is often a challenge. According to the N.Y. Times, "[s]imple supplies like pads and tampons can become bargaining chips, used to maintain control by correction officers, or traded among incarcerated women, according to former inmates and advocates on the issue." Zoe Greenberg, "In Jail, Pads and Tampons as Bargaining Chips," *N.Y. Times* (Apr. 20, 2017).

NOTES ON REPRODUCTIVE CARE IN PRISON

1. *Access to Abortions in Prison.* One type of reproductive health care that is particularly difficult to obtain while incarcerated is access to abortion services. As discussed above, inmates do not shed all of their constitutional rights at the prison door. One fundamental right that courts have held is retained by inmates is the right to terminate a pregnancy. *See, e.g., Roe v. Crawford*, 514 F.3d 789 (8th Cir. 2008) (holding that state policy of refusing to provide transportation for off-site elective abortions violated the Due Process Clause, but rejecting the plaintiffs' claim that this policy also violated the Eighth Amendment). *See also* Diana Kasdan, "Abortion Access for Incarcerated Women: Are Correctional Health Practices in Conflict with Constitutional Standards," 41 *Viewpoint* 59, 60 (2009).

That said, greater restrictions are permissible in the prison setting than would be the case outside that setting. Many prisons require the pregnant inmate to first obtain a court order. The case law is mixed as to whether such a policy is constitutionally permissible. *See, e.g., Doe v. Arpaio*, 150 P.3d 1258 (Ariz. Ct. App. 2007) (holding that county jail policy requiring court order for inmates to be transported to off-site location for elective abortion was unconstitutional); *contra Victoria W. v. Larpenter*, 369 F.3d 475 (5th Cir. 2004) (holding that a prison policy requiring a court order in order to obtain an elective abortion was constitutionally permissible under the *Turner* standard). These kinds of policies have been challenged both under the Due Process Clause, on the ground that they impermissibly infringe a fundamental right, and under the Eighth Amendment, on the ground that they constitute cruel and unusual punishment. Courts have been most receptive to the Due Process claims, but some courts have also found Eighth Amendment violations. *See, e.g., Monmouth Cnty. Corr. Instit. Inmates v. Lanzaro*, 834 F.2d 326, 349 (3d Cir. 1987).

Even if abortions are technically available, they may be out of reach as a practical matter for many female prisoners as the inmates are usually required to pay not only for the abortion itself, but also for the costs associated with transportation to the off-site facility. *See, e.g.*, Rachel Roth, "Obstructing Justice: Prisons as Barriers to Medical Care for Pregnant Women," 18 *UCLA Women's L.J.* 79, 85 (2010). Finally, the bureaucratic hurdles often take so long that by the time the woman has completed all of the necessary steps, an abortion is no longer available to her.

On the other end of the spectrum, "[o]ther women have reported being pressured to have an abortion, especially when the person who got them pregnant is a prison employee. Other women have reported being sterilized without their consent, or even without their knowledge." *Id.* at 84–85.

2. *(Lack of) Reproductive Care and Miscarriages and Stillbirths.* Many women report having difficulty accessing adequate medical care during their pregnancies. Prisons "typically do not have on-site physicians trained in obstetrics and gynecology." Sandy de Sauvage & Kelly Head, "Correctional Facilities," 17 *Geo. J. Gender & L.* 175, 191 (2016). In some more extreme cases, some inmates have had miscarriages or delivered stillborn babies, allegedly after being denied access to adequate care. Some of these women have sued, claiming, among other things, a violation of the Eighth Amendment.

Such a claim was made in *Clifton v. Eubank*, 418 F. Supp. 2d 1243 (D. Colo. 2006). In the morning on December 25, 1998, Pamela Clifton, an inmate who was eight months pregnant, went into labor. Clifton told one of the guards that she was in labor and needed medical assistance. Instead of providing medical assistance, the guard sent her back to her unit. Later that day, Clifton told another guard that she was in labor. That guard also declined to provide medical assistance and also sent her back to her unit. The same thing happened a third time, later that same day. Clifton was later evaluated by a nurse at the facility. The nurse found that Clifton's water had not broken and sent her back to her unit, even though Clifton told the nurse that during past deliveries her water had to be manually broken. The next day, a different guard noticed that Clifton was in distress and had her sent to the medical unit. At this point it was discovered that the fetus was dead. Clifton sued, alleging violations of the Eighth and Fourteenth Amendments.

Prison officials in the case argued that Clifton's claims were barred by PLRA's requirement that the inmate have experienced a physical injury. *Clifton v. Eubank*, 418 F. Supp. 2d 1243, 1245 (D. Colo. 2006) ("Defendants argue the loss of a fetus requiring the mother to undergo a stillbirth does not constitute a physical injury that satisfies the physical injury requirement of the PLRA."). The court rejected this argument, concluding that what the plaintiff had experienced "far surpassed" what had been held to be a sufficient "physical injury" in other cases.

The court then ruled for Clifton on the merits, finding that "a reasonable juror could find each Defendant was deliberately indifferent to Clifton's serious medical needs, thus violating her Eighth Amendment constitutional rights," and that the defendants were not entitled to qualified immunity.

Clifton v. Eubank, 2006 WL 3746694 (D. Colo. 2006). *See also Pool v. Sebastian Cty., Ark*, 418 F.3d 934 (8th Cir. 2005) (denying defendants' motion for summary judgment in a case where the inmate suffered a miscarriage after informing officials that she was pregnant, bleeding, passing clots of blood, and suffering from extreme pain). *Contra Norton v. Greene Cty., Tenn.*, 2013 WL 791154 (E.D. Tenn. 2013) (ruling for defendants in case brought by female inmate who suffered a miscarriage while in custody); *Croskey v. Cty. Of St. Louis*, 2014 WL 3956617 (E.D. Mo. 2014) (same).

3. *Shackling During Labor.* Another issue that has gotten a fair amount of attention in recent years is the issue of shackling pregnant inmates during labor. Both the American Medical Association and the American College of Obstetricians and Gynecologists have policy positions opposing the shackling of women prisoners in most situations. *See, e.g., Villegas v. Metropolitan Gov't of Nashville*, 709 F.3d 563 (6th Cir. 2012) (discussing policies).

The following case grapples with the constitutionality of shackling.

Juana Villegas v. Metropolitan Gov't of Nashville, et al.

United States Court of Appeals for the Sixth Circuit, 2012.
709 F.3d 563.

■ CLAY, J.,

Plaintiff Juana Villegas brought suit under 42 U.S.C. § 1983, claiming violations of her Eighth Amendment rights (made applicable to pretrial detainees through the Fourteenth Amendment) as a result of her being restrained and shackled prior to and following giving birth while in the custody of law enforcement authorities * * *. On cross-motions for summary judgment, the district court granted summary judgment to Plaintiff as to liability on * * * her shackling * * * claim[ ]. * * * For the reasons that follow, we **REVERSE** the district court's grant of summary judgment to Plaintiff and **REMAND** for further proceedings.

[**Background**] Plaintiff Juana Villegas's saga began on July 3, 2008 when her car was stopped by Berry Hill, Tennessee police officer Tim Coleman. At the time of the stop, Plaintiff was nine months pregnant. When Plaintiff failed to produce a valid driver's license, Coleman arrested Plaintiff and transported her to the jail operated by the Davison County Sheriff's Office ("the jail"). Once there, a jail employee, working as an agent of the United States through Immigration and Customs Enforcement's 287(g) program, *see* 8 U.S.C. § 1357(g), inquired into Plaintiff's immigration status and determined that Plaintiff was not lawfully in the United States. Due to her illegal status, a detainer was placed on Plaintiff, which meant that federal immigration officials would delay taking any action until after resolution of Plaintiff's then-pending state charges. After being unable to post bond, Plaintiff was, as a result of the immigration detainer, classified as a medium-security inmate.

Plaintiff was held in the jail from Thursday, July 3, 2008 until late on Saturday, July 5, 2008. At 10:00 p.m. on July 5, 2008, Plaintiff informed a jail guard that her amniotic fluid (or "water") had "broke" and that she was about to have her baby. Plaintiff was transported to the jail infirmary where a nurse confirmed that Plaintiff's water had broken and summoned an ambulance to take Plaintiff to Nashville General Hospital (the "Hospital"). For transportation in the ambulance, Plaintiff was placed on a stretcher with her wrists handcuffed together in front of her body and her legs restrained together. According to Defendant Metropolitan Government of Nashville and Davidson County, because hospitals are "conducive to security breaches including escape," medium-security inmates at hospitals remain shackled until they return to jail. Two male officers (Matthew Barshaw and Thomas Farragher) accompanied Plaintiff in the ambulance to the Hospital * * * .

Upon arriving at the Hospital, Farragher removed Plaintiff's shackles at the request of Hospital staff so that Plaintiff could change into a hospital gown. * * * [A]fter she finished, they again restrained her. Shortly after Plaintiff arrived at the Hospital, officer Brandi Moore arrived to relieve Barshaw and Farragher. * * * After Farragher and Barshaw left, Moore removed Plaintiff's handcuffs but kept one of Plaintiff's legs restrained to the hospital bed.

* * * At 11:20 p.m., a Hospital doctor signed a physician's order stating: "Please remove shackles," and this order was placed in Plaintiff's hospital file, though never specifically given to any officer. Moore was relieved by officer David Peralta at 11:00 p.m. on June 5th and told Peralta to "be prepared for a no restraint order."

Shortly after the shift change, Peralta removed Plaintiff's restraints. According to hospital records, when the shackles were removed, Plaintiff had only dilated to 3 centimeters ("cm"). Plaintiff did not become dilated to 4 cm, a point that Defendant contends is medically relevant, until 11:45 p.m. It was around this time that Plaintiff also first requested pain medication, which she received in the form of an epidural. Plaintiff gave birth without any complications at approximately 1:00 a.m. on July 6, 2008—roughly two hours after Peralta removed her shackles. Plaintiff remained unshackled until shortly before Peralta's shift ended at 7:00 a.m., when he re-restrained Plaintiff to the bed at one of her ankles. Plaintiff was never handcuffed postpartum. * * *

In March 2009, Plaintiff filed suit * * * . On April 27, 2011, the district court granted Plaintiff's partial summary judgment motion on the basis that Defendant was deliberately indifferent to Plaintiff's medical needs by shackling her while she was in labor and postpartum * * *. Defendant timely appealed * * *.

[**Discussion**] Plaintiff * * * claims that by shackling her while she was in labor and postpartum, in the manner it did, Defendant was deliberately indifferent to her need to be unrestrained during this time. * * *

[**I.B**]   "The Eighth Amendment prohibition on cruel and unusual punishment protects prisoners from the 'unnecessary and wanton infliction of pain.' " * * * Pretrial detainee claims, though they sound in the Due Process Clause of the Fourteenth Amendment rather than the Eighth Amendment, * * * are analyzed under the same rubric as Eighth Amendment claims brought by prisoners. * * * . Fundamentally, the " 'concept underlying the Eighth Amendment . . . is nothing less than the dignity of [hu]man[kind].' " * * *

Proving an Eighth Amendment claim requires that the plaintiff make a showing of deliberate indifference. * * * Deliberate indifference has two components to it: objective and subjective. * * * The * * * objective component of deliberate indifference is met upon a showing that a detainee faced a substantial risk of serious harm and that such a risk is one that society chooses not to tolerate.

As to the subjective component, a plaintiff must show that the defendant had "a sufficiently culpable state of mind." * * * This state of mind is shown "where 'the official knows of and disregards' " the substantial risk of serious harm facing the detainee. * * *

[**I.C.1**]   In dealing with deliberate indifference claims in the past, this Court has enumerated some specific types of claims for factual scenarios that frequently arise. These types include, but are not limited to, conditions-of-confinement, excessive-force, and medical-needs. * * * The district court as well as the parties in their briefing discuss this as a medical-needs claim, * * * but as we explain below, the nature of Plaintiff's claim does not quite square with our medical-needs jurisprudence nor our other refinements of the general deliberate indifference principles.

A typical medical-needs claim deals with a deprivation of medical care like the one at issue in *Blackmore v. Kalamazoo County*, 390 F.3d 890 (6th Cir.2004). In that case, a detainee requested medical care after experiencing over twenty-four hours of "sharp" and "extreme" pain in his lower abdomen. Id. at 894 (internal quotation marks omitted). No care was given to the detainee, despite multiple further complaints, until two days after the detainee's first complaint. Id. After three days of pain, a jail nurse diagnosed the plaintiff-detainee with appendicitis. Id. * * *

In light of [this] common factual scenario[ ], this Court has stated that the objective component of deliberate indifference in a medical-needs case is met where a plaintiff produces evidence of a "serious medical need." *Blackmore v. Kalamazoo Cnty.*, 390 F.3d 890, 896 (6th Cir.2004). * * * The problem with viewing a shackling claim, like Plaintiff's, solely as a medical-needs claim is that it does not quite square with either of the typical factual scenarios or the definition of "serious medical need" from * * * *Blackmore*. A shackling claim does not necessarily involve the denial of or interference with medical treatment; rather, it may be premised on the notion that the shackles increase Plaintiff's risk of medical complications. * * *

This problem led one court to analyze the shackling claim it faced as a conditions-of-confinement claim. *See Women Prisoners of D.C. Dep't of Corr. v. Dist. of Columbia*, 877 F.Supp. 634, 668–69 (D.D.C.1994), *modified in part on other ground* s, 899 F.Supp. 659 (1995), *vacated in part and remanded on other grounds,* (93 F.3d 910 (D.C.Cir.1996)). Under our case law, the objective component of a conditions-of-confinement claim is proven where the detainee or prisoner is denied "the minimal civilized measure of life's necessities." * * * This includes deprivations of "adequate food, clothing, shelter, [medical care, and safety]." *Farmer*, 511 U.S. at 832, 114 S.Ct. 1970. A typical conditions-of-confinement case is *Spencer v. Bouchard*, 449 F.3d 721 (6th Cir.2006), *abrogated on other grounds by Jones v. Bock*, 549 U.S. 199, 127 S.Ct. 910, 166 L.Ed.2d 798 (2007), where the prisoner complained of being held in an unbearably cold and leaky cell. Id. at 728–29. While a shackling claim does in some respects resemble some of our conditions-of-confinement cases, * * *, the nature of the medical proof offered by Plaintiff is different than we have previously addressed in the conditions-of-confinement context.

Similarly, we believe that the excessive-force type of claim is also not well adapted for analysis of Plaintiff's claim. The inquiry in excessive-force cases is about " 'whether force was applied in a good-faith effort to maintain or restore discipline, or maliciously and sadistically to cause harm,' " a formulation that does not harmonize with the way Plaintiff has presented her claim. In sum, it seems to us that none of the refinements we have made to the general deliberate indifference principles in order to more easily analyze common factual scenarios are particularly well-suited to the theory and proof offered by Plaintiff.

The Eighth Circuit in *Nelson v. Correctional Medical Services*, 583 F.3d 522 (8th Cir.2009) (en banc), seems to have similarly recognized the crossover nature of a pregnant shackling claim. In dealing with such a claim the Eighth Circuit identified the "relevant questions" as: "(1) whether [the plaintiff] had a serious medical need or whether a substantial risk to her health or safety existed, and (2) whether [the official] had knowledge of such serious medical need or substantial risk to [the plaintiff's] health or safety but nevertheless disregarded it." Id. at 529. This formulation used by the *Nelson* court combines both medical-needs language ("serious medical need") as well as language that points to conditions-of-confinement ("substantial risk to health or safety"). In light of this language, rather than attempt to pigeonhole Plaintiff's shackling claim into a more specific subcategory of deliberate indifference claims, we think it best to analyze her claim under the general deliberate indifference principles. * * *

Consistent with the general principles discussed above, we analyze Plaintiff's claim in two steps, addressing first the objective component and then the subjective one. On the objective component, we ask whether shackling pregnant detainees in the manner and under the circumstances in which Plaintiff was shackled creates a substantial risk of serious harm that society chooses not to tolerate. On the subjective component, the inquiry is whether the officers were aware and understood (or should have been aware and understood) that they were exposing Plaintiff to a substantial risk of serious harm.

[**I.C.2.a**] In attempting to prove the objective component of her shackling claim, Plaintiff points us to prior pregnancy shackling cases, like Nelson, as well as statements from notable public health organizations. Turning first to the case law, each of the three courts to deal with a deliberate indifference shackling claim found the practice of shackling women in labor to be violative of contemporary standards of decency.

In the 1994 *Women Prisoners* case, the District Court for the District of Columbia * * * stated that it understood that prisons "may need to shackle a woman prisoner who has a history of assaultive behavior or escapes. In general, however, the physical limitations of a woman in the third trimester of pregnancy and the pain involved in delivery make complete shackling redundant and unacceptable in light of the risk of injury to a woman and baby." Id.

Next, in 2009, the en banc Eighth Circuit determined that summary judgment was inappropriately granted to a prison where a pregnant woman was shackled "well into the final stage of labor" (7–8 cm dilated). *Nelson*, 583 F.3d at 525–27 & n. 1. * * *

Similarly, in *Brawley v. Washington*, 712 F.Supp.2d 1208 (W.D. Wash.2010), a district court held that fact issues precluded summary judgment, id. at 1220–21, where a prisoner was restrained until "just prior to" her "emergency cesarean" and was re-restrained "right after surgery," id. at 1214. Before doing so, the *Brawley* court concluded that "[c]ommon sense, and the [department of corrections'] own policy, tells us that it is not good practice to shackle women to a hospital bed while they are in labor," id. at 1219 * * *.

All of these courts found that shackling the pregnant women under the circumstances of their respective cases violated the Eighth Amendment. In addition to these analogous cases, as the Eighth Amendment " 'must draw its meaning from the evolving standards of decency that mark the progress of a maturing society,' . . . an assessment of contemporary values concerning the infliction of a challenged sanction is relevant." In this vein, Plaintiff has adduced evidence from the American Medical Association, the American College of Obstetricians and Gynecologists, the United Nations, and Amnesty International decrying the practice of shackling pregnant women, especially while in labor. * * *

However, as the United Nations and American Medical Association recognize, Amnesty International's policy also recognizes that there may be "rare instances" that deviations may be warranted—specifically, "where there are serious and imminent grounds to believe that a woman may attempt to harm herself or others or presents a credible risk of escape that cannot be contained through other methods." *Id.*

Two things are clear from Plaintiff's evidence on the objective component. First, the shackling of pregnant detainees while in labor offends contemporary standards of human decency such that the practice violates the Eighth Amendment's prohibition against the "unnecessary and wanton infliction of pain"—i.e., it poses a substantial risk of serious harm. *See Gamble,* 429 U.S. at 104, 97 S.Ct. 285. The universal consensus from the courts to have addressed this issue as well as the chorus of prominent organizations condemning the practice demonstrates that, without any extenuating circumstances, shackling women during labor runs afoul of the protections of the Eighth Amendment.

Second, it is equally clear, however, from both courts and commentators that the right to be free from shackling during labor is not unqualified. The sources establishing the potential violation also recognize that in certain circumstances, despite the fact that the woman is in labor, shackles may nonetheless be tolerated by society. [The court notes that these sources recognize "potential exceptions where the pregnant detainee presents a danger to herself or others and where the detainee poses a flight risk."]

These same caveats are found in the cases applying the Eighth Amendment to shackled pregnant detainees. The court in the Women Prisoners case left the door open for a situation where a prison "may need to shackle a woman prisoner who has a history of assaultive behavior or escapes." 877 F.Supp. at 668. Additionally, Nelson stated that Eighth Amendment would not afford a detainee a claim where a jail put forth "clear evidence that she is a security or flight risk." 583 F.3d at 534. Therefore, we must consider whether there is evidence in the record of the instant case that supports Defendant's claim that Plaintiff was a flight risk. [The court concludes that because there were disputed issues of material fact on that issue, summary judgment was inappropriate.]

[I.C.2.b] Turning to the subjective component, as stated above, the question is whether the officers had knowledge of the substantial risk, recognized the serious harm that such a risk could cause, and, nonetheless, disregarded it. * * *

Plaintiff attempts to establish that Defendant was subjectively aware of the risks that the shackles posed by virtue of the fact that Hospital staff ordered the shackles removed. Knowledge of such a "no restraint order" would, at minimum, evince knowledge of a substantial risk of serious harm. * * * [But a]lthough it is clear from the record that a no restraint order was placed in Plaintiff's file at 11:20 p.m., no testimony reveals that Defendant or its officers ever knew about the existence of this order. * * *

Both sides also presented expert testimony as to the specific harm faced by Plaintiff and the potential obviousness of this harm to Defendant's officers. * * * Plaintiff offered two different witnesses: a gynecologist, Dr. Sandra Torrente, to opine on the physical risks associated with shackling, and a psychiatrist, Dr. Jill DeBona, to opine on the psychological risks. Defendant also presented a gynecologist, Dr. Bennett Spetalnick.

[Defendant's witness,] Spetalnick, who is the head of Obstetrics and Gynecology at Vanderbilt University Medical Center, opined that "[a]lthough the risk of a DVT (deep venous thrombosis) and PE (pulmonary embolism) is increased with pregnancy and postpartum, my medical opinion, based on the literature and personal experience, is that these risks are not enhanced by a leg restraint and/or handcuffs." * * *

[Plaintiff's witness] Torrente, an assistant professor of Obstetrics and Gynecology at Meharry Medical College, on the other hand, stated: "Placing a pregnant woman in leg irons or shackles increases her risk of developing a potentially life-threatening blood clot. This risk is increased and present throughout a woman's entire pregnancy; however, it is at the greatest risk post-partum," and therefore women should be "ambulatory . . . as often as possible" during this period. Additionally, Torrente detailed the importance of being unrestrained due to "potential occurrence of umbilical cord prolapse" and "the increased risk in falling due to a pregnant woman's impaired balance." Finally, restraints would create "discomfort" and would not allow the woman to "safely handle a newborn child." Torrente further opined that Plaintiff was shackled during "active labor" and because she had previously given birth, "the risk created by shackling her during labor are even greater because of her potential to begin giving birth much sooner following the onset of labor than the average woman in labor." Specifically in response to Spetalnick, she disagreed "that there was no significant risk to [Plaintiff] because she happened to be unshackled two hours before she delivered[, and] . . . Spetalnick is incorrect that [Defendant's] conduct did not substantially elevate [Plaintiff's] risk of DVT and PE."

Lastly, psychiatrist DeBona, in detailing the various "episode[s] of shackling" that Plaintiff experienced, described the psychological effects of the shackling on Plaintiff * * *.

As is the case with many claims of deliberate indifference, we find that there are fact issues that preclude the grant of summary judgment to Plaintiff. * * *

In light of the material factual disputes surrounding whether Plaintiff was shown to be a flight risk, whether Defendant's officers had any knowledge about a no restraint order, and the conflicting expert testimony about the ill effects of Plaintiff's shackling, we conclude that the district court improperly granted summary judgment to Plaintiff on her shackling claim. On remand, a jury will need to determine whether Plaintiff was a flight risk in her condition and whether Defendant had knowledge of the substantial risk, recognized the serious harm that such a risk could cause, and, nonetheless, disregarded it, recognizing that such knowledge may be established through the obviousness of the risk. * * *

■ HELENE N. WHITE, CIRCUIT JUDGE, dissenting.

I respectfully dissent. * * *

Villegas established that shackling created an objectively substantial risk of serious harm in two ways; by showing that her condition as a laboring and then lactating woman 1) resulted in medically prescribed treatment and 2) was obvious to lay persons as a serious medical need. * * *

The majority observes that Villegas's right to be free from shackling during labor must be balanced against Defendant's penological interest, and concludes that a question of material fact remained whether Villegas was a flight risk. I disagree.

First, deliberate indifference to a prisoner's serious medical need "can typically be established or disproved without the necessity of balancing competing institutional concerns for the safety of prison staff." * * *

Here, Defendant maintained that Villegas's restraints were "consistent with" her medium-security designation and that illegal immigrants *in general* pose a danger of flight. But Villegas's medium-security designation did not take into account her late-term pregnancy or that she had gone into labor, nor was it based on any assessment of flight risk or risk of harm—it was automatic because of the Immigration and Customs Enforcement (ICE) detainer. Villegas was not being held for a crime of violence and had not been convicted of any crime. She was not individually assessed for flight risk or risk of harm to herself or others, and she had not engaged in any conduct evidencing such. * * *

Defendant's asserted penological interest in shackling Villegas while she was being transported to and then hospitalized, to maintain control over her in an *unsecured* facility, suffers from another flaw. It is undisputed that at least one armed officer was present in the ambulance, at least one armed officer was present in the hospital room or outside the room at all times, and the maternity ward at Metro General Hospital is locked down at all times, that is, a nurse must unlock the doors and authorize persons to enter and exit. In order to flee or pose a threat, Villegas would have had to harm or elude armed officer(s) and the nurse authorizing entry and exit from the maternity ward charged with unlocking the doors.

Finally, I note that even though Villegas went through labor and gave birth without threat of escape or harm to anyone, Defendant's officers shackled her legs *together* postpartum while she walked, showered and used the toilet. This despite the fact that before the birth, a physician had ordered in writing that the shackles be removed. R. 86–17; PID 1609.

In sum, Defendant made no showing, and the facts belied, that shackling Villegas at any time was necessary, whether to effect their purported penological interest or otherwise.

Villegas satisfied the subjective component by demonstrating that Defendant's officers acted with deliberate indifference to her serious medical needs, i.e., knew of and disregarded the substantial risk of harm posed by shackling her during labor and postpartum. An Eighth Amendment claimant "need not show that a prison official acted or failed to act believing that harm actually would befall an inmate; it is enough to that the official acted or failed to act despite his knowledge of a substantial risk of serious harm."

The district court's opinion sets forth the evidence establishing that Defendant's officers were aware of the substantial medical risks posed by shackling women while in labor and during postpartum recovery and disregarded it. * * *

The majority also concludes that conflicting expert testimony about the ill effects of Villegas's shackling raised a material factual dispute. I disagree. Given the long-established law on shackling during labor and postpartum and the undisputed facts, I agree with the district court that the declaration of defense expert Dr. Spetalnick did not raise an issue of *material* fact.

* * * The subjective component of a deliberate indifference claim goes to whether Defendant's officers were deliberately indifferent to substantial risks of serious harm posed by shackling. Defendant's experts did not address several of the serious medical risks to which Villegas's experts attested and did not rebut that shackling Villegas while en route to the hospital, during labor and postpartum, increased the medical risks of serious harm to Villegas and her unborn child. I agree with the district court that no genuine or material factual dispute remained regarding whether Defendant's officers knew of and disregarded the substantial risks of harm posed by shackling Villegas during labor and postpartum * * * .

NOTES ON *VILLEGAS*

1. *Legality of Shackling Pregnant Inmates.* Although the practice of shackling pregnant female inmates in labor continues to be utilized by some prison officials, all courts that have considered the question have concluded that, at least based on the facts of the particular cases presented to them, shackling pregnant women in labor violates the Eighth Amendment. *See, e.g., Nelson v. Corr. Med. Serv.*, 583 F.3d 522, 531 (8th Cir. 2009); *Brawley v. Washington*, 712 F. Supp. 2d 1208, 1221 (W.D. Wash. 2010).

About 20 states have enacted statutes prohibiting the practice. *See, e.g.,* Heather Schultz, "An Anti-Shackling Wake-Up Call," *The Ctr. For Am. Progress* (May 22, 2014), https://www.americanprogress.org/issues/women/news/2014/05/22/90306/an-anti-shackling-wake-up-call/ (stating that, as of May 2014, the following states had enacted anti-shackling legislation:

Arizona, California, Colorado, Delaware, Florida, Hawaii, Idaho, Illinois, Louisiana, Maryland, Massachusetts, Minnesota, Nevada, New Mexico, New York, Pennsylvania, Rhode Island, Texas, Vermont, Washington, and West Virginia).

For scholarly considerations of shackling pregnant inmates, see, e.g., Priscilla A. Ocen, "Punishing Pregnancy: Race, Incarceration, and the Shackling of Pregnant Prisoners," 100 *Cal. L. Rev.* 1239 (2012); Robin Levi, et al, "Creating the 'Bad Mother:' How the U.S. Approach to Pregnancy in Prison Violates the Right to be a Mother," 18 *UCLA Women's L.J.* 1 (2010); Dana Sussman, "Bound by Injustice: Challenging the Use of Shackles on Incarcerated Pregnant Women," 15 *Cardozo J.L. & Gender* 477 (2009).

Professor Ocen argues that "[w]hen place[d] in [the context of racial subjugation], we can see the continuities between the degradation and devaluation of Black women during slavery, convict leasing, and chain gains, and the dehumanization of female prisoners through the use of shackles during childbirth. The constructions of Black women as masculine, deviant, and dangerous constitute the metaphorical scaffolding of women's prisons, framing experiences within institutions and justifying the application of harsh conditions upon all imprisoned women." Ocen, *supra,* at 1310.

2.   *Mothers in Prison.* Whether or not they were shackled in labor, many women give birth while incarcerated. "Approximately 70,000 incarcerated women are mothers, 2,000 entered prison pregnant, and more than 1,000 will give birth while incarcerated." Zakiya Luna & Kristin Luker, "Reproductive Justice," 9 *Ann. Rev. L. & Soc. Sci.* 327, 341 (2013). But "[o]f the more than 100 women's prisons in the U.S., there are only eight nurseries." Colleen Long, "Babies Behind Bars," *Post Standard* (May 30, 2016), 2016 WLNR 16533721. "Research demonstrates that these programs can yield effective outcomes for mothers and their children." The Rebecca Project for Human Rights & National Women's Law Center, "Mothers Behind Bars: A state-by-state report card and analysis of federal policies on conditions of confinement for pregnant and parenting women and the effect on their children" 13 (2010), https://www.nwlc.org/sites/default/files/pdfs/mothersbehindbars2010.pdf. But because there are so few prison nursery programs, in most cases, children born to incarcerated women are placed with a relative or in foster care almost immediately after birth. *Id.* Indeed, "some mothers are denied the ability to nurse the newborn, stay with the newborn for any length of time, or introduce the newborn to other family members." Deborah Ahrens, "Incarcerated Childbirth and Broader 'Birth Control': Autonomy, Regulation, and the State," 80 *Mo. L. Rev.* 1, 30 (2015).

For a comprehensive review of policies affecting mothers in prison, see The Rebecca Project for Human Rights & National Women's Law Center, "Mothers Behind Bars: A state-by-state report card and analysis of federal policies on conditions of confinement for pregnant and parenting women and the effect on their children" (2010), https://www.nwlc.org/sites/default/files/pdfs/mothersbehindbars2010.pdf.

APPENDIX 1

INDIVIDUAL RIGHTS PROVISIONS FROM THE AMENDMENTS TO THE CONSTITUTION OF THE UNITED STATES

Amendment I [1791]

Congress shall make no law respecting an establishment of religion, or prohibiting the free exercise thereof; or abridging the freedom of speech, or of the press; or the right of the people peaceably to assemble, and to petition the Government for a redress of grievances.

Amendment II [1791]

A well regulated Militia, being necessary to the security of a free State, the right of the people to keep and bear Arms, shall not be infringed.

Amendment III [1791]

No Soldier shall, in time of peace be quartered in any house, without the consent of the Owner, nor in time of war, but in a manner to be prescribed by law.

Amendment IV [1791]

The right of the people to be secure in their persons, houses, papers, and effects, against unreasonable searches and seizures, shall not be violated, and no Warrants shall issue, but upon probable cause, supported by Oath or affirmation, and particularly describing the place to be searched, and the persons or things to be seized.

Amendment V [1791]

No person shall be held to answer for a capital, or otherwise infamous crime, unless on a presentment or indictment of a Grand Jury, except in cases arising in the land or naval forces, or in the Militia, when in actual service in time of War or public danger; nor shall any person be subject for the same offence to be twice put in jeopardy of life or limb; nor shall be compelled in any criminal case to be a witness against himself, nor be deprived of life, liberty, or property, without due process of law; nor shall private property be taken for public use, without just compensation.

Amendment VI [1791]

In all criminal prosecutions, the accused shall enjoy the right to a speedy and public trial, by an impartial jury of the State and district wherein the crime shall have been committed, which district shall have been previously ascertained by law, and to be informed of the nature and cause of the accusation; to be confronted with the witnesses against him; to have compulsory process for obtaining witnesses in his favor, and to have the Assistance of Counsel for his defence.

Amendment VII [1791]

In Suits at common law, where the value in controversy shall exceed twenty dollars, the right of trial by jury shall be preserved, and no fact tried by a jury, shall be otherwise re-examined in any Court of the United States, than according to the rules of the common law.

Amendment VIII [1791]

Excessive bail shall not be required, nor excessive fines imposed, nor cruel and unusual punishments inflicted.

Amendment IX [1791]

The enumeration in the Constitution, of certain rights, shall not be construed to deny or disparage others retained by the people.

Amendment X [1791]

The powers not delegated to the United States by the Constitution, nor prohibited by it to the States, are reserved to the States respectively, or to the people.

* * *

Amendment XIII [1865]

Section 1.   Neither slavery nor involuntary servitude, except as a punishment for crime whereof the party shall have been duly convicted, shall exist within the United States, or any place subject to their jurisdiction.

Section 2.   Congress shall have power to enforce this article by appropriate legislation.

Amendment XIV [1868]

Section 1.   All persons born or naturalized in the United States, and subject to the jurisdiction thereof, are citizens of the United States and of the State wherein they reside. No State shall make or enforce any law which shall abridge the privileges or immunities of citizens of the United States; nor shall any State deprive any person of life, liberty, or property, without due process of law; nor deny to any person within its jurisdiction the equal protection of the laws.

* * *

Section 5.   The Congress shall have power to enforce, by appropriate legislation, the provisions of this article.

Amendment XV [1870]

Section 1.   The right of citizens of the United States to vote shall not be denied or abridged by the United States or by any State on account of race, color, or previous condition of servitude.

Section 2.   The Congress shall have power to enforce this article by appropriate legislation.

* * *

Amendment XIX [1920]

[1]   The right of citizens of the United States to vote shall not be denied or abridged by the United States or by any State on account of sex.

[2]   Congress shall have power to enforce this article by appropriate legislation.

* * *

APPENDIX 2

TITLE VII OF THE CIVIL RIGHTS ACT OF 1964 AS AMENDED (EXCERPTS)

DEFINITIONS

SEC. 2000e [of 42 U.S. Code and] *Section 701 [of the original legislation]*

For the purposes of this subchapter—* * *

(b) The term "employer" means a person engaged in an industry affecting commerce who has fifteen or more employees for each working day in each of twenty or more calendar weeks in the current or preceding calendar year, and any agent of such a person, but such term does not include (1) the United States, a corporation wholly owned by the Government of the United States, an Indian tribe, or any department or agency of the District of Columbia subject by statute to procedures of the competitive service (as defined in section 2102 of Title 5 *[United States Code]*), or

(2) a bona fide private membership club (other than a labor organization) which is exempt from taxation under section 501(c) of Title 26 *[the Internal Revenue Code of 1986]* * * *

(c) The term "employment agency" means any person regularly undertaking with or without compensation to procure employees for an employer or to procure for employees opportunities to work for an employer and includes an agent of such a person.

(d) The term "labor organization" means a labor organization engaged in an industry affecting commerce, and any agent of such an organization * * *

(e) A labor organization shall be deemed to be engaged in an industry affecting commerce if (1) it maintains or operates a hiring hall or hiring office which procures employees for an employer or procures for employees opportunities to work for an employer, or (2) the number of members * * * is * * * fifteen or more * * *

(f) The term "employee" means an individual employed by except that the term "employee" shall not include any pe public office in any State or political subdivision of qualified voters thereof, or any person chosen by officer's personal staff, or an appointee on immediate adviser with respect to th legal powers of the office [unless service laws].

(g) The term "commerce" means trade, traffic, commerce, transportation, transmission, or communication among the several States; or between a State and any place outside thereof; or within the District of Columbia, or a possession of the United States; or between points in the same State but through a point outside thereof.

(h) The term "industry affecting commerce" means any activity, business, or industry in commerce or in which a labor dispute would hinder or obstruct commerce or the free flow of commerce and includes any activity or industry "affecting commerce" within the meaning of the Labor-Management Reporting and Disclosure Act of 1959 *[29 U.S.C. 401 et seq.]*, and further includes any governmental industry, business, or activity. * * *

(j)   The term "religion" includes all aspects of religious observance and practice, as well as belief, unless an employer demonstrates that he is unable to reasonably accommodate to an employee's or prospective employee's religious observance or practice without undue hardship on the conduct of the employer's business.

(k)   The terms "because of sex" or "on the basis of sex" include, but are not limited to, because of or on the basis of pregnancy, childbirth, or related medical conditions; and women affected by pregnancy, childbirth, or related medical conditions shall be treated the same for all employment-related purposes, including receipt of benefits under fringe benefit programs, as other persons not so affected but similar in their ability or inability to work, and nothing in section 2000e–2(h) of this title *[section 703(h)]* shall be interpreted to permit otherwise. This subsection shall not require an employer to pay for health insurance benefits for abortion, except where the life of the mother would be endangered if the fetus were carried to term, or except where medical complications have arisen from an abortion: Provided, That nothing herein shall preclude an employer from providing abortion benefits or otherwise affect bargaining agreements in regard to abortion.

The term "complaining party" means the Commission, the Attorney

(a)   person who may bring an action or proceeding under this

It shall be

(1)   to fail or re
to discriminate agai

urdens of production

TICES

loyer—

l, or otherwise
mpensation,

terms, conditions, or privileges of employment, because of such individual's race, color, religion, sex, or national origin; or

(2) to limit, segregate, or classify his employees or applicants for employment in any way which would deprive or tend to deprive any individual of employment opportunities or otherwise adversely affect his status as an employee, because of such individual's race, color, religion, sex, or national origin.

(b) Employment agency practices

It shall be an unlawful employment practice for an employment agency to fail or refuse to refer for employment, or otherwise to discriminate against, any individual because of his race, color, religion, sex, or national origin, or to classify or refer for employment any individual on the basis of his race, color, religion, sex, or national origin.

(c) Labor organization practices

It shall be an unlawful employment practice for a labor organization—

(1) to exclude or to expel from its membership, or otherwise to discriminate against, any individual because of his race, color, religion, sex, or national origin;

(2) to limit, segregate, or classify its membership or applicants for membership, or to classify or fail or refuse to refer for employment any individual, in any way which would deprive or tend to deprive any individual of employment opportunities, or would limit such employment opportunities or otherwise adversely affect his status as an employee or as an applicant for employment, because of such individual's race, color, religion, sex, or national origin; or

(3) to cause or attempt to cause an employer to discriminate against an individual in violation of this section.

(d) Training programs

It shall be an unlawful employment practice for any employer, labor organization, or joint labor-management committee controlling apprenticeship or other training or retraining, including on-the-job training programs to discriminate against any individual because of his race, color, religion, sex, or national origin in admission to, or employment in, any program established to provide apprenticeship or other training.

(e) Businesses or enterprises with personnel qualified on basis of religion, sex, or national origin; educational institutions with personnel of particular religion

Notwithstanding any other provision of this subchapter, (1) it shall not be an unlawful employment practice for an employer to hire and employ employees [or entity controlling] training * * * programs to admit or employ any individual in any such program, on the basis of his religion, sex, or national origin in those certain instances where religion, sex, or national origin is a bona fide occupational qualification reasonably necessary to the normal operation of that particular business or enterprise, and (2) it shall not be an unlawful employment practice for a school, college, university, or other educational institution or institution of learning to hire and employ employees of a particular religion if such school, college, university, or other educational institution or institution of learning is, in whole or in substantial part, owned, supported, controlled, or managed by a particular religion or by a particular religious corporation, association, or society, or if the curriculum of such school, college, university, or other educational institution or institution of learning is directed toward the propagation of a particular religion.

(f)   Members of Communist Party or Communist-action or Communist-front organizations

As used in this subchapter, the phrase "unlawful employment practice" shall not be deemed to include any action or measure taken * * * with respect to an individual who is a member of the Communist Party of the United States or of any other organization required to register as a Communist-action or Communist-front organization by final order of the Subversive Activities Control Board pursuant to the Subversive Activities Control Act of 1950 *[50 U.S.C. 781 et seq.].*

(g)   National security

Notwithstanding any other provision of this subchapter, it shall not be an unlawful employment practice for an employer to fail or refuse to hire and employ any individual for any position, for an employer to discharge any individual from any position, or for an employment agency to fail or refuse to refer any individual for employment in any position, or for a labor organization to fail or refuse to refer any individual for employment in any position, if—

(1)   the occupancy of such position, or access to the premises in or upon which any part of the duties of such position is performed or is to be performed, is subject to any requirement imposed in the interest of the national security of the United States under any security program in effect pursuant to or administered under any statute of the United States or any Executive order of the President; and

(2)   such individual has not fulfilled or has ceased to fulfill that requirement.

(h)   Seniority or merit system; quantity or quality of production; ability tests; compensation based on sex and authorized by minimum wage provisions

Notwithstanding any other provision of this subchapter, it shall not be an unlawful employment practice for an employer to apply different standards of compensation, or different terms, conditions, or privileges of employment pursuant to a bona fide seniority or merit system, or a system which measures earnings by quantity or quality of production or to employees who work in different locations, provided that such differences are not the result of an intention to discriminate because of race, color, religion, sex, or national origin, nor shall it be an unlawful employment practice for an employer to give and to act upon the results of any professionally developed ability test provided that such test, its administration or action upon the results is not designed, intended or used to discriminate because of race, color, religion, sex or national origin. It shall not be an unlawful employment practice under this subchapter for any employer to differentiate upon the basis of sex in determining the amount of the wages or compensation paid or to be paid to employees of such employer if such differentiation is authorized by the provisions of section 206(d) of Title 29 *[section 6(d) of the Labor Standards Act of 1938, as amended]*. * * *.

(j)   Preferential treatment not to be granted on account of existing number or percentage imbalance

Nothing contained in this subchapter shall be interpreted to require any employer * * * to grant preferential treatment to any individual or to any group because of the race, color, religion, sex, or national origin of such individual or group on account of an imbalance which may exist with respect to the total number or percentage of persons of any race, color, religion, sex, or national origin employed by any employer * * * in comparison with the total number or percentage of persons of such race, color, religion, sex, or national origin in any community, State, section, or other area, or in the available work force in any community, State, section, or other area.

(k)   Burden of proof in disparate impact cases

(1)(A)   An unlawful employment practice based on disparate impact is established under this subchapter only if—

(i)   a complaining party demonstrates that a respondent uses a particular employment practice that causes a disparate impact on the basis of race, color, religion, sex, or national origin and the respondent fails to demonstrate that the challenged practice is job related for the position in question and consistent with business necessity; or

(ii) the complaining party makes the demonstration described in subparagraph (C) with respect to an alternative employment practice and the respondent refuses to adopt such alternative employment practice.

(B)(i)   With respect to demonstrating that a particular employment practice causes a disparate impact as described in subparagraph (A)(i), the complaining party shall demonstrate that each particular challenged employment practice causes a disparate impact, except that if the complaining party can demonstrate to the court that the elements of a respondent's decisionmaking process are not capable of separation for analysis, the decisionmaking process may be analyzed as one employment practice.

(ii) If the respondent demonstrates that a specific employment practice does not cause the disparate impact, the respondent shall not be required to demonstrate that such practice is required by business necessity. * * *

(2) A demonstration that an employment practice is required by business necessity may not be used as a defense against a claim of intentional discrimination under this subchapter.

(3) Notwithstanding any other provision of this subchapter, a rule barring the employment of an individual who currently and knowingly uses or possesses a controlled substance [unless under medical supervision] shall be considered an unlawful employment practice under this subchapter only if such rule is adopted or applied with an intent to discriminate because of race, color, religion, sex, or national origin.

(*l*) Prohibition of discriminatory use of test scores

It shall be an unlawful employment practice for a respondent, in connection with the selection or referral of applicants or candidates for employment or promotion, to adjust the scores of, use different cutoff scores for, or otherwise alter the results of, employment related tests on the basis of race, color, religion, sex, or national origin.

(m) Impermissible consideration of race, color, religion, sex, or national origin in employment practices

Except as otherwise provided in this subchapter, an unlawful employment practice is established when the complaining party demonstrates that race, color, religion, sex, or national origin was a motivating factor for any employment practice, even though other factors also motivated the practice. * * *

OTHER UNLAWFUL EMPLOYMENT PRACTICES

SEC. 2000e–3. *[Section 704]*

(a) Discrimination for making charges, testifying, assisting, or participating in enforcement proceedings

It shall be an unlawful employment practice for an employer to discriminate against any of his employees * * * to discriminate against any individual, or for a labor organization to discriminate against any member thereof or applicant for membership, because he has opposed any practice made an unlawful employment practice by this subchapter, or because he has made a charge, testified, assisted, or participated in any manner in an investigation, proceeding, or hearing under this subchapter.

(b) Printing or publication of notices or advertisements indicating prohibited preference, limitation, specification, or discrimination; occupational qualification exception

It shall be an unlawful employment practice for an employer * * * to print or publish or cause to be printed or published any notice or advertisement relating to employment by such an employer * * * indicating any preference, limitation, specification, or discrimination, based on race, color, religion, sex, or national origin, except that such a notice or advertisement may indicate a preference, limitation, specification, or discrimination based on religion, sex, or national origin when religion, sex, or national origin is a bona fide occupational qualification for employment.

EQUAL EMPLOYMENT OPPORTUNITY COMMISSION

SEC. 2000e–4. *[Section 705]*

(a) Creation; composition; political representation; appointment; term; vacancies; Chairman and Vice Chairman; duties of Chairman; appointment of personnel; compensation of personnel

There is hereby created a Commission to be known as the Equal Employment Opportunity Commission, which shall be composed of five members, not more than three of whom shall be members of the same political party. Members of the Commission shall be appointed by the President by and with the advice and consent of the Senate for a term of five years. * * *

(b) General Counsel; appointment; term; duties; representation by attorneys and Attorney General

(1) There shall be a General Counsel of the Commission appointed by the President, by and with the advice and consent of the Senate, for a term of four years. * * *

EFFECT ON STATE LAWS

SEC. 2000e–7. *[Section 708]*

Nothing in this subchapter shall be deemed to exempt or relieve any person from any liability, duty, penalty, or punishment provided by any present or future law of any State or political subdivision of a State, other than any such law which purports to require or permit the doing of any act which would be an unlawful employment practice under this subchapter. * * *

APPENDIX 3

THE PROPOSED EQUALITY ACT (EXCERPTS)

115th CONGRESS

1st Session

H.R. 2282

IN THE HOUSE OF REPRESENTATIVES

May 2, 2017

A BILL

To prohibit discrimination on the basis of sex, gender identity, and sexual orientation, and for other purposes.

Be it enacted by the Senate and House of Representatives of the United States of America in Congress assembled,

SECTION 1. SHORT TITLE.

This Act may be cited as the "Equality Act".

SEC. 2. FINDINGS AND PURPOSE.

(a) Findings.—Congress finds the following:

(1) Discrimination can occur on the basis of the sex, sexual orientation, gender identity, or pregnancy, childbirth, or a related medical condition of an individual, as well as because of sex-based stereotypes. Each of these factors alone can serve as the basis for discrimination, and each is a form of sex discrimination.

(2) A single instance of discrimination may have more than one basis. For example, discrimination against a married same-sex couple could be based on the sex stereotype that marriage should only be between heterosexual couples, the sexual orientation of the two individuals in the couple, or both. Discrimination against a pregnant lesbian could be based on her sex, her sexual orientation, her pregnancy, or on the basis of multiple factors.

(3) Lesbian, gay, bisexual, and transgender (referred to as "LGBT") people commonly experience discrimination in securing access to public accommodations—including restaurants, stores, places of or establishments that provide entertainment, and transportation. Forms of discrimination include the exclusion and denial of entry, unequal or unfair treatment, harassment, and violence. This discrimination prevents the full participation of LGBT people in society and disrupts the free flow of commerce.

(4) Women also face discrimination, in establishments such as stores and restaurants, and places or establishments that provide other goods or services, such as entertainment or transportation, including sexual harassment, differential pricing, and denial of services because they are pregnant or breastfeeding.

(5) Regular and ongoing discrimination against LGBT people, as well as women, in accessing public accommodations contributes to negative social and economic outcomes.

(6) The discredited practice known as "conversion therapy" is a form of discrimination that harms LGBT people by undermining individuals' sense of self worth, increasing suicide ideation and substance abuse, exacerbating family conflict, and contributing to second class status.

(7) Both LGBT people and women face widespread discrimination in employment and various services, including by entities that receive Federal financial assistance. * * *

(8) Workers who are LGBT, or are perceived to be LGBT, have been subjected to a history and pattern of persistent, widespread, and pervasive discrimination on the bases of sexual orientation and gender identity by private sector employers and Federal, State, and local government employers.

(9) Numerous provisions of Federal law expressly prohibit discrimination on the basis of sex, and Federal agencies and courts have correctly interpreted these prohibitions on sex discrimination to include discrimination based on sexual orientation, gender identity, and sex stereotypes. In particular, the Equal Employment Opportunity Commission correctly interpreted title VII of the Civil Rights Act of 1964 in Macy v. Holder, Baldwin v. Foxx, and Lusardi v. McHugh.

(10) The absence of explicit prohibitions of discrimination on the basis of sexual orientation and gender identity under Federal statutory law, as well as the existence of legislative proposals that would have provided such explicit prohibitions, has led some courts to conclude incorrectly that current Federal laws prohibiting sex discrimination do not prohibit discrimination on the basis of sexual orientation and gender identity. It has also created uncertainty for employers and other entities covered by Federal nondiscrimination laws and caused unnecessary hardships for LGBT individuals.

(11) LGBT people often face discrimination when seeking to rent or purchase housing, as well as in every other aspect of obtaining and maintaining housing. LGBT people in same-sex relationships are often discriminated against when two names associated with one gender appear on a housing application, and transgender people often encounter discrimination when credit checks or inquiries reveal a former name.

(12) National surveys, including a study commissioned by the Department of Housing and Urban Development, show that housing discrimination against LGBT people is very prevalent. * * *

(13) As a result of the absence of explicit prohibitions against discrimination on the basis of sexual orientation and gender identity, credit applicants who are LGBT, or perceived to be LGBT, have unequal opportunities to establish credit. * * *

(14) Numerous studies demonstrate that LGBT people, especially transgender people and women, are economically disadvantaged and at a higher risk for poverty compared with other groups of people.

(15) The right to an impartial jury of one's peers and the reciprocal right to jury service are fundamental to the free and democratic system of justice in the United States and are based in the Bill of Rights. There is, however, an unfortunate and long-documented history in the United States of attorneys discriminating against LGBT individuals, or those perceived to be LGBT, in jury selection. * * *

(b)   Purpose.—It is the purpose of this Act to expand as well as clarify, confirm and create greater consistency in the protections against discrimination on the basis of all covered characteristics and to provide guidance and notice to individuals, organizations, corporations, and agencies regarding their obligations under the law.

SEC. 3. PUBLIC ACCOMMODATIONS.

(a) Prohibition on Discrimination or Segregation in Public Accommodations.—Section 201 of the Civil Rights Act of 1964 (42 U.S.C. 2000a) is amended—

(1) in subsection (a), by inserting "sex, sexual orientation, gender identity," before "or national origin"; and

(2) in subsection (b)—

> (A) in paragraph (3), by striking "stadium" and all that follows and inserting "stadium or other place of or establishment that provides exhibition, entertainment, recreation, exercise, amusement, gathering, or display"; * * * and

> (C) by inserting after paragraph (3) the following:

> "(4) any establishment that provides a good, service, or program, including a store, shopping center, online retailer or service provider, salon, bank, gas station, food bank, service or care center, shelter, travel agency, or funeral parlor, or establishment that provides health care, accounting, or legal services;

> "(5) any train service, bus service, car service, taxi service, airline service, station, depot, or other place of or establishment that provides transportation service;" * * *

SEC. 4. DESEGREGATION OF PUBLIC FACILITIES.

Section 301(a) of the Civil Rights Act of 1964 (42 U.S.C. 2000b(a)) is amended by inserting "sex, sexual orientation, gender identity," before "or national origin".

SEC. 5. DESEGREGATION OF PUBLIC EDUCATION.

[Subsections (a), (b), and (c) amend Sections 401(b), 407 and 410 of the Civil Rights Act of 1964 by inserting ", sexual orientation, gender identity," before "or national origin".

SEC. 6. FEDERAL FUNDING.

Section 601 of the Civil Rights Act of 1964 (42 U.S.C. 2000d) is amended by inserting "sex, sexual orientation, gender identity," before "or national origin,".

SEC. 7. EMPLOYMENT.

* * *

(b) Unlawful Employment Practices.—[Sections 703 and 704(b)] of the Civil Rights Act of 1964 (42 U.S.C. 2000e–2) [are] amended—

(1) in the section header, by striking "sex," and inserting "sex, sexual orientation, gender identity,";

(2) * * * by striking "sex," each place it appears and inserting "sex, sexual orientation, gender identity,";

(3) * * * by striking "enterprise," and inserting "enterprise, if, in a situation in which sex is a bona fide occupational qualification, individuals are recognized as qualified in accordance with their gender identity,"; * * *

(e) Employment by Federal Government.—Section 717 of the Civil Rights Act of 1964 (42 U.S.C. 2000e–16) is amended [by inserting sex, sexual orientation and gender identity in subsections (a) and (c)] * * *

SEC. 9. MISCELLANEOUS.

Title XI of the Civil Rights Act of 1964 is amended * * *

(2) by inserting after the title heading the following:

"SEC. 1101. DEFINITIONS AND RULES.

"(a) Definitions * * *

"(1) Race; color; religion; sex; sexual orientation; gender identity; national origin.—The term 'race', 'color', 'religion', 'sex', 'sexual orientation', 'gender identity', or 'national origin', used with respect to an individual, includes—

"(A) the race, color, religion, sex, sexual orientation, gender identity, or national origin, respectively, of another person with whom the individual is associated or has been associated; and

"(B) a perception or belief, even if inaccurate, concerning the race, color, religion, sex, sexual orientation, gender identity, or national origin, respectively, of the individual.

"(2) Gender identity.—The term 'gender identity' means the gender-related identity, appearance, mannerisms, or other gender-related characteristics of an individual, regardless of the individual's designated sex at birth. * * *

"(4) Sex.—The term 'sex' includes—

"(A) a sex stereotype;

"(B) pregnancy, childbirth, or a related medical condition; and

"(C) sexual orientation or gender identity.

"(5) Sexual orientation.—The term 'sexual orientation' means homosexuality, heterosexuality, or bisexuality.

"(b) Rules.—In a covered title referred to in subsection (a)—

"(1) (with respect to sex) pregnancy, childbirth, or a related medical condition shall not receive less favorable treatment than other physical conditions; and

"(2) (with respect to gender identity) an individual shall not be denied access to a shared facility, including a restroom, a locker room, and a dressing room, that is in accordance with the individual's gender identity."; * * *

"SEC. 1107. CLAIMS.

"The Religious Freedom Restoration Act of 1993 (42 U.S.C. 2000bb et seq.) shall not provide a claim concerning, or a defense to a claim under, a covered title, or provide a basis for challenging the application or enforcement of a covered title.".

SEC. 10. HOUSING.

(a) Fair Housing Act.—The Fair Housing Act (42 U.S.C. 3601 et seq.) is amended [to insert the same protected classifications that prior sections of this bill have added to other components of the 1964 Civil Rights Act.] * * *

SEC. 11. EQUAL CREDIT OPPORTUNITY.

(a) Prohibited Discrimination.—Section 701(a)(1) of the Equal Credit Opportunity Act (15 U.S.C. 1691(a)(1)) is amended [to insert the same protected classifications that prior sections of this bill have added to other components of the 1964 Civil Rights Act.] * * *

SEC. 12. JURIES.

(a) In General.—Chapter 121 of title 28, United States Code, is amended [to insert the same protected classifications that prior sections of this bill have added to other components of the 1964 Civil Rights Act.] * * *

APPENDIX 4

THE ATTORNEY GENERAL'S LETTER SUPPORTING HEIGHTENED SCRUTINY FOR SEXUAL ORIENTATION DISCRIMINATION

February 23, 2011

Letter from the Attorney General to Congress on Litigation Involving the Defense of Marriage Act

The Honorable John A. Boehner

Speaker
U.S. House of Representatives

Washington, DC 20515

Re: Defense of Marriage Act

Dear Mr. Speaker:

After careful consideration, including review of a recommendation from me, the President of the United States has made the determination that Section 3 of the Defense of Marriage Act ("DOMA"), 1 U.S.C. § 7,[i] as applied to same-sex couples who are legally married under state law, violates the equal protection component of the Fifth Amendment. Pursuant to 28 U.S.C. § 530D, I am writing to advise you of the Executive Branch's determination and to inform you of the steps the Department will take in two pending DOMA cases to implement that determination.

While the Department has previously defended DOMA against legal challenges involving legally married same-sex couples, recent lawsuits that challenge the constitutionality of DOMA Section 3 have caused the President and the Department to conduct a new examination of the defense of this provision. In particular, in November 2010, plaintiffs filed two new lawsuits challenging the constitutionality of Section 3 of DOMA in jurisdictions without precedent on whether sexual-orientation classifications are subject to rational basis review or whether they must satisfy some form of heightened scrutiny. *Windsor v. United States*, No.

---

[i] DOMA Section 3 states: "In determining the meaning of any Act of Congress, or of any ruling, regulation, or interpretation of the various administrative bureaus and agencies of the United States, the word 'marriage' means only a legal union between one man and one woman as husband and wife, and the word 'spouse' refers only to a person of the opposite sex who is a husband or a wife."

1:10-cv-8435 (S.D.N.Y.); *Pedersen v. OPM*, No. 3:10-cv-1750 (D. Conn.). Previously, the Administration has defended Section 3 in jurisdictions where circuit courts have already held that classifications based on sexual orientation are subject to rational basis review, and it has advanced arguments to defend DOMA Section 3 under the binding standard that has applied in those cases.[ii]

These new lawsuits, by contrast, will require the Department to take an affirmative position on the level of scrutiny that should be applied to DOMA Section 3 in a circuit without binding precedent on the issue. As described more fully below, the President and I have concluded that classifications based on sexual orientation warrant heightened scrutiny and that, as applied to same-sex couples legally married under state law, Section 3 of DOMA is unconstitutional.

Standard of Review

The Supreme Court has yet to rule on the appropriate level of scrutiny for classifications based on sexual orientation. It has, however, rendered a number of decisions that set forth the criteria that should inform this and any other judgment as to whether heightened scrutiny applies: (1) whether the group in question has suffered a history of discrimination; (2) whether individuals "exhibit obvious, immutable, or distinguishing characteristics that define them as a discrete group"; (3) whether the group is a minority or is politically powerless; and (4) whether the characteristics distinguishing the group have little relation to legitimate policy objectives or to an individual's "ability to perform or contribute to society." *See Bowen v. Gilliard*, 483 U.S. 587, 602–03 (1987); *City of Cleburne v. Cleburne Living Ctr.*, 473 U.S. 432, 441–42 (1985).

Each of these factors counsels in favor of being suspicious of classifications based on sexual orientation. First and most importantly, there is, regrettably, a significant history of purposeful discrimination against gay and lesbian people, by governmental as well as private entities, based on prejudice and stereotypes that continue to have ramifications today. Indeed, until very recently, states have "demean[ed] the[ ] existence" of gays and lesbians "by making their private sexual conduct a crime." *Lawrence v. Texas*, 539 U.S. 558, 578 (2003).[iii]

[ii] *See, e.g., Dragovich v. U.S. Department of the Treasury*, 2011 WL 175502 (N.D. Cal. Jan. 18, 2011); *Gill v. Office of Personnel Management*, 699 F. Supp. 2d 374 (D. Mass. 2010); *Smelt v. County of Orange*, 374 F. Supp. 2d 861, 880 (C.D. Cal.,2005); *Wilson v. Ake*, 354 F.Supp.2d 1298, 1308 (M.D. Fla. 2005); *;In re Kandu*, 315 B.R. 123, 145 (Bkrtcy. W.D. Wash. 2004) *In re Levenson*, 587 F.3d 925, 931 (9th Cir. E.D.R. Plan Administrative Ruling 2009).

[iii] While significant, that history of discrimination is different in some respects from the discrimination that burdened African-Americans and women. *See Adarand Constructors, Inc. v. Pena*, 515 U.S. 200, 216 (1995) (classifications based on race "must be viewed in light of the historical fact that the central purpose of the Fourteenth Amendment was to eliminate racial discrimination emanating from official sources in the States," and "[t]his strong policy renders racial classifications 'constitutionally suspect.' "); *United States v. Virginia*, 518 U.S. 515, 531 (1996) (observing that " 'our Nation has had a long and unfortunate history of sex discrimination' " and pointing out the denial of the right to vote to women until 1920). In the

Second, while sexual orientation carries no visible badge, a growing scientific consensus accepts that sexual orientation is a characteristic that is immutable, *see* Richard A. Posner, Sex and Reason 101 (1992); it is undoubtedly unfair to require sexual orientation to be hidden from view to avoid discrimination, *see* Don't Ask, Don't Tell Repeal Act of 2010, Pub. L. No. 111–321, 124 Stat. 3515 (2010).

Third, the adoption of laws like those at issue in *Romer v. Evans,* 517 U.S. 620 (1996), and *Lawrence,* the longstanding ban on gays and lesbians in the military, and the absence of federal protection for employment discrimination on the basis of sexual orientation show the group to have limited political power and "ability to attract the [favorable] attention of the lawmakers." *Cleburne,* 473 U.S. at 445. And while the enactment of the Matthew Shepard Act and pending repeal of Don't Ask, Don't Tell indicate that the political process is not closed *entirely* to gay and lesbian people, that is not the standard by which the Court has judged "political powerlessness." Indeed, when the Court ruled that gender-based classifications were subject to heightened scrutiny, women already had won major political victories such as the Nineteenth Amendment (right to vote) and protection under Title VII (employment discrimination).

Finally, there is a growing acknowledgment that sexual orientation "bears no relation to ability to perform or contribute to society." *Frontiero v. Richardson*, 411 U.S. 677, 686 (1973) (plurality). Recent evolutions in legislation (including the pending repeal of Don't Ask, Don't Tell), in community practices and attitudes, in case law (including the Supreme Court's holdings in *Lawrence* and *Romer*), and in social science regarding sexual orientation all make clear that sexual orientation is not a characteristic that generally bears on legitimate policy objectives. *See, e.g.,* Statement by the President on the Don't Ask, Don't Tell Repeal Act of 2010 ("It is time to recognize that sacrifice, valor and integrity are no more defined by sexual orientation than they are by race or gender, religion or creed.")

To be sure, there is substantial circuit court authority applying rational basis review to sexual-orientation classifications. We have carefully examined each of those decisions. Many of them reason only that if consensual same-sex sodomy may be criminalized under *Bowers v. Hardwick*, then it follows that no heightened review is appropriate—a line of reasoning that does not survive the overruling of *Bowers* in *Lawrence v. Texas*, 538 U.S. 558 (2003).[iv] Others rely on claims regarding

---

case of sexual orientation, some of the discrimination has been based on the incorrect belief that sexual orientation is a behavioral characteristic that can be changed or subject to moral approbation. *Cf. Cleburne*, 473 U.S. at 441 (heightened scrutiny may be warranted for characteristics "beyond the individual's control" and that "very likely reflect outmoded notions of the relative capabilities of" the group at issue); *Boy Scouts of America v. Dale*, 530 U.S. 640 (2000) (Stevens, J., dissenting) ("Unfavorable opinions about homosexuals 'have ancient roots.' " (quoting *Bowers*, 478 U.S. at 192)).

[iv] *See Equality Foundation v. City of Cincinnati*, 54 F.3d 261, 266–67 & n. 2. (6th Cir. 1995); *Steffan v. Perry*, 41 F.3d 677, 685 (D.C. Cir. 1994); *Woodward v. United States*, 871 F.2d

"procreational responsibility" that the Department has disavowed already in litigation as unreasonable, or claims regarding the immutability of sexual orientation that we do not believe can be reconciled with more recent social science understandings.[v] And none engages in an examination of all the factors that the Supreme Court has identified as relevant to a decision about the appropriate level of scrutiny. Finally, many of the more recent decisions have relied on the fact that the Supreme Court has not recognized that gays and lesbians constitute a suspect class or the fact that the Court has applied rational basis review in its most recent decisions addressing classifications based on sexual orientation, *Lawrence* and *Romer*.[vi] But neither of those decisions reached, let alone resolved, the level of scrutiny issue because in both the Court concluded that the laws could not even survive the more deferential rational basis standard.

Application to Section 3 of DOMA

In reviewing a legislative classification under heightened scrutiny, the government must establish that the classification is "substantially related to an important government objective." *Clark v. Jeter*, 486 U.S. 456, 461 (1988). Under heightened scrutiny, "a tenable justification must describe actual state purposes, not rationalizations for actions in fact differently grounded." *United States v. Virginia*, 518 U.S. 515, 535–36 (1996). "The justification must be genuine, not hypothesized or invented post hoc in response to litigation." *Id.* at 533.

In other words, under heightened scrutiny, the United States cannot defend Section 3 by advancing hypothetical rationales, independent of the legislative record, as it has done in circuits where precedent mandates application of rational basis review. Instead, the United States can defend Section 3 only by invoking Congress' actual justifications for the law.

Moreover, the legislative record underlying DOMA's passage contains discussion and debate that undermines any defense under heightened scrutiny. The record contains numerous expressions reflecting moral disapproval of gays and lesbians and their intimate and family relationships—precisely the kind of stereotype-based thinking

---

1068, 1076 (Fed. Cir. 1989); *Ben-Shalom v. Marsh*, 881 F.2d 454, 464 (7th Cir. 1989); *Padula v. Webster*, 822 F.2d 97, 103 (D.C. Cir. 1987).

[v]   See, e.g., *Lofton v. Secretary of the Dep't of Children & Family Servs.*, 358 F.3d 804, 818 (11th Cir. 2004) (discussing child-rearing rationale); *High Tech Gays v. Defense Indust. Sec. Clearance Office*, 895 F.2d 563, 571 (9th Cir. 1990) (discussing immutability). As noted, this Administration has already disavowed in litigation the argument that DOMA serves a governmental interest in "responsible procreation and child-rearing." H.R. Rep. No. 104-664, at 13. As the Department has explained in numerous filings, since the enactment of DOMA, many leading medical, psychological, and social welfare organizations have concluded, based on numerous studies, that children raised by gay and lesbian parents are as likely to be well-adjusted as children raised by heterosexual parents.

[vi]   See *Cook v. Gates*, 528 F.3d 42, 61 (1st Cir. 2008); *Citizens for Equal Prot. v. Bruning*, 455 F.3d 859, 866 (8th Cir. 2006); *Johnson v. Johnson*, 385 F.3d 503, 532 (5th Cir. 2004); *Veney v. Wyche*, 293 F.3d 726, 732 (4th Cir. 2002); *Equality Foundation of Greater Cincinnati, Inc. v. City of Cincinnati*, 128 F.3d 289, 292–94 (6th Cir. 1997).

and animus the Equal Protection Clause is designed to guard against.[vii] *See Cleburne*, 473 U.S. at 448 ("mere negative attitudes, or fear" are not permissible bases for discriminatory treatment); *see also Romer*, 517 U.S. at 635 (rejecting rationale that law was supported by "the liberties of landlords or employers who have personal or religious objections to homosexuality"); *Palmore v. Sidoti*, 466 U.S. 429, 433 (1984) ("Private biases may be outside the reach of the law, but the law cannot, directly or indirectly, give them effect.").

Application to Second Circuit Cases

After careful consideration, including a review of my recommendation, the President has concluded that given a number of factors, including a documented history of discrimination, classifications based on sexual orientation should be subject to a heightened standard of scrutiny. The President has also concluded that Section 3 of DOMA, as applied to legally married same-sex couples, fails to meet that standard and is therefore unconstitutional. Given that conclusion, the President has instructed the Department not to defend the statute in *Windsor* and *Pedersen*, now pending in the Southern District of New York and the District of Connecticut. I concur in this determination.

Notwithstanding this determination, the President has informed me that Section 3 will continue to be enforced by the Executive Branch. To that end, the President has instructed Executive agencies to continue to comply with Section 3 of DOMA, consistent with the Executive's obligation to take care that the laws be faithfully executed, unless and until Congress repeals Section 3 or the judicial branch renders a definitive verdict against the law's constitutionality. This course of action respects the actions of the prior Congress that enacted DOMA, and it recognizes the judiciary as the final arbiter of the constitutional claims raised.

As you know, the Department has a longstanding practice of defending the constitutionality of duly-enacted statutes if reasonable arguments can be made in their defense, a practice that accords the respect appropriately due to a coequal branch of government. However, the Department in the past has declined to defend statutes despite the availability of professionally responsible arguments, in part because the Department does not consider every plausible argument to be a

---

[vii] *See, e.g.,* H.R. Rep. at 15–16 ("judgment [opposing same-sex marriage] entails both moral disapproval of homosexuality and a moral conviction that heterosexuality better comports with traditional (especially Judeo-Christian) morality"); *id.* at 16 (same-sex marriage "legitimates a public union, a legal status that most people . . . feel ought to be illegitimate" and "put[s] a stamp of approval . . . on a union that many people . . . think is immoral"); *id.* at 15 ("Civil laws that permit only heterosexual marriage reflect and honor a collective moral judgment about human sexuality"); *id.* (reasons behind heterosexual marriage—procreation and child-rearing—are "in accord with nature and hence have a moral component"); *id.* at 31 (favorably citing the holding in *Bowers* that an "anti-sodomy law served the rational purpose of expressing the presumed belief . . . that homosexual sodomy is immoral and unacceptable"); *id.* at 17 n.56 (favorably citing statement in dissenting opinion in *Romer* that "[t]his Court has no business . . . pronouncing that 'animosity' toward homosexuality is evil").

"reasonable" one. "[D]ifferent cases can raise very different issues with respect to statutes of doubtful constitutional validity," and thus there are "a variety of factors that bear on whether the Department will defend the constitutionality of a statute." Letter to Hon. Orrin G. Hatch from Assistant Attorney General Andrew Fois at 7 (Mar. 22, 1996). This is the rare case where the proper course is to forgo the defense of this statute. Moreover, the Department has declined to defend a statute "in cases in which it is manifest that the President has concluded that the statute is unconstitutional," as is the case here. Seth P. Waxman, *Defending Congress*, 79 N.C. L.Rev. 1073, 1083 (2001).

In light of the foregoing, I will instruct the Department's lawyers to immediately inform the district courts in *Windsor* and *Pedersen* of the Executive Branch's view that heightened scrutiny is the appropriate standard of review and that, consistent with that standard, Section 3 of DOMA may not be constitutionally applied to same-sex couples whose marriages are legally recognized under state law. If asked by the district courts in the Second Circuit for the position of the United States in the event those courts determine that the applicable standard is rational basis, the Department will state that, consistent with the position it has taken in prior cases, a reasonable argument for Section 3's constitutionality may be proffered under that permissive standard. Our attorneys will also notify the courts of our interest in providing Congress a full and fair opportunity to participate in the litigation in those cases. We will remain parties to the case and continue to represent the interests of the United States throughout the litigation.

Furthermore, pursuant to the President's instructions, and upon further notification to Congress, I will instruct Department attorneys to advise courts in other pending DOMA litigation of the President's and my conclusions that a heightened standard should apply, that Section 3 is unconstitutional under that standard and that the Department will cease defense of Section 3.

A motion to dismiss in the *Windsor* and *Pedersen* cases would be due on March 11, 2011. Please do not hesitate to contact us if you have any questions.

Sincerely yours,
Eric H. Holder, Jr.
Attorney General

APPENDIX 5

THE DISTRICT OF COLUMBIA HUMAN RIGHTS ACT (EXCERPTS)

Subchapter I

§ 2–1401.01 Intent of Council.

It is the intent of the Council of the District of Columbia, in enacting this chapter, to secure an end in the District of Columbia to discrimination for any reason other than that of individual merit, including, but not limited to, discrimination by reason of race, color, religion, national origin, sex, age, marital status, personal appearance, sexual orientation, gender identity or expression, familial status, family responsibilities, matriculation, political affiliation, genetic information, disability, source of income, status as a victim of an intrafamily offense, and place of residence or business.

§ 2–1401.02 Definitions.

The following words and terms when used in this chapter have the following meanings: * * *

(2) "Age" means 18 years of age or older. * * *

(4) "Commission" means the Commission on Human Rights, as established under subchapter IV of Unit A of this chapter.* * *

(5A) "Disability" means a physical or mental impairment that substantially limits one or more of the major life activities of an individual having a record of such an impairment or being regarded as having such an impairment. * * *

(7A) "Domestic partner" shall have the same meaning as provided in

(8) "Educational institution" means any public or private institution including an academy, college, elementary or secondary school, extension course, kindergarten, nursery, school system or university; and a business, nursing, professional, secretarial, technical, or vocational school; and includes an agent of an educational institution. * * *

(10) "Employer" means any person who, for compensation, employs an individual, except for the employer's parent, spouse, children or domestic servants, engaged in work in and about the employer's household; any person acting in the interest of such employer, directly or indirectly; and any professional association. * * *

(15) "Labor organization" means any organization, agency, employee representation committee, group, association, or plan in which employees participate directly or indirectly; and which exists for the purpose, in whole or in part, of dealing with employers, or any agent thereof, concerning grievances, labor disputes, wages, rates of pay, hours, or other terms, conditions, or privileges of employment; and any conference, general committee, joint or system board, or joint council, which is subordinate to a national or international organization. * * *

(17) "Marital status" means the state of being married, single, divorced, separated, or widowed and the usual conditions associated therewith, including pregnancy or parenthood. * * *

(21) "Person" means any individual, firm, partnership, mutual company, joint-stock company, corporation, association, organization, unincorporated organization, labor union, government agency, incorporated society, statutory or common-law trust, estate, executor, administrator, receiver, trustee, conservator, liquidator, trustee in bankruptcy, committee, assignee, officer, employee, principal or agent, legal or personal representative, real estate broker or salesman or any agent or representative of any of the foregoing.

(22) "Personal appearance" means the outward appearance of any person, irrespective of sex, with regard to bodily condition or characteristics, manner or style of dress, and manner or style of personal grooming, including, but not limited to, hair style and beards. It shall not relate, however, to the requirement of cleanliness, uniforms, or prescribed standards, when uniformly applied for admittance to a public accommodation, or when uniformly applied to a class of employees for a reasonable business purpose; or when such bodily conditions or characteristics, style or manner of dress or personal grooming presents a danger to the health, welfare or safety of any individual. * * *

(24) "Place of public accommodation" means all places included in the meaning of such terms as inns, taverns, road houses, hotels, motels, whether conducted for the entertainment of transient guests or for the accommodation of those seeking health, recreation or rest; restaurants or eating houses, or any place where food is sold for consumption on the premises; buffets, saloons, barrooms, or any store, park or enclosure where spirituous or malt liquors are sold; ice cream parlors, confectionaries, soda fountains and all stores where ice cream, ice and fruit preparation or their derivatives, or where beverages of any kind are retailed for consumption on the premises; wholesale and retail stores, and establishments dealing with goods or services of any kind, including, but not limited to, the credit facilities thereof; banks, savings and loan associations, establishments of mortgage bankers and brokers, all other financial institutions, and credit information bureaus; insurance companies and establishments of insurance policy brokers; dispensaries, clinics, hospitals, bath-houses, swimming pools, laundries and all other cleaning establishments; barber shops, beauty parlors, theaters, motion

picture houses, airdromes, roof gardens, music halls, race courses, skating rinks, amusement and recreation parks, trailer camps, resort camps, fairs, bowling alleys, golf courses, gymnasiums, shooting galleries, billiards and pool parlors; garages, all public conveyances operated on land or water or in the air, as well as the stations and terminals thereof; travel or tour advisory services, agencies or bureaus; public halls and public elevators of buildings and structures, occupied by 2 or more tenants, or by the owner and 1 or more tenants. Such term shall not include any institution, club, or place of accommodation which is in its nature distinctly private except, that any such institution, club or place of accommodation shall be subject to the provisions of § 2–1402.67. A place of accommodation, institution, or club shall not be considered in its nature distinctly private if the place of accommodation, institution, or club:

(A) Has 350 or more members;

(B) Serves meals on a regular basis; and

(C) Regularly receives payment for dues, fees, use of space, facilities, services, meals, or beverages directly or indirectly from or on behalf of nonmembers for the furtherance of trade or business. * * *

(28) "Sexual orientation" means male or female homosexuality, heterosexuality and bisexuality, by preference or practice.

(29) "Source of income" means the point, the cause, or the form of the origination, or transmittal of gains of property accruing to a person in a stated period of time; including, but not limited to, money and property secured from any occupation, profession or activity, from any contract, agreement or settlement, from federal payments, court-ordered payments, from payments received as gifts, bequests, annuities, life insurance policies and compensation for illness or injury, except in a case where conflict of interest may exist. * * *

(31) "Unlawful discriminatory practice" means those discriminatory practices which are so specified in subchapter II of Unit A of this chapter.

"Unlawful discriminatory practice" shall include harassment engaged in for discriminatory reasons specified in § 2.1402.11(a).

Subchapter II

§ 2–1402.01 Equal opportunities.

Every individual shall have an equal opportunity to participate fully in the economic, cultural and intellectual life of the District and to have an equal opportunity to participate in all aspects of life, including, but not limited to, in employment, in places of public accommodation, resort or amusement, in educational institutions, in public service, and in housing and commercial space accommodations.

§ 2–1402.11 Unlawful discriminatory practices in employment.

(a) General.—It shall be an unlawful discriminatory practice to do any of the following acts, wholly or partially for a discriminatory reason based upon the actual or perceived: race, color, religion, national origin, sex, age, marital status, personal appearance, sexual orientation, family responsibilities, disability, matriculation, or political affiliation of any individual:

(1) By an employer.—To fail or refuse to hire, or to discharge, any individual; or otherwise to discriminate against any individual, with respect to his compensation, terms, conditions, or privileges of employment, including promotion; or to limit, segregate, or classify his employees in any way which would deprive or tend to deprive any individual of employment opportunities, or otherwise adversely affect his status as an employee;

(2) By an employment agency.—To fail or refuse to refer for employment, or to classify or refer for employment, any individual, or otherwise to discriminate against, any individual; or

(3) By a labor organization.—To exclude or to expel from its membership, or otherwise to discriminate against, any individual; or to limit, segregate, or classify its membership; or to classify, or fail, or refuse to refer for employment any individual in any way, which would deprive such individual of employment opportunities, or would limit such employment opportunities, or otherwise adversely affect his status as an employee or as an applicant for employment; or

(4) By an employer, employment agency or labor organization—

(A) To discriminate against any individual in admission to or the employment in, any program established to provide apprenticeship or other training or retraining, including an on-the-job training program;

(B) To print or publish, or cause to be printed or published, any notice or advertisement, or use any publication form, relating to employment by such an employer, or to membership in, or any classification or referral for employment by such a labor organization, or to any classification or referral for employment by such an employment agency, unlawfully indicating any preference, limitation, specification, or distinction, based on the race, color, religion, national origin, sex, age, marital status, personal appearance, sexual orientation, family responsibilities, matriculation, disability, or political affiliation of any individual.

(b) Subterfuge.—It shall further be an unlawful discriminatory practice to do any of the above said acts for any reason that would not have been asserted but for, wholly or partially, a discriminatory reason based on the actual or perceived: race, color, religion, national origin, sex, age, marital status, personal appearance, sexual orientation, family responsibilities, matriculation, disability, or political affiliation of any individual.

(c) Accommodation for religious observance.—(1) It shall further be an unlawful discriminatory practice for an employer to refuse to make a reasonable accommodation for an employee's religious observance by permitting the employee to make up work time lost due to such observance, unless such an accommodation would cause the employer undue hardship. An accommodation would cause an employer undue hardship when it would cause the employer to incur more than de minimis costs.

(2) Such an accommodation may be made by permitting the employee to work:

(A) During the employee's scheduled lunch time or other work breaks;

(B) Before or after the employee's usual working hours;

(C) Outside of the employer's normal business hours;

(D) During the employee's paid vacation days;

(E) During another employee's working hours as part of a voluntary swap with such other employee; or

(F) In any other manner that is mutually agreeable to the employer and employee.

(3) When an employee's request for a particular form of accommodation would cause undue hardship to the employer, the employer shall reasonably accommodate the employee in a manner that does not cause undue hardship to the employer. Where other means of accommodation would cause undue hardship to the employer, an employee shall have the option of taking leave without pay if granting leave without pay would not cause undue hardship to the employer.

(4) An employee shall notify the employer of the need for an accommodation at least 10 working days prior to the day or days for which the accommodation is needed, unless the need for the accommodation cannot reasonably be foreseen.

(5) In any proceeding brought under this section, the employer shall have the burden of establishing that it would be unable reasonably to accommodate an employee's religious observance without incurring an undue hardship, provided, however, that in the case of an employer that employs more than 5 but fewer than 15 full-time employees, or where accommodation of an employee's observance of a religious practice would require the employee to take more than 3 consecutive days off from work, the employee shall have the burden of establishing that the employer could reasonably accommodate the employee's religious observance without incurring an undue hardship; and provided further, that it shall be considered an undue hardship if an employer would be required to pay any additional compensation to an employee by reason of an

accommodation for an employee's religious observance. The mere assumption that other employees with the same religious beliefs might also request accommodation shall not be considered evidence of undue hardship. An employer that employs 5 or fewer full-time employees shall be exempt from the provisions of this subsection.

§ 2–1402.31 Unlawful discriminatory practices in public accommodations.

(a) General.—It shall be an unlawful discriminatory practice to do any of the following acts, wholly or partially for a discriminatory reason based on the actual or perceived: race, color, religion, national origin, sex, age, marital status, personal appearance, sexual orientation, familial status, family responsibilities, disability, matriculation, political affiliation, source of income, or place of residence or business of any individual:

(1) To deny, directly or indirectly, any person the full and equal enjoyment of the goods, services, facilities, privileges, advantages, and accommodations of any place of public accommodations;

(2) To print, circulate, post, or mail, or otherwise cause, directly or indirectly, to be published a statement, advertisement, or sign which indicates that the full and equal enjoyment of the goods, services, facilities, privileges, advantages, and accommodations of a place of public accommodation will be unlawfully refused, withheld from or denied an individual; or that an individual's patronage of, or presence at, a place of public accommodation is objectional, unwelcome, unacceptable, or undesirable.

(b) Subterfuge.—It is further unlawful to do any of the above said acts for any reason that would not have been asserted but for, wholly or partially, a discriminatory reason based on the actual or perceived: race, color, religion, national origin, sex, age, marital status, personal appearance, sexual orientation, familial status, family responsibilities, disability, matriculation, political affiliation, source of income, or place of residence or business of any individual.

§ 2–1402.41 Unlawful discriminatory practices in educational institutions.

It is an unlawful discriminatory practice, subject to the exemptions in § 2–1401.03(b), for an educational institution:

(1) To deny, restrict, or to abridge or condition the use of, or access to, any of its facilities, services, programs, or benefits of any program or activity to any person otherwise qualified, wholly or partially, for a discriminatory reason, based upon the actual or perceived: race, color, religion, national origin, sex, age, marital status, personal appearance, sexual orientation, familial status, family responsibilities, political affiliation, source of income, or disability of any individual; or

(2)   To make or use a written or oral inquiry, or form of application for admission, that elicits or attempts to elicit information, or to make or keep a record, concerning the race, color, religion, or national origin of an applicant for admission, except as permitted by regulations of the Office.

(3)   Notwithstanding any other provision of the laws of the District of Columbia, it shall not be an unlawful discriminatory practice in the District of Columbia for any educational institution that is affiliated with a religious organization or closely associated with the tenets of a religious organization to deny, restrict, abridge, or condition—

(A)   the use of any fund, service, facility, or benefit; or

(B)   the granting of any endorsement, approval, or recognition,

to any person or persons that are organized for, or engaged in, promoting, encouraging, or condoning any homosexual act, lifestyle, orientation, or belief.

§ 2–1402.62 Aiding or abetting.

It shall be an unlawful discriminatory practice for any person to aid, abet, invite, compel, or coerce the doing of any of the acts forbidden under the provisions of this chapter or to attempt to do so.

§ 2–1402.67 Compliance with chapter prerequisite for licenses.

All permits, licenses, franchises, benefits, exemptions, or advantages issued by or on behalf of the government of the District of Columbia, shall specifically require and be conditioned upon full compliance with the provisions of this chapter; and shall further specify that the failure or refusal to comply with any provision of this chapter shall be a proper basis for revocation of such permit, license, franchise, benefit, exemption, or advantage.

§ 2–1402.68 Discriminatory effects of practices.

Any practice which has the effect or consequence of violating any of the provisions of this chapter shall be deemed to be an unlawful discriminatory practice.

§ 2–1403.16 Private cause of action.

(a)   Any person claiming to be aggrieved by an unlawful discriminatory practice shall have a cause of action in any court of competent jurisdiction for damages and such other remedies as may be appropriate, unless such person has filed a complaint hereunder; provided, that where the Office has dismissed such complaint on the grounds of administrative convenience, or where the complainant has withdrawn a complaint, such person shall maintain all rights to bring suit as if no complaint had been filed. No person who maintains, in a court of competent jurisdiction, any action based upon an act which would be an unlawful discriminatory practice under this chapter may file the same complaint with the Office. A private cause of action pursuant to this chapter shall be filed in a court of competent jurisdiction within one year of the unlawful discriminatory act, or the discovery thereof, except that the limitation shall be within 2 years of the unlawful discriminatory act, or the discovery thereof, for complaints of unlawful discrimination in real estate transactions brought pursuant to this chapter or the FHA. The timely filing of a complaint with the Office, or under the administrative procedures established by the Mayor pursuant to § 2–1403.03, shall the running of the statute of limitations while the complaint is pending.

(b) The court may grant any relief it deems appropriate, including the relief provided in §§ 2–1403.07 and 2–1403.13(a).

* * *

APPENDIX 6

TEXAS SEX CRIMES STATUTES

VERNON'S TEXAS STATUTES AND CODES ANNOTATED PENAL CODE
TITLE 5. OFFENSES AGAINST THE PERSON
CHAPTER 21. SEXUAL OFFENSES * * *

Section 21.06. Homosexual Conduct

(a) A person commits an offense if he engages in deviate sexual intercourse with another individual of the same sex.

(b) An offense under this section is a Class C misdemeanor.

Section 21.07. Public Lewdness

(a) A person commits an offense if he knowingly engages in any of the following acts in a public place or, if not in a public place, he is reckless about whether another is present who will be offended or alarmed by his:

(1) act of sexual intercourse;

(2) act of deviate sexual intercourse;

(3) act of sexual contact; or

(4) act involving contact between the person's mouth or genitals and the anus or genitals of an animal or fowl.

(b) An offense under this section is a Class A misdemeanor.

Section 21.08. Indecent Exposure

(a) A person commits an offense if he exposes his anus or any part of his genitals with intent to arouse or gratify the sexual desire of any person, and he is reckless about whether another is present who will be offended or alarmed by his act.

(b) An offense under this section is a Class B misdemeanor.

Section 21.11. Indecency With a Child

(a) A person commits an offense if, with a child younger than 17 years and not the person's spouse, whether the child is of the same or opposite sex, the person:

(1) engages in sexual contact with the child or causes the child to engage in sexual contact; or

(2) with intent to arouse or gratify the sexual desire of any person:

(A) exposes the person's anus or any part of the person's genitals, knowing the child is present; or

(B) causes the child to expose the child's anus or any part of the child's genitals.

(b) It is an affirmative defense to prosecution under this section that the actor:

(1) was not more than three years older than the victim and of the opposite sex;

(2) did not use duress, force, or a threat against the victim at the time of the offense; and

(3) at the time of the offense:

(A) was not required under Chapter 62, Code of Criminal Procedure, to register for life as a sex offender; or

(B) was not a person who under Chapter 62 had a reportable conviction or adjudication for an offense under this section.

(c) In this section, "sexual contact" means the following acts, if committed with the intent to arouse or gratify the sexual desire of any person:

(1) any touching by a person, including touching through clothing, of the anus, breast, or any part of the genitals of a child; or

(2) any touching of any part of the body of a child, including touching through clothing, with the anus, breast, or any part of the genitals of a person.

(d) An offense under Subsection (a)(1) is a felony of the second degree and an offense under Subsection (a)(2) is a felony of the third degree.

CHAPTER 22. ASSAULTIVE OFFENSES

Section 22.01.   Assault

(a) A person commits an offense if the person:

(1) intentionally, knowingly, or recklessly causes bodily injury to another, including the person's spouse;

(2) intentionally or knowingly threatens another with imminent bodily injury, including the person's spouse; or

(3) intentionally or knowingly causes physical contact with another when the person knows or should reasonably believe that the other will regard the contact as offensive or provocative.

(b) An offense under Subsection (a)(1) is a Class A misdemeanor * * *.

(c) An offense under Subsection (a)(2) or (3) is a Class C misdemeanor * * *.

[We have omitted provisions setting forth special rules to govern assaults on public servants, household members, the elderly/disabled, security officers, and sports competitors.]

Section 22.011. Sexual Assault

(a) A person commits an offense if the person:

(1) intentionally or knowingly:

(A) causes the penetration of the anus or sexual organ of another person by any means, without that person's consent;

(B) causes the penetration of the mouth of another person by the sexual organ of the actor, without that person's consent; or

(C) causes the sexual organ of another person, without that person's consent, to contact or penetrate the mouth, anus, or sexual organ of another person, including the actor; or

(2) intentionally or knowingly:

(A) causes the penetration of the anus or sexual organ of a child by any means;

(B) causes the penetration of the mouth of a child by the sexual organ of the actor;

(C) causes the sexual organ of a child to contact or penetrate the mouth, anus, or sexual organ of another person, including the actor;

(D) causes the anus of a child to contact the mouth, anus, or sexual organ of another person, including the actor; or

(E) causes the mouth of a child to contact the anus or sexual organ of another person, including the actor.

(b) A sexual assault under Subsection (a)(1) is without the consent of the other person if:

(1) the actor compels the other person to submit or participate by the use of physical force or violence;

(2) the actor compels the other person to submit or participate by threatening to use force or violence against the other person, and the other person believes that the actor has the present ability to execute the threat;

(3) the other person has not consented and the actor knows the other person is unconscious or physically unable to resist;

(4) the actor knows that as a result of mental disease or defect the other person is at the time of the sexual assault incapable either of appraising the nature of the act or of resisting it;

(5) the other person has not consented and the actor knows the other person is unaware that the sexual assault is occurring;

(6) the actor has intentionally impaired the other person's power to appraise or control the other person's conduct by administering any substance without the other person's knowledge;

(7)   the actor compels the other person to submit or participate by threatening to use force or violence against any person, and the other person believes that the actor has the ability to execute the threat; or

(8)   the actor is a public servant who coerces the other person to submit or participate;

(9)   the actor is a mental health services provider or a health care services provider who causes the other person, who is a patient or former patient of the actor, to submit or participate by exploiting the other person's emotional dependency on the actor;

(10) the actor is a clergyman who causes the other person to submit or participate by exploiting the other person's emotional dependency on the clergyman in the clergyman's professional character as spiritual adviser; or

(11) the actor is an employee of a facility where the other person is a resident, unless the employee and resident are formally or informally married to each other under Chapter 2, Family Code.

(c)   In this section:

(1)   "Child" means a person younger than 17 years of age who is not the spouse of the actor.

(2)   "Spouse" means a person who is legally married to another.
* * *

(d)   It is a defense to prosecution under Subsection (a)(2) that the conduct consisted of medical care for the child and did not include any contact between the anus or sexual organ of the child and the mouth, anus, or sexual organ of the actor or a third party.

(e)   It is an affirmative defense to prosecution under Subsection (a)(2) that:

(1)   the actor was not more than three years older than the victim and at the time of the offense:

(A)   was not required under Chapter 62, Code of Criminal Procedure, as added by Chapter 668, Acts of the 75th Legislature, Regular Session, 1997, to register for life as a sex offender; or

(B)   was not a person who under Chapter 62 had a reportable conviction or adjudication for an offense under this section; and

(2)   the victim was a child of 14 years of age or older.

(f)   An offense under this section is a felony of the second degree.
* * *

Section 22.06.   Consent as Defense to Assaultive Conduct

The victim's effective consent or the actor's reasonable belief that the victim consented to the actor's conduct is a defense to prosecution under

Section 22.01 (Assault), 22.02 (Aggravated Assault), or 22.05 (Deadly Conduct) if:

(1) the conduct did not threaten or inflict serious bodily injury; or

(2) the victim knew the conduct was a risk of:

(A) his occupation;

(B) recognized medical treatment; or

(C) a scientific experiment conducted by recognized methods. * * *

TITLE 9. OFFENSES AGAINST PUBLIC ORDER AND DECENCY

CHAPTER 42. DISORDERLY CONDUCT AND RELATED OFFENSES

Section 42.01. Disorderly Conduct

(a) A person commits an offense if he intentionally or knowingly:

(1) uses abusive, indecent, profane, or vulgar language in a public place, and the language by its very utterance tends to incite an immediate breach of the peace;

(2) makes an offensive gesture or display in a public place, and the gesture or display tends to incite an immediate breach of the peace;

(3) creates, by chemical means, a noxious and unreasonable odor in a public place;

(4) abuses or threatens a person in a public place in an obviously offensive manner;

(5) makes unreasonable noise in a public place other than a sport shooting range, as defined by Section 250.001, Local Government Code, or in or near a private residence that he has no right to occupy;

(6) fights with another in a public place;

(7) discharges a firearm in a public place other than a public road or a sport shooting range, as defined by Section 250.001, Local Government Code;

(8) displays a firearm or other deadly weapon in a public place in a manner calculated to alarm;

(9) discharges a firearm on or across a public road; or

(10) exposes his anus or genitals in a public place and is reckless about whether another may be present who will be offended or alarmed by his act; or

(11) for a lewd or unlawful purpose:

(A) enters on the property of another and looks into a dwelling on the property through any window or other opening in the dwelling;

(B) while on the premises of a hotel or comparable establishment, looks into a guest room not the person's own through a window or other opening in the room; or

(C) while on the premises of a public place, looks into an area such as a restroom or shower stall or changing or dressing room that is designed to provide privacy to a person using the area.

(b) It is a defense to prosecution under Subsection (a)(4) that the actor had significant provocation for his abusive or threatening conduct.

(c) For purposes of this section:

(1) an act is deemed to occur in a public place or near a private residence if it produces its offensive or proscribed consequences in the public place or near a private residence; * * *

(d) An offense under this section is a Class C misdemeanor unless committed under Subsection (a)(7) or (a)(8), in which event it is a Class B misdemeanor. * * *

CHAPTER 43. PUBLIC INDECENCY
SUBCHAPTER A. PROSTITUTION

Section 43.01.   Definitions

In this subchapter:

(1) "Deviate sexual intercourse" means any contact between the genitals of one person and the mouth or anus of another person.

(2) "Prostitution" means the offense defined in Section 43.02.

(3) "Sexual contact" means any touching of the anus, breast, or any part of the genitals of another person with intent to arouse or gratify the sexual desire of any person.

(4) "Sexual conduct" includes deviate sexual intercourse, sexual contact, and sexual intercourse.

(5) "Sexual intercourse" means any penetration of the female sex organ by the male sex organ.

Section 43.02.   Prostitution

(a) A person commits an offense if he knowingly:

(1) offers to engage, agrees to engage, or engages in sexual conduct for a fee; or

(2) solicits another in a public place to engage with him in sexual conduct for hire.

(b) An offense is established under Subsection (a)(1) whether the actor is to receive or pay a fee. An offense is established under Subsection (a)(2) whether the actor solicits a person to hire him or offers to hire the person solicited.

(c) An offense under this section is a Class B misdemeanor, unless the actor has previously been convicted one or two times of an offense under this section, in which event it is a Class A misdemeanor. If the actor has previously been convicted three or more times of an offense under this section, the offense is a state jail felony.

Section 43.03. *Promotion of Prostitution*

(a) A person commits an offense if, acting other than as a prostitute receiving compensation for personally rendered prostitution services, he or she knowingly:

(1) receives money or other property pursuant to an agreement to participate in the proceeds of prostitution; or

(2) solicits another to engage in sexual conduct with another person for compensation.

(b) An offense under this section is a Class A misdemeanor.

Section 43.04. Aggravated Promotion of Prostitution

(a) A person commits an offense if he knowingly owns, invests in, finances, controls, supervises, or manages a prostitution enterprise that uses two or more prostitutes.

(b) An offense under this section is a felony of the third degree.

Section 43.05. Compelling Prostitution

(a) A person commits an offense if he knowingly:

(1) causes another by force, threat, or fraud to commit prostitution; or

(2) causes by any means a person younger than 17 years to commit prostitution.

(b) An offense under this section is a felony of the second degree.

* * *

SUBCHAPTER B. OBSCENITY

Section 43.21. *Definitions*

(a) In this subchapter:

(1) "Obscene" means material or a performance that:

(A) the average person, applying contemporary community standards, would find that taken as a whole appeals to the prurient interest in sex;

(B) depicts or describes:

(i) patently offensive representations or descriptions of ultimate sexual acts, normal or perverted, actual or simulated, including sexual intercourse, sodomy, and sexual bestiality; or

(ii) patently offensive representations or descriptions of masturbation, excretory functions, sadism, masochism, lewd exhibition of the genitals, the male or female genitals in a state of sexual stimulation or arousal, covered male genitals in a discernibly turgid state or a device designed and marketed as useful primarily for stimulation of the human genital organs; and

(C) taken as a whole, lacks serious literary, artistic, political, and scientific value.

(2) "Material" means anything tangible that is capable of being used or adapted to arouse interest, whether through the medium of reading, observation, sound, or in any other manner, but does not include an actual three dimensional obscene device.

(3) "Performance" means a play, motion picture, dance, or other exhibition performed before an audience.

(4) "Patently offensive" means so offensive on its face as to affront current community standards of decency.

(5) "Promote" means to manufacture, issue, sell, give, provide, lend, mail, deliver, transfer, transmit, publish, distribute, circulate, disseminate, present, exhibit, or advertise, or to offer or agree to do the same.

(6) "Wholesale promote" means to manufacture, issue, sell, provide, mail, deliver, transfer, transmit, publish, distribute, circulate, disseminate, or to offer or agree to do the same for purpose of resale.

(7) "Obscene device" means a device including a dildo or artificial vagina, designed or marketed as useful primarily for the stimulation of human genital organs.

(b) If any of the depictions or descriptions of sexual conduct described in this section are declared by a court of competent jurisdiction to be unlawfully included herein, this declaration shall not invalidate this section as to other patently offensive sexual conduct included herein.

Section 43.22.   Obscene Display or Distribution

(a) A person commits an offense if he intentionally or knowingly displays or distributes an obscene photograph, drawing, or similar visual representation or other obscene material and is reckless about whether a person is present who will be offended or alarmed by the display or distribution.

(b) An offense under this section is a Class C misdemeanor.

Section 43.23.   Obscenity

(a) A person commits an offense if, knowing its content and character, he wholesale promotes or possesses with intent to wholesale promote any obscene material or obscene device.

(b) Except as provided by Subsection (h), an offense under Subsection (a) is a state jail felony.

(c) A person commits an offense if, knowing its content and character, he:

(1) promotes or possesses with intent to promote any obscene material or obscene device; or

(2) produces, presents, or directs an obscene performance or participates in a portion thereof that is obscene or that contributes to its obscenity.

(d) Except as provided under Subsection (h), an offense under Subsection (c) is a Class A misdemeanor.

(e) A person who promotes or wholesale promotes obscene material or an obscene device or possesses the same with intent to promote or wholesale promote it in the course of his business is presumed to do so with knowledge of its content and character.

(f) A person who possesses six or more obscene devices or identical or similar obscene articles is presumed to possess them with intent to promote the same.

(g) It is an affirmative defense to prosecution under this section that the person who possesses or promotes material or a device proscribed by this section does so for a bona fide medical, psychiatric, judicial, legislative, or law enforcement purpose.

(h) The punishment for an offense under Subsection (a) is increased to the punishment for a felony of the third degree and the punishment for an offense under Subsection (c) is increased to the punishment for a state jail felony if it is shown on the trial of the offense that obscene material that is the subject of the offense visually depicts activities described by Section 43.21(a)(1)(B) engaged in by:

(1) a child younger than 18 years of age at the time the image of the child was made;

(2) an image that to a reasonable person would be virtually indistinguishable from the image of a child younger than 18 years of age; or

(3) an image created, adapted, or modified to be the image of an identifiable child.

(i) In this section, "identifiable child" means a person, recognizable as an actual person by the person's face, likeness, or other distinguishing characteristic, such as a unique birthmark or other recognizable feature:

(1) who was younger than 18 years of age at the time the visual depiction was created, adapted or modified; or

(2) whose image as a person younger than 18 years of age was used in creating, adapting, or modifying the visual depiction.

(j) An attorney representing the State who seeks an increase in punishment under Subsection (h)(3) is not required to prove the actual identity of an identifiable child.

Section 43.24.   Sale, Distribution, or Display of Harmful Material to Minor

(a) For purposes of this section:

(1) "Minor" means an individual younger than 18 years.

(2) "Harmful material" means material whose dominant theme taken as a whole:

(A) appeals to the prurient interest of a minor, in sex, nudity, or excretion;

(B) is patently offensive to prevailing standards in the adult community as a whole with respect to what is suitable for minors; and

(C) is utterly without redeeming social value for minors.

(b) A person commits an offense if, knowing that the material is harmful:

(1) and knowing the person is a minor, he sells, distributes, exhibits, or possesses for sale, distribution, or exhibition to a minor harmful material;

(2) he displays harmful material and is reckless about whether a minor is present who will be offended or alarmed by the display; or

(3) he hires, employs, or uses a minor to do or accomplish or assist in doing or accomplishing any of the acts prohibited in Subsection (b)(1) or (b)(2).

(c) It is a defense to prosecution under this section that:

(1) the sale, distribution, or exhibition was by a person having scientific, educational, governmental, or other similar justification; or

(2) the sale, distribution, or exhibition was to a minor who was accompanied by a consenting parent, guardian, or spouse.

(d) An offense under this section is a Class A misdemeanor unless it is committed under Subsection (b)(3) in which event it is a felony of the third degree.

Section 43.25.   Sexual Performance by a Child

(a) In this section:

(1) "Sexual performance" means any performance or part thereof that includes sexual conduct by a child younger than 18 years of age.

(2) "Sexual conduct" means sexual contact, actual or simulated sexual intercourse, deviate sexual intercourse, sexual bestiality, masturbation, sado-masochistic abuse, or lewd exhibition of the genitals, the anus, or any portion of the female breast below the top of the areola.

(3) "Performance" means any play, motion picture, photograph, dance, or other visual representation that can be exhibited before an audience of one or more persons.

(4) "Produce" with respect to a sexual performance includes any conduct that directly contributes to the creation or manufacture of the sexual performance.

(5) "Promote" means to procure, manufacture, issue, sell, give, provide, lend, mail, deliver, transfer, transmit, publish, distribute, circulate, disseminate, present, exhibit, or advertise or to offer or agree to do any of the above.

(6) "Simulated" means the explicit depiction of sexual conduct that creates the appearance of actual sexual conduct and during which a person engaging in the conduct exhibits any uncovered portion of the breasts, genitals, or buttocks.

(7) "Deviate sexual intercourse" and "sexual contact" have the meanings assigned by Section 43.01.

(b) A person commits an offense if, knowing the character and content thereof, he employs, authorizes, or induces a child younger than 18 years of age to engage in sexual conduct or a sexual performance. A parent or legal guardian or custodian of a child younger than 18 years of age commits an offense if he consents to the participation by the child in a sexual performance.

(c) An offense under Subsection (b) is a felony of the second degree.

(d) A person commits an offense if, knowing the character and content of the material, he produces, directs, or promotes a performance that includes sexual conduct by a child younger than 18 years of age.

(e) An offense under Subsection (d) is a felony of the third degree.

(f) It is an affirmative defense to a prosecution under this section that:

(1) the defendant was the spouse of the child at the time of the offense;

(2) the conduct was for a bona fide educational, medical, psychological, psychiatric, judicial, law enforcement, or legislative purpose; or

(3) the defendant is not more than two years older than the child.

(g) When it becomes necessary for the purposes of this section or Section 43.26 to determine whether a child who participated in sexual conduct was younger than 18 years of age, the court or jury may make this determination by any of the following methods:

(1) personal inspection of the child;

(2) inspection of the photograph or motion picture that shows the child engaging in the sexual performance;

(3) oral testimony by a witness to the sexual performance as to the age of the child based on the child's appearance at the time;

(4) expert medical testimony based on the appearance of the child engaging in the sexual performance; or

(5) any other method authorized by law or by the rules of evidence at common law.

Section 43.251. *Employment Harmful to Children*

(a) In this section:

(1) "Child" means a person younger than 18 years of age.

(2) "Massage" has the meaning assigned to the term "massage therapy" by Section 455.001, Occupations Code.

(3) "Massage establishment" has the meaning assigned by Section 455.001, Occupations Code.

(4) "Nude" means a child who is:

(A) entirely unclothed; or

(B) clothed in a manner that leaves uncovered or visible through less than fully opaque clothing any portion of the breasts below the top of the areola of the breasts, if the child is female, or any portion of the genitals or buttocks.

(5) "Sexually oriented commercial activity" means a massage establishment, nude studio, modeling studio, love parlor, or other similar commercial enterprise the primary business of which is the offering of a service that is intended to provide sexual stimulation or sexual gratification to the customer.

(6) "Topless" means a female child clothed in a manner that leaves uncovered or visible through less than fully opaque clothing any portion of her breasts below the top of the areola.

(b) A person commits an offense if the person employs, authorizes, or induces a child to work:

(1) in a sexually oriented commercial activity; or

(2) in any place of business permitting, requesting, or requiring a child to work nude or topless.

(c) An offense under this section is a Class A misdemeanor.

Section 43.26. *Possession or Promotion of Child Pornography*

(a) A person commits an offense if:

(1) the person knowingly or intentionally possesses visual material that visually depicts a child younger than 18 years of age at the time the image of the child was made who is engaging in sexual conduct; and

(2) the person knows that the material depicts the child as described by Subdivision (1).

(b)   In this section:

(1) "Promote" has the meaning assigned by Section 43.25.

(2) "Sexual conduct" has the meaning assigned by Section 43.25.

(3) "Visual material" means:

(A) any film, photograph, videotape, negative, or slide or any photographic reproduction that contains or incorporates in any manner any film, photograph, videotape, negative, or slide; or

(B) any disk, diskette, or other physical medium that allows an image to be displayed on a computer or other video screen and any image transmitted to a computer or other video screen by telephone line, cable, satellite transmission, or other method.

(c)   The affirmative defenses provided by Section 43.25(f) also apply to a prosecution under this section.

(d)   An offense under this section is a felony of the third degree.

(e)   A person commits an offense if:

(1) the person knowingly or intentionally promotes or possesses with intent to promote material described by Subsection (a)(1); and

(2) the person knows that the material depicts the child as described by Subsection (a)(1).

(f)   A person who possesses visual material that contains six or more identical visual depictions of a child as described by Subsection (a)(1) is presumed to possess the film images with the intent to promote the material.

(g)   An offense under Subsection (e) is a felony of the second degree.
* * *

THE BALLOT PAMPHLET SUPPORTING AMENDMENT 2 TO THE COLORADO CONSTITUTION (1992)

Equal Rights—Not Special Rights!

If you do one thing to prepare yourself for this November 3rd election — please. . . arm yourself with the facts about Amendment 2. Militant homosexuals have flooded Colorado's media with claims that they're only after "equal protection". Truth is, they already share that with all Americans. What they really want will shock and alarm you. Please — read this tabloid carefully, cover to cover. We've packed it with astonishing, fully-documented reports on the actual goals of homosexual extremists. Information they — and their friends in the press — desperately want to keep from you. So please read on. Because an educated decision on Amendment 2 may be the most important contribution you can give to the future of civil rights in Colorado . . . and the future of our children.

TURN INSIDE FOR THE SHOCKING TRUTH!

Gay propaganda in the schools .... p. 2

Target: children .... p. 2

Lies from the laboratory .... p. 4

Attacks on Colorado .... p. 5

Home rule and Amendment 2 .... p. 3

Homosexual affluence .... p. 1

Free speech — an endangered right! .... p. 7

Attack on the Family .... p. 4

Businesses lose their rights .... p. 6

Churches attacked nationwide .... p. 5

Homosexual behavior and you .... p. 4

The truth about "discrimination" .... p. 3

Hate Really Isn't A Family Value! .... p. 3

Ethnic "Civil Rights" Destroyed! .... p. 1

Colorado civil rights leaders say "YES!" on Amendment 2.

Question: *How does special class status for gays threaten the hard-won gains of disadvantaged minorities?*

Mr. Ignacio Rodriguez
Former Chairman of the
Colorado Civil Rights Commission
"For many years, there were hard-fought battles to establish minority status and protection under civil rights law for certain identifiable groups of people. . . If we include a group of people who are generally identified as a deviant group sexually, it would erode, and seriously damage the legitimate civil rights protections that have been gained by ethnic minorities."

Mr. Tom Duran
Well-known state civil rights professional
"I don't see gay ghettos. I don't see the gay homeless. I don't see the gays being disadvantaged politically or economically. I don't think that they are in the same class as the traditional minority groups, Hispanic or Indian women.

John Franklin
Former chairman and 8-year commissioner,
Colorado Civil Rights Commission
"Making sexual preference a protected class does a disservice to all those people presently being discriminated against or mistreated, by diluting the significance of civil rights protection. I hate to see resources taken away from those who are truly in need of protection."

QUESTION: *"Does denying protected class status to homosexuals endanger in any way the legitimate rights of Colorado's minorities?"*

Mr. Rodriguez
"I think the reverse is true. I think that if gays and lesbians are afforded protected status, it will erode civil rights the way it exists today.

Mr. Duran
". . . This movement would negatively impact people already receiving protection."

Mr. Franklin
"I have been an attorney for almost 18 years and have been involved heavily in civil rights issues for the last 12 years. It's an insult to me to say that because I am in favor of this amendment that I will be in favor of further erosion of civil rights laws. The laws of this country are very clear as to protections that have been placed upon the economically disavantaged citizens of this country. We are not asking people to take a step backwards." ∎

Are homosexuals a "disadvantaged" minority? You decide!

Records show that even now, not only are gays not economically disadvantaged, they're actually one of the most affluent groups in America!

✔ On July 18, 1991, the Wall Street Journal reported the results of a nation-wide marketing survey about gay income levels. The survey reported that gays' average income was more than $30,000 over that of the average Americans'. Gays were over three times more likely to be college graduates. Three times as likely to hold professional or managerial positions. Four times as likely to be overseas travelers. These are people with tons of discretionary income!

please turn to page 2

	AVERAGE HOUSEHOLD INCOME	% COLLEGE GRADS	% PROFESSIONAL/ MANAGERIAL POSITIONS	% W/ OVERSEAS VACATIONS
GAYS	$55,430	60%	49%	66%
NAT'L AVERAGE	$32,286	18%	16%	14%
DISADVANTAGED AFR. AMERICANS	$12,166	less than 5%	less than 1%	less than 1%

VOTE YES! ON AMENDMENT 2.

EQUAL RIGHTS—NOT SPECIAL RIGHTS!

Sound like an oppressed minority to you? Judge for yourself — Take a look at the hardships Black Americans have had to face. Then see if homosexuals compare. Special rights for homosexuals just isn't fair — especially to disadvantaged minorities in Colorado. Please vote YES! on Amendment 2.

HISTORICALLY ACCEPTED EVIDENCES OF DISCRIMINATION	BLACK AMERICANS	HOMOSEXUALS
Ever denied the right to vote?	Yes	No
Ever faced legal segregation?	Yes	No
Ever denied access by law to public drinking fountains, restrooms	Yes	No
Ever denied access by law to businesses, restaurants, barber shops, etc.?	Yes	No
Evidence of systematic discrimination in housing and jobs in Colorado today?	Yes	No
Verifiable economic hardship as a result of discrimination? (see page 3)	Yes	No

TARGET: CHILDREN

Lately, America's been hearing alot about the subject of childhood sexual abuse. This terrible epidemic has scarred countless young lives and destroyed thousands of families. But what militant homosexuals don't want you to know is the large role they play in this epidemic. In fact, pedophilia (the sexual molestation of children) is actually an accepted part of the homosexual community!

✔ David Thorstad, founding member of the gay organization called the North American Man-Boy Love Association, a group whose motto is "Sex by eight, or it's too late" and a former president of the Gay Activist Alliance of New York, writes:

"The issue of man-boy love has intersected the gay movement since the late nineteenth century." Thorstad complains that pedophilia is being swept under the rug by the gay-rights movement, which "... seeks to sanitize the image of homosexuality to facilitate its entrance into the social mainstream."

"Man-Boy Love and the American Gay Movement" from The Journal of Homosexuality, 20, 1990, pp. 251-252).

✔ Two homosexual researchers writing in *The Gay Report* reported that 73% of homosexuals surveyed had at some time had sex with boys sixteen to nineteen years of age or younger!

✔ The British Journal of Sexual Medicine (April 1987) published a study in which homosexuals are statistically about 18 times more likely to engage in sex with minors than heterosexuals.

The North American Man-Boy Love Association, an accepted member of the homosexual community, proudly waves its motto at gay-pride parades: "Sex by Eight, or It's Too Late". And they're dedicated to repealing age-of-consent laws!

✔ *Psychological Reports* (1986, #58, pp. 327-337) published a report revealing that homosexuals, who represent perhaps 2% of the population, perpetrate more than one-third of all reported child molestations!

✔ The 1972 Gay Rights Platform, which has not changed or been rescinded in twenty years, calls for (1) "Repeal of all state laws prohibiting private sexual acts involving consenting persons" (not consenting adults) and (2) "Repeal of all laws governing the age of sexual consent."

Don't let gay militant double-talk hide their true intentions. Sexual molestation of children is a large part of many homosexuals' lifestyle — part of the very lifestyle "gay-rights" activists want government to give special class, ethnic status! Say no to sexual perversion with children — vote YES! on Amendment 2! ■

Homosexual indoctrination in the schools?
IT'S HAPPENING IN COLORADO!

Here's a frightening example of the "gay-rights" agenda right here in our state: a 1992 Denver Public Schools Health and Science Education teachers' guide entitled "Gay and Lesbian Youth Tools for Educators", presented to teachers by gay instructors during a taxpayer-funded continuing education course. This guide contains a questionnaire designed to be answered by heterosexual junior high and high school students. It asks, among others, these questions:

3. *Is it possible your heterosexuality is just a phase you may outgrow?*

5. *Is it possible that all you need is a good gay lover?*

7. *If you have never slept with a person of the same sex, how do you know that you would not prefer to do so?*

14. *How can you hope to become a whole person if you limit yourself to an exclusive heterosexual object choice and remain unwilling to explore and develop your normal, natural, healthy homosexual potential?*

And the brochure goes on — aggressively promoting acceptance of homosexuality, bisexuality, lesbianism, and condom use, complete with graphic, "how-to" descriptions. It also suggests that teachers distribute to children pamphlets containing phone numbers of possible adult gay mentors, who may encourage children to experiment with gay behavior. Imagine your tax money being spent to try and convince children — maybe even your own — that they should consider homosexuality! In the public schools! This is the true, sinister face of "gay-rights". Please — vote "YES" on Amendment 2, or you may be denied the chance to protest outrages like this one! ■

VOTE YES! ON AMENDMENT 2!

2

EQUAL RIGHTS — NOT SPECIAL RIGHTS!

Does Amendment 2 "write discrmination" into the Constitution?

No way! All Amendment 2 does is say "loud and clear" that special, protected civil rights are reserved for legitimate ethnic minorities who are truly disadvantaged. It says that not everybody who wants special treatment from society is entitled to get it. That's not discrimination, it's fairness. Amendment 2 upholds America's common-sense civil rights laws and Supreme Court decisions, which say that people who want protected class status have to show they need it, in three fair, logical ways:

1. A group wanting true minority rights must show that it's discriminated against to the point that its members can't earn average income, get an adequate education, or enjoy a fulfilling cultural life.

2. The group must be clearly identifiable by unchangeable physical characteristics like skin color, gender, handicap, etc. (not behavior).

3. The group must clearly show that it is politically powerless.

As you can clearly see, gays flunk all three requirements! And no group that fails to meet these requirements is entitled to make discrimination claims. These requirements are the heart and soul of civil rights protections. African/Americans, Hispanics, women, etc. all met them. For gays to get minority status, we'd have to throw these requirements out, and that would mean rewriting the whole book on civil rights!

Please, don't turn the tables on this country. Homosexuals deserve human rights — not special rights. Vote YES! on Amendment 2. ■

Hate is not a family value — we agree 100 percent!

Opponents of Amendment 2 have been plastering the state with posters saying that "Hate Is Not A Family Value". But Colorado for Family Values, sponsor of Amendment 2, agree with that statement 100 percent! That's exactly why we've filled this tabloid with "just the facts"; because facts don't hate, they just are.

We agree that Hate Is Not A Family Value so much, nearly a year ago we announced and implemented the statewide "No Room for Hatred" campaign, to let every Coloradan know loud and clear that there's no room on either side of this debate for hatred of any kind.

Unfortunately, our opponents didn't get the message. Although we invited them to join us in sending a strong, unified no-hatred statement to the people of Colorado, after one letter suggesting an interest, they continuously refused to respond to our repeated attempts to follow through. Obviously, coming out against hatred wasn't on their agenda back then:

✔ Soon after that, crude, obviously forged "hate" literature supposedly written by us, started being circulated by our opponents.

✔ Militant gays started shouting obscenities at CFV meetings.

✔ Men in drag started showing up outside our meetings, soliciting money in CFV's name.

✔ Sabotage and threatening posters started becoming daily occurences at our headquarters.

✔ One EPOC leader repeated her frequently-expressed hope that we all "rot in hell" and threatened, "we're gonna get you [expletive deleted]'s."

Colorado for Family Values, on the other hand, made "No Room for Hatred" a cornerstone of our successful and completely peaceful, petition drive:

✔ We've declined to attend rallies where the chance of unpleasantness existed.

✔ We encouraged gay-rights opponents to stay away from so-called "pride" parades to ensure that the peace was kept.

✔ We published a Resolution In Support of Principled Debate, which EPOC received and ignored.

✔ We've stuck to the facts. We've delivered on our promise to make our case logically and honestly to the people of Colorado. And we continue today. We've filled this tabloid with facts about the militant gay agenda not to make you hate them, but to warn you about the danger their goals represent to you and your children's rights. As proof that the gay lifestyle has nothing in common with the kinds of traits and behaviors America has protected in its civil rights laws. And as proof that it isn't the kind of behavior society needs to reward with special class status. So please — if you stand with us against hatred toward any fellow Coloradans — vote YES! November 3rd on Amendment 2. ■

The truth about "home rule" and a "Yes!" vote on Amendment 2.

Home rule" has always been an important, legitimate part of how Coloradans govern themselves. But lately, militant gays have been crying that Amendment 2 would violate this important concept. They want you to believe that voting "Yes" on Amendment 2 means no one will ever be able to vote on a local issue again.

That's ridiculous. Here's a little truth about Amendment 2 and the home rule issue:

✔ Everyone knows some issues are "home rule" in nature, and some aren't. It's common sense: some are local in scope, others are statewide or national. If the people had no right to vote their conscience on a statewide or national level, then why would we have a State Legislature or a U.S. Congress?

✔ The hateful "Jim Crow" laws that once oppressed African/Americans in the South were "home rule" laws — enacted locally, by racist city and county officials, to keep people of color "in their place". Thankfully, the Civil Rights Act of 1964 said "No" to "Jim Crow" laws and declared loud and clear that civil rights aren't a local, "home rule" issue. They're for a whole state, even a whole nation, to decide on. Should local authorities regain complete control over civil rights?

✔ Militant homosexuals don't care a hoot for "home rule". They've been lobbying the U.S. Congress, the Courts and the Colorado Legislature on their agenda for years. Do those sound like local, "home rule" institutions to you? Of course not. When they lobbied the U.S. Congress for a national "gay-rights" law, do you think gay extremists planned to give every town in America a choice on whether to go along? Of course not. "Home rule" is a red herring, meant to confuse the issue. They've ignored "home rule" themselves for years.

✔ Gay extremists actually want you to believe there's something undemocratic, unrepresentative about YOU having a vote on this issue! What's more democratic than gathering petition signatures, then giving Coloradans a voice at the ballot box?

Amendment 2 does give everyone the right to vote their conscience about "gay-rights". That's what we'll all do on November 3rd. And if a "gay-rights" supporter tries to tell you "home rule" should prevail, just ask them this question: "Should a town in Colorado have the right to vote 'Jim Crow' laws back into existence again if they want?" We think you'll agree that that's a terrible idea. ■

In Laguna Beach, California, a city with one of the country's largest gay communities and strongest "gay-rights" ordinances, a three-year old boy entered a public park restroom. What he saw there traumatized him severely. Three grown gay men were engaging in group sex, right there in the bathroom. When he ran out to his mother, crying and upset, she attempted to file a complaint with the Laguna Beach Police Department. Their reply: with a "gay-rights" ordinance in place, there was nothing they could do. You can stop this from happening in Colorado with your "YES" vote on Amendment 2.

VOTE YES! ON AMENDMENT 2.

EQUAL RIGHTS—NOT SPECIAL RIGHTS!

Homosexual behavior — should government protect *this*?

Militant gays want government to give their lifestyle special class status — but we think it's important to know just what kind of lifestyle they want your tax dollars to endorse. You may already know that the sexual practices of gays differ drastically from those of most of Colorado's population. But how much those practices differ — and the dangerous perversions they involve — may shock you!

✔ Let's start with number of sexual partners. 1982 U.S. Centers for Disease Control figures put the lifetime total for typical homosexuals interviewed at 500. AIDS sufferers individually studied: 1,100. In a Kinsey Institute survey, 43% of white male homosexuals estimated 500 or more, 75% 100 or more, 28% over 1,000. 79% said over half of their partners were strangers. A survey by two homosexual researchers reports 38% of lesbians having between 11 and over 300 lifetime partners.

✔ "Monogamy" is virtually unknown in the gay lifestyle. One university-published study shows that 3% of homosexuals have had fewer than 10 lifetime partners. Only 2% could be classified as either monogamous or semi-monogamous (although "monogamy" in gay terms is hardly permanent — lasting anywhere between 9 to 60 months).

✔ Gays' have been unwilling (or unable) to curb their voracious, unsafe sex practices in the face of AIDS. A 1985 study of 655 San Francisco gay men in the *American Journal of Public Health* reported that "knowledge of health guidelines was quite high, but this knowledge had no relation to sexual behavior." 59% had been unprotected, passive recipients of anal intercourse in the month before the survey. The Washington Post (June 1990) and Time Magazine (July 1990) both report that despite the threat of AIDS, gays have not restrained themselves. The Journal reported last October a study in which 45% of gay men remained sexually active after learning that they were HIV+, and incredibly, 52% of them *did not inform their partners!*

✔ Overall, surveys show that 90% of gay men engage in anal intercourse — the most high-risk sexual behavior in society today. (No wonder 83% of Colorado AIDS cases have occurred in gay males — it's a tragedy, but it's true.) About 80% of gay men surveyed have engaged in oral sex upon the anus of partners. Well over a third of gays in 1977 admitted to "fisting". In the largest study of gay men ever conducted, 29% admitted participating in "golden showers".

✔ Gays live shorter lives. In a survey of 6,211 obituaries from gay journals compared to obituaries from regular newspapers, gays who did not die of AIDS had a median age of death of 42 years old! (And 39 if AIDS was the cause.) The lesbians surveyed had a median age of death of 45.

Is this the kind of lifestyle we want to reward with special protection, and protected ethnic status? Gay activists want you to think they're "just like you" — but these statistics point out how false that is. So please remember — gays deserve, and have, human rights. But there's no way this lifestyle deserves special rights. Please vote YES! on Amendment 2. ■

OBJECTIVE: DESTROY THE FAMILY

If you value the role of family in the fabric of Colorado, then you have reason to fear the true agenda of "gay-rights" militants. To this angry, alienated minority, the family is the symbol of everything they attack. Consider these facts:

✔ The 1972 Gay Rights Platform called for "... Repeal of all laws governing the age of consent... of all legislative provisions that restrict the sex or number of persons entering into a marriage unit; and the extension of legal benefits to all persons who cohabit regardless of sex or numbers."

✔ Manifestoes in prominent gay-authored books (The Gay Militants, The Gay Crusaders and Out of the Closets) demand: "That all organized religions be condemned for helping in the genocide of homosexuals... That the family as we now know it be abolished... That children be placed in communal areas away from their parents, with boys and girls reared the same and cared for by adults who are under the direction of lesbian women."

✔ Gay activist Michael Swift writes "[The family unit] is a spawning ground of lies, betrayal, mediocrity, hypocrisy and violence — and will be abolished."

So if you value the family, show the militant "anti-family" activists that you stand for its protection. Your "YES" vote on Amendment 2 will keep the anti-family onslaught from getting official government approval in Colorado. ■

"We shall sodomize your sons, emblems of your feeble masculinity, of your shallow dreams and vulgar lies. We shall seduce them in your schools, in your dormitories, in your gymnasiums, in your locker rooms, in your sports arenas, in your seminaries, in your youth groups...

... The family unit — which only dampens imaginations and curbs free will, must be eliminated.

... All churches who condemn us will be closed. Our only gods are handsome young men."

— Michael Swift, "Gay Revolutionary" writing in Gay Community News
Don't let this kind of hatred prevail in Colorado. Tell this angry minority they deserve equal rights — but not special rights. Vote YES! on Amendment 2 this November 3rd.

Don't believe lies from the laboratory

Homosexuality isn't something you "are", it's something you "do".

Are gays born, or made? It's a question on a lot of people's minds. And militant gays, in order to strengthen their demand for special class status, are desperate to manufacture evidence that homosexuality is a genetic condition. Their strategy: flood the media with reports of so-called "discoveries", knowing full-well the average person isn't trained in telling true scientific evidence from false.

So first, here are some conclusions from impartial, neutral scientists:

✔ "Homosexuality is not innate... there is no inevitable genetically inborn propensity toward the choice of a partner of either the same or opposite sex" (Socarides, C.W., "Homosexuality: Basic Concepts and Psychodynamics," *International Journal of Psychiatry*, Vol. 10 [March 1972, p. 118].

✔ "The genetic theory of homosexuality has been generally discarded today... no serious scientist today suggests that a simple cause-effect relationship applies" (Masters, Johnson and Kolodny, *Human Sexuality*, Boston: Little, Brown & Co., 1984, p. 319).

✔ "We're born man, woman and sexual beings. We learn our sexual preferences and orientations" (Masters and Johnson, interview, UPI, April 23, 1979)

✔ "There is little evidence of the existence of such a thing as innate perversity..." (Alfred Kinsey, as reported by W.B. Pomeroy, Dr. Kinsey and the Institute for Sex Research, New York: Harper & Row, 1972, p. 273).

So what about the so-called "gay brains" study? Or the "gay twins" study—both of which got so much widespread, unquestioning media coverage? The "gay brain" study, which claimed to find a difference in brain chemistry between the corpses of gays and heterosexuals...

✔ ... ignored the fact that the brain cells in question have never been proven to actually work together in any way whatsoever!

✔ ... as a gay writer himself pointed out, "It turns out that LeVay doesn't know anything about the sexual orientation of his control group, the 16 corpses 'presumed heterosexual.' A sloppy control like this is... enough by itself to invalidate the study." (Michael Botkin, Salk and Pepper, Bay Area Reporter, September 5, 1991, pp. 21-24)

✔ ...most important of all: do these supposed differences point to a *cause* or a *result* of homosexuality? "Scientist" LeVay, an avowed homosexual who has now become a gay activist himself, answered, on national television: "I can't say. But I'll bet the house that it's the cause." How's that for scientific fairness?

✔ ...the "gay twins" study, which claims to show that identical twins are more likely to both become homosexual, ignores the fact that identical twins share their environments even more closely than other twins, and actually recruited its subjects from gay magazines! More damaging still, when the study's subjects actually spoke for themselves, there was no difference between fraternal twins and adopted brothers!

We could go on, but you get the point: these "scientific studies" are nothing more than political propaganda, laboratory-style — "research" twisted to fit a pre-arranged conclusion. Don't let fake science fool you — being gay isn't like being born Black or Hispanic, or a Woman, or even being physically disabled. That's yet another reason why they don't deserve protected class status! Please — to safeguard civil rights for the truly disadvantaged, vote YES! on Amendment 2 ■

VOTE YES! ON AMENDMENT 2

EQUAL RIGHTS—NOT SPECIAL RIGHTS!

"Gay-rights" destroys basic freedoms!

Ann Lockwood should have known better. Assuming that freedom of association was still allowed in Madison, Wisconsin, Ann put a notice in the classifieds for a second roommate.

But Ann didn't count on Madison's "gay-rights" ordinance. When an open lesbian answered Ann's ad and was politely declined by Ann and her heterosexual roommate, the lesbian filed a complaint. And "gay rights" suddenly showed their true colors.

Ann and her roommate were:

✔ summoned before a "fact-finding" board

✔ interrogated for hours

✔ assessed fines totalling $1500

✔ assigned to "sensitivity" classes, taught by lesbians, designed to realign their "politically incorrect" views on homosexuality.

Ann pleaded that the fines would bankrupt her. "That's not our problem," she was told.

✔ Finally, both were ordered to report periodically to the city for monitoring of their lifestyle — for the next three years.

But this isn't just some exceptional, "one-in-a-million" tale of justice betrayed:

✔ In Minnesota, the Catholic Archdiocese was assessed $35,000 in fines and damages for refusing to open Church facilities to a homosexual club.

✔ In Hawaii, churches have been warned that regardless of their beliefs, all staff positions save the pastorate must be made available to homosexuals.

✔ Again in Minnesota, a Catholic priest was sued, in a case that dragged on for years, simply for refusing to hire a homosexual to teach in a Catholic school!

✔ A 1992 "gay-rights" statute in New Jersey prohibits employers from discriminating on the basis of sexual orientation in hiring and firing. The same law could force churches to unite homosexuals in marriage.

✔ In Minneapolis, Big Brothers was prosecuted for merely telling one mother that a prospective Big Brother was homosexual. After years of legal harassment, Big Brothers has adopted a national policy of "accepting gay men as prospective Big Brothers to fatherless youths."

✔ Constitutional attorneys estimate the cost of fighting charges filed under "gay-rights" legislation to a Supreme Court decision as nearly $250,000.

It goes on and on. Cut through the gushy slogans about "tolerance" and "freedom" militant gays cloak themselves in, and you discover actions saying exactly the opposite. Actions revealing a concerted attack on the right of any American to hold, speak or live out non–"politically correct" beliefs.

Amendment 2 will safeguard your right to disagree with the militant gay mindset. Please — vote "YES" on 2 November 3rd. ■

Churches attacked nationwide!

In the related article "Gay-rights destroys basic freedoms" we tell you how churches in "gay-rights" cities and states are being forced to violate their beliefs in their hiring practices, or face legal retaliation. But in many places, churches are actually being physically attacked by militant gays, services invaded, clergy assaulted. Here's just a few instances of this unreported outrage:

✔ New York's St. Patrick's Cathedral was attacked in 1989 by extremists from ACT-UP!, the gay shock-troop organization. The chanting and shouting homosexuals paraded down the aisles of the Cathedral, incensed at Cardinal John O'Connor's stand against homosexuality. They pelted the congregation with condoms, and defiled the communion elements, completely bringing the Mass to a halt before having to be forcibly removed from the service.

✔ In Costa Mesa, California, militant gays angry at Calvary Chapel's ministry outreach to the Orange County gay community invaded that church during Sunday morning services. The church that launched the "Jesus People" movement of the sixties had its aisles filled with gays shouting and fondling themselves in full view of families in the congregation. Attempts to remove them nearly resulted in serious violence.

✔ On Saturday, November 16, 1991, a group of AIDS demonstrators dressed in suits and ties infiltrated a Family Concerns Conference at the First Baptist Church of Atlanta, then peppered the diners with hundreds of condoms, all the while chanting, "safer sex saves lives."

If "gay-rights" succeed and homosexuals gain protected class status, this kind of abuse will continue, even increase. Protect your right to worship and believe as you choose — vote "YES" on Amendment 2. ■

Gay-rights abuses here in Colorado!

Already, here in our state, various "gay-rights" ordinances and policies are violating the rights of our citizens. Please read for the untold story:

✔ Last year's statewide proposed "Ethnic Harassment Bill" would have made it a hate crime for any Colorado citizen to speak negatively about homosexuality. A pastor or member of the clergy could haved face felony charges for saying what he/she believes!

Thankfully, this outrage was defeated in committee.

✔ This year, the Student Association of Metro State College ordered all campus religious groups to admit homosexuals or face expulsion. Menorah Ministries, a small Christian organization on campus, became the target of an intimidation campaign merely because, in accordance with its beliefs, it declined to admit homosexual members.

✔ Already in Boulder, apartment dwellers and dorm-residing students alike are being told they are legally prohibited from asking if a prospective roommate is gay. Furthermore, if they've been lied to and want to change roommates, the financial burden is on them!

Imagine being the parent of a CU/Boulder student: your child is uncomfortable with the thought of living with a homosexual, but is prohibited from learning about the lifestyle of his/her roommate. Three months into the term, the roommate "comes out" and begins living an active gay lifestyle, in close quarters with your child. What can you or your child do about it? According to the "law" in Boulder, nothing — unless you want to undergo the severe inconvenience and thousands of dollars in expenses involved in changing roommates mid-semester, and launching into the difficult search for a new one.

Whether you're a student or an apartment resident, the result is the same. You can ask a prospective roommate any question you want, but if you ask "Are you gay?", you face charges from the city. If you decide to change roommates, you face thousands of dollars in expenses.

Don't let these abuses of civil rights come to your town — vote "YES" on Amendment 2 and protect your freedom of conscience! ■

DAY-CARE CENTER

RESUME

I'M SORRY SIR. YOUR CREDENTIALS ARE PERFECT--BUT WE HAVEN'T FILLED OUR QUOTA OF HOMOSEXUALS!

VOTE YES! ON AMENDMENT 2!

EQUAL RIGHTS—NOT SPECIAL RIGHTS!

Under "gay-rights", free-speech becomes an endangered species!

✔ You probably remember the orchestrated attack that gay militants and their supporters hurled on Coach McCartney this year for speaking his mind. Simply for stating his beliefs, in response to reporters' constant questions, he was subjected to a wave of media and pro gay-rights abuse. It was as if the First Amendment has suddenly been suspended in the state of Colorado! But don't think that was an isolated occurence:

✔ Last year, an ethnic harassment bill (which was thankfully defeated in committee) would have made it a felony hate crime to speak negatively about homosexuality! Even a member of the clergy could have faced criminal penalties for preaching against the homosexual lifestyle. Yes, it can happen in America.

✔ Several public figures who have made known their support for Amendment 2 have received specific, serious death threats. Others have been threatened in their careers. Some have been forced to move from offices or homes. Others have had to hire extra security — all because they spoke in favor of Amendment 2.

Don't let this attack on the free-speech rights of all Coloradans succeed! Stand up for freedom of speech by voting "YES!" on Amendment 2. ■

Amendment 2 doesn't hinge on religion or morality. And it *certainly* isn't about hatred.

It's about fairness.

What's fair about an affluent group gaining minority privileges simply for what they do in bed? What's fair about making someone's opinion illegal just because it isn't "politically correct"? What's fair about people who enjoy all the rights and privileges of American citizenship asking for special status — just because they're unhappy with the rights they already have?

Nothing, we say. If you agree with us, we ask you to please Vote "Yes" on Amendment 2 in November. ■

Businesses: one more burden to bear

If you own or manage a business, you already know how many rules and regulations make your job so difficult already. But "gay-rights" adds another substantial layer of liability and responsibility in favor of a group that already enjoys substantial income and professional privileges! Consider just a few of the burdens you'll face under "gay-rights":

✔ How do you know if a job applicant is "gay"? Does saying so make it a fact? What would keep a would-be employee from claiming to be homosexual in order to gain an advantage over other applicants?

✔ Under state or municipal ordinances, an employer charged with discrimination pays not only for his own defense, but, through taxation, for its own prosecution. Even if you win, you can still face exorbitant attorney's fees.

✔ Will homosexual employees — who are now starting to think of themselves as a brand-new "gender", demand their own separate bathrooms? How will you afford to build them if the demand is made — backed up by law?

✔ Will you be hampered in potential disciplinary actions when a homosexual employee harasses or propositions others around him/her? If they claim the activity is a part of their "lifestyle", will you feel confident in taking action to protect your employees' morale?

Remember: you don't have to be guilty to be sued. In anticipation of brisk activity, publishers are already advertising "Sexual Orientation" litigation guides to lawyers. Already, homosexuals are bringing million-dollar verdicts against employers, even when their behavior has violated the conditions of their employment.

Keep this added burden from overwhelming Colorado's business community. Vote "YES!" on Amendment 2 this November. ■

AMENDMENT 2 will *not* keep gays from legal recourse, or equal protection!

In fine fear-mongering form, EPOC is claiming that after Amendment 2's passage, homosexuals will be ". . . legislatively barred from asking for or receiving protection from even basic discrimination." Sound scary? It's designed to. It's also complete nonsense.

✔ Amendment 2 will only prohibit discrimination claims *based on* sexual orientation. Homosexuals as individuals will still have legal recourse: recourse based on factors like the fact that they were good employees, minding their own business, etc. They won't — as American citizens — be "barred" from the courts.

To argue that membership in a particular group shouldn't form the basis of a discrimination claim — that's different from barring that group's members from ever making a claim on any basis. EPOC members exploit this distinction — apparently hoping it will prove beyond the understanding of the "Average Coloradan".

Example: young-Caucasian-males-without-disabilities aren't a protected class. Claims of discrimination are not accepted on the basis of being a Caucasian-male-without-disabilities. But does that mean that someone belonging to this group has no legal recourse? Of course not. Just ask a Caucasian-male, Alan Bakke. If he hadn't had legal recourse, there wouldn't be a famous Supreme Court reverse-discrimination case named after him. For Bakke to get that recourse, however, we didn't have to make Caucasian-males a specially protected class, or declare them, as a group, immune from discrimination. That would have destroyed the whole meaning of civil-rights. And so will protected status for homosexuals.

✔ Once more for the record: anti-discrimination laws were written to protect specially protected classes — groups who've proven they need help. Caucasian-males-under-forty aren't protected by them. Millionaires-born-that-way can't file claims based on being millionaires-born-that-way. Neither should an affluent, well-educated and politically powerful group, based only on the gender of their sex partners. Anti-discrimination laws were made to protect people based on what they clearly "are", not how they behave, what kind of sexual "inclinations" they proclaim, and not, God forbid, what kind of person they sleep with. Your "YES" vote will not deprive homosexuals of a single basic right — or access to the courts. ■

Making sense out of "discrimination"

Historically, anti-discrimination laws were written for specially protected classes — and nobody else. Caucasian males under forty aren't protected by those laws. Millionaires born that way aren't protected by those laws. These laws were made to protect disadvantaged, politically powerless people not because of how they behave or what kind of kinky desires they have. If you're not politically powerless, if there's no sign that you're actually oppressed, you don't have the privilege of claiming discrimination just because people don't like your behavior or desires.

Militant gays want to create a whole new category of anti-discrimination protections. Now they want rich, "horny", political power brokers to enjoy special protection from discrimination.

They're counting on Americans to not know what "discrimination" really means. Show the gay extremists that you know — *vote YES on Amendment 2.*

VOTE YES ON AMENDMENT 2.

EQUAL RIGHTS—NOT SPECIAL RIGHTS!

Homosexuals' drive to grab "protected class" status threatens more Coloradans than any other political issue today. " gay-rights" threaten. . .

✔ Parents, who fear the influence of homosexuals on their children

✔ School administrators and teachers, both public and private, against whom enormous pressure is now being exerted, both to hire gay teachers and to teach children that homosexuality is "normal and healthy"

✔ Employees, forced by their companies to "value" homosexuals, in violation of their convictions, or lose their jobs

✔ Health care providers and workers, vulnerable to disease because of "privacy" given AIDS as a disease with "civil rights"

✔ Banks and insurance companies, compelled to endorse and protect homosexual behavior financially

✔ Disadvantaged minority groups, who stand to lose status and benefits by associating their ethnicity with homosexuality

✔ Landlords, forced to rent to homosexuals no matter what their personal beliefs may be on sexuality

✔ Day-care owners, compelled to hire homosexuals for care-giving of small children

✔ Churches, pastors, congregations, and parachurch ministries, threatened with having to hire homosexuals and with severe consequences if they dare to speak out against homosexuality

✔ Government workers, compelled to promote homosexuals and their agenda on all levels of government.

Homosexuals deserve equal rights — not special rights. Please: on November 3rd, **vote "YES" on Amendment 2.** ∎

Published and Distributed by
**COLORADO FOR
FAMILY VALUES**
Colorado Springs, CO

*with the help of local
concerned citizens*

Will Perkins, Chairman, Executive Board • Kevin Tebedo, Director
© 1992 Colorado for Family Values

Why "Gay-rights" threaten your Church.

If you weren't sure whether so-called "gay rights" actually threaten you and this fellowship, please consider the following:

✔ A church in Minnesota was assessed over $35,000 in fines and damages — all because it declined to rent out its basement for a homosexual activist group to hold its meetings in.

✔ In Hawaii, the Attorney General handed down an advisory opinion stating that from now on in the state, only the post of pastor could be withheld from a homosexual without breaking the law. All other posts — from children's Sunday School teacher to Youth Director — could not be legally withheld from someone on the ground of sexual "orientation".

✔ Two women in Madison, Wisconsin were interrogated by police, fined $1,500, ordered to write a letter of apology, report to a local homosexual group for "sensitivity" classes, and submit to monitoring of their lifestyle by the city for three years — all because they did not invite to become their roommate a lesbian who had answered their newspaper ad.

✔ Here in Colorado last summer, wording proposed for the Ethnic Anti-Harassment Bill would have made it a felony "hate crime" to voice any views critical of gays. Your spiritual leader could have been subject to arrest for even reading negative towards homosexuality from the pulpit!

Please don't write these off as random events, or shake your head and think,

"These kinds of things don't really happen in America." These outrages are not random occurrences; they're part of a stated campaign to take away our rights to believe, express and live out our Christian views on sexuality. And these things really are happening. They're already scheduled for Colorado, unless we do something about it.

Amendment 2 *will* do something about it. It won't remove, limit or infringe a single fundamental freedom gays enjoy with the rest of us; it simply upholds what the Supreme Court and federal courts have upheld for years: that sexual behavior just isn't a proper reason to give a group special, extraordinary legal status.

Remember this shocking incident, from our article on page 3 about militant gay attacks on churches:

✔ Recently, the Calvary Chapel of Costa Mesa, California had its morning worship service interrupted by an invasion of chanting, condom-throwing militant gays — all because the church had an evangelistic outreach program to Southern California's gay community.

Any religious outreach to gays could soon become illegal if we fail to act. And our right to personal conviction on the issue may be considered a crime.

Won't you help? Your "YES" vote for Amendment 2 will put a crucial safeguard in our constitution — a safeguard, among others things, for religious freedoms — yours and mine. ∎

"WHAT HOMOSEXUALS DO AMONG THEMSELVES IN PRIVATE, THAT'S UP TO THEM. I JUST DON'T THINK IT OUGHT TO GET 'EM SPECIAL RIGHTS, THAT'S ALL."

—That's what one crusty Coloradan told us during out petition drive. We couldn't have put it better outselves. Coloradans understand that protected class status shouldn't be given to just anyone who asks for it. That wouldn't be fair.

Amendment 2 says basically one thing: that homosexuals, like all Americans, deserve *equal rights*. But nothing about their circumstances, their lifestyle or their political power rates them as a group in need of *special* rights. Don't let "political correctness" and Hollywood values carry the day. **Vote "YES" on Amendment 2** and cast a vote for the true meaning of civil rights.

VOTE YES! ON AMENDMENT 2.

APPENDIX 8

PROPOSITION 8 BALLOT MATERIALS

Proposition 8 Official Voter Information Guide

PROPOSITION **8**	ELIMINATES RIGHT OF SAME-SEX COUPLES TO MARRY. INITIATIVE CONSTITUTIONAL AMENDMENT.

OFFICIAL TITLE AND SUMMARY	PREPARED BY THE ATTORNEY GENERAL

ELIMINATES RIGHT OF SAME-SEX COUPLES TO MARRY. INITIATIVE CONSTITUTIONAL AMENDMENT.

- Changes the California Constitution to eliminate the right of same-sex couples to marry in California.
- Provides that only marriage between a man and a woman is valid or recognized in California.

Summary of Legislative Analyst's Estimate of Net State and Local Government Fiscal Impact:

- Over the next few years, potential revenue loss, mainly from sales taxes, totaling in the several tens of millions of dollars, to state and local governments.
- In the long run, likely little fiscal impact on state and local governments.

PROP 8   ELIMINATES RIGHT OF SAME-SEX COUPLES TO MARRY.
INITIATIVE CONSTITUTIONAL AMENDMENT.

ANALYSIS BY THE LEGISLATIVE ANALYST

BACKGROUND

In March 2000, California voters passed Proposition 22 to specify in state law that only marriage between a man and a woman is valid or recognized in California. In May 2008, the California Supreme Court ruled that the statute enacted by Proposition 22 and other statutes that limit marriage to a relationship between a man and a woman violated the equal protection clause of the California Constitution. It also held that individuals of the same sex have the right to marry under the California Constitution. As a result of the ruling, marriage between individuals of the same sex is currently valid or recognized in the state.

PROPOSAL

This measure amends the California Constitution to specify that only marriage between a man and a woman is valid or recognized in California. As a result, notwithstanding the California Supreme Court ruling of May 2008, marriage would be limited to individuals of the opposite sex, and individuals of the same sex would not have the right to marry in California.

FISCAL EFFECTS

Because marriage between individuals of the same sex is currently valid in California, there would likely be an increase in spending on weddings by same-sex couples in California over the next few years. This would result in increased revenue, primarily sales tax revenue, to state and local governments.

By specifying that marriage between individuals of the same sex is not valid or recognized, this measure could result in revenue loss, mainly from sales taxes, to state and local governments. Over the next few years, this loss could potentially total in the several tens of millions of dollars. Over the long run, this measure would likely have little fiscal impact on state and local governments.

PROP
8
ELIMINATES RIGHT OF SAME-SEX COUPLES TO MARRY.
INITIATIVE CONSTITUTIONAL AMENDMENT.

★ ARGUMENT IN FAVOR OF PROPOSITION 8 ★

Proposition 8 is simple and straightforward. It contains the same 14 words that were previously approved in 2000 by over 61% of California voters: "Only marriage between a man and a woman is valid or recognized in California."

Because four activist judges in San Francisco wrongly overturned the people's vote, we need to pass this measure as a constitutional amendment to RESTORE THE DEFINITION OF MARRIAGE as a man and a woman.

Proposition 8 is about preserving marriage; *it's not an attack on the gay lifestyle.* Proposition 8 doesn't take away any rights or benefits of gay or lesbian domestic partnerships. Under California law, "domestic partners shall have the same rights, protections, and benefits" as married spouses. (Family Code § 297.5.) There are NO exceptions. Proposition 8 WILL NOT change this.

YES on Proposition 8 does three simple things:

It restores the definition of marriage to what the vast majority of California voters already approved and human history has understood marriage to be.

It overturns the outrageous decision of four activist Supreme Court judges who ignored the will of the people.

It protects our children from being taught in public schools that "same-sex marriage" is the same as traditional marriage.

Proposition 8 protects marriage as an essential institution of society. While death, divorce, or other circumstances may prevent the ideal, the best situation for a child is to be raised by a married mother and father.

The narrow decision of the California Supreme Court isn't just about "live and let live." State law may require teachers to instruct children as young as kindergarteners about marriage. (Education Code § 51890.) If the gay marriage ruling is not overturned, TEACHERS COULD BE REQUIRED to teach young children there is *no difference* between gay marriage and traditional marriage.

We should not accept a court decision that may result in public schools teaching our kids that gay marriage is okay. That is an issue for parents to discuss with their children according to their own values and beliefs. *It shouldn't be forced on us against our will.*

Some will try to tell you that Proposition 8 takes away legal rights of gay domestic partnerships. That is false. Proposition 8 DOES NOT take away any of those rights and does not interfere with gays living the lifestyle they choose.

However, while gays have the right to their private lives, *they do not have the right to redefine marriage* for everyone else.

CALIFORNIANS HAVE NEVER VOTED FOR SAME-SEX MARRIAGE. If gay activists want to legalize gay marriage, they should put it on the ballot. Instead, they have gone behind the backs of voters and convinced four activist judges in San Francisco to redefine marriage for the rest of society. That is the wrong approach.

Voting YES on Proposition 8 RESTORES the definition of marriage that was approved by over 61% of voters. Voting YES overturns the decision of four activist judges. Voting YES *protects our children.*

Please vote YES on Proposition 8 to RESTORE the meaning of marriage.

RON PRENTICE, President
California Family Council
ROSEMARIE "ROSIE" AVILA, Governing Board Member
Santa Ana Unified School District
BISHOP GEORGE McKINNEY, Director
Coalition of African American Pastors

★ REBUTTAL TO ARGUMENT IN FAVOR OF PROPOSITION 8 ★

Don't be tricked by scare tactics.

• PROP. 8 DOESN'T HAVE ANYTHING TO DO WITH SCHOOLS

There's NOT ONE WORD IN 8 ABOUT EDUCATION. In fact, local school districts and parents—not the state—develop health education programs for their schools.

NO CHILD CAN BE FORCED, AGAINST THE WILL OF THEIR PARENTS, TO BE TAUGHT ANYTHING about health and family issues. CALIFORNIA LAW PROHIBITS IT.

And NOTHING IN STATE LAW REQUIRES THE MENTION OF MARRIAGE IN KINDERGARTEN!

It's a smokescreen.

• DOMESTIC PARTNERSHIPS and MARRIAGE AREN'T THE SAME.

CALIFORNIA STATUTES CLEARLY IDENTIFY NINE REAL DIFFERENCES BETWEEN MARRIAGE AND DOMESTIC PARTNERSHIPS. Only marriage provides the security that spouses provide one another—it's why people get married in the first place!

Think about it. Married couples depend on spouses when they're sick, hurt, or aging. They accompany them into ambulances or hospital rooms, and help make life-and-death decisions, with no questions asked. ONLY MARRIAGE ENDS

THE CONFUSION AND GUARANTEES THE CERTAINTY COUPLES CAN COUNT ON IN TIMES OF GREATEST NEED.

Regardless of how you feel about this issue, we should guarantee the same fundamental freedoms to every Californian.

• PROP. 8 TAKES AWAY THE RIGHTS OF GAY AND LESBIAN COUPLES AND TREATS THEM DIFFERENTLY UNDER THE LAW.

Equality under the law is one of the basic foundations of our society.

Prop. 8 means one class of citizens can enjoy the dignity and responsibility of marriage, and another cannot. That's unfair.

PROTECT FUNDAMENTAL FREEDOMS. SAY NO TO PROP. 8.

www.NoonProp8.com

ELLYNE BELL, School Board Member
Sacramento City Schools
RACHAEL SALCIDO, Associate Professor of Law
McGeorge School of Law
DELAINE EASTIN
Former California State Superintendent of Public Instruction

★ ARGUMENT AGAINST PROPOSITION 8 ★

OUR CALIFORNIA CONSTITUTION—the law of our land—SHOULD GUARANTEE THE SAME FREEDOMS AND RIGHTS TO EVERYONE—NO ONE group SHOULD be singled out to BE TREATED DIFFERENTLY.

In fact, our nation was founded on the principle that all people should be treated equally. EQUAL PROTECTION UNDER THE LAW IS THE FOUNDATION OF AMERICAN SOCIETY.

That's what this election is about—equality, freedom, and fairness, for all.

Marriage is the institution that conveys dignity and respect to the lifetime commitment of any couple. PROPOSITION 8 WOULD DENY LESBIAN AND GAY COUPLES that same DIGNITY AND RESPECT.

That's why Proposition 8 is wrong for California.

Regardless of how you feel about this issue, the freedom to marry is fundamental to our society, just like the freedoms of religion and speech.

PROPOSITION 8 MANDATES ONE SET OF RULES FOR GAY AND LESBIAN COUPLES AND ANOTHER SET FOR EVERYONE ELSE. That's just not fair. OUR LAWS SHOULD TREAT EVERYONE EQUALLY.

In fact, the government has no business telling people who can and cannot get married. Just like government has no business telling us what to read, watch on TV, or do in our private lives. We don't need Prop. 8; WE DON'T NEED MORE GOVERNMENT IN OUR LIVES.

REGARDLESS OF HOW ANYONE FEELS ABOUT MARRIAGE FOR GAY AND LESBIAN COUPLES, PEOPLE SHOULD NOT BE SINGLED OUT FOR UNFAIR TREATMENT UNDER THE LAWS OF OUR STATE. Those committed and loving couples who want to accept the responsibility that comes with marriage should be treated like everyone else.

DOMESTIC PARTNERSHIPS ARE NOT MARRIAGE. When you're married and your spouse is sick or hurt, there is no confusion: you get into the ambulance or hospital room with no questions asked. IN EVERYDAY LIFE, AND ESPECIALLY IN EMERGENCY SITUATIONS, DOMESTIC PARTNERSHIPS ARE SIMPLY NOT ENOUGH. Only marriage provides the certainty and the security that people know they can count on in their times of greatest need.

EQUALITY UNDER THE LAW IS A FUNDAMENTAL CONSTITUTIONAL GUARANTEE. Prop. 8 separates one group of Californians from another and excludes them from enjoying the same rights as other loving couples.

Forty-six years ago I married my college sweetheart, Julia. We raised three children—two boys and one girl. The boys are married, with children of their own. Our daughter, Liz, a lesbian, can now also be married—if she so chooses.

All we have ever wanted for our daughter is that she be treated with the same dignity and respect as her brothers—with the same freedoms and responsibilities as every other Californian.

My wife and I never treated our children differently, we never loved them any differently, and now the law doesn't treat them differently, either.

Each of our children now has the same rights as the others, to choose the person to love, commit to, and to marry.

Don't take away the equality, freedom, and fairness that everyone in California—straight, gay, or lesbian—deserves.

Please join us in voting NO on Prop. 8.

SAMUEL THORON, Former President
Parents, Families and Friends of Lesbians and Gays
JULIA MILLER THORON, Parent

★ REBUTTAL TO ARGUMENT AGAINST PROPOSITION 8 ★

Proposition 8 is about traditional marriage; it is not an attack on gay relationships. Under California law gay and lesbian domestic partnerships are treated equally; they already have the same rights as married couples. Proposition 8 does not change that.

What Proposition 8 does is restore the meaning of marriage to what human history has understood it to be and over 61% of California voters approved just a few years ago.

Your YES vote ensures that the will of the people is respected. It overturns the flawed legal reasoning of four judges in San Francisco who wrongly disregarded the people's vote, and ensures that gay marriage can be legalized only through a vote of the people.

Your YES vote ensures that parents can teach their children about marriage according to their own values and beliefs without conflicting messages being forced on young children in public schools that gay marriage is okay.

Your YES vote on Proposition 8 means that only marriage between a man and a woman will be valid or recognized in California, regardless of when or where performed. But Prop. 8 will NOT take away any other rights or benefits of gay couples.

Gays and lesbians have the right to live the lifestyle they choose, but they do not have the right to redefine marriage for everyone else. Proposition 8 respects the rights of gays while still reaffirming traditional marriage.

Please vote YES on Proposition 8 to RESTORE the definition of marriage that the voters already approved.

DR. JANE ANDERSON, M.D., Fellow
American College of Pediatricians
ROBERT BOLINGBROKE, Council Commissioner
San Diego-Imperial Council, Boy Scouts of America
JERALEE SMITH, Director of Education/California
Parents and Friends of Ex-Gays and Gays (PFOX)

PROPOSITION 8

This initiative measure is submitted to the people in accordance with the provisions of Article II, Section 8, of the California Constitution.

This initiative measure expressly amends the California Constitution by adding a section thereto; therefore, new provisions proposed to be added are printed in *italic type* to indicate that they are new.

SECTION 1. Title

This measure shall be known and may be cited as the "California Marriage Protection Act."

SECTION 2. Section 7.5 is added to Article I of the California Constitution, to read:

Sec. 7.5. Only marriage between a man and a woman is valid or recognized in California.

Proposition 8 "In Plain English"

Frames from the video created by the
"Yes on Proposition 8" campaign.

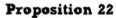

In the year 2000, Californians voted "Yes" on legislation to define marriage as being between a man and a woman.

In May 2008, four San Francisco judges overturned this legislation, ruling it unconstitutional.

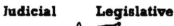

Suddenly, same sex marriage was legal in California. But have the courts gone too far? And is same sex marriage the right choice for California?

On November 4, Californians will have the chance to make their voices heard once more. This is Proposition 8, in plain English.

Proposition 8 is a measure on the November ballot which will amend the California constitution by adding these fourteen words: "Only marriage between a man and a woman is valid or recognized in California."

A "Yes" vote will reverse the Supreme Court's decision and restore traditional marriage to California.

A "No" vote will affirm the Supreme Court's decision and allow same sex marriage to continue in California.

As with most political issues, there are strong feelings on both sides. Those in favor of the amendment argue that strong families are fundamental to society and legalizing same sex marriage could have harmful consequences. Those opposed to the amendment argue that same sex marriage is a right and won't harm anyone. There are also many people in the middle who aren't quite sure what to think.

Meet Jan and Tom. Jan and Tom have two children and a dog. They own a minivan. Tom mows his lawn on Saturday. Jan likes to cook.

Jan and Tom live next door to Dan and Michael, a same sex couple. Jan and Tom have been good friends with Dan and Michael for years. When Jan and Tom were on vacation, Dan and Michael watched their dog. When Dan was sick, Jan brought him soup.

When they first heard about Proposition 8, Tom and Jan felt torn. On the one hand, they believed in and wanted to teach their children traditional values. On the other hand, they felt Dan and Michael should be treated fairly and equally, regardless of their lifestyle choice. Tom and Jan wondered, "Will same sex marriage affect us and our children?" They decided to find out.

After a few minutes on the Internet, Tom discovered section 297 of the California Family Code. "That's interesting," Tom thought as he read it. "It appears that same sex couples like Dan and Michael, who are in a domestic partnership, already have the same legal rights and privileges as married couples."

"If this isn't about rights and equality, then what is it about? And why is changing the definition of marriage such a big deal?" At that very moment, Jan was on the phone with her sister Nancy, who lives in Massachusetts, the only other state in the U.S. to legalize same sex marriage. Here's what Jan learned. Fact: In 2004, Massachusetts legalized same sex marriage.

FACT:

Fact: in 2006, a Massachusetts teacher read the story "King and King" to her 2nd grade class, which tells the story of a prince marrying a prince.

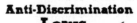

When parents objected, courts ruled that parents had no right to receive advanced notice that their children would be taught about gay marriage, nor could they pull their children from class.

Fact: In 2006, Catholic Charities ended its adoption work in Massachusetts after more than one hundred years of service

because the state's anti-discrimination laws required adoption
agencies to place children in same sex homes.

Tom was now starting to understand. Changing the definition
of marriage was a big deal and could have some very serious
consequences: consequences that could affect not only
their children but also their community.

If Proposition 8 were to fail, would their church be required to
perform same sex marriages? What would their children be
taught at school? Could anti-discrimination laws force
citizens to compromise their values and beliefs in the
name of tolerance? Was same sex marriage really
the right choice for California?

Tom and Jan decided there was far too much at stake to leave
these questions to chance. Tom and Jan are still good friends
with Dan and Michael. In fact, they're having a barbeque
together right now. You see, being a good neighbor is
important, but Tom and Jan have come to an important
realization: they can respect Dan and Michael's lifestyle
choice without affirming and embracing their lifestyle.

whatisprop8.com

Tom and Jan will be voting "Yes" this November on Proposition 8, and we hope you'll do the same.

Church Bulletin

Flier distributed by the "Yes on Proposition 8" campaign.

Questions and Answers Handout

Printed and published online by the
"Yes on Proposition 8" campaign.

ProtectMarriage.com

Questions & Answers
About Proposition 8

What is Proposition 8?

Proposition 8 is a simple and straightforward voter initiative. It contains the same 14 words that were previously approved in 2000 by over 61% of California voters: "Only marriage between a man and a woman is valid or recognized in California."

Because four activist judges in San Francisco wrongly overturned the people's vote, we need to pass this measure as a constitutional amendment to restore the definition of marriage as between a man and a woman.

What does a YES vote on Proposition 8 mean?

Voting YES on Proposition 8 does 3 simple things:

- It restores the definition of marriage to what the vast majority of California voters already approved and human history has understood marriage to be.
- It overturns the outrageous decision of four activist Supreme Court judges who ignored the will of the people.
- It protects our children from being taught in public schools that "same-sex marriage" is the same as traditional marriage.

What does a NO vote on Proposition 8 mean?

If Proposition 8 is defeated, the sanctity of marriage will be destroyed and its powerful influence on the betterment of society will be lost. The defeat of Prop. 8 would result in the very meaning of marriage being transformed into nothing more than a contractual relationship between adults. No longer will the interests of children and families even be a consideration. We will no longer celebrate marriage as a union of husband and wife, but rather a relationship between 'Party A' and 'Party B.' The marriage of a man and a woman has been at the heart of society since the beginning of time. It promotes the ideal opportunity for children to be raised by a mother and father in a family held together by the

Paid for by ProtectMarriage.com – Yes on 8, a Project of California Renewal.
915 L Street, Suite C-259, Sacramento, CA 95814. 916/446-2956.
Major funding by National Organization for Marriage California Committee, Fieldstead & Co., and Focus on the Family.

legal, communal and spiritual bonds of marriage. And while divorce and death too frequently disrupt the ideal, as a society we should put the best interests of children first, and that is traditional marriage. Voting No on Proposition 8 would destroy marriage as we know it and cause profound harm to society.

Will Proposition 8 take away any rights for gay and lesbian domestic partners?

No. Proposition 8 is about preserving marriage; it's not an attack on the gay lifestyle. Proposition 8 doesn't take away any rights or benefits from gays or lesbians in domestic partnerships. Under California law, "domestic partners shall have the same rights, protections and benefits" as married spouses. (Family Code §297.5.) There are no exceptions. Proposition 8 will not change this.

If Proposition 8 passes, what will happen to the same-sex marriages that have already taken place?

Under Proposition 8, the validity and recognition of *all* marriage in California would be limited to a man and a woman, including past and future marriages, as well as marriages from other states or countries. The rights and obligations of same-sex couples who obtained marriage licenses before Proposition 8 passes will be up to the Courts to decide.

If Proposition 8 does not pass, will my children be forced to learn about gay marriage at school?

Yes. In health education classes, state law requires teachers to instruct children as young as kindergarteners about marriage. (Education Code §51890.) If the same-sex marriage ruling is not overturned, teachers will be required to teach young children that there is no difference between gay marriage and traditional marriage.

Why is Proposition 8 needed? Didn't we already vote on this issue?

In 2000, over 61% of Californians voted to reaffirm the traditional definition of marriage as only between a man and a woman (Proposition 22). However, because this language wasn't put into the California Constitution, four activist judges from San Francisco wrongly overturned the people's vote in a closely divided 4-3 decision. Proposition 8 reverses the court's decision by restoring the definition of marriage as a man and a woman in the state Constitution.

Could the California Supreme Court overturn the people's vote again and declare Proposition 8 unconstitutional?

No. By amending the state Constitution directly, the court cannot declare Proposition 8 to be unconstitutional, as it did with Proposition 22. Proposition 22 added a regular statute to the California Family Code. Regular statutes are a "lower" law than the state Constitution. By adding the language of Proposition 8 to the state Constitution, which is the highest source of law in the state, the California courts would be required to uphold traditional marriage.

▣ Who supports this initiative?

A wide range of national, state and local pro-family organizations, churches and individuals have formed a broad-based coalition to support Proposition 8. To date, the coalition represents over one million people in California. To view a list of supporters, visit www.ProtectMarriage.com.

▣ What will happen to the domestic partnership laws if Proposition 8 is enacted?

Nothing. All laws on the books regarding domestic partnerships will remain intact. Gays and lesbians in domestic partnerships will continue to enjoy all the legal rights and benefits that married couples enjoy. Proposition 8 does not affect those rights and benefits.

▣ Where can I find more information about Proposition 8 or get involved in the campaign?

You can visit the Proposition 8 Web site at www.ProtectMarriage.com or call (916) 446-2956. There are a number of ways to get involved with the campaign, including volunteering, donating and helping to spread the word about the importance of voting YES on Proposition 8.

Vote Yes on Proposition 8!

www.ProtectMarriage.com

ProtectMarriage.com

TOPIC INDEX

References are to Pages

ABORTION, 22–29
Education, 1042–1043, 1059
Health reform law and, 29
Hyde Amendment, 28
Parental consent and notification, 273–275
Sex equality and, 26, 199–200

ACADEMIC FREEDOM
See also Education
Solomon Amendment, 182

ACQUIRED IMMUNO-DEFICIENCY SYNDROME (AIDS)
See also Americans with Disabilities Act
Adoption and child custody, 877–879
Disease and epidemic as a social construction, 455–462
Speech, 1080

ADOPTION, 877–896
Lesbian and gay, 877–887
Second-parent, 887–896
Transracial, 893

ADULTERY, 11, 252

AFRICAN-AMERICANS
See Critical Race Theory; Race and Sexuality

AMERICAN PSYCHIATRIC ASSOCIATION, 33–34, 109–110

AMERICANS WITH DISABILITIES ACT (ADA)
Exclusion of transsexuals, 111–112
Homosexuality and, 98

ARMED FORCES
See Military

BIRTH CONTROL, 4–14
Minors and, 18–21
Race and, 7

BISEXUALITY, 33, 479–482

CHILD CUSTODY AND VISITATION, 857–871
Race, 858
Sexual orientation, 858–875
Spousal disputes, 859–864

CHILD SEXUAL ABUSE, 272–275, 435–442
Intergenerational sex as, 272–273
Pornography as, 138–141, 147
State age-of-consent laws (list and description), 272–273

CIVIL RIGHTS ACT OF 1964, TITLE VII
See Employment Discrimination

COHABITATION OUTSIDE OF MARRIAGE, 760–787
Contractual obligations, 790–796
Same-sex relationships, 795
Interracial, 22, 277–295
Legitimacy of nonmarital children, 71–76
New legal categories, 751–757, 807–852
Privacy right, Preface
Third-party obligations, 805–806

COMSTOCK LAW, 4–5

CONSENT, SEXUAL, 267–271, 1241–1243 (Texas)
See also Rape
Coercion
    Economic, 252–254
    Physical, 252–254, 1241–1243 (Texas)
    Psychological, 267–271, 1241–1243 (Texas)
History of, 267–271
Sodomy, consensual, 29–34
Theory, 267–271

CONSUMERISM
Commercial sex, 252–267
Surrogacy, 911–919

CRIMINAL LAWS REGULATING SEXUALITY AND GENDER DEVIANCE
Adultery, 11, 252
Child molestation and pornography, 147
Cross-dressing and masquerade, 106–108
Disorderly conduct, 1243–1244
Fornication, 11, 30, 252–267
Incest, 11, 435–440
Indecent conduct with minor, 1241–1243 (Texas)
Indecent exposure, 1241 (Texas)
Obscenity, 11, 17–18, 1245–1247 (Texas)
Prostitution, 252–267, 1244–1245 (Texas)
Public indecency and lewdness, 11, 1239 (Texas)
Rape (sexual assault), 11, 267–271, 1241–1243 (Texas)
Sex toys, 250, 1246–1247 (Texas)
Sex with minors, 272–75, 1248–1251 (Texas)
    Romeo and Juliet exception, 275
Sexual psychopath laws, 31–34
Sodomy, 11, 29–47, 250–251, 1239 (Texas)
Solicitation, 1244 (Texas)

CRITICAL RACE THEORY, 148–151, 649
See also Race and Sexuality
Segregation and manhood (Kenneth Karst), 1085–1086

DISPARATE IMPACT (TITLE VII), 57–58

DISPARATE TREATMENT (TITLE VII), 293–295

DIVORCE, 363
See also Marriage

DUE PROCESS CLAUSE
Equal protection component, Preface
Liberty interest in sexual relations, 9–11
Privacy rights, Preface, 1–47

ECONOMIC THEORIES OF SEXUALITY AND GENDER, 370–377
Chicago school theory (Gary Becker, Richard Posner), 370–377
Evolutionary psychology (Edward O. Wilson), 360–364
Feminist theory (Carol Rose, Debra Satz), 377–380

EDUCATION, 971–1081
Abortion, 1045–1046
AIDS and other sexually transmitted diseases, 1045–1069, 1075–1079
Educational need, 1060–1061
Sexual harassment and AIDS education, 1068–1069
State laws (survey), 1045–1046
Athletic teams, sex discrimination, 419–420
"No promotion of homosexuality" policies
Federal, 1075–1079
State, 1058–1059, 1070–1075
Pregnancy and family planning advice, 1045–1070
Prom night, 974–976
Sex education, 1045–1079
Sex segregation
All-female schools, 1036–1044
All-male schools, 1042–1044
Sexual harassment in schools, 991–1044
Sexually harassing speech, 1067–1068
Speech (general), 973–985
Teachers and sexuality
Bisexuality, 479–489
Theories of, 971–972, 981–984
University, 130–134

EMPLOYMENT DISCRIMINATION, 601–749
See also Americans with Disabilities Act; Disparate Impact; Disparate Treatment
Dress, 442–449
Gender, 442–449, 601–613, 621–650
Intersectional, 616, 641
Marital status, 442–449

Sex discrimination, 442–449, 613–619
Private sector discrimination, 613–619
Civil Rights Act of 1964, Title VII, 613–650
District of Columbia Human Rights Act, Appendix 4
EEOC's Sexual Harassment Guidelines, 659–678
Pregnancy Discrimination Act of 1978, 621–630
State and federal agency discrimination, 442–449
Armed forces
Combat exclusion, 1096–1141
Sexual harassment, 659–684
Pregnancy, 621–650
Sexual orientation discrimination, 613–619
Private sector discrimination
District of Columbia Human Rights Act, Appendix 4
Employment Non-Discrimination Act, (proposed), Appendix 5
State and federal agency discrimination, 613–619
Armed forces, 1105–1132
Federal civil service, 1105–1132
Transgendered people, discrimination against, 112–115, 709–742

EQUAL ACCESS ACT, 985–986

EQUAL EDUCATION OPPORTUNITY ACT OF 1974, 1034–1040

EQUAL PROTECTION CLAUSE,
Preface, 50–123
Race discrimination, Preface, 277–279, 1085–1096
Sex discrimination, Preface, 50–123, 1096–1141
Relationship to sex discrimination and theory for strict scrutiny, 50–123
Sexual orientation discrimination, Preface, 1105–1132
Theories for strict scrutiny, 280–281

EQUAL RIGHTS AMENDMENT
State constitutions, Preface (listing states)

FEMINIST THEORY, 384–412
See also Marriage; Queer Theory; Rape; Social Construction Theory; Surrogate Motherhood
Deconstruction and feminism (Eve Sedgwick), 471–478
Feminism and Foucault (Judith Butler, Vicki Bell), 437–442

Liberal feminism (Wendy Webster Williams, Ruth Bader Ginsburg, Jana Singer), 50–61
Mutuality feminism, 399–401
Radical feminism, 384–391
    Marriage critics (Paula Ettelbrick), 337–338
    Prosex (Gayle Rubin),391–399
Rational choice feminism (Carol Rose), 377–380

FIRST AMENDMENT, Preface, 125–181
    See also Academic Freedom; Free Exercise Clause; Freedom of Association; Obscenity; Outing
Birth control advice and advocacy, 6–8
Coming out speech, 130–138
Exclusions, Preface (general survey)
    Obscenity, 7, 141–148 et seq.
Forums, Preface (general survey)
    Adult theatres, 151–153
    Colleges and universities, 564–576, 1014–1018, 1040–1041
    Libraries, 1047–1053
    Music lyrics, 148–157
    Secondary schools, 971–982, 1034–1040
    Sex education and reproductive rights materials, 68, 1075–1079
General theory and introduction, Preface
Identity expression, 130–138, 564–576, 984–985
No promo homo restrictions, 1069–1079
Political versus sexual speech, 134–136, 1069–1079
Sexually harassing speech, 1014–1018
Rights of
    Association, 157–181
    Marching, 157–164
    Publication, 138–153
    Sexual expression, 1075–1079
    Speech, 130–157

FORNICATION, 251

FOUCAULDIAN THEORY, 424–429, 437–440
See also Social Constructionist Theory

FREE EXERCISE CLAUSE
See First Amendment

FREEDOM OF ASSOCIATION, 165–181
See also First Amendment

GENDER, 70–76

GENDER IDENTITY DISCRIMINATION, 741–742

GENETICS
Homosexuality (the "hard-wired homos" thesis), 100–102
Intersexuality, 108–112

HATE CRIMES, 401–402

HERMAPHRODITES
See Intersexuals

HUMAN IMMUNO-DEFICIENCY VIRUS (HIV)
See Acquired Immuno-Deficiency Syndrome (AIDS)

IMMIGRATION LAW, 32–34

INCEST, 435–440

INDECENCY, 163–164, 1239–1240 (Texas)

INITIATIVES AND REFERENDA (ANTI-GAY)
Colorado's Amendment 2, Appendix 3
Proposition 8 (California), Appendix 6

INTERSEXUALS, 71–74

LIBERTARIAN THEORY (JOHN STUART MILL), 16

MANN ACT OF 1910, 253–254

MARITAL STATUS DISCRIMINATION, 645–657
District of Columbia Human Rights Act, Appendix 4

MARRIAGE, 277–343, 751–852
Alternative forms of state recognition, 807–852
Constitutional right to marry, 277–297
Covenant marriages, 770–777
Deregulation proposals, 751–757, 789–790
Divorce, 771–773
Limits imposed by the state, and legal challenges thereto
    Age, 272–275
    Mental disability, 789–800
    Number of spouses, 358–359
    Poverty, Preface
    Race, 277–279
    Sex, 277–343
Natural law theory of, 351–364
Polygamy, 358–359
Privatization of marital rights and obligations
    Contract rights of cohabitants, 760–796
    Feminist critiques of privatization, 792–796
Same-sex marriage, 277–343
    Critics
        Traditionalists, 349–364

MARXIST THEORY, 384–387
MacKinnon's parallel feminist theory, 384–387

MEDICALIZATION OF SEXUALITY REGULATION
Abortion, 22–29
Contraception, 4–22
Homosexuality, 32–34
Transgender, 108–112

MILITARY, 1083–1145
Discriminations according to
    Race, 1083–1096
    Sex, 1096–1141
    Sexual orientation, 1105–1145
Don't Ask, Don't Tell repeal, 1111–1131
Manhood and military service, 1083–1084
Sexual harassment, 1136–1145
Unit cohesion and morale, 1094–1096,
    1111–1131

MINORS SEX BY AND WITH, 272–275
Statutory rape laws, 272–275, 1248–1250
    (Texas)
    Intergenerational sex, 272–275
    Sex between minors, 272–275
Theory and critique
    Foucauldian defense and feminist
        response, 437–440

MISCEGENATION, 277–279

MODEL PENAL CODE
Sodomy (consensual, deregulation), 231

**MODERNIZATION OF
    JUSTIFICATION (FOR
    SUBORDINATING WOMEN
    AND GAYS),** 864
Anti-gay adoption rules, 878–887
Bars to same-sex marriage, 511–512

NATURAL LAW THEORY, 29, 351–364

NO PROMO HOMO POLICIES
Marriage, 277–343

NONMARITAL CHILDREN, 71–74

OBSCENITY, 1, 6–8, 127–130
See also First Amendment; Indecency

OUTING, 480–482, 493

PARENTING, 853–970
    See also Adoption; Surrogacy;
        Polyparenting
Best interests of the child test, 853–855,
    919–949
Child custody, 857–872
    Homosexuality or bisexuality, 862–
        872
    Race, 858
    Transgender, 868–872
Child visitation, 861–862
De facto parenthood (psychological
    parenthood), 897
Nuclear family, decline of, 853–855
Parental rights, 853–855

POLYGAMY, 96–98, 358–360

POLYPARENTING, 957–970

PORNOGRAPHY, 138–147
    See also Obscenity
Child, 147
Electronic, 147–148
Feminist debate over, 148–153, 384–387
Race issues, 148–151

PREGNANCY, 57–59, 621–641
See also Employment Discrimination

PRISONS, 112, 370–372, 418

PRIVACY, Preface, 1–27
Decisional (body, etc.), 22–27
Relational
    Child-rearing (parental), 14–22
    Marriage, 9–11, 14–16, 277–280,
        281–297
    Sexual intimacy, 4, 18–22, 246
Spatial, 14

PROSTITUTION, 252–255, 1244–1245
    (Texas)

PUBLIC-PRIVATE DICHOTOMY, 3–
    28, 151–187, 225–275
Abortion, 22–29
Contraception, 4–22
Public sexuality, 151–187, 225–275
Sodomy, 29–47
Source of eroticism, 151–153

QUEER THEORY
    See also Social Construction Theory
Deconstructive theory (Eve Sedgwick),
    471–478
Pro-sex feminism (Gayle Rubin, Pat
    Califia, Duggan-Hunter-Vance),
    391–399

RACE AND SEXUALITY
    See also Critical Race Theory
Adoption, 877–887, 893
Armed forces segregation, 1083–1096
Censorship
    Library books, 1047–1053
    Rap music, 148–157
Child custody, 858
Employment, 645–649
Marriage and cohabitation, 277–279

RAPE, 267–275

RELIGION, 642–645
    See also Free Exercise Clause;
        Religious Freedom
        Restoration Act
Christianity, 345–364
    Employment discrimination because
        of pregnancy, 642–645
    Same-sex marriage, 363
    Sodomy, 349–358

**RELIGIOUS FREEDOM
    RESTORATION ACT,** 510

SADOMASOCHISM, 267–271
See also Feminist Theory

SAME-SEX MARRIAGE, 277–343, 349–
    364
See also Marriage

SEX DISCRIMINATION, 613–619
    See also Equal Protection Clause;
        Sexual Harassment
Gender stereotyping as, 611–613, 625–626

Hostile school environment as, 991–1043
Pregnancy discrimination as, 621–641
Sexual harassment as, 679–684
Sexual orientation discrimination as, 613–
    619, 679–684

SEXUAL HARASSMENT, 601–613,
    679–684
Within sexualized workplace, 601–613

**SEXUAL ORIENTATION
    DISCRIMINATION,** 49–123
Adoption and foster parenting, 877–879
Employment, 601–613
    State and federal anti-gay
        discrimination, 442–449,
        1111–1131
        Federal armed forces, 659–
            679, 1111–1131
    Laws protecting against private
        anti-gay discrimination
        District of Columbia Human
            Rights Act, Appendix 4
        Employment Non-
            Discrimination Act
            (proposed) Appendix 5
Equal protection claims (general), 49–123
Immigration, 611–613
Initiatives repealing pro-gay laws,
    Appendix 3, Appendix 6
Marriage, 104–106, 277–343
Military exclusion, 1105–1145
Sodomy laws, 29–47

SEX WORK, 252–255, 1244–1245 (Texas)
See also Prostitution

SOCIAL CONSTRUCTION THEORY
Basic theory (Michel Foucault), 424–429
Examples and applications
    Binarism of sex and gender
        critiqued (Judith Butler,
        Katherine Franke), 70–71
    Compulsory heterosexuality
        (Adrienne Rich, Catherine
        MacKinnon), 384–391
    Disease and epidemics (Linda
        Singer), 455–460
    Hostile or discouraging workplaces
        (Rosemary Pringle, Vicki
        Schultz), 606–613
    Identity politics (William Eskridge),
        449–451
    Incest taboos (Foucault, Vicki Bell),
        437–440
    Pornography as sexy because taboo
        (David Cole), 151–153
    Privacy as resistance to state
        totalization (Jed Rubenfeld),
        44–47
    Rape as especially injurious, 440
    Sexual orientation and
        homosexuality as a modern
        creation (Mary McIntosh),
        424–492
Feminism and (Judith Butler, Vicki Bell,
    Katherine Franke), 429–451

Globalization and (Sonia Katyal), 484–488
Law as an agent (Ellen Ross and Rayna
    Rapp), 489–491

**SOCIAL MOVEMENTS AND
    AMERICAN
    CONSTITUTIONALISM**
Birth control movement and the right to
    privacy, 1–22
Choice movement and the right to an
    abortion, 22–28
Equal rights for women movement, 49–
    123
Gay rights movement and sexual
    freedoms, 31–181

SODOMY LAWS
Constitutionality, 29–31
History, 11, 29–47
Normative critique
    Deconstructionist (Janet Halley), 42
    Historical (Anne Goldstein, William
        Eskridge), 41–42
    Importance of intimacy (Michael
        Sandel), 43–44
    Social constructionist (Jed
        Rubenfeld), 44–47

SOLOMON AMENDMENT, 182–187

SPEECH-CONDUCT DISTINCTION,
    134–136

STATUS-CONDUCT DEBATE, 158–
    181

STATUTORY RAPE, 59–61, 272–275
    434–435, 437–440
See also Minors, Sex with

SURROGACY CONTRACTS, 911–919
Economic defense, 916
Feminist debate, 917
Gestational surrogacy, 912–916
Statutes prohibiting or regulating, 912–
    916

**TITLE VII CIVIL RIGHTS ACT OF
    1964**
See Employment Discrimination

**TITLE IX OF THE EDUCATION
    AMENDMENTS OF 1972**
See Education

TRANSGENDER, TRANSSEXUALS
Child custody, support, and visitation,
    868–872
Criminalization, 106–108
Defined, 106
Medicalization, 108–110, 112–113
Military service and, 1083, 1128–1132
Parents, 872–873, 868–872
Prisons, 491–496
Transsexualism and, 108–112

VAGUENESS, Preface
Abortion laws, 201–208
Sodomy laws, 29, 32–34

VIOLENCE
Against gays and lesbians, 1011, 1123
Against transsexuals, 1004
Against women, 148–151, 256–261

VIOLENCE AGAINST WOMEN ACT,
69, 390

WORKPLACE DISCRIMINATION
See Employment Discrimination